THE

COMPLETE OXFORD

SHAKESPEARE

VOLUME II · COMEDIES

General Editors

STANLEY WELLS AND GARY TAYLOR

Editors

STANLEY WELLS, GARY TAYLOR

JOHN JOWETT, AND WILLIAM MONTGOMERY

With Introductions by

STANLEY WELLS

OXFORD UNIVERSITY PRESS

Oxford University Press, Walton Street, Oxford OX2 6DP

Oxford New York Toronto
Delhi Bombay Calcutta Madras Karachi
Kuala Lumpur Singapore Hong Kong Tokyo
Nairobi Dar es Salaam Cape Town
Melbourne Auckland Madrid
and associated companies in
Berlin Ibadan

Oxford is a trade mark of Oxford University Press

Published in the United States
by Oxford University Press Inc., New York

© Oxford University Press 1987

First published 1987
Reprinted 1988, 1989 (twice), 1990
First published in paperback 1994

British Library Cataloguing in Publication Data
Shakespeare, William
[Works]. The Oxford library: the complete
works of William Shakespeare.
I. Title   II. Wells, Stanley, 1930–
III. Taylor, Gary   IV. William Shakespeare, the complete works
822.3'3   PR2754
ISBN 0–19–818273–2 (Pbk)

Library of Congress Cataloging in Publication Data
Shakespeare, William, 1564–1616.
The complete Oxford Shakespeare.
Contents: v. 1. The histories—v. 2. The comedies—v. 3. The tragedies.
I. Wells, Stanley, W., 1930– . II. Taylor, Gary.
III. Title   IV. Series.
PR2754.W45 1987 822.3'3 87–7850
ISBN 0–19–818273–2 (Pbk)

Printed in Spain
by Printer Industria Gráfica SA

CONTENTS

ILLUSTRATIONS

THE TWO GENTLEMEN OF VERONA

THE accomplished elegance of the lyrical verse in *The Two Gentlemen of Verona*, as well as the skilful, theatrically effective prose of Lance's monologues, demonstrates that Shakespeare had already developed his writing skills when he composed this play. Nevertheless—and although the earliest mention of it is by Francis Meres in 1598—it may be his first work for the stage; for its dramatic structure is comparatively unambitious, and while some of its scenes are expertly constructed, those involving more than, at the most, four characters betray an uncertainty of technique suggestive of inexperience. It was first printed in the 1623 Folio.

The friendship of the 'two gentlemen'—Valentine and Proteus—is strained when both fall in love with Silvia. Proteus has followed Valentine from Verona to Milan, leaving behind his beloved Julia, who in turn follows him, disguised as a boy. At the climax of the action Valentine displays the depth of his friendship by offering Silvia to Proteus. The conflicting claims of love and friendship illustrated in this plot had been treated in a considerable body of English literature written by the time Shakespeare wrote his play, probably in the late 1580s. John Lyly's didactic fiction *Euphues* (1578) was an immensely popular example; and Lyly's earliest plays, such as *Campaspe* (1584) and *Endimion* (1588), influenced Shakespeare's style as well as his subject matter. Shakespeare was writing in a fashionable mode, but his story of Proteus and Julia is specifically (though perhaps indirectly) indebted to a prose fiction, *Diana*, written in Spanish by the Portuguese Jorge de Montemayor and first published in 1559. Many other influences on the young dramatist may be discerned: his idealized portrayal of Silvia and her relationship with Valentine derives from the medieval tradition of courtly love; Arthur Brooke's long poem *The Tragical History of Romeus and Juliet* (1562) provided some details of the plot; and the comic commentary on the romantic action supplied by the page-boy Speed and the more rustic clown Lance has dramatic antecedents in English plays such as Lyly's early comedies.

Though the play was presumably acted in Shakespeare's time, its first recorded performance is in 1762, in a rewritten version at Drury Lane. Later performances have been sparse, and the play has succeeded best when subjected to adaptation, increasing its musical content, adjusting the emphasis of the last scene so as to reduce the shock of Valentine's donation of Silvia to Proteus, and updating the setting. It can be seen as a dramatic laboratory in which Shakespeare first experimented with conventions of romantic comedy which he would later treat with a more subtle complexity, but it has its own charm. If the whole is not greater than the parts, some of the parts—such as Lance's brilliant monologues, and the delightful scene (4.2) in which Proteus serenades his new love with 'Who is Silvia?' while his disguised old love, Julia, looks wistfully on—are wholly successful. And Lance's dog, Crab, has the most scene-stealing non-speaking role in the canon: this is an experiment that Shakespeare did not repeat.

THE PERSONS OF THE PLAY

DUKE of Milan
SILVIA, his daughter

PROTEUS, a gentleman of Verona
LANCE, his clownish servant

VALENTINE, a gentleman of Verona
SPEED, his clownish servant
THURIO, a foolish rival to Valentine

ANTONIO, father of Proteus
PANTHINO, his servant

JULIA, beloved of Proteus
LUCETTA, her waiting-woman
HOST, where Julia lodges

EGLAMOUR, agent for Silvia in her escape

OUTLAWS

Servants, musicians

The Two Gentlemen of Verona

1.1   *Enter Valentine and Proteus*

VALENTINE
Cease to persuade, my loving Proteus.
Home-keeping youth have ever homely wits.
Were't not affection chains thy tender days
To the sweet glances of thy honoured love,
I rather would entreat thy company   5
To see the wonders of the world abroad
Than, living dully sluggardized at home,
Wear out thy youth with shapeless idleness.
But since thou lov'st, love still, and thrive therein—
Even as I would, when I to love begin.   10

PROTEUS
Wilt thou be gone? Sweet Valentine, adieu.
Think on thy Proteus when thou haply seest
Some rare noteworthy object in thy travel.
Wish me partaker in thy happiness
When thou dost meet good hap; and in thy danger—
If ever danger do environ thee—   16
Commend thy grievance to my holy prayers;
For I will be thy beadsman, Valentine.

VALENTINE
And on a love-book pray for my success?

PROTEUS
Upon some book I love I'll pray for thee.   20

VALENTINE
That's on some shallow story of deep love—
How young Leander crossed the Hellespont.

PROTEUS
That's a deep story of a deeper love,
For he was more than over-shoes in love.

VALENTINE
'Tis true, for you are over-boots in love,   25
And yet you never swam the Hellespont.

PROTEUS
Over the boots? Nay, give me not the boots.

VALENTINE
No, I will not; for it boots thee not.

PROTEUS   What?

VALENTINE
To be in love, where scorn is bought with groans,
Coy looks with heart-sore sighs, one fading moment's
         mirth   30
With twenty watchful, weary, tedious nights.
If haply won, perhaps a hapless gain;
If lost, why then a grievous labour won;
However, but a folly bought with wit,
Or else a wit by folly vanquishèd.   35

PROTEUS
So by your circumstance you call me fool.

VALENTINE
So by your circumstance I fear you'll prove.

PROTEUS
'Tis love you cavil at. I am not love.

VALENTINE
Love is your master, for he masters you,
And he that is so yokèd by a fool   40
Methinks should not be chronicled for wise.

PROTEUS
Yet writers say 'As in the sweetest bud
The eating canker dwells, so doting love
Inhabits in the finest wits of all.'

VALENTINE
And writers say 'As the most forward bud   45
Is eaten by the canker ere it blow,
Even so by love the young and tender wit
Is turned to folly, blasting in the bud,
Losing his verdure even in the prime,
And all the fair effects of future hopes.'   50
But wherefore waste I time to counsel thee
That art a votary to fond desire?
Once more adieu. My father at the road
Expects my coming, there to see me shipped.

PROTEUS
And thither will I bring thee, Valentine.   55

VALENTINE
Sweet Proteus, no. Now let us take our leave.
To Milan let me hear from thee by letters
Of thy success in love, and what news else
Betideth here in absence of thy friend;
And I likewise will visit thee with mine.   60

PROTEUS
All happiness bechance to thee in Milan.

VALENTINE
As much to you at home; and so farewell.   *Exit*

PROTEUS
He after honour hunts, I after love.
He leaves his friends to dignify them more,
I leave myself, my friends, and all, for love.   65
Thou, Julia, thou hast metamorphosed me,
Made me neglect my studies, lose my time,
War with good counsel, set the world at naught;
Made wit with musing weak, heart sick with thought.
         Enter Speed

SPEED
Sir Proteus, save you. Saw you my master?   70

PROTEUS
But now he parted hence to embark for Milan.

SPEED
Twenty to one, then, he is shipped already,
And I have played the sheep in losing him.

PROTEUS
Indeed, a sheep doth very often stray,
An if the shepherd be a while away.   75

SPEED
  You conclude that my master is a shepherd, then,
    and I a sheep?
PROTEUS I do.
SPEED
  Why then, my horns are his horns, whether I wake
    or sleep.
PROTEUS A silly answer, and fitting well a sheep.
SPEED This proves me still a sheep.   80
PROTEUS True, and thy master a shepherd.
SPEED Nay, that I can deny by a circumstance.
PROTEUS It shall go hard but I'll prove it by another.
SPEED The shepherd seeks the sheep, and not the sheep
  the shepherd. But I seek my master, and my master
  seeks not me. Therefore I am no sheep.   86
PROTEUS The sheep for fodder follow the shepherd, the
  shepherd for food follows not the sheep. Thou for wages
  followest thy master, thy master for wages follows not
  thee. Therefore thou art a sheep.   90
SPEED Such another proof will make me cry 'baa'.
PROTEUS But dost thou hear: gav'st thou my letter to
  Julia?
SPEED Ay, sir. I, a lost mutton, gave your letter to her, a
  laced mutton, and she, a laced mutton, gave me, a lost
  mutton, nothing for my labour.   96
PROTEUS Here's too small a pasture for such store of
  muttons.
SPEED If the ground be overcharged, you were best stick
  her.   100
PROTEUS Nay, in that you are astray. 'Twere best pound
  you.
SPEED Nay sir, less than a pound shall serve me for
  carrying your letter.
PROTEUS You mistake. I mean the pound, a pinfold. 105
SPEED
  From a pound to a pin? Fold it over and over
  'Tis threefold too little for carrying a letter to your
    lover.
PROTEUS But what said she?
SPEED (nods, then says) Ay.
PROTEUS Nod-ay? Why, that's 'noddy'.   110
SPEED You mistook, sir. I say she did nod, and you ask
  me if she did nod, and I say 'Ay'.
PROTEUS And that set together is 'noddy'.
SPEED Now you have taken the pains to set it together,
  take it for your pains.   115
PROTEUS No, no. You shall have it for bearing the letter.
SPEED Well, I perceive I must be fain to bear with you.
PROTEUS Why, sir, how do you bear with me?
SPEED Marry, sir, the letter very orderly, having nothing
  but the word 'noddy' for my pains.   120
PROTEUS Beshrew me but you have a quick wit.
SPEED And yet it cannot overtake your slow purse.
PROTEUS Come, come, open the matter in brief. What said
  she?
SPEED Open your purse, that the money and the matter
  may be both at once delivered.   126

PROTEUS (giving money) Well, sir, here is for your pains.
  What said she?
SPEED Truly, sir, I think you'll hardly win her.   129
PROTEUS Why? Couldst thou perceive so much from her?
SPEED Sir, I could perceive nothing at all from her, no,
  not so much as a ducat for delivering your letter. And
  being so hard to me, that brought your mind, I fear
  she'll prove as hard to you in telling your mind. Give
  her no token but stones, for she's as hard as steel. 135
PROTEUS What said she? Nothing?
SPEED No, not so much as 'Take this for thy pains'. To
  testify your bounty, I thank you, you have testerned
  me; in requital whereof, henceforth carry your letters
  yourself. And so, sir, I'll commend you to my master.
                                                   ⌜Exit⌝
PROTEUS
  Go, go, be gone, to save your ship from wreck,
  Which cannot perish having thee aboard,
  Being destined to a drier death on shore.
  I must go send some better messenger.
  I fear my Julia would not deign my lines,   145
  Receiving them from such a worthless post.   Exit

1.2   Enter Julia and Lucetta
JULIA
  But say, Lucetta, now we are alone—
  Wouldst thou then counsel me to fall in love?
LUCETTA
  Ay, madam, so you stumble not unheedfully.
JULIA
  Of all the fair resort of gentlemen
  That every day with parle encounter me,   5
  In thy opinion which is worthiest love?
LUCETTA
  Please you repeat their names, I'll show my mind
  According to my shallow simple skill.
JULIA
  What think'st thou of the fair Sir Eglamour?
LUCETTA
  As of a knight well spoken, neat, and fine,   10
  But were I you, he never should be mine.
JULIA
  What think'st thou of the rich Mercatio?
LUCETTA
  Well of his wealth, but of himself, so-so.
JULIA
  What think'st thou of the gentle Proteus?
LUCETTA
  Lord, lord, to see what folly reigns in us!   15
JULIA
  How now? What means this passion at his name?
LUCETTA
  Pardon, dear madam, 'tis a passing shame
  That I, unworthy body as I am,
  Should censure thus on lovely gentlemen.
JULIA
  Why not on Proteus, as of all the rest?   20

LUCETTA
Then thus: of many good, I think him best.
JULIA Your reason?
LUCETTA
I have no other but a woman's reason:
I think him so because I think him so.
JULIA
And wouldst thou have me cast my love on him?   25
LUCETTA
Ay, if you thought your love not cast away.
JULIA
Why, he of all the rest hath never moved me.
LUCETTA
Yet he of all the rest I think best loves ye.
JULIA
His little speaking shows his love but small.
LUCETTA
Fire that's closest kept burns most of all.   30
JULIA
They do not love that do not show their love.
LUCETTA
O, they love least that let men know their love.
JULIA
I would I knew his mind.
LUCETTA (giving Proteus' letter)
Peruse this paper, madam.
JULIA
'To Julia'—say, from whom?   35
LUCETTA
That the contents will show.
JULIA
Say, say—who gave it thee?
LUCETTA
Sir Valentine's page; and sent, I think, from Proteus.
He would have given it you, but I being in the way
Did in your name receive it. Pardon the fault, I pray.
JULIA
Now, by my modesty, a goodly broker.   41
Dare you presume to harbour wanton lines?
To whisper, and conspire against my youth?
Now trust me, 'tis an office of great worth,
And you an officer fit for the place.   45
There. Take the paper.
    She gives Lucetta the letter
                        See it be returned,
Or else return no more into my sight.
LUCETTA
To plead for love deserves more fee than hate.
JULIA
Will ye be gone?
LUCETTA   That you may ruminate.   *Exit*
JULIA
And yet I would I had o'erlooked the letter.   50
It were a shame to call her back again
And pray her to a fault for which I chid her.
What fool is she, that knows I am a maid
And would not force the letter to my view,
Since maids in modesty say 'No' to that   55

Which they would have the profferer construe 'Ay'.
Fie, fie, how wayward is this foolish love
That like a testy babe will scratch the nurse
And presently, all humbled, kiss the rod.
How churlishly I chid Lucetta hence   60
When willingly I would have had her here.
How angerly I taught my brow to frown
When inward joy enforced my heart to smile.
My penance is to call Lucetta back
And ask remission for my folly past.   65
What ho! Lucetta!
    Enter Lucetta
LUCETTA   What would your ladyship?
JULIA
Is't near dinner-time?
LUCETTA   I would it were,
That you might kill your stomach on your meat
And not upon your maid.
    She drops and picks up the letter
JULIA   What is't that you
Took up so gingerly?   70
LUCETTA Nothing.
JULIA Why didst thou stoop then?
LUCETTA
To take a paper up that I let fall.
JULIA
And is that paper nothing?
LUCETTA
Nothing concerning me.   75
JULIA
Then let it lie for those that it concerns.
LUCETTA
Madam, it will not lie where it concerns,
Unless it have a false interpreter.
JULIA
Some love of yours hath writ to you in rhyme.
LUCETTA
That I might sing it, madam, to a tune,   80
Give me a note. Your ladyship can set.
JULIA
As little by such toys as may be possible.
Best sing it to the tune of 'Light o' love'.
LUCETTA
It is too heavy for so light a tune.
JULIA
Heavy? Belike it hath some burden, then?   85
LUCETTA
Ay, and melodious were it, would you sing it.
JULIA
And why not you?
LUCETTA   I cannot reach so high.
JULIA
Let's see your song.
    She tries to take the letter
                        How now, minion!
LUCETTA
Keep tune there still. So you will sing it out.
And yet methinks I do not like this tune.   90

JULIA You do not?

LUCETTA
No, madam, 'tis too sharp.

JULIA
You, minion, are too saucy.

LUCETTA
Nay, now you are too flat,
And mar the concord with too harsh a descant.   95
There wanteth but a mean to fill your song.

JULIA
The mean is drowned with your unruly bass.

LUCETTA
Indeed, I bid the base for Proteus.

JULIA
This bauble shall not henceforth trouble me.
Here is a coil with protestation.   100

She tears the letter and drops the pieces
Go, get you gone, and let the papers lie.
You would be fing'ring them to anger me.

LUCETTA (*aside*)
She makes it strange, but she would be best pleased
To be so angered with another letter.   *Exit*

JULIA
Nay, would I were so angered with the same.   105
O hateful hands, to tear such loving words;
Injurious wasps, to feed on such sweet honey
And kill the bees that yield it with your stings.
I'll kiss each several paper for amends.

She picks up some of the pieces of paper
Look, here is writ 'Kind Julia'—unkind Julia,   110
As in revenge of thy ingratitude
I throw thy name against the bruising stones,
Trampling contemptuously on thy disdain.
And here is writ 'Love-wounded Proteus'.
Poor wounded name, my bosom as a bed   115
Shall lodge thee till thy wound be throughly healed;
And thus I search it with a sovereign kiss.
But twice or thrice was 'Proteus' written down.
Be calm, good wind, blow not a word away
Till I have found each letter in the letter   120
Except mine own name. That, some whirlwind bear
Unto a ragged, fearful, hanging rock
And throw it thence into the raging sea.
Lo, here in one line is his name twice writ:
'Poor forlorn Proteus', 'passionate Proteus',   125
'To the sweet Julia'—that I'll tear away.
And yet I will not, sith so prettily
He couples it to his complaining names.
Thus will I fold them, one upon another.
Now kiss, embrace, contend, do what you will.   130

Enter Lucetta

LUCETTA
Madam, dinner is ready, and your father stays.

JULIA Well, let us go.

LUCETTA
What, shall these papers lie like telltales here?

JULIA
If you respect them, best to take them up.

LUCETTA
Nay, I was taken up for laying them down.   135
Yet here they shall not lie, for catching cold.

JULIA
I see you have a month's mind to them.

LUCETTA
Ay, madam, you may say what sights you see.
I see things too, although you judge I wink.   139

JULIA Come, come, will't please you go?   *Exeunt*

1.3   *Enter Antonio and Panthino*

ANTONIO
Tell me, Panthino, what sad talk was that
Wherewith my brother held you in the cloister?

PANTHINO
'Twas of his nephew Proteus, your son.

ANTONIO
Why, what of him?

PANTHINO   He wondered that your lordship
Would suffer him to spend his youth at home   5
While other men, of slender reputation,
Put forth their sons to seek preferment out—
Some to the wars, to try their fortune there,
Some to discover islands far away,
Some to the studious universities.   10
For any or for all these exercises
He said that Proteus your son was meet,
And did request me to importune you
To let him spend his time no more at home,
Which would be great impeachment to his age   15
In having known no travel in his youth.

ANTONIO
Nor need'st thou much importune me to that
Whereon this month I have been hammering.
I have considered well his loss of time,
And how he cannot be a perfect man,   20
Not being tried and tutored in the world.
Experience is by industry achieved,
And perfected by the swift course of time.
Then tell me, whither were I best to send him?

PANTHINO
I think your lordship is not ignorant   25
How his companion, youthful Valentine,
Attends the Emperor in his royal court.

ANTONIO I know it well.

PANTHINO
'Twere good, I think, your lordship sent him thither.
There shall he practise tilts and tournaments,   30
Hear sweet discourse, converse with noblemen,
And be in eye of every exercise
Worthy his youth and nobleness of birth.

ANTONIO
I like thy counsel. Well hast thou advised,
And that thou mayst perceive how well I like it,   35
The execution of it shall make known.
Even with the speediest expedition
I will dispatch him to the Emperor's court.

PANTHINO
Tomorrow, may it please you, Don Alfonso,

With other gentlemen of good esteem,   40
Are journeying to salute the Emperor
And to commend their service to his will.
ANTONIO
Good company. With them shall Proteus go.
   Enter Proteus with a letter. He does not see Antonio
   and Panthino
And in good time. Now will we break with him.
PROTEUS Sweet love, sweet lines, sweet life!   45
Here is her hand, the agent of her heart.
Here is her oath for love, her honour's pawn.
O that our fathers would applaud our loves
To seal our happiness with their consents.
O heavenly Julia!   50
ANTONIO
How now, what letter are you reading there?
PROTEUS
May't please your lordship, 'tis a word or two
Of commendations sent from Valentine,
Delivered by a friend that came from him.
ANTONIO
Lend me the letter. Let me see what news.   55
PROTEUS
There is no news, my lord, but that he writes
How happily he lives, how well beloved
And daily gracèd by the Emperor,
Wishing me with him, partner of his fortune.
ANTONIO
And how stand you affected to his wish?   60
PROTEUS
As one relying on your lordship's will,
And not depending on his friendly wish.
ANTONIO
My will is something sorted with his wish.
Muse not that I thus suddenly proceed,
For what I will, I will, and there an end.   65
I am resolved that thou shalt spend some time
With Valentinus in the Emperor's court.
What maintenance he from his friends receives,
Like exhibition thou shalt have from me.
Tomorrow be in readiness to go.   70
Excuse it not, for I am peremptory.
PROTEUS
My lord, I cannot be so soon provided.
Please you deliberate a day or two.
ANTONIO
Look what thou want'st shall be sent after thee.
No more of stay. Tomorrow thou must go.   75
Come on, Panthino. You shall be employed
To hasten on his expedition.
   Exeunt Antonio and Panthino
PROTEUS
Thus have I shunned the fire for fear of burning
And drenched me in the sea where I am drowned.
I feared to show my father Julia's letter   80
Lest he should take exceptions to my love,
And with the vantage of mine own excuse
Hath he excepted most against my love.

O, how this spring of love resembleth
The uncertain glory of an April day,   85
Which now shows all the beauty of the sun,
And by and by a cloud takes all away.
   Enter Panthino
PANTHINO
Sir Proteus, your father calls for you.
He is in haste, therefore I pray you go.
PROTEUS
Why, this it is. My heart accords thereto,   90
And yet a thousand times it answers 'No'.   *Exeunt*

2.1   *Enter Valentine and Speed*
SPEED (*offering Valentine a glove*)
   Sir, your glove.
VALENTINE   Not mine. My gloves are on.
SPEED
Why then, this may be yours, for this is but one.
VALENTINE
Ha, let me see. Ay, give it me, it's mine—
Sweet ornament, that decks a thing divine.
Ah, Silvia, Silvia!   5
SPEED Madam Silvia, Madam Silvia!
VALENTINE How now, sirrah?
SPEED She is not within hearing, sir.
VALENTINE Why, sir, who bade you call her?
SPEED Your worship, sir, or else I mistook.   10
VALENTINE Well, you'll still be too forward.
SPEED And yet I was last chidden for being too slow.
VALENTINE Go to, sir. Tell me, do you know Madam
Silvia?
SPEED She that your worship loves?   15
VALENTINE Why, how know you that I am in love?
SPEED Marry, by these special marks: first, you have
learned, like Sir Proteus, to wreath your arms, like a
malcontent; to relish a love-song, like a robin redbreast;
to walk alone, like one that had the pestilence; to sigh,
like a schoolboy that had lost his ABC; to weep, like a
young wench that had buried her grandam; to fast,
like one that takes diet; to watch, like one that fears
robbing; to speak puling, like a beggar at Hallowmas.
You were wont, when you laughed, to crow like a
cock; when you walked, to walk like one of the lions.
When you fasted, it was presently after dinner; when
you looked sadly, it was for want of money. And now
you are metamorphosed with a mistress, that when I
look on you I can hardly think you my master.   30
VALENTINE Are all these things perceived in me?
SPEED They are all perceived without ye.
VALENTINE Without me? They cannot.
SPEED Without you? Nay, that's certain, for without you
were so simple, none else would. But you are so without
these follies that these follies are within you, and shine
through you like the water in an urinal, that not an
eye that sees you but is a physician to comment on
your malady.   39
VALENTINE But tell me, dost thou know my lady Silvia?
SPEED She that you gaze on so as she sits at supper?

VALENTINE Hast thou observed that? Even she I mean.

SPEED Why sir, I know her not.

VALENTINE Dost thou know her by my gazing on her, and
yet know'st her not?   45

SPEED Is she not hard-favoured, sir?

VALENTINE Not so fair, boy, as well favoured.

SPEED Sir, I know that well enough.

VALENTINE What dost thou know?

SPEED That she is not so fair as of you well favoured.   50

VALENTINE I mean that her beauty is exquisite but her
favour infinite.

SPEED That's because the one is painted and the other
out of all count.

VALENTINE How painted? And how out of count?   55

SPEED Marry, sir, so painted to make her fair that no man
counts of her beauty.

VALENTINE How esteem'st thou me? I account of her
beauty.

SPEED You never saw her since she was deformed.   60

VALENTINE How long hath she been deformed?

SPEED Ever since you loved her.

VALENTINE I have loved her ever since I saw her, and still
I see her beautiful.

SPEED If you love her you cannot see her.   65

VALENTINE Why?

SPEED Because love is blind. O that you had mine eyes,
or your own eyes had the lights they were wont to
have when you chid at Sir Proteus for going ungartered.

VALENTINE What should I see then?   70

SPEED Your own present folly and her passing deformity;
for he being in love could not see to garter his hose,
and you being in love cannot see to put on your hose.

VALENTINE Belike, boy, then you are in love, for last
morning you could not see to wipe my shoes.   75

SPEED True, sir. I was in love with my bed. I thank you,
you swinged me for my love, which makes me the
bolder to chide you for yours.

VALENTINE In conclusion, I stand affected to her.

SPEED I would you were set. So your affection would
cease.   81

VALENTINE Last night she enjoined me to write some lines
to one she loves.

SPEED And have you?

VALENTINE I have.   85

SPEED Are they not lamely writ?

VALENTINE No, boy, but as well as I can do them. Peace,
here she comes.

Enter Silvia

SPEED (*aside*) O excellent motion! O exceeding puppet!
Now will he interpret to her.   90

VALENTINE
Madam and mistress, a thousand good-morrows.

SPEED (*aside*) O, give ye good e'en! Here's a million of
manners.

SILVIA
Sir Valentine and servant, to you two thousand.

SPEED (*aside*) He should give her interest, and she gives it
him.   96

VALENTINE
As you enjoined me, I have writ your letter
Unto the secret, nameless friend of yours;
Which I was much unwilling to proceed in
But for my duty to your ladyship.   100

He gives her a letter

SILVIA
I thank you, gentle servant. 'Tis very clerkly done.

VALENTINE
Now trust me, madam, it came hardly off;
For being ignorant to whom it goes
I writ at random, very doubtfully.

SILVIA
Perchance you think too much of so much pains?

VALENTINE
No, madam. So it stead you I will write—   106
Please you command—a thousand times as much.
And yet . . .

SILVIA
A pretty period. Well, I guess the sequel.
And yet I will not name it. And yet I care not.   110
And yet, take this again.

She offers him the letter
                                          And yet I thank you,
Meaning henceforth to trouble you no more.

SPEED (*aside*)
And yet you will, and yet another yet.

VALENTINE
What means your ladyship? Do you not like it?

SILVIA
Yes, yes. The lines are very quaintly writ,   115
But since unwillingly, take them again.

She presses the letter upon him
Nay, take them.

VALENTINE   Madam, they are for you.

SILVIA
Ay, ay. You writ them, sir, at my request,
But I will none of them. They are for you.
I would have had them writ more movingly.   120

VALENTINE
Please you, I'll write your ladyship another.

SILVIA
And when it's writ, for my sake read it over,
And if it please you, so. If not, why, so.

VALENTINE
If it please me, madam? What then?

SILVIA
Why, if it please you, take it for your labour.   125
And so good morrow, servant.   *Exit*

SPEED (*aside*)
O jest unseen, inscrutable, invisible
As a nose on a man's face or a weathercock on a
steeple.
My master sues to her, and she hath taught her suitor,
He being her pupil, to become her tutor.   130
O excellent device! Was there ever heard a better?—
That my master, being scribe, to himself should write
the letter.

VALENTINE How now, sir—what, are you reasoning with yourself?

SPEED Nay, I was rhyming. 'Tis you that have the reason.

VALENTINE To do what?

SPEED To be a spokesman from Madam Silvia.

VALENTINE To whom?

SPEED To yourself. Why, she woos you by a figure.

VALENTINE What figure?   140

SPEED By a letter, I should say.

VALENTINE Why, she hath not writ to me.

SPEED What need she, when she hath made you write to yourself? Why, do you not perceive the jest?

VALENTINE No, believe me.   145

SPEED No believing you indeed, sir. But did you perceive her earnest?

VALENTINE She gave me none, except an angry word.

SPEED Why, she hath given you a letter.

VALENTINE That's the letter I writ to her friend.   150

SPEED And that letter hath she delivered, and there an end.

VALENTINE I would it were no worse.

SPEED I'll warrant you, for often have you writ to her, and she in modesty 155
Or else for want of idle time could not again reply,
Or fearing else some messenger that might her mind discover,
Herself hath taught her love himself to write unto her lover.
—All this I speak in print, for in print I found it. Why muse you, sir? 'Tis dinner-time.   160

VALENTINE I have dined.

SPEED Ay, but hearken, sir. Though the chameleon love can feed on the air, I am one that am nourished by my victuals, and would fain have meat. O, be not like your mistress—be moved, be moved!   *Exeunt*

2.2   *Enter Proteus and Julia*

PROTEUS
Have patience, gentle Julia.

JULIA
I must where is no remedy.

PROTEUS
When possibly I can I will return.

JULIA
If you turn not, you will return the sooner.
    She gives him a ring
Keep this remembrance for thy Julia's sake.   5

PROTEUS
Why then, we'll make exchange. Here, take you this.
    He gives her a ring

JULIA
And seal the bargain with a holy kiss.

⌈*They kiss*⌉

PROTEUS
Here is my hand for my true constancy.
And when that hour o'erslips me in the day
Wherein I sigh not, Julia, for thy sake,   10
The next ensuing hour some foul mischance

Torment me for my love's forgetfulness.
My father stays my coming. Answer not.
The tide is now. (*Julia weeps*) Nay, not thy tide of tears,
That tide will stay me longer than I should.   15
Julia, farewell.   *Exit Julia*
                What, gone without a word?
Ay, so true love should do. It cannot speak,
For truth hath better deeds than words to grace it.
    Enter Panthino

PANTHINO
Sir Proteus, you are stayed for.

PROTEUS   Go, I come, I come.—
Alas, this parting strikes poor lovers dumb.   *Exeunt*

2.3   *Enter Lance with his dog Crab*

LANCE (*to the audience*) Nay, 'twill be this hour ere I have done weeping. All the kind of the Lances have this very fault. I have received my proportion, like the prodigious son, and am going with Sir Proteus to the Imperial's court. I think Crab, my dog, be the sourest-natured dog that lives. My mother weeping, my father wailing, my sister crying, our maid howling, our cat wringing her hands, and all our house in a great perplexity, yet did not this cruel-hearted cur shed one tear. He is a stone, a very pebble-stone, and has no more pity in him than a dog. A Jew would have wept to have seen our parting. Why, my grandam, having no eyes, look you, wept herself blind at my parting. Nay, I'll show you the manner of it. This shoe is my father. No, this left shoe is my father. No, no, this left shoe is my mother. Nay, that cannot be so, neither. Yes, it is so, it is so, it hath the worser sole. This shoe with the hole in it is my mother, and this my father. A vengeance on't, there 'tis. Now, sir, this staff is my sister, for, look you, she is as white as a lily and as small as a wand. This hat is Nan our maid. I am the dog. No, the dog is himself, and I am the dog. O, the dog is me, and I am myself. Ay, so, so. Now come I to my father. 'Father, your blessing.' Now should not the shoe speak a word for weeping. Now should I kiss my father. Well, he weeps on. Now come I to my mother. O that she could speak now, like a moved woman. Well, I kiss her. Why, there 'tis. Here's my mother's breath up and down. Now come I to my sister. Mark the moan she makes.—Now the dog all this while sheds not a tear nor speaks a word. But see how I lay the dust with my tears.   32
    Enter Panthino

PANTHINO Lance, away, away, aboard. Thy master is shipped, and thou art to post after with oars. What's the matter? Why weep'st thou, man? Away, ass, you'll lose the tide if you tarry any longer.   36

LANCE It is no matter if the tied were lost, for it is the unkindest tied that ever any man tied.

PANTHINO What's the unkindest tide?

LANCE Why, he that's tied here, Crab my dog.   40

PANTHINO Tut, man, I mean thou'lt lose the flood, and in losing the flood, lose thy voyage, and in losing thy

voyage, lose thy master, and in losing thy master, lose
thy service, and in losing thy service—
Lance puts his hand over Panthino's mouth
Why dost thou stop my mouth?   45
LANCE For fear thou shouldst lose thy tongue.
PANTHINO Where should I lose my tongue?
LANCE In thy tale.
PANTHINO In thy tail!   49
LANCE Lose the tide, and the voyage, and the master, and
the service, and the tied? Why, man, if the river were
dry, I am able to fill it with my tears. If the wind were
down, I could drive the boat with my sighs.
PANTHINO Come, come away, man. I was sent to call
thee.   55
LANCE Sir, call me what thou darest.
PANTHINO Wilt thou go?
LANCE Well, I will go.   *Exeunt*

2.4   *Enter Valentine, Silvia, Thurio, and Speed*
SILVIA Servant!
VALENTINE Mistress?
SPEED (*to Valentine*) Master, Sir Thurio frowns on you.
VALENTINE Ay, boy, it's for love.
SPEED Not of you.   5
VALENTINE Of my mistress, then.
SPEED 'Twere good you knocked him.
SILVIA (*to Valentine*) Servant, you are sad.
VALENTINE Indeed, madam, I seem so.
THURIO Seem you that you are not?   10
VALENTINE Haply I do.
THURIO So do counterfeits.
VALENTINE So do you.
THURIO What seem I that I am not?
VALENTINE Wise.   15
THURIO What instance of the contrary?
VALENTINE Your folly.
THURIO And how quote you my folly?
VALENTINE I quote it in your jerkin.
THURIO My 'jerkin' is a doublet.   20
VALENTINE Well then, I'll double your folly.
THURIO How!
SILVIA What, angry, Sir Thurio? Do you change colour?
VALENTINE Give him leave, madam, he is a kind of chame-
leon.   25
THURIO That hath more mind to feed on your blood than
live in your air.
VALENTINE You have said, sir.
THURIO Ay, sir, and done too, for this time.
VALENTINE I know it well, sir, you always end ere you
begin.   31
SILVIA A fine volley of words, gentlemen, and quickly
shot off.
VALENTINE 'Tis indeed, madam, we thank the giver.
SILVIA Who is that, servant?   35
VALENTINE Yourself, sweet lady, for you gave the fire. Sir
Thurio borrows his wit from your ladyship's looks, and
spends what he borrows kindly in your company.
THURIO Sir, if you spend word for word with me, I shall
make your wit bankrupt.   40

VALENTINE I know it well, sir. You have an exchequer of
words, and, I think, no other treasure to give your
followers. For it appears by their bare liveries that they
live by your bare words.
SILVIA No more, gentlemen, no more. Here comes my
father.   46
Enter the Duke
DUKE
Now, daughter Silvia, you are hard beset.
Sir Valentine, your father is in good health,
What say you to a letter from your friends
Of much good news?
VALENTINE   My lord, I will be thankful   50
To any happy messenger from thence.
DUKE
Know ye Don Antonio, your countryman?
VALENTINE
Ay, my good lord, I know the gentleman
To be of worth, and worthy estimation,
And not without desert so well reputed.   55
DUKE Hath he not a son?
VALENTINE
Ay, my good lord, a son that well deserves
The honour and regard of such a father.
DUKE You know him well?
VALENTINE
I knew him as myself, for from our infancy   60
We have conversed, and spent our hours together.
And though myself have been an idle truant,
Omitting the sweet benefit of time
To clothe mine age with angel-like perfection,
Yet hath Sir Proteus—for that's his name—   65
Made use and fair advantage of his days:
His years but young, but his experience old;
His head unmellowed, but his judgement ripe.
And in a word—for far behind his worth
Comes all the praises that I now bestow—   70
He is complete, in feature and in mind,
With all good grace to grace a gentleman.
DUKE
Beshrew me, sir, but if he make this good
He is as worthy for an empress' love
As meet to be an emperor's counsellor.   75
Well, sir, this gentleman is come to me
With commendation from great potentates,
And here he means to spend his time awhile.
I think 'tis no unwelcome news to you.
VALENTINE
Should I have wished a thing it had been he.   80
DUKE
Welcome him then according to his worth.
Silvia, I speak to you, and you, Sir Thurio;
For Valentine, I need not cite him to it.
I will send him hither to you presently.   *Exit*
VALENTINE
This is the gentleman I told your ladyship   85
Had come along with me, but that his mistress
Did hold his eyes locked in her crystal looks.

SILVIA
Belike that now she hath enfranchised them
Upon some other pawn for fealty.
VALENTINE
Nay, sure, I think she holds them prisoners still. 90
SILVIA
Nay, then he should be blind, and being blind
How could he see his way to seek out you?
VALENTINE
Why, lady, love hath twenty pair of eyes.
THURIO
They say that love hath not an eye at all.
VALENTINE
To see such lovers, Thurio, as yourself. 95
Upon a homely object love can wink.
SILVIA
Have done, have done. Here comes the gentleman.
Enter Proteus
VALENTINE
Welcome, dear Proteus. Mistress, I beseech you
Confirm his welcome with some special favour.
SILVIA
His worth is warrant for his welcome hither, 100
If this be he you oft have wished to hear from.
VALENTINE
Mistress, it is. Sweet lady, entertain him
To be my fellow-servant to your ladyship.
SILVIA
Too low a mistress for so high a servant.
PROTEUS
Not so, sweet lady, but too mean a servant 105
To have a look of such a worthy mistress.
VALENTINE
Leave off discourse of disability.
Sweet lady, entertain him for your servant.
PROTEUS
My duty will I boast of, nothing else.
SILVIA
And duty never yet did want his meed. 110
Servant, you are welcome to a worthless mistress.
PROTEUS
I'll die on him that says so but yourself.
SILVIA
That you are welcome?
PROTEUS   That you are worthless.
⌈*Enter a Servant*⌉
⌈SERVANT⌉
Madam, my lord your father would speak with you.
SILVIA
I wait upon his pleasure.   ⌈*Exit the Servant*⌉
         Come, Sir Thurio, 115
Go with me. Once more, new servant, welcome.
I'll leave you to confer of home affairs.
When you have done, we look to hear from you.
PROTEUS
We'll both attend upon your ladyship.
         Exeunt Silvia and Thurio

VALENTINE
Now tell me, how do all from whence you came? 120
PROTEUS
Your friends are well, and have them much
    commended.
VALENTINE
And how do yours?
PROTEUS   I left them all in health.
VALENTINE
How does your lady, and how thrives your love?
PROTEUS
My tales of love were wont to weary you.
I know you joy not in a love-discourse. 125
VALENTINE
Ay, Proteus, but that life is altered now.
I have done penance for contemning love,
Whose high imperious thoughts have punished me
With bitter fasts, with penitential groans,
With nightly tears and daily heart-sore sighs. 130
For in revenge of my contempt of love
Love hath chased sleep from my enthrallèd eyes,
And made them watchers of mine own heart's sorrow.
O gentle Proteus, love's a mighty lord,
And hath so humbled me as I confess 135
There is no woe to his correction,
Nor to his service no such joy on earth.
Now, no discourse except it be of love.
Now can I break my fast, dine, sup, and sleep
Upon the very naked name of love. 140
PROTEUS
Enough. I read your fortune in your eye.
Was this the idol that you worship so?
VALENTINE
Even she; and is she not a heavenly saint?
PROTEUS
No, but she is an earthly paragon.
VALENTINE
Call her divine.
PROTEUS   I will not flatter her. 145
VALENTINE
O flatter me; for love delights in praises.
PROTEUS
When I was sick you gave me bitter pills,
And I must minister the like to you.
VALENTINE
Then speak the truth by her; if not divine,
Yet let her be a principality, 150
Sovereign to all the creatures on the earth.
PROTEUS
Except my mistress.
VALENTINE   Sweet, except not any,
Except thou wilt except against my love.
PROTEUS
Have I not reason to prefer mine own?
VALENTINE
And I will help thee to prefer her, too. 155
She shall be dignified with this high honour,

To bear my lady's train, lest the base earth
Should from her vesture chance to steal a kiss
And, of so great a favour growing proud,
Disdain to root the summer-swelling flower,   160
And make rough winter everlastingly.

PROTEUS
Why, Valentine, what braggartism is this?

VALENTINE
Pardon me, Proteus, all I can is nothing
To her whose worth makes other worthies nothing.
She is alone.

PROTEUS   Then let her alone.   165

VALENTINE
Not for the world. Why man, she is mine own,
And I as rich in having such a jewel
As twenty seas, if all their sand were pearl,
The water nectar, and the rocks pure gold.
Forgive me that I do not dream on thee   170
Because thou seest me dote upon my love.
My foolish rival, that her father likes
Only for his possessions are so huge,
Is gone with her along, and I must after;
For love, thou know'st, is full of jealousy.   175

PROTEUS But she loves you?

VALENTINE
Ay, and we are betrothed. Nay more, our marriage
    hour,
With all the cunning manner of our flight,
Determined of: how I must climb her window,
The ladder made of cords, and all the means   180
Plotted and 'greed on for my happiness.
Good Proteus, go with me to my chamber
In these affairs to aid me with thy counsel.

PROTEUS
Go on before. I shall enquire you forth.
I must unto the road, to disembark   185
Some necessaries that I needs must use,
And then I'll presently attend you.

VALENTINE Will you make haste?

PROTEUS I will.   *Exit Valentine*

Even as one heat another heat expels,   190
Or as one nail by strength drives out another,
So the remembrance of my former love
Is by a newer object quite forgotten.
Is it mine eye, or Valentine's praise,
Her true perfection, or my false transgression   195
That makes me, reasonless, to reason thus?
She is fair, and so is Julia that I love—
That I did love, for now my love is thawed,
Which like a waxen image 'gainst a fire
Bears no impression of the thing it was.   200
Methinks my zeal to Valentine is cold,
And that I love him not as I was wont.
O, but I love his lady too-too much,
And that's the reason I love him so little.
How shall I dote on her with more advice,   205
That thus without advice begin to love her?
'Tis but her picture I have yet beheld,

And that hath dazzled my reason's light.
But when I look on her perfections
There is no reason but I shall be blind.   210
If I can check my erring love I will,
If not, to compass her I'll use my skill.   *Exit*

2.5   *Enter Speed, and Lance with his dog Crab*

SPEED Lance, by mine honesty, welcome to Milan.

LANCE Forswear not thyself, sweet youth, for I am not
welcome. I reckon this always, that a man is never
undone till he be hanged, nor never welcome to a place
till some certain shot be paid and the hostess say
'Welcome'.   6

SPEED Come on, you madcap. I'll to the alehouse with
you presently, where, for one shot of five pence, thou
shalt have five thousand welcomes. But sirrah, how
did thy master part with Madam Julia?   10

LANCE Marry, after they closed in earnest they parted
very fairly in jest.

SPEED But shall she marry him?

LANCE No.

SPEED How then, shall he marry her?   15

LANCE No, neither.

SPEED What, are they broken?

LANCE No, they are both as whole as a fish.

SPEED Why then, how stands the matter with them?

LANCE Marry, thus: when it stands well with him it
stands well with her.   21

SPEED What an ass art thou! I understand thee not.

LANCE What a block art thou, that thou canst not! My
staff understands me.

SPEED What thou sayst?   25

LANCE Ay, and what I do too. Look thee, I'll but lean,
and my staff under-stands me.

SPEED It stands under thee indeed.

LANCE Why, stand-under and under-stand is all one.

SPEED But tell me true, will't be a match?   30

LANCE Ask my dog. If he say 'Ay', it will. If he say 'No',
it will. If he shake his tail and say nothing, it will.

SPEED The conclusion is, then, that it will.

LANCE Thou shalt never get such a secret from me but
by a parable.   35

SPEED 'Tis well that I get it so. But Lance, how sayst thou
that my master is become a notable lover?

LANCE I never knew him otherwise.

SPEED Than how?

LANCE A notable lubber, as thou reportest him to be.   40

SPEED Why, thou whoreson ass, thou mistak'st me.

LANCE Why, fool, I meant not thee, I meant thy master.

SPEED I tell thee my master is become a hot lover.

LANCE Why, I tell thee I care not, though he burn himself
in love. If thou wilt, go with me to the alehouse. If not,
thou art an Hebrew, a Jew, and not worth the name
of a Christian.   47

SPEED Why?

LANCE Because thou hast not so much charity in thee as
to go to the ale with a Christian. Wilt thou go?   50

SPEED At thy service.   *Exeunt*

2.6   *Enter Proteus*

PROTEUS

To leave my Julia shall I be forsworn;
To love fair Silvia shall I be forsworn;
To wrong my friend I shall be much forsworn.
And e'en that power which gave me first my oath
Provokes me to this three-fold perjury.   5
Love bade me swear, and love bids me forswear.
O sweet-suggesting love, if thou hast sinned
Teach me, thy tempted subject, to excuse it.
At first I did adore a twinkling star,
But now I worship a celestial sun.   10
Unheedful vows may heedfully be broken,
And he wants wit that wants resolvèd will
To learn his wit t'exchange the bad for better.
Fie, fie, unreverent tongue, to call her bad
Whose sovereignty so oft thou hast preferred   15
With twenty thousand soul-confirming oaths.
I cannot leave to love, and yet I do.
But there I leave to love where I should love.
Julia I lose, and Valentine I lose.
If I keep them I needs must lose myself.   20
If I lose them, thus find I by their loss
For Valentine, myself, for Julia, Silvia.
I to myself am dearer than a friend,
For love is still most precious in itself,
And Silvia—witness heaven that made her fair—   25
Shows Julia but a swarthy Ethiope.
I will forget that Julia is alive,
Rememb'ring that my love to her is dead,
And Valentine I'll hold an enemy,
Aiming at Silvia as a sweeter friend.   30
I cannot now prove constant to myself
Without some treachery used to Valentine.
This night he meaneth with a corded ladder
To climb celestial Silvia's chamber-window,
Myself in counsel his competitor.   35
Now presently I'll give her father notice
Of their disguising and pretended flight,
Who, all enraged, will banish Valentine;
For Thurio he intends shall wed his daughter.
But Valentine being gone, I'll quickly cross   40
By some sly trick blunt Thurio's dull proceeding.
Love, lend me wings to make my purpose swift,
As thou hast lent me wit to plot this drift.   *Exit*

2.7   *Enter Julia and Lucetta*

JULIA

Counsel, Lucetta. Gentle girl, assist me,
And e'en in kind love I do conjure thee,
Who art the table wherein all my thoughts
Are visibly charactered and engraved,
To lesson me, and tell me some good mean   5
How with my honour I may undertake
A journey to my loving Proteus.

LUCETTA

Alas, the way is wearisome and long.

JULIA

A true-devoted pilgrim is not weary
To measure kingdoms with his feeble steps.   10
Much less shall she that hath love's wings to fly,
And when the flight is made to one so dear,
Of such divine perfection as Sir Proteus.

LUCETTA

Better forbear till Proteus make return.

JULIA

O, know'st thou not his looks are my soul's food?   15
Pity the dearth that I have pinèd in
By longing for that food so long a time.
Didst thou but know the inly touch of love
Thou wouldst as soon go kindle fire with snow
As seek to quench the fire of love with words.   20

LUCETTA

I do not seek to quench your love's hot fire,
But qualify the fire's extreme rage,
Lest it should burn above the bounds of reason.

JULIA

The more thou damm'st it up, the more it burns.
The current that with gentle murmur glides,   25
Thou know'st, being stopped, impatiently doth rage.
But when his fair course is not hinderèd
He makes sweet music with th'enamelled stones,
Giving a gentle kiss to every sedge
He overtaketh in his pilgrimage.   30
And so by many winding nooks he strays
With willing sport to the wild ocean.
Then let me go, and hinder not my course.
I'll be as patient as a gentle stream,
And make a pastime of each weary step   35
Till the last step have brought me to my love.
And there I'll rest as after much turmoil
A blessèd soul doth in Elysium.

LUCETTA

But in what habit will you go along?

JULIA

Not like a woman, for I would prevent   40
The loose encounters of lascivious men.
Gentle Lucetta, fit me with such weeds
As may beseem some well-reputed page.

LUCETTA

Why then, your ladyship must cut your hair.

JULIA

No, girl, I'll knit it up in silken strings   45
With twenty odd-conceited true-love knots.
To be fantastic may become a youth
Of greater time than I shall show to be.

LUCETTA

What fashion, madam, shall I make your breeches?

JULIA

That fits as well as 'Tell me, good my lord,   50
What compass will you wear your farthingale?'
Why, e'en what fashion thou best likes, Lucetta.

LUCETTA

You must needs have them with a codpiece, madam.

JULIA
    Out, out, Lucetta. That will be ill-favoured.

LUCETTA
    A round hose, madam, now's not worth a pin   55
    Unless you have a codpiece to stick pins on.

JULIA
    Lucetta, as thou lov'st me let me have
    What thou think'st meet and is most mannerly.
    But tell me, wench, how will the world repute me
    For undertaking so unstaid a journey?   60
    I fear me it will make me scandalized.

LUCETTA
    If you think so, then stay at home, and go not.

JULIA Nay, that I will not.

LUCETTA
    Then never dream on infamy, but go.
    If Proteus like your journey when you come,   65
    No matter who's displeased when you are gone.
    I fear me he will scarce be pleased withal.

JULIA
    That is the least, Lucetta, of my fear.
    A thousand oaths, an ocean of his tears,
    And instances of infinite of love   70
    Warrant me welcome to my Proteus.

LUCETTA
    All these are servants to deceitful men.

JULIA
    Base men, that use them to so base effect.
    But truer stars did govern Proteus' birth.
    His words are bonds, his oaths are oracles,   75
    His love sincere, his thoughts immaculate,
    His tears pure messengers sent from his heart,
    His heart as far from fraud as heaven from earth.

LUCETTA
    Pray heaven he prove so when you come to him.

JULIA
    Now, as thou lov'st me, do him not that wrong   80
    To bear a hard opinion of his truth.
    Only deserve my love by loving him,
    And presently go with me to my chamber
    To take a note of what I stand in need of
    To furnish me upon my longing journey.   85
    All that is mine I leave at thy dispose,
    My goods, my lands, my reputation;
    Only in lieu thereof dispatch me hence.
    Come, answer not, but to it presently.
    I am impatient of my tarriance.   *Exeunt*

3.1 *Enter Duke, Thurio, and Proteus*

DUKE
    Sir Thurio, give us leave, I pray, awhile.
    We have some secrets to confer about.   *Exit Thurio*
    Now tell me, Proteus, what's your will with me?

PROTEUS
    My gracious lord, that which I would discover
    The law of friendship bids me to conceal.   5
    But when I call to mind your gracious favours
    Done to me, undeserving as I am,

My duty pricks me on to utter that
Which else no worldly good should draw from me.
Know, worthy prince, Sir Valentine my friend   10
This night intends to steal away your daughter.
Myself am one made privy to the plot.
I know you have determined to bestow her
On Thurio, whom your gentle daughter hates,
And should she thus be stol'n away from you   15
It would be much vexation to your age.
Thus, for my duty's sake, I rather chose
To cross my friend in his intended drift
Than by concealing it heap on your head
A pack of sorrows which would press you down,   20
Being unprevented, to your timeless grave.

DUKE
    Proteus, I thank thee for thine honest care,
    Which to requite command me while I live.
    This love of theirs myself have often seen,
    Haply, when they have judged me fast asleep,   25
    And oftentimes have purposed to forbid
    Sir Valentine her company and my court.
    But fearing lest my jealous aim might err,
    And so unworthily disgrace the man—
    A rashness that I ever yet have shunned—   30
    I gave him gentle looks, thereby to find
    That which thyself hast now disclosed to me.
    And that thou mayst perceive my fear of this,
    Knowing that tender youth is soon suggested,
    I nightly lodge her in an upper tower,   35
    The key whereof myself have ever kept;
    And thence she cannot be conveyed away.

PROTEUS
    Know, noble lord, they have devised a mean
    How he her chamber-window will ascend,
    And with a corded ladder fetch her down,   40
    For which the youthful lover now is gone,
    And this way comes he with it presently,
    Where, if it please you, you may intercept him.
    But, good my lord, do it so cunningly
    That my discovery be not aimèd at;   45
    For love of you, not hate unto my friend,
    Hath made me publisher of this pretence.

DUKE
    Upon mine honour, he shall never know
    That I had any light from thee of this.

PROTEUS
    Adieu, my lord. Sir Valentine is coming.   *Exit*
                    Enter Valentine

DUKE
    Sir Valentine, whither away so fast?

VALENTINE
    Please it your grace, there is a messenger
    That stays to bear my letters to my friends,
    And I am going to deliver them.

DUKE Be they of much import?   55

VALENTINE
    The tenor of them doth but signify
    My health and happy being at your court.

DUKE
Nay then, no matter. Stay with me awhile.
I am to break with thee of some affairs
That touch me near, wherein thou must be secret. 60
'Tis not unknown to thee that I have sought
To match my friend Sir Thurio to my daughter.
VALENTINE
I know it well, my lord; and sure the match
Were rich and honourable. Besides, the gentleman
Is full of virtue, bounty, worth, and qualities 65
Beseeming such a wife as your fair daughter.
Cannot your grace win her to fancy him?
DUKE
No, trust me. She is peevish, sullen, froward,
Proud, disobedient, stubborn, lacking duty,
Neither regarding that she is my child 70
Nor fearing me as if I were her father.
And may I say to thee, this pride of hers
Upon advice hath drawn my love from her,
And where I thought the remnant of mine age
Should have been cherished by her child-like duty, 75
I now am full resolved to take a wife,
And turn her out to who will take her in.
Then let her beauty be her wedding dower,
For me and my possessions she esteems not.
VALENTINE
What would your grace have me to do in this? 80
DUKE
There is a lady of Verona here
Whom I affect, but she is nice, and coy,
And naught esteems my agèd eloquence.
Now therefore would I have thee to my tutor—
For long agone I have forgot to court, 85
Besides, the fashion of the time is changed—
How and which way I may bestow myself
To be regarded in her sun-bright eye.
VALENTINE
Win her with gifts if she respect not words.
Dumb jewels often in their silent kind 90
More than quick words do move a woman's mind.
DUKE
But she did scorn a present that I sent her.
VALENTINE
A woman sometime scorns what best contents her.
Send her another. Never give her o'er,
For scorn at first makes after-love the more. 95
If she do frown, 'tis not in hate of you,
But rather to beget more love in you.
If she do chide, 'tis not to have you gone,
Forwhy the fools are mad if left alone.
Take no repulse, whatever she doth say: 100
For 'Get you gone' she doth not mean 'Away'.
Flatter and praise, commend, extol their graces;
Though ne'er so black, say they have angels' faces.
That man that hath a tongue I say is no man
If with his tongue he cannot win a woman. 105
DUKE
But she I mean is promised by her friends

Unto a youthful gentleman of worth,
And kept severely from resort of men,
That no man hath access by day to her.
VALENTINE
Why then I would resort to her by night. 110
DUKE
Ay, but the doors be locked and keys kept safe,
That no man hath recourse to her by night.
VALENTINE
What lets but one may enter at her window?
DUKE
Her chamber is aloft, far from the ground,
And built so shelving that one cannot climb it 115
Without apparent hazard of his life.
VALENTINE
Why then, a ladder quaintly made of cords
To cast up, with a pair of anchoring hooks,
Would serve to scale another Hero's tower,
So bold Leander would adventure it. 120
DUKE
Now as thou art a gentleman of blood,
Advise me where I may have such a ladder.
VALENTINE
When would you use it? Pray sir, tell me that.
DUKE
This very night; for love is like a child
That longs for everything that he can come by. 125
VALENTINE
By seven o'clock I'll get you such a ladder.
DUKE
But hark thee: I will go to her alone.
How shall I best convey the ladder thither?
VALENTINE
It will be light, my lord, that you may bear it
Under a cloak that is of any length. 130
DUKE
A cloak as long as thine will serve the turn?
VALENTINE
Ay, my good lord.
DUKE   Then let me see thy cloak,
I'll get me one of such another length.
VALENTINE
Why, any cloak will serve the turn, my lord.
DUKE
How shall I fashion me to wear a cloak? 135
I pray thee let me feel thy cloak upon me.
    He lifts Valentine's cloak and finds a letter and a
    rope-ladder
What letter is this same? What's here? 'To Silvia'?
And here an engine fit for my proceeding.
I'll be so bold to break the seal for once.
(*Reads*)
'My thoughts do harbour with my Silvia nightly, 140
    And slaves they are to me, that send them flying.
O, could their master come and go as lightly,
    Himself would lodge where, senseless, they are
        lying.

My herald thoughts in thy pure bosom rest them,
  While I, their king, that thither them importune,
Do curse the grace that with such grace hath blessed
  them,   146
  Because myself do want my servants' fortune.
I curse myself for they are sent by me,
  That they should harbour where their lord should
  be.'
What's here?   150
'Silvia, this night I will enfranchise thee'?
'Tis so, and here's the ladder for the purpose.
Why, Phaëton, for thou art Merops' son
Wilt thou aspire to guide the heavenly car,
And with thy daring folly burn the world?   155
Wilt thou reach stars because they shine on thee?
Go, base intruder, over-weening slave,
Bestow thy fawning smiles on equal mates,
And think my patience, more than thy desert,
Is privilege for thy departure hence.   160
Thank me for this more than for all the favours
Which, all too much, I have bestowed on thee.
But if thou linger in my territories
Longer than swiftest expedition
Will give thee time to leave our royal court,   165
By heaven, my wrath shall far exceed the love
I ever bore my daughter or thyself.
Be gone. I will not hear thy vain excuse,
But as thou lov'st thy life, make speed from hence.
                                                                   Exit

VALENTINE
And why not death, rather than living torment?   170
To die is to be banished from myself,
And Silvia is my self. Banished from her
Is self from self, a deadly banishment.
What light is light, if Silvia be not seen?
What joy is joy, if Silvia be not by—   175
Unless it be to think that she is by,
And feed upon the shadow of perfection.
Except I be by Silvia in the night
There is no music in the nightingale.
Unless I look on Silvia in the day   180
There is no day for me to look upon.
She is my essence, and I leave to be
If I be not by her fair influence
Fostered, illumined, cherished, kept alive.
I fly not death to fly his deadly doom.   185
Tarry I here I but attend on death,
But fly I hence, I fly away from life.
      Enter Proteus and Lance
PROTEUS Run, boy, run, run, and seek him out.
LANCE So-ho, so-ho!
PROTEUS What seest thou?   190
LANCE Him we go to find. There's not a hair on's head
  but 'tis a Valentine.
PROTEUS Valentine?
VALENTINE No.
PROTEUS Who then—his spirit?   195
VALENTINE Neither.

PROTEUS What then?
VALENTINE Nothing.
LANCE Can nothing speak?
      He threatens Valentine
  Master, shall I strike?   200
PROTEUS Who wouldst thou strike?
LANCE Nothing.
PROTEUS Villain, forbear.
LANCE Why, sir, I'll strike nothing. I pray you—
PROTEUS
  Sirrah, I say forbear. Friend Valentine, a word.   205
VALENTINE
My ears are stopped, and cannot hear good news,
So much of bad already hath possessed them.
PROTEUS
Then in dumb silence will I bury mine,
For they are harsh, untuneable, and bad.
VALENTINE
Is Silvia dead?
PROTEUS   No, Valentine.   210
VALENTINE
No Valentine indeed, for sacred Silvia.
Hath she forsworn me?
PROTEUS   No, Valentine.
VALENTINE
No Valentine, if Silvia have forsworn me.
What is your news?   214
LANCE Sir, there is a proclamation that you are vanished.
PROTEUS
That thou art banished. O that's the news:
From hence, from Silvia, and from me thy friend.
VALENTINE
O, I have fed upon this woe already,
And now excess of it will make me surfeit.
Doth Silvia know that I am banishèd?   220
PROTEUS
Ay, ay; and she hath offered to the doom,
Which unreversed stands in effectual force,
A sea of melting pearl, which some call tears.
Those at her father's churlish feet she tendered,
With them, upon her knees, her humble self,   225
Wringing her hands, whose whiteness so became them
As if but now they waxèd pale, for woe.
But neither bended knees, pure hands held up,
Sad sighs, deep groans, nor silver-shedding tears
Could penetrate her uncompassionate sire,   230
But Valentine, if he be ta'en, must die.
Besides, her intercession chafed him so
When she for thy repeal was suppliant
That to close prison he commanded her,
With many bitter threats of biding there.   235
VALENTINE
No more, unless the next word that thou speak'st
Have some malignant power upon my life.
If so I pray thee breathe it in mine ear,
As ending anthem of my endless dolour.
PROTEUS
Cease to lament for that thou canst not help,   240

And study help for that which thou lament'st.
Time is the nurse and breeder of all good.
Here if thou stay thou canst not see thy love.
Besides, thy staying will abridge thy life.
Hope is a lover's staff. Walk hence with that,   245
And manage it against despairing thoughts.
Thy letters may be here, though thou art hence,
Which, being writ to me, shall be delivered
Even in the milk-white bosom of thy love.
The time now serves not to expostulate.   250
Come, I'll convey thee through the city gate,
And ere I part with thee confer at large
Of all that may concern thy love affairs.
As thou lov'st Silvia, though not for thyself,
Regard thy danger, and along with me.   255

VALENTINE
I pray thee, Lance, an if thou seest my boy
Bid him make haste, and meet me at the North Gate.

PROTEUS
Go, sirrah, find him out. Come, Valentine.

VALENTINE
O my dear Silvia! Hapless Valentine.
                    Exeunt Proteus and Valentine

LANCE I am but a fool, look you, and yet I have the wit
to think my master is a kind of a knave. But that's
all one, if he be but one knave. He lives not now that
knows me to be in love, yet I am in love, but a team
of horse shall not pluck that from me, nor who 'tis I
love; and yet 'tis a woman, but what woman I will
not tell myself; and yet 'tis a milkmaid; yet 'tis not a
maid, for she hath had gossips; yet 'tis a maid, for she
is her master's maid, and serves for wages. She hath
more qualities than a water-spaniel, which is much in
a bare Christian.   270
    He takes out a paper
Here is the catalogue of her conditions. 'Imprimis, she
can fetch and carry'—why, a horse can do no more.
Nay, a horse cannot fetch, but only carry, therefore is
she better than a jade. '*Item*, she can milk.' Look you,
a sweet virtue in a maid with clean hands.   275
    Enter Speed
SPEED How now, Signor Lance, what news with your
mastership?

LANCE With my master's ship? Why, it is at sea.

SPEED Well, your old vice still, mistake the word. What
news then in your paper?   280

LANCE The blackest news that ever thou heard'st.

SPEED Why, man, how 'black'?

LANCE Why, as black as ink.

SPEED Let me read them.

LANCE Fie on thee, jolt-head, thou canst not read.   285

SPEED Thou liest. I can.

LANCE I will try thee. Tell me this: who begot thee?

SPEED Marry, the son of my grandfather.

LANCE O illiterate loiterer, it was the son of thy grandmother. This proves that thou canst not read.   290

SPEED Come, fool, come. Try me in thy paper.

LANCE (*giving Speed the paper*) There: and Saint Nicholas
be thy speed.

SPEED '*Imprimis*, she can milk.'

LANCE Ay, that she can.   295

SPEED '*Item*, she brews good ale.'

LANCE And thereof comes the proverb 'Blessing of your
heart, you brew good ale'.

SPEED '*Item*, she can sew.'

LANCE That's as much as to say 'Can she so?'   300

SPEED '*Item*, she can knit.'

LANCE What need a man care for a stock with a wench
when she can knit him a stock?

SPEED '*Item*, she can wash and scour.'

LANCE A special virtue, for then she need not be washed
and scoured.   306

SPEED '*Item*, she can spin.'

LANCE Then may I set the world on wheels, when she
can spin for her living.

SPEED '*Item*, she hath many nameless virtues.'   310

LANCE That's as much as to say 'bastard virtues', that
indeed know not their fathers, and therefore have no
names.

SPEED Here follows her vices.

LANCE Close at the heels of her virtues.   315

SPEED '*Item*, she is not to be broken with fasting, in
respect of her breath.'

LANCE Well, that fault may be mended with a breakfast.
Read on.

SPEED '*Item*, she hath a sweet mouth.'   320

LANCE That makes amends for her sour breath.

SPEED '*Item*, she doth talk in her sleep.'

LANCE It's no matter for that, so she sleep not in her talk.

SPEED '*Item*, she is slow in words.'   324

LANCE O villain, that set this down among her vices! To
be slow in words is a woman's only virtue. I pray thee
out with't, and place it for her chief virtue.

SPEED '*Item*, she is proud.'

LANCE Out with that, too. It was Eve's legacy, and cannot
be ta'en from her.   330

SPEED '*Item*, she hath no teeth.'

LANCE I care not for that, neither, because I love crusts.

SPEED '*Item*, she is curst.'

LANCE Well, the best is, she hath no teeth to bite.

SPEED '*Item*, she will often praise her liquor.'   335

LANCE If her liquor be good, she shall. If she will not, I
will; for good things should be praised.

SPEED '*Item*, she is too liberal.'

LANCE Of her tongue she cannot, for that's writ down
she is slow of. Of her purse she shall not, for that I'll
keep shut. Now of another thing she may, and that
cannot I help. Well, proceed.

SPEED '*Item*, she hath more hair than wit, and more faults
than hairs, and more wealth than faults.'   344

LANCE Stop there. I'll have her. She was mine and not
mine twice or thrice in that last article. Rehearse that
once more.

SPEED '*Item*, she hath more hair than wit'—

LANCE 'More hair than wit.' It may be. I'll prove it: the cover of the salt hides the salt, and therefore it is more than the salt. The hair that covers the wit is more than the wit, for the greater hides the less. What's next?

SPEED 'And more faults than hairs'—

LANCE That's monstrous. O that that were out!

SPEED 'And more wealth than faults.'   355

LANCE Why, that word makes the faults gracious. Well, I'll have her, and if it be a match—as nothing is impossible—

SPEED What then?

LANCE Why then will I tell thee that thy master stays for thee at the North Gate.

SPEED For me?

LANCE For thee? Ay, who art thou? He hath stayed for a better man than thee.

SPEED And must I go to him?   365

LANCE Thou must run to him, for thou hast stayed so long that going will scarce serve the turn.

SPEED Why didst not tell me sooner? Pox of your love letters!   *Exit*

LANCE Now will he be swinged for reading my letter. An unmannerly slave, that will thrust himself into secrets. I'll after, to rejoice in the boy's correction.   *Exit*

3.2   *Enter the Duke and Thurio*

DUKE
Sir Thurio, fear not but that she will love you
Now Valentine is banished from her sight.

THURIO
Since his exile she hath despised me most,
Forsworn my company, and railed at me,
That I am desperate of obtaining her.   5

DUKE
This weak impress of love is as a figure
Trenchèd in ice, which with an hour's heat
Dissolves to water and doth lose his form.
A little time will melt her frozen thoughts,
And worthless Valentine shall be forgot.   10
Enter Proteus
How now, Sir Proteus, is your countryman,
According to our proclamation, gone?

PROTEUS Gone, my good lord.

DUKE
My daughter takes his going grievously?

PROTEUS
A little time, my lord, will kill that grief.   15

DUKE
So I believe, but Thurio thinks not so.
Proteus, the good conceit I hold of thee—
For thou hast shown some sign of good desert—
Makes me the better to confer with thee.

PROTEUS
Longer than I prove loyal to your grace   20
Let me not live to look upon your grace.

DUKE
Thou know'st how willingly I would effect
The match between Sir Thurio and my daughter?

PROTEUS I do, my lord.

DUKE
And also, I think, thou art not ignorant   25
How she opposes her against my will?

PROTEUS
She did, my lord, when Valentine was here.

DUKE
Ay, and perversely she persevers so.
What might we do to make the girl forget
The love of Valentine, and love Sir Thurio?   30

PROTEUS
The best way is to slander Valentine
With falsehood, cowardice, and poor descent,
Three things that women highly hold in hate.

DUKE
Ay, but she'll think that it is spoke in hate.

PROTEUS
Ay, if his enemy deliver it.   35
Therefore it must with circumstance be spoken
By one whom she esteemeth as his friend.

DUKE
Then you must undertake to slander him.

PROTEUS
And that, my lord, I shall be loath to do.
'Tis an ill office for a gentleman,   40
Especially against his very friend.

DUKE
Where your good word cannot advantage him
Your slander never can endamage him.
Therefore the office is indifferent,
Being entreated to it by your friend.   45

PROTEUS
You have prevailed, my lord. If I can do it
By aught that I can speak in his dispraise
She shall not long continue love to him.
But say this weed her love from Valentine,
It follows not that she will love Sir Thurio.   50

THURIO
Therefore, as you unwind her love from him,
Lest it should ravel and be good to none
You must provide to bottom it on me;
Which must be done by praising me as much
As you in worth dispraise Sir Valentine.   55

DUKE
And Proteus, we dare trust you in this kind
Because we know, on Valentine's report,
You are already love's firm votary,
And cannot soon revolt, and change your mind.
Upon this warrant shall you have access   60
Where you with Silvia may confer at large.
For she is lumpish, heavy, melancholy,
And for your friend's sake will be glad of you;
Where you may temper her, by your persuasion,
To hate young Valentine and love my friend.   65

PROTEUS
As much as I can do, I will effect.
But you, Sir Thurio, are not sharp enough.
You must lay lime to tangle her desires

By wailful sonnets, whose composèd rhymes
Should be full-fraught with serviceable vows. 70

DUKE

Ay, much is the force of heaven-bred poesy.

PROTEUS

Say that upon the altar of her beauty
You sacrifice your tears, your sighs, your heart.
Write till your ink be dry, and with your tears
Moist it again; and frame some feeling line 75
That may discover such integrity;
For Orpheus' lute was strung with poets' sinews,
Whose golden touch could soften steel and stones,
Make tigers tame, and huge leviathans
Forsake unsounded deeps to dance on sands. 80
After your dire-lamenting elegies,
Visit by night your lady's chamber-window
With some sweet consort. To their instruments
Tune a deploring dump. The night's dead silence
Will well become such sweet-complaining grievance.
This, or else nothing, will inherit her. 86

DUKE

This discipline shows thou hast been in love.

THURIO

And thy advice this night I'll put in practice.
Therefore, sweet Proteus, my direction-giver,
Let us into the city presently 90
To sort some gentlemen well skilled in music.
I have a sonnet that will serve the turn
To give the onset to thy good advice.

DUKE About it, gentlemen.

PROTEUS

We'll wait upon your grace till after supper, 95
And afterward determine our proceedings.

DUKE

Even now about it. I will pardon you.

Exeunt Thurio and Proteus at one door, and the
Duke at another

4.1   *Enter the Outlaws*

FIRST OUTLAW

Fellows, stand fast. I see a passenger.

SECOND OUTLAW

If there be ten, shrink not, but down with 'em.

Enter Valentine and Speed

THIRD OUTLAW

Stand, sir, and throw us that you have about ye.
If not, we'll make you sit, and rifle you.

SPEED (*to Valentine*)

Sir, we are undone. These are the villains 5
That all the travellers do fear so much.

VALENTINE (*to the Outlaws*) My friends.

FIRST OUTLAW

That's not so, sir. We are your enemies.

SECOND OUTLAW Peace. We'll hear him.

THIRD OUTLAW Ay, by my beard will we. For he is a proper
man. 11

VALENTINE

Then know that I have little wealth to lose.
A man I am, crossed with adversity.

My riches are these poor habiliments,
Of which if you should here disfurnish me 15
You take the sum and substance that I have.

SECOND OUTLAW Whither travel you?

VALENTINE To Verona.

FIRST OUTLAW Whence came you?

VALENTINE From Milan. 20

THIRD OUTLAW Have you long sojourned there?

VALENTINE

Some sixteen months, and longer might have stayed
If crooked fortune had not thwarted me.

FIRST OUTLAW

What, were you banished thence?

VALENTINE   I was.

SECOND OUTLAW   For what offence?

VALENTINE

For that which now torments me to rehearse. 25
I killed a man, whose death I much repent,
But yet I slew him manfully, in fight,
Without false vantage or base treachery.

FIRST OUTLAW

Why, ne'er repent it, if it were done so.
But were you banished for so small a fault? 30

VALENTINE

I was, and held me glad of such a doom.

SECOND OUTLAW Have you the tongues?

VALENTINE

My youthful travel therein made me happy,
Or else I had been often miserable.

THIRD OUTLAW

By the bare scalp of Robin Hood's fat friar, 35
This fellow were a king for our wild faction.

FIRST OUTLAW

We'll have him. Sirs, a word.

The Outlaws confer

SPEED (*to Valentine*)   Master, be one of them.
It's an honourable kind of thievery.

VALENTINE Peace, villain.

SECOND OUTLAW

Tell us this: have you anything to take to? 40

VALENTINE Nothing but my fortune.

THIRD OUTLAW

Know, then, that some of us are gentlemen
Such as the fury of ungoverned youth
Thrust from the company of aweful men.
Myself was from Verona banishèd 45
For practising to steal away a lady,
An heir, and near allied unto the Duke.

SECOND OUTLAW

And I from Mantua, for a gentleman
Who, in my mood, I stabbed unto the heart.

FIRST OUTLAW

And I, for suchlike petty crimes as these. 50
But to the purpose, for we cite our faults
That they may hold excused our lawless lives.
And partly seeing you are beautified
With goodly shape, and by your own report
A linguist, and a man of such perfection 55
As we do in our quality much want—

SECOND OUTLAW
Indeed because you are a banished man,
Therefore above the rest we parley to you.
Are you content to be our general,
To make a virtue of necessity   60
And live as we do in this wilderness?
THIRD OUTLAW
What sayst thou? Wilt thou be of our consort?
Say 'Ay', and be the captain of us all.
We'll do thee homage, and be ruled by thee,
Love thee as our commander and our king.   65
FIRST OUTLAW
But if thou scorn our courtesy, thou diest.
SECOND OUTLAW
Thou shalt not live to brag what we have offered.
VALENTINE
I take your offer, and will live with you,
Provided that you do no outrages
On silly women or poor passengers.   70
THIRD OUTLAW
No, we detest such vile, base practices.
Come, go with us. We'll bring thee to our crews
And show thee all the treasure we have got,
Which, with ourselves, all rest at thy dispose.   *Exeunt*

4.2   *Enter Proteus*
PROTEUS
Already have I been false to Valentine,
And now I must be as unjust to Thurio.
Under the colour of commending him
I have access my own love to prefer.
But Silvia is too fair, too true, too holy   5
To be corrupted with my worthless gifts.
When I protest true loyalty to her
She twits me with my falsehood to my friend.
When to her beauty I commend my vows
She bids me think how I have been forsworn   10
In breaking faith with Julia, whom I loved.
And notwithstanding all her sudden quips,
The least whereof would quell a lover's hope,
Yet, spaniel-like, the more she spurns my love,
The more it grows and fawneth on her still.   15
But here comes Thurio. Now must we to her window,
And give some evening music to her ear.
Enter Thurio with Musicians
THURIO
How now, Sir Proteus, are you crept before us?
PROTEUS
Ay, gentle Thurio, for you know that love
Will creep in service where it cannot go.   20
THURIO
Ay, but I hope, sir, that you love not here.
PROTEUS
Sir, but I do, or else I would be hence.
THURIO
Who, Silvia?
PROTEUS   Ay, Silvia—for your sake.

THURIO
I thank you for your own. Now, gentlemen,
Let's tune, and to it lustily awhile.   25
Enter the Host, and Julia dressed as a page-boy.
They talk apart
HOST Now, my young guest, methinks you're allycholly.
I pray you, why is it?
JULIA Marry, mine host, because I cannot be merry.
HOST Come, we'll have you merry. I'll bring you where
you shall hear music, and see the gentleman that you
asked for.   31
JULIA But shall I hear him speak?
HOST Ay, that you shall.
JULIA That will be music.
HOST Hark, hark.   35
JULIA Is he among these?
HOST Ay. But peace, let's hear 'em.

Song

Who is Silvia? What is she,
    That all our swains commend her?
Holy, fair, and wise is she.   40
    The heaven such grace did lend her
That she might admirèd be.

Is she kind as she is fair?
    For beauty lives with kindness.
Love doth to her eyes repair   45
    To help him of his blindness,
And, being helped, inhabits there.

Then to Silvia let us sing
    That Silvia is excelling.
She excels each mortal thing   50
    Upon the dull earth dwelling.
To her let us garlands bring.

HOST How now, are you sadder than you were before?
How do you, man? The music likes you not.
JULIA You mistake. The musician likes me not.   55
HOST Why, my pretty youth?
JULIA He plays false, father.
HOST How, out of tune on the strings?
JULIA Not so, but yet so false that he grieves my very
heart-strings.   60
HOST You have a quick ear.
JULIA Ay, I would I were deaf. It makes me have a slow
heart.
HOST I perceive you delight not in music.
JULIA Not a whit when it jars so.   65
HOST Hark what fine change is in the music.
JULIA Ay, that 'change' is the spite.
HOST You would have them always play but one thing?
JULIA I would always have one play but one thing. But
host, doth this Sir Proteus that we talk on often resort
unto this gentlewoman?   71
HOST I tell you what Lance his man told me, he loved
her out of all nick.

JULIA Where is Lance?   74
HOST Gone to seek his dog, which tomorrow, by his
    master's command, he must carry for a present to his
    lady.
JULIA Peace, stand aside. The company parts.
PROTEUS
    Sir Thurio, fear not you. I will so plead
    That you shall say my cunning drift excels.   80
THURIO
    Where meet we?
PROTEUS   At Saint Gregory's well.
THURIO   Farewell.
            Exeunt Thurio and the Musicians
        Enter Silvia, above
PROTEUS
    Madam, good even to your ladyship.
SILVIA
    I thank you for your music, gentlemen.
    Who is that that spake?
PROTEUS
    One, lady, if you knew his pure heart's truth   85
    You would quickly learn to know him by his voice.
SILVIA Sir Proteus, as I take it.
PROTEUS
    Sir Proteus, gentle lady, and your servant.
SILVIA
    What's your will?
PROTEUS   That I may compass yours.
SILVIA
    You have your wish. My will is even this,   90
    That presently you hie you home to bed.
    Thou subtle, perjured, false, disloyal man,
    Think'st thou I am so shallow, so conceitless
    To be seducèd by thy flattery,
    That hast deceived so many with thy vows?   95
    Return, return, and make thy love amends.
    For me—by this pale queen of night I swear—
    I am so far from granting thy request
    That I despise thee for thy wrongful suit,
    And by and by intend to chide myself   100
    Even for this time I spend in talking to thee.
PROTEUS
    I grant, sweet love, that I did love a lady,
    But she is dead.
JULIA (*aside*)   'Twere false if I should speak it,
    For I am sure she is not burièd.
SILVIA
    Say that she be, yet Valentine, thy friend,   105
    Survives, to whom, thyself art witness,
    I am betrothed. And art thou not ashamed
    To wrong him with thy importunacy?
PROTEUS
    I likewise hear that Valentine is dead.
SILVIA
    And so suppose am I, for in his grave,   110
    Assure thyself, my love is burièd.
PROTEUS
    Sweet lady, let me rake it from the earth.

SILVIA
    Go to thy lady's grave and call hers thence,
    Or at the least, in hers sepulchre thine.
JULIA (*aside*) He heard not that.   115
PROTEUS
    Madam, if your heart be so obdurate,
    Vouchsafe me yet your picture for my love,
    The picture that is hanging in your chamber.
    To that I'll speak, to that I'll sigh and weep;
    For since the substance of your perfect self   120
    Is else devoted, I am but a shadow,
    And to your shadow will I make true love.
JULIA (*aside*)
    If 'twere a substance, you would sure deceive it
    And make it but a shadow, as I am.
SILVIA
    I am very loath to be your idol, sir,   125
    But since your falsehood shall become you well
    To worship shadows and adore false shapes,
    Send to me in the morning, and I'll send it.
    And so, good rest.   *Exit*
PROTEUS   As wretches have o'ernight,   129
    That wait for execution in the morn.   *Exit*
JULIA Host, will you go?
HOST By my halidom, I was fast asleep.
JULIA Pray you, where lies Sir Proteus?
HOST Marry, at my house. Trust me, I think 'tis almost
    day.   135
JULIA
    Not so; but it hath been the longest night
    That e'er I watched, and the most heaviest. *Exeunt*

4.3   *Enter Sir Eglamour*
EGLAMOUR
    This is the hour that Madam Silvia
    Entreated me to call, and know her mind.
    There's some great matter she'd employ me in.
    Madam, madam!
        Enter Silvia ⌈above⌉
SILVIA   Who calls?
EGLAMOUR   Your servant, and your friend.
    One that attends your ladyship's command.   5
SILVIA
    Sir Eglamour, a thousand times good morrow!
EGLAMOUR
    As many, worthy lady, to yourself.
    According to your ladyship's impose
    I am thus early come, to know what service
    It is your pleasure to command me in.   10
SILVIA
    O Eglamour, thou art a gentleman—
    Think not I flatter, for I swear I do not—
    Valiant, wise, remorseful, well accomplished.
    Thou art not ignorant what dear good will
    I bear unto the banished Valentine,   15
    Nor how my father would enforce me marry
    Vain Thurio, whom my very soul abhors.
    Thyself hast loved, and I have heard thee say

473

No grief did ever come so near thy heart
As when thy lady and thy true love died,   20
Upon whose grave thou vowed'st pure chastity.
Sir Eglamour, I would to Valentine,
To Mantua, where I hear he makes abode;
And for the ways are dangerous to pass
I do desire thy worthy company,   25
Upon whose faith and honour I repose.
Urge not my father's anger, Eglamour,
But think upon my grief, a lady's grief,
And on the justice of my flying hence
To keep me from a most unholy match,   30
Which heaven and fortune still rewards with plagues.
I do desire thee, even from a heart
As full of sorrows as the sea of sands,
To bear me company and go with me.
If not, to hide what I have said to thee   35
That I may venture to depart alone.

EGLAMOUR

Madam, I pity much your grievances,
Which, since I know they virtuously are placed,
I give consent to go along with you,
Recking as little what betideth me   40
As much I wish all good befortune you.
When will you go?

SILVIA   This evening coming.

EGLAMOUR

Where shall I meet you?

SILVIA   At Friar Patrick's cell,
Where I intend holy confession.

EGLAMOUR

I will not fail your ladyship.   45
Good morrow, gentle lady.

SILVIA

Good morrow, kind Sir Eglamour.   *Exeunt*

4.4   *Enter Lance and his dog Crab*

LANCE (*to the audience*) When a man's servant shall play
the cur with him, look you, it goes hard. One that I
brought up of a puppy, one that I saved from drowning
when three or four of his blind brothers and sisters
went to it. I have taught him, even as one would say
precisely 'Thus I would teach a dog'. I was sent to
deliver him as a present to Mistress Silvia from my
master, and I came no sooner into the dining-chamber
but he steps me to her trencher and steals her capon's
leg. O, 'tis a foul thing when a cur cannot keep himself
in all companies. I would have, as one should say, one
that takes upon him to be a dog indeed, to be, as it
were, a dog at all things. If I had not had more wit
than he, to take a fault upon me that he did, I think
verily he had been hanged for't. Sure as I live, he had
suffered for't. You shall judge. He thrusts me himself
into the company of three or four gentleman-like dogs
under the Duke's table. He had not been there—bless
the mark—a pissing-while but all the chamber smelled
him. 'Out with the dog,' says one. 'What cur is that?'

says another. 'Whip him out,' says the third. 'Hang
him up,' says the Duke. I, having been acquainted with
the smell before, knew it was Crab, and goes me to the
fellow that whips the dogs. 'Friend,' quoth I, 'you mean
to whip the dog.' 'Ay, marry do I,' quoth he. 'You do
him the more wrong,' quoth I, ''twas I did the thing
you wot of.' He makes me no more ado, but whips me
out of the chamber. How many masters would do this
for his servant? Nay, I'll be sworn I have sat in the
stocks for puddings he hath stolen, otherwise he had
been executed. I have stood on the pillory for geese he
hath killed, otherwise he had suffered for't. (*To Crab*)
Thou think'st not of this now. Nay, I remember the
trick you served me when I took my leave of Madam
Silvia. Did not I bid thee still mark me, and do as I do?
When didst thou see me heave up my leg and make
water against a gentlewoman's farthingale? Didst thou
ever see me do such a trick?

Enter Proteus, with Julia dressed as a page-boy

PROTEUS (*to Julia*)

Sebastian is thy name? I like thee well,
And will employ thee in some service presently.   40

JULIA

In what you please. I'll do what I can.

PROTEUS

I hope thou wilt.—How now, you whoreson peasant,
Where have you been these two days loitering?

LANCE Marry, sir, I carried Mistress Silvia the dog you
bade me.   45

PROTEUS And what says she to my little jewel?

LANCE Marry, she says your dog was a cur, and tells you
currish thanks is good enough for such a present.

PROTEUS But she received my dog?

LANCE No indeed did she not. Here have I brought him
back again.   51

PROTEUS What, didst thou offer her this from me?

LANCE Ay, sir. The other squirrel was stolen from me by
the hangman boys in the market place, and then I
offered her mine own, who is a dog as big as ten of
yours, and therefore the gift the greater.   56

PROTEUS

Go, get thee hence, and find my dog again,
Or ne'er return again into my sight.
Away, I say. Stay'st thou to vex me here?

Exit Lance with Crab

A slave, that still on end turns me to shame.   60
Sebastian, I have entertainèd thee
Partly that I have need of such a youth
That can with some discretion do my business,
For 'tis no trusting to yon foolish lout,
But chiefly for thy face and thy behaviour,   65
Which, if my augury deceive me not,
Witness good bringing up, fortune, and truth.
Therefore know thou, for this I entertain thee.
Go presently, and take this ring with thee.
Deliver it to Madam Silvia.   70
She loved me well delivered it to me.

JULIA
It seems you loved not her, to leave her token.
She is dead belike?
PROTEUS   Not so. I think she lives.
JULIA
Alas.
PROTEUS Why dost thou cry 'Alas'?
JULIA
I cannot choose but pity her.   75
PROTEUS
Wherefore shouldst thou pity her?
JULIA
Because methinks that she loved you as well
As you do love your lady Silvia.
She dreams on him that has forgot her love;
You dote on her that cares not for your love.   80
'Tis pity love should be so contrary,
And thinking on it makes me cry 'Alas'.
PROTEUS
Well, give her that ring, and therewithal
This letter. (*Pointing*) That's her chamber. Tell my
    lady
I claim the promise for her heavenly picture.   85
Your message done, hie home unto my chamber,
Where thou shalt find me sad and solitary.   *Exit*
JULIA
How many women would do such a message?
Alas, poor Proteus, thou hast entertained
A fox to be the shepherd of thy lambs.   90
Alas, poor fool, why do I pity him
That with his very heart despiseth me?
Because he loves her, he despiseth me.
Because I love him, I must pity him.
This ring I gave him when he parted from me,   95
To bind him to remember my good will.
And now am I, unhappy messenger,
To plead for that which I would not obtain;
To carry that which I would have refused;
To praise his faith, which I would have dispraised. 100
I am my master's true-confirmèd love,
But cannot be true servant to my master
Unless I prove false traitor to myself.
Yet will I woo for him, but yet so coldly
As, heaven it knows, I would not have him speed. 105
    Enter Silvia
Gentlewoman, good day. I pray you be my mean
To bring me where to speak with Madam Silvia.
SILVIA
What would you with her, if that I be she?
JULIA
If you be she, I do entreat your patience
To hear me speak the message I am sent on.   110
SILVIA From whom?
JULIA
From my master, Sir Proteus, madam.
SILVIA O, he sends you for a picture?
JULIA Ay, madam.
SILVIA Ursula, bring my picture there.   115

⌈An attendant brings a picture⌉
Go, give your master this. Tell him from me
One Julia, that his changing thoughts forget,
Would better fit his chamber than this shadow.
JULIA
Madam, please you peruse this letter.
    She gives Silvia a letter
Pardon me, madam, I have unadvised   120
Delivered you a paper that I should not.
    *She takes back the letter and gives Silvia another
    letter*
This is the letter to your ladyship.
SILVIA
I pray thee, let me look on that again.
JULIA
It may not be. Good madam, pardon me.
SILVIA
There, hold. I will not look upon your master's lines.
I know they are stuffed with protestations,   126
And full of new-found oaths, which he will break
As easily as I do tear his paper.
    She tears the letter
JULIA
Madam, he sends your ladyship this ring.
    She offers Silvia a ring
SILVIA
The more shame for him, that he sends it me;   130
For I have heard him say a thousand times
His Julia gave it him at his departure.
Though his false finger have profaned the ring,
Mine shall not do his Julia so much wrong.
JULIA She thanks you.   135
SILVIA What sayst thou?
JULIA
I thank you, madam, that you tender her.
Poor gentlewoman, my master wrongs her much.
SILVIA Dost thou know her?
JULIA
Almost as well as I do know myself.   140
To think upon her woes I do protest
That I have wept a hundred several times.
SILVIA
Belike she thinks that Proteus hath forsook her?
JULIA
I think she doth; and that's her cause of sorrow.
SILVIA Is she not passing fair?   145
JULIA
She hath been fairer, madam, than she is.
When she did think my master loved her well
She, in my judgement, was as fair as you.
But since she did neglect her looking-glass,
And threw her sun-expelling mask away,   150
The air hath starved the roses in her cheeks
And pinched the lily tincture of her face,
That now she is become as black as I.
SILVIA How tall was she?
JULIA
About my stature; for at Pentecost,   155

When all our pageants of delight were played,
Our youth got me to play the woman's part,
And I was trimmed in Madam Julia's gown,
Which servèd me as fit, by all men's judgements,
As if the garment had been made for me;   160
Therefore I know she is about my height.
And at that time I made her weep agood,
For I did play a lamentable part.
Madam, 'twas Ariadne, passioning
For Theseus' perjury and unjust flight;   165
Which I so lively acted with my tears
That my poor mistress, movèd therewithal,
Wept bitterly; and would I might be dead
If I in thought felt not her very sorrow.

SILVIA
She is beholden to thee, gentle youth.   170
Alas, poor lady, desolate and left.
I weep myself to think upon thy words.
Here, youth. There is my purse. I give thee this
For thy sweet mistress' sake, because thou lov'st her.
Farewell.   *Exit*

JULIA
And she shall thank you for't, if e'er you know her.—
A virtuous gentlewoman, mild, and beautiful.   177
I hope my master's suit will be but cold,
Since she respects 'my mistress'' love so much.
Alas, how love can trifle with itself.   180
Here is her picture. Let me see, I think
If I had such a tire, this face of mine
Were full as lovely as is this of hers.
And yet the painter flattered her a little,
Unless I flatter with myself too much.   185
Her hair is auburn, mine is perfect yellow.
If that be all the difference in his love,
I'll get me such a coloured periwig.
Her eyes are grey as glass, and so are mine.
Ay, but her forehead's low, and mine's as high.   190
What should it be that he respects in her
But I can make respective in myself,
If this fond love were not a blinded god?
Come, shadow, come, and take this shadow up,
For 'tis thy rival.
    She picks up the portrait
    O thou senseless form,   195
Thou shalt be worshipped, kissed, loved, and adored;
And were there sense in his idolatry
My substance should be statue in thy stead.
I'll use thee kindly, for thy mistress' sake,
That used me so; or else, by Jove I vow,   200
I should have scratched out your unseeing eyes,
To make my master out of love with thee.   *Exit*

5.1   *Enter Sir Eglamour*

EGLAMOUR
The sun begins to gild the western sky,
And now it is about the very hour
That Silvia at Friar Patrick's cell should meet me.
She will not fail; for lovers break not hours,

Unless it be to come before their time,   5
So much they spur their expedition.
    Enter Silvia
See where she comes. Lady, a happy evening!

SILVIA
Amen, amen. Go on, good Eglamour,
Out at the postern by the abbey wall.
I fear I am attended by some spies.   10

EGLAMOUR
Fear not. The forest is not three leagues off.
If we recover that, we are sure enough.   *Exeunt*

    Enter Thurio, Proteus, and Julia dressed as a page-
5.2   *boy*

THURIO
Sir Proteus, what says Silvia to my suit?

PROTEUS
O sir, I find her milder than she was,
And yet she takes exceptions at your person.

THURIO
What? That my leg is too long?

PROTEUS
No, that it is too little.   5

THURIO
I'll wear a boot, to make it somewhat rounder.

JULIA (*aside*)
But love will not be spurred to what it loathes.

THURIO
What says she to my face?

PROTEUS
She says it is a fair one.

THURIO
Nay, then, the wanton lies. My face is black.   10

PROTEUS
But pearls are fair; and the old saying is,
'Black men are pearls in beauteous ladies' eyes'.

JULIA (*aside*)
'Tis true, such pearls as put out ladies' eyes,
For I had rather wink than look on them.

THURIO
How likes she my discourse?   15

PROTEUS
Ill, when you talk of war.

THURIO
But well when I discourse of love and peace.

JULIA (*aside*)
But better indeed when you hold your peace.

THURIO
What says she to my valour?

PROTEUS
O sir, she makes no doubt of that.   20

JULIA (*aside*)
She needs not, when she knows it cowardice.

THURIO
What says she to my birth?

PROTEUS
That you are well derived.

JULIA (*aside*)
True: from a gentleman to a fool.

THURIO
Considers she my possessions?   25
PROTEUS
O ay, and pities them.
THURIO Wherefore?
JULIA (aside)
That such an ass should owe them.
PROTEUS
That they are out by lease.
JULIA   Here comes the Duke.
    Enter the Duke
DUKE
How now, Sir Proteus. How now, Thurio.   30
Which of you saw Eglamour of late?
THURIO
Not I.
PROTEUS Nor I.
DUKE   Saw you my daughter?
PROTEUS   Neither.
DUKE
Why then, she's fled unto that peasant Valentine,
And Eglamour is in her company.
'Tis true, for Friar Laurence met them both   35
As he in penance wandered through the forest.
Him he knew well, and guessed that it was she,
But being masked, he was not sure of it.
Besides, she did intend confession
At Patrick's cell this even, and there she was not.   40
These likelihoods confirm her flight from hence;
Therefore I pray you stand not to discourse,
But mount you presently, and meet with me
Upon the rising of the mountain foot
That leads toward Mantua, whither they are fled.   45
Dispatch, sweet gentlemen, and follow me.   Exit
THURIO
Why, this it is to be a peevish girl,
That flies her fortune when it follows her.
I'll after, more to be revenged on Eglamour   49
Than for the love of reckless Silvia.   ⌈Exit⌉
PROTEUS
And I will follow, more for Silvia's love
Than hate of Eglamour that goes with her.   ⌈Exit⌉
JULIA
And I will follow, more to cross that love
Than hate for Silvia, that is gone for love.   ⌈Exit⌉

5.3   Enter the Outlaws with Silvia captive
FIRST OUTLAW
Come, come, be patient. We must bring you to our
    captain.
SILVIA
A thousand more mischances than this one
Have learned me how to brook this patiently.
SECOND OUTLAW Come, bring her away.
FIRST OUTLAW
Where is the gentleman that was with her?   5
THIRD OUTLAW
Being nimble-footed he hath outrun us;

But Moses and Valerius follow him.
Go thou with her to the west end of the wood.
There is our captain. We'll follow him that's fled.
The thicket is beset, he cannot scape.   10
                Exeunt the Second and Third Outlaws
FIRST OUTLAW (to Silvia)
Come, I must bring you to our captain's cave.
Fear not. He bears an honourable mind,
And will not use a woman lawlessly.
SILVIA (aside)
O Valentine! This I endure for thee.   Exeunt

5.4   Enter Valentine
VALENTINE
How use doth breed a habit in a man!
This shadowy desert, unfrequented woods
I better brook than flourishing peopled towns.
Here can I sit alone, unseen of any,
And to the nightingale's complaining notes   5
Tune my distresses and record my woes.
O thou that dost inhabit in my breast,
Leave not the mansion so long tenantless
Lest, growing ruinous, the building fall
And leave no memory of what it was.   10
Repair me with thy presence, Silvia.
Thou gentle nymph, cherish thy forlorn swain.
What hallooing and what stir is this today?
These are my mates, that make their wills their law,
Have some unhappy passenger in chase.   15
They love me well, yet I have much to do
To keep them from uncivil outrages.
Withdraw thee, Valentine. Who's this comes here?
    He stands aside.
    Enter Proteus, Silvia, and Julia dressed as a page-
    boy
PROTEUS
Madam, this service I have done for you—
Though you respect not aught your servant doth—   20
To hazard life, and rescue you from him
That would have forced your honour and your love.
Vouchsafe me for my meed but one fair look.
A smaller boon than this I cannot beg,
And less than this I am sure you cannot give.   25
VALENTINE (aside)
How like a dream is this I see and hear!
Love lend me patience to forbear awhile.
SILVIA
O miserable, unhappy that I am!
PROTEUS
Unhappy were you, madam, ere I came.
But by my coming I have made you happy.   30
SILVIA
By thy approach thou mak'st me most unhappy.
JULIA (aside)
And me, when he approacheth to your presence.
SILVIA
Had I been seizèd by a hungry lion
I would have been a breakfast to the beast

Rather than have false Proteus rescue me.   35
O heaven be judge how I love Valentine,
Whose life's as tender to me as my soul.
And full as much, for more there cannot be,
I do detest false perjured Proteus.
Therefore be gone, solicit me no more.   40

PROTEUS
What dangerous action, stood it next to death,
Would I not undergo for one calm look!
O, 'tis the curse in love, and still approved,
When women cannot love where they're beloved.

SILVIA
When Proteus cannot love where he's beloved.   45
Read over Julia's heart, thy first, best love,
For whose dear sake thou didst then rend thy faith
Into a thousand oaths, and all those oaths
Descended into perjury to love me.
Thou hast no faith left now, unless thou'dst two,   50
And that's far worse than none. Better have none
Than plural faith, which is too much by one,
Thou counterfeit to thy true friend.

PROTEUS   In love
Who respects friend?

SILVIA   All men but Proteus.

PROTEUS
Nay, if the gentle spirit of moving words   55
Can no way change you to a milder form
I'll woo you like a soldier, at arm's end,
And love you 'gainst the nature of love: force ye.

SILVIA
O heaven!

PROTEUS (assailing her) I'll force thee yield to my desire.

VALENTINE (coming forward)
Ruffian, let go that rude uncivil touch,   60
Thou friend of an ill fashion.

PROTEUS .   Valentine!

VALENTINE
Thou common friend, that's without faith or love,
For such is a friend now. Treacherous man,
Thou hast beguiled my hopes. Naught but mine eye
Could have persuaded me. Now I dare not say   65
I have one friend alive. Thou wouldst disprove me.
Who should be trusted, when one's right hand
Is perjured to the bosom? Proteus,
I am sorry I must never trust thee more,
But count the world a stranger for thy sake.   70
The private wound is deepest. O time most accursed,
'Mongst all foes that a friend should be the worst!

PROTEUS My shame and guilt confounds me.
Forgive me, Valentine. If hearty sorrow
Be a sufficient ransom for offence,   75
I tender't here. I do as truly suffer
As e'er I did commit.

VALENTINE   Then I am paid,
And once again I do receive thee honest.
Who by repentance is not satisfied
Is nor of heaven nor earth. For these are pleased;   80
By penitence th' Eternal's wrath's appeased.

And that my love may appear plain and free,
All that was mine in Silvia I give thee.

JULIA
O me unhappy!
          She faints

PROTEUS   Look to the boy.

VALENTINE   Why, boy!
Why wag, how now? What's the matter? Look up.
          Speak.   85

JULIA O good sir, my master charged me to deliver a ring
to Madam Silvia, which out of my neglect was never
done.

PROTEUS Where is that ring, boy?

JULIA Here 'tis. This is it.   90
          She gives Proteus the ring

PROTEUS How, let me see!
Why, this is the ring I gave to Julia.

JULIA
O, cry you mercy, sir, I have mistook.
          She offers Proteus another ring
This is the ring you sent to Silvia.

PROTEUS
But how cam'st thou by this ring? At my depart   95
I gave this unto Julia.

JULIA
And Julia herself did give it me,
And Julia herself hath brought it hither.

PROTEUS How? Julia?

JULIA
Behold her that gave aim to all thy oaths   100
And entertained 'em deeply in her heart.
How oft hast thou with perjury cleft the root?
O Proteus, let this habit make thee blush.
Be thou ashamed that I have took upon me
Such an immodest raiment, if shame live   105
In a disguise of love.
It is the lesser blot, modesty finds,
Women to change their shapes than men their minds.

PROTEUS
Than men their minds! 'Tis true. O heaven, were man
But constant, he were perfect. That one error   110
Fills him with faults, makes him run through all th'
          sins;
Inconstancy falls off ere it begins.
What is in Silvia's face but I may spy
More fresh in Julia's, with a constant eye?

VALENTINE Come, come, a hand from either.   115
Let me be blessed to make this happy close.
'Twere pity two such friends should be long foes.
          Julia and Proteus join hands

PROTEUS
Bear witness, heaven, I have my wish for ever.

JULIA
And I mine.
          Enter the Outlaws with the Duke and Thurio as
          captives

OUTLAWS   A prize, a prize, a prize!

VALENTINE

Forbear, forbear, I say. It is my lord the Duke.   120
The Outlaws release the Duke and Thurio
(*To the Duke*) Your grace is welcome to a man
    disgraced,
Banishèd Valentine.

DUKE   Sir Valentine!

THURIO

Yonder is Silvia, and Silvia's mine.

VALENTINE

Thurio, give back, or else embrace thy death.
Come not within the measure of my wrath.   125
Do not name Silvia thine. If once again,
Verona shall not hold thee. Here she stands.
Take but possession of her with a touch—
I dare thee but to breathe upon my love.

THURIO

Sir Valentine, I care not for her, I.   130
I hold him but a fool that will endanger
His body for a girl that loves him not.
I claim her not, and therefore she is thine.

DUKE

The more degenerate and base art thou
To make such means for her as thou hast done,   135
And leave her on such slight conditions.
Now by the honour of my ancestry
I do applaud thy spirit, Valentine,
And think thee worthy of an empress' love.
Know then I here forget all former griefs,   140
Cancel all grudge, repeal thee home again,
Plead a new state in thy unrivalled merit,
To which I thus subscribe: Sir Valentine,
Thou art a gentleman, and well derived.
Take thou thy Silvia, for thou hast deserved her.   145

VALENTINE

I thank your grace. The gift hath made me happy.
I now beseech you, for your daughter's sake,
To grant one boon that I shall ask of you.

DUKE

I grant it, for thine own, whate'er it be.

VALENTINE

These banished men that I have kept withal   150
Are men endowed with worthy qualities.
Forgive them what they have committed here,
And let them be recalled from their exile.
They are reformèd, civil, full of good,
And fit for great employment, worthy lord.   155

DUKE

Thou hast prevailed. I pardon them and thee.
Dispose of them as thou know'st their deserts.
Come, let us go. We will include all jars
With triumphs, mirth, and rare solemnity.

VALENTINE

And as we walk along I dare be bold   160
With our discourse to make your grace to smile.
What think you of this page, my lord?

DUKE

I think the boy hath grace in him. He blushes.

VALENTINE

I warrant you, my lord, more grace than boy.

DUKE What mean you by that saying?   165

VALENTINE

Please you, I'll tell you as we pass along,
That you will wonder what hath fortunèd.
Come, Proteus, 'tis your penance but to hear
The story of your loves discoverèd.
That done, our day of marriage shall be yours,   170
One feast, one house, one mutual happiness.   *Exeunt*

THE TAMING OF THE SHREW

The Taming of the Shrew was first published in the 1623 Folio, but a related play, shorter and simpler, with the title *The Taming of a Shrew*, had appeared in print in 1594. The exact relationship of these plays is disputed. *A Shrew* has sometimes been regarded as the source for *The Shrew*; some scholars have believed that both plays derive independently from an earlier play, now lost; it has even been suggested that Shakespeare wrote both plays. In our view Shakespeare's play was written first, not necessarily on the foundation of an earlier play, and *A Shrew* is an anonymous imitation, written in the hope of capitalizing on the success of Shakespeare's play. The difference between the titles is probably no more significant than the fact that *The Winter's Tale* is even now often loosely referred to as *A Winter's Tale*, or *The Comedy of Errors* as *A Comedy of Errors*.

The plot of *The Taming of the Shrew* has three main strands. First comes the Induction showing how a drunken tinker, Christopher Sly, is made to believe himself a lord for whose entertainment a play is to be presented. This resembles an episode in *The Arabian Nights*, in which Caliph Haroun al Raschid plays a similar trick on Abu Hassan. A Latin version of this story was known in Shakespeare's England; it may also have circulated by word of mouth. Second comes the principal plot of the play performed for Sly, in which the shrewish Katherine is wooed, won, and tamed by the fortune-hunting Petruccio. This is a popular narrative theme; Shakespeare may have known a ballad called 'A merry jest of a shrewd and curst wife lapped in morel's skin for her good behaviour', printed around 1550. The third strand of the play involves Lucentio, Gremio, and Hortensio, all of them suitors for the hand of Katherine's sister, Bianca. This is based on the first English prose comedy, George Gascoigne's *Supposes*, translated from Ludovico Ariosto's *I Suppositi* (1509), acted in 1566, and published in 1573. In *The Taming of the Shrew* as printed in the 1623 Folio Christopher Sly fades out after Act 1, Scene 1; in *A Shrew* he makes other appearances, and rounds off the play. These episodes may derive from a version of Shakespeare's play different from that preserved in the Folio; we print them as Additional Passages.

The adapting of Shakespeare's play that seems to have occurred early in its career foreshadows its later history on the stage. Seven versions appeared during the seventeenth and eighteenth centuries, culminating in David Garrick's *Catharine and Petruchio*, first performed in 1754. This version, omitting Christopher Sly and concentrating on the taming story, held the stage almost unchallenged until late in the nineteenth century. In various incarnations *The Taming of the Shrew* has always been popular on the stage, but its reputation as a robust comedy verging on farce has often obscured its more subtle and imaginative aspects, brutalizing Petruccio and trivializing Kate. The Induction, finely written, establishes a fundamentally serious concern with the powers of persuasion to change not merely appearance but reality, and this theme is acted out at different levels in both strands of the subsequent action.

THE PERSONS OF THE PLAY

In the Induction

CHRISTOPHER SLY, beggar and tinker

A HOSTESS

A LORD

BARTHOLOMEW, his page

HUNTSMEN

SERVANTS

PLAYERS

In the play-within-the-play

BAPTISTA Minola, a gentleman of Padua

KATHERINE, his elder daughter

BIANCA, his younger daughter

PETRUCCIO, a gentleman of Verona, suitor of Katherine

GRUMIO }
CURTIS } his servants

GREMIO, a rich old man of Padua, suitor of Bianca

HORTENSIO, another suitor, who disguises himself as Licio, a teacher

LUCENTIO, from Pisa, who disguises himself as Cambio, a teacher

TRANIO }
BIONDELLO } his servants

VINCENTIO, Lucentio's father

A PEDANT (schoolmaster), from Mantua

A WIDOW

A TAILOR

A HABERDASHER

An OFFICER

SERVINGMEN, including NATHANIEL, PHILIP, JOSEPH, and PETER

Other servants of Baptista and Petruccio

The Taming of the Shrew

Induction 1

Enter Christopher Sly the beggar, and the Hostess

SLY I'll feeze you, in faith.

HOSTESS A pair of stocks, you rogue.

SLY You're a baggage. The Slys are no rogues. Look in the Chronicles—we came in with Richard Conqueror, therefore *paucas palabras*, let the world slide. Sessa! 5

HOSTESS You will not pay for the glasses you have burst?

SLY No, not a denier. Go by, Saint Jeronimy! Go to thy cold bed and warm thee.

HOSTESS I know my remedy, I must go fetch the headborough. *Exit*

SLY Third or fourth or fifth borough, I'll answer him by law. I'll not budge an inch, boy. Let him come, and kindly.

He falls asleep.

Horns sound. Enter a Lord from hunting, with his train

LORD
Huntsman, I charge thee, tender well my hounds.
Breathe Merriman—the poor cur is embossed— 15
And couple Clowder with the deep-mouthed brach.
Saw'st thou not, boy, how Silver made it good
At the hedge corner, in the coldest fault?
I would not lose the dog for twenty pound.

FIRST HUNTSMAN
Why, Belman is as good as he, my lord. 20
He cried upon it at the merest loss,
And twice today picked out the dullest scent.
Trust me, I take him for the better dog.

LORD
Thou art a fool. If Echo were as fleet
I would esteem him worth a dozen such. 25
But sup them well, and look unto them all.
Tomorrow I intend to hunt again.

FIRST HUNTSMAN I will, my lord.

LORD *(seeing Sly)*
What's here? One dead, or drunk? See, doth he breathe?

SECOND HUNTSMAN
He breathes, my lord. Were he not warmed with ale
This were a bed but cold to sleep so soundly. 31

LORD
O monstrous beast! How like a swine he lies.
Grim death, how foul and loathsome is thine image.
Sirs, I will practise on this drunken man.
What think you: if he were conveyed to bed, 35
Wrapped in sweet clothes, rings put upon his fingers,
A most delicious banquet by his bed,
And brave attendants near him when he wakes—
Would not the beggar then forget himself?

FIRST HUNTSMAN
Believe me, lord, I think he cannot choose. 40

SECOND HUNTSMAN
It would seem strange unto him when he waked.

LORD
Even as a flatt'ring dream or worthless fancy.
Then take him up, and manage well the jest.
Carry him gently to my fairest chamber,
And hang it round with all my wanton pictures. 45
Balm his foul head in warm distillèd waters,
And burn sweet wood to make the lodging sweet.
Procure me music ready when he wakes
To make a dulcet and a heavenly sound,
And if he chance to speak be ready straight, 50
And with a low submissive reverence
Say 'What is it your honour will command?'
Let one attend him with a silver basin
Full of rose-water and bestrewed with flowers;
Another bear the ewer, the third a diaper, 55
And say 'Will't please your lordship cool your hands?'
Someone be ready with a costly suit,
And ask him what apparel he will wear.
Another tell him of his hounds and horse,
And that his lady mourns at his disease. 60
Persuade him that he hath been lunatic,
And when he says he is, say that he dreams,
For he is nothing but a mighty lord.
This do, and do it kindly, gentle sirs.
It will be pastime passing excellent, 65
If it be husbanded with modesty.

FIRST HUNTSMAN
My lord, I warrant you we will play our part
As he shall think by our true diligence
He is no less than what we say he is.

LORD
Take him up gently, and to bed with him; 70
And each one to his office when he wakes.

Servingmen carry Sly out

Trumpets sound

Sirrah, go see what trumpet 'tis that sounds.

Exit a Servingman

Belike some noble gentleman that means,
Travelling some journey, to repose him here. 74

Enter a Servingman

How now? Who is it?

SERVINGMAN An't please your honour, players
That offer service to your lordship.

Enter Players

LORD
Bid them come near. Now fellows, you are welcome.

PLAYERS We thank your honour.

LORD
Do you intend to stay with me tonight?

A PLAYER
So please your lordship to accept our duty. 80

LORD

With all my heart. This fellow I remember
Since once he played a farmer's eldest son.
'Twas where you wooed the gentlewoman so well.
I have forgot your name, but sure that part
Was aptly fitted and naturally performed.   85

ANOTHER PLAYER

I think 'twas Soto that your honour means.

LORD

'Tis very true. Thou didst it excellent.
Well, you are come to me in happy time,
The rather for I have some sport in hand
Wherein your cunning can assist me much.   90
There is a lord will hear you play tonight;
But I am doubtful of your modesties
Lest, over-eyeing of his odd behaviour—
For yet his honour never heard a play—
You break into some merry passion,   95
And so offend him; for I tell you, sirs,
If you should smile he grows impatient.

A PLAYER

Fear not, my lord, we can contain ourselves
Were he the veriest antic in the world.

LORD (to a Servingman)

Go, sirrah, take them to the buttery   100
And give them friendly welcome every one.
Let them want nothing that my house affords.

Exit one with the Players

(To a Servingman) Sirrah, go you to Barthol'mew, my
        page,
And see him dressed in all suits like a lady.
That done, conduct him to the drunkard's chamber
And call him 'madam', do him obeisance.   106
Tell him from me, as he will win my love,
He bear himself with honourable action
Such as he hath observed in noble ladies
Unto their lords by them accomplishèd.   110
Such duty to the drunkard let him do
With soft low tongue and lowly courtesy,
And say 'What is't your honour will command
Wherein your lady and your humble wife
May show her duty and make known her love?'   115
And then with kind embracements, tempting kisses,
And with declining head into his bosom
Bid him shed tears, as being overjoyed
To see her noble lord restored to health,
Who for this seven years hath esteemèd him   120
No better than a poor and loathsome beggar.
And if the boy have not a woman's gift
To rain a shower of commanded tears,
An onion will do well for such a shift,
Which, in a napkin being close conveyed,   125
Shall in despite enforce a watery eye.
See this dispatched with all the haste thou canst.
Anon I'll give thee more instructions.

Exit a Servingman

I know the boy will well usurp the grace,
Voice, gait, and action of a gentlewoman.   130

I long to hear him call the drunkard husband,
And how my men will stay themselves from laughter
When they do homage to this simple peasant.
I'll in to counsel them. Haply my presence
May well abate the over-merry spleen
Which otherwise would grow into extremes.   *Exeunt*

Induction 2 *Enter aloft Sly, the drunkard, with attendants,
        some with apparel, basin, and ewer, and other
        appurtenances; and Lord*

SLY For God's sake, a pot of small ale!

FIRST SERVINGMAN

Will't please your lordship drink a cup of sack?

SECOND SERVINGMAN

Will't please your honour taste of these conserves?

THIRD SERVINGMAN

What raiment will your honour wear today?   4

SLY I am Christophero Sly. Call not me 'honour' nor
'lordship'. I ne'er drank sack in my life, and if you give
me any conserves, give me conserves of beef. Ne'er ask
me what raiment I'll wear, for I have no more doublets
than backs, no more stockings than legs, nor no more
shoes than feet—nay, sometime more feet than shoes,
or such shoes as my toes look through the over-leather.

LORD

Heaven cease this idle humour in your honour.   12
O that a mighty man of such descent,
Of such possessions and so high esteem,
Should be infusèd with so foul a spirit.

SLY What, would you make me mad? Am not I
Christopher Sly—old Sly's son of Burton Heath, by
birth a pedlar, by education a cardmaker, by transmuta-
tion a bearherd, and now by present profession a
tinker? Ask Marian Hacket, the fat alewife of Wincot,
if she know me not. If she say I am not fourteen pence
on the score for sheer ale, score me up for the lying'st
knave in Christendom. What, I am not bestraught;
here's—

THIRD SERVINGMAN

O, this it is that makes your lady mourn.   25

SECOND SERVINGMAN

O, this is it that makes your servants droop.

LORD

Hence comes it that your kindred shuns your house,
As beaten hence by your strange lunacy.
O noble lord, bethink thee of thy birth.
Call home thy ancient thoughts from banishment,   30
And banish hence these abject lowly dreams.
Look how thy servants do attend on thee,
Each in his office, ready at thy beck.
Wilt thou have music?   *Music*
                    Hark, Apollo plays,
And twenty cagèd nightingales do sing.   35
Or wilt thou sleep? We'll have thee to a couch
Softer and sweeter than the lustful bed
On purpose trimmed up for Semiramis.
Say thou wilt walk, we will bestrew the ground.
Or wilt thou ride, thy horses shall be trapped,   40

Their harness studded all with gold and pearl.
Dost thou love hawking? Thou hast hawks will soar
Above the morning lark. Or wilt thou hunt,
Thy hounds shall make the welkin answer them
And fetch shrill echoes from the hollow earth.   45
FIRST SERVINGMAN
Say thou wilt course, thy greyhounds are as swift
As breathèd stags, ay, fleeter than the roe.
SECOND SERVINGMAN
Dost thou love pictures? We will fetch thee straight
Adonis painted by a running brook,
And Cytherea all in sedges hid,   50
Which seem to move and wanton with her breath
Even as the waving sedges play wi'th' wind.
LORD
We'll show thee Io as she was a maid,
And how she was beguilèd and surprised,
As lively painted as the deed was done.   55
THIRD SERVINGMAN
Or Daphne roaming through a thorny wood,
Scratching her legs that one shall swear she bleeds,
And at that sight shall sad Apollo weep,
So workmanly the blood and tears are drawn.
LORD
Thou art a lord, and nothing but a lord.   60
Thou hast a lady far more beautiful
Than any woman in this waning age.
FIRST SERVINGMAN
And till the tears that she hath shed for thee
Like envious floods o'errun her lovely face
She was the fairest creature in the world;   65
And yet she is inferior to none.
SLY
Am I a lord, and have I such a lady?
Or do I dream? Or have I dreamed till now?
I do not sleep. I see, I hear, I speak.
I smell sweet savours, and I feel soft things.   70
Upon my life, I am a lord indeed,
And not a tinker, nor Christopher Sly.
Well, bring our lady hither to our sight,
And once again a pot o'th' smallest ale.
SECOND SERVINGMAN
Will't please your mightiness to wash your hands?   75
O, how we joy to see your wit restored!
O that once more you knew but what you are!
These fifteen years you have been in a dream,
Or when you waked, so waked as if you slept.
SLY
These fifteen years—by my fay, a goodly nap.   80
But did I never speak of all that time?
FIRST SERVINGMAN
O yes, my lord, but very idle words,
For though you lay here in this goodly chamber
Yet would you say ye were beaten out of door,
And rail upon the hostess of the house,   85
And say you would present her at the leet
Because she brought stone jugs and no sealed quarts.
Sometimes you would call out for Cicely Hacket.

SLY Ay, the woman's maid of the house.
THIRD SERVINGMAN
Why, sir, you know no house, nor no such maid,   90
Nor no such men as you have reckoned up,
As Stephen Sly, and old John Naps of Greet,
And Peter Turf, and Henry Pimpernel,
And twenty more such names and men as these,
Which never were, nor no man ever saw.   95
SLY
Now Lord be thankèd for my good amends.
ALL Amen.
SLY I thank thee. Thou shalt not lose by it.
        Enter Bartholomew the Page, as Lady, with
        attendants
BARTHOLOMEW
How fares my noble lord?
SLY   Marry, I fare well,
For here is cheer enough. Where is my wife?   100
BARTHOLOMEW
Here, noble lord. What is thy will with her?
SLY
Are you my wife, and will not call me husband?
My men should call me lord. I am your goodman.
BARTHOLOMEW
My husband and my lord, my lord and husband;
I am your wife in all obedience.   105
SLY
I know it well. (*To the Lord*) What must I call her?
LORD   Madam.
SLY Al'ce Madam or Joan Madam?
LORD
Madam, and nothing else. So lords call ladies.
SLY
Madam wife, they say that I have dreamed,
And slept above some fifteen year or more.   110
BARTHOLOMEW
Ay, and the time seems thirty unto me,
Being all this time abandoned from your bed.
SLY
'Tis much. Servants, leave me and her alone.
        Exeunt ⌈Lord and⌉ attendants
Madam, undress you and come now to bed.
BARTHOLOMEW
Thrice-noble lord, let me entreat of you   115
To pardon me yet for a night or two,
Or if not so, until the sun be set,
For your physicians have expressly charged,
In peril to incur your former malady,
That I should yet absent me from your bed.   120
I hope this reason stands for my excuse.
SLY Ay, it stands so that I may hardly tarry so long. But
I would be loath to fall into my dreams again. I will
therefore tarry in despite of the flesh and the blood.
        Enter a Messenger
MESSENGER
Your honour's players, hearing your amendment,   125
Are come to play a pleasant comedy,
For so your doctors hold it very meet,

Seeing too much sadness hath congealed your blood,
And melancholy is the nurse of frenzy.
Therefore they thought it good you hear a play   130
And frame your mind to mirth and merriment,
Which bars a thousand harms and lengthens life.

SLY

Marry, I will let them play it. Is not a comonty
A Christmas gambol, or a tumbling trick?

BARTHOLOMEW

No, my good lord, it is more pleasing stuff.   135

SLY

What, household stuff?

BARTHOLOMEW   It is a kind of history.

SLY

Well, we'll see't. Come, madam wife, sit by my side
And let the world slip. We shall ne'er be younger.
    Bartholomew sits

1.1   *Flourish. Enter Lucentio and his man, Tranio*

LUCENTIO

Tranio, since for the great desire I had
To see fair Padua, nursery of arts,
I am arrived fore fruitful Lombardy,
The pleasant garden of great Italy,
And by my father's love and leave am armed   5
With his good will and thy good company,
My trusty servant, well approved in all,
Here let us breathe, and haply institute
A course of learning and ingenious studies.
Pisa, renownèd for grave citizens,   10
Gave me my being, and my father first—
A merchant of great traffic through the world,
Vincentio, come of the Bentivolii.
Vincentio's son, brought up in Florence,
It shall become to serve all hopes conceived   15
To deck his fortune with his virtuous deeds.
And therefore, Tranio, for the time I study,
Virtue and that part of philosophy
Will I apply that treats of happiness
By virtue specially to be achieved.   20
Tell me thy mind, for I have Pisa left
And am to Padua come as he that leaves
A shallow plash to plunge him in the deep,
And with satiety seeks to quench his thirst.

TRANIO

Mi *perdonate*, gentle master mine.   25
I am in all affected as yourself,
Glad that you thus continue your resolve
To suck the sweets of sweet philosophy.
Only, good master, while we do admire
This virtue and this moral discipline,   30
Let's be no stoics nor no stocks, I pray,
Or so devote to Aristotle's checks
As Ovid be an outcast quite abjured.
Balk logic with acquaintance that you have,
And practise rhetoric in your common talk.   35
Music and poesy use to quicken you;
The mathematics and the metaphysics,

Fall to them as you find your stomach serves you.
No profit grows where is no pleasure ta'en.
In brief, sir, study what you most affect.   40

LUCENTIO

Gramercies, Tranio, well dost thou advise.
If, Biondello, thou wert come ashore,
We could at once put us in readiness
And take a lodging fit to entertain
Such friends as time in Padua shall beget.   45
But stay a while, what company is this?

TRANIO

Master, some show to welcome us to town.
    Enter Baptista with his two daughters, Katherine
    and Bianca; Gremio, a pantaloon; Hortensio,
    suitor to Bianca. Lucentio and Tranio stand by

BAPTISTA

Gentlemen, importune me no farther,
For how I firmly am resolved you know:
That is, not to bestow my youngest daughter   50
Before I have a husband for the elder.
If either of you both love Katherina,
Because I know you well and love you well
Leave shall you have to court her at your pleasure.

GREMIO

To cart her rather. She's too rough for me.   55
There, there, Hortensio. Will you any wife?

KATHERINE (*to Baptista*)

I pray you, sir, is it your will
To make a stale of me amongst these mates?

HORTENSIO

'Mates', maid? How mean you that? No mates for
    you
Unless you were of gentler, milder mould.   60

KATHERINE

I'faith, sir, you shall never need to fear.
Iwis it is not half-way to her heart,
But if it were, doubt not her care should be
To comb your noddle with a three-legged stool,
And paint your face, and use you like a fool.   65

HORTENSIO

From all such devils, good Lord deliver us.

GREMIO And me too, good Lord.

TRANIO (*aside to Lucentio*)

Husht, master, here's some good pastime toward.
That wench is stark mad or wonderful froward.

LUCENTIO (*aside to Tranio*)

But in the other's silence do I see   70
Maid's mild behaviour and sobriety.
Peace, Tranio.

TRANIO (*aside to Lucentio*)

Well said, master. Mum, and gaze your fill.

BAPTISTA

Gentlemen, that I may soon make good
What I have said—Bianca, get you in.   75
And let it not displease thee, good Bianca,
For I will love thee ne'er the less, my girl.

KATHERINE A pretty peat! It is best
Put finger in the eye, an she knew why.

BIANCA
    Sister, content you in my discontent.   80
    (*To Baptista*) Sir, to your pleasure humbly I subscribe.
    My books and instruments shall be my company,
    On them to look and practise by myself.
LUCENTIO (*aside to Tranio*)
    Hark, Tranio, thou mayst hear Minerva speak.
HORTENSIO
    Signor Baptista, will you be so strange?   85
    Sorry am I that our good will effects
    Bianca's grief.
GREMIO   Why will you mew her up,
    Signor Baptista, for this fiend of hell,
    And make her bear the penance of her tongue?
BAPTISTA
    Gentlemen, content ye. I am resolved.   90
    Go in, Bianca.   *Exit Bianca*
    And for I know she taketh most delight
    In music, instruments, and poetry,
    Schoolmasters will I keep within my house
    Fit to instruct her youth. If you, Hortensio,   95
    Or, Signor Gremio, you know any such,
    Prefer them hither; for to cunning men
    I will be very kind, and liberal
    To mine own children in good bringing up.
    And so farewell. Katherina, you may stay,   100
    For I have more to commune with Bianca.   *Exit*
KATHERINE Why, and I trust I may go too, may I not?
    What, shall I be appointed hours, as though belike I
    knew not what to take and what to leave? Ha!   *Exit*
GREMIO You may go to the devil's dam. Your gifts are so
    good here's none will hold you. Their love is not so
    great, Hortensio, but we may blow our nails together
    and fast it fairly out. Our cake's dough on both sides.
    Farewell. Yet for the love I bear my sweet Bianca, if I
    can by any means light on a fit man to teach her that
    wherein she delights, I will wish him to her father.
HORTENSIO So will I, Signor Gremio. But a word, I pray.
    Though the nature of our quarrel yet never brooked
    parle, know now, upon advice, it toucheth us both—
    that we may yet again have access to our fair mistress
    and be happy rivals in Bianca's love—to labour and
    effect one thing specially.
GREMIO What's that, I pray?
HORTENSIO Marry, sir, to get a husband for her sister.
GREMIO A husband?—a devil!   120
HORTENSIO I say a husband.
GREMIO I say a devil. Think'st thou, Hortensio, though
    her father be very rich, any man is so very a fool to
    be married to hell?
HORTENSIO Tush, Gremio. Though it pass your patience
    and mine to endure her loud alarums, why, man, there
    be good fellows in the world, an a man could light on
    them, would take her with all faults, and money
    enough.   129
GREMIO I cannot tell, but I had as lief take her dowry
    with this condition: to be whipped at the high cross
    every morning.

HORTENSIO Faith, as you say, there's small choice in rotten
    apples. But come, since this bar in law makes us friends,
    it shall be so far forth friendly maintained till by helping
    Baptista's eldest daughter to a husband we set his
    youngest free for a husband, and then have to't afresh.
    Sweet Bianca! Happy man be his dole. He that runs
    fastest gets the ring. How say you, Signor Gremio?
GREMIO I am agreed, and would I had given him the best
    horse in Padua to begin his wooing that would
    thoroughly woo her, wed her, and bed her, and rid the
    house of her. Come on.
          Exeunt Hortensio and Gremio. Tranio and
                                        Lucentio remain
TRANIO
    I pray, sir, tell me: is it possible
    That love should of a sudden take such hold?   145
LUCENTIO
    O Tranio, till I found it to be true
    I never thought it possible or likely.
    But see, while idly I stood looking on
    I found the effect of love in idleness,
    And now in plainness do confess to thee,   150
    That art to me as secret and as dear
    As Anna to the Queen of Carthage was,
    Tranio, I burn, I pine, I perish, Tranio,
    If I achieve not this young modest girl.
    Counsel me, Tranio, for I know thou canst.   155
    Assist me, Tranio, for I know thou wilt.
TRANIO
    Master, it is no time to chide you now.
    Affection is not rated from the heart.
    If love have touched you, naught remains but so—
    Redime te captum quam queas minimo.   160
LUCENTIO
    Gramercies, lad. Go forward, this contents.
    The rest will comfort, for thy counsel's sound.
TRANIO
    Master, you looked so longly on the maid
    Perhaps you marked not what's the pith of all.
LUCENTIO
    O yes, I saw sweet beauty in her face,   165
    Such as the daughter of Agenor had,
    That made great Jove to humble him to her hand
    When with his knees he kissed the Cretan strand.
TRANIO
    Saw you no more? Marked you not how her sister
    Began to scold and raise up such a storm   170
    That mortal ears might hardly endure the din?
LUCENTIO
    Tranio, I saw her coral lips to move,
    And with her breath she did perfume the air.
    Sacred and sweet was all I saw in her.
TRANIO (*aside*)
    Nay, then 'tis time to stir him from his trance.   175
    (*To Lucentio*) I pray, awake, sir. If you love the maid,
    Bend thoughts and wits to achieve her. Thus it
          stands:
    Her elder sister is so curst and shrewd

That till the father rid his hands of her,
Master, your love must live a maid at home,   180
And therefore has he closely mewed her up
Because she will not be annoyed with suitors.

LUCENTIO
Ah, Tranio, what a cruel father's he!
But art thou not advised he took some care
To get her cunning schoolmasters to instruct her?   185

TRANIO
Ay, marry am I, sir, and now 'tis plotted.

LUCENTIO
I have it, Tranio.

TRANIO   Master, for my hand,
Both our inventions meet and jump in one.

LUCENTIO
Tell me thine first.

TRANIO   You will be schoolmaster
And undertake the teaching of the maid.   190
That's your device.

LUCENTIO   It is. May it be done?

TRANIO
Not possible; for who shall bear your part,
And be in Padua here Vincentio's son,
Keep house, and ply his book, welcome his friends,
Visit his countrymen, and banquet them?   195

LUCENTIO
Basta, content thee, for I have it full.
We have not yet been seen in any house,
Nor can we be distinguished by our faces
For man or master. Then it follows thus:
Thou shalt be master, Tranio, in my stead;   200
Keep house, and port, and servants, as I should.
I will some other be, some Florentine,
Some Neapolitan, or meaner man of Pisa.
'Tis hatched, and shall be so. Tranio, at once
Uncase theè. Take my coloured hat and cloak.   205
When Biondello comes he waits on thee,
But I will charm him first to keep his tongue.

TRANIO So had you need.
          [*They exchange clothes*]
In brief, sir, sith it your pleasure is,
And I am tied to be obedient—   210
For so your father charged me at our parting,
'Be serviceable to my son,' quoth he,
Although I think 'twas in another sense—
I am content to be Lucentio
Because so well I love Lucentio.   215

LUCENTIO
Tranio, be so, because Lucentio loves,
And let me be a slave t'achieve that maid
Whose sudden sight hath thralled my wounded eye.
          Enter Biondello
Here comes the rogue. Sirrah, where have you been?

BIONDELLO Where have *I* been? Nay, how now, where
are *you*? Master, has my fellow Tranio stolen your
clothes, or you stolen his, or both? Pray, what's the
news?

LUCENTIO
Sirrah, come hither. 'Tis no time to jest,
And therefore frame your manners to the time.   225
Your fellow Tranio here, to save my life
Puts my apparel and my count'nance on,
And I for my escape have put on his,
For in a quarrel since I came ashore
I killed a man, and fear I was descried.   230
Wait you on him, I charge you, as becomes,
While I make way from hence to save my life.
You understand me?

BIONDELLO   I sir? Ne'er a whit.

LUCENTIO
And not a jot of Tranio in your mouth.
Tranio is changed into Lucentio.   235

BIONDELLO
The better for him. Would I were so too.

TRANIO
So could I, faith, boy, to have the next wish after—
That Lucentio indeed had Baptista's youngest
          daughter.
But sirrah, not for my sake but your master's I advise
You use your manners discreetly in all kind of
          companies.   240
When I am alone, why then I am Tranio,
But in all places else your master, Lucentio.

LUCENTIO Tranio, let's go.
One thing more rests that thyself execute—
To make one among these wooers. If thou ask me
          why,   245
Sufficeth my reasons are both good and weighty.
                              Exeunt

          The presenters above speak

FIRST SERVINGMAN
My lord, you nod. You do not mind the play.

SLY Yes, by Saint Anne do I. A good matter, surely.
Comes there any more of it?

BARTHOLOMEW My lord, 'tis but begun.   250

SLY 'Tis a very excellent piece of work, madam lady.
Would 'twere done.
          They sit and mark

1.2   *Enter Petruccio and his man, Grumio*

PETRUCCIO
Verona, for a while I take my leave
To see my friends in Padua; but of all
My best-belovèd and approvèd friend
Hortensio, and I trow this is his house.
Here, șirrah Grumio, knock, I say.   5

GRUMIO Knock, sir? Whom should I knock? Is there any
man has rebused your worship?

PETRUCCIO Villain, I say, knock me here soundly.

GRUMIO Knock you here, sir? Why, sir, what am I, sir,
that I should knock you here, sir?   10

PETRUCCIO
Villain, I say, knock me at this gate,
And rap me well or I'll knock your knave's pate.

GRUMIO
My master is grown quarrelsome. I should knock you
first,
And then I know after who comes by the worst.
PETRUCCIO Will it not be?   15
Faith, sirrah, an you'll not knock, I'll ring it.
I'll try how you can sol-fa and sing it.
He wrings him by the ears. ⌈Grumio kneels⌉
GRUMIO Help, masters, help! My master is mad.
PETRUCCIO Now knock when I bid you, sirrah villain.
Enter Hortensio
HORTENSIO How now, what's the matter? My old friend
Grumio and my good friend Petruccio? How do you all
at Verona?
PETRUCCIO
Signor Hortensio, come you to part the fray?
Con tutto il cuore ben trovato, may I say.   24
HORTENSIO *Alla nostra casa ben venuto, molto onorato signor
mio Petruccio.*
Rise, Grumio, rise. We will compound this quarrel.
Grumio rises
GRUMIO Nay, 'tis no matter, sir, what he 'leges in Latin.
If this be not a lawful cause for me to leave his service—
look you, sir: he bid me knock him and rap him
soundly, sir. Well, was it fit for a servant to use his
master so, being perhaps, for aught I see, two-and-
thirty, a pip out?
Whom would to God I had well knocked at first,
Then had not Grumio come by the worst.   35
PETRUCCIO
A senseless villain. Good Hortensio,
I bade the rascal knock upon your gate,
And could not get him for my heart to do it.
GRUMIO Knock at the gate? O heavens, spake you not
these words plain? 'Sirrah, knock me here, rap me
here, knock me well, and knock me soundly'? And
come you now with knocking at the gate?
PETRUCCIO
Sirrah, be gone, or talk not, I advise you.
HORTENSIO
Petruccio, patience. I am Grumio's pledge.
Why this' a heavy chance 'twixt him and you,   45
Your ancient, trusty, pleasant servant Grumio.
And tell me now, sweet friend, what happy gale
Blows you to Padua here from old Verona?
PETRUCCIO
Such wind as scatters young men through the world
To seek their fortunes farther than at home,   50
Where small experience grows. But in a few,
Signor Hortensio, thus it stands with me:
Antonio, my father, is deceased,
And I have thrust myself into this maze
Happily to wive and thrive as best I may.   55
Crowns in my purse I have, and goods at home,
And so am come abroad to see the world.
HORTENSIO
Petruccio, shall I then come roundly to thee
And wish thee to a shrewd, ill-favoured wife?

Thou'dst thank me but a little for my counsel,   60
And yet I'll promise thee she shall be rich,
And very rich. But thou'rt too much my friend,
And I'll not wish thee to her.
PETRUCCIO
Signor Hortensio, 'twixt such friends as we
Few words suffice; and therefore, if thou know   65
One rich enough to be Petruccio's wife—
As wealth is burden of my wooing dance—
Be she as foul as was Florentius' love,
As old as Sibyl, and as curst and shrewd
As Socrates' Xanthippe or a worse,   70
She moves me not—or not removes at least
Affection's edge in me, were she as rough
As are the swelling Adriatic seas.
I come to wive it wealthily in Padua;
If wealthily, then happily in Padua.   75
GRUMIO (*to Hortensio*) Nay, look you, sir, he tells you flatly
what his mind is. Why, give him gold enough and
marry him to a puppet or an aglet-baby, or an old trot
with ne'er a tooth in her head, though she have as
many diseases as two-and-fifty horses. Why, nothing
comes amiss so money comes withal.   81
HORTENSIO
Petruccio, since we are stepped thus far in,
I will continue that I broached in jest.
I can, Petruccio, help thee to a wife
With wealth enough, and young and beauteous,   85
Brought up as best becomes a gentlewoman.
Her only fault—and that is faults enough—
Is that she is intolerable curst,
And shrewd and froward so beyond all measure
That, were my state far worser than it is,   90
I would not wed her for a mine of gold.
PETRUCCIO
Hortensio, peace. Thou know'st not gold's effect.
Tell me her father's name and 'tis enough,
For I will board her though she chide as loud
As thunder when the clouds in autumn crack.   95
HORTENSIO
Her father is Baptista Minola,
An affable and courteous gentleman.
Her name is Katherina Minola,
Renowned in Padua for her scolding tongue.
PETRUCCIO
I know her father, though I know not her,   100
And he knew my deceasèd father well.
I will not sleep, Hortensio, till I see her,
And therefore let me be thus bold with you
To give you over at this first encounter,
Unless you will accompany me thither.   105
GRUMIO I pray you, sir, let him go while the humour
lasts. O' my word, an she knew him as well as I do
she would think scolding would do little good upon
him. She may perhaps call him half a score knaves or
so. Why, that's nothing; an he begin once he'll rail in
his rope-tricks. I'll tell you what, sir, an she stand him
but a little he will throw a figure in her face and so

disfigure her with it that she shall have no more eyes
to see withal than a cat. You know him not, sir.

HORTENSIO
Tarry, Petruccio, I must go with thee,   115
For in Baptista's keep my treasure is.
He hath the jewel of my life in hold,
His youngest daughter, beautiful Bianca,
And her withholds from me and other more,
Suitors to her and rivals in my love,   120
Supposing it a thing impossible,
For those defects I have before rehearsed,
That ever Katherina will be wooed.
Therefore this order hath Baptista ta'en:
That none shall have access unto Bianca   125
Till Katherine the curst have got a husband.

GRUMIO Katherine the curst—
A title for a maid of all titles the worst.

HORTENSIO
Now shall my friend Petruccio do me grace,
And offer me disguised in sober robes   130
To old Baptista as a schoolmaster
Well seen in music, to instruct Bianca,
That so I may by this device at least
Have leave and leisure to make love to her,
And unsuspected court her by herself.   135

Enter Gremio with a paper, and Lucentio disguised
as a schoolmaster

GRUMIO Here's no knavery. See, to beguile the old folks,
how the young folks lay their heads together. Master,
master, look about you. Who goes there, ha?

HORTENSIO
Peace, Grumio, it is the rival of my love.
Petruccio, stand by a while.   140

GRUMIO
A proper stripling, and an amorous!

Petruccio, Hortensio, and Grumio stand aside

GREMIO (*to Lucentio*)
O, very well—I have perused the note.
Hark you, sir, I'll have them very fairly bound—
All books of love, see that at any hand—
And see you read no other lectures to her.   145
You understand me. Over and beside
Signor Baptista's liberality,
I'll mend it with a largess. Take your paper, too,
And let me have them very well perfumed,
For she is sweeter than perfume itself   150
To whom they go to. What will you read to her?

LUCENTIO
Whate'er I read to her, I'll plead for you
As for my patron, stand you so assured,
As firmly as yourself were still in place—
Yea, and perhaps with more successful words   155
Than you, unless you were a scholar, sir.

GREMIO
O this learning, what a thing it is!

GRUMIO (*aside*)
O this woodcock, what an ass it is!

PETRUCCIO Peace, sirrah.

HORTENSIO
Grumio, mum. (*Coming forward*) God save you, Signor
Gremio.   160

GREMIO
And you are well met, Signor Hortensio.
Trow you whither I am going? To Baptista Minola.
I promised to enquire carefully
About a schoolmaster for the fair Bianca,   165
And by good fortune I have lighted well
On this young man, for learning and behaviour
Fit for her turn, well read in poetry
And other books—good ones, I warrant ye.

HORTENSIO
'Tis well, and I have met a gentleman   170
Hath promised me to help me to another,
A fine musician, to instruct our mistress.
So shall I no whit be behind in duty
To fair Bianca, so beloved of me.

GREMIO
Beloved of me, and that my deeds shall prove.   175

GRUMIO (*aside*) And that his bags shall prove.

HORTENSIO
Gremio, 'tis now no time to vent our love.
Listen to me, and if you speak me fair
I'll tell you news indifferent good for either.
Here is a gentleman whom by chance I met,   180
Upon agreement from us to his liking
Will undertake to woo curst Katherine,
Yea, and to marry her, if her dowry please.

GREMIO So said, so done, is well.
Hortensio, have you told him all her faults?   185

PETRUCCIO
I know she is an irksome brawling scold.
If that be all, masters, I hear no harm.

GREMIO
No, sayst me so, friend? What countryman?

PETRUCCIO
Born in Verona, old Antonio's son.
My father dead, his fortune lives for me,   190
And I do hope good days and long to see.

GREMIO O sir, such a life with such a wife were strange.
But if you have a stomach, to't, a' God's name.
You shall have me assisting you in all.
But will you woo this wildcat?

PETRUCCIO   Will I live!   195

GRUMIO
Will he woo her? Ay, or I'll hang her.

PETRUCCIO
Why came I hither but to that intent?
Think you a little din can daunt mine ears?
Have I not in my time heard lions roar?
Have I not heard the sea, puffed up with winds,   200
Rage like an angry boar chafèd with sweat?
Have I not heard great ordnance in the field,
And heaven's artillery thunder in the skies?
Have I not in a pitchèd battle heard   204
Loud 'larums, neighing steeds, and trumpets' clang?

And do you tell me of a woman's tongue,
That gives not half so great a blow to hear
As will a chestnut in a farmer's fire?
Tush, tush—fear boys with bugs.
GRUMIO For he fears none.   210
GREMIO Hortensio, hark.
    This gentleman is happily arrived,
    My mind presumes, for his own good and ours.
HORTENSIO
    I promised we would be contributors,
    And bear his charge of wooing, whatsoe'er.   215
GREMIO
    And so we will, provided that he win her.
GREMIO
    I would I were as sure of a good dinner.
        Enter Tranio, brave, as Lucentio, and Biondello
TRANIO Gentlemen, God save you. If I may be bold, tell
    me, I beseech you, which is the readiest way to the
    house of Signor Baptista Minola?   220
BIONDELLO He that has the two fair daughters—is't he
    you mean?
TRANIO Even he, Biondello.
GREMIO
    Hark you, sir, you mean not her to—
TRANIO
    Perhaps him and her, sir. What have you to do?   225
PETRUCCIO
    Not her that chides, sir, at any hand, I pray.
TRANIO
    I love no chiders, sir. Biondello, let's away.
LUCENTIO (*aside*)
    Well begun, Tranio.
HORTENSIO   Sir, a word ere you go.
    Are you a suitor to the maid you talk of—yea or no?
TRANIO
    And if I be, sir, is it any offence?   230
GREMIO
    No, if without more words you will get you hence.
TRANIO
    Why, sir, I pray, are not the streets as free
    For me as for you?
GREMIO   But so is not she.
TRANIO
    For what reason, I beseech you?
GREMIO
    For this reason, if you'll know—   235
    That she's the choice love of Signor Gremio.
HORTENSIO
    That she's the chosen of Signor Hortensio.
TRANIO
    Softly, my masters. If you be gentlemen,
    Do me this right, hear me with patience.
    Baptista is a noble gentleman   240
    To whom my father is not all unknown,
    And were his daughter fairer than she is
    She may more suitors have, and me for one.
    Fair Leda's daughter had a thousand wooers;
    Then well one more may fair Bianca have,   245

And so she shall. Lucentio shall make one,
    Though Paris came, in hope to speed alone.
GREMIO
    What, this gentleman will out-talk us all!
LUCENTIO
    Sir, give him head, I know he'll prove a jade.
PETRUCCIO
    Hortensio, to what end are all these words?   250
HORTENSIO
    Sir, let me be so bold as ask you,
    Did you yet ever see Baptista's daughter?
TRANIO
    No, sir, but hear I do that he hath two,
    The one as famous for a scolding tongue
    As is the other for beauteous modesty.   255
PETRUCCIO
    Sir, sir, the first's for me. Let her go by.
GREMIO
    Yea, leave that labour to great Hercules,
    And let it be more than Alcides' twelve.
PETRUCCIO
    Sir, understand you this of me in sooth,
    The youngest daughter whom you hearken for   260
    Her father keeps from all access of suitors,
    And will not promise her to any man
    Until the elder sister first be wed.
    The younger then is free, and not before.
TRANIO
    If it be so, sir, that you are the man   265
    Must stead us all, and me amongst the rest,
    And if you break the ice and do this feat,
    Achieve the elder, set the younger free
    For our access, whose hap shall be to have her
    Will not so graceless be to be ingrate.   270
HORTENSIO
    Sir, you say well, and well you do conceive;
    And since you do profess to be a suitor
    You must, as we do, gratify this gentleman,
    To whom we all rest generally beholden.
TRANIO
    Sir, I shall not be slack. In sign whereof,   275
    Please ye we may contrive this afternoon,
    And quaff carouses to our mistress' health,
    And do as adversaries do in law—
    Strive mightily, but eat and drink as friends.
GRUMIO *and* BIONDELLO
    O excellent motion! Fellows, let's be gone.   280
HORTENSIO
    The motion's good indeed, and be it so.
    Petruccio, I shall be your *ben venuto*.   *Exeunt*

2.1   *Enter Katherina and Bianca, her hands bound*
BIANCA
    Good sister, wrong me not, nor wrong yourself
    To make a bondmaid and a slave of me.
    That I disdain, but for these other goods,
    Unbind my hands, I'll pull them off myself,
    Yea, all my raiment to my petticoat,   5

Or what you will command me will I do,
So well I know my duty to my elders.
KATHERINE
Of all thy suitors here I charge thee tell
Whom thou lov'st best. See thou dissemble not.
BIANCA
Believe me, sister, of all the men alive   10
I never yet beheld that special face
Which I could fancy more than any other.
KATHERINE
Minion, thou liest. Is't not Hortensio?
BIANCA
If you affect him, sister, here I swear
I'll plead for you myself but you shall have him.   15
KATHERINE
O then, belike you fancy riches more.
You will have Gremio to keep you fair.
BIANCA
Is it for him you do envy me so?
Nay, then, you jest, and now I well perceive
You have but jested with me all this while.   20
I prithee, sister Kate, untie my hands.
KATHERINE (*strikes her*)
If that be jest, then all the rest was so.
          Enter Baptista
BAPTISTA
Why, how now, dame, whence grows this insolence?
Bianca, stand aside.—Poor girl, she weeps.—
Go ply thy needle, meddle not with her.   25
(*To Katherine*) For shame, thou hilding of a devilish
          spirit,
Why dost thou wrong her that did ne'er wrong thee?
When did she cross thee with a bitter word?
KATHERINE
Her silence flouts me, and I'll be revenged.
          She flies after Bianca
BAPTISTA
What, in my sight? Bianca, get thee in.   *Exit Bianca*
KATHERINE
What, will you not suffer me? Nay, now I see
She is your treasure, she must have a husband.
I must dance barefoot on her wedding day,
And for your love to her lead apes in hell.
Talk not to me. I will go sit and weep   35
Till I can find occasion of revenge.   *Exit*
BAPTISTA
Was ever gentleman thus grieved as I?
But who comes here?
          *Enter Gremio, Lucentio as a schoolmaster in the
          habit of a mean man, Petruccio with Hortensio as
          a musician, Tranio as Lucentio, with Biondello his
          boy bearing a lute and books*
GREMIO Good morrow, neighbour Baptista.
BAPTISTA Good morrow, neighbour Gremio. God save you,
gentlemen.   41
PETRUCCIO
And you, good sir. Pray, have you not a daughter
Called Katherina, fair and virtuous?

BAPTISTA
I have a daughter, sir, called Katherina.
GREMIO
You are too blunt. Go to it orderly.   45
PETRUCCIO
You wrong me, Signor Gremio. Give me leave.
(*To Baptista*) I am a gentleman of Verona, sir,
That hearing of her beauty and her wit,
Her affability and bashful modesty,
Her wondrous qualities and mild behaviour,   50
Am bold to show myself a forward guest
Within your house to make mine eye the witness
Of that report which I so oft have heard,
And for an entrance to my entertainment
I do present you with a man of mine (*presenting
          Hortensio*)   55
Cunning in music and the mathematics
To instruct her fully in those sciences,
Whereof I know she is not ignorant.
Accept of him, or else you do me wrong.
His name is Licio, born in Mantua.   60
BAPTISTA
You're welcome, sir, and he for your good sake.
But for my daughter, Katherine, this I know:
She is not for your turn, the more my grief.
PETRUCCIO
I see you do not mean to part with her,
Or else you like not of my company.   65
BAPTISTA
Mistake me not, I speak but as I find.
Whence are you, sir? What may I call your name?
PETRUCCIO
Petruccio is my name, Antonio's son,
A man well known throughout all Italy.
BAPTISTA
I know him well. You are welcome for his sake.   70
GREMIO
Saving your tale, Petruccio, I pray
Let us that are poor petitioners speak too.
Baccare, you are marvellous forward.
PETRUCCIO
O pardon me, Signor Gremio, I would fain be doing.
GREMIO
I doubt it not, sir. But you will curse your wooing.   75
(*To Baptista*) Neighbour, this is a gift very grateful, I
am sure of it. To express the like kindness, myself, that
have been more kindly beholden to you than any,
freely give unto you this young scholar (*presenting
Lucentio*) that hath been long studying at Rheims, as
cunning in Greek, Latin, and other languages as the
other in music and mathematics. His name is Cambio.
Pray accept his service.
BAPTISTA A thousand thanks, Signor Gremio. Welcome,
good Cambio. (*To Tranio*) But, gentle sir, methinks you
walk like a stranger. May I be so bold to know the
cause of your coming?   87
TRANIO
Pardon me, sir, the boldness is mine own
That, being a stranger in this city here,

Do make myself a suitor to your daughter,   90
Unto Bianca, fair and virtuous.
Nor is your firm resolve unknown to me
In the preferment of the eldest sister.
This liberty is all that I request:
That upon knowledge of my parentage   95
I may have welcome 'mongst the rest that woo,
And free access and favour as the rest.
And toward the education of your daughters
I here bestow a simple instrument,
And this small packet of Greek and Latin books.   100
If you accept them, then their worth is great.
BAPTISTA
Lucentio is your name—of whence, I pray?
TRANIO
Of Pisa, sir, son to Vincentio.
BAPTISTA
A mighty man of Pisa. By report
I know him well. You are very welcome, sir.   105
(*To Hortensio*) Take you the lute, (*to Lucentio*) and you
  the set of books.
You shall go see your pupils presently.
Holla, within!
          Enter a Servant
                    Sirrah, lead these gentlemen
To my daughters, and tell them both
These are their tutors. Bid them use them well.   110
          Exit Servant with Lucentio and Hortensio,
                    ⌈*Biondello following*⌉
(*To Petruccio*) We will go walk a little in the orchard,
And then to dinner. You are passing welcome—
And so I pray you all to think yourselves.
PETRUCCIO
Signor Baptista, my business asketh haste,
And every day I cannot come to woo.   115
You knew my father well, and in him me,
Left solely heir to all his lands and goods,
Which I have bettered rather than decreased.
Then tell me, if I get your daughter's love,
What dowry shall I have with her to wife?   120
BAPTISTA
After my death the one half of my lands,
And in possession twenty thousand crowns.
PETRUCCIO
And for that dowry I'll assure her of
Her widowhood, be it that she survive me,
In all my lands and leases whatsoever.   125
Let specialties be therefore drawn between us,
That covenants may be kept on either hand.
BAPTISTA
Ay, when the special thing is well obtained—
That is her love, for that is all in all.
PETRUCCIO
Why, that is nothing, for I tell you, father,   130
I am as peremptory as she proud-minded,
And where two raging fires meet together
They do consume the thing that feeds their fury.
Though little fire grows great with little wind,

Yet extreme gusts will blow out fire and all.   135
So I to her, and so she yields to me,
For I am rough, and woo not like a babe.
BAPTISTA
Well mayst thou woo, and happy be thy speed.
But be thou armed for some unhappy words.
PETRUCCIO
Ay, to the proof, as mountains are for winds,   140
That shakes not though they blow perpetually.
          Enter Hortensio with his head broke
BAPTISTA
How now, my friend, why dost thou look so pale?
HORTENSIO
For fear, I promise you, if I look pale.
BAPTISTA
What, will my daughter prove a good musician?
HORTENSIO
I think she'll sooner prove a soldier.   145
Iron may hold with her, but never lutes.
BAPTISTA
Why then, thou canst not break her to the lute?
HORTENSIO
Why no, for she hath broke the lute to me.
I did but tell her she mistook her frets,
And bowed her hand to teach her fingering,   150
When, with a most impatient devilish spirit,
'Frets, call you these?' quoth she, 'I'll fume with
  them,'
And with that word she struck me on the head,
And through the instrument my pate made way,
And there I stood amazèd for a while,   155
As on a pillory, looking through the lute,
While she did call me rascal, fiddler,
And twangling jack, with twenty such vile terms,
As had she studied to misuse me so.
PETRUCCIO
Now, by the world, it is a lusty wench!   160
I love her ten times more than e'er I did.
O, how I long to have some chat with her!
BAPTISTA (*to Hortensio*)
Well, go with me, and be not so discomfited.
Proceed in practice with my younger daughter.
She's apt to learn, and thankful for good turns.   165
Signor Petruccio, will you go with us,
Or shall I send my daughter Kate to you?
PETRUCCIO
I pray you, do.   *Exeunt all but Petruccio*
          I'll attend her here,
And woo her with some spirit when she comes.
Say that she rail, why then I'll tell her plain   170
She sings as sweetly as a nightingale.
Say that she frown, I'll say she looks as clear
As morning roses newly washed with dew.
Say she be mute and will not speak a word,
Then I'll commend her volubility,   175
And say she uttereth piercing eloquence.
If she do bid me pack, I'll give her thanks
As though she bid me stay by her a week.

If she deny to wed, I'll crave the day
When I shall ask the banns, and when be marrièd. 180
But here she comes, and now, Petruccio, speak.
Enter Katherina
Good morrow, Kate, for that's your name, I hear.

KATHERINE
Well have you heard, but something hard of hearing.
They call me Katherine that do talk of me.

PETRUCCIO
You lie, in faith, for you are called plain Kate,   185
And bonny Kate, and sometimes Kate the curst,
But Kate, the prettiest Kate in Christendom,
Kate of Kate Hall, my super-dainty Kate—
For dainties are all cates, and therefore 'Kate'—
Take this of me, Kate of my consolation: 190
Hearing thy mildness praised in every town,
Thy virtues spoke of, and thy beauty sounded—
Yet not so deeply as to thee belongs—
Myself am moved to woo thee for my wife.

KATHERINE
Moved? In good time. Let him that moved you hither
Re-move you hence. I knew you at the first   196
You were a movable.

PETRUCCIO   Why, what's a movable?

KATHERINE
A joint-stool.

PETRUCCIO   Thou hast hit it. Come, sit on me.

KATHERINE
Asses are made to bear, and so are you.

PETRUCCIO
Women are made to bear, and so are you.   200

KATHERINE
No such jade as you, if me you mean.

PETRUCCIO
Alas, good Kate, I will not burden thee,
For knowing thee to be but young and light.

KATHERINE
Too light for such a swain as you to catch,
And yet as heavy as my weight should be.   205

PETRUCCIO
Should be?—should buzz.

KATHERINE   Well ta'en, and like a buzzard.

PETRUCCIO
O slow-winged turtle, shall a buzzard take thee?

KATHERINE
Ay, for a turtle, as he takes a buzzard.

PETRUCCIO
Come, come, you wasp, i'faith you are too angry.

KATHERINE
If I be waspish, best beware my sting.   210

PETRUCCIO
My remedy is then to pluck it out.

KATHERINE
Ay, if the fool could find it where it lies.

PETRUCCIO
Who knows not where a wasp does wear his sting?
In his tail.

KATHERINE   In his tongue.

PETRUCCIO   Whose tongue?

KATHERINE
Yours, if you talk of tales, and so farewell.   215

PETRUCCIO
What, with my tongue in your tail? Nay, come again,
Good Kate, I am a gentleman.

KATHERINE   That I'll try.
She strikes him

PETRUCCIO
I swear I'll cuff you if you strike again.

KATHERINE So may you lose your arms.
If you strike me you are no gentleman,   220
And if no gentleman, why then, no arms.

PETRUCCIO
A herald, Kate? O, put me in thy books.

KATHERINE What is your crest—a coxcomb?

PETRUCCIO
A combless cock, so Kate will be my hen.

KATHERINE
No cock of mine. You crow too like a craven.   225

PETRUCCIO
Nay, come, Kate, come. You must not look so sour.

KATHERINE
It is my fashion when I see a crab.

PETRUCCIO
Why, here's no crab, and therefore look not sour.

KATHERINE There is, there is.

PETRUCCIO Then show it me.   230

KATHERINE Had I a glass I would.

PETRUCCIO
What, you mean my face?

KATHERINE   Well aimed, of such a young one.

PETRUCCIO
Now, by Saint George, I am too young for you.

KATHERINE
Yet you are withered.

PETRUCCIO   'Tis with cares.

KATHERINE   I care not.

PETRUCCIO
Nay, hear you, Kate. In sooth, you scape not so.   235

KATHERINE
I chafe you if I tarry. Let me go.

PETRUCCIO
No, not a whit. I find you passing gentle.
'Twas told me you were rough, and coy, and sullen,
And now I find report a very liar,   239
For thou art pleasant, gamesome, passing courteous,
But slow in speech, yet sweet as springtime flowers.
Thou canst not frown. Thou canst not look askance,
Nor bite the lip, as angry wenches will,
Nor hast thou pleasure to be cross in talk,
But thou with mildness entertain'st thy wooers,   245
With gentle conference, soft, and affable.
Why does the world report that Kate doth limp?
O sland'rous world! Kate like the hazel twig
Is straight and slender, and as brown in hue
As hazelnuts, and sweeter than the kernels.   250
O let me see thee walk. Thou dost not halt.

KATHERINE
Go, fool, and whom thou keep'st command.

PETRUCCIO
Did ever Dian so become a grove
As Kate this chamber with her princely gait?
O, be thou Dian, and let her be Kate,   255
And then let Kate be chaste and Dian sportful.

KATHERINE
Where did you study all this goodly speech?

PETRUCCIO
It is extempore, from my mother-wit.

KATHERINE
A witty mother, witless else her son.

PETRUCCIO
Am I not wise?

KATHERINE   Yes, keep you warm.   260

PETRUCCIO
Marry, so I mean, sweet Katherine, in thy bed.
And therefore setting all this chat aside,
Thus in plain terms: your father hath consented
That you shall be my wife, your dowry 'greed on,
And will you, nill you, I will marry you.   265
Now, Kate, I am a husband for your turn,
For by this light, whereby I see thy beauty—
Thy beauty that doth make me like thee well—
Thou must be married to no man but me,
        Enter Baptista, Gremio, and Tranio as Lucentio
For I am he am born to tame you, Kate,   270
And bring you from a wild Kate to a Kate
Conformable as other household Kates.
Here comes your father. Never make denial.
I must and will have Katherine to my wife.

BAPTISTA Now, Signor Petruccio, how speed you with my
daughter?   276

PETRUCCIO How but well, sir, how but well?
It were impossible I should speed amiss.

BAPTISTA
Why, how now, daughter Katherine—in your dumps?

KATHERINE
Call you me daughter? Now I promise you   280
You have showed a tender fatherly regard,
To wish me wed to one half-lunatic,
A madcap ruffian and a swearing Jack,
That thinks with oaths to face the matter out.

PETRUCCIO
Father, 'tis thus: yourself and all the world   285
That talked of her have talked amiss of her.
If she be curst, it is for policy,
For she's not froward, but modest as the dove.
She is not hot, but temperate as the morn.
For patience she will prove a second Grissel,   290
And Roman Lucrece for her chastity.
And to conclude, we have 'greed so well together
That upon Sunday is the wedding day.

KATHERINE
I'll see thee hanged on Sunday first.

GREMIO Hark, Petruccio, she says she'll see thee hanged
first.   296

TRANIO
Is this your speeding? Nay then, goodnight our part.

PETRUCCIO
Be patient, gentlemen. I choose her for myself.
If she and I be pleased, what's that to you?
'Tis bargained 'twixt us twain, being alone,   300
That she shall still be curst in company.
I tell you, 'tis incredible to believe
How much she loves me. O, the kindest Kate!
She hung about my neck, and kiss on kiss
She vied so fast, protesting oath on oath,   305
That in a twink she won me to her love.
O, you are novices. 'Tis a world to see
How tame, when men and women are alone,
A meacock wretch can make the curstest shrew.
Give me thy hand, Kate. I will unto Venice,   310
To buy apparel 'gainst the wedding day.
Provide the feast, father, and bid the guests.
I will be sure my Katherine shall be fine.

BAPTISTA
I know not what to say, but give me your hands.
God send you joy, Petruccio! 'Tis a match.   315

GREMIO *and* TRANIO
Amen, say we. We will be witnesses.

PETRUCCIO
Father, and wife, and gentlemen, adieu.
I will to Venice. Sunday comes apace.
We will have rings, and things, and fine array;
And kiss me, Kate. We will be married o' Sunday.   320
        Exeunt Petruccio and Katherine, severally

GREMIO
Was ever match clapped up so suddenly?

BAPTISTA
Faith, gentlemen, now I play a merchant's part,
And venture madly on a desperate mart.

TRANIO
'Twas a commodity lay fretting by you.
'Twill bring you gain, or perish on the seas.   325

BAPTISTA
The gain I seek is quiet in the match.

GREMIO
No doubt but he hath got a quiet catch.
But now, Baptista, to your younger daughter.
Now is the day we long have looked for.
I am your neighbour, and was suitor first.   330

TRANIO
And I am one that love Bianca more
Than words can witness, or your thoughts can guess.

GREMIO
Youngling, thou canst not love so dear as I.

TRANIO
Greybeard, thy love doth freeze.

GREMIO   But thine doth fry.
Skipper, stand back. 'Tis age that nourisheth.   335

TRANIO
But youth in ladies' eyes that flourisheth.

BAPTISTA
Content you, gentlemen. I will compound this strife.
'Tis deeds must win the prize, and he of both
That can assure my daughter greatest dower

Shall have my Bianca's love.
Say, Signor Gremio, what can you assure her? 340

GREMIO
First, as you know, my house within the city
Is richly furnishèd with plate and gold,
Basins and ewers to lave her dainty hands;
My hangings all of Tyrian tapestry. 345
In ivory coffers I have stuffed my crowns,
In cypress chests my arras counterpoints,
Costly apparel, tents and canopies,
Fine linen, Turkey cushions bossed with pearl,
Valance of Venice gold in needlework, 350
Pewter, and brass, and all things that belongs
To house or housekeeping. Then at my farm
I have a hundred milch-kine to the pail,
Six score fat oxen standing in my stalls,
And all things answerable to this portion. 355
Myself am struck in years, I must confess,
And if I die tomorrow this is hers,
If whilst I live she will be only mine.

TRANIO
That 'only' came well in. Sir, list to me.
I am my father's heir and only son. 360
If I may have your daughter to my wife
I'll leave her houses three or four as good,
Within rich Pisa walls, as any one
Old Signor Gremio has in Padua,
Besides two thousand ducats by the year 365
Of fruitful land, all which shall be her jointure.
What, have I pinched you, Signor Gremio?

GREMIO
Two thousand ducats by the year of land—
My land amounts not to so much in all.
That she shall have; besides, an argosy 370
That now is lying in Marseilles road.
What, have I choked you with an argosy?

TRANIO
Gremio, 'tis known my father hath no less
Than three great argosies, besides two galliasses
And twelve tight galleys. These I will assure her, 375
And twice as much whate'er thou off'rest next.

GREMIO
Nay, I have offered all. I have no more,
And she can have no more than all I have.
If you like me, she shall have me and mine.

TRANIO
Why then, the maid is mine from all the world. 380
By your firm promise Gremio is out-vied.

BAPTISTA
I must confess your offer is the best,
And let your father make her the assurance,
She is your own. Else, you must pardon me,
If you should die before him, where's her dower? 385

TRANIO
That's but a cavil. He is old, I young.

GREMIO
And may not young men die as well as old?

BAPTISTA Well, gentlemen,

I am thus resolved. On Sunday next, you know,
My daughter Katherine is to be married. 390
(To Tranio) Now, on the Sunday following shall
    Bianca
Be bride to you, if you make this assurance;
If not, to Signor Gremio.
And so I take my leave, and thank you both.

GREMIO
Adieu, good neighbour.   Exit Baptista
                        Now I fear thee not. 395
Sirrah, young gamester, your father were a fool
To give thee all, and in his waning age
Set foot under thy table. Tut, a toy!
An old Italian fox is not so kind, my boy.   Exit

TRANIO
A vengeance on your crafty withered hide! 400
Yet I have faced it with a card of ten.
'Tis in my head to do my master good.
I see no reason but supposed Lucentio
Must get a father called supposed Vincentio—
And that's a wonder; fathers commonly 405
Do get their children, but in this case of wooing
A child shall get a sire, if I fail not of my cunning.
                                            Exit

3.1   Enter Lucentio with books, as Cambio, Hortensio
        with a lute, as Licio, and Bianca

LUCENTIO
Fiddler, forbear. You grow too forward, sir.
Have you so soon forgot the entertainment
Her sister Katherine welcomed you withal?

HORTENSIO
But, wrangling pedant, this Bianca is,
The patroness of heavenly harmony. 5
Then give me leave to have prerogative,
And when in music we have spent an hour
Your lecture shall have leisure for as much.

LUCENTIO
Preposterous ass, that never read so far
To know the cause why music was ordained! 10
Was it not to refresh the mind of man
After his studies or his usual pain?
Then give me leave to read philosophy,
And while I pause, serve in your harmony.

HORTENSIO
Sirrah, I will not bear these braves of thine. 15

BIANCA
Why, gentlemen, you do me double wrong
To strive for that which resteth in my choice.
I am no breeching scholar in the schools.
I'll not be tied to hours nor 'pointed times,
But learn my lessons as I please myself; 20
And to cut off all strife, here sit we down.
(To Hortensio) Take you your instrument, play you the
    whiles.
His lecture will be done ere you have tuned.

HORTENSIO
You'll leave his lecture when I am in tune?

LUCENTIO
  That will be never. Tune your instrument.   25
    Hortensio tunes his lute. Lucentio opens a book
BIANCA Where left we last?
LUCENTIO Here, madam.
    (*Reads*) '*Hic ibat Simois, hic est Sigeia tellus,*
        Hic steterat Priami regia celsa senis.'
BIANCA Construe them.   30
LUCENTIO '*Hic ibat*', as I told you before—'*Simois*', I am
  Lucentio—'*hic est*', son unto Vincentio of Pisa—'*Sigeia*
  tellus', disguised thus to get your love—'*hic steterat*',
  and that Lucentio that comes a-wooing—'*Priami*', is
  my man Tranio—'*regia*', bearing my port—'*celsa senis*',
  that we might beguile the old pantaloon.   36
HORTENSIO Madam, my instrument's in tune.
BIANCA Let's hear. (*Hortensio plays*) O fie, the treble jars.
LUCENTIO Spit in the hole, man, and tune again.
    Hortensio tunes his lute again
BIANCA Now let me see if I can construe it. '*Hic ibat*
  Simois', I know you not—'*hic est Sigeia tellus*', I trust
  you not—'*hic steterat Priami*', take heed he hear us
  not—'*regia*', presume not—'*celsa senis*', despair not.
HORTENSIO
  Madam, 'tis now in tune.
LUCENTIO   All but the bass.
HORTENSIO
  The bass is right, 'tis the base knave that jars.   45
  (*Aside*) How fiery and forward our pedant is!
  Now, for my life, the knave doth court my love.
  Pedascule, I'll watch you better yet.
BIANCA (*to Lucentio*)
  In time I may believe; yet, I mistrust.
LUCENTIO
  Mistrust it not, for sure Aeacides   50
  Was Ajax, called so from his grandfather.
BIANCA
  I must believe my master, else, I promise you,
  I should be arguing still upon that doubt.
  But let it rest. Now Licio, to you.
  Good master, take it not unkindly, pray,   55
  That I have been thus pleasant with you both.
HORTENSIO (*to Lucentio*)
  You may go walk and give me leave awhile.
  My lessons make no music in three parts.
LUCENTIO
  Are you so formal, sir? Well, I must wait.
  (*Aside*) And watch withal, for but I be deceived   60
  Our fine musician groweth amorous.
HORTENSIO
  Madam, before you touch the instrument
  To learn the order of my fingering,
  I must begin with rudiments of art,
  To teach you gamut in a briefer sort,   65
  More pleasant, pithy, and effectual
  Than hath been taught by any of my trade;
  And there it is in writing, fairly drawn.
    He gives a paper
BIANCA
  Why, I am past my gamut long ago.

HORTENSIO
  Yet read the gamut of Hortensio.   70
BIANCA (*reads*)
  '*Gam-ut* I am, the ground of all accord,
    A—*re*—to plead Hortensio's passion.
    B—*mi*—Bianca, take him for thy lord,
    C—*fa, ut*—that loves with all affection.
    D—*sol, re*—one clef, two notes have I,   75
    E—*la, mi*—show pity, or I die.'
  Call you this gamut? Tut, I like it not.
  Old fashions please me best. I am not so nice
  To change true rules for odd inventions.
    Enter a Messenger
MESSENGER
  Mistress, your father prays you leave your books   80
  And help to dress your sister's chamber up.
  You know tomorrow is the wedding day.
BIANCA
  Farewell, sweet masters both. I must be gone.
LUCENTIO
  Faith, mistress, then I have no cause to stay.
    Exeunt Bianca, Messenger, and Lucentio
HORTENSIO
  But I have cause to pry into this pedant.   85
  Methinks he looks as though he were in love.
  Yet if thy thoughts, Bianca, be so humble
  To cast thy wand'ring eyes on every stale,
  Seize thee that list. If once I find thee ranging,
  Hortensio will be quit with thee by changing. *Exit* 90

3.2   *Enter Baptista, Gremio, Tranio as Lucentio,*
        Katherine, Bianca, and others, attendants
BAPTISTA (*to Tranio*)
  Signor Lucentio, this is the 'pointed day
  That Katherine and Petruccio should be married,
  And yet we hear not of our son-in-law.
  What will be said, what mockery will it be,
  To want the bridegroom when the priest attends   5
  To speak the ceremonial rites of marriage?
  What says Lucentio to this shame of ours?
KATHERINE
  No shame but mine. I must forsooth be forced
  To give my hand opposed against my heart
  Unto a mad-brain rudesby full of spleen,   10
  Who wooed in haste and means to wed at leisure.
  I told you, I, he was a frantic fool,
  Hiding his bitter jests in blunt behaviour,
  And to be noted for a merry man
  He'll woo a thousand, 'point the day of marriage,   15
  Make friends, invite them, and proclaim the banns,
  Yet never means to wed where he hath wooed.
  Now must the world point at poor Katherine
  And say 'Lo, there is mad Petruccio's wife,
  If it would please him come and marry her.'   20
TRANIO
  Patience, good Katherine, and Baptista, too.
  Upon my life, Petruccio means but well.
  Whatever fortune stays him from his word,

Though he be blunt, I know him passing wise;
Though he be merry, yet withal he's honest.   25
KATHERINE
Would Katherine had never seen him, though.
Exit weeping
BAPTISTA
Go, girl. I cannot blame thee now to weep.
For such an injury would vex a very saint,
Much more a shrew of thy impatient humour.
Enter Biondello
BIONDELLO Master, master, news—old news, and such
news as you never heard of.   31
BAPTISTA Is it new and old too? How may that be?
BIONDELLO Why, is it not news to hear of Petruccio's
coming?
BAPTISTA Is he come?   35
BIONDELLO Why, no, sir.
BAPTISTA What then?
BIONDELLO He is coming.
BAPTISTA When will he be here?
BIONDELLO When he stands where I am and sees you
there.   41
TRANIO But say, what to thine old news?
BIONDELLO Why, Petruccio is coming in a new hat and
an old jerkin, a pair of old breeches thrice-turned, a
pair of boots that have been candle-cases, one buckled,
another laced, an old rusty sword ta'en out of the town
armoury with a broken hilt, and chapeless, with two
broken points, his horse hipped, with an old mothy
saddle and stirrups of no kindred, besides, possessed
with the glanders and like to mose in the chine, troubled
with the lampass, infected with the fashions, full of
windgalls, sped with spavins, rayed with the yellows,
past cure of the fives, stark spoiled with the staggers,
begnawn with the bots, weighed in the back and
shoulder-shotten, near-legged before and with a half-
cheeked bit and a headstall of sheep's leather which,
being restrained to keep him from stumbling, hath been
often burst and now repaired with knots, one girth six
times pieced, and a woman's crupper of velour which
hath two letters for her name fairly set down in studs,
and here and there pieced with packthread.   61
BAPTISTA Who comes with him?
BIONDELLO O sir, his lackey, for all the world caparisoned
like the horse, with a linen stock on one leg and a
kersey boot-hose on the other, gartered with a red and
blue list; an old hat, and the humour of forty fancies
pricked in't for a feather—a monster, a very monster
in apparel, and not like a Christian footboy or a
gentleman's lackey.
TRANIO
'Tis some odd humour pricks him to this fashion;   70
Yet oftentimes he goes but mean-apparelled.
BAPTISTA
I am glad he's come, howsoe'er he comes.
BIONDELLO Why, sir, he comes not.
BAPTISTA Didst thou not say he comes?
BIONDELLO Who? That Petruccio came?   75
BAPTISTA Ay, that Petruccio came.

BIONDELLO No, sir. I say his horse comes with him on his
back.
BAPTISTA Why, that's all one.
BIONDELLO   Nay, by Saint Jamy,   80
I hold you a penny,
A horse and a man
Is more than one,
And yet not many.
Enter Petruccio and Grumio, fantastically dressed
PETRUCCIO Come, where be these gallants? Who's at
home?   86
BAPTISTA You are welcome, sir.
PETRUCCIO And yet I come not well.
BAPTISTA And yet you halt not.
TRANIO
Not so well apparelled as I wish you were.   90
PETRUCCIO
Were it not better I should rush in thus—
But where is Kate? Where is my lovely bride?
How does my father? Gentles, methinks you frown.
And wherefore gaze this goodly company
As if they saw some wondrous monument,   95
Some comet or unusual prodigy?
BAPTISTA
Why, sir, you know this is your wedding day.
First were we sad, fearing you would not come;
Now sadder that you come so unprovided.
Fie, doff this habit, shame to your estate,   100
An eyesore to our solemn festival.
TRANIO
And tell us what occasion of import
Hath all so long detained you from your wife
And sent you hither so unlike yourself?
PETRUCCIO
Tedious it were to tell, and harsh to hear.   105
Sufficeth I am come to keep my word,
Though in some part enforcèd to digress,
Which at more leisure I will so excuse
As you shall well be satisfied withal.
But where is Kate? I stay too long from her.   110
The morning wears, 'tis time we were at church.
TRANIO
See not your bride in these unreverent robes.
Go to my chamber, put on clothes of mine.
PETRUCCIO
Not I, believe me. Thus I'll visit her.
BAPTISTA
But thus, I trust, you will not marry her.   115
PETRUCCIO
Good sooth, even thus. Therefore ha' done with
words.
To me she's married, not unto my clothes.
Could I repair what she will wear in me
As I can change these poor accoutrements,
'Twere well for Kate and better for myself.   120
But what a fool am I to chat with you
When I should bid good morrow to my bride,
And seal the title with a lovely kiss!
Exit ⌈with Grumio⌉

TRANIO
He hath some meaning in his mad attire.
We will persuade him, be it possible,   125
To put on better ere he go to church.
                             ⌜Exit with Gremio⌝
BAPTISTA
I'll after him, and see the event of this.   ⌜Exeunt⌝

3.3   ⌜Enter Lucentio as Cambio, and Tranio as Lucentio⌝
TRANIO
But, sir, to love concerneth us to add
Her father's liking, which to bring to pass,
As I before imparted to your worship,
I am to get a man—whate'er he be
It skills not much, we'll fit him to our turn—   5
And he shall be Vincentio of Pisa,
And make assurance here in Padua
Of greater sums than I have promisèd.
So shall you quietly enjoy your hope,
And marry sweet Bianca with consent.   10
LUCENTIO
Were it not that my fellow schoolmaster
Doth watch Bianca's steps so narrowly,
'Twere good, methinks, to steal our marriage,
Which once performed, let all the world say no,
I'll keep mine own, despite of all the world.   15
TRANIO
That by degrees we mean to look into,
And watch our vantage in this business.
We'll overreach the greybeard Gremio,
The narrow-prying father Minola,
The quaint musician, amorous Licio,   20
All for my master's sake, Lucentio.
      Enter Gremio
Signor Gremio, came you from the church?
GREMIO
As willingly as e'er I came from school.
TRANIO
And is the bride and bridegroom coming home?
GREMIO
A bridegroom, say you? 'Tis a groom indeed—   25
A grumbling groom, and that the girl shall find.
TRANIO
Curster than she? Why, 'tis impossible.
GREMIO
Why, he's a devil, a devil, a very fiend.
TRANIO
Why, she's a devil, a devil, the devil's dam.
GREMIO
Tut, she's a lamb, a dove, a fool to him.   30
I'll tell you, Sir Lucentio: when the priest
Should ask if Katherine should be his wife,
'Ay, by Gog's woun's,' quoth he, and swore so loud
That all amazed the priest let fall the book,
And as he stooped again to take it up   35
This mad-brained bridegroom took him such a cuff
That down fell priest, and book, and book, and priest.
'Now take them up,' quoth he, 'if any list.'

TRANIO
What said the vicar when he rose again?
GREMIO
Trembled and shook, forwhy he stamped and swore   40
As if the vicar meant to cozen him.
But after many ceremonies done
He calls for wine. 'A health,' quoth he, as if
He had been aboard, carousing to his mates
After a storm; quaffed off the muscatel   45
And threw the sops all in the sexton's face,
Having no other reason
But that his beard grew thin and hungerly
And seemed to ask him sops as he was drinking.
This done, he took the bride about the neck   50
And kissed her lips with such a clamorous smack
That at the parting all the church did echo,
And I seeing this came thence for very shame,
And after me, I know, the rout is coming.
Such a mad marriage never was before.   55
      Music plays
Hark, hark, I hear the minstrels play.
      Enter Petruccio, Katherine, Bianca, Hortensio as
      Licio, Baptista, Grumio, and others, attendants
PETRUCCIO
Gentlemen and friends, I thank you for your pains.
I know you think to dine with me today,
And have prepared great store of wedding cheer.
But so it is my haste doth call me hence,   60
And therefore here I mean to take my leave.
BAPTISTA
Is't possible you will away tonight?
PETRUCCIO
I must away today, before night come.
Make it no wonder. If you knew my business,
You would entreat me rather go than stay.   65
And, honest company, I thank you all
That have beheld me give away myself
To this most patient, sweet, and virtuous wife.
Dine with my father, drink a health to me,
For I must hence; and farewell to you all.   70
TRANIO
Let us entreat you stay till after dinner.
PETRUCCIO
It may not be.
GREMIO   Let me entreat you.
PETRUCCIO
It cannot be.
KATHERINE   Let me entreat you.
PETRUCCIO
I am content.
KATHERINE   Are you content to stay?
PETRUCCIO
I am content you shall entreat me stay,   75
But yet not stay, entreat me how you can.
KATHERINE
Now, if you love me, stay.
PETRUCCIO   Grumio, my horse.

GRUMIO Ay, sir, they be ready. The oats have eaten the
horses.

KATHERINE
Nay, then, do what thou canst, I will not go today, 80
No, nor tomorrow—not till I please myself.
The door is open, sir, there lies your way.
You may be jogging whiles your boots are green.
For me, I'll not be gone till I please myself.
'Tis like you'll prove a jolly, surly groom,   85
That take it on you at the first so roundly.

PETRUCCIO
O Kate, content thee. Prithee, be not angry.

KATHERINE
I will be angry. What hast thou to do?
Father, be quiet. He shall stay my leisure.

GREMIO
Ay, marry, sir. Now it begins to work.   90

KATHERINE
Gentlemen, forward to the bridal dinner.
I see a woman may be made a fool
If she had not a spirit to resist.

PETRUCCIO
They shall go forward, Kate, at thy command.
Obey the bride, you that attend on her.   95
Go to the feast, revel and domineer,
Carouse full measure to her maidenhead.
Be mad and merry, or go hang yourselves.
But for my bonny Kate, she must with me.
Nay, look not big, nor stamp, nor stare, nor fret. 100
I will be master of what is mine own.
She is my goods, my chattels. She is my house,
My household-stuff, my field, my barn,
My horse, my ox, my ass, my anything,
And here she stands, touch her whoever dare.   105
I'll bring mine action on the proudest he
That stops my way in Padua. Grumio,
Draw forth thy weapon, we are beset with thieves.
Rescue thy mistress if thou be a man.
Fear not, sweet wench. They shall not touch thee,
Kate.   110
I'll buckler thee against a million.

Exeunt Petruccio, Katherine, and Grumio

BAPTISTA
Nay, let them go—a couple of quiet ones!

GREMIO
Went they not quickly I should die with laughing.

TRANIO
Of all mad matches never was the like.

LUCENTIO
Mistress, what's your opinion of your sister?   115

BIANCA
That being mad herself she's madly mated.

GREMIO
I warrant him, Petruccio is Kated.

BAPTISTA
Neighbours and friends, though bride and bridegroom
wants

For to supply the places at the table,
You know there wants no junkets at the feast.   120
Lucentio, you shall supply the bridegroom's place,
And let Bianca take her sister's room.

TRANIO
Shall sweet Bianca practise how to bride it?

BAPTISTA
She shall, Lucentio. Come, gentlemen, let's go.

Exeunt

4.1   *Enter Grumio*

GRUMIO Fie, fie on all tired jades, on all mad masters, and
all foul ways. Was ever man so beaten? Was ever man
so rayed? Was ever man so weary? I am sent before
to make a fire, and they are coming after to warm
them. Now were not I a little pot and soon hot, my
very lips might freeze to my teeth, my tongue to the
roof of my mouth, my heart in my belly ere I should
come by a fire to thaw me. But I with blowing the fire
shall warm myself, for considering the weather, a taller
man than I will take cold. Holla! Hoa, Curtis!   10

Enter Curtis

CURTIS Who is that calls so coldly?

GRUMIO A piece of ice. If thou doubt it, thou mayst slide
from my shoulder to my heel with no greater a run
but my head and my neck. A fire, good Curtis!

CURTIS Is my master and his wife coming, Grumio?   15

GRUMIO O ay, Curtis, ay, and therefore fire, fire! Cast on
no water.

CURTIS Is she so hot a shrew as she's reported?

GRUMIO She was, good Curtis, before this frost; but thou
know'st, winter tames man, woman, and beast, for it
hath tamed my old master, and my new mistress, and
myself, fellow Curtis.   22

CURTIS Away, you three-inch fool. I am no beast.

GRUMIO Am I but three inches? Why, thy horn is a foot,
and so long am I, at the least. But wilt thou make a
fire, or shall I complain on thee to our mistress, whose
hand—she being now at hand—thou shalt soon feel to
thy cold comfort, for being slow in thy hot office.

CURTIS I prithee, good Grumio, tell me—how goes the
world?   30

GRUMIO A cold world, Curtis, in every office but thine.
And therefore fire, do thy duty, and have thy duty, for
my master and mistress are almost frozen to death.

CURTIS There's fire ready, and therefore, good Grumio,
the news.   35

GRUMIO Why, 'Jack boy, ho boy!', and as much news as
wilt thou.

CURTIS Come, you are so full of cony-catching.

GRUMIO Why, therefore fire, for I have caught extreme
cold. Where's the cook? Is supper ready, the house
trimmed, rushes strewed, cobwebs swept, the servingmen in their new fustian, the white stockings, and
every officer his wedding garment on? Be the Jacks fair
within, the Jills fair without, the carpets laid, and
everything in order?   45

CURTIS All ready, and therefore, I pray thee, news.

GRUMIO First, know my horse is tired, my master and mistress fallen out.

CURTIS How?

GRUMIO Out of their saddles into the dirt, and thereby hangs a tale. 51

CURTIS Let's ha't, good Grumio.

GRUMIO Lend thine ear.

CURTIS Here.

GRUMIO (cuffing him) There. 55

CURTIS This 'tis to feel a tale, not to hear a tale.

GRUMIO And therefore 'tis called a sensible tale, and this cuff was but to knock at your ear and beseech listening. Now I begin. Inprimis, we came down a foul hill, my master riding behind my mistress. 60

CURTIS Both of one horse?

GRUMIO What's that to thee?

CURTIS Why, a horse.

GRUMIO Tell thou the tale. But hadst thou not crossed me thou shouldst have heard how her horse fell and she under her horse; thou shouldst have heard in how miry a place, how she was bemoiled, how he left her with the horse upon her, how he beat me because her horse stumbled, how she waded through the dirt to pluck him off me, how he swore, how she prayed that never prayed before, how I cried, how the horses ran away, how her bridle was burst, how I lost my crupper, with many things of worthy memory which now shall die in oblivion, and thou return unexperienced to thy grave. 75

CURTIS By this reckoning he is more shrew than she.

GRUMIO Ay, and that thou and the proudest of you all shall find when he comes home. But what talk I of this? Call forth Nathaniel, Joseph, Nicholas, Philip, Walter, Sugarsop, and the rest. Let their heads be sleekly combed, their blue coats brushed, and their garters of an indifferent knit. Let them curtsy with their left legs and not presume to touch a hair of my master's horse-tail till they kiss their hands. Are they all ready?

CURTIS They are. 85

GRUMIO Call them forth.

CURTIS (calling) Do you hear, ho? You must meet my master to countenance my mistress.

GRUMIO Why, she hath a face of her own.

CURTIS Who knows not that? 90

GRUMIO Thou, it seems, that calls for company to countenance her.

CURTIS I call them forth to credit her.
Enter four or five servingmen

GRUMIO Why, she comes to borrow nothing of them.

NATHANIEL Welcome home, Grumio! 95

PHILIP How now, Grumio?

JOSEPH What, Grumio?

NICHOLAS Fellow Grumio!

NATHANIEL How now, old lad!

GRUMIO Welcome you, how now you, what you, fellow you, and thus much for greeting. Now, my spruce companions, is all ready and all things neat? 102

NATHANIEL All things is ready. How near is our master?

GRUMIO E'en at hand, alighted by this, and therefore be not—Cock's passion, silence! I hear my master. 105
Enter Petruccio and Katherine

PETRUCCIO
Where be these knaves? What, no man at door
To hold my stirrup nor to take my horse?
Where is Nathaniel, Gregory, Philip?

ALL SERVANTS Here, here sir, here sir.

PETRUCCIO
Here sir, here sir, here sir, here sir! 110
You logger-headed and unpolished grooms,
What! No attendance! No regard! No duty!
Where is the foolish knave I sent before?

GRUMIO
Here, sir, as foolish as I was before.

PETRUCCIO
You peasant swain, you whoreson, malthorse drudge,
Did I not bid thee meet me in the park 116
And bring along these rascal knaves with thee?

GRUMIO
Nathaniel's coat, sir, was not fully made,
And Gabriel's pumps were all unpinked i'th' heel.
There was no link to colour Peter's hat, 120
And Walter's dagger was not come from sheathing.
There were none fine but Adam, Ralph, and Gregory.
The rest were ragged, old, and beggarly.
Yet as they are, here are they come to meet you.

PETRUCCIO
Go, rascals, go and fetch my supper in. 125
Exeunt servants

(Sings) 'Where is the life that late I led?
              Where are those—'
Sit down, Kate, and welcome. Soud, soud, soud, soud.
Enter servants with supper
Why, when, I say?—Nay, good sweet Kate, be merry.—
Off with my boots, you rogues, you villains. When?

(Sings) 'It was the friar of orders gray, 131
              As he forth walkèd on his way.'
Out, you rogue, you pluck my foot awry.
(Kicking a servant) Take that, and mend the plucking of the other.
Be merry, Kate. (Calling) Some water, here. What, hoa! 135
Enter one with water
Where's my spaniel Troilus? Sirrah, get you hence,
And bid my cousin Ferdinand come hither—
One, Kate, that you must kiss and be acquainted with.
(Calling) Where are my slippers? Shall I have some water?
Come, Kate, and wash, and welcome heartily. 140
⌈A servant drops water⌉
You whoreson villain, will you let it fall?

KATHERINE
Patience, I pray you, 'twas a fault unwilling.

PETRUCCIO
A whoreson, beetle-headed, flap-eared knave.

Come, Kate, sit down, I know you have a stomach.
Will you give thanks, sweet Kate, or else shall I?   145
What's this—mutton?
FIRST SERVINGMAN   Ay.
PETRUCCIO   Who brought it?
PETER   I.
PETRUCCIO
'Tis burnt, and so is all the meat.
What dogs are these? Where is the rascal cook?
How durst you villains bring it from the dresser
And serve it thus to me that love it not?   150
There, (*throwing food*) take it to you, trenchers, cups,
          and all,
You heedless jolt-heads and unmannered slaves.
What, do you grumble? I'll be with you straight.
          He chases the servants away
KATHERINE
I pray you, husband, be not so disquiet.
The meat was well, if you were so contented.   155
PETRUCCIO
I tell thee, Kate, 'twas burnt and dried away,
And I expressly am forbid to touch it,
For it engenders choler, planteth anger,
And better 'twere that both of us did fast,
Since of ourselves ourselves are choleric,   160
Than feed it with such overroasted flesh.
Be patient, tomorrow't shall be mended,
And for this night we'll fast for company.
Come, I will bring thee to thy bridal chamber.   *Exeunt*
          Enter servants severally
NATHANIEL Peter, didst ever see the like?   165
PETER He kills her in her own humour.
          Enter Curtis, a servant
GRUMIO Where is he?
CURTIS In her chamber,
Making a sermon of continency to her,
And rails, and swears, and rates, that she, poor soul,
Knows not which way to stand, to look, to speak,   171
And sits as one new risen from a dream.
Away, away, for he is coming hither.   *Exeunt*
          Enter Petruccio
PETRUCCIO
Thus have I politicly begun my reign,
And 'tis my hope to end successfully.   175
My falcon now is sharp and passing empty,
And till she stoop she must not be full-gorged,
For then she never looks upon her lure.
Another way I have to man my haggard,
To make her come and know her keeper's call—   180
That is, to watch her as we watch these kites
That bate and beat, and will not be obedient.
She ate no meat today, nor none shall eat.
Last night she slept not, nor tonight she shall not.
As with the meat, some undeservèd fault   185
I'll find about the making of the bed,
And here I'll fling the pillow, there the bolster,
This way the coverlet, another way the sheets,
Ay, and amid this hurly I intend
That all is done in reverent care of her,   190

And in conclusion she shall watch all night,
And if she chance to nod I'll rail and brawl
And with the clamour keep her still awake.
This is a way to kill a wife with kindness,
And thus I'll curb her mad and headstrong humour.
He that knows better how to tame a shrew,
Now let him speak. 'Tis charity to show.   *Exit*

4.2   *Enter Tranio as Lucentio, and Hortensio as Licio*
TRANIO
Is't possible, friend Licio, that Mistress Bianca
Doth fancy any other but Lucentio?
I tell you, sir, she bears me fair in hand.
HORTENSIO
Sir, to satisfy you in what I have said,
Stand by, and mark the manner of his teaching.   5
          They stand aside
          Enter Bianca, and Lucentio as Cambio
LUCENTIO
Now, mistress, profit you in what you read?
BIANCA
What, master, read you? First resolve me that.
LUCENTIO
I read that I profess, *The Art to Love*.
BIANCA
And may you prove, sir, master of your art.
LUCENTIO
While you, sweet dear, prove mistress of my heart.   10
          They stand aside
HORTENSIO
Quick proceeders, marry! Now tell me, I pray,
You that durst swear that your mistress Bianca
Loved none in the world so well as Lucentio.
TRANIO
O despiteful love, unconstant womankind!
I tell thee, Licio, this is wonderful.   15
HORTENSIO
Mistake no more, I am not Licio,
Nor a musician as I seem to be,
But one that scorn to live in this disguise
For such a one as leaves a gentleman
And makes a god of such a cullion.   20
Know, sir, that I am called Hortensio.
TRANIO
Signor Hortensio, I have often heard
Of your entire affection to Bianca,
And since mine eyes are witness of her lightness
I will with you, if you be so contented,   25
Forswear Bianca and her love for ever.
HORTENSIO
See how they kiss and court. Signor Lucentio,
Here is my hand, and here I firmly vow
Never to woo her more, but do forswear her
As one unworthy all the former favours   30
That I have fondly flattered her withal.
TRANIO
And here I take the like unfeignèd oath
Never to marry with her, though she would entreat.
Fie on her, see how beastly she doth court him!

HORTENSIO
Would all the world but he had quite forsworn. 35
For me, that I may surely keep mine oath
I will be married to a wealthy widow
Ere three days pass, which hath as long loved me
As I have loved this proud disdainful haggard.
And so farewell, Signor Lucentio. 40
Kindness in women, not their beauteous looks,
Shall win my love; and so I take my leave,
In resolution as I swore before.   *Exit*

TRANIO
Mistress Bianca, bless you with such grace
As 'longeth to a lover's blessèd case. 45
Nay, I have ta'en you napping, gentle love,
And have forsworn you with Hortensio.

BIANCA
Tranio, you jest. But have you both forsworn me?

TRANIO
Mistress, we have.

LUCENTIO   Then we are rid of Licio.

TRANIO
I'faith, he'll have a lusty widow now, 50
That shall be wooed and wedded in a day.

BIANCA God give him joy.

TRANIO Ay, and he'll tame her.

BIANCA He says so, Tranio.

TRANIO
Faith, he is gone unto the taming-school. 55

BIANCA
The taming-school—what, is there such a place?

TRANIO
Ay, mistress, and Petruccio is the master,
That teacheth tricks eleven-and-twenty long
To tame a shrew and charm her chattering tongue.
                    Enter Biondello

BIONDELLO
O, master, master, I have watched so long 60
That I am dog-weary, but at last I spied
An ancient angel coming down the hill
Will serve the turn.

TRANIO   What is he, Biondello?

BIONDELLO
Master, a marcantant or a pedant,
I know not what, but formal in apparel, 65
In gait and countenance surely like a father.

LUCENTIO And what of him, Tranio?

TRANIO
If he be credulous and trust my tale,
I'll make him glad to seem Vincentio
And give assurance to Baptista Minola 70
As if he were the right Vincentio.
Take in your love, and then let me alone.
                    Exeunt Lucentio and Bianca
                    Enter a Pedant

PEDANT
God save you, sir.

TRANIO   And you, sir. You are welcome.
Travel you farre on, or are you at the farthest?

PEDANT
Sir, at the farthest for a week or two, 75
But then up farther and as far as Rome,
And so to Tripoli, if God lend me life.

TRANIO
What countryman, I pray?

PEDANT   Of Mantua.

TRANIO
Of Mantua, sir? Marry, God forbid,
And come to Padua careless of your life! 80

PEDANT
My life, sir? How, I pray? For that goes hard.

TRANIO
'Tis death for anyone in Mantua
To come to Padua. Know you not the cause?
Your ships are stayed at Venice, and the Duke,
For private quarrel 'twixt your Duke and him, 85
Hath published and proclaimed it openly.
'Tis marvel, but that you are but newly come,
You might have heard it else proclaimed about.

PEDANT
Alas, sir, it is worse for me than so,
For I have bills for money by exchange 90
From Florence, and must here deliver them.

TRANIO
Well, sir, to do you courtesy
This will I do, and this I will advise you.
First tell me, have you ever been at Pisa?

PEDANT
Ay, sir, in Pisa have I often been, 95
Pisa renownèd for grave citizens.

TRANIO
Among them know you one Vincentio?

PEDANT
I know him not, but I have heard of him,
A merchant of incomparable wealth.

TRANIO
He is my father, sir, and sooth to say, 100
In count'nance somewhat doth resemble you.

BIONDELLO (*aside*) As much as an apple doth an oyster,
and all one.

TRANIO
To save your life in this extremity
This favour will I do you for his sake, 105
And think it not the worst of all your fortunes
That you are like to Sir Vincentio.
His name and credit shall you undertake,
And in my house you shall be friendly lodged.
Look that you take upon you as you should. 110
You understand me, sir? So shall you stay
Till you have done your business in the city.
If this be courtesy, sir, accept of it.

PEDANT
O sir, I do, and will repute you ever
The patron of my life and liberty. 115

TRANIO
Then go with me to make the matter good.
This, by the way, I let you understand—

My father is here looked for every day
To pass assurance of a dower in marriage
'Twixt me and one Baptista's daughter here.   120
In all these circumstances I'll instruct you.
Go with me to clothe you as becomes you.   *Exeunt*

4.3   *Enter Katherine and Grumio*

GRUMIO
No, no, forsooth. I dare not, for my life.

KATHERINE
The more my wrong, the more his spite appears.
What, did he marry me to famish me?
Beggars that come unto my father's door
Upon entreaty have a present alms,   5
If not, elsewhere they meet with charity.
But I, who never knew how to entreat,
Nor never needed that I should entreat,
Am starved for meat, giddy for lack of sleep,
With oaths kept waking and with brawling fed,   10
And that which spites me more than all these wants,
He does it under name of perfect love,
As who should say if I should sleep or eat
'Twere deadly sickness, or else present death.
I prithee, go and get me some repast.   15
I care not what, so it be wholesome food.

GRUMIO What say you to a neat's foot?

KATHERINE
'Tis passing good. I prithee, let me have it.

GRUMIO
I fear it is too choleric a meat.
How say you to a fat tripe finely broiled?   20

KATHERINE
I like it well. Good Grumio, fetch it me.

GRUMIO
I cannot tell, I fear 'tis choleric.
What say you to a piece of beef, and mustard?

KATHERINE
A dish that I do love to feed upon.

GRUMIO
Ay, but the mustard is too hot a little.   25

KATHERINE
Why then, the beef, and let the mustard rest.

GRUMIO
Nay, then I will not. You shall have the mustard,
Or else you get no beef of Grumio.

KATHERINE
Then both, or one, or anything thou wilt.

GRUMIO
Why then, the mustard without the beef.   30

KATHERINE
Go, get thee gone, thou false, deluding slave,
(*Beating him*) That feed'st me with the very name of
          meat.
Sorrow on thee and all the pack of you,
That triumph thus upon my misery.
Go, get thee gone, I say.   35
          Enter Petruccio and Hortensio, with meat

PETRUCCIO
How fares my Kate? What, sweeting, all amort?

HORTENSIO
Mistress, what cheer?

KATHERINE   Faith, as cold as can be.

PETRUCCIO
Pluck up thy spirits, look cheerfully upon me.
Here, love, thou seest how diligent I am
To dress thy meat myself and bring it thee.   40
I am sure, sweet Kate, this kindness merits thanks.
What, not a word? Nay then, thou lov'st it not,
And all my pains is sorted to no proof.
Here, take away this dish.

KATHERINE   I pray you, let it stand.

PETRUCCIO
The poorest service is repaid with thanks,   45
And so shall mine before you touch the meat.

KATHERINE I thank you, sir.

HORTENSIO
Signor Petruccio, fie, you are to blame.
Come, Mistress Kate, I'll bear you company.

PETRUCCIO (*aside*)
Eat it up all, Hortensio, if thou lov'st me.   50
(*To Katherine*) Much good do it unto thy gentle heart.
Kate, eat apace; and now, my honey love,
Will we return unto thy father's house,
And revel it as bravely as the best,
With silken coats, and caps, and golden rings,   55
With ruffs, and cuffs, and farthingales, and things,
With scarves, and fans, and double change of
          bravery,
With amber bracelets, beads, and all this knavery.
What, hast thou dined? The tailor stays thy leisure,
To deck thy body with his ruffling treasure.   60
          Enter Tailor with a gown
Come, tailor, let us see these ornaments.
Lay forth the gown.
          Enter Haberdasher with a cap
                    What news with you, sir?

HABERDASHER
Here is the cap your worship did bespeak.

PETRUCCIO
Why, this was moulded on a porringer—
A velvet dish. Fie, fie, 'tis lewd and filthy.   65
Why, 'tis a cockle or a walnut-shell,
A knack, a toy, a trick, a baby's cap.
Away with it! Come, let me have a bigger.

KATHERINE
I'll have no bigger. This doth fit the time,
And gentlewomen wear such caps as these.   70

PETRUCCIO
When you are gentle you shall have one, too,
And not till then.

HORTENSIO (*aside*)   That will not be in haste.

KATHERINE
Why, sir, I trust I may have leave to speak,
And speak I will. I am no child, no babe.
Your betters have endured me say my mind,   75
And if you cannot, best you stop your ears.
My tongue will tell the anger of my heart,
Or else my heart concealing it will break,

And rather than it shall I will be free
Even to the uttermost as I please in words.   80

PETRUCCIO
Why, thou sayst true. It is a paltry cap,
A custard-coffin, a bauble, a silken pie.
I love thee well in that thou lik'st it not.

KATHERINE
Love me or love me not, I like the cap
And it I will have, or I will have none.   85

[Exit Haberdasher]

PETRUCCIO
Thy gown? Why, ay. Come, tailor, let us see't.
O mercy, God, what masquing stuff is here?
What's this—a sleeve? 'Tis like a demi-cannon.
What, up and down carved like an apple-tart?
Here's snip, and nip, and cut, and slish and slash,   90
Like to a scissor in a barber's shop.
Why, what o' devil's name, tailor, call'st thou this?

HORTENSIO (aside)
I see she's like to have nor cap nor gown.

TAILOR
You bid me make it orderly and well,
According to the fashion and the time.   95

PETRUCCIO
Marry, and did, but if you be remembered
I did not bid you mar it to the time.
Go hop me over every kennel home,
For you shall hop without my custom, sir.
I'll none of it. Hence, make your best of it.   100

KATHERINE
I never saw a better fashioned gown,
More quaint, more pleasing, nor more commendable.
Belike you mean to make a puppet of me.

PETRUCCIO
Why true, he means to make a puppet of thee.

TAILOR She says your worship means to make a puppet
of her.

PETRUCCIO
O monstrous arrogance! Thou liest, thou thread, thou
thimble,
Thou yard, three-quarters, half-yard, quarter, nail,
Thou flea, thou nit, thou winter-cricket, thou.
Braved in mine own house with a skein of thread!   110
Away, thou rag, thou quantity, thou remnant,
Or I shall so bemete thee with thy yard
As thou shalt think on prating whilst thou liv'st.
I tell thee, I, that thou hast marred her gown.

TAILOR
Your worship is deceived. The gown is made   115
Just as my master had direction.
Grumio gave order how it should be done.

GRUMIO
I gave him no order, I gave him the stuff.

TAILOR
But how did you desire it should be made?

GRUMIO Marry, sir, with needle and thread.   120

TAILOR
But did you not request to have it cut?

GRUMIO Thou hast faced many things.

TAILOR I have.

GRUMIO Face not me. Thou hast braved many men. Brave
not me. I will neither be faced nor braved. I say unto
thee I bid thy master cut out the gown, but I did not
bid him cut it to pieces. *Ergo* thou liest.

TAILOR (showing a paper) Why, here is the note of the
fashion, to testify.

PETRUCCIO Read it.   130

GRUMIO The note lies in's throat if he say I said so.

TAILOR (reads) 'Imprimis, a loose-bodied gown.'

GRUMIO Master, if ever I said loose-bodied gown, sew me
in the skirts of it and beat me to death with a bottom
of brown thread. I said a gown.   135

PETRUCCIO Proceed.

TAILOR (reads) 'With a small compassed cape.'

GRUMIO I confess the cape.

TAILOR (reads) 'With a trunk sleeve.'

GRUMIO I confess two sleeves.   140

TAILOR (reads) 'The sleeves curiously cut.'

PETRUCCIO Ay, there's the villany.

GRUMIO Error i'th' bill, sir, error i'th' bill. I commanded
the sleeves should be cut out and sewed up again, and
that I'll prove upon thee though thy little finger be
armed in a thimble.   146

TAILOR This is true that I say. An I had thee in place
where, thou shouldst know it.

GRUMIO I am for thee straight. Take thou the bill, give
me thy mete-yard, and spare not me.   150

HORTENSIO Godamercy, Grumio, then he shall have no
odds.

PETRUCCIO
Well, sir, in brief, the gown is not for me.

GRUMIO You are i'th' right, sir. 'Tis for my mistress.

PETRUCCIO (to the Tailor)
Go, take it up unto thy master's use.   155

GRUMIO (to the Tailor) Villain, not for thy life. Take up my
mistress' gown for thy master's use!

PETRUCCIO Why, sir, what's your conceit in that?

GRUMIO O, sir, the conceit is deeper than you think for.
'Take up my mistress' gown to his master's use'—O
fie, fie, fie!   161

PETRUCCIO (aside)
Hortensio, say thou wilt see the tailor paid.
(To the Tailor) Go, take it hence. Be gone, and say no
more.

HORTENSIO (aside to the Tailor)
Tailor, I'll pay thee for thy gown tomorrow.
Take no unkindness of his hasty words.   165
Away, I say. Commend me to thy master.   *Exit Tailor*

PETRUCCIO
Well, come, my Kate. We will unto your father's
Even in these honest, mean habiliments.
Our purses shall be proud, our garments poor,
For 'tis the mind that makes the body rich,   170
And as the sun breaks through the darkest clouds,
So honour peereth in the meanest habit.
What, is the jay more precious than the lark

Because his feathers are more beautiful?
Or is the adder better than the eel　　　　175
Because his painted skin contents the eye?
O no, good Kate, neither art thou the worse
For this poor furniture and mean array.
If thou account'st it shame, lay it on me,
And therefore frolic; we will hence forthwith　　　　180
To feast and sport us at thy father's house.
Go call my men, and let us straight to him,
And bring our horses unto Long Lane end.
There will we mount, and thither walk on foot.
Let's see, I think 'tis now some seven o'clock,　　　　185
And well we may come there by dinner-time.

KATHERINE
I dare assure you, sir, 'tis almost two,
And 'twill be supper-time ere you come there.

PETRUCCIO
It shall be seven ere I go to horse.
Look what I speak, or do, or think to do,　　　　190
You are still crossing it. Sirs, let't alone.
I will not go today, and ere I do
It shall be what o'clock I say it is.

HORTENSIO (aside)
Why, so this gallant will command the sun.　　　　Exeunt

4.4　　*Enter Tranio as Lucentio, and the Pedant dressed*
　　　　like Vincentio, booted and bare-headed

TRANIO
Sir, this is the house. Please it you that I call?

PEDANT
Ay, what else. And but I be deceived,
Signor Baptista may remember me
Near twenty years ago in Genoa—

TRANIO
Where we were lodgers at the Pegasus.—　　　　5
'Tis well, and hold your own in any case
With such austerity as 'longeth to a father.
　　　　Enter Biondello

PEDANT
I warrant you. But sir, here comes your boy.
'Twere good he were schooled.

TRANIO
Fear you not him. Sirrah Biondello,　　　　10
Now do your duty throughly, I advise you.
Imagine 'twere the right Vincentio.

BIONDELLO Tut, fear not me.

TRANIO
But hast thou done thy errand to Baptista?

BIONDELLO
I told him that your father was at Venice　　　　15
And that you looked for him this day in Padua.

TRANIO (*giving money*)
Thou'rt a tall fellow. Hold thee that to drink.
Here comes Baptista. Set your countenance, sir.
　　　　Enter Baptista, and Lucentio as Cambio

TRANIO
Signor Baptista, you are happily met.　　　　19
(*To the Pedant*) Sir, this is the gentleman I told you of.

I pray you stand good father to me now.
Give me Bianca for my patrimony.

PEDANT
Soft, son. (*To Baptista*) Sir, by your leave, having
　　　　come to Padua
To gather in some debts, my son Lucentio
Made me acquainted with a weighty cause　　　　25
Of love between your daughter and himself,
And for the good report I hear of you,
And for the love he beareth to your daughter,
And she to him, to stay him not too long
I am content in a good father's care　　　　30
To have him matched, and if you please to like
No worse than I, upon some agreement
Me shall you find ready and willing
With one consent to have her so bestowed,
For curious I cannot be with you,　　　　35
Signor Baptista, of whom I hear so well.

BAPTISTA
Sir, pardon me in what I have to say.
Your plainness and your shortness please me well.
Right true it is your son Lucentio here
Doth love my daughter, and she loveth him,　　　　40
Or both dissemble deeply their affections.
And therefore if you say no more than this,
That like a father you will deal with him
And pass my daughter a sufficient dower,
The match is made, and all is done.　　　　45
Your son shall have my daughter with consent.

TRANIO
I thank you, sir. Where then do you know best
We be affied, and such assurance ta'en
As shall with either part's agreement stand?

BAPTISTA
Not in my house, Lucentio, for you know　　　　50
Pitchers have ears, and I have many servants.
Besides, old Gremio is heark'ning still,
And happily we might be interrupted.

TRANIO
Then at my lodging, an it like you.
There doth my father lie, and there this night　　　　55
We'll pass the business privately and well.
Send for your daughter by your servant here.
My boy shall fetch the scrivener presently.
The worst is this, that at so slender warning
You are like to have a thin and slender pittance.　　　　60

BAPTISTA
It likes me well. Cambio, hie you home
And bid Bianca make her ready straight,
And if you will, tell what hath happened—
Lucentio's father is arrived in Padua—
And how she's like to be Lucentio's wife.　　　　65
　　　　⌈*Exit Lucentio*⌉

BIONDELLO
I pray the gods she may with all my heart.

TRANIO
Dally not with the gods, but get thee gone.
　　　　⌈*Exit Biondello*⌉

Signor Baptista, shall I lead the way?
Welcome. One mess is like to be your cheer.
Come, sir, we will better it in Pisa.   70
BAPTISTA I follow you.   *Exeunt*

4.5   *Enter Lucentio and Biondello*
BIONDELLO Cambio.
LUCENTIO What sayst thou, Biondello?
BIONDELLO You saw my master wink and laugh upon
   you?
LUCENTIO Biondello, what of that?   5
BIONDELLO Faith, nothing, but he's left me here behind to
   expound the meaning or moral of his signs and tokens.
LUCENTIO I pray thee, moralize them.
BIONDELLO Then thus: Baptista is safe, talking with the
   deceiving father of a deceitful son.   10
LUCENTIO And what of him?
BIONDELLO His daughter is to be brought by you to the
   supper.
LUCENTIO And then?
BIONDELLO The old priest at Saint Luke's church is at your
   command at all hours.   16
LUCENTIO And what of all this?
BIONDELLO I cannot tell, except they are busied about a
   counterfeit assurance. Take you assurance of her *cum*
   privilegio ad imprimendum solum—to th' church take the
   priest, clerk, and some sufficient honest witnesses. 21
   If this be not that you look for, I have no more to
   say,
   But bid Bianca farewell for ever and a day.
LUCENTIO Hear'st thou, Biondello?   24
BIONDELLO I cannot tarry, I knew a wench married in an
   afternoon as she went to the garden for parsley to stuff
   a rabbit, and so may you, sir, and so adieu, sir. My
   master hath appointed me to go to Saint Luke's to bid
   the priest be ready t'attend against you come with your
   appendix.   *Exit*
LUCENTIO
   I may and will, if she be so contented.   31
   She will be pleased, then wherefore should I doubt?
   Hap what hap may, I'll roundly go about her.
   It shall go hard if Cambio go without her.   *Exit*

4.6   *Enter Petruccio, Katherine, Hortensio, and servants*
PETRUCCIO
   Come on, i' God's name. Once more toward our
      father's.
   Good Lord, how bright and goodly shines the moon!
KATHERINE
   The moon?—the sun. It is not moonlight now.
PETRUCCIO
   I say it is the moon that shines so bright.
KATHERINE
   I know it is the sun that shines so bright.   5
PETRUCCIO
   Now, by my mother's son—and that's myself—
   It shall be moon, or star, or what I list
   Or ere I journey to your father's house.

Go on, and fetch our horses back again.
Evermore crossed and crossed, nothing but crossed. 10
HORTENSIO (*to Katherine*)
   Say as he says or we shall never go.
KATHERINE
   Forward, I pray, since we have come so far,
   And be it moon or sun or what you please,
   And if you please to call it a rush-candle
   Henceforth I vow it shall be so for me.   15
PETRUCCIO
   I say it is the moon.
KATHERINE
   I know it is the moon.
PETRUCCIO
   Nay then you lie, it is the blessèd sun.
KATHERINE
   Then God be blessed, it is the blessèd sun,
   But sun it is not when you say it is not,   20
   And the moon changes even as your mind.
   What you will have it named, even that it is,
   And so it shall be still for Katherine.
HORTENSIO
   Petruccio, go thy ways. The field is won.
PETRUCCIO
   Well, forward, forward. Thus the bowl should run, 25
   And not unluckily against the bias.
   But soft, company is coming here.
      Enter old Vincentio
   (*To Vincentio*) Good morrow, gentle mistress, where
      away?
   Tell me, sweet Kate, and tell me truly too,
   Hast thou beheld a fresher gentlewoman,   30
   Such war of white and red within her cheeks?
   What stars do spangle heaven with such beauty
   As those two eyes become that heavenly face?
   Fair lovely maid, once more good day to thee.
   Sweet Kate, embrace her for her beauty's sake.   35
HORTENSIO A will make the man mad to make the woman
   of him.
KATHERINE
   Young budding virgin, fair, and fresh, and sweet,
   Whither away, or where is thy abode?
   Happy the parents of so fair a child,   40
   Happier the man whom favourable stars
   Allots thee for his lovely bedfellow.
PETRUCCIO
   Why, how now, Kate, I hope thou art not mad.
   This is a man, old, wrinkled, faded, withered,
   And not a maiden as thou sayst he is.   45
KATHERINE
   Pardon, old father, my mistaking eyes
   That have been so bedazzled with the sun
   That everything I look on seemeth green.
   Now I perceive thou art a reverend father.
   Pardon, I pray thee, for my mad mistaking.   50
PETRUCCIO
   Do, good old grandsire, and withal make known

Which way thou travell'st. If along with us,
We shall be joyful of thy company.

VINCENTIO
Fair sir, and you, my merry mistress,
That with your strange encounter much amazed me,
My name is called Vincentio, my dwelling Pisa,   56
And bound I am to Padua, there to visit
A son of mine which long I have not seen.

PETRUCCIO
What is his name?

VINCENTIO   Lucentio, gentle sir.

PETRUCCIO
Happily met, the happier for thy son.   60
And now by law as well as reverend age
I may entitle thee my loving father.
The sister to my wife, this gentlewoman,
Thy son by this hath married. Wonder not,
Nor be not grieved. She is of good esteem,   65
Her dowry wealthy, and of worthy birth,
Beside, so qualified as may beseem
The spouse of any noble gentleman.
Let me embrace with old Vincentio,
And wander we to see thy honest son,   70
Who will of thy arrival be full joyous.

He embraces Vincentio

VINCENTIO
But is this true, or is it else your pleasure
Like pleasant travellers to break a jest
Upon the company you overtake?

HORTENSIO
I do assure thee, father, so it is.   75

PETRUCCIO
Come, go along, and see the truth hereof,
For our first merriment hath made thee jealous.

Exeunt all but Hortensio

HORTENSIO
Well, Petruccio, this has put me in heart.
Have to my widow, and if she be froward,
Then hast thou taught Hortensio to be untoward.   80

Exit

5.1   *Enter Biondello, Lucentio, and Bianca. Gremio is out
before*

BIONDELLO Softly and swiftly, sir, for the priest is ready.

LUCENTIO I fly, Biondello; but they may chance to need
thee at home, therefore leave us.

BIONDELLO Nay, faith, I'll see the church a' your back
and then come back to my master's as soon as I can. 5

Exeunt Lucentio, Bianca, and Biondello

GREMIO
I marvel Cambio comes not all this while.

*Enter Petruccio, Katherine, Vincentio, Grumio, with
attendants*

PETRUCCIO
Sir, here's the door. This is Lucentio's house.
My father's bears more toward the market-place.
Thither must I, and here I leave you, sir.

VINCENTIO
You shall not choose but drink before you go.   10
I think I shall command your welcome here,
And by all likelihood some cheer is toward.

He knocks

GREMIO They're busy within. You were best knock louder.

*Vincentio knocks again. The Pedant looks out of the
window*

PEDANT What's he that knocks as he would beat down
the gate?   15

VINCENTIO Is Signor Lucentio within, sir?

PEDANT He's within, sir, but not to be spoken withal.

VINCENTIO What if a man bring him a hundred pound or
two to make merry withal?

PEDANT Keep your hundred pounds to yourself. He shall
need none so long as I live.   21

PETRUCCIO (*to Vincentio*) Nay, I told you your son was well
beloved in Padua. (*To the Pedant*) Do you hear, sir, to
leave frivolous circumstances, I pray you tell Signor
Lucentio that his father is come from Pisa and is here
at the door to speak with him.   26

PEDANT Thou liest. His father is come from Padua and
here looking out at the window.

VINCENTIO Art thou his father?   29

PEDANT Ay, sir, so his mother says, if I may believe her.

PETRUCCIO (*to Vincentio*) Why, how now, gentleman? Why,
this is flat knavery, to take upon you another man's
name.

PEDANT Lay hands on the villain. I believe a means to
cozen somebody in this city under my countenance.

Enter Biondello

BIONDELLO (*aside*) I have seen them in the church together,
God send 'em good shipping. But who is here? Mine
old master, Vincentio—now we are undone and
brought to nothing.

VINCENTIO (*to Biondello*) Come hither, crackhemp.   40

BIONDELLO I hope I may choose, sir.

VINCENTIO Come hither, you rogue. What, have you forgot
me?

BIONDELLO Forgot you? No, sir, I could not forget you,
for I never saw you before in all my life.   45

VINCENTIO What, you notorious villain, didst thou never
see thy master's father, Vincentio?

BIONDELLO What, my old worshipful old master? Yes,
marry, sir, see where he looks out of the window.

VINCENTIO Is't so indeed?   50

He beats Biondello

BIONDELLO Help, help, help! Here's a madman will murder
me.   *Exit*

PEDANT Help, son! Help, Signor Baptista!   *Exit above*

PETRUCCIO Prithee, Kate, let's stand aside and see the end
of this controversy.   55

They stand aside.

*Enter Pedant with servants, Baptista, Tranio as
Lucentio*

TRANIO (*to Vincentio*) Sir, what are you that offer to beat
my servant?

VINCENTIO What am I, sir? Nay, what are you, sir? O
immortal gods, O fine villain, a silken doublet, a velvet
hose, a scarlet cloak, and a copintank hat—O, I am
undone, I am undone! While I play the good husband
at home, my son and my servant spend all at the
university.

TRANIO How now, what's the matter?

BAPTISTA What, is the man lunatic?   65

TRANIO Sir, you seem a sober, ancient gentleman by your
habit, but your words show you a madman. Why sir,
what 'cerns it you if I wear pearl and gold? I thank
my good father, I am able to maintain it.

VINCENTIO Thy father! O villain, he is a sailmaker in
Bergamo.   71

BAPTISTA You mistake, sir, you mistake, sir. Pray what
do you think is his name?

VINCENTIO His name? As if I knew not his name—I have
brought him up ever since he was three years old, and
his name is Tranio.   76

PEDANT Away, away, mad ass. His name is Lucentio, and
he is mine only son, and heir to the lands of me, Signor
Vincentio.

VINCENTIO Lucentio? O, he hath murdered his master!
Lay hold on him, I charge you, in the Duke's name. O
my son, my son! Tell me, thou villain, where is my
son Lucentio?

TRANIO Call forth an officer.

    Enter an Officer

Carry this mad knave to the jail. Father Baptista, I
charge you see that he be forthcoming.   86

VINCENTIO Carry me to the jail?

GREMIO Stay, officer, he shall not go to prison.

BAPTISTA Talk not, Signor Gremio. I say he shall go to
prison.   90

GREMIO Take heed, Signor Baptista, lest you be cony-
catched in this business. I dare swear this is the right
Vincentio.

PEDANT Swear if thou dar'st.

GREMIO Nay, I dare not swear it.   95

TRANIO Then thou wert best say that I am not Lucentio.

GREMIO Yes, I know thee to be Signor Lucentio.

BAPTISTA Away with the dotard. To the jail with him.

    Enter Biondello, Lucentio, and Bianca

VINCENTIO Thus strangers may be haled and abused. O
monstrous villain!   100

BIONDELLO O, we are spoiled and—yonder he is. Deny
him, forswear him, or else we are all undone.

    *Exeunt Biondello, Tranio, and Pedant, as fast as
                                           may be*

LUCENTIO (*to Vincentio*) Pardon, sweet father.

    He kneels

VINCENTIO Lives my sweet son?

BIANCA (*to Baptista*) Pardon, dear father.   105

BAPTISTA
How hast thou offended? Where is Lucentio?

LUCENTIO
Here's Lucentio, right son to the right Vincentio,

That have by marriage made thy daughter mine,
While counterfeit supposes bleared thine eyne.

GREMIO
Here's packing with a witness, to deceive us all.   110

VINCENTIO
Where is that damnèd villain Tranio,
That faced and braved me in this matter so?

BAPTISTA
Why, tell me, is not this my Cambio?

BIANCA
Cambio is changed into Lucentio.

LUCENTIO
Love wrought these miracles. Bianca's love   115
Made me exchange my state with Tranio
While he did bear my countenance in the town,
And happily I have arrived at the last
Unto the wishèd haven of my bliss.
What Tranio did, myself enforced him to.   120
Then pardon him, sweet father, for my sake.

VINCENTIO I'll slit the villain's nose that would have sent
me to the jail.

BAPTISTA But do you hear, sir, have you married my
daughter without asking my good will?   125

VINCENTIO Fear not, Baptista. We will content you. Go to,
but I will in to be revenged for this villainy.   *Exit*

BAPTISTA And I to sound the depth of this knavery.
                                                        Exit

LUCENTIO Look not pale, Bianca. Thy father will not frown.
                                   Exeunt Lucentio and Bianca

GREMIO
My cake is dough, but I'll in among the rest,   130
Out of hope of all but my share of the feast.   *Exit*

KATHERINE (*coming forward*) Husband, let's follow to see
the end of this ado.

PETRUCCIO First kiss me, Kate, and we will.

KATHERINE What, in the midst of the street?   135

PETRUCCIO What, art thou ashamed of me?

KATHERINE No, sir, God forbid; but ashamed to kiss.

PETRUCCIO
Why then, let's home again. Come sirrah, let's away.

KATHERINE
Nay, I will give thee a kiss. Now pray thee love, stay.
    They kiss

PETRUCCIO
Is not this well? Come, my sweet Kate.   140
Better once than never, for never too late.   *Exeunt*

5.2   *Enter Baptista, Vincentio, Gremio, the Pedant,
        Lucentio and Bianca, Petruccio, Katherine, and
        Hortensio, Tranio, Biondello, Grumio, and the
        Widow, the servingmen with Tranio bringing in a
        banquet*

LUCENTIO
At last, though long, our jarring notes agree,
And time it is when raging war is done
To smile at scapes and perils overblown.
My fair Bianca, bid my father welcome,

While I with selfsame kindness welcome thine.   5
Brother Petruccio, sister Katherina,
And thou, Hortensio, with thy loving widow,
Feast with the best, and welcome to my house.
My banquet is to close our stomachs up
After our great good cheer. Pray you, sit down,   10
For now we sit to chat as well as eat.
          They sit

PETRUCCIO
Nothing but sit, and sit, and eat, and eat.

BAPTISTA
Padua affords this kindness, son Petruccio.

PETRUCCIO
Padua affords nothing but what is kind.

HORTENSIO
For both our sakes I would that word were true.   15

PETRUCCIO
Now, for my life, Hortensio fears his widow.

WIDOW
Then never trust me if I be afeard.

PETRUCCIO
You are very sensible, and yet you miss my sense.
I mean Hortensio is afeard of you.

WIDOW
He that is giddy thinks the world turns round.   20

PETRUCCIO Roundly replied.

KATHERINE Mistress, how mean you that?

WIDOW Thus I conceive by him.

PETRUCCIO
Conceives by me! How likes Hortensio that?

HORTENSIO
My widow says thus she conceives her tale.   25

PETRUCCIO Very well mended. Kiss him for that, good
widow.

KATHERINE
'He that is giddy thinks the world turns round'—
I pray you tell me what you meant by that.

WIDOW
Your husband, being troubled with a shrew,   30
Measures my husband's sorrow by his woe.
And now you know my meaning.

KATHERINE
A very mean meaning.

WIDOW   Right, I mean you.

KATHERINE
And I am mean indeed respecting you.

PETRUCCIO To her, Kate!   35

HORTENSIO To her, widow!

PETRUCCIO
A hundred marks my Kate does put her down.

HORTENSIO That's my office.

PETRUCCIO
Spoke like an officer! Ha' to thee, lad.
          He drinks to Hortensio

BAPTISTA
How likes Gremio these quick-witted folks?   40

GREMIO
Believe me, sir, they butt together well.

BIANCA
Head and butt? An hasty-witted body
Would say your head and butt were head and horn.

VINCENTIO
Ay, mistress bride, hath that awakened you?

BIANCA
Ay, but not frighted me, therefore I'll sleep again.   45

PETRUCCIO
Nay, that you shall not. Since you have begun,
Have at you for a better jest or two.

BIANCA
Am I your bird? I mean to shift my bush,
And then pursue me as you draw your bow.
You are welcome all.   50
          Exit Bianca with Katherine and the Widow

PETRUCCIO
She hath prevented me here, Signor Tranio.
This bird you aimed at, though you hit her not.
Therefore a health to all that shot and missed.

TRANIO
O sir, Lucentio slipped me like his greyhound,
Which runs himself and catches for his master.   55

PETRUCCIO
A good swift simile, but something currish.

TRANIO
'Tis well, sir, that you hunted for yourself.
'Tis thought your deer does hold you at a bay.

BAPTISTA
O, O, Petruccio, Tranio hits you now.

LUCENTIO
I thank thee for that gird, good Tranio.   60

HORTENSIO
Confess, confess, hath he not hit you here?

PETRUCCIO
A has a little galled me, I confess,
And as the jest did glance away from me,
'Tis ten to one it maimed you two outright.

BAPTISTA
Now in good sadness, son Petruccio,   65
I think thou hast the veriest shrew of all.

PETRUCCIO
Well, I say no.—And therefore, Sir Assurance,
Let's each one send unto his wife,
And he whose wife is most obedient
To come at first when he doth send for her   70
Shall win the wager which we will propose.

HORTENSIO Content. What's the wager?

LUCENTIO Twenty crowns.

PETRUCCIO Twenty crowns!
I'll venture so much of my hawk or hound,   75
But twenty times so much upon my wife.

LUCENTIO A hundred, then.

HORTENSIO Content.

PETRUCCIO A match, 'tis done.

HORTENSIO Who shall begin?   80

LUCENTIO That will I.
          Go, Biondello, bid your mistress come to me.

BIONDELLO I go.   *Exit*

BAPTISTA
Son, I'll be your half Bianca comes.

LUCENTIO
I'll have no halves, I'll bear it all myself.   85
  Enter Biondello
How now, what news?

BIONDELLO   Sir, my mistress sends you word
That she is busy and she cannot come.

PETRUCCIO
How? She's busy and she cannot come?
Is that an answer?

GREMIO   Ay, and a kind one, too.
Pray God, sir, your wife send you not a worse.   90

PETRUCCIO
I hope, better.

HORTENSIO   Sirrah Biondello,
Go and entreat my wife to come to me forthwith.
                                    Exit Biondello

PETRUCCIO
O ho, 'entreat' her—nay, then she must needs come.

HORTENSIO
I am afraid, sir, do what you can,
  Enter Biondello
Yours will not be entreated. Now, where's my wife? 95

BIONDELLO
She says you have some goodly jest in hand.
She will not come. She bids you come to her.

PETRUCCIO
Worse and worse! She will not come—O vile,
Intolerable, not to be endured!
Sirrah Grumio, go to your mistress.   100
Say I command her come to me.   *Exit Grumio*

HORTENSIO
I know her answer.

PETRUCCIO   What?

HORTENSIO   She will not.

PETRUCCIO
The fouler fortune mine, and there an end.
  Enter Katherine

BAPTISTA
Now by my halidom, here comes Katherina.

KATHERINE (*to Petruccio*)
What is your will, sir, that you send for me?   105

PETRUCCIO
Where is your sister and Hortensio's wife?

KATHERINE
They sit conferring by the parlour fire.

PETRUCCIO
Go, fetch them hither. If they deny to come,
Swinge me them soundly forth unto their husbands.
Away, I say, and bring them hither straight.   110
                                    Exit Katherine

LUCENTIO
Here is a wonder, if you talk of wonders.

HORTENSIO
And so it is. I wonder what it bodes.

PETRUCCIO
Marry, peace it bodes, and love, and quiet life;
An aweful rule and right supremacy,
And, to be short, what not that's sweet and happy.

BAPTISTA
Now fair befall thee, good Petruccio,   116
The wager thou hast won, and I will add
Unto their losses twenty thousand crowns,
Another dowry to another daughter,
For she is changed as she had never been.   120

PETRUCCIO
Nay, I will win my wager better yet,
And show more sign of her obedience,
Her new-built virtue and obedience.
  Enter Katherine, Bianca, and the Widow
See where she comes, and brings your froward wives
As prisoners to her womanly persuasion.   125
Katherine, that cap of yours becomes you not.
Off with that bauble, throw it underfoot.
  Katherine throws down her cap

WIDOW
Lord, let me never have a cause to sigh
Till I be brought to such a silly pass.

BIANCA
Fie, what a foolish duty call you this?   130

LUCENTIO
I would your duty were as foolish, too.
The wisdom of your duty, fair Bianca,
Hath cost me a hundred crowns since supper-time.

BIANCA
The more fool you for laying on my duty.

PETRUCCIO
Katherine, I charge thee tell these headstrong women
What duty they do owe their lords and husbands.   136

WIDOW
Come, come, you're mocking. We will have no telling.

PETRUCCIO
Come on, I say, and first begin with her.

WIDOW She shall not.

PETRUCCIO
I say she shall: and first begin with her.   140

KATHERINE
Fie, fie, unknit that threat'ning, unkind brow,
And dart not scornful glances from those eyes
To wound thy lord, thy king, thy governor.
It blots thy beauty as frosts do bite the meads,
Confounds thy fame as whirlwinds shake fair buds, 145
And in no sense is meet or amiable.
A woman moved is like a fountain troubled,
Muddy, ill-seeming, thick, bereft of beauty,
And while it is so, none so dry or thirsty
Will deign to sip or touch one drop of it.   150
Thy husband is thy lord, thy life, thy keeper,
Thy head, thy sovereign, one that cares for thee,
And for thy maintenance commits his body
To painful labour both by sea and land,
To watch the night in storms, the day in cold,   155

Whilst thou liest warm at home, secure and safe,
And craves no other tribute at thy hands
But love, fair looks, and true obedience,
Too little payment for so great a debt.
Such duty as the subject owes the prince,   160
Even such a woman oweth to her husband,
And when she is froward, peevish, sullen, sour,
And not obedient to his honest will,
What is she but a foul contending rebel,
And graceless traitor to her loving lord?   165
I am ashamed that women are so simple
To offer war where they should kneel for peace,
Or seek for rule, supremacy, and sway
When they are bound to serve, love, and obey.
Why are our bodies soft, and weak, and smooth,   170
Unapt to toil and trouble in the world,
But that our soft conditions and our hearts
Should well agree with our external parts?
Come, come, you froward and unable worms,
My mind hath been as big as one of yours,   175
My heart as great, my reason haply more,
To bandy word for word and frown for frown;
But now I see our lances are but straws,
Our strength as weak, our weakness past compare,
That seeming to be most which we indeed least are.   180

Then vail your stomachs, for it is no boot,
And place your hands below your husband's foot,
In token of which duty, if he please,
My hand is ready, may it do him ease.   184
PETRUCCIO
Why, there's a wench! Come on, and kiss me, Kate.
        They kiss
LUCENTIO
Well, go thy ways, old lad, for thou shalt ha't.
VINCENTIO
'Tis a good hearing when children are toward.
LUCENTIO
But a harsh hearing when women are froward.
PETRUCCIO Come, Kate, we'll to bed.
We three are married, but you two are sped.   190
'Twas I won the wager, though (*to Lucentio*) you hit
        the white,
And being a winner, God give you good night.
        Exit Petruccio with Katherine
HORTENSIO
Now go thy ways, thou hast tamed a curst shrew.
LUCENTIO
'Tis a wonder, by your leave, she will be tamed so.
        Exeunt

ADDITIONAL PASSAGES

The Taming of A Shrew, printed in 1594 and believed to derive from Shakespeare's play as performed, contains episodes continuing and rounding off the Christopher Sly framework which may echo passages written by Shakespeare but not printed in the Folio. They are given below.

A. The following exchange occurs at a point for which there is no exact equivalent in Shakespeare's play. It could come at the end of 2.1. The 'fool' of the first line is Sander, the counterpart of Grumio.

        Then Sly speaks
SLY Sim, when will the fool come again?
LORD He'll come again, my lord, anon.
SLY Gi's some more drink here. Zounds, where's the
        tapster? Here, Sim, eat some of these things.
LORD So I do, my lord.   5
SLY Here, Sim, I drink to thee.
LORD My lord, here comes the players again.
SLY O brave, here's two fine gentlewomen.

B. This passage comes between 4.5 and 4.6. If it originates with Shakespeare it implies that Grumio accompanies Petruccio at the beginning of 4.6.

SLY Sim, must they be married now?
LORD Ay, my lord.

        Enter Ferando and Kate and Sander
SLY Look, Sim, the fool is come again now.

C. Sly interrupts the action of the play-within-play. This is at 5.1.102 of Shakespeare's play.

        Phylotus and Valeria runs away.
        Then Sly speaks
SLY I say we'll have no sending to prison.
LORD My lord, this is but the play. They're but in jest.
SLY I tell thee, Sim, we'll have no sending to prison, that's
        flat. Why, Sim, am not I Don Christo Vary? Therefore I
        say they shall not go to prison.   5
LORD No more they shall not, my lord. They be run away.
SLY Are they run away, Sim? That's well. Then gi's some
        more drink, and let them play again.
LORD Here, my lord.
        Sly drinks and then falls asleep

D. Sly is carried off between 5.1 and 5.2.

        Exeunt omnes
        Sly sleeps
LORD
Who's within there? Come hither, sirs, my lord's
Asleep again. Go take him easily up
And put him in his own apparel again,
And lay him in the place where we did find him

Just underneath the alehouse side below. 5
But see you wake him not in any case.

BOY

It shall be done, my lord. Come help to bear him hence.

Exit

E. The conclusion.

Then enter two bearing of Sly in his own apparel again
and leaves him where they found him and then goes
out.

Then enter the Tapster

TAPSTER

Now that the darksome night is overpast
And dawning day appears in crystal sky,
Now must I haste abroad. But soft, who's this?
What, Sly! O wondrous, hath he lain here all night?
I'll wake him. I think he's starved by this, 5
But that his belly was so stuffed with ale.
What ho, Sly, awake, for shame!

SLY Sim, gi's some more wine. What, 's all the players
gone? Am not I a lord?

TAPSTER

A lord with a murrain! Come, art thou drunken still?

SLY

Who's this? Tapster? O Lord, sirrah, I have had 11
The bravest dream tonight that ever thou
Heardest in all thy life.

TAPSTER

Ay, marry, but you had best get you home,
For your wife will course you for dreaming here tonight.

SLY

Will she? I know now how to tame a shrew. 16
I dreamt upon it all this night till now,
And thou hast waked me out of the best dream
That ever I had in my life. But I'll to my
Wife presently and tame her too, 20
An if she anger me.

TAPSTER

Nay, tarry, Sly, for I'll go home with thee
And hear the rest that thou hast dreamt tonight.

Exeunt omnes

THE COMEDY OF ERRORS

On the night of 28 December 1594, the Christmas revels at Gray's Inn—one of London's law schools—became so uproarious that one performance planned for the occasion had to be abandoned. Eventually 'it was thought good not to offer anything of account saving dancing and revelling with gentlewomen; and after such sports a comedy of errors (like to Plautus his *Menaechmus*) was played by the players. So that night was begun, and continued to the end, in nothing but confusion and errors; whereupon it was ever afterwards called "The Night of Errors".'

This sounds like a reference to Shakespeare's play, first printed in the 1623 Folio, which is certainly based in large part on the Roman dramatist Plautus' comedy *Menaechmi*. As Shakespeare's shortest play, it would have been especially suited to late-night performance; there is no evidence that it was written for the occasion, but it may well have been new in 1594.

The comedy in *Menaechmi* derives from the embarrassment experienced by a man in search of his long-lost twin brother when various people intimately acquainted with that twin—including his wife, his mistress, and his father—mistake the one for the other. Shakespeare greatly increases the possibilities of comic confusion by giving the brothers (both called Antipholus) servants (both called Dromio) who themselves are long-separated twins. An added episode in which Antipholus of Ephesus' wife, Adriana, bars him from his own house in which she is entertaining his brother is based on another play by Plautus, *Amphitruo*. Shakespeare sets the comic action within a more serious framework, opening with a scene in which the twin masters' old father, Egeon, who has arrived at Ephesus in search of them, is shown under imminent sentence of death unless he finds someone to redeem him. This strand of the plot, as well as the surprising revelation that brings about the resolution of the action, is based on the story of Apollonius of Tyre which Shakespeare was to use again, many years later, in *Pericles*.

The Comedy of Errors is a kind of diploma piece, as if Shakespeare were displaying his ability to outshine both his classical progenitors and their English imitators. Along with *The Tempest*, it is his most classically constructed play: all the action takes place within a few hours and in a single place. Moreover, it seems to make use of the conventionalized arcade setting of academic drama, with three 'houses'—the Phoenix, the Porcupine, and the Priory—represented by doors and signs on stage. The working out of the complexities inherent in the basic situation represents a considerable intellectual feat. But the comedy is humanized by the interweaving of romantic elements, such as Egeon's initial plight, the love between the visiting Antipholus and his twin brother's wife's sister, Luciana, and the entirely serious portrayal of Egeon's suffering when his own son fails to recognize him at the moment of his greatest need. From time to time the comic tension is relaxed by the presence of discursive set pieces, none more memorable than Dromio of Syracuse's description of Nell, the kitchen wench who is 'spherical, like a globe'.

THE PERSONS OF THE PLAY

Solinus, DUKE of Ephesus

EGEON, a merchant of Syracuse, father of the Antipholus twins

ANTIPHOLUS OF EPHESUS ⎱ twin brothers, sons of Egeon
ANTIPHOLUS OF SYRACUSE ⎰

DROMIO OF EPHESUS ⎱ twin brothers, and bondmen of the
DROMIO OF SYRACUSE ⎰ Antipholus twins

ADRIANA, wife of Antipholus of Ephesus

LUCIANA, her sister

NELL, Adriana's kitchen-maid

ANGELO, a goldsmith

BALTHASAR, a merchant

A COURTESAN

Doctor PINCH, a schoolmaster and exorcist

MERCHANT OF EPHESUS, a friend of Antipholus of Syracuse

SECOND MERCHANT, Angelo's creditor

EMILIA, an abbess at Ephesus

Jailer, messenger, headsman, officers, and other attendants

The Comedy of Errors

Enter Solinus, the Duke of Ephesus, with Egeon the
Merchant of Syracuse, Jailer, and other attendants

EGEON

Proceed, Solinus, to procure my fall,
And by the doom of death end woes and all.

DUKE

Merchant of Syracusa, plead no more.
I am not partial to infringe our laws.
The enmity and discord which of late   5
Sprung from the rancorous outrage of your Duke
To merchants, our well-dealing countrymen,
Who, wanting guilders to redeem their lives,
Have sealed his rigorous statutes with their bloods,
Excludes all pity from our threat'ning looks.   10
For since the mortal and intestine jars
'Twixt thy seditious countrymen and us,
It hath in solemn synods been decreed,
Both by the Syracusians and ourselves,
To admit no traffic to our adverse towns.   15
Nay more: if any born at Ephesus
Be seen at Syracusian marts and fairs;
Again, if any Syracusian born
Come to the bay of Ephesus—he dies,
His goods confiscate to the Duke's dispose,   20
Unless a thousand marks be levièd
To quit the penalty and ransom him.
Thy substance, valued at the highest rate,
Cannot amount unto a hundred marks.
Therefore by law thou art condemned to die.   25

EGEON

Yet this my comfort: when your words are done,
My woes end likewise with the evening sun.

DUKE

Well, Syracusian, say in brief the cause
Why thou departed'st from thy native home,
And for what cause thou cam'st to Ephesus.   30

EGEON

A heavier task could not have been imposed
Than I to speak my griefs unspeakable.
Yet, that the world may witness that my end
Was wrought by nature, not by vile offence,
I'll utter what my sorrow gives me leave.   35
In Syracusa was I born, and wed
Unto a woman happy but for me,
And by me happy, had not our hap been bad.
With her I lived in joy, our wealth increased
By prosperous voyages I often made   40
To Epidamnum, till my factor's death,
And the great care of goods at random left,
Drew me from kind embracements of my spouse,
From whom my absence was not six months old
Before herself—almost at fainting under   45
The pleasing punishment that women bear—
Had made provision for her following me,

And soon and safe arrivèd where I was.
There had she not been long but she became
A joyful mother of two goodly sons;   50
And, which was strange, the one so like the other
As could not be distinguished but by names.
That very hour, and in the selfsame inn,
A mean-born woman was deliverèd
Of such a burden male, twins both alike.   55
Those, for their parents were exceeding poor,
I bought, and brought up to attend my sons.
My wife, not meanly proud of two such boys,
Made daily motions for our home return.
Unwilling, I agreed. Alas! Too soon   60
We came aboard.
A league from Epidamnum had we sailed
Before the always-wind-obeying deep
Gave any tragic instance of our harm.
But longer did we not retain much hope,   65
For what obscurèd light the heavens did grant
Did but convey unto our fearful minds
A doubtful warrant of immediate death,
Which though myself would gladly have embraced,
Yet the incessant weepings of my wife—   70
Weeping before for what she saw must come—
And piteous plainings of the pretty babes,
That mourned for fashion, ignorant what to fear,
Forced me to seek delays for them and me.
And this it was—for other means was none: 75
The sailors sought for safety by our boat,
And left the ship, then sinking-ripe, to us.
My wife, more careful for the latter-born,
Had fastened him unto a small spare mast
Such as seafaring men provide for storms.   80
To him one of the other twins was bound,
Whilst I had been like heedful of the other.
The children thus disposed, my wife and I,
Fixing our eyes on whom our care was fixed,
Fastened ourselves at either end the mast,   85
And floating straight, obedient to the stream,
Was carried towards Corinth, as we thought.
At length the sun, gazing upon the earth,
Dispersed those vapours that offended us,
And by the benefit of his wishèd light   90
The seas waxed calm, and we discoverèd
Two ships from far, making amain to us:
Of Corinth that, of Epidaurus this.
But ere they came—O let me say no more!
Gather the sequel by that went before.   95

DUKE

Nay, forward, old man; do not break off so,
For we may pity though not pardon thee.

EGEON

O, had the gods done so, I had not now
Worthily termed them merciless to us.

For, ere the ships could meet by twice five leagues,
We were encountered by a mighty rock,   101
Which being violently borne upon,
Our helpful ship was splitted in the midst,
So that in this unjust divorce of us
Fortune had left to both of us alike   105
What to delight in, what to sorrow for.
Her part, poor soul, seeming as burdenèd
With lesser weight but not with lesser woe,
Was carried with more speed before the wind,
And in our sight they three were taken up   110
By fishermen of Corinth, as we thought.
At length another ship had seized on us,
And, knowing whom it was their hap to save,
Gave healthful welcome to their shipwrecked guests,
And would have reft the fishers of their prey   115
Had not their barque been very slow of sail;
And therefore homeward did they bend their course.
Thus have you heard me severed from my bliss,
That by misfortunes was my life prolonged
To tell sad stories of my own mishaps.   120

DUKE
And for the sake of them thou sorrow'st for,
Do me the favour to dilate at full
What have befall'n of them and thee till now.

EGEON
My youngest boy, and yet my eldest care,
At eighteen years became inquisitive   125
After his brother, and importuned me
That his attendant—so his case was like,
Reft of his brother, but retained his name—
Might bear him company in the quest of him;
Whom whilst I laboured of a love to see,   130
I hazarded the loss of whom I loved.
Five summers have I spent in farthest Greece,
Roaming clean through the bounds of Asia,
And coasting homeward came to Ephesus,
Hopeless to find, yet loath to leave unsought   135
Or that or any place that harbours men.
But here must end the story of my life,
And happy were I in my timely death
Could all my travels warrant me they live.

DUKE
Hapless Egeon, whom the fates have marked   140
To bear the extremity of dire mishap,
Now trust me, were it not against our laws—
Which princes, would they, may not disannul—
Against my crown, my oath, my dignity,
My soul should sue as advocate for thee.   145
But though thou art adjudgèd to the death,
And passèd sentence may not be recalled
But to our honour's great disparagement,
Yet will I favour thee in what I can.
Therefore, merchant, I'll limit thee this day   150
To seek thy health by beneficial help.
Try all the friends thou hast in Ephesus:
Beg thou or borrow to make up the sum,

And live. If no, then thou art doomed to die.
Jailer, take him to thy custody.   155

JAILER I will, my lord.

EGEON
Hopeless and helpless doth Egeon wend,
But to procrastinate his lifeless end.   *Exeunt*

1.2   Enter [*from the bay*] *Antipholus of Syracuse,*
         Merchant [*of Ephesus*], *and Dromio of Syracuse*

MERCHANT [OF EPHESUS]
Therefore give out you are of Epidamnum,
Lest that your goods too soon be confiscate.
This very day a Syracusian merchant
Is apprehended for arrival here,
And, not being able to buy out his life,   5
According to the statute of the town
Dies ere the weary sun set in the west.
There is your money that I had to keep.

ANTIPHOLUS OF SYRACUSE (*to Dromio*)
Go bear it to the Centaur, where we host,
And stay there, Dromio, till I come to thee.   10
Within this hour it will be dinner-time.
Till that I'll view the manners of the town,
Peruse the traders, gaze upon the buildings,
And then return and sleep within mine inn;
For with long travel I am stiff and weary.   15
Get thee away.

DROMIO OF SYRACUSE
Many a man would take you at your word,
And go indeed, having so good a mean.   *Exit*

ANTIPHOLUS OF SYRACUSE
A trusty villain, sir, that very oft,
When I am dull with care and melancholy,   20
Lightens my humour with his merry jests.
What, will you walk with me about the town,
And then go to my inn and dine with me?

MERCHANT [OF EPHESUS]
I am invited, sir, to certain merchants
Of whom I hope to make much benefit.   25
I crave your pardon. Soon at five o'clock,
Please you, I'll meet with you upon the mart,
And afterward consort you till bedtime.
My present business calls me from you now.

ANTIPHOLUS OF SYRACUSE
Farewell till then. I will go lose myself,   30
And wander up and down to view the city.

MERCHANT [OF EPHESUS]
Sir, I commend you to your own content.   *Exit*

ANTIPHOLUS OF SYRACUSE
He that commends me to mine own content
Commends me to the thing I cannot get.
I to the world am like a drop of water   35
That in the ocean seeks another drop,
Who, falling there to find his fellow forth,
Unseen, inquisitive, confounds himself.
So I, to find a mother and a brother,
In quest of them, unhappy, lose myself.   40

Enter Dromio of Ephesus
Here comes the almanac of my true date.
What now? How chance thou art returned so soon?
DROMIO OF EPHESUS
Returned so soon? Rather approached too late.
The capon burns, the pig falls from the spit.
The clock hath strucken twelve upon the bell;   45
My mistress made it one upon my cheek.
She is so hot because the meat is cold.
The meat is cold because you come not home.
You come not home because you have no stomach.
You have no stomach, having broke your fast;   50
But we that know what 'tis to fast and pray
Are penitent for your default today.
ANTIPHOLUS OF SYRACUSE
Stop in your wind, sir. Tell me this, I pray:
Where have you left the money that I gave you?
DROMIO OF EPHESUS
O—sixpence that I had o' Wednesday last   55
To pay the saddler for my mistress' crupper?
The saddler had it, sir; I kept it not.
ANTIPHOLUS OF SYRACUSE
I am not in a sportive humour now.
Tell me, and dally not: where is the money?
We being strangers here, how dar'st thou trust   60
So great a charge from thine own custody?
DROMIO OF EPHESUS
I pray you, jest, sir, as you sit at dinner.
I from my mistress come to you in post.
If I return I shall be post indeed,
For she will scour your fault upon my pate.   65
Methinks your maw, like mine, should be your clock,
And strike you home without a messenger.
ANTIPHOLUS OF SYRACUSE
Come, Dromio, come, these jests are out of season.
Reserve them till a merrier hour than this.
Where is the gold I gave in charge to thee?   70
DROMIO OF EPHESUS
To me, sir? Why, you gave no gold to me.
ANTIPHOLUS OF SYRACUSE
Come on, sir knave, have done your foolishness,
And tell me how thou hast disposed thy charge.
DROMIO OF EPHESUS
My charge was but to fetch you from the mart
Home to your house, the Phoenix, sir, to dinner.   75
My mistress and her sister stays for you.
ANTIPHOLUS OF SYRACUSE
Now, as I am a Christian, answer me
In what safe place you have bestowed my money,
Or I shall break that merry sconce of yours
That stands on tricks when I am undisposed.   80
Where is the thousand marks thou hadst of me?
DROMIO OF EPHESUS
I have some marks of yours upon my pate,
Some of my mistress' marks upon my shoulders,
But not a thousand marks between you both.
If I should pay your worship those again,   85
Perchance you will not bear them patiently.

ANTIPHOLUS OF SYRACUSE
Thy mistress' marks? What mistress, slave, hast thou?
DROMIO OF EPHESUS
Your worship's wife, my mistress, at the Phoenix:
She that doth fast till you come home to dinner,
And prays that you will hie you home to dinner.   90
ANTIPHOLUS OF SYRACUSE
What, wilt thou flout me thus unto my face,
Being forbid? There, take you that, sir knave!
He beats Dromio
DROMIO OF EPHESUS
What mean you, sir? For God's sake, hold your hands!
Nay, an you will not, sir, I'll take my heels.   *Exit*
ANTIPHOLUS OF SYRACUSE
Upon my life, by some device or other   95
The villain is o'er-raught of all my money.
They say this town is full of cozenage,
As nimble jugglers that deceive the eye,
Dark-working sorcerers that change the mind,
Soul-killing witches that deform the body,   100
Disguisèd cheaters, prating mountebanks,
And many suchlike libertines of sin.
If it prove so, I will be gone the sooner.
I'll to the Centaur to go seek this slave.   104
I greatly fear my money is not safe.   *Exit*

❦

2.1   *Enter ⌈from the Phoenix⌉ Adriana, wife of*
        Antipholus of Ephesus, with Luciana, her sister
ADRIANA
Neither my husband nor the slave returned
That in such haste I sent to seek his master?
Sure, Luciana, it is two o'clock.
LUCIANA
Perhaps some merchant hath invited him,
And from the mart he's somewhere gone to dinner.   5
Good sister, let us dine, and never fret.
A man is master of his liberty.
Time is their mistress, and when they see time
They'll go or come. If so, be patient, sister.
ADRIANA
Why should their liberty than ours be more?   10
LUCIANA
Because their business still lies out o' door.
ADRIANA
Look when I serve him so, he takes it ill.
LUCIANA
O, know he is the bridle of your will.
ADRIANA
There's none but asses will be bridled so.
LUCIANA
Why, headstrong liberty is lashed with woe.   15
There's nothing situate under heaven's eye
But hath his bound in earth, in sea, in sky.
The beasts, the fishes, and the wingèd fowls
Are their males' subjects and at their controls.
Man, more divine, the master of all these,   20
Lord of the wide world and wild wat'ry seas,

Indued with intellectual sense and souls,
Of more pre-eminence than fish and fowls,
Are masters to their females, and their lords.
Then let your will attend on their accords.   25

ADRIANA
This servitude makes you to keep unwed.

LUCIANA
Not this, but troubles of the marriage bed.

ADRIANA
But were you wedded, you would bear some sway.

LUCIANA
Ere I learn love, I'll practise to obey.

ADRIANA
How if your husband start some otherwhere?   30

LUCIANA
Till he come home again, I would forbear.

ADRIANA
Patience unmoved! No marvel though she pause:
They can be meek that have no other cause.
A wretched soul, bruised with adversity,
We bid be quiet when we hear it cry.   35
But were we burdened with like weight of pain,
As much or more we should ourselves complain.
So thou, that hast no unkind mate to grieve thee,
With urging helpless patience would relieve me.
But if thou live to see like right bereft,   40
This fool-begged patience in thee will be left.

LUCIANA
Well, I will marry one day, but to try.
Enter Dromio of Ephesus
Here comes your man. Now is your husband nigh.

ADRIANA
Say, is your tardy master now at hand?

DROMIO OF EPHESUS Nay, he's at two hands with me, and
that my two ears can witness.   46

ADRIANA
Say, didst thou speak with him? Know'st thou his
mind?

DROMIO OF EPHESUS
I? Ay, he told his mind upon mine ear.
Beshrew his hand, I scarce could understand it.

LUCIANA
Spake he so doubtfully thou couldst not feel his
meaning?   50

DROMIO OF EPHESUS Nay, he struck so plainly I could too
well feel his blows, and withal so doubtfully that I
could scarce under-stand them.

ADRIANA
But say, I prithee, is he coming home?
It seems he hath great care to please his wife.   55

DROMIO OF EPHESUS
Why, mistress, sure my master is horn-mad.

ADRIANA Horn-mad, thou villain?

DROMIO OF EPHESUS
I mean not cuckold-mad, but sure he is stark mad.
When I desired him to come home to dinner,
He asked me for a thousand marks in gold.   60
''Tis dinner-time,' quoth I. 'My gold,' quoth he.

'Your meat doth burn,' quoth I. 'My gold,' quoth he.
'Will you come home?' quoth I. 'My gold,' quoth he;
'Where is the thousand marks I gave thee, villain?'
'The pig,' quoth I, 'is burned.' 'My gold!' quoth he.
'My mistress, sir—' quoth I. 'Hang up thy mistress!
I know thy mistress not. Out on thy mistress!'

LUCIANA Quoth who?

DROMIO OF EPHESUS Quoth my master.
'I know', quoth he, 'no house, no wife, no mistress.'
So that my errand, due unto my tongue,   71
I thank him, I bare home upon my shoulders;
For, in conclusion, he did beat me there.

ADRIANA
Go back again, thou slave, and fetch him home.

DROMIO OF EPHESUS
Go back again and be new beaten home?   75
For God's sake, send some other messenger.

ADRIANA
Back, slave, or I will break thy pate across.

DROMIO OF EPHESUS
An he will bless that cross with other beating,
Between you I shall have a holy head.

ADRIANA
Hence, prating peasant. Fetch thy master home.   80
She beats Dromio

DROMIO OF EPHESUS
Am I so round with you as you with me,
That like a football you do spurn me thus?
You spurn me hence, and he will spurn me hither.
If I last in this service, you must case me in leather.
         Exit

LUCIANA (*to Adriana*)
Fie, how impatience loureth in your face!   85

ADRIANA
His company must do his minions grace,
Whilst I at home starve for a merry look.
Hath homely age th'alluring beauty took
From my poor cheek? Then he hath wasted it.
Are my discourses dull? Barren my wit?   90
If voluble and sharp discourse be marred,
Unkindness blunts it more than marble hard.
Do their gay vestments his affections bait?
That's not my fault: he's master of my state.
What ruins are in me that can be found   95
By him not ruined? Then is he the ground
Of my defeatures. My decayèd fair
A sunny look of his would soon repair.
But, too unruly deer, he breaks the pale,
And feeds from home. Poor I am but his stale.   100

LUCIANA
Self-harming jealousy! Fie, beat it hence.

ADRIANA
Unfeeling fools can with such wrongs dispense.
I know his eye doth homage otherwhere,
Or else what lets it but he would be here?
Sister, you know he promised me a chain.   105
Would that alone o' love he would detain,
So he would keep fair quarter with his bed.

I see the jewel best enamellèd
Will lose her beauty. Yet the gold bides still
That others touch; and often touching will   110
Wear gold, and yet no man that hath a name
By falsehood and corruption doth it shame.
Since that my beauty cannot please his eye,
I'll weep what's left away, and weeping die.
LUCIANA
How many fond fools serve mad jealousy!   115

⌜Exeunt into the Phoenix⌝

2.2   *Enter Antipholus of Syracuse*
ANTIPHOLUS OF SYRACUSE
The gold I gave to Dromio is laid up
Safe at the Centaur, and the heedful slave
Is wandered forth in care to seek me out.
By computation and mine host's report,
I could not speak with Dromio since at first   5
I sent him from the mart! See, here he comes.
Enter Dromio of Syracuse
How now, sir, is your merry humour altered?
As you love strokes, so jest with me again.
You know no Centaur? You received no gold?
Your mistress sent to have me home to dinner?   10
My house was at the Phoenix?—Wast thou mad,
That thus so madly thou didst answer me?
DROMIO OF SYRACUSE
What answer, sir? When spake I such a word?
ANTIPHOLUS OF SYRACUSE
Even now, even here, not half an hour since.
DROMIO OF SYRACUSE
I did not see you since you sent me hence   15
Home to the Centaur with the gold you gave me.
ANTIPHOLUS OF SYRACUSE
Villain, thou didst deny the gold's receipt,
And told'st me of a mistress and a dinner,
For which I hope thou felt'st I was displeased.
DROMIO OF SYRACUSE
I am glad to see you in this merry vein.   20
What means this jest? I pray you, master, tell me.
ANTIPHOLUS OF SYRACUSE
Yea, dost thou jeer and flout me in the teeth?
Think'st thou I jest? Hold, take thou that, and that.
He beats Dromio
DROMIO OF SYRACUSE
Hold, sir, for God's sake—now your jest is earnest!
Upon what bargain do you give it me?   25
ANTIPHOLUS OF SYRACUSE
Because that I familiarly sometimes
Do use you for my fool, and chat with you,
Your sauciness will jest upon my love,
And make a common of my serious hours.
When the sun shines, let foolish gnats make sport, 30
But creep in crannies when he hides his beams.
If you will jest with me, know my aspect,
And fashion your demeanour to my looks,
Or I will beat this method in your sconce.   34
DROMIO OF SYRACUSE 'Sconce' call you it? So you would
leave battering, I had rather have it a head. An you

use these blows long, I must get a sconce for my head,
and ensconce it too, or else I shall seek my wit in my
shoulders. But I pray, sir, why am I beaten?
ANTIPHOLUS OF SYRACUSE Dost thou not know?   40
DROMIO OF SYRACUSE Nothing, sir, but that I am beaten.
ANTIPHOLUS OF SYRACUSE Shall I tell you why?
DROMIO OF SYRACUSE Ay, sir, and wherefore; for they say
every why hath a wherefore.
ANTIPHOLUS OF SYRACUSE
'Why' first: for flouting me; and then 'wherefore': 45
For urging it the second time to me.
DROMIO OF SYRACUSE
Was there ever any man thus beaten out of season,
When in the why and the wherefore is neither rhyme
   nor reason?—
Well, sir, I thank you.
ANTIPHOLUS OF SYRACUSE Thank me, sir, for what?
DROMIO OF SYRACUSE Marry, sir, for this something that
you gave me for nothing.   51
ANTIPHOLUS OF SYRACUSE I'll make you amends next, to
give you nothing for something. But say, sir, is it
dinner-time?
DROMIO OF SYRACUSE No, sir, I think the meat wants that
I have.   56
ANTIPHOLUS OF SYRACUSE In good time, sir. What's that?
DROMIO OF SYRACUSE Basting.
ANTIPHOLUS OF SYRACUSE Well, sir, then 'twill be dry.
DROMIO OF SYRACUSE If it be, sir, I pray you eat none of it.
ANTIPHOLUS OF SYRACUSE Your reason?   61
DROMIO OF SYRACUSE Lest it make you choleric and
purchase me another dry basting.
ANTIPHOLUS OF SYRACUSE Well, sir, learn to jest in good
time. There's a time for all things.   65
DROMIO OF SYRACUSE I durst have denied that before you
were so choleric.
ANTIPHOLUS OF SYRACUSE By what rule, sir?
DROMIO OF SYRACUSE Marry, sir, by a rule as plain as the
plain bald pate of Father Time himself.   70
ANTIPHOLUS OF SYRACUSE Let's hear it.
DROMIO OF SYRACUSE There's no time for a man to recover
his hair that grows bald by nature.
ANTIPHOLUS OF SYRACUSE May he not do it by fine and
recovery?   75
DROMIO OF SYRACUSE Yes, to pay a fine for a periwig, and
recover the lost hair of another man.
ANTIPHOLUS OF SYRACUSE Why is Time such a niggard of
hair, being, as it is, so plentiful an excrement?   79
DROMIO OF SYRACUSE Because it is a blessing that he
bestows on beasts, and what he hath scanted men in
hair he hath given them in wit.
ANTIPHOLUS OF SYRACUSE Why, but there's many a man
hath more hair than wit.
DROMIO OF SYRACUSE Not a man of those but he hath the
wit to lose his hair.   86
ANTIPHOLUS OF SYRACUSE Why, thou didst conclude hairy
men plain dealers, without wit.
DROMIO OF SYRACUSE The plainer dealer, the sooner lost.
Yet he loseth it in a kind of jollity.   90
ANTIPHOLUS OF SYRACUSE For what reason?

DROMIO OF SYRACUSE For two, and sound ones too.

ANTIPHOLUS OF SYRACUSE Nay, not sound, I pray you.

DROMIO OF SYRACUSE Sure ones, then.

ANTIPHOLUS OF SYRACUSE Nay, not sure, in a thing falsing.

DROMIO OF SYRACUSE Certain ones, then. 96

ANTIPHOLUS OF SYRACUSE Name them.

DROMIO OF SYRACUSE The one, to save the money that he spends in tiring; the other, that at dinner they should not drop in his porridge. 100

ANTIPHOLUS OF SYRACUSE You would all this time have proved there is no time for all things.

DROMIO OF SYRACUSE Marry, and did, sir: namely, e'en no time to recover hair lost by nature.

ANTIPHOLUS OF SYRACUSE But your reason was not substantial, why there is no time to recover. 106

DROMIO OF SYRACUSE Thus I mend it: Time himself is bald, and therefore to the world's end will have bald followers.

ANTIPHOLUS OF SYRACUSE I knew 'twould be a bald conclusion. 111

    Enter ⌈from the Phoenix⌉ Adriana and Luciana

But soft—who wafts us yonder?

ADRIANA

Ay, ay, Antipholus, look strange and frown:
Some other mistress hath thy sweet aspects.
I am not Adriana, nor thy wife. 115
The time was once when thou unurged wouldst vow
That never words were music to thine ear,
That never object pleasing in thine eye,
That never touch well welcome to thy hand,
That never meat sweet-savoured in thy taste, 120
Unless I spake, or looked, or touched, or carved to thee.
How comes it now, my husband, O how comes it
That thou art then estrangèd from thyself?—
Thy 'self' I call it, being strange to me
That, undividable, incorporate, 125
Am better than thy dear self's better part.
Ah, do not tear away thyself from me;
For know, my love, as easy mayst thou fall
A drop of water in the breaking gulf,
And take unmingled thence that drop again 130
Without addition or diminishing,
As take from me thyself, and not me too.
How dearly would it touch thee to the quick
Shouldst thou but hear I were licentious,
And that this body, consecrate to thee, 135
By ruffian lust should be contaminate?
Wouldst thou not spit at me, and spurn at me,
And hurl the name of husband in my face,
And tear the stained skin off my harlot brow,
And from my false hand cut the wedding ring, 140
And break it with a deep-divorcing vow?
I know thou canst, and therefore see thou do it!
I am possessed with an adulterate blot;
My blood is mingled with the crime of lust.
For if we two be one, and thou play false, 145
I do digest the poison of thy flesh,

Being strumpeted by thy contagion.
Keep then fair league and truce with thy true bed,
I live unstained, thou undishonourèd.

ANTIPHOLUS OF SYRACUSE

Plead you to *me*, fair dame? I know you not. 150
In Ephesus I am but two hours old,
As strange unto your town as to your talk,
Who, every word by all my wit being scanned,
Wants wit in all one word to understand.

LUCIANA

Fie, brother, how the world is changed with you! 155
When were you wont to use my sister thus?
She sent for you by Dromio home to dinner.

ANTIPHOLUS OF SYRACUSE By Dromio?

DROMIO OF SYRACUSE By me?

ADRIANA

By thee; and this thou didst return from him— 160
That he did buffet thee, and in his blows
Denied my house for his, me for his wife.

ANTIPHOLUS OF SYRACUSE

Did you converse, sir, with this gentlewoman?
What is the course and drift of your compact?

DROMIO OF SYRACUSE

I, sir? I never saw her till this time. 165

ANTIPHOLUS OF SYRACUSE

Villain, thou liest; for even her very words
Didst thou deliver to me on the mart.

DROMIO OF SYRACUSE

I never spake with her in all my life.

ANTIPHOLUS OF SYRACUSE

How can she thus then call us by our names?—
Unless it be by inspiration. 170

ADRIANA

How ill agrees it with your gravity
To counterfeit thus grossly with your slave,
Abetting him to thwart me in my mood!
Be it my wrong you are from me exempt,
But wrong not that wrong with a more contempt. 175
Come, I will fasten on this sleeve of thine.
Thou art an elm, my husband; I a vine,
Whose weakness, married to thy stronger state,
Makes me with thy strength to communicate.
If aught possess thee from me, it is dross, 180
Usurping ivy, brier, or idle moss,
Who, all for want of pruning, with intrusion
Infect thy sap, and live on thy confusion.

ANTIPHOLUS OF SYRACUSE *(aside)*

To me she speaks, she moves me for her theme.
What, was I married to her in my dream? 185
Or sleep I now, and think I hear all this?
What error drives our eyes and ears amiss?
Until I know this sure uncertainty,
I'll entertain the offered fallacy.

LUCIANA

Dromio, go bid the servants spread for dinner. 190

DROMIO OF SYRACUSE *(aside)*

O, for my beads! I cross me for a sinner.

This is the fairy land. O spite of spites,
We talk with goblins, oafs, and sprites.
If we obey them not, this will ensue:
They'll suck our breath or pinch us black and blue.

LUCIANA
Why prat'st thou to thyself, and answer'st not?   196
Dromio, thou drone, thou snail, thou slug, thou sot.

DROMIO OF SYRACUSE (to Antipholus)
I am transformèd, master, am not I?

ANTIPHOLUS OF SYRACUSE
I think thou art in mind, and so am I.

DROMIO OF SYRACUSE
Nay, master, both in mind and in my shape.   200

ANTIPHOLUS OF SYRACUSE
Thou hast thine own form.

DROMIO OF SYRACUSE   No, I am an ape.

LUCIANA
If thou art changed to aught, 'tis to an ass.

DROMIO OF SYRACUSE [to Antipholus]
'Tis true she rides me, and I long for grass.
'Tis so, I am an ass; else it could never be
But I should know her as well as she knows me.   205

ADRIANA
Come, come, no longer will I be a fool,
To put the finger in the eye and weep
Whilst man and master laughs my woes to scorn.
(To Antipholus) Come, sir, to dinner.—Dromio, keep
        the gate.—
Husband, I'll dine above with you today,   210
And shrive you of a thousand idle pranks.—
Sirrah, if any ask you for your master,
Say he dines forth, and let no creature enter.—
Come, sister.—Dromio, play the porter well.

ANTIPHOLUS OF SYRACUSE (aside)
Am I in earth, in heaven, or in hell?   215
Sleeping or waking? Mad or well advised?
Known unto these, and to myself disguised!
I'll say as they say, and persever so,
And in this mist at all adventures go.

DROMIO OF SYRACUSE
Master, shall I be porter at the gate?   220

ADRIANA
Ay, and let none enter, lest I break your pate.

LUCIANA
Come, come, Antipholus, we dine too late.

                    Exeunt [into the Phoenix]

                        ✸

3.1   Enter Antipholus of Ephesus, his man Dromio,
        Angelo the goldsmith, and Balthasar the merchant

ANTIPHOLUS OF EPHESUS
Good Signor Angelo, you must excuse us all.
My wife is shrewish when I keep not hours.
Say that I lingered with you at your shop
To see the making of her carcanet,
And that tomorrow you will bring it home.—   5
But here's a villain that would face me down
He met me on the mart, and that I beat him,

And charged him with a thousand marks in gold,
And that I did deny my wife and house.
Thou drunkard, thou, what didst thou mean by this?

DROMIO OF EPHESUS
Say what you will, sir, but I know what I know—   11
That you beat me at the mart I have your hand to
    show.
If the skin were parchment, and the blows you gave
    were ink,
Your own handwriting would tell you what I think.

ANTIPHOLUS OF EPHESUS
I think thou art an ass.

DROMIO OF EPHESUS   Marry, so it doth appear   15
By the wrongs I suffer and the blows I bear.
I should kick being kicked, and, being at that pass,
You would keep from my heels, and beware of an ass.

ANTIPHOLUS OF EPHESUS
You're sad, Signor Balthasar. Pray God our cheer
May answer my good will, and your good welcome
    here.   20

BALTHASAR
I hold your dainties cheap, sir, and your welcome dear.

ANTIPHOLUS OF EPHESUS
O, Signor Balthasar, either at flesh or fish
A table full of welcome makes scarce one dainty dish.

BALTHASAR
Good meat, sir, is common; that every churl affords.

ANTIPHOLUS OF EPHESUS
And welcome more common, for that's nothing but
    words.   25

BALTHASAR
Small cheer and great welcome makes a merry feast.

ANTIPHOLUS OF EPHESUS
Ay, to a niggardly host and more sparing guest.
But though my cates be mean, take them in good part.
Better cheer may you have, but not with better heart.
But soft, my door is locked. (To Dromio) Go bid them
    let us in.   30

DROMIO OF EPHESUS (calling,
Maud, Bridget, Marian, Cicely, Gillian, Ginn!
    [Enter Dromio of Syracuse within the Phoenix]

DROMIO OF SYRACUSE (within the Phoenix)
Mome, malt-horse, capon, coxcomb, idiot, patch!
Either get thee from the door or sit down at the hatch.
Dost thou conjure for wenches, that thou call'st for
    such store
When one is one too many? Go, get thee from the
    door.   35

DROMIO OF EPHESUS
What patch is made our porter? My master stays in
    the street.

DROMIO OF SYRACUSE (within)
Let him walk from whence he came, lest he catch
    cold on's feet.

ANTIPHOLUS OF EPHESUS
Who talks within there? Ho, open the door!

DROMIO OF SYRACUSE (within the Phoenix)
Right, sir, I'll tell you when, an you'll tell me wherefore.

ANTIPHOLUS OF EPHESUS
Wherefore? For my dinner—I have not dined today.

DROMIO OF SYRACUSE (*within the Phoenix*)
Nor today here you must not. Come again when you
    may.   41

ANTIPHOLUS OF EPHESUS
What art thou that keep'st me out from the house I
    owe?

DROMIO OF SYRACUSE (*within the Phoenix*)
The porter for this time, sir, and my name is Dromio.

DROMIO OF EPHESUS
O villain, thou hast stol'n both mine office and my
    name.
The one ne'er got me credit, the other mickle blame.
If thou hadst been Dromio today in my place,   46
Thou wouldst have changed thy pate for an aim, or
    thy name for an ass.
    Enter Nell within the Phoenix

NELL (*within the Phoenix*)
What a coil is there, Dromio? Who are those at the
    gate?

DROMIO OF EPHESUS
Let my master in, Nell.

NELL (*within the Phoenix*) Faith no, he comes too late;
And so tell your master.

DROMIO OF EPHESUS   O Lord, I must laugh.   50
Have at you with a proverb: 'Shall I set in my staff?'

NELL (*within the Phoenix*)
Have at you with another—that's 'When? Can you
    tell?'

DROMIO OF SYRACUSE (*within the Phoenix*)
If thy name be called Nell, Nell, thou hast answered
    him well.
   ⌜   ⌝

ANTIPHOLUS OF EPHESUS (*to Nell*)
Do you hear, you minion? You'll let us in, I hope?

NELL (*within the Phoenix*)
I thought to have asked you.

DROMIO OF SYRACUSE (*within*)   And you said no.   56

DROMIO OF EPHESUS
So, come help.
    ⌜*He and Antipholus beat the door*⌝
           Well struck! There was blow for blow.

ANTIPHOLUS OF EPHESUS (*to Nell*)
Thou baggage, let me in.

NELL (*within the Phoenix*)   Can you tell for whose sake?

DROMIO OF EPHESUS
Master, knock the door hard.

NELL (*within the Phoenix*)   Let him knock till it ache.

ANTIPHOLUS OF EPHESUS
You'll cry for this, minion, if I beat the door down.   60

NELL (*within the Phoenix*)
What needs all that, and a pair of stocks in the town?
    Enter Adriana within the Phoenix

ADRIANA (*within the Phoenix*)
Who is that at the door that keeps all this noise?

DROMIO OF SYRACUSE (*within the Phoenix*)
By my troth, your town is troubled with unruly boys.

ANTIPHOLUS OF EPHESUS (*to Adriana*)
Are you there, wife? You might have come before.

ADRIANA (*within the Phoenix*)
Your wife, sir knave? Go, get you from the door.   65
                             Exit with Nell

DROMIO OF EPHESUS (*to Antipholus*)
If you went in pain, master, this knave would go sore.

ANGELO (*to Antipholus*)
Here is neither cheer, sir, nor welcome; we would
    fain have either.

BALTHASAR
In debating which was best, we shall part with neither.

DROMIO OF EPHESUS (*to Antipholus*)
They stand at the door, master. Bid them welcome
    hither.   69

ANTIPHOLUS OF EPHESUS
There is something in the wind, that we cannot get in.

DROMIO OF EPHESUS
You would say so, master, if your garments were thin.
Your cake here is warm within: you stand here in the
    cold.
It would make a man mad as a buck to be so bought
    and sold.

ANTIPHOLUS OF EPHESUS
Go fetch me something. I'll break ope the gate.

DROMIO OF SYRACUSE (*within the Phoenix*)
Break any breaking here, and I'll break your knave's
    pate.   75

DROMIO OF EPHESUS
A man may break a word with you, sir, and words
    are but wind;
Ay, and break it in your face, so he break it not
    behind.

DROMIO OF SYRACUSE (*within the Phoenix*)
It seems thou want'st breaking. Out upon thee, hind!

DROMIO OF EPHESUS
Here's too much 'Out upon thee!' I pray thee, let me
    in.

DROMIO OF SYRACUSE (*within the Phoenix*)
Ay, when fowls have no feathers, and fish have no fin.

ANTIPHOLUS OF EPHESUS
Well, I'll break in.—Go borrow me a crow.   81

DROMIO OF EPHESUS
A crow without feather? Master, mean you so?
For a fish without a fin, there's a fowl without a feather.
(*To Dromio of Syracuse*)
If a crow help us in, sirrah, we'll pluck a crow together.

ANTIPHOLUS OF EPHESUS
Go, get thee gone. Fetch me an iron crow.   85

BALTHASAR
Have patience, sir. O, let it not be so!
Herein you war against your reputation,
And draw within the compass of suspect
Th'unviolated honour of your wife.
Once this: your long experience of her wisdom,   90
Her sober virtue, years, and modesty,
Plead on her part some cause to you unknown;
And doubt not, sir, but she will well excuse

Why at this time the doors are made against you.
Be ruled by me. Depart in patience,   95
And let us to the Tiger all to dinner,
And about evening come yourself alone
To know the reason of this strange restraint.
If by strong hand you offer to break in
Now in the stirring passage of the day,   100
A vulgar comment will be made of it,
And that supposèd by the common rout
Against your yet ungallèd estimation,
That may with foul intrusion enter in
And dwell upon your grave when you are dead.   105
For slander lives upon succession,
For ever housed where once it gets possession.

ANTIPHOLUS OF EPHESUS
You have prevailed. I will depart in quiet,
And in despite of mirth mean to be merry.
I know a wench of excellent discourse,   110
Pretty and witty; wild, and yet, too, gentle.
There will we dine. This woman that I mean,
My wife—but, I protest, without desert—
Hath oftentimes upbraided me withal.
To her will we to dinner. (To Angelo) Get you home 115
And fetch the chain. By this, I know, 'tis made.
Bring it, I pray you, to the Porcupine,
For there's the house. That chain will I bestow—
Be it for nothing but to spite my wife—
Upon mine hostess there. Good sir, make haste: 120
Since mine own doors refuse to entertain me,
I'll knock elsewhere, to see if they'll disdain me.

ANGELO
I'll meet you at that place some hour hence.

ANTIPHOLUS OF EPHESUS
Do so.   ⌜Exit Angelo⌝
      This jest shall cost me some expense.
                  Exeunt ⌜Dromio of Syracuse within the
                  Phoenix, and the others into the Porcupine⌝

3.2   Enter ⌜from the Phoenix⌝ Luciana with Antipholus
         of Syracuse

LUCIANA
And may it be that you have quite forgot
A husband's office? Shall, Antipholus,
Even in the spring of love thy love-springs rot?
   Shall love, in building, grow so ruinous?
If you did wed my sister for her wealth,   5
   Then for her wealth's sake use her with more
      kindness;
Or if you like elsewhere, do it by stealth:
   Muffle your false love with some show of blindness.
Let not my sister read it in your eye.
   Be not thy tongue thy own shame's orator.   10
Look sweet, speak fair, become disloyalty;
   Apparel vice like virtue's harbinger.
Bear a fair presence, though your heart be tainted:
   Teach sin the carriage of a holy saint.
Be secret-false. What need she be acquainted?   15
   What simple thief brags of his own attaint?

'Tis double wrong to truant with your bed,
   And let her read it in thy looks at board.
Shame hath a bastard fame, well managèd;
   Ill deeds is doubled with an evil word.   20
Alas, poor women, make us but believe—
   Being compact of credit—that you love us.
Though others have the arm, show us the sleeve.
   We in your motion turn, and you may move us.
Then, gentle brother, get you in again.   25
   Comfort my sister, cheer her, call her wife:
'Tis holy sport to be a little vain
   When the sweet breath of flattery conquers strife.

ANTIPHOLUS OF SYRACUSE
Sweet mistress—what your name is else I know not,
   Nor by what wonder you do hit of mine.   30
Less in your knowledge and your grace you show not
   Than our earth's wonder, more than earth divine.
Teach me, dear creature, how to think and speak.
   Lay open to my earthy gross conceit,
Smothered in errors, feeble, shallow, weak,   35
   The folded meaning of your words' deceit.
Against my soul's pure truth why labour you
   To make it wander in an unknown field?
Are you a god? Would you create me new?
   Transform me, then, and to your power I'll yield. 40
But if that I am I, then well I know
   Your weeping sister is no wife of mine,
Nor to her bed no homage do I owe.
   Far more, far more, to you do I decline.
O, train me not, sweet mermaid, with thy note   45
   To drown me in thy sister's flood of tears.
Sing, siren, for thyself, and I will dote.
   Spread o'er the silver waves thy golden hairs,
And as a bed I'll take them, and there lie,
   And in that glorious supposition think   50
He gains by death that hath such means to die.
   Let love, being light, be drownèd if she sink.

LUCIANA
What, are you mad, that you do reason so?

ANTIPHOLUS OF SYRACUSE
Not mad, but mated—how, I do not know.

LUCIANA
It is a fault that springeth from your eye.   55

ANTIPHOLUS OF SYRACUSE
For gazing on your beams, fair sun, being by.

LUCIANA
Gaze where you should, and that will clear your
      sight.

ANTIPHOLUS OF SYRACUSE
As good to wink, sweet love, as look on night.

LUCIANA
Why call you me 'love'? Call my sister so.

ANTIPHOLUS OF SYRACUSE
Thy sister's sister.

LUCIANA   That's my sister.

ANTIPHOLUS OF SYRACUSE   No,   60
It is thyself, mine own self's better part,
Mine eye's clear eye, my dear heart's dearer heart,

My food, my fortune, and my sweet hope's aim,
My sole earth's heaven, and my heaven's claim.

LUCIANA
All this my sister is, or else should be.   65

ANTIPHOLUS OF SYRACUSE
Call thyself sister, sweet, for I am thee.
Thee will I love, and with thee lead my life.
Thou hast no husband yet, nor I no wife.
Give me thy hand.

LUCIANA   O soft, sir, hold you still;
I'll fetch my sister to get her good will.   70

Exit ⌈into the Phoenix⌉

Enter ⌈from the Phoenix⌉ Dromio of Syracuse

ANTIPHOLUS OF SYRACUSE Why, how now, Dromio! Where
runn'st thou so fast?

DROMIO OF SYRACUSE Do you know me, sir? Am I Dromio?
Am I your man? Am I myself?

ANTIPHOLUS OF SYRACUSE Thou art Dromio, thou art my
man, thou art thyself.

DROMIO OF SYRACUSE I am an ass, I am a woman's man,
and besides myself.

ANTIPHOLUS OF SYRACUSE What woman's man? And how
besides thyself?   80

DROMIO OF SYRACUSE Marry, sir, besides myself I am due
to a woman: one that claims me, one that haunts me,
one that will have me.

ANTIPHOLUS OF SYRACUSE What claim lays she to thee?   84

DROMIO OF SYRACUSE Marry, sir, such claim as you would
lay to your horse; and she would have me as a beast—
not that, I being a beast, she would have me, but that
she, being a very beastly creature, lays claim to me.

ANTIPHOLUS OF SYRACUSE What is she?   89

DROMIO OF SYRACUSE A very reverend body; ay, such a
one as a man may not speak of without he say 'sir-
reverence'. I have but lean luck in the match, and yet
is she a wondrous fat marriage.

ANTIPHOLUS OF SYRACUSE How dost thou mean, a fat
marriage?   95

DROMIO OF SYRACUSE Marry, sir, she's the kitchen wench,
and all grease; and I know not what use to put her to
but to make a lamp of her, and run from her by her
own light. I warrant her rags and the tallow in them
will burn a Poland winter. If she lives till doomsday,
she'll burn a week longer than the whole world.

ANTIPHOLUS OF SYRACUSE What complexion is she of?   102

DROMIO OF SYRACUSE Swart like my shoe, but her face
nothing like so clean kept. For why?—She sweats a
man may go overshoes in the grime of it.   105

ANTIPHOLUS OF SYRACUSE That's a fault that water will
mend.

DROMIO OF SYRACUSE No, sir, 'tis in grain. Noah's flood
could not do it.

ANTIPHOLUS OF SYRACUSE What's her name?   110

DROMIO OF SYRACUSE Nell, sir. But her name and three-
quarters—that's an ell and three-quarters—will not
measure her from hip to hip.

ANTIPHOLUS OF SYRACUSE Then she bears some breadth?

DROMIO OF SYRACUSE No longer from head to foot than
from hip to hip. She is spherical, like a globe. I could
find out countries in her.

ANTIPHOLUS OF SYRACUSE In what part of her body stands
Ireland?

DROMIO OF SYRACUSE Marry, sir, in her buttocks. I found
it out by the bogs.   121

ANTIPHOLUS OF SYRACUSE Where Scotland?

DROMIO OF SYRACUSE I found it by the barrenness, hard
in the palm of her hand.

ANTIPHOLUS OF SYRACUSE Where France?   125

DROMIO OF SYRACUSE In her forehead, armed and reverted,
making war against her heir.

ANTIPHOLUS OF SYRACUSE Where England?

DROMIO OF SYRACUSE I looked for the chalky cliffs, but I
could find no whiteness in them. But I guess it stood
in her chin, by the salt rheum that ran between France
and it.   132

ANTIPHOLUS OF SYRACUSE Where Spain?

DROMIO OF SYRACUSE Faith, I saw it not, but I felt it hot
in her breath.   135

ANTIPHOLUS OF SYRACUSE Where America, the Indies?

DROMIO OF SYRACUSE O, sir, upon her nose, all o'er
embellished with rubies, carbuncles, sapphires,
declining their rich aspect to the hot breath of Spain,
who sent whole armadas of carracks to be ballast at
her nose.   141

ANTIPHOLUS OF SYRACUSE Where stood Belgia, the
Netherlands?

DROMIO OF SYRACUSE O, sir, I did not look so low. To
conclude, this drudge or diviner laid claim to me, called
me Dromio, swore I was assured to her, told me what
privy marks I had about me—as the mark of my
shoulder, the mole in my neck, the great wart on my
left arm—that I, amazed, ran from her as a witch. And
I think if my breast had not been made of faith, and
my heart of steel, she had transformed me to a curtal
dog, and made me turn i'th' wheel.   152

ANTIPHOLUS OF SYRACUSE
Go, hie thee presently. Post to the road.
An if the wind blow any way from shore,
I will not harbour in this town tonight.
If any barque put forth, come to the mart,
Where I will walk till thou return to me.
If everyone knows us, and we know none,
'Tis time, I think, to trudge, pack, and be gone.

DROMIO OF SYRACUSE
As from a bear a man would run for life,   160
So fly I from her that would be my wife.

Exit ⌈to the bay⌉

ANTIPHOLUS OF SYRACUSE
There's none but witches do inhabit here,
And therefore 'tis high time that I were hence.
She that doth call me husband, even my soul
Doth for a wife abhor. But her fair sister,   165
Possessed with such a gentle sovereign grace,
Of such enchanting presence and discourse,
Hath almost made me traitor to myself.
But lest myself be guilty to self-wrong,
I'll stop mine ears against the mermaid's song.   170

Enter Angelo with the chain

ANGELO
  Master Antipholus.

ANTIPHOLUS OF SYRACUSE Ay, that's my name.

ANGELO
  I know it well, sir. Lo, here's the chain.
  I thought to have ta'en you at the Porcupine.
  The chain unfinished made me stay thus long.

ANTIPHOLUS OF SYRACUSE (*taking the chain*)
  What is your will that I shall do with this?   175

ANGELO
  What please yourself, sir. I have made it for you.

ANTIPHOLUS OF SYRACUSE
  Made it for me, sir? I bespoke it not.

ANGELO
  Not once, nor twice, but twenty times you have.
  Go home with it, and please your wife withal,
  And soon at supper-time I'll visit you,   180
  And then receive my money for the chain.

ANTIPHOLUS OF SYRACUSE
  I pray you, sir, receive the money now,
  For fear you ne'er see chain nor money more.

ANGELO
  You are a merry man, sir. Fare you well.   *Exit*

ANTIPHOLUS OF SYRACUSE
  What I should think of this I cannot tell.   185
  But this I think: there's no man is so vain
  That would refuse so fair an offered chain.
  I see a man here needs not live by shifts,
  When in the streets he meets such golden gifts.
  I'll to the mart, and there for Dromio stay.   190
  If any ship put out, then straight away!   *Exit*

❀

4.1   *Enter Second Merchant, Angelo the goldsmith, and*
      an Officer

SECOND MERCHANT (*to Angelo*)
  You know since Pentecost the sum is due,
  And since I have not much importuned you;
  Nor now I had not, but that I am bound
  To Persia, and want guilders for my voyage.
  Therefore make present satisfaction,   5
  Or I'll attach you by this officer.

ANGELO
  Even just the sum that I do owe to you
  Is growing to me by Antipholus,
  And in the instant that I met with you
  He had of me a chain. At five o'clock   10
  I shall receive the money for the same.
  Pleaseth you walk with me down to his house,
  I will discharge my bond, and thank you too.

      Enter Antipholus of Ephesus and Dromio of Ephesus
      from the Courtesan's house (the Porcupine)

OFFICER
  That labour may you save. See where he comes.

ANTIPHOLUS OF EPHESUS (*to Dromio*)
  While I go to the goldsmith's house, go thou   15
  And buy a rope's end. That will I bestow

Among my wife and her confederates
For locking me out of my doors by day.
But soft, I see the goldsmith. Get thee gone.
Buy thou a rope, and bring it home to me.   20

DROMIO OF EPHESUS
  I buy a thousand pound a year, I buy a rope.   *Exit*

ANTIPHOLUS OF EPHESUS (*to Angelo*)
  A man is well holp up that trusts to you!
  I promisèd your presence and the chain,
  But neither chain nor goldsmith came to me.
  Belike you thought our love would last too long   25
  If it were chained together, and therefore came not.

ANGELO
  Saving your merry humour, here's the note
  How much your chain weighs to the utmost carat,
  The fineness of the gold, and chargeful fashion,
  Which doth amount to three odd ducats more   30
  Than I stand debted to this gentleman.
  I pray you see him presently discharged,
  For he is bound to sea, and stays but for it.

ANTIPHOLUS OF EPHESUS
  I am not furnished with the present money.
  Besides, I have some business in the town.   35
  Good signor, take the stranger to my house,
  And with you take the chain, and bid my wife
  Disburse the sum on the receipt thereof.
  Perchance I will be there as soon as you.

ANGELO
  Then you will bring the chain to her yourself?   40

ANTIPHOLUS OF EPHESUS
  No, bear it with you, lest I come not time enough.

ANGELO
  Well, sir, I will. Have you the chain about you?

ANTIPHOLUS OF EPHESUS
  An if I have not, sir, I hope you have;
  Or else you may return without your money.

ANGELO
  Nay, come, I pray you, sir, give me the chain.   45
  Both wind and tide stays for this gentleman,
  And I, to blame, have held him here too long.

ANTIPHOLUS OF EPHESUS
  Good Lord! You use this dalliance to excuse
  Your breach of promise to the Porcupine.
  I should have chid you for not bringing it,   50
  But like a shrew you first begin to brawl.

SECOND MERCHANT (*to Angelo*)
  The hour steals on. I pray you, sir, dispatch.

ANGELO (*to Antipholus*)
  You hear how he importunes me. The chain!

ANTIPHOLUS OF EPHESUS
  Why, give it to my wife, and fetch your money.

ANGELO
  Come, come, you know I gave it you even now.   55
  Either send the chain, or send me by some token.

ANTIPHOLUS OF EPHESUS
  Fie, now you run this humour out of breath.
  Come, where's the chain? I pray you let me see it.

SECOND MERCHANT
  My business cannot brook this dalliance.

Good sir, say whe'er you'll answer me or no;   60
If not, I'll leave him to the officer.

ANTIPHOLUS OF EPHESUS
I answer you? What should I answer you?

ANGELO
The money that you owe me for the chain.

ANTIPHOLUS OF EPHESUS
I owe you none till I receive the chain.

ANGELO
You know I gave it you half an hour since.   65

ANTIPHOLUS OF EPHESUS
You gave me none. You wrong me much to say so

ANGELO
You wrong me more, sir, in denying it.
Consider how it stands upon my credit.

SECOND MERCHANT
Well, officer, arrest him at my suit.

OFFICER (to Angelo)
I do, and charge you in the Duke's name to obey me.

ANGELO (to Antipholus)
This touches me in reputation.   71
Either consent to pay this sum for me,
Or I attach you by this officer.

ANTIPHOLUS OF EPHESUS
Consent to pay thee that I never had?
Arrest me, foolish fellow, if thou dar'st.   75

ANGELO
Here is thy fee: arrest him, officer.
I would not spare my brother in this case
If he should scorn me so apparently.

OFFICER (to Antipholus)
I do arrest you, sir. You hear the suit.

ANTIPHOLUS OF EPHESUS
I do obey thee till I give thee bail.   80
(To Angelo) But, sirrah, you shall buy this sport as dear
As all the metal in your shop will answer.

ANGELO
Sir, sir, I shall have law in Ephesus,
To your notorious shame, I doubt it not.

Enter Dromio of Syracuse, from the bay

DROMIO OF SYRACUSE
Master, there's a barque of Epidamnum   85
That stays but till her owner comes aboard,
And then she bears away. Our freightage, sir,
I have conveyed aboard, and I have bought
The oil, the balsamum, and aqua-vitae.
The ship is in her trim; the merry wind   90
Blows fair from land. They stay for naught at all
But for their owner, master, and yourself.

ANTIPHOLUS OF EPHESUS
How now? A madman? Why, thou peevish sheep,
What ship of Epidamnum stays for me?

DROMIO OF SYRACUSE
A ship you sent me to, to hire waftage.   95

ANTIPHOLUS OF EPHESUS
Thou drunken slave, I sent thee for a rope,
And told thee to what purpose and what end.

DROMIO OF SYRACUSE
You sent me for a rope's end as soon.
You sent me to the bay, sir, for a barque.

ANTIPHOLUS OF EPHESUS
I will debate this matter at more leisure,   100
And teach your ears to list me with more heed.
To Adriana, villain, hie thee straight.
Give her this key, and tell her in the desk
That's covered o'er with Turkish tapestry
There is a purse of ducats. Let her send it.   105
Tell her I am arrested in the street,
And that shall bail me. Hie thee, slave. Be gone!—
On, officer, to prison, till it come.

Exeunt all but Dromio of Syracuse

DROMIO OF SYRACUSE
To Adriana. That is where we dined,
Where Dowsabel did claim me for her husband.   110
She is too big, I hope, for me to compass.
Thither I must, although against my will;
For servants must their masters' minds fulfil.   *Exit*

4.2   *Enter ⌈from the Phoenix⌉ Adriana and Luciana*

ADRIANA
Ah, Luciana, did he tempt thee so?
   Mightst thou perceive austerely in his eye
That he did plead in earnest, yea or no?
   Looked he or red or pale, or sad or merrily?
What observation mad'st thou in this case   5
Of his heart's meteors tilting in his face?

LUCIANA
First he denied you had in him no right.

ADRIANA
He meant he did me none, the more my spite.

LUCIANA
Then swore he that he was a stranger here.

ADRIANA
And true he swore, though yet forsworn he were.   10

LUCIANA
Then pleaded I for you.

ADRIANA   And what said he?

LUCIANA
That love I begged for you, he begged of me.

ADRIANA
With what persuasion did he tempt thy love?

LUCIANA
With words that in an honest suit might move.
First he did praise my beauty, then my speech.   15

ADRIANA
Didst speak him fair?

LUCIANA   Have patience, I beseech.

ADRIANA
I cannot, nor I will not, hold me still.
My tongue, though not my heart, shall have his will.
He is deformèd, crookèd, old, and sere,
Ill-faced, worse-bodied, shapeless everywhere,   20
Vicious, ungentle, foolish, blunt, unkind,
Stigmatical in making, worse in mind.

LUCIANA
Who would be jealous, then, of such a one?
No evil lost is wailed when it is gone.
ADRIANA
Ah, but I think him better than I say,   25
And yet would herein others' eyes were worse.
Far from her nest the lapwing cries away.
My heart prays for him, though my tongue do curse.
    Enter Dromio of Syracuse running
DROMIO OF SYRACUSE
Here, go—the desk, the purse! Sweet now, make haste!
LUCIANA
How? Hast thou lost thy breath?
DROMIO OF SYRACUSE   By running fast.   30
ADRIANA
Where is thy master, Dromio? Is he well?
DROMIO OF SYRACUSE
No, he's in Tartar limbo, worse than hell.
A devil in an everlasting garment hath him,
One whose hard heart is buttoned up with steel;
A fiend, a fairy, pitiless and rough;   35
A wolf, nay worse, a fellow all in buff;
A back-friend, a shoulder-clapper, one that
    countermands
The passages of alleys, creeks, and narrow launds;
A hound that runs counter, and yet draws dryfoot
    well;
One that before the Judgement carries poor souls to
    hell.   40
ADRIANA Why, man, what is the matter?
DROMIO OF SYRACUSE
I do not know the matter, he is 'rested on the case.
ADRIANA
What, is he arrested? Tell me at whose suit.
DROMIO OF SYRACUSE
I know not at whose suit he is arrested well,
But is in a suit of buff which 'rested him, that can I
    tell.   45
Will you send him, mistress, redemption—the money
    in his desk?
ADRIANA
Go fetch it, sister.   *Exit Luciana ⌈into the Phoenix⌉*
    This I wonder at,
That he unknown to me should be in debt.
Tell me, was he arrested on a bond?
DROMIO OF SYRACUSE
Not on a bond but on a stronger thing: 50
A chain, a chain—do you not hear it ring?
ADRIANA
What, the chain?
DROMIO OF SYRACUSE
    No, no, the bell. 'Tis time that I were gone:
It was two ere I left him, and now the clock strikes
    one.
ADRIANA
The hours come back! That did I never hear.
DROMIO OF SYRACUSE
O yes, if any hour meet a sergeant, a turns back for
    very fear.   55

ADRIANA
As if time were in debt. How fondly dost thou reason!
DROMIO OF SYRACUSE
Time is a very bankrupt, and owes more than he's
    worth to season.
Nay, he's a thief too. Have you not heard men say
That time comes stealing on by night and day?
If a be in debt and theft, and a sergeant in the way, 60
Hath he not reason to turn back an hour in a day?
    Enter Luciana ⌈from the Phoenix⌉ with the money
ADRIANA
Go, Dromio, there's the money. Bear it straight,
And bring thy master home immediately.
    ⌈*Exit Dromio*⌉
Come, sister, I am pressed down with conceit:
Conceit, my comfort and my injury.   65
    Exeunt ⌈into the Phoenix⌉

4.3   *Enter Antipholus of Syracuse, wearing the chain*
ANTIPHOLUS OF SYRACUSE
There's not a man I meet but doth salute me
As if I were their well-acquainted friend,
And everyone doth call me by my name.
Some tender money to me, some invite me,
Some other give me thanks for kindnesses.   5
Some offer me commodities to buy.
Even now a tailor called me in his shop,
And showed me silks that he had bought for me,
And therewithal took measure of my body.
Sure, these are but imaginary wiles,   10
And Lapland sorcerers inhabit here.
    Enter Dromio of Syracuse with the money
DROMIO OF SYRACUSE Master, here's the gold you sent me
for. What, have you got redemption from the picture
of old Adam new apparelled?
ANTIPHOLUS OF SYRACUSE
What gold is this? What Adam dost thou mean?   15
DROMIO OF SYRACUSE Not that Adam that kept the
Paradise, but that Adam that keeps the prison—he that
goes in the calf's skin, that was killed for the Prodigal;
he that came behind you, sir, like an evil angel, and
bid you forsake your liberty.   20
ANTIPHOLUS OF SYRACUSE I understand thee not.
DROMIO OF SYRACUSE No? Why, 'tis a plain case: he that
went like a bass viol in a case of leather; the man, sir,
that when gentlemen are tired gives them a sob and
'rests them; he, sir, that takes pity on decayed men
and gives them suits of durance; he that sets up his
rest to do more exploits with his mace than a Moorish
pike.
ANTIPHOLUS OF SYRACUSE What, thou mean'st an officer?
DROMIO OF SYRACUSE Ay, sir, the sergeant of the band: he
that brings any man to answer it that breaks his bond;
one that thinks a man always going to bed, and says
'God give you good rest.'   33
ANTIPHOLUS OF SYRACUSE Well, sir, there rest in your
foolery. Is there any ships puts forth tonight? May we
be gone?   36

DROMIO OF SYRACUSE Why, sir, I brought you word an
hour since that the barque *Expedition* put forth tonight,
and then were you hindered by the sergeant to tarry
for the hoy *Delay*. Here are the angels that you sent
for to deliver you.   41
ANTIPHOLUS OF SYRACUSE
The fellow is distraught, and so am I,
And here we wander in illusions.
Some blessèd power deliver us from hence.
        Enter a Courtesan [from the Porcupine]
COURTESAN
Well met, well met, Master Antipholus.   45
I see, sir, you have found the goldsmith now.
Is that the chain you promised me today?
ANTIPHOLUS OF SYRACUSE
Satan, avoid! I charge thee, tempt me not!
DROMIO OF SYRACUSE Master, is this Mistress Satan?
ANTIPHOLUS OF SYRACUSE It is the devil.   50
DROMIO OF SYRACUSE Nay, she is worse, she is the devil's
dam; and here she comes in the habit of a light wench.
And thereof comes that the wenches say 'God damn
me'—that's as much to say, 'God make me a light
wench.' It is written they appear to men like angels of
light. Light is an effect of fire, and fire will burn. Ergo,
light wenches will burn. Come not near her.   57
COURTESAN
Your man and you are marvellous merry, sir.
Will you go with me? We'll mend our dinner here.
DROMIO OF SYRACUSE Master, if you do, expect spoon-meat,
and bespeak a long spoon.   61
ANTIPHOLUS OF SYRACUSE Why, Dromio?
DROMIO OF SYRACUSE Marry, he must have a long spoon
that must eat with the devil.
ANTIPHOLUS OF SYRACUSE (*to Courtesan*)
Avoid, thou fiend! What tell'st thou me of supping?
Thou art, as you are all, a sorceress.   66
I conjure thee to leave me and be gone.
COURTESAN
Give me the ring of mine you had at dinner,
Or for my diamond the chain you promised,
And I'll be gone, sir, and not trouble you.   70
DROMIO OF SYRACUSE
Some devils ask but the parings of one's nail,
A rush, a hair, a drop of blood, a pin,
A nut, a cherry-stone;
But she, more covetous, would have a chain.
Master, be wise; an if you give it her,   75
The devil will shake her chain, and fright us with it.
COURTESAN (*to Antipholus*)
I pray you, sir, my ring, or else the chain.
I hope you do not mean to cheat me so?
ANTIPHOLUS OF SYRACUSE
Avaunt, thou witch!—Come, Dromio, let us go.   79
DROMIO OF SYRACUSE
'Fly pride' says the peacock. Mistress, that you know.
        Exeunt Antipholus of Syracuse
        and Dromio of Syracuse

COURTESAN
Now, out of doubt, Antipholus is mad;
Else would he never so demean himself.
A ring he hath of mine worth forty ducats,
And for the same he promised me a chain.
Both one and other he denies me now.   85
The reason that I gather he is mad,
Besides this present instance of his rage,
Is a mad tale he told today at dinner
Of his own doors being shut against his entrance.
Belike his wife, acquainted with his fits,   90
On purpose shut the doors against his way.
My way is now to hie home to his house,
And tell his wife that, being lunatic,
He rushed into my house, and took perforce
My ring away. This course I fittest choose,   95
For forty ducats is too much to lose.   *Exit*

4.4   *Enter Antipholus of Ephesus with the Officer*
ANTIPHOLUS OF EPHESUS
Fear me not, man, I will not break away.
I'll give thee ere I leave thee so much money
To warrant thee as I am 'rested for.
My wife is in a wayward mood today,
And will not lightly trust the messenger   5
That I should be attached in Ephesus.
I tell you 'twill sound harshly in her ears.
        Enter Dromio of Ephesus with a rope's end
Here comes my man. I think he brings the money.—
How now, sir? Have you that I sent you for?
DROMIO OF EPHESUS
Here's that, I warrant you, will pay them all.   10
ANTIPHOLUS OF EPHESUS But where's the money?
DROMIO OF EPHESUS
Why, sir, I gave the money for the rope.
ANTIPHOLUS OF EPHESUS
Five hundred ducats, villain, for a rope?
DROMIO OF EPHESUS
I'll serve you, sir, five hundred at the rate.
ANTIPHOLUS OF EPHESUS
To what end did I bid thee hie thee home?   15
DROMIO OF EPHESUS To a rope's end, sir, and to that end
am I returned.
ANTIPHOLUS OF EPHESUS
And to that end, sir, I will welcome you.
        He beats Dromio
OFFICER Good sir, be patient.
DROMIO OF EPHESUS Nay, 'tis for me to be patient: I am
in adversity.   21
OFFICER Good now, hold thy tongue.
DROMIO OF EPHESUS Nay, rather persuade *him* to hold his
hands.   24
ANTIPHOLUS OF EPHESUS Thou whoreson, senseless villain!
DROMIO OF EPHESUS I would I were senseless, sir, that I
might not feel your blows.
ANTIPHOLUS OF EPHESUS Thou art sensible in nothing but
blows, and so is an ass.

DROMIO OF EPHESUS I am an ass indeed. You may prove
it by my long ears.—I have served him from the hour
of my nativity to this instant, and have nothing at his
hands for my service but blows. When I am cold, he
heats me with beating. When I am warm, he cools me
with beating. I am waked with it when I sleep, raised
with it when I sit, driven out of doors with it when I
go from home, welcomed home with it when I return.
Nay, I bear it on my shoulders, as a beggar wont her
brat, and I think when he hath lamed me I shall beg
with it from door to door.   40
    Enter Adriana, Luciana, Courtesan, and a
    schoolmaster called Pinch
ANTIPHOLUS OF EPHESUS
Come, go along: my wife is coming yonder.
DROMIO OF EPHESUS (*to Adriana*) Mistress, *respice finem*—
respect your end—or rather, to prophesy like the parrot,
'Beware the rope's end'.
ANTIPHOLUS OF EPHESUS Wilt thou still talk?   45
    He beats Dromio
COURTESAN (*to Adriana*)
How say you now? Is not your husband mad?
ADRIANA
His incivility confirms no less.—
Good Doctor Pinch, you are a conjurer.
Establish him in his true sense again,
And I will please you what you will demand.   50
LUCIANA
Alas, how fiery and how sharp he looks!
COURTESAN
Mark how he trembles in his ecstasy.
PINCH (*to Antipholus*)
Give me your hand, and let me feel your pulse.
ANTIPHOLUS OF EPHESUS
There is my hand, and let it feel your ear.
    He strikes Pinch
PINCH
I charge thee, Satan, housed within this man,   55
To yield possession to my holy prayers,
And to thy state of darkness hie thee straight:
I conjure thee by all the saints in heaven.
ANTIPHOLUS OF EPHESUS
Peace, doting wizard, peace! I am not mad.
ADRIANA
O that thou wert not, poor distressèd soul.   60
ANTIPHOLUS OF EPHESUS
You minion, you, are these your customers?
Did this companion with the saffron face
Revel and feast it at my house today,
Whilst upon me the guilty doors were shut,
And I denied to enter in my house?   65
ADRIANA
O husband, God doth know you dined at home,
Where would you had remained until this time,
Free from these slanders and this open shame.
ANTIPHOLUS OF EPHESUS
Dined at home?
(*To Dromio*)   Thou villain, what sayst thou?

DROMIO OF EPHESUS
Sir, sooth to say, you did not dine at home.   70
ANTIPHOLUS OF EPHESUS
Were not my doors locked up, and I shut out?
DROMIO OF EPHESUS
Pardie, your doors were locked, and you shut out.
ANTIPHOLUS OF EPHESUS
And did not she herself revile me there?
DROMIO OF EPHESUS
Sans fable, she herself reviled you there.
ANTIPHOLUS OF EPHESUS
Did not her kitchen-maid rail, taunt, and scorn me?
DROMIO OF EPHESUS
Certes she did. The kitchen vestal scorned you.   76
ANTIPHOLUS OF EPHESUS
And did not I in rage depart from thence?
DROMIO OF EPHESUS
In verity you did. My bones bears witness,
That since have felt the vigour of his rage.
ADRIANA (*aside to Pinch*)
Is't good to soothe him in these contraries?   80
PINCH (*aside to Adriana*)
It is no shame. The fellow finds his vein,
And, yielding to him, humours well his frenzy.
ANTIPHOLUS OF EPHESUS (*to Adriana*)
Thou hast suborned the goldsmith to arrest me.
ADRIANA
Alas, I sent you money to redeem you,
By Dromio here, who came in haste for it.   85
DROMIO OF EPHESUS
Money by me? Heart and good will you might,
But surely, master, not a rag of money.
ANTIPHOLUS OF EPHESUS
Went'st not thou to her for a purse of ducats?
ADRIANA
He came to me, and I delivered it.
LUCIANA
And I am witness with her that she did.   90
DROMIO OF EPHESUS
God and the ropemaker bear me witness
That I was sent for nothing but a rope.
PINCH (*aside to Adriana*)
Mistress, both man and master is possessed.
I know it by their pale and deadly looks.
They must be bound and laid in some dark room.   95
ANTIPHOLUS OF EPHESUS (*to Adriana*)
Say wherefore didst thou lock me forth today,
(*To Dromio*) And why dost thou deny the bag of gold?
ADRIANA
I did not, gentle husband, lock thee forth.
DROMIO OF EPHESUS
And, gentle master, I received no gold.
But I confess, sir, that we were locked out.   100
ADRIANA
Dissembling villain, thou speak'st false in both.
ANTIPHOLUS OF EPHESUS
Dissembling harlot, thou art false in all,
And art confederate with a damnèd pack

To make a loathsome abject scorn of me.
But with these nails I'll pluck out those false eyes, 105
That would behold in me this shameful sport.
[He reaches for Adriana; she shrieks.]
Enter three or four, and offer to bind him. He strives
ADRIANA
O, bind him, bind him. Let him not come near me.
PINCH
More company! The fiend is strong within him.
LUCIANA
Ay me, poor man, how pale and wan he looks.
ANTIPHOLUS OF EPHESUS
What, will you murder me?—Thou, jailer, thou, 110
I am thy prisoner. Wilt thou suffer them
To make a rescue?
OFFICER   Masters, let him go.
He is my prisoner, and you shall not have him.
PINCH
Go, bind his man, for he is frantic too.
They bind Dromio
ADRIANA
What wilt thou do, thou peevish officer? 115
Hast thou delight to see a wretched man
Do outrage and displeasure to himself?
OFFICER
He is my prisoner. If I let him go,
The debt he owes will be required of me.
ADRIANA
I will discharge thee ere I go from thee. 120
Bear me forthwith unto his creditor,
And, knowing how the debt grows, I will pay it.—
Good Master Doctor, see him safe conveyed
Home to my house. O most unhappy day!
ANTIPHOLUS OF EPHESUS O most unhappy strumpet! 125
DROMIO OF EPHESUS
Master, I am here entered in bond for you.
ANTIPHOLUS OF EPHESUS
Out on thee, villain! Wherefore dost thou mad me?
DROMIO OF EPHESUS
Will you be bound for nothing? Be mad, good master—
Cry, 'The devil!'
LUCIANA
God help, poor souls, how idly do they talk! 130
ADRIANA
Go bear him hence. Sister, go you with me.
Exeunt [into the Phoenix], Pinch and others
carrying off Antipholus of Ephesus and Dromio of
Ephesus. The Officer, Adriana, Luciana, and the
Courtesan remain
(To the Officer) Say now, whose suit is he arrested at?
OFFICER
One Angelo, a goldsmith. Do you know him?
ADRIANA
I know the man. What is the sum he owes?
OFFICER
Two hundred ducats.
ADRIANA   Say, how grows it due? 135

OFFICER
Due for a chain your husband had of him.
ADRIANA
He did bespeak a chain for me, but had it not.
COURTESAN
Whenas your husband all in rage today
Came to my house, and took away my ring—
The ring I saw upon his finger now— 140
Straight after did I meet him with a chain.
ADRIANA
It may be so, but I did never see it.
Come, jailer, bring me where the goldsmith is.
I long to know the truth hereof at large.
Enter Antipholus of Syracuse (wearing the chain)
and Dromio of Syracuse with their rapiers drawn
LUCIANA
God, for thy mercy, they are loose again! 145
ADRIANA
And come with naked swords. Let's call more help
To have them bound again.
OFFICER   Away, they'll kill us!
All but Antipholus and Dromio run out, as fast as
may be, frighted
ANTIPHOLUS OF SYRACUSE
I see these witches are afraid of swords.
DROMIO OF SYRACUSE
She that would be your wife now ran from you.
ANTIPHOLUS OF SYRACUSE
Come to the Centaur. Fetch our stuff from thence. 150
I long that we were safe and sound aboard.
DROMIO OF SYRACUSE Faith, stay here this night. They will
surely do us no harm. You saw they speak us fair, give
us gold. Methinks they are such a gentle nation that,
but for the mountain of mad flesh that claims marriage
of me, I could find in my heart to stay here still, and
turn witch.
ANTIPHOLUS OF SYRACUSE
I will not stay tonight for all the town.
Therefore away, to get our stuff aboard.   *Exeunt*

❦

5.1   *Enter Second Merchant and Angelo the goldsmith*
ANGELO
I am sorry, sir, that I have hindered you,
But I protest he had the chain of me,
Though most dishonestly he doth deny it.
SECOND MERCHANT
How is the man esteemed here in the city?
ANGELO
Of very reverend reputation, sir, 5
Of credit infinite, highly beloved,
Second to none that lives here in the city.
His word might bear my wealth at any time.
SECOND MERCHANT
Speak softly. Yonder, as I think, he walks.
Enter Antipholus of Syracuse, wearing the chain,
and Dromio of Syracuse again

ANGELO

'Tis so, and that self chain about his neck   10
Which he forswore most monstrously to have.
Good sir, draw near to me. I'll speak to him.—
Signor Antipholus, I wonder much
That you would put me to this shame and trouble,
And not without some scandal to yourself,   15
With circumstance and oaths so to deny
This chain, which now you wear so openly.
Beside the charge, the shame, imprisonment,
You have done wrong to this my honest friend,
Who, but for staying on our controversy,
Had hoisted sail and put to sea today.   20
This chain you had of me. Can you deny it?

ANTIPHOLUS OF SYRACUSE

I think I had. I never did deny it.

SECOND MERCHANT

Yes, that you did, sir, and forswore it too.

ANTIPHOLUS OF SYRACUSE

Who heard me to deny it or forswear it?   25

SECOND MERCHANT

These ears of mine, thou know'st, did hear thee.
Fie on thee, wretch! 'Tis pity that thou liv'st
To walk where any honest men resort.

ANTIPHOLUS OF SYRACUSE

Thou art a villain to impeach me thus.
I'll prove mine honour and mine honesty   30
Against thee presently, if thou dar'st stand.

SECOND MERCHANT

I dare, and do defy thee for a villain.

They draw. Enter Adriana, Luciana, Courtesan,
and others ⌈from the Phoenix⌉

ADRIANA

Hold, hurt him not, for God's sake; he is mad.
Some get within him, take his sword away.
Bind Dromio too, and bear them to my house.   35

DROMIO OF SYRACUSE

Run, master, run! For God's sake take a house.
This is some priory—in, or we are spoiled.

Exeunt Antipholus of Syracuse and
Dromio of Syracuse to the priory

Enter ⌈from the priory⌉ the Lady Abbess

ABBESS

Be quiet, people. Wherefore throng you hither?

ADRIANA

To fetch my poor distracted husband hence.
Let us come in, that we may bind him fast,   40
And bear him home for his recovery.

ANGELO

I knew he was not in his perfect wits.

SECOND MERCHANT

I am sorry now that I did draw on him.

ABBESS

How long hath this possession held the man?

ADRIANA

This week he hath been heavy, sour, sad,   45
And much, much different from the man he was;

But till this afternoon his passion
Ne'er brake into extremity of rage.

ABBESS

Hath he not lost much wealth by wreck at sea?
Buried some dear friend? Hath not else his eye   50
Strayed his affection in unlawful love—
A sin prevailing much in youthful men,
Who give their eyes the liberty of gazing?
Which of these sorrows is he subject to?

ADRIANA

To none of these, except it be the last,   55
Namely some love that drew him oft from home.

ABBESS

You should for that have reprehended him.

ADRIANA

Why, so I did.

ABBESS   Ay, but not rough enough.

ADRIANA

As roughly as my modesty would let me.

ABBESS Haply in private.   60

ADRIANA And in assemblies too.

ABBESS Ay, but not enough.

ADRIANA

It was the copy of our conference.
In bed he slept not for my urging it.
At board he fed not for my urging it.   65
Alone, it was the subject of my theme.
In company I often glancèd it.
Still did I tell him it was vile and bad.

ABBESS

And thereof came it that the man was mad.
The venom clamours of a jealous woman   70
Poisons more deadly than a mad dog's tooth.
It seems his sleeps were hindered by thy railing,
And thereof comes it that his head is light.
Thou sayst his meat was sauced with thy upbraidings.
Unquiet meals make ill digestions.   75
Thereof the raging fire of fever bred,
And what's a fever but a fit of madness?
Thou sayst his sports were hindered by thy brawls.
Sweet recreation barred, what doth ensue
But moody and dull melancholy,   80
Kinsman to grim and comfortless despair,
And at her heels a huge infectious troop
Of pale distemperatures and foes to life?
In food, in sport, and life-preserving rest
To be disturbed would mad or man or beast.   85
The consequence is, then, thy jealous fits
Hath scared thy husband from the use of wits.

LUCIANA

She never reprehended him but mildly
When he demeaned himself rough, rude, and wildly.
(To Adriana) Why bear you these rebukes, and answer
not?   90

ADRIANA

She did betray me to my own reproof.—
Good people, enter, and lay hold on him.

ABBESS
No, not a creature enters in my house.
ADRIANA
Then let your servants bring my husband forth.
ABBESS
Neither. He took this place for sanctuary,   95
And it shall privilege him from your hands
Till I have brought him to his wits again,
Or lose my labour in essaying it.
ADRIANA
I will attend my husband, be his nurse,
Diet his sickness, for it is my office,   100
And will have no attorney but myself.
And therefore let me have him home with me.
ABBESS
Be patient, for I will not let him stir
Till I have used the approvèd means I have,
With wholesome syrups, drugs, and holy prayers   105
To make of him a formal man again.
It is a branch and parcel of mine oath,
A charitable duty of my order.
Therefore depart, and leave him here with me.
ADRIANA
I will not hence, and leave my husband here;   110
And ill it doth beseem your holiness
To separate the husband and the wife.
ABBESS
Be quiet and depart. Thou shalt not have him.
                                    ⌈Exit into the priory⌉
LUCIANA (to Adriana)
Complain unto the Duke of this indignity.
ADRIANA
Come, go, I will fall prostrate at his feet,   115
And never rise until my tears and prayers
Have won his grace to come in person hither
And take perforce my husband from the Abbess.
SECOND MERCHANT
By this, I think, the dial point's at five.
Anon, I'm sure, the Duke himself in person   120
Comes this way to the melancholy vale,
The place of death and sorry execution,
Behind the ditches of the abbey here.
ANGELO Upon what cause?
SECOND MERCHANT
To see a reverend Syracusian merchant,   125
Who put unluckily into this bay
Against the laws and statutes of this town,
Beheaded publicly for his offence.
ANGELO
See where they come. We will behold his death.
LUCIANA
Kneel to the Duke before he pass the abbey.   130
        Enter Solinus Duke of Ephesus, and Egeon the
        merchant of Syracuse, bareheaded, with the
        headsman and other officers
DUKE
Yet once again proclaim it publicly:
If any friend will pay the sum for him,
He shall not die, so much we tender him.

ADRIANA (kneeling)
Justice, most sacred Duke, against the Abbess!
DUKE
She is a virtuous and a reverend lady.   135
It cannot be that she hath done thee wrong.
ADRIANA
May it please your grace, Antipholus my husband,
Who I made lord of me and all I had
At your important letters—this ill day
A most outrageous fit of madness took him,   140
That desp'rately he hurried through the street,
With him his bondman, all as mad as he,
Doing displeasure to the citizens
By rushing in their houses, bearing thence
Rings, jewels, anything his rage did like.   145
Once did I get him bound, and sent him home,
Whilst to take order for the wrongs I went
That here and there his fury had committed.
Anon, I wot not by what strong escape,
He broke from those that had the guard of him,   150
And with his mad attendant and himself,
Each one with ireful passion, with drawn swords,
Met us again, and, madly bent on us,
Chased us away; till, raising of more aid,
We came again to bind them. Then they fled   155
Into this abbey, whither we pursued them,
And here the Abbess shuts the gates on us,
And will not suffer us to fetch him out,
Nor send him forth that we may bear him hence.
Therefore, most gracious Duke, with thy command 160
Let him be brought forth, and borne hence for help.
DUKE ⌈raising Adriana⌉
Long since, thy husband served me in my wars,
And I to thee engaged a prince's word,
When thou didst make him master of thy bed,
To do him all the grace and good I could.—   165
Go, some of you, knock at the abbey gate,
And bid the Lady Abbess come to me.
I will determine this before I stir.
        Enter a Messenger ⌈from the Phoenix⌉
MESSENGER (to Adriana)
O mistress, mistress, shift and save yourself!
My master and his man are both broke loose,   170
Beaten the maids a-row, and bound the Doctor,
Whose beard they have singed off with brands of fire,
And ever as it blazed they threw on him
Great pails of puddled mire to quench the hair.
My master preaches patience to him, and the while
His man with scissors nicks him like a fool;
And sure—unless you send some present help—
Between them they will kill the conjurer.
ADRIANA
Peace, fool. Thy master and his man are here,
And that is false thou dost report to us.   180
MESSENGER
Mistress, upon my life I tell you true.
I have not breathed almost since I did see it.
He cries for you, and vows, if he can take you,
To scorch your face and to disfigure you.

Cry within

Hark, hark, I hear him, mistress. Fly, be gone!   185

DUKE (*to Adriana*)

Come stand by me. Fear nothing. Guard with halberds!

Enter Antipholus of Ephesus and Dromio of Ephesus
[from the Phoenix]

ADRIANA

Ay me, it is my husband! Witness you

That he is borne about invisible.

Even now we housed him in the abbey here,

And now he's there, past thought of human reason.

ANTIPHOLUS OF EPHESUS

Justice, most gracious Duke, O grant me justice,

Even for the service that long since I did thee,

When I bestrid thee in the wars, and took

Deep scars to save thy life; even for the blood

That then I lost for thee, now grant me justice!   195

EGEON (*aside*)

Unless the fear of death doth make me dote,

I see my son Antipholus, and Dromio.

ANTIPHOLUS OF EPHESUS

Justice, sweet prince, against that woman there,

She whom thou gav'st to me to be my wife,

That hath abusèd and dishonoured me   200

Even in the strength and height of injury.

Beyond imagination is the wrong

That she this day hath shameless thrown on me.

DUKE

Discover how, and thou shalt find me just.

ANTIPHOLUS OF EPHESUS

This day, great Duke, she shut the doors upon me   205

While she with harlots feasted in my house.

DUKE

A grievous fault!—Say, woman, didst thou so?

ADRIANA

No, my good lord. Myself, he, and my sister

Today did dine together. So befall my soul

As this is false he burdens me withal.   210

LUCIANA

Ne'er may I look on day nor sleep on night

But she tells to your highness simple truth.

ANGELO (*aside*)

O perjured woman! They are both forsworn.

In this the madman justly chargeth them.

ANTIPHOLUS OF EPHESUS

My liege, I am advisèd what I say,   215

Neither disturbed with the effect of wine,

Nor heady-rash provoked with raging ire,

Albeit my wrongs might make one wiser mad.

This woman locked me out this day from dinner.

That goldsmith there, were he not packed with her,

Could witness it, for he was with me then,   221

Who parted with me to go fetch a chain,

Promising to bring it to the Porcupine,

Where Balthasar and I did dine together.

Our dinner done, and he not coming thither,   225

I went to seek him. In the street I met him,

And in his company that gentleman.

He points to the Second Merchant

There did this perjured goldsmith swear me down

That I this day of him received the chain,

Which, God he knows, I saw not. For the which   230

He did arrest me with an officer.

I did obey, and sent my peasant home

For certain ducats. He with none returned.

Then fairly I bespoke the officer

To go in person with me to my house.   235

By th' way, we met my wife, her sister, and a rabble
more

Of vile confederates. Along with them

They brought one Pinch, a hungry lean-faced villain,

A mere anatomy, a mountebank,

A threadbare juggler, and a fortune-teller,   240

A needy, hollow-eyed, sharp-looking wretch,

A living dead man. This pernicious slave,

Forsooth, took on him as a conjurer,

And gazing in mine eyes, feeling my pulse,

And with no face, as 'twere, outfacing me,   245

Cries out I was possessed. Then all together

They fell upon me, bound me, bore me thence,

And in a dark and dankish vault at home

There left me and my man, both bound together,

Till, gnawing with my teeth my bonds in sunder,   250

I gained my freedom, and immediately

Ran hither to your grace, whom I beseech

To give me ample satisfaction

For these deep shames and great indignities.

ANGELO

My lord, in truth, thus far I witness with him: 255

That he dined not at home, but was locked out.

DUKE

But had he such a chain of thee, or no?

ANGELO

He had, my lord, and when he ran in here

These people saw the chain about his neck.

SECOND MERCHANT (*to Antipholus*)

Besides, I will be sworn these ears of mine   260

Heard you confess you had the chain of him,

After you first forswore it on the mart,

And thereupon I drew my sword on you;

And then you fled into this abbey here,

From whence I think you are come by miracle.   265

ANTIPHOLUS OF EPHESUS

I never came within these abbey walls,

Nor ever didst thou draw thy sword on me.

I never saw the chain, so help me heaven,

And this is false you burden me withal.

DUKE

Why, what an intricate impeach is this!   270

I think you all have drunk of Circe's cup.

If here you housed him, here he would have been.

If he were mad, he would not plead so coldly.

(*To Adriana*) You say he dined at home, the goldsmith
here

Denies that saying. (*To Dromio*) Sirrah, what say you?

DROMIO OF EPHESUS (*pointing out the Courtesan*)

Sir, he dined with her there, at the Porcupine.   276

COURTESAN
 He did, and from my finger snatched that ring.
ANTIPHOLUS OF EPHESUS
 'Tis true, my liege, this ring I had of her.
DUKE (*to Courtesan*)
 Saw'st thou him enter at the abbey here?
COURTESAN
 As sure, my liege, as I do see your grace.   280
DUKE
 Why, this is strange. Go call the Abbess hither.
 I think you are all mated, or stark mad.
                                        Exit one to the priory
EGEON (*coming forward*)
 Most mighty Duke, vouchsafe me speak a word.
 Haply I see a friend will save my life,
 And pay the sum that may deliver me.   285
DUKE
 Speak freely, Syracusian, what thou wilt.
EGEON (*to Antipholus*)
 Is not your name, sir, called Antipholus?
 And is not that your bondman Dromio?
DROMIO OF EPHESUS
 Within this hour I was his bondman, sir,
 But he, I thank him, gnawed in two my cords.   290
 Now am I Dromio, and his man, unbound.
EGEON
 I am sure you both of you remember me.
DROMIO OF EPHESUS
 Ourselves we do remember, sir, by you;
 For lately we were bound as you are now.
 You are not Pinch's patient, are you, sir?   295
EGEON
 Why look you strange on me? You know me well.
ANTIPHOLUS OF EPHESUS
 I never saw you in my life till now.
EGEON
 O, grief hath changed me since you saw me last,
 And careful hours with time's deformèd hand
 Have written strange defeatures in my face.   300
 But tell me yet, dost thou not know my voice?
ANTIPHOLUS OF EPHESUS Neither.
EGEON Dromio, nor thou?
DROMIO OF EPHESUS No, trust me sir, nor I.
EGEON I am sure thou dost.   305
DROMIO OF EPHESUS Ay, sir, but I am sure I do not, and
 whatsoever a man denies, you are now bound to believe
 him.
EGEON
 Not know my voice? O time's extremity,
 Hast thou so cracked and splitted my poor tongue   310
 In seven short years that here my only son
 Knows not my feeble key of untuned cares?
 Though now this grainèd face of mine be hid
 In sap-consuming winter's drizzled snow,
 And all the conduits of my blood froze up,   315
 Yet hath my night of life some memory,
 My wasting lamps some fading glimmer left,
 My dull deaf ears a little use to hear.

 All these old witnesses, I cannot err,
 Tell me thou art my son Antipholus.   320
ANTIPHOLUS OF EPHESUS
 I never saw my father in my life.
EGEON
 But seven years since, in Syracusa bay,
 Thou know'st we parted. But perhaps, my son,
 Thou sham'st to acknowledge me in misery.
ANTIPHOLUS OF EPHESUS
 The Duke, and all that know me in the city,   325
 Can witness with me that it is not so.
 I ne'er saw Syracusa in my life.
DUKE (*to Egeon*)
 I tell thee, Syracusian, twenty years
 Have I been patron to Antipholus,
 During which time he ne'er saw Syracusa.   330
 I see thy age and dangers make thee dote.
                Enter ⌈from the priory⌉ the Abbess, with Antipholus
                of Syracuse, wearing the chain, and Dromio of
                Syracuse
ABBESS
 Most mighty Duke, behold a man much wronged.
                All gather to see them
ADRIANA
 I see two husbands, or mine eyes deceive me.
DUKE
 One of these men is *genius* to the other:
 And so of these, which is the natural man,   335
 And which the spirit? Who deciphers them?
DROMIO OF SYRACUSE
 I, sir, am Dromio. Command him away.
DROMIO OF EPHESUS
 I, sir, am Dromio. Pray let me stay.
ANTIPHOLUS OF SYRACUSE
 Egeon, art thou not? Or else his ghost.
DROMIO OF SYRACUSE
 O, my old master, who hath bound him here?   340
ABBESS
 Whoever bound him, I will loose his bonds,
 And gain a husband by his liberty.
 Speak, old Egeon, if thou beest the man
 That hadst a wife once called Emilia,
 That bore thee at a burden two fair sons.   345
 O, if thou beest the same Egeon, speak,
 And speak unto the same Emilia.
DUKE
 Why, here begins his morning story right:
 These two Antipholus', these two so like,
 And these two Dromios, one in semblance—   350
 Besides his urging of her wreck at sea.
 These are the parents to these children,
 Which accidentally are met together.
EGEON
 If I dream not, thou art Emilia.
 If thou art she, tell me, where is that son   355
 That floated with thee on the fatal raft?
ABBESS
 By men of Epidamnum he and I

536

And the twin Dromio all were taken up.
But, by and by, rude fishermen of Corinth
By force took Dromio and my son from them,   360
And me they left with those of Epidamnum.
What then became of them I cannot tell;
I, to this fortune that you see me in.

DUKE (*to Antipholus of Syracuse*)
Antipholus, thou cam'st from Corinth first.

ANTIPHOLUS OF SYRACUSE
No, sir, not I. I came from Syracuse.   365

DUKE
Stay, stand apart. I know not which is which.

ANTIPHOLUS OF EPHESUS
I came from Corinth, my most gracious lord.

DROMIO OF EPHESUS And I with him.

ANTIPHOLUS OF EPHESUS
Brought to this town by that most famous warrior,
Duke Menaphon, your most renownèd uncle.   370

ADRIANA
Which of you two did dine with me today?

ANTIPHOLUS OF SYRACUSE I, gentle mistress.

ADRIANA And are not you my husband?

ANTIPHOLUS OF EPHESUS No, I say nay to that.

ANTIPHOLUS OF SYRACUSE
And so do I. Yet did she call me so;   375
And this fair gentlewoman, her sister here,
Did call me brother. (*To Luciana*) What I told you then
I hope I shall have leisure to make good,
If this be not a dream I see and hear.

ANGELO
That is the chain, sir, which you had of me.   380

ANTIPHOLUS OF SYRACUSE
I think it be, sir. I deny it not.

ANTIPHOLUS OF EPHESUS (*to Angelo*)
And you, sir, for this chain arrested me.

ANGELO
I think I did, sir. I deny it not.

ADRIANA (*to Antipholus of Ephesus*)
I sent you money, sir, to be your bail,
By Dromio, but I think he brought it not.   385

DROMIO OF EPHESUS No, none by me.

ANTIPHOLUS OF SYRACUSE (*to Adriana*)
This purse of ducats I received from you,
And Dromio my man did bring them me.
I see we still did meet each other's man,
And I was ta'en for him, and he for me,   390
And thereupon these errors are arose.

ANTIPHOLUS OF EPHESUS
These ducats pawn I for my father here.

DUKE
It shall not need. Thy father hath his life.

COURTESAN
Sir, I must have that diamond from you.

ANTIPHOLUS OF EPHESUS
There, take it, and much thanks for my good cheer.

ABBESS
Renownèd Duke, vouchsafe to take the pains   396
To go with us into the abbey here,
And hear at large discoursèd all our fortunes,
And all that are assembled in this place,
That by this sympathizèd one day's error   400
Have suffered wrong. Go, keep us company,
And we shall make full satisfaction.
Thirty-three years have I but gone in travail
Of you, my sons, and till this present hour
My heavy burden ne'er deliverèd.   405
The Duke, my husband, and my children both,
And you the calendars of their nativity,
Go to a gossips' feast, and joy with me.
After so long grief, such festivity!

DUKE
With all my heart I'll gossip at this feast.   410
                *Exeunt ⌈into the priory⌉ all but the two
                Dromios and two brothers Antipholus*

DROMIO OF SYRACUSE (*to Antipholus of Ephesus*)
Master, shall I fetch your stuff from shipboard?

ANTIPHOLUS OF EPHESUS
Dromio, what stuff of mine hast thou embarked?

DROMIO OF SYRACUSE
Your goods that lay at host, sir, in the Centaur.

ANTIPHOLUS OF SYRACUSE
He speaks to me.—I am your master, Dromio.
Come, go with us. We'll look to that anon.   415
Embrace thy brother there; rejoice with him.
                Exeunt the brothers Antipholus

DROMIO OF SYRACUSE
There is a fat friend at your master's house,
That kitchened me for you today at dinner.
She now shall be my sister, not my wife.

DROMIO OF EPHESUS
Methinks you are my glass and not my brother.   420
I see by you I am a sweet-faced youth.
Will you walk in to see their gossiping?

DROMIO OF SYRACUSE Not I, sir, you are my elder.

DROMIO OF EPHESUS That's a question. How shall we try
    it?   425

DROMIO OF SYRACUSE We'll draw cuts for the senior. Till
    then, lead thou first.

DROMIO OF EPHESUS Nay, then thus:
    We came into the world like brother and brother,   429
    And now let's go hand in hand, not one before
            another.   *Exeunt ⌈to the priory⌉*

LOVE'S LABOUR'S LOST

THE 1598 edition of *Love's Labour's Lost* is the first play text to carry Shakespeare's name on the title-page, which also refers to performance before the Queen 'this last Christmas'. The play is said to be 'Newly corrected and augmented', so perhaps an earlier edition has failed to survive. Even so, the text shows every sign of having been printed from Shakespeare's working papers, since it includes some passages in draft as well as in revised form. We print the drafts as Additional Passages. The play was probably written some years before publication, in 1593 or 1594.

The setting is Navarre—a kingdom straddling the border between Spain and France—where the young King and three of his friends vow to devote the following three years to austere self-improvement, forgoing the company of women. But they have forgotten the imminent arrival on a diplomatic mission of the Princess of France with, as it happens, three of her ladies; much comedy derives from, first, the men's embarrassed attempts to conceal from one another that they are falling in love, and second, the girls' practical joke in exchanging identities when the men, disguised as Russians, come to entertain and to woo them. Shakespeare seems to have picked up the King's friends' names—Biron, Dumaine, and Longueville—from leading figures in contemporary France, but to have invented the plot himself. He counterpoints the main action with events involving characters based in part on the type-figures of Italian commedia dell'arte who reflect facets of the lords' personalities. Costard, an unsophisticated, open-hearted yokel, and his girl-friend Jaquenetta are sexually uninhibited; Don Adriano de Armado, 'a refinèd traveller of Spain' who also, though covertly, loves Jaquenetta, is full of pompous affectation; and Holofernes, a schoolmaster (seen always with his admiring companion, the curate Sir Nathaniel), demonstrates the avid pedantry into which the young men's verbal brilliance could degenerate. Much of the play's language is highly sophisticated (this is, as the title-page claims, a 'conceited comedy'), in keeping with its subject matter. But the action reaches its climax when a messenger brings news which is communicated entirely without verbal statement. This is a theatrical masterstroke which also signals Shakespeare's most daring experiment with comic form. 'The scene begins to cloud'; in the play's closing minutes the lords and ladies seek to readjust themselves to the new situation, and the play ends in subdued fashion with a third entertainment, the songs of the owl and the cuckoo.

Love's Labour's Lost was for long regarded as a play of excessive verbal sophistication, of interest mainly because of a series of supposed topical allusions; but a number of distinguished twentieth-century productions have revealed its theatrical mastery.

THE PERSONS OF THE PLAY

Ferdinand, KING of Navarre

BIRON
LONGUEVILLE ⎫ lords attending on the King
DUMAINE

Don Adriano de ARMADO, an affected Spanish braggart
MOTE, his page

PRINCESS of France

ROSALINE
CATHERINE ⎫ ladies attending on the Princess
MARIA

BOYET ⎫ attending on the Princess
Two other LORDS

COSTARD, a Clown
JAQUENETTA, a country wench

Sir NATHANIEL, a curate
HOLOFERNES, a schoolmaster
Anthony DULL, a constable

MERCADÉ, a messenger

A FORESTER

Love's Labour's Lost

Enter Ferdinand, King of Navarre, Biron,
Longueville, and Dumaine

KING

Let fame, that all hunt after in their lives,
Live registered upon our brazen tombs,
And then grace us in the disgrace of death
When, spite of cormorant devouring time,
Th'endeavour of this present breath may buy   5
That honour which shall bate his scythe's keen edge
And make us heirs of all eternity.
Therefore, brave conquerors—for so you are,
That war against your own affections
And the huge army of the world's desires—   10
Our late edict shall strongly stand in force.
Navarre shall be the wonder of the world.
Our court shall be a little academe,
Still and contemplative in living art.
You three—Biron, Dumaine, and Longueville—   15
Have sworn for three years' term to live with me
My fellow scholars, and to keep those statutes
That are recorded in this schedule here.
Your oaths are passed; and now subscribe your
names,
That his own hand may strike his honour down   20
That violates the smallest branch herein.
If you are armed to do as sworn to do,
Subscribe to your deep oaths, and keep it, too.

LONGUEVILLE

I am resolved. 'Tis but a three years' fast.
The mind shall banquet, though the body pine.   25
Fat paunches have lean pates, and dainty bits
Make rich the ribs but bankrupt quite the wits.

He signs

DUMAINE

My loving lord, Dumaine is mortified.
The grosser manner of these world's delights
He throws upon the gross world's baser slaves.   30
To love, to wealth, to pomp I pine and die,
With all these living in philosophy.

He signs

BIRON

I can but say their protestation over.
So much, dear liege, I have already sworn:
That is, to live and study here three years.   35
But there are other strict observances,
As not to see a woman in that term,
Which I hope well is not enrollèd there;
And one day in a week to touch no food,
And but one meal on every day beside,   40
The which I hope is not enrollèd there;
And then to sleep but three hours in the night,
And not be seen to wink of all the day,
When I was wont to think no harm all night,
And make a dark night too of half the day,   45
Which I hope well is not enrollèd there.
O, these are barren tasks, too hard to keep—
Not to see ladies, study, fast, not sleep.

KING

Your oath is passed to pass away from these.

BIRON

Let me say no, my liege, an if you please.   50
I only swore to study with your grace,
And stay here in your court, for three years' space.

LONGUEVILLE

You swore to that, Biron, and to the rest.

BIRON

By yea and nay, sir, then I swore in jest.
What is the end of study, let me know?   55

KING

Why, that to know which else we should not know.

BIRON

Things hid and barred, you mean, from common
sense.

KING

Ay, that is study's god-like recompense.

BIRON

Come on, then, I will swear to study so
To know the thing I am forbid to know,   60
As thus: to study where I well may dine
When I to feast expressly am forbid;
Or study where to meet some mistress fine
When mistresses from common sense are hid;
Or having sworn too hard a keeping oath,   65
Study to break it and not break my troth.
If study's gain be thus, and this be so,
Study knows that which yet it doth not know.
Swear me to this, and I will ne'er say no.

KING

These be the stops that hinder study quite,   70
And train our intellects to vain delight.

BIRON

Why, all delights are vain, but that most vain
Which, with pain purchased, doth inherit pain;
As painfully to pore upon a book
To seek the light of truth while truth the while   75
Doth falsely blind the eyesight of his look.
Light, seeking light, doth light of light beguile;
So ere you find where light in darkness lies
Your light grows dark by losing of your eyes.
Study me how to please the eye indeed   80
By fixing it upon a fairer eye,
Who dazzling so, that eye shall be his heed,
And give him light that it was blinded by.
Study is like the heavens' glorious sun,
That will not be deep searched with saucy looks.   85
Small have continual plodders ever won
Save base authority from others' books.

These earthly godfathers of heaven's lights,
   That give a name to every fixèd star,
Have no more profit of their shining nights   90
   Than those that walk and wot not what they are.
Too much to know is to know naught but fame,
And every godfather can give a name.
KING
How well he's read, to reason against reading!
DUMAINE
Proceeded well, to stop all good proceeding.   95
LONGUEVILLE
He weeds the corn and still lets grow the weeding.
BIRON
The spring is near when green geese are a-breeding.
DUMAINE
How follows that?
BIRON   Fit in his place and time.
DUMAINE
In reason nothing.
BIRON   Something then in rhyme.
KING
Biron is like an envious sneaping frost,   100
   That bites the first-born infants of the spring.
BIRON
Well, say I am! Why should proud summer boast
   Before the birds have any cause to sing?
Why should I joy in any abortive birth?
At Christmas I no more desire a rose   105
Than wish a snow in May's new-fangled shows,
But like of each thing that in season grows,
So you to study, now it is too late,
Climb o'er the house to unlock the little gate.
KING
Well, sit you out. Go home, Biron. Adieu.   110
BIRON
No, my good lord, I have sworn to stay with you.
And though I have for barbarism spoke more
   Than for that angel knowledge you can say,
Yet confident I'll keep what I have sworn,
   And bide the penance of each three years' day.   115
Give me the paper. Let me read the same,
And to the strict'st decrees I'll write my name.
KING (*giving a paper*)
How well this yielding rescues thee from shame!
BIRON (*reads*) 'Item: that no woman shall come within a
mile of my court.' Hath this been proclaimed?   120
LONGUEVILLE Four days ago.
BIRON Let's see the penalty. 'On pain of losing her tongue.'
Who devised this penalty?
LONGUEVILLE Marry, that did I.
BIRON Sweet lord, and why?   125
LONGUEVILLE
To fright them hence with that dread penalty.
BIRON
A dangerous law against gentility.
'Item: if any man be seen to talk with a woman within
the term of three years, he shall endure such public
shame as the rest of the court can possible devise.'

This article, my liege, yourself must break;
   For well you know here comes in embassy
The French King's daughter with yourself to speak—
   A maid of grace and complete majesty—
About surrender-up of Aquitaine   135
   To her decrepit, sick, and bedrid father.
Therefore this article is made in vain,
   Or vainly comes th'admirèd Princess hither.
KING
What say you, lords? Why, this was quite forgot.
BIRON
So study evermore is overshot.   140
While it doth study to have what it would,
   It doth forget to do the thing it should;
And when it hath the thing it hunteth most,
   'Tis won as towns with fire—so won, so lost.
KING
We must of force dispense with this decree.   145
She must lie here, on mere necessity.
BIRON
Necessity will make us all forsworn
   Three thousand times within this three years' space;
For every man with his affects is born,
   Not by might mastered, but by special grace.   150
If I break faith, this word shall speak for me:
I am forsworn on mere necessity.
So to the laws at large I write my name,
   And he that breaks them in the least degree
Stands in attainder of eternal shame.   155
   He signs
Suggestions are to other as to me,
But I believe, although I seem so loath,
I am the last that will last keep his oath.
But is there no quick recreation granted?
KING
Ay, that there is. Our court, you know, is haunted   160
   With a refinèd traveller of Spain,
A man in all the world's new fashion planted,
   That hath a mint of phrases in his brain.
One who the music of his own vain tongue
   Doth ravish like enchanting harmony;   165
A man of complements, whom right and wrong
   Have chose as umpire of their mutiny.
This child of fancy, that Armado hight,
   For interim to our studies shall relate
In high-borne words the worth of many a knight   170
   From tawny Spain lost in the world's debate.
How you delight, my lords, I know not, I;
   But I protest I love to hear him lie,
And I will use him for my minstrelsy.
BIRON
Armado is a most illustrious wight,   175
A man of fire-new words, fashion's own knight.
LONGUEVILLE
Costard the swain and he shall be our sport,
And so to study three years is but short.
   Enter a constable, Anthony Dull, with Costard with
   a letter

DULL Which is the Duke's own person?

BIRON This, fellow. What wouldst? 180

DULL I myself reprehend his own person, for I am his grace's farborough. But I would see his own person in flesh and blood.

BIRON This is he.

DULL Señor Arm—Arm—commends you. There's villainy abroad. This letter will tell you more. 186

COSTARD Sir, the contempts thereof are as touching me.

KING A letter from the magnificent Armado.

BIRON How low soever the matter, I hope in God for high words.

LONGUEVILLE A high hope for a low heaven. God grant us patience. 192

BIRON To hear, or forbear laughing?

LONGUEVILLE To hear meekly, sir, and to laugh moderately, or to forbear both. 195

BIRON Well, sir, be it as the style shall give us cause to climb in the merriness.

COSTARD The matter is to me, sir, as concerning Jaquenetta. The manner of it is, I was taken with the manner. 200

BIRON In what manner?

COSTARD In manner and form following, sir—all those three. I was seen with her in the manor house, sitting with her upon the form, and taken following her into the park; which put together is 'in manner and form following'. Now, sir, for the manner: it is the manner of a man to speak to a woman. For the form: in some form.

BIRON For the 'following', sir? 209

COSTARD As it shall follow in my correction; and God defend the right.

KING Will you hear this letter with attention? 212

BIRON As we would hear an oracle.

COSTARD Such is the simplicity of man to hearken after the flesh. 215

KING (reads) 'Great deputy, the welkin's vicegerent and sole dominator of Navarre, my soul's earth's god, and body's fostering patron'—

COSTARD Not a word of Costard yet.

KING 'So it is'— 220

COSTARD It may be so; but if he say it is so, he is, in telling true, but so.

KING Peace!

COSTARD Be to me and every man that dares not fight.

KING No words! 225

COSTARD Of other men's secrets, I beseech you.

KING 'So it is, besieged with sable-coloured melancholy, I did commend the black-oppressing humour to the most wholesome physic of thy health-giving air, and, as I am a gentleman, betook myself to walk. The time when? About the sixth hour, when beasts most graze, birds best peck, and men sit down to that nourishment which is called supper. So much for the time when. Now for the ground which—which, I mean, I walked upon. It is yclept thy park. Then for the place where—where, I mean, I did encounter that obscene and most

preposterous event that draweth from my snow-white pen the ebon-coloured ink which here thou viewest, beholdest, surveyest, or seest. But to the place where. It standeth north-north-east and by east from the west corner of thy curious-knotted garden. There did I see that low-spirited swain, that base minnow of thy mirth'—

COSTARD Me?

KING 'That unlettered, small-knowing soul'— 245

COSTARD Me?

KING 'That shallow vassal'—

COSTARD Still me?

KING 'Which, as I remember, hight Costard'—

COSTARD O, me! 250

KING 'Sorted and consorted, contrary to thy established proclaimed edict and continent canon, with, with, O with—but with this I passion to say wherewith'—

COSTARD With a wench.

KING 'With a child of our grandmother Eve, a female, or for thy more sweet understanding a woman. Him I, as my ever-esteemed duty pricks me on, have sent to thee, to receive the meed of punishment, by thy sweet grace's officer Anthony Dull, a man of good repute, carriage, bearing, and estimation.' 260

DULL Me, an't shall please you. I am Anthony Dull.

KING 'For Jaquenetta—so is the weaker vessel called— which I apprehended with the aforesaid swain, I keep her as a vessel of thy law's fury, and shall at the least of thy sweet notice bring her to trial. Thine in all compliments of devoted and heartburning heat of duty,
      Don Adriano de Armado.'

BIRON This is not so well as I looked for, but the best that ever I heard.

KING Ay, the best for the worst. (To Costard) But, sirrah, what say you to this? 271

COSTARD Sir, I confess the wench.

KING Did you hear the proclamation?

COSTARD I do confess much of the hearing it, but little of the marking of it. 275

KING It was proclaimed a year's imprisonment to be taken with a wench.

COSTARD I was taken with none, sir. I was taken with a damsel.

KING Well, it was proclaimed 'damsel'. 280

COSTARD This was no damsel, neither, sir. She was a virgin.

⌈KING⌉ It is so varied, too, for it was proclaimed 'virgin'.

COSTARD If it were, I deny her virginity. I was taken with a maid. 285

KING This 'maid' will not serve your turn, sir.

COSTARD This maid will serve my turn, sir.

KING Sir, I will pronounce your sentence. You shall fast a week with bran and water.

COSTARD I had rather pray a month with mutton and porridge. 291

KING
And Don Armado shall be your keeper.
My lord Biron, see him delivered o'er,

And go we, lords, to put in practice that
　Which each to other hath so strongly sworn.　295
　　　Exeunt the King, Longueville, and Dumaine
BIRON
I'll lay my head to any good man's hat
　These oaths and laws will prove an idle scorn.
　Sirrah, come on.
COSTARD I suffer for the truth, sir; for true it is I was
taken with Jaquenetta, and Jaquenetta is a true girl,
and therefore, welcome the sour cup of prosperity,
affliction may one day smile again; and till then, sit
thee down, sorrow.　　　　　　　　　　　*Exeunt*

1.2　*Enter Armado and Mote, his page*

ARMADO Boy, what sign is it when a man of great spirit
grows melancholy?
MOTE A great sign, sir, that he will look sad.
ARMADO Why, sadness is one and the selfsame thing,
dear imp.　　　　　　　　　　　　　　　　5
MOTE No, no, O Lord, sir, no.
ARMADO How canst thou part sadness and melancholy,
my tender juvenal?
MOTE By a familiar demonstration of the working, my
tough señor.　　　　　　　　　　　　　10
ARMADO Why 'tough señor'? Why 'tough señor'?
MOTE Why 'tender juvenal'? Why 'tender juvenal'?
ARMADO I spoke it, tender juvenal, as a congruent
epitheton appertaining to thy young days, which we
may nominate 'tender'.　　　　　　　　　15
MOTE And I, tough señor, as an appertinent title to your
old time, which we may name 'tough'.
ARMADO Pretty and apt.
MOTE How mean you, sir? I 'pretty' and my saying 'apt'?
Or I 'apt' and my saying 'pretty'?　　　　20
ARMADO Thou 'pretty', because little.
MOTE Little pretty, because little. Wherefore 'apt'?
ARMADO And therefore 'apt' because quick.
MOTE Speak you this in my praise, master?
ARMADO In thy condign praise.　　　　　　25
MOTE I will praise an eel with the same praise.
ARMADO What—that an eel is ingenious?
MOTE That an eel is quick.
ARMADO I do say thou art quick in answers. Thou heatest
my blood.　　　　　　　　　　　　　30
MOTE I am answered, sir.
ARMADO I love not to be crossed.
MOTE (*aside*) He speaks the mere contrary—crosses love
not him.
ARMADO I have promised to study three years with the
Duke.　　　　　　　　　　　　　　　36
MOTE You may do it in an hour, sir.
ARMADO Impossible.
MOTE How many is one, thrice told?
ARMADO I am ill at reckoning; it fitteth the spirit of a
tapster.　　　　　　　　　　　　　　41
MOTE You are a gentleman and a gamester, sir.
ARMADO I confess both. They are both the varnish of a
complete man.

MOTE Then I am sure you know how much the gross
sum of deuce-ace amounts to.　　　　　　46
ARMADO It doth amount to one more than two.
MOTE Which the base vulgar do call three.
ARMADO True.　　　　　　　　　　　49
MOTE Why, sir, is this such a piece of study? Now here
is 'three' studied ere ye'll thrice wink, and how easy it
is to put 'years' to the word 'three' and study 'three
years' in two words, the dancing horse will tell you.
ARMADO A most fine figure.
MOTE (*aside*) To prove you a cipher.　　　　55
ARMADO I will hereupon confess I am in love; and as it
is base for a soldier to love, so am I in love with a base
wench. If drawing my sword against the humour of
affection would deliver me from the reprobate thought
of it, I would take desire prisoner and ransom him to
any French courtier for a new-devised curtsy. I think
scorn to sigh. Methinks I should outswear Cupid.
Comfort me, boy. What great men have been in love?
MOTE Hercules, master.　　　　　　　　64
ARMADO Most sweet Hercules! More authority, dear boy.
Name more—and, sweet my child, let them be men of
good repute and carriage.
MOTE Samson, master; he was a man of good carriage,
great carriage, for he carried the town-gates on his
back like a porter, and he was in love.　　70
ARMADO O well-knit Samson, strong-jointed Samson! I do
excel thee in my rapier as much as thou didst me in
carrying gates. I am in love, too. Who was Samson's
love, my dear Mote?
MOTE A woman, master.　　　　　　　75
ARMADO Of what complexion?
MOTE Of all the four, or the three, or the two, or one of
the four.
ARMADO Tell me precisely of what complexion?
MOTE Of the sea-water green, sir.　　　　80
ARMADO Is that one of the four complexions?
MOTE As I have read, sir; and the best of them, too.
ARMADO Green indeed is the colour of lovers, but to have
a love of that colour, methinks Samson had small
reason for it. He surely affected her for her wit.　85
MOTE It was so, sir, for she had a green wit.
ARMADO My love is most immaculate white and red.
MOTE Most maculate thoughts, master, are masked under
such colours.
ARMADO Define, define, well-educated infant.　90
MOTE My father's wit and my mother's tongue assist me!
ARMADO Sweet invocation of a child!—most pretty and
pathetical.
MOTE　　　If she be made of white and red
　　　Her faults will ne'er be known,　　　95
　　For blushing cheeks by faults are bred
　　　And fears by pale white shown.
　　Then if she fear or be to blame,
　　　By this you shall not know;
　　For still her cheeks possess the same　　100
　　　Which native she doth owe.
A dangerous rhyme, master, against the reason of
white and red.

ARMADO Is there not a ballad, boy, of the King and the
Beggar?   105
MOTE The world was very guilty of such a ballad some
three ages since, but I think now 'tis not to be found;
or if it were, it would neither serve for the writing nor
the tune.
ARMADO I will have that subject newly writ o'er, that I
may example my digression by some mighty precedent.
Boy, I do love that country girl that I took in the park
with the rational hind Costard. She deserves well.
MOTE (aside) To be whipped—and yet a better love than
my master.   115
ARMADO Sing, boy. My spirit grows heavy in love.
MOTE And that's great marvel, loving a light wench.
ARMADO I say, sing.
MOTE Forbear till this company be past.

Enter Costard the clown, Constable Dull, and
Jaquenetta, a wench

DULL (to Armado) Sir, the Duke's pleasure is that you keep
Costard safe, and you must suffer him to take no
delight, nor no penance, but a must fast three days a
week. For this damsel, I must keep her at the park. She
is allowed for the dey-woman. Fare you well.   124
ARMADO (aside) I do betray myself with blushing.—Maid.
JAQUENETTA Man.
ARMADO I will visit thee at the lodge.
JAQUENETTA That's hereby.
ARMADO I know where it is situate.
JAQUENETTA Lord, how wise you are!   130
ARMADO I will tell thee wonders.
JAQUENETTA With that face?
ARMADO I love thee.
JAQUENETTA So I heard you say.
ARMADO And so farewell.   135
JAQUENETTA Fair weather after you.
⌈DULL⌉ Come, Jaquenetta, away.
                        ⌈*Exeunt Dull and Jaquenetta*⌉
ARMADO Villain, thou shalt fast for thy offences ere thou
be pardoned.
COSTARD Well, sir, I hope when I do it I shall do it on a
full stomach.   141
ARMADO Thou shalt be heavily punished.
COSTARD I am more bound to you than your fellows, for
they are but lightly rewarded.
ARMADO Take away this villain. Shut him up.   145
MOTE Come, you transgressing slave. Away!
COSTARD Let me not be pent up, sir. I will fast, being
loose.
MOTE No, sir. That were fast and loose. Thou shalt to
prison.   150
COSTARD Well, if ever I do see the merry days of desolation
that I have seen, some shall see.
MOTE What shall some see?
COSTARD Nay, nothing, Master Mote, but what they look
upon. It is not for prisoners to be too silent in their
words, and therefore I will say nothing. I thank God I
have as little patience as another man, and therefore I
can be quiet.   *Exeunt Mote and Costard*
ARMADO I do affect the very ground—which is base—

where her shoe—which is baser—guided by her foot—
which is basest—doth tread. I shall be forsworn—which
is a great argument of falsehood—if I love. And how
can that be true love which is falsely attempted? Love
is a familiar; love is a devil. There is no evil angel but
love. Yet was Samson so tempted, and he had an
excellent strength. Yet was Solomon so seduced, and
he had a very good wit. Cupid's butt-shaft is too hard
for Hercules' club, and therefore too much odds for a
Spaniard's rapier. The first and second cause will not
serve my turn: the passado he respects not, the duello
he regards not. His disgrace is to be called boy, but his
glory is to subdue men. Adieu, valour; rust, rapier; be
still, drum: for your manager is in love; yea, he loveth.
Assist me, some extemporal god of rhyme, for I am
sure I shall turn sonnet. Devise wit, write pen, for I
am for whole volumes, in folio.   *Exit*

2.1   *Enter the Princess of France with three attending*
       ladies—Maria, Catherine, and Rosaline—and three
       lords, one named Boyet
BOYET
Now, madam, summon up your dearest spirits.
Consider who the King your father sends,
To whom he sends, and what's his embassy:
Yourself, held precious in the world's esteem,
To parley with the sole inheritor   5
Of all perfections that a man may owe,
Matchless Navarre; the plea of no less weight
Than Aquitaine, a dowry for a queen.
Be now as prodigal of all dear grace
As nature was in making graces dear   10
When she did starve the general world beside
And prodigally gave them all to you.
PRINCESS
Good Lord Boyet, my beauty, though but mean,
Needs not the painted flourish of your praise.
Beauty is bought by judgement of the eye,   15
Not uttered by base sale of chapmen's tongues.
I am less proud to hear you tell my worth
Than you much willing to be counted wise
In spending your wit in the praise of mine.
But now to task the tasker: good Boyet,   20
You are not ignorant all-telling fame
Doth noise abroad Navarre hath made a vow
Till painful study shall outwear three years
No woman may approach his silent court.
Therefore to's seemeth it a needful course,   25
Before we enter his forbidden gates,
To know his pleasure; and in that behalf,
Bold of your worthiness, we single you
As our best-moving fair solicitor.
Tell him the daughter of the King of France   30
On serious business, craving quick dispatch,
Importunes personal conference with his grace.
Haste, signify so much while we attend,
Like humble-visaged suitors, his high will.
BOYET
Proud of employment, willingly I go.   35

PRINCESS
    All pride is willing pride, and yours is so.   *Exit Boyet*
    Who are the votaries, my loving lords,
    That are vow-fellows with this virtuous duke?
A LORD
    Lord Longueville is one.
PRINCESS   Know you the man?
MARIA
    I know him, madam. At a marriage feast   40
    Between Lord Périgord and the beauteous heir
    Of Jaques Fauconbridge solemnizèd
    In Normandy saw I this Longueville.
    A man of sovereign parts he is esteemed,
    Well fitted in arts, glorious in arms.   45
    Nothing becomes him ill that he would well.
    The only soil of his fair virtue's gloss—
    If virtue's gloss will stain with any soil—
    Is a sharp wit matched with too blunt a will,
    Whose edge hath power to cut, whose will still wills
    It should none spare that come within his power.   51
PRINCESS
    Some merry mocking lord, belike—is't so?
MARIA
    They say so most that most his humours know.
PRINCESS
    Such short-lived wits do wither as they grow.
    Who are the rest?   55
CATHERINE
    The young Dumaine, a well-accomplished youth,
    Of all that virtue love for virtue loved.
    Most power to do most harm, least knowing ill,
    For he hath wit to make an ill shape good,
    And shape to win grace, though he had no wit.   60
    I saw him at the Duke Alençon's once,
    And much too little of that good I saw
    Is my report to his great worthiness.
ROSALINE
    Another of these students at that time
    Was there with him, if I have heard a truth.   65
    Biron they call him, but a merrier man,
    Within the limit of becoming mirth,
    I never spent an hour's talk withal.
    His eye begets occasion for his wit,
    For every object that the one doth catch   70
    The other turns to a mirth-moving jest,
    Which his fair tongue, conceit's expositor,
    Delivers in such apt and gracious words
    That agèd ears play truant at his tales,
    And younger hearings are quite ravishèd,   75
    So sweet and voluble is his discourse.
PRINCESS
    God bless my ladies, are they all in love,
    That every one her own hath garnishèd
    With such bedecking ornaments of praise?
A LORD
    Here comes Boyet.
        Enter Boyet
PRINCESS   Now, what admittance, lord?   80

BOYET
    Navarre had notice of your fair approach,
    And he and his competitors in oath
    Were all addressed to meet you, gentle lady,
    Before I came. Marry, thus much I have learnt:
    He rather means to lodge you in the field,   85
    Like one that comes here to besiege his court,
    Than seek a dispensation for his oath
    To let you enter his unpeopled house.
        Enter Navarre, Longueville, Dumaine, and Biron
    Here comes Navarre.
KING Fair Princess, welcome to the court of Navarre.   90
PRINCESS 'Fair' I give you back again, and welcome I
    have not yet. The roof of this court is too high to be
    yours, and welcome to the wide fields too base to be
    mine.
KING
    You shall be welcome, madam, to my court.   95
PRINCESS
    I will be welcome, then. Conduct me thither.
KING
    Hear me, dear lady. I have sworn an oath—
PRINCESS
    Our Lady help my lord! He'll be forsworn.
KING
    Not for the world, fair madam, by my will.
PRINCESS
    Why, will shall break it—will and nothing else.   100
KING
    Your ladyship is ignorant what it is.
PRINCESS
    Were my lord so his ignorance were wise,
    Where now his knowledge must prove ignorance.
    I hear your grace hath sworn out housekeeping.
    'Tis deadly sin to keep that oath, my lord,   105
    And sin to break it.
    But pardon me, I am too sudden-bold.
    To teach a teacher ill beseemeth me.
    Vouchsafe to read the purpose of my coming,
    And suddenly resolve me in my suit.   110
        She gives him a paper
KING
    Madam, I will, if suddenly I may.
PRINCESS
    You will the sooner that I were away,
    For you'll prove perjured if you make me stay.
        Navarre reads the paper
BIRON (*to Rosaline*)
    Did not I dance with you in Brabant once?
⌈ROSALINE⌉
    Did not I dance with you in Brabant once?   115
BIRON
    I know you did.
⌈ROSALINE⌉   How needless was it then
    To ask the question!
BIRON   You must not be so quick.
⌈ROSALINE⌉
    'Tis 'long of you, that spur me with such questions.

BIRON
  Your wit's too hot, it speeds too fast, 'twill tire.
⌐ROSALINE⌐
  Not till it leave the rider in the mire.   120
BIRON
  What time o' day?
⌐ROSALINE⌐
  The hour that fools should ask.
BIRON
  Now fair befall your mask.
⌐ROSALINE⌐
  Fair fall the face it covers.
BIRON
  And send you many lovers.   125
⌐ROSALINE⌐
  Amen, so you be none.
BIRON
  Nay, then will I be gone.
KING (to the Princess)
  Madam, your father here doth intimate
  The payment of a hundred thousand crowns,
  Being but the one-half of an entire sum   130
  Disbursèd by my father in his wars.
  But say that he or we—as neither have—
  Received that sum, yet there remains unpaid
  A hundred thousand more, in surety of the which
  One part of Aquitaine is bound to us,   135
  Although not valued to the money's worth.
  If then the King your father will restore
  But that one half which is unsatisfied,
  We will give up our right in Aquitaine
  And hold fair friendship with his majesty.   140
  But that, it seems, he little purposeth,
  For here he doth demand to have repaid
  A hundred thousand crowns, and not demands,
  On payment of a hundred thousand crowns,
  To have his title live in Aquitaine,   145
  Which we much rather had depart withal,
  And have the money by our father lent,
  Than Aquitaine, so gelded as it is.
  Dear Princess, were not his requests so far
  From reason's yielding, your fair self should make   150
  A yielding 'gainst some reason in my breast,
  And go well satisfied to France again.
PRINCESS
  You do the King my father too much wrong,
  And wrong the reputation of your name,
  In so unseeming to confess receipt   155
  Of that which hath so faithfully been paid.
KING
  I do protest I never heard of it,
  And if you prove it I'll repay it back
  Or yield up Aquitaine.
PRINCESS   We arrest your word.
  Boyet, you can produce acquittances   160
  For such a sum from special officers
  Of Charles, his father.
KING   Satisfy me so.

BOYET
  So please your grace, the packet is not come
  Where that and other specialties are bound.
  Tomorrow you shall have a sight of them.   165
KING
  It shall suffice me, at which interview
  All liberal reason I will yield unto.
  Meantime receive such welcome at my hand
  As honour, without breach of honour, may
  Make tender of to thy true worthiness.   170
  You may not come, fair princess, within my gates,
  But here without you shall be so received
  As you shall deem yourself lodged in my heart,
  Though so denied fair harbour in my house.
  Your own good thoughts excuse me, and farewell. 175
  Tomorrow shall we visit you again.
PRINCESS
  Sweet health and fair desires consort your grace.
KING
  Thy own wish wish I thee in every place.
              Exit with Longueville and Dumaine
BIRON (to Rosaline) Lady, I will commend you to mine
  own heart.   180
ROSALINE Pray you, do my commendations. I would be
  glad to see it.
BIRON I would you heard it groan.
ROSALINE Is the fool sick?
BIRON Sick at the heart.   185
ROSALINE
  Alack, let it blood.
BIRON
  Would that do it good?
ROSALINE
  My physic says 'Ay'.
BIRON
  Will you prick't with your eye?
ROSALINE
  Non point, with my knife.   190
BIRON
  Now God save thy life.
ROSALINE
  And yours, from long living.
BIRON
  I cannot stay thanksgiving.   *Exit*
          Enter Dumaine
DUMAINE (to Boyet)
  Sir, I pray you a word. What lady is that same?
BOYET
  The heir of Alençon, Catherine her name.   195
DUMAINE
  A gallant lady. Monsieur, fare you well.   *Exit*
          Enter Longueville
LONGUEVILLE (to Boyet)
  I beseech you a word, what is she in the white?
BOYET
  A woman sometimes, an you saw her in the light.
LONGUEVILLE
  Perchance light in the light. I desire her name.

BOYET
She hath but one for herself; to desire that were a
shame.   200
LONGUEVILLE
Pray you, sir, whose daughter?
BOYET
Her mother's, I have heard.
LONGUEVILLE
God's blessing on your beard!
BOYET
Good sir, be not offended.
She is an heir of Fauconbridge.   205
LONGUEVILLE
Nay, my choler is ended.
She is a most sweet lady.
BOYET
Not unlike, sir. That may be.   *Exit Longueville*
            Enter Biron
BIRON
What's her name in the cap?
BOYET
Rosaline, by good hap.   210
BIRON
Is she wedded or no?
BOYET
To her will, sir, or so.
BIRON
O, you are welcome, sir. Adieu.
BOYET
Farewell to me, sir, and welcome to you.   *Exit Biron*
MARIA
That last is Biron, the merry madcap lord.   215
Not a word with him but a jest.
BOYET   And every jest but a word.
PRINCESS
It was well done of you to take him at his word.
BOYET
I was as willing to grapple as he was to board.
⌈CATHERINE⌉
Two hot sheeps, marry.
BOYET   And wherefore not ships?
No sheep, sweet lamb, unless we feed on your lips. 220
⌈CATHERINE⌉
You sheep and I pasture—shall that finish the jest?
BOYET
So you grant pasture for me.
⌈CATHERINE⌉   Not so, gentle beast.
My lips are no common, though several they be.
BOYET
Belonging to whom?
⌈CATHERINE⌉   To my fortunes and me.
PRINCESS
Good wits will be jangling; but, gentles, agree.   225
This civil war of wits were much better used
On Navarre and his bookmen, for here 'tis abused.
BOYET
If my observation, which very seldom lies,
By the heart's still rhetoric disclosèd with eyes,
Deceive me not now, Navarre is infected.   230

PRINCESS With what?
BOYET
With that which we lovers entitle 'affected'.
PRINCESS Your reason?
BOYET
Why, all his behaviours did make their retire
To the court of his eye, peeping thorough desire.   235
His heart like an agate with your print impressed,
Proud with his form, in his eye pride expressed.
His tongue, all impatient to speak and not see,
Did stumble with haste in his eyesight to be.
All senses to that sense did make their repair,   240
To feel only looking on fairest of fair.
Methought all his senses were locked in his eye,
As jewels in crystal, for some prince to buy,
Who, tendering their own worth from where they
       were glassed,
Did point you to buy them along as you passed.   245
His face's own margin did quote such amazes
That all eyes saw his eyes enchanted with gazes.
I'll give you Aquitaine and all that is his
An you give him for my sake but one loving kiss.
PRINCESS
Come, to our pavilion. Boyet is disposed.   250
BOYET
But to speak that in words which his eye hath
       disclosed.
I only have made a mouth of his eye
By adding a tongue, which I know will not lie.
⌈ROSALINE⌉
Thou art an old love-monger, and speak'st skilfully.
⌈MARIA⌉
He is Cupid's grandfather, and learns news of him. 255
⌈CATHERINE⌉
Then was Venus like her mother, for her father is but
       grim.
BOYET
Do you hear, my mad wenches?
⌈MARIA⌉   No.
BOYET   What then, do you see?
⌈CATHERINE⌉
Ay—our way to be gone.
BOYET   You are too hard for me.
                                                                            Exeunt

3.1   *Enter Armado the braggart, and Mote his boy*
ARMADO Warble, child; make passionate my sense of
       hearing.
MOTE (*sings*) Concolinel.
ARMADO Sweet air! Go, tenderness of years, take this key.
       Give enlargement to the swain. Bring him festinately
       hither. I must employ him in a letter to my love.   6
MOTE Master, will you win your love with a French
       brawl?
ARMADO How meanest thou—brawling in French?   9
MOTE No, my complete master; but to jig off a tune at
       the tongue's end, canary to it with your feet, humour
       it with turning up your eyelids, sigh a note and sing
       a note, sometime through the throat as if you swallowed

love with singing love, sometime through the nose as if you snuffed up love by smelling love, with your hat penthouse-like o'er the shop of your eyes, with your arms crossed on your thin-belly doublet like a rabbit on a spit, or your hands in your pocket like a man after the old painting, and keep not too long in one tune, but a snip and away. These are complements, these are humours; these betray nice wenches that would be betrayed without these, and make them men of note—do you note? *men*—that most are affected to these.

ARMADO How hast thou purchased this experience?   25

MOTE By my penny of observation.

ARMADO But O, but O—

MOTE 'The hobby-horse is forgot.'

ARMADO Call'st thou my love hobby-horse?   29

MOTE No, master, the hobby-horse is but a colt, and your love perhaps a hackney. But have you forgot your love?

ARMADO Almost I had.

MOTE Negligent student, learn her by heart.

ARMADO By heart and in heart, boy.

MOTE And out of heart, master. All those three I will prove.   36

ARMADO What wilt thou prove?

MOTE A man, if I live; and this, 'by', 'in', and 'without', upon the instant: 'by' heart you love her because your heart cannot come *by* her; 'in' heart you love her because your heart is *in* love with her; and 'out' of heart you love her, being *out* of heart that you cannot enjoy her.

ARMADO I am all these three.   44

MOTE (*aside*) And three times as much more, and yet nothing at all.

ARMADO Fetch hither the swain. He must carry me a letter.

MOTE (*aside*) A message well sympathized—a horse to be ambassador for an ass.   50

ARMADO Ha, ha! What sayst thou?

MOTE Marry, sir, you must send the ass upon the horse, for he is very slow-gaited. But I go.

ARMADO The way is but short. Away!

MOTE As swift as lead, sir.   55

ARMADO The meaning, pretty ingenious?
Is not lead a metal heavy, dull, and slow?

MOTE
Minime, honest master—or rather, master, no.

ARMADO
I say lead is slow.

MOTE   You are too swift, sir, to say so.
Is that lead slow which is fired from a gun?   60

ARMADO Sweet smoke of rhetoric!
He reputes me a cannon, and the bullet, that's he.
I shoot thee at the swain.

MOTE   Thump, then, and I flee.

                           Exit

ARMADO
A most acute juvenal—voluble and free of grace.   64
By thy favour, sweet welkin, I must sigh in thy face.

Most rude melancholy, valour gives thee place.   66
My herald is returned.

     Enter Mote the page, and Costard the clown

MOTE
A wonder, master—here's a costard broken in a shin.

ARMADO
Some enigma, some riddle; come, thy *l'envoi*. Begin.

COSTARD No egma, no riddle, no *l'envoi*, no salve in the mail, sir. O sir, plantain, a plain plantain—no *l'envoi*, no *l'envoi*, no salve, sir, but a plantain.

ARMADO By virtue, thou enforcest laughter—thy silly thought my spleen. The heaving of my lungs provokes me to ridiculous smiling. O pardon me, my stars! Doth the inconsiderate take salve for *l'envoi*, and the word *l'envoi* for a salve?   77

MOTE
Do the wise think them other? Is not *l'envoi* a salve?

ARMADO
No, page, it is an epilogue or discourse to make plain
Some obscure precedence that hath tofore been sain.
I will example it.   81
     The fox, the ape, and the humble-bee
     Were still at odds, being but three.
There's the moral. Now the *l'envoi*.

MOTE I will add the *l'envoi*. Say the moral again.   85

ARMADO   The fox, the ape, and the humble-bee
     Were still at odds, being but three.

MOTE   Until the goose came out of door
     And stayed the odds by adding four.
Now will I begin your moral, and do you follow with my *l'envoi*.
     The fox, the ape, and the humble-bee
     Were still at odds, being but three.

ARMADO   Until the goose came out of door,
     Staying the odds by adding four.   95

MOTE A good *l'envoi*, ending in the goose. Would you desire more?

COSTARD
The boy hath sold him a bargain—a goose, that's flat.
Sir, your pennyworth is good an your goose be fat.
To sell a bargain well is as cunning as fast and loose.
Let me see, a fat *l'envoi*—ay, that's a fat goose.   101

ARMADO
Come hither, come hither. How did this argument
     begin?

MOTE
By saying that a costard was broken in a shin.
Then called you for the *l'envoi*.   104

COSTARD True, and I for a plantain. Thus came your argument in. Then the boy's fat *l'envoi*, the goose that you bought, and he ended the market.

ARMADO But tell me, how was there a costard broken in a shin?

MOTE I will tell you sensibly.   110

COSTARD Thou hast no feeling of it. Mote, I will speak that *l'envoi*.
I, Costard, running out, that was safely within,
Fell over the threshold and broke my shin.

ARMADO We will talk no more of this matter.   115

COSTARD Till there be more matter in the shin.

ARMADO Sirrah Costard, I will enfranchise thee.

COSTARD O, marry me to one Frances! I smell some *l'envoi*,
some goose, in this.   119

ARMADO By my sweet soul, I mean setting thee at liberty,
enfreedoming thy person. Thou wert immured,
restrained, captivated, bound.

COSTARD True, true, and now you will be my purgation
and let me loose.   124

ARMADO I give thee thy liberty, set thee from durance,
and in lieu thereof impose on thee nothing but this:
bear this significant to the country maid, Jaquenetta.
(*Giving him a letter*) There is remuneration (*giving him
money*), for the best ward of mine honour is rewarding
my dependants. Mote, follow.   *Exit*

MOTE

Like the sequel, I. Signor Costard, adieu.   *Exit*

COSTARD

My sweet ounce of man's flesh, my incony Jew!   132
Now will I look to his remuneration. Remuneration—
O, that's the Latin word for three-farthings. Three-
farthings—remuneration. 'What's the price of this
inkle?' 'One penny.' 'No, I'll give you a remuneration.'
Why, it carries it! Remuneration! Why, it is a fairer
name than French crown. I will never buy and sell out
of this word.

Enter Biron

BIRON My good knave Costard, exceedingly well met. 140

COSTARD Pray you, sir, how much carnation ribbon may
a man buy for a remuneration?

BIRON What is a remuneration?

COSTARD Marry, sir, halfpenny-farthing.

BIRON Why, then, three-farthing-worth of silk.   145

COSTARD I thank your worship. God be wi' you.

BIRON Stay, slave, I must employ thee.

As thou wilt win my favour, good my knave,
Do one thing for me that I shall entreat.

COSTARD When would you have it done, sir?   150

BIRON This afternoon.

COSTARD Well, I will do it, sir. Fare you well.

BIRON Thou knowest not what it is.

COSTARD I shall know, sir, when I have done it.

BIRON Why, villain, thou must know first.   155

COSTARD I will come to your worship tomorrow morning.

BIRON

It must be done this afternoon. Hark, slave,
It is but this:
The Princess comes to hunt here in the park,
And in her train there is a gentle lady.   160
When tongues speak sweetly, then they name her
name,
And Rosaline they call her. Ask for her,
And to her white hand see thou do commend
This sealed-up counsel. There's thy guerdon (*giving
him a letter and money*), go.   164

COSTARD Guerdon! O sweet guerdon!—better than
remuneration, elevenpence-farthing better—most sweet

guerdon! I will do it, sir, in print. Guerdon—
remuneration.   *Exit*

BIRON

And I, forsooth, in love—I that have been love's whip,
A very beadle to a humorous sigh,   170
A critic, nay, a night-watch constable,
A domineering pedant o'er the boy,
Than whom no mortal so magnificent.
This wimpled, whining, purblind, wayward boy,
This Signor Junior, giant dwarf, Dan Cupid,   175
Regent of love-rhymes, lord of folded arms,
Th'anointed sovereign of sighs and groans,
Liege of all loiterers and malcontents,
Dread prince of plackets, king of codpieces,
Sole imperator and great general   180
Of trotting paritors—O my little heart!
And I to be a corporal of his field,
And wear his colours like a tumbler's hoop!
What? I love, I sue, I seek a wife?—
A woman, that is like a German clock,   185
Still a-repairing, ever out of frame,
And never going aright, being a watch,
But being watched that it may still go right.
Nay, to be perjured, which is worst of all,
And among three to love the worst of all—   190
A whitely wanton with a velvet brow,
With two pitch-balls stuck in her face for eyes—
Ay, and, by heaven, one that will do the deed
Though Argus were her eunuch and her guard.
And I to sigh for her, to watch for her,   195
To pray for her—go to, it is a plague
That Cupid will impose for my neglect
Of his almighty dreadful little might.
Well, I will love, write, sigh, pray, sue, groan:
Some men must love my lady, and some Joan.   *Exit*

4.1   *Enter the Princess, a Forester, her ladies—Rosaline,
Maria, and Catherine—and her lords, among them
Boyet*

PRINCESS

Was that the King that spurred his horse so hard
Against the steep uprising of the hill?

⌈BOYET⌉

I know not, but I think it was not he.

PRINCESS

Whoe'er a was, a showed a mounting mind.
Well, lords, today we shall have our dispatch.   5
Ere Saturday we will return to France.
Then, forester my friend, where is the bush
That we must stand and play the murderer in?

FORESTER

Hereby, upon the edge of yonder coppice—
A stand where you may make the fairest shoot.   10

PRINCESS

I thank my beauty, I am fair that shoot,
And thereupon thou speak'st 'the fairest shoot'.

FORESTER

Pardon me, madam, for I meant not so.

PRINCESS

  What, what? First praise me, and again say no?

  O short-lived pride! Not fair? Alack, for woe!   15

FORESTER

  Yes, madam, fair.

PRINCESS   Nay, never paint me now.

  Where fair is not, praise cannot mend the brow.

  Here, good my glass, take this for telling true.

    She gives him money

  Fair payment for foul words is more than due.

FORESTER

  Nothing but fair is that which you inherit.   20

PRINCESS

  See, see, my beauty will be saved by merit!

  O heresy in fair, fit for these days—

  A giving hand, though foul, shall have fair praise.

  But come, the bow. Now mercy goes to kill,

  And shooting well is then accounted ill.   25

  Thus will I save my credit in the shoot,

  Not wounding—pity would not let me do't.

  If wounding, then it was to show my skill,

  That more for praise than purpose meant to kill.

  And, out of question, so it is sometimes—   30

  Glory grows guilty of detested crimes

  When for fame's sake, for praise, an outward part,

  We bend to that the working of the heart,

  As I for praise alone now seek to spill

  The poor deer's blood that my heart means no ill. 35

BOYET

  Do not curst wives hold that self-sovereignty

  Only for praise' sake when they strive to be

  Lords o'er their lords?

PRINCESS

  Only for praise, and praise we may afford

  To any lady that subdues a lord.   40

    Enter Costard the clown

BOYET

  Here comes a member of the commonwealth.

COSTARD God dig-you-de'en, all. Pray you, which is the

  head lady?

PRINCESS Thou shalt know her, fellow, by the rest that

  have no heads.   45

COSTARD Which is the greatest lady, the highest?

PRINCESS The thickest and the tallest.

COSTARD

  The thickest and the tallest—it is so, truth is truth.

  An your waist, mistress, were as slender as my wit

  One o' these maids' girdles for your waist should be fit.

  Are not you the chief woman? You are the thickest

  here.   51

PRINCESS What's your will, sir? What's your will?

COSTARD

  I have a letter from Monsieur Biron to one Lady

  Rosaline.

PRINCESS

  O, thy letter, thy letter! (*She takes it*) He's a good

  friend of mine.

  (*To Costard*) Stand aside, good bearer. Boyet, you can

  carve.   55

  Break up this capon.

    She gives the letter to Boyet

BOYET   I am bound to serve.

  This letter is mistook. It importeth none here.

  It is writ to Jaquenetta.

PRINCESS   We will read it, I swear.

  Break the neck of the wax, and everyone give ear. 59

BOYET (*reads*) 'By heaven, that thou art fair is most

infallible, true that thou art beauteous, truth itself that

thou art lovely. More fairer than fair, beautiful than

beauteous, truer than truth itself, have commiseration

on thy heroical vassal. The magnanimous and most

illustrate King Cophetua set's eye upon the penurious

and indubitate beggar Zenelophon, and he it was that

might rightly say "*Veni, vidi, vici*", which to

annothanize in the vulgar—O base and obscure

vulgar!—*videlicet* "He came, see, and overcame." He

came, one; see, two; overcame, three. Who came? The

King. Why did he come? To see. Why did he see? To

overcome. To whom came he? To the beggar. What

saw he? The beggar. Who overcame he? The beggar.

The conclusion is victory. On whose side? The King's.

The captive is enriched. On whose side? The beggar's.

The catastrophe is a nuptial. On whose side? The

King's—no, on both in one, or one in both. I am the

King—for so stands the comparison—thou the beggar,

for so witnesseth thy lowliness. Shall I command thy

love? I may. Shall I enforce thy love? I could. Shall I

entreat thy love? I will. What shalt thou exchange for

rags? Robes. For tittles? Titles. For thyself? Me. Thus,

expecting thy reply, I profane my lips on thy foot, my

eyes on thy picture, and my heart on thy every part.

    Thine in the dearest design of industry,   85

          Don Adriano de Armado.

Thus dost thou hear the Nemean lion roar

'Gainst thee, thou lamb, that standest as his prey.

Submissive fall his princely feet before,

  And he from forage will incline to play.   90

But if thou strive, poor soul, what art thou then?

Food for his rage, repasture for his den.'

PRINCESS

  What plume of feathers is he that indited this letter?

  What vane? What weathercock? Did you ever hear

  better?

BOYET

  I am much deceived but I remember the style.   95

PRINCESS

  Else your memory is bad, going o'er it erewhile.

BOYET

  This Armado is a Spaniard that keeps here in court,

  A phantasim, a Monarcho, and one that makes sport

  To the Prince and his bookmates.

PRINCESS (*to Costard*)   Thou, fellow, a word.

  Who gave thee this letter?

COSTARD   I told you—my lord.   100

PRINCESS
To whom shouldst thou give it?
COSTARD　　　　　　　From my lord to my lady.
PRINCESS
From which lord to which lady?
COSTARD
From my lord Biron, a good master of mine,
To a lady of France that he called Rosaline.
PRINCESS
Thou hast mistaken his letter. Come, lords, away.　105
(To Rosaline, giving her the letter)
Here, sweet, put up this, 'twill be thine another day.
　　　　　　　　　　　　　　　　　Exit attended
BOYET
Who is the suitor? Who is the suitor?
ROSALINE　　　　　　　Shall I teach you to know?
BOYET
Ay, my continent of beauty.
ROSALINE　　　　　　　Why, she that bears the bow.
Finely put off.
BOYET
My lady goes to kill horns, but if thou marry,　　110
Hang me by the neck if horns that year miscarry.
Finely put on.
ROSALINE
Well then, I am the shooter.
BOYET　　　　　　　　And who is your deer?
ROSALINE
If we choose by the horns, yourself come not near.
Finely put on indeed!　　　　　　　　　　115
MARIA
You still wrangle with her, Boyet, and she strikes at
　the brow.
BOYET
But she herself is hit lower—have I hit her now?
ROSALINE Shall I come upon thee with an old saying that
was a man when King Pépin of France was a little boy,
as touching the hit it?　　　　　　　　　　120
BOYET So I may answer thee with one as old that was a
woman when Queen Guinevere of Britain was a little
wench, as touching the hit it.
ROSALINE (sings)
　　　Thou canst not hit it, hit it, hit it,
　　　Thou canst not hit it, my good man.　　125
BOYET (sings)
　　　An I cannot, cannot, cannot,
　　　An I cannot, another can.　　Exit Rosaline
COSTARD
By my troth, most pleasant! How both did fit it!
MARIA
A mark marvellous well shot, for they both did hit it.
BOYET
A mark—O mark but that mark! A mark, says my
　lady.　　　　　　　　　　　　　130
Let the mark have a prick in't to mete at, if it may be.
MARIA
Wide o' the bow hand—i'faith, your hand is out.
COSTARD
Indeed, a must shoot nearer, or he'll ne'er hit the clout.

BOYET
An if my hand be out, then belike your hand is in.
COSTARD
Then will she get the upshoot by cleaving the pin.　135
MARIA
Come, come, you talk greasily, your lips grow foul.
COSTARD
She's too hard for you at pricks, sir. Challenge her to
　bowl.
BOYET
I fear too much rubbing. Goodnight, my good owl.
　　　　　　Exeunt Boyet, Maria, ⌈and Catherine⌉
COSTARD
By my soul, a swain, a most simple clown.
Lord, Lord, how the ladies and I have put him down!
O' my troth, most sweet jests, most incony vulgar　141
　wit,
When it comes so smoothly off, so obscenely, as it
　were, so fit!
Armado o'th' t'other side—O, a most dainty man!—
To see him walk before a lady and to bear her fan!
To see him kiss his hand, and how most sweetly a
　will swear,　　　　　　　　　　　145
And his page o' t'other side, that handful of wit—
Ah heavens, it is a most pathetical nit!
　　　Shout within
Sola, sola!　　　　　　　　　　　　　Exit

4.2　Enter Dull, Holofernes the pedant, and Nathaniel the
　　　curate
NATHANIEL Very reverend sport, truly, and done in the
testimony of a good conscience.
HOLOFERNES The deer was, as you know—sanguis—in
blood, ripe as the pomewater who now hangeth like a
jewel in the ear of caelo, the sky, the welkin, the heaven,
and anon falleth like a crab on the face of terra, the
soil, the land, the earth.
NATHANIEL Truly, Master Holofernes, the epithets are
sweetly varied, like a scholar at the least. But, sir, I
assure ye it was a buck of the first head.　　10
HOLOFERNES Sir Nathaniel, haud credo.
DULL 'Twas not a 'auld grey doe', 'twas a pricket.
HOLOFERNES Most barbarous intimation! Yet a kind of
insinuation, as it were in via, in way, of explication,
facere, as it were, replication, or rather ostentare, to
show, as it were, his inclination after his undressed,
unpolished, uneducated, unpruned, untrained, or
rather unlettered, or ratherest unconfirmed, fashion, to
insert again my 'haud credo' for a deer.
DULL I said the deer was not a 'auld grey doe', 'twas a
pricket.　　　　　　　　　　　　　21
HOLOFERNES Twice-sod simplicity, bis coctus!
O thou monster ignorance, how deformed dost thou
　look!
NATHANIEL
Sir, he hath never fed of the dainties that are bred in
　a book.
He hath not eat paper, as it were, he hath not drunk
ink. His intellect is not replenished, he is only an

animal, only sensible in the duller parts,
And such barren plants are set before us that we
   thankful should be,
Which we of taste and feeling are, for those parts that
   do fructify in us more than he.
For as it would ill become me to be vain, indiscreet,
   or a fool,   30
So were there a patch set on learning to see *him* in a
   school.
But *omne bene* say I, being of an old father's mind:
'Many can brook the weather that love not the wind.'
DULL
  You two are bookmen. Can you tell me by your wit
  What was a month old at Cain's birth that's not five
   weeks old as yet?   35
HOLOFERNES *Dictynna*, Goodman Dull, *Dictynna*, Goodman
  Dull.
DULL What is '*Dictima*'?
NATHANIEL A title to Phoebe, to *luna*, to the moon.
HOLOFERNES
  The moon was a month old when Adam was no
   more,   40
  And raught not to five weeks when he came to five
   score.
  Th'allusion holds in the exchange.
DULL 'Tis true, indeed, the collusion holds in the
  exchange.
HOLOFERNES God comfort thy capacity, I say th'allusion
  holds in the exchange.   46
DULL And I say the pollution holds in the exchange, for
  the moon is never but a month old—and I say beside
  that 'twas a pricket that the Princess killed.
HOLOFERNES Sir Nathaniel, will you hear an extemporal
  epitaph on the death of the deer? And to humour the
  ignorant call I the deer the Princess killed a pricket.
NATHANIEL *Perge*, good Master Holofernes, *perge*, so it
  shall please you to abrogate scurrility.
HOLOFERNES I will something affect the letter, for it argues
  facility.   56
  The preyful Princess pierced and pricked a pretty
   pleasing pricket.
    Some say a sore, but not a sore till now made sore
    with shooting.
  The dogs did yell; put 'l' to 'sore', then 'sorel' jumps
   from thicket—
    Or pricket sore, or else sorel. The people fall a-
    hooting.   60
  If sore be sore, then 'l' to 'sore' makes fifty sores—O
   sore 'l'!
  Of one sore I an hundred make by adding but one
   more 'l'.
NATHANIEL A rare talent!
DULL If a talent be a claw, look how he claws him with
  a talent.   65
HOLOFERNES This is a gift that I have, simple, simple—a
  foolish extravagant spirit, full of forms, figures, shapes,
  objects, ideas, apprehensions, motions, revolutions.
  These are begot in the ventricle of memory, nourished

in the womb of *pia mater*, and delivered upon the
mellowing of occasion. But the gift is good in those in
whom it is acute, and I am thankful for it.   72
NATHANIEL Sir, I praise the Lord for you, and so may my
  parishioners; for their sons are well tutored by you,
  and their daughters profit very greatly under you. You
  are a good member of the commonwealth.   76
HOLOFERNES *Mehercle*, if their sons be ingenious they shall
  want no instruction; if their daughters be capable, I
  will put it to them. But *Vir sapit qui pauca loquitur*; a
  soul feminine saluteth us.   80
    Enter Jaquenetta, and Costard the clown
JAQUENETTA God give you good-morrow, Master Parson.
HOLOFERNES Master Parson, *quasi* 'pierce one'? And if one
  should be pierced, which is the one?
COSTARD Marry, Master Schoolmaster, he that is likeliest
  to a hogshead.   85
HOLOFERNES 'Of piercing a hogshead'—a good lustre of
  conceit in a turf of earth, fire enough for a flint, pearl
  enough for a swine—'tis pretty, it is well.
JAQUENETTA Good Master Parson, be so good as read me
  this letter. It was given me by Costard, and sent me
  from Don Armado. I beseech you read it.   91
    She gives the letter to Nathaniel, who reads it
HOLOFERNES (*to himself*) 'Facile precor gelida quando pecas
  omnia sub umbra ruminat', and so forth. Ah, good old
  Mantuan! I may speak of thee as the traveller doth of
  Venice: 95
    Venezia, Venezia,
    Chi non ti vede, chi non ti prezia.
  Old Mantuan, old Mantuan—who understandeth thee
  not, loves thee not. (*He sings*) Ut, re, sol, la, mi, fa. (*To
  Nathaniel*) Under pardon, sir, what are the contents?
  Or rather, as Horace says in his—what, my soul—
  verses?
NATHANIEL Ay, sir, and very learned.
HOLOFERNES Let me hear a staff, a stanza, a verse. *Lege,*
  domine.   105
NATHANIEL (*reads*)
  'If love make me forsworn, how shall I swear to love?
    Ah, never faith could hold, if not to beauty vowed.
  Though to myself forsworn, to thee I'll faithful prove.
    Those thoughts to me were oaks, to thee like osiers
    bowed.
  Study his bias leaves, and makes his book thine eyes,
    Where all those pleasures live that art would   111
    comprehend.
  If knowledge be the mark, to know thee shall suffice.
    Well learnèd is that tongue that well can thee
    commend;
  All ignorant that soul that sees thee without wonder;
    Which is to me some praise that I thy parts admire.
  Thy eye Jove's lightning bears, thy voice his dreadful
    thunder,   116
    Which, not to anger bent, is music and sweet fire.
  Celestial as thou art, O pardon, love, this wrong,
    That singeth heaven's praise with such an earthly
    tongue.'

HOLOFERNES You find not the apostrophus, and so miss the accent. Let me supervise the canzonet. Here are only numbers ratified, but for the elegancy, facility, and golden cadence of poesy—*caret*. Ovidius Naso was the man. And why indeed 'Naso' but for smelling out the odoriferous flowers of fancy, the jerks of invention? *Imitari* is nothing. So doth the hound his master, the ape his keeper, the tired horse his rider. But *domicella*—virgin—was this directed to you?   128

JAQUENETTA Ay, sir.

HOLOFERNES I will overglance the superscript. 'To the snow-white hand of the most beauteous Lady Rosaline.' I will look again on the intellect of the letter for the nomination of the party writing to the person written unto. 'Your ladyship's in all desired employment, Biron.' Sir Nathaniel, this Biron is one of the votaries with the King, and here he hath framed a letter to a sequent of the stranger Queen's, which, accidentally or by the way of progression, hath miscarried. (*To Jaquenetta*) Trip and go, my sweet, deliver this paper into the royal hand of the King. It may concern much. Stay not thy compliment, I forgive thy duty. Adieu.

JAQUENETTA Good Costard, go with me.—Sir, God save your life.

COSTARD Have with thee, my girl.   *Exit with Jaquenetta*

NATHANIEL Sir, you have done this in the fear of God very religiously, and, as a certain father saith—   146

HOLOFERNES Sir, tell not me of the father; I do fear colourable colours. But to return to the verses—did they please you, Sir Nathaniel?

NATHANIEL Marvellous well for the pen.   150

HOLOFERNES I do dine today at the father's of a certain pupil of mine where, if before repast it shall please you to gratify the table with a grace, I will on my privilege I have with the parents of the foresaid child or pupil undertake your *ben venuto*, where I will prove those verses to be very unlearned, neither savouring of poetry, wit, nor invention. I beseech your society.

NATHANIEL And thank you too, for society, saith the text, is the happiness of life.   159

HOLOFERNES And certes the text most infallibly concludes it. (*To Dull*) Sir, I do invite you too. You shall not say me nay. *Pauca verba*. Away, the gentles are at their game, and we will to our recreation.   *Exeunt*

4.3   *Enter Biron with a paper in his hand, alone*

BIRON The King, he is hunting the deer. I am coursing myself. They have pitched a toil, I am toiling in a pitch—pitch that defiles. Defile—a foul word. Well, set thee down, sorrow; for so they say the fool said, and so say I, and I the fool. Well proved, wit! By the Lord, this love is as mad as Ajax, it kills sheep, it kills me, I a sheep—well proved again o' my side. I will not love. If I do, hang me; i'faith, I will not. O, but her eye! By this light, but for her eye I would not love her. Yes, for her two eyes. Well, I do nothing in the world but lie, and lie in my throat. By heaven, I do love, and it

hath taught me to rhyme and to be melancholy, and here (*showing a paper*) is part of my rhyme, and here (*touching his breast*) my melancholy. Well, she hath one o' my sonnets already. The clown bore it, the fool sent it, and the lady hath it. Sweet clown, sweeter fool, sweetest lady. By the world, I would not care a pin if the other three were in. Here comes one with a paper. God give him grace to groan.

He stands aside. The King entereth with a paper

KING Ay me!   20

BIRON (*aside*) Shot, by heaven! Proceed, sweet Cupid, thou hast thumped him with thy birdbolt under the left pap. In faith, secrets.

KING (*reads*)

'So sweet a kiss the golden sun gives not
    To those fresh morning drops upon the rose   25
As thy eyebeams when their fresh rays have smote
    The night of dew that on my cheeks down flows.
Nor shines the silver moon one-half so bright
    Through the transparent bosom of the deep   29
As doth thy face through tears of mine give light.
    Thou shin'st in every tear that I do weep.
No drop but as a coach doth carry thee,
    So ridest thou triumphing in my woe.
Do but behold the tears that swell in me
    And they thy glory through my grief will show.
But do not love thyself; then thou wilt keep   36
My tears for glasses, and still make me weep.
O Queen of queens, how far dost thou excel,
No thought can think nor tongue of mortal tell.'

How shall she know my griefs? I'll drop the paper. Sweet leaves, shade folly. Who is he comes here?   41

Enter Longueville with papers. The King steps aside

What, Longueville, and reading—listen, ear!

BIRON (*aside*)

Now in thy likeness one more fool appear!

LONGUEVILLE Ay me! I am forsworn.

BIRON (*aside*)

Why, he comes in like a perjure, wearing papers.

KING (*aside*)

In love, I hope! Sweet fellowship in shame.   46

BIRON (*aside*)

One drunkard loves another of the name.

LONGUEVILLE

Am I the first that have been perjured so?

BIRON (*aside*)

I could put thee in comfort, not by two that I know.
Thou makest the triumviry, the corner-cap of society,
The shape of love's Tyburn, that hangs up simplicity.

LONGUEVILLE

I fear these stubborn lines lack power to move.   52
O sweet Maria, empress of my love,
These numbers will I tear, and write in prose.

BIRON (*aside*)

O, rhymes are guards on wanton Cupid's hose,   55
Disfigure not his slop.

LONGUEVILLE   This same shall go.

He reads the sonnet
'Did not the heavenly rhetoric of thine eye,
  'Gainst whom the world cannot hold argument,
Persuade my heart to this false perjury?
  Vows for thee broke deserve not punishment.   60
A woman I forswore, but I will prove,
  Thou being a goddess, I forswore not thee.
My vow was earthly, thou a heavenly love.
  Thy grace being gained cures all disgrace in me.
Vows are but breath, and breath a vapour is.   65
  Then thou, fair sun, which on my earth dost shine,
Exhal'st this vapour-vow; in thee it is.
  If broken then, it is no fault of mine.
If by me broke, what fool is not so wise
To lose an oath to win a paradise?'   70
BIRON (*aside*)
This is the liver vein, which makes flesh a deity,
A green goose a goddess, pure, pure idolatry.
God amend us, God amend: we are much out o'th'
  way.
    Enter Dumaine with a paper
LONGUEVILLE (*aside*)
By whom shall I send this? Company? Stay.
    He steps aside
BIRON (*aside*)
All hid, all hid—an old infant play.   75
Like a demigod here sit I in the sky,
And wretched fools' secrets heedfully o'er-eye.
More sacks to the mill! O heavens, I have my wish.
Dumaine transformed—four woodcocks in a dish!
DUMAINE O most divine Kate!   80
BIRON (*aside*) O most profane coxcomb!
DUMAINE
By heaven, the wonder in a mortal eye!
BIRON (*aside*)
By earth, she is not, corporal; there you lie.
DUMAINE
Her amber hairs for foul hath amber quoted.
BIRON (*aside*)
An amber-coloured raven was well noted.   85
DUMAINE
As upright as the cedar.
BIRON (*aside*)   Stoop, I say.
Her shoulder is with child.
DUMAINE   As fair as day.
BIRON (*aside*)
Ay, as some days; but then no sun must shine.
DUMAINE O that I had my wish!
LONGUEVILLE (*aside*) And I had mine!   90
KING (*aside*) And I mine too, good Lord!
BIRON (*aside*)
Amen, so I had mine. Is not that a good word?
DUMAINE
I would forget her, but a fever she
Reigns in my blood and will remembered be.
BIRON (*aside*)
A fever in your blood—why then, incision   95
Would let her out in saucers—sweet misprision.

DUMAINE
Once more I'll read the ode that I have writ.
BIRON (*aside*)
Once more I'll mark how love can vary wit.
    Dumaine reads his sonnet
DUMAINE
    'On a day—alack the day—
    Love, whose month is ever May,   100
    Spied a blossom passing fair
    Playing in the wanton air.
    Through the velvet leaves the wind
    All unseen can passage find,
    That the lover, sick to death,   105
    Wished himself the heavens' breath.
    "Air", quoth he, "thy cheeks may blow;
    Air, would I might triumph so.
    But, alack, my hand is sworn
    Ne'er to pluck thee from thy thorn—   110
    Vow, alack, for youth unmeet,
    Youth so apt to pluck a sweet.
    Do not call it sin in me
    That I am forsworn for thee,
    Thou for whom great Jove would swear   115
    Juno but an Ethiop were,
    And deny himself for Jove,
    Turning mortal for thy love."''
This will I send, and something else more plain,
That shall express my true love's fasting pain.   120
O, would the King, Biron, and Longueville
Were lovers too! Ill to example ill
Would from my forehead wipe a perjured note,
For none offend where all alike do dote.
LONGUEVILLE (*coming forward*)
Dumaine, thy love is far from charity,   125
That in love's grief desir'st society.
You may look pale, but I should blush, I know,
To be o'erheard and taken napping so.
KING (*coming forward*)
Come, sir, you blush. As his, your case is such.
You chide at him, offending twice as much.   130
You do not love Maria? Longueville
Did never sonnet for her sake compile,
Nor never lay his wreathèd arms athwart
His loving bosom to keep down his heart?
I have been closely shrouded in this bush,   135
And marked you both, and for you both did blush.
I heard your guilty rhymes, observed your fashion,
Saw sighs reek from you, noted well your passion.
'Ay me!' says one, 'O Jove!' the other cries.
One, her hairs were gold; crystal the other's eyes.   140
(*To Longueville*) You would for paradise break faith and
  troth,
(*To Dumaine*) And Jove for your love would infringe an
  oath.
What will Biron say when that he shall hear
Faith so infringèd, which such zeal did swear?
How will he scorn, how will he spend his wit!   145
How will he triumph, leap, and laugh at it!

For all the wealth that ever I did see
I would not have him know so much by me.
BIRON (*coming forward*)
Now step I forth to whip hypocrisy.
Ah, good my liege, I pray thee pardon me.   150
Good heart, what grace hast thou thus to reprove
These worms for loving, that art most in love?
Your eyes do make no coaches. In your tears
There is no certain princess that appears.
You'll not be perjured, 'tis a hateful thing;   155
Tush, none but minstrels like of sonneting!
But are you not ashamed, nay, are you not,
All three of you, to be thus much o'ershot?
(*To Longueville*) You found his mote, the King your
    mote did see,
But I a beam do find in each of three.   160
O, what a scene of fool'ry have I seen,
Of sighs, of groans, of sorrow, and of teen!
O me, with what strict patience have I sat,
To see a king transformèd to a gnat!
To see great Hercules whipping a gig,   165
And profound Solomon to tune a jig,
And Nestor play at pushpin with the boys,
And critic Timon laugh at idle toys!
Where lies thy grief, O tell me, good Dumaine?
And, gentle Longueville, where lies thy pain?   170
And where my liege's? All about the breast.
A caudle, ho!
KING   Too bitter is thy jest.
Are we betrayed thus to thy over-view?
BIRON
Not you to me, but I betrayed by you.
I that am honest, I that hold it sin   175
To break the vow I am engagèd in.
I am betrayed by keeping company
With men like you, men of inconstancy.
When shall you see me write a thing in rhyme,
Or groan for Joan, or spend a minute's time   180
In pruning me? When shall you hear that I
Will praise a hand, a foot, a face, an eye,
A gait, a state, a brow, a breast, a waist,
A leg, a limb?
KING   Soft, whither away so fast?
A true man or a thief, that gallops so?   185
BIRON
I post from love; good lover, let me go.
    Enter Jaquenetta with a letter, and Costard the
    clown
JAQUENETTA
God bless the King!
KING   What present hast thou there?
COSTARD
Some certain treason.
KING   What makes treason here?
COSTARD
Nay, it makes nothing, sir.
KING   If it mar nothing neither,
The treason and you go in peace away together!   190

JAQUENETTA
I beseech your grace, let this letter be read.
Our parson misdoubts it; 'twas treason, he said.
KING Biron, read it over.
    Biron takes and reads the letter
    (*To Jaquenetta*) Where hadst thou it?
JAQUENETTA Of Costard.   195
KING (*to Costard*) Where hadst thou it?
COSTARD Of Dun Adramadio, Dun Adramadio.
    Biron tears the letter
KING (*to Biron*)
How now, what is in you? Why dost thou tear it?
BIRON
A toy, my liege, a toy. Your grace needs not fear it.
LONGUEVILLE
It did move him to passion, and therefore let's hear it.
DUMAINE (*taking up a piece of the letter*)
It is Biron's writing, and here is his name.   201
BIRON (*to Costard*)
Ah, you whoreson loggerhead, you were born to do
    me shame!
Guilty, my lord, guilty! I confess, I confess.
KING What?
BIRON
That you three fools lacked me fool to make up the
    mess.   205
He, he, and you—e'en you, my liege—and I
Are pickpurses in love, and we deserve to die.
O, dismiss this audience, and I shall tell you more.
DUMAINE
Now the number is even.
BIRON   True, true; we are four.
Will these turtles be gone?
KING   Hence, sirs; away.   210
COSTARD
Walk aside the true folk, and let the traitors stay.
    Exeunt Costard and Jaquenetta
BIRON
Sweet lords, sweet lovers!—O, let us embrace.   216
    As true we are as flesh and blood can be.
The sea will ebb and flow, heaven show his face.
    Young blood doth not obey an old decree.   215
We cannot cross the cause why we were born,
Therefore of all hands must we be forsworn.
KING
What, did these rent lines show some love of thine
BIRON
'Did they', quoth you? Who sees the heavenly
    Rosaline
That, like a rude and savage man of Ind   220
    At the first op'ning of the gorgeous east,
Bows not his vassal head and, strucken blind,
    Kisses the base ground with obedient breast?
What peremptory eagle-sighted eye
    Dares look upon the heaven of her brow   225
That is not blinded by her majesty?
KING
    What zeal, what fury hath inspired thee now?

My love, her mistress, is a gracious moon,
  She an attending star, scarce seen a light.
BIRON
My eyes are then no eyes, nor I Biron.   230
  O, but for my love, day would turn to night.
Of all complexions the culled sovereignty
  Do meet as at a fair in her fair cheek,
Where several worthies make one dignity,
  Where nothing wants that want itself doth seek. 235
Lend me the flourish of all gentle tongues—
  Fie, painted rhetoric! O, she needs it not.
To things of sale a seller's praise belongs.
  She passes praise—then praise too short doth blot.
A withered hermit fivescore winters worn   240
  Might shake off fifty, looking in her eye.
Beauty doth varnish age as if new-born,
  And gives the crutch the cradle's infancy.
O, 'tis the sun that maketh all things shine.
KING
By heaven, thy love is black as ebony.   245
BIRON
Is ebony like her? O word divine!
  A wife of such wood were felicity.
O, who can give an oath? Where is a book,
  That I may swear beauty doth beauty lack
If that she learn not of her eye to look?   250
  No face is fair that is not full so black.
KING
O paradox! Black is the badge of hell,
  The hue of dungeons and the style of night,
And beauty's crest becomes the heavens well.
BIRON
Devils soonest tempt, resembling spirits of light. 255
  O, if in black my lady's brows be decked,
It mourns that painting and usurping hair
  Should ravish doters with a false aspect,
And therefore is she born to make black fair.
  Her favour turns the fashion of the days,   260
For native blood is counted painting now,
  And therefore red that would avoid dispraise
Paints itself black to imitate her brow.
DUMAINE
To look like her are chimney-sweepers black.
LONGUEVILLE
And since her time are colliers counted bright. 265
KING
And Ethiops of their sweet complexion crack.
DUMAINE
Dark needs no candles now, for dark is light.
BIRON
Your mistresses dare never come in rain,
  For fear their colours should be washed away.
KING
'Twere good yours did; for, sir, to tell you plain, 270
  I'll find a fairer face not washed today.
BIRON
I'll prove her fair, or talk till doomsday here.
KING
No devil will fright thee then so much as she.

DUMAINE
I never knew man hold vile stuff so dear.
LONGUEVILLE (showing his foot)
Look, here's thy love—my foot and her face see. 275
BIRON
O, if the streets were pavèd with thine eyes
  Her feet were much too dainty for such tread.
DUMAINE
O vile! Then as she goes, what upward lies
  The street should see as she walked overhead.
KING
But what of this? Are we not all in love?   280
BIRON
Nothing so sure, and thereby all forsworn.
KING
Then leave this chat and, good Biron, now prove
  Our loving lawful and our faith not torn.
DUMAINE
Ay, marry there, some flattery for this evil.
LONGUEVILLE
O, some authority how to proceed,   285
  Some tricks, some quillets how to cheat the devil.
DUMAINE
Some salve for perjury.
BIRON   O, 'tis more than need.
Have at you, then, affection's men-at-arms.
Consider what you first did swear unto:
To fast, to study, and to see no woman—   290
Flat treason 'gainst the kingly state of youth.
Say, can you fast? Your stomachs are too young,
And abstinence engenders maladies.
O, we have made a vow to study, lords,
And in that vow we have forsworn our books;   295
For when would you, my liege, or you, or you
In leaden contemplation have found out
Such fiery numbers as the prompting eyes
Of beauty's tutors have enriched you with?
Other slow arts entirely keep the brain,   300
And therefore, finding barren practisers,
Scarce show a harvest of their heavy toil.
But love, first learnèd in a lady's eyes,
Lives not alone immurèd in the brain,
But with the motion of all elements   305
Courses as swift as thought in every power,
And gives to every power a double power
Above their functions and their offices.
It adds a precious seeing to the eye—
A lover's eyes will gaze an eagle blind.   310
A lover's ear will hear the lowest sound
When the suspicious head of theft is stopped.
Love's feeling is more soft and sensible
Than are the tender horns of cockled snails.
Love's tongue proves dainty Bacchus gross in taste. 315
For valour, is not love a Hercules,
Still climbing trees in the Hesperides?
Subtle as Sphinx, as sweet and musical
As bright Apollo's lute strung with his hair;
And when love speaks, the voice of all the gods 320
Make heaven drowsy with the harmony.

Never durst poet touch a pen to write
Until his ink were tempered with love's sighs.
O, then his lines would ravish savage ears,
And plant in tyrants mild humility.   325
From women's eyes this doctrine I derive.
They sparkle still the right Promethean fire.
They are the books, the arts, the academes
That show, contain, and nourish all the world,
Else none at all in aught proves excellent.   330
Then fools you were these women to forswear,
Or keeping what is sworn, you will prove fools.
For wisdom's sake—a word that all men love—
Or for love's sake—a word that loves all men—
Or for men's sake—the authors of these women—   335
Or women's sake—by whom we men are men—
Let us once lose our oaths to find ourselves,
Or else we lose ourselves to keep our oaths.
It is religion to be thus forsworn,
For charity itself fulfils the law,   340
And who can sever love from charity?

KING
Saint Cupid, then, and, soldiers, to the field!

BIRON
Advance your standards, and upon them, lords.
Pell-mell, down with them; but be first advised
In conflict that you get the sun of them.   345

LONGUEVILLE
Now to plain dealing. Lay these glozes by.
Shall we resolve to woo these girls of France?

KING
And win them, too! Therefore let us devise
Some entertainment for them in their tents.

BIRON
First, from the park let us conduct them thither;   350
Then homeward every man attach the hand
Of his fair mistress. In the afternoon
We will with some strange pastime solace them,
Such as the shortness of the time can shape,
For revels, dances, masques, and merry hours   355
Forerun fair love, strewing her way with flowers.

KING
Away, away, no time shall be omitted
That will be time, and may by us be fitted.

BIRON
Allons, allons! Sowed cockle reaped no corn,
And justice always whirls in equal measure.   360
Light wenches may prove plagues to men forsworn.
If so, our copper buys no better treasure.   *Exeunt*

5.1 *Enter Holofernes the pedant, Nathaniel the curate,*
        and Anthony Dull

HOLOFERNES *Satis quid sufficit.*

NATHANIEL I praise God for you, sir. Your reasons at
dinner have been sharp and sententious, pleasant
without scurrility, witty without affection, audacious
without impudency, learned without opinion, and
strange without heresy. I did converse this quondam
day with a companion of the King's who is intituled,
nominated, or called Don Adriano de Armado.   8

HOLOFERNES *Novi hominum tanquam te.* His humour is
lofty, his discourse peremptory, his tongue filed, his eye
ambitious, his gait majestical, and his general
behaviour vain, ridiculous, and thrasonical. He is too
picked, too spruce, too affected, too odd, as it were, too
peregrinate, as I may call it.

NATHANIEL A most singular and choice epithet.   15
        He draws out his table-book

HOLOFERNES He draweth out the thread of his verbosity
finer than the staple of his argument. I abhor such
fanatical phantasims, such insociable and point-device
companions, such rackers of orthography as to speak
'dout', *sine* 'b', when he should say 'doubt'; 'det' when
he should pronounce 'debt'—'d, e, b, t', not 'd, e, t'.
He clepeth a calf 'cauf', half 'hauf', neighbour
vocatur 'nebour'—'neigh' abbreviated 'ne'. This is
abhominable—which he would call 'abominable'. It
insinuateth me of *insanire—ne intelligis, domine?*—to
make frantic, lunatic.   26

NATHANIEL *Laus deo, bone intelligo.*

HOLOFERNES *Bone? Bon, fort bon*—Priscian a little
scratched—'twill serve.
        Enter Armado the braggart, Mote his boy, and
        Costard the clown

NATHANIEL *Videsne quis venit?*   30

HOLOFERNES *Video, et gaudio.*

ARMADO (*to Mote*) Chirrah.

HOLOFERNES (*to Nathaniel*) *Quare* 'chirrah', not 'sirrah'?

ARMADO Men of peace, well encountered.

HOLOFERNES Most military sir, salutation!   35

MOTE (*aside to Costard*) They have been at a great feast of
languages and stolen the scraps.

COSTARD (*aside to Mote*) O, they have lived long on the
alms-basket of words. I marvel thy master hath not
eaten thee for a word, for thou art not so long by
the head as *honorificabilitudinitatibus.* Thou art easier
swallowed than a flapdragon.

MOTE (*aside to Costard*) Peace, the peal begins.

ARMADO (*to Holofernes*) Monsieur, are you not lettered?

MOTE Yes, yes, he teaches boys the horn-book. What is
'a, b' spelled backward, with the horn on his head? 46

HOLOFERNES Ba, *pueritia*, with a horn added.

MOTE Ba, most silly sheep, with a horn! You hear his
learning.

HOLOFERNES *Quis, quis*, thou consonant?   50

MOTE The last of the five vowels if you repeat them, or
the fifth if I.

HOLOFERNES I will repeat them: a, e, i—

MOTE The sheep. The other two concludes it: o, u.   54

ARMADO Now by the salt wave of the *Mediterraneum* a
sweet touch, a quick venue of wit; snip, snap, quick,
and home. It rejoiceth my intellect—true wit.

MOTE Offered by a child to an old man, which is
'wit-old'.

HOLOFERNES What is the figure? What is the figure? 60

MOTE Horns.

HOLOFERNES Thou disputes like an infant. Go whip thy
gig.

MOTE Lend me your horn to make one, and I will whip

about your infamy *circum circa*—a gig of a cuckold's
horn.   66
COSTARD An I had but one penny in the world, thou
shouldst have it to buy gingerbread. (*Giving money*)
Hold, there is the very remuneration I had of thy
master, thou halfpenny purse of wit, thou pigeon-egg
of discretion. O, an the heavens were so pleased that
thou wert but my bastard, what a joyful father wouldst
thou make me! Go to, thou hast it *ad dunghill*, at the
fingers' ends, as they say.   74
HOLOFERNES O, I smell false Latin—'dunghill' for *unguem*.
ARMADO Arts-man, *preambulate*. We will be singled from
the barbarous. Do you not educate youth at the charge-
house on the top of the mountain?
HOLOFERNES Or *mons*, the hill.
ARMADO At your sweet pleasure, for the mountain.   80
HOLOFERNES I do, sans question.
ARMADO Sir, it is the King's most sweet pleasure and
affection to congratulate the Princess at her pavilion
in the posteriors of this day, which the rude multitude
call the afternoon.   85
HOLOFERNES The posterior of the day, most generous sir,
is liable, congruent, and measurable for the afternoon.
The word is well culled, choice, sweet, and apt, I do
assure you, sir, I do assure.   89
ARMADO Sir, the King is a noble gentleman, and my
familiar, I do assure ye, very good friend. For what is
inward between us, let it pass. I do beseech thee,
remember thy courtesy. I beseech thee, apparel thy
head. And, among other important and most serious
designs, and of great import indeed, too—but let that
pass, for I must tell thee it will please his grace, by the
world, sometime to lean upon my poor shoulder and
with his royal finger thus dally with my excrement,
with my mustachio. But, sweetheart, let that pass. By
the world, I recount no fable. Some certain special
honours it pleaseth his greatness to impart to Armado,
a soldier, a man of travel, that hath seen the world.
But let that pass. The very all of all is—but, sweetheart,
I do implore secrecy—that the King would have me
present the Princess—sweet chuck—with some delightful ostentation, or show, or pageant, or antic, or
firework. Now, understanding that the curate and your
sweet self are good at such eruptions and sudden
breaking-out of mirth, as it were, I have acquainted
you withal to the end to crave your assistance.   110
HOLOFERNES Sir, you shall present before her the Nine
Worthies. Sir Nathaniel, as concerning some entertainment of time, some show in the posterior of this
day to be rendered by our assistance, the King's
command, and this most gallant, illustrate, and learned
gentleman before the Princess, I say none so fit as to
present the Nine Worthies.
NATHANIEL Where will you find men worthy enough to
present them?   119
HOLOFERNES Joshua, yourself; myself, Judas Maccabeus;
and this gallant gentleman, Hector. This swain, because
of his great limb or joint, shall pass Pompey the Great;
the page, Hercules.

ARMADO Pardon, sir, error! He is not quantity enough
for that Worthy's thumb. He is not so big as the end
of his club.   126
HOLOFERNES Shall I have audience? He shall present
Hercules in minority. His enter and exit shall be
strangling a snake, and I will have an apology for that
purpose.   130
MOTE An excellent device! So, if any of the audience hiss,
you may cry 'Well done, Hercules, now thou crushest
the snake!'—that is the way to make an offence
gracious, though few have the grace to do it.
ARMADO For the rest of the Worthies?   135
HOLOFERNES I will play three myself.
MOTE Thrice-worthy gentleman!
ARMADO Shall I tell you a thing?
HOLOFERNES We attend.
ARMADO We will have, if this fadge not, an antic. I
beseech you, follow.   141
HOLOFERNES *Via*, goodman Dull! Thou hast spoken no
word all this while.
DULL Nor understood none neither, sir.
HOLOFERNES *Allons*! We will employ thee.   145
DULL I'll make one in a dance or so, or I will play on the
tabor to the Worthies, and let them dance the hay.
HOLOFERNES Most dull, honest Dull! To our sport, away.
                                                                Exeunt

5.2   *Enter the Princess and her ladies: Rosaline, Maria,*
         and Catherine
PRINCESS
  Sweethearts, we shall be rich ere we depart,
  If fairings come thus plentifully in.
  A lady walled about with diamonds—
  Look you what I have from the loving King.
ROSALINE
  Madam, came nothing else along with that?   5
PRINCESS
  Nothing but this?—yes, as much love in rhyme
  As would be crammed up in a sheet of paper
  Writ o' both sides the leaf, margin and all,
  That he was fain to seal on Cupid's name.
ROSALINE
  That was the way to make his godhead wax,   10
  For he hath been five thousand year a boy.
CATHERINE
  Ay, and a shrewd unhappy gallows, too.
ROSALINE
  You'll ne'er be friends with him, a killed your sister.
CATHERINE
  He made her melancholy, sad, and heavy,
  And so she died. Had she been light like you,   15
  Of such a merry, nimble, stirring spirit,
  She might ha' been a grandam ere she died;
  And so may you, for a light heart lives long.
ROSALINE
  What's your dark meaning, mouse, of this light
        word?
CATHERINE
  A light condition in a beauty dark.   20

ROSALINE
We need more light to find your meaning out.
CATHERINE
You'll mar the light by taking it in snuff,
Therefore I'll darkly end the argument.
ROSALINE
Look what you do, you do it still i'th' dark.
CATHERINE
So do not you, for you are a light wench.   25
ROSALINE
Indeed I weigh not you, and therefore light.
CATHERINE
You weigh me not? O, that's you care not for me.
ROSALINE
Great reason, for past care is still past cure.
PRINCESS
Well bandied, both; a set of wit well played.
But Rosaline, you have a favour, too.   30
Who sent it? And what is it?
ROSALINE   I would you knew.
An if my face were but as fair as yours
My favour were as great, be witness this.
Nay, I have verses, too, I thank Biron,
The numbers true, and were the numb'ring, too,   35
I were the fairest goddess on the ground.
I am compared to twenty thousand fairs.
O, he hath drawn my picture in his letter.
PRINCESS Anything like?
ROSALINE
Much in the letters, nothing in the praise.   40
PRINCESS
Beauteous as ink—a good conclusion.
CATHERINE
Fair as a text B in a copy-book.
ROSALINE
Ware pencils, ho! Let me not die your debtor,
My red dominical, my golden letter.
O, that your face were not so full of O's!   45
PRINCESS
A pox of that jest; I beshrew all shrews.
But Catherine, what was sent to you from fair
  Dumaine?
CATHERINE
Madam, this glove.
PRINCESS   Did he not send you twain?
CATHERINE Yes, madam; and moreover,
Some thousand verses of a faithful lover.   50
A huge translation of hypocrisy
Vilely compiled, profound simplicity.
MARIA
This and these pearls to me sent Longueville.
The letter is too long by half a mile.
PRINCESS
I think no less. Dost thou not wish in heart   55
The chain were longer and the letter short?
MARIA
Ay, or I would these hands might never part.

PRINCESS
We are wise girls to mock our lovers so.
ROSALINE
They are worse fools to purchase mocking so.
That same Biron I'll torture ere I go.   60
O that I knew he were but in by th' week!—
How I would make him fawn, and beg, and seek,
And wait the season, and observe the times,
And spend his prodigal wits in bootless rhymes,
And shape his service wholly to my hests,   65
And make him proud to make me proud that jests!
So pursuivant-like would I o'ersway his state
That he should be my fool, and I his fate.
PRINCESS
None are so surely caught when they are catched
As wit turned fool. Folly in wisdom hatched   70
Hath wisdom's warrant, and the help of school,
And wit's own grace, to grace a learnèd fool.
ROSALINE
The blood of youth burns not with such excess
As gravity's revolt to wantonness.
MARIA
Folly in fools bears not so strong a note   75
As fool'ry in the wise when wit doth dote,
Since all the power thereof it doth apply
To prove, by wit, worth in simplicity.
            Enter Boyet
PRINCESS
Here comes Boyet, and mirth is in his face.
BOYET
O, I am stabbed with laughter! Where's her grace? 80
PRINCESS
Thy news, Boyet?
BOYET   Prepare, madam, prepare.
Arm, wenches, arm. Encounters mounted are
Against your peace. Love doth approach disguised,
Armèd in arguments. You'll be surprised.
Muster your wits, stand in your own defence,   85
Or hide your heads like cowards and fly hence.
PRINCESS
Saint Denis to Saint Cupid! What are they
That charge their breath against us? Say, scout, say.
BOYET
Under the cool shade of a sycamore
I thought to close mine eyes some half an hour   90
When lo, to interrupt my purposed rest
Toward that shade I might behold addressed
The King and his companions. Warily
I stole into a neighbour thicket by
And overheard what you shall overhear: 95
That by and by disguised they will be here.
Their herald is a pretty knavish page
That well by heart hath conned his embassage.
Action and accent did they teach him there.
'Thus must thou speak', and 'thus thy body bear'. 100
And ever and anon they made a doubt
Presence majestical would put him out,

'For', quoth the King, 'an angel shalt thou see,
Yet fear not thou, but speak audaciously.'
The boy replied, 'An angel is not evil.   105
I should have feared her had she been a devil.'
With that all laughed and clapped him on the
   shoulder,
Making the bold wag by their praises bolder.
One rubbed his elbow thus, and fleered, and swore
A better speech was never spoke before.   110
Another with his finger and his thumb
Cried '*Via*, we will do't, come what will come!'
The third he capered and cried 'All goes well!'
The fourth turned on the toe and down he fell.
With that they all did tumble on the ground   115
With such a zealous laughter, so profound,
That in this spleen ridiculous appears,
To check their folly, passion's solemn tears.

PRINCESS
But what, but what—come they to visit us?

BOYET
They do, they do, and are apparelled thus   120
⌈   ⌉
Like Muscovites or Russians, as I guess.
Their purpose is to parley, to court and dance,
And every one his love-suit will advance
Unto his several mistress, which they'll know   125
By favours several which they did bestow.

PRINCESS
And will they so? The gallants shall be tasked,
For, ladies, we will every one be masked,
And not a man of them shall have the grace,
Despite of suit, to see a lady's face.   130
(*To Rosaline*) Hold, take thou this, my sweet, and give
   me thine.
So shall Biron take me for Rosaline.
   She changes favours with Rosaline
(*To Catherine and Maria*)
And change you favours, too. So shall your loves
Woo contrary, deceived by these removes.
   Catherine and Maria change favours

ROSALINE
Come on, then, wear the favours most in sight.   135

CATHERINE
But in this changing what is your intent?

PRINCESS
The effect of my intent is to cross theirs.
They do it but in mockery-merriment,
And mock for mock is only my intent.
Their several counsels they unbosom shall   140
To loves mistook, and so be mocked withal
Upon the next occasion that we meet
With visages displayed to talk and greet.

ROSALINE
But shall we dance if they desire us to't?

PRINCESS
No, to the death we will not move a foot,   145
Nor to their penned speech render we no grace,
But while 'tis spoke each turn away her face.

BOYET
Why, that contempt will kill the speaker's heart,
And quite divorce his memory from his part.

PRINCESS
Therefore I do it; and I make no doubt   150
The rest will ne'er come in if he be out.
There's no such sport as sport by sport o'erthrown,
To make theirs ours, and ours none but our own.
So shall we stay, mocking intended game,
And they well mocked depart away with shame.   155
   A trumpet sounds

BOYET
The trumpet sounds, be masked, the masquers come.
   The ladies mask.
   Enter blackamoors with music; the boy Mote with
   a speech; the King and his lords, disguised as
   Russians

MOTE
All hail, the richest beauties on the earth!

BIRON (*aside*)
Beauties no richer than rich taffeta.

MOTE
A holy parcel of the fairest dames—
   The ladies turn their backs to him
That ever turned their—backs to mortal views.   160

BIRON 'Their eyes', villain, 'their eyes'!

MOTE
That ever turned their eyes to mortal views.
Out . . .

BOYET True, out indeed!

MOTE
Out of your favours, heavenly spirits, vouchsafe   165
Not to behold—

BIRON 'Once to behold', rogue!

MOTE
Once to behold with your sun-beamèd eyes—
With your sun-beamèd eyes—

BOYET
They will not answer to that epithet.   170
You were best call it 'daughter-beamèd' eyes.

MOTE
They do not mark me, and that brings me out.

BIRON
Is this your perfectness? Be gone, you rogue!
                        Exit Mote

ROSALINE (*as the Princess*)
What would these strangers? Know their minds, Boyet.
If they do speak our language, 'tis our will   175
That some plain man recount their purposes.
Know what they would.

BOYET   What would you with the Princess?

BIRON
Nothing but peace and gentle visitation.

ROSALINE What would they, say they?

BOYET
Nothing but peace and gentle visitation.   180

ROSALINE
Why, that they have, and bid them so be gone.

BOYET
She says you have it, and you may be gone.
KING
Say to her we have measured many miles
To tread a measure with her on this grass.
BOYET
They say that they have measured many a mile   185
To tread a measure with you on this grass.
ROSALINE
It is not so. Ask them how many inches
Is in one mile. If they have measured many,
The measure then of one is easily told.
BOYET
If to come hither you have measured miles,   190
And many miles, the Princess bids you tell
How many inches doth fill up one mile.
BIRON
Tell her we measure them by weary steps.
BOYET
She hears herself.
ROSALINE   How many weary steps
Of many weary miles you have o'ergone   195
Are numbered in the travel of one mile?
BIRON
We number nothing that we spend for you.
Our duty is so rich, so infinite,
That we may do it still without account.
Vouchsafe to show the sunshine of your face   200
That we, like savages, may worship it.
ROSALINE
My face is but a moon, and clouded, too.
KING
Blessed are clouds to do as such clouds do.
Vouchsafe, bright moon, and these thy stars, to shine,
Those clouds removed, upon our watery eyne.   205
ROSALINE
O vain petitioner, beg a greater matter.
Thou now requests but moonshine in the water.
KING
Then in our measure do but vouchsafe one change.
Thou bid'st me beg; this begging is not strange.
ROSALINE
Play, music, then.
          ⌜Music plays⌝
                    Nay, you must do it soon.   210
Not yet?—no dance! Thus change I like the moon.
KING
Will you not dance? How come you thus estranged?
ROSALINE
You took the moon at full, but now she's changed.
KING
Yet still she is the moon, and I the man.
⌜   ⌝   215
The music plays, vouchsafe some motion to it.
ROSALINE
Our ears vouchsafe it.
KING   But your legs should do it.

ROSALINE
Since you are strangers and come here by chance
We'll not be nice. Take hands. We will not dance.
KING
Why take we hands, then?
ROSALINE   Only to part friends.   220
Curtsy, sweethearts, and so the measure ends.
KING
More measure of this measure, be not nice.
ROSALINE
We can afford no more at such a price.
KING
Price you yourselves. What buys your company?
ROSALINE
Your absence only.
KING   That can never be.   225
ROSALINE
Then cannot we be bought, and so adieu—
Twice to your visor, and half once to you.
KING
If you deny to dance, let's hold more chat.
ROSALINE
In private, then.
KING   I am best pleased with that.
          The King and Rosaline talk apart
BIRON (to the Princess, taking her for Rosaline)
White-handed mistress, one sweet word with thee.   230
PRINCESS
Honey and milk and sugar—there is three.
BIRON
Nay then, two treys, an if you grow so nice—
Metheglin, wort, and malmsey—well run, dice!
There's half-a-dozen sweets.
PRINCESS   Seventh sweet, adieu.
Since you can cog, I'll play no more with you.   235
BIRON
One word in secret.
PRINCESS   Let it not be sweet.
BIRON
Thou griev'st my gall.
PRINCESS   Gall—bitter!
BIRON   Therefore meet.
          Biron and the Princess talk apart
DUMAINE (to Maria, taking her for Catherine)
Will you vouchsafe with me to change a word?
MARIA
Name it.
DUMAINE   Fair lady—
MARIA   Say you so? Fair lord—
Take that for your 'fair lady'.
DUMAINE   Please it you,   240
As much in private, and I'll bid adieu.
          Dumaine and Maria talk apart
CATHERINE
What, was your visor made without a tongue?
LONGUEVILLE (taking Catherine for Maria)
I know the reason, lady, why you ask.

CATHERINE
  O, for your reason! Quickly, sir, I long.
LONGUEVILLE
    You have a double tongue within your mask,   245
  And would afford my speechless visor half.
CATHERINE
  'Veal', quoth the Dutchman. Is not veal a calf?
LONGUEVILLE
  A calf, fair lady?
CATHERINE   No, a fair lord calf.
LONGUEVILLE
  Let's part the word.
CATHERINE   No, I'll not be your half.
  Take all and wean it, it may prove an ox.   250
LONGUEVILLE
  Look how you butt yourself in these sharp mocks!
  Will you give horns, chaste lady? Do not so.
CATHERINE
  Then die a calf before your horns do grow.
LONGUEVILLE
  One word in private with you ere I die.
CATHERINE
  Bleat softly, then. The butcher hears you cry.   255
    Longueville and Catherine talk apart
BOYET
  The tongues of mocking wenches are as keen
    As is the razor's edge invisible,
  Cutting a smaller hair than may be seen,
    Above the sense of sense; so sensible   259
  Seemeth their conference. Their conceits have wings
  Fleeter than arrows, bullets, wind, thought, swifter
    things.
ROSALINE
  Not one word more, my maids. Break off, break off.
BIRON
  By heaven, all dry-beaten with pure scoff!
KING
  Farewell, mad wenches, you have simple wits.
        Exeunt the King, lords, and blackamoors
  ⌈*The ladies unmask*⌉
PRINCESS
  Twenty adieus, my frozen Muscovites.   265
  Are these the breed of wits so wondered at?
BOYET
  Tapers they are, with your sweet breaths puffed
    out.
ROSALINE
  Well-liking wits they have; gross, gross; fat, fat.
PRINCESS
  O poverty in wit, kingly-poor flout!
  Will they not, think you, hang themselves tonight, 270
  Or ever but in visors show their faces?
  This pert Biron was out of count'nance quite.
ROSALINE
  Ah, they were all in lamentable cases.
  The King was weeping-ripe for a good word.
PRINCESS
  Biron did swear himself out of all suit.   275

MARIA
  Dumaine was at my service, and his sword.
  '*Non point*,' quoth I. My servant straight was mute.
CATHERINE
  Lord Longueville said I came o'er his heart,
    And trow you what he called me?
PRINCESS   'Qualm', perhaps.
CATHERINE
  Yes, in good faith.
PRINCESS   Go, sickness as thou art.   281
ROSALINE
  Well, better wits have worn plain statute-caps.
  But will you hear? The King is my love sworn.
PRINCESS
  And quick Biron hath plighted faith to me.
CATHERINE
  And Longueville was for my service born.   285
MARIA
  Dumaine is mine, as sure as bark on tree.
BOYET
  Madam, and pretty mistresses, give ear.
  Immediately they will again be here
  In their own shapes, for it can never be
  They will digest this harsh indignity.   290
PRINCESS
  Will they return?
BOYET   They will, they will, God knows,
  And leap for joy, though they are lame with blows.
  Therefore change favours, and when they repair,
  Blow like sweet roses in this summer air.
PRINCESS
  How 'blow'? How 'blow'? Speak to be understood. 295
BOYET
  Fair ladies masked are roses in their bud;
  Dismasked, their damask sweet commixture shown,
  Are angels vailing clouds, or roses blown.
PRINCESS
  Avaunt, perplexity! What shall we do
  If they return in their own shapes to woo?   300
ROSALINE
  Good madam, if by me you'll be advised,
  Let's mock them still, as well known as disguised.
  Let us complain to them what fools were here,
  Disguised like Muscovites in shapeless gear,
  And wonder what they were, and to what end   305
  Their shallow shows, and prologue vilely penned,
  And their rough carriage so ridiculous,
  Should be presented at our tent to us.
BOYET
  Ladies, withdraw. The gallants are at hand.
PRINCESS
  Whip, to our tents, as roes run over land!   310
        Exeunt the ladies
    Enter the King, Biron, Dumaine, and Longueville, as
    themselves
KING
  Fair sir, God save you. Where's the Princess?

BOYET
Gone to her tent. Please it your majesty
Command me any service to her thither?
KING
That she vouchsafe me audience for one word.
BOYET
I will, and so will she, I know, my lord.   *Exit*   315
BIRON
This fellow pecks up wit as pigeons peas,
And utters it again when God doth please.
He is wit's pedlar, and retails his wares
At wakes and wassails, meetings, markets, fairs.
And we that sell by gross, the Lord doth know,   320
Have not the grace to grace it with such show.
This gallant pins the wenches on his sleeve.
Had he been Adam, he had tempted Eve.
A can carve too, and lisp, why, this is he
That kissed his hand away in courtesy.   325
This is the ape of form, Monsieur the Nice,
That when he plays at tables chides the dice
In honourable terms. Nay, he can sing
A mean most meanly, and in ushering
Mend him who can. The ladies call him sweet.   330
The stairs as he treads on them kiss his feet.
This is the flower that smiles on everyone
To show his teeth as white as whales' bone,
And consciences that will not die in debt
Pay him the due of 'honey-tongued' Boyet.   335
KING
A blister on his sweet tongue with my heart,
That put Armado's page out of his part!
    Enter the ladies and Boyet
BIRON
See where it comes. Behaviour, what wert thou
Till this madman showed thee, and what art thou
    now?
KING
All hail, sweet madam, and fair time of day!   340
PRINCESS
'Fair' in 'all hail' is foul, as I conceive.
KING
Construe my speeches better, if you may.
PRINCESS
Then wish me better. I will give you leave.
KING
We came to visit you, and purpose now
To lead you to our court. Vouchsafe it, then.   345
PRINCESS
This field shall hold me, and so hold your vow.
Nor God nor I delights in perjured men.
KING
Rebuke me not for that which you provoke.
The virtue of your eye must break my oath.
PRINCESS
You nickname virtue. 'Vice' you should have spoke,
For virtue's office never breaks men's troth.   351
Now by my maiden honour, yet as pure
As the unsullied lily, I protest,

A world of torments though I should endure,
I would not yield to be your house's guest,   355
So much I hate a breaking cause to be
Of heavenly oaths, vowed with integrity.
KING
O, you have lived in desolation here,
Unseen, unvisited, much to our shame.
PRINCESS
Not so, my lord. It is not so, I swear.   360
We have had pastimes here, and pleasant game.
A mess of Russians left us but of late.
KING
How, madam? Russians?
PRINCESS   Ay, in truth, my lord.
Trim gallants, full of courtship and of state.
ROSALINE
Madam, speak true.—It is not so, my lord.   365
My lady, to the manner of the days,
In courtesy gives undeserving praise.
We four indeed confronted were with four
In Russian habit. Here they stayed an hour,
And talked apace, and in that hour, my lord,   370
They did not bless us with one happy word.
I dare not call them fools, but this I think:
When they are thirsty, fools would fain have drink.
BIRON
This jest is dry to me. Gentle sweet,
Your wits makes wise things foolish. When we greet,
With eyes' best seeing, heaven's fiery eye,   376
By light we lose light. Your capacity
Is of that nature that to your huge store
Wise things seem foolish, and rich things but poor.
ROSALINE
This proves you wise and rich, for in my eye—   380
BIRON
I am a fool, and full of poverty.
ROSALINE
But that you take what doth to you belong
It were a fault to snatch words from my tongue.
BIRON
O, I am yours, and all that I possess.
ROSALINE
All the fool mine!
BIRON   I cannot give you less.   385
ROSALINE
Which of the visors was it that you wore?
BIRON
Where? When? What visor? Why demand you this?
ROSALINE
There, then, that visor, that superfluous case,
That hid the worse and showed the better face.
KING (*aside to the lords*)
We were descried. They'll mock us now, downright.
DUMAINE (*aside to the King*)
Let us confess, and turn it to a jest.   391
PRINCESS
Amazed, my lord? Why looks your highness sad?

ROSALINE
Help, hold his brows, he'll swoon. Why look you
   pale?
Seasick, I think, coming from Muscovy.
BIRON
Thus pour the stars down plagues for perjury.   395
   Can any face of brass hold longer out?
Here stand I, lady. Dart thy skill at me—
   Bruise me with scorn, confound me with a flout,
Thrust thy sharp wit quite through my ignorance,
   Cut me to pieces with thy keen conceit,   400
And I will wish thee nevermore to dance,
   Nor nevermore in Russian habit wait.
O, never will I trust to speeches penned,
   Nor to the motion of a schoolboy's tongue,
Nor never come in visor to my friend,   405
   Nor woo in rhyme, like a blind harper's song.
Taffeta phrases, silken terms precise,
   Three-piled hyperboles, spruce affectation,
Figures pedantical—these summer flies
   Have blown me full of maggot ostentation.   410
I do forswear them, and I here protest,
   By this white glove—how white the hand, God
   knows!—
Henceforth my wooing mind shall be expressed
   In russet yeas, and honest kersey noes.
And to begin, wench, so God help me, law!   415
   My love to thee is sound, sans crack or flaw.
ROSALINE
Sans 'sans', I pray you.
BIRON   Yet I have a trick
Of the old rage. Bear with me, I am sick.
I'll leave it by degrees. Soft, let us see.
Write 'Lord have mercy on us' on those three.   420
They are infected, in their hearts it lies.
They have the plague, and caught it of your eyes.
These lords are visited, you are not free;
For the Lord's tokens on you do I see.
PRINCESS
No, they are free that gave these tokens to us.   425
BIRON
Our states are forfeit. Seek not to undo us.
ROSALINE
It is not so, for how can this be true,
That you stand forfeit, being those that sue?
BIRON
Peace, for I will not have to do with you.
ROSALINE
Nor shall not, if I do as I intend.   430
BIRON (to the lords)
Speak for yourselves. My wit is at an end.
KING
Teach us, sweet madam, for our rude transgression
Some fair excuse.
PRINCESS   The fairest is confession.
Were not you here but even now disguised?
KING
Madam, I was.
PRINCESS   And were you well advised?   435

KING
I was, fair madam.
PRINCESS   When you then were here,
What did you whisper in your lady's ear?
KING
That more than all the world I did respect her.
PRINCESS
When she shall challenge this, you will reject her.
KING
Upon mine honour, no.
PRINCESS   Peace, peace, forbear.   440
Your oath once broke, you force not to forswear.
KING
Despise me when I break this oath of mine.
PRINCESS
I will, and therefore keep it. Rosaline,
What did the Russian whisper in your ear?
ROSALINE
Madam, he swore that he did hold me dear   445
As precious eyesight, and did value me
Above this world, adding thereto moreover
That he would wed me, or else die my lover.
PRINCESS
God give thee joy of him! The noble lord
Most honourably doth uphold his word.   450
KING
What mean you, madam? By my life, my troth,
I never swore this lady such an oath.
ROSALINE
By heaven, you did, and to confirm it plain,
You gave me this. But take it, sir, again.
KING
My faith and this the Princess I did give.   455
I knew her by this jewel on her sleeve.
PRINCESS
Pardon me, sir, *this* jewel did she wear,
And Lord Biron, I thank him, is my dear.
(*To Biron*) What, will you have me, or your pearl
   again?
BIRON
Neither of either. I remit both twain.   460
I see the trick on't. Here was a consent,
Knowing aforehand of our merriment,
To dash it like a Christmas comedy.
Some carry-tale, some please-man, some slight zany,
Some mumble-news, some trencher-knight, some Dick
That smiles his cheek in years, and knows the trick
To make my lady laugh when she's disposed,
Told our intents before, which once disclosed,
The ladies did change favours, and then we,
Following the signs, wooed but the sign of she.   470
Now, to our perjury to add more terror,
We are again forsworn, in will and error.
Much upon this 'tis, (*to Boyet*) and might not you
Forestall our sport, to make us thus untrue?
Do not you know my lady's foot by th' square,   475
   And laugh upon the apple of her eye,
And stand between her back, sir, and the fire,
   Holding a trencher, jesting merrily?

You put our page out. Go, you are allowed.
Die when you will, a smock shall be your shroud.   480
You leer upon me, do you? There's an eye
Wounds like a leaden sword.
BOYET   Full merrily
Hath this brave manège, this career been run.
BIRON
Lo, he is tilting straight. Peace, I have done.
Enter Costard the clown
Welcome, pure wit. Thou partest a fair fray.   485
COSTARD
O Lord, sir, they would know
Whether the three Worthies shall come in or no.
BIRON
What, are there but three?
COSTARD   No, sir, but it is vara fine,
For everyone pursents three.
BIRON   And three times thrice is nine.
COSTARD
Not so, sir, under correction, sir, I hope it is not so.
You cannot beg us, sir. I can assure you, sir, we   491
    know what we know.
I hope, sir, three times thrice, sir—
BIRON   Is not nine?
COSTARD Under correction, sir, we know whereuntil it
    doth amount.
BIRON By Jove, I always took three threes for nine.   495
COSTARD O Lord, sir, it were pity you should get your
    living by reck'ning, sir.
BIRON How much is it?
COSTARD O Lord, sir, the parties themselves, the actors,
    sir, will show whereuntil it doth amount. For mine
    own part, I am, as they say, but to parfect one man
    in one poor man, Pompion the Great, sir.   502
BIRON Art thou one of the Worthies?
COSTARD It pleased them to think me worthy of Pompey
    the Great. For mine own part, I know not the degree
    of the Worthy, but I am to stand for him.   506
BIRON Go, bid them prepare.
COSTARD
We will turn it finely off, sir. We will take some care.
                                            Exit
KING
Biron, they will shame us. Let them not approach.
BIRON
We are shame-proof, my lord, and 'tis some policy   510
To have one show worse than the King's and his
    company.
KING I say they shall not come.
PRINCESS
Nay, my good lord, let me o'errule you now.
That sport best pleases that doth least know how.
Where zeal strives to content, and the contents   515
Dies in the zeal of that which it presents,
There form confounded makes most form in mirth,
When great things labouring perish in their birth.
BIRON
A right description of our sport, my lord.

Enter Armado the braggart
ARMADO (*to the King*) Anointed, I implore so much expense
    of thy royal sweet breath as will utter a brace of words.
    ⌈*Armado and the King speak apart*⌉
PRINCESS Doth this man serve God?   522
BIRON Why ask you?
PRINCESS
A speaks not like a man of God his making.
ARMADO That is all one, my fair sweet honey monarch,
    for, I protest, the schoolmaster is exceeding fantastical,
    too-too vain, too-too vain. But we will put it, as they
    say, to *fortuna de la guerra*. I wish you the peace of
    mind, most royal couplement.   *Exit*
KING Here is like to be a good presence of Worthies. He
    presents Hector of Troy, the swain Pompey the Great,
    the parish curate Alexander, Armado's page Hercules,
    the pedant Judas Maccabeus,
And if these four Worthies in their first show thrive,
These four will change habits and present the other
    five.   535
BIRON
There is five in the first show.
KING
You are deceived, 'tis not so.
BIRON
The pedant, the braggart, the hedge-priest, the fool,
    and the boy,
Abate throw at novum and the whole world again
Cannot pick out five such, take each one in his vein.
KING
The ship is under sail, and here she comes amain.   541
Enter Costard the clown as Pompey
COSTARD (*as Pompey*)
I Pompey am—
BIRON   You lie, you are not he.
COSTARD (*as Pompey*)
I Pompey am—
BOYET   With leopard's head on knee.
BIRON
Well said, old mocker. I must needs be friends with
    thee.
COSTARD (*as Pompey*)
I Pompey am, Pompey surnamed the Big.   545
DUMAINE 'The Great'.
COSTARD It is 'Great', sir—
    (*As Pompey*) Pompey surnamed the Great,
That oft in field with targe and shield did make my
    foe to sweat,
And travelling along this coast I here am come by
    chance,   550
And lay my arms before the legs of this sweet lass of
    France.—
If your ladyship would say 'Thanks, Pompey', I had
    done.
⌈PRINCESS⌉ Great thanks, great Pompey.
COSTARD 'Tis not so much worth, but I hope I was perfect.
    I made a little fault in 'great'.   556

BIRON My hat to a halfpenny Pompey proves the best
Worthy.
    Costard stands aside.
    Enter Nathaniel the curate as Alexander
NATHANIEL (*as Alexander*)
When in the world I lived I was the world's
  commander.
  By east, west, north, and south, I spread my
    conquering might.   560
My scutcheon plain declares that I am Alisander.
BOYET
Your nose says no, you are not, for it stands too
  right.
BIRON (*to Boyet*)
Your nose smells 'no' in this, most tender-smelling
  knight.
PRINCESS
The conqueror is dismayed. Proceed, good Alexander.
NATHANIEL (*as Alexander*)
When in the world I lived I was the world's
  commander.   565
BOYET
Most true, 'tis right, you were so, Alisander.
BIRON (*to Costard*) Pompey the Great.
COSTARD Your servant, and Costard.
BIRON Take away the conqueror, take away Alisander.
COSTARD (*to Nathaniel*) O, sir, you have overthrown
Alisander the Conqueror. You will be scraped out of
the painted cloth for this. Your lion that holds his pole-
axe sitting on a close-stool will be given to Ajax. He
will be the ninth Worthy. A conqueror and afeard to
speak? Run away for shame, Alisander.   575
    ⌈*Exit Nathaniel the curate*⌉
There, an't shall please you, a foolish mild man, an
honest man, look you, and soon dashed. He is a
marvellous good neighbour, faith, and a very good
bowler, but for Alisander—alas, you see how 'tis—a
little o'erparted. But there are Worthies a-coming will
speak their mind in some other sort.   581
PRINCESS Stand aside, good Pompey.
    Enter Holofernes the pedant as Judas, and the boy
    Mote as Hercules
HOLOFERNES
Great Hercules is presented by this imp,
  Whose club killed Cerberus, that three-headed
    canus,
And when he was a babe, a child, a shrimp,   585
  Thus did he strangle serpents in his *manus.*
Quoniam he seemeth in minority,
Ergo I come with this apology.
(*To Mote*) Keep some state in thy exit, and vanish.
         Exit Mote
HOLOFERNES (*as Judas*)
Judas I am—
         590
DUMAINE A Judas?
HOLOFERNES Not Iscariot, sir.
(*As Judas*) Judas I am, yclept Maccabeus.
DUMAINE Judas Maccabeus clipped is plain Judas.

BIRON A kissing traitor. How art thou proved Judas? 595
HOLOFERNES (*as Judas*)
  Judas I am—
DUMAINE The more shame for you, Judas.
HOLOFERNES What mean you, sir?
BOYET To make Judas hang himself.
HOLOFERNES Begin, sir. You are my elder.   600
BIRON Well followed—Judas was hanged on an elder.
HOLOFERNES I will not be put out of countenance.
BIRON Because thou hast no face.
HOLOFERNES What is this?
BOYET A cittern-head.   605
DUMAINE The head of a bodkin.
BIRON A death's face in a ring.
LONGUEVILLE The face of an old Roman coin, scarce s
BOYET The pommel of Caesar's falchion.
DUMAINE The carved-bone face on a flask.   610
BIRON Saint George's half-cheek in a brooch.
DUMAINE Ay, and in a brooch of lead.
BIRON Ay, and worn in the cap of a tooth-drawer. And
  now forward, for we have put thee in countenance.
HOLOFERNES You have put me out of countenance. 615
BIRON False, we have given thee faces.
HOLOFERNES But you have outfaced them all.
BIRON
  An thou wert a lion, we would do so.
BOYET
  Therefore, as he is an ass, let him go.
And so adieu, sweet Jude. Nay, why dost thou stay?
DUMAINE For the latter end of his name.   621
BIRON
  For the ass to the Jude. Give it him. Jud-as, away.
HOLOFERNES
  This is not generous, not gentle, not humble.
BOYET
  A light for Monsieur Judas. It grows dark, he may
    stumble.   *Exit Holofernes*
PRINCESS Alas, poor Maccabeus, how hath he been baited!
    Enter Armado the braggart as Hector
BIRON Hide thy head, Achilles, here comes Hector in
  arms.
DUMAINE Though my mocks come home by me, I will
  now be merry.
KING Hector was but a Trojan in respect of this. 630
BOYET But is this Hector?
KING I think Hector was not so clean-timbered.
LONGUEVILLE His leg is too big for Hector's.
DUMAINE More calf, certain.
BOYET No, he is best endowed in the small. 635
BIRON This cannot be Hector.
DUMAINE He's a god, or a painter, for he makes faces.
ARMADO (*as Hector*)
  The armipotent Mars, of lances the almighty,
    Gave Hector a gift—
DUMAINE A gilt nutmeg.   640
BIRON A lemon.
LONGUEVILLE Stuck with cloves.
DUMAINE No, cloven.

ARMADO Peace!
(*As Hector*) The armipotent Mars, of lances the
  almighty,   645
  Gave Hector a gift, the heir of Ilion,
A man so breathèd that certain he would fight, yea,
  From morn till night, out of his pavilion.
I am that flower—
DUMAINE   That mint.
LONGUEVILLE   That colombine.
ARMADO Sweet Lord Longueville, rein thy tongue.   650
LONGUEVILLE I must rather give it the rein, for it runs
  against Hector.
DUMAINE Ay, and Hector's a greyhound.
ARMADO The sweet war-man is dead and rotten. Sweet
chucks, beat not the bones of the buried. When he
breathed he was a man. But I will forward with my
device. (*To the Princess*) Sweet royalty, bestow on me
the sense of hearing.
   Biron steps forth
PRINCESS
  Speak, brave Hector, we are much delighted.
ARMADO I do adore thy sweet grace's slipper.   660
BOYET Loves her by the foot.
DUMAINE He may not by the yard.
ARMADO (*as Hector*)
  This Hector far surmounted Hannibal.
⌈   ⌉
ARMADO The party is gone.   665
COSTARD Fellow Hector, she is gone, she is two months
  on her way.
ARMADO What meanest thou?
COSTARD Faith, unless you play the honest Trojan the
poor wench is cast away. She's quick. The child brags
in her belly already. 'Tis yours.   671
ARMADO Dost thou infamonize me among potentates?
  Thou shalt die.
COSTARD Then shall Hector be whipped for Jaquenetta
that is quick by him, and hanged for Pompey that is
dead by him.   676
DUMAINE Most rare Pompey!
BOYET Renowned Pompey!
BIRON Greater than great—great, great, great Pompey,
  Pompey the Huge.   680
DUMAINE Hector trembles.
BIRON Pompey is moved. More Ates, more Ates—stir them
  on, stir them on!
DUMAINE Hector will challenge him.
BIRON Ay, if a have no more man's blood in his belly
  than will sup a flea.   686
ARMADO By the North Pole, I do challenge thee.
COSTARD I will not fight with a pole, like a northern man.
I'll slash, I'll do it by the sword. I bepray you, let me
borrow my arms again.   690
DUMAINE Room for the incensed Worthies.
COSTARD I'll do it in my shirt.
DUMAINE Most resolute Pompey.
MOTE (*aside to Armado*) Master, let me take you a button-
hole lower. Do you not see Pompey is uncasing for the

combat? What mean you? You will lose your
reputation.
ARMADO Gentlemen and soldiers, pardon me. I will not
combat in my shirt.
DUMAINE You may not deny it, Pompey hath made the
challenge.   701
ARMADO Sweet bloods, I both may and will.
BIRON What reason have you for't?
ARMADO The naked truth of it is, I have no shirt. I go
woolward for penance.   705
⌈MOTE⌉ True, and it was enjoined him in Rome for want
of linen, since when I'll be sworn he wore none but a
dish-clout of Jaquenetta's, and that a wears next his
heart, for a favour.
   Enter a messenger, Monsieur Mercadé
MERCADÉ
  God save you, madam.
PRINCESS   Welcome, Mercadé,   710
  But that thou interrupt'st our merriment.
MERCADÉ
  I am sorry, madam, for the news I bring
  Is heavy in my tongue. The King your father—
PRINCESS
  Dead, for my life.
MERCADÉ   Even so. My tale is told.
BIRON
  Worthies, away. The scene begins to cloud.   715
ARMADO For mine own part, I breathe free breath. I have
seen the day of wrong through the little hole of
discretion, and I will right myself like a soldier.
                  Exeunt the Worthies
KING How fares your majesty?
QUEEN
  Boyet, prepare. I will away tonight.   720
KING
  Madam, not so, I do beseech you stay.
QUEEN
  Prepare, I say. I thank you, gracious lords,
  For all your fair endeavours, and entreat,
  Out of a new-sad soul, that you vouchsafe
  In your rich wisdom to excuse or hide   725
  The liberal opposition of our spirits.
  If overboldly we have borne ourselves
  In the converse of breath, your gentleness
  Was guilty of it. Farewell, worthy lord.
  A heavy heart bears not a nimble tongue.   730
  Excuse me so coming too short of thanks,
  For my great suit so easily obtained.
KING
  The extreme parts of time extremely forms
  All causes to the purpose of his speed,
  And often at his very loose decides   735
  That which long process could not arbitrate.
  And though the mourning brow of progeny
  Forbid the smiling courtesy of love
  The holy suit which fain it would convince,
  Yet since love's argument was first on foot,   740
  Let not the cloud of sorrow jostle it

From what it purposed, since to wail friends lost
Is not by much so wholesome-profitable
As to rejoice at friends but newly found.

QUEEN
I understand you not. My griefs are double.   745

BIRON
Honest plain words best pierce the ear of grief,
And by these badges understand the King.
For your fair sakes have we neglected time,
Played foul play with our oaths. Your beauty, ladies,
Hath much deformed us, fashioning our humours
Even to the opposèd end of our intents,
And what in us hath seemed ridiculous—
As love is full of unbefitting strains,
All wanton as a child, skipping and vain,
Formed by the eye and therefore like the eye,   755
Full of strange shapes, of habits and of forms,
Varying in subjects as the eye doth roll
To every varied object in his glance;
Which parti-coated presence of loose love
Put on by us, if in your heavenly eyes   760
Have misbecomed our oaths and gravities,
Those heavenly eyes that look into these faults
Suggested us to make them. Therefore, ladies,
Our love being yours, the error that love makes
Is likewise yours. We to ourselves prove false   765
By being once false for ever to be true
To those that make us both—fair ladies, you.
And even that falsehood, in itself a sin,
Thus purifies itself and turns to grace.

QUEEN
We have received your letters full of love,   770
Your favours the ambassadors of love,
And in our maiden council rated them
At courtship, pleasant jest, and courtesy,
As bombast and as lining to the time.
But more devout than this in our respects   775
Have we not been, and therefore met your loves
In their own fashion, like a merriment.

DUMAINE
Our letters, madam, showed much more than jest.

LONGUEVILLE
So did our looks.

ROSALINE   We did not quote them so.

KING
Now, at the latest minute of the hour,   780
Grant us your loves.

QUEEN   A time, methinks, too short
To make a world-without-end bargain in.
No, no, my lord, your grace is perjured much,
Full of dear guiltiness, and therefore this:
If for my love—as there is no such cause—   785
You will do aught, this shall you do for me:
Your oath I will not trust, but go with speed
To some forlorn and naked hermitage
Remote from all the pleasures of the world.
There stay until the twelve celestial signs   790
Have brought about the annual reckoning.
If this austere, insociable life

Change not your offer made in heat of blood;
If frosts and fasts, hard lodging and thin weeds
Nip not the gaudy blossoms of your love,   795
But that it bear this trial and last love,
Then at the expiration of the year
Come challenge me, challenge me by these deserts,
And, by this virgin palm now kissing thine,
I will be thine, and till that instance shut   800
My woeful self up in a mourning house,
Raining the tears of lamentation
For the remembrance of my father's death.
If this thou do deny, let our hands part,
Neither entitled in the other's heart.   805

KING
If this, or more than this, I would deny,
To flatter up these powers of mine with rest
The sudden hand of death close up mine eye.
Hence, hermit, then. My heart is in thy breast.
They talk apart

DUMAINE (*to Catherine*)
But what to me, my love? But what to me?   810
A wife?

CATHERINE A beard, fair health, and honesty.
With three-fold love I wish you all these three.

DUMAINE
O, shall I say 'I thank you, gentle wife'?

CATHERINE
Not so, my lord. A twelvemonth and a day
I'll mark no words that smooth-faced wooers say.   815
Come when the King doth to my lady come;
Then if I have much love, I'll give you some.

DUMAINE
I'll serve thee true and faithfully till then.

CATHERINE
Yet swear not, lest ye be forsworn again.
They talk apart

LONGUEVILLE
What says Maria?

MARIA   At the twelvemonth's end   820
I'll change my black gown for a faithful friend.

LONGUEVILLE
I'll stay with patience; but the time is long.

MARIA
The liker you—few taller are so young.
They talk apart

BIRON (*to Rosaline*)
Studies my lady? Mistress, look on me.
Behold the window of my heart, mine eye,   825
What humble suit attends thy answer there.
Impose some service on me for thy love.

ROSALINE
Oft have I heard of you, my lord Biron,
Before I saw you; and the world's large tongue
Proclaims you for a man replete with mocks,   830
Full of comparisons and wounding flouts,
Which you on all estates will execute
That lie within the mercy of your wit.
To weed this wormwood from your fruitful brain,
And therewithal to win me if you please,   835

Without the which I am not to be won,
You shall this twelvemonth term from day to day
Visit the speechless sick and still converse
With groaning wretches, and your task shall be
With all the fierce endeavour of your wit   840
To enforce the painèd impotent to smile.

BIRON
To move wild laughter in the throat of death?—
It cannot be, it is impossible.
Mirth cannot move a soul in agony.

ROSALINE
Why, that's the way to choke a gibing spirit,   845
Whose influence is begot of that loose grace
Which shallow laughing hearers give to fools.
A jest's prosperity lies in the ear
Of him that hears it, never in the tongue
Of him that makes it. Then if sickly ears,   850
Deafed with the clamours of their own dear groans,
Will hear your idle scorns, continue then,
And I will have you and that fault withal.
But if they will not, throw away that spirit,
And I shall find you empty of that fault,   855
Right joyful of your reformation.

BIRON
A twelvemonth? Well, befall what will befall,
I'll jest a twelvemonth in an hospital.

QUEEN (to the King)
Ay, sweet my lord, and so I take my leave.

KING
No, madam, we will bring you on your way.   860

BIRON
Our wooing doth not end like an old play.
Jack hath not Jill. These ladies' courtesy
Might well have made our sport a comedy.

KING
Come, sir, it wants a twelvemonth an' a day,
And then 'twill end.

BIRON   That's too long for a play.   865

Enter Armado the braggart

ARMADO (to the King) Sweet majesty, vouchsafe me.

QUEEN Was not that Hector?

DUMAINE The worthy knight of Troy.

ARMADO
I will kiss thy royal finger and take leave.
I am a votary, I have vowed to Jaquenetta   870
To hold the plough for her sweet love three year.
But, most esteemed greatness, will you hear the
dialogue that the two learned men have compiled in
praise of the owl and the cuckoo? It should have
followed in the end of our show.   875

KING Call them forth quickly, we will do so.

ARMADO
Holla, approach!

Enter Holofernes, Nathaniel, Costard, Mote, Dull,
Jaquenetta, and others
                         This side is Hiems, winter,
This Ver, the spring, the one maintained by the owl,
The other by the cuckoo. Ver, begin.

SPRING (sings)
When daisies pied and violets blue,   880
    And lady-smocks, all silver-white,
And cuckoo-buds of yellow hue
    Do paint the meadows with delight,
The cuckoo then on every tree
Mocks married men, for thus sings he: 885
    Cuckoo!
Cuckoo, cuckoo—O word of fear,
Unpleasing to a married ear.

When shepherds pipe on oaten straws,
    And merry larks are ploughmen's clocks;   890
When turtles tread, and rooks and daws,
    And maidens bleach their summer smocks,
The cuckoo then on every tree
Mocks married men, for thus sings he:
    Cuckoo!   895
Cuckoo, cuckoo—O word of fear,
Unpleasing to a married ear.

WINTER (sings)
When icicles hang by the wall,
    And Dick the shepherd blows his nail,
And Tom bears logs into the hall,   900
    And milk comes frozen home in pail;
When blood is nipped, and ways be foul,
Then nightly sings the staring owl:
Tu-whit, tu-whoo!—a merry note,
While greasy Joan doth keel the pot.   905

When all aloud the wind doth blow,
    And coughing drowns the parson's saw,
And birds sit brooding in the snow,
    And Marian's nose looks red and raw;
When roasted crabs hiss in the bowl,   910
Then nightly sings the staring owl:
Tu-whit, tu-whoo!—a merry note,
While greasy Joan doth keel the pot.

⌈ARMADO⌉ The words of Mercury are harsh after the songs
of Apollo. You that way, we this way.   915

                         Exeunt, severally

ADDITIONAL PASSAGES

A. The following lines found after 4.3.293 in the First Quarto represent an unrevised version of parts of Biron's long speech, 4.3.287–341. The first six lines form the basis of 4.3.294–9; the next three are revised at 4.3.326–30; the next four at 4.3.300–2; the last nine are less directly related to the revised version.

And where that you have vowed to study, lords,
In that each of you have forsworn his book,
Can you still dream, and pore, and thereon look?
For when would you, my lord, or you, or you,
Have found the ground of study's excellence   5
Without the beauty of a woman's face?
From women's eyes this doctrine I derive.
They are the ground, the books, the academes,
From whence doth spring the true Promethean fire.
Why, universal plodding poisons up   10
The nimble spirits in the arteries,
As motion and long-during action tires
The sinewy vigour of the traveller.
Now, for not looking on a woman's face
You have in that forsworn the use of eyes,   15
And study, too, the causer of your vow.
For where is any author in the world

Teaches such beauty as a woman's eye?
Learning is but an adjunct to ourself,
And where we are, our learning likewise is.   20
Then when ourselves we see in ladies' eyes
With ourselves.
Do we not likewise see our learning there?

B. The following two lines, spoken by the Princess and found after 5.2.130 in the First Quarto, seem to represent a first draft of 5.2.131–2.

Hold, Rosaline. This favour thou shalt wear,
And then the King will court thee for his dear.

C. The following lines found after 5.2.809 in the First Quarto represent a draft version of 5.2.824–41.

BIRON
And what to me, my love? And what to me?
ROSALINE
You must be purgèd, too. Your sins are rank.
You are attaint with faults and perjury.
Therefore if you my favour mean to get
A twelvemonth shall you spend, and never rest   5
But seek the weary beds of people sick.

LOVE'S LABOUR'S WON

A BRIEF ACCOUNT

IN 1598, Francis Meres called as witnesses to Shakespeare's excellence in comedy 'his *Gêtlemē of Verona*, his *Errors*, his *Loue labors lost*, his *Loue labours wonne*, his *Midsummers night dreame*, & his *Merchant of Venice*'. This was the only evidence that Shakespeare wrote a play called *Love's Labour's Won* until the discovery in 1953 of a fragment of a bookseller's list that had been used in the binding of a volume published in 1637/8. The fragment itself appears to record items sold from 9 to 17 August 1603 by a book dealer in the south of England. Among items headed '[inte]rludes & tragedyes' are

> marchant of vennis
> taming of a shrew
> knak to know a knave
> knak to know an honest man
> loves labor lost
> loves labor won

No author is named for any of the items. All the plays named in the list except *Love's Labour's Won* are known to have been printed by 1600; all were written by 1596-7. Taken together, Meres's reference in 1598 and the 1603 fragment appear to demonstrate that a play by Shakespeare called *Love's Labour's Won* had been performed by the time Meres wrote and was in print by August 1603. Conceivably the phrase served as an alternative title for one of Shakespeare's other comedies, though the only one believed to have been written by 1598 but not listed by Meres is *The Taming of the Shrew*, which is named (as *The Taming of A Shrew*) in the bookseller's fragment. Otherwise we must suppose that *Love's Labour's Won* is the title of a lost play by Shakespeare, that no copy of the edition mentioned in the bookseller's list is extant, and that Heminges and Condell failed to include it in the 1623 Folio.

None of these suppositions is implausible. We know of at least one other lost play attributed to Shakespeare (see *Cardenio*, below), and of many lost works by contemporary playwrights. No copy of the first edition of *Titus Andronicus* was known until 1904; for *1 Henry IV* and *The Passionate Pilgrim* only a fragment of the first edition survives. And we now know that *Troilus and Cressida* was almost omitted from the 1623 Folio (probably for copyright reasons) despite its evident authenticity. It is also possible that, like most of the early editions of Shakespeare's plays, the lost edition of *Love's Labour's Won* did not name him on the title-page, and this omission might go some way to explaining the failure of the edition to survive, or (if it does still survive) to be noticed. *Love's Labour's Won* stands a much better chance of having survived, somewhere, than *Cardenio*: because it was printed, between 500 and 1,500 copies were once in circulation, whereas for *Cardenio* we know of only a single manuscript.

The evidence for the existence of the lost play (unlike that for *Cardenio*) gives us little indication of its content. Meres explicitly states, and the title implies, that it was a comedy. Its titular pairing with *Love's Labour's Lost* suggests that they may have been written at about the same time. Both Meres and the bookseller's catalogue place it after *Love's Labour's Lost*; although neither list is necessarily chronological, Meres's does otherwise agree with our own view of the order of composition of Shakespeare's comedies.

A MIDSUMMER NIGHT'S DREAM

FRANCIS MERES mentions *A Midsummer Night's Dream* in his *Palladis Tamia*, of 1598, and it was first printed in 1600. It has often been thought that Shakespeare wrote the play for an aristocratic wedding, but there is no evidence to support this speculation, and the 1600 title-page states that it had been 'sundry times publicly acted' by the Lord Chamberlain's Men. In stylistic variation it resembles *Love's Labour's Lost*: both plays employ a wide variety of verse measures and rhyme schemes, along with prose that is sometimes (as in Bottom's account of his dream, 4.1.202-15) rhetorically patterned. Probably it was written in 1594 or 1595, either just before or just after *Romeo and Juliet*.

Shakespeare built his own plot from diverse elements of literature, drama, legend, and folklore, supplemented by his imagination and observation. There are four main strands. One, which forms the basis of the action, shows the preparations for the marriage of Theseus, Duke of Athens, to Hippolyta, Queen of the Amazons, and (in the last act) its celebration. This is indebted to Chaucer's *Knight's Tale*, as is the play's second strand, the love story of Lysander and Hermia (who elope to escape her father's opposition) and of Demetrius. In Chaucer, two young men fall in love with the same girl and quarrel over her; Shakespeare adds the comic complication of another girl (Helena) jilted by, but still loving, one of the young men. A third strand shows the efforts of a group of Athenian workmen—the 'mechanicals'—led by Bottom the Weaver to prepare a play, *Pyramus and Thisbe* (based mainly on Arthur Golding's translation of Ovid's *Metamorphoses*) for performance at the Duke's wedding. The mechanicals themselves belong rather to Elizabethan England than to ancient Greece. Bottom's partial transformation into an ass has many literary precedents. Fourthly, Shakespeare depicts a quarrel between Oberon and Titania, King and Queen of the Fairies. Oberon's attendant, Robin Goodfellow, a puck (or pixie), interferes mischievously in the workmen's rehearsals and the affairs of the lovers. The fairy part of the play owes something to both folklore and literature; Robin Goodfellow was a well-known figure about whom Shakespeare could have read in Reginald Scot's *Discovery of Witchcraft* (1586).

A Midsummer Night's Dream offers a glorious celebration of the powers of the human imagination while also making comic capital out of its limitations. It is one of Shakespeare's most polished achievements, a poetic drama of exquisite grace, wit, and humanity. In performance, its imaginative unity has sometimes been violated, but it has become one of Shakespeare's most popular plays, with a special appeal for the young.

THE PERSONS OF THE PLAY

THESEUS, Duke of Athens

HIPPOLYTA, Queen of the Amazons, betrothed to Theseus

EGEUS, father of Hermia

HERMIA, daughter of Egeus, in love with Lysander

LYSANDER, loved by Hermia

DEMETRIUS, suitor to Hermia

HELENA, in love with Demetrius

OBERON, King of Fairies

TITANIA, Queen of Fairies

ROBIN GOODFELLOW, a puck

PEASEBLOSSOM
COBWEB
MOTE
MUSTARDSEED } fairies

Peter QUINCE, a carpenter

Nick BOTTOM, a weaver

Francis FLUTE, a bellows-mender

Tom SNOUT, a tinker

SNUG, a joiner

Robin STARVELING, a tailor

Attendant lords and fairies

A Midsummer Night's Dream

1.1 *Enter Theseus, Hippolyta, and Philostrate, with
others*

THESEUS

Now, fair Hippolyta, our nuptial hour
Draws on apace. Four happy days bring in
Another moon—but O, methinks how slow
This old moon wanes! She lingers my desires
Like to a stepdame or a dowager   5
Long withering out a young man's revenue.

HIPPOLYTA

Four days will quickly steep themselves in night,
Four nights will quickly dream away the time;
And then the moon, like to a silver bow
New bent in heaven, shall behold the night   10
Of our solemnities.

THESEUS   Go, Philostrate,
Stir up the Athenian youth to merriments.
Awake the pert and nimble spirit of mirth.
Turn melancholy forth to funerals—
The pale companion is not for our pomp.   15

⌈Exit Philostrate⌉

Hippolyta, I wooed thee with my sword,
And won thy love doing thee injuries.
But I will wed thee in another key—
With pomp, with triumph, and with revelling.

*Enter Egeus and his daughter Hermia, and Lysander
and Demetrius*

EGEUS

Happy be Theseus, our renownèd Duke.   20

THESEUS

Thanks, good Egeus. What's the news with thee?

EGEUS

Full of vexation come I, with complaint
Against my child, my daughter Hermia.—
Stand forth Demetrius.—My noble lord,
This man hath my consent to marry her.—   25
Stand forth Lysander.—And, my gracious Duke,
This hath bewitched the bosom of my child.
Thou, thou, Lysander, thou hast given her rhymes,
And interchanged love tokens with my child.
Thou hast by moonlight at her window sung   30
With feigning voice verses of feigning love,
And stol'n the impression of her fantasy
With bracelets of thy hair, rings, gauds, conceits,
Knacks, trifles, nosegays, sweetmeats—messengers
Of strong prevailment in unhardened youth.   35
With cunning hast thou filched my daughter's heart,
Turned her obedience which is due to me
To stubborn harshness. And, my gracious Duke,
Be it so she will not here before your grace
Consent to marry with Demetrius,   40
I beg the ancient privilege of Athens:
As she is mine, I may dispose of her,

Which shall be either to this gentleman
Or to her death, according to our law
Immediately provided in that case.   45

THESEUS

What say you, Hermia? Be advised, fair maid.
To you your father should be as a god,
One that composed your beauties, yea, and one
To whom you are but as a form in wax,
By him imprinted, and within his power   50
To leave the figure or disfigure it.
Demetrius is a worthy gentleman.

HERMIA

So is Lysander.

THESEUS   In himself he is,
But in this kind, wanting your father's voice,
The other must be held the worthier.   55

HERMIA

I would my father looked but with my eyes.

THESEUS

Rather your eyes must with his judgement look.

HERMIA

I do entreat your grace to pardon me.
I know not by what power I am made bold,
Nor how it may concern my modesty   60
In such a presence here to plead my thoughts,
But I beseech your grace that I may know
The worst that may befall me in this case
If I refuse to wed Demetrius.

THESEUS

Either to die the death, or to abjure   65
For ever the society of men.
Therefore, fair Hermia, question your desires.
Know of your youth, examine well your blood,
Whether, if you yield not to your father's choice,
You can endure the livery of a nun,   70
For aye to be in shady cloister mewed,
To live a barren sister all your life,
Chanting faint hymns to the cold fruitless moon.
Thrice blessèd they that master so their blood
To undergo such maiden pilgrimage;   75
But earthlier happy is the rose distilled
Than that which, withering on the virgin thorn,
Grows, lives, and dies in single blessedness.

HERMIA

So will I grow, so live, so die, my lord,
Ere I will yield my virgin patent up   80
Unto his lordship whose unwishèd yoke
My soul consents not to give sovereignty.

THESEUS

Take time to pause, and by the next new moon—
The sealing day betwixt my love and me
For everlasting bond of fellowship—   85
Upon that day either prepare to die

For disobedience to your father's will,
Or else to wed Demetrius, as he would,
Or on Diana's altar to protest
For aye austerity and single life.   90

DEMETRIUS
Relent, sweet Hermia; and, Lysander, yield
Thy crazèd title to my certain right.

LYSANDER
You have her father's love, Demetrius;
Let me have Hermia's. Do you marry him.

EGEUS
Scornful Lysander! True, he hath my love;   95
And what is mine my love shall render him,
And she is mine, and all my right of her
I do estate unto Demetrius.

LYSANDER ⌈to Theseus⌉
I am, my lord, as well derived as he,
As well possessed. My love is more than his,   100
My fortunes every way as fairly ranked,
If not with vantage, as Demetrius;
And—which is more than all these boasts can be—
I am beloved of beauteous Hermia.
Why should not I then prosecute my right?   105
Demetrius—I'll avouch it to his head—
Made love to Nedar's daughter, Helena,
And won her soul, and she, sweet lady, dotes,
Devoutly dotes, dotes in idolatry
Upon this spotted and inconstant man.   110

THESEUS
I must confess that I have heard so much,
And with Demetrius thought to have spoke thereof;
But, being over-full of self affairs,
My mind did lose it. But, Demetrius, come;
And come, Egeus. You shall go with me.   115
I have some private schooling for you both.
For you, fair Hermia, look you arm yourself
To fit your fancies to your father's will,
Or else the law of Athens yields you up—
Which by no means we may extenuate—   120
To death or to a vow of single life.
Come, my Hippolyta; what cheer, my love?—
Demetrius and Egeus, go along.
I must employ you in some business
Against our nuptial, and confer with you   125
Of something nearly that concerns yourselves.

EGEUS
With duty and desire we follow you.

Exeunt all but Lysander and Hermia

LYSANDER
How now, my love? Why is your cheek so pale?
How chance the roses there do fade so fast?

HERMIA
Belike for want of rain, which I could well   130
Beteem them from the tempest of my eyes.

LYSANDER
Ay me, for aught that I could ever read,
Could ever hear by tale or history,
The course of true love never did run smooth,
But either it was different in blood—   135

HERMIA
O cross!—too high to be enthralled to low.

LYSANDER
Or else misgrafted in respect of years—

HERMIA
O spite!—too old to be engaged to young.

LYSANDER
Or merit stood upon the choice of friends—

HERMIA
O hell!—to choose love by another's eyes.   140

LYSANDER
Or if there were a sympathy in choice,
War, death, or sickness did lay siege to it,
Making it momentany as a sound,
Swift as a shadow, short as any dream,
Brief as the lightning in the collied night,   145
That, in a spleen, unfolds both heaven and earth,
And, ere a man hath power to say 'Behold!',
The jaws of darkness do devour it up.
So quick bright things come to confusion.

HERMIA
If then true lovers have been ever crossed,   150
It stands as an edict in destiny.
Then let us teach our trial patience,
Because it is a customary cross,
As due to love as thoughts, and dreams, and sighs,
Wishes, and tears, poor fancy's followers.   155

LYSANDER
A good persuasion. Therefore hear me, Hermia.
I have a widow aunt, a dowager
Of great revenue, and she hath no child,
And she respects me as her only son.
From Athens is her house remote seven leagues.   160
There, gentle Hermia, may I marry thee,
And to that place the sharp Athenian law
Cannot pursue us. If thou lov'st me then,
Steal forth thy father's house tomorrow night,
And in the wood, a league without the town,   165
Where I did meet thee once with Helena
To do observance to a morn of May,
There will I stay for thee.

HERMIA   My good Lysander,
I swear to thee by Cupid's strongest bow,
By his best arrow with the golden head,   170
By the simplicity of Venus' doves,
By that which knitteth souls and prospers loves,
And by that fire which burned the Carthage queen
When the false Trojan under sail was seen;
By all the vows that ever men have broke—   175
In number more than ever women spoke—
In that same place thou hast appointed me
Tomorrow truly will I meet with thee.

LYSANDER
Keep promise, love. Look, here comes Helena.
Enter Helena

HERMIA
God speed, fair Helena. Whither away?   180

HELENA
Call you me fair? That 'fair' again unsay.
Demetrius loves your fair—O happy fair!
Your eyes are lodestars, and your tongue's sweet air
More tuneable than lark to shepherd's ear
When wheat is green, when hawthorn buds appear.
Sickness is catching. O, were favour so!   186
Your words I catch, fair Hermia; ere I go,
My ear should catch your voice, my eye your eye,
My tongue should catch your tongue's sweet melody.
Were the world mine, Demetrius being bated,   190
The rest I'd give to be to you translated.
O, teach me how you look, and with what art
You sway the motion of Demetrius' heart.

HERMIA
I frown upon him, yet he loves me still.

HELENA
O that your frowns would teach my smiles such skill!

HERMIA
I give him curses, yet he gives me love.   196

HELENA
O that my prayers could such affection move!

HERMIA
The more I hate, the more he follows me.

HELENA
The more I love, the more he hateth me.

HERMIA
His folly, Helen, is no fault of mine.   200

HELENA
None but your beauty; would that fault were mine!

HERMIA
Take comfort. He no more shall see my face.
Lysander and myself will fly this place.
Before the time I did Lysander see
Seemed Athens as a paradise to me.   205
O then, what graces in my love do dwell,
That he hath turned a heaven unto a hell?

LYSANDER
Helen, to you our minds we will unfold.
Tomorrow night, when Phoebe doth behold
Her silver visage in the wat'ry glass,   210
Decking with liquid pearl the bladed grass—
A time that lovers' sleights doth still conceal—
Through Athens' gates have we devised to steal.

HERMIA
And in the wood where often you and I
Upon faint primrose beds were wont to lie,   215
Emptying our bosoms of their counsel sweet,
There my Lysander and myself shall meet,
And thence from Athens turn away our eyes
To seek new friends and stranger companies.
Farewell, sweet playfellow. Pray thou for us,   220
And good luck grant thee thy Demetrius.—
Keep word, Lysander. We must starve our sight
From lovers' food till morrow deep midnight.

LYSANDER
I will, my Hermia.   *Exit Hermia*
Helena, adieu.
As you on him, Demetrius dote on you.   *Exit*

HELENA
How happy some o'er other some can be!   226
Through Athens I am thought as fair as she.
But what of that? Demetrius thinks not so.
He will not know what all but he do know.
And as he errs, doting on Hermia's eyes,   230
So I, admiring of his qualities,
Things base and vile, holding no quantity,
Love can transpose to form and dignity.
Love looks not with the eyes, but with the mind,
And therefore is winged Cupid painted blind.   235
Nor hath love's mind of any judgement taste;
Wings and no eyes figure unheedy haste.
And therefore is love said to be a child
Because in choice he is so oft beguiled.
As waggish boys in game themselves forswear,   240
So the boy Love is perjured everywhere.
For ere Demetrius looked on Hermia's eyne
He hailed down oaths that he was only mine,
And when this hail some heat from Hermia felt,
So he dissolved, and showers of oaths did melt.   245
I will go tell him of fair Hermia's flight.
Then to the wood will he tomorrow night
Pursue her, and for this intelligence
If I have thanks it is a dear expense.
But herein mean I to enrich my pain,   250
To have his sight thither and back again.   *Exit*

1.2   *Enter Quince the carpenter, and Snug the joiner,*
    and Bottom the weaver, and Flute the bellows-
    mender, and Snout the tinker, and Starveling the
    tailor

QUINCE Is all our company here?

BOTTOM You were best to call them generally, man by
man, according to the scrip.

QUINCE Here is the scroll of every man's name which is
thought fit through all Athens to play in our interlude
before the Duke and the Duchess on his wedding day
at night.   7

BOTTOM First, good Peter Quince, say what the play treats
on; then read the names of the actors; and so grow to
a point.   10

QUINCE Marry, our play is *The Most Lamentable Comedy
and Most Cruel Death of Pyramus and Thisbe.*

BOTTOM A very good piece of work, I assure you, and a
merry. Now, good Peter Quince, call forth your actors
by the scroll. Masters, spread yourselves.   15

QUINCE Answer as I call you. Nick Bottom, the weaver?

BOTTOM Ready. Name what part I am for, and proceed.

QUINCE You, Nick Bottom, are set down for Pyramus.

BOTTOM What is Pyramus? A lover or a tyrant?

QUINCE A lover, that kills himself most gallant for love.   20

BOTTOM That will ask some tears in the true performing

of it. If I do it, let the audience look to their eyes. I will
move stones. I will condole, in some measure. To the
rest.—Yet my chief humour is for a tyrant. I could play
'erc'les rarely, or a part to tear a cat in, to make all
split.   26

       The raging rocks
       And shivering shocks
       Shall break the locks
         Of prison gates,   30
       And Phibus' car
       Shall shine from far
       And make and mar
         The foolish Fates.   34

This was lofty. Now name the rest of the players.—
This is 'erc'les' vein, a tyrant's vein. A lover is more
condoling.

QUINCE Francis Flute, the bellows-mender?

FLUTE Here, Peter Quince.

QUINCE Flute, you must take Thisbe on you.   40

FLUTE What is Thisbe? A wand'ring knight?

QUINCE It is the lady that Pyramus must love.

FLUTE Nay, faith, let not me play a woman. I have a
beard coming.

QUINCE That's all one. You shall play it in a mask, and
you may speak as small as you will.   46

BOTTOM An I may hide my face, let me play Thisbe too.
I'll speak in a monstrous little voice: 'Thisne, Thisne!'—
'Ah Pyramus, my lover dear, thy Thisbe dear and lady
dear.'   50

QUINCE No, no, you must play Pyramus; and Flute, you
Thisbe.

BOTTOM Well, proceed.

QUINCE Robin Starveling, the tailor?

STARVELING Here, Peter Quince.   55

QUINCE Robin Starveling, you must play Thisbe's mother.
Tom Snout, the tinker?

SNOUT Here, Peter Quince.

QUINCE You, Pyramus' father; myself, Thisbe's father.
Snug the joiner, you the lion's part; and I hope here
is a play fitted.   61

SNUG Have you the lion's part written? Pray you, if it be,
give it me; for I am slow of study.

QUINCE You may do it extempore, for it is nothing but
roaring.   65

BOTTOM Let me play the lion too. I will roar that I will
do any man's heart good to hear me. I will roar that I
will make the Duke say 'Let him roar again; let him
roar again'.

QUINCE An you should do it too terribly you would fright
the Duchess and the ladies that they would shriek, and
that were enough to hang us all.   72

ALL THE REST That would hang us, every mother's son.

BOTTOM I grant you, friends, if you should fright the ladies
out of their wits they would have no more discretion
but to hang us, but I will aggravate my voice so that
I will roar you as gently as any sucking dove. I will
roar you an 'twere any nightingale.   78

QUINCE You can play no part but Pyramus; for Pyramus

is a sweet-faced man; a proper man as one shall see
in a summer's day; a most lovely, gentlemanlike man.
Therefore you must needs play Pyramus.

BOTTOM Well, I will undertake it. What beard were I best
to play it in?

QUINCE Why, what you will.   85

BOTTOM I will discharge it in either your straw-colour
beard, your orange-tawny beard, your purple-in-grain
beard, or your French-crown-colour beard, your perfect
yellow.   89

QUINCE Some of your French crowns have no hair at all,
and then you will play bare faced. But masters, here
are your parts, and I am to entreat you, request you,
and desire you to con them by tomorrow night, and
meet me in the palace wood a mile without the town
by moonlight. There will we rehearse; for if we meet
in the city we shall be dogged with company, and our
devices known. In the meantime I will draw a bill of
properties such as our play wants. I pray you fail me
not.   99

BOTTOM We will meet, and there we may rehearse most
obscenely and courageously. Take pains; be perfect.
Adieu.

QUINCE At the Duke's oak we meet.

BOTTOM Enough. Hold, or cut bowstrings.   *Exeunt*

2.1 *Enter a Fairy at one door and Robin Goodfellow, a
puck, at another*

ROBIN
How now, spirit, whither wander you?

FAIRY
    Over hill, over dale,
      Thorough bush, thorough brier,
    Over park, over pale,
      Thorough flood, thorough fire: 5
    I do wander everywhere
    Swifter than the moonës sphere,
    And I serve the Fairy Queen
    To dew her orbs upon the green.
    The cowslips tall her pensioners be.   10
    In their gold coats spots you see;
    Those be rubies, fairy favours;
    In those freckles live their savours.
    I must go seek some dewdrops here,
    And hang a pearl in every cowslip's ear.   15
Farewell, thou lob of spirits; I'll be gone.
Our Queen and all her elves come here anon.

ROBIN
The King doth keep his revels here tonight.
Take heed the Queen come not within his sight,
For Oberon is passing fell and wroth   20
Because that she, as her attendant, hath
A lovely boy stol'n from an Indian king.
She never had so sweet a changeling;
And jealous Oberon would have the child
Knight of his train, to trace the forests wild.   25
But she perforce withholds the lovèd boy,
Crowns him with flowers, and makes him all her joy.

And now they never meet in grove, or green,
By fountain clear, or spangled starlight sheen,
But they do square, that all their elves for fear   30
Creep into acorn cups, and hide them there.

FAIRY
Either I mistake your shape and making quite
Or else you are that shrewd and knavish sprite
Called Robin Goodfellow. Are not you he
That frights the maidens of the villag'ry,   35
Skim milk, and sometimes labour in the quern,
And bootless make the breathless housewife churn,
And sometime make the drink to bear no barm—
Mislead night wanderers, laughing at their harm?
Those that 'hobgoblin' call you, and 'sweet puck',   40
You do their work, and they shall have good luck.
Are not you he?

ROBIN   Thou speak'st aright;
I am that merry wanderer of the night.
I jest to Oberon, and make him smile
When I a fat and bean-fed horse beguile,   45
Neighing in likeness of a filly foal;
And sometime lurk I in a gossip's bowl
In very likeness of a roasted crab,
And when she drinks, against her lips I bob,
And on her withered dewlap pour the ale.   50
The wisest aunt telling the saddest tale
Sometime for three-foot stool mistaketh me;
Then slip I from her bum. Down topples she,
And 'tailor' cries, and falls into a cough,
And then the whole choir hold their hips, and laugh,
And waxen in their mirth, and sneeze, and swear   56
A merrier hour was never wasted there.—

Enter Oberon the King of Fairies at one door, with
his train, and Titania the Queen at another, with hers
But make room, fairy: here comes Oberon.

FAIRY
And here my mistress. Would that he were gone.

OBERON
Ill met by moonlight, proud Titania.   60

TITANIA
What, jealous Oberon?—Fairies, skip hence.
I have forsworn his bed and company.

OBERON
Tarry, rash wanton. Am not I thy lord?

TITANIA
Then I must be thy lady; but I know
When thou hast stol'n away from fairyland   65
And in the shape of Corin sat all day,
Playing on pipes of corn, and versing love
To amorous Phillida. Why art thou here
Come from the farthest step of India,
But that, forsooth, the bouncing Amazon,   70
Your buskined mistress and your warrior love,
To Theseus must be wedded, and you come
To give their bed joy and prosperity?

OBERON
How canst thou thus for shame, Titania,
Glance at my credit with Hippolyta,   75

Knowing I know thy love to Theseus?
Didst not thou lead him through the glimmering night
From Perigouna whom he ravishèd,
And make him with fair Aegles break his faith,
With Ariadne and Antiopa?   80

TITANIA
These are the forgeries of jealousy,
And never since the middle summer's spring
Met we on hill, in dale, forest, or mead,
By pavèd fountain or by rushy brook,
Or in the beachèd margin of the sea   85
To dance our ringlets to the whistling wind,
But with thy brawls thou hast disturbed our sport.
Therefore the winds, piping to us in vain,
As in revenge have sucked up from the sea
Contagious fogs which, falling in the land,   90
Hath every pelting river made so proud
That they have overborne their continents.
The ox hath therefore stretched his yoke in vain,
The ploughman lost his sweat, and the green corn
Hath rotted ere his youth attained a beard.   95
The fold stands empty in the drownèd field,
And crows are fatted with the murrain flock,
The nine men's morris is filled up with mud,
And the quaint mazes in the wanton green
For lack of tread are undistinguishable.   100
The human mortals want their winter cheer.
No night is now with hymn or carol blessed.
Therefore the moon, the governess of floods,
Pale in her anger washes all the air,
That rheumatic diseases do abound;   105
And thorough this distemperature we see
The seasons alter: hoary-headed frosts
Fall in the fresh lap of the crimson rose,
And on old Hiems' thin and icy crown
An odorous chaplet of sweet summer buds   110
Is, as in mock'ry, set. The spring, the summer,
The childing autumn, angry winter change
Their wonted liveries, and the mazèd world
By their increase now knows not which is which;
And this same progeny of evils comes   115
From our debate, from our dissension.
We are their parents and original.

OBERON
Do you amend it, then. It lies in you.
Why should Titania cross her Oberon?
I do but beg a little changeling boy   120
To be my henchman.

TITANIA   Set your heart at rest.
The fairyland buys not the child of me.
His mother was a vot'ress of my order,
And in the spicèd Indian air by night
Full often hath she gossiped by my side,   125
And sat with me on Neptune's yellow sands,
Marking th'embarkèd traders on the flood,
When we have laughed to see the sails conceive
And grow big-bellied with the wanton wind,
Which she with pretty and with swimming gait   130

Following, her womb then rich with my young squire,
Would imitate, and sail upon the land
To fetch me trifles, and return again
As from a voyage, rich with merchandise.
But she, being mortal, of that boy did die;   135
And for her sake do I rear up her boy;
And for her sake I will not part with him.

OBERON
How long within this wood intend you stay?

TITANIA
Perchance till after Theseus' wedding day.
If you will patiently dance in our round,   140
And see our moonlight revels, go with us.
If not, shun me, and I will spare your haunts.

OBERON
Give me that boy and I will go with thee.

TITANIA
Not for thy fairy kingdom.—Fairies, away.
We shall chide downright if I longer stay.   145
Exeunt Titania and her train

OBERON
Well, go thy way. Thou shalt not from this grove
Till I torment thee for this injury.—
My gentle puck, come hither. Thou rememb'rest
Since once I sat upon a promontory
And heard a mermaid on a dolphin's back   150
Uttering such dulcet and harmonious breath
That the rude sea grew civil at her song
And certain stars shot madly from their spheres
To hear the sea-maid's music?

ROBIN   I remember.

OBERON
That very time I saw, but thou couldst not,   155
Flying between the cold moon and the earth
Cupid, all armed. A certain aim he took
At a fair vestal thronèd by the west,
And loosed his love-shaft smartly from his bow
As it should pierce a hundred thousand hearts.   160
But I might see young Cupid's fiery shaft
Quenched in the chaste beams of the wat'ry moon
And the imperial vot'ress passèd on,
In maiden meditation, fancy-free.
Yet marked I where the bolt of Cupid fell.   165
It fell upon a little western flower—
Before, milk-white; now, purple with love's wound—
And maidens call it love-in-idleness.
Fetch me that flower; the herb I showed thee once.
The juice of it on sleeping eyelids laid   170
Will make or man or woman madly dote
Upon the next live creature that it sees.
Fetch me this herb, and be thou here again
Ere the leviathan can swim a league.

ROBIN
I'll put a girdle round about the earth   175
In forty minutes.   *Exit*

OBERON   Having once this juice
I'll watch Titania when she is asleep,

And drop the liquor of it in her eyes.
The next thing then she waking looks upon—
Be it on lion, bear, or wolf, or bull,   180
On meddling monkey, or on busy ape—
She shall pursue it with the soul of love.
And ere I take this charm from off her sight—
As I can take it with another herb—
I'll make her render up her page to me.   185
But who comes here? I am invisible,
And I will overhear their conference.
Enter Demetrius, Helena following him

DEMETRIUS
I love thee not, therefore pursue me not.
Where is Lysander, and fair Hermia?
The one I'll slay, the other slayeth me.   190
Thou told'st me they were stol'n unto this wood,
And here am I, and wood within this wood
Because I cannot meet my Hermia.
Hence, get thee gone, and follow me no more.

HELENA
You draw me, you hard-hearted adamant,   195
But yet you draw not iron; for my heart
Is true as steel. Leave you your power to draw,
And I shall have no power to follow you.

DEMETRIUS
Do I entice you? Do I speak you fair?
Or rather do I not in plainest truth   200
Tell you I do not nor I cannot love you?

HELENA
And even for that do I love you the more.
I am your spaniel, and, Demetrius,
The more you beat me I will fawn on you.
Use me but as your spaniel: spurn me, strike me,   205
Neglect me, lose me; only give me leave,
Unworthy as I am, to follow you.
What worser place can I beg in your love—
And yet a place of high respect with me—
Than to be usèd as you use your dog?   210

DEMETRIUS
Tempt not too much the hatred of my spirit;
For I am sick when I do look on thee.

HELENA
And I am sick when I look not on you.

DEMETRIUS
You do impeach your modesty too much,
To leave the city and commit yourself   215
Into the hands of one that loves you not;
To trust the opportunity of night,
And the ill counsel of a desert place,
With the rich worth of your virginity.

HELENA
Your virtue is my privilege, for that   220
It is not night when I do see your face;
Therefore I think I am not in the night,
Nor doth this wood lack worlds of company;
For you in my respect are all the world.
Then how can it be said I am alone,   225
When all the world is here to look on me?

DEMETRIUS

  I'll run from thee, and hide me in the brakes,

  And leave thee to the mercy of wild beasts.

HELENA

  The wildest hath not such a heart as you.

  Run when you will. The story shall be changed: 230

  Apollo flies, and Daphne holds the chase.

  The dove pursues the griffin, the mild hind

  Makes speed to catch the tiger: bootless speed,

  When cowardice pursues, and valour flies.

DEMETRIUS

  I will not stay thy questions. Let me go;   235

  Or if thou follow me, do not believe

  But I shall do thee mischief in the wood.

HELENA

  Ay, in the temple, in the town, the field,

  You do me mischief. Fie, Demetrius,

  Your wrongs do set a scandal on my sex.   240

  We cannot fight for love as men may do;

  We should be wooed, and were not made to woo.

  I'll follow thee, and make a heaven of hell,

  To die upon the hand I love so well.

         ⌐Exit Demetrius, Helena following him⌐

OBERON

  Fare thee well, nymph. Ere he do leave this grove   245

  Thou shalt fly him, and he shall seek thy love.

       Enter Robin Goodfellow the puck

  Hast thou the flower there? Welcome, wanderer.

ROBIN

  Ay, there it is.

OBERON   I pray thee give it me.

  I know a bank where the wild thyme blows,

  Where oxlips and the nodding violet grows,   250

  Quite overcanopied with luscious woodbine,

  With sweet musk-roses, and with eglantine.

  There sleeps Titania sometime of the night,

  Lulled in these flowers with dances and delight;

  And there the snake throws her enamelled skin,   255

  Weed wide enough to wrap a fairy in;

  And with the juice of this I'll streak her eyes,

  And make her full of hateful fantasies.

  Take thou some of it, and seek through this grove.

  A sweet Athenian lady is in love   260

  With a disdainful youth. Anoint his eyes;

  But do it when the next thing he espies

  May be the lady. Thou shalt know the man

  By the Athenian garments he hath on.

  Effect it with some care, that he may prove   265

  More fond on her than she upon her love;

  And look thou meet me ere the first cock crow.

ROBIN

  Fear not, my lord. Your servant shall do so.

               Exeunt severally

2.2   *Enter Titania, Queen of Fairies, with her train*

TITANIA

  Come, now a roundel and a fairy song,

  Then for the third part of a minute hence:

Some to kill cankers in the musk-rose buds,

Some war with reremice for their leathern wings

To make my small elves coats, and some keep back   5

The clamorous owl, that nightly hoots and wonders

At our quaint spirits. Sing me now asleep;

Then to your offices, and let me rest.

       She lies down. Fairies sing

⌐FIRST FAIRY⌐

  You spotted snakes with double tongue,

    Thorny hedgehogs, be not seen;   10

  Newts and blindworms, do no wrong;

    Come not near our Fairy Queen.

⌐CHORUS⌐ ⌐*dancing*⌐

    Philomel with melody,

    Sing in our sweet lullaby;

  Lulla, lulla, lullaby; lulla, lulla, lullaby.   15

      Never harm

      Nor spell nor charm

    Come our lovely lady nigh.

    So good night, with lullaby.

FIRST FAIRY

  Weaving spiders, come not here;   20

    Hence, you long-legged spinners, hence;

  Beetles black, approach not near;

    Worm nor snail do no offence.

⌐CHORUS⌐ ⌐*dancing*⌐

    Philomel with melody,

    Sing in our sweet lullaby;   25

  Lulla, lulla, lullaby; lulla, lulla, lullaby.

      Never harm

      Nor spell nor charm

    Come our lovely lady nigh.

    So good night, with lullaby.   30

       Titania sleeps

SECOND FAIRY

  Hence, away. Now all is well.

  One aloof stand sentinel.

         Exeunt all but Titania ⌐*and the sentinel*⌐

       Enter Oberon. He drops the juice on Titania's

       eyelids

OBERON

  What thou seest when thou dost wake,

  Do it for thy true love take;

  Love and languish for his sake.   •   35

  Be it ounce, or cat, or bear,

  Pard, or boar with bristled hair,

  In thy eye that shall appear

  When thou wak'st, it is thy dear.   39

  Wake when some vile thing is near.   *Exit*

       Enter Lysander and Hermia

LYSANDER

  Fair love, you faint with wand'ring in the wood,

    And, to speak truth, I have forgot our way.

  We'll rest us, Hermia, if you think it good,

    And tarry for the comfort of the day.

HERMIA

Be it so, Lysander. Find you out a bed;   45
For I upon this bank will rest my head.
⌈*She lies down*⌉

LYSANDER

One turf shall serve as pillow for us both;
One heart, one bed; two bosoms, and one troth.

HERMIA

Nay, good Lysander; for my sake, my dear,
Lie further off yet; do not lie so near.   50

LYSANDER

O, take the sense, sweet, of my innocence!
Love takes the meaning in love's conference —
I mean that my heart unto yours is knit,
So that but one heart we can make of it.
Two bosoms interchainèd with an oath;   55
So, then, two bosoms and a single troth.
Then by your side no bed-room me deny;
For lying so, Hermia, I do not lie.

HERMIA

Lysander riddles very prettily.
Now much beshrew my manners and my pride   60
If Hermia meant to say Lysander lied.
But, gentle friend, for love and courtesy,
Lie further off, in humane modesty.
Such separation as may well be said
Becomes a virtuous bachelor and a maid,   65
So far be distant; and good night, sweet friend.
Thy love ne'er alter till thy sweet life end.

LYSANDER

Amen, amen, to that fair prayer say I;
And then end life when I end loyalty.
Here is my bed; sleep give thee all his rest.   70
He lies down

HERMIA

With half that wish the wisher's eyes be pressed.
They sleep apart.
Enter Robin Goodfellow the puck

ROBIN

Through the forest have I gone,
But Athenian found I none
On whose eyes I might approve
This flower's force in stirring love.   75
Night and silence. Who is here?
Weeds of Athens he doth wear.
This is he my master said
Despisèd the Athenian maid —
And here the maiden, sleeping sound   80
On the dank and dirty ground.
Pretty soul, she durst not lie
Near this lack-love, this kill-courtesy.
Churl, upon thy eyes I throw
All the power this charm doth owe.   85
He drops the juice on Lysander's eyelids
When thou wak'st, let love forbid
Sleep his seat on thy eyelid.
So, awake when I am gone.
For I must now to Oberon.   *Exit*

Enter Demetrius and Helena, running

HELENA

Stay, though thou kill me, sweet Demetrius.   90

DEMETRIUS

I charge thee hence, and do not haunt me thus.

HELENA

O, wilt thou darkling leave me? Do not so.

DEMETRIUS

Stay, on thy peril; I alone will go.   *Exit*

HELENA

O, I am out of breath in this fond chase.
The more my prayer, the lesser is my grace.   95
Happy is Hermia, wheresoe'er she lies;
For she hath blessèd and attractive eyes.
How came her eyes so bright? Not with salt tears —
If so, my eyes are oft'ner washed than hers.
No, no; I am as ugly as a bear,   100
For beasts that meet me run away for fear.
Therefore no marvel though Demetrius
Do, as a monster, fly my presence thus.
What wicked and dissembling glass of mine
Made me compare with Hermia's sphery eyne!   105
But who is here? Lysander, on the ground?
Dead, or asleep? I see no blood, no wound.
Lysander, if you live, good sir, awake.

LYSANDER (*awaking*)

And run through fire I will for thy sweet sake.
Transparent Helena, nature shows art   110
That through thy bosom makes me see thy heart.
Where is Demetrius? O, how fit a word
Is that vile name to perish on my sword!

HELENA

Do not say so, Lysander; say not so.
What though he love your Hermia? Lord, what
though?   115
Yet Hermia still loves you; then be content.

LYSANDER

Content with Hermia? No, I do repent
The tedious minutes I with her have spent.
Not Hermia but Helena I love.
Who will not change a raven for a dove?   120
The will of man is by his reason swayed,
And reason says you are the worthier maid.
Things growing are not ripe until their season,
So I, being young, till now ripe not to reason.
And, touching now the point of human skill,   125
Reason becomes the marshal to my will,
And leads me to your eyes, where I o'erlook
Love's stories written in love's richest book.

HELENA

Wherefore was I to this keen mockery born?
When at your hands did I deserve this scorn?   130
Is't not enough, is't not enough, young man,
That I did never — no, nor never can —
Deserve a sweet look from Demetrius' eye,
But you must flout my insufficiency?
Good troth, you do me wrong; good sooth, you do,
In such disdainful manner me to woo.   136

But fare you well. Perforce I must confess
I thought you lord of more true gentleness.
O, that a lady of one man refused
Should of another therefore be abused!   *Exit*

LYSANDER
She sees not Hermia. Hermia, sleep thou there,   141
And never mayst thou come Lysander near;
For as a surfeit of the sweetest things
The deepest loathing to the stomach brings,
Or as the heresies that men do leave   145
Are hated most of those they did deceive,
So thou, my surfeit and my heresy,
Of all be hated, but the most of me;
And all my powers, address your love and might
To honour Helen, and to be her knight.   *Exit*

HERMIA (*awaking*)
Help me, Lysander, help me! Do thy best   151
To pluck this crawling serpent from my breast!
Ay me, for pity. What a dream was here?
Lysander, look how I do quake with fear.
Methought a serpent ate my heart away,   155
And you sat smiling at his cruel prey.
Lysander—what, removed? Lysander, lord—
What, out of hearing, gone? No sound, no word?
Alack, where are you? Speak an if you hear,
Speak, of all loves. I swoon almost with fear.   160
No? Then I well perceive you are not nigh.
Either death or you I'll find immediately.   *Exit*

3.1   *Enter the clowns: Quince, Snug, Bottom, Flute,*
          Snout, and Starveling
BOTTOM Are we all met?
QUINCE Pat, pat; and here's a marvellous convenient
place for our rehearsal. This green plot shall be our
stage, this hawthorn brake our tiring-house, and we
will do it in action as we will do it before the Duke.   5
BOTTOM Peter Quince?
QUINCE What sayst thou, bully Bottom?
BOTTOM There are things in this comedy of Pyramus and
Thisbe that will never please. First, Pyramus must draw
a sword to kill himself, which the ladies cannot abide.
How answer you that?   11
SNOUT By'r la'kin, a parlous fear.
STARVELING I believe we must leave the killing out, when
all is done.   14
BOTTOM Not a whit. I have a device to make all well.
Write me a prologue, and let the prologue seem to say
we will do no harm with our swords, and that Pyramus
is not killed indeed; and for the more better assurance,
tell them that I, Pyramus, am not Pyramus, but Bottom
the weaver. This will put them out of fear.   20
QUINCE Well, we will have such a prologue; and it shall
be written in eight and six.
BOTTOM No, make it two more: let it be written in eight
and eight.
SNOUT Will not the ladies be afeard of the lion?   25
STARVELING I fear it, I promise you.
BOTTOM Masters, you ought to consider with yourself, to

bring in—God shield us—a lion among ladies is a most
dreadful thing; for there is not a more fearful wild fowl
than your lion living, and we ought to look to't.   30
SNOUT Therefore another prologue must tell he is not a
lion.
BOTTOM Nay, you must name his name, and half his face
must be seen through the lion's neck, and he himself
must speak through, saying thus or to the same defect:
'ladies', or 'fair ladies, I would wish you' or 'I would
request you' or 'I would entreat you not to fear, not
to tremble. My life for yours. If you think I come hither
as a lion, it were pity of my life. No, I am no such
thing. I am a man, as other men are'—and there,
indeed, let him name his name, and tell them plainly
he is Snug the joiner.
QUINCE Well, it shall be so; but there is two hard things:
that is, to bring the moonlight into a chamber—for
you know Pyramus and Thisbe meet by moonlight.   45
⌈SNOUT⌉ Doth the moon shine that night we play our
play?
BOTTOM A calendar, a calendar—look in the almanac,
find out moonshine, find out moonshine.
          ⌈*Enter Robin Goodfellow the puck, invisible*⌉
QUINCE ⌈*with a book*⌉ Yes, it doth shine that night.   50
BOTTOM Why, then may you leave a casement of the great
chamber window where we play open, and the moon
may shine in at the casement.
QUINCE Ay, or else one must come in with a bush of
thorns and a lantern and say he comes to disfigure, or
to present, the person of Moonshine. Then there is
another thing: we must have a wall in the great
chamber; for Pyramus and Thisbe, says the story, did
talk through the chink of a wall.
SNOUT You can never bring in a wall. What say you,
Bottom?   61
BOTTOM Some man or other must present Wall; and let
him have some plaster, or some loam, or some roughcast about him, to signify 'wall'; and let him hold his
fingers thus, and through that cranny shall Pyramus
and Thisbe whisper.   66
QUINCE If that may be, then all is well. Come, sit down
every mother's son, and rehearse your parts. Pyramus,
you begin. When you have spoken your speech, enter
into that brake; and so everyone according to his cue.
ROBIN (*aside*)
What hempen homespuns have we swagg'ring here
So near the cradle of the Fairy Queen?
What, a play toward? I'll be an auditor—
An actor, too, perhaps, if I see cause.
QUINCE Speak, Pyramus. Thisbe, stand forth.   75
BOTTOM (*as Pyramus*)
Thisbe, the flowers of odious savours sweet.
QUINCE Odours, odours.
BOTTOM (*as Pyramus*)   Odours savours sweet:
So hath thy breath, my dearest Thisbe dear.
But hark, a voice. Stay thou but here a while,   80
And by and by I will to thee appear.   *Exit*
⌈ROBIN⌉ (*aside*)
A stranger Pyramus than e'er played here.   *Exit*

FLUTE Must I speak now?

QUINCE Ay, marry must you. For you must understand he goes but to see a noise that he heard, and is to come again. 86

FLUTE (*as Thisbe*)
Most radiant Pyramus, most lily-white of hue,
Of colour like the red rose on triumphant brier;
Most bristly juvenile, and eke most lovely Jew,
 As true as truest horse that yet would never tire: 90
I'll meet thee, Pyramus, at Ninny's tomb.

QUINCE Ninus' tomb, man!—Why, you must not speak that yet. That you answer to Pyramus. You speak all your part at once, cues and all.—Pyramus, enter: your cue is past; it is 'never tire'. 95

FLUTE O.
 (*As Thisbe*) As true as truest horse that yet would never tire.
 Enter ⌈Robin leading⌉ Bottom with the ass-head

BOTTOM (*as Pyramus*)
 If I were fair, Thisbe, I were only thine.

QUINCE O monstrous! O strange! We are haunted. Pray, masters; fly, masters: help! *⌈The clowns all exeunt⌉*

ROBIN
 I'll follow you, I'll lead you about a round, 101
 Through bog, through bush, through brake, through brier.
Sometime a horse I'll be, sometime a hound,
A hog, a headless bear, sometime a fire, 104
And neigh, and bark, and grunt, and roar, and burn,
Like horse, hound, hog, bear, fire, at every turn. *Exit*
 ⌈Enter Bottom again, with the ass-head⌉

BOTTOM Why do they run away? This is a knavery of them to make me afeard.
 Enter Snout

SNOUT O Bottom, thou art changed. What do I see on thee? 110

BOTTOM What do you see? You see an ass-head of your own, do you? *⌈Exit Snout⌉*
 Enter Quince

QUINCE Bless thee, Bottom, bless thee. Thou art translated.
 Exit

BOTTOM I see their knavery. This is to make an ass of me, to fright me, if they could; but I will not stir from this place, do what they can. I will walk up and down here, and I will sing, that they shall hear I am not afraid.
 (*Sings*)
 The ousel cock so black of hue,
  With orange-tawny bill;
 The throstle with his note so true, 120
  The wren with little quill.

TITANIA (*awaking*)
 What angel wakes me from my flow'ry bed?

BOTTOM (*sings*)
 The finch, the sparrow, and the lark,
  The plainsong cuckoo grey,
 Whose note full many a man doth mark, 125
 And dares not answer 'Nay'—

for indeed, who would set his wit to so foolish a bird? Who would give a bird the lie, though he cry 'Cuckoo' never so?

TITANIA
 I pray thee, gentle mortal, sing again. 130
 Mine ear is much enamoured of thy note;
 So is mine eye enthrallèd to thy shape;
 And thy fair virtue's force perforce doth move me
 On the first view to say, to swear, I love thee. 134

BOTTOM Methinks, mistress, you should have little reason for that. And yet, to say the truth, reason and love keep little company together nowadays—the more the pity that some honest neighbours will not make them friends. Nay, I can gleek upon occasion.

TITANIA
 Thou art as wise as thou art beautiful. 140

BOTTOM Not so, neither; but if I had wit enough to get out of this wood, I have enough to serve mine own turn.

TITANIA
 Out of this wood do not desire to go.
 Thou shalt remain here, whether thou wilt or no. 145
 I am a spirit of no common rate:
 The summer still doth tend upon my state;
 And I do love thee. Therefore go with me.
 I'll give thee fairies to attend on thee,
 And they shall fetch thee jewels from the deep, 150
 And sing while thou on pressèd flowers dost sleep;
 And I will purge thy mortal grossness so
 That thou shalt like an airy spirit go.
 Peaseblossom, Cobweb, Mote, and Mustardseed!
 Enter four fairies: Peaseblossom, Cobweb, Mote, and Mustardseed

A FAIRY
 Ready.

ANOTHER And I.

ANOTHER   And I.

ANOTHER   And I.

⌈ALL FOUR⌉   Where shall we go? 155

TITANIA
 Be kind and courteous to this gentleman.
 Hop in his walks, and gambol in his eyes.
 Feed him with apricots and dewberries,
 With purple grapes, green figs, and mulberries;
 The honeybags steal from the humble-bees, 160
 And for night tapers crop their waxen thighs
 And light them at the fiery glow-worms' eyes
 To have my love to bed, and to arise;
 And pluck the wings from painted butterflies
 To fan the moonbeams from his sleeping eyes. 165
 Nod to him, elves, and do him courtesies.

A FAIRY Hail, mortal.

⌈ANOTHER⌉ Hail.

ANOTHER Hail.

ANOTHER Hail. 170

BOTTOM I cry your worships mercy, heartily.—I beseech your worship's name.

COBWEB Cobweb.

BOTTOM I shall desire you of more acquaintance, good
  Master Cobweb. If I cut my finger, I shall make bold
  with you.—Your name, honest gentleman?   176

PEASEBLOSSOM Peaseblossom.

BOTTOM I pray you commend me to Mistress Squash, your
  mother, and to Master Peascod, your father. Good
  Master Peaseblossom, I shall desire you of more
  acquaintance, too.—Your name, I beseech you, sir?

MUSTARDSEED Mustardseed.   182

BOTTOM Good Master Mustardseed, I know your patience
  well. That same cowardly giantlike ox-beef hath
  devoured many a gentleman of your house. I promise
  you your kindred hath made my eyes water ere now.
  I desire you of more acquaintance, good Master
  Mustardseed.   188

TITANIA (to the Fairies)
  Come, wait upon him, lead him to my bower.
    The moon, methinks, looks with a wat'ry eye,   190
  And when she weeps, weeps every little flower,
    Lamenting some enforcèd chastity.
  Tie up my love's tongue; bring him silently.   Exeunt

3.2   Enter Oberon, King of Fairies
OBERON
  I wonder if Titania be awaked,
  Then what it was that next came in her eye,
  Which she must dote on in extremity.
    Enter Robin Goodfellow
  Here comes my messenger. How now, mad spirit?
  What nightrule now about this haunted grove?   5
ROBIN
  My mistress with a monster is in love.
  Near to her close and consecrated bower
  While she was in her dull and sleeping hour
  A crew of patches, rude mechanicals
  That work for bread upon Athenian stalls,   10
  Were met together to rehearse a play
  Intended for great Theseus' nuptial day.
  The shallowest thickskin of that barren sort,
  Who Pyramus presented, in their sport
  Forsook his scene and entered in a brake,   15
  When I did him at this advantage take.
  An ass's nole I fixèd on his head.
  Anon his Thisbe must be answerèd,
  And forth my mimic comes. When they him spy—
  As wild geese that the creeping fowler eye,   20
  Or russet-pated choughs, many in sort,
  Rising and cawing at the gun's report,
  Sever themselves and madly sweep the sky—
  So, at his sight, away his fellows fly,
  And at our stamp here o'er and o'er one falls.   25
  He 'Murder' cries, and help from Athens calls.
  Their sense thus weak, lost with their fears thus
      strong,
  Made senseless things begin to do them wrong.
  For briers and thorns at their apparel snatch;   29
  Some sleeves, some hats—from yielders all things catch.

  I led them on in this distracted fear,
  And left sweet Pyramus translated there;
  When in that moment, so it came to pass,
  Titania waked and straightway loved an ass.
OBERON
  This falls out better than I could devise.   35
  But hast thou yet latched the Athenian's eyes
  With the love juice, as I did bid thee do?
ROBIN
  I took him sleeping; that is finished, too;
  And the Athenian woman by his side,
  That when he waked of force she must be eyed.   40
    Enter Demetrius and Hermia
OBERON
  Stand close. This is the same Athenian.
ROBIN
  This is the woman, but not this the man.
    [They stand apart]
DEMETRIUS
  O, why rebuke you him that loves you so?
  Lay breath so bitter on your bitter foe.
HERMIA
  Now I but chide, but I should use thee worse;   45
  For thou, I fear, hast given me cause to curse.
  If thou hast slain Lysander in his sleep,
  Being o'er shoes in blood, plunge in the deep,
  And kill me too.
  The sun was not so true unto the day   50
  As he to me. Would he have stolen away
  From sleeping Hermia? I'll believe as soon
  This whole earth may be bored, and that the moon
  May through the centre creep, and so displease
  Her brother's noontide with th'Antipodes.   55
  It cannot be but thou hast murdered him.
  So should a murderer look—so dead, so grim.
DEMETRIUS
  So should the murdered look, and so should I,
  Pierced through the heart with your stern cruelty.
  Yet you, the murderer, look as bright, as clear   60
  As yonder Venus in her glimmering sphere.
HERMIA
  What's this to my Lysander? Where is he?
  Ah, good Demetrius, wilt thou give him me?
DEMETRIUS
  I had rather give his carcass to my hounds.
HERMIA
  Out, dog; out, cur. Thou driv'st me past the bounds
  Of maiden's patience. Hast thou slain him then?   66
  Henceforth be never numbered among men.
  O, once tell true; tell true, even for my sake.
  Durst thou have looked upon him being awake,
  And hast thou killed him sleeping? O brave touch!   70
  Could not a worm, an adder do so much?—
  An adder did it, for with doubler tongue
  Than thine, thou serpent, never adder stung.
DEMETRIUS
  You spend your passion on a misprised mood.
  I am not guilty of Lysander's blood,   75
  Nor is he dead, for aught that I can tell.

HERMIA
I pray thee, tell me then that he is well.
DEMETRIUS
And if I could, what should I get therefor?
HERMIA
A privilege never to see me more;
And from thy hated presence part I so.   80
See me no more, whether he be dead or no.   *Exit*
DEMETRIUS
There is no following her in this fierce vein.
Here therefore for a while I will remain.
So sorrow's heaviness doth heavier grow
For debt that bankrupt sleep doth sorrow owe,   85
Which now in some slight measure it will pay,
If for his tender here I make some stay.
He lies down and sleeps
OBERON (*to Robin*)
What hast thou done? Thou hast mistaken quite,
And laid the love juice on some true love's sight.
Of thy misprision must perforce ensue   90
Some true love turned, and not a false turned true.
ROBIN
Then fate o'errules, that, one man holding troth,
A million fail, confounding oath on oath.
OBERON
About the wood go swifter than the wind,
And Helena of Athens look thou find.   95
All fancy-sick she is, and pale of cheer
With sighs of love that costs the fresh blood dear.
By some illusion see thou bring her here.
I'll charm his eyes against she do appear.
ROBIN
I go, I go—look how I go,   100
Swifter than arrow from the Tartar's bow.   *Exit*
OBERON
Flower of this purple dye,
Hit with Cupid's archery,
Sink in apple of his eye.
He drops the juice on Demetrius' eyelids
When his love he doth espy,   105
Let her shine as gloriously
As the Venus of the sky.
When thou wak'st, if she be by,
Beg of her for remedy.
Enter Robin Goodfellow, the puck
ROBIN
Captain of our fairy band,   110
Helena is here at hand,
And the youth mistook by me,
Pleading for a lover's fee.
Shall we their fond pageant see?
Lord, what fools these mortals be!   115
OBERON
Stand aside. The noise they make
Will cause Demetrius to awake.
ROBIN
Then will two at once woo one.
That must needs be sport alone;

And those things do best please me   120
That befall prepost'rously.
[They stand apart.]
Enter Helena, Lysander [following her]
LYSANDER
Why should you think that I should woo in scorn?
Scorn and derision never come in tears.
Look when I vow, I weep; and vows so born,
In their nativity all truth appears.   125
How can these things in me seem scorn to you,
Bearing the badge of faith to prove them true?
HELENA
You do advance your cunning more and more,
When truth kills truth—O devilish holy fray!
These vows are Hermia's. Will you give her o'er   130
Weigh oath with oath, and you will nothing weigh.
Your vows to her and me put in two scales
Will even weigh, and both as light as tales.
LYSANDER
I had no judgement when to her I swore.
HELENA
Nor none, in my mind, now you give her o'er.   135
LYSANDER
Demetrius loves her, and he loves not you.
[HELENA]
┌   ┐
DEMETRIUS (*awaking*)
O Helen, goddess, nymph, perfect, divine!
To what, my love, shall I compare thine eyne?
Crystal is muddy. O, how ripe in show   140
Thy lips, those kissing cherries, tempting grow!
That pure congealèd white—high Taurus' snow,
Fanned with the eastern wind—turns to a crow
When thou hold'st up thy hand. O, let me kiss
This princess of pure white, this seal of bliss!   145
HELENA
O spite! O hell! I see you all are bent
To set against me for your merriment.
If you were civil, and knew courtesy,
You would not do me thus much injury.
Can you not hate me—as I know you do—   150
But you must join in souls to mock me too?
If you were men, as men you are in show,
You would not use a gentle lady so,
To vow and swear and superpraise my parts
When I am sure you hate me with your hearts.   155
You both are rivals and love Hermia,
And now both rivals to mock Helena.
A trim exploit, a manly enterprise—
To conjure tears up in a poor maid's eyes
With your derision. None of noble sort   160
Would so offend a virgin, and extort
A poor soul's patience, all to make you sport.
LYSANDER
You are unkind, Demetrius. Be not so.
For you love Hermia; this you know I know.
And here with all good will, with all my heart,   165
In Hermia's love I yield you up my part;

And yours of Helena to me bequeath,
Whom I do love, and will do till my death.
HELENA
Never did mockers waste more idle breath.
DEMETRIUS
Lysander, keep thy Hermia. I will none.   170
If e'er I loved her, all that love is gone.
My heart to her but as guestwise sojourned
And now to Helen is it home returned,
There to remain.
LYSANDER   Helen, it is not so.
DEMETRIUS
Disparage not the faith thou dost not know,   175
Lest to thy peril thou aby it dear.
      Enter Hermia
Look where thy love comes; yonder is thy dear.
HERMIA
Dark night, that from the eye his function takes,
The ear more quick of apprehension makes.
Wherein it doth impair the seeing sense,   180
It pays the hearing double recompense.
Thou art not by mine eye, Lysander, found;
Mine ear, I thank it, brought me to thy sound.
But why unkindly didst thou leave me so?
LYSANDER
Why should he stay whom love doth press to go?   185
HERMIA
What love could press Lysander from my side?
LYSANDER
Lysander's love, that would not let him bide:
Fair Helena, who more engilds the night
Than all yon fiery O's and eyes of light.
Why seek'st thou me? Could not this make thee know
The hate I bare thee made me leave thee so?   191
HERMIA
You speak not as you think. It cannot be.
HELENA [*aside*]
Lo, she is one of this confederacy.
Now I perceive they have conjoined all three
To fashion this false sport in spite of me.—   195
Injurious Hermia, most ungrateful maid,
Have you conspired, have you with these contrived
To bait me with this foul derision?
Is all the counsel that we two have shared—
The sisters' vows, the hours that we have spent   200
When we have chid the hasty-footed time
For parting us—O, is all quite forgot?
All schooldays' friendship, childhood innocence?
We, Hermia, like two artificial gods
Have with our needles created both one flower,   205
Both on one sampler, sitting on one cushion,
Both warbling of one song, both in one key,
As if our hands, our sides, voices, and minds
Had been incorporate. So we grew together,
Like to a double cherry: seeming parted,   210
But yet an union in partition,
Two lovely berries moulded on one stem.
So, with two seeming bodies but one heart,
Two of the first—like coats in heraldry,

Due but to one and crownèd with one crest.   215
And will you rend our ancient love asunder,
To join with men in scorning your poor friend?
It is not friendly, 'tis not maidenly.
Our sex as well as I may chide you for it,
Though I alone do feel the injury.   220
HERMIA
I am amazèd at your passionate words.
I scorn you not. It seems that you scorn me.
HELENA
Have you not set Lysander, as in scorn,
To follow me, and praise my eyes and face?
And made your other love, Demetrius—   225
Who even but now did spurn me with his foot—
To call me goddess, nymph, divine, and rare,
Precious, celestial? Wherefore speaks he this
To her he hates? And wherefore doth Lysander
Deny your love so rich within his soul,   230
And tender me, forsooth, affection,
But by your setting on, by your consent?
What though I be not so in grace as you,
So hung upon with love, so fortunate,
But miserable most, to love unloved—   235
This you should pity rather than despise.
HERMIA
I understand not what you mean by this.
HELENA
Ay, do. Persever, counterfeit sad looks,
Make mouths upon me when I turn my back,
Wink each at other, hold the sweet jest up.   240
This sport well carried shall be chronicled.
If you have any pity, grace, or manners,
You would not make me such an argument.
But fare ye well. 'Tis partly my own fault,
Which death or absence soon shall remedy.   245
LYSANDER
Stay, gentle Helena, hear my excuse,
My love, my life, my soul, fair Helena.
HELENA
O excellent!
HERMIA (*to Lysander*) Sweet, do not scorn her so.
DEMETRIUS (*to Lysander*)
If she cannot entreat I can compel.
LYSANDER
Thou canst compel no more than she entreat.   250
Thy threats have no more strength than her weak
      prayers.—
Helen, I love thee; by my life I do.
I swear by that which I will lose for thee
To prove him false that says I love thee not.
DEMETRIUS (*to Helena*)
I say I love thee more than he can do.   255
LYSANDER
If thou say so, withdraw, and prove it too.
DEMETRIUS
Quick, come.
HERMIA   Lysander, whereto tends all this?
      [*She takes him by the arm*]

LYSANDER
  Away, you Ethiope.
DEMETRIUS   No, no, sir, yield.
  Seem to break loose, take on as you would follow,
  But yet come not. You are a tame man; go.   260
LYSANDER (*to Hermia*)
  Hang off, thou cat, thou burr; vile thing, let loose,
  Or I will shake thee from me like a serpent.
HERMIA
  Why are you grown so rude? What change is this,
  Sweet love?
LYSANDER   Thy love? Out, tawny Tartar, out;
  Out, loathèd med'cine; O hated potion, hence.   265
HERMIA
  Do you not jest?
HELENA   Yes, sooth, and so do you.
LYSANDER
  Demetrius, I will keep my word with thee.
DEMETRIUS
  I would I had your bond, for I perceive
  A weak bond holds you. I'll not trust your word.
LYSANDER
  What, should I hurt her, strike her, kill her dead? 270
  Although I hate her, I'll not harm her so.
HERMIA
  What, can you do me greater harm than hate?
  Hate me—wherefore? O me, what news, my love?
  Am not I Hermia? Are not you Lysander?
  I am as fair now as I was erewhile.   275
  Since night you loved me, yet since night you left me.
  Why then, you left me—O, the gods forbid—
  In earnest, shall I say?
LYSANDER   Ay, by my life,
  And never did desire to see thee more.
  Therefore be out of hope, of question, doubt.   280
  Be certain, nothing truer; 'tis no jest
  That I do hate thee and love Helena.
HERMIA (*to Helena*)
  O me, you juggler, you canker blossom,
  You thief of love—what, have you come by night
  And stol'n my love's heart from him?
HELENA   Fine, i'faith. 285
  Have you no modesty, no maiden shame,
  No touch of bashfulness? What, will you tear
  Impatient answers from my gentle tongue?
  Fie, fie, you counterfeit, you puppet, you!
HERMIA
  Puppet? Why, so! Ay, that way goes the game.   290
  Now I perceive that she hath made compare
  Between our statures; she hath urged her height,
  And with her personage, her tall personage,
  Her height, forsooth, she hath prevailed with him—
  And are you grown so high in his esteem   295
  Because I am so dwarfish and so low?
  How low am I, thou painted maypole? Speak,
  How low am I? I am not yet so low
  But that my nails can reach unto thine eyes.
HELENA (*to Demetrius and Lysander*)
  I pray you, though you mock me, gentlemen,   300

  Let her not hurt me. I was never curst.
  I have no gift at all in shrewishness.
  I am a right maid for my cowardice.
  Let her not strike me. You perhaps may think
  Because she is something lower than myself   305
  That I can match her—
HERMIA   Lower? Hark again.
HELENA
  Good Hermia, do not be so bitter with me.
  I evermore did love you, Hermia,
  Did ever keep your counsels, never wronged you—
  Save that in love unto Demetrius   310
  I told him of your stealth unto this wood.
  He followed you; for love I followed him.
  But he hath chid me hence, and threatened me
  To strike me, spurn me, nay, to kill me too.
  And now, so you will let me quiet go,   315
  To Athens will I bear my folly back,
  And follow you no further. Let me go.
  You see how simple and how fond I am.
HERMIA
  Why, get you gone. Who is't that hinders you?
HELENA
  A foolish heart that I leave here behind.   320
HERMIA
  What, with Lysander?
HELENA   With Demetrius. •
LYSANDER
  Be not afraid; she shall not harm thee, Helena.
DEMETRIUS
  No, sir, she shall not, though you take her part.
HELENA
  O, when she is angry she is keen and shrewd.
  She was a vixen when she went to school,   325
  And though she be but little, she is fierce.
HERMIA
  Little again? Nothing but 'low' and 'little'?—
  Why will you suffer her to flout me thus?
  Let me come to her.
LYSANDER   Get you gone, you dwarf,
  You *minimus* of hind'ring knot-grass made,   330
  You bead, you acorn.
DEMETRIUS   You are too officious
  In her behalf that scorns your services.
  Let her alone. Speak not of Helena.
  Take not her part. For if thou dost intend
  Never so little show of love to her,   335
  Thou shalt aby it.
LYSANDER   Now she holds me not.
  Now follow, if thou dar'st, to try whose right,
  Of thine or mine, is most in Helena.
DEMETRIUS
  Follow? Nay, I'll go with thee, cheek by jowl.
                  Exeunt Lysander and Demetrius
HERMIA
  You, mistress, all this coil is long of you.   340
  Nay, go not back.
HELENA   I will not trust you, I,
  Nor longer stay in your curst company.

Your hands than mine are quicker for a fray;
My legs are longer, though, to run away.   *Exit*

HERMIA
I am amazed, and know not what to say.   *Exit*
    ⌜*Oberon and Robin come forward*⌝

OBERON
This is thy negligence. Still thou mistak'st,
Or else commit'st thy knaveries wilfully.

ROBIN
Believe me, king of shadows, I mistook.
Did not you tell me I should know the man
By the Athenian garments he had on?—   350
And so far blameless proves my enterprise
That I have 'nointed an Athenian's eyes;
And so far am I glad it so did sort
As this their jangling I esteem a sport.

OBERON
Thou seest these lovers seek a place to fight.   355
Hie therefore, Robin, overcast the night;
The starry welkin cover thou anon
With drooping fog as black as Acheron,
And lead these testy rivals so astray
As one come not within another's way.   360
Like to Lysander sometime frame thy tongue,
Then stir Demetrius up with bitter wrong;
And sometime rail thou like Demetrius,
And from each other look thou lead them thus
Till o'er their brows death-counterfeiting sleep   365
With leaden legs and batty wings doth creep.
Then crush this herb into Lysander's eye—
Whose liquor hath this virtuous property,
To take from thence all error with his might,
And make his eyeballs roll with wonted sight.   370
When they next wake, all this derision
Shall seem a dream and fruitless vision,
And back to Athens shall the lovers wend
With league whose date till death shall never end.
Whiles I in this affair do thee employ,   375
I'll to my queen and beg her Indian boy;
And then I will her charmèd eye release
From monster's view, and all things shall be peace.

ROBIN
My fairy lord, this must be done with haste,
For night's swift dragons cut the clouds full fast,   380
And yonder shines Aurora's harbinger,
At whose approach ghosts, wand'ring here and there,
Troop home to churchyards; damnèd spirits all
That in cross-ways and floods have burial
Already to their wormy beds are gone,   385
For fear lest day should look their shames upon.
They wilfully themselves exiled from light,
And must for aye consort with black-browed night.

OBERON
But we are spirits of another sort.
I with the morning's love have oft made sport,   390
And like a forester the groves may tread
Even till the eastern gate, all fiery red,
Opening on Neptune with fair blessèd beams
Turns into yellow gold his salt green streams.

But notwithstanding, haste, make no delay;   395
We may effect this business yet ere day.   *Exit*

ROBIN
    Up and down, up and down,
    I will lead them up and down.
    I am feared in field and town.
    Goblin, lead them up and down.   400
Here comes one.
        Enter Lysander

LYSANDER
    Where art thou, proud Demetrius? Speak thou now.

ROBIN ⌜*shifting place*⌝
    Here, villain, drawn and ready. Where art thou?

LYSANDER
    I will be with thee straight.

ROBIN ⌜*shifting place*⌝   Follow me then
    To plainer ground.   ⌜*Exit Lysander*⌝
        Enter Demetrius

DEMETRIUS ⌜*shifting place*⌝ Lysander, speak again.   405
    Thou runaway, thou coward, art thou fled?
    Speak! In some bush? Where dost thou hide thy head?

ROBIN ⌜*shifting place*⌝
    Thou coward, art thou bragging to the stars,
    Telling the bushes that thou look'st for wars,
    And wilt not come? Come, recreant; come, thou child,
    I'll whip thee with a rod. He is defiled   411
    That draws a sword on thee.

DEMETRIUS ⌜*shifting place*⌝   Yea, art thou there?

ROBIN ⌜*shifting place*⌝
    Follow my voice; we'll try no manhood here.   *Exeunt*

3.3   ⌜*Enter Lysander*⌝

LYSANDER
    He goes before me, and still dares me on;
    When I come where he calls, then he is gone.
    The villain is much lighter heeled than I;
    I followed fast, but faster he did fly,
    That fallen am I in dark uneven way,   5
    And here will rest me.
        He lies down
                Come, thou gentle day;
    For if but once thou show me thy grey light,
    I'll find Demetrius, and revenge this spite.   *He sleeps*
        Enter Robin Goodfellow and Demetrius

ROBIN ⌜*shifting place*⌝
    Ho, ho, ho, coward, why com'st thou not?

DEMETRIUS
    Abide me if thou dar'st, for well I wot   10
    Thou runn'st before me, shifting every place,
    And dar'st not stand nor look me in the face.
    Where art thou now?

ROBIN ⌜*shifting place*⌝   Come hither, I am here.

DEMETRIUS
    Nay, then thou mock'st me. Thou shalt buy this dear
    If ever I thy face by daylight see.   15
    Now go thy way. Faintness constraineth me
    To measure out my length on this cold bed.
        He lies down
    By day's approach look to be visited.   *He sleeps*

Enter Helena

HELENA

O weary night, O long and tedious night,
  Abate thy hours; shine comforts from the east   20
That I may back to Athens by daylight
From these that my poor company detest;
And sleep, that sometimes shuts up sorrow's eye,
Steal me a while from mine own company.
  She lies down and sleeps

ROBIN

  Yet but three? Come one more,   25
  Two of both kinds makes up four.
    ⌐Enter Hermia⌐
  Here she comes, curst and sad.
  Cupid is a knavish lad
  Thus to make poor females mad.

HERMIA

Never so weary, never so in woe,   30
  Bedabbled with the dew, and torn with briers,
I can no further crawl, no further go.
  My legs can keep no pace with my desires.
Here will I rest me till the break of day.
  She lies down
Heavens shield Lysander, if they mean a fray.   35
  She sleeps

ROBIN   On the ground sleep sound.
  I'll apply to your eye,
    Gentle lover, remedy.
  He drops the juice on Lysander's eyelids
  When thou wak'st thou tak'st
    True delight in the sight   40
    Of thy former lady's eye,
  And the country proverb known,
  That 'every man should take his own',
  In your waking shall be shown.
    Jack shall have Jill,   45
    Naught shall go ill,

the man shall have his mare again, and all shall be
well.   *Exit*

4.1 *Enter Titania, Queen of Fairies, and Bottom the*
        clown with the ass-head, and fairies: Peaseblossom,
        Cobweb, Mote, and Mustardseed

TITANIA (*to Bottom*)

Come, sit thee down upon this flow'ry bed,
  While I thy amiable cheeks do coy,
And stick musk-roses in thy sleek smooth head,
  And kiss thy fair large ears, my gentle joy.

BOTTOM Where's Peaseblossom?   5

PEASEBLOSSOM Ready.

BOTTOM Scratch my head, Peaseblossom. Where's Monsieur Cobweb?

COBWEB Ready.   9

BOTTOM Monsieur Cobweb, good monsieur, get you your
weapons in your hand and kill me a red-hipped humble-
bee on the top of a thistle; and, good monsieur, bring
me the honeybag. Do not fret yourself too much in the

action, monsieur; and, good monsieur, have a care the
honeybag break not. I would be loath to have you
overflowen with a honeybag, signor.   ⌐*Exit Cobweb*⌐
Where's Monsieur Mustardseed?   17

MUSTARDSEED Ready.

BOTTOM Give me your neaf, Monsieur Mustardseed. Pray
you, leave your courtesy, good monsieur.   20

MUSTARDSEED What's your will?

BOTTOM Nothing, good monsieur, but to help Cavaliery
Peaseblossom to scratch. I must to the barber's,
monsieur, for methinks I am marvellous hairy about
the face; and I am such a tender ass, if my hair do but
tickle me I must scratch.   26

TITANIA

What, wilt thou hear some music, my sweet love?

BOTTOM I have a reasonable good ear in music. Let's have
the tongs and the bones.
    ⌐*Rural music*⌐

TITANIA

Or say, sweet love, what thou desir'st to eat.   30

BOTTOM Truly, a peck of provender. I could munch your
good dry oats. Methinks I have a great desire to a bottle
of hay. Good hay, sweet hay, hath no fellow.

TITANIA

I have a venturous fairy that shall seek
  The squirrel's hoard, and fetch thee off new nuts.   35

BOTTOM I had rather have a handful or two of dried peas.
But I pray you, let none of your people stir me. I have
an exposition of sleep come upon me.

TITANIA

Sleep thou, and I will wind thee in my arms.
Fairies, be gone, and be all ways away.   40
                                    Exeunt Fairies
So doth the woodbine the sweet honeysuckle
Gently entwist; the female ivy so
Enrings the barky fingers of the elm.
O how I love thee, how I dote on thee!
  They sleep.
  Enter Robin Goodfellow ⌐*and Oberon, meeting*⌐

OBERON

Welcome, good Robin. Seest thou this sweet sight?   45
Her dotage now I do begin to pity,
For meeting her of late behind the wood,
Seeking sweet favours for this hateful fool,
I did upbraid her and fall out with her,
For he his hairy temples then had rounded   50
With coronet of fresh and fragrant flowers,
And that same dew which sometime on the buds
Was wont to swell like round and orient pearls
Stood now within the pretty flow'rets' eyes,
Like tears that did their own disgrace bewail.   55
When I had at my pleasure taunted her,
And she in mild terms begged my patience,
I then did ask of her her changeling child,
Which straight she gave me, and her fairy sent
To bear him to my bower in fairyland.   60
And now I have the boy, I will undo

This hateful imperfection of her eyes.
And, gentle puck, take this transformèd scalp
From off the head of this Athenian swain,
That he, awaking when the other do,   65
May all to Athens back again repair,
And think no more of this night's accidents
But as the fierce vexation of a dream.
But first I will release the Fairy Queen.
   He drops the juice on Titania's eyelids
      Be as thou wast wont to be,   70
      See as thou wast wont to see.
      Dian's bud o'er Cupid's flower
      Hath such force and blessèd power.
   Now, my Titania, wake you, my sweet queen.
TITANIA (*awaking*)
   My Oberon, what visions have I seen!   75
   Methought I was enamoured of an ass.
OBERON
   There lies your love.
TITANIA   How came these things to pass?
   O, how mine eyes do loathe his visage now!
OBERON
   Silence a while.—Robin, take off this head.—
   Titania, music call, and strike more dead   80
   Than common sleep of all these five the sense.
TITANIA
   Music, ho—music such as charmeth sleep.
   ⌈*Still music*⌉
ROBIN (*taking the ass-head off Bottom*)
   Now when thou wak'st with thine own fool's eyes
      peep.
OBERON
   Sound music.
   ⌈*The music changes*⌉
            Come, my queen, take hands with me,
   And rock the ground whereon these sleepers be.   85
   Oberon and Titania dance
   Now thou and I are new in amity,
   And will tomorrow midnight solemnly
   Dance in Duke Theseus' house, triumphantly,
   And bless it to all fair prosperity.
   There shall the pairs of faithful lovers be   90
   Wedded with Theseus, all in jollity.
ROBIN
   Fairy King, attend and mark.
   I do hear the morning lark.
OBERON
   Then, my queen, in silence sad
   Trip we after nightès shade.   95
   We the globe can compass soon,
   Swifter than the wand'ring moon.
TITANIA
   Come, my lord, and in our flight
   Tell me how it came this night
   That I sleeping here was found   100
   With these mortals on the ground.
            Exeunt Oberon, Titania, and
            Robin. The sleepers lie still

   Wind horns within. Enter Theseus with Egeus,
   Hippolyta, and all his train
THESEUS
   Go, one of you, find out the forester,
   For now our observation is performed;
   And since we have the vanguard of the day,
   My love shall hear the music of my hounds.   105
   Uncouple in the western valley; let them go.
   Dispatch, I say, and find the forester.   *Exit one*
   We will, fair Queen, up to the mountain's top,
   And mark the musical confusion
   Of hounds and echo in conjunction.   110
HIPPOLYTA
   I was with Hercules and Cadmus once
   When in a wood of Crete they bayed the bear
   With hounds of Sparta. Never did I hear
   Such gallant chiding; for besides the groves,
   The skies, the fountains, every region near   115
   Seemed all one mutual cry. I never heard
   So musical a discord, such sweet thunder.
THESEUS
   My hounds are bred out of the Spartan kind,
   So flewed, so sanded; and their heads are hung
   With ears that sweep away the morning dew,   120
   Crook-kneed, and dewlapped like Thessalian bulls,
   Slow in pursuit, but matched in mouth like bells,
   Each under each. A cry more tuneable
   Was never holla'd to nor cheered with horn
   In Crete, in Sparta, nor in Thessaly.   125
   Judge when you hear. But soft: what nymphs are
      these?
EGEUS
   My lord, this is my daughter here asleep,
   And this Lysander; this Demetrius is;
   This Helena, old Nedar's Helena.
   I wonder of their being here together.   130
THESEUS
   No doubt they rose up early to observe
   The rite of May, and, hearing our intent,
   Came here in grace of our solemnity.
   But speak, Egeus: is not this the day
   That Hermia should give answer of her choice?   135
EGEUS It is, my lord.
THESEUS
   Go bid the huntsmen wake them with their horns.
                              ⌈*Exit one*⌉
   Shout within: wind horns. The lovers all start up
   Good morrow, friends. Saint Valentine is past.
   Begin these wood-birds but to couple now?
LYSANDER
   Pardon, my lord.
   The lovers kneel
THESEUS   I pray you all stand up.   140
   The lovers stand
   (*To Demetrius and Lysander*) I know you two are rival
      enemies.
   How comes this gentle concord in the world,

That hatred is so far from jealousy
To sleep by hate, and fear no enmity?

LYSANDER

My lord, I shall reply amazèdly,   145
Half sleep, half waking. But as yet, I swear,
I cannot truly say how I came here,
But as I think—for truly would I speak,
And, now I do bethink me, so it is—
I came with Hermia hither. Our intent   150
Was to be gone from Athens where we might,
Without the peril of the Athenian law—

EGEUS (to Theseus)

Enough, enough, my lord, you have enough.
I beg the law, the law upon his head.—
They would have stol'n away, they would, Demetrius,
Thereby to have defeated you and me—   156
You of your wife, and me of my consent,
Of my consent that she should be your wife.

DEMETRIUS (to Theseus)

My lord, fair Helen told me of their stealth,
Of this their purpose hither to this wood,   160
And I in fury hither followed them,
Fair Helena in fancy following me.
But, my good lord, I wot not by what power—
But by some power it is—my love to Hermia,
Melted as the snow, seems to me now   165
As the remembrance of an idle gaud
Which in my childhood I did dote upon,
And all the faith, the virtue of my heart,
The object and the pleasure of mine eye
Is only Helena. To her, my lord,   170
Was I betrothed ere I see Hermia;
But like in sickness did I loathe this food;
But, as in health come to my natural taste,
Now I do wish it, love it, long for it,
And will for evermore be true to it.   175

THESEUS

Fair lovers, you are fortunately met.
Of this discourse we more will hear anon.—
Egeus, I will overbear your will,
For in the temple by and by with us
These couples shall eternally be knit.—   180
And, for the morning now is something worn,
Our purposed hunting shall be set aside.
Away with us to Athens. Three and three,
We'll hold a feast in great solemnity.
Come, Hippolyta.   185
          Exit Duke Theseus with Hippolyta, Egeus,
                              and all his train

DEMETRIUS

These things seem small and undistinguishable,
Like far-off mountains turnèd into clouds.

HERMIA

Methinks I see these things with parted eye,
When everything seems double.

HELENA   So methinks,
And I have found Demetrius like a jewel,   190
Mine own and not mine own.

DEMETRIUS   It seems to me

That yet we sleep, we dream. Do not you think
The Duke was here and bid us follow him?

HERMIA

Yea, and my father.

HELENA   And Hippolyta.

LYSANDER

And he did bid us follow to the temple.   195

DEMETRIUS

Why then, we are awake. Let's follow him,
And by the way let us recount our dreams.
                              Exeunt the lovers
          Bottom wakes

BOTTOM When my cue comes, call me, and I will answer.
My next is 'most fair Pyramus'. Heigh-ho. Peter Quince?
Flute the bellows-mender? Snout the tinker?
Starveling? God's my life! Stolen hence, and left me
asleep?—I have had a most rare vision. I have had a
dream past the wit of man to say what dream it was.
Man is but an ass if he go about t'expound this dream.
Methought I was—there is no man can tell what.
Methought I was, and methought I had—but man is
but a patched fool if he will offer to say what methought
I had. The eye of man hath not heard, the ear of man
hath not seen, man's hand is not able to taste, his
tongue to conceive, nor his heart to report what my
dream was. I will get Peter Quince to write a ballad of
this dream. It shall be called 'Bottom's Dream', because
it hath no bottom, and I will sing it in the latter end
of a play, before the Duke. Peradventure, to make it
the more gracious, I shall sing it at her death.   *Exit*

4.2   *Enter Quince, Flute, Snout, and Starveling*

QUINCE Have you sent to Bottom's house? Is he come
home yet?

STARVELING He cannot be heard of. Out of doubt he is
transported.

FLUTE If he come not, then the play is marred. It goes
not forward. Doth it?   6

QUINCE It is not possible. You have not a man in all
Athens able to discharge Pyramus but he.

FLUTE No, he hath simply the best wit of any handicraft-
man in Athens.   10

QUINCE Yea, and the best person, too; and he is a very
paramour for a sweet voice.

FLUTE You must say 'paragon'. A paramour is, God bless
us, a thing of naught.
          Enter Snug the joiner

SNUG Masters, the Duke is coming from the temple, and
there is two or three lords and ladies more married. If
our sport had gone forward we had all been made men.

FLUTE O sweet bully Bottom! Thus hath he lost sixpence
a day during his life. He could not have scaped sixpence
a day. An the Duke had not given him sixpence a day
for playing Pyramus, I'll be hanged. He would have
deserved it. Sixpence a day in Pyramus, or nothing. 22
          Enter Bottom

BOTTOM Where are these lads? Where are these hearts?

QUINCE Bottom! O most courageous day! O most happy
hour!   25

BOTTOM Masters, I am to discourse wonders; but ask me
not what. For if I tell you, I am no true Athenian. I
will tell you everything right as it fell out.

QUINCE Let us hear, sweet Bottom.   29

BOTTOM Not a word of me. All that I will tell you is that
the Duke hath dined. Get your apparel together, good
strings to your beards, new ribbons to your pumps.
Meet presently at the palace; every man look o'er his
part. For the short and the long is, our play is preferred.
In any case let Thisbe have clean linen, and let not
him that plays the lion pare his nails, for they shall
hang out for the lion's claws. And, most dear actors,
eat no onions nor garlic, for we are to utter sweet
breath, and I do not doubt but to hear them say it is
a sweet comedy. No more words. Away, go, away! 40

Exeunt

5.1   *Enter Theseus, Hippolyta, ⌈Egeus⌉, and attendant
       lords*

HIPPOLYTA
'Tis strange, my Theseus, that these lovers speak of.

THESEUS
More strange than true. I never may believe
These antique fables, nor these fairy toys.
Lovers and madmen have such seething brains,
Such shaping fantasies, that apprehend   5
More than cool reason ever comprehends.
The lunatic, the lover, and the poet
Are of imagination all compact.
One sees more devils than vast hell can hold:
That is the madman. The lover, all as frantic, 10
Sees Helen's beauty in a brow of Egypt.
The poet's eye, in a fine frenzy rolling,
Doth glance from heaven to earth, from earth to
       heaven,
And as imagination bodies forth
The forms of things unknown, the poet's pen   15
Turns them to shapes, and gives to airy nothing
A local habitation and a name.
Such tricks hath strong imagination
That if it would but apprehend some joy
It comprehends some bringer of that joy;   20
Or in the night, imagining some fear,
How easy is a bush supposed a bear!

HIPPOLYTA
But all the story of the night told over,
And all their minds transfigured so together,
More witnesseth than fancy's images,   25
And grows to something of great constancy;
But howsoever, strange and admirable.

       *Enter the lovers: Lysander, Demetrius, Hermia,
       and Helena*

THESEUS
Here come the lovers, full of joy and mirth.
Joy, gentle friends—joy and fresh days of love
Accompany your hearts.

LYSANDER   More than to us   30
Wait in your royal walks, your board, your bed.

THESEUS
Come now, what masques, what dances shall we have
To wear away this long age of three hours
Between our after-supper and bed-time?
Where is our usual manager of mirth?   35
What revels are in hand? Is there no play
To ease the anguish of a torturing hour?
Call Egeus.

⌈EGEUS⌉   Here, mighty Theseus.

THESEUS
Say, what abridgement have you for this evening?
What masque, what music? How shall we beguile 40
The lazy time if not with some delight?

⌈EGEUS⌉
There is a brief how many sports are ripe.
Make choice of which your highness will see first.

⌈LYSANDER⌉ (*reads*)
'The battle with the centaurs, to be sung
By an Athenian eunuch to the harp.'   45

THESEUS
We'll none of that. That have I told my love
In glory of my kinsman Hercules.

⌈LYSANDER⌉ (*reads*)
'The riot of the tipsy bacchanals
Tearing the Thracian singer in their rage.'

THESEUS
That is an old device, and it was played   50
When I from Thebes came last a conqueror.

⌈LYSANDER⌉ (*reads*)
'The thrice-three muses mourning for the death
Of learning, late deceased in beggary.'

THESEUS
That is some satire, keen and critical,
Not sorting with a nuptial ceremony.   55

⌈LYSANDER⌉ (*reads*)
'A tedious brief scene of young Pyramus
And his love Thisbe: very tragical mirth.'

THESEUS
'Merry' *and* 'tragical'? 'Tedious' *and* 'brief'?—
That is, hot ice and wondrous strange black snow.
How shall we find the concord of this discord? 60

⌈EGEUS⌉
A play there is, my lord, some ten words long,
Which is as 'brief' as I have known a play;
But by ten words, my lord, it is too long,
Which makes it 'tedious'; for in all the play
There is not one word apt, one player fitted.   65
And 'tragical', my noble lord, it is,
For Pyramus therein doth kill himself;
Which when I saw rehearsed, I must confess,
Made mine eyes water; but more merry tears
The passion of loud laughter never shed.   70

THESEUS What are they that do play it?

⌈EGEUS⌉
Hard-handed men that work in Athens here,
Which never laboured in their minds till now,
And now have toiled their unbreathed memories
With this same play against your nuptial.   75

THESEUS
And we will hear it.
⌈EGEUS⌉   No, my noble lord,
It is not for you. I have heard it over,
And it is nothing, nothing in the world,
Unless you can find sport in their intents
Extremely stretched, and conned with cruel pain   80
To do you service.
THESEUS   I will hear that play;
For never anything can be amiss
When simpleness and duty tender it.
Go, bring them in; and take your places, ladies.
                              Exit ⌈Egeus⌉
HIPPOLYTA
I love not to see wretchedness o'ercharged,   85
And duty in his service perishing.
THESEUS
Why, gentle sweet, you shall see no such thing.
HIPPOLYTA
He says they can do nothing in this kind.
THESEUS
The kinder we, to give them thanks for nothing.
Our sport shall be to take what they mistake,   90
And what poor duty cannot do,
Noble respect takes it in might, not merit.
Where I have come, great clerks have purposèd
To greet me with premeditated welcomes,
Where I have seen them shiver and look pale,   95
Make periods in the midst of sentences,
Throttle their practised accent in their fears,
And in conclusion dumbly have broke off,
Not paying me a welcome. Trust me, sweet,
Out of this silence yet I picked a welcome,   100
And in the modesty of fearful duty
I read as much as from the rattling tongue
Of saucy and audacious eloquence.
Love, therefore, and tongue-tied simplicity
In least speak most, to my capacity.   105
          Enter ⌈Egeus⌉
⌈EGEUS⌉
So please your grace, the Prologue is addressed.
THESEUS Let him approach.
          ⌈Flourish trumpets.⌉ Enter ⌈Quince as⌉ the Prologue
⌈QUINCE⌉ (as Prologue)
If we offend, it is with our good will.
  That you should think: we come not to offend
But with good will. To show our simple skill,   110
  That is the true beginning of our end.
Consider then we come but in despite.
  We do not come as minding to content you,
Our true intent is. All for your delight
  We are not here. That you should here repent you
The actors are at hand, and by their show   116
You shall know all that you are like to know.
THESEUS This fellow doth not stand upon points.
LYSANDER He hath rid his prologue like a rough colt: he
knows not the stop. A good moral, my lord: it is not
enough to speak, but to speak true.   121

HIPPOLYTA Indeed, he hath played on this prologue like
a child on a recorder—a sound, but not in government.
THESEUS His speech was like a tangled chain—nothing
impaired, but all disordered. Who is next?   125
          Enter ⌈with a trumpeter before them⌉ Bottom as
          Pyramus, Flute as Thisbe, Snout as Wall, Starveling
          as Moonshine, and Snug as Lion, for the dumb show
⌈QUINCE⌉ (as Prologue)
Gentles, perchance you wonder at this show,
  But wonder on, till truth make all things plain.
This man is Pyramus, if you would know;
  This beauteous lady Thisbe is, certain.
This man with lime and roughcast doth present   130
  Wall, that vile wall which did these lovers sunder;
And through Wall's chink, poor souls, they are content
  To whisper; at the which let no man wonder.
This man, with lantern, dog, and bush of thorn,
  Presenteth Moonshine. For if you will know,   135
By moonshine did these lovers think no scorn
  To meet at Ninus' tomb, there, there to woo.
This grizzly beast, which 'Lion' hight by name,
  The trusty Thisbe coming first by night
Did scare away, or rather did affright;   140
And as she fled, her mantle she did fall,
  Which Lion vile with bloody mouth did stain.
Anon comes Pyramus, sweet youth and tall,
  And finds his trusty Thisbe's mantle slain;
Whereat with blade—with bloody, blameful blade—
  He bravely broached his boiling bloody breast;   146
And Thisbe, tarrying in mulberry shade,
  His dagger drew and died. For all the rest,
Let Lion, Moonshine, Wall, and lovers twain
  At large discourse, while here they do remain.   150
          ⌈Exeunt all the clowns but Snout as Wall⌉
THESEUS I wonder if the lion be to speak.
DEMETRIUS No wonder, my lord—one lion may when
many asses do.
⌈SNOUT⌉ (as Wall)
In this same interlude it doth befall
  That I, one Snout by name, present a wall;   155
And such a wall as I would have you think
  That had in it a crannied hole or chink,
Through which the lovers Pyramus and Thisbe
  Did whisper often, very secretly.
This loam, this roughcast, and this stone doth show
  That I am that same wall; the truth is so.   161
And this the cranny is, right and sinister,
  Through which the fearful lovers are to whisper.
THESEUS Would you desire lime and hair to speak better?
DEMETRIUS It is the wittiest partition that ever I heard
discourse, my lord.   166
          Enter Bottom as Pyramus
THESEUS Pyramus draws near the wall. Silence.
BOTTOM (as Pyramus)
O grim-looked night, O night with hue so black,
  O night which ever art when day is not;
O night, O night, alack, alack, alack,   170
  I fear my Thisbe's promise is forgot.

And thou, O wall, O sweet O lovely wall,
    That stand'st between her father's ground and mine,
Thou wall, O wall, O sweet and lovely wall,
    Show me thy chink, to blink through with mine
    eyne.   175
    Wall shows his chink
Thanks, courteous wall. Jove shield thee well for this.
But what see I? No Thisbe do I see.
O wicked wall, through whom I see no bliss,
Cursed be thy stones for thus deceiving me.
THESEUS The wall methinks, being sensible, should curse
    again.   181
BOTTOM (*to Theseus*) No, in truth, sir, he should not.
'Deceiving me' is Thisbe's cue. She is to enter now,
and I am to spy her through the wall. You shall see,
it will fall pat as I told you.   185
    Enter Flute as Thisbe
Yonder she comes.
FLUTE (*as Thisbe*)
    O wall, full often hast thou heard my moans
    For parting my fair Pyramus and me.
My cherry lips have often kissed thy stones,
    Thy stones with lime and hair knit up in thee.   190
BOTTOM (*as Pyramus*)
    I see a voice. Now will I to the chink
    To spy an I can hear my Thisbe's face.
    Thisbe?
FLUTE (*as Thisbe*) My love—thou art my love, I think.
BOTTOM (*as Pyramus*)
    Think what thou wilt, I am thy lover's grace,
    And like Lemander am I trusty still.   195
FLUTE (*as Thisbe*)
    And I like Helen, till the fates me kill.
BOTTOM (*as Pyramus*)
    Not Shaphalus to Procrus was so true.
FLUTE (*as Thisbe*)
    As Shaphalus to Procrus, I to you.
BOTTOM (*as Pyramus*)
    O kiss me through the hole of this vile wall.
FLUTE (*as Thisbe*)
    I kiss the wall's hole, not your lips at all.   200
BOTTOM (*as Pyramus*)
    Wilt thou at Ninny's tomb meet me straightway?
FLUTE (*as Thisbe*)
    Tide life, tide death, I come without delay.
                Exeunt Bottom and Flute severally
SNOUT (*as Wall*)
    Thus have I, Wall, my part dischargèd so;
    And being done, thus Wall away doth go.   *Exit*
THESEUS Now is the wall down between the two
    neighbours.   206
DEMETRIUS No remedy, my lord, when walls are so wilful
    to hear without warning.
HIPPOLYTA This is the silliest stuff that ever I heard.
THESEUS The best in this kind are but shadows, and the
    worst are no worse if imagination amend them.   211
HIPPOLYTA It must be your imagination, then, and not
    theirs.
THESEUS If we imagine no worse of them than they of

themselves, they may pass for excellent men. Here
come two noble beasts in: a man and a lion.   216
    Enter Snug as Lion, and Starveling as Moonshine
    with a lantern, thorn bush, and dog
SNUG (*as Lion*)
    You, ladies, you whose gentle hearts do fear
        The smallest monstrous mouse that creeps on floor,
    May now perchance both quake and tremble here
        When lion rough in wildest rage doth roar.   220
    Then know that I as Snug the joiner am
    A lion fell, nor else no lion's dam.
    For if I should as Lion come in strife
    Into this place, 'twere pity on my life.
THESEUS A very gentle beast, and of a good conscience.
DEMETRIUS The very best at a beast, my lord, that e'er I
    saw.
LYSANDER This lion is a very fox for his valour.
THESEUS True, and a goose for his discretion.
DEMETRIUS Not so, my lord, for his valour cannot carry
    his discretion, and the fox carries the goose.   231
THESEUS His discretion, I am sure, cannot carry his valour,
    for the goose carries not the fox. It is well. Leave it to
    his discretion, and let us listen to the moon.
STARVELING (*as Moonshine*)
    This lantern doth the hornèd moon present.   235
DEMETRIUS He should have worn the horns on his head.
THESEUS He is no crescent, and his horns are invisible
    within the circumference.
STARVELING (*as Moonshine*)
    This lantern doth the hornèd moon present.
    Myself the man i'th' moon do seem to be.   240
THESEUS This is the greatest error of all the rest—the man
    should be put into the lantern. How is it else the man
    i'th' moon?
DEMETRIUS He dares not come there for the candle; for
    you see it is already in snuff.   245
HIPPOLYTA I am aweary of this moon. Would he would
    change.
THESEUS It appears by his small light of discretion that he
    is in the wane; but yet in courtesy, in all reason, we
    must stay the time.   250
LYSANDER Proceed, Moon.
STARVELING All that I have to say is to tell you that the
    lantern is the moon, I the man i'th' moon, this thorn
    bush my thorn bush, and this dog my dog.   254
DEMETRIUS Why, all these should be in the lantern, for
    all these are in the moon. But silence; here comes
    Thisbe.
    Enter Flute as Thisbe
FLUTE (*as Thisbe*)
    This is old Ninny's tomb. Where is my love?
SNUG (*as Lion*) O.
    Lion roars. Thisbe drops her mantle and runs off
DEMETRIUS Well roared, Lion.   260
THESEUS Well run, Thisbe.
HIPPOLYTA Well shone, Moon.—Truly, the moon shines
    with a good grace.
    Lion worries Thisbe's mantle
THESEUS Well moused, Lion.

DEMETRIUS And then came Pyramus.   265
 ⌈*Enter Bottom as Pyramus*⌉
LYSANDER And so the lion vanished.   ⌈*Exit Lion*⌉
BOTTOM (*as Pyramus*)
 Sweet moon, I thank thee for thy sunny beams.
  I thank thee, moon, for shining now so bright;
 For by thy gracious, golden, glittering gleams
  I trust to take of truest Thisbe sight.   270
   But stay, O spite!
   But mark, poor knight,
  What dreadful dole is here?
   Eyes, do you see?
   How can it be?   275
  O dainty duck, O dear!
   Thy mantle good,
   What, stained with blood?
  Approach, ye furies fell.
   O fates, come, come,   280
   Cut thread and thrum,
  Quail, crush, conclude, and quell.
THESEUS This passion—and the death of a dear friend—
 would go near to make a man look sad.
HIPPOLYTA Beshrew my heart, but I pity the man.   285
BOTTOM (*as Pyramus*)
 O wherefore, nature, didst thou lions frame,
  Since lion vile hath here deflowered my dear?—
 Which is—no, no, which *was*—the fairest dame
  That lived, that loved, that liked, that looked, with
   cheer.
  Come tears, confound;   290
  Out sword, and wound
 The pap of Pyramus.
  Ay, that left pap,
  Where heart doth hop.
 Thus die I: thus, thus, thus.   295
  He stabs himself
  Now am I dead,
  Now am I fled,
 My soul is in the sky.
  Tongue, lose thy light;
  Moon, take thy flight.   ⌈*Exit Moonshine*⌉
 Now die, die, die, die, die.   *He dies*
DEMETRIUS No die but an ace for him; for he is but one.
LYSANDER Less than an ace, man; for he is dead; he is
 nothing.
THESEUS With the help of a surgeon he might yet recover
 and prove an ass.   306
HIPPOLYTA How chance Moonshine is gone before Thisbe
 comes back and finds her lover.
THESEUS She will find him by starlight.
 ⌈*Enter Flute as Thisbe*⌉
 Here she comes, and her passion ends the play.   310
HIPPOLYTA Methinks she should not use a long one for
 such a Pyramus. I hope she will be brief.
DEMETRIUS A mote will turn the balance which Pyramus,
 which Thisbe, is the better—he for a man, God warrant
 us; she for a woman, God bless us.   315
LYSANDER She hath spied him already with those sweet
 eyes.

DEMETRIUS And thus she means, videlicet:
FLUTE (*as Thisbe*)
 Asleep, my love?
  What, dead, my dove?   320
 O Pyramus, arise.
  Speak, speak. Quite dumb?
  Dead, dead? A tomb
 Must cover thy sweet eyes.
  These lily lips,   325
  This cherry nose,
 These yellow cowslip cheeks
  Are gone, are gone.
  Lovers, make moan.
 His eyes were green as leeks.   330
  O sisters three,
  Come, come to me
 With hands as pale as milk.
  Lay them in gore,
  Since you have shore   335
 With shears his thread of silk.
  Tongue, not a word.
  Come, trusty sword,
 Come, blade, my breast imbrue.
  She stabs herself
  And farewell friends,   340
  Thus Thisbe ends.
 Adieu, adieu, adieu.   *She dies*
THESEUS Moonshine and Lion are left to bury the dead.
DEMETRIUS Ay, and Wall too.   344
⌈BOTTOM⌉ No, I assure you, the wall is down that parted
 their fathers. Will it please you to see the epilogue or
 to hear a bergamask dance between two of our
 company?
THESEUS No epilogue, I pray you; for your play needs no
 excuse. Never excuse; for when the players are all dead
 there need none to be blamed. Marry, if he that writ
 it had played Pyramus and hanged himself in Thisbe's
 garter it would have been a fine tragedy; and so it is,
 truly, and very notably discharged. But come, your
 bergamask. Let your epilogue alone.   355
 ⌈*Bottom and Flute*⌉ *dance a bergamask, then exeunt*
 The iron tongue of midnight hath told twelve.
 Lovers, to bed; 'tis almost fairy time.
 I fear we shall outsleep the coming morn
 As much as we this night have overwatched.
 This palpable-gross play hath well beguiled   360
 The heavy gait of night. Sweet friends, to bed.
 A fortnight hold we this solemnity
 In nightly revels and new jollity.   *Exeunt*

5.2   *Enter Robin Goodfellow with a broom*
ROBIN
 Now the hungry lion roars,
  And the wolf behowls the moon,
 Whilst the heavy ploughman snores,
  All with weary task fordone.
 Now the wasted brands do glow   5
  Whilst the screech-owl, screeching loud,
 Puts the wretch that lies in woe

In remembrance of a shroud.
Now it is the time of night
That the graves, all gaping wide,   10
Every one lets forth his sprite
In the churchway paths to glide;
And we fairies that do run
By the triple Hecate's team
From the presence of the sun,   15
Following darkness like a dream,
Now are frolic. Not a mouse
Shall disturb this hallowed house.
I am sent with broom before
To sweep the dust behind the door.   20

Enter Oberon and Titania, King and Queen of
Fairies, with all their train

OBERON
Through the house give glimmering light.
By the dead and drowsy fire
Every elf and fairy sprite
Hop as light as bird from brier,
And this ditty after me   25
Sing, and dance it trippingly.

TITANIA
First rehearse your song by rote,
To each word a warbling note.
Hand in hand with fairy grace
Will we sing and bless this place.   30

⌈*The song. The fairies dance*⌉

OBERON
Now until the break of day
Through this house each fairy stray.
To the best bride bed will we,
Which by us shall blessèd be,
And the issue there create   35
Ever shall be fortunate.

So shall all the couples three
Ever true in loving be,
And the blots of nature's hand
Shall not in their issue stand.   40
Never mole, harelip, nor scar,
Nor mark prodigious such as are
Despisèd in nativity
Shall upon their children be.
With this field-dew consecrate   45
Every fairy take his gait
And each several chamber bless
Through this palace with sweet peace;
And the owner of it blessed
Ever shall in safety rest.   50
Trip away, make no stay,
Meet me all by break of day. *Exeunt all but Robin*

Epilogue

ROBIN
If we shadows have offended,
Think but this, and all is mended:
That you have but slumbered here,
While these visions did appear;
And this weak and idle theme,   5
No more yielding but a dream,
Gentles, do not reprehend.
If you pardon, we will mend.
And as I am an honest puck,
If we have unearnèd luck   10
Now to 'scape the serpent's tongue,
We will make amends ere long,
Else the puck a liar call.
So, good night unto you all.
Give me your hands, if we be friends,   15
And Robin shall restore amends.

ADDITIONAL PASSAGES

An unusual quantity and kind of mislineation in the first edition has persuaded most scholars that the text at the beginning of 5.1 was revised, with new material written in the margins. We here offer a reconstruction of the passage as originally drafted, which can be compared with 5.1.1–86 of the edited text.

5.1 *Enter Theseus, Hippolyta, and Philostrate*

HIPPOLYTA
'Tis strange, my Theseus, that these lovers speak of.

THESEUS
More strange than true. I never may believe
These antique fables, nor these fairy toys.
Lovers and mad men have such seething brains.
One sees more devils than vast hell can hold: 5
That is the madman. The lover, all as frantic,
Sees Helen's beauty in a brow of Egypt.
Such tricks hath strong imagination
That if it would but apprehend some joy
It comprehends some bringer of that joy;   10
Or in the night, imagining some fear,
How easy is a bush supposed a bear!

HIPPOLYTA
But all the story of the night told over,
And all their minds transfigured so together,
More witnesseth than fancy's images,   15
And grows to something of great constancy;
But howsoever, strange and admirable.

Enter the lovers: Lysander, Demetrius, Hermia, and
Helena

THESEUS
Here come the lovers, full of joy and mirth.
Come now, what masques, what dances shall we
   have
To ease the anguish of a torturing hour?   20
Call Philostrate.

PHILOSTRATE   Here mighty Theseus.
THESEUS
  Say, what abridgement have you for this evening?
  What masque, what music? How shall we beguile
  The lazy time if not with some delight?
PHILOSTRATE
  There is a brief how many sports are ripe.   25
  Make choice of which your highness will see first.
THESEUS
  'The battle with the centaurs to be sung
  By an Athenian eunuch to the harp.'
  We'll none of that. That have I told my love
  In glory of my kinsman Hercules.   30
  'The riot of the tipsy Bacchanals
  Tearing the Thracian singer in their rage.'
  That is an old device, and it was played
  When I from Thebes came last a conquerer.
  'The thrice-three Muses mourning for the death   35
  Of learning, late deceased in beggary.'
  That is some satire, keen and critical,
  Not sorting with a nuptial ceremony.

  'A tedious brief scene of young Pyramus
  And his love Thisby.' 'Tedious' *and* 'brief'?   40
PHILOSTRATE
  A play there is, my lord, some ten words long,
  Which is as 'brief' as I have known a play;
  But by ten words, my lord, it is too long,
  Which makes it 'tedious'; for in all the play
  There is not one word apt, one player fitted.   45
THESEUS What are they that do play it?
PHILOSTRATE
  Hard-handed men that work in Athens here,
  Which never laboured in their minds till now,
  And now have toiled their unbreathed memories
  With this same play against your nuptial.   50
THESEUS
  Go, bring them in; and take your places, ladies.
                                      Exit Philostrate
HIPPOLYTA
  I love not to see wretchedness o'ercharged
  And duty in his service perishing.

THE MERCHANT OF VENICE

ENTRY of 'a book of *The Merchant of Venice* or otherwise called *The Jew of Venice*' in the Stationers' Register on 22 July 1598 probably represents an attempt by Shakespeare's company to prevent the unauthorized printing of a popular play: it eventually appeared in print as '*The Comical History of the Merchant of Venice*' in 1600, when it was said to have 'been divers times acted by the Lord Chamberlain his servants'; probably Shakespeare wrote it in 1596 or 1597. The alternative title—*The Jew of Venice*—probably reflects Shylock's impact on the play's first audiences.

The play is constructed on the basis of two romantic tales using motifs well known to sixteenth-century readers. The story of Giannetto (Shakespeare's Bassanio) and the Lady (Portia) of Belmont comes from an Italian collection of fifty stories published under the title of *Il Pecorone* ('the big sheep', or 'dunce') and attributed to one Ser Giovanni of Florence. Written in the later part of the fourteenth century, the volume did not appear until 1558. No sixteenth-century translation is known, so (unless there was a lost intermediary) Shakespeare must have read it in Italian. It gave him the main outline of the plot involving Antonio (the merchant), Bassanio (the wooer), Portia, and the Jew (Shylock). The pound of flesh motif was available also in other versions, one of which, in Alexander Silvayn's *The Orator* (translated 1596), influenced the climactic scene (4.1) in which Shylock attempts to exact the full penalty of his bond.

In the story from *Il Pecorone* the lady (a widow) challenges her suitors to seduce her, on pain of the forfeiture of their wealth, and thwarts them by drugging their wine. Shakespeare more romantically shows a maiden required by her father's will to accept only a wooer who will forswear marriage if he fails to make the right choice among caskets of gold, silver, and lead. The story of the caskets was readily available in versions by John Gower (in his *Confessio Amantis*) and Giovanni Boccaccio (in his *Decameron*), and in an anonymous anthology (the *Gesta Romanorum*). Shakespeare added the character of Jessica, Shylock's daughter who elopes with the Christian Lorenzo—perhaps influenced by episodes in Christopher Marlowe's play *The Jew of Malta* (c.1589)—and made many adjustments to the stories from which he borrowed.

The Merchant of Venice is a natural development from Shakespeare's earlier comedies, especially *The Two Gentlemen of Verona*, with its heroine disguised as a boy and its portrayal of the competing demands of love and friendship. But Portia is the first of his great romantic heroines, and Shylock his first great comic antagonist. Though the play grew out of fairy tales, its moral scheme is not entirely clear cut: the Christians are open to criticism, the Jew is true to his own code of conduct. The response of twentieth-century audiences has been complicated by racial issues; in any case, the role of Shylock affords such strong opportunities for an actor capable of arousing an undercurrent of sympathy for a vindictive character that it has sometimes unbalanced the play in performance. But the so-called trial scene (4.1) is unfailing in its impact on audiences, and the closing episodes modulate skilfully from romantic lyricism to high comedy, while sustaining the play's concern with true and false values.

THE PERSONS OF THE PLAY

ANTONIO, a merchant of Venice

BASSANIO, his friend and Portia's suitor

LEONARDO, Bassanio's servant

LORENZO ⎫
GRAZIANO ⎪
SALERIO ⎬ friends of Antonio and Bassanio
SOLANIO ⎭

SHYLOCK, a Jew

JESSICA, his daughter

TUBAL, a Jew

LANCELOT, a clown, first Shylock's servant and then Bassanio's

GOBBO, his father

PORTIA, an heiress

NERISSA, her waiting-gentlewoman

BALTHASAR ⎫
STEFANO ⎬ Portia's servants

Prince of MOROCCO ⎫
Prince of ARAGON ⎬ Portia's suitors

DUKE of Venice

Magnificoes of Venice

A jailer, attendants, and servants

The Comical History of the Merchant of Venice, or Otherwise Called the Jew of Venice

1.1 *Enter Antonio, Salerio, and Solanio*

ANTONIO

In sooth, I know not why I am so sad.
It wearies me, you say it wearies you,
But how I caught it, found it, or came by it,
What stuff 'tis made of, whereof it is born,
I am to learn; 5
And such a want-wit sadness makes of me
That I have much ado to know myself.

SALERIO

Your mind is tossing on the ocean,
There where your argosies with portly sail,
Like signors and rich burghers on the flood— 10
Or as it were the pageants of the sea—
Do overpeer the petty traffickers
That curtsy to them, do them reverence,
As they fly by them with their woven wings.

SOLANIO (*to Antonio*)

Believe me, sir, had I such venture forth 15
The better part of my affections would
Be with my hopes abroad. I should be still
Plucking the grass to know where sits the wind,
Peering in maps for ports and piers and roads,
And every object that might make me fear 20
Misfortune to my ventures out of doubt
Would make me sad.

SALERIO   My wind cooling my broth
Would blow me to an ague when I thought
What harm a wind too great might do at sea.
I should not see the sandy hour-glass run 25
But I should think of shallows and of flats,
And see my wealthy Andrew, decks in sand,
Vailing her hightop lower than her ribs
To kiss her burial. Should I go to church
And see the holy edifice of stone 30
And not bethink me straight of dangerous rocks
Which, touching but my gentle vessel's side,
Would scatter all her spices on the stream,
Enrobe the roaring waters with my silks,
And, in a word, but even now worth this, 35
And now worth nothing? Shall I have the thought
To think on this, and shall I lack the thought
That such a thing bechanced would make me sad?
But tell not me. I know Antonio
Is sad to think upon his merchandise. 40

ANTONIO

Believe me, no. I thank my fortune for it,
My ventures are not in one bottom trusted,
Nor to one place; nor is my whole estate
Upon the fortune of this present year.
Therefore my merchandise makes me not sad. 45

SOLANIO

Why then, you are in love.

ANTONIO   Fie, fie.

SOLANIO

Not in love neither? Then let us say you are sad
Because you are not merry, and 'twere as easy
For you to laugh, and leap, and say you are merry
Because you are not sad. Now, by two-headed Janus,
Nature hath framed strange fellows in her time: 51
Some that will evermore peep through their eyes
And laugh like parrots at a bagpiper,
And other of such vinegar aspect
That they'll not show their teeth in way of smile 55
Though Nestor swear the jest be laughable.

Enter Bassanio, Lorenzo, and Graziano

Here comes Bassanio, your most noble kinsman,
Graziano, and Lorenzo. Fare ye well.
We leave you now with better company.

SALERIO

I would have stayed till I had made you merry 60
If worthier friends had not prevented me.

ANTONIO

Your worth is very dear in my regard.
I take it your own business calls on you,
And you embrace th'occasion to depart.

SALERIO Good morrow, my good lords. 65

BASSANIO

Good signors both, when shall we laugh? Say, when?
You grow exceeding strange. Must it be so?

SALERIO

We'll make our leisures to attend on yours.

Exeunt Salerio and Solanio

LORENZO

My lord Bassanio, since you have found Antonio,
We two will leave you; but at dinner-time 70
I pray you have in mind where we must meet.

BASSANIO I will not fail you.

GRAZIANO

You look not well, Signor Antonio.
You have too much respect upon the world.
They lose it that do buy it with much care. 75
Believe me, you are marvellously changed.

ANTONIO

I hold the world but as the world, Graziano—
A stage where every man must play a part,
And mine a sad one.

GRAZIANO   Let me play the fool.
With mirth and laughter let old wrinkles come, 80
And let my liver rather heat with wine
Than my heart cool with mortifying groans.
Why should a man whose blood is warm within

Sit like his grandsire cut in alabaster,
Sleep when he wakes, and creep into the jaundice   85
By being peevish? I tell thee what, Antonio—
I love thee, and 'tis my love that speaks—
There are a sort of men whose visages
Do cream and mantle like a standing pond,
And do a wilful stillness entertain   90
With purpose to be dressed in an opinion
Of wisdom, gravity, profound conceit,
As who should say 'I am Sir Oracle,
And when I ope my lips, let no dog bark.'
O my Antonio, I do know of these   95
That therefore only are reputed wise
For saying nothing, when I am very sure,
If they should speak, would almost damn those ears
Which, hearing them, would call their brothers fools.
I'll tell thee more of this another time.   100
But fish not with this melancholy bait
For this fool gudgeon, this opinion.—
Come, good Lorenzo.—Fare ye well a while.
I'll end my exhortation after dinner.

LORENZO (to Antonio and Bassanio)
Well, we will leave you then till dinner-time.   105
I must be one of these same dumb wise men,
For Graziano never lets me speak.

GRAZIANO
Well, keep me company but two years more
Thou shalt not know the sound of thine own tongue.

ANTONIO
Fare you well. I'll grow a talker for this gear.   110

GRAZIANO
Thanks, i'faith, for silence is only commendable
In a neat's tongue dried and a maid not vendible.
                    Exeunt Graziano and Lorenzo

ANTONIO Yet is that anything now?

BASSANIO Graziano speaks an infinite deal of nothing,
more than any man in all Venice. His reasons are as
two grains of wheat hid in two bushels of chaff: you
shall seek all day ere you find them, and when you
have them they are not worth the search.

ANTONIO
Well, tell me now what lady is the same
To whom you swore a secret pilgrimage,   120
That you today promised to tell me of.

BASSANIO
'Tis not unknown to you, Antonio,
How much I have disabled mine estate
By something showing a more swelling port
Than my faint means would grant continuance,   125
Nor do I now make moan to be abridged
From such a noble rate; but my chief care
Is to come fairly off from the great debts
Wherein my time, something too prodigal,
Hath left me gaged. To you, Antonio,   130
I owe the most in money and in love,
And from your love I have a warranty
To unburden all my plots and purposes
How to get clear of all the debts I owe.

ANTONIO
I pray you, good Bassanio, let me know it,   135
And if it stand as you yourself still do,
Within the eye of honour, be assured
My purse, my person, my extremest means
Lie all unlocked to your occasions.

BASSANIO
In my schooldays, when I had lost one shaft,   140
I shot his fellow of the selfsame flight
The selfsame way, with more advisèd watch,
To find the other forth; and by adventuring both,
I oft found both. I urge this childhood proof
Because what follows is pure innocence.   145
I owe you much, and, like a wilful youth,
That which I owe is lost; but if you please
To shoot another arrow that self way
Which you did shoot the first, I do not doubt,
As I will watch the aim, or to find both   150
Or bring your latter hazard back again,
And thankfully rest debtor for the first.

ANTONIO
You know me well, and herein spend but time
To wind about my love with circumstance;
And out of doubt you do me now more wrong   155
In making question of my uttermost
Than if you had made waste of all I have.
Then do but say to me what I should do
That in your knowledge may by me be done,
And I am pressed unto it. Therefore speak.   160

BASSANIO
In Belmont is a lady richly left,
And she is fair, and, fairer than that word,
Of wondrous virtues. Sometimes from her eyes
I did receive fair speechless messages.
Her name is Portia, nothing undervalued   165
To Cato's daughter, Brutus' Portia;
Nor is the wide world ignorant of her worth,
For the four winds blow in from every coast
Renownèd suitors, and her sunny locks
Hang on her temples like a golden fleece,   170
Which makes her seat of Belmont Colchis' strand,
And many Jasons come in quest of her.
O my Antonio, had I but the means
To hold a rival place with one of them,
I have a mind presages me such thrift   175
That I should questionless be fortunate.

ANTONIO
Thou know'st that all my fortunes are at sea,
Neither have I money nor commodity
To raise a present sum. Therefore go forth—
Try what my credit can in Venice do;   180
That shall be racked even to the uttermost
To furnish thee to Belmont, to fair Portia.
Go presently enquire, and so will I,
Where money is; and I no question make
To have it of my trust or for my sake.   185
                    Exeunt ⌜severally⌝

1.2   *Enter Portia with Nerissa, her waiting-woman*

PORTIA By my troth, Nerissa, my little body is aweary of this great world.

NERISSA You would be, sweet madam, if your miseries were in the same abundance as your good fortunes are; and yet, for aught I see, they are as sick that surfeit with too much as they that starve with nothing. It is no mean happiness, therefore, to be seated in the mean. Superfluity comes sooner by white hairs, but competency lives longer.

PORTIA Good sentences, and well pronounced.   10

NERISSA They would be better if well followed.

PORTIA If to do were as easy as to know what were good to do, chapels had been churches, and poor men's cottages princes' palaces. It is a good divine that follows his own instructions. I can easier teach twenty what were good to be done than to be one of the twenty to follow mine own teaching. The brain may devise laws for the blood, but a hot temper leaps o'er a cold decree. Such a hare is madness, the youth, to skip o'er the meshes of good counsel, the cripple. But this reasoning is not in the fashion to choose me a husband. O me, the word 'choose'! I may neither choose who I would nor refuse who I dislike; so is the will of a living daughter curbed by the will of a dead father. Is it not hard, Nerissa, that I cannot choose one nor refuse none?   26

NERISSA Your father was ever virtuous, and holy men at their death have good inspirations; therefore the lottery that he hath devised in these three chests of gold, silver, and lead, whereof who chooses his meaning chooses you, will no doubt never be chosen by any rightly but one who you shall rightly love. But what warmth is there in your affection towards any of these princely suitors that are already come?   34

PORTIA I pray thee overname them, and as thou namest them I will describe them; and according to my description, level at my affection.

NERISSA First there is the Neapolitan prince.   38

PORTIA Ay, that's a colt indeed, for he doth nothing but talk of his horse, and he makes it a great appropriation to his own good parts that he can shoe him himself. I am much afeard my lady his mother played false with a smith.

NERISSA Then is there the County Palatine.   44

PORTIA He doth nothing but frown, as who should say 'An you will not have me, choose'. He hears merry tales and smiles not. I fear he will prove the weeping philosopher when he grows old, being so full of unmannerly sadness in his youth. I had rather be married to a death's-head with a bone in his mouth than to either of these. God defend me from these two!

NERISSA How say you by the French lord, Monsieur le Bon?   53

PORTIA God made him, and therefore let him pass for a man. In truth, I know it is a sin to be a mocker, but he—why, he hath a horse better than the Neapolitan's, a better bad habit of frowning than the Count Palatine. He is every man in no man. If a throstle sing, he falls straight a-cap'ring. He will fence with his own shadow. If I should marry him, I should marry twenty husbands. If he would despise me, I would forgive him, for if he love me to madness, I shall never requite him.   62

NERISSA What say you then to Falconbridge, the young baron of England?

PORTIA You know I say nothing to him, for he understands not me, nor I him. He hath neither Latin, French, nor Italian, and you will come into the court and swear that I have a poor pennyworth in the English. He is a proper man's picture, but alas, who can converse with a dumb show? How oddly he is suited! I think he bought his doublet in Italy, his round hose in France, his bonnet in Germany, and his behaviour everywhere. ,   73

NERISSA What think you of the Scottish lord, his neighbour?

PORTIA That he hath a neighbourly charity in him, for he borrowed a box of the ear of the Englishman and swore he would pay him again when he was able. I think the Frenchman became his surety, and sealed under for another.   80

NERISSA How like you the young German, the Duke of Saxony's nephew?

PORTIA Very vilely in the morning when he is sober, and most vilely in the afternoon when he is drunk. When he is best he is a little worse than a man, and when he is worst he is little better than a beast. An the worst fall that ever fell, I hope I shall make shift to go without him.   88

NERISSA If he should offer to choose, and choose the right casket, you should refuse to perform your father's will if you should refuse to accept him.

PORTIA Therefore, for fear of the worst, I pray thee set a deep glass of Rhenish wine on the contrary casket; for if the devil be within and that temptation without, I know he will choose it. I will do anything, Nerissa, ere I will be married to a sponge.   96

NERISSA You need not fear, lady, the having any of these lords. They have acquainted me with their determinations, which is indeed to return to their home and to trouble you with no more suit unless you may be won by some other sort than your father's imposition depending on the caskets.   102

PORTIA If I live to be as old as Sibylla I will die as chaste as Diana unless I be obtained by the manner of my father's will. I am glad this parcel of wooers are so reasonable, for there is not one among them but I dote on his very absence; and I pray God grant them a fair departure.   108

NERISSA Do you not remember, lady, in your father's time, a Venetian, a scholar and a soldier, that came hither in company of the Marquis of Montferrat?

PORTIA Yes, yes, it was Bassanio—as I think, so was he called.

NERISSA True, madam. He of all the men that ever my
foolish eyes looked upon was the best deserving a fair
lady.   116
PORTIA I remember him well, and I remember him worthy
of thy praise.

Enter a Servingman

How now, what news?   119
SERVINGMAN The four strangers seek for you, madam, to
take their leave, and there is a forerunner come from
a fifth, the Prince of Morocco, who brings word the
Prince his master will be here tonight.   123
PORTIA If I could bid the fifth welcome with so good heart
as I can bid the other four farewell, I should be glad
of his approach. If he have the condition of a saint and
the complexion of a devil, I had rather he should shrive
me than wive me.   128
Come, Nerissa. (*To the Servingman*) Sirrah, go before.
Whiles we shut the gate upon one wooer,
Another knocks at the door.   *Exeunt*

1.3   *Enter Bassanio with Shylock the Jew*
SHYLOCK Three thousand ducats. Well.
BASSANIO Ay, sir, for three months.
SHYLOCK For three months. Well.
BASSANIO For the which, as I told you, Antonio shall be
bound.   5
SHYLOCK Antonio shall become bound. Well.
BASSANIO May you stead me? Will you pleasure me? Shall
I know your answer?
SHYLOCK Three thousand ducats for three months, and
Antonio bound.   10
BASSANIO Your answer to that.
SHYLOCK Antonio is a good man.
BASSANIO Have you heard any imputation to the
contrary?   14
SHYLOCK Ho, no, no, no, no! My meaning in saying he
is a good man is to have you understand me that he
is sufficient. Yet his means are in supposition. He hath
an argosy bound to Tripolis, another to the Indies. I
understand moreover upon the Rialto he hath a third
at Mexico, a fourth for England, and other ventures he
hath squandered abroad. But ships are but boards,
sailors but men. There be land rats and water rats,
water thieves and land thieves—I mean pirates—and
then there is the peril of waters, winds, and rocks. The
man is, notwithstanding, sufficient. Three thousand
ducats. I think I may take his bond.   26
BASSANIO Be assured you may.
SHYLOCK I will be assured I may, and that I may be
assured, I will bethink me. May I speak with Antonio?
BASSANIO If it please you to dine with us.   30
SHYLOCK ⌈*aside*⌉ Yes, to smell pork, to eat of the habitation
which your prophet the Nazarite conjured the devil
into! I will buy with you, sell with you, talk with you,
walk with you, and so following, but I will not eat
with you, drink with you, nor pray with you.   35

Enter Antonio

⌈*To Antonio*⌉ What news on the Rialto? ⌈*To Bassanio*⌉
Who is he comes here?
BASSANIO This is Signor Antonio.
    ⌈*Bassanio and Antonio speak silently to one another*⌉
SHYLOCK (*aside*)
How like a fawning publican he looks.
I hate him for he is a Christian;   40
But more, for that in low simplicity
He lends out money gratis, and brings down
The rate of usance here with us in Venice.
If I can catch him once upon the hip
I will feed fat the ancient grudge I bear him.   45
He hates our sacred nation, and he rails,
Even there where merchants most do congregate,
On me, my bargains, and my well-won thrift—
Which he calls interest. Cursèd be my tribe
If I forgive him.
BASSANIO   Shylock, do you hear?   50
SHYLOCK
I am debating of my present store,
And by the near guess of my memory
I cannot instantly raise up the gross
Of full three thousand ducats. What of that?
Tubal, a wealthy Hebrew of my tribe,   55
Will furnish me. But soft—how many months
Do you desire? ⌈*To Antonio*⌉ Rest you fair, good signor.
Your worship was the last man in our mouths.
ANTONIO
Shylock, albeit I neither lend nor borrow
By taking nor by giving of excess,   60
Yet to supply the ripe wants of my friend
I'll break a custom. (*To Bassanio*) Is he yet possessed
How much ye would?
SHYLOCK Ay, ay, three thousand ducats.
ANTONIO And for three months.   65
SHYLOCK
I had forgot—three months. (*To Bassanio*) You told me
so.—
Well then, your bond; and let me see—but hear you,
Methoughts you said you neither lend nor borrow
Upon advantage.
ANTONIO   I do never use it.
SHYLOCK
When Jacob grazed his uncle Laban's sheep—   70
This Jacob from our holy Abram was,
As his wise mother wrought in his behalf,
The third possessor; ay, he was the third—
ANTONIO
And what of him? Did he take interest?
SHYLOCK
No, not take interest, not, as you would say,   75
Directly int'rest. Mark what Jacob did:
When Laban and himself were compromised
That all the eanlings which were streaked and pied
Should fall as Jacob's hire, the ewes, being rank,
In end of autumn turnèd to the rams,   80
And when the work of generation was

Between these woolly breeders in the act,
The skilful shepherd peeled me certain wands,
And in the doing of the deed of kind
He stuck them up before the fulsome ewes   85
Who, then conceiving, did in eaning time
Fall parti-coloured lambs; and those were Jacob's.
This was a way to thrive; and he was blest;
And thrift is blessing, if men steal it not.

ANTONIO

This was a venture, sir, that Jacob served for—   90
A thing not in his power to bring to pass,
But swayed and fashioned by the hand of heaven.
Was this inserted to make interest good,
Or is your gold and silver ewes and rams?

SHYLOCK

I cannot tell. I make it breed as fast.   95
But note me, signor—

ANTONIO   Mark you this, Bassanio?
The devil can cite Scripture for his purpose.
An evil soul producing holy witness
Is like a villain with a smiling cheek,
A goodly apple rotten at the heart.   100
O, what a goodly outside falsehood hath!

SHYLOCK

Three thousand ducats. 'Tis a good round sum.
Three months from twelve—then let me see the rate.

ANTONIO

Well, Shylock, shall we be beholden to you?

SHYLOCK

Signor Antonio, many a time and oft   105
In the Rialto you have rated me
About my moneys and my usances.
Still have I borne it with a patient shrug,
For suff'rance is the badge of all our tribe.
You call me misbeliever, cut-throat, dog,   110
And spit upon my Jewish gaberdine,
And all for use of that which is mine own.
Well then, it now appears you need my help.
Go to, then. You come to me, and you say
'Shylock, we would have moneys'—you say so,   115
You, that did void your rheum upon my beard,
And foot me as you spurn a stranger cur
Over your threshold. Moneys is your suit.
What should I say to you? Should I not say
'Hath a dog money? Is it possible   120
A cur can lend three thousand ducats?' Or
Shall I bend low, and in a bondman's key,
With bated breath and whisp'ring humbleness
Say this: 'Fair sir, you spat on me on Wednesday last;
You spurned me such a day; another time   125
You called me dog; and for these courtesies
I'll lend you thus much moneys'?

ANTONIO

I am as like to call thee so again,
To spit on thee again, to spurn thee too.
If thou wilt lend this money, lend it not   130
As to thy friends; for when did friendship take
A breed for barren metal of his friend?

But lend it rather to thine enemy,
Who if he break, thou mayst with better face
Exact the penalty.

SHYLOCK   Why, look you, how you storm!   135
I would be friends with you, and have your love,
Forget the shames that you have stained me with,
Supply your present wants, and take no doit
Of usance for my moneys; and you'll not hear me.
This is kind I offer.   140

BASSANIO This were kindness.

SHYLOCK This kindness will I show.
Go with me to a notary, seal me there
Your single bond, and, in a merry sport,
If you repay me not on such a day,   145
In such a place, such sum or sums as are
Expressed in the condition, let the forfeit
Be nominated for an equal pound
Of your fair flesh to be cut off and taken
In what part of your body pleaseth me.   150

ANTONIO

Content, in faith. I'll seal to such a bond,
And say there is much kindness in the Jew.

BASSANIO

You shall not seal to such a bond for me.
I'll rather dwell in my necessity.

ANTONIO

Why, fear not, man; I will not forfeit it.   155
Within these two months—that's a month before
This bond expires—I do expect return
Of thrice three times the value of this bond.

SHYLOCK

O father Abram, what these Christians are,
Whose own hard dealings teaches them suspect   160
The thoughts of others! (*To Bassanio*) Pray you tell me
    this:
If he should break his day, what should I gain
By the exaction of the forfeiture?
A pound of man's flesh taken from a man
Is not so estimable, profitable neither,   165
As flesh of muttons, beeves, or goats. I say,
To buy his favour I extend this friendship.
If he will take it, so. If not, adieu,
And, for my love, I pray you wrong me not.

ANTONIO

Yes, Shylock, I will seal unto this bond.   170

SHYLOCK

Then meet me forthwith at the notary's.
Give him direction for this merry bond,
And I will go and purse the ducats straight,
See to my house—left in the fearful guard
Of an unthrifty knave—and presently   175
I'll be with you.

ANTONIO   Hie thee, gentle Jew.   *Exit Shylock*
The Hebrew will turn Christian; he grows kind.

BASSANIO

I like not fair terms and a villain's mind.

ANTONIO

Come on. In this there can be no dismay.   179
My ships come home a month before the day.   *Exeunt*

2.1 ⌈*Flourish of cornetts.*⌉ *Enter the Prince of Morocco,*
     a tawny Moor all in white, and three or four
     followers accordingly, with Portia, Nerissa, and
     their train

MOROCCO (*to Portia*)
  Mislike me not for my complexion,
  The shadowed livery of the burnished sun,
  To whom I am a neighbour and near bred.
  Bring me the fairest creature northward born,
  Where Phoebus' fire scarce thaws the icicles,   5
  And let us make incision for your love
  To prove whose blood is reddest, his or mine.
  I tell thee, lady, this aspect of mine
  Hath feared the valiant. By my love I swear,
  The best regarded virgins of our clime   10
  Have loved it too. I would not change this hue
  Except to steal your thoughts, my gentle queen.
PORTIA
  In terms of choice I am not solely led
  By nice direction of a maiden's eyes.
  Besides, the lott'ry of my destiny   15
  Bars me the right of voluntary choosing.
  But if my father had not scanted me,
  And hedged me by his wit to yield myself
  His wife who wins me by that means I told you,
  Yourself, renownèd Prince, then stood as fair   20
  As any comer I have looked on yet
  For my affection.
MOROCCO   Even for that I thank you.
  Therefore I pray you lead me to the caskets
  To try my fortune. By this scimitar,
  That slew the Sophy and a Persian prince   25
  That won three fields of Sultan Suleiman,
  I would o'erstare the sternest eyes that look,
  Outbrave the heart most daring on the earth,
  Pluck the young sucking cubs from the she-bear,
  Yea, mock the lion when a roars for prey,   30
  To win the lady. But alas the while,
  If Hercules and Lichas play at dice
  Which is the better man, the greater throw
  May turn by fortune from the weaker hand.
  So is Alcides beaten by his rage,   35
  And so may I, blind Fortune leading me,
  Miss that which one unworthier may attain,
  And die with grieving.
PORTIA   You must take your chance,
  And either not attempt to choose at all,
  Or swear before you choose, if you choose wrong   40
  Never to speak to lady afterward
  In way of marriage. Therefore be advised.
MOROCCO
  Nor will not. Come, bring me unto my chance.
PORTIA
  First, forward to the temple. After dinner
  Your hazard shall be made.
MOROCCO   Good fortune then,   45
  To make me blest or cursèd'st among men.
                    ⌈*Flourish of cornetts.*⌉ *Exeunt*

2.2 *Enter Lancelot the clown*

LANCELOT Certainly my conscience will serve me to run
from this Jew my master. The fiend is at mine elbow
and tempts me, saying to me 'Gobbo, Lancelot Gobbo,
good Lancelot,' or 'good Gobbo,' or 'good Lancelot
Gobbo—use your legs, take the start, run away.' My
conscience says 'No, take heed, honest Lancelot, take
heed, honest Gobbo,' or, as aforesaid, 'honest Lancelot
Gobbo—do not run, scorn running with thy heels.'
Well, the most courageous fiend bids me pack. '*Via!*'
says the fiend; 'Away!' says the fiend. 'For the heavens,
rouse up a brave mind,' says the fiend, 'and run.' Well,
my conscience hanging about the neck of my heart
says very wisely to me, 'My honest friend Lancelot'—
being an honest man's son, or rather an honest
woman's son, for indeed my father did something
smack, something grow to; he had a kind of taste—
well, my conscience says, 'Lancelot, budge not';
'Budge!' says the fiend; 'Budge not', says my
conscience. 'Conscience,' say I, 'you counsel well';
'Fiend,' say I, 'you counsel well.' To be ruled by my
conscience I should stay with the Jew my master who,
God bless the mark, is a kind of devil; and to run away
from the Jew I should be ruled by the fiend who, saving
your reverence, is the devil himself. Certainly the Jew
is the very devil incarnation; and in my conscience,
my conscience is but a kind of hard conscience to offer
to counsel me to stay with the Jew. The fiend gives the
more friendly counsel. I will run, fiend. My heels are
at your commandment. I will run.   29
          Enter old Gobbo, ⌈*blind,*⌉ *with a basket*
GOBBO Master young man, you, I pray you, which is the
way to Master Jew's?
LANCELOT (*aside*) O heavens, this is my true-begotten father
who, being more than sand-blind—high-gravel-blind—
knows me not. I will try confusions with him.   34
GOBBO Master young gentleman, I pray you which is the
way to Master Jew's?
LANCELOT Turn up on your right hand at the next turning,
but at the next turning of all on your left, marry at
the very next turning, turn of no hand but turn down
indirectly to the Jew's house.   40
GOBBO By God's sonties, 'twill be a hard way to hit. Can
you tell me whether one Lancelot that dwells with him
dwell with him or no?
LANCELOT Talk you of young Master Lancelot? (*Aside*)
Mark me now, now will I raise the waters. (*To Gobbo*)
Talk you of young Master Lancelot?   46
GOBBO No master, sir, but a poor man's son. His father,
though I say't, is an honest exceeding poor man, and,
God be thanked, well to live.
LANCELOT Well, let his father be what a will, we talk of
young Master Lancelot.   51
GOBBO Your worship's friend, and Lancelot, sir.
LANCELOT But I pray you, *ergo* old man, *ergo* I beseech
you, talk you of young Master Lancelot?
GOBBO Of Lancelot, an't please your mastership.   55
LANCELOT *Ergo* Master Lancelot. Talk not of Master

Lancelot, father, for the young gentleman, according to fates and destinies and such odd sayings—the sisters three and such branches of learning—is indeed deceased; or, as you would say in plain terms, gone to heaven.   61
GOBBO Marry, God forbid! The boy was the very staff of my age, my very prop.
LANCELOT ⌈aside⌉ Do I look like a cudgel or a hovel-post, a staff or a prop? (To Gobbo) Do you know me, father?
GOBBO Alack the day, I know you not, young gentleman. But I pray you tell me, is my boy—God rest his soul—alive or dead?
LANCELOT Do you not know me, father?
GOBBO Alack, sir, I am sand-blind. I know you not.   70
LANCELOT Nay, indeed, if you had your eyes you might fail of the knowing me. It is a wise father that knows his own child. Well, old man, I will tell you news of your son. (Kneeling) Give me your blessing. Truth will come to light; murder cannot be hid long—a man's son may, but in the end truth will out.   76
GOBBO Pray you, sir, stand up. I am sure you are not Lancelot, my boy.
LANCELOT Pray you, let's have no more fooling about it, but give me your blessing. I am Lancelot, your boy that was, your son that is, your child that shall be.
GOBBO I cannot think you are my son.
LANCELOT I know not what I shall think of that, but I am Lancelot the Jew's man, and I am sure Margery your wife is my mother.   85
GOBBO Her name is Margery indeed. I'll be sworn, if thou be Lancelot thou art mine own flesh and blood.
  He feels Lancelot's head
Lord worshipped might he be, what a beard hast thou got! Thou hast got more hair on thy chin than Dobbin my fill-horse has on his tail.   90
LANCELOT It should seem then that Dobbin's tail grows backward. I am sure he had more hair of his tail than I have of my face when I last saw him.
GOBBO Lord, how art thou changed! How dost thou and thy master agree? I have brought him a present. How 'gree you now?   96
LANCELOT Well, well; but for mine own part, as I have set up my rest to run away, so I will not rest till I have run some ground. My master's a very Jew. Give him a present?—give him a halter! I am famished in his service. You may tell every finger I have with my ribs. Father, I am glad you are come. Give me your present to one Master Bassanio, who indeed gives rare new liveries. If I serve not him, I will run as far as God has any ground.   105
  Enter Bassanio with Leonardo and followers
O rare fortune! Here comes the man. To him, father, for I am a Jew if I serve the Jew any longer.
BASSANIO (to one of his men) You may do so, but let it be so hasted that supper be ready at the farthest by five of the clock. See these letters delivered, put the liveries to making, and desire Graziano to come anon to my lodging.   *Exit one*

LANCELOT (to Gobbo) To him, father.
GOBBO (to Bassanio) God bless your worship.
BASSANIO Gramercy. Wouldst thou aught with me?   115
GOBBO Here's my son, sir, a poor boy—
LANCELOT (to Bassanio) Not a poor boy, sir, but the rich Jew's man that would, sir, as my father shall specify.
GOBBO (to Bassanio) He hath a great infection, sir, as one would say, to serve—   120
LANCELOT Indeed, the short and the long is, I serve the Jew, and have a desire as my father shall specify.
GOBBO (to Bassanio) His master and he, saving your worship's reverence, are scarce cater-cousins.   124
LANCELOT (to Bassanio) To be brief, the very truth is that the Jew, having done me wrong, doth cause me, as my father—being, I hope, an old man—shall frutify unto you.   128
GOBBO (to Bassanio) I have here a dish of doves that I would bestow upon your worship, and my suit is—
LANCELOT (to Bassanio) In very brief, the suit is impertinent to myself, as your worship shall know by this honest old man; and though I say it, though old man, yet, poor man, my father.
BASSANIO One speak for both. What would you?   135
LANCELOT Serve you, sir.
GOBBO (to Bassanio) That is the very defect of the matter, sir.
BASSANIO (to Lancelot)
I know thee well. Thou hast obtained thy suit.
Shylock thy master spoke with me this day,   140
And hath preferred thee, if it be preferment
To leave a rich Jew's service to become
The follower of so poor a gentleman.
LANCELOT The old proverb is very well parted between my master Shylock and you, sir: you have the grace of God, sir, and he hath enough.   146
BASSANIO
Thou speak'st it well. (To Gobbo) Go, father, with thy son.
(To Lancelot) Take leave of thy old master and enquire
My lodging out. (To one of his men) Give him a livery
More guarded than his fellows'. See it done.   150
LANCELOT (to Gobbo) Father, in. I cannot get a service, no, I have ne'er a tongue in my head—well!
  He looks at his palm
If any man in Italy have a fairer table which doth offer to swear upon a book, I shall have good fortune. Go to, here's a simple line of life, here's a small trifle of wives—alas, fifteen wives is nothing. Eleven widows and nine maids is a simple coming-in for one man, and then to scape drowning thrice, and to be in peril of my life with the edge of a featherbed—here are simple scapes. Well, if Fortune be a woman, she's a good wench for this gear. Father, come. I'll take my leave of the Jew in the twinkling.   *Exit with old Gobbo*
BASSANIO
I pray thee, good Leonardo, think on this.
These things being bought and orderly bestowed,
Return in haste, for I do feast tonight   165
My best-esteemed acquaintance. Hie thee. Go.

LEONARDO
My best endeavours shall be done herein.
He begins to leave. Enter Graziano
GRAZIANO (*to Leonardo*)
Where's your master?
LEONARDO   Yonder, sir, he walks.   *Exit*
GRAZIANO
Signor Bassanio.
BASSANIO   Graziano.
GRAZIANO
I have a suit to you.
BASSANIO   You have obtained it.   170
GRAZIANO
You must not deny me. I must go with you to
    Belmont.
BASSANIO
Why then, you must. But hear thee, Graziano,
Thou art too wild, too rude and bold of voice—
Parts that become thee happily enough,
And in such eyes as ours appear not faults;   175
But where thou art not known, why, there they show
Something too liberal. Pray thee, take pain
To allay with some cold drops of modesty
Thy skipping spirit, lest through thy wild behaviour
I be misconstered in the place I go to,   180
And lose my hopes.
GRAZIANO   Signor Bassanio, hear me.
If I do not put on a sober habit,
Talk with respect, and swear but now and then,
Wear prayer books in my pocket, look demurely—
Nay more, while grace is saying hood mine eyes   185
Thus with my hat, and sigh, and say 'Amen',
Use all the observance of civility,
Like one well studied in a sad ostent
To please his grandam, never trust me more.
BASSANIO Well, we shall see your bearing.   190
GRAZIANO
Nay, but I bar tonight. You shall not gauge me
By what we do tonight.
BASSANIO   No, that were pity.
I would entreat you rather to put on
Your boldest suit of mirth, for we have friends
That purpose merriment. But fare you well.   195
I have some business.
GRAZIANO
And I must to Lorenzo and the rest.
But we will visit you at supper-time.   *Exeunt severally*

2.3   *Enter Jessica and Lancelot, the clown*
JESSICA
I am sorry thou wilt leave my father so.
Our house is hell, and thou, a merry devil,
Didst rob it of some taste of tediousness.
But fare thee well. There is a ducat for thee.
And, Lancelot, soon at supper shalt thou see   5
Lorenzo, who is thy new master's guest.
Give him this letter, do it secretly;
And so farewell. I would not have my father
See me in talk with thee.

LANCELOT Adieu. Tears exhibit my tongue, most beautiful
pagan; most sweet Jew; if a Christian do not play the
knave and get thee, I am much deceived. But adieu.
These foolish drops do something drown my manly
spirit. Adieu.
JESSICA Farewell, good Lancelot.   *Exit Lancelot*
Alack, what heinous sin is it in me   16
To be ashamed to be my father's child!
But though I am a daughter to his blood,
I am not to his manners. O Lorenzo,
If thou keep promise I shall end this strife,   20
Become a Christian and thy loving wife.   *Exit*

2.4   *Enter Graziano, Lorenzo, Salerio, and Salanio*
LORENZO
Nay, we will slink away in supper-time,
Disguise us at my lodging, and return
All in an hour.
GRAZIANO
We have not made good preparation.
SALERIO
We have not spoke as yet of torchbearers.   5
SOLANIO
'Tis vile, unless it may be quaintly ordered,
And better in my mind not undertook.
LORENZO
'Tis now but four o'clock. We have two hours
To furnish us.
    Enter Lancelot with a letter
            Friend Lancelot, what's the news?
LANCELOT (*presenting the letter*) An it shall please you to
break up this, it shall seem to signify.   11
LORENZO (*taking the letter*)
I know the hand. In faith, 'tis a fair hand,
And whiter than the paper it writ on
Is the fair hand that writ.
GRAZIANO   Love-news, in faith.
LANCELOT ⌈*to Lorenzo*⌉ By your leave, sir.   15
LORENZO Whither goest thou?
LANCELOT Marry, sir, to bid my old master the Jew to sup
tonight with my new master the Christian.
LORENZO
Hold, here, take this. (*Giving money*) Tell gentle Jessica
I will not fail her. Speak it privately.   20
Go.   *Exit Lancelot*
    Gentlemen,
Will you prepare you for this masque tonight?
I am provided of a torchbearer.
SALERIO
Ay, marry, I'll be gone about it straight.
SOLANIO
And so will I.
LORENZO   Meet me and Graziano   25
    At Graziano's lodging some hour hence.
SALERIO 'Tis good we do so.   *Exit with Solanio*
GRAZIANO
Was not that letter from fair Jessica?
LORENZO
I must needs tell thee all. She hath directed

How I shall take her from her father's house,   30
What gold and jewels she is furnished with,
What page's suit she hath in readiness.
If e'er the Jew her father come to heaven
It will be for his gentle daughter's sake;
And never dare misfortune cross her foot   35
Unless she do it under this excuse:
That she is issue to a faithless Jew.
Come, go with me. Peruse this as thou goest.
He gives Graziano the letter
Fair Jessica shall be my torchbearer.   *Exeunt*

2.5   *Enter Shylock the Jew and his man that was,*
         Lancelot the clown

SHYLOCK
Well, thou shalt see, thy eyes shall be thy judge,
The difference of old Shylock and Bassanio.
(*Calling*) What, Jessica! (*To Lancelot*) Thou shalt not
   gormandize
As thou hast done with me. (*Calling*) What, Jessica!
(*To Lancelot*) And sleep and snore and rend apparel
   out.   5
(*Calling*) Why, Jessica, I say!
LANCELOT (*calling*)   Why, Jessica!
SHYLOCK
Who bids thee call? I do not bid thee call.
LANCELOT Your worship was wont to tell me I could do
nothing without bidding.
   Enter Jessica
JESSICA (*to Shylock*) Call you? What is your will?   10
SHYLOCK
I am bid forth to supper, Jessica.
There are my keys. But wherefore should I go?
I am not bid for love. They flatter me,
But yet I'll go in hate, to feed upon
The prodigal Christian. Jessica, my girl,   15
Look to my house. I am right loath to go.
There is some ill a-brewing towards my rest,
For I did dream of money-bags tonight.
LANCELOT I beseech you, sir, go. My young master doth
expect your reproach.   20
SHYLOCK So do I his.
LANCELOT And they have conspired together. I will not
say you shall see a masque, but if you do, then it was
not for nothing that my nose fell a-bleeding on Black
Monday last at six o'clock i'th' morning, falling out
that year on Ash Wednesday was four year in
th'afternoon.
SHYLOCK
What, are there masques? Hear you me, Jessica,
Lock up my doors; and when you hear the drum
And the vile squealing of the wry-necked fife,   30
Clamber not you up to the casements then,
Nor thrust your head into the public street
To gaze on Christian fools with varnished faces,
But stop my house's ears—I mean my casements.
Let not the sound of shallow fopp'ry enter   35
My sober house. By Jacob's staff I swear

I have no mind of feasting forth tonight.
But I will go. (*To Lancelot*) Go you before me, sirrah.
Say I will come.
LANCELOT   I will go before, sir.
(*Aside to Jessica*)
Mistress, look out at window for all this.   40
   There will come a Christian by
   Will be worth a Jewès eye.   *Exit*
SHYLOCK (*to Jessica*)
What says that fool of Hagar's offspring, ha?
JESSICA
His words were 'Farewell, mistress'; nothing else.
SHYLOCK
The patch is kind enough, but a huge feeder,   45
Snail-slow in profit, and he sleeps by day
More than the wildcat. Drones hive not with me;
Therefore I part with him, and part with him
To one that I would have him help to waste
His borrowed purse. Well, Jessica, go in.   50
Perhaps I will return immediately.
Do as I bid you. Shut doors after you.
Fast bind, fast find—
A proverb never stale in thrifty mind.
                                        Exit at one door
JESSICA
Farewell; and if my fortune be not crossed,   55
I have a father, you a daughter lost.
                                        Exit at another door

2.6   *Enter the masquers, Graziano and Salerio, ⌈with*
         torchbearers⌉

GRAZIANO
This is the penthouse under which Lorenzo
Desired us to make stand.
SALERIO   His hour is almost past.
GRAZIANO
And it is marvel he outdwells his hour,
For lovers ever run before the clock.
SALERIO
O, ten times faster Venus' pigeons fly   5
To seal love's bonds new made than they are wont
To keep obligèd faith unforfeited.
GRAZIANO
That ever holds. Who riseth from a feast
With that keen appetite that he sits down?
Where is the horse that doth untread again   10
His tedious measures with the unbated fire
That he did pace them first? All things that are
Are with more spirit chasèd than enjoyed.
How like a younker or a prodigal
The scarfèd barque puts from her native bay,   15
Hugged and embracèd by the strumpet wind!
How like the prodigal doth she return,
With over-weathered ribs and raggèd sails,
Lean, rent, and beggared by the strumpet wind!
   Enter Lorenzo, ⌈with a torch⌉
SALERIO
Here comes Lorenzo. More of this hereafter.   20

LORENZO

Sweet friends, your patience for my long abode.
Not I but my affairs have made you wait.
When you shall please to play the thieves for wives
I'll watch as long for you therein. Approach.   24
Here dwells my father Jew. (*Calling*) Ho, who's within?
        Enter Jessica above in boy's apparel

JESSICA

Who are you? Tell me for more certainty,
Albeit I'll swear that I do know your tongue.

LORENZO Lorenzo, and thy love.

JESSICA

Lorenzo, certain, and my love indeed,
For who love I so much? And now who knows   30
But you, Lorenzo, whether I am yours?

LORENZO

Heaven and thy thoughts are witness that thou art.

JESSICA

Here, catch this casket. It is worth the pains.
I am glad 'tis night, you do not look on me,
For I am much ashamed of my exchange;   35
But love is blind, and lovers cannot see
The pretty follies that themselves commit;
For if they could, Cupid himself would blush
To see me thus transformèd to a boy.

LORENZO

Descend, for you must be my torchbearer.   40

JESSICA

What, must I hold a candle to my shames?
They in themselves, good sooth, are too too light.
Why, 'tis an office of discovery, love,
And I should be obscured.

LORENZO   So are you, sweet,
Even in the lovely garnish of a boy.   45
But come at once,
For the close night doth play the runaway,
And we are stayed for at Bassanio's feast.

JESSICA

I will make fast the doors, and gild myself
With some more ducats, and be with you straight. 50
        Exit above

GRAZIANO

Now, by my hood, a gentile, and no Jew.

LORENZO

Beshrew me but I love her heartily,
For she is wise, if I can judge of her;
And fair she is, if that mine eyes be true;
And true she is, as she hath proved herself;   55
And therefore like herself, wise, fair, and true,
Shall she be placèd in my constant soul.
        Enter Jessica below
What, art thou come? On, gentlemen, away.
Our masquing mates by this time for us stay.
        Exit with Jessica and Salerio
        Enter Antonio

ANTONIO

Who's there?

GRAZIANO   Signor Antonio?   60

ANTONIO

Fie, fie, Graziano, where are all the rest?
'Tis nine o'clock. Our friends all stay for you.
No masque tonight. The wind is come about.
Bassanio presently will go aboard.
I have sent twenty out to seek for you.   65

GRAZIANO

I am glad on't. I desire no more delight
Than to be under sail and gone tonight.   *Exeunt*

2.7   ⌈*Flourish of cornetts.*⌉ *Enter Portia with Morocco*
        and both their trains

PORTIA

Go, draw aside the curtains, and discover
The several caskets to this noble prince.
        The curtains are drawn aside, revealing three caskets
(*To Morocco*) Now make your choice.

MOROCCO

This first of gold, who this inscription bears:
'Who chooseth me shall gain what many men desire.'
The second silver, which this promise carries: 6
'Who chooseth me shall get as much as he deserves.'
This third dull lead, with warning all as blunt:
'Who chooseth me must give and hazard all he hath.'
How shall I know if I do choose the right?   10

PORTIA

The one of them contains my picture, Prince.
If you choose that, then I am yours withal.

MOROCCO

Some god direct my judgement! Let me see.
I will survey th'inscriptions back again.
What says this leaden casket?   15
'Who chooseth me must give and hazard all he hath.'
Must give, for what? For lead? Hazard for lead?
This casket threatens. Men that hazard all
Do it in hope of fair advantages.
A golden mind stoops not to shows of dross.   20
I'll then nor give nor hazard aught for lead.
What says the silver with her virgin hue?
'Who chooseth me shall get as much as he deserves.'
'As much as he deserves': pause there, Morocco,
And weigh thy value with an even hand.   25
If thou beest rated by thy estimation
Thou dost deserve enough, and yet 'enough'
May not extend so far as to the lady.
And yet to be afeard of my deserving
Were but a weak disabling of myself.   30
As much as I deserve—why, that's the lady!
I do in birth deserve her, and in fortunes,
In graces, and in qualities of breeding;
But more than these, in love I do deserve.
What if I strayed no farther, but chose here?   35
Let's see once more this saying graved in gold:
'Who chooseth me shall gain what many men desire.'
Why, that's the lady! All the world desires her.
From the four corners of the earth they come
To kiss this shrine, this mortal breathing saint.   40
The Hyrcanian deserts and the vasty wilds

Of wide Arabia are as throughfares now
For princes to come view fair Portia.
The watery kingdom, whose ambitious head
Spits in the face of heaven, is no bar   45
To stop the foreign spirits, but they come
As o'er a brook to see fair Portia.
One of these three contains her heavenly picture.
Is't like that lead contains her? 'Twere damnation
To think so base a thought. It were too gross   50
To rib her cerecloth in the obscure grave.
Or shall I think in silver she's immured,
Being ten times undervalued to tried gold?
O sinful thought! Never so rich a gem
Was set in worse than gold. They have in England   55
A coin that bears the figure of an angel
Stamped in gold, but that's insculped upon;
But here an angel in a golden bed
Lies all within. Deliver me the key.
Here do I choose, and thrive I as I may.   60
He is given a key
PORTIA
There, take it, Prince; and if my form lie there,
Then I am yours.
Morocco opens the golden casket
MOROCCO   O hell! What have we here?
A carrion death, within whose empty eye
There is a written scroll. I'll read the writing.
'All that glisters is not gold;   65
Often have you heard that told.
Many a man his life hath sold
But my outside to behold.
Gilded tombs do worms infold.
Had you been as wise as bold,   70
Young in limbs, in judgement old,
Your answer had not been enscrolled.
Fare you well; your suit is cold.'
Cold indeed, and labour lost.
Then farewell heat, and welcome frost.   75
Portia, adieu. I have too grieved a heart
To take a tedious leave. Thus losers part.
⌐*Flourish of cornetts.*⌐ *Exit with his train*
PORTIA
A gentle riddance. Draw the curtains, go.
Let all of his complexion choose me so.
The curtains are drawn. Exeunt

2.8   *Enter Salerio and Solanio*
SALERIO
Why, man, I saw Bassanio under sail.
With him is Graziano gone along,
And in their ship I am sure Lorenzo is not.
SOLANIO
The villain Jew with outcries raised the Duke,
Who went with him to search Bassanio's ship.   5
SALERIO
He came too late. The ship was under sail.
But there the Duke was given to understand
That in a gondola were seen together

Lorenzo and his amorous Jessica.
Besides, Antonio certified the Duke   10
They were not with Bassanio in his ship.
SOLANIO
I never heard a passion so confused,
So strange, outrageous, and so variable
As the dog Jew did utter in the streets.
'My daughter! O, my ducats! O, my daughter!   15
Fled with a Christian! O, my Christian ducats!
Justice! The law! My ducats and my daughter!
A sealèd bag, two sealèd bags of ducats,
Of double ducats, stol'n from me by my daughter!
And jewels, two stones, two rich and precious stones,
Stol'n by my daughter! Justice! Find the girl!   21
She hath the stones upon her, and the ducats!'
SALERIO
Why, all the boys in Venice follow him,
Crying, 'His stones, his daughter, and his ducats!'
SOLANIO
Let good Antonio look he keep his day,   25
Or he shall pay for this.
SALERIO   Marry, well remembered.
I reasoned with a Frenchman yesterday,
Who told me in the narrow seas that part
The French and English there miscarrièd
A vessel of our country, richly fraught.   30
I thought upon Antonio when he told me,
And wished in silence that it were not his.
SOLANIO
You were best to tell Antonio what you hear—
Yet do not suddenly, for it may grieve him.
SALERIO
A kinder gentleman treads not the earth.   35
I saw Bassanio and Antonio part.
Bassanio told him he would make some speed
Of his return. He answered, 'Do not so.
Slubber not business for my sake, Bassanio,
But stay the very riping of the time;   40
And for the Jew's bond which he hath of me,
Let it not enter in your mind of love.
Be merry, and employ your chiefest thoughts
To courtship and such fair ostents of love
As shall conveniently become you there.'   45
And even there, his eye being big with tears,
Turning his face, he put his hand behind him
And, with affection wondrous sensible,
He wrung Bassanio's hand; and so they parted.
SOLANIO
I think he only loves the world for him.   50
I pray thee let us go and find him out,
And quicken his embracèd heaviness
With some delight or other.
SALERIO   Do we so.   *Exeunt*

2.9   *Enter Nerissa and a servitor*
NERISSA
Quick, quick, I pray thee, draw the curtain straight.
The Prince of Aragon hath ta'en his oath,
And comes to his election presently.

*The servitor draws aside the curtain, revealing the
three caskets. ⌈Flourish of cornetts.⌉ Enter Aragon,
his train, and Portia*

PORTIA
Behold, there stand the caskets, noble Prince.
If you choose that wherein I am contained,   5
Straight shall our nuptial rites be solemnized.
But if you fail, without more speech, my lord,
You must be gone from hence immediately.

ARAGON
I am enjoined by oath to observe three things:
First, never to unfold to anyone   10
Which casket 'twas I chose. Next, if I fail
Of the right casket, never in my life
To woo a maid in way of marriage.
Lastly, if I do fail in fortune of my choice,
Immediately, to leave you and be gone.   15

PORTIA
To these injunctions everyone doth swear
That comes to hazard for my worthless self.

ARAGON
And so have I addressed me. Fortune now
To my heart's hope! Gold, silver, and base lead.
    He reads the leaden casket
'Who chooseth me must give and hazard all he hath.'
You shall look fairer ere I give or hazard.   21
What says the golden chest? Ha, let me see.
'Who chooseth me shall gain what many men desire.'
'What many men desire'—that 'many' may be meant
By the fool multitude, that choose by show,   25
Not learning more than the fond eye doth teach,
Which pries not to th'interior but, like the martlet,
Builds in the weather on the outward wall
Even in the force and road of casualty.
I will not choose what many men desire,   30
Because I will not jump with common spirits
And rank me with the barbarous multitudes.
Why then, to thee, thou silver treasure-house.
Tell me once more what title thou dost bear.
'Who chooseth me shall get as much as he deserves'—
And well said too, for who shall go about   36
To cozen fortune, and be honourable
Without the stamp of merit? Let none presume
To wear an undeservèd dignity.
O, that estates, degrees, and offices   40
Were not derived corruptly, and that clear honour
Were purchased by the merit of the wearer!
How many then should cover that stand bare,
How many be commanded that command?
How much low peasantry would then be gleaned   45
From the true seed of honour, and how much honour
Picked from the chaff and ruin of the times
To be new varnished? Well; but to my choice.
'Who chooseth me shall get as much as he deserves.'
I will assume desert. Give me a key for this,   50
And instantly unlock my fortunes here.
    He is given a key. ⌈He⌉ opens the silver casket

PORTIA
Too long a pause for that which you find there.

ARAGON
What's here? The portrait of a blinking idiot
Presenting me a schedule. I will read it.
How much unlike art thou to Portia!   55
How much unlike my hopes and my deservings!
'Who chooseth me shall have as much as he deserves.'
Did I deserve no more than a fool's head?
Is that my prize? Are my deserts no better?

PORTIA
To offend and judge are distinct offices,   60
And of opposèd natures.

ARAGON   What is here?
    He reads the schedule
'The fire seven times tried this;
Seven times tried that judgement is
That did never choose amiss.
Some there be that shadows kiss;   65
Such have but a shadow's bliss.
There be fools alive, iwis,
Silvered o'er; and so was this.
Take what wife you will to bed,
I will ever be your head.   70
So be gone; you are sped.'
Still more fool I shall appear
By the time I linger here.
With one fool's head I came to woo,
But I go away with two.   ·75
Sweet, adieu. I'll keep my oath
Patiently to bear my wroth.
    ⌈Flourish of cornetts.⌉ Exit with his train

PORTIA
Thus hath the candle singed the moth.
O, these deliberate fools! When they do choose
They have the wisdom by their wit to lose.   80

NERISSA
The ancient saying is no heresy:
Hanging and wiving goes by destiny.

PORTIA
Come, draw the curtain, Nerissa.
    Nerissa draws the curtain.
    Enter a Messenger

MESSENGER
Where is my lady?

PORTIA   Here. What would my lord?

MESSENGER
Madam, there is alighted at your gate   85
A young Venetian, one that comes before
To signify th'approaching of his lord,
From whom he bringeth sensible regreets,
To wit, besides commends and courteous breath,
Gifts of rich value. Yet I have not seen   90
So likely an ambassador of love.
A day in April never came so sweet
To show how costly summer was at hand
As this fore-spurrer comes before his lord.

PORTIA
No more, I pray thee, I am half afeard   95
Thou wilt say anon he is some kin to thee,
Thou spend'st such high-day wit in praising him.

Come, come, Nerissa, for I long to see
Quick Cupid's post that comes so mannerly.   99

NERISSA
Bassanio, Lord Love, if thy will it be!   *Exeunt*

3.1   *Enter Solanio and Salerio*
SOLANIO
Now, what news on the Rialto?

SALERIO Why, yet it lives there unchecked that Antonio
hath a ship of rich lading wrecked on the narrow
seas—the Goodwins I think they call the place—a very
dangerous flat, and fatal, where the carcasses of many
a tall ship lie buried, as they say, if my gossip Report
be an honest woman of her word.   7

SOLANIO I would she were as lying a gossip in that as
ever knapped ginger or made her neighbours believe
she wept for the death of a third husband. But it is
true, without any slips of prolixity or crossing the plain
highway of talk, that the good Antonio, the honest
Antonio—O that I had a title good enough to keep his
name company—

SALERIO Come, the full stop.   15

SOLANIO Ha, what sayst thou? Why, the end is he hath
lost a ship.

SALERIO I would it might prove the end of his losses.

SOLANIO Let me say amen betimes, lest the devil cross my
prayer—   20
     Enter Shylock
for here he comes in the likeness of a Jew. How now,
Shylock, what news among the merchants?

SHYLOCK You knew, none so well, none so well as you,
of my daughter's flight.

SALERIO That's certain. I for my part knew the tailor that
made the wings she flew withal.   26

SOLANIO And Shylock for his own part knew the bird was
fledge, and then it is the complexion of them all to
leave the dam.

SHYLOCK She is damned for it.   30

SALERIO That's certain, if the devil may be her judge.

SHYLOCK My own flesh and blood to rebel!

SOLANIO Out upon it, old carrion, rebels it at these years?

SHYLOCK I say my daughter is my flesh and my blood.

SALERIO There is more difference between thy flesh and
hers than between jet and ivory; more between your
bloods than there is between red wine and Rhenish.
But tell us, do you hear whether Antonio have had
any loss at sea or no?   39

SHYLOCK There I have another bad match. A bankrupt, a
prodigal, who dare scarce show his head on the Rialto;
a beggar, that was used to come so smug upon the
mart. Let him look to his bond. He was wont to call
me usurer: let him look to his bond. He was wont to
lend money for a Christian courtesy: let him look to
his bond.   46

SALERIO Why, I am sure if he forfeit thou wilt not take
his flesh. What's that good for?

SHYLOCK To bait fish withal. If it will feed nothing else it
will feed my revenge. He hath disgraced me, and
hindered me half a million; laughed at my losses,
mocked at my gains, scorned my nation, thwarted my
bargains, cooled my friends, heated mine enemies, and
what's his reason?—I am a Jew. Hath not a Jew eyes?
Hath not a Jew hands, organs, dimensions, senses,
affections, passions; fed with the same food, hurt with
the same weapons, subject to the same diseases, healed
by the same means, warmed and cooled by the same
winter and summer as a Christian is? If you prick us
do we not bleed? If you tickle us do we not laugh? If
you poison us do we not die? And if you wrong us
shall we not revenge? If we are like you in the rest,
we will resemble you in that. If a Jew wrong a Christian,
what is his humility? Revenge. If a Christian wrong a
Jew, what should his sufferance be by Christian
example? Why, revenge. The villainy you teach me I
will execute, and it shall go hard but I will better the
instruction.   68
     Enter a Man from Antonio
MAN (*to Solanio and Salerio*) Gentlemen, my master Antonio
is at his house and desires to speak with you both.   70

SALERIO We have been up and down to seek him.
     Enter Tubal
SOLANIO Here comes another of the tribe. A third cannot
be matched unless the devil himself turn Jew.
     Exeunt Solanio and Salerio, with Antonio's Man
SHYLOCK How now, Tubal? What news from Genoa? Hast
thou found my daughter?   75

TUBAL I often came where I did hear of her, but cannot
find her.

SHYLOCK Why, there, there, there, there. A diamond gone
cost me two thousand ducats in Frankfurt. The curse
never fell upon our nation till now—I never felt it till
now. Two thousand ducats in that and other precious,
precious jewels. I would my daughter were dead at my
foot and the jewels in her ear! Would she were hearsed
at my foot and the ducats in her coffin! No news of
them? Why, so. And I know not what's spent in the
search. Why thou, loss upon loss: the thief gone with
so much, and so much to find the thief, and no
satisfaction, no revenge, nor no ill luck stirring but
what lights o' my shoulders, no sighs but o' my
breathing, no tears but o' my shedding.   90

TUBAL Yes, other men have ill luck too. Antonio, as I
heard in Genoa—

SHYLOCK What, what, what? Ill luck, ill luck?

TUBAL Hath an argosy cast away coming from Tripolis.

SHYLOCK I thank God, I thank God! Is it true, is it true?

TUBAL I spoke with some of the sailors that escaped the
wreck.

SHYLOCK I thank thee, good Tubal. Good news, good
news! Ha, ha—heard in Genoa?

TUBAL Your daughter spent in Genoa, as I heard, one
night fourscore ducats.   101

SHYLOCK Thou stick'st a dagger in me. I shall never see
my gold again. Fourscore ducats at a sitting? Fourscore
ducats?   104

TUBAL There came divers of Antonio's creditors in my
company to Venice that swear he cannot choose but
break.

SHYLOCK I am very glad of it. I'll plague him, I'll torture
him. I am glad of it.

TUBAL One of them showed me a ring that he had of your
daughter for a monkey.   111

SHYLOCK Out upon her! Thou torturest me, Tubal. It was
my turquoise. I had it of Leah when I was a bachelor.
I would not have given it for a wilderness of monkeys.

TUBAL But Antonio is certainly undone.   115

SHYLOCK Nay, that's true, that's very true. Go, Tubal, fee
me an officer. Bespeak him a fortnight before. I will
have the heart of him if he forfeit, for were he out of
Venice I can make what merchandise I will. Go, Tubal,
and meet me at our synagogue. Go, good Tubal; at
our synagogue, Tubal.   *Exeunt severally*

3.2 *Enter Bassanio, Portia, Nerissa, Graziano, and all
their trains. ⌈The curtains are drawn aside
revealing the three caskets⌉*

PORTIA (*to Bassanio*)
I pray you tarry. Pause a day or two
Before you hazard, for in choosing wrong
I lose your company. Therefore forbear a while.
There's something tells me—but it is not love—
I would not lose you; and you know yourself   5
Hate counsels not in such a quality.
But lest you should not understand me well—
And yet a maiden hath no tongue but thought—
I would detain you here some month or two
Before you venture for me. I could teach you   10
How to choose right, but then I am forsworn.
So will I never be; so may you miss me.
But if you do, you'll make me wish a sin,
That I had been forsworn. Beshrew your eyes,
They have o'erlooked me and divided me.   15
One half of me is yours, the other half yours—
Mine own, I would say, but if mine, then yours,
And so all yours. O, these naughty times
Puts bars between the owners and their rights;
And so, though yours, not yours. Prove it so,   20
Let fortune go to hell for it, not I.
I speak too long, but 'tis to piece the time,
To eke it, and to draw it out in length
To stay you from election.
BASSANIO   Let me choose,
For as I am, I live upon the rack.   25
PORTIA
Upon the rack, Bassanio? Then confess
What treason there is mingled with your love.
BASSANIO
None but that ugly treason of mistrust
Which makes me fear th'enjoying of my love.
There may as well be amity and life   30
'Tween snow and fire as treason and my love.
PORTIA
Ay, but I fear you speak upon the rack,
Where men enforcèd do speak anything.
BASSANIO
Promise me life and I'll confess the truth.

PORTIA
Well then, confess and live.
BASSANIO   'Confess and love'   35
Had been the very sum of my confession.
O happy torment, when my torturer
Doth teach me answers for deliverance!
But let me to my fortune and the caskets.
PORTIA
Away then. I am locked in one of them.   40
If you do love me, you will find me out.
Nerissa and the rest, stand all aloof.
Let music sound while he doth make his choice.
Then if he lose he makes a swanlike end,
Fading in music. That the comparison   45
May stand more proper, my eye shall be the stream
And wat'ry deathbed for him. He may win,
And what is music then? Then music is
Even as the flourish when true subjects bow
To a new-crownèd monarch. Such it is   50
As are those dulcet sounds in break of day
That creep into the dreaming bridegroom's ear
And summon him to marriage. Now he goes,
With no less presence but with much more love
Than young Alcides when he did redeem   55
The virgin tribute paid by howling Troy
To the sea-monster. I stand for sacrifice.
The rest aloof are the Dardanian wives,
With blearèd visages come forth to view
The issue of th'exploit. Go, Hercules.   60
Live thou, I live. With much much more dismay
I view the fight than thou that mak'st the fray.
        ⌈*Here music.*⌉ *A song the whilst Bassanio comments
        on the caskets to himself*

⌈ONE FROM PORTIA'S TRAIN⌉
        Tell me where is fancy bred,
        Or in the heart, or in the head?
        How begot, how nourishèd?   65
⌈ALL⌉   Reply, reply.

⌈ONE FROM PORTIA'S TRAIN⌉
        It is engendered in the eyes,
        With gazing fed; and fancy dies
        In the cradle where it lies.
        Let us all ring fancy's knell.   70
        I'll begin it: ding, dong, bell.
ALL   Ding, dong, bell.

BASSANIO (*aside*)
So may the outward shows be least themselves.
The world is still deceived with ornament.
In law, what plea so tainted and corrupt   75
But, being seasoned with a gracious voice,
Obscures the show of evil? In religion,
What damnèd error but some sober brow
Will bless it and approve it with a text,
Hiding the grossness with fair ornament?   80
There is no vice so simple but assumes
Some mark of virtue on his outward parts.

How many cowards whose hearts are all as false
As stairs of sand, wear yet upon their chins
The beards of Hercules and frowning Mars,   85
Who, inward searched, have livers white as milk?
And these assume but valour's excrement
To render them redoubted. Look on beauty
And you shall see 'tis purchased by the weight,
Which therein works a miracle in nature,   90
Making them lightest that wear most of it.
So are those crispèd, snaky, golden locks
Which makes such wanton gambols with the wind
Upon supposèd fairness, often known
To be the dowry of a second head,   95
The skull that bred them in the sepulchre.
Thus ornament is but the guilèd shore
To a most dangerous sea, the beauteous scarf
Veiling an Indian beauty; in a word,
The seeming truth which cunning times put on   100
To entrap the wisest. (*Aloud*) Therefore, thou gaudy
       gold,
Hard food for Midas, I will none of thee.
(*To the silver casket*) Nor none of thee, thou pale and
       common drudge
'Tween man and man. But thou, thou meagre lead,
Which rather threaten'st than dost promise aught,
Thy paleness moves me more than eloquence,   106
And here choose I. Joy be the consequence!
PORTIA (*aside*)
How all the other passions fleet to air,
As doubtful thoughts, and rash-embraced despair,
And shudd'ring fear, and green-eyed jealousy.   110
O love, be moderate! Allay thy ecstasy.
In measure rain thy joy; scant this excess.
I feel too much thy blessing: make it less,
For fear I surfeit.
       Bassanio opens the leaden casket
BASSANIO   What find I here?
Fair Portia's counterfeit. What demi-god   115
Hath come so near creation? Move these eyes?
Or whether, riding on the balls of mine,
Seem they in motion? Here are severed lips
Parted with sugar breath. So sweet a bar   119
Should sunder such sweet friends. Here in her hairs
The painter plays the spider, and hath woven
A golden mesh t'untrap the hearts of men
Faster than gnats in cobwebs. But her eyes—
How could he see to do them? Having made one,
Methinks it should have power to steal both his   125
And leave itself unfurnished. Yet look how far
The substance of my praise doth wrong this shadow
In underprizing it, so far this shadow
Doth limp behind the substance. Here's the scroll,
The continent and summary of my fortune.   130
       'You that choose not by the view
       Chance as fair and choose as true.
       Since this fortune falls to you,
       Be content, and seek no new.
       If you be well pleased with this,   135
       And hold your fortune for your bliss,

       Turn you where your lady is,
       And claim her with a loving kiss.'
A gentle scroll. Fair lady, by your leave,
I come by note to give and to receive,   140
Like one of two contending in a prize,
That thinks he hath done well in people's eyes,
Hearing applause and universal shout,
Giddy in spirit, still gazing in a doubt
Whether those peals of praise be his or no.   145
So, thrice-fair lady, stand I even so,
As doubtful whether what I see be true
Until confirmed, signed, ratified by you.
PORTIA
You see me, Lord Bassanio, where I stand,
Such as I am. Though for myself alone   150
I would not be ambitious in my wish
To wish myself much better, yet for you
I would be trebled twenty times myself,
A thousand times more fair, ten thousand times more
       rich,
That only to stand high in your account   155
I might in virtues, beauties, livings, friends,
Exceed account. But the full sum of me
Is sum of something which, to term in gross,
Is an unlessoned girl, unschooled, unpractisèd,
Happy in this, she is not yet so old   160
But she may learn; happier than this,
She is not bred so dull but she can learn;
Happiest of all is that her gentle spirit
Commits itself to yours to be directed
As from her lord, her governor, her king.   165
Myself and what is mine to you and yours
Is now converted. But now I was the lord
Of this fair mansion, master of my servants,
Queen o'er myself; and even now, but now,
This house, these servants, and this same myself   170
Are yours, my lord's. I give them with this ring,
Which when you part from, lose, or give away,
Let it presage the ruin of your love,
And be my vantage to exclaim on you.
BASSANIO
Madam, you have bereft me of all words.   175
Only my blood speaks to you in my veins,
And there is such confusion in my powers
As after some oration fairly spoke
By a belovèd prince there doth appear
Among the buzzing pleasèd multitude,   180
Where every something being blent together
Turns to a wild of nothing save of joy,
Expressed and not expressed. But when this ring
Parts from this finger, then parts life from hence.
O, then be bold to say Bassanio's dead.   185
NERISSA
My lord and lady, it is now our time
That have stood by and seen our wishes prosper
To cry 'Good joy, good joy, my lord and lady!'
GRAZIANO
My lord Bassanio, and my gentle lady,
I wish you all the joy that you can wish,   190

For I am sure you can wish none from me.
And when your honours mean to solemnize
The bargain of your faith, I do beseech you
Even at that time I may be married too.

BASSANIO
With all my heart, so thou canst get a wife.   195

GRAZIANO
I thank your lordship, you have got me one.
My eyes, my lord, can look as swift as yours.
You saw the mistress, I beheld the maid.
You loved, I loved; for intermission
No more pertains to me, my lord, than you.   200
Your fortune stood upon the caskets there,
And so did mine too, as the matter falls;
For wooing here until I sweat again,
And swearing till my very roof was dry
With oaths of love, at last—if promise last—   205
I got a promise of this fair one here
To have her love, provided that your fortune
Achieved her mistress.

PORTIA   Is this true, Nerissa?

NERISSA
Madam, it is, so you stand pleased withal.

BASSANIO
And do you, Graziano, mean good faith?   210

GRAZIANO Yes, faith, my lord.

BASSANIO
Our feast shall be much honoured in your marriage.

GRAZIANO (to Nerissa)
We'll play with them the first boy for a thousand
     ducats.

NERISSA What, and stake down?

GRAZIANO
No, we shall ne'er win at that sport and stake down.
     Enter Lorenzo, Jessica, and Salerio, a messenger
     from Venice
But who comes here? Lorenzo and his infidel!   216
What, and my old Venetian friend Salerio!

BASSANIO
Lorenzo and Salerio, welcome hither,
If that the youth of my new int'rest here
Have power to bid you welcome. (*To Portia*) By your
     leave,   220
I bid my very friends and countrymen,
Sweet Portia, welcome.

PORTIA
So do I, my lord. They are entirely welcome.

LORENZO
I thank your honour. For my part, my lord,
My purpose was not to have seen you here,   225
But meeting with Salerio by the way
He did entreat me past all saying nay
To come with him along.

SALERIO   I did, my lord,
And I have reason for it. Signor Antonio
Commends him to you.
     He gives Bassanio a letter

BASSANIO   Ere I ope his letter   230
I pray you tell me how my good friend doth.

SALERIO
Not sick, my lord, unless it be in mind;
Nor well, unless in mind. His letter there
Will show you his estate.
     Bassanio opens the letter and reads

GRAZIANO
Nerissa, (*indicating Jessica*) cheer yon stranger. Bid her
     welcome.   235
Your hand, Salerio. What's the news from Venice?
How doth that royal merchant good Antonio?
I know he will be glad of our success.
We are the Jasons; we have won the fleece.

SALERIO
I would you had won the fleece that he hath lost.   240

PORTIA
There are some shrewd contents in yon same paper
That steals the colour from Bassanio's cheek.
Some dear friend dead, else nothing in the world
Could turn so much the constitution
Of any constant man. What, worse and worse?   245
With leave, Bassanio, I am half yourself,
And I must freely have the half of anything
That this same paper brings you.

BASSANIO   O sweet Portia,
Here are a few of the unpleasant'st words
That ever blotted paper. Gentle lady,   250
When I did first impart my love to you
I freely told you all the wealth I had
Ran in my veins: I was a gentleman;
And then I told you true; and yet, dear lady,
Rating myself at nothing, you shall see   255
How much I was a braggart. When I told you
My state was nothing, I should then have told you
That I was worse than nothing, for indeed
I have engaged myself to a dear friend,
Engaged my friend to his mere enemy,   260
To feed my means. Here is a letter, lady,
The paper as the body of my friend,
And every word in it a gaping wound
Issuing life-blood. But is it true, Salerio?
Hath all his ventures failed? What, not one hit?   265
From Tripolis, from Mexico, and England,
From Lisbon, Barbary, and India,
And not one vessel scape the dreadful touch
Of merchant-marring rocks?

SALERIO   Not one, my lord.
Besides, it should appear that if he had   270
The present money to discharge the Jew
He would not take it. Never did I know
A creature that did bear the shape of man
So keen and greedy to confound a man.
He plies the Duke at morning and at night,   275
And doth impeach the freedom of the state
If they deny him justice. Twenty merchants,
The Duke himself, and the magnificoes
Of greatest port, have all persuaded with him,
But none can drive him from the envious plea   280
Of forfeiture, of justice, and his bond.

JESSICA
When I was with him I have heard him swear
To Tubal and to Cush, his countrymen,
That he would rather have Antonio's flesh
Than twenty times the value of the sum   285
That he did owe him; and I know, my lord,
If law, authority, and power deny not,
It will go hard with poor Antonio.

PORTIA (to Bassanio)
Is it your dear friend that is thus in trouble?

BASSANIO
The dearest friend to me, the kindest man,   290
The best-conditioned and unwearied spirit
In doing courtesies, and one in whom
The ancient Roman honour more appears
Than any that draws breath in Italy.

PORTIA What sum owes he the Jew?   295

BASSANIO
For me, three thousand ducats.

PORTIA   What, no more?
Pay him six thousand and deface the bond.
Double six thousand, and then treble that,
Before a friend of this description
Shall lose a hair thorough Bassanio's fault.   300
First go with me to church and call me wife,
And then away to Venice to your friend;
For never shall you lie by Portia's side
With an unquiet soul. You shall have gold
To pay the petty debt twenty times over.   305
When it is paid, bring your true friend along.
My maid Nerissa and myself meantime
Will live as maids and widows. Come, away,
For you shall hence upon your wedding day.
Bid your friends welcome, show a merry cheer.   310
Since you are dear bought, I will love you dear.
But let me hear the letter of your friend.

⌈BASSANIO⌉ (reads) 'Sweet Bassanio, my ships have all
miscarried, my creditors grow cruel, my estate is very
low, my bond to the Jew is forfeit, and since in paying
it, it is impossible I should live, all debts are cleared
between you and I if I might but see you at my death.
Notwithstanding, use your pleasure. If your love do
not persuade you to come, let not my letter.'

PORTIA
O, love! Dispatch all business, and be gone.   320

BASSANIO
Since I have your good leave to go away
I will make haste, but till I come again
No bed shall e'er be guilty of my stay
Nor rest be interposer 'twixt us twain.   Exeunt

3.3   Enter Shylock the Jew, Solanio, Antonio, and the
      jailer

SHYLOCK
Jailer, look to him. Tell not me of mercy.
This is the fool that lent out money gratis.
Jailer, look to him.

ANTONIO   Hear me yet, good Shylock.

SHYLOCK
I'll have my bond. Speak not against my bond.
I have sworn an oath that I will have my bond.   5
Thou called'st me dog before thou hadst a cause,
But since I am a dog, beware my fangs.
The Duke shall grant me justice. I do wonder,
Thou naughty jailer, that thou art so fond
To come abroad with him at his request.   10

ANTONIO I pray thee hear me speak.

SHYLOCK
I'll have my bond. I will not hear thee speak.
I'll have my bond, and therefore speak no more.
I'll not be made a soft and dull-eyed fool
To shake the head, relent, and sigh, and yield   15
To Christian intercessors. Follow not.
I'll have no speaking. I will have my bond.   Exit

SOLANIO
It is the most impenetrable cur
That ever kept with men.

ANTONIO   Let him alone.
I'll follow him no more with bootless prayers.   20
He seeks my life. His reason well I know:
I oft delivered from his forfeitures
Many that have at times made moan to me.
Therefore he hates me.

SOLANIO   I am sure the Duke
Will never grant this forfeiture to hold.   25

ANTONIO
The Duke cannot deny the course of law,
For the commodity that strangers have
With us in Venice, if it be denied,
Will much impeach the justice of the state,
Since that the trade and profit of the city   30
Consisteth of all nations. Therefore go.
These griefs and losses have so bated me
That I shall hardly spare a pound of flesh
Tomorrow to my bloody creditor.
Well, jailer, on. Pray God Bassanio come   35
To see me pay his debt, and then I care not.   Exeunt

3.4   Enter Portia, Nerissa, Lorenzo, Jessica, and
      Balthasar, a man of Portia's

LORENZO (to Portia)
Madam, although I speak it in your presence,
You have a noble and a true conceit
Of godlike amity, which appears most strongly
In bearing thus the absence of your lord.
But if you knew to whom you show this honour,   5
How true a gentleman you send relief,
How dear a lover of my lord your husband,
I know you would be prouder of the work
Than customary bounty can enforce you.

PORTIA
I never did repent for doing good,   10
Nor shall not now; for in companions
That do converse and waste the time together,
Whose souls do bear an equal yoke of love,
There must be needs a like proportion

Of lineaments, of manners, and of spirit,   15
Which makes me think that this Antonio,
Being the bosom lover of my lord,
Must needs be like my lord. If it be so,
How little is the cost I have bestowed
In purchasing the semblance of my soul   20
From out the state of hellish cruelty.
This comes too near the praising of myself,
Therefore no more of it. Hear other things:
Lorenzo, I commit into your hands
The husbandry and manage of my house   25
Until my lord's return. For mine own part,
I have toward heaven breathed a secret vow
To live in prayer and contemplation,
Only attended by Nerissa here,
Until her husband and my lord's return.   30
There is a monastery two miles off,
And there we will abide. I do desire you
Not to deny this imposition,
The which my love and some necessity
Now lays upon you.
LORENZO   Madam, with all my heart,   35
I shall obey you in all fair commands.
PORTIA
My people do already know my mind,
And will acknowledge you and Jessica
In place of Lord Bassanio and myself.
So fare you well till we shall meet again.   40
LORENZO
Fair thoughts and happy hours attend on you!
JESSICA
I wish your ladyship all heart's content.
PORTIA
I thank you for your wish, and am well pleased
To wish it back on you. Fare you well, Jessica.
                        Exeunt Lorenzo and Jessica
Now, Balthasar,   45
As I have ever found thee honest-true,
So let me find thee still. Take this same letter,
And use thou all th'endeavour of a man
In speed to Padua. See thou render this
Into my cousin's hands, Doctor Bellario,   50
And look what notes and garments he doth give thee,
Bring them, I pray thee, with imagined speed
Unto the traject, to the common ferry
Which trades to Venice. Waste no time in words,
But get thee gone. I shall be there before thee.   55
BALTHASAR
Madam, I go with all convenient speed.   *Exit*
PORTIA
Come on, Nerissa. I have work in hand
That you yet know not of. We'll see our husbands
Before they think of us.
NERISSA   Shall they see us?
PORTIA
They shall, Nerissa, but in such a habit   60
That they shall think we are accomplishèd

With that we lack. I'll hold thee any wager,
When we are both accoutered like young men
I'll prove the prettier fellow of the two,
And wear my dagger with the braver grace,   65
And speak between the change of man and boy
With a reed voice, and turn two mincing steps
Into a manly stride, and speak of frays
Like a fine bragging youth, and tell quaint lies
How honourable ladies sought my love,   70
Which I denying, they fell sick and died.
I could not do withal. Then I'll repent,
And wish for all that that I had not killed them;
And twenty of these puny lies I'll tell,
That men shall swear I have discontinued school   75
Above a twelvemonth. I have within my mind
A thousand raw tricks of these bragging Jacks
Which I will practise.
NERISSA Why, shall we turn to men?
PORTIA Fie, what a question's that   80
If thou wert near a lewd interpreter!
But come, I'll tell thee all my whole device
When I am in my coach, which stays for us
At the park gate; and therefore haste away,
For we must measure twenty miles today.   *Exeunt*

3.5   *Enter Lancelot the clown, and Jessica*

LANCELOT Yes, truly; for look you, the sins of the father
are to be laid upon the children, therefore I promise
you I fear you. I was always plain with you, and so
now I speak my agitation of the matter, therefore be
o' good cheer, for truly I think you are damned. There
is but one hope in it that can do you any good, and
that is but a kind of bastard hope, neither.
JESSICA And what hope is that, I pray thee?
LANCELOT Marry, you may partly hope that your father
got you not, that you are not the Jew's daughter.   10
JESSICA That were a kind of bastard hope indeed. So the
sins of my mother should be visited upon me.
LANCELOT Truly then, I fear you are damned both by
father and mother. Thus, when I shun Scylla your
father, I fall into Charybdis your mother. Well, you are
gone both ways.   16
JESSICA I shall be saved by my husband. He hath made
me a Christian.
LANCELOT Truly, the more to blame he! We were
Christians enough before, e'en as many as could well
live one by another. This making of Christians will
raise the price of hogs. If we grow all to be pork-eaters
we shall not shortly have a rasher on the coals for
money.   24
        Enter Lorenzo
JESSICA I'll tell my husband, Lancelot, what you say. Here
he comes.
LORENZO I shall grow jealous of you shortly, Lancelot, if
you thus get my wife into corners.   28
JESSICA Nay, you need not fear us, Lorenzo. Lancelot and
I are out. He tells me flatly there's no mercy for me in

heaven because I am a Jew's daughter, and he says
you are no good member of the commonwealth, for in
converting Jews to Christians you raise the price of
pork.   34
LORENZO (*to Lancelot*) I shall answer that better to the
commonwealth than you can the getting up of the
Negro's belly. The Moor is with child by you, Lancelot.
LANCELOT It is much that the Moor should be more than
reason, but if she be less than an honest woman, she
is indeed more than I took her for.   40
LORENZO How every fool can play upon the word! I think
the best grace of wit will shortly turn into silence, and
discourse grow commendable in none only but parrots.
Go in, sirrah, bid them prepare for dinner.
LANCELOT That is done, sir. They have all stomachs.   45
LORENZO Goodly Lord, what a wit-snapper are you! Then
bid them prepare dinner.
LANCELOT That is done too, sir; only 'cover' is the word.
LORENZO Will you cover then, sir?
LANCELOT Not so, sir, neither. I know my duty.   50
LORENZO Yet more quarrelling with occasion! Wilt thou
show the whole wealth of thy wit in an instant? I pray
thee understand a plain man in his plain meaning. Go
to thy fellows; bid them cover the table, serve in the
meat, and we will come in to dinner.   55
LANCELOT For the table, sir, it shall be served in. For the
meat, sir, it shall be covered. For your coming in to
dinner, sir, why, let it be as humours and conceits
shall govern.   *Exit*
LORENZO
O dear discretion, how his words are suited!   60
The fool hath planted in his memory
An army of good words, and I do know
A many fools that stand in better place,
Garnished like him, that for a tricksy word
Defy the matter. How cheer'st thou, Jessica?   65
And now, good sweet, say thy opinion:
How dost thou like the Lord Bassanio's wife?
JESSICA
Past all expressing. It is very meet
The Lord Bassanio live an upright life,
For, having such a blessing in his lady,   70
He finds the joys of heaven here on earth,
And if on earth he do not merit it,
In reason he should never come to heaven.
Why, if two gods should play some heavenly match
And on the wager lay two earthly women,   75
And Portia one, there must be something else
Pawned with the other; for the poor rude world
Hath not her fellow.
LORENZO   Even such a husband
Hast thou of me as she is for a wife.
JESSICA
Nay, but ask my opinion too of that!   80
LORENZO
I will anon. First let us go to dinner.
JESSICA
Nay, let me praise you while I have a stomach.

LORENZO
No, pray thee, let it serve for table-talk.
Then, howsome'er thou speak'st, 'mong other things
I shall digest it.
JESSICA   Well, I'll set you forth.   *Exeunt*

4.1   *Enter the Duke, the magnificoes, Antonio, Bassanio,*
          Graziano, and Salerio
DUKE
What, is Antonio here?
ANTONIO   Ready, so please your grace.
DUKE
I am sorry for thee. Thou art come to answer
A stony adversary, an inhuman wretch
Uncapable of pity, void and empty
From any dram of mercy.
ANTONIO   I have heard   5
Your grace hath ta'en great pains to qualify
His rigorous course, but since he stands obdurate,
And that no lawful means can carry me
Out of his envy's reach, I do oppose
My patience to his fury, and am armed   10
To suffer with a quietness of spirit
The very tyranny and rage of his.
DUKE
Go one, and call the Jew into the court.
SALERIO
He is ready at the door. He comes, my lord.
          Enter Shylock
DUKE
Make room, and let him stand before our face.   15
Shylock, the world thinks—and I think so too—
That thou but lead'st this fashion of thy malice
To the last hour of act, and then 'tis thought
Thou'lt show thy mercy and remorse more strange
Than is thy strange apparent cruelty,   20
And where thou now exacts the penalty—
Which is a pound of this poor merchant's flesh—
Thou wilt not only loose the forfeiture,
But, touched with human gentleness and love,
Forgive a moiety of the principal,   25
Glancing an eye of pity on his losses,
That have of late so huddled on his back
Enough to press a royal merchant down
And pluck commiseration of his state
From brassy bosoms and rough hearts of flint,   30
From stubborn Turks and Tartars never trained
To offices of tender courtesy.
We all expect a gentle answer, Jew.
SHYLOCK
I have possessed your grace of what I purpose,
And by our holy Sabbath have I sworn   35
To have the due and forfeit of my bond.
If you deny it, let the danger light
Upon your charter and your city's freedom.
You'll ask me why I rather choose to have
A weight of carrion flesh than to receive   40
Three thousand ducats. I'll not answer that,

But say it is my humour. Is it answered?
What if my house be troubled with a rat,
And I be pleased to give ten thousand ducats
To have it baned? What, are you answered yet?   45
Some men there are love not a gaping pig,
Some that are mad if they behold a cat,
And others when the bagpipe sings i'th' nose
Cannot contain their urine; for affection,
Mistress of passion, sways it to the mood   50
Of what it likes or loathes. Now for your answer:
As there is no firm reason to be rendered
Why he cannot abide a gaping pig,
Why he a harmless necessary cat,
Why he a woollen bagpipe, but of force   55
Must yield to such inevitable shame
As to offend himself being offended,
So can I give no reason, nor I will not,
More than a lodged hate and a certain loathing
I bear Antonio, that I follow thus   60
A losing suit against him. Are you answered?

BASSANIO
This is no answer, thou unfeeling man,
To excuse the current of thy cruelty.

SHYLOCK
I am not bound to please thee with my answers.

BASSANIO
Do all men kill the things they do not love?   65

SHYLOCK
Hates any man the thing he would not kill?

BASSANIO
Every offence is not a hate at first.

SHYLOCK
What, wouldst thou have a serpent sting thee twice?

ANTONIO
I pray you think you question with the Jew.
You may as well go stand upon the beach   70
And bid the main flood bate his usual height;
You may as well use question with the wolf
Why he hath made the ewe bleat for the lamb;   .
You may as well forbid the mountain pines
To wag their high tops and to make no noise   75
When they are fretten with the gusts of heaven,
You may as well do anything most hard
As seek to soften that—than which what's harder?—
His Jewish heart. Therefore, I do beseech you,
Make no more offers, use no farther means,   80
But with all brief and plain conveniency
Let me have judgement and the Jew his will.

BASSANIO (to Shylock)
For thy three thousand ducats here is six.

SHYLOCK
If every ducat in six thousand ducats
Were in six parts, and every part a ducat,   85
I would not draw them. I would have my bond.

DUKE
How shalt thou hope for mercy, rend'ring none?

SHYLOCK
What judgement shall I dread, doing no wrong?

You have among you many a purchased slave
Which, like your asses and your dogs and mules,   90
You use in abject and in slavish parts
Because you bought them. Shall I say to you
'Let them be free, marry them to your heirs.
Why sweat they under burdens? Let their beds
Be made as soft as yours, and let their palates   95
Be seasoned with such viands.' You will answer
'The slaves are ours.' So do I answer you.
The pound of flesh which I demand of him
Is dearly bought. 'Tis mine, and I will have it.
If you deny me, fie upon your law: 100
There is no force in the decrees of Venice.
I stand for judgement. Answer: shall I have it?

DUKE
Upon my power I may dismiss this court
Unless Bellario, a learnèd doctor
Whom I have sent for to determine this,   105
Come here today.

SALERIO   My lord, here stays without
A messenger with letters from the doctor,
New come from Padua.

DUKE
Bring us the letters. Call the messenger.   ⌐Exit Salerio⌐

BASSANIO
Good cheer, Antonio. What, man, courage yet!   110
The Jew shall have my flesh, blood, bones, and all
Ere thou shalt lose for me one drop of blood.

ANTONIO
I am a tainted wether of the flock,
Meetest for death. The weakest kind of fruit
Drops earliest to the ground; and so let me.   115
You cannot better be employed, Bassanio,
Than to live still and write mine epitaph.

*Enter ⌐Salerio, with⌐ Nerissa apparelled as a judge's
clerk*

DUKE
Came you from Padua, from Bellario?

NERISSA
From both, my lord. Bellario greets your grace.
She gives a letter to the Duke.
Shylock whets his knife on his shoe

BASSANIO (to Shylock)
Why dost thou whet thy knife so earnestly?   120

SHYLOCK
To cut the forfeit from that bankrupt there.

GRAZIANO
Not on thy sole but on thy soul, harsh Jew,
Thou mak'st thy knife keen. But no metal can,
No, not the hangman's axe, bear half the keenness
Of thy sharp envy. Can no prayers pierce thee?   125

SHYLOCK
No, none that thou hast wit enough to make.

GRAZIANO
O, be thou damned, inexorable dog,
And for thy life let justice be accused!
Thou almost mak'st me waver in my faith
To hold opinion with Pythagoras   130

That souls of animals infuse themselves
Into the trunks of men. Thy currish spirit
Governed a wolf who, hanged for human slaughter,
Even from the gallows did his fell soul fleet,
And, whilst thou lay'st in thy unhallowed dam,   135
Infused itself in thee; for thy desires
Are wolvish, bloody, starved, and ravenous.

SHYLOCK
Till thou canst rail the seal from off my bond
Thou but offend'st thy lungs to speak so loud.
Repair thy wit, good youth, or it will fall   140
To cureless ruin. I stand here for law.

DUKE
This letter from Bellario doth commend
A young and learnèd doctor to our court.
Where is he?

NERISSA   He attendeth here hard by
To know your answer, whether you'll admit him.   145

DUKE
With all my heart. Some three or four of you
Go give him courteous conduct to this place.

Exeunt three or four

Meantime the court shall hear Bellario's letter.
(*Reads*) 'Your grace shall understand that at the receipt
of your letter I am very sick, but in the instant that
your messenger came, in loving visitation was with me
a young doctor of Rome; his name is Balthasar. I
acquainted him with the cause in controversy between
the Jew and Antonio, the merchant. We turned o'er
many books together. He is furnished with my opinion
which, bettered with his own learning—the greatness
whereof I cannot enough commend—comes with him
at my importunity to fill up your grace's request in my
stead. I beseech you let his lack of years. be no
impediment to let him lack a reverend estimation, for
I never knew so young a body with so old a head. I
leave him to your gracious acceptance, whose trial
shall better publish his commendation.'

Enter ⌈three or four with⌉ Portia as Balthasar

You hear the learn'd Bellario, what he writes;
And here, I take it, is the doctor come.   165
(*To Portia*) Give me your hand. Come you from old
Bellario?

PORTIA
I did, my lord.

DUKE   You are welcome. Take your place.
Are you acquainted with the difference
That holds this present question in the court?

PORTIA
I am informèd throughly of the cause.   170
Which is the merchant here, and which the Jew?

DUKE
Antonio and old Shylock, both stand forth.

Antonio and Shylock stand forth

PORTIA
Is your name Shylock?

SHYLOCK   Shylock is my name.

PORTIA
Of a strange nature is the suit you follow,
Yet in such rule that the Venetian law   175
Cannot impugn you as you do proceed.
(*To Antonio*) You stand within his danger, do you not?

ANTONIO
Ay, so he says.

PORTIA   Do you confess the bond?

ANTONIO
I do.

PORTIA Then must the Jew be merciful.

SHYLOCK
On what compulsion must I? Tell me that.   180

PORTIA
The quality of mercy is not strained.
It droppeth as the gentle rain from heaven
Upon the place beneath. It is twice blest:
It blesseth him that gives, and him that takes.
'Tis mightiest in the mightiest. It becomes   185
The thronèd monarch better than his crown.
His sceptre shows the force of temporal power,
The attribute to awe and majesty,
Wherein doth sit the dread and fear of kings;
But mercy is above this sceptred sway.   190
It is enthronèd in the hearts of kings;
It is an attribute to God himself,
And earthly power doth then show likest God's
When mercy seasons justice. Therefore, Jew,
Though justice be thy plea, consider this: 195
That in the course of justice none of us
Should see salvation. We do pray for mercy,
And that same prayer doth teach us all to render
The deeds of mercy. I have spoke thus much
To mitigate the justice of thy plea,   200
Which if thou follow, this strict court of Venice
Must needs give sentence 'gainst the merchant there.

SHYLOCK
My deeds upon my head! I crave the law,
The penalty and forfeit of my bond.

PORTIA
Is he not able to discharge the money?   205

BASSANIO
Yes, here I tender it for him in the court,
Yea, twice the sum. If that will not suffice
I will be bound to pay it ten times o'er
On forfeit of my hands, my head, my heart.
If this will not suffice, it must appear   210
That malice bears down truth. And, I beseech you,
Wrest once the law to your authority.
To do a great right, do a little wrong,
And curb this cruel devil of his will.

PORTIA
It must not be. There is no power in Venice   215
Can alter a decree establishèd.
'Twill be recorded for a precedent,
And many an error by the same example
Will rush into the state. It cannot be.

SHYLOCK
A Daniel come to judgement, yea, a Daniel!　　220
O wise young judge, how I do honour thee!

PORTIA
I pray you let me look upon the bond.

SHYLOCK
Here 'tis, most reverend doctor, here it is.

PORTIA
Shylock, there's thrice thy money offered thee.

SHYLOCK
An oath, an oath! I have an oath in heaven.　　225
Shall I lay perjury upon my soul?
No, not for Venice.

PORTIA　　　　　　　　Why, this bond is forfeit,
And lawfully by this the Jew may claim
A pound of flesh, to be by him cut off
Nearest the merchant's heart. (To Shylock) Be merciful.
Take thrice thy money. Bid me tear the bond.　　231

SHYLOCK
When it is paid according to the tenor.
It doth appear you are a worthy judge.
You know the law. Your exposition
Hath been most sound. I charge you, by the law　　235
Whereof you are a well-deserving pillar,
Proceed to judgement. By my soul I swear
There is no power in the tongue of man
To alter me. I stay here on my bond.

ANTONIO
Most heartily I do beseech the court　　240
To give the judgement.

PORTIA　　　　　　　Why, then thus it is:
You must prepare your bosom for his knife—

SHYLOCK
O noble judge, O excellent young man!

PORTIA
For the intent and purpose of the law
Hath full relation to the penalty　　245
Which here appeareth due upon the bond.

SHYLOCK
'Tis very true. O wise and upright judge!
How much more elder art thou than thy looks!

PORTIA (to Antonio)
Therefore lay bare your bosom.

SHYLOCK　　　　　　　Ay, his breast.
So says the bond, doth it not, noble judge?　　250
'Nearest his heart'—those are the very words.

PORTIA
It is so. Are there balance here to weigh the flesh?

SHYLOCK I have them ready.

PORTIA
Have by some surgeon, Shylock, on your charge
To stop his wounds, lest he do bleed to death.　　255

SHYLOCK
Is it so nominated in the bond?

PORTIA
It is not so expressed, but what of that?
'Twere good you do so much for charity.

SHYLOCK
I cannot find it. 'Tis not in the bond.

PORTIA (to Antonio)
You, merchant, have you anything to say?　　260

ANTONIO
But little. I am armed and well prepared.
Give me your hand, Bassanio; fare you well.
Grieve not that I am fall'n to this for you,
For herein Fortune shows herself more kind
Than is her custom; it is still her use　　265
To let the wretched man outlive his wealth
To view with hollow eye and wrinkled brow
An age of poverty, from which ling'ring penance
Of such misery doth she cut me off.
Commend me to your honourable wife.　　270
Tell her the process of Antonio's end.
Say how I loved you. Speak me fair in death,
And when the tale is told, bid her be judge
Whether Bassanio had not once a love.
Repent but you that you shall lose your friend,　　275
And he repents not that he pays your debt;
For if the Jew do cut but deep enough,
I'll pay it instantly, with all my heart.

BASSANIO
Antonio, I am married to a wife
Which is as dear to me as life itself,　　280
But life itself, my wife, and all the world
Are not with me esteemed above thy life.
I would lose all, ay, sacrifice them all
Here to this devil, to deliver you.

PORTIA ⌈aside⌉
Your wife would give you little thanks for that　　285
If she were by to hear you make the offer.

GRAZIANO
I have a wife who, I protest, I love.
I would she were in heaven so she could
Entreat some power to change this currish Jew.

NERISSA ⌈aside⌉
'Tis well you offer it behind her back;　　290
The wish would make else an unquiet house.

SHYLOCK ⌈aside⌉
These be the Christian husbands. I have a daughter.
Would any of the stock of Barabbas
Had been her husband rather than a Christian.
(Aloud) We trifle time. I pray thee pursue sentence.　295

PORTIA
A pound of that same merchant's flesh is thine.
The court awards it, and the law doth give it.

SHYLOCK Most rightful judge!

PORTIA
And you must cut this flesh from off his breast.
The law allows it, and the court awards it.　　300

SHYLOCK
Most learnèd judge! A sentence: (to Antonio) come,
prepare.

PORTIA
Tarry a little. There is something else.
This bond doth give thee here no jot of blood.

The words expressly are 'a pound of flesh'.
Take then thy bond. Take thou thy pound of flesh. 305
But in the cutting it, if thou dost shed
One drop of Christian blood, thy lands and goods
Are by the laws of Venice confiscate
Unto the state of Venice.
GRAZIANO   O upright judge!
Mark, Jew! O learnèd judge!   310
SHYLOCK Is that the law?
PORTIA Thyself shalt see the act;
For as thou urgest justice, be assured
Thou shalt have justice more than thou desir'st.
GRAZIANO
O learnèd judge! Mark, Jew—a learnèd judge!   315
SHYLOCK
I take this offer, then. Pay the bond thrice,
And let the Christian go.
BASSANIO   Here is the money.
PORTIA
Soft, the Jew shall have all justice. Soft, no haste.
He shall have nothing but the penalty.
GRAZIANO
O Jew, an upright judge, a learnèd judge!   320
PORTIA (to Shylock)
Therefore prepare thee to cut off the flesh.
Shed thou no blood, nor cut thou less nor more
But just a pound of flesh. If thou tak'st more
Or less than a just pound, be it but so much
As makes it light or heavy in the substance   325
Or the division of the twentieth part
Of one poor scruple—nay, if the scale do turn
But in the estimation of a hair,
Thou diest, and all thy goods are confiscate.
GRAZIANO
A second Daniel, a Daniel, Jew!   330
Now, infidel, I have you on the hip.
PORTIA
Why doth the Jew pause? Take thy forfeiture.
SHYLOCK
Give me my principal, and let me go.
BASSANIO
I have it ready for thee. Here it is.
PORTIA
He hath refused it in the open court.   335
He shall have merely justice and his bond.
GRAZIANO
A Daniel, still say I, a second Daniel!
I thank thee, Jew, for teaching me that word.
SHYLOCK
Shall I not have barely my principal?
PORTIA
Thou shalt have nothing but the forfeiture   340
To be so taken at thy peril, Jew.
SHYLOCK
Why then, the devil give him good of it.
I'll stay no longer question.
PORTIA   Tarry, Jew.
The law hath yet another hold on you.

It is enacted in the laws of Venice,   345
If it be proved against an alien
That by direct or indirect attempts
He seek the life of any citizen,
The party 'gainst the which he doth contrive
Shall seize one half his goods; the other half   350
Comes to the privy coffer of the state,
And the offender's life lies in the mercy
Of the Duke only, 'gainst all other voice—
In which predicament I say thou stand'st,
For it appears by manifest proceeding   355
That indirectly, and directly too,
Thou hast contrived against the very life
Of the defendant, and thou hast incurred
The danger formerly by me rehearsed.
Down, therefore, and beg mercy of the Duke.   360
GRAZIANO (to Shylock)
Beg that thou mayst have leave to hang thyself—
And yet, thy wealth being forfeit to the state,
Thou hast not left the value of a cord.
Therefore thou must be hanged at the state's charge.
DUKE (to Shylock)
That thou shalt see the difference of our spirit, 365
I pardon thee thy life before thou ask it.
For half thy wealth, it is Antonio's.
The other half comes to the general state,
Which humbleness may drive unto a fine.
PORTIA
Ay, for the state, not for Antonio.   370
SHYLOCK
Nay, take my life and all, pardon not that.
You take my house when you do take the prop
That doth sustain my house; you take my life
When you do take the means whereby I live.
PORTIA
What mercy can you render him, Antonio?   375
GRAZIANO
A halter, gratis. Nothing else, for God's sake.
ANTONIO
So please my lord the Duke and all the court
To quit the fine for one half of his goods,
I am content, so he will let me have
The other half in use, to render it   380
Upon his death unto the gentleman
That lately stole his daughter.
Two things provided more: that for this favour
He presently become a Christian;
The other, that he do record a gift   385
Here in the court of all he dies possessed
Unto his son, Lorenzo, and his daughter.
DUKE
He shall do this, or else I do recant
The pardon that I late pronouncèd here.
PORTIA
Art thou contented, Jew? What dost thou say?   390
SHYLOCK
I am content.
PORTIA (to Nerissa) Clerk, draw a deed of gift.

SHYLOCK
I pray you give me leave to go from hence.
I am not well. Send the deed after me,
And I will sign it.
DUKE   Get thee gone, but do it.
GRAZIANO (*to Shylock*)
In christ'ning shalt thou have two godfathers.   395
Had I been judge thou shouldst have had ten more,
To bring thee to the gallows, not the font.
                                Exit Shylock
DUKE (*to Portia*)
Sir, I entreat you home with me to dinner.
PORTIA
I humbly do desire your grace of pardon.
I must away this night toward Padua,   400
And it is meet I presently set forth.
DUKE
I am sorry that your leisure serves you not.
Antonio, gratify this gentleman,
For in my mind you are much bound to him.
                          Exit Duke and his train
BASSANIO (*to Portia*)
Most worthy gentleman, I and my friend   405
Have by your wisdom been this day acquitted
Of grievous penalties, in lieu whereof
Three thousand ducats due unto the Jew
We freely cope your courteous pains withal.
ANTONIO
And stand indebted over and above   410
In love and service to you evermore.
PORTIA
He is well paid that is well satisfied,
And I, delivering you, am satisfied,
And therein do account myself well paid.
My mind was never yet more mercenary.   415
I pray you know me when we meet again.
I wish you well; and so I take my leave.
BASSANIO
Dear sir, of force I must attempt you further.
Take some remembrance of us as a tribute,
Not as fee. Grant me two things, I pray you: 420
Not to deny me, and to pardon me.
PORTIA
You press me far, and therefore I will yield.
⌈*To Antonio*⌉ Give me your gloves. I'll wear them for
      your sake.
(*To Bassanio*) And for your love I'll take this ring from
      you.
Do not draw back your hand. I'll take no more,   425
And you in love shall not deny me this.
BASSANIO
This ring, good sir? Alas, it is a trifle.
I will not shame myself to give you this.
PORTIA
I will have nothing else, but only this;
And now, methinks, I have a mind to it.   430
BASSANIO
There's more depends on this than on the value.
The dearest ring in Venice will I give you,

And find it out by proclamation.
Only for this, I pray you pardon me.
PORTIA
I see, sir, you are liberal in offers.   435
You taught me first to beg, and now methinks
You teach me how a beggar should be answered.
BASSANIO
Good sir, this ring was given me by my wife,
And when she put it on she made me vow
That I should neither sell, nor give, nor lose it.   440
PORTIA
That 'scuse serves many men to save their gifts.
An if your wife be not a madwoman,
And know how well I have deserved this ring,
She would not hold out enemy for ever
For giving it to me. Well, peace be with you.   445
                          Exeunt Portia and Nerissa
ANTONIO
My lord Bassanio, let him have the ring.
Let his deservings and my love withal
Be valued 'gainst your wife's commandëment.
BASSANIO
Go, Graziano, run and overtake him.
Give him the ring, and bring him, if thou canst,   450
Unto Antonio's house. Away, make haste.
                                Exit Graziano
Come, you and I will thither presently,
And in the morning early will we both
Fly toward Belmont. Come, Antonio.   *Exeunt*

4.2   *Enter Portia and Nerissa, still disguised*
PORTIA
Enquire the Jew's house out, give him this deed,
And let him sign it. We'll away tonight,
And be a day before our husbands home.
This deed will be well welcome to Lorenzo.
                          Enter Graziano
GRAZIANO Fair sir, you are well o'erta'en.   5
My lord Bassanio upon more advice
Hath sent you here this ring, and doth entreat
Your company at dinner.
PORTIA   That cannot be.
His ring I do accept most thankfully,
And so I pray you tell him. Furthermore,   10
I pray you show my youth old Shylock's house.
GRAZIANO
That will I do.
NERISSA   Sir, I would speak with you.
(*Aside to Portia*) I'll see if I can get my husband's ring
Which I did make him swear to keep for ever.
PORTIA (*aside to Nerissa*)
Thou mayst; I warrant we shall have old swearing 15
That they did give the rings away to men.
But we'll outface them, and outswear them too.
Away, make haste. Thou know'st where I will tarry.
                              Exit ⌈at one door⌉
NERISSA (*to Graziano*)
Come, good sir, will you show me to this house?
                          Exeunt ⌈at another door⌉

5.1   *Enter Lorenzo and Jessica*

LORENZO
The moon shines bright. In such a night as this,
When the sweet wind did gently kiss the trees
And they did make no noise—in such a night
Troilus, methinks, mounted the Trojan walls,
And sighed his soul toward the Grecian tents   5
Where Cressid lay that night.

JESSICA   In such a night
Did Thisbe fearfully o'ertrip the dew
And saw the lion's shadow ere himself,
And ran dismayed away.

LORENZO   In such a night
Stood Dido with a willow in her hand   10
Upon the wild sea banks, and waft her love
To come again to Carthage.

JESSICA   In such a night
Medea gathèred the enchanted herbs
That did renew old Aeson.

LORENZO   In such a night
Did Jessica steal from the wealthy Jew,   15
And with an unthrift love did run from Venice
As far as Belmont.

JESSICA   In such a night
Did young Lorenzo swear he loved her well,
Stealing her soul with many vows of faith,
And ne'er a true one.

LORENZO   In such a night   20
Did pretty Jessica, like a little shrew,
Slander her love, and he forgave it her.

JESSICA
I would outnight you, did nobody come.
But hark, I hear the footing of a man.

Enter Stefano, a messenger

LORENZO
Who comes so fast in silence of the night?   25

STEFANO A friend.

LORENZO
A friend—what friend? Your name, I pray you, friend?

STEFANO
Stefano is my name, and I bring word
My mistress will before the break of day
Be here at Belmont. She doth stray about   30
By holy crosses, where she kneels and prays
For happy wedlock hours.

LORENZO   Who comes with her?

STEFANO
None but a holy hermit and her maid.
I pray you, is my master yet returned?

LORENZO
He is not, nor we have not heard from him.   35
But go we in, I pray thee, Jessica,
And ceremoniously let us prepare
Some welcome for the mistress of the house.

Enter Lancelot, the clown

LANCELOT (*calling*) Sola, sola! Wo, ha, ho! Sola, sola!

LORENZO Who calls?   40

LANCELOT (*calling*) Sola!—Did you see Master Lorenzo?
(*Calling*) Master Lorenzo! Sola, sola!

LORENZO Leave hollering, man: here.

LANCELOT (*calling*) Sola! —Where, where?

LORENZO Here.   45

LANCELOT Tell him there's a post come from my master
with his horn full of good news. My master will be here
ere morning.   *Exit*

LORENZO (*to Jessica*)
Sweet soul, let's in, and there expect their coming.
And yet no matter. Why should we go in?   50
My friend Stefano, signify, I pray you,
Within the house your mistress is at hand,
And bring your music forth into the air.   *Exit Stefano*
How sweet the moonlight sleeps upon this bank!
Here will we sit, and let the sounds of music   55
Creep in our ears. Soft stillness and the night
Become the touches of sweet harmony.
Sit, Jessica.
        ⌈*They*⌉ *sit*
                Look how the floor of heaven
Is thick inlaid with patens of bright gold.
There's not the smallest orb which thou behold'st   60
But in his motion like an angel sings,
Still choiring to the young-eyed cherubins.
Such harmony is in immortal souls,
But whilst this muddy vesture of decay
Doth grossly close it in, we cannot hear it.   65
        ⌈*Enter Musicians*⌉
(*To the Musicians*) Come, ho, and wake Diana with a
        hymn.
With sweetest touches pierce your mistress' ear,
And draw her home with music.
The Musicians play

JESSICA
I am never merry when I hear sweet music.

LORENZO
The reason is your spirits are attentive,   70
For do but note a wild and wanton herd
Or race of youthful and unhandled colts,
Fetching mad bounds, bellowing and neighing loud,
Which is the hot condition of their blood,
If they but hear perchance a trumpet sound,   75
Or any air of music touch their ears,
You shall perceive them make a mutual stand,
Their savage eyes turned to a modest gaze
By the sweet power of music. Therefore the poet
Did feign that Orpheus drew trees, stones, and floods,
Since naught so stockish, hard, and full of rage
But music for the time doth change his nature.
The man that hath no music in himself,
Nor is not moved with concord of sweet sounds,
Is fit for treasons, stratagems, and spoils.   85
The motions of his spirit are dull as night,
And his affections dark as Erebus.
Let no such man be trusted. Mark the music.
Enter Portia and Nerissa, as themselves

PORTIA
That light we see is burning in my hall.
How far that little candle throws his beams—   90
So shines a good deed in a naughty world.

NERISSA
When the moon shone we did not see the candle.

PORTIA
So doth the greater glory dim the less.
A substitute shines brightly as a king
Until a king be by, and then his state   95
Empties itself as doth an inland brook
Into the main of waters. Music, hark.

NERISSA
It is your music, madam, of the house.

PORTIA
Nothing is good, I see, without respect.
Methinks it sounds much sweeter than by day.   100

NERISSA
Silence bestows that virtue on it, madam.

PORTIA
The crow doth sing as sweetly as the lark
When neither is attended, and I think
The nightingale, if she should sing by day,
When every goose is cackling, would be thought   105
No better a musician than the wren.
How many things by season seasoned are
To their right praise and true perfection!
          ⌈She sees Lorenzo and Jessica⌉
Peace, ho!
          ⌈Music ceases⌉
                    The moon sleeps with Endymion,
And would not be awaked.

LORENZO ⌈rising⌉   That is the voice,   110
Or I am much deceived, of Portia.

PORTIA
He knows me as the blind man knows the cuckoo—
By the bad voice.

LORENZO   Dear lady, welcome home.

PORTIA
We have been praying for our husbands' welfare,
Which speed we hope the better for our words.   115
Are they returned?

LORENZO   Madam, they are not yet,
But there is come a messenger before
To signify their coming.

PORTIA   Go in, Nerissa.
Give order to my servants that they take
No note at all of our being absent hence;   120
Nor you, Lorenzo; Jessica, nor you.
          ⌈A tucket sounds⌉

LORENZO
Your husband is at hand. I hear his trumpet.
We are no tell-tales, madam. Fear you not.

PORTIA
This night, methinks, is but the daylight sick.
It looks a little paler. 'Tis a day   125
Such as the day is when the sun is hid.
          Enter Bassanio, Antonio, Graziano, and their
          followers. Graziano and Nerissa speak silently to
          one another

BASSANIO
We should hold day with the Antipodes
If you would walk in absence of the sun.

PORTIA
Let me give light, but let me not be light;
For a light wife doth make a heavy husband,   130
And never be Bassanio so for me.
But God sort all. You are welcome home, my lord.

BASSANIO
I thank you, madam. Give welcome to my friend.
This is the man, this is Antonio,
To whom I am so infinitely bound.   135

PORTIA
You should in all sense be much bound to him,
For as I hear he was much bound for you.

ANTONIO
No more than I am well acquitted of.

PORTIA
Sir, you are very welcome to our house.
It must appear in other ways than words,   140
Therefore I scant this breathing courtesy.

GRAZIANO (*to Nerissa*)
By yonder moon I swear you do me wrong.
In faith, I gave it to the judge's clerk.
Would he were gelt that had it for my part,
Since you do take it, love, so much at heart.   145

PORTIA
A quarrel, ho, already! What's the matter?

GRAZIANO
About a hoop of gold, a paltry ring
That she did give me, whose posy was
For all the world like cutlers' poetry
Upon a knife—'Love me and leave me not'.   150

NERISSA
What talk you of the posy or the value?
You swore to me when I did give it you
That you would wear it till your hour of death,
And that it should lie with you in your grave.
Though not for me, yet for your vehement oaths   155
You should have been respective and have kept it.
Gave it a judge's clerk?—no, God's my judge,
The clerk will ne'er wear hair on's face that had it.

GRAZIANO
He will an if he live to be a man.

NERISSA
Ay, if a woman live to be a man.   160

GRAZIANO
Now by this hand, I gave it to a youth,
A kind of boy, a little scrubbèd boy
No higher than thyself, the judge's clerk,
A prating boy that begged it as a fee.
I could not for my heart deny it him.   165

PORTIA
You were to blame, I must be plain with you,
To part so slightly with your wife's first gift,
A thing stuck on with oaths upon your finger,
And so riveted with faith unto your flesh.
I gave my love a ring, and made him swear   170
Never to part with it, and here he stands.
I dare be sworn for him he would not leave it,
Nor pluck it from his finger for the wealth
That the world masters. Now, in faith, Graziano,

You give your wife too unkind a cause of grief. 175
An 'twere to me, I should be mad at it.

BASSANIO (*aside*)
Why, I were best to cut my left hand off
And swear I lost the ring defending it.

GRAZIANO ⌈*to Portia*⌉
My lord Bassanio gave his ring away
Unto the judge that begged it, and indeed 180
Deserved it, too, and then the boy his clerk,
That took some pains in writing, he begged mine,
And neither man nor master would take aught
But the two rings.

PORTIA (*to Bassanio*) What ring gave you, my lord?
Not that, I hope, which you received of me. 185

BASSANIO
If I could add a lie unto a fault
I would deny it; but you see my finger
Hath not the ring upon it. It is gone.

PORTIA
Even so void is your false heart of truth.
By heaven, I will ne'er come in your bed 190
Until I see the ring.

NERISSA (*to Graziano*) Nor I in yours
Till I again see mine.

BASSANIO Sweet Portia,
If you did know to whom I gave the ring,
If you did know for whom I gave the ring,
And would conceive for what I gave the ring, 195
And how unwillingly I left the ring
When naught would be accepted but the ring,
You would abate the strength of your displeasure.

PORTIA
If you had known the virtue of the ring,
Or half her worthiness that gave the ring, 200
Or your own honour to contain the ring,
You would not then have parted with the ring.
What man is there so much unreasonable,
If you had pleased to have defended it
With any terms of zeal, wanted the modesty 205
To urge the thing held as a ceremony?
Nerissa teaches me what to believe.
I'll die for't but some woman had the ring.

BASSANIO
No, by my honour, madam, by my soul,
No woman had it, but a civil doctor 210
Which did refuse three thousand ducats of me,
And begged the ring, the which I did deny him,
And suffered him to go displeased away,
Even he that had held up the very life
Of my dear friend. What should I say, sweet lady? 215
I was enforced to send it after him.
I was beset with shame and courtesy.
My honour would not let ingratitude
So much besmear it. Pardon me, good lady,
For by these blessèd candles of the night, 220
Had you been there I think you would have begged
The ring of me to give the worthy doctor.

PORTIA
Let not that doctor e'er come near my house.

Since he hath got the jewel that I loved,
And that which you did swear to keep for me, 225
I will become as liberal as you.
I'll not deny him anything I have,
No, not my body nor my husband's bed.
Know him I shall, I am well sure of it.
Lie not a night from home. Watch me like Argus. 230
If you do not, if I be left alone,
Now by mine honour, which is yet mine own,
I'll have that doctor for my bedfellow.

NERISSA (*to Graziano*)
And I his clerk, therefore be well advised
How you do leave me to mine own protection. 235

GRAZIANO
Well, do you so. Let not me take him then,
For if I do, I'll mar the young clerk's pen.

ANTONIO
I am th'unhappy subject of these quarrels.

PORTIA
Sir, grieve not you. You are welcome
notwithstanding.

BASSANIO
Portia, forgive me this enforcèd wrong, 240
And in the hearing of these many friends
I swear to thee, even by thine own fair eyes,
Wherein I see myself—

PORTIA Mark you but that?
In both my eyes he doubly sees himself,
In each eye one. Swear by your double self, 245
And there's an oath of credit.

BASSANIO Nay, but hear me.
Pardon this fault, and by my soul I swear
I never more will break an oath with thee.

ANTONIO (*to Portia*)
I once did lend my body for his wealth
Which, but for him that had your husband's ring, 250
Had quite miscarried. I dare be bound again,
My soul upon the forfeit, that your lord
Will never more break faith advisedly.

PORTIA
Then you shall be his surety. Give him this,
And bid him keep it better than the other. 255

ANTONIO
Here, Lord Bassanio, swear to keep this ring.

BASSANIO
By heaven, it is the same I gave the doctor!

PORTIA
I had it of him. Pardon me, Bassanio,
For by this ring, the doctor lay with me.

NERISSA
And pardon me, my gentle Graziano, 260
For that same scrubbèd boy, the doctor's clerk,
In lieu of this last night did lie with me.

GRAZIANO
Why, this is like the mending of highways
In summer where the ways are fair enough!
What, are we cuckolds ere we have deserved it? 265

PORTIA
Speak not so grossly. You are all amazed.

Here is a letter. Read it at your leisure.
It comes from Padua, from Bellario.
There you shall find that Portia was the doctor,
Nerissa there her clerk. Lorenzo here   270
Shall witness I set forth as soon as you,
And even but now returned. I have not yet
Entered my house. Antonio, you are welcome,
And I have better news in store for you
Than you expect. Unseal this letter soon.   275
There you shall find three of your argosies
Are richly come to harbour suddenly.
You shall not know by what strange accident
I chancèd on this letter.

ANTONIO   I am dumb!

BASSANIO (*to Portia*)
Were you the doctor and I knew you not?   280

GRAZIANO (*to Nerissa*)
Were you the clerk that is to make me cuckold?

NERISSA
Ay, but the clerk that never means to do it
Unless he live until he be a man.

BASSANIO (*to Portia*)
Sweet doctor, you shall be my bedfellow.
When I am absent, then lie with my wife.   285

ANTONIO (*to Portia*)
Sweet lady, you have given me life and living,

For here I read for certain that my ships
Are safely come to road.

PORTIA   How now, Lorenzo?
My clerk hath some good comforts, too, for you.

NERISSA
Ay, and I'll give them him without a fee.   290
There do I give to you and Jessica
From the rich Jew a special deed of gift,
After his death, of all he dies possessed of.

LORENZO
Fair ladies, you drop manna in the way
Of starvèd people.

PORTIA   It is almost morning,   295
And yet I am sure you are not satisfied
Of these events at full. Let us go in,
And charge us there upon inter'gatories,
And we will answer all things faithfully.

GRAZIANO
Let it be so. The first inter'gatory   300
That my Nerissa shall be sworn on is
Whether till the next night she had rather stay,
Or go to bed now, being two hours to day.
But were the day come, I should wish it dark
Till I were couching with the doctor's clerk.   305
Well, while I live I'll fear no other thing
So sore as keeping safe Nerissa's ring.   *Exeunt*

THE MERRY WIVES OF WINDSOR

A LEGEND dating from 1702 claims that Shakespeare wrote *The Merry Wives of Windsor* in fourteen days and by command of Queen Elizabeth; in 1709 she was said to have wished particularly to see Falstaff in love. Whether or not this is true, a passage towards the end of the play alluding directly to the ceremonies of the Order of the Garter, Britain's highest order of chivalry, encourages the belief that the play has a direct connection with a specific occasion. In 1597 George Carey, Lord Hunsdon, Lord Chamberlain and patron of Shakespeare's company, was installed at Windsor as a Knight of the Garter. The Queen was not present at the installation but had attended the Garter Feast at the Palace of Westminster on St George's Day (23 April). Shakespeare's play was probably performed in association with this occasion, and may have been written especially for it. It was first printed, in a corrupt text, in 1602; a better text appears in the 1623 Folio.

Some of the characters—Sir John Falstaff, Mistress Quickly, Pistol, Nim, Justice Shallow—appear also in *1* and *2 Henry IV* and *Henry V*, but in spite of a reference to 'the wild Prince and Poins' at 3.2.66–7, this is essentially an Elizabethan comedy, the only one that Shakespeare set firmly in England. The play is full of details that would have been familiar to Elizabethan Londoners, and the language is colloquial and up to date. The plot, however, is made up of conventional situations whose ancestry is literary rather than realistic. There are many analogues in medieval and other tales to Shakespeare's basic plot situations, some in books that he probably or certainly knew. The central story, of Sir John's unsuccessful attempts to seduce Mistress Page and Mistress Ford, and of Master Ford's unfounded jealousy, is in the tradition of the Italian *novella*, and may have been suggested by Ser Giovanni Fiorentino's *Il Pecorone* (1558). Alongside it Shakespeare places the comical but finally romantic love story of Anne Page, wooed by the foolish but rich Abraham Slender and the irascible French Doctor Caius, but won by the young and handsome Fenton. The play contains a higher proportion of prose to verse than any other play by Shakespeare, and the action is often broadly comic; but it ends, after the midnight scene in Windsor Forest during which Sir John is frightened out of his lechery, in forgiveness and love.

The play is known to have been acted for James I on 4 November 1604, and for Charles I in 1638. It was revived soon after the theatres reopened, in 1660; at first it was not particularly popular, but since 1720 it has consistently pleased audiences. Many artists have illustrated it, and it forms the basis for a number of operas, including Otto Nicolai's *Die lustigen Weiben von Windsor* (1848) and Giuseppe Verdi's comic masterpiece, *Falstaff* (1893).

THE PERSONS OF THE PLAY

MISTRESS Margaret PAGE
Master George PAGE, her husband
ANNE Page, their daughter
WILLIAM Page, their son

citizens of Windsor

MISTRESS Alice FORD
Master Frank FORD, her husband

JOHN
ROBERT } their servants

SIR JOHN Falstaff

BARDOLPH
PISTOL
NIM } Sir John's followers

ROBIN, Sir John's page

The HOST of the Garter Inn

Sir Hugh EVANS, a Welsh parson

Doctor CAIUS, a French physician
MISTRESS QUICKLY, his housekeeper
John RUGBY, his servant

Master FENTON, a young gentleman, in love with Anne Page

Master Abraham SLENDER
Robert SHALLOW, his uncle, a Justice
Peter SIMPLE, Slender's servant

Children of Windsor, appearing as fairies

632

The Merry Wives of Windsor

1.1 *Enter Justice Shallow, Master Slender, and Sir Hugh
Evans*

SHALLOW Sir Hugh, persuade me not. I will make a Star
Chamber matter of it. If he were twenty Sir John
Falstaffs, he shall not abuse Robert Shallow, Esquire.

SLENDER In the county of Gloucester, Justice of Peace and
Coram.   5

SHALLOW Ay, cousin Slender, and Custalorum.

SLENDER Ay, and Ratolorum too; and a gentleman born,
Master Parson, who writes himself 'Armigero' in any
bill, warrant, quittance, or obligation: 'Armigero'.

SHALLOW Ay, that I do, and have done any time these
three hundred years.   11

SLENDER All his successors gone before him hath done't,
and all his ancestors that come after him may. They
may give the dozen white luces in their coat.

SHALLOW It is an old coat.   15

EVANS The dozen white louses do become an old coad
well. It agrees well passant: it is a familiar beast to
man, and signifies love.

SHALLOW The luce is the fresh fish; the salt fish is an old
cod.   20

SLENDER I may quarter, coz.

SHALLOW You may, by marrying.

EVANS It is marring indeed if he quarter it.

SHALLOW Not a whit.   24

EVANS Yes, py'r Lady. If he has a quarter of your coat,
there is but three skirts for yourself, in my simple
conjectures. But that is all one. If Sir John Falstaff have
committed disparagements unto you, I am of the
Church, and will be glad to do my benevolence to make
atonements and compromises between you.   30

SHALLOW The Council shall hear it; it is a riot.

EVANS It is not meet the Council hear a riot. There is no
fear of Got in a riot. The Council, look you, shall desire
to hear the fear of Got, and not to hear a riot. Take
your 'visaments in that.   35

SHALLOW Ha! O' my life, if I were young again, the sword
should end it.

EVANS It is petter that friends is the sword and end it.
And there is also another device in my prain, which
peradventure prings goot discretions with it. There is
Anne Page which is daughter to Master George Page,
which is pretty virginity.

SLENDER Mistress Anne Page? She has brown hair, and
speaks small like a woman?   44

EVANS It is that fery person for all the 'orld, as just as
you will desire. And seven hundred pounds of moneys,
and gold and silver, is her grandsire upon his death's-
bed—Got deliver to a joyful resurrections—give, when
she is able to overtake seventeen years old. It were a
goot motion if we leave our pribbles and prabbles, and
desire a marriage between Master Abraham and
Mistress Anne Page.   52

SLENDER Did her grandsire leave her seven hundred
pound?

EVANS Ay, and her father is make her a petter penny.   55

[SHALLOW] I know the young gentlewoman. She has good
gifts.

EVANS Seven hundred pounds and possibilities is goot
gifts.

SHALLOW Well, let us see honest Master Page. Is Falstaff
there?   61

EVANS Shall I tell you a lie? I do despise a liar as I do
despise one that is false, or as I despise one that is not
true. The knight Sir John is there, and I beseech you
be ruled by your well-willers. I will peat the door for
Master Page.   66

He knocks on the door

What ho! Got pless your house here!

PAGE [*within*] Who's there?

EVANS Here is Got's plessing and your friend, and Justice
Shallow, and here young Master Slender, that perad-
ventures shall tell you another tale if matters grow to
your likings.   72

[*Enter Master Page*]

PAGE I am glad to see your worships well. I thank you
for my venison, Master Shallow.

SHALLOW Master Page, I am glad to see you. Much good
do it your good heart! I wished your venison better; it
was ill killed.—How doth good Mistress Page?—And I
thank you always with my heart, la, with my heart.

PAGE Sir, I thank you.

SHALLOW Sir, I thank you. By yea and no, I do.   80

PAGE I am glad to see you, good Master Slender.

SLENDER How does your fallow greyhound, sir? I heard
say he was outrun on Cotswold.

PAGE It could not be judged, sir.

SLENDER You'll not confess, you'll not confess.   85

SHALLOW That he will not. 'Tis your fault, 'tis your fault.
(*To Page*) 'Tis a good dog.

PAGE A cur, sir.

SHALLOW Sir, he's a good dog and a fair dog. Can there
be more said? He is good and fair. Is Sir John Falstaff
here?   91

PAGE Sir, he is within; and I would I could do a good
office between you.

EVANS It is spoke as a Christians ought to speak.

SHALLOW He hath wronged me, Master Page.   95

PAGE Sir, he doth in some sort confess it.

SHALLOW If it be confessed, it is not redressed. Is not that
so, Master Page? He hath wronged me; indeed he
hath; at a word, he hath. Believe me, Robert Shallow,
Esquire, saith he is wronged.   100

Enter Sir John Falstaff, Bardolph, Nim, and Pistol

PAGE Here comes Sir John.

SIR JOHN Now, Master Shallow, you'll complain of me to
the King?

SHALLOW Knight, you have beaten my men, killed my
  deer, and broke open my lodge.   105
SIR JOHN But not kissed your keeper's daughter?
SHALLOW Tut, a pin. This shall be answered.
SIR JOHN I will answer it straight: I have done all this.
  That is now answered.
SHALLOW The Council shall know this.   110
SIR JOHN 'Twere better for you if it were known in counsel.
  You'll be laughed at.
EVANS *Pauca verba*, Sir John, good worts.
SIR JOHN Good worts? Good cabbage!—Slender, I broke
  your head. What matter have you against me?   115
SLENDER Marry, sir, I have matter in my head against
  you, and against your cony-catching rascals, Bardolph,
  Nim, and Pistol.
BARDOLPH You Banbury cheese!
SLENDER Ay, it is no matter.   120
PISTOL How now, Mephistopheles?
SLENDER Ay, it is no matter.
NIM Slice, I say *pauca, pauca*. Slice, that's my humour.
SLENDER (*to Shallow*) Where's Simple, my man? Can you
  tell, cousin?   125
EVANS Peace, I pray you. Now let us understand. There
  is three umpires in this matter, as I understand: that
  is, Master Page, fidelicet Master Page; and there is
  myself, fidelicet myself; and the three party is, lastly
  and finally, mine Host of the Garter.   130
PAGE We three to hear it, and end it between them.
EVANS Fery goot. I will make a prief of it in my notebook,
  and we will afterwards 'ork upon the cause with as
  great discreetly as we can.
SIR JOHN Pistol.   135
PISTOL He hears with ears.
EVANS The tevil and his tam! What phrase is this? 'He
  hears with ear'! Why, it is affectations.
SIR JOHN Pistol, did you pick Master Slender's purse? 139
SLENDER Ay, by these gloves did he—or I would I might
  never come in mine own great chamber again else—
  of seven groats in mill-sixpences, and two Edward
  shovel-boards that cost me two shilling and twopence
  apiece of Ed Miller. By these gloves.
SIR JOHN Is this true, Pistol?   145
EVANS No, it is false, if it is a pickpurse.
PISTOL
  Ha, thou mountain-foreigner! Sir John and master
    mine,
  I combat challenge of this latten bilbo.—
  Word of denial in thy *labras* here,
  Word of denial: froth and scum, thou liest.   150
SLENDER (*pointing to Nim*) By these gloves, then, 'twas he.
NIM Be advised, sir, and pass good humours. I will say
  'marry, trap with you' if you run the nuthook's humour
  on me. That is the very note of it.
SLENDER By this hat, then, he in the red face had it. For
  though I cannot remember what I did when you made
  me drunk, yet I am not altogether an ass.   157
SIR JOHN (*to Bardolph*) What say you, Scarlet and John?

BARDOLPH Why, sir, for my part I say the gentleman had
  drunk himself out of his five sentences.   160
EVANS It is 'his five senses'. Fie, what the ignorance is!
BARDOLPH And being fap, sir, was, as they say, cashiered.
  And so conclusions passed the careers.
SLENDER Ay, you spake in Latin then, too. But 'tis no
  matter. I'll ne'er be drunk, whilst I live, again, but in
  honest, civil, godly company, for this trick. If I be
  drunk, I'll be drunk with those that have the fear of
  God, and not with drunken knaves.
EVANS So Got 'udge me, that is a virtuous mind.
SIR JOHN You hear all these matters denied, gentlemen,
  you hear it.   171
      Enter Anne Page, with wine
PAGE Nay, daughter, carry the wine in; we'll drink
  within.   *Exit Anne*
SLENDER O heaven, this is Mistress Anne Page!
      ⌈*Enter at another door Mistress Ford and Mistress
      Page*⌉
PAGE How now, Mistress Ford?   175
SIR JOHN Mistress Ford, by my troth, you are very well
  met. By your leave, good mistress.
      ⌈*He kisses her*⌉
PAGE Wife, bid these gentlemen welcome.—Come, we
  have a hot venison pasty to dinner. Come, gentlemen,
  I hope we shall drink down all unkindness.   180
      Exeunt all but Slender
SLENDER I had rather than forty shillings I had my book
  of songs and sonnets here.
      Enter Simple
  How now, Simple, where have you been? I must wait
  on myself, must I? You have not the book of riddles
  about you, have you?   185
SIMPLE Book of riddles? Why, did you not lend it to Alice
  Shortcake upon Allhallowmas last, a fortnight afore
  Michaelmas?
      Enter Shallow and Evans
SHALLOW (*to Slender*) Come, coz; come, coz; we stay for
  you. (*Aside to him*) A word with you, coz.   190
      He draws Slender aside
  Marry, this, coz: there is, as 'twere, a tender, a kind
  of tender, made afar off by Sir Hugh here. Do you
  understand me?
SLENDER Ay, sir, you shall find me reasonable. If it be so,
  I shall do that that is reason.   195
SHALLOW Nay, but understand me.
SLENDER So I do, sir.
EVANS Give ear to his motions. Master Slender, I will
  description the matter to you, if you be capacity of it.
SLENDER Nay, I will do as my cousin Shallow says. I pray
  you pardon me. He's a Justice of Peace in his country,
  simple though I stand here.
EVANS But that is not the question. The question is
  concerning your marriage.
SHALLOW Ay, there's the point, sir.   205
EVANS Marry, is it, the very point of it—to Mistress Anne
  Page.

SLENDER Why, if it be so, I will marry her upon any reasonable demands.   209

EVANS But can you affection the 'oman? Let us command to know that of your mouth, or of your lips—for divers philosophers hold that the lips is parcel of the mouth. Therefore, precisely, can you carry your good will to the maid?   214

SHALLOW Cousin Abraham Slender, can you love her?

SLENDER I hope, sir, I will do as it shall become one that would do reason.

EVANS Nay, Got's lords and his ladies, you must speak positable if you can carry her your desires towards her.

SHALLOW That you must. Will you, upon good dowry, marry her?   221

SLENDER I will do a greater thing than that upon your request, cousin, in any reason.

SHALLOW Nay, conceive me, conceive me, sweet coz. What I do is to pleasure you, coz. Can you love the maid?   226

SLENDER I will marry her, sir, at your request. But if there be no great love in the beginning, yet heaven may decrease it upon better acquaintance, when we are married and have more occasion to know one another. I hope upon familiarity will grow more contempt. But if you say 'marry her', I will marry her. That I am freely dissolved, and dissolutely.

EVANS It is a fery discretion answer, save the faul' is in the 'ord 'dissolutely'. The 'ort is, according to our meaning, 'resolutely'. His meaning is good.   236

SHALLOW Ay, I think my cousin meant well.

SLENDER Ay, or else I would I might be hanged, la.

Enter Anne Page

SHALLOW Here comes fair Mistress Anne.—Would I were young for your sake, Mistress Anne.   240

ANNE The dinner is on the table. My father desires your worships' company.

SHALLOW I will wait on him, fair Mistress Anne. ,

EVANS 'Od's plessed will, I will not be absence at the grace.   *Exeunt Shallow and Evans*

ANNE (*to Slender*) Will't please your worship to come in, sir?

SLENDER No, I thank you, forsooth, heartily; I am very well.

ANNE The dinner attends you, sir.   250

SLENDER I am not a-hungry, I thank you, forsooth. (*To Simple*) Go, sirrah; for all you are my man, go wait upon my cousin Shallow.   *Exit Simple*
A Justice of Peace sometime may be beholden to his friend for a man. I keep but three men and a boy yet, till my mother be dead. But what though? Yet I live like a poor gentleman born.   257

ANNE I may not go in without your worship. They will not sit till you come.

SLENDER I'faith, I'll eat nothing. I thank you as much as though I did.   261

ANNE I pray you, sir, walk in.

⌈*Dogs bark within*⌉

SLENDER I had rather walk here, I thank you. I bruised my shin th'other day, with playing at sword and dagger with a master of fence—three veneys for a dish of stewed prunes—and, by my troth, I cannot abide the smell of hot meat since. Why do your dogs bark so? Be there bears i'th' town?   268

ANNE I think there are, sir. I heard them talked of.

SLENDER I love the sport well—but I shall as soon quarrel at it as any man in England. You are afraid if you see the bear loose, are you not?   272

ANNE Ay, indeed, sir.

SLENDER That's meat and drink to me, now. I have seen Sackerson loose twenty times, and have taken him by the chain. But I warrant you, the women have so cried and shrieked at it that it passed. But women, indeed, cannot abide 'em. They are very ill-favoured, rough things.

Enter Page

PAGE Come, gentle Master Slender, come. We stay for you.   281

SLENDER I'll eat nothing, I thank you, sir.

PAGE By cock and pie, you shall not choose, sir. Come, come.

SLENDER Nay, pray you lead the way.   285

PAGE Come on, sir.

SLENDER Mistress Anne, yourself shall go first.

ANNE Not I, sir. Pray you keep on.

SLENDER Truly, I will not go first, truly, la. I will not do you that wrong.   290

ANNE I pray you, sir.

SLENDER I'll rather be unmannerly than troublesome. You do yourself wrong, indeed, la.

Exeunt ⌈Slender first, the others following⌉

1.2   *Enter Sir Hugh Evans and Simple, ⌈from dinner⌉*

EVANS Go your ways, and ask of Doctor Caius' house which is the way. And there dwells one Mistress Quickly, which is in the manner of his 'oman, or his dry-nurse, or his cook, or his laundry, his washer, and his wringer.   5

SIMPLE Well, sir.

EVANS Nay, it is petter yet. Give her this letter, for it is a 'oman that altogethers acquaintance with Mistress Anne Page. And the letter is to desire and require her to solicit your master's desires to Mistress Anne Page. I pray you be gone.   ⌈*Exit Simple*⌉
I will make an end of my dinner; there's pippins and cheese to come.   *Exit*

1.3   *Enter Sir John Falstaff, Bardolph, Nim, Pistol, and Robin*

SIR JOHN Mine Host of the Garter!

Enter the Host of the Garter

HOST What says my bully rook? Speak scholarly and wisely.

SIR JOHN Truly, mine Host, I must turn away some of my followers.   5

HOST Discard, bully Hercules, cashier. Let them wag. Trot, trot.

SIR JOHN I sit at ten pounds a week.

HOST Thou'rt an emperor: Caesar, kaiser, and pheezer. I will entertain Bardolph. He shall draw, he shall tap. Said I well, bully Hector?   11

SIR JOHN Do so, good mine Host.

HOST I have spoke; let him follow. (*To Bardolph*) Let me see thee froth and lime. I am at a word: follow.   *Exit*

SIR JOHN Bardolph, follow him. A tapster is a good trade. An old cloak makes a new jerkin; a withered servingman a fresh tapster. Go; adieu.   17

BARDOLPH It is a life that I have desired. I will thrive.

⌈*Exit*⌉

PISTOL

O base Hungarian wight, wilt thou the spigot wield?

NIM He was gotten in drink; his mind is not heroic. Is not the humour conceited?   21

SIR JOHN I am glad I am so acquit of this tinderbox. His thefts were too open. His filching was like an unskilful singer: he kept not time.

NIM The good humour is to steal at a minute's rest.   25

PISTOL

'Convey' the wise it call. 'Steal'? Foh, a fico for the phrase!

SIR JOHN Well, sirs, I am almost out at heels.

PISTOL Why then, let kibes ensue.

SIR JOHN There is no remedy: I must cony-catch, I must shift.   30

PISTOL Young ravens must have food.

SIR JOHN Which of you know Ford of this town?

PISTOL I ken the wight. He is of substance good.

SIR JOHN My honest lads, I will tell you what I am about.

PISTOL Two yards and more.   35

SIR JOHN No quips now, Pistol. Indeed, I am in the waist two yards about. But I am now about no waste; I am about thrift. Briefly, I do mean to make love to Ford's wife. I spy entertainment in her. She discourses, she carves, she gives the leer of invitation. I can construe the action of her familiar style; and the hardest voice of her behaviour, to be Englished rightly, is 'I am Sir John Falstaff's'.

PISTOL He hath studied her well, and translated her will: out of honesty, into English.   45

NIM The anchor is deep. Will that humour pass?

SIR JOHN Now, the report goes, she has all the rule of her husband's purse; he hath a legion of angels.

PISTOL

As many devils entertain, and 'To her, boy!' say I.   49

NIM The humour rises; it is good. Humour me the angels!

SIR JOHN (*showing letters*) I have writ me here a letter to her—and here another to Page's wife, who even now gave me good eyes too, examined my parts with most judicious oeillades; sometimes the beam of her view gilded my foot, sometimes my portly belly.   55

PISTOL

Then did the sun on dunghill shine.

NIM I thank thee for that humour.

SIR JOHN O, she did so course o'er my exteriors, with such a greedy intention, that the appetite of her eye did

seem to scorch me up like a burning-glass! Here's another letter to her. She bears the purse too. She is a region in Guiana, all gold and bounty. I will be cheaters to them both, and they shall be exchequers to me. They shall be my East and West Indies, and I will trade to them both. (*Giving a letter to Pistol*) Go bear thou this letter to Mistress Page, (*giving a letter to Nim*) and thou this to Mistress Ford. We will thrive, lads, we will thrive.   68

PISTOL (*returning the letter*)

Shall I Sir Pandarus of Troy become,

And by my side wear steel? Then Lucifer take all.

NIM (*returning the letter*) I will run no base humour. Here, take the humour-letter. I will keep the haviour of reputation.

SIR JOHN (*to Robin*)

Hold, sirrah. Bear you these letters tightly.

Sail like my pinnace to these golden shores.   75

He gives Robin the letters

Rogues, hence, avaunt! Vanish like hailstones! Go!

Trudge, plod, away o'th' hoof, seek shelter, pack!

Falstaff will learn the humour of the age:

French thrift, you rogues—myself and skirted page.

Exeunt Sir John and Robin

PISTOL

Let vultures gripe thy guts!—for gourd and fullam holds,   80

And high and low beguiles the rich and poor.

Tester I'll have in pouch when thou shalt lack,

Base Phrygian Turk!

NIM

I have operations which be humours of revenge.

PISTOL

Wilt thou revenge?

NIM   By welkin and her stars!   85

PISTOL

With wit or steel?

NIM   With both the humours, I.

I will discuss the humour of this love to Ford.

PISTOL

And I to Page shall eke unfold

How Falstaff, varlet vile,

His dove will prove, his gold will hold,   90

And his soft couch defile.

NIM My humour shall not cool. I will incense Ford to deal with poison; I will possess him with yellowness; for this revolt of mine is dangerous. That is my true humour.   95

PISTOL

Thou art the Mars of malcontents.

I second thee. Troop on.   *Exeunt*

1.4   *Enter Mistress Quickly and Simple*

MISTRESS QUICKLY What, John Rugby!

Enter John Rugby

I pray thee, go to the casement and see if you can see my master, Master Doctor Caius, coming. If he do, i'faith, and find anybody in the house, here will be an

old abusing of God's patience and the King's English. 5
RUGBY I'll go watch.
MISTRESS QUICKLY Go; and we'll have a posset for't soon
at night, in faith, at the latter end of a seacoal fire.
                                                    Exit Rugby
An honest, willing, kind fellow as ever servant shall
come in house withal; and, I warrant you, no telltale,
nor no breedbate. His worst fault is that he is given to
prayer; he is something peevish that way—but nobody
but has his fault. But let that pass. Peter Simple you
say your name is?
SIMPLE Ay, for fault of a better.   15
MISTRESS QUICKLY And Master Slender's your master?
SIMPLE Ay, forsooth.
MISTRESS QUICKLY Does he not wear a great round beard,
like a glover's paring-knife?
SIMPLE No, forsooth; he hath but a little whey face, with
a little yellow beard, a Cain-coloured beard.   21
MISTRESS QUICKLY A softly spirited man, is he not?
SIMPLE Ay, forsooth; but he is as tall a man of his hands
as any is between this and his head. He hath fought
with a warrener.   25
MISTRESS QUICKLY How say you?—O, I should remember
him: does he not hold up his head, as it were, and
strut in his gait?
SIMPLE Yes, indeed does he.
MISTRESS QUICKLY Well, heaven send Anne Page no worse
fortune! Tell Master Parson Evans I will do what I can
for your master. Anne is a good girl, and I wish—
            Enter Rugby
RUGBY Out, alas, here comes my master!   ⌈*Exit*⌉
MISTRESS QUICKLY We shall all be shent. Run in here, good
young man; for God's sake, go into this closet. He will
not stay long.   36
            Simple steps into the closet
What, John Rugby! John! What, John, I say!
            ⌈*Enter Rugby*⌉
⌈*Speaking loudly*⌉ Go, John, go enquire for my master. I
doubt he be not well, that he comes not home.
                                          ⌈*Exit Rugby*⌉
(*Singing*) 'And down, down, adown-a' (*etc.*)   40
            Enter Doctor Caius
CAIUS Vat is you sing? I do not like dese toys. Pray you
go and vetch me in my closet *un boîtier vert*—a box, a
green-a box. Do intend vat I speak? A green-a box.
MISTRESS QUICKLY Ay, forsooth, I'll fetch it you. (*Aside*) I
am glad he went not in himself. If he had found the
young man, he would have been horn-mad.   46
            She goes to fetch the box
CAIUS *Fe, fe, fe, fe! Ma foi, il fait fort chaud! Je m'en vais à
la cour. La grande affaire.*
MISTRESS QUICKLY Is it this, sir?
CAIUS *Oui. Mets-le à ma pochette. Dépêche*, quickly! Vere is
dat knave Rugby?   51
MISTRESS QUICKLY What, John Rugby! John!
            ⌈*Enter Rugby*⌉
RUGBY Here, sir.
CAIUS You are John Rugby, and you are Jack Rugby.

Come, take-a your rapier, and come after my heel to
the court.   56
RUGBY 'Tis ready, sir, here in the porch.
            He fetches the rapier
CAIUS By my trot, I tarry too long. 'Od's me, *qu'ai-j'
oublié?* Dere is some simples in my closet dat I vill not
for the varld I shall leave behind.   60
MISTRESS QUICKLY (*aside*)· Ay me, he'll find the young man
there, and be mad.
CAIUS (*discovering Simple*) O *diable, diable!* Vat is in my
closet? Villainy, *larron!* Rugby, my rapier!
            He takes the rapier
MISTRESS QUICKLY Good master, be content.   65
CAIUS Wherefore shall I be content-a?
MISTRESS QUICKLY The young man is an honest man.
CAIUS What shall de honest man do in my closet? Dere
is no honest man dat shall come in my closet.   69
MISTRESS QUICKLY I beseech you, be not so phlegmatic.
Hear the truth of it. He came of an errand to me from
Parson Hugh.
CAIUS Vell.
SIMPLE Ay, forsooth, to desire her to—
MISTRESS QUICKLY Peace, I pray you.   75
CAIUS Peace-a your tongue. (*To Simple*) Speak-a your tale.
SIMPLE To desire this honest gentlewoman, your maid, to
speak a good word to Mistress Anne Page for my master
in the way of marriage.
MISTRESS QUICKLY This is all, indeed, la; but I'll ne'er put
my finger in the fire an need not.   81
CAIUS Sir Hugh send-a you?—Rugby, *baile* me some
paper.
            Rugby brings paper
(*To Simple*) Tarry you a little-a while.
            Caius writes
MISTRESS QUICKLY (*aside to Simple*) I am glad he is so quiet.
If he had been throughly moved, you should have
heard him so loud and so melancholy. But
notwithstanding, man, I'll do your master what good
I can. And the very yea and the no is, the French
doctor, my master—I may call him my master, look
you, for I keep his house, and I wash, wring, brew,
bake, scour, dress meat and drink, make the beds, and
do all myself—
SIMPLE (*aside to Mistress Quickly*) 'Tis a great charge to
come under one body's hand.   95
MISTRESS QUICKLY (*aside to Simple*) Are you advised o' that?
You shall find it a great charge—and to be up early,
and down late. But notwithstanding, to tell you in your
ear—I would have no words of it—my master himself
is in love with Mistress Anne Page. But notwithstanding
that, I know Anne's mind: that's neither here nor
there.   102
CAIUS (*giving the letter to Simple*) You, jack'nape, give-a
this letter to Sir Hugh. By Gar, it is a shallenge. I will
cut his troat in de Park, and I will teach a scurvy
jackanape priest to meddle or make. You may be gone.
It is not good you tarry here. By Gar, I will cut all his
two stones. By Gar, he shall not have a stone to throw
at his dog.   *Exit Simple*

MISTRESS QUICKLY Alas, he speaks but for his friend. 110

CAIUS It is no matter-a ver dat. Do not you tell-a me dat I shall have Anne Page for myself? By Gar, I vill kill de jack-priest. And I have appointed mine Host of de Jarteer to measure our weapon. By Gar, I will myself have Anne Page. 115

MISTRESS QUICKLY Sir, the maid loves you, and all shall be well. We must give folks leave to prate, what the goodyear!

CAIUS Rugby, come to the court with me. (*To Mistress Quickly*) By Gar, if I have not Anne Page, I shall turn your head out of my door. Follow my heels, Rugby.

MISTRESS QUICKLY You shall have Anne— 122

Exeunt Caius and Rugby

—ass-head of your own. No, I know Anne's mind for that. Never a woman in Windsor knows more of Anne's mind than I do, nor can do more than I do with her, I thank heaven. 126

FENTON (*within*) Who's within there, ho!

MISTRESS QUICKLY Who's there, I trow?—Come near the house, I pray you.

Enter Master Fenton

FENTON How now, good woman, how dost thou? 130

MISTRESS QUICKLY The better that it pleases your good worship to ask.

FENTON What news? How does pretty Mistress Anne?

MISTRESS QUICKLY In truth, sir, and she is pretty, and honest, and gentle, and one that is your friend. I can tell you that by the way, I praise heaven for it. 136

FENTON Shall I do any good, thinkest thou? Shall I not lose my suit?

MISTRESS QUICKLY Troth, sir, all is in His hands above. But notwithstanding, Master Fenton, I'll be sworn on a book she loves you. Have not your worship a wart above your eye? 142

FENTON Yes, marry, have I. What of that?

MISTRESS QUICKLY Well, thereby hangs a tale. Good faith, it is such another Nan!—But I detest, an honest maid as ever broke bread.—We had an hour's talk of that wart. I shall never laugh but in that maid's company.— But indeed she is given too much to allicholy and musing.—But for you—well—go to! 149

FENTON Well, I shall see her today. Hold, there's money for thee. Let me have thy voice in my behalf. If thou seest her before me, commend me.

MISTRESS QUICKLY Will I? I'faith, that I will. And I will tell your worship more of the wart the next time we have confidence, and of other wooers. 155

FENTON Well, farewell. I am in great haste now.

MISTRESS QUICKLY Farewell to your worship.

Exit Fenton

Truly, an honest gentleman; but Anne loves him not, for I know Anne's mind as well as another does.—Out upon't, what have I forgot? *Exit*

2.1 *Enter Mistress Page, with a letter*

MISTRESS PAGE What, have I scaped love-letters in the holiday time of my beauty, and am I now a subject for them? Let me see. 163

She reads

'Ask me no reason why I love you, for though Love use Reason for his precision, he admits him not for his counsellor. You are not young; no more am I. Go to, then, there's sympathy. You are merry; so am I. Ha, ha, then, there's more sympathy. You love sack, and so do I. Would you desire better sympathy? Let it suffice thee, Mistress Page, at the least if the love of soldier can suffice, that I love thee. I will not say "pity me"— 'tis not a soldier-like phrase—but I say "love me". 12
> By me, thine own true knight,
> By day or night
> Or any kind of light, 15
> With all his might
> For thee to fight,
>   John Falstaff.'

What a Herod of Jewry is this! O, wicked, wicked world! One that is well-nigh worn to pieces with age, to show himself a young gallant! What an unweighed behaviour hath this Flemish drunkard picked, i'th' devil's name, out of my conversation, that he dares in this manner assay me? Why, he hath not been thrice in my company. What should I say to him? I was then frugal of my mirth, heaven forgive me. Why, I'll exhibit a bill in the Parliament for the putting down of men. O God, that I knew how to be revenged on him! For revenged I will be, as sure as his guts are made of puddings. 30

Enter Mistress Ford

MISTRESS FORD Mistress Page! By my faith, I was going to your house.

MISTRESS PAGE And by my faith, I was coming to you. You look very ill.

MISTRESS FORD Nay, I'll ne'er believe that: I have to show to the contrary. 36

MISTRESS PAGE Faith, but you do, in my mind.

MISTRESS FORD Well, I do, then. Yet I say I could show you to the contrary. O Mistress Page, give me some counsel. 40

MISTRESS PAGE What's the matter, woman?

MISTRESS FORD O woman, if it were not for one trifling respect, I could come to such honour!

MISTRESS PAGE Hang the trifle, woman; take the honour. What is it? Dispense with trifles. What is it? 45

MISTRESS FORD If I would but go to hell for an eternal moment or so, I could be knighted.

MISTRESS PAGE What? Thou liest! Sir Alice Ford? These knights will hack, and so thou shouldst not alter the article of thy gentry. 50

MISTRESS FORD We burn daylight. Here: read, read.

She gives Mistress Page a letter

Perceive how I might be knighted.

Mistress Page reads

I shall think the worse of fat men as long as I have an eye to make difference of men's liking. And yet he would not swear, praised women's modesty, and gave such orderly and well-behaved reproof to all uncomeliness that I would have sworn his disposition would have gone to the truth of his words. But they do no more adhere and keep place together than the hundred and fifty psalms to the tune of 'Greensleeves'. What tempest, I trow, threw this whale, with so many tuns of oil in his belly, ashore at Windsor? How shall I be revenged on him? I think the best way were to entertain him with hope, till the wicked fire of lust have melted him in his own grease. Did you ever hear the like? 66

MISTRESS PAGE Letter for letter, but that the name of Page and Ford differs.

She gives Mistress Ford her letter

To thy great comfort in this mystery of ill opinions, here's the twin brother of thy letter. But let thine inherit first, for I protest mine never shall. I warrant he hath a thousand of these letters, writ with blank space for different names—sure, more, and these are of the second edition. He will print them, out of doubt—for he cares not what he puts into the press when he would put us two. I had rather be a giantess, and lie under Mount Pelion. Well, I will find you twenty lascivious turtles ere one chaste man.

MISTRESS FORD Why, this is the very same: the very hand, the very words. What doth he think of us? 80

MISTRESS PAGE Nay, I know not. It makes me almost ready to wrangle with mine own honesty. I'll entertain myself like one that I am not acquainted withal; for, sure, unless he know some strain in me that I know not myself, he would never have boarded me in this fury.

MISTRESS FORD 'Boarding' call you it? I'll be sure to keep him above deck. 87

MISTRESS PAGE So will I. If he come under my hatches, I'll never to sea again. Let's be revenged on him. Let's appoint him a meeting, give him a show of comfort in his suit, and lead him on with a fine baited delay till he hath pawned his horses to mine Host of the Garter.

MISTRESS FORD Nay, I will consent to act any villainy against him that may not sully the chariness of our honesty. O that my husband saw this letter! It would give eternal food to his jealousy. 96

Enter Master Ford with Pistol, and Master Page with Nim

MISTRESS PAGE Why, look where he comes, and my goodman too. He's as far from jealousy as I am from giving him cause; and that, I hope, is an unmeasurable distance. 100

MISTRESS FORD You are the happier woman.

MISTRESS PAGE Let's consult together against this greasy knight. Come hither.

They withdraw.

FORD Well, I hope it be not so.

PISTOL

Hope is a curtal dog in some affairs. 105
Sir John affects thy wife.

FORD Why, sir, my wife is not young.

PISTOL

He woos both high and low, both rich and poor,
Both young and old, one with another, Ford.
He loves the gallimaufry, Ford. Perpend. 110

FORD Love my wife?

PISTOL

With liver burning hot. Prevent,
Or go thou like Sir Actaeon, he,
With Ringwood at thy heels.
O, odious is the name! 115

FORD What name, sir?

PISTOL The horn, I say. Farewell.
Take heed; have open eye; for thieves do foot by night.
Take heed ere summer comes, or cuckoo-birds do
sing.— 119
Away, Sir Corporal Nim!—Believe it, Page; he speaks
sense. *Exit*

FORD (*aside*) I will be patient. I will find out this.

NIM (*to Page*) And this is true. I like not the humour of lying. He hath wronged me in some humours. I should have borne the humoured letter to her; but I have a sword, and it shall bite upon my necessity. He loves your wife. There's the short and the long. 126

My name is Corporal Nim. I speak and I avouch 'tis true.

My name is Nim, and Falstaff loves your wife. Adieu.
I love not the humour of bread and cheese. Adieu.

Exit

PAGE (*aside*) The humour of it, quoth a? Here's a fellow frights English out of his wits. 131

FORD (*aside*) I will seek out Falstaff.

PAGE (*aside*) I never heard such a drawling, affecting rogue.

FORD (*aside*) If I do find it—well. 135

PAGE (*aside*) I will not believe such a Cathayan though the priest o'th' town commended him for a true man.

FORD (*aside*) 'Twas a good, sensible fellow. Well.

Mistress Page and Mistress Ford come forward

PAGE How now, Meg?

MISTRESS PAGE Whither go you, George? Hark you. 140

They talk apart

MISTRESS FORD How now, sweet Frank? Why art thou melancholy?

FORD I melancholy? I am not melancholy. Get you home, go.

MISTRESS FORD Faith, thou hast some crotchets in thy head now. Will you go, Mistress Page? 146

MISTRESS PAGE Have with you.—You'll come to dinner, George?

Enter Mistress Quickly

(*Aside to Mistress Ford*) Look who comes yonder. She shall be our messenger to this paltry knight. 150

MISTRESS FORD (*aside to Mistress Page*) Trust me, I thought on her. She'll fit it.

MISTRESS PAGE (*to Mistress Quickly*) You are come to see my daughter Anne?

MISTRESS QUICKLY Ay, forsooth; and I pray how does good Mistress Anne? 156

MISTRESS PAGE Go in with us and see. We have an hour's talk with you.

Exeunt Mistress Page, Mistress Ford, and Mistress Quickly

PAGE How now, Master Ford?

FORD You heard what this knave told me, did you not?

PAGE Yes, and you heard what the other told me?   161

FORD Do you think there is truth in them?

PAGE Hang 'em, slaves! I do not think the knight would offer it. But these that accuse him in his intent towards our wives are a yoke of his discarded men—very rogues, now they be out of service.   166

FORD Were they his men?

PAGE Marry, were they.

FORD I like it never the better for that. Does he lie at the Garter?   170

PAGE Ay, marry, does he. If he should intend this voyage toward my wife, I would turn her loose to him; and what he gets more of her than sharp words, let it lie on my head.   174

FORD I do not misdoubt my wife, but I would be loath to turn them together. A man may be too confident. I would have nothing lie on my head. I cannot be thus satisfied.

Enter the Host of the Garter

PAGE Look where my ranting Host of the Garter comes. There is either liquor in his pate or money in his purse when he looks so merrily.—How now, mine Host?   181

HOST God bless you, bully rook, God bless you! Thou'rt a gentleman.

Enter Shallow

Cavaliero Justice, I say!   184

SHALLOW I follow, mine Host, I follow.—Good even and twenty, good Master Page. Master Page, will you go with us? We have sport in hand.

HOST Tell him, Cavaliero Justice, tell him, bully rook.

SHALLOW Sir, there is a fray to be fought between Sir Hugh, the Welsh priest, and Caius, the French doctor.

FORD Good mine Host o'th' Garter, a word with you.

HOST What sayst thou, my bully rook?

They talk apart

SHALLOW (*to Page*) Will you go with us to behold it? My merry Host hath had the measuring of their weapons, and, I think, hath appointed them contrary places. For, believe me, I hear the parson is no jester. Hark, I will tell you what our sport shall be.   197

They talk apart

HOST (*to Ford*) Hast thou no suit against my knight, my guest cavaliero?   199

⌈FORD⌉ None, I protest. But I'll give you a pottle of burnt sack to give you recourse to him and tell him my name is Brooke—only for a jest.

HOST My hand, bully. Thou shalt have egress and regress—said I well?—and thy name shall be Brooke. It is a merry knight. (*To Shallow and Page*) Will you go, mijn'heers?   206

SHALLOW Have with you, mine Host.

PAGE I have heard the Frenchman hath good skill in his rapier.   209

SHALLOW Tut, sir, I could have told you more. In these times you stand on distance—your passes, stoccados, and I know not what. 'Tis the heart, Master Page;

⌈*showing his rapier-passes*⌉ 'tis here, 'tis here. I have seen the time with my long sword I would have made you four tall fellows skip like rats.   215

HOST Here, boys; here, here! Shall we wag?

PAGE Have with you. I had rather hear them scold than fight.   *Exeunt Host, Shallow, and Page*

FORD Though Page be a secure fool and stands so firmly on his wife's frailty, yet I cannot put off my opinion so easily. She was in his company at Page's house, and what they made there I know not. Well, I will look further into't; and I have a disguise to sound Falstaff. If I find her honest, I lose not my labour. If she be otherwise, 'tis labour well bestowed.   *Exit*

2.2   *Enter Sir John Falstaff and Pistol*

SIR JOHN I will not lend thee a penny.

PISTOL

I will retort the sum in equipage.

SIR JOHN Not a penny.

PISTOL ⌈*drawing his sword*⌉ Why then, the world's mine oyster, which I with sword will open.   5

SIR JOHN Not a penny. I have been content, sir, you should lay my countenance to pawn. I have grated upon my good friends for three reprieves for you and your coach-fellow Nim, or else you had looked through the grate like a gemini of baboons. I am damned in hell for swearing to gentlemen my friends you were good soldiers and tall fellows. And when Mistress Bridget lost the handle of her fan, I took't upon mine honour thou hadst it not.

PISTOL

Didst not thou share? Hadst thou not fifteen pence?   15

SIR JOHN Reason, you rogue, reason. Thinkest thou I'll endanger my soul gratis? At a word, hang no more about me. I am no gibbet for you. Go, a short knife and a throng, to your manor of Pickt-hatch, go. You'll not bear a letter for me, you rogue? You stand upon your honour? Why, thou unconfinable baseness, it is as much as I can do to keep the terms of my honour precise. Ay, ay, I myself sometimes, leaving the fear of God on the left hand, and hiding mine honour in my necessity, am fain to shuffle, to hedge, and to lurch; and yet you, you rogue, will ensconce your rags, your cat-a-mountain looks, your red-lattice phrases, and your bold beating oaths, under the shelter of your honour! You will not do it, you?

PISTOL ⌈*sheathing his sword*⌉

I do relent. What wouldst thou more of man?   30

Enter Robin

ROBIN Sir, here's a woman would speak with you.

SIR JOHN Let her approach.

Enter Mistress Quickly

MISTRESS QUICKLY Give your worship good morrow.

SIR JOHN Good morrow, goodwife.

MISTRESS QUICKLY Not so, an't please your worship.   35

SIR JOHN Good maid, then.

MISTRESS QUICKLY I'll be sworn: as my mother was the first hour I was born.

SIR JOHN I do believe the swearer. What with me?

MISTRESS QUICKLY Shall I vouchsafe your worship a word or two?   41

SIR JOHN Two thousand, fair woman, and I'll vouchsafe thee the hearing.

MISTRESS QUICKLY There is one Mistress Ford, sir—I pray come a little nearer this ways.   45

She draws Sir John aside

I myself dwell with Master Doctor Caius—

SIR JOHN Well, on. Mistress Ford, you say.

MISTRESS QUICKLY Your worship says very true. I pray your worship come a little nearer this ways.

SIR JOHN I warrant thee nobody hears. Mine own people, mine own people.   51

MISTRESS QUICKLY Are they so? God bless them and make them His servants!

SIR JOHN Well, Mistress Ford: what of her?   54

MISTRESS QUICKLY Why, sir, she's a good creature. Lord, Lord, your worship's a wanton! Well, heaven forgive you, and all of us, I pray—

SIR JOHN Mistress Ford; come, Mistress Ford.   58

MISTRESS QUICKLY Marry, this is the short and the long of it. You have brought her into such a canaries as 'tis wonderful. The best courtier of them all, when the court lay at Windsor, could never have brought her to such a canary. Yet there has been knights, and lords, and gentlemen, with their coaches; I warrant you, coach after coach, letter after letter, gift after gift, smelling so sweetly, all musk; and so rustling, I warrant you, in silk and gold, and in such aligant terms, and in such wine and sugar of the best and the fairest, that would have won any woman's heart; and, I warrant you, they could never get an eye-wink of her. I had myself twenty angels given me this morning—but I defy all angels, in any such sort, as they say, but in the way of honesty. And, I warrant you, they could never get her so much as sip on a cup with the proudest of them all. And yet there has been earls, nay, which is more, pensioners. But, I warrant you, all is one with her.

SIR JOHN But what says she to me? Be brief, my good she-Mercury.   79

MISTRESS QUICKLY Marry, she hath received your letter, for the which she thanks you a thousand times, and she gives you to notify that her husband will be absence from his house between ten and eleven.

SIR JOHN Ten and eleven.   84

MISTRESS QUICKLY Ay, forsooth, and then you may come and see the picture, she says, that you wot of. Master Ford, her husband, will be from home. Alas, the sweet woman leads an ill life with him. He's a very jealousy man. She leads a very frampold life with him, good heart.

SIR JOHN Ten and eleven. Woman, commend me to her. I will not fail her.   92

MISTRESS QUICKLY Why, you say well. But I have another messenger to your worship. Mistress Page hath her hearty commendations to you too; and, let me tell you

in your ear, she's as fartuous a civil modest wife, and one, I tell you, that will not miss you morning nor evening prayer, as any is in Windsor, whoe'er be the other; and she bade me tell your worship that her husband is seldom from home, but she hopes there will come a time. I never knew a woman so dote upon a man. Surely I think you have charms, la; yes, in truth.

SIR JOHN Not I, I assure thee. Setting the attraction of my good parts aside, I have no other charms.

MISTRESS QUICKLY Blessing on your heart for't!   105

SIR JOHN But I pray thee tell me this: has Ford's wife and Page's wife acquainted each other how they love me?

MISTRESS QUICKLY O God no, sir; that were a jest indeed! They have not so little grace, I hope. That were a trick indeed! But Mistress Page would desire you to send her your little page of all loves. Her husband has a marvellous infection to the little page; and, truly, Master Page is an honest man. Never a wife in Windsor leads a better life than she does. Do what she will; say what she will; take all, pay all; go to bed when she list; rise when she list; all is as she will. And, truly, she deserves it, for if there be a kind woman in Windsor, she is one. You must send her your page, no remedy.

SIR JOHN Why, I will.   119

MISTRESS QUICKLY Nay, but do so, then; and, look you, he may come and go between you both. And in any case have a nay-word, that you may know one another's mind, and the boy never need to understand anything—for 'tis not good that children should know any wickedness. Old folks, you know, have discretion, as they say, and know the world.   126

SIR JOHN Fare thee well. Commend me to them both. There's my purse; I am yet thy debtor.—Boy, go along with this woman.

Exeunt Mistress Quickly and Robin

(*Aside*) This news distracts me.   130

PISTOL (*aside*)

This punk is one of Cupid's carriers.

Clap on more sails! Pursue! Up with your sights!

Give fire! She is my prize, or ocean whelm them all!

Exit

SIR JOHN Sayst thou so, old Jack? Go thy ways! I'll make more of thy old body than I have done. Will they yet look after thee? Wilt thou, after the expense of so much money, be now a gainer? Good body, I thank thee. Let them say 'tis grossly done; so it be fairly done, no matter.   139

Enter Bardolph, ⌈*with sack*⌉

BARDOLPH Sir John, there's one Master Brooke below would fain speak with you and be acquainted with you, and hath sent your worship a morning's draught of sack.

SIR JOHN Brooke is his name?

BARDOLPH Ay, sir.   145

SIR JOHN Call him in. ⌈*Drinking sack*⌉ Such Brookes are welcome to me, that o'erflows such liquor.

Exit Bardolph

Aha, Mistress Ford and Mistress Page, have I encompassed you? ⌜*Drinking*⌝ Go to. Via!

Enter Bardolph, and Master Ford disguised as Brooke

FORD God bless you, sir.   150

SIR JOHN And you, sir. Would you speak with me?

FORD I make bold to press with so little preparation upon you.

SIR JOHN You're welcome. What's your will? (*To Bardolph*) Give us leave, drawer.   *Exit Bardolph*

FORD Sir, I am a gentleman that have spent much. My name is Brooke.   157

SIR JOHN Good Master Brooke, I desire more acquaintance of you.

FORD Good Sir John, I sue for yours—not to charge you, for I must let you understand I think myself in better plight for a lender than you are; the which hath something emboldened me to this unseasoned intrusion; for they say if money go before, all ways do lie open.   165

SIR JOHN Money is a good soldier, sir, and will on.

FORD Troth, and I have a bag of money here troubles me. If you will help to bear it, Sir John, take half, or all, for easing me of the carriage.

SIR JOHN Sir, I know not how I may deserve to be your porter.   171

FORD I will tell you, sir, if you will give me the hearing.

SIR JOHN Speak, good Master Brooke. I shall be glad to be your servant.   174

FORD Sir, I hear you are a scholar—I will be brief with you—and you have been a man long known to me, though I had never so good means as desire to make myself acquainted with you. I shall discover a thing to you wherein I must very much lay open mine own imperfection; but, good Sir John, as you have one eye upon my follies, as you hear them unfolded, turn another into the register of your own, that I may pass with a reproof the easier, sith you yourself know how easy it is to be such an offender.

SIR JOHN Very well, sir, proceed.   185

FORD There is a gentlewoman in this town; her husband's name is Ford.

SIR JOHN Well, sir.

FORD I have long loved her, and, I protest to you, bestowed much on her, followed her with a doting observance, engrossed opportunities to meet her, fee'd every slight occasion that could but niggardly give me sight of her; not only bought many presents to give her, but have given largely to many to know what she would have given. Briefly, I have pursued her as love hath pursued me, which hath been on the wing of all occasions. But, whatsoever I have merited, either in my mind or in my means, meed I am sure I have received none, unless experience be a jewel. That I have purchased at an infinite rate, and that hath taught me to say this:
'Love like a shadow flies when substance love pursues,
Pursuing that that flies, and flying what pursues.'   202

SIR JOHN Have you received no promise of satisfaction at her hands?

FORD Never.   205

SIR JOHN Have you importuned her to such a purpose?

FORD Never.

SIR JOHN Of what quality was your love then?

FORD Like a fair house built on another man's ground, so that I have lost my edifice by mistaking the place where I erected it.   211

SIR JOHN To what purpose have you unfolded this to me?

FORD When I have told you that, I have told you all. Some say that though she appear honest to me, yet in other places she enlargeth her mirth so far that there is shrewd construction made of her. Now, Sir John, here is the heart of my purpose. You are a gentleman of excellent breeding, admirable discourse, of great admittance, authentic in your place and person, generally allowed for your many warlike, court-like, and learned preparations.   221

SIR JOHN O sir!

FORD Believe it, for you know it. There is money.

⌜*He offers money*⌝

Spend it, spend it; spend more; spend all I have; only give me so much of your time in exchange of it as to lay an amiable siege to the honesty of this Ford's wife. Use your art of wooing, win her to consent to you. If any man may, you may as soon as any.   228

SIR JOHN Would it apply well to the vehemency of your affection that I should win what you would enjoy? Methinks you prescribe to yourself very preposterously.

FORD O, understand my drift. She dwells so securely on the excellency of her honour that the folly of my soul dares not present itself. She is too bright to be looked against. Now, could I come to her with any detection in my hand, my desires had instance and argument to commend themselves. I could drive her then from the ward of her purity, her reputation, her marriage vow, and a thousand other her defences which now are too too strongly embattled against me. What say you to't, Sir John?   241

SIR JOHN Master Brooke, I will first make bold with your money.

⌜*He takes the money*⌝

Next, give me your hand.

He takes his hand

And last, as I am a gentleman, you shall, if you will, enjoy Ford's wife.   246

FORD O, good sir!

SIR JOHN I say you shall.

FORD Want no money, Sir John, you shall want none.

SIR JOHN Want no Mistress Ford, Master Brooke, you shall want none. I shall be with her, I may tell you, by her own appointment. Even as you came in to me, her spokesmate, or go-between, parted from me. I say I shall be with her between ten and eleven, for at that time the jealous rascally knave her husband will be forth. Come you to me at night; you shall know how I speed.   257

FORD I am blessed in your acquaintance. Do you know
    Ford, sir?   259
SIR JOHN Hang him, poor cuckoldly knave, I know him
    not. Yet I wrong him to call him poor. They say the
    jealous wittolly knave hath masses of money, for the
    which his wife seems to me well favoured. I will use
    her as the key of the cuckoldly rogue's coffer, and
    there's my harvest-home.   265
FORD I would you knew Ford, sir, that you might avoid
    him if you saw him.
SIR JOHN Hang him, mechanical salt-butter rogue! I will
    stare him out of his wits. I will awe him with my
    cudgel; it shall hang like a meteor o'er the cuckold's
    horns. Master Brooke, thou shalt know I will
    predominate over the peasant, and thou shalt lie with
    his wife. Come to me soon at night. Ford's a knave,
    and I will aggravate his style: thou, Master Brooke,
    shalt know him for knave and cuckold. Come to me
    soon at night.   *Exit*
FORD What a damned epicurean rascal is this! My heart
    is ready to crack with impatience. Who says this is
    improvident jealousy? My wife hath sent to him, the
    hour is fixed, the match is made. Would any man have
    thought this? See the hell of having a false woman!
    My bed shall be abused, my coffers ransacked, my
    reputation gnawn at, and I shall not only receive this
    villainous wrong, but stand under the adoption of
    abominable terms, and by him that does me this wrong.
    Terms! Names! 'Amaimon' sounds well, 'Lucifer' well,
    'Barbason' well; yet they are devils' additions, the
    names of fiends. But 'cuckold', 'wittol'! 'Cuckold'—the
    devil himself hath not such a name. Page is an ass, a
    secure ass. He will trust his wife, he will not be jealous.
    I will rather trust a Fleming with my butter, Parson
    Hugh the Welshman with my cheese, an Irishman with
    my aqua-vitae bottle, or a thief to walk my ambling
    gelding, than my wife with herself. Then she plots,
    then she ruminates, then she devises; and what they
    think in their hearts they may effect, they will break
    their hearts but they will effect. God be praised for my
    jealousy! Eleven o'clock the hour. I will prevent this,
    detect my wife, be revenged on Falstaff, and laugh at
    Page. I will about it. Better three hours too soon than
    a minute too late. God's my life: cuckold, cuckold,
    cuckold!   *Exit*

2.3   *Enter Doctor Caius and John Rugby, with rapiers*
CAIUS Jack Rugby!
RUGBY Sir.
CAIUS Vat is the clock, Jack?
RUGBY 'Tis past the hour, sir, that Sir Hugh promised to
    meet.   5
CAIUS By Gar, he has save his soul dat he is no come;
    he has pray his Pible well dat he is no come. By Gar,
    Jack Rugby, he is dead already if he be come.
RUGBY He is wise, sir, he knew your worship would kill
    him if he came.   10

CAIUS ⌈*drawing his rapier*⌉ By Gar, de herring is no dead
    so as I vill kill him. Take your rapier, Jack. I vill tell
    you how I vill kill him.
RUGBY Alas, sir, I cannot fence.
CAIUS Villainy, take your rapier.   15
RUGBY Forbear: here's company.
      ⌈*Caius sheathes his rapier.*⌉
      Enter the Host of the Garter, Justice Shallow,
      Master Page, and Master Slender
HOST God bless thee, bully Doctor.
SHALLOW God save you, Master Doctor Caius.
PAGE Now, good Master Doctor.
SLENDER Give you good morrow, sir.   20
CAIUS Vat be all you, one, two, tree, four, come for?
HOST To see thee fight, to see thee foin, to see thee
    traverse, to see thee here, to see thee there; to see thee
    pass thy punto, thy stock, thy reverse, thy distance,
    thy montant. Is he dead, my Ethiopian? Is he dead, my
    Francisco? Ha, bully? What says my Aesculapius, my
    Galen, my heart of elder, ha? Is he dead, bully stale?
    Is he dead?   28
CAIUS By Gar, he is de coward jack-priest of de vorld. He
    is not show his face.   30
HOST Thou art a Castalian King Urinal, Hector of Greece,
    my boy.
CAIUS I pray you bear witness that me have stay six or
    seven, two, tree hours for him, and he is no come. 34
SHALLOW He is the wiser man, Master Doctor. He is a
    curer of souls, and you a curer of bodies. If you should
    fight you go against the hair of your professions. Is it
    not true, Master Page?
PAGE Master Shallow, you have yourself been a great
    fighter, though now a man of peace.   40
SHALLOW Bodykins, Master Page, though I now be old
    and of the peace, if I see a sword out my finger itches
    to make one. Though we are justices and doctors and
    churchmen, Master Page, we have some salt of our
    youth in us. We are the sons of women, Master Page.
PAGE 'Tis true, Master Shallow.   46
SHALLOW It will be found so, Master Page.—Master Doctor
    Caius, I am come to fetch you home. I am sworn of
    the peace. You have showed yourself a wise physician,
    and Sir Hugh hath shown himself a wise and patient
    churchman. You must go with me, Master Doctor. 51
HOST Pardon, guest Justice. (*To Caius*) A word, Monsieur
    Mockwater.
CAIUS Mockvater? Vat is dat?   54
HOST Mockwater, in our English tongue, is valour, bully.
CAIUS By Gar, then I have as much mockvater as de
    Englishman. Scurvy jack-dog priest! By Gar, me vill
    cut his ears.
HOST He will clapper-claw thee tightly, bully.
CAIUS Clapper-de-claw? Vat is dat?   60
HOST That is, he will make thee amends.
CAIUS By Gar, me do look he shall clapper-de-claw me,
    for, by Gar, me vill have it.
HOST And I will provoke him to't, or let him wag.

CAIUS Me tank you for dat.   65

HOST And moreover, bully— (*Aside to the others*) But first, master guest and Master Page, and eke Cavaliero Slender, go you through the town to Frogmore.

PAGE Sir Hugh is there, is he?

HOST He is there. See what humour he is in, and I will bring the Doctor about by the fields. Will it do well? 71

SHALLOW We will do it.

⌈PAGE, SHALLOW, *and* SLENDER⌉ Adieu, good Master Doctor.
                    Exeunt Page, Shallow, and Slender

CAIUS ⌈*drawing his rapier*⌉ By Gar, me vill kill de priest, for he speak for a jackanape to Anne Page.   75

HOST Let him die. Sheathe thy impatience; throw cold water on thy choler. Go about the fields with me through Frogmore. I will bring thee where Mistress Anne Page is, at a farmhouse a-feasting; and thou shalt woo her. Cried game? Said I well?   80

CAIUS ⌈*sheathing his rapier*⌉ By Gar, me dank you vor dat. By Gar, I love you, and I shall procure-a you de good guest: de earl, de knight, de lords, de gentlemen, my patiences.

HOST For the which I will be thy adversary toward Anne Page. Said I well?   86

CAIUS By Gar, 'tis good. Vell said.

HOST Let us wag, then.

CAIUS Come at my heels, Jack Rugby.   *Exeunt*

3.1   *Enter Sir Hugh Evans* ⌈*with a rapier, and bearing a book*⌉ *and Simple* ⌈*bearing Evans's gown*⌉

EVANS I pray you now, good Master Slender's servingman, and friend Simple by your name, which way have you looked for Master Caius, that calls himself Doctor of Physic?   4

SIMPLE Marry, sir, the Petty Ward, the Park Ward, every way; old Windsor way, and every way but the town way.

EVANS I most fehemently desire you you will also look that way.   9

SIMPLE I will, sir.   ⌈*Exit*⌉

EVANS ⌈*opening the book*⌉ Jeshu pless me, how full of cholers I am, and trempling of mind! I shall be glad if he have deceived me. How melancholies I am! I will knog his urinals about his knave's costard when I have good opportunities for the 'ork. Pless my soul!—   15

(*Singing*)
    To shallow rivers, to whose falls
    Melodious birds sings madrigals.
    There will we make our peds of roses,
    And a thousand fragrant posies.
    To shallow—   20

Mercy on me! I have a great dispositions to cry.—

(*Singing*)
    Melodious birds sing madrigals.—
    When as I sat in Pabylon—
    And a thousand vagram posies.
    To shallow (*etc.*)   25

⌈*Enter Simple*⌉

SIMPLE Yonder he is coming. This way, Sir Hugh.

EVANS He's welcome.
    (*Singing*) 'To shallow rivers to whose falls—'
    God prosper the right! What weapons is he?   29

SIMPLE No weapons, sir. There comes my master, Master Shallow, and another gentleman, from Frogmore, over the stile this way.

EVANS Pray you give me my gown—or else keep it in your arms.
                                        ⌈*He reads.*⌉
    Enter Justice Shallow, Master Slender, and Master Page

SHALLOW How now, Master Parson? Good morrow, good Sir Hugh. Keep a gamester from the dice and a good student from his book, and it is wonderful.   37

SLENDER (*aside*) Ah, sweet Anne Page!

PAGE God save you, good Sir Hugh.

EVANS God pless you from his mercy sake, all of you. 40

SHALLOW What, the sword and the Word? Do you study them both, Master Parson?

PAGE And youthful still: in your doublet and hose this raw, rheumatic day!

EVANS There is reasons and causes for it.   45

PAGE We are come to you to do a good office, Master Parson.

EVANS Fery well. What is it?

PAGE Yonder is a most reverend gentleman, who, belike having received wrong by some person, is at most odds with his own gravity and patience that ever you saw.

SHALLOW I have lived fourscore years and upward; I never heard a man of his place, gravity, and learning so wide of his own respect.

EVANS What is he?   55

PAGE I think you know him: Master Doctor Caius, the renowned French physician.

EVANS Got's will and his passion of my heart! I had as lief you would tell me of a mess of pottage.

PAGE Why?   60

EVANS He has no more knowledge in Hibbocrates and Galen, and he is a knave besides—a cowardly knave as you would desires to be acquainted withal.

PAGE ⌈*to Shallow*⌉ I warrant you, he's the man should fight with him.   65

SLENDER (*aside*) O sweet Anne Page!

SHALLOW It appears so by his weapons.
    Enter the Host of the Garter, Doctor Caius, and John Rugby.
    Keep them asunder—here comes Doctor Caius.
    Evans and Caius draw and offer to fight

PAGE Nay, good Master Parson, keep in your weapon.

SHALLOW So do you, good Master Doctor.   70

HOST Disarm them and let them question. Let them keep their limbs whole, and hack our English.
    Shallow and Page take Caius's and Evans's rapiers

CAIUS (*to Evans*) I pray you let-a me speak a word with your ear. Wherefore vill you not meet-a me?

EVANS ⌈*aside to Caius*⌉ Pray you use your patience. ⌈*Aloud*⌉
In good time! 76

CAIUS By Gar, you are de coward, de jack-dog, john-ape.

EVANS (*aside to Caius*) Pray you let us not be laughing-
stocks to other men's humours. I desire you in
friendship, and I will one way or other make you
amends. (*Aloud*) By Jeshu, I will knog your urinal about
your knave's cogscomb.

CAIUS *Diable!* Jack Rugby, mine Host de Jarteer, have I
not stay for him to kill him? Have I not, at de place I
did appoint? 85

EVANS As I am a Christians soul, now look you, this is
the place appointed. I'll be judgement by mine Host of
the Garter.

HOST Peace, I say, Gallia and Gaul, French and Welsh,
soul-curer and body-curer. 90

CAIUS Ay, dat is very good, *excellent*.

HOST Peace, I say. Hear mine Host of the Garter. Am I
politic? Am I subtle? Am I a Machiavel? Shall I lose
my doctor? No, he gives me the potions and the
motions. Shall I lose my parson, my priest, my Sir
Hugh? No, he gives me the Proverbs and the No-verbs.
(*To Caius*) Give me thy hand terrestrial—so. (*To Evans*)
Give me thy hand celestial—so. Boys of art, I have
deceived you both, I have directed you to wrong places.
Your hearts are mighty, your skins are whole, and let
burnt sack be the issue. (*To Shallow and Page*) Come,
lay their swords to pawn. (*To Caius and Evans*) Follow
me, lads of peace, follow, follow, follow. *Exit*

SHALLOW Afore God, a mad host! Follow, gentlemen,
follow. *Exeunt Shallow and Page*

SLENDER (*aside*) O sweet Anne Page! *Exit*

CAIUS Ha, do I perceive dat? Have you make-a de sot of
us, ha, ha? 108

EVANS This is well: he has made us his vlouting-stog. I
desire you that we may be friends, and let us knog our
prains together to be revenge on this same scall, scurvy,
cogging companion, the Host of the Garter.

CAIUS By Gar, with all my heart. He promise to bring me
where is Anne Page. By Gar, he deceive me too.

EVANS Well, I will smite his noddles. Pray you follow. 115
Exeunt

3.2 *Enter Robin, followed by Mistress Page*

MISTRESS PAGE Nay, keep your way, little gallant. You
were wont to be a follower, but now you are a leader.
Whether had you rather, lead mine eyes, or eye your
master's heels?

ROBIN I had rather, forsooth, go before you like a man
than follow him like a dwarf. 6

MISTRESS PAGE O, you are a flattering boy! Now I see
you'll be a courtier.

Enter Master Ford

FORD
Well met, Mistress Page. Whither go you? 9

MISTRESS PAGE Truly, sir, to see your wife. Is she at home?

FORD Ay, and as idle as she may hang together, for want
of company. I think if your husbands were dead you
two would marry.

MISTRESS PAGE Be sure of that—two other husbands.

FORD Where had you this pretty weathercock? 15

MISTRESS PAGE I cannot tell what the dickens his name is
my husband had him of.—What do you call your
knight's name, sirrah?

ROBIN Sir John Falstaff.

FORD Sir John Falstaff? 20

MISTRESS PAGE He, he; I can never hit on's name. There
is such a league between my goodman and he! Is your
wife at home indeed?

FORD Indeed she is. 24

MISTRESS PAGE By your leave, sir, I am sick till I see her.
Exeunt Robin and Mistress Page

FORD Has Page any brains? Hath he any eyes? Hath he
any thinking? Sure they sleep; he hath no use of them.
Why, this boy will carry a letter twenty mile, as easy
as a cannon will shoot point-blank twelve score. He
pieces out his wife's inclination; he gives her folly
motion and advantage. And now she's going to my
wife, and Falstaff's boy with her. A man may hear this
shower sing in the wind. And Falstaff's boy with her.
Good plots—they are laid; and our revolted wives share
damnation together. Well, I will take him; then torture
my wife, pluck the borrowed veil of modesty from the
so-seeming Mistress Page, divulge Page himself for a
secure and wilful Actaeon, and to these violent
proceedings all my neighbours shall cry aim. 39
⌈*Clock strikes*⌉
The clock gives me my cue, and my assurance bids me
search. There I shall find Falstaff. I shall be rather
praised for this than mocked, for it is as positive as the
earth is firm that Falstaff is there. I will go.

*Enter Master Page, Justice Shallow, Master Slender,
the Host of the Garter, Sir Hugh Evans, Doctor
Caius, and John Rugby*

SHALLOW, PAGE, *etc.* Well met, Master Ford.

FORD (*aside*) By my faith, a good knot! (*To them*) I have
good cheer at home, and I pray you all go with me. 46

SHALLOW I must excuse myself, Master Ford.

SLENDER And so must I, sir. We have appointed to dine
with Mistress Anne, and I would not break with her
for more money than I'll speak of. 50

SHALLOW We have lingered about a match between Anne
Page and my cousin Slender, and this day we shall
have our answer.

SLENDER I hope I have your good will, father Page. 54

PAGE You have, Master Slender: I stand wholly for you.
(*To Caius*) But my wife, Master Doctor, is for you
altogether.

CAIUS Ay, be Gar, and de maid is love-a me. My nursh-a
Quickly tell me so mush. 59

HOST (*to Page*) What say you to young Master Fenton?
He capers, he dances, he has eyes of youth; he writes
verses, he speaks holiday, he smells April and May. He
will carry't, he will carry't; 'tis in his buttons he will
carry't. 64

PAGE Not by my consent, I promise you. The gentleman
is of no having. He kept company with the wild Prince

and Poins. He is of too high a region; he knows too much. No, he shall not knit a knot in his fortunes with the finger of my substance. If he take her, let him take her simply: the wealth I have waits on my consent, and my consent goes not that way.   71

FORD I beseech you heartily, some of you go home with me to dinner. Besides your cheer, you shall have sport: I will show you a monster. Master Doctor, you shall go. So shall you, Master Page, and you, Sir Hugh.   75

SHALLOW Well, God be with you! ⌜Aside to Slender⌝ We shall have the freer wooing at Master Page's.
Exeunt Shallow and Slender

CAIUS Go home, John Rugby; I come anon.   *Exit Rugby*

HOST Farewell, my hearts. I will to my honest knight Falstaff, and drink canary with him.   *Exit*

FORD (*aside*) I think I shall drink in pipe-wine first with him: I'll make him dance. (*To Page, Caius, and Evans*) Will you go, gentles?   83

⌜PAGE, CAIUS, *and* EVANS⌝ Have with you to see this monster.   *Exeunt*

3.3   *Enter Mistress Ford and Mistress Page*

MISTRESS FORD What, John! What, Robert!

MISTRESS PAGE Quickly, quickly! Is the buck-basket—

MISTRESS FORD I warrant.—What, Robert, I say!

MISTRESS PAGE Come, come, come!

Enter John and Robert, with a buck-basket

MISTRESS FORD Here, set it down.   5

MISTRESS PAGE Give your men the charge. We must be brief.

MISTRESS FORD Marry, as I told you before, John and Robert, be ready here hard by in the brew-house; and when I suddenly call you, come forth, and without any pause or staggering take this basket on your shoulders. That done, trudge with it in all haste, and carry it among the whitsters in Datchet Mead, and there empty it in the muddy ditch close by the Thames' side.

MISTRESS PAGE (*to John and Robert*) You will do it?   15

MISTRESS FORD I ha' told them over and over; they lack no direction.—Be gone, and come when you are called.
Exeunt John and Robert

Enter Robin

MISTRESS PAGE Here comes little Robin.

MISTRESS FORD How now, my eyas-musket, what news with you?   20

ROBIN My master Sir John is come in at your back door, Mistress Ford, and requests your company.

MISTRESS PAGE You little Jack-a-Lent, have you been true to us?   24

ROBIN Ay, I'll be sworn. My master knows not of your being here, and hath threatened to put me into everlasting liberty if I tell you of it; for he swears he'll turn me away.

MISTRESS PAGE Thou'rt a good boy. This secrecy of thine shall be a tailor to thee, and shall make thee a new doublet and hose.—I'll go hide me.   31

MISTRESS FORD Do so. (*To Robin*) Go tell thy master I am alone.   *Exit Robin*

Mistress Page, remember you your cue.   34

MISTRESS PAGE I warrant thee. If I do not act it, hiss me.

MISTRESS FORD Go to, then.   ⌜*Exit Mistress Page*⌝ We'll use this unwholesome humidity, this gross watery pumpkin. We'll teach him to know turtles from jays.

Enter Sir John Falstaff

SIR JOHN Have I caught thee, my heavenly jewel? Why, now let me die, for I have lived long enough. This is the period of my ambition. O, this blessed hour!   41

MISTRESS FORD O sweet Sir John!

SIR JOHN Mistress Ford, I cannot cog; I cannot prate, Mistress Ford. Now shall I sin in my wish: I would thy husband were dead. I'll speak it before the best lord. I would make thee my lady.   46

MISTRESS FORD I your lady, Sir John? Alas, I should be a pitiful lady.

SIR JOHN Let the court of France show me such another. I see how thine eye would emulate the diamond. Thou hast the right arched beauty of the brow that becomes the ship-tire, the tire-valiant, or any tire of Venetian admittance.

MISTRESS FORD A plain kerchief, Sir John—my brows become nothing else, nor that well neither.   55

SIR JOHN By the Lord, thou art a tyrant to say so. Thou wouldst make an absolute courtier, and the firm fixture of thy foot would give an excellent motion to thy gait in a semicircled farthingale. I see what thou wert if fortune, thy foe, were, with nature, thy friend. Come, thou canst not hide it.   61

MISTRESS FORD Believe me, there's no such thing in me.

SIR JOHN What made me love thee? Let that persuade thee there's something extraordinary in thee. Come, I cannot cog and say thou art this and that, like a-many of these lisping hawthorn-buds that come like women in men's apparel and smell like Bucklersbury in simple time; I cannot. But I love thee, none but thee; and thou deservest it.

MISTRESS FORD Do not betray me, sir. I fear you love Mistress Page.   71

SIR JOHN Thou mightst as well say I love to walk by the Counter gate, which is as hateful to me as the reek of a lime-kiln.

MISTRESS FORD Well, heaven knows how I love you; and you shall one day find it.   76

SIR JOHN Keep in that mind. I'll deserve it.

MISTRESS FORD Nay, I must tell you, so you do; or else I could not be in that mind.

Enter Robin

ROBIN Mistress Ford, Mistress Ford! Here's Mistress Page at the door, sweating and blowing, and looking wildly, and would needs speak with you presently.   82

SIR JOHN She shall not see me. I will ensconce me behind the arras.

MISTRESS FORD Pray you do so; she's a very tattling woman.   86

Sir John hides behind the arras.
Enter Mistress Page
What's the matter? How now?

MISTRESS PAGE O Mistress Ford, what have you done?
You're shamed, you're overthrown, you're undone for
ever.   90
MISTRESS FORD What's the matter, good Mistress Page?
MISTRESS PAGE O well-a-day, Mistress Ford! Having an
honest man to your husband, to give him such cause
of suspicion!
MISTRESS FORD What cause of suspicion?   95
MISTRESS PAGE What cause of suspicion? Out upon you!
How am I mistook in you!
MISTRESS FORD Why, alas, what's the matter?
MISTRESS PAGE Your husband's coming hither, woman,
with all the officers in Windsor, to search for a
gentleman that he says is here now in the house, by
your consent, to take an ill advantage of his absence.
You are undone.
MISTRESS FORD 'Tis not so, I hope.   104
MISTRESS PAGE Pray heaven it be not so that you have
such a man here! But 'tis most certain your husband's
coming, with half Windsor at his heels, to search for
such a one. I come before to tell you. If you know
yourself clear, why, I am glad of it; but if you have a
friend here, convey, convey him out. Be not amazed.
Call all your senses to you. Defend your reputation, or
bid farewell to your good life for ever.   112
MISTRESS FORD What shall I do? There is a gentleman,
my dear friend; and I fear not mine own shame so
much as his peril. I had rather than a thousand pound
he were out of the house.   116
MISTRESS PAGE For shame, never stand 'you had rather'
and 'you had rather'. Your husband's here at hand.
Bethink you of some conveyance: in the house you
cannot hide him. O, how have you deceived me! Look,
here is a basket. If he be of any reasonable stature, he
may creep in here; and throw foul linen upon him as
if it were going to bucking. Or—it is whiting time—
send him by your two men to Datchet Mead.
MISTRESS FORD He's too big to go in there. What shall I
do?   126
SIR JOHN (coming forward) Let me see't, let me see't, O let
me see't! I'll in, I'll in. Follow your friend's counsel;
I'll in.
MISTRESS PAGE What, Sir John Falstaff! (Aside to him) Are
these your letters, knight?   131
SIR JOHN (aside to Mistress Page) I love thee. Help me
away. Let me creep in here.
          He goes into the basket
I'll never—
          Mistress Page and Mistress Ford put foul clothes
          over him
MISTRESS PAGE (to Robin) Help to cover your master, boy.—
Call your men, Mistress Ford. ⌈Aside to Sir John⌉ You
dissembling knight!   137
MISTRESS FORD What, John! Robert, John!
          Enter John and Robert
Go take up these clothes here quickly. Where's the
cowl-staff?   140
          John and Robert fit the cowl-staff

Look how you drumble! Carry them to the laundress
in Datchet Mead. Quickly, come!
          They lift the basket and start to leave.
          Enter Master Ford, Master Page, Doctor Caius, and
          Sir Hugh Evans
FORD (to Page, Caius, and Evans) Pray you come near. If I
suspect without cause, why then, make sport at me;
then let me be your jest—I deserve it. (To John and
Robert) How now? Whither bear you this?   146
⌈JOHN⌉ To the laundress, forsooth.
MISTRESS FORD Why, what have you to do whither they
bear it? You were best meddle with buck-washing!
FORD Buck? I would I could wash myself of the buck!
Buck, buck, buck? Ay, buck, I warrant you, buck. And
of the season too, it shall appear.   152
          ⌈Exeunt John and Robert, with the basket⌉
Gentlemen, I have dreamt tonight. I'll tell you my
dream. Here, here, here be my keys. Ascend my
chambers, search, seek, find out. I'll warrant we'll
unkennel the fox. Let me stop this way first.   156
          He locks the door
So, now, uncoop.
PAGE Good Master Ford, be contented. You wrong yourself
too much.   159
FORD True, Master Page.—Up, gentlemen! You shall see
sport anon. Follow me, gentlemen.   Exit
EVANS This is fery fantastical humours and jealousies.
CAIUS By Gar, 'tis no the fashion of France; it is not
jealous in France.   164
PAGE Nay, follow him, gentlemen. See the issue of his
search.   Exeunt Caius, Evans, and Page
MISTRESS PAGE Is there not a double excellency in this?
MISTRESS FORD I know not which pleases me better: that
my husband is deceived, or Sir John.
MISTRESS PAGE What a taking was he in when your
husband asked what was in the basket!   171
MISTRESS FORD I am half afraid he will have need of
washing, so throwing him into the water will do him
a benefit.
MISTRESS PAGE Hang him, dishonest rascal! I would all of
the same strain were in the same distress.   176
MISTRESS FORD I think my husband hath some special
suspicion of Falstaff's being here, for I never saw him
so gross in his jealousy till now.
MISTRESS PAGE I will lay a plot to try that, and we will
yet have more tricks with Falstaff. His dissolute disease
will scarce obey this medicine.
MISTRESS FORD Shall we send that foolish carrion Mistress
Quickly to him, and excuse his throwing into the water,
and give him another hope, to betray him to another
punishment?   186
MISTRESS PAGE We will do it. Let him be sent for tomorrow
eight o'clock, to have amends.
          Enter Ford, Page, Caius, and Evans
FORD I cannot find him. Maybe the knave bragged of that
he could not compass.   190
MISTRESS PAGE (aside to Mistress Ford) Heard you that?
MISTRESS FORD You use me well, Master Ford, do you?

FORD Ay, I do so.

MISTRESS FORD Heaven make me better than your
thoughts!　　　195

FORD Amen.

MISTRESS PAGE You do yourself mighty wrong, Master
Ford.

FORD Ay, ay, I must bear it.　　　199

EVANS If there be anypody in the house, and in the
chambers, and in the coffers, and in the presses, heaven
forgive my sins at the day of judgement!

CAIUS Be Gar, nor I too. There is nobodies.

PAGE Fie, fie, Master Ford, are you not ashamed? What
spirit, what devil suggests this imagination? I would
not ha' your distemper in this kind for the wealth of
Windsor Castle.　　　207

FORD 'Tis my fault, Master Page. I suffer for it.

EVANS You suffer for a pad conscience. Your wife is as
honest a 'omans as I will desires among five thousand,
and five hundred too.　　　211

CAIUS By Gar, I see 'tis an honest woman.

FORD Well, I promised you a dinner. Come, come, walk
in the park. I pray you pardon me. I will hereafter
make known to you why I have done this.—Come,
wife; come, Mistress Page. I pray you pardon me. Pray
heartily pardon me.　　　217

PAGE (to Caius and Evans) Let's go in, gentlemen. (Aside
to them) But trust me, we'll mock him. (To Ford, Caius,
and Evans) I do invite you tomorrow morning to my
house to breakfast. After, we'll a-birding together. I
have a fine hawk for the bush. Shall it be so?　　　222

FORD Anything.

EVANS If there be one, I shall make two in the company.

CAIUS If there be one or two, I shall make-a the turd.

FORD Pray you go, Master Page.　　　226

Exeunt ⌈all but Evans and Caius⌉

EVANS I pray you now, remembrance tomorrow on the
lousy knave mine Host.

CAIUS Dat is good, by Gar; with all my heart.　　　229

EVANS A lousy knave, to have his gibes and his mockeries.

Exeunt

3.4　*Enter Master Fenton and Anne Page*

FENTON

I see I cannot get thy father's love;
Therefore no more turn me to him, sweet Nan.

ANNE

Alas, how then?

FENTON　　　　　Why, thou must be thyself.
He doth object I am too great of birth,
And that, my state being galled with my expense,　　5
I seek to heal it only by his wealth.
Besides these, other bars he lays before me—
My riots past, my wild societies;
And tells me 'tis a thing impossible
I should love thee but as a property.　　　10

ANNE Maybe he tells you true.

⌈FENTON⌉

No, heaven so speed me in my time to come!

Albeit I will confess thy father's wealth
Was the first motive that I wooed thee, Anne,
Yet, wooing thee, I found thee of more value　　15
Than stamps in gold or sums in sealèd bags;
And 'tis the very riches of thyself
That now I aim at.

ANNE　　　　　Gentle Master Fenton,
Yet seek my father's love, still seek it, sir.
If opportunity and humblest suit　　　20
Cannot attain it, why then—

*Enter Justice Shallow, Master Slender ⌈richly
dressed⌉, and Mistress Quickly*

　　　　　　　　　Hark you hither.

They talk apart

SHALLOW Break their talk, Mistress Quickly. My kinsman
shall speak for himself.

SLENDER I'll make a shaft or a bolt on't. 'Slid, 'tis but
venturing.　　　25

SHALLOW
Be not dismayed.

SLENDER　　　　　No, she shall not dismay me.
I care not for that, but that I am afeard.

MISTRESS QUICKLY (to Anne) Hark ye, Master Slender would
speak a word with you.

ANNE
I come to him. (To Fenton) This is my father's choice.
O, what a world of vile ill-favoured faults　　　31
Looks handsome in three hundred pounds a year!

MISTRESS QUICKLY And how does good Master Fenton?
Pray you, a word with you.

She draws Fenton aside

SHALLOW She's coming. To her, coz! O boy, thou hadst
a father!　　　36

SLENDER I had a father, Mistress Anne; my uncle can tell
you good jests of him.—Pray you, uncle, tell Mistress
Anne the jest how my father stole two geese out of a
pen, good uncle.　　　40

SHALLOW Mistress Anne, my cousin loves you.

SLENDER Ay, that I do, as well as I love any woman in
Gloucestershire.

SHALLOW He will maintain you like a gentlewoman.

SLENDER Ay, by God, that I will, come cut and long-tail,
under the degree of a squire.　　　46

SHALLOW He will make you a hundred and fifty pounds
jointure.

ANNE Good Master Shallow, let him woo for himself.

SHALLOW Marry, I thank you for it, I thank you for that
good comfort.—She calls you, coz. I'll leave you.　　51

He stands aside

ANNE Now, Master Slender.

SLENDER Now, good Mistress Anne.

ANNE What is your will?　　　54

SLENDER My will? 'Od's heartlings, that's a pretty jest
indeed! I ne'er made my will yet, I thank God; I am
not such a sickly creature, I give God praise.

ANNE I mean, Master Slender, what would you with me?

SLENDER Truly, for mine own part, I would little or
nothing with you. Your father and my uncle hath

made motions. If it be my luck, so. If not, happy man be his dole. They can tell you how things go better than I can.

Enter Master Page and Mistress Page

You may ask your father: here he comes.

PAGE

Now, Master Slender.—Love him, daughter Anne.— 65
Why, how now? What does Master Fenton here?
You wrong me, sir, thus still to haunt my house.
I told you, sir, my daughter is disposed of.

FENTON

Nay, Master Page, be not impatient.

MISTRESS PAGE

Good Master Fenton, come not to my child.   70

PAGE She is no match for you.

FENTON Sir, will you hear me?

PAGE No, good Master Fenton.—
Come, Master Shallow; come, son Slender, in.—
Knowing my mind, you wrong me, Master Fenton. 75

Exeunt Page, Shallow, and Slender

MISTRESS QUICKLY (*to Fenton*) Speak to Mistress Page.

FENTON

Good Mistress Page, for that I love your daughter
In such a righteous fashion as I do,
Perforce against all checks, rebukes, and manners
I must advance the colours of my love,   80
And not retire. Let me have your good will.

ANNE Good mother, do not marry me to yon fool.

MISTRESS PAGE I mean it not; I seek you a better husband.

MISTRESS QUICKLY ⌈*aside to Anne*⌉ That's my master, Master Doctor.   85

ANNE

Alas, I had rather be set quick i'th' earth
And bowled to death with turnips.

MISTRESS PAGE

Come, trouble not yourself, good Master Fenton.
I will not be your friend nor enemy.
My daughter will I question how she loves you, 90
And as I find her, so am I affected.
Till then, farewell, sir. She must needs go in.
Her father will be angry.

FENTON

Farewell, gentle mistress.—Farewell, Nan.   94

Exeunt Mistress Page and Anne

MISTRESS QUICKLY This is my doing now. 'Nay', said I, 'will you cast away your child on a fool and a physician? Look on Master Fenton.' This is my doing.

FENTON

I thank thee, (*giving her a ring*) and I pray thee, once tonight
Give my sweet Nan this ring. (*Giving money*) There's for thy pains.   99

MISTRESS QUICKLY Now heaven send thee good fortune!

Exit Fenton

A kind heart he hath. A woman would run through fire and water for such a kind heart. But yet I would my master had Mistress Anne; or I would Master Slender had her; or, in sooth, I would Master Fenton

had her. I will do what I can for them all three, for so I have promised, and I'll be as good as my word—but speciously for Master Fenton. Well, I must of another errand to Sir John Falstaff from my two mistresses. What a beast am I to slack it!   *Exit*

3.5   *Enter Sir John Falstaff*

SIR JOHN Bardolph, I say!

Enter Bardolph

BARDOLPH Here, sir.

SIR JOHN Go fetch me a quart of sack; put a toast in't.

Exit Bardolph

Have I lived to be carried in a basket like a barrow of butcher's offal, and to be thrown in the Thames? Well, if I be served such another trick, I'll have my brains ta'en out and buttered, and give them to a dog for a New Year's gift. 'Sblood, the rogues slighted me into the river with as little remorse as they would have drowned a blind bitch's puppies, fifteen i'th' litter! And you may know by my size that I have a kind of alacrity in sinking. If the bottom were as deep as hell, I should down. I had been drowned, but that the shore was shelvy and shallow—a death that I abhor, for the water swells a man, and what a thing should I have been when I had been swelled? By the Lord, a mountain of mummy!   17

Enter Bardolph, with ⌈two large cups of⌉ sack

BARDOLPH Here's Mistress Quickly, sir, to speak with you.

SIR JOHN Come, let me pour in some sack to the Thames' water, for my belly's as cold as if I had swallowed snowballs for pills to cool the reins.   21

He drinks

Call her in.

BARDOLPH Come in, woman!

Enter Mistress Quickly

MISTRESS QUICKLY (*to Sir John*) By your leave; I cry you mercy. Give your worship good morrow!   25

SIR JOHN (⌈*drinking, then*⌉ *speaking to Bardolph*) Take away these chalices. Go brew me a pottle of sack, finely.

BARDOLPH With eggs, sir?

SIR JOHN Simple of itself. I'll no pullet-sperms in my brewage.   *Exit Bardolph, ⌈with cups⌉*
How now?   31

MISTRESS QUICKLY Marry, sir, I come to your worship from Mistress Ford.

SIR JOHN Mistress Ford? I have had ford enough: I was thrown into the ford, I have my belly full of ford.   35

MISTRESS QUICKLY Alas the day, good heart, that was not her fault. She does so take on with her men; they mistook their erection.

SIR JOHN So did I mine, to build upon a foolish woman's promise.   40

MISTRESS QUICKLY Well, she laments, sir, for it, that it would yearn your heart to see it. Her husband goes this morning a-birding. She desires you once more to come to her, between eight and nine. I must carry her word quickly. She'll make you amends, I warrant you.

SIR JOHN Well, I will visit her. Tell her so, and bid her

think what a man is; let her consider his frailty, and
then judge of my merit.

MISTRESS QUICKLY I will tell her.

SIR JOHN Do so. Between nine and ten, sayst thou? 50

MISTRESS QUICKLY Eight and nine, sir.

SIR JOHN Well, be gone. I will not miss her.

MISTRESS QUICKLY Peace be with you, sir.   *Exit*

SIR JOHN I marvel I hear not of Master Brooke; he sent
me word to stay within. I like his money well. 55

    Enter Master Ford, disguised as Brooke

By the mass, here he comes.

FORD God bless you, sir.

SIR JOHN Now, Master Brooke, you come to know what
hath passed between me and Ford's wife.

FORD That indeed, Sir John, is my business. 60

SIR JOHN Master Brooke, I will not lie to you. I was at
her house the hour she appointed me.

FORD And sped you, sir?

SIR JOHN Very ill-favouredly, Master Brooke.

FORD How so, sir? Did she change her determination? 65

SIR JOHN No, Master Brooke, but the peaking cornuto her
husband, Master Brooke, dwelling in a continual 'larum
of jealousy, comes me in the instant of our encounter—
after we had embraced, kissed, protested, and, as it
were, spoke the prologue of our comedy—and at his
heels a rabble of his companions, thither provoked and
instigated by his distemper, and, forsooth, to search his
house for his wife's love.

FORD What, while you were there?

SIR JOHN While I was there. 75

FORD And did he search for you, and could not find you?

SIR JOHN You shall hear. As God would have it, comes
in one Mistress Page, gives intelligence of Ford's
approach, and, by her invention and Ford's wife's
distraction, they conveyed me into a buck-basket— 80

FORD A buck-basket?

SIR JOHN By the Lord, a buck-basket!—rammed me in
with foul shirts and smocks, socks, foul stockings,
greasy napkins, that, Master Brooke, there was the
rankest compound of villainous smell that ever offended
nostril. 86

FORD And how long lay you there?

SIR JOHN Nay, you shall hear, Master Brooke, what I have
suffered to bring this woman to evil, for your good.
Being thus crammed in the basket, a couple of Ford's
knaves, his hinds, were called forth by their mistress,
to carry me, in the name of foul clothes, to Datchet
Lane. They took me on their shoulders, met the jealous
knave their master in the door, who asked them once
or twice what they had in their basket. I quaked for
fear lest the lunatic knave would have searched it, but
fate, ordaining he should be a cuckold, held his hand.
Well, on went he for a search, and away went I for
foul clothes. But mark the sequel, Master Brooke. I
suffered the pangs of three several deaths. First, an
intolerable fright, to be detected with a jealous rotten
bell-wether. Next, to be compassed like a good bilbo in
the circumference of a peck, hilt to point, heel to head.

And then, to be stopped in, like a strong distillation,
with stinking clothes that fretted in their own grease.
Think of that—a man of my kidney—think of that—
that am as subject to heat as butter, a man of continual
dissolution and thaw. It was a miracle to scape
suffocation. And in the height of this bath, when I was
more than half stewed in grease like a Dutch dish, to
be thrown into the Thames and cooled, glowing-hot,
in that surge, like a horseshoe. Think of that—hissing
hot—think of that, Master Brooke! 113

FORD In good sadness, sir, I am sorry that for my sake
you have suffered all this. My suit then is desperate.
You'll undertake her no more?

SIR JOHN Master Brooke, I will be thrown into Etna as I
have been into Thames ere I will leave her thus. Her
husband is this morning gone a-birding. I have received
from her another embassy of meeting. 'Twixt eight and
nine is the hour, Master Brooke. 121

FORD 'Tis past eight already, sir.

SIR JOHN Is it? I will then address me to my appointment.
Come to me at your convenient leisure, and you shall
know how I speed; and the conclusion shall be crowned
with your enjoying her. Adieu. You shall have her,
Master Brooke; Master Brooke, you shall cuckold Ford.
    Exit

FORD Hum! Ha! Is this a vision? Is this a dream? Do I
sleep? Master Ford, awake! Awake, Master Ford!
There's a hole made in your best coat, Master Ford.
This 'tis to be married! This 'tis to have linen and
buck-baskets! Well, I will proclaim myself what I am.
I will now take the lecher. He is at my house. He
cannot scape me; 'tis impossible he should. He cannot
creep into a halfpenny purse, nor into a pepperbox.
But lest the devil that guides him should aid him, I will
search impossible places. Though what I am I cannot
avoid, yet to be what I would not shall not make me
tame. If I have horns to make one mad, let the proverb
go with me: I'll be horn-mad.   *Exit*

4.1 *Enter Mistress Page, Mistress Quickly, and William
Page*

MISTRESS PAGE Is he at Mistress Ford's already, thinkest
thou?

MISTRESS QUICKLY Sure he is by this, or will be presently.
But truly he is very courageous-mad about his throwing
into the water. Mistress Ford desires you to come
suddenly. 6

MISTRESS PAGE I'll be with her by and by. I'll but bring
my young man here to school.

    Enter Sir Hugh Evans

Look where his master comes. 'Tis a playing day, I
see.—How now, Sir Hugh, no school today? 10

EVANS No, Master Slender is let the boys leave to play.

MISTRESS QUICKLY Blessing of his heart!

MISTRESS PAGE Sir Hugh, my husband says my son profits
nothing in the world at his book. I pray you ask him
some questions in his accidence. 15

EVANS Come hither, William. Hold up your head. Come.

MISTRESS PAGE Come on, sirrah. Hold up your head. Answer your master; be not afraid.

EVANS William, how many numbers is in nouns?

WILLIAM Two. 20

MISTRESS QUICKLY Truly, I thought there had been one number more, because they say "Od's nouns".

EVANS Peace your tattlings!—What is 'fair', William?

WILLIAM *'Pulcher'.*

MISTRESS QUICKLY Polecats? There are fairer things than polecats, sure. 26

EVANS You are a very simplicity 'oman. I pray you peace.—What is 'lapis', William?

WILLIAM A stone.

EVANS And what is 'a stone', William? 30

WILLIAM A pebble.

EVANS No, it is 'lapis'. I pray you remember in your prain.

WILLIAM *'Lapis'.*

EVANS That is a good William. What is he, William, that does lend articles? 35

WILLIAM Articles are borrowed of the pronoun, and be thus declined. *Singulariter nominativo: 'hic, haec, hoc'.*

EVANS *Nominativo: 'hig, hag, hog'.* Pray you mark: *genitivo: 'huius'.* Well, what is your accusative case?

WILLIAM *Accusativo: 'hinc'—* 40

EVANS I pray you have your remembrance, child. *Accusativo: 'hing, hang, hog'.*

MISTRESS QUICKLY 'Hang-hog' is Latin for bacon, I warrant you.

EVANS Leave your prabbles, 'oman!—What is the focative case, William? 46

WILLIAM *O—vocativo,* O—

EVANS Remember, William, focative is *caret.*

MISTRESS QUICKLY And that's a good root.

EVANS 'Oman, forbear. 50

MISTRESS PAGE (to Mistress Quickly) Peace.

EVANS What is your genitive case plural, William?

WILLIAM Genitive case?

EVANS Ay.

WILLIAM *Genitivo: 'horum, harum, horum'.* 55

MISTRESS QUICKLY Vengeance of Jenny's case! Fie on her! Never name her, child, if she be a whore.

EVANS For shame, 'oman!

MISTRESS QUICKLY You do ill to teach the child such words. He teaches him to hick and to hack, which they'll do fast enough of themselves, and to call 'whorum'. Fie upon you! 62

EVANS 'Oman, art thou lunatics? Hast thou no understandings for thy cases, and the numbers of the genders? Thou art as foolish Christian creatures as I would desires. 66

MISTRESS PAGE (to Mistress Quickly) Prithee, hold thy peace.

EVANS Show me now, William, some declensions of your pronouns.

WILLIAM Forsooth, I have forgot. 70

EVANS It is 'qui, que, quod'. If you forget your 'qui's, your 'que's, and your 'quod's, you must be preeches. Go your ways and play; go.

MISTRESS PAGE He is a better scholar than I thought he was. 75

EVANS He is a good sprag memory. Farewell, Mistress Page.

MISTRESS PAGE Adieu, good Sir Hugh.   *Exit Evans*
Get you home, boy.   *Exit William*
(*To Mistress Quickly*) Come, we stay too long. |*Exeunt*

4.2   *Enter Sir John Falstaff and Mistress Ford*

SIR JOHN Mistress Ford, your sorrow hath eaten up my sufferance. I see you are obsequious in your love, and I profess requital to a hair's breadth: not only, Mistress Ford, in the simple office of love, but in all the accoutrement, complement, and ceremony of it. But are you sure of your husband now? 6

MISTRESS FORD He's a-birding, sweet Sir John.

MISTRESS PAGE (*within*) What ho, gossip Ford, what ho!

MISTRESS FORD Step into th' chamber, Sir John.
    Sir John steps into the chamber
    Enter Mistress Page

MISTRESS PAGE How now, sweetheart, who's at home besides yourself? 11

MISTRESS FORD Why, none but mine own people.

MISTRESS PAGE Indeed?

MISTRESS FORD No, certainly. (*Aside to her*) Speak louder.

MISTRESS PAGE Truly, I am so glad you have nobody here.

MISTRESS FORD Why? 16

MISTRESS PAGE Why, woman, your husband is in his old lines again. He so takes on yonder with my husband, so rails against all married mankind, so curses all Eve's daughters of what complexion soever, and so buffets himself on the forehead, crying 'Peer out, peer out!', that any madness I ever yet beheld seemed but tameness, civility, and patience to this his distemper he is in now. I am glad the fat knight is not here.

MISTRESS FORD Why, does he talk of him? 25

MISTRESS PAGE Of none but him; and swears he was carried out, the last time he searched for him, in a basket, protests to my husband he is now here, and hath drawn him and the rest of their company from their sport to make another experiment of his suspicion. But I am glad the knight is not here. Now he shall see his own foolery. 32

MISTRESS FORD How near is he, Mistress Page?

MISTRESS PAGE Hard by at street end. He will be here anon. 35

MISTRESS FORD I am undone: the knight is here.

MISTRESS PAGE Why then, you are utterly shamed, and he's but a dead man. What a woman are you! Away with him, away with him! Better shame than murder.

MISTRESS FORD Which way should he go? How should I bestow him? Shall I put him into the basket again? 41
    Sir John comes forth from the chamber

SIR JOHN No, I'll come no more i'th' basket. May I not go out ere he come?

MISTRESS PAGE Alas, three of Master Ford's brothers watch the door with pistols, that none shall issue out.

Otherwise you might slip away ere he came. But what
make you here?

SIR JOHN What shall I do? I'll creep up into the chimney.

MISTRESS FORD There they always use to discharge their
birding-pieces.   50

⌜MISTRESS PAGE⌝ Creep into the kiln-hole.

SIR JOHN Where is it?

MISTRESS FORD He will seek there, on my word. Neither
press, coffer, chest, trunk, well, vault, but he hath an
abstract for the remembrance of such places, and goes
to them by his note. There is no hiding you in the
house.   57

SIR JOHN I'll go out, then.

MISTRESS ⌜PAGE⌝ If you go out in your own semblance,
you die, Sir John—unless you go out disguised.   60

MISTRESS FORD How might we disguise him?

MISTRESS PAGE Alas the day, I know not. There is no
woman's gown big enough for him; otherwise he might
put on a hat, a muffler, and a kerchief, and so escape.

SIR JOHN Good hearts, devise something. Any extremity
rather than a mischief.   66

MISTRESS FORD My maid's aunt, the fat woman of Brentford, has a gown above.

MISTRESS PAGE On my word, it will serve him; she's as
big as he is; and there's her thrummed hat, and her
muffler too.—Run up, Sir John.   71

MISTRESS FORD Go, go, sweet Sir John. Mistress Page and
I will look some linen for your head.

MISTRESS PAGE Quick, quick! We'll come dress you
straight. Put on the gown the while.   *Exit Sir John*

MISTRESS FORD I would my husband would meet him in
this shape. He cannot abide the old woman of Brentford.
He swears she's a witch, forbade her my house, and
hath threatened to beat her.

MISTRESS PAGE Heaven guide him to thy husband's cudgel,
and the devil guide his cudgel afterwards!   81

MISTRESS FORD But is my husband coming?

MISTRESS PAGE Ay, in good sadness is he, and talks of the
basket too, howsoever he hath had intelligence.   84

MISTRESS FORD We'll try that, for I'll appoint my men to
carry the basket again, to meet him at the door with
it as they did last time.

MISTRESS PAGE Nay, but he'll be here presently. Let's go
dress him like the witch of Brentford.   89

MISTRESS FORD I'll first direct my men what they shall do
with the basket. Go up; I'll bring linen for him straight.

MISTRESS PAGE Hang him, dishonest varlet! We cannot
misuse him enough.   ⌜*Exit Mistress Ford*⌝
We'll leave a proof by that which we will do,
Wives may be merry, and yet honest, too.   95
We do not act that often jest and laugh.
'Tis old but true: 'Still swine eats all the draff'.   *Exit*
      Enter ⌜*Mistress Ford, with*⌝ *John and Robert*

MISTRESS FORD Go, sirs, take the basket again on your
shoulders. Your master is hard at door. If he bid you
set it down, obey him. Quickly, dispatch!   *Exit*

⌜JOHN⌝ Come, come, take it up.   101

⌜ROBERT⌝ Pray heaven it be not full of knight again.

⌜JOHN⌝ I hope not; I had as lief bear so much lead.
      They lift the basket.
      Enter Master Ford, Master Page, Doctor Caius, Sir
      Hugh Evans, and Justice Shallow

FORD
Ay, but if it prove true, Master Page, have you any
way then to unfool me again? (*To John and Robert*) Set
down the basket, villains.   106
      John and Robert set down the basket
Somebody call my wife. Youth in a basket! O, you
panderly rascals! There's a knot, a gang, a pack, a
conspiracy against me. Now shall the devil be
shamed.—What, wife, I say! Come, come forth! Behold
what honest clothes you send forth to bleaching.   111

PAGE Why, this passes, Master Ford. You are not to go
loose any longer; you must be pinioned.

EVANS Why, this is lunatics; this is mad as a mad dog.

SHALLOW Indeed, Master Ford, this is not well, indeed.

FORD So say I too, sir.   116
      Enter Mistress Ford
Come hither, Mistress Ford! Mistress Ford, the honest
woman, the modest wife, the virtuous creature, that
hath the jealous fool to her husband! I suspect without
cause, mistress, do I?   120

MISTRESS FORD God be my witness you do, if you suspect
me in any dishonesty.

FORD Well said, brazen-face; hold it out.
      He opens the basket and starts to take out clothes
Come forth, sirrah!

PAGE This passes.   125

MISTRESS FORD (*to Ford*) Are you not ashamed? Let the
clothes alone.

FORD I shall find you anon.

EVANS 'Tis unreasonable: will you take up your wife's
clothes? Come, away.   130

FORD ⌜*to John and Robert*⌝ Empty the basket, I say.

⌜PAGE⌝ Why, man, why?

FORD Master Page, as I am a man, there was one conveyed
out of my house yesterday in this basket. Why may
not he be there again? In my house I am sure he is.
My intelligence is true, my jealousy is reasonable. ⌜*To*
John and Robert⌝ Pluck me out all the linen.   137
      He takes out clothes

MISTRESS FORD If you find a man there, he shall die a
flea's death.

PAGE Here's no man.   140

SHALLOW By my fidelity, this is not well, Master Ford.
This wrongs you.

EVANS Master Ford, you must pray, and not follow the
imaginations of your own heart. This is jealousies.

FORD Well, he's not here I seek for.   145

PAGE No, nor nowhere else but in your brain.

FORD Help to search my house this one time. If I find not
what I seek, show no colour for my extremity; let me
for ever be your table-sport; let them say of me, 'As
jealous as Ford, that searched a hollow walnut for his
wife's leman'. Satisfy me once more; once more search
with me.   ⌜*Exeunt John and Robert with the basket*⌝

MISTRESS FORD What ho, Mistress Page! Come you and the old woman down. My husband will come into the chamber. 155

FORD Old woman? What old woman's that?

MISTRESS FORD Why, it is my maid's Aunt of Brentford.

FORD A witch, a quean, an old, cozening quean! Have I not forbid her my house? She comes of errands, does she? We are simple men; we do not know what's brought to pass under the profession of fortune-telling. She works by charms, by spells, by th' figure, and such daubery as this is, beyond our element. We know nothing.—Come down, you witch, you hag, you! Come down, I say! 165

   ⌈*Enter Mistress Page, and Sir John Falstaff,*
   disguised as an old woman.⌉
   ⌈*Ford makes towards them*⌉

MISTRESS FORD Nay, good sweet husband!—Good gentlemen, let him not strike the old woman.

MISTRESS PAGE (*to Sir John*) Come, Mother Prat. Come, give me your hand.

FORD I'll prat her! 170

   He beats Sir John

Out of my door, you witch, you rag, you baggage, you polecat, you runnion! Out, out! I'll conjure you, I'll fortune-tell you!   *Exit Sir John*

MISTRESS PAGE Are you not ashamed? I think you have killed the poor woman. 175

MISTRESS FORD Nay, he will do it.—'Tis a goodly credit for you!

FORD Hang her, witch!

EVANS By Jeshu, I think the 'oman is a witch indeed. I like not when a 'oman has a great peard. I spy a great peard under his muffler. 181

FORD Will you follow, gentlemen? I beseech you, follow. See but the issue of my jealousy. If I cry out thus upon no trail, never trust me when I open again.

PAGE Let's obey his humour a little further. Come, gentlemen.   *Exeunt the men*

MISTRESS PAGE By my troth, he beat him most pitifully.

MISTRESS FORD Nay, by th' mass, that he did not—he beat him most unpitifully, methought.

MISTRESS PAGE I'll have the cudgel hallowed and hung o'er the altar. It hath done meritorious service. 191

MISTRESS FORD What think you—may we, with the warrant of womanhood and the witness of a good conscience, pursue him with any further revenge?

MISTRESS PAGE The spirit of wantonness is sure scared out of him. If the devil have him not in fee-simple, with fine and recovery, he will never, I think, in the way of waste attempt us again.

MISTRESS FORD Shall we tell our husbands how we have served him? 200

MISTRESS PAGE Yes, by all means, if it be but to scrape the figures out of your husband's brains. If they can find in their hearts the poor, unvirtuous, fat knight shall be any further afflicted, we two will still be the ministers. 205

MISTRESS FORD I'll warrant they'll have him publicly shamed, and methinks there would be no period to the jest should he not be publicly shamed.

MISTRESS PAGE Come, to the forge with it, then shape it. I would not have things cool.   *Exeunt*

4.3   *Enter the Host of the Garter and Bardolph*

BARDOLPH Sir, the Germans desire to have three of your horses. The Duke himself will be tomorrow at court, and they are going to meet him.

HOST What duke should that be comes so secretly? I hear not of him in the court. Let me speak with the gentlemen. They speak English? 6

BARDOLPH Ay, sir. I'll call them to you.

HOST They shall have my horses, but I'll make them pay; I'll sauce them. They have had my house a week at command; I have turned away my other guests. They must come off: I'll sauce them. Come.   *Exeunt*

4.4   *Enter Master Page, Master Ford, Mistress Page,*
       Mistress Ford, and Sir Hugh Evans

EVANS 'Tis one of the best discretions of a 'oman as ever I did look upon.

PAGE And did he send you both these letters at an instant?

MISTRESS PAGE Within a quarter of an hour.

FORD
Pardon me, wife. Henceforth do what thou wilt. 5
I rather will suspect the sun with cold
Than thee with wantonness. Now doth thy honour stand,
In him that was of late an heretic,
As firm as faith.

PAGE   'Tis well, 'tis well; no more.
Be not as extreme in submission 10
As in offence.
But let our plot go forward. Let our wives
Yet once again, to make us public sport,
Appoint a meeting with this old fat fellow,
Where we may take him and disgrace him for it. 15

FORD
There is no better way than that they spoke of.

PAGE
How, to send him word they'll meet him in the Park
At midnight? Fie, fie, he'll never come.

EVANS You say he has been thrown in the rivers, and has been grievously peaten as an old 'oman. Methinks there should be terrors in him, that he should not come. Methinks his flesh is punished; he shall have no desires.

PAGE So think I too.

⌈MISTRESS⌉ FORD
Devise but how you'll use him when he comes, 25
And let us two devise to bring him thither.

MISTRESS PAGE
There is an old tale goes that Herne the hunter,
Sometime a keeper here in Windsor Forest,
Doth all the winter time at still midnight
Walk round about an oak with great ragg'd horns; 30

And there he blasts the trees, and takes the cattle,
And makes milch-kine yield blood, and shakes a chain
In a most hideous and dreadful manner.
You have heard of such a spirit, and well you know
The superstitious idle-headed eld   35
Received, and did deliver to our age,
This tale of Herne the hunter for a truth.

PAGE
Why, yet there want not many that do fear
In deep of night to walk by this Herne's Oak.
But what of this?

MISTRESS FORD   Marry, this is our device: 40
That Falstaff at that oak shall meet with us,
Disguised like Herne, with huge horns on his head.

PAGE
Well, let it not be doubted but he'll come,
And in this shape. When you have brought him
     thither
What shall be done with him? What is your plot?   45

MISTRESS PAGE
That likewise have we thought upon, and thus.
Nan Page my daughter, and my little son,
And three or four more of their growth, we'll dress
Like urchins, oafs, and fairies, green and white,
With rounds of waxen tapers on their heads,   50
And rattles in their hands. Upon a sudden,
As Falstaff, she, and I are newly met,
Let them from forth a saw-pit rush at once,
With some diffusèd song. Upon their sight
We two in great amazèdness will fly.   55
Then let them all encircle him about,
And, fairy-like, to pinch the unclean knight,
And ask him why, that hour of fairy revel,
In their so sacred paths he dares to tread
In shape profane.

⌈MISTRESS⌉ FORD   And till he tell the truth,   60
Let the supposèd fairies pinch him sound,
And burn him with their tapers.

MISTRESS PAGE   The truth being known,
We'll all present ourselves, dis-horn the spirit,
And mock him home to Windsor.

FORD   ·   The children must
Be practised well to this, or they'll ne'er do't.   65

EVANS I will teach the children their behaviours, and I
will be like a jackanapes also, to burn the knight with
my taber.

FORD
That will be excellent. I'll go buy them vizors.

MISTRESS PAGE
My Nan shall be the Queen of all the Fairies,   70
Finely attirèd in a robe of white.

PAGE
That silk will I go buy— (aside) and in that tire
Shall Master Slender steal my Nan away,
And marry her at Eton. (To Mistress Page) Go send to
     Falstaff straight.

FORD
Nay, I'll to him again in name of Brooke.   75
He'll tell me all his purpose. Sure he'll come.

MISTRESS PAGE
Fear not you that. (To Page, Ford, and Evans) Go get us
     properties
And tricking for our fairies.

EVANS Let us about it. It is admirable pleasures, and fery
honest knaveries.   Exeunt Ford, Page, and Evans

MISTRESS PAGE   Go, Mistress Ford,   80
Send quickly to Sir John, to know his mind.
                                        Exit Mistress Ford
I'll to the Doctor. He hath my good will,
And none but he, to marry with Nan Page.
That Slender, though well landed, is an idiot;
And he my husband best of all affects.   85
The Doctor is well moneyed, and his friends
Potent at court. He, none but he, shall have her,
Though twenty thousand worthier come to crave her.
                                                    Exit

4.5   *Enter the Host of the Garter and Simple*

HOST What wouldst thou have, boor? What, thick-skin?
Speak, breathe, discuss. Brief, short, quick, snap.

SIMPLE Marry, sir, I come to speak with Sir John Falstaff,
from Master Slender.   4

HOST There's his chamber, his house, his castle, his
standing-bed and truckle-bed. 'Tis painted about with
the story of the Prodigal, fresh and new. Go knock and
call. He'll speak like an Anthropophaginian unto thee.
Knock, I say.   9

SIMPLE There's an old woman, a fat woman, gone up
into his chamber. I'll be so bold as stay, sir, till she
come down. I come to speak with her, indeed.

HOST Ha, a fat woman? The knight may be robbed. I'll
call.—Bully knight, bully Sir John! Speak from thy
lungs military! Art thou there? It is thine Host, thine
Ephesian, calls.   16

SIR JOHN (within) How now, mine Host?

HOST Here's a Bohemian Tartar tarries the coming down
of thy fat woman. Let her descend, bully, let her
descend. My chambers are honourable. Fie, privacy!
Fie!   21

Enter Sir John Falstaff

SIR JOHN There was, mine Host, an old fat woman even
now with me; but she's gone.

SIMPLE Pray you, sir, was't not the wise woman of
Brentford?   25

SIR JOHN Ay, marry was it, mussel-shell. What would you
with her?

SIMPLE My master, sir, my master Slender, sent to her,
seeing her go through the streets, to know, sir, whether
one Nim, sir, that beguiled him of a chain, had the
chain or no.   31

SIR JOHN I spake with the old woman about it.

SIMPLE And what says she, I pray, sir?

SIR JOHN Marry, she says that the very same man that
beguiled Master Slender of his chain cozened him of it.

SIMPLE I would I could have spoken with the woman
herself. I had other things to have spoken with her,
too, from him.   38

SIR JOHN What are they? Let us know.
HOST Ay, come, quick.   40
⌈SIMPLE⌉ I may not conceal them, sir.
HOST Conceal them, or thou diest.
SIMPLE Why, sir, they were nothing but about Mistress
   Anne Page, to know if it were my master's fortune to
   have her or no.   45
SIR JOHN 'Tis, 'tis his fortune.
SIMPLE What, sir?
SIR JOHN To have her or no. Go say the woman told me
   so.
SIMPLE May I be bold to say so, sir?   50
SIR JOHN Ay, Sir Tike; who more bold?
SIMPLE I thank your worship. I shall make my master
   glad with these tidings.   *Exit*
HOST Thou art clerkly, thou art clerkly, Sir John. Was
   there a wise woman with thee?   55
SIR JOHN Ay, that there was, mine Host, one that hath
   taught me more wit than ever I learned before in my
   life. And I paid nothing for it, neither, but was paid for
   my learning.
      Enter Bardolph, ⌈muddy⌉
BARDOLPH O Lord, sir, cozenage, mere cozenage!   60
HOST Where be my horses? Speak well of them, varletto.
BARDOLPH Run away with the cozeners. For so soon as I
   came beyond Eton, they threw me off from behind one
   of them, in a slough of mire, and set spurs and away,
   like three German devils, three Doctor Faustuses.   65
HOST They are gone but to meet the Duke, villain. Do not
   say they be fled. Germans are honest men.
      Enter Sir Hugh Evans
EVANS Where is mine Host?
HOST What is the matter, sir?   69
EVANS Have a care of your entertainments. There is a
   friend of mine come to town tells me there is three
   cozen Garmombles that has cozened all the hosts of
   Reading, of Maidenhead, of Colnbrook, of horses and
   money. I tell you for good will, look you. You are wise,
   and full of gibes and vlouting-stocks, and 'tis not
   convenient you should be cozened. Fare you well.   76
                                                       Exit
      Enter Doctor Caius
CAIUS Vere is mine Host de Jarteer?
HOST Here, Master Doctor, in perplexity and doubtful
   dilemma.   79
CAIUS I cannot tell vat is dat, but it is tell-a me dat you
   make grand preparation for a duke de Jamany. By my
   trot, der is no duke that the court is know to come. I
   tell you for good will. Adieu.   *Exit*
HOST (*to Bardolph*) Hue and cry, villain, go! (*To Sir John*)
   Assist me, knight. I am undone. (*To Bardolph*) Fly, run,
   hue and cry, villain. I am undone.   86
      Exeunt Host and Bardolph ⌈severally⌉
SIR JOHN I would all the world might be cozened, for I
   have been cozened, and beaten too. If it should come
   to the ear of the court how I have been transformed,
   and how my transformation hath been washed and
   cudgelled, they would melt me out of my fat, drop by

drop, and liquor fishermen's boots with me. I warrant
they would whip me with their fine wits till I were as
crestfallen as a dried pear. I never prospered since I
forswore myself at primero. Well, if my wind were but
long enough, I would repent.   96
      Enter Mistress Quickly
Now; whence come you?
MISTRESS QUICKLY From the two parties, forsooth.
SIR JOHN The devil take one party, and his dam the other,
   and so they shall be both bestowed. I have suffered
   more for their sakes, more than the villainous
   inconstancy of man's disposition is able to bear.   102
MISTRESS QUICKLY O Lord, sir, and have not they suffered?
   Yes, I warrant, speciously one of them. Mistress Ford,
   good heart, is beaten black and blue, that you cannot
   see a white spot about her.   106
SIR JOHN What tellest thou me of black and blue? I was
   beaten myself into all the colours of the rainbow, and
   I was like to be apprehended for the witch of Brentford.
   But that my admirable dexterity of wit, my
   counterfeiting the action of an old woman, delivered
   me, the knave constable had set me i'th' stocks, i'th'
   common stocks, for a witch.   113
MISTRESS QUICKLY Sir, let me speak with you in your
   chamber. You shall hear how things go, and, I warrant,
   to your content. Here is a letter will say somewhat.
   Good hearts, what ado here is to bring you together!
   Sure one of you does not serve heaven well, that you
   are so crossed.   119
SIR JOHN Come up into my chamber.   *Exeunt*

4.6   *Enter Master Fenton and the Host of the Garter*
HOST Master Fenton, talk not to me. My mind is heavy.
   I will give over all.
FENTON
   Yet hear me speak. Assist me in my purpose,
   And, as I am a gentleman, I'll give thee
   A hundred pound in gold more than your loss.   5
HOST I will hear you, Master Fenton, and I will at the
   least keep your counsel.
FENTON
   From time to time I have acquainted you
   With the dear love I bear to fair Anne Page,
   Who mutually hath answered my affection,   10
   So far forth as herself might be her chooser,
   Even to my wish. I have a letter from her
   Of such contents as you will wonder at,
   The mirth whereof so larded with my matter
   That neither singly can be manifested   15
   Without the show of both. Fat Falstaff
   Hath a great scene. The image of the jest
   I'll show you here at large. Hark, good mine Host.
   Tonight at Herne's Oak, just 'twixt twelve and one,
   Must my sweet Nan present the Fairy Queen—   20
      ⌈*Showing the letter*⌉
   The purpose why is here—in which disguise,
   While other jests are something rank on foot,
   Her father hath commanded her to slip

Away with Slender, and with him at Eton
Immediately to marry. She hath consented.   25
Now, sir, her mother, ever strong against that match
And firm for Doctor Caius, hath appointed
That he shall likewise shuffle her away,
While other sports are tasking of their minds,
And at the dean'ry, where a priest attends,   30
Straight marry her. To this her mother's plot
She, seemingly obedient, likewise hath
Made promise to the Doctor. Now, thus it rests.
Her father means she shall be all in white;
And in that habit, when Slender sees his time   35
To take her by the hand and bid her go,
She shall go with him. Her mother hath intended,
The better to denote her to the Doctor—
For they must all be masked and visorèd—
That quaint in green she shall be loose enrobed,   40
With ribbons pendant flaring 'bout her head;
And when the Doctor spies his vantage ripe,
To pinch her by the hand, and on that token
The maid hath given consent to go with him.
HOST
   Which means she to deceive, father or mother?   45
FENTON
   Both, my good Host, to go along with me.
And here it rests: that you'll procure the vicar
To stay for me at church 'twixt twelve and one,
And, in the lawful name of marrying,
To give our hearts united ceremony.   50
HOST
   Well, husband your device. I'll to the vicar.
Bring you the maid, you shall not lack a priest.
FENTON
   So shall I evermore be bound to thee.
Besides, I'll make a present recompense.
                        Exeunt ⌈severally⌉

5.1   *Enter Sir John Falstaff and Mistress Quickly*
SIR JOHN Prithee, no more prattling; go; I'll hold. This is
   the third time; I hope good luck lies in odd numbers.
   Away, go! They say there is divinity in odd numbers,
   either in nativity, chance, or death. Away!   4
MISTRESS QUICKLY I'll provide you a chain, and I'll do
   what I can to get you a pair of horns.   6
SIR JOHN Away, I say! Time wears. Hold up your head,
   and mince.   *Exit Mistress Quickly*
   Enter Master Ford, disguised as Brooke
   How now, Master Brooke? Master Brooke, the matter
   will be known tonight or never. Be you in the Park
   about midnight at Herne's Oak, and you shall see
   wonders.
FORD Went you not to her yesterday, sir, as you told me
   you had appointed?   14
SIR JOHN I went to her, Master Brooke, as you see, like
   a poor old man; but I came from her, Master Brooke,
   like a poor old woman. That same knave Ford, her
   husband, hath the finest mad devil of jealousy in him,

Master Brooke, that ever governed frenzy. I will tell
you, he beat me grievously in the shape of a woman—
for in the shape of man, Master Brooke, I fear not
Goliath with a weaver's beam, because I know also life
is a shuttle. I am in haste. Go along with me; I'll tell
you all, Master Brooke. Since I plucked geese, played
truant, and whipped top, I knew not what 'twas to be
beaten till lately. Follow me. I'll tell you strange things
of this knave Ford, on whom tonight I will be revenged,
and I will deliver his wife into your hand. Follow.
Strange things in hand, Master Brooke. Follow.   29
                        Exeunt

5.2   *Enter Master Page, Justice Shallow, and Master
          Slender*
PAGE Come, come, we'll couch i'th' Castle ditch till we
   see the light of our fairies. Remember, son Slender, my
   daughter.
SLENDER Ay, forsooth. I have spoke with her, and we
   have a nay-word how to know one another. I come to
   her in white and cry 'mum'; she cries 'budget'; and
   by that we know one another.   7
SHALLOW That's good, too. But what needs either your
   'mum' or her 'budget'? The white will decipher her
   well enough. (*To Page*) It hath struck ten o'clock.   10
PAGE The night is dark; lights and spirits will become it
   well. God prosper our sport! No man means evil but
   the devil, and we shall know him by his horns. Let's
   away. Follow me.   *Exeunt*

5.3   *Enter Mistress Page, Mistress Ford, and Doctor
          Caius*
MISTRESS PAGE Master Doctor, my daughter is in green.
   When you see your time, take her by the hand, away
   with her to the deanery, and dispatch it quickly. Go
   before into the Park. We two must go together.
CAIUS I know vat I have to do. Adieu.   5
MISTRESS PAGE Fare you well, sir.   *Exit Caius*
   My husband will not rejoice so much at the abuse of
   Falstaff as he will chafe at the doctor's marrying my
   daughter. But 'tis no matter. Better a little chiding than
   a great deal of heartbreak.   10
MISTRESS FORD Where is Nan now, and her troop of fairies,
   and the Welsh devil Hugh?
MISTRESS PAGE They are all couched in a pit hard by
   Herne's Oak, with obscured lights, which, at the very
   instant of Falstaff's and our meeting, they will at once
   display to the night.   16
MISTRESS FORD That cannot choose but amaze him.
MISTRESS PAGE If he be not amazed, he will be mocked. If
   he be amazed, he will every way be mocked.
MISTRESS FORD We'll betray him finely.   20
MISTRESS PAGE
   Against such lewdsters and their lechery
   Those that betray them do no treachery.
MISTRESS FORD The hour draws on. To the Oak, to the
   Oak!   *Exeunt*

5.4   *Enter Sir Hugh Evans, ⌈disguised as a satyr,⌉ and*
       ⌈William Page and other⌉ children, disguised as
       fairies

EVANS Trib, trib, fairies! Come! And remember your parts.
Be pold, I pray you. Follow me into the pit, and when
I give the watch'ords, do as I pid you. Come, come;
trib, trib!   *Exeunt*

5.5   *Enter Sir John Falstaff, disguised as Herne, ⌈with*
       horns on his head, and bearing a chain⌉

SIR JOHN The Windsor bell hath struck twelve; the minute
draws on. Now the hot-blooded gods assist me!
Remember, Jove, thou wast a bull for thy Europa; love
set on thy horns. O powerful love, that in some respects
makes a beast a man; in some other, a man a beast!
You were also, Jupiter, a swan, for the love of Leda. O
omnipotent love! How near the god drew to the
complexion of a goose! A fault done first in the form
of a beast—O Jove, a beastly fault!—and then another
fault in the semblance of a fowl—think on't, Jove, a
foul fault! When gods have hot backs, what shall poor
men do? For me, I am here a Windsor stag, and the
fattest, I think, i'th' forest. Send me a cool rut-time,
Jove, or who can blame me to piss my tallow?

Enter Mistress Ford ⌈followed by⌉ Mistress Page

Who comes here? My doe!   15

MISTRESS FORD Sir John! Art thou there, my deer, my
male deer?

SIR JOHN My doe with the black scut! Let the sky rain
potatoes, let it thunder to the tune of 'Greensleeves',
hail kissing-comfits, and snow eringoes; let there come
a tempest of provocation, I will shelter me here.   21

       ⌈He embraces her⌉

MISTRESS FORD Mistress Page is come with me, sweetheart.

SIR JOHN Divide me like a bribed buck, each a haunch. I
will keep my sides to myself, my shoulders for the fellow
of this walk, and my horns I bequeath your husbands.
Am I a woodman, ha? Speak I like Herne the hunter?
Why, now is Cupid a child of conscience; he makes
restitution. As I am a true spirit, welcome!

       ⌈A noise within⌉

MISTRESS PAGE Alas, what noise?

MISTRESS FORD God forgive our sins!   30

SIR JOHN What should this be?

MISTRESS FORD *and* MISTRESS PAGE Away, away!

       Exeunt Mistress Ford and Mistress Page,
       ⌈running⌉

SIR JOHN I think the devil will not have me damned, lest
the oil that's in me should set hell on fire. He would
never else cross me thus.   35

       Enter Sir Hugh Evans, ⌈William Page,⌉ and
       children, disguised as before, with tapers; Mistress
       Quickly, disguised as the Fairy Queen; Anne Page,
       disguised as a fairy; and one disguised as
       Hobgoblin

MISTRESS QUICKLY
Fairies black, grey, green, and white,
You moonshine revellers, and shades of night,

You orphan heirs of fixèd destiny,
Attend your office and your quality.—
Crier hobgoblin, make the fairy oyes.   40

⌈HOBGOBLIN⌉
Elves, list your names. Silence, you airy toys.
Cricket, to Windsor chimneys shalt thou leap.
Where fires thou find'st unraked and hearths unswept,
There pinch the maids as blue as bilberry.
Our radiant Queen hates sluts and sluttery.   45

SIR JOHN (*aside*)
They are fairies. He that speaks to them shall die.
I'll wink and couch; no man their works must eye.
       He lies down, and hides his face

EVANS
Where's Bead? Go you, and, where you find a maid
That ere she sleep has thrice her prayers said,
Raise up the organs of her fantasy,   50
Sleep she as sound as careless infancy.
But those as sleep and think not on their sins,
Pinch them, arms, legs, backs, shoulders, sides, and
       shins.

MISTRESS QUICKLY About, about!
Search Windsor Castle, elves, within and out.   55
Strew good luck, oafs, on every sacred room,
That it may stand till the perpetual doom
In state as wholesome as in state 'tis fit,
Worthy the owner, and the owner it.
The several chairs of order look you scour   60
With juice of balm and every precious flower.
Each fair instalment, coat, and sev'ral crest
With loyal blazon evermore be blessed;
And nightly, meadow-fairies, look you sing,
Like to the Garter's compass, in a ring.   65
Th'expressure that it bears, green let it be,
More fertile-fresh than all the field to see;
And 'Honi soit qui mal y pense' write
In em'rald tufts, flowers purple, blue, and white,
Like sapphire, pearl, and rich embroidery,   70
Buckled below fair knighthood's bending knee—
Fairies use flowers for their charactery.
Away, disperse!—But till 'tis one o'clock
Our dance of custom, round about the oak
Of Herne the hunter, let us not forget.   75

EVANS
Pray you, lock hand in hand; yourselves in order set;
And twenty glow-worms shall our lanterns be
To guide our measure round about the tree.—
But stay; I smell a man of middle earth.

SIR JOHN (*aside*)
God defend me from that Welsh fairy,   80
Lest he transform me to a piece of cheese!

⌈HOBGOBLIN⌉ (*to Sir John*)
Vile worm, thou wast o'erlooked even in thy birth.

MISTRESS QUICKLY (*to fairies*)
With trial-fire, touch me his finger-end.
If he be chaste, the flame will back descend,
And turn him to no pain; but if he start,   85
It is the flesh of a corrupted heart.

⌈HOBGOBLIN⌉
  A trial, come!
EVANS   Come, will this wood take fire?
  They burn Sir John with tapers
SIR JOHN O, O, O!
MISTRESS QUICKLY
  Corrupt, corrupt, and tainted in desire.
  About him, fairies; sing a scornful rhyme;   90
  And, as you trip, still pinch him to your time.
  They dance around Sir John, pinching him and
  singing:

FAIRIES   Fie on sinful fantasy!
      Fie on lust and luxury!
      Lust is but a bloody fire,
      Kindled with unchaste desire,   95
      Fed in heart, whose flames aspire,
      As thoughts do blow them, higher and higher.
      Pinch him, fairies, mutually.
      Pinch him for his villainy.
  Pinch him, and burn him, and turn him about, 100
  Till candles and starlight and moonshine be out.

During the song, enter Doctor Caius one way, and
exit stealing away a fairy in green; enter Master
Slender another way, and exit stealing away a fairy
in white; enter Master Fenton, and exit stealing
away Anne Page. After the song, a noise of hunting
within. Exeunt Mistress Quickly, Evans, Hobgoblin,
and fairies, running. Sir John rises, and starts to
run away. Enter Master Page, Master Ford,
Mistress Page, and Mistress Ford
PAGE
  Nay, do not fly. I think we have watched you now.
  Will none but Herne the hunter serve your turn?
MISTRESS PAGE
  I pray you, come, hold up the jest no higher.
  Now, good Sir John, how like you Windsor wives? 105
  (*Pointing to Falstaff's horns*)
  See you these, husband? Do not these fair yokes
  Become the forest better than the town?
FORD (*to Sir John*) Now, sir, who's a cuckold now? Master
  Brooke, Falstaff's a knave, a cuckoldly knave. Here are
  his horns, Master Brooke. And, Master Brooke, he hath
  enjoyed nothing of Ford's but his buck-basket, his
  cudgel, and twenty pounds of money which must be
  paid to Master Brooke; his horses are arrested for it,
  Master Brooke.   114
MISTRESS FORD Sir John, we have had ill luck. We could
  never mate. I will never take you for my love again,
  but I will always count you my deer.
SIR JOHN I do begin to perceive that I am made an ass.
  ⌈*He takes off the horns*⌉
FORD Ay, and an ox, too. Both the proofs are extant. 119
SIR JOHN And these are not fairies? By the Lord, I was
  three or four times in the thought they were not fairies,
  and yet the guiltiness of my mind, the sudden surprise
  of my powers, drove the grossness of the foppery into
  a received belief—in despite of the teeth of all rhyme

and reason—that they were fairies. See now how wit
may be made a Jack-a-Lent when 'tis upon ill
employment!   127
EVANS Sir John Falstaff, serve Got and leave your desires,
  and fairies will not pinse you.
FORD Well said, Fairy Hugh.   130
EVANS And leave you your jealousies too, I pray you.
FORD I will never mistrust my wife again till thou art able
  to woo her in good English.
SIR JOHN Have I laid my brain in the sun and dried it,
  that it wants matter to prevent so gross o'er-reaching
  as this? Am I ridden with a Welsh goat too? Shall I
  have a coxcomb of frieze? 'Tis time I were choked with
  a piece of toasted cheese.
EVANS Seese is not good to give putter; your belly is all
  putter.   140
SIR JOHN 'Seese' and 'putter'? Have I lived to stand at
  the taunt of one that makes fritters of English? This is
  enough to be the decay of lust and late walking through
  the realm.   144
MISTRESS PAGE Why, Sir John, do you think, though we
  would have thrust virtue out of our hearts by the head
  and shoulders, and have given ourselves without
  scruple to hell, that ever the devil could have made
  you our delight?
FORD What, a hodge-pudding, a bag of flax?   150
MISTRESS PAGE A puffed man?
PAGE Old, cold, withered, and of intolerable entrails?
FORD And one that is as slanderous as Satan?
PAGE And as poor as Job?
FORD And as wicked as his wife?   155
EVANS And given to fornications, and to taverns, and
  sack, and wine, and metheglins; and to drinkings, and
  swearings, and starings, pribbles and prabbles?
SIR JOHN Well, I am your theme; you have the start of
  me. I am dejected. I am not able to answer the Welsh
  flannel. Ignorance itself is a plummet o'er me. Use me
  as you will.   162
FORD Marry, sir, we'll bring you to Windsor, to one
  Master Brooke, that you have cozened of money, to
  whom you should have been a pander. Over and above
  that you have suffered, I think to repay that money
  will be a biting affliction.   167
PAGE Yet be cheerful, knight. Thou shalt eat a posset
  tonight at my house, where I will desire thee to laugh
  at my wife that now laughs at thee. Tell her Master
  Slender hath married her daughter.   171
MISTRESS PAGE (*aside*) Doctors doubt that! If Anne Page
  be my daughter, she is, by this, Doctor Caius's wife.
        Enter Master Slender
SLENDER Whoa, ho, ho, father Page!
PAGE Son, how now? How now, son? Have you
  dispatched?   176
SLENDER Dispatched? I'll make the best in Gloucestershire
  know on't; would I were hanged, la, else.
PAGE Of what, son?   179
SLENDER I came yonder at Eton to marry Mistress Anne
  Page, and she's a great lubberly boy. If it had not been

i'th' church, I would have swinged him, or he should
have swinged me. If I did not think it had been Anne
Page, would I might never stir; and 'tis a postmaster's
boy.   185

PAGE Upon my life, then, you took the wrong.

SLENDER What need you tell me that? I think so, when I
took a boy for a girl. If I had been married to him, for
all he was in woman's apparel, I would not have had
him.   190

PAGE Why, this is your own folly. Did not I tell you how
you should know my daughter by her garments?

SLENDER I went to her in white and cried 'mum', and she
cried 'budget', as Anne and I had appointed; and yet
it was not Anne, but a postmaster's boy.   195

MISTRESS PAGE Good George, be not angry. I knew of your
purpose, turned my daughter into green, and indeed
she is now with the Doctor at the deanery, and there
married.

Enter Doctor Caius

CAIUS Ver is Mistress Page? By Gar, I am cozened! I ha'
married *un garçon*, a boy, *un paysan*, by Gar. A boy! It
is not Anne Page, by Gar. I am cozened.

PAGE Why, did you take her in green?

CAIUS Ay, be Gar, and 'tis a boy. Be Gar, I'll raise all
Windsor.   205

FORD This is strange. Who hath got the right Anne?

Enter Master Fenton and Anne

PAGE
My heart misgives me: here comes Master Fenton. —
How now, Master Fenton?

ANNE
Pardon, good father. Good my mother, pardon.

PAGE
Now, mistress, how chance you went not with Master
Slender?   210

⌈MISTRESS⌉ PAGE
Why went you not with Master Doctor, maid?

FENTON
You do amaze her. Hear the truth of it.
You would have married her, most shamefully,
Where there was no proportion held in love.
The truth is, she and I, long since contracted,   215
Are now so sure that nothing can dissolve us.
Th'offence is holy that she hath committed,
And this deceit loses the name of craft,
Of disobedience, or unduteous title,
Since therein she doth evitate and shun   220
A thousand irreligious cursèd hours
Which forcèd marriage would have brought upon her.

FORD (*to Page and Mistress Page*)
Stand not amazed. Here is no remedy.
In love the heavens themselves do guide the state;
Money buys lands, and wives are sold by fate.   225

SIR JOHN I am glad, though you have ta'en a special
stand to strike at me, that your arrow hath glanced.

PAGE
Well, what remedy? Fenton, heaven give thee joy!
What cannot be eschewed must be embraced.

SIR JOHN
When night-dogs run, all sorts of deer are chased.   230

MISTRESS PAGE
Well, I will muse no further. Master Fenton,
Heaven give you many, many merry days!
Good husband, let us every one go home,
And laugh this sport o'er by a country fire,
Sir John and all.

FORD   Let it be so, Sir John.   235
To Master Brooke you yet shall hold your word,
For he tonight shall lie with Mistress Ford.   *Exeunt*

MUCH ADO ABOUT NOTHING

Much Ado About Nothing is not mentioned in the list of plays by Shakespeare given by Francis Meres in his *Palladis Tamia*, published in the autumn of 1598. Certain speech-prefixes of the first edition, published in 1600, suggest that as Shakespeare wrote he had in mind for the role of Dogberry the comic actor Will Kemp, who is believed to have left the Lord Chamberlain's Men during 1599. Probably Shakespeare wrote the play between summer 1598 and spring 1599.

The action is set in Sicily, where Don Pedro, Prince of Aragon, has recently defeated his half-brother, the bastard Don John, in a military engagement. Apparently reconciled, they return to the capital, Messina, as guests of the Governor, Leonato. There Count Claudio, a young nobleman serving in Don Pedro's army, falls in love with Hero, Leonato's daughter, whom Don Pedro woos on his behalf. The play's central plot, written mainly in verse, shows how Don John maliciously deceives Claudio into believing that Hero has taken a lover on the eve of her marriage, causing Claudio to repudiate her publicly, at the altar. This is a variation on an old tale that existed in many versions; it had been told in Italian verse by Ariosto, in his *Orlando Furioso* (1516, translated into English verse by Sir John Harington, 1591), in Italian prose by Matteo Bandello in his *Novelle* (1554, adapted into French by P. de Belleforest, 1569), in English prose by George Whetstone (*The Rock of Regard*, 1576), in English verse by Edmund Spenser (*The Faerie Queene*, Book 2, canto 4, 1590), and in a number of plays including Luigi Pasqualigo's *Il Fedele* (1579), adapted into English—perhaps by Anthony Munday—as *Fedele and Fortunio* (published in 1583). Shakespeare, whose plot is an independent reworking of the traditional story, seems to owe most to Ariosto and Bandello, perhaps indirectly.

Don John's deception, with its tragicomical resolution, is offset by a parallel plot written mainly in prose, portraying another, more light-hearted deception, by which Hero's cousin, Beatrice, and Benedick—friend of Don Pedro and Claudio—are tricked into acknowledging, first to themselves and then to each other, that they are in love. This part of the play seems to be of Shakespeare's invention: the juxtaposition of this clever, sophisticated, apparently unillusioned pair with the more naïve Claudio and Hero recalls Shakespeare's earlier contrast of romantic and antiromantic attitudes to love and marriage in *The Taming of the Shrew*. The play's third main strand is provided by Constable Dogberry, his partner Verges, and the Watchmen, clearly English rather than Sicilian in origin. Although Benedick and Beatrice are, technically, subordinate characters, they have dominated the imagination of both readers and playgoers.

THE PERSONS OF THE PLAY

DON PEDRO, Prince of Aragon

BENEDICK, of Padua ⎫
CLAUDIO, of Florence ⎬ lords, companions of Don Pedro

BALTHASAR, attendant on Don Pedro, a singer

DON JOHN, the bastard brother of Don Pedro

BORACHIO ⎫
CONRAD ⎬ followers of Don John

LEONATO, Governor of Messina

HERO, his daughter

BEATRICE, an orphan, his niece

ANTONIO, an old man, brother of Leonato

MARGARET ⎫
URSULA ⎬ waiting-gentlewomen attendant on Hero

FRIAR Francis

DOGBERRY, the Constable in charge of the Watch

VERGES, the Headborough, Dogberry's partner

A SEXTON

WATCHMEN

A BOY, serving Benedick

Attendants and messengers

Much Ado About Nothing

1.1 *Enter Leonato, governor of Messina, Hero his*
daughter, and Beatrice his niece, with a Messenger

LEONATO I learn in this letter that Don Pedro of Aragon comes this night to Messina.

MESSENGER He is very near by this. He was not three leagues off when I left him.

LEONATO How many gentlemen have you lost in this action? 6

MESSENGER But few of any sort, and none of name.

LEONATO A victory is twice itself when the achiever brings home full numbers. I find here that Don Pedro hath bestowed much honour on a young Florentine called Claudio. 11

MESSENGER Much deserved on his part, and equally remembered by Don Pedro. He hath borne himself beyond the promise of his age, doing in the figure of a lamb the feats of a lion. He hath indeed better bettered expectation than you must expect of me to tell you how. 17

LEONATO He hath an uncle here in Messina will be very much glad of it.

MESSENGER I have already delivered him letters, and there appears much joy in him—even so much that joy could not show itself modest enough without a badge of bitterness.

LEONATO Did he break out into tears?

MESSENGER In great measure. 25

LEONATO A kind overflow of kindness, there are no faces truer than those that are so washed. How much better is it to weep at joy than to joy at weeping!

BEATRICE I pray you, is Signor Montanto returned from the wars, or no? 30

MESSENGER I know none of that name, lady. There was none such in the army, of any sort.

LEONATO What is he that you ask for, niece?

HERO My cousin means Signor Benedick of Padua.

MESSENGER O, he's returned, and as pleasant as ever he was. 36

BEATRICE He set up his bills here in Messina, and challenged Cupid at the flight; and my uncle's fool, reading the challenge, subscribed for Cupid and challenged him at the bird-bolt. I pray you, how many hath he killed and eaten in these wars? But how many hath he killed? For indeed I promised to eat all of his killing.

LEONATO Faith, niece, you tax Signor Benedick too much. But he'll be meet with you, I doubt it not. 45

MESSENGER He hath done good service, lady, in these wars.

BEATRICE You had musty victual, and he hath holp to eat it. He is a very valiant trencherman, he hath an excellent stomach. 50

MESSENGER And a good soldier too, lady.

BEATRICE And a good soldier to a lady, but what is he to a lord?

MESSENGER A lord to a lord, a man to a man, stuffed with all honourable virtues. 55

BEATRICE It is so, indeed. He is no less than a stuffed man. But for the stuffing—well, we are all mortal.

LEONATO You must not, sir, mistake my niece. There is a kind of merry war betwixt Signor Benedick and her. They never meet but there's a skirmish of wit between them. 61

BEATRICE Alas, he gets nothing by that. In our last conflict four of his five wits went halting off, and now is the whole man governed with one, so that if he have wit enough to keep himself warm, let him bear it for a difference between himself and his horse, for it is all the wealth that he hath left to be known a reasonable creature. Who is his companion now? He hath every month a new sworn brother.

MESSENGER Is't possible? 70

BEATRICE Very easily possible. He wears his faith but as the fashion of his hat, it ever changes with the next block.

MESSENGER I see, lady, the gentleman is not in your books.

BEATRICE No. An he were, I would burn my study. But I pray you, who is his companion? Is there no young squarer now that will make a voyage with him to the devil?

MESSENGER He is most in the company of the right noble Claudio. 80

BEATRICE O Lord, he will hang upon him like a disease. He is sooner caught than the pestilence, and the taker runs presently mad. God help the noble Claudio. If he have caught the Benedick, it will cost him a thousand pound ere a be cured. 85

MESSENGER I will hold friends with you, lady.

BEATRICE Do, good friend.

LEONATO You will never run mad, niece.

BEATRICE No, not till a hot January.

MESSENGER Don Pedro is approached. 90

Enter Don Pedro, Claudio, Benedick, Balthasar, and
Don John the bastard

DON PEDRO Good Signor Leonato, are you come to meet your trouble? The fashion of the world is to avoid cost, and you encounter it.

LEONATO Never came trouble to my house in the likeness of your grace; for trouble being gone, comfort should remain, but when you depart from me, sorrow abides and happiness takes his leave.

DON PEDRO You embrace your charge too willingly. I think this is your daughter.

LEONATO Her mother hath many times told me so. 100

BENEDICK Were you in doubt, sir, that you asked her?

LEONATO Signor Benedick, no, for then were you a child.

DON PEDRO You have it full, Benedick. We may guess by this what you are, being a man. Truly, the lady fathers herself. Be happy, lady, for you are like an honourable father. 106

BENEDICK If Signor Leonato be her father, she would not have his head on her shoulders for all Messina, as like him as she is.

BEATRICE I wonder that you will still be talking, Signor Benedick. Nobody marks you. 111

BENEDICK What, my dear Lady Disdain! Are you yet living?

BEATRICE Is it possible disdain should die while she hath such meet food to feed it as Signor Benedick? Courtesy itself must convert to disdain if you come in her presence.

BENEDICK Then is courtesy a turncoat. But it is certain I am loved of all ladies, only you excepted. And I would I could find in my heart that I had not a hard heart, for truly I love none. 121

BEATRICE A dear happiness to women. They would else have been troubled with a pernicious suitor. I thank God and my cold blood I am of your humour for that. I had rather hear my dog bark at a crow than a man swear he loves me. 126

BENEDICK God keep your ladyship still in that mind. So some gentleman or other shall scape a predestinate scratched face.

BEATRICE Scratching could not make it worse an 'twere such a face as yours were. 131

BENEDICK Well, you are a rare parrot-teacher.

BEATRICE A bird of my tongue is better than a beast of yours.

BENEDICK I would my horse had the speed of your tongue, and so good a continuer. But keep your way, o' God's name. I have done.

BEATRICE You always end with a jade's trick. I know you of old. 139

DON PEDRO That is the sum of all, Leonato. Signor Claudio and Signor Benedick, my dear friend Leonato hath invited you all. I tell him we shall stay here at the least a month, and he heartily prays some occasion may detain us longer. I dare swear he is no hypocrite, but prays from his heart. 145

LEONATO If you swear, my lord, you shall not be forsworn. (*To Don John*) Let me bid you welcome, my lord. Being reconciled to the Prince your brother, I owe you all duty.

DON JOHN I thank you. I am not of many words, but I thank you. 151

LEONATO (*to Don Pedro*) Please it your grace lead on?

DON PEDRO Your hand, Leonato. We will go together.

Exeunt all but Benedick and Claudio

CLAUDIO Benedick, didst thou note the daughter of Signor Leonato? 155

BENEDICK I noted her not, but I looked on her.

CLAUDIO Is she not a modest young lady?

BENEDICK Do you question me as an honest man should do, for my simple true judgement, or would you have me speak after my custom, as being a professed tyrant to their sex? 161

CLAUDIO No, I pray thee speak in sober judgement.

BENEDICK Why, i'faith, methinks she's too low for a high praise, too brown for a fair praise, and too little for a great praise. Only this commendation I can afford her, that were she other than she is she were unhandsome, and being no other but as she is, I do not like her.

CLAUDIO Thou thinkest I am in sport. I pray thee tell me truly how thou likest her.

BENEDICK Would you buy her, that you enquire after her?

CLAUDIO Can the world buy such a jewel? 171

BENEDICK Yea, and a case to put it into. But speak you this with a sad brow, or do you play the flouting jack, to tell us Cupid is a good hare-finder and Vulcan a rare carpenter? Come, in what key shall a man take you to go in the song? 176

CLAUDIO In mine eye she is the sweetest lady that ever I looked on.

BENEDICK I can see yet without spectacles, and I see no such matter. There's her cousin, an she were not possessed with a fury, exceeds her as much in beauty as the first of May doth the last of December. But I hope you have no intent to turn husband, have you?

CLAUDIO I would scarce trust myself though I had sworn the contrary, if Hero would be my wife. 185

BENEDICK Is't come to this? In faith, hath not the world one man but he will wear his cap with suspicion? Shall I never see a bachelor of three-score again? Go to, i'faith, an thou wilt needs thrust thy neck into a yoke, wear the print of it, and sigh away Sundays. Look, Don Pedro is returned to seek you. 191

Enter Don Pedro

DON PEDRO What secret hath held you here that you followed not to Leonato's?

BENEDICK I would your grace would constrain me to tell.

DON PEDRO I charge thee on thy allegiance. 195

BENEDICK You hear, Count Claudio? I can be secret as a dumb man, I would have you think so. But on my allegiance, mark you this, on my allegiance! He is in love. With who? Now that is your grace's part. Mark how short his answer is: with Hero, Leonato's short daughter. 201

CLAUDIO If this were so, so were it uttered.

BENEDICK Like the old tale, my lord—it is not so, nor 'twas not so, but indeed, God forbid it should be so.

CLAUDIO If my passion change not shortly, God forbid it should be otherwise. 206

DON PEDRO Amen, if you love her, for the lady is very well worthy.

CLAUDIO You speak this to fetch me in, my lord.

DON PEDRO By my troth, I speak my thought. 210

CLAUDIO And in faith, my lord, I spoke mine.

BENEDICK And by my two faiths and troths, my lord, I spoke mine.

CLAUDIO That I love her, I feel.

DON PEDRO That she is worthy, I know. 215

BENEDICK That I neither feel how she should be loved nor

know how she should be worthy is the opinion that fire cannot melt out of me. I will die in it at the stake.

DON PEDRO Thou wast ever an obstinate heretic in the despite of beauty.   220

CLAUDIO And never could maintain his part but in the force of his will.

BENEDICK That a woman conceived me, I thank her. That she brought me up, I likewise give her most humble thanks. But that I will have a recheat winded in my forehead, or hang my bugle in an invisible baldric, all women shall pardon me. Because I will not do them the wrong to mistrust any, I will do myself the right to trust none. And the fine is—for the which I may go the finer—I will live a bachelor.   230

DON PEDRO I shall see thee ere I die look pale with love.

BENEDICK With anger, with sickness, or with hunger, my lord; not with love. Prove that ever I lose more blood with love than I will get again with drinking, pick out mine eyes with a ballad-maker's pen and hang me up at the door of a brothel house for the sign of blind Cupid.

DON PEDRO Well, if ever thou dost fall from this faith thou wilt prove a notable argument.   239

BENEDICK If I do, hang me in a bottle like a cat, and shoot at me, and he that hits me, let him be clapped on the shoulder and called Adam.

DON PEDRO Well, as time shall try. 'In time the savage bull doth bear the yoke.'   244

BENEDICK The savage bull may, but if ever the sensible Benedick bear it, pluck off the bull's horns and set them in my forehead, and let me be vilely painted, and in such great letters as they write 'Here is good horse to hire' let them signify under my sign 'Here you may see Benedick, the married man'.   250

CLAUDIO If this should ever happen thou wouldst be horn-mad.

DON PEDRO Nay, if Cupid have not spent all his quiver in Venice thou wilt quake for this shortly.

BENEDICK I look for an earthquake too, then.   255

DON PEDRO Well, you will temporize with the hours. In the mean time, good Signor Benedick, repair to Leonato's, commend me to him, and tell him I will not fail him at supper, for indeed he hath made great preparation.   260

BENEDICK I have almost matter enough in me for such an embassage. And so I commit you—

CLAUDIO To the tuition of God, from my house if I had it—

DON PEDRO The sixth of July,   265
                     Your loving friend,
                                          Benedick.

BENEDICK Nay, mock not, mock not. The body of your discourse is sometime guarded with fragments, and the guards are but slightly basted on neither. Ere you flout old ends any further, examine your conscience. And so I leave you.   *Exit*

CLAUDIO

My liege, your highness now may do me good.

DON PEDRO

My love is thine to teach. Teach it but how
And thou shalt see how apt it is to learn   275
Any hard lesson that may do thee good.

CLAUDIO

Hath Leonato any son, my lord?

DON PEDRO

No child but Hero. She's his only heir.
Dost thou affect her, Claudio?

CLAUDIO   O my lord,
When you went onward on this ended action   280
I looked upon her with a soldier's eye,
That liked, but had a rougher task in hand
Than to drive liking to the name of love.
But now I am returned, and that war-thoughts
Have left their places vacant, in their rooms   285
Come thronging soft and delicate desires,
All prompting me how fair young Hero is,
Saying I liked her ere I went to wars.

DON PEDRO

Thou wilt be like a lover presently,
And tire the hearer with a book of words.   290
If thou dost love fair Hero, cherish it,
And I will break with her, and with her father,
And thou shalt have her. Was't not to this end
That thou began'st to twist so fine a story?

CLAUDIO

How sweetly you do minister to love,   295
That know love's grief by his complexion!
But lest my liking might too sudden seem
I would have salved it with a longer treatise.

DON PEDRO

What need the bridge much broader than the flood?
The fairest grant is the necessity.   300
Look what will serve is fit. 'Tis once: thou lovest,
And I will fit thee with the remedy.
I know we shall have revelling tonight.
I will assume thy part in some disguise,
And tell fair Hero I am Claudio.   305
And in her bosom I'll unclasp my heart
And take her hearing prisoner with the force
And strong encounter of my amorous tale.
Then after to her father will I break,
And the conclusion is, she shall be thine.   310
In practice let us put it presently.   *Exeunt*

1.2   *Enter Leonato and Antonio, an old man brother to*
       Leonato, severally

LEONATO How now, brother, where is my cousin, your son? Hath he provided this music?

ANTONIO He is very busy about it. But brother, I can tell you strange news that you yet dreamt not of.

LEONATO Are they good?   5

ANTONIO As the event stamps them. But they have a good cover, they show well outward. The Prince and Count Claudio, walking in a thick-pleached alley in mine orchard, were thus much overheard by a man of mine: the Prince discovered to Claudio that he loved my niece, your daughter, and meant to acknowledge it this night in a dance, and if he found her accordant he meant to take the present time by the top and instantly break with you of it.

LEONATO Hath the fellow any wit that told you this?   15

ANTONIO A good sharp fellow. I will send for him, and question him yourself.

LEONATO No, no. We will hold it as a dream till it appear itself. But I will acquaint my daughter withal, that she may be the better prepared for an answer if peradventure this be true. Go you and tell her of it.   21

⌈Enter attendants⌉

Cousins, you know what you have to do. O, I cry you mercy, friend. Go you with me and I will use your skill.—Good cousin, have a care this busy time.

Exeunt

1.3   *Enter Don John the bastard and Conrad, his companion*

CONRAD What the goodyear, my lord, why are you thus out of measure sad?

DON JOHN There is no measure in the occasion that breeds it, therefore the sadness is without limit.

CONRAD You should hear reason.   5

DON JOHN And when I have heard it, what blessing brings it?

CONRAD If not a present remedy, at least a patient sufferance.   9

DON JOHN I wonder that thou—being, as thou sayst thou art, born under Saturn—goest about to apply a moral medicine to a mortifying mischief. I cannot hide what I am. I must be sad when I have cause, and smile at no man's jests; eat when I have stomach, and wait for no man's leisure; sleep when I am drowsy, and tend on no man's business; laugh when I am merry, and claw no man in his humour.   17

CONRAD Yea, but you must not make the full show of this till you may do it without controlment. You have of late stood out against your brother, and he hath ta'en you newly into his grace, where it is impossible you should take true root but by the fair weather that you make yourself. It is needful that you frame the season for your own harvest.   24

DON JOHN I had rather be a canker in a hedge than a rose in his grace, and it better fits my blood to be disdained of all than to fashion a carriage to rob love from any. In this, though I cannot be said to be a flattering honest man, it must not be denied but I am a plain-dealing villain. I am trusted with a muzzle, and enfranchised with a clog. Therefore I have decreed not to sing in my cage. If I had my mouth I would bite. If I had my liberty I would do my liking. In the mean time, let me be that I am, and seek not to alter me.

CONRAD Can you make no use of your discontent?   35

DON JOHN I make all use of it, for I use it only. Who comes here?

Enter Borachio

What news, Borachio?

BORACHIO I came yonder from a great supper. The Prince your brother is royally entertained by Leonato, and I can give you intelligence of an intended marriage.   41

DON JOHN Will it serve for any model to build mischief on? What is he for a fool that betroths himself to unquietness?

BORACHIO Marry, it is your brother's right hand.   45

DON JOHN Who, the most exquisite Claudio?

BORACHIO Even he.

DON JOHN A proper squire. And who, and who? Which way looks he?

BORACHIO Marry, on Hero, the daughter and heir of Leonato.   51

DON JOHN A very forward March chick. How came you to this?

BORACHIO Being entertained for a perfumer, as I was smoking a musty room comes me the Prince and Claudio hand in hand, in sad conference. I whipped me behind the arras, and there heard it agreed upon that the Prince should woo Hero for himself and, having obtained her, give her to Count Claudio.   59

DON JOHN Come, come, let us thither. This may prove food to my displeasure. That young start-up hath all the glory of my overthrow. If I can cross him any way I bless myself every way. You are both sure, and will assist me?

CONRAD To the death, my lord.   65

DON JOHN Let us to the great supper. Their cheer is the greater that I am subdued. Would the cook were o' my mind. Shall we go prove what's to be done?

BORACHIO We'll wait upon your lordship.   *Exeunt*

2.1   *Enter Leonato, Antonio his brother, Hero his daughter, Beatrice his niece, ⌈Margaret, and Ursula⌉*

LEONATO Was not Count John here at supper?

ANTONIO I saw him not.

BEATRICE How tartly that gentleman looks. I never can see him but I am heartburned an hour after.

HERO He is of a very melancholy disposition.   5

BEATRICE He were an excellent man that were made just in the midway between him and Benedick. The one is too like an image and says nothing, and the other too like my lady's eldest son, evermore tattling.   9

LEONATO Then half Signor Benedick's tongue in Count John's mouth, and half Count John's melancholy in Signor Benedick's face—

BEATRICE With a good leg and a good foot, uncle, and money enough in his purse—such a man would win any woman in the world, if a could get her good will.

LEONATO By my troth, niece, thou wilt never get thee a husband if thou be so shrewd of thy tongue.

ANTONIO In faith, she's too curst.

BEATRICE Too curst is more than curst. I shall lessen God's sending that way, for it is said God sends a curst cow short horns, but to a cow too curst he sends none.   21

LEONATO So, by being too curst, God will send you no horns.

BEATRICE Just, if he send me no husband, for the which

blessing I am at him upon my knees every morning
and evening. Lord, I could not endure a husband with
a beard on his face. I had rather lie in the woollen.   27
LEONATO You may light on a husband that hath no beard.
BEATRICE What should I do with him—dress him in my
apparel and make him my waiting gentlewoman? He
that hath a beard is more than a youth, and he that
hath no beard is less than a man; and he that is more
than a youth is not for me, and he that is less than a
man, I am not for him. Therefore I will even take
sixpence in earnest of the bearherd and lead his apes
into hell.   36
LEONATO Well then, go you into hell?
BEATRICE No, but to the gate, and there will the devil
meet me like an old cuckold with horns on his head,
and say, 'Get you to heaven, Beatrice, get you to
heaven. Here's no place for you maids.' So deliver I up
my apes and away to Saint Peter fore the heavens. He
shows me where the bachelors sit, and there live we
as merry as the day is long.
ANTONIO (to Hero) Well, niece, I trust you will be ruled
by your father.   46
BEATRICE Yes, faith, it is my cousin's duty to make curtsy
and say, 'Father, as it please you.' But yet for all that,
cousin, let him be a handsome fellow, or else make
another curtsy and say, 'Father, as it please me.'   50
LEONATO Well, niece, I hope to see you one day fitted
with a husband.
BEATRICE Not till God make men of some other mettle
than earth. Would it not grieve a woman to be
overmastered with a piece of valiant dust?—to make
an account of her life to a clod of wayward marl? No,
uncle, I'll none. Adam's sons are my brethren, and
truly I hold it a sin to match in my kindred.
LEONATO (to Hero) Daughter, remember what I told you.
If the Prince do solicit you in that kind, you know your
answer.   61
BEATRICE The fault will be in the music, cousin, if you be
not wooed in good time. If the Prince be too important,
tell him there is measure in everything, and so dance
out the answer. For hear me, Hero, wooing, wedding,
and repenting is as a Scotch jig, a measure, and a
cinquepace. The first suit is hot and hasty, like a Scotch
jig—and full as fantastical; the wedding mannerly
modest, as a measure, full of state and ancientry. And
then comes repentance, and with his bad legs falls into
the cinquepace faster and faster till he sink into his
grave.   72
LEONATO Cousin, you apprehend passing shrewdly.
BEATRICE I have a good eye, uncle. I can see a church by
daylight.   75
LEONATO The revellers are entering, brother. Make good
room.
    Enter Don Pedro, Claudio, Benedick, and Balthasar,
    all masked, Don John, and Borachio, ⌈with a
    drummer⌉
DON PEDRO (to Hero) Lady, will you walk a bout with your
friend?   79
HERO So you walk softly, and look sweetly, and say

nothing, I am yours for the walk; and especially when
I walk away.
DON PEDRO With me in your company?
HERO I may say so when I please.
DON PEDRO And when please you to say so?   85
HERO When I like your favour; for God defend the lute
should be like the case.
DON PEDRO
My visor is Philemon's roof. Within the house is Jove.
HERO
Why, then, your visor should be thatched.
DON PEDRO   Speak low if you speak love.
    They move aside
⌈BALTHASAR⌉ (to Margaret) Well, I would you did like me.
MARGARET So would not I, for your own sake, for I have
many ill qualities.
⌈BALTHASAR⌉ Which is one?
MARGARET I say my prayers aloud.
⌈BALTHASAR⌉ I love you the better—the hearers may cry
amen.   96
MARGARET God match me with a good dancer.
BALTHASAR Amen.
MARGARET And God keep him out of my sight when the
dance is done. Answer, clerk.   100
BALTHASAR No more words. The clerk is answered.
    They move aside
URSULA (to Antonio) I know you well enough, you are
Signor Antonio.
ANTONIO At a word, I am not.
URSULA I know you by the waggling of your head.   105
ANTONIO To tell you true, I counterfeit him.
URSULA You could never do him so ill-well unless you
were the very man. Here's his dry hand up and down.
You are he, you are he.
ANTONIO At a word, I am not.   110
URSULA Come, come, do you think I do not know you by
your excellent wit? Can virtue hide itself? Go to, mum,
you are he. Graces will appear, and there's an end.
    They move aside
BEATRICE (to Benedick) Will you not tell me who told you
so?   115
BENEDICK No, you shall pardon me.
BEATRICE Nor will you not tell me who you are?
BENEDICK Not now.
BEATRICE That I was disdainful, and that I had my good
wit out of the Hundred Merry Tales—well, this was
Signor Benedick that said so.   121
BENEDICK What's he?
BEATRICE I am sure you know him well enough.
BENEDICK Not I, believe me.
BEATRICE Did he never make you laugh?   125
BENEDICK I pray you, what is he?
BEATRICE Why, he is the Prince's jester, a very dull fool.
Only his gift is in devising impossible slanders. None
but libertines delight in him, and the commendation is
not in his wit but in his villainy, for he both pleases
men and angers them, and then they laugh at him,
and beat him. I am sure he is in the fleet. I would he
had boarded me.

BENEDICK When I know the gentleman, I'll tell him what you say.   135

BEATRICE Do, do. He'll but break a comparison or two on me, which peradventure not marked, or not laughed at, strikes him into melancholy, and then there's a partridge wing saved, for the fool will eat no supper that night.   140

⌜Music⌝

We must follow the leaders.

BENEDICK In every good thing.

BEATRICE Nay, if they lead to any ill I will leave them at the next turning.   144

Dance. Exeunt all but Don John, Borachio, and Claudio

DON JOHN (*aside to Borachio*) Sure my brother is amorous on Hero, and hath withdrawn her father to break with him about it. The ladies follow her, and but one visor remains.

BORACHIO (*aside to Don John*) And that is Claudio. I know him by his bearing.   150

DON JOHN Are not you Signor Benedick?

CLAUDIO You know me well. I am he.

DON JOHN Signor, you are very near my brother in his love. He is enamoured on Hero. I pray you dissuade him from her. She is no equal for his birth. You may do the part of an honest man in it.   156

CLAUDIO How know you he loves her?

DON JOHN I heard him swear his affection.

BORACHIO So did I, too, and he swore he would marry her tonight.   160

DON JOHN Come, let us to the banquet.

Exeunt all but Claudio

CLAUDIO
Thus answer I in name of Benedick,
But hear these ill news with the ears of Claudio.
'Tis certain so, the Prince woos for himself.
Friendship is constant in all other things   165
Save in the office and affairs of love.
Therefore all hearts in love use their own tongues.
Let every eye negotiate for itself,
And trust no agent; for beauty is a witch
Against whose charms faith melteth into blood.   170
This is an accident of hourly proof,
Which I mistrusted not. Farewell, therefore, Hero.

Enter Benedick

BENEDICK Count Claudio?

CLAUDIO Yea, the same.

BENEDICK Come, will you go with me?   175

CLAUDIO Whither?

BENEDICK Even to the next willow, about your own business, County. What fashion will you wear the garland of? About your neck, like an usurer's chain? Or under your arm, like a lieutenant's scarf? You must wear it one way, for the Prince hath got your Hero.

CLAUDIO I wish him joy of her.

BENEDICK Why, that's spoken like an honest drover; so they sell bullocks. But did you think the Prince would have served you thus?   185

CLAUDIO I pray you leave me.

BENEDICK Ho, now you strike like the blind man—'twas the boy that stole your meat, and you'll beat the post.

CLAUDIO If it will not be, I'll leave you.   *Exit*

BENEDICK Alas, poor hurt fowl, now will he creep into sedges. But that my Lady Beatrice should know me, and not know me! The Prince's fool! Ha, it may be I go under that title because I am merry. Yea, but so I am apt to do myself wrong. I am not so reputed. It is the base, though bitter, disposition of Beatrice that puts the world into her person, and so gives me out. Well, I'll be revenged as I may.

Enter Don Pedro the Prince

DON PEDRO Now, signor, where's the Count? Did you see him?   199

BENEDICK Troth, my lord, I have played the part of Lady Fame. I found him here as melancholy as a lodge in a warren. I told him—and I think I told him true—that your grace had got the good will of this young lady, and I offered him my company to a willow tree, either to make him a garland, as being forsaken, or to bind him up a rod, as being worthy to be whipped.   206

DON PEDRO To be whipped—what's his fault?

BENEDICK The flat transgression of a schoolboy who, being overjoyed with finding a bird's nest, shows it his companion, and he steals it.   210

DON PEDRO Wilt thou make a trust a transgression? The transgression is in the stealer.

BENEDICK Yet it had not been amiss the rod had been made, and the garland too, for the garland he might have worn himself, and the rod he might have bestowed on you, who, as I take it, have stolen his bird's nest.

DON PEDRO I will but teach them to sing, and restore them to the owner.

BENEDICK If their singing answer your saying, by my faith you say honestly.   220

DON PEDRO The Lady Beatrice hath a quarrel to you. The gentleman that danced with her told her she is much wronged by you.   223

BENEDICK O, she misused me past the endurance of a block. An oak but with one green leaf on it would have answered her. My very visor began to assume life and scold with her. She told me—not thinking I had been myself—that I was the Prince's jester, that I was duller than a great thaw, huddling jest upon jest with such impossible conveyance upon me that I stood like a man at a mark, with a whole army shooting at me. She speaks poniards, and every word stabs. If her breath were as terrible as her terminations, there were no living near her, she would infect to the North Star. I would not marry her though she were endowed with all that Adam had left him before he transgressed. She would have made Hercules have turned spit, yea, and have cleft his club to make the fire, too. Come, talk not of her. You shall find her the infernal Ate in good apparel. I would to God some scholar would conjure her, for certainly, while she is here a man may live as quiet in hell as in a sanctuary, and people sin upon purpose because they would go thither, so indeed all disquiet, horror, and perturbation follows her.

Enter Claudio and Beatrice, ⌜and Leonato with Hero⌝

DON PEDRO Look, here she comes.   245

BENEDICK Will your grace command me any service to the world's end? I will go on the slightest errand now to the Antipodes that you can devise to send me on. I will fetch you a tooth-picker now from the furthest inch of Asia, bring you the length of Prester John's foot, fetch you a hair off the Great Cham's beard, do you any embassage to the pigmies, rather than hold three words' conference with this harpy. You have no employment for me?

DON PEDRO None but to desire your good company.   255

BENEDICK O God, sir, here's a dish I love not. I cannot endure my Lady Tongue.   *Exit*

DON PEDRO Come, lady, come, you have lost the heart of Signor Benedick.   259

BEATRICE Indeed, my lord, he lent it me a while, and I gave him use for it, a double heart for his single one. Marry, once before he won it of me, with false dice. Therefore your grace may well say I have lost it.

DON PEDRO You have put him down, lady, you have put him down.   265

BEATRICE So I would not he should do me, my lord, lest I should prove the mother of fools. I have brought Count Claudio, whom you sent me to seek.

DON PEDRO Why, how now, Count, wherefore are you sad?   270

CLAUDIO Not sad, my lord.

DON PEDRO How then? Sick?

CLAUDIO Neither, my lord.

BEATRICE The Count is neither sad, nor sick, nor merry, nor well, but civil count, civil as an orange, and something of that jealous complexion.   276

DON PEDRO I'faith, lady, I think your blazon to be true, though I'll be sworn, if he be so, his conceit is false. Here, Claudio, I have wooed in thy name, and fair Hero is won. I have broke with her father and his good will obtained. Name the day of marriage, and God give thee joy.

LEONATO Count, take of me my daughter, and with her my fortunes. His grace hath made the match, and all grace say amen to it.   285

BEATRICE Speak, Count, 'tis your cue.

CLAUDIO Silence is the perfectest herald of joy. I were but little happy if I could say how much. (*To Hero*) Lady, as you are mine, I am yours. I give away myself for you, and dote upon the exchange.   290

BEATRICE (*to Hero*) Speak, cousin. Or, if you cannot, stop his mouth with a kiss, and let not him speak, neither.

DON PEDRO In faith, lady, you have a merry heart.

BEATRICE Yea, my lord, I thank it. Poor fool, it keeps on the windy side of care.—My cousin tells him in his ear that he is in her heart.   296

CLAUDIO And so she doth, cousin.

BEATRICE Good Lord, for alliance! Thus goes everyone to the world but I, and I am sunburnt. I may sit in a corner and cry 'Heigh-ho for a husband'.   300

DON PEDRO Lady Beatrice, I will get you one.

BEATRICE I would rather have one of your father's getting. Hath your grace ne'er a brother like you? Your father got excellent husbands if a maid could come by them.

DON PEDRO Will you have me, lady?   305

BEATRICE No, my lord, unless I might have another for working days. Your grace is too costly to wear every day. But I beseech your grace, pardon me. I was born to speak all mirth and no matter.   309

DON PEDRO Your silence most offends me, and to be merry best becomes you; for out o' question, you were born in a merry hour.

BEATRICE No, sure, my lord, my mother cried. But then there was a star danced, and under that was I born. (*To Hero and Claudio*) Cousins, God give you joy.   315

LEONATO Niece, will you look to those things I told you of?

BEATRICE I cry you mercy, uncle. (*To Don Pedro*) By your grace's pardon.   *Exit Beatrice*

DON PEDRO By my troth, a pleasant-spirited lady.   320

LEONATO There's little of the melancholy element in her, my lord. She is never sad but when she sleeps, and not ever sad then; for I have heard my daughter say she hath often dreamt of unhappiness and waked herself with laughing.   325

DON PEDRO She cannot endure to hear tell of a husband.

LEONATO O, by no means. She mocks all her wooers out of suit.

DON PEDRO She were an excellent wife for Benedick.

LEONATO O Lord, my lord, if they were but a week married they would talk themselves mad.   331

DON PEDRO County Claudio, when mean you to go to church?

CLAUDIO Tomorrow, my lord. Time goes on crutches till love have all his rites.   335

LEONATO Not till Monday, my dear son, which is hence a just sevennight, and a time too brief, too, to have all things answer my mind.

DON PEDRO Come, you shake the head at so long a breathing, but I warrant thee, Claudio, the time shall not go dully by us. I will in the interim undertake one of Hercules' labours, which is to bring Signor Benedick and the Lady Beatrice into a mountain of affection th'one with th'other. I would fain have it a match, and I doubt not but to fashion it, if you three will but minister such assistance as I shall give you direction.

LEONATO My lord, I am for you, though it cost me ten nights' watchings.

CLAUDIO And I, my lord.

DON PEDRO And you too, gentle Hero?   350

HERO I will do any modest office, my lord, to help my cousin to a good husband.

DON PEDRO And Benedick is not the unhopefullest husband that I know. Thus far can I praise him: he is of a noble

strain, of approved valour and confirmed honesty. I
will teach you how to humour your cousin that she
shall fall in love with Benedick, and I, with your two
helps, will so practise on Benedick that, in despite of
his quick wit and his queasy stomach, he shall fall in
love with Beatrice. If we can do this, Cupid is no longer
an archer; his glory shall be ours, for we are the only
love-gods. Go in with me, and I will tell you my drift.

                                                  Exeunt

2.2   *Enter Don John and Borachio*

DON JOHN It is so. The Count Claudio shall marry the
   daughter of Leonato.

BORACHIO Yea, my lord, but I can cross it.

DON JOHN Any bar, any cross, any impediment will be
   medicinable to me. I am sick in displeasure to him, and
   whatsoever comes athwart his affection ranges evenly
   with mine. How canst thou cross this marriage?

BORACHIO Not honestly, my lord, but so covertly that no
   dishonesty shall appear in me.

DON JOHN Show me briefly how.   10

BORACHIO I think I told your lordship a year since how
   much I am in the favour of Margaret, the waiting
   gentlewoman to Hero.

DON JOHN I remember.   14

BORACHIO I can at any unseasonable instant of the night
   appoint her to look out at her lady's chamber window.

DON JOHN What life is in that to be the death of this
   marriage?

BORACHIO The poison of that lies in you to temper. Go
   you to the Prince your brother. Spare not to tell him
   that he hath wronged his honour in marrying the
   renowned Claudio—whose estimation do you mightily
   hold up—to a contaminated stale, such a one as Hero.

DON JOHN What proof shall I make of that?   24

BORACHIO Proof enough to misuse the Prince, to vex
   Claudio, to undo Hero, and kill Leonato. Look you for
   any other issue?

DON JOHN Only to despite them I will endeavour anything.

BORACHIO Go then. Find me a meet hour to draw Don
   Pedro and the Count Claudio alone. Tell them that you
   know that Hero loves me. Intend a kind of zeal both
   to the Prince and Claudio as in love of your brother's
   honour who hath made this match, and his friend's
   reputation who is thus like to be cozened with the
   semblance of a maid, that you have discovered thus.
   They will scarcely believe this without trial. Offer them
   instances, which shall bear no less likelihood than to
   see me at her chamber window, hear me call Margaret
   Hero, hear Margaret term me Claudio. And bring them
   to see this the very night before the intended wedding,
   for in the mean time I will so fashion the matter that
   Hero shall be absent, and there shall appear such
   seeming truth of Hero's disloyalty that jealousy shall
   be called assurance, and all the preparation overthrown.   45

DON JOHN Grow this to what adverse issue it can, I will
   put it in practice. Be cunning in the working this, and
   thy fee is a thousand ducats.

BORACHIO Be you constant in the accusation, and my
   cunning shall not shame me.   50

DON JOHN I will presently go learn their day of marriage.

                                                  Exeunt

2.3   *Enter Benedick*

BENEDICK Boy!

             ⌈*Enter Boy*⌉

BOY Signor?

BENEDICK In my chamber window lies a book. Bring it
   hither to me in the orchard.

BOY I am here already, sir.   5

BENEDICK I know that, but I would have thee hence and
   here again.   ⌈*Exit Boy*⌉
I do much wonder that one man, seeing how much
another man is a fool when he dedicates his behaviours
to love, will, after he hath laughed at such shallow
follies in others, become the argument of his own scorn
by falling in love. And such a man is Claudio. I have
known when there was no music with him but the
drum and the fife, and now had he rather hear the
tabor and the pipe. I have known when he would have
walked ten mile afoot to see a good armour, and now
will he lie ten nights awake carving the fashion of a
new doublet. He was wont to speak plain and to the
purpose, like an honest man and a soldier, and now is
he turned orthography. His words are a very fantastical
banquet, just so many strange dishes. May I be so
converted, and see with these eyes? I cannot tell. I
think not. I will not be sworn but love may transform
me to an oyster, but I'll take my oath on it, till he
have made an oyster of me he shall never make me
such a fool. One woman is fair, yet I am well. Another
is wise, yet I am well. Another virtuous, yet I am well.
But till all graces be in one woman, one woman shall
not come in my grace. Rich she shall be, that's certain.
Wise, or I'll none. Virtuous, or I'll never cheapen her.
Fair, or I'll never look on her. Mild, or come not near
me. Noble, or not I for an angel. Of good discourse, an
excellent musician, and her hair shall be of what colour
it please God. Ha! The Prince and Monsieur Love. I
will hide me in the arbour.   35

    He hides.

    Enter Don Pedro the Prince, Leonato, and Claudio

DON PEDRO Come, shall we hear this music?

CLAUDIO

Yea, my good lord. How still the evening is,

As hushed on purpose to grace harmony.

DON PEDRO (*aside*)

See you where Benedick hath hid himself?

CLAUDIO (*aside*)

O, very well, my lord. The music ended,   40

We'll fit the hid-fox with a pennyworth.

    Enter Balthasar with music

DON PEDRO

Come, Balthasar, we'll hear that song again.

BALTHASAR

O good my lord, tax not so bad a voice

To slander music any more than once.

DON PEDRO
  It is the witness still of excellency   45
  To put a strange face on his own perfection.
  I pray thee sing, and let me woo no more.
BALTHASAR
  Because you talk of wooing I will sing,
  Since many a wooer doth commence his suit
  To her he thinks not worthy, yet he woos,   50
  Yet will he swear he loves.
DON PEDRO   Nay pray thee, come;
  Or if thou wilt hold longer argument,
  Do it in notes.
BALTHASAR   Note this before my notes:
  There's not a note of mine that's worth the noting.
DON PEDRO
  Why, these are very crotchets that he speaks—   55
  Note notes, forsooth, and nothing!
    The accompaniment begins
BENEDICK Now, divine air! Now is his soul ravished. Is it
  not strange that sheep's guts should hale souls out of
  men's bodies? Well, a horn for my money, when all's
  done.   60

BALTHASAR (*sings*)
      Sigh no more, ladies, sigh no more.
        Men were deceivers ever,
      One foot in sea, and one on shore,
        To one thing constant never.
      Then sigh not so, but let them go,   65
        And be you blithe and bonny,
      Converting all your sounds of woe
        Into hey nonny, nonny.

      Sing no more ditties, sing no more
        Of dumps so dull and heavy.   70
      The fraud of men was ever so
        Since summer first was leafy.
      Then sigh not so, but let them go,
        And be you blithe and bonny,
      Converting all your sounds of woe   75
        Into hey nonny, nonny.

DON PEDRO By my troth, a good song.
BALTHASAR And an ill singer, my lord.
DON PEDRO Ha, no, no, faith. Thou singest well enough
  for a shift.   80
BENEDICK (*aside*) An he had been a dog that should have
  howled thus, they would have hanged him; and I pray
  God his bad voice bode no mischief. I had as lief have
  heard the night-raven, come what plague could have
  come after it.   85
DON PEDRO Yea, marry, dost thou hear, Balthasar? I pray
  thee get us some excellent music, for tomorrow night
  we would have it at the Lady Hero's chamber window.
BALTHASAR The best I can, my lord.   *Exit*
DON PEDRO Do so. Farewell. Come hither, Leonato. What
  was it you told me of today, that your niece Beatrice
  was in love with Signor Benedick?   92
CLAUDIO (*aside*) O, ay, stalk on, stalk on. The fowl sits.—
  I did never think that lady would have loved any man.

LEONATO No, nor I neither. But most wonderful that she
  should so dote on Signor Benedick, whom she hath in
  all outward behaviours seemed ever to abhor.
BENEDICK (*aside*) Is't possible? Sits the wind in that corner?
LEONATO By my troth, my lord, I cannot tell what to
  think of it. But that she loves him with an enraged
  affection, it is past the infinite of thought.   101
DON PEDRO Maybe she doth but counterfeit.
CLAUDIO Faith, like enough.
LEONATO O God! Counterfeit? There was never counterfeit
  of passion came so near the life of passion as she
  discovers it.   106
DON PEDRO Why, what effects of passion shows she?
CLAUDIO (*aside*) Bait the hook well. This fish will bite.
LEONATO What effects, my lord? She will sit you—you
  heard my daughter tell you how.   110
CLAUDIO She did indeed.
DON PEDRO How, how, I pray you? You amaze me. I
  would have thought her spirit had been invincible
  against all assaults of affection.
LEONATO I would have sworn it had, my lord, especially
  against Benedick.   116
BENEDICK (*aside*) I should think this a gull, but that the
  white-bearded fellow speaks it. Knavery cannot, sure,
  hide himself in such reverence.
CLAUDIO (*aside*) He hath ta'en th'infection. Hold it up. 120
DON PEDRO Hath she made her affection known to
  Benedick?
LEONATO No, and swears she never will. That's her
  torment.   124
CLAUDIO 'Tis true, indeed, so your daughter says. 'Shall
  I,' says she, 'that have so oft encountered him with
  scorn, write to him that I love him?'
LEONATO This says she now when she is beginning to
  write to him, for she'll be up twenty times a night, and
  there will she sit in her smock till she have writ a sheet
  of paper. My daughter tells us all.   131
CLAUDIO Now you talk of a sheet of paper, I remember a
  pretty jest your daughter told us of.
LEONATO O, when she had writ it and was reading it over,
  she found Benedick and Beatrice between the sheet.
CLAUDIO That.   136
LEONATO O, she tore the letter into a thousand halfpence,
  railed at herself that she should be so immodest to
  write to one that she knew would flout her. 'I measure
  him,' says she, 'by my own spirit, for I should flout
  him if he writ to me, yea, though I love him I should.'
CLAUDIO Then down upon her knees she falls, weeps,
  sobs, beats her heart, tears her hair, prays, curses, 'O
  sweet Benedick, God give me patience.'   144
LEONATO She doth indeed, my daughter says, and so the
  ecstasy hath so much overborne her that my daughter
  is sometime afeard she will do a desperate outrage to
  herself. It is very true.
DON PEDRO It were good that Benedick knew of it by some
  other, if she will not discover it.   150
CLAUDIO To what end? He would make but a sport of it
  and torment the poor lady worse.
DON PEDRO An he should, it were an alms to hang him.

She's an excellent sweet lady, and, out of all suspicion, she is virtuous.   155

CLAUDIO And she is exceeding wise.

DON PEDRO In everything but in loving Benedick.

LEONATO O my lord, wisdom and blood combating in so tender a body, we have ten proofs to one that blood hath the victory. I am sorry for her, as I have just cause, being her uncle and her guardian.   161

DON PEDRO I would she had bestowed this dotage on me. I would have doffed all other respects and made her half myself. I pray you tell Benedick of it, and hear what a will say.   165

LEONATO Were it good, think you?

CLAUDIO Hero thinks surely she will die, for she says she will die if he love her not, and she will die ere she make her love known, and she will die if he woo her, rather than she will bate one breath of her accustomed crossness.   171

DON PEDRO She doth well. If she should make tender of her love 'tis very possible he'll scorn it, for the man, as you know all, hath a contemptible spirit.

CLAUDIO He is a very proper man.   175

DON PEDRO He hath indeed a good outward happiness.

CLAUDIO Before God; and in my mind, very wise.

DON PEDRO He doth indeed show some sparks that are like wit.

CLAUDIO And I take him to be valiant.   180

DON PEDRO As Hector, I assure you; and in the managing of quarrels you may say he is wise, for either he avoids them with great discretion or undertakes them with a most Christianlike fear.   184

LEONATO If he do fear God, a must necessarily keep peace. If he break the peace, he ought to enter into a quarrel with fear and trembling.

DON PEDRO And so will he do, for the man doth fear God, howsoever it seems not in him by some large jests he will make. Well, I am sorry for your niece. Shall we go seek Benedick and tell him of her love?   191

CLAUDIO Never tell him, my lord. Let her wear it out with good counsel.

LEONATO Nay, that's impossible. She may wear her heart out first.   195

DON PEDRO Well, we will hear further of it by your daughter. Let it cool the while. I love Benedick well, and I could wish he would modestly examine himself to see how much he is unworthy so good a lady.

LEONATO My lord, will you walk? Dinner is ready.   200

CLAUDIO (aside) If he do not dote on her upon this, I will never trust my expectation.

DON PEDRO (aside) Let there be the same net spread for her, and that must your daughter and her gentlewomen carry. The sport will be when they hold one an opinion of another's dotage, and no such matter. That's the scene that I would see, which will be merely a dumb show. Let us send her to call him in to dinner.

Exeunt Don Pedro, Claudio, and Leonato

BENEDICK (coming forward) This can be no trick. The conference was sadly borne. They have the truth of this from Hero. They seem to pity the lady. It seems

her affections have their full bent. Love me! Why, it must be requited. I hear how I am censured. They say I will bear myself proudly if I perceive the love come from her. They say too that she will rather die than give any sign of affection. I did never think to marry. I must not seem proud. Happy are they that hear their detractions and can put them to mending. They say the lady is fair. 'Tis a truth, I can bear them witness. And virtuous—'tis so, I cannot reprove it. And wise, but for loving me. By my troth, it is no addition to her wit—nor no great argument of her folly, for I will be horribly in love with her. I may chance have some odd quirks and remnants of wit broken on me because I have railed so long against marriage; but doth not the appetite alter? A man loves the meat in his youth that he cannot endure in his age. Shall quips and sentences and these paper bullets of the brain awe a man from the career of his humour? No. The world must be peopled. When I said I would die a bachelor, I did not think I should live till I were married. Here comes Beatrice.   232

Enter Beatrice

By this day, she's a fair lady. I do spy some marks of love in her.

BEATRICE Against my will I am sent to bid you come in to dinner.   236

BENEDICK
Fair Beatrice, I thank you for your pains.

BEATRICE I took no more pains for those thanks than you take pains to thank me. If it had been painful I would not have come.   240

BENEDICK You take pleasure, then, in the message?

BEATRICE Yea, just so much as you may take upon a knife's point and choke a daw withal. You have no stomach, signor? Fare you well.   *Exit*

BENEDICK Ha! 'Against my will I am sent to bid you come in to dinner.' There's a double meaning in that. 'I took no more pains for those thanks than you took pains to thank me.' That's as much as to say 'Any pains that I take for you is as easy as thanks.'—If I do not take pity of her I am a villain. If I do not love her I am a Jew. I will go get her picture.   *Exit*

3.1   *Enter Hero and two gentlewomen, Margaret and Ursula*

HERO
Good Margaret, run thee to the parlour.
There shalt thou find my cousin Beatrice
Proposing with the Prince and Claudio.
Whisper her ear, and tell her I and Ursula
Walk in the orchard, and our whole discourse   5
Is all of her. Say that thou overheard'st us,
And bid her steal into the pleachèd bower
Where honeysuckles, ripened by the sun,
Forbid the sun to enter—like favourites
Made proud by princes, that advance their pride   10
Against that power that bred it. There will she hide her
To listen our propose. This is thy office.
Bear thee well in it, and leave us alone.

MARGARET
I'll make her come, I warrant you, presently. *Exit*

HERO
Now, Ursula, when Beatrice doth come,   15
As we do trace this alley up and down
Our talk must only be of Benedick.
When I do name him, let it be thy part
To praise him more than ever man did merit.
My talk to thee must be how Benedick   20
Is sick in love with Beatrice. Of this matter
Is little Cupid's crafty arrow made,
That only wounds by hearsay.
        Enter Beatrice
                                    Now begin,
For look where Beatrice like a lapwing runs
Close by the ground to hear our conference.   25

URSULA
The pleasant'st angling is to see the fish
Cut with her golden oars the silver stream
And greedily devour the treacherous bait.
So angle we for Beatrice, who even now
Is couchèd in the woodbine coverture.   30
Fear you not my part of the dialogue.

HERO
Then go we near her, that her ear lose nothing
Of the false-sweet bait that we lay for it.—
        They approach Beatrice's hiding-place
No, truly, Ursula, she is too disdainful.
I know her spirits are as coy and wild   35
As haggards of the rock.

URSULA   But are you sure
That Benedick loves Beatrice so entirely?

HERO
So says the Prince and my new trothèd lord.

URSULA
And did they bid you tell her of it, madam?

HERO
They did entreat me to acquaint her of it,   40
But I persuaded them, if they loved Benedick,
To wish him wrestle with affection
And never to let Beatrice know of it.

URSULA
Why did you so? Doth not the gentleman
Deserve as full as fortunate a bed   45
As ever Beatrice shall couch upon?

HERO
O god of love! I know he doth deserve
As much as may be yielded to a man.
But nature never framed a woman's heart
Of prouder stuff than that of Beatrice.   50
Disdain and scorn ride sparkling in her eyes,
Misprising what they look on, and her wit
Values itself so highly that to her
All matter else seems weak. She cannot love,
Nor take no shape nor project of affection,   55
She is so self-endearèd.

URSULA   Sure, I think so.
And therefore certainly it were not good
She knew his love, lest she'll make sport at it.

HERO
Why, you speak truth. I never yet saw man,
How wise, how noble, young, how rarely featured,
But she would spell him backward. If fair-faced, 61
She would swear the gentleman should be her sister.
If black, why nature, drawing of an antic,
Made a foul blot. If tall, a lance ill headed;
If low, an agate very vilely cut;   65
If speaking, why, a vane blown with all winds;
If silent, why, a block movèd with none.
So turns she every man the wrong side out,
And never gives to truth and virtue that
Which simpleness and merit purchaseth.   70

URSULA
Sure, sure, such carping is not commendable.

HERO
No, not to be so odd and from all fashions
As Beatrice is cannot be commendable.
But who dare tell her so? If I should speak
She would mock me into air, O, she would laugh me
Out of myself, press me to death with wit.   76
Therefore let Benedick, like covered fire,
Consume away in sighs, waste inwardly.
It were a better death than die with mocks,
Which is as bad as die with tickling.   80

URSULA
Yet tell her of it, hear what she will say.

HERO
No. Rather I will go to Benedick
And counsel him to fight against his passion.
And truly, I'll devise some honest slanders
To stain my cousin with. One doth not know   85
How much an ill word may empoison liking.

URSULA
O, do not do your cousin such a wrong.
She cannot be so much without true judgement,
Having so swift and excellent a wit
As she is prized to have, as to refuse   90
So rare a gentleman as Signor Benedick.

HERO
He is the only man of Italy,
Always excepted my dear Claudio.

URSULA
I pray you be not angry with me, madam,
Speaking my fancy. Signor Benedick,   95
For shape, for bearing, argument, and valour
Goes foremost in report through Italy.

HERO
Indeed, he hath an excellent good name.

URSULA
His excellence did earn it ere he had it.
When are you married, madam?   100

HERO
Why, every day, tomorrow. Come, go in.
I'll show thee some attires and have thy counsel
Which is the best to furnish me tomorrow.

URSULA (*aside*)
She's limed, I warrant you. We have caught her,
        madam.

HERO (*aside*)
  If it prove so, then loving goes by haps.   105
  Some Cupid kills with arrows, some with traps.
                    Exeunt Hero and Ursula

BEATRICE (*coming forward*)
  What fire is in mine ears? Can this be true?
    Stand I condemned for pride and scorn so much?
  Contempt, farewell; and maiden pride, adieu.
    No glory lives behind the back of such.   110
  And, Benedick, love on. I will requite thee,
    Taming my wild heart to thy loving hand.
  If thou dost love, my kindness shall incite thee
    To bind our loves up in a holy band.
  For others say thou dost deserve, and I   115
  Believe it better than reportingly.   *Exit*

3.2   *Enter Don Pedro the Prince, Claudio, Benedick, and*
    Leonato

DON PEDRO I do but stay till your marriage be consummate, and then go I toward Aragon.

CLAUDIO I'll bring you thither, my lord, if you'll vouchsafe
  me.   4

DON PEDRO Nay, that would be as great a soil in the new
  gloss of your marriage as to show a child his new coat
  and forbid him to wear it. I will only be bold with
  Benedick for his company, for from the crown of his
  head to the sole of his foot he is all mirth. He hath
  twice or thrice cut Cupid's bow-string, and the little
  hangman dare not shoot at him. He hath a heart as
  sound as a bell, and his tongue is the clapper, for what
  his heart thinks his tongue speaks.

BENEDICK Gallants, I am not as I have been.

LEONATO So say I. Methinks you are sadder.   15

CLAUDIO I hope he be in love.

DON PEDRO Hang him, truant! There's no true drop of
  blood in him to be truly touched with love. If he be
  sad, he wants money.

BENEDICK I have the toothache.   20

DON PEDRO Draw it.

BENEDICK Hang it.

CLAUDIO You must hang it first and draw it afterwards.

DON PEDRO What? Sigh for the toothache?

LEONATO Where is but a humour or a worm.   25

BENEDICK Well, everyone can master a grief but he that
  has it.

CLAUDIO Yet say I he is in love.

DON PEDRO There is no appearance of fancy in him, unless
  it be a fancy that he hath to strange disguises, as to
  be a Dutchman today, a Frenchman tomorrow, or in
  the shape of two countries at once, as a German from
  the waist downward, all slops, and a Spaniard from
  the hip upward, no doublet. Unless he have a fancy to
  this foolery, as it appears he hath, he is no fool for
  fancy, as you would have it appear he is.   36

CLAUDIO If he be not in love with some woman there is
  no believing old signs. A brushes his hat o' mornings,
  what should that bode?

DON PEDRO Hath any man seen him at the barber's?   40

CLAUDIO No, but the barber's man hath been seen with
  him, and the old ornament of his cheek hath already
  stuffed tennis balls.

LEONATO Indeed, he looks younger than he did by the
  loss of a beard.   45

DON PEDRO Nay, a rubs himself with civet. Can you smell
  him out by that?

CLAUDIO That's as much as to say the sweet youth's in
  love.

DON PEDRO The greatest note of it is his melancholy.   50

CLAUDIO And when was he wont to wash his face?

DON PEDRO Yea, or to paint himself?—for the which I
  hear what they say of him.

CLAUDIO Nay, but his jesting spirit, which is now crept
  into a lute-string, and now governed by stops.   55

DON PEDRO Indeed, that tells a heavy tale for him.
  Conclude, conclude, he is in love.

CLAUDIO Nay, but I know who loves him.

DON PEDRO That would I know, too. I warrant, one that
  knows him not.   60

CLAUDIO Yes, and his ill conditions, and in despite of all,
  dies for him.

DON PEDRO She shall be buried with her face upwards.

BENEDICK Yet is this no charm for the toothache. Old
  signor, walk aside with me. I have studied eight or
  nine wise words to speak to you which these hobby-
  horses must not hear.   *Exeunt Benedick and Leonato*

DON PEDRO For my life, to break with him about Beatrice.

CLAUDIO 'Tis even so. Hero and Margaret have by this
  played their parts with Beatrice, and then the two bears
  will not bite one another when they meet.   71

    Enter Don John the bastard

DON JOHN My lord, and brother, God save you.

DON PEDRO Good-e'en, brother.

DON JOHN If your leisure served I would speak with you.

DON PEDRO In private?   75

DON JOHN If it please you. Yet Count Claudio may hear,
  for what I would speak of concerns him.

DON PEDRO What's the matter?

DON JOHN (*to Claudio*) Means your lordship to be married
  tomorrow?   80

DON PEDRO You know he does.

DON JOHN I know not that when he knows what I know.

CLAUDIO If there be any impediment, I pray you discover
  it.   84

DON JOHN You may think I love you not. Let that appear
  hereafter, and aim better at me by that I now will
  manifest. For my brother, I think he holds you well
  and in dearness of heart hath holp to effect your
  ensuing marriage—surely suit ill spent, and labour ill
  bestowed.   90

DON PEDRO Why, what's the matter?

DON JOHN I came hither to tell you, and, circumstances
  shortened—for she has been too long a-talking of—the
  lady is disloyal.

CLAUDIO Who, Hero?   95

DON JOHN Even she. Leonato's Hero, your Hero, every
  man's Hero.

CLAUDIO Disloyal?

DON JOHN The word is too good to paint out her wickedness. I could say she were worse. Think you of a worse title, and I will fit her to it. Wonder not till further warrant. Go but with me tonight, you shall see her chamber window entered, even the night before her wedding day. If you love her then, tomorrow wed her. But it would better fit your honour to change your mind.   106

CLAUDIO May this be so?

DON PEDRO I will not think it.

DON JOHN If you dare not trust that you see, confess not that you know. If you will follow me I will show you enough, and when you have seen more and heard more, proceed accordingly.

CLAUDIO If I see anything tonight why I should not marry her, tomorrow, in the congregation where I should wed, there will I shame her.   115

DON PEDRO And as I wooed for thee to obtain her, I will join with thee to disgrace her.

DON JOHN I will disparage her no farther till you are my witnesses. Bear it coldly but till midnight, and let the issue show itself.   120

DON PEDRO O day untowardly turned!

CLAUDIO O mischief strangely thwarting!

DON JOHN O plague right well prevented!—So will you say when you have seen the sequel.   *Exeunt*

3.3   *Enter Dogberry and his compartner Verges, with the Watch*

DOGBERRY Are you good men and true?

VERGES Yea, or else it were pity but they should suffer salvation, body and soul.

DOGBERRY Nay, that were a punishment too good for them if they should have any allegiance in them, being chosen for the Prince's watch.   6

VERGES Well, give them their charge, neighbour Dogberry.

DOGBERRY First, who think you the most desertless man to be constable?

SECOND WATCHMAN Hugh Oatcake, sir, or George Seacoal, for they can write and read.   11

DOGBERRY Come hither, neighbour Seacoal, God hath blest you with a good name. To be a well-favoured man is the gift of fortune, but to write and read comes by nature.   15

FIRST WATCHMAN Both which, Master Constable—

DOGBERRY You have. I knew it would be your answer. Well, for your favour, sir, why, give God thanks, and make no boast of it. And for your writing and reading, let that appear when there is no need of such vanity. You are thought here to be the most senseless and fit man for the constable of the watch, therefore bear you the lantern. This is your charge: you shall comprehend all vagrom men. You are to bid any man stand, in the Prince's name.   25

FIRST WATCHMAN How if a will not stand?

DOGBERRY Why then take no note of him, but let him go, and presently call the rest of the watch together, and thank God you are rid of a knave.

VERGES If he will not stand when he is bidden he is none of the Prince's subjects.   31

DOGBERRY True, and they are to meddle with none but the Prince's subjects.—You shall also make no noise in the streets, for for the watch to babble and to talk is most tolerable and not to be endured.   35

A WATCHMAN We will rather sleep than talk. We know what belongs to a watch.

DOGBERRY Why, you speak like an ancient and most quiet watchman, for I cannot see how sleeping should offend. Only have a care that your bills be not stolen. Well, you are to call at all the alehouses and bid those that are drunk get them to bed.

A WATCHMAN How if they will not?

DOGBERRY Why then, let them alone till they are sober. If they make you not then the better answer, you may say they are not the men you took them for.   46

A WATCHMAN Well, sir.

DOGBERRY If you meet a thief you may suspect him, by virtue of your office, to be no true man; and for such kind of men, the less you meddle or make with them why, the more is for your honesty.   51

A WATCHMAN If we know him to be a thief, shall we not lay hands on him?

DOGBERRY Truly, by your office you may, but I think they that touch pitch will be defiled. The most peaceable way for you if you do take a thief is to let him show himself what he is, and steal out of your company.

VERGES You have been always called a merciful man, partner.

DOGBERRY Truly, I would not hang a dog by my will, much more a man who hath any honesty in him.   61

VERGES If you hear a child cry in the night you must call to the nurse and bid her still it.

A WATCHMAN How if the nurse be asleep and will not hear us?   65

DOGBERRY Why then, depart in peace and let the child wake her with crying, for the ewe that will not hear her lamb when it baes will never answer a calf when he bleats.

VERGES 'Tis very true.   70

DOGBERRY This is the end of the charge. You, constable, are to present the Prince's own person. If you meet the Prince in the night you may stay him.

VERGES Nay, by'r Lady, that I think a cannot.   74

DOGBERRY Five shillings to one on't with any man that knows the statutes he may stay him. Marry, not without the Prince be willing, for indeed the watch ought to offend no man, and it is an offence to stay a man against his will.

VERGES By'r Lady, I think it be so.   80

DOGBERRY Ha ha ha! Well, masters, good night. An there be any matter of weight chances, call up me. Keep your fellows' counsels, and your own, and good night. Come, neighbour.

⌈FIRST⌉ WATCHMAN Well, masters, we hear our charge. Let us go sit here upon the church bench till two, and then all to bed.

DOGBERRY One word more, honest neighbours. I pray you watch about Signor Leonato's door, for the wedding being there tomorrow, there is a great coil tonight. Adieu. Be vigitant, I beseech you.   91

Exeunt Dogberry and Verges. ⌈The Watch sit⌉
Enter Borachio and Conrad

BORACHIO What, Conrad!

⌈FIRST⌉ WATCHMAN (*aside*) Peace, stir not.

BORACHIO Conrad, I say.

CONRAD Here, man, I am at thy elbow.   95

BORACHIO Mass, an my elbow itched, I thought there would a scab follow.

CONRAD I will owe thee an answer for that. And now, forward with thy tale.   99

BORACHIO Stand thee close, then, under this penthouse, for it drizzles rain, and I will, like a true drunkard, utter all to thee.

A WATCHMAN (*aside*) Some treason, masters. Yet stand close.

BORACHIO Therefore, know I have earned of Don John a thousand ducats.

CONRAD Is it possible that any villainy should be so dear?

BORACHIO Thou shouldst rather ask if it were possible any villainy should be so rich. For when rich villains have need of poor ones, poor ones may make what price they will.   111

CONRAD I wonder at it.

BORACHIO That shows thou art unconfirmed. Thou knowest that the fashion of a doublet, or a hat, or a cloak is nothing to a man.   115

CONRAD Yes, it is apparel.

BORACHIO I mean the fashion.

CONRAD Yes, the fashion is the fashion.

BORACHIO Tush, I may as well say the fool's the fool. But seest thou not what a deformed thief this fashion is?

A WATCHMAN (*aside*) I know that Deformed. A has been a vile thief this seven year. A goes up and down like a gentleman. I remember his name.

BORACHIO Didst thou not hear somebody?

CONRAD No, 'twas the vane on the house.   125

BORACHIO Seest thou not, I say, what a deformed thief this fashion is, how giddily a turns about all the hot-bloods between fourteen and five-and-thirty, sometimes fashioning them like Pharaoh's soldiers in the reechy painting, sometime like god Bel's priests in the old church window, sometime like the shaven Hercules in the smirched, worm-eaten tapestry, where his codpiece seems as massy as his club?   133

CONRAD All this I see, and I see that the fashion wears out more apparel than the man. But art not thou thyself giddy with the fashion, too, that thou hast shifted out of thy tale into telling me of the fashion?

BORACHIO Not so, neither. But know that I have tonight wooed Margaret, the Lady Hero's gentlewoman, by the name of Hero. She leans me out at her mistress' chamber window, bids me a thousand times good

night—I tell this tale vilely, I should first tell thee how the Prince, Claudio, and my master, planted and placed and possessed by my master, Don John, saw afar off in the orchard this amiable encounter.   145

CONRAD And thought they Margaret was Hero?

BORACHIO Two of them did, the Prince and Claudio, but the devil my master knew she was Margaret, and partly by his oaths, which first possessed them, partly by the dark night, which did deceive them, but chiefly by my villainy, which did confirm any slander that Don John had made, away went Claudio enraged, swore he would meet her as he was appointed next morning at the temple, and there, before the whole congregation, shame her with what he saw o'ernight, and send her home again without a husband.   156

⌈FIRST⌉ WATCHMAN (*coming forward*) We charge you in the Prince's name. Stand.

⌈A WATCHMAN⌉ Call up the right Master Constable. We have here recovered the most dangerous piece of lechery that ever was known in the commonwealth.

⌈FIRST⌉ WATCHMAN And one Deformed is one of them. I know him—a wears a lock.

CONRAD Masters, masters!

⌈A WATCHMAN⌉ You'll be made bring Deformed forth, I warrant you.   166

⌈CONRAD⌉ Masters—

⌈A WATCHMAN⌉ Never speak. We charge you. Let us obey you to go with us.

BORACHIO (*to Conrad*) We are like to prove a goodly commodity, being taken up of these men's bills.   171

CONRAD A commodity in question, I warrant you. Come, we'll obey you.   *Exeunt*

3.4   *Enter Hero, Margaret, and Ursula*

HERO Good Ursula, wake my cousin Beatrice, and desire her to rise.

URSULA I will, lady.

HERO And bid her come hither.

URSULA Well.   *Exit*

MARGARET Troth, I think your other rebato were better.

HERO No, pray thee, good Meg, I'll wear this.

MARGARET By my troth, 's not so good, and I warrant your cousin will say so.

HERO My cousin's a fool, and thou art another: I'll wear none but this.   11

MARGARET I like the new tire within excellently, if the hair were a thought browner. And your gown's a most rare fashion, i'faith. I saw the Duchess of Milan's gown that they praise so.   15

HERO O, that exceeds, they say.

MARGARET By my troth, 's but a night-gown in respect of yours—cloth o' gold, and cuts, and laced with silver, set with pearls, down sleeves, side sleeves, and skirts round underborne with a bluish tinsel. But for a fine, quaint, graceful, and excellent fashion, yours is worth ten on't.

HERO God give me joy to wear it, for my heart is exceeding heavy.   24

MARGARET 'Twill be heavier soon by the weight of a man.

HERO Fie upon thee, art not ashamed?

MARGARET Of what, lady? Of speaking honourably? Is not marriage honourable in a beggar? Is not your lord honourable without marriage? I think you would have me say 'saving your reverence, a husband'. An bad thinking do not wrest true speaking, I'll offend nobody. Is there any harm in 'the heavier for a husband'? None, I think, an it be the right husband and the right wife—otherwise 'tis light and not heavy. Ask my Lady Beatrice else. Here she comes.   35

Enter Beatrice

HERO Good morrow, coz.

BEATRICE Good morrow, sweet Hero.

HERO Why, how now? Do you speak in the sick tune?

BEATRICE I am out of all other tune, methinks.

MARGARET Clap 's into 'Light o' love'. That goes without a burden. Do you sing it, and I'll dance it.   41

BEATRICE Ye light o' love with your heels. Then if your husband have stables enough, you'll see he shall lack no barns.

MARGARET O illegitimate construction! I scorn that with my heels.   46

BEATRICE (*to Hero*) 'Tis almost five o'clock, cousin. 'Tis time you were ready. By my troth, I am exceeding ill. Heigh-ho!

MARGARET For a hawk, a horse, or a husband?   50

BEATRICE For the letter that begins them all—h.

MARGARET Well, an you be not turned Turk, there's no more sailing by the star.

BEATRICE What means the fool, trow?

MARGARET Nothing, I. But God send everyone their heart's desire.   56

HERO These gloves the Count sent me, they are an excellent perfume.

BEATRICE I am stuffed, cousin. I cannot smell.

MARGARET A maid, and stuffed! There's goodly catching of cold.   61

BEATRICE O, God help me, God help me. How long have you professed apprehension?

MARGARET Ever since you left it. Doth not my wit become me rarely?   65

BEATRICE It is not seen enough. You should wear it in your cap. By my troth, I am sick.

MARGARET Get you some of this distilled *carduus benedictus*, and lay it to your heart. It is the only thing for a qualm.   70

HERO There thou prickest her with a thistle.

BEATRICE Benedictus—why Benedictus? You have some moral in this Benedictus.

MARGARET Moral? No, by my troth, I have no moral meaning. I meant plain holy-thistle. You may think perchance that I think you are in love. Nay, by'r Lady, I am not such a fool to think what I list, nor I list not to think what I can, nor indeed I cannot think, if I would think my heart out of thinking, that you are in love, or that you will be in love, or that you can be in love. Yet Benedick was such another, and now is he become a man. He swore he would never marry, and

yet now in despite of his heart he eats his meat without grudging. And how you may be converted I know not, but methinks you look with your eyes, as other women do.   86

BEATRICE What pace is this that thy tongue keeps?

MARGARET Not a false gallop.

Enter Ursula

URSULA (*to Hero*) Madam, withdraw. The Prince, the Count, Signor Benedick, Don John, and all the gallants of the town are come to fetch you to church.   91

HERO Help to dress me, good coz, good Meg, good Ursula.

Exeunt

3.5 *Enter Leonato, and Dogberry the constable, and Verges the headborough*

LEONATO What would you with me, honest neighbour?

DOGBERRY Marry, sir, I would have some confidence with you that decerns you nearly.

LEONATO Brief I pray you, for you see it is a busy time with me.   5

DOGBERRY Marry, this it is, sir.

VERGES Yes, in truth it is, sir.

LEONATO What is it, my good friends?

DOGBERRY Goodman Verges, sir, speaks a little off the matter—an old man, sir, and his wits are not so blunt as, God help, I would desire they were. But in faith, honest as the skin between his brows.

VERGES Yes, I thank God, I am as honest as any man living that is an old man and no honester than I.

DOGBERRY Comparisons are odorous. Palabras, neighbour Verges.   16

LEONATO Neighbours, you are tedious.

DOGBERRY It pleases your worship to say so, but we are the poor Duke's officers. But truly, for mine own part, if I were as tedious as a king I could find in my heart to bestow it all of your worship.   21

LEONATO All thy tediousness on me, ah?

DOGBERRY Yea, an 'twere a thousand pound more than 'tis, for I hear as good exclamation on your worship as of any man in the city, and though I be but a poor man, I am glad to hear it.   26

VERGES And so am I.

LEONATO I would fain know what you have to say.

VERGES Marry, sir, our watch tonight, excepting your worship's presence, ha' ta'en a couple of as arrant knaves as any in Messina.   31

DOGBERRY A good old man, sir. He will be talking. As they say, when the age is in, the wit is out. God help us, it is a world to see. Well said, i'faith, neighbour Verges. Well, God's a good man. An two men ride of a horse, one must ride behind. An honest soul, i'faith, sir, by my troth he is, as ever broke bread. But, God is to be worshipped, all men are not alike, alas, good neighbour.

LEONATO Indeed, neighbour, he comes too short of you.

DOGBERRY Gifts that God gives!   41

LEONATO I must leave you.

DOGBERRY One word, sir. Our watch, sir, have indeed

comprehended two auspicious persons, and we would
have them this morning examined before your worship.

LEONATO Take their examination yourself, and bring it
me. I am now in great haste, as it may appear unto
you.

DOGBERRY It shall be suffigance.

LEONATO Drink some wine ere you go. Fare you well.   50
Enter a Messenger

MESSENGER My lord, they stay for you to give your
daughter to her husband.

LEONATO I'll wait upon them, I am ready.
Exeunt Leonato and Messenger

DOGBERRY Go, good partner, go get you to Francis Seacoal,
bid him bring his pen and inkhorn to the jail. We are
now to examination these men.   56

VERGES And we must do it wisely.

DOGBERRY We will spare for no wit, I warrant you. Here's
that shall drive some of them to a non-com. Only get
the learned writer to set down our excommunication,
and meet me at the jail.   *Exeunt*

4.1   *Enter Don Pedro the Prince, Don John the bastard,*
Leonato, Friar Francis, Claudio, Benedick, Hero,
and Beatrice

LEONATO Come, Friar Francis, be brief. Only to the plain
form of marriage, and you shall recount their particular
duties afterwards.

FRIAR (*to Claudio*) You come hither, my lord, to marry
this lady?   5

CLAUDIO No.

LEONATO To be married to her. Friar, you come to marry
her.

FRIAR (*to Hero*) Lady, you come hither to be married to
this count?   10

HERO I do.

FRIAR If either of you know any inward impediment why
you should not be conjoined, I charge you on your
souls to utter it.

CLAUDIO Know you any, Hero?   15

HERO None, my lord.

FRIAR Know you any, Count?

LEONATO I dare make his answer—none.

CLAUDIO O, what men dare do! What men may do! What
men daily do, not knowing what they do!   20

BENEDICK How now! Interjections? Why then, some be of
laughing, as 'ah, ha, he!'

CLAUDIO
Stand thee by, Friar. Father, by your leave,
Will you with free and unconstrainèd soul
Give me this maid, your daughter?   25

LEONATO
As freely, son, as God did give her me.

CLAUDIO
And what have I to give you back whose worth
May counterpoise this rich and precious gift?

DON PEDRO
Nothing, unless you render her again.

CLAUDIO
Sweet Prince, you learn me noble thankfulness.   30
There, Leonato, take her back again.
Give not this rotten orange to your friend.
She's but the sign and semblance of her honour.
Behold how like a maid she blushes here!
O, what authority and show of truth   35
Can cunning sin cover itself withal!
Comes not that blood as modest evidence
To witness simple virtue? Would you not swear,
All you that see her, that she were a maid,
By these exterior shows? But she is none.   40
She knows the heat of a luxurious bed.
Her blush is guiltiness, not modesty.

LEONATO
What do you mean, my lord?

CLAUDIO   Not to be married,
Not to knit my soul to an approvèd wanton.

LEONATO
Dear my lord, if you in your own proof   45
Have vanquished the resistance of her youth
And made defeat of her virginity—

CLAUDIO
I know what you would say. If I have known her,
You will say she did embrace me as a husband,
And so extenuate the forehand sin.   50
No, Leonato,
I never tempted her with word too large,
But as a brother to his sister showed
Bashful sincerity and comely love.

HERO
And seemed I ever otherwise to you?   55

CLAUDIO
Out on thee, seeming! I will write against it.
You seem to me as Dian in her orb,
As chaste as is the bud ere it be blown.
But you are more intemperate in your blood
Than Venus or those pampered animals   60
That rage in savage sensuality.

HERO
Is my lord well that he doth speak so wide?

LEONATO
Sweet Prince, why speak not you?

DON PEDRO   What should I speak?
I stand dishonoured, that have gone about
To link my dear friend to a common stale.   65

LEONATO
Are these things spoken, or do I but dream?

DON JOHN
Sir, they are spoken, and these things are true.

BENEDICK This looks not like a nuptial.

HERO 'True'! O God!

CLAUDIO Leonato, stand I here?   70
Is this the Prince? Is this the Prince's brother?
Is this face Hero's? Are our eyes our own?

LEONATO
All this is so. But what of this, my lord?

CLAUDIO
Let me but move one question to your daughter,
And by that fatherly and kindly power   75
That you have in her, bid her answer truly.

LEONATO (*to Hero*)
I charge thee do so, as thou art my child.

HERO
O God defend me, how am I beset!
What kind of catechizing call you this?

CLAUDIO
To make you answer truly to your name.   80

HERO
Is it not Hero? Who can blot that name
With any just reproach?

CLAUDIO   Marry, that can Hero.
Hero itself can blot out Hero's virtue.
What man was he talked with you yesternight
Out at your window betwixt twelve and one?   85
Now if you are a maid, answer to this.

HERO
I talked with no man at that hour, my lord.

DON PEDRO
Why, then are you no maiden. Leonato,
I am sorry you must hear. Upon mine honour,
Myself, my brother, and this grievèd Count   90
Did see her, hear her, at that hour last night
Talk with a ruffian at her chamber window,
Who hath indeed, most like a liberal villain,
Confessed the vile encounters they have had
A thousand times in secret.

DON JOHN   Fie, fie, they are   95
Not to be named, my lord, not to be spoke of.
There is not chastity enough in language
Without offence to utter them. Thus, pretty lady,
I am sorry for thy much misgovernment.

CLAUDIO
O Hero! What a Hero hadst thou been   100
If half thy outward graces had been placed
About thy thoughts and counsels of thy heart!
But fare thee well, most foul, most fair, farewell
Thou pure impiety and impious purity.
For thee I'll lock up all the gates of love,   105
And on my eyelids shall conjecture hang
To turn all beauty into thoughts of harm,
And never shall it more be gracious.

LEONATO
Hath no man's dagger here a point for me?
    Hero falls to the ground

BEATRICE
Why, how now, cousin, wherefore sink you down? 110

DON JOHN
Come. Let us go. These things come thus to light
Smother her spirits up.
    Exeunt Don Pedro, Don John, and Claudio

BENEDICK
How doth the lady?

BEATRICE   Dead, I think. Help, uncle.
Hero, why Hero! Uncle, Signor Benedick, Friar—

LEONATO
O fate, take not away thy heavy hand.   115
Death is the fairest cover for her shame
That may be wished for.

BEATRICE   How now, cousin Hero?

FRIAR (*to Hero*) Have comfort, lady.

LEONATO (*to Hero*) Dost thou look up?

FRIAR Yea, wherefore should she not?   120

LEONATO
Wherefore? Why, doth not every earthly thing
Cry shame upon her? Could she here deny
The story that is printed in her blood?
Do not live, Hero, do not ope thine eyes,
For did I think thou wouldst not quickly die,   125
Thought I thy spirits were stronger than thy shames,
Myself would on the rearward of reproaches
Strike at thy life. Grieved I I had but one?
Chid I for that at frugal nature's frame?
O one too much by thee! Why had I one?   130
Why ever wast thou lovely in my eyes?
Why had I not with charitable hand
Took up a beggar's issue at my gates,
Who smirchèd thus and mired with infamy,
I might have said 'No part of it is mine,   135
This shame derives itself from unknown loins.'
But mine, and mine I loved, and mine I praised,
And mine that I was proud on, mine so much
That I myself was to myself not mine,
Valuing of her—why she, O she is fallen   140
Into a pit of ink, that the wide sea
Hath drops too few to wash her clean again,
And salt too little which may season give
To her foul tainted flesh.

BENEDICK   Sir, sir, be patient.
For my part, I am so attired in wonder   145
I know not what to say.

BEATRICE
O, on my soul, my cousin is belied.

BENEDICK
Lady, were you her bedfellow last night?

BEATRICE
No, truly not, although until last night
I have this twelvemonth been her bedfellow.   150

LEONATO
Confirmed, confirmed. O, that is stronger made
Which was before barred up with ribs of iron.
Would the two princes lie? And Claudio lie,
Who loved her so that, speaking of her foulness,
Washed it with tears? Hence from her, let her die. 155

FRIAR Hear me a little,
For I have only been silent so long
And given way unto this course of fortune
┌   ┐
By noting of the lady. I have marked   160
A thousand blushing apparitions
To start into her face, a thousand innocent shames
In angel whiteness beat away those blushes,
And in her eye there hath appeared a fire
To burn the errors that these princes hold   165

Against her maiden truth. Call me a fool,
Trust not my reading nor my observations,
Which with experimental seal doth warrant
The tenor of my book. Trust not my age,
My reverence, calling, nor divinity,   170
If this sweet lady lie not guiltless here
Under some biting error.
LEONATO   Friar, it cannot be.
Thou seest that all the grace that she hath left
Is that she will not add to her damnation
A sin of perjury. She not denies it.   175
Why seek'st thou then to cover with excuse
That which appears in proper nakedness?
FRIAR (to Hero)
Lady, what man is he you are accused of?
HERO
They know that do accuse me. I know none.
If I know more of any man alive   180
Than that which maiden modesty doth warrant,
Let all my sins lack mercy. O my father,
Prove you that any man with me conversed
At hours unmeet, or that I yesternight
Maintained the change of words with any creature, 185
Refuse me, hate me, torture me to death.
FRIAR
There is some strange misprision in the princes.
BENEDICK
Two of them have the very bent of honour,
And if their wisdoms be misled in this
The practice of it lives in John the bastard,   190
Whose spirits toil in frame of villainies.
LEONATO
I know not. If they speak but truth of her
These hands shall tear her. If they wrong her honour
The proudest of them shall well hear of it.
Time hath not yet so dried this blood of mine,   195
Nor age so eat up my invention,
Nor fortune made such havoc of my means,
Nor my bad life reft me so much of friends,
But they shall find awaked in such a kind
Both strength of limb and policy of mind,   200
Ability in means, and choice of friends,
To quit me of them throughly.
FRIAR   Pause awhile,
And let my counsel sway you in this case.
Your daughter here the princes left for dead,
Let her a while be secretly kept in,   205
And publish it that she is dead indeed.
Maintain a mourning ostentation,
And on your family's old monument
Hang mournful epitaphs, and do all rites
That appertain unto a burial.   210
LEONATO
What shall become of this? What will this do?
FRIAR
Marry, this, well carried, shall on her behalf
Change slander to remorse. That is some good.

But not for that dream I on this strange course,
But on this travail look for greater birth.   215
She—dying, as it must be so maintained,
Upon the instant that she was accused—
Shall be lamented, pitied, and excused
Of every hearer. For it so falls out
That what we have, we prize not to the worth   220
Whiles we enjoy it, but, being lacked and lost,
Why then we rack the value, then we find
The virtue that possession would not show us
Whiles it was ours. So will it fare with Claudio.
When he shall hear she died upon his words,   225
Th'idea of her life shall sweetly creep
Into his study of imagination,
And every lovely organ of her life
Shall come apparelled in more precious habit,
More moving-delicate, and full of life,   230
Into the eye and prospect of his soul
Than when she lived indeed. Then shall he mourn,
If ever love had interest in his liver,
And wish he had not so accusèd her,
No, though he thought his accusation true.   235
Let this be so, and doubt not but success
Will fashion the event in better shape
Than I can lay it down in likelihood.
But if all aim but this be levelled false,
The supposition of the lady's death   240
Will quench the wonder of her infamy.
And if it sort not well, you may conceal her,
As best befits her wounded reputation,
In some reclusive and religious life,
Out of all eyes, tongues, minds, and injuries.   245
BENEDICK
Signor Leonato, let the Friar advise you.
And though you know my inwardness and love
Is very much unto the Prince and Claudio,
Yet, by mine honour, I will deal in this
As secretly and justly as your soul   250
Should with your body.
LEONATO Being that I flow in grief,
The smallest twine may lead me.
FRIAR
'Tis well consented. Presently away,
For to strange sores strangely they strain the cure. 255
(To Hero) Come, lady, die to live. This wedding day
Perhaps is but prolonged. Have patience, and endure.
               Exeunt all but Beatrice and Benedick
BENEDICK Lady Beatrice, have you wept all this while?
BEATRICE Yea, and I will weep a while longer.
BENEDICK I will not desire that.   260
BEATRICE You have no reason, I do it freely.
BENEDICK Surely I do believe your fair cousin is wronged.
BEATRICE Ah, how much might the man deserve of me
   that would right her!
BENEDICK Is there any way to show such friendship?   265
BEATRICE A very even way, but no such friend.
BENEDICK May a man do it?

BEATRICE It is a man's office, but not yours.

BENEDICK I do love nothing in the world so well as you. Is not that strange? 270

BEATRICE As strange as the thing I know not. It were as possible for me to say I loved nothing so well as you, but believe me not, and yet I lie not. I confess nothing nor I deny nothing. I am sorry for my cousin.

BENEDICK By my sword, Beatrice, thou lovest me. 275

BEATRICE Do not swear and eat it.

BENEDICK I will swear by it that you love me, and I will make him eat it that says I love not you.

BEATRICE Will you not eat your word?

BENEDICK With no sauce that can be devised to it. I protest I love thee. 281

BEATRICE Why then, God forgive me.

BENEDICK What offence, sweet Beatrice?

BEATRICE You have stayed me in a happy hour. I was about to protest I loved you. 285

BENEDICK And do it with all thy heart.

BEATRICE I love you with so much of my heart that none is left to protest.

BENEDICK Come, bid me do anything for thee.

BEATRICE Kill Claudio. 290

BENEDICK Ha! Not for the wide world.

BEATRICE You kill me to deny it. Farewell.

BENEDICK Tarry, sweet Beatrice.

BEATRICE I am gone though I am here. There is no love in you.—Nay, I pray you, let me go. 295

BENEDICK Beatrice.

BEATRICE In faith, I will go.

BENEDICK We'll be friends first.

BEATRICE You dare easier be friends with me than fight with mine enemy. 300

BENEDICK Is Claudio thine enemy?

BEATRICE Is a not approved in the height a villain, that hath slandered, scorned, dishonoured my kinswoman? O that I were a man! What, bear her in hand until they come to take hands, and then with public accusation, uncovered slander, unmitigated rancour— O God that I were a man! I would eat his heart in the market place.

BENEDICK Hear me, Beatrice.

BEATRICE Talk with a man out at a window—a proper saying! 311

BENEDICK Nay, but Beatrice.

BEATRICE Sweet Hero, she is wronged, she is slandered, she is undone.

BENEDICK Beat— 315

BEATRICE Princes and counties! Surely a princely testimony, a goodly count, Count Comfit, a sweet gallant, surely. O that I were a man for his sake! Or that I had any friend would be a man for my sake! But manhood is melted into courtesies, valour into compliment, and men are only turned into tongue, and trim ones, too. He is now as valiant as Hercules that only tells a lie and swears it. I cannot be a man with wishing, therefore I will die a woman with grieving. 324

BENEDICK Tarry, good Beatrice. By this hand, I love thee.

BEATRICE Use it for my love some other way than swearing by it.

BENEDICK Think you in your soul the Count Claudio hath wronged Hero?

BEATRICE Yea, as sure as I have a thought or a soul. 330

BENEDICK Enough, I am engaged, I will challenge him. I will kiss your hand, and so I leave you. By this hand, Claudio shall render me a dear account. As you hear of me, so think of me. Go comfort your cousin. I must say she is dead. And so, farewell. *Exeunt*

4.2 *Enter Dogberry and Verges the constables, and the Sexton, in gowns, and the Watch, with Conrad and Borachio*

DOGBERRY Is our whole dissembly appeared?

VERGES O, a stool and a cushion for the Sexton.

SEXTON ⌈*sits*⌉ Which be the malefactors?

DOGBERRY Marry, that am I, and my partner.

VERGES Nay, that's certain, we have the exhibition to examine. 6

SEXTON But which are the offenders that are to be examined? Let them come before Master Constable.

DOGBERRY Yea, marry, let them come before me. What is your name, friend? 10

BORACHIO Borachio.

DOGBERRY (*to the Sexton*) Pray write down 'Borachio'. (*To Conrad*) Yours, sirrah?

CONRAD I am a gentleman, sir, and my name is Conrad.

DOGBERRY Write down 'Master Gentleman Conrad'.— Masters, do you serve God? 16

CONRAD *and* BORACHIO Yea, sir, we hope.

DOGBERRY Write down that they hope they serve God. And write 'God' first, for God defend but God should go before such villains. Masters, it is proved already that you are little better than false knaves, and it will go near to be thought so shortly. How answer you for yourselves?

CONRAD Marry, sir, we say we are none. 24

DOGBERRY A marvellous witty fellow, I assure you, but I will go about with him. Come you hither, sirrah. A word in your ear, sir. I say to you it is thought you are false knaves.

BORACHIO Sir, I say to you we are none.

DOGBERRY Well, stand aside. Fore God, they are both in a tale. Have you writ down that they are none? 31

SEXTON Master Constable, you go not the way to examine. You must call forth the watch that are their accusers.

DOGBERRY Yea, marry, that's the eftest way. Let the watch come forth. Masters, I charge you in the Prince's name accuse these men. 36

FIRST WATCHMAN This man said, sir, that Don John, the Prince's brother, was a villain.

DOGBERRY Write down Prince John a villain. Why, this is flat perjury, to call a prince's brother villain. 40

BORACHIO Master Constable.

DOGBERRY Pray thee, fellow, peace. I do not like thy look, I promise thee.

SEXTON What heard you him say else?

SECOND WATCHMAN Marry, that he had received a
thousand ducats of Don John for accusing the Lady
Hero wrongfully.

DOGBERRY Flat burglary, as ever was committed.

VERGES Yea, by mass, that it is.

SEXTON What else, fellow?   50

FIRST WATCHMAN And that Count Claudio did mean upon
his words to disgrace Hero before the whole assembly,
and not marry her.

DOGBERRY O villain! Thou wilt be condemned into everlasting redemption for this.   55

SEXTON What else?

WATCH This is all.

SEXTON And this is more, masters, than you can deny.
Prince John is this morning secretly stolen away. Hero
was in this manner accused, in this very manner
refused, and upon the grief of this suddenly died. Master
Constable, let these men be bound and brought to
Leonato's. I will go before and show him their
examination.   *Exit*

DOGBERRY Come, let them be opinioned.   65

VERGES Let them be, in the hands—

⌜CONRAD⌝ Off, coxcomb!

DOGBERRY God's my life, where's the Sexton? Let him
write down the Prince's officer coxcomb. Come, bind
them. Thou naughty varlet!   70

CONRAD Away, you are an ass, you are an ass.

DOGBERRY Dost thou not suspect my place? Dost thou not
suspect my years? O that he were here to write me
down an ass! But masters, remember that I am an ass.
Though it be not written down, yet forget not that I
am an ass. No, thou villain, thou art full of piety, as
shall be proved upon thee by good witness. I am a wise
fellow, and which is more, an officer, and which is
more, a householder, and which is more, as pretty a
piece of flesh as any is in Messina, and one that knows
the law, go to, and a rich fellow enough, go to, and a
fellow that hath had losses, and one that hath two
gowns, and everything handsome about him. Bring
him away. O that I had been writ down an ass!

Exeunt

5.1   *Enter Leonato and Antonio his brother*

ANTONIO
If you go on thus, you will kill yourself,
And 'tis not wisdom thus to second grief
Against yourself.

LEONATO   I pray thee cease thy counsel,
Which falls into mine ears as profitless
As water in a sieve. Give not me counsel,   5
Nor let no comforter delight mine ear
But such a one whose wrongs do suit with mine.
Bring me a father that so loved his child,
Whose joy of her is overwhelmed like mine,
And bid him speak of patience.   10
Measure his woe the length and breadth of mine,
And let it answer every strain for strain,
As thus for thus, and such a grief for such,

In every lineament, branch, shape, and form.
If such a one will smile and stroke his beard,   15
Bid sorrow wag, cry 'hem' when he should groan,
Patch grief with proverbs, make misfortune drunk
With candle-wasters, bring him yet to me,
And I of him will gather patience.
But there is no such man, for, brother, men   20
Can counsel and speak comfort to that grief
Which they themselves not feel, but tasting it
Their counsel turns to passion, which before
Would give preceptial medicine to rage,
Fetter strong madness in a silken thread,   25
Charm ache with air and agony with words.
No, no, 'tis all men's office to speak patience
To those that wring under the load of sorrow,
But no man's virtue nor sufficiency
To be so moral when he shall endure   30
The like himself. Therefore give me no counsel.
My griefs cry louder than advertisement.

ANTONIO
Therein do men from children nothing differ.

LEONATO
I pray thee peace, I will be flesh and blood,
For there was never yet philosopher   35
That could endure the toothache patiently,
However they have writ the style of gods,
And made a pish at chance and sufferance.

ANTONIO
Yet bend not all the harm upon yourself.
Make those that do offend you suffer, too.   40

LEONATO
There thou speak'st reason, nay I will do so.
My soul doth tell me Hero is belied,
And that shall Claudio know, so shall the Prince,
And all of them that thus dishonour her.

Enter Don Pedro the Prince and Claudio

ANTONIO
Here comes the Prince and Claudio hastily.   45

DON PEDRO
Good e'en, good e'en.

CLAUDIO   Good day to both of you.

LEONATO
Hear you, my lords?

DON PEDRO   We have some haste, Leonato.

LEONATO
Some haste, my lord! Well, fare you well, my lord.
Are you so hasty now? Well, all is one.

DON PEDRO
Nay, do not quarrel with us, good old man.   50

ANTONIO
If he could right himself with quarrelling,
Some of us would lie low.

CLAUDIO   Who wrongs him?

LEONATO
Marry, thou dost wrong me, thou dissembler, thou.
Nay, never lay thy hand upon thy sword,
I fear thee not.

CLAUDIO   Marry, beshrew my hand   55

If it should give your age such cause of fear.
In faith, my hand meant nothing to my sword.
LEONATO
  Tush, tush, man, never fleer and jest at me.
  I speak not like a dotard nor a fool,
  As under privilege of age to brag   60
  What I have done being young, or what would do
  Were I not old. Know Claudio to thy head,
  Thou hast so wronged mine innocent child and me
  That I am forced to lay my reverence by
  And with grey hairs and bruise of many days   65
  Do challenge thee to trial of a man.
  I say thou hast belied mine innocent child.
  Thy slander hath gone through and through her heart,
  And she lies buried with her ancestors,
  O, in a tomb where never scandal slept   70
  Save this of hers, framed by thy villainy.
CLAUDIO
  My villainy?
LEONATO   Thine, Claudio, thine I say.
DON PEDRO
  You say not right, old man.
LEONATO   My lord, my lord,
  I'll prove it on his body if he dare,
  Despite his nice fence and his active practice,   75
  His May of youth and bloom of lustihood.
CLAUDIO
  Away, I will not have to do with you.
LEONATO
  Canst thou so doff me? Thou hast killed my child.
  If thou kill'st me, boy, thou shalt kill a man.
ANTONIO
  He shall kill two of us, and men indeed.   80
  But that's no matter, let him kill one first.
  Win me and wear me. Let him answer me.
  Come follow me boy, come sir boy, come follow me,
  Sir boy, I'll whip you from your foining fence.
  Nay, as I am a gentleman, I will.   85
LEONATO Brother.
ANTONIO
  Content yourself. God knows, I loved my niece,
  And she is dead, slandered to death by villains
  That dare as well answer a man
  As I dare take a serpent by the tongue.   90
  Boys, apes, braggarts, jacks, milksops!
LEONATO Brother Antony—
ANTONIO
  Hold you content. What, man, I know them, yea
  And what they weigh, even to the utmost scruple.
  Scambling, outfacing, fashion-monging boys,   95
  That lie, and cog, and flout, deprave, and slander,
  Go anticly, and show an outward hideousness,
  And speak off half a dozen dangerous words,
  How they might hurt their enemies, if they durst,
  And this is all.   100
LEONATO But brother Antony—
ANTONIO Come, 'tis no matter,
  Do not you meddle, let me deal in this.

DON PEDRO
  Gentlemen both, we will not wake your patience.
  My heart is sorry for your daughter's death,   105
  But on my honour she was charged with nothing
  But what was true and very full of proof.
LEONATO
  My lord, my lord—
DON PEDRO   I will not hear you.
LEONATO
  No? Come brother, away. I will be heard.
ANTONIO
  And shall, or some of us will smart for it.   110
                 Exeunt Leonato and Antonio
    Enter Benedick
DON PEDRO
  See, see, here comes the man we went to seek.
CLAUDIO Now signor, what news?
BENEDICK (*to Don Pedro*) Good day, my lord.
DON PEDRO Welcome, signor. You are almost come to part
  almost a fray.   115
CLAUDIO We had liked to have had our two noses snapped
  off with two old men without teeth.
DON PEDRO Leonato and his brother. What thinkest thou?
  Had we fought, I doubt we should have been too young
  for them.   120
BENEDICK In a false quarrel there is no true valour. I came
  to seek you both.
CLAUDIO We have been up and down to seek thee, for we
  are high-proof melancholy and would fain have it
  beaten away. Wilt thou use thy wit?   125
BENEDICK It is in my scabbard. Shall I draw it?
DON PEDRO Dost thou wear thy wit by thy side?
CLAUDIO Never any did so, though very many have been
  beside their wit. I will bid thee draw as we do the
  minstrels, draw to pleasure us.   130
DON PEDRO As I am an honest man he looks pale. Art
  thou sick, or angry?
CLAUDIO What, courage, man. What though care killed
  a cat, thou hast mettle enough in thee to kill care. 134
BENEDICK Sir, I shall meet your wit in the career an you
  charge it against me. I pray you choose another subject.
CLAUDIO Nay then, give him another staff. This last was
  broke cross.
DON PEDRO By this light, he changes more and more. I
  think he be angry indeed.   140
CLAUDIO If he be, he knows how to turn his girdle.
BENEDICK (*aside to Claudio*) Shall I speak a word in your
  ear?
CLAUDIO God bless me from a challenge.
BENEDICK You are a villain. I jest not. I will make it good
  how you dare, with what you dare, and when you
  dare. Do me right, or I will protest your cowardice.
  You have killed a sweet lady, and her death shall fall
  heavy on you. Let me hear from you.
CLAUDIO Well, I will meet you, so I may have good cheer.
DON PEDRO What, a feast, a feast?   151
CLAUDIO I'faith, I thank him, he hath bid me to a calf's
  head and a capon, the which if I do not carve most

curiously, say my knife's naught. Shall I not find a woodcock too?   155

BENEDICK Sir, your wit ambles well, it goes easily.

DON PEDRO I'll tell thee how Beatrice praised thy wit the other day. I said thou hadst a fine wit. 'True,' said she, 'a fine little one.' 'No,' said I, 'a great wit.' 'Right,' says she, 'a great gross one.' 'Nay,' said I, 'a good wit.' 'Just,' said she, 'it hurts nobody.' 'Nay,' said I, 'the gentleman is wise.' 'Certain,' said she, 'a wise gentleman.' 'Nay,' said I, 'he hath the tongues.' 'That I believe,' said she, 'for he swore a thing to me on Monday night which he forswore on Tuesday morning. There's a double tongue, there's two tongues.' Thus did she an hour together trans-shape thy particular virtues, yet at last she concluded with a sigh thou wast the properest man in Italy.

CLAUDIO For the which she wept heartily and said she cared not.   171

DON PEDRO Yea, that she did. But yet for all that, an if she did not hate him deadly she would love him dearly. The old man's daughter told us all.

CLAUDIO All, all. And moreover, God saw him when he was hid in the garden.   176

DON PEDRO But when shall we set the savage bull's horns on the sensible Benedick's head?

CLAUDIO Yea, and text underneath, 'Here dwells Benedick the married man'.   180

BENEDICK Fare you well, boy, you know my mind. I will leave you now to your gossip-like humour. You break jests as braggarts do their blades which, God be thanked, hurt not. (*To Don Pedro*) My lord, for your many courtesies I thank you. I must discontinue your company. Your brother the bastard is fled from Messina. You have among you killed a sweet and innocent lady. For my lord Lackbeard there, he and I shall meet, and till then, peace be with him.   *Exit*

DON PEDRO He is in earnest.   190

CLAUDIO In most profound earnest, and, I'll warrant you, for the love of Beatrice.

DON PEDRO And hath challenged thee.

CLAUDIO Most sincerely.

DON PEDRO What a pretty thing man is when he goes in his doublet and hose and leaves off his wit!   196

Enter Dogberry and Verges the constables, the Watch, Conrad, and Borachio

CLAUDIO He is then a giant to an ape. But then is an ape a doctor to such a man.

DON PEDRO But soft you, let me be. Pluck up, my heart, and be sad. Did he not say my brother was fled?   200

DOGBERRY Come you sir, if justice cannot tame you, she shall ne'er weigh more reasons in her balance. Nay, an you be a cursing hypocrite once, you must be looked to.

DON PEDRO How now, two of my brother's men bound? Borachio one.   205

CLAUDIO Hearken after their offence, my lord.

DON PEDRO Officers, what offence have these men done?

DOGBERRY Marry, sir, they have committed false report, moreover they have spoken untruths, secondarily they are slanders, sixth and lastly they have belied a lady, thirdly they have verified unjust things, and to conclude, they are lying knaves.

DON PEDRO First I ask thee what they have done, thirdly I ask thee what's their offence, sixth and lastly why they are committed, and to conclude, what you lay to their charge.   216

CLAUDIO Rightly reasoned, and in his own division. And by my troth there's one meaning well suited.

DON PEDRO (*to Conrad and Borachio*) Who have you offended, masters, that you are thus bound to your answer? This learned constable is too cunning to be understood. What's your offence?   222

BORACHIO Sweet Prince, let me go no farther to mine answer. Do you hear me, and let this Count kill me. I have deceived even your very eyes. What your wisdoms could not discover, these shallow fools have brought to light, who in the night overheard me confessing to this man how Don John your brother incensed me to slander the Lady Hero, how you were brought into the orchard and saw me court Margaret in Hero's garments, how you disgraced her when you should marry her. My villainy they have upon record, which I had rather seal with my death than repeat over to my shame. The lady is dead upon mine and my master's false accusation, and briefly, I desire nothing but the reward of a villain.   236

DON PEDRO (*to Claudio*)
Runs not this speech like iron through your blood?

CLAUDIO
I have drunk poison whiles he uttered it.

DON PEDRO (*to Borachio*)
But did my brother set thee on to this?

BORACHIO
Yea, and paid me richly for the practice of it.   240

DON PEDRO
He is composed and framed of treachery,
And fled he is upon this villainy.

CLAUDIO
Sweet Hero, now thy image doth appear
In the rare semblance that I loved it first.   244

DOGBERRY Come, bring away the plaintiffs. By this time our Sexton hath reformed Signor Leonato of the matter. And masters, do not forget to specify, when time and place shall serve, that I am an ass.

VERGES Here, here comes Master Signor Leonato, and the Sexton, too.   250

Enter Leonato, Antonio his brother, and the Sexton

LEONATO
Which is the villain? Let me see his eyes,
That when I note another man like him
I may avoid him. Which of these is he?

BORACHIO
If you would know your wronger, look on me.

LEONATO
Art thou the slave that with thy breath hast killed 255
Mine innocent child?

BORACHIO   Yea, even I alone.

LEONATO
No, not so, villain, thou beliest thyself.
Here stand a pair of honourable men.
A third is fled that had a hand in it.
I thank you, Princes, for my daughter's death.   260
Record it with your high and worthy deeds.
'Twas bravely done, if you bethink you of it.

CLAUDIO
I know not how to pray your patience,
Yet I must speak. Choose your revenge yourself,
Impose me to what penance your invention   265
Can lay upon my sin. Yet sinned I not
But in mistaking.

DON PEDRO   By my soul, nor I,
And yet to satisfy this good old man
I would bend under any heavy weight
That he'll enjoin me to.   270

LEONATO
I cannot bid you bid my daughter live—
That were impossible—but I pray you both
Possess the people in Messina here
How innocent she died, and if your love
Can labour aught in sad invention,   275
Hang her an epitaph upon her tomb
And sing it to her bones, sing it tonight.
Tomorrow morning come you to my house,
And since you could not be my son-in-law,
Be yet my nephew. My brother hath a daughter,   280
Almost the copy of my child that's dead,
And she alone is heir to both of us.
Give her the right you should have giv'n her cousin,
And so dies my revenge.

CLAUDIO   O noble sir!
Your overkindness doth wring tears from me.   285
I do embrace your offer; and dispose
For henceforth of poor Claudio.

LEONATO
Tomorrow then I will expect your coming.
Tonight I take my leave. This naughty man
Shall face to face be brought to Margaret,   290
Who I believe was packed in all this wrong,
Hired to it by your brother.

BORACHIO   No, by my soul, she was not,
Nor knew not what she did when she spoke to me,
But always hath been just and virtuous
In anything that I do know by her.   295

DOGBERRY (to Leonato) Moreover, sir, which indeed is not
under white and black, this plaintiff here, the offender,
did call me ass. I beseech you let it be remembered in
his punishment. And also the watch heard them talk
of one Deformed. They say he wears a key in his ear
and a lock hanging by it, and borrows money in God's
name, the which he hath used so long and never paid
that now men grow hard-hearted and will lend nothing
for God's sake. Pray you examine him upon that point.

LEONATO
I thank thee for thy care and honest pains.   305

DOGBERRY Your worship speaks like a most thankful and
reverend youth, and I praise God for you.
LEONATO (giving him money) There's for thy pains.
DOGBERRY God save the foundation.
LEONATO Go. I discharge thee of thy prisoner, and I thank
thee.   311
DOGBERRY I leave an arrant knave with your worship,
which I beseech your worship to correct yourself, for
the example of others. God keep your worship, I wish
your worship well. God restore you to health. I humbly
give you leave to depart, and if a merry meeting may
be wished, God prohibit it. Come, neighbour.
          Exeunt Dogberry and Verges
LEONATO
Until tomorrow morning, lords, farewell.
ANTONIO
Farewell, my lords. We look for you tomorrow.
DON PEDRO
We will not fail.
CLAUDIO   Tonight I'll mourn with Hero.   320
LEONATO (to the Watch)
Bring you these fellows on.—We'll talk with Margaret
How her acquaintance grew with this lewd fellow.
          Exeunt

5.2   *Enter Benedick and Margaret*
BENEDICK Pray thee, sweet Mistress Margaret, deserve well
at my hands by helping me to the speech of Beatrice.
MARGARET Will you then write me a sonnet in praise of
my beauty?   4
BENEDICK In so high a style, Margaret, that no man living
shall come over it, for in most comely truth, thou
deservest it.
MARGARET To have no man come over me—why, shall I
always keep below stairs?
BENEDICK Thy wit is as quick as the greyhound's mouth,
it catches.   11
MARGARET And yours as blunt as the fencer's foils, which
hit but hurt not.
BENEDICK A most manly wit, Margaret, it will not hurt a
woman. And so I pray thee call Beatrice. I give thee
the bucklers.   16
MARGARET Give us the swords. We have bucklers of our
own.
BENEDICK If you use them, Margaret, you must put in the
pikes with a vice—and they are dangerous weapons
for maids.   21
MARGARET Well, I will call Beatrice to you, who I think
hath legs.   *Exit*
BENEDICK And therefore will come.
(*Sings*)   The god of love   25
          That sits above,
          And knows me, and knows me,
          How pitiful I deserve—
I mean in singing; but in loving, Leander the good
swimmer, Troilus the first employer of panders, and a
whole book full of these quondam carpet-mongers

whose names yet run smoothly in the even road of a
blank verse, why they were never so truly turned over
and over as my poor self in love. Marry, I cannot show
it in rhyme. I have tried. I can find out no rhyme to
'lady' but 'baby', an innocent rhyme; for 'scorn' 'horn',
a hard rhyme; for 'school' 'fool', a babbling rhyme.
Very ominous endings. No, I was not born under a
rhyming planet, nor I cannot woo in festival terms.

Enter Beatrice

Sweet Beatrice, wouldst thou come when I called thee?
BEATRICE Yea, signor, and depart when you bid me.   41
BENEDICK O, stay but till then.
BEATRICE 'Then' is spoken. Fare you well now. And yet
ere I go, let me go with that I came for, which is with
knowing what hath passed between you and Claudio.
BENEDICK Only foul words, and thereupon I will kiss thee.
BEATRICE Foul words is but foul wind, and foul wind is
but foul breath, and foul breath is noisome, therefore
I will depart unkissed.   49
BENEDICK Thou hast frighted the word out of his right
sense, so forcible is thy wit. But I must tell thee plainly,
Claudio undergoes my challenge, and either I must
shortly hear from him or I will subscribe him a coward.
And I pray thee now tell me, for which of my bad parts
didst thou first fall in love with me?   55
BEATRICE For them all together, which maintain so politic
a state of evil that they will not admit any good part
to intermingle with them. But for which of my good
parts did you first suffer love for me?
BENEDICK Suffer love—a good epithet. I do suffer love
indeed, for I love thee against my will.   61
BEATRICE In spite of your heart, I think. Alas, poor heart.
If you spite it for my sake I will spite it for yours, for I
will never love that which my friend hates.
BENEDICK Thou and I are too wise to woo peaceably.   65
BEATRICE It appears not in this confession. There's not
one wise man among twenty that will praise himself.
BENEDICK An old, an old instance, Beatrice, that lived in
the time of good neighbours. If a man do not erect in
this age his own tomb ere he dies, he shall live no
longer in monument than the bell rings and the widow
weeps.
BEATRICE And how long is that, think you?
BENEDICK Question—why, an hour in clamour and a
quarter in rheum. Therefore is it most expedient for the
wise, if Don Worm—his conscience—find no impediment to the contrary, to be the trumpet of his own
virtues, as I am to myself. So much for praising myself
who, I myself will bear witness, is praiseworthy. And
now tell me, how doth your cousin?   80
BEATRICE Very ill.
BENEDICK And how do you?
BEATRICE Very ill too.
BENEDICK Serve God, love me, and mend. There will I
leave you too, for here comes one in haste.   85

Enter Ursula

URSULA Madam, you must come to your uncle. Yonder's
old coil at home. It is proved my lady Hero hath been
falsely accused, the Prince and Claudio mightily abused,
and Don John is the author of all, who is fled and gone.
Will you come presently?   90
BEATRICE Will you go hear this news, signor?
BENEDICK I will live in thy heart, die in thy lap, and be
buried in thy eyes. And moreover, I will go with thee
to thy uncle's.   *Exeunt*

5.3   *Enter Claudio, Don Pedro the Prince, and three or*
      four with tapers, all in black
CLAUDIO
Is this the monument of Leonato?
A LORD
It is, my lord.
⌈CLAUDIO (*reading from a scroll*)⌉
      Done to death by slanderous tongues
         Was the Hero that here lies.
      Death in guerdon of her wrongs   5
         Gives her fame which never dies.
      So the life that died with shame
      Lives in death with glorious fame.

He hangs the epitaph on the tomb

      Hang thou there upon the tomb,
      Praising her when I am dumb.   10

Now music sound, and sing your solemn hymn.

            Song

      Pardon, goddess of the night,
      Those that slew thy virgin knight,
      For the which with songs of woe
      Round about her tomb they go.   15
      Midnight, assist our moan,
      Help us to sigh and groan,
            Heavily, heavily.
      Graves yawn, and yield your dead
      Till death be utterèd,   20
            Heavily, heavily.

⌈CLAUDIO⌉
Now, unto thy bones good night.
Yearly will I do this rite.
DON PEDRO
Good morrow, masters, put your torches out.
   The wolves have preyed, and look, the gentle day 25
Before the wheels of Phoebus round about
   Dapples the drowsy east with spots of grey.
Thanks to you all, and leave us. Fare you well.
CLAUDIO
Good morrow, masters. Each his several way.
DON PEDRO
Come, let us hence, and put on other weeds,   30
   And then to Leonato's we will go.
CLAUDIO
And Hymen now with luckier issue speed 's
   Than this for whom we rendered up this woe.
                                           Exeunt

5.4 *Enter Leonato, Antonio, Benedick, Beatrice,*
    Margaret, Ursula, Friar Francis, and Hero

FRIAR
Did I not tell you she was innocent?
LEONATO
So are the Prince and Claudio who accused her
Upon the error that you heard debated.
But Margaret was in some fault for this,
Although against her will as it appears   5
In the true course of all the question.
ANTONIO
Well, I am glad that all things sorts so well.
BENEDICK
And so am I, being else by faith enforced
To call young Claudio to a reckoning for it.
LEONATO
Well, daughter, and you gentlewomen all,   10
Withdraw into a chamber by yourselves,
And when I send for you come hither masked.
    Exeunt Beatrice, Hero, Margaret, and Ursula
The Prince and Claudio promised by this hour
To visit me. You know your office, brother,
You must be father to your brother's daughter,   15
And give her to young Claudio.
ANTONIO
Which I will do with confirmed countenance.
BENEDICK
Friar, I must entreat your pains, I think.
FRIAR To do what, signor?
BENEDICK
To bind me or undo me, one of them.   20
Signor Leonato, truth it is, good signor,
Your niece regards me with an eye of favour.
LEONATO
That eye my daughter lent her, 'tis most true.
BENEDICK
And I do with an eye of love requite her.
LEONATO
The sight whereof I think you had from me,   25
From Claudio and the Prince. But what's your will?
BENEDICK
Your answer, sir, is enigmatical.
But for my will, my will is your good will
May stand with ours this day to be conjoined
In the state of honourable marriage,   30
In which, good Friar, I shall desire your help.
LEONATO
My heart is with your liking.
FRIAR   And my help.
Here comes the Prince and Claudio.
    Enter Don Pedro and Claudio with attendants
DON PEDRO
Good morrow to this fair assembly.
LEONATO
Good morrow, Prince. Good morrow, Claudio.   35
We here attend you. Are you yet determined
Today to marry with my brother's daughter?

CLAUDIO
I'll hold my mind, were she an Ethiope.
LEONATO
Call her forth, brother, here's the Friar ready.
    Exit Antonio
DON PEDRO
Good morrow, Benedick. Why, what's the matter   40
That you have such a February face,
So full of frost, of storm and cloudiness?
CLAUDIO
I think he thinks upon the savage bull.
Tush, fear not, man, we'll tip thy horns with gold,
And all Europa shall rejoice at thee   45
As once Europa did at lusty Jove
When he would play the noble beast in love.
BENEDICK
Bull Jove, sir, had an amiable low,
And some such strange bull leapt your father's cow
And got a calf in that same noble feat   50
Much like to you, for you have just his bleat.
    Enter Antonio with Hero, Beatrice, Margaret, and
    Ursula, masked
CLAUDIO
For this I owe you. Here comes other reck'nings.
Which is the lady I must seize upon?
⌜ANTONIO⌝
This same is she, and I do give you her.
CLAUDIO
Why then, she's mine. Sweet, let me see your face. 55
LEONATO
No, that you shall not till you take her hand
Before this Friar and swear to marry her.
CLAUDIO (*to Hero*)
Give me your hand before this holy friar.
I am your husband if you like of me.
HERO (*unmasking*)
And when I lived I was your other wife;   60
And when you loved, you were my other husband.
CLAUDIO
Another Hero!
HERO   Nothing certainer.
One Hero died defiled, but I do live,
And surely as I live, I am a maid.
DON PEDRO
The former Hero, Hero that is dead!   65
LEONATO
She died, my lord, but whiles her slander lived.
FRIAR
All this amazement can I qualify
When after that the holy rites are ended
I'll tell you largely of fair Hero's death.
Meantime, let wonder seem familiar,   70
And to the chapel let us presently.
BENEDICK
Soft and fair, Friar, which is Beatrice?
BEATRICE (*unmasking*)
I answer to that name, what is your will?

BENEDICK
Do not you love me?
BEATRICE   Why no, no more than reason.
BENEDICK
Why then, your uncle and the Prince and Claudio
Have been deceived. They swore you did.
BEATRICE
Do not you love me?
BENEDICK   Troth no, no more than reason.
BEATRICE
Why then, my cousin, Margaret, and Ursula
Are much deceived, for they did swear you did.
BENEDICK
They swore that you were almost sick for me.   80
BEATRICE
They swore that you were wellnigh dead for me.
BENEDICK
'Tis no such matter. Then you do not love me?
BEATRICE
No, truly, but in friendly recompense.
LEONATO
Come, cousin, I am sure you love the gentleman.
CLAUDIO
And I'll be sworn upon't that he loves her,   85
For here's a paper written in his hand,
A halting sonnet of his own pure brain,
Fashioned to Beatrice.
HERO   And here's another,
Writ in my cousin's hand, stol'n from her pocket,
Containing her affection unto Benedick.   90
BENEDICK A miracle! Here's our own hands against our
hearts. Come, I will have thee, but by this light, I take
thee for pity.
BEATRICE I would not deny you, but by this good day, I
yield upon great persuasion, and partly to save your
life, for I was told you were in a consumption.   96

BENEDICK (kissing her) Peace, I will stop your mouth.
DON PEDRO
How dost thou, Benedick the married man?
BENEDICK I'll tell thee what, Prince: a college of wit-
crackers cannot flout me out of my humour. Dost thou
think I care for a satire or an epigram? No, if a man
will be beaten with brains, a shall wear nothing
handsome about him. In brief, since I do purpose to
marry, I will think nothing to any purpose that the
world can say against it, and therefore never flout at
me for what I have said against it. For man is a giddy
thing, and this is my conclusion. For thy part, Claudio,
I did think to have beaten thee, but in that thou art
like to be my kinsman, live unbruised, and love my
cousin.   110
CLAUDIO I had well hoped thou wouldst have denied
Beatrice, that I might have cudgelled thee out of thy
single life to make thee a double dealer, which out of
question thou wilt be, if my cousin do not look
exceeding narrowly to thee.   115
BENEDICK Come, come, we are friends, let's have a dance
ere we are married, that we may lighten our own
hearts and our wives' heels.
LEONATO We'll have dancing afterward.   119
BENEDICK First, of my word. Therefore play, music. (To
Don Pedro) Prince, thou art sad, get thee a wife, get
thee a wife. There is no staff more reverend than one
tipped with horn.
          Enter Messenger
MESSENGER
My lord, your brother John is ta'en in flight,
And brought with armèd men back to Messina.   125
BENEDICK Think not on him till tomorrow, I'll devise thee
brave punishments for him. Strike up, pipers.
          Dance, and exeunt

AS YOU LIKE IT

As You Like It is first heard of in the Stationers' Register on 4 August 1600, and was probably written not long before. In spite of its early entry for publication, it was not printed until 1623. This play, with its contrasts between court and country, its bucolic as well as its aristocratic characters, its inset songs and poems, its predominantly woodland setting, its conscious artifice and its romantic ending, is the one in which Shakespeare makes most use of the conventions of pastoral literature, though he does not wholly endorse them.

The story of the love between a high-born maiden—Rosalind—oppressed by the uncle—Duke Frederick—who has usurped his elder brother's dukedom, and Orlando, the third and youngest son of Duke Frederick's old enemy Sir Rowland de Bois, himself oppressed by his tyrannical eldest brother Oliver, derives from Thomas Lodge's *Rosalynde*, a prose romance interspersed with verses, which first appeared in 1590 and was several times reprinted. There are many indications that Shakespeare thought of the action as taking place in the Ardenne area of France, as in *Rosalynde*, even though there was also a Forest of Arden in Warwickshire. Like Lodge, Shakespeare counterpoints the developing love between Rosalind—who for much of the action is disguised as a boy, Ganymede—with the idealized pastoral romance of Silvius and Phoebe; he adds the down-to-earth, unromantic affair between the jester Touchstone and Audrey. Once Rosalind and her cousin Celia (also disguised) reach the forest, plot is virtually suspended in favour of a series of scintillating conversations making much use of prose. The sudden flowering of love between Celia and Orlando's brother Oliver, newly converted to virtue, is based on *Rosalynde*, but Shakespeare alters the climax of the story, bringing Hymen, the god of marriage, on stage to resolve all complications. As well as Touchstone, Shakespeare added the melancholy courtier Jaques, both of whom act as commentators, though from very different standpoints.

The first performances of Shakespeare's text after his own time were given in 1740. It rapidly established itself in the theatrical repertoire, and has also been appreciated for its literary qualities. It has usually been played in picturesque settings, often since the late nineteenth century in the open air. Rosalind (written originally, of course, for a boy actor) is the dominant character, but other roles, especially Jaques, Touchstone, Audrey, Corin, and—in his single scene—William, have proved particularly effective when played by performers with a strong sense of their latent individuality.

THE PERSONS OF THE PLAY

DUKE SENIOR, living in banishment

ROSALIND, his daughter, later disguised as Ganymede

AMIENS
JAQUES } Lords attending on him

TWO PAGES

DUKE FREDERICK

CELIA, his daughter, later disguised as Aliena

LE BEAU, a courtier attending on him

CHARLES, Duke Frederick's wrestler

TOUCHSTONE, a jester

OLIVER, eldest son of Sir Rowland de Bois

JAQUES
ORLANDO } his younger brothers

ADAM, a former servant of Sir Rowland

DENIS, Oliver's servant

SIR OLIVER MARTEXT, a country clergyman

CORIN, an old shepherd

SILVIUS, a young shepherd, in love with Phoebe

PHOEBE, a shepherdess

WILLIAM, a countryman, in love with Audrey

AUDREY, a goatherd, betrothed to Touchstone

HYMEN, god of marriage

Lords, pages, and other attendants

As You Like It

1.1 *Enter Orlando and Adam*

ORLANDO As I remember, Adam, it was upon this fashion bequeathed me by will but poor a thousand crowns, and, as thou sayst, charged my brother on his blessing to breed me well—and there begins my sadness. My brother Jaques he keeps at school, and report speaks goldenly of his profit. For my part, he keeps me rustically at home—or, to speak more properly, stays me here at home unkept; for call you that keeping for a gentleman of my birth, that differs not from the stalling of an ox? His horses are bred better, for besides that they are fair with their feeding, they are taught their manège, and to that end riders dearly hired. But I, his brother, gain nothing under him but growth, for the which his animals on his dunghills are as much bound to him as I. Besides this nothing that he so plentifully gives me, the something that nature gave me his countenance seems to take from me. He lets me feed with his hinds, bars me the place of a brother, and as much as in him lies, mines my gentility with my education. This is it, Adam, that grieves me; and the spirit of my father, which I think is within me, begins to mutiny against this servitude. I will no longer endure it, though yet I know no wise remedy how to avoid it. 23

Enter Oliver

ADAM Yonder comes my master, your brother.

ORLANDO Go apart, Adam, and thou shalt hear how he will shake me up. 26

Adam stands aside

OLIVER Now, sir, what make you here?

ORLANDO Nothing. I am not taught to make anything.

OLIVER What mar you then, sir? 29

ORLANDO Marry, sir, I am helping you to mar that which God made, a poor unworthy brother of yours, with idleness.

OLIVER Marry, sir, be better employed, and be nought awhile. 34

ORLANDO Shall I keep your hogs, and eat husks with them? What prodigal portion have I spent, that I should come to such penury?

OLIVER Know you where you are, sir?

ORLANDO O sir, very well; here in your orchard.

OLIVER Know you before whom, sir? 40

ORLANDO Ay, better than him I am before knows me. I know you are my eldest brother, and in the gentle condition of blood you should so know me. The courtesy of nations allows you my better, in that you are the first-born; but the same tradition takes not away my blood, were there twenty brothers betwixt us. I have as much of my father in me as you, albeit I confess your coming before me is nearer to his reverence.

OLIVER (*assailing him*) What, boy!

ORLANDO (*seizing him by the throat*) Come, come, elder brother, you are too young in this. 51

OLIVER Wilt thou lay hands on me, villain?

ORLANDO I am no villein. I am the youngest son of Sir Rowland de Bois. He was my father, and he is thrice a villain that says such a father begot villeins. Wert thou not my brother, I would not take this hand from thy throat till this other had pulled out thy tongue for saying so. Thou hast railed on thyself.

ADAM (*coming forward*) Sweet masters, be patient. For your father's remembrance, be at accord. 60

OLIVER (*to Orlando*) Let me go, I say.

ORLANDO I will not till I please. You shall hear me. My father charged you in his will to give me good education. You have trained me like a peasant, obscuring and hiding from me all gentleman-like qualities. The spirit of my father grows strong in me, and I will no longer endure it. Therefore allow me such exercises as may become a gentleman, or give me the poor allottery my father left me by testament. With that I will go buy my fortunes. 70

OLIVER And what wilt thou do—beg when that is spent? Well, sir, get you in. I will not long be troubled with you. You shall have some part of your will. I pray you, leave me.

ORLANDO I will no further offend you than becomes me for my good. 76

OLIVER (*to Adam*) Get you with him, you old dog.

ADAM Is 'old dog' my reward? Most true, I have lost my teeth in your service. God be with my old master, he would not have spoke such a word. 80

Exeunt Orlando and Adam

OLIVER Is it even so? Begin you to grow upon me? I will physic your rankness, and yet give no thousand crowns neither. Holla, Denis!

Enter Denis

DENIS Calls your worship?

OLIVER Was not Charles, the Duke's wrestler, here to speak with me? 86

DENIS So please you, he is here at the door, and importunes access to you.

OLIVER Call him in. *Exit Denis*

'Twill be a good way. And tomorrow the wrestling is.

Enter Charles

CHARLES Good morrow to your worship. 91

OLIVER Good Monsieur Charles—what's the new news at the new court?

CHARLES There's no news at the court, sir, but the old news: that is, the old Duke is banished by his younger brother, the new Duke, and three or four loving lords have put themselves into voluntary exile with him, whose lands and revenues enrich the new Duke; therefore he gives them good leave to wander.

OLIVER Can you tell if Rosalind, the Duke's daughter, be banished with her father? 101

CHARLES O no; for the Duke's daughter her cousin so

loves her, being ever from their cradles bred together, that she would have followed her exile, or have died to stay behind her. She is at the court, and no less beloved of her uncle than his own daughter; and never two ladies loved as they do.   107

OLIVER Where will the old Duke live?

CHARLES They say he is already in the forest of Ardenne, and a many merry men with him; and there they live like the old Robin Hood of England. They say many young gentlemen flock to him every day, and fleet the time carelessly, as they did in the golden world.

OLIVER What, you wrestle tomorrow before the new Duke?   115

CHARLES Marry do I, sir, and I came to acquaint you with a matter. I am given, sir, secretly to understand that your younger brother, Orlando, hath a disposition to come in disguised against me to try a fall. Tomorrow, sir, I wrestle for my credit, and he that escapes me without some broken limb, shall acquit him well. Your brother is but young and tender, and for your love I would be loath to foil him, as I must for my own honour if he come in. Therefore out of my love to you I came hither to acquaint you withal, that either you might stay him from his intendment, or brook such disgrace well as he shall run into, in that it is a thing of his own search, and altogether against my will.   128

OLIVER Charles, I thank thee for thy love to me, which thou shalt find I will most kindly requite. I had myself notice of my brother's purpose herein, and have by underhand means laboured to dissuade him from it; but he is resolute. I'll tell thee, Charles, it is the stubbornest young fellow of France, full of ambition, an envious emulator of every man's good parts, a secret and villainous contriver against me his natural brother. Therefore use thy discretion. I had as lief thou didst break his neck as his finger. And thou wert best look to't; for if thou dost him any slight disgrace, or if he do not mightily grace himself on thee, he will practise against thee by poison, entrap thee by some treacherous device, and never leave thee till he hath ta'en thy life by some indirect means or other. For I assure thee— and almost with tears I speak it—there is not one so young and so villainous this day living. I speak but brotherly of him, but should I anatomize him to thee as he is, I must blush and weep, and thou must look pale and wonder.   148

CHARLES I am heartily glad I came hither to you. If he come tomorrow I'll give him his payment. If ever he go alone again, I'll never wrestle for prize more. And so God keep your worship.   152

OLIVER Farewell, good Charles.   *Exit Charles*

Now will I stir this gamester. I hope I shall see an end of him, for my soul—yet I know not why—hates nothing more than he. Yet he's gentle; never schooled, and yet learned; full of noble device; of all sorts enchantingly beloved; and, indeed, so much in the heart of the world, and especially of my own people, who best know him, that I am altogether misprized.

But it shall be not so long. This wrestler shall clear all. Nothing remains but that I kindle the boy thither, which now I'll go about.   *Exit*

1.2   *Enter Rosalind and Celia*

CELIA I pray thee Rosalind, sweet my coz, be merry.

ROSALIND Dear Celia, I show more mirth than I am mistress of; and would you yet I were merrier? Unless you could teach me to forget a banished father you must not learn me how to remember any extraordinary pleasure.   6

CELIA Herein I see thou lovest me not with the full weight that I love thee. If my uncle, thy banished father, had banished thy uncle, the Duke my father, so thou hadst been still with me I could have taught my love to take thy father for mine. So wouldst thou, if the truth of thy love to me were so righteously tempered as mine is to thee.   13

ROSALIND Well, I will forget the condition of my estate to rejoice in yours.   15

CELIA You know my father hath no child but I, nor none is like to have. And truly, when he dies thou shalt be his heir; for what he hath taken away from thy father perforce, I will render thee again in affection. By mine honour I will, and when I break that oath, let me turn monster. Therefore, my sweet Rose, my dear Rose, be merry.   22

ROSALIND From henceforth I will, coz, and devise sports. Let me see, what think you of falling in love?   24

CELIA Marry, I prithee do, to make sport withal; but love no man in good earnest, nor no further in sport neither than with safety of a pure blush thou mayst in honour come off again.

ROSALIND What shall be our sport, then?   29

CELIA Let us sit and mock the good housewife Fortune from her wheel, that her gifts may henceforth be bestowed equally.

ROSALIND I would we could do so, for her benefits are mightily misplaced; and the bountiful blind woman doth most mistake in her gifts to women.   35

CELIA 'Tis true; for those that she makes fair she scarce makes honest, and those that she makes honest she makes very ill-favouredly.

ROSALIND Nay, now thou goest from Fortune's office to Nature's. Fortune reigns in gifts of the world, not in the lineaments of nature.   41

Enter Touchstone the clown

CELIA No. When Nature hath made a fair creature, may she not by Fortune fall into the fire? Though Nature hath given us wit to flout at Fortune, hath not Fortune sent in this fool to cut off the argument?   45

ROSALIND Indeed, there is Fortune too hard for Nature, when Fortune makes Nature's natural the cutter-off of Nature's wit.

CELIA Peradventure this is not Fortune's work, neither, but Nature's, who perceiveth our natural wits too dull to reason of such goddesses, and hath sent this natural for our whetstone; for always the dullness of the fool is the whetstone of the wits. How now, wit: whither wander you?

TOUCHSTONE Mistress, you must come away to your father.

CELIA Were you made the messenger?   56

TOUCHSTONE No, by mine honour, but I was bid to come for you.

ROSALIND Where learned you that oath, fool?   59

TOUCHSTONE Of a certain knight that swore 'by his honour' they were good pancakes, and swore 'by his honour' the mustard was naught. Now I'll stand to it the pancakes were naught and the mustard was good, and yet was not the knight forsworn.

CELIA How prove you that in the great heap of your knowledge?   66

ROSALIND Ay, marry, now unmuzzle your wisdom.

TOUCHSTONE Stand you both forth now. Stroke your chins, and swear by your beards that I am a knave.

CELIA By our beards—if we had them—thou art.   70

TOUCHSTONE By my knavery—if I had it—then I were; but if you swear by that that is not, you are not forsworn. No more was this knight, swearing by his honour, for he never had any; or if he had, he had sworn it away before ever he saw those pancakes or that mustard.   76

CELIA Prithee, who is't that thou meanest?

TOUCHSTONE One that old Frederick, your father, loves.

⌜CELIA⌝ My father's love is enough to honour him. Enough, speak no more of him; you'll be whipped for taxation one of these days.   81

TOUCHSTONE The more pity that fools may not speak wisely what wise men do foolishly.

CELIA By my troth, thou sayst true; for since the little wit that fools have was silenced, the little foolery that wise men have makes a great show. Here comes Monsieur Le Beau.   87

Enter Le Beau

ROSALIND With his mouth full of news.

CELIA Which he will put on us as pigeons feed their young.   90

ROSALIND Then shall we be news-crammed.

CELIA All the better: we shall be the more marketable. *Bonjour*, Monsieur Le Beau, what's the news?

LE BEAU Fair princess, you have lost much good sport.

CELIA Sport? Of what colour?   95

LE BEAU What colour, madam? How shall I answer you?

ROSALIND As wit and fortune will.

TOUCHSTONE Or as the destinies decrees.

CELIA Well said. That was laid on with a trowel.

TOUCHSTONE Nay, if I keep not my rank—   100

ROSALIND Thou losest thy old smell.

LE BEAU You amaze me, ladies. I would have told you of good wrestling, which you have lost the sight of.

ROSALIND Yet tell us the manner of the wrestling.   104

LE BEAU I will tell you the beginning, and if it please your ladyships you may see the end, for the best is yet to do, and here, where you are, they are coming to perform it.

CELIA Well, the beginning that is dead and buried.

LE BEAU There comes an old man and his three sons—

CELIA I could match this beginning with an old tale.   111

LE BEAU Three proper young men, of excellent growth and presence.

ROSALIND With bills on their necks: 'Be it known unto all men by these presents'—   115

LE BEAU The eldest of the three wrestled with Charles, the Duke's wrestler, which Charles in a moment threw him, and broke three of his ribs, that there is little hope of life in him. So he served the second, and so the third. Yonder they lie, the poor old man their father making such pitiful dole over them that all the beholders take his part with weeping.

ROSALIND Alas!

TOUCHSTONE But what is the sport, monsieur, that the ladies have lost?   125

LE BEAU Why, this that I speak of.

TOUCHSTONE Thus men may grow wiser every day. It is the first time that ever I heard breaking of ribs was sport for ladies.

CELIA Or I, I promise thee.   130

ROSALIND But is there any else longs to see this broken music in his sides? Is there yet another dotes upon rib-breaking? Shall we see this wrestling, cousin?

LE BEAU You must if you stay here, for here is the place appointed for the wrestling, and they are ready to perform it.   136

CELIA Yonder sure they are coming. Let us now stay and see it.

Flourish. Enter Duke Frederick, Lords, Orlando, Charles, and attendants

DUKE FREDERICK Come on. Since the youth will not be entreated, his own peril on his forwardness.   140

ROSALIND Is yonder the man?

LE BEAU Even he, madam.

CELIA Alas, he is too young. Yet he looks successfully.

DUKE FREDERICK How now, daughter and cousin; are you crept hither to see the wrestling?   145

ROSALIND Ay, my liege, so please you give us leave.

DUKE FREDERICK You will take little delight in it, I can tell you, there is such odds in the man. In pity of the challenger's youth I would fain dissuade him, but he will not be entreated. Speak to him, ladies; see if you can move him.   151

CELIA Call him hither, good Monsieur Le Beau.

DUKE FREDERICK Do so. I'll not be by.

He stands aside

LE BEAU (*to Orlando*) Monsieur the challenger, the Princess calls for you.   155

ORLANDO I attend them with all respect and duty.

ROSALIND Young man, have you challenged Charles the wrestler?

ORLANDO No, fair Princess. He is the general challenger; I come but in as others do, to try with him the strength of my youth.   161

CELIA Young gentleman, your spirits are too bold for your years. You have seen cruel proof of this man's strength. If you saw yourself with your eyes, or knew yourself

with your judgement, the fear of your adventure would
counsel you to a more equal enterprise. We pray you
for your own sake to embrace your own safety and
give over this attempt.   168

ROSALIND Do, young sir. Your reputation shall not
therefore be misprized. We will make it our suit to the
Duke that the wrestling might not go forward.   171

ORLANDO I beseech you, punish me not with your hard
thoughts, wherein I confess me much guilty to deny
so fair and excellent ladies anything. But let your fair
eyes and gentle wishes go with me to my trial, wherein
if I be foiled, there is but one shamed that was never
gracious, if killed, but one dead that is willing to be so.
I shall do my friends no wrong, for I have none to
lament me; the world no injury, for in it I have nothing.
Only in the world I fill up a place which may be better
supplied when I have made it empty.   181

ROSALIND The little strength that I have, I would it were
with you.

CELIA And mine, to eke out hers.

ROSALIND Fare you well. Pray heaven I be deceived in
you.   186

CELIA Your heart's desires be with you.

CHARLES Come, where is this young gallant that is so
desirous to lie with his mother earth?

ORLANDO Ready, sir; but his will hath in it a more modest
working.   191

DUKE FREDERICK You shall try but one fall.

CHARLES No, I warrant your grace you shall not entreat
him to a second that have so mightily persuaded him
from a first.   195

ORLANDO You mean to mock me after; you should not
have mocked me before. But come your ways.

ROSALIND (to Orlando) Now Hercules be thy speed, young
man!

CELIA I would I were invisible, to catch the strong fellow
by the leg.   201

Charles and Orlando wrestle

ROSALIND O excellent young man!

CELIA If I had a thunderbolt in mine eye, I can tell who
should down.

Orlando throws Charles. Shout

DUKE FREDERICK
No more, no more.

ORLANDO   Yes, I beseech your grace.   205
I am not yet well breathed.

DUKE FREDERICK How dost thou, Charles?

LE BEAU He cannot speak, my lord.

DUKE FREDERICK Bear him away.

Attendants carry Charles off

What is thy name, young man?   210

ORLANDO Orlando, my liege, the youngest son of Sir
Rowland de Bois.

DUKE FREDERICK
I would thou hadst been son to some man else.
The world esteemed thy father honourable,
But I did find him still mine enemy.   215

Thou shouldst have better pleased me with this deed
Hadst thou descended from another house.
But fare thee well, thou art a gallant youth.
I would thou hadst told me of another father.

*Exeunt Duke Frederick, Le Beau, ⌐Touchstone,¬
Lords, and attendants*

CELIA (to Rosalind)
Were I my father, coz, would I do this?   220

ORLANDO
I am more proud to be Sir Rowland's son,
His youngest son, and would not change that calling
To be adopted heir to Frederick.

ROSALIND
My father loved Sir Rowland as his soul,
And all the world was of my father's mind.   225
Had I before known this young man his son
I should have given him tears unto entreaties
Ere he should thus have ventured.

CELIA   Gentle cousin,
Let us go thank him, and encourage him.
My father's rough and envious disposition   230
Sticks me at heart.—Sir, you have well deserved.
If you do keep your promises in love
But justly, as you have exceeded all promise,
Your mistress shall be happy.

ROSALIND (giving him a chain from her neck) Gentleman,
Wear this for me—one out of suits with fortune, 235
That could give more but that her hand lacks means.
Shall we go, coz?

CELIA   Ay. Fare you well, fair gentleman.

Rosalind and Celia turn to go

ORLANDO (aside)
Can I not say 'I thank you'? My better parts
Are all thrown down, and that which here stands up
Is but a quintain, a mere lifeless block.   240

ROSALIND (to Celia)
He calls us back. My pride fell with my fortunes,
I'll ask him what he would.—Did you call, sir?
Sir, you have wrestled well, and overthrown
More than your enemies.

CELIA Will you go, coz?   245

ROSALIND Have with you. (To Orlando) Fare you well.

Exeunt Rosalind and Celia

ORLANDO
What passion hangs these weights upon my tongue?
I cannot speak to her, yet she urged conference.

Enter Le Beau

O poor Orlando! Thou art overthrown.
Or Charles or something weaker masters thee.   250

LE BEAU
Good sir, I do in friendship counsel you
To leave this place. Albeit you have deserved
High commendation, true applause, and love,
Yet such is now the Duke's condition
That he misconsters all that you have done.   255
The Duke is humorous. What he is indeed
More suits you to conceive than I to speak of.

ORLANDO
I thank you, sir. And pray you tell me this,
Which of the two was daughter of the Duke
That here was at the wrestling?   260
LE BEAU
Neither his daughter, if we judge by manners—
But yet indeed the shorter is his daughter.
The other is daughter to the banished Duke,
And here detained by her usurping uncle
To keep his daughter company, whose loves   265
Are dearer than the natural bond of sisters.
But I can tell you that of late this Duke
Hath ta'en displeasure 'gainst his gentle niece,
Grounded upon no other argument
But that the people praise her for her virtues   270
And pity her for her good father's sake.
And, on my life, his malice 'gainst the lady
Will suddenly break forth. Sir, fare you well.
Hereafter, in a better world than this,
I shall desire more love and knowledge of you.   275
ORLANDO
I rest much bounden to you. Fare you well.
                                              Exit Le Beau
Thus must I from the smoke into the smother,
From tyrant Duke unto a tyrant brother.—
But heavenly Rosalind!   *Exit*

1.3   *Enter Celia and Rosalind*
CELIA Why cousin, why Rosalind—Cupid have mercy, not a word?
ROSALIND Not one to throw at a dog.
CELIA No, thy words are too precious to be cast away upon curs. Throw some of them at me. Come, lame me with reasons.   6
ROSALIND Then there were two cousins laid up, when the one should be lamed with reasons and the other mad without any.
CELIA But is all this for your father?   10
ROSALIND No, some of it is for my child's father. O how full of briers is this working-day world!
CELIA They are but burs, cousin, thrown upon thee in holiday foolery. If we walk not in the trodden paths our very petticoats will catch them.   15
ROSALIND I could shake them off my coat. These burs are in my heart.
CELIA Hem them away.
ROSALIND I would try, if I could cry 'hem' and have him.
CELIA Come, come, wrestle with thy affections.   20
ROSALIND O, they take the part of a better wrestler than myself.
CELIA O, a good wish upon you! You will try in time, in despite of a fall. But turning these jests out of service, let us talk in good earnest. Is it possible on such a sudden you should fall into so strong a liking with old Sir Rowland's youngest son?   27
ROSALIND The Duke my father loved his father dearly.
CELIA Doth it therefore ensue that you should love his son dearly? By this kind of chase I should hate him,

for my father hated his father dearly; yet I hate not Orlando.
ROSALIND No, faith, hate him not, for my sake.
CELIA Why should I not? Doth he not deserve well?
                Enter Duke Frederick, with Lords
ROSALIND Let me love him for that, and do you love him because I do. Look, here comes the Duke.   36
CELIA With his eyes full of anger.
DUKE FREDERICK *(to Rosalind)*
Mistress, dispatch you with your safest haste,
And get you from our court.
ROSALIND Me, uncle?   40
DUKE FREDERICK You, cousin.
Within these ten days if that thou beest found
So near our public court as twenty miles,
Thou diest for it.
ROSALIND   I do beseech your grace
Let me the knowledge of my fault bear with me.   45
If with myself I hold intelligence,
Or have acquaintance with mine own desires,
If that I do not dream, or be not frantic—
As I do trust I am not—then, dear uncle,
Never so much as in a thought unborn   50
Did I offend your highness.
DUKE FREDERICK   Thus do all traitors.
If their purgation did consist in words
They are as innocent as grace itself.
Let it suffice thee that I trust thee not.
ROSALIND
Yet your mistrust cannot make me a traitor.   55
Tell me whereon the likelihood depends?
DUKE FREDERICK
Thou art thy father's daughter—there's enough.
ROSALIND
So was I when your highness took his dukedom;
So was I when your highness banished him.
Treason is not inherited, my lord,   60
Or if we did derive it from our friends,
What's that to me? My father was no traitor.
Then, good my liege, mistake me not so much
To think my poverty is treacherous.
CELIA Dear sovereign, hear me speak.   65
DUKE FREDERICK
Ay, Celia, we stayed her for your sake,
Else had she with her father ranged along.
CELIA
I did not then entreat to have her stay.
It was your pleasure, and your own remorse.
I was too young that time to value her,   70
But now I know her. If she be a traitor,
Why, so am I. We still have slept together,
Rose at an instant, learned, played, eat together,
And wheresoe'er we went, like Juno's swans
Still we went coupled and inseparable.   75
DUKE FREDERICK
She is too subtle for thee, and her smoothness,
Her very silence, and her patience
Speak to the people, and they pity her.

Thou art a fool. She robs thee of thy name,
And thou wilt show more bright and seem more
    virtuous   80
When she is gone. Then open not thy lips.
Firm and irrevocable is my doom
Which I have passed upon her. She is banished.

CELIA
Pronounce that sentence then on me, my liege.
I cannot live out of her company.   85

DUKE FREDERICK
You are a fool.—You, niece, provide yourself.
If you outstay the time, upon mine honour
And in the greatness of my word, you die.
      Exit Duke Frederick, with Lords

CELIA
O my poor Rosalind, whither wilt thou go?
Wilt thou change fathers? I will give thee mine.   90
I charge thee, be not thou more grieved than I am.

ROSALIND
I have more cause.

CELIA   Thou hast not, cousin.
Prithee, be cheerful. Know'st thou not the Duke
Hath banished me, his daughter?

ROSALIND   That he hath not.

CELIA
No, hath not? Rosalind, lack'st thou then the love 95
Which teacheth thee that thou and I am one?
Shall we be sundered? Shall we part, sweet girl?
No. Let my father seek another heir.
Therefore devise with me how we may fly,
Whither to go, and what to bear with us,   100
And do not seek to take your change upon you,
To bear your griefs yourself, and leave me out.
For by this heaven, now at our sorrows pale,
Say what thou canst, I'll go along with thee.

ROSALIND Why, whither shall we go?   105

CELIA
To seek my uncle in the forest of Ardenne.

ROSALIND
Alas, what danger will it be to us,
Maids as we are, to travel forth so far!
Beauty provoketh thieves sooner than gold.

CELIA
I'll put myself in poor and mean attire,   110
And with a kind of umber smirch my face.
The like do you, so shall we pass along
And never stir assailants.

ROSALIND   Were it not better,
Because that I am more than common tall,
That I did suit me all points like a man,   115
A gallant curtal-axe upon my thigh,
A boar-spear in my hand, and in my heart,
Lie there what hidden woman's fear there will.
We'll have a swashing and a martial outside,
As many other mannish cowards have,   120
That do outface it with their semblances.

CELIA
What shall I call thee when thou art a man?

ROSALIND
I'll have no worse a name than Jove's own page,
And therefore look you call me Ganymede.
But what will you be called?   125

CELIA
Something that hath a reference to my state.
No longer Celia, but Aliena.

ROSALIND
But cousin, what if we essayed to steal
The clownish fool out of your father's court.
Would he not be a comfort to our travel?   130

CELIA
He'll go along o'er the wide world with me.
Leave me alone to woo him. Let's away,
And get our jewels and our wealth together,
Devise the fittest time and safest way
To hide us from pursuit that will be made   135
After my flight. Now go we in content,
To liberty, and not to banishment.   *Exeunt*

2.1   *Enter Duke Senior, Amiens, and two or three Lords*
      dressed as foresters

DUKE SENIOR
Now, my co-mates and brothers in exile,
Hath not old custom made this life more sweet
Than that of painted pomp? Are not these woods
More free from peril than the envious court?
Here feel we not the penalty of Adam,   5
The seasons' difference, as the icy fang
And churlish chiding of the winter's wind,
Which when it bites and blows upon my body
Even till I shrink with cold, I smile, and say
'This is no flattery. These are counsellors   10
That feelingly persuade me what I am.'
Sweet are the uses of adversity
Which, like the toad, ugly and venomous,
Wears yet a precious jewel in his head;
And this our life, exempt from public haunt,   15
Finds tongues in trees, books in the running brooks,
Sermons in stones, and good in everything.

AMIENS
I would not change it. Happy is your grace
That can translate the stubbornness of fortune
Into so quiet and so sweet a style.   20

DUKE SENIOR
Come, shall we go and kill us venison?
And yet it irks me the poor dappled fools,
Being native burghers of this desert city,
Should in their own confines with forkèd heads
Have their round haunches gored.

FIRST LORD   Indeed, my lord, 25
The melancholy Jaques grieves at that,
And in that kind swears you do more usurp
Than doth your brother that hath banished you.
Today my lord of Amiens and myself
Did steal behind him as he lay along   30
Under an oak, whose antic root peeps out
Upon the brook that brawls along this wood,

To the which place a poor sequestered stag
That from the hunter's aim had ta'en a hurt
Did come to languish. And indeed, my lord,   35
The wretched animal heaved forth such groans
That their discharge did stretch his leathern coat
Almost to bursting, and the big round tears
Coursed one another down his innocent nose
In piteous chase. And thus the hairy fool,   40
Much markèd of the melancholy Jaques,
Stood on th'extremest verge of the swift brook,
Augmenting it with tears.
DUKE SENIOR   But what said Jaques?
Did he not moralize this spectacle?
FIRST LORD
O yes, into a thousand similes.   45
First, for his weeping into the needless stream;
'Poor deer,' quoth he, 'thou mak'st a testament
As worldlings do, giving thy sum of more
To that which had too much.' Then being there
    alone,
Left and abandoned of his velvet friend,   50
''Tis right,' quoth he, 'thus misery doth part
The flux of company.' Anon a careless herd
Full of the pasture jumps along by him
And never stays to greet him. 'Ay,' quoth Jaques,
'Sweep on, you fat and greasy citizens,   55
'Tis just the fashion. Wherefore should you look
Upon that poor and broken bankrupt there?'
Thus most invectively he pierceth through
The body of the country, city, court,
Yea, and of this our life, swearing that we   60
Are mere usurpers, tyrants, and what's worse,
To fright the animals and to kill them up
In their assigned and native dwelling place.
DUKE SENIOR
And did you leave him in this contemplation?
SECOND LORD
We did, my lord, weeping and commenting   65
Upon the sobbing deer.
DUKE SENIOR   Show me the place.
I love to cope him in these sullen fits,
For then he's full of matter.
FIRST LORD   I'll bring you to him straight.
                                   Exeunt

2.2   *Enter Duke Frederick, with Lords*
DUKE FREDERICK
Can it be possible that no man saw them?
It cannot be. Some villains of my court
Are of consent and sufferance in this.
FIRST LORD
I cannot hear of any that did see her.
The ladies her attendants of her chamber   5
Saw her abed, and in the morning early
They found the bed untreasured of their mistress.
SECOND LORD
My lord, the roynish clown at whom so oft
Your grace was wont to laugh is also missing.
Hisperia, the Princess' gentlewoman,   10

Confesses that she secretly o'erheard
Your daughter and her cousin much commend
The parts and graces of the wrestler
That did but lately foil the sinewy Charles,
And she believes wherever they are gone   15
That youth is surely in their company.
DUKE FREDERICK
Send to his brother; fetch that gallant hither.
If he be absent, bring his brother to me,
I'll make him find him. Do this suddenly,
And let not search and inquisition quail   20
To bring again these foolish runaways.
                               Exeunt severally

2.3   *Enter Orlando and Adam, meeting*
ORLANDO Who's there?
ADAM
What, my young master, O my gentle master,
O my sweet master, O you memory
Of old Sir Rowland, why, what make you here!
Why are you virtuous? Why do people love you?   5
And wherefore are you gentle, strong, and valiant?
Why would you be so fond to overcome
The bonny prizer of the humorous Duke?
Your praise is come too swiftly home before you.
Know you not, master, to some kind of men   10
Their graces serve them but as enemies?
No more do yours. Your virtues, gentle master,
Are sanctified and holy traitors to you.
O, what a world is this, when what is comely
Envenoms him that bears it!   15
ORLANDO Why, what's the matter?
ADAM O, unhappy youth,
Come not within these doors. Within this roof
The enemy of all your graces lives,
Your brother—no, no brother—yet the son—   20
Yet not the son, I will not call him son—
Of him I was about to call his father,
Hath heard your praises, and this night he means
To burn the lodging where you use to lie,
And you within it. If he fail of that,   25
He will have other means to cut you off.
I overheard him and his practices.
This is no place, this house is but a butchery.
Abhor it, fear it, do not enter it.
ORLANDO
Why, whither, Adam, wouldst thou have me go?   30
ADAM
No matter whither, so you come not here.
ORLANDO
What, wouldst thou have me go and beg my food,
Or with a base and boisterous sword enforce
A thievish living on the common road?
This I must do, or know not what to do.   35
Yet this I will not do, do how I can.
I rather will subject me to the malice
Of a diverted blood and bloody brother.
ADAM
But do not so. I have five hundred crowns,

The thrifty hire I saved under your father,   40
Which I did store to be my foster-nurse
When service should in my old limbs lie lame,
And unregarded age in corners thrown.
Take that, and he that doth the ravens feed,
Yea providently caters for the sparrow,   45
Be comfort to my age. Here is the gold.
All this I give you. Let me be your servant.
Though I look old, yet I am strong and lusty,
For in my youth I never did apply
Hot and rebellious liquors in my blood,   50
Nor did not with unbashful forehead woo
The means of weakness and debility.
Therefore my age is as a lusty winter,
Frosty but kindly. Let me go with you,
I'll do the service of a younger man   55
In all your business and necessities.

ORLANDO
O good old man, how well in thee appears
The constant service of the antique world,
When service sweat for duty, not for meed!
Thou art not for the fashion of these times,   60
Where none will sweat but for promotion,
And having that do choke their service up
Even with the having. It is not so with thee.
But, poor old man, thou prun'st a rotten tree,
That cannot so much as a blossom yield   65
In lieu of all thy pains and husbandry.
But come thy ways. We'll go along together,
And ere we have thy youthful wages spent,
We'll light upon some settled low content.

ADAM
Master, go on, and I will follow thee   70
To the last gasp with truth and loyalty.
From seventeen years till now almost fourscore
Here livèd I, but now live here no more.
At seventeen years, many their fortunes seek,
But at fourscore, it is too late a week.   75
Yet fortune cannot recompense me better
Than to die well, and not my master's debtor.   *Exeunt*

2.4   *Enter Rosalind in man's clothes as Ganymede; Celia*
      as Aliena, a shepherdess; and Touchstone the
      clown

ROSALIND O Jupiter, how weary are my spirits!
TOUCHSTONE I care not for my spirits, if my legs were not
  weary.
ROSALIND I could find in my heart to disgrace my man's
  apparel and to cry like a woman. But I must comfort
  the weaker vessel, as doublet and hose ought to show
  itself courageous to petticoat; therefore, courage, good
  Aliena!   8
CELIA I pray you, bear with me. I cannot go no further.
TOUCHSTONE For my part, I had rather bear with you than
  bear you. Yet I should bear no cross if I did bear you,
  for I think you have no money in your purse.   12
ROSALIND Well, this is the forest of Ardenne.
TOUCHSTONE Ay, now am I in Ardenne; the more fool I.

When I was at home I was in a better place; but
travellers must be content.   16
      Enter Corin and Silvius
ROSALIND Ay, be so, good Touchstone. Look you, who
  comes here—a young man and an old in solemn talk.
CORIN *(to Silvius)*
That is the way to make her scorn you still.
SILVIUS
O Corin, that thou knew'st how I do love her!   20
CORIN
I partly guess; for I have loved ere now.
SILVIUS
No, Corin, being old thou canst not guess,
Though in thy youth thou wast as true a lover
As ever sighed upon a midnight pillow.
But if thy love were ever like to mine—   25
As sure I think did never man love so—
How many actions most ridiculous
Hast thou been drawn to by thy fantasy?
CORIN
Into a thousand that I have forgotten.
SILVIUS
O, thou didst then never love so heartily.   30
If thou rememberest not the slightest folly
That ever love did make thee run into,
Thou hast not loved.
Or if thou hast not sat as I do now,
Wearing thy hearer in thy mistress' praise,   35
Thou hast not loved.
Or if thou hast not broke from company
Abruptly, as my passion now makes me,
Thou hast not loved.
O, Phoebe, Phoebe, Phoebe!   *Exit*
ROSALIND
Alas, poor shepherd, searching of thy wound,   41
I have by hard adventure found mine own.
TOUCHSTONE And I mine. I remember when I was in love
  I broke my sword upon a stone and bid him take that
  for coming a-night to Jane Smile, and I remember the
  kissing of her batlet, and the cow's dugs that her pretty
  chapped hands had milked; and I remember the wooing
  of a peascod instead of her, from whom I took two
  cods, and giving her them again, said with weeping
  tears, 'Wear these for my sake.' We that are true lovers
  run into strange capers. But as all is mortal in nature,
  so is all nature in love mortal in folly.   52
ROSALIND Thou speak'st wiser than thou art ware of.
TOUCHSTONE Nay, I shall ne'er be ware of mine own wit
  till I break my shins against it.   55
ROSALIND
Jove, Jove, this shepherd's passion
Is much upon my fashion.
TOUCHSTONE And mine, but it grows something stale with
  me.
CELIA
I pray you, one of you question yon man   60
If he for gold will give us any food.
I faint almost to death.

TOUCHSTONE (*to Corin*) Holla, you clown!
ROSALIND Peace, fool, he's not thy kinsman.
CORIN Who calls? 65
TOUCHSTONE Your betters, sir.
CORIN Else are they very wretched.
ROSALIND (*to Touchstone*)
  Peace, I say. (*To Corin*) Good even to you, friend.
CORIN
  And to you, gentle sir, and to you all.
ROSALIND
  I prithee, shepherd, if that love or gold 70
  Can in this desert place buy entertainment,
  Bring us where we may rest ourselves, and feed.
  Here's a young maid with travel much oppressed,
  And faints for succour.
CORIN   Fair sir, I pity her,
  And wish, for her sake more than for mine own, 75
  My fortunes were more able to relieve her.
  But I am shepherd to another man,
  And do not shear the fleeces that I graze.
  My master is of churlish disposition,
  And little recks to find the way to heaven 80
  By doing deeds of hospitality.
  Besides, his cot, his flocks, and bounds of feed
  Are now on sale, and at our sheepcote now
  By reason of his absence there is nothing
  That you will feed on. But what is, come see, 85
  And in my voice most welcome shall you be.
ROSALIND
  What is he that shall buy his flock and pasture?
CORIN
  That young swain that you saw here but erewhile,
  That little cares for buying anything.
ROSALIND
  I pray thee, if it stand with honesty,
  Buy thou the cottage, pasture, and the flock, 90
  And thou shalt have to pay for it of us.
CELIA
  And we will mend thy wages. I like this place,
  And willingly could waste my time in it.
CORIN
  Assuredly the thing is to be sold.
  Go with me. If you like upon report 95
  The soil, the profit, and this kind of life,
  I will your very faithful feeder be,
  And buy it with your gold right suddenly.   *Exeunt*

2.5   *Enter Amiens, Jaques, and other Lords dressed as
          foresters*

⌈AMIENS⌉ (*sings*)
          Under the greenwood tree
          Who loves to lie with me,
          And turn his merry note
          Unto the sweet bird's throat,
      Come hither, come hither, come hither. 5
          Here shall he see
          No enemy
      But winter and rough weather.

JAQUES More, more, I prithee, more. 9
AMIENS It will make you melancholy, Monsieur Jaques.
JAQUES I thank it. More, I prithee, more. I can suck
  melancholy out of a song as a weasel sucks eggs. More,
  I prithee, more.
AMIENS My voice is ragged, I know I cannot please you.
JAQUES I do not desire you to please me, I do desire you
  to sing. Come, more; another stanza. Call you 'em
  stanzas? 17
AMIENS What you will, Monsieur Jaques.
JAQUES Nay, I care not for their names, they owe me
  nothing. Will you sing? 20
AMIENS More at your request than to please myself.
JAQUES Well then, if ever I thank any man, I'll thank
  you. But that they call compliment is like th'encounter
  of two dog-apes, and when a man thanks me heartily
  methinks I have given him a penny and he renders me
  the beggarly thanks. Come, sing; and you that will
  not, hold your tongues. 27
AMIENS Well, I'll end the song.—Sirs, cover the while.
          Lords prepare food and drink
  The Duke will drink under this tree. (*To Jaques*) He hath
  been all this day to look you. 30
JAQUES And I have been all this day to avoid him. He is
  too disputable for my company. I think of as many
  matters as he, but I give heaven thanks, and make no
  boast of them. Come, warble, come.

ALL (*sing*)   Who doth ambition shun, 35
          And loves to live i'th' sun,
          Seeking the food he eats
          And pleased with what he gets,
      Come hither, come hither, come hither.
          Here shall he see 40
          No enemy
      But winter and rough weather.

JAQUES I'll give you a verse to this note that I made
  yesterday in despite of my invention.
AMIENS And I'll sing it. 45
JAQUES Thus it goes:
          If it do come to pass
          That any man turn ass,
          Leaving his wealth and ease
          A stubborn will to please, 50
          Ducdame, ducdame, ducdame.
          Here shall he see
          Gross fools as he,
          An if he will come to me.
AMIENS What's that 'ducdame'? 55
JAQUES 'Tis a Greek invocation to call fools into a circle.
  I'll go sleep if I can. If I cannot, I'll rail against all the
  firstborn of Egypt.
AMIENS And I'll go seek the Duke; his banquet is prepared.
          Exeunt

2.6   *Enter Orlando and Adam*
ADAM Dear master, I can go no further. O, I die for food.
  Here lie I down and measure out my grave. Farewell,
  kind master.

ORLANDO Why, how now, Adam? No greater heart in
thee? Live a little, comfort a little, cheer thyself a little.
If this uncouth forest yield anything savage I will either
be food for it or bring it for food to thee. Thy conceit
is nearer death than thy powers. For my sake be
comfortable. Hold death awhile at the arm's end. I will
here be with thee presently, and if I bring thee not
something to eat, I will give thee leave to die. But if
thou diest before I come, thou art a mocker of my
labour. Well said. Thou lookest cheerly, and I'll be with
thee quickly. Yet thou liest in the bleak air. Come, I
will bear thee to some shelter, and thou shalt not die
for lack of a dinner if there live anything in this desert.
Cheerly, good Adam.   *Orlando carries Adam off*

2.7   *Enter Duke Senior and Lords dressed as outlaws*
DUKE SENIOR
  I think he be transformed into a beast,
  For I can nowhere find him like a man.
FIRST LORD
  My lord, he is but even now gone hence.
  Here was he merry, hearing of a song.
DUKE SENIOR
  If he, compact of jars, grow musical   5
  We shall have shortly discord in the spheres.
  Go seek him. Tell him I would speak with him.
         Enter Jaques
FIRST LORD
  He saves my labour by his own approach.
DUKE SENIOR
  Why, how now, monsieur, what a life is this,
  That your poor friends must woo your company!   10
  What, you look merrily.
JAQUES
  A fool, a fool, I met a fool i'th' forest,
  A motley fool—a miserable world!—
  As I do live by food, I met a fool,
  Who laid him down and basked him in the sun,   15
  And railed on Lady Fortune in good terms,
  In good set terms, and yet a motley fool.
  'Good morrow, fool,' quoth I. 'No, sir,' quoth he,
  'Call me not fool till heaven hath sent me fortune.'
  And then he drew a dial from his poke,   20
  And looking on it with lack-lustre eye
  Says very wisely 'It is ten o'clock.'
  'Thus we may see', quoth he, 'how the world wags.
  'Tis but an hour ago since it was nine,
  And after one hour more 'twill be eleven.   25
  And so from hour to hour we ripe and ripe,
  And then from hour to hour we rot and rot;
  And thereby hangs a tale.' When I did hear
  The motley fool thus moral on the time
  My lungs began to crow like chanticleer,   30
  That fools should be so deep-contemplative,
  And I did laugh sans intermission
  An hour by his dial. O noble fool,
  A worthy fool—motley's the only wear.

DUKE SENIOR What fool is this?   35
JAQUES
  O worthy fool!—One that hath been a courtier,
  And says 'If ladies be but young and fair
  They have the gift to know it.' And in his brain,
  Which is as dry as the remainder biscuit
  After a voyage, he hath strange places crammed   40
  With observation, the which he vents
  In mangled forms. O that I were a fool,
  I am ambitious for a motley coat.
DUKE SENIOR
  Thou shalt have one.
JAQUES   It is my only suit,
  Provided that you weed your better judgements   45
  Of all opinion that grows rank in them
  That I am wise. I must have liberty
  Withal, as large a charter as the wind,
  To blow on whom I please, for so fools have;
  And they that are most gallèd with my folly,   50
  They most must laugh. And why, sir, must they so?
  The why is plain as way to parish church:
  He that a fool doth very wisely hit
  Doth very foolishly, although he smart,
  Seem aught but senseless of the bob. If not,   55
  The wise man's folly is anatomized
  Even by the squandering glances of the fool.
  Invest me in my motley. Give me leave
  To speak my mind, and I will through and through
  Cleanse the foul body of th'infected world,   60
  If they will patiently receive my medicine.
DUKE SENIOR
  Fie on thee, I can tell what thou wouldst do.
JAQUES
  What, for a counter, would I do but good?
DUKE SENIOR
  Most mischievous foul sin, in chiding sin;
  For thou thyself hast been a libertine,   65
  As sensual as the brutish sting itself,
  And all th'embossèd sores and headed evils
  That thou with licence of free foot hast caught
  Wouldst thou disgorge into the general world.
JAQUES Why, who cries out on pride   70
  That can therein tax any private party?
  Doth it not flow as hugely as the sea,
  Till that the weary very means do ebb?
  What woman in the city do I name
  When that I say the city-woman bears   75
  The cost of princes on unworthy shoulders?
  Who can come in and say that I mean her
  When such a one as she, such is her neighbour?
  Or what is he of basest function,
  That says his bravery is not on my cost,   80
  Thinking that I mean him, but therein suits
  His folly to the mettle of my speech?
  There then, how then, what then, let me see wherein
  My tongue hath wronged him. If it do him right,
  Then he hath wronged himself. If he be free,   85

Why then my taxing like a wild goose flies,
Unclaimed of any man. But who comes here?
Enter Orlando, with sword drawn

ORLANDO
Forbear, and eat no more!

JAQUES   Why, I have eat none yet.

ORLANDO
Nor shalt not till necessity be served.

JAQUES Of what kind should this cock come of?   90

DUKE SENIOR
Art thou thus boldened, man, by thy distress?
Or else a rude despiser of good manners,
That in civility thou seem'st so empty?

ORLANDO
You touched my vein at first. The thorny point
Of bare distress hath ta'en from me the show   95
Of smooth civility. Yet am I inland bred,
And know some nurture. But forbear, I say.
He dies that touches any of this fruit
Till I and my affairs are answerèd.

JAQUES An you will not be answered with reason, I must
die.   101

DUKE SENIOR
What would you have? Your gentleness shall force
More than your force move us to gentleness.

ORLANDO
I almost die for food; and let me have it.

DUKE SENIOR
Sit down and feed, and welcome to our table.   105

ORLANDO
Speak you so gently? Pardon me, I pray you.
I thought that all things had been savage here,
And therefore put I on the countenance
Of stern commandment. But whate'er you are
That in this desert inaccessible,   110
Under the shade of melancholy boughs,
Lose and neglect the creeping hours of time,
If ever you have looked on better days,
If ever been where bells have knolled to church,
If ever sat at any good man's feast,   115
If ever from your eyelids wiped a tear,
And know what 'tis to pity, and be pitied,
Let gentleness my strong enforcement be.
In the which hope I blush, and hide my sword.

DUKE SENIOR
True is it that we have seen better days,   120
And have with holy bell been knolled to church,
And sat at good men's feasts, and wiped our eyes
Of drops that sacred pity hath engendered.
And therefore sit you down in gentleness,
And take upon command what help we have   125
That to your wanting may be ministered.

ORLANDO
Then but forbear your food a little while
Whiles, like a doe, I go to find my fawn
And give it food. There is an old poor man
Who after me hath many a weary step   130
Limped in pure love. Till he be first sufficed,

Oppressed with two weak evils, age and hunger,
I will not touch a bit.

DUKE SENIOR   Go find him out,
And we will nothing waste till you return.

ORLANDO
I thank ye; and be blessed for your good comfort!   135
Exit

DUKE SENIOR
Thou seest we are not all alone unhappy.
This wide and universal theatre
Presents more woeful pageants than the scene
Wherein we play in.

JAQUES   All the world's a stage,
And all the men and women merely players.   140
They have their exits and their entrances,
And one man in his time plays many parts,
His acts being seven ages. At first the infant,
Mewling and puking in the nurse's arms.
Then the whining schoolboy with his satchel   145
And shining morning face, creeping like snail
Unwillingly to school. And then the lover,
Sighing like furnace, with a woeful ballad
Made to his mistress' eyebrow. Then, a soldier,
Full of strange oaths, and bearded like the pard,   150
Jealous in honour, sudden, and quick in quarrel,
Seeking the bubble reputation
Even in the cannon's mouth. And then the justice,
In fair round belly with good capon lined,
With eyes severe and beard of formal cut,   155
Full of wise saws and modern instances;
And so he plays his part. The sixth age shifts
Into the lean and slippered pantaloon,
With spectacles on nose and pouch on side,
His youthful hose, well saved, a world too wide   160
For his shrunk shank, and his big, manly voice,
Turning again toward childish treble, pipes
And whistles in his sound. Last scene of all,
That ends this strange, eventful history,
Is second childishness and mere oblivion,   165
Sans teeth, sans eyes, sans taste, sans everything.
Enter Orlando bearing Adam

DUKE SENIOR
Welcome. Set down your venerable burden
And let him feed.

ORLANDO I thank you most for him.

ADAM So had you need;   170
I scarce can speak to thank you for myself.

DUKE SENIOR
Welcome. Fall to. I will not trouble you
As yet to question you about your fortunes.
Give us some music, and, good cousin, sing.

⌈AMIENS⌉ (*sings*)
    Blow, blow, thou winter wind,   175
    Thou art not so unkind
        As man's ingratitude.
    Thy tooth is not so keen,
    Because thou art not seen,
        Although thy breath be rude.   180

Hey-ho, sing hey-ho, unto the green holly.
Most friendship is feigning, most loving, mere folly.
　Then hey-ho, the holly;
　This life is most jolly.

　Freeze, freeze, thou bitter sky,　　　　185
　That dost not bite so nigh
　　As benefits forgot.
　Though thou the waters warp,
　Thy sting is not so sharp
　　As friend remembered not.　　　　　190
Hey-ho, sing hey-ho, unto the green holly.
Most friendship is feigning, most loving, mere folly.
　Then hey-ho, the holly;
　This life is most jolly.

DUKE SENIOR (*to Orlando*)
If that you were the good Sir Rowland's son,　195
As you have whispered faithfully you were,
And as mine eye doth his effigies witness
Most truly limned and living in your face,
Be truly welcome hither. I am the Duke　　199
That loved your father. The residue of your fortune,
Go to my cave and tell me. (*To Adam*) Good old man,
Thou art right welcome, as thy master is.—
(*To Lords*) Support him by the arm. (*To Orlando*) Give
　me your hand,
And let me all your fortunes understand.　　*Exeunt*

3.1　*Enter Duke Frederick, Lords, and Oliver*
DUKE FREDERICK
Not see him since? Sir, sir, that cannot be.
But were I not the better part made mercy,
I should not seek an absent argument
Of my revenge, thou present. But look to it:
Find out thy brother wheresoe'er he is.　　　5
Seek him with candle. Bring him, dead or living,
Within this twelvemonth, or turn thou no more
To seek a living in our territory.
Thy lands, and all things that thou dost call thine
Worth seizure, do we seize into our hands　　10
Till thou canst quit thee by thy brother's mouth
Of what we think against thee.
OLIVER
O that your highness knew my heart in this.
I never loved my brother in my life.
DUKE FREDERICK
More villain thou. (*To Lords*) Well, push him out of
　doors,　　　　　　　　　　　　　　　15
And let my officers of such a nature
Make an extent upon his house and lands.
Do this expediently, and turn him going.
　　　　　　　　　　　　　　　Exeunt severally

3.2　*Enter Orlando with a paper*
ORLANDO
Hang there, my verse, in witness of my love;
　And thou thrice-crownèd queen of night, survey

With thy chaste eye, from thy pale sphere above,
　Thy huntress' name that my full life doth sway.
O Rosalind, these trees shall be my books,　　5
　And in their barks my thoughts I'll character
That every eye which in this forest looks
　Shall see thy virtue witnessed everywhere.
Run, run, Orlando; carve on every tree
The fair, the chaste, and unexpressive she.　*Exit*
　　Enter Corin and Touchstone the clown
CORIN And how like you this shepherd's life, Master
　Touchstone?
TOUCHSTONE Truly, shepherd, in respect of itself, it is a
　good life; but in respect that it is a shepherd's life, it
　is naught. In respect that it is solitary, I like it very
　well; but in respect that it is private, it is a very vile
　life. Now in respect it is in the fields, it pleaseth me
　well; but in respect it is not in the court, it is tedious.
　As it is a spare life, look you, it fits my humour well;
　but as there is no more plenty in it, it goes much
　against my stomach. Hast any philosophy in thee,
　shepherd?　　　　　　　　　　　　　22
CORIN No more but that I know the more one sickens,
　the worse at ease he is, and that he that wants money,
　means, and content is without three good friends; that
　the property of rain is to wet, and fire to burn; that
　good pasture makes fat sheep; and that a great cause
　of the night is lack of the sun; that he that hath learned
　no wit by nature nor art may complain of good breeding
　or comes of a very dull kindred.
TOUCHSTONE Such a one is a natural philosopher. Wast
　ever in court, shepherd?　　　　　　　32
CORIN No, truly.
TOUCHSTONE Then thou art damned.
CORIN Nay, I hope.
TOUCHSTONE Truly thou art damned, like an ill-roasted
　egg, all on one side.　　　　　　　　37
CORIN For not being at court? Your reason?
TOUCHSTONE Why, if thou never wast at court thou never
　sawest good manners. If thou never sawest good
　manners, then thy manners must be wicked, and
　wickedness is sin, and sin is damnation. Thou art in a
　parlous state, shepherd.　　　　　　　43
CORIN Not a whit, Touchstone. Those that are good
　manners at the court are as ridiculous in the country
　as the behaviour of the country is most mockable at
　the court. You told me you salute not at the court but
　you kiss your hands. That courtesy would be uncleanly
　if courtiers were shepherds.
TOUCHSTONE Instance, briefly; come, instance.　　50
CORIN Why, we are still handling our ewes, and their
　fells, you know, are greasy.
TOUCHSTONE Why, do not your courtier's hands sweat?
　And is not the grease of a mutton as wholesome as the
　sweat of a man? Shallow, shallow. A better instance,
　I say. Come.　　　　　　　　　　56
CORIN Besides, our hands are hard.
TOUCHSTONE Your lips will feel them the sooner. Shallow
　again. A more sounder instance. Come.

CORIN And they are often tarred over with the surgery of our sheep; and would you have us kiss tar? The courtier's hands are perfumed with civet.   62

TOUCHSTONE Most shallow, man. Thou worms' meat in respect of a good piece of flesh indeed, learn of the wise, and perpend: civet is of a baser birth than tar, the very uncleanly flux of a cat. Mend the instance, shepherd.   67

CORIN You have too courtly a wit for me. I'll rest.

TOUCHSTONE Wilt thou rest damned? God help thee, shallow man. God make incision in thee, thou art raw.

CORIN Sir, I am a true labourer. I earn that I eat, get that I wear; owe no man hate, envy no man's happiness; glad of other men's good, content with my harm; and the greatest of my pride is to see my ewes graze and my lambs suck.   75

TOUCHSTONE That is another simple sin in you, to bring the ewes and the rams together, and to offer to get your living by the copulation of cattle; to be bawd to a bell-wether, and to betray a she-lamb of a twelve-month to a crooked-pated old cuckoldly ram, out of all reasonable match. If thou beest not damned for this, the devil himself will have no shepherds. I cannot see else how thou shouldst scape.

CORIN Here comes young Master Ganymede, my new mistress's brother.   85

Enter Rosalind as Ganymede

ROSALIND (*reads*)
    'From the east to western Ind
    No jewel is like Rosalind.
    Her worth being mounted on the wind
    Through all the world bears Rosalind.
    All the pictures fairest lined   90
    Are but black to Rosalind.
    Let no face be kept in mind
    But the fair of Rosalind.'

TOUCHSTONE I'll rhyme you so eight years together, dinners, and suppers, and sleeping-hours excepted. It is the right butter-women's rank to market.

ROSALIND Out, fool.

TOUCHSTONE For a taste:
    If a hart do lack a hind,
    Let him seek out Rosalind.   100
    If the cat will after kind,
    So, be sure, will Rosalind.
    Wintered garments must be lined,
    So must slender Rosalind.
    They that reap must sheaf and bind,   105
    Then to cart with Rosalind.
    'Sweetest nut hath sourest rind',
    Such a nut is Rosalind.
    He that sweetest rose will find
    Must find love's prick, and Rosalind.   110
This is the very false gallop of verses. Why do you infect yourself with them?

ROSALIND Peace, you dull fool, I found them on a tree.

TOUCHSTONE Truly, the tree yields bad fruit.   114

ROSALIND I'll graft it with you, and then I shall graft it with a medlar; then it will be the earliest fruit i'th' country, for you'll be rotten ere you be half-ripe, and that's the right virtue of the medlar.

TOUCHSTONE You have said; but whether wisely or no, let the forest judge.   120

Enter Celia, as Aliena, with a writing

ROSALIND
Peace, here comes my sister, reading. Stand aside.

CELIA (*reads*)
    'Why should this a desert be?
    For it is unpeopled? No.
    Tongues I'll hang on every tree,
    That shall civil sayings show.   125
    Some, how brief the life of man
    Runs his erring pilgrimage,
    That the stretching of a span
    Buckles in his sum of age.
    Some of violated vows   130
    'Twixt the souls of friend and friend.
    But upon the fairest boughs,
    Or at every sentence end,
    Will I 'Rosalinda' write,
    Teaching all that read to know   135
    The quintessence of every sprite
    Heaven would in little show.
    Therefore heaven nature charged
    That one body should be filled
    With all graces wide-enlarged.   140
    Nature presently distilled
    Helen's cheek, but not her heart,
    Cleopatra's majesty,
    Atalanta's better part,
    Sad Lucretia's modesty.   145
    Thus Rosalind of many parts
    By heavenly synod was devised
    Of many faces, eyes, and hearts
    To have the touches dearest prized.
    Heaven would that she these gifts should have 150
    And I to live and die her slave.'

ROSALIND O most gentle Jupiter! What tedious homily of love have you wearied your parishioners withal, and never cried 'Have patience, good people.'

CELIA How now, back, friends. Shepherd, go off a little. Go with him, sirrah.   156

TOUCHSTONE Come, shepherd, let us make an honourable retreat, though not with bag and baggage, yet with scrip and scrippage.   *Exit with Corin*

CELIA Didst thou hear these verses?   160

ROSALIND O yes, I heard them all, and more, too, for some of them had in them more feet than the verses would bear.

CELIA That's no matter; the feet might bear the verses.

ROSALIND Ay, but the feet were lame, and could not bear themselves without the verse, and therefore stood lamely in the verse.   167

CELIA But didst thou hear without wondering how thy name should be hanged and carved upon these trees?

ROSALIND I was seven of the nine days out of the wonder before you came; for look here what I found on a palm-tree; (*showing Celia the verses*) I was never so berhymed since Pythagoras' time that I was an Irish rat, which I can hardly remember.

CELIA Trow you who hath done this? 175

ROSALIND Is it a man?

CELIA And a chain that you once wore about his neck. Change you colour?

ROSALIND I prithee, who? 179

CELIA O Lord, Lord, it is a hard matter for friends to meet. But mountains may be removed with earthquakes, and so encounter.

ROSALIND Nay, but who is it?

CELIA Is it possible?

ROSALIND Nay, I prithee now with most petitionary vehemence, tell me who it is. 186

CELIA O wonderful, wonderful, and most wonderful-wonderful, and yet again wonderful, and after that out of all whooping! 189

ROSALIND Good my complexion! Dost thou think, though I am caparisoned like a man, I have a doublet and hose in my disposition? One inch of delay more is a South Sea of discovery. I prithee tell me who is it quickly, and speak apace. I would thou couldst stammer, that thou mightst pour this concealed man out of thy mouth as wine comes out of a narrow-mouthed bottle—either too much at once, or none at all. I prithee, take the cork out of thy mouth, that I may drink thy tidings.

CELIA So you may put a man in your belly. 200

ROSALIND Is he of God's making? What manner of man? Is his head worth a hat? Or his chin worth a beard?

CELIA Nay, he hath but a little beard.

ROSALIND Why, God will send more, if the man will be thankful. Let me stay the growth of his beard, if thou delay me not the knowledge of his chin. 206

CELIA It is young Orlando, that tripped up the wrestler's heels and your heart both in an instant.

ROSALIND Nay, but the devil take mocking. Speak sad brow and true maid. 210

CELIA I'faith, coz, 'tis he.

ROSALIND Orlando?

CELIA Orlando.

ROSALIND Alas the day, what shall I do with my doublet and hose! What did he when thou sawest him? What said he? How looked he? Wherein went he? What makes he here? Did he ask for me? Where remains he? How parted he with thee? And when shalt thou see him again? Answer me in one word. 219

CELIA You must borrow me Gargantua's mouth first, 'tis a word too great for any mouth of this age's size. To say ay and no to these particulars is more than to answer in a catechism.

ROSALIND But doth he know that I am in this forest, and in man's apparel? Looks he as freshly as he did the day he wrestled? 226

CELIA It is as easy to count atomies as to resolve the

propositions of a lover; but take a taste of my finding him, and relish it with good observance. I found him under a tree, like a dropped acorn— 230

ROSALIND It may well be called Jove's tree when it drops forth such fruit.

CELIA Give me audience, good madam.

ROSALIND Proceed.

CELIA There lay he, stretched along like a wounded knight— 236

ROSALIND Though it be pity to see such a sight, it well becomes the ground.

CELIA Cry 'holla' to thy tongue, I prithee: it curvets unseasonably.—He was furnished like a hunter— 240

ROSALIND O ominous—he comes to kill my heart.

CELIA I would sing my song without a burden; thou bringest me out of tune.

ROSALIND Do you not know I am a woman? When I think, I must speak.—Sweet, say on. 245

Enter Orlando and Jaques

CELIA You bring me out. Soft, comes he not here?

ROSALIND 'Tis he. Slink by, and note him.

Rosalind and Celia stand aside

JAQUES (*to Orlando*) I thank you for your company, but, good faith, I had as lief have been myself alone.

ORLANDO And so had I. But yet for fashion' sake, I thank you too for your society. 251

JAQUES God b'wi'you; let's meet as little as we can.

ORLANDO I do desire we may be better strangers.

JAQUES I pray you mar no more trees with writing love-songs in their barks. 255

ORLANDO I pray you mar no more of my verses with reading them ill-favouredly.

JAQUES Rosalind is your love's name?

ORLANDO Yes, just.

JAQUES I do not like her name. 260

ORLANDO There was no thought of pleasing you when she was christened.

JAQUES What stature is she of?

ORLANDO Just as high as my heart. 264

JAQUES You are full of pretty answers. Have you not been acquainted with goldsmiths' wives, and conned them out of rings?

ORLANDO Not so; but I answer you right painted cloth, from whence you have studied your questions. 269

JAQUES You have a nimble wit; I think 'twas made of Atalanta's heels. Will you sit down with me, and we two will rail against our mistress the world, and all our misery?

ORLANDO I will chide no breather in the world but myself, against whom I know most faults. 275

JAQUES The worst fault you have is to be in love.

ORLANDO 'Tis a fault I will not change for your best virtue. I am weary of you.

JAQUES By my troth, I was seeking for a fool when I found you. 280

ORLANDO He is drowned in the brook. Look but in, and you shall see him.

JAQUES There I shall see mine own figure.

ORLANDO Which I take to be either a fool or a cipher.

JAQUES I'll tarry no longer with you. Farewell, good Signor Love.   286

ORLANDO I am glad of your departure. Adieu, good Monsieur Melancholy.   *Exit Jaques*

ROSALIND (*to Celia*) I will speak to him like a saucy lackey, and under that habit play the knave with him. (*To Orlando*) Do you hear, forester?   291

ORLANDO Very well. What would you?

ROSALIND I pray you, what is't o'clock?

ORLANDO You should ask me what time o' day. There's no clock in the forest.   295

ROSALIND Then there is no true lover in the forest, else sighing every minute and groaning every hour would detect the lazy foot of time as well as a clock.

ORLANDO And why not the swift foot of time? Had not that been as proper?   300

ROSALIND By no means, sir. Time travels in divers paces with divers persons. I'll tell you who time ambles withal, who time trots withal, who time gallops withal, and who he stands still withal.

ORLANDO I prithee, who doth he trot withal?   305

ROSALIND Marry, he trots hard with a young maid between the contract of her marriage and the day it is solemnized. If the interim be but a se'nnight, time's pace is so hard that it seems the length of seven year.

ORLANDO Who ambles time withal?   310

ROSALIND With a priest that lacks Latin, and a rich man that hath not the gout; for the one sleeps easily because he cannot study, and the other lives merrily because he feels no pain, the one lacking the burden of lean and wasteful learning, the other knowing no burden of heavy tedious penury. These time ambles withal.

ORLANDO Who doth he gallop withal?

ROSALIND With a thief to the gallows; for though he go as softly as foot can fall, he thinks himself too soon there.   320

ORLANDO Who stays it still withal?

ROSALIND With lawyers in the vacation; for they sleep between term and term, and then they perceive not how time moves.

ORLANDO Where dwell you, pretty youth?   325

ROSALIND With this shepherdess, my sister, here in the skirts of the forest, like fringe upon a petticoat.

ORLANDO Are you native of this place?

ROSALIND As the coney that you see dwell where she is kindled.   330

ORLANDO Your accent is something finer than you could purchase in so removed a dwelling.

ROSALIND I have been told so of many; but indeed an old religious uncle of mine taught me to speak, who was in his youth an inland man; one that knew courtship too well, for there he fell in love. I have heard him read many lectures against it, and I thank God I am not a woman, to be touched with so many giddy offences as he hath generally taxed their whole sex withal.   340

ORLANDO Can you remember any of the principal evils that he laid to the charge of women?

ROSALIND There were none principal; they were all like one another as halfpence are, every one fault seeming monstrous till his fellow-fault came to match it.   345

ORLANDO I prithee, recount some of them.

ROSALIND No. I will not cast away my physic but on those that are sick. There is a man haunts the forest that abuses our young plants with carving Rosalind on their barks; hangs odes upon hawthorns and elegies on brambles; all, forsooth, deifying the name of Rosalind. If I could meet that fancy-monger, I would give him some good counsel, for he seems to have the quotidian of love upon him.

ORLANDO I am he that is so love-shaked. I pray you, tell me your remedy.   356

ROSALIND There is none of my uncle's marks upon you. He taught me how to know a man in love, in which cage of rushes I am sure you are not prisoner.

ORLANDO What were his marks?   360

ROSALIND A lean cheek, which you have not; a blue eye and sunken, which you have not; an unquestionable spirit, which you have not; a beard neglected, which you have not—but I pardon you for that, for simply your having in beard is a younger brother's revenue. Then your hose should be ungartered, your bonnet unbanded, your sleeve unbuttoned, your shoe untied, and everything about you demonstrating a careless desolation. But you are no such man. You are rather point-device in your accoutrements, as loving yourself than seeming the lover of any other.   371

ORLANDO Fair youth, I would I could make thee believe I love.

ROSALIND Me believe it? You may as soon make her that you love believe it, which I warrant she is apter to do than to confess she does. That is one of the points in the which women still give the lie to their consciences. But in good sooth, are you he that hangs the verses on the trees wherein Rosalind is so admired?

ORLANDO I swear to thee, youth, by the white hand of Rosalind, I am that he, that unfortunate he.   381

ROSALIND But are you so much in love as your rhymes speak?

ORLANDO Neither rhyme nor reason can express how much.   385

ROSALIND Love is merely a madness, and I tell you, deserves as well a dark house and a whip as madmen do; and the reason why they are not so punished and cured is that the lunacy is so ordinary that the whippers are in love too. Yet I profess curing it by counsel. 390

ORLANDO Did you ever cure any so?

ROSALIND Yes, one; and in this manner. He was to imagine me his love, his mistress; and I set him every day to woo me. At which time would I, being but a moonish youth, grieve, be effeminate, changeable, longing and liking, proud, fantastical, apish, shallow, inconstant, full of tears, full of smiles; for every passion something, and for no passion truly anything, as boys and women are for the most part cattle of this colour—would now like him, now loathe him; then entertain him, then forswear him; now weep for him, then spit at him, that I drave my suitor from his mad humour of love to a living humour of madness, which was to forswear the full stream of the world and to live in a nook merely monastic. And thus I cured him, and this way will I take upon me to wash your liver as clean as a sound sheep's heart, that there shall not be one spot of love in't.   408

ORLANDO I would not be cured, youth.

ROSALIND I would cure you if you would but call me Rosalind and come every day to my cot, and woo me.

ORLANDO Now by the faith of my love, I will. Tell me where it is.   413

ROSALIND Go with me to it, and I'll show it you. And by the way you shall tell me where in the forest you live. Will you go?

ORLANDO With all my heart, good youth.

ROSALIND Nay, you must call me Rosalind.—Come, sister. Will you go?   *Exeunt*

3.3   *Enter Touchstone the clown and Audrey, followed by Jaques*

TOUCHSTONE Come apace, good Audrey. I will fetch up your goats, Audrey. And how, Audrey, am I the man yet? Doth my simple feature content you?   3

AUDREY Your features, Lord warrant us—what features?

TOUCHSTONE I am here with thee and thy goats as the most capricious poet honest Ovid was among the Goths.

JAQUES (*aside*) O knowledge ill-inhabited; worse than Jove in a thatched house.

TOUCHSTONE When a man's verses cannot be understood, nor a man's good wit seconded with the forward child, understanding, it strikes a man more dead than a great reckoning in a little room. Truly, I would the gods had made thee poetical.

AUDREY I do not know what 'poetical' is. Is it honest in deed and word? Is it a true thing?   15

TOUCHSTONE No, truly; for the truest poetry is the most feigning, and lovers are given to poetry; and what they swear in poetry it may be said, as lovers, they do feign.

AUDREY Do you wish, then, that the gods had made me poetical?   20

TOUCHSTONE I do, truly; for thou swearest to me thou art honest. Now if thou wert a poet, I might have some hope thou didst feign.

AUDREY Would you not have me honest?

TOUCHSTONE No, truly, unless thou wert hard-favoured; for honesty coupled to beauty is to have honey a sauce to sugar.   27

JAQUES (*aside*) A material fool.

AUDREY Well, I am not fair, and therefore I pray the gods make me honest.   30

TOUCHSTONE Truly, and to cast away honesty upon a foul slut were to put good meat into an unclean dish.

AUDREY I am not a slut, though I thank the gods I am foul.   34

TOUCHSTONE Well, praised be the gods for thy foulness. Sluttishness may come hereafter. But be it as it may be, I will marry thee; and to that end I have been with Sir Oliver Martext, the vicar of the next village, who hath promised to meet me in this place of the forest, and to couple us.   40

JAQUES (*aside*) I would fain see this meeting.

AUDREY Well, the gods give us joy.

TOUCHSTONE Amen.—A man may, if he were of a fearful heart, stagger in this attempt; for here we have no temple but the wood, no assembly but horn-beasts. But what though? Courage. As horns are odious, they are necessary. It is said many a man knows no end of his goods. Right: many a man has good horns, and knows no end of them. Well, that is the dowry of his wife, 'tis none of his own getting. Horns? Even so. Poor men alone? No, no; the noblest deer hath them as huge as the rascal. Is the single man therefore blessed? No. As a walled town is more worthier than a village, so is the forehead of a married man more honourable than the bare brow of a bachelor. And by how much defence is better than no skill, by so much is a horn more precious than to want.   57

Enter Sir Oliver Martext

Here comes Sir Oliver.—Sir Oliver Martext, you are well met. Will you dispatch us here under this tree, or shall we go with you to your chapel?   60

SIR OLIVER MARTEXT Is there none here to give the woman?

TOUCHSTONE I will not take her on gift of any man.

SIR OLIVER MARTEXT Truly she must be given, or the marriage is not lawful.

JAQUES (*coming forward*) Proceed, proceed. I'll give her.   65

TOUCHSTONE Good even, good Monsieur What-ye-call't. How do you, sir? You are very well met. God'ield you for your last company. I am very glad to see you. Even a toy in hand here, sir.

Jaques removes his hat

Nay, pray be covered.   70

JAQUES Will you be married, motley?

TOUCHSTONE As the ox hath his bow, sir, the horse his curb, and the falcon her bells, so man hath his desires; and as pigeons bill, so wedlock would be nibbling.   74

JAQUES And will you, being a man of your breeding, be married under a bush, like a beggar? Get you to church, and have a good priest that can tell you what marriage is. This fellow will but join you together as they join wainscot; then one of you will prove a shrunk panel and, like green timber, warp, warp.   80

TOUCHSTONE I am not in the mind but I were better to be married of him than of another, for he is not like to marry me well, and not being well married, it will be a good excuse for me hereafter to leave my wife.

JAQUES Go thou with me, and let me counsel thee.   85

TOUCHSTONE

Come, sweet Audrey.

We must be married, or we must live in bawdry.

Farewell, good Master Oliver. Not

O, sweet Oliver,
O, brave Oliver,   90
Leave me not behind thee

but

Wind away,
Begone, I say,
I will not to wedding with thee.   95

SIR OLIVER MARTEXT (*aside*) 'Tis no matter. Ne'er a fantastical knave of them all shall flout me out of my calling.   *Exeunt*

3.4   *Enter Rosalind as Ganymede and Celia as Aliena*

ROSALIND Never talk to me. I will weep.

CELIA Do, I prithee, but yet have the grace to consider that tears do not become a man.

ROSALIND But have I not cause to weep?

CELIA As good cause as one would desire; therefore weep.

ROSALIND His very hair is of the dissembling colour.   6

CELIA Something browner than Judas's. Marry, his kisses are Judas's own children.

ROSALIND I'faith, his hair is of a good colour.

CELIA An excellent colour. Your chestnut was ever the only colour.   11

ROSALIND And his kissing is as full of sanctity as the touch of holy bread.

CELIA He hath bought a pair of cast lips of Diana. A nun of winter's sisterhood kisses not more religiously. The very ice of chastity is in them.   16

ROSALIND But why did he swear he would come this morning, and comes not?

CELIA Nay, certainly, there is no truth in him.

ROSALIND Do you think so?   20

CELIA Yes. I think he is not a pick-purse, nor a horse-stealer; but for his verity in love, I do think him as concave as a covered goblet, or a worm-eaten nut.

ROSALIND Not true in love?

CELIA Yes, when he is in. But I think he is not in.   25

ROSALIND You have heard him swear downright he was.

CELIA 'Was' is not 'is'. Besides, the oath of a lover is no stronger than the word of a tapster. They are both the confirmer of false reckonings. He attends here in the forest on the Duke your father.   30

ROSALIND I met the Duke yesterday, and had much question with him. He asked me of what parentage I was. I told him, of as good as he, so he laughed and let me go. But what talk we of fathers when there is such a man as Orlando?   35

CELIA O that's a brave man. He writes brave verses, speaks brave words, swears brave oaths, and breaks them bravely, quite traverse, athwart the heart of his lover, as a puny tilter that spurs his horse but on one side breaks his staff, like a noble goose. But all's brave that youth mounts, and folly guides. Who comes here?

Enter Corin

CORIN

Mistress and master, you have oft enquired   42

After the shepherd that complained of love
Who you saw sitting by me on the turf,
Praising the proud disdainful shepherdess   45
That was his mistress.

CELIA   Well, and what of him?

CORIN

If you will see a pageant truly played
Between the pale complexion of true love
And the red glow of scorn and proud disdain,
Go hence a little, and I shall conduct you,   50
If you will mark it.

ROSALIND (*to Celia*)   O come, let us remove.
The sight of lovers feedeth those in love.
(*To Corin*) Bring us to this sight, and you shall say
I'll prove a busy actor in their play.   *Exeunt*

3.5   *Enter Silvius and Phoebe*

SILVIUS

Sweet Phoebe, do not scorn me, do not, Phoebe.
Say that you love me not, but say not so
In bitterness. The common executioner,
Whose heart th'accustomed sight of death makes hard,
Falls not the axe upon the humbled neck   5
But first begs pardon. Will you sterner be
Than he that dies and lives by bloody drops?
    *Enter Rosalind as Ganymede, Celia as Aliena, and
    Corin, and stand aside*

PHOEBE (*to Silvius*)

I would not be thy executioner.
I fly thee for I would not injure thee.
Thou tell'st me there is murder in mine eye.   10
'Tis pretty, sure, and very probable
That eyes, that are the frail'st and softest things,
Who shut their coward gates on atomies,
Should be called tyrants, butchers, murderers.
Now I do frown on thee with all my heart,   15
And if mine eyes can wound, now let them kill thee.
Now counterfeit to swoon, why now fall down;
Or if thou canst not, O, for shame, for shame,
Lie not, to say mine eyes are murderers.
Now show the wound mine eye hath made in thee.   20
Scratch thee but with a pin, and there remains
Some scar of it. Lean upon a rush,
The cicatrice and capable impressure
Thy palm some moment keeps. But now mine eyes,
Which I have darted at thee, hurt thee not;   25
Nor I am sure there is no force in eyes
That can do hurt.

SILVIUS O dear Phoebe,
If ever—as that ever may be near—
You meet in some fresh cheek the power of fancy, 30
Then shall you know the wounds invisible
That love's keen arrows make.

PHOEBE   But till that time
Come not thou near me. And when that time comes,
Afflict me with thy mocks, pity me not,
As till that time I shall not pity thee.   35

ROSALIND (*coming forward*)
  And why, I pray you? Who might be your mother,
  That you insult, exult, and all at once,
  Over the wretched? What though you have no
      beauty—
  As, by my faith, I see no more in you
  Than without candle may go dark to bed—   40
  Must you be therefore proud and pitiless?
  Why, what means this? Why do you look on me?
  I see no more in you than in the ordinary
  Of nature's sale-work.—'Od's my little life,
  I think she means to tangle my eyes, too.   45
  No, faith, proud mistress, hope not after it.
  'Tis not your inky brows, your black silk hair,
  Your bugle eyeballs, nor your cheek of cream,
  That can entame my spirits to your worship.
  (*To Silvius*) You, foolish shepherd, wherefore do you
      follow her   50
  Like foggy south, puffing with wind and rain?
  You are a thousand times a properer man
  Than she a woman. 'Tis such fools as you
  That makes the world full of ill-favoured children.
  'Tis not her glass but you that flatters her,   55
  And out of you she sees herself more proper
  Than any of her lineaments can show her.
  (*To Phoebe*) But, mistress, know yourself; down on
      your knees
  And thank heaven, fasting, for a good man's love;
  For I must tell you friendly in your ear,   60
  Sell when you can. You are not for all markets.
  Cry the man mercy, love him, take his offer;
  Foul is most foul, being foul to be a scoffer.—
  So, take her to thee, shepherd. Fare you well.
PHOEBE
  Sweet youth, I pray you chide a year together.   65
  I had rather hear you chide than this man woo.
ROSALIND (*to Phoebe*) He's fallen in love with your foulness
  (*to Silvius*) and she'll fall in love with my anger. If it
  be so, as fast as she answers thee with frowning looks,
  I'll sauce her with bitter words.   70
  (*To Phoebe*) Why look you so upon me?
PHOEBE
  For no ill will I bear you.
ROSALIND
  I pray you do not fall in love with me,
  For I am falser than vows made in wine.
  Besides, I like you not. If you will know my house, 75
  'Tis at the tuft of olives, here hard by.
  (*To Celia*) Will you go, sister? (*To Silvius*) Shepherd,
      ply her hard.—
  Come, sister. (*To Phoebe*) Shepherdess, look on him
      better,
  And be not proud. Though all the world could see,
  None could be so abused in sight as he.—   80
  Come, to our flock.   *Exeunt Rosalind, Celia, and Corin*
PHOEBE (*aside*)
  Dead shepherd, now I find thy saw of might:
  'Who ever loved that loved not at first sight?'

SILVIUS
  Sweet Phoebe—
PHOEBE   Ha, what sayst thou, Silvius?
SILVIUS Sweet Phoebe, pity me.   85
PHOEBE
  Why, I am sorry for thee, gentle Silvius.
SILVIUS
  Wherever sorrow is, relief would be.
  If you do sorrow at my grief in love,
  By giving love your sorrow and my grief
  Were both extermined.   90
PHOEBE
  Thou hast my love, is not that neighbourly?
SILVIUS
  I would have you.
PHOEBE   Why, that were covetousness.
  Silvius, the time was that I hated thee;
  And yet it is not that I bear thee love.
  But since that thou canst talk of love so well,   95
  Thy company, which erst was irksome to me,
  I will endure; and I'll employ thee, too.
  But do not look for further recompense
  Than thine own gladness that thou art employed.
SILVIUS
  So holy and so perfect is my love,   100
  And I in such a poverty of grace,
  That I shall think it a most plenteous crop
  To glean the broken ears after the man
  That the main harvest reaps. Loose now and then
  A scattered smile, and that I'll live upon.   105
PHOEBE
  Know'st thou the youth that spoke to me erewhile?
SILVIUS
  Not very well, but I have met him oft,
  And he hath bought the cottage and the bounds
  That the old Carlot once was master of.
PHOEBE
  Think not I love him, though I ask for him.   110
  'Tis but a peevish boy. Yet he talks well.
  But what care I for words? Yet words do well
  When he that speaks them pleases those that hear.
  It is a pretty youth—not very pretty—
  But sure he's proud; and yet his pride becomes him.
  He'll make a proper man. The best thing in him   116
  Is his complexion; and faster than his tongue
  Did make offence, his eye did heal it up.
  He is not very tall; yet for his years he's tall.
  His leg is but so-so; and yet 'tis well.   120
  There was a pretty redness in his lip,
  A little riper and more lusty-red
  Than that mixed in his cheek. 'Twas just the
      difference
  Betwixt the constant red and mingled damask.
  There be some women, Silvius, had they marked him
  In parcels as I did, would have gone near   126
  To fall in love with him; but for my part,
  I love him not, nor hate him not. And yet
  Have I more cause to hate him than to love him,

For what had he to do to chide at me?   130
He said mine eyes were black, and my hair black,
And now I am remembered, scorned at me.
I marvel why I answered not again.
But that's all one. Omittance is no quittance.
I'll write to him a very taunting letter,   135
And thou shalt bear it. Wilt thou, Silvius?

SILVIUS
Phoebe, with all my heart.

PHOEBE   I'll write it straight.
The matter's in my head and in my heart.
I will be bitter with him, and passing short.
Go with me, Silvius.   *Exeunt*

4.1   *Enter Rosalind as Ganymede, Celia as Aliena, and*
      Jaques

JAQUES I prithee, pretty youth, let me be better acquainted
with thee.

ROSALIND They say you are a melancholy fellow.

JAQUES I am so. I do love it better than laughing.

ROSALIND Those that are in extremity of either are
abominable fellows, and betray themselves to every
modern censure worse than drunkards.   7

JAQUES Why, 'tis good to be sad and say nothing.

ROSALIND Why then, 'tis good to be a post.

JAQUES I have neither the scholar's melancholy, which is
emulation, nor the musician's, which is fantastical, nor
the courtier's, which is proud, nor the soldier's, which
is ambitious, nor the lawyer's, which is politic, nor the
lady's, which is nice, nor the lover's, which is all these;
but it is a melancholy of mine own, compounded of
many simples, extracted from many objects, and indeed
the sundry contemplation of my travels, in which my
often rumination wraps me in a most humorous
sadness.   19

ROSALIND A traveller! By my faith, you have great reason
to be sad. I fear you have sold your own lands to see
other men's. Then to have seen much and to have
nothing is to have rich eyes and poor hands.

JAQUES Yes, I have gained my experience.

    Enter Orlando

ROSALIND And your experience makes you sad. I had
rather have a fool to make me merry than experience
to make me sad—and to travel for it too!   27

ORLANDO
Good day and happiness, dear Rosalind.

JAQUES Nay then, God b'wi'you an you talk in blank
verse.   30

ROSALIND Farewell, Monsieur Traveller. Look you lisp,
and wear strange suits; disable all the benefits of your
own country; be out of love with your nativity, and
almost chide God for making you that countenance
you are, or I will scarce think you have swam in a
gondola.   ⌜*Exit Jaques*⌝
Why, how now, Orlando? Where have you been all
this while? You a lover? An you serve me such another
trick, never come in my sight more.

ORLANDO My fair Rosalind, I come within an hour of my
promise.   41

ROSALIND Break an hour's promise in love! He that will
divide a minute into a thousand parts and break but a
part of the thousand part of a minute in the affairs of
love, it may be said of him that Cupid hath clapped
him o'th' shoulder, but I'll warrant him heartwhole.

ORLANDO Pardon me, dear Rosalind.   47

ROSALIND Nay, an you be so tardy, come no more in my
sight. I had as lief be wooed of a snail.

ORLANDO Of a snail?   50

ROSALIND Ay, of a snail; for though he comes slowly, he
carries his house on his head—a better jointure, I think,
than you make a woman. Besides, he brings his destiny
with him.

ORLANDO What's that?   55

ROSALIND Why, horns, which such as you are fain to be
beholden to your wives for. But he comes armed in his
fortune, and prevents the slander of his wife.

ORLANDO Virtue is no hornmaker, and my Rosalind is
virtuous.   60

ROSALIND And I am your Rosalind.

CELIA It pleases him to call you so; but he hath a Rosalind
of a better leer than you.

ROSALIND Come, woo me, woo me, for now I am in a
holiday humour, and like enough to consent. What
would you say to me now an I were your very, very
Rosalind?   67

ORLANDO I would kiss before I spoke.

ROSALIND Nay, you were better speak first, and when you
were gravelled for lack of matter you might take
occasion to kiss. Very good orators, when they are out,
they will spit; and for lovers, lacking—God warr'nt
us—matter, the cleanliest shift is to kiss.   73

ORLANDO How if the kiss be denied?

ROSALIND Then she puts you to entreaty, and there begins
new matter.   76

ORLANDO Who could be out, being before his beloved
mistress?

ROSALIND Marry, that should you if I were your mistress,
or I should think my honesty ranker than my wit.   80

ORLANDO What, of my suit?

ROSALIND Not out of your apparel, and yet out of your
suit. Am not I your Rosalind?

ORLANDO I take some joy to say you are because I would
be talking of her.   85

ROSALIND Well, in her person I say I will not have you.

ORLANDO Then in mine own person I die.

ROSALIND No, faith; die by attorney. The poor world is
almost six thousand years old, and in all this time there
was not any man died in his own person, videlicet, in
a love-cause. Troilus had his brains dashed out with a
Grecian club, yet he did what he could to die before,
and he is one of the patterns of love. Leander, he would
have lived many a fair year though Hero had turned
nun if it had not been for a hot midsummer night, for,
good youth, he went but forth to wash him in the
Hellespont and, being taken with the cramp, was
drowned; and the foolish chroniclers of that age found
it was Hero of Sestos. But these are all lies. Men have

died from time to time, and worms have eaten them, but not for love. 101

ORLANDO I would not have my right Rosalind of this mind, for I protest her frown might kill me.

ROSALIND By this hand, it will not kill a fly. But come, now I will be your Rosalind in a more coming-on disposition; and ask me what you will, I will grant it.

ORLANDO Then love me, Rosalind. 107

ROSALIND Yes, faith, will I, Fridays and Saturdays and all.

ORLANDO And wilt thou have me? 110

ROSALIND Ay, and twenty such.

ORLANDO What sayst thou?

ROSALIND Are you not good?

ORLANDO I hope so.

ROSALIND Why then, can one desire too much of a good thing? (*To Celia*) Come, sister, you shall be the priest and marry us.—Give me your hand, Orlando.—What do you say, sister? 118

ORLANDO (*to Celia*) Pray thee, marry us.

CELIA I cannot say the words. 120

ROSALIND You must begin, 'Will you, Orlando'—

CELIA Go to. Will you, Orlando, have to wife this Rosalind?

ORLANDO I will.

ROSALIND Ay, but when? 125

ORLANDO Why now, as fast as she can marry us.

ROSALIND Then you must say, 'I take thee, Rosalind, for wife.'

ORLANDO I take thee, Rosalind, for wife. 129

ROSALIND I might ask you for your commission; but I do take thee, Orlando, for my husband. There's a girl goes before the priest; and certainly a woman's thought runs before her actions.

ORLANDO So do all thoughts; they are winged.

ROSALIND Now tell me how long you would have her after you have possessed her? 136

ORLANDO For ever and a day.

ROSALIND Say a day without the ever. No, no, Orlando; men are April when they woo, December when they wed. Maids are May when they are maids, but the sky changes when they are wives. I will be more jealous of thee than a Barbary cock-pigeon over his hen, more clamorous than a parrot against rain, more new-fangled than an ape, more giddy in my desires than a monkey. I will weep for nothing, like Diana in the fountain, and I will do that when you are disposed to be merry. I will laugh like a hyena, and that when thou art inclined to sleep. 148

ORLANDO But will my Rosalind do so?

ROSALIND By my life, she will do as I do.

ORLANDO O, but she is wise.

ROSALIND Or else she could not have the wit to do this. The wiser, the waywarder. Make the doors upon a woman's wit, and it will out at the casement. Shut that, and 'twill out at the key-hole. Stop that, 'twill fly with the smoke out at the chimney. 156

ORLANDO A man that had a wife with such a wit, he might say 'Wit, whither wilt?'

ROSALIND Nay, you might keep that check for it till you met your wife's wit going to your neighbour's bed. 160

ORLANDO And what wit could wit have to excuse that?

ROSALIND Marry, to say she came to seek you there. You shall never take her without her answer unless you take her without her tongue. O, that woman that cannot make her fault her husband's occasion, let her never nurse her child herself, for she will breed it like a fool. 167

ORLANDO For these two hours, Rosalind, I will leave thee.

ROSALIND Alas, dear love, I cannot lack thee two hours.

ORLANDO I must attend the Duke at dinner. By two o'clock I will be with thee again. 171

ROSALIND Ay, go your ways, go your ways. I knew what you would prove; my friends told me as much, and I thought no less. That flattering tongue of yours won me. 'Tis but one cast away, and so, come, death! Two o'clock is your hour? 176

ORLANDO Ay, sweet Rosalind.

ROSALIND By my troth, and in good earnest, and so God mend me, and by all pretty oaths that are not dangerous, if you break one jot of your promise or come one minute behind your hour, I will think you the most pathetical break-promise, and the most hollow lover, and the most unworthy of her you call Rosalind that may be chosen out of the gross band of the unfaithful. Therefore beware my censure, and keep your promise. 186

ORLANDO With no less religion than if thou wert indeed my Rosalind. So, adieu.

ROSALIND Well, Time is the old justice that examines all such offenders; and let Time try. Adieu.   *Exit Orlando*

CELIA You have simply misused our sex in your love-prate. We must have your doublet and hose plucked over your head, and show the world what the bird hath done to her own nest. 194

ROSALIND O coz, coz, coz, my pretty little coz, that thou didst know how many fathom deep I am in love. But it cannot be sounded. My affection hath an unknown bottom, like the Bay of Portugal.

CELIA Or rather bottomless, that as fast as you pour affection in, it runs out. 200

ROSALIND No, that same wicked bastard of Venus, that was begot of thought, conceived of spleen, and born of madness, that blind rascally boy that abuses everyone's eyes because his own are out, let him be judge how deep I am in love. I'll tell thee, Aliena, I cannot be out of the sight of Orlando. I'll go find a shadow and sigh till he come. 207

CELIA And I'll sleep.   *Exeunt*

4.2   *Enter Jaques and Lords dressed as foresters*

JAQUES Which is he that killed the deer?

FIRST LORD Sir, it was I.

JAQUES (*to the others*) Let's present him to the Duke like

a Roman conqueror. And it would do well to set the
deer's horns upon his head for a branch of victory.
Have you no song, forester, for this purpose?   6
SECOND LORD Yes, sir.
JAQUES Sing it. 'Tis no matter how it be in tune, so it
make noise enough.

LORDS (sing)
    What shall he have that killed the deer?   10
    His leather skin and horns to wear.
    Then sing him home; the rest shall bear
      This burden.
    Take thou no scorn to wear the horn;
    It was a crest ere thou wast born.   15
      Thy father's father wore it,
      And thy father bore it.
    The horn, the horn, the lusty horn
    Is not a thing to laugh to scorn.   *Exeunt*

4.3   *Enter Rosalind as Ganymede and Celia as Aliena*
ROSALIND How say you now? Is it not past two o'clock?
And here much Orlando.
CELIA I warrant you, with pure love and troubled brain
he hath ta'en his bow and arrows and is gone forth to
sleep.   5
    ⌈*Enter Silvius*⌉
Look who comes here.
SILVIUS (*to Rosalind*)
My errand is to you, fair youth.
My gentle Phoebe did bid me give you this.
    He offers Rosalind a letter, which she takes
    and reads
I know not the contents, but as I guess
By the stern brow and waspish action   10
Which she did use as she was writing of it,
It bears an angry tenor. Pardon me;
I am but as a guiltless messenger.
ROSALIND
Patience herself would startle at this letter,
And play the swaggerer. Bear this, bear all.   15
She says I am not fair, that I lack manners;
She calls me proud, and that she could not love me
Were man as rare as Phoenix. 'Od's my will,
Her love is not the hare that I do hunt.
Why writes she so to me? Well, shepherd, well,   20
This is a letter of your own device.
SILVIUS
No, I protest; I know not the contents.
Phoebe did write it.
ROSALIND   Come, come, you are a fool,
And turned into the extremity of love.
I saw her hand. She has a leathern hand,   25
A free-stone coloured hand. I verily did think
That her old gloves were on; but 'twas her hands.
She has a housewife's hand—but that's no matter.
I say she never did invent this letter.
This is a man's invention, and his hand.   30
SILVIUS Sure, it is hers.

ROSALIND
Why, 'tis a boisterous and a cruel style,
A style for challengers. Why, she defies me,
Like Turk to Christian. Women's gentle brain
Could not drop forth such giant-rude invention,   35
Such Ethiop words, blacker in their effect
Than in their countenance. Will you hear the letter?
SILVIUS
So please you, for I never heard it yet,
Yet heard too much of Phoebe's cruelty.
ROSALIND
She Phoebes me. Mark how the tyrant writes: 40
(*reads*) 'Art thou god to shepherd turned,
    That a maiden's heart hath burned?'
Can a woman rail thus?
SILVIUS Call you this railing?
ROSALIND (*reads*)
    'Why, thy godhead laid apart,   45
    Warr'st thou with a woman's heart?'
Did you ever hear such railing?
    'Whiles the eye of man did woo me
    That could do no vengeance to me.'—
Meaning me a beast.   50
    'If the scorn of your bright eyne
    Have power to raise such love in mine,
    Alack, in me what strange effect
    Would they work in mild aspect?
    Whiles you chid me I did love;   55
    How then might your prayers move?
    He that brings this love to thee
    Little knows this love in me,
    And by him seal up thy mind
    Whether that thy youth and kind   60
    Will the faithful offer take
    Of me, and all that I can make,
    Or else by him my love deny,
    And then I'll study how to die.'
SILVIUS Call you this chiding?   65
CELIA Alas, poor shepherd.
ROSALIND Do you pity him? No, he deserves no pity. (*To
Silvius*) Wilt thou love such a woman? What, to make
thee an instrument, and play false strains upon thee?—
not to be endured. Well, go your way to her—for I see
love hath made thee a tame snake—and say this to
her: that if she love me, I charge her to love thee. If
she will not, I will never have her unless thou entreat
for her. If you be a true lover, hence, and not a word;
for here comes more company.   *Exit Silvius*
    Enter Oliver
OLIVER
Good morrow, fair ones. Pray you, if you know,   76
Where in the purlieus of this forest stands
A sheepcote fenced about with olive trees?
CELIA
West of this place, down in the neighbour bottom.
The rank of osiers by the murmuring stream   80
Left on your right hand brings you to the place.

But at this hour the house doth keep itself.
There's none within.

OLIVER
If that an eye may profit by a tongue,
Then should I know you by description.   85
Such garments, and such years. 'The boy is fair,
Of female favour, and bestows himself
Like a ripe sister. The woman low
And browner than her brother.' Are not you
The owner of the house I did enquire for?   90

CELIA
It is no boast, being asked, to say we are.

OLIVER
Orlando doth commend him to you both,
And to that youth he calls his Rosalind
He sends this bloody napkin. Are you he?

ROSALIND
I am. What must we understand by this?   95

OLIVER
Some of my shame, if you will know of me
What man I am, and how, and why, and where
This handkerchief was stained.

CELIA   I pray you tell it.

OLIVER
When last the young Orlando parted from you,
He left a promise to return again   100
Within an hour, and pacing through the forest,
Chewing the food of sweet and bitter fancy,
Lo what befell. He threw his eye aside,
And mark what object did present itself.
Under an old oak, whose boughs were mossed with
          age   105
And high top bald with dry antiquity,
A wretched, ragged man, o'ergrown with hair,
Lay sleeping on his back. About his neck
A green and gilded snake had wreathed itself,
Who with her head, nimble in threats, approached 110
The opening of his mouth. But suddenly
Seeing Orlando, it unlinked itself,
And with indented glides did slip away
Into a bush, under which bush's shade
A lioness, with udders all drawn dry,   115
Lay couching, head on ground, with catlike watch
When that the sleeping man should stir. For 'tis
The royal disposition of that beast
To prey on nothing that doth seem as dead.
This seen, Orlando did approach the man   120
And found it was his brother, his elder brother.

CELIA
O, I have heard him speak of that same brother,
And he did render him the most unnatural
That lived amongst men.

OLIVER   And well he might so do,
For well I know he was unnatural.   125

ROSALIND
But to Orlando. Did he leave him there,
Food to the sucked and hungry lioness?

OLIVER
Twice did he turn his back, and purposed so.
But kindness, nobler ever than revenge,
And nature, stronger than his just occasion,   130
Made him give battle to the lioness,
Who quickly fell before him; in which hurtling
From miserable slumber I awaked.

CELIA
Are you his brother?

ROSALIND   Was't you he rescued?

CELIA
Was't you that did so oft contrive to kill him?   135

OLIVER
'Twas I, but 'tis not I. I do not shame
To tell you what I was, since my conversion
So sweetly tastes, being the thing I am.

ROSALIND
But for the bloody napkin?

OLIVER   By and by.
When from the first to last betwixt us two   140
Tears our recountments had most kindly bathed—
As how I came into that desert place—
I' brief, he led me to the gentle Duke,
Who gave me fresh array, and entertainment,
Committing me unto my brother's love,   145
Who led me instantly unto his cave,
There stripped himself, and here upon his arm
The lioness had torn some flesh away,
Which all this while had bled. And now he fainted,
And cried in fainting upon Rosalind.   150
Brief, I recovered him, bound up his wound,
And after some small space, being strong at heart,
He sent me hither, stranger as I am,
To tell this story, that you might excuse
His broken promise, and to give this napkin,   155
Dyed in his blood, unto the shepherd youth
That he in sport doth call his Rosalind.

          Rosalind faints

CELIA
Why, how now, Ganymede, sweet Ganymede!

OLIVER
Many will swoon when they do look on blood.

CELIA
There is more in it. Cousin Ganymede!   160

OLIVER Look, he recovers.

ROSALIND I would I were at home.

CELIA We'll lead you thither.
          (*To Oliver*) I pray you, will you take him by the arm?

OLIVER Be of good cheer, youth. You a man? You lack a
          man's heart.   166

ROSALIND I do so, I confess it. Ah, sirrah, a body would
          think this was well counterfeited. I pray you, tell your
          brother how well I counterfeited. Heigh-ho!

OLIVER This was not counterfeit. There is too great
          testimony in your complexion that it was a passion of
          earnest.   172

ROSALIND Counterfeit, I assure you.

OLIVER Well then, take a good heart, and counterfeit to
be a man.   175
ROSALIND So I do; but, i'faith, I should have been a
woman by right.
CELIA Come, you look paler and paler. Pray you, draw
homewards. Good sir, go with us.
OLIVER
That will I, for I must bear answer back   180
How you excuse my brother, Rosalind.
ROSALIND I shall devise something. But I pray you
commend my counterfeiting to him. Will you go?
                                                        Exeunt

5.1   *Enter Touchstone the clown and Audrey*

TOUCHSTONE We shall find a time, Audrey. Patience, gentle
Audrey.
AUDREY Faith, the priest was good enough, for all the old
gentleman's saying.   4
TOUCHSTONE A most wicked Sir Oliver, Audrey, a most
vile Martext. But, Audrey, there is a youth here in the
forest lays claim to you.
AUDREY Ay, I know who 'tis. He hath no interest in me
in the world. Here comes the man you mean.   9
            Enter William
TOUCHSTONE It is meat and drink to me to see a clown.
By my troth, we that have good wits have much to
answer for. We shall be flouting; we cannot hold.
WILLIAM Good ev'n, Audrey.
AUDREY God ye good ev'n, William.
WILLIAM (*to Touchstone*) And good ev'n to you, sir.   15
TOUCHSTONE Good ev'n, gentle friend. Cover thy head,
cover thy head. Nay, prithee, be covered. How old are
you, friend?
WILLIAM Five-and-twenty, sir.
TOUCHSTONE A ripe age. Is thy name William?   20
WILLIAM William, sir.
TOUCHSTONE A fair name. Wast born i'th' forest here?
WILLIAM Ay, sir, I thank God.
TOUCHSTONE Thank God—a good answer. Art rich?
WILLIAM Faith, sir, so-so.   25
TOUCHSTONE So-so is good, very good, very excellent good.
And yet it is not, it is but so-so. Art thou wise?
WILLIAM Ay, sir, I have a pretty wit.
TOUCHSTONE Why, thou sayst well. I do now remember a
saying: 'The fool doth think he is wise, but the wise
man knows himself to be a fool.' The heathen
philosopher, when he had a desire to eat a grape,
would open his lips when he put it into his mouth,
meaning thereby that grapes were made to eat, and
lips to open. You do love this maid?   35
WILLIAM I do, sir.
TOUCHSTONE Give me your hand. Art thou learned?
WILLIAM No, sir.
TOUCHSTONE Then learn this of me: to have is to have.
For it is a figure in rhetoric that drink, being poured
out of a cup into a glass, by filling the one doth empty
the other. For all your writers do consent that *ipse* is
he. Now you are not *ipse*, for I am he.

WILLIAM Which he, sir?   44
TOUCHSTONE He, sir, that must marry this woman.
Therefore, you clown, abandon—which is in the vulgar,
leave—the society—which in the boorish is company—
of this female—which in the common is woman; which
together is, abandon the society of this female, or,
clown, thou perishest; or, to thy better understanding,
diest; or, to wit, I kill thee, make thee away, translate
thy life into death, thy liberty into bondage. I will deal
in poison with thee, or in bastinado, or in steel. I will
bandy with thee in faction, I will o'errun thee with
policy. I will kill thee a hundred and fifty ways.
Therefore tremble, and depart.   56
AUDREY Do, good William.
WILLIAM God rest you merry, sir.   *Exit*
            Enter Corin
CORIN Our master and mistress seeks you. Come, away,
away.   60
TOUCHSTONE Trip, Audrey, trip, Audrey. (*To Corin*) I
attend, I attend.   *Exeunt*

5.2   *Enter Orlando and Oliver*

ORLANDO Is't possible that on so little acquaintance you
should like her? That but seeing, you should love her?
And loving, woo? And wooing, she should grant? And
will you persevere to enjoy her?   4
OLIVER Neither call the giddiness of it in question, the
poverty of her, the small acquaintance, my sudden
wooing, nor her sudden consenting; but say with me,
'I love Aliena'; say with her, that she loves me; consent
with both that we may enjoy each other. It shall be to
your good, for my father's house and all the revenue
that was old Sir Rowland's will I estate upon you, and
here live and die a shepherd.   12
            Enter Rosalind as Ganymede
ORLANDO You have my consent. Let your wedding be
tomorrow. Thither will I invite the Duke and all's
contented followers. Go you, and prepare Aliena; for
look you, here comes my Rosalind.   16
ROSALIND God save you, brother.
OLIVER And you, fair sister.   *Exit*
ROSALIND O, my dear Orlando, how it grieves me to see
thee wear thy heart in a scarf.   20
ORLANDO It is my arm.
ROSALIND I thought thy heart had been wounded with
the claws of a lion.
ORLANDO Wounded it is, but with the eyes of a lady.
ROSALIND Did your brother tell you how I counterfeited
to swoon when he showed me your handkerchief?   26
ORLANDO Ay, and greater wonders than that.
ROSALIND O, I know where you are. Nay, 'tis true. There
was never anything so sudden but the fight of two
rams, and Caesar's thrasonical brag of 'I came, saw,
and overcame', for your brother and my sister no
sooner met but they looked; no sooner looked but they
loved; no sooner loved but they sighed; no sooner
sighed but they asked one another the reason; no
sooner knew the reason but they sought the remedy;

and in these degrees have they made a pair of stairs to marriage, which they will climb incontinent, or else be incontinent before marriage. They are in the very wrath of love, and they will together. Clubs cannot part them.

ORLANDO They shall be married tomorrow, and I will bid the Duke to the nuptial. But O, how bitter a thing it is to look into happiness through another man's eyes. By so much the more shall I tomorrow be at the height of heart-heaviness by how much I shall think my brother happy in having what he wishes for.   45

ROSALIND Why, then, tomorrow I cannot serve your turn for Rosalind?

ORLANDO I can live no longer by thinking.   48

ROSALIND I will weary you then no longer with idle talking. Know of me then—for now I speak to some purpose—that I know you are a gentleman of good conceit. I speak not this that you should bear a good opinion of my knowledge, insomuch I say I know you are; neither do I labour for a greater esteem than may in some little measure draw a belief from you to do yourself good, and not to grace me. Believe then, if you please, that I can do strange things. I have since I was three year old conversed with a magician, most profound in his art, and yet not damnable. If you do love Rosalind so near the heart as your gesture cries it out, when your brother marries Aliena shall you marry her. I know into what straits of fortune she is driven, and it is not impossible to me, if it appear not inconvenient to you, to set her before your eyes tomorrow, human as she is, and without any danger.

ORLANDO Speakest thou in sober meanings?   66

ROSALIND By my life, I do, which I tender dearly, though I say I am a magician. Therefore put you in your best array, bid your friends: for if you will be married tomorrow, you shall; and to Rosalind if you will.   70

Enter Silvius and Phoebe

Look, here comes a lover of mine and a lover of hers.

PHOEBE (*to Rosalind*)
    Youth, you have done me much ungentleness,
    To show the letter that I writ to you.

ROSALIND
    I care not if I have. It is my study
    To seem despiteful and ungentle to you.   75
    You are there followed by a faithful shepherd.
    Look upon him; love him; he worships you.

PHOEBE (*to Silvius*)
    Good shepherd, tell this youth what 'tis to love.

SILVIUS
    It is to be all made of sighs and tears,
    And so am I for Phoebe.   80

PHOEBE And I for Ganymede.
ORLANDO And I for Rosalind.
ROSALIND And I for no woman.

SILVIUS
    It is to be all made of faith and service,
    And so am I for Phoebe.   85

PHOEBE And I for Ganymede.
ORLANDO And I for Rosalind.
ROSALIND And I for no woman.

SILVIUS
    It is to be all made of fantasy,
    All made of passion, and all made of wishes,   90
    All adoration, duty, and observance,
    All humbleness, all patience and impatience,
    All purity, all trial, all obedience,
    And so am I for Phoebe.

PHOEBE And so am I for Ganymede.   95
ORLANDO And so am I for Rosalind.
ROSALIND And so am I for no woman.

PHOEBE (*to Rosalind*)
    If this be so, why blame you me to love you?

SILVIUS (*to Phoebe*)
    If this be so, why blame you me to love you?

ORLANDO
    If this be so, why blame you me to love you?   100

ROSALIND Why do you speak too, 'Why blame you me to love you?'

ORLANDO
    To her that is not here nor doth not hear.

ROSALIND Pray you, no more of this, 'tis like the howling of Irish wolves against the moon. (*To Silvius*) I will help you if I can. (*To Phoebe*) I would love you if I could.—Tomorrow meet me all together. (*To Phoebe*) I will marry you if ever I marry woman, and I'll be married tomorrow. (*To Orlando*) I will satisfy you if ever I satisfy man, and you shall be married tomorrow. (*To Silvius*) I will content you if what pleases you contents you, and you shall be married tomorrow. (*To Orlando*) As you love Rosalind, meet. (*To Silvius*) As you love Phoebe, meet. And as I love no woman, I'll meet. So fare you well. I have left you commands.   115

SILVIUS I'll not fail, if I live.
PHOEBE Nor I.
ORLANDO Nor I.   *Exeunt severally*

5.3   *Enter Touchstone the clown and Audrey*

TOUCHSTONE Tomorrow is the joyful day, Audrey, tomorrow will we be married.

AUDREY I do desire it with all my heart; and I hope it is no dishonest desire to desire to be a woman of the world. Here come two of the banished Duke's pages.   5

Enter two Pages

FIRST PAGE Well met, honest gentleman.

TOUCHSTONE By my troth, well met. Come, sit, sit, and a song.

SECOND PAGE We are for you. Sit i'th' middle.   9

FIRST PAGE Shall we clap into't roundly, without hawking, or spitting, or saying we are hoarse, which are the only prologues to a bad voice?

SECOND PAGE I'faith, i'faith, and both in a tune, like two gipsies on a horse.

BOTH PAGES (*sing*)
        It was a lover and his lass,   15
            With a hey, and a ho, and a hey-nonny-no,
        That o'er the green cornfield did pass
            In spring-time, the only pretty ring-time,
        When birds do sing, hey ding-a-ding ding,
        Sweet lovers love the spring.   20

Between the acres of the rye,
  With a hey, and a ho, and a hey-nonny-no,
These pretty country folks would lie,
  In spring-time, the only pretty ring-time,
When birds do sing, hey ding-a-ding ding,   25
Sweet lovers love the spring.

This carol they began that hour,
  With a hey, and a ho, and a hey-nonny-no,
How that a life was but a flower,
  In spring-time, the only pretty ring-time,   30
When birds do sing, hey ding-a-ding ding,
Sweet lovers love the spring.

And therefore take the present time,
  With a hey, and a ho, and a hey-nonny-no,
For love is crownèd with the prime,   35
  In spring time, the only pretty ring-time,
When birds do sing, hey ding-a-ding ding,
Sweet lovers love the spring.

TOUCHSTONE Truly, young gentlemen, though there was
no great matter in the ditty, yet the note was very
untunable.   41
FIRST PAGE You are deceived, sir, we kept time, we lost
not our time.
TOUCHSTONE By my troth, yes, I count it but time lost to
hear such a foolish song. God b'wi'you, and God mend
your voices. Come, Audrey.   *Exeunt severally*

5.4   *Enter Duke Senior, Amiens, Jaques, Orlando, Oliver,
and Celia as Aliena*
DUKE SENIOR
Dost thou believe, Orlando, that the boy
Can do all this that he hath promisèd?
ORLANDO
I sometimes do believe, and sometimes do not,
As those that fear they hope, and know they fear.
    *Enter Rosalind as Ganymede, with Silvius and
    Phoebe*
ROSALIND
Patience once more, whiles our compact is urged.   5
(*To the Duke*) You say if I bring in your Rosalind
You will bestow her on Orlando here?
DUKE SENIOR
That would I, had I kingdoms to give with her.
ROSALIND (*to Orlando*)
And you say you will have her when I bring her?
ORLANDO
That would I, were I of all kingdoms king.   10
ROSALIND (*to Phoebe*)
You say you'll marry me if I be willing?
PHOEBE
That will I, should I die the hour after.
ROSALIND
But if you do refuse to marry me
You'll give yourself to this most faithful shepherd?
PHOEBE So is the bargain.   15
ROSALIND (*to Silvius*)
You say that you'll have Phoebe if she will.

SILVIUS
Though to have her and death were both one thing.
ROSALIND
I have promised to make all this matter even.
Keep you your word, O Duke, to give your daughter.
You yours, Orlando, to receive his daughter.   20
Keep your word, Phoebe, that you'll marry me,
Or else refusing me to wed this shepherd.
Keep your word, Silvius, that you'll marry her
If she refuse me; and from hence I go
To make these doubts all even.   25
    Exeunt Rosalind and Celia
DUKE SENIOR
I do remember in this shepherd boy
Some lively touches of my daughter's favour.
ORLANDO
My lord, the first time that I ever saw him,
Methought he was a brother to your daughter.
But, my good lord, this boy is forest-born,   30
And hath been tutored in the rudiments
Of many desperate studies by his uncle,
Whom he reports to be a great magician
Obscurèd in the circle of this forest.   34
    ⌈*Enter Touchstone the clown and Audrey*⌉
JAQUES There is sure another flood toward, and these
couples are coming to the ark. Here comes a pair of
very strange beasts, which in all tongues are called
fools.
TOUCHSTONE Salutation and greeting to you all.   39
JAQUES (*to the Duke*) Good my lord, bid him welcome. This
is the motley-minded gentleman that I have so often
met in the forest. He hath been a courtier, he swears.
TOUCHSTONE If any man doubt that, let him put me to my
purgation. I have trod a measure, I have flattered a
lady, I have been politic with my friend, smooth with
mine enemy, I have undone three tailors, I have had
four quarrels, and like to have fought one.   47
JAQUES And how was that ta'en up?
TOUCHSTONE Faith, we met, and found the quarrel was
upon the seventh cause.   50
JAQUES How, seventh cause?—Good my lord, like this
fellow.
DUKE SENIOR I like him very well.
TOUCHSTONE God'ield you, sir, I desire you of the like. I
press in here, sir, amongst the rest of the country
copulatives, to swear, and to forswear, according as
marriage binds and blood breaks. A poor virgin, sir, an
ill-favoured thing, sir, but mine own. A poor humour
of mine, sir, to take that that no man else will. Rich
honesty dwells like a miser, sir, in a poor house, as
your pearl in your foul oyster.   61
DUKE SENIOR By my faith, he is very swift and sententious.
TOUCHSTONE According to the fool's bolt, sir, and such
dulcet diseases.
JAQUES But for the seventh cause. How did you find the
quarrel on the seventh cause?   66
TOUCHSTONE Upon a lie seven times removed.—Bear your
body more seeming, Audrey.—As thus, sir: I did dislike

the cut of a certain courtier's beard. He sent me word
if I said his beard was not cut well, he was in the mind
it was. This is called the Retort Courteous. If I sent him
word again it was not well cut, he would send me
word he cut it to please himself. This is called the Quip
Modest. If again it was not well cut, he disabled my
judgement. This is called the Reply Churlish. If again
it was not well cut, he would answer I spake not true.
This is called the Reproof Valiant. If again it was not
well cut, he would say I lie. This is called the
Countercheck Quarrelsome. And so to the Lie Circumstantial, and the Lie Direct.   80

JAQUES And how oft did you say his beard was not well
cut?

TOUCHSTONE I durst go no further than the Lie
Circumstantial, nor he durst not give me the Lie Direct;
and so we measured swords, and parted.   85

JAQUES Can you nominate in order now the degrees of
the lie?

TOUCHSTONE O sir, we quarrel in print, by the book, as
you have books for good manners. I will name you the
degrees. The first, the Retort Courteous; the second,
the Quip Modest; the third, the Reply Churlish; the
fourth, the Reproof Valiant; the fifth, the Countercheck
Quarrelsome; the sixth, the Lie with Circumstance; the
seventh, the Lie Direct. All these you may avoid but
the Lie Direct; and you may avoid that, too, with an
'if'. I knew when seven justices could not take up a
quarrel, but when the parties were met themselves,
one of them thought but of an 'if', as 'If you said so,
then I said so', and they shook hands and swore
brothers. Your 'if' is the only peacemaker; much virtue
in 'if'.   101

JAQUES (to the Duke) Is not this a rare fellow, my lord?
He's as good at anything, and yet a fool.

DUKE SENIOR He uses his folly like a stalking-horse, and
under the presentation of that he shoots his wit.   105
⌈Still music.⌉ Enter Hymen with Rosalind and Celia
as themselves

HYMEN   Then is there mirth in heaven
         When earthly things made even
             Atone together.
         Good Duke, receive thy daughter;
         Hymen from heaven brought her,   110
             Yea, brought her hither,
         That thou mightst join her hand with his
         Whose heart within his bosom is.

ROSALIND (to the Duke)
         To you I give myself, for I am yours.
         (To Orlando) To you I give myself, for I am yours. 115

DUKE SENIOR
         If there be truth in sight, you are my daughter.

ORLANDO
         If there be truth in sight, you are my Rosalind.

PHOEBE
         If sight and shape be true,
         Why then, my love adieu!

ROSALIND (to the Duke)
         I'll have no father if you be not he.   120
         (To Orlando) I'll have no husband if you be not he,
         (To Phoebe) Nor ne'er wed woman if you be not she.

HYMEN   Peace, ho, I bar confusion.
             'Tis I must make conclusion
                 Of these most strange events.   125
             Here's eight that must take hands
             To join in Hymen's bands,
                 If truth holds true contents.
         (To Orlando and Rosalind)
             You and you no cross shall part.
         (To Oliver and Celia)
             You and you are heart in heart.   130
         (To Phoebe)
             You to his love must accord,
             Or have a woman to your lord.
         (To Touchstone and Audrey)
             You and you are sure together
             As the winter to foul weather.—
             Whiles a wedlock hymn we sing,   135
             Feed yourselves with questioning,
             That reason wonder may diminish
             How thus we met, and these things finish.

                        Song
             Wedding is great Juno's crown,
                 O blessèd bond of board and bed.   140
             'Tis Hymen peoples every town.
                 High wedlock then be honourèd.
             Honour, high honour and renown
             To Hymen, god of every town.

DUKE SENIOR (to Celia)
         O my dear niece, welcome thou art to me,   145
         Even daughter; welcome in no less degree.

PHOEBE (to Silvius)
         I will not eat my word. Now thou art mine,
         Thy faith my fancy to thee doth combine.
             Enter Jaques de Bois, the second brother

JAQUES DE BOIS
         Let me have audience for a word or two.
         I am the second son of old Sir Rowland,   150
         That bring these tidings to this fair assembly.
         Duke Frederick, hearing how that every day
         Men of great worth resorted to this forest,
         Addressed a mighty power, which were on foot,
         In his own conduct, purposely to take   155
         His brother here, and put him to the sword.
         And to the skirts of this wild wood he came
         Where, meeting with an old religious man,
         After some question with him was converted
         Both from his enterprise and from the world, 160
         His crown bequeathing to his banished brother,
         And all their lands restored to them again
         That were with him exiled. This to be true
         I do engage my life.

DUKE SENIOR   Welcome, young man.
         Thou offer'st fairly to thy brothers' wedding: 165
         To one his lands withheld, and to the other

A land itself at large, a potent dukedom.
First, in this forest let us do those ends
That here were well begun, and well begot.
And after, every of this happy number   170
That have endured shrewd days and nights with us
Shall share the good of our returnèd fortune
According to the measure of their states.
Meantime, forget this new-fallen dignity
And fall into our rustic revelry.   175
Play, music, and you brides and bridegrooms all,
With measure heaped in joy to th' measures fall.

JAQUES
Sir, by your patience. (*To Jaques de Bois*) If I heard you
rightly
The Duke hath put on a religious life
And thrown into neglect the pompous court.   180

JAQUES DE BOIS He hath.

JAQUES
To him will I. Out of these convertites
There is much matter to be heard and learned.
(*To the Duke*)
You to your former honour I bequeath;
Your patience and your virtue well deserves it.   185
(*To Orlando*)
You to a love that your true faith doth merit;
(*To Oliver*)
You to your land, and love, and great allies;
(*To Silvius*)
You to a long and well-deservèd bed;
(*To Touchstone*)
And you to wrangling, for thy loving voyage
Is but for two months victualled.—So, to your
pleasures;   190
I am for other than for dancing measures.

DUKE SENIOR Stay, Jaques, stay.

JAQUES
To see no pastime, I. What you would have
I'll stay to know at your abandoned cave.   *Exit*

DUKE SENIOR
Proceed, proceed. We'll so begin these rites   195
As we do trust they'll end, in true delights.
⌈*They dance; then⌉ exeunt all but Rosalind*

Epilogue

ROSALIND (*to the audience*) It is not the fashion to see the
lady the epilogue; but it is no more unhandsome than
to see the lord the prologue. If it be true that good
wine needs no bush, 'tis true that a good play needs
no epilogue. Yet to good wine they do use good bushes,
and good plays prove the better by the help of good
epilogues. What a case am I in then, that am neither
a good epilogue nor cannot insinuate with you in the
behalf of a good play! I am not furnished like a beggar,
therefore to beg will not become me. My way is to
conjure you; and I'll begin with the women. I charge
you, O women, for the love you bear to men, to like
as much of this play as please you. And I charge you,
O men, for the love you bear to women—as I perceive
by your simpering none of you hates them—that
between you and the women the play may please. If I
were a woman I would kiss as many of you as had
beards that pleased me, complexions that liked me, and
breaths that I defied not. And I am sure, as many as
have good beards, or good faces, or sweet breaths will
for my kind offer, when I make curtsy, bid me farewell.
                                                        Exit

TWELFTH NIGHT

TWELFTH NIGHT, the end of the Christmas season, was traditionally a time of revelry and topsy-turvydom; Shakespeare's title for a play in which a servant aspires to his mistress's hand has no more specific reference. It was thought appropriate to the festive occasion of Candlemas (2 February) 1602 when, in the first known allusion to it, John Manningham, a law student of the Middle Temple in London, noted 'at our feast we had a play called *Twelfth Night, or What You Will*'. References to 'the Sophy'— the Shah of Persia (2.5.174; 3.4.271)—probably post-date Sir Robert Shirley's return from Persia, in a ship named *The Sophy*, in 1599; and 'the new map with the augmentation of the Indies' (3.2.75) appears to be one published in 1599 and reissued in 1600. Shakespeare may have picked up the name Orsino for his young duke from a Tuscan nobleman whom Queen Elizabeth entertained at Whitehall with a play performed by Shakespeare's company on Twelfth Night 1601. Probably he wrote *Twelfth Night* during that year.

Twelfth Night's romantic setting is Illyria, the Greek and Roman name for Adriatic territory roughly corresponding to modern Yugoslavia. Manningham had noted that the play was 'much like *The Comedy of Errors* or *Menaechmi* in Plautus', thinking no doubt of the confusions created by identical twins. Shakespeare may also have known an anonymous Italian comedy, *Gl'Ingannati* (*The Deceived Ones*), acted in 1531 and first printed in 1537, which influenced a number of other plays and prose tales including Barnaby Riche's story of Apolonius and Silla printed as part of *Riche's Farewell to Military Profession* (1581). Riche gave Shakespeare his main plot of a shipwrecked girl (Viola) who, disguised as a boy (Cesario), serves a young Duke (Orsino) and undertakes love-errands on his behalf to a noble lady (Olivia) who falls in love with her but mistakenly marries her twin brother (Sebastian). Shakespeare idealizes Riche's characters and purges the story of some its explicit sexuality: Riche's Olivia, for example, is pregnant before marriage, and his Viola reveals her identity, in a manner impractical for a boy actor, by stripping to the waist. Shakespeare complicates the plot by giving Olivia a reprobate uncle, Sir Toby Belch, and two additional suitors, the asinine Sir Andrew Aguecheek and her steward, Malvolio, tricked by members of her household into believing that she loves him. More important to the play than to the plot is the entirely Shakespearian clown, Feste, a wry and oblique commentator whose wit in folly is opposed to Malvolio's folly in wit.

Twelfth Night is the consummation of Shakespeare's romantic comedy, a play of wide emotional range, extending from the robust, brilliantly orchestrated humour of the scene of midnight revelry (2.2) to the rapt wonder of the antiphon of recognition (5.1.224–56) between the reunited twins. In performance the balance shifts, favouring sometimes the exposure and celebration of folly, at other times the poignancy of unattained love and of unheeded wisdom; but few other plays have so consistently provided theatrical pleasure of so high an order.

THE PERSONS OF THE PLAY

ORSINO, Duke of Illyria

VALENTINE
CURIO   } attending on Orsino

FIRST OFFICER

SECOND OFFICER

VIOLA, a lady, later disguised as Cesario

A CAPTAIN

SEBASTIAN, her twin brother

ANTONIO, another sea-captain

OLIVIA, a Countess

MARIA, her waiting-gentlewoman

SIR TOBY Belch, Olivia's kinsman

SIR ANDREW Aguecheek, companion of Sir Toby

MALVOLIO, Olivia's steward

FABIAN, a member of Olivia's household

FESTE the Clown, her jester

A PRIEST

A SERVANT of Olivia

Musicians, sailors, lords, attendants

Twelfth Night, or What You Will

1.1 *Music. Enter Orsino Duke of Illyria, Curio, and*
other lords

ORSINO
If music be the food of love, play on,
Give me excess of it that, surfeiting,
The appetite may sicken and so die.
That strain again, it had a dying fall.
O, it came o'er my ear like the sweet sound   5
That breathes upon a bank of violets,
Stealing and giving odour. Enough, no more,
'Tis not so sweet now as it was before.
⌐Music ceases⌐
O spirit of love, how quick and fresh art thou
That, notwithstanding thy capacity   10
Receiveth as the sea, naught enters there,
Of what validity and pitch so e'er,
But falls into abatement and low price
Even in a minute! So full of shapes is fancy
That it alone is high fantastical.   15
CURIO
Will you go hunt, my lord?
ORSINO   What, Curio?
CURIO   The hart.
ORSINO
Why so I do, the noblest that I have.
O, when mine eyes did see Olivia first
Methought she purged the air of pestilence;
That instant was I turned into a hart,   20
And my desires, like fell and cruel hounds,
E'er since pursue me.
Enter Valentine
How now, what news from her?
VALENTINE
So please my lord, I might not be admitted,
But from her handmaid do return this answer:
The element itself till seven years' heat   25
Shall not behold her face at ample view,
But like a cloistress she will veilèd walk
And water once a day her chamber round
With eye-offending brine—all this to season
A brother's dead love, which she would keep fresh 30
And lasting in her sad remembrance.
ORSINO
O, she that hath a heart of that fine frame
To pay this debt of love but to a brother,
How will she love when the rich golden shaft
Hath killed the flock of all affections else   35
That live in her—when liver, brain, and heart,
These sovereign thrones, are all supplied, and filled
Her sweet perfections with one self king!
Away before me to sweet beds of flowers.
Love-thoughts lie rich when canopied with bowers. 40
Exeunt

1.2   *Enter Viola, a Captain, and sailors*
VIOLA
What country, friends, is this?
CAPTAIN   This is Illyria, lady.
VIOLA
And what should I do in Illyria?
My brother, he is in Elysium.
Perchance he is not drowned. What think you sailors?
CAPTAIN
It is perchance that you yourself were saved.   5
VIOLA
O my poor brother!—and so perchance may he be.
CAPTAIN
True, madam, and to comfort you with chance,
Assure yourself, after our ship did split,
When you and those poor number savèd with you
Hung on our driving boat, I saw your brother,   10
Most provident in peril, bind himself—
Courage and hope both teaching him the practice—
To a strong mast that lived upon the sea,
Where, like Arion on the dolphin's back,
I saw him hold acquaintance with the waves   15
So long as I could see.
VIOLA (*giving money*)   For saying so, there's gold.
Mine own escape unfoldeth to my hope,
Whereto thy speech serves for authority,
The like of him. Know'st thou this country?
CAPTAIN
Ay, madam, well, for I was bred and born   20
Not three hours' travel from this very place.
VIOLA
Who governs here?
CAPTAIN   A noble duke, in nature
As in name.
VIOLA   What is his name?
CAPTAIN   Orsino.
VIOLA
Orsino. I have heard my father name him.
He was a bachelor then.   25
CAPTAIN
And so is now, or was so very late,
For but a month ago I went from hence,
And then 'twas fresh in murmur—as, you know,
What great ones do the less will prattle of—
That he did seek the love of fair Olivia.   30
VIOLA What's she?
CAPTAIN
A virtuous maid, the daughter of a count
That died some twelvemonth since, then leaving her
In the protection of his son, her brother,
Who shortly also died, for whose dear love,   35
They say, she hath abjured the sight
And company of men.
VIOLA   O that I served that lady,

And might not be delivered to the world
Till I had made mine own occasion mellow,
What my estate is.

CAPTAIN   That were hard to compass,   40
Because she will admit no kind of suit,
No, not the Duke's.

VIOLA
There is a fair behaviour in thee, captain,
And though that nature with a beauteous wall
Doth oft close in pollution, yet of thee   45
I will believe thou hast a mind that suits
With this thy fair and outward character.
I pray thee—and I'll pay thee bounteously—
Conceal me what I am, and be my aid
For such disguise as haply shall become   50
The form of my intent. I'll serve this duke.
Thou shalt present me as an eunuch to him.
It may be worth thy pains, for I can sing,
And speak to him in many sorts of music
That will allow me very worth his service.   55
What else may hap, to time I will commit.
Only shape thou thy silence to my wit.

CAPTAIN
Be you his eunuch, and your mute I'll be.
When my tongue blabs, then let mine eyes not see. 59

VIOLA
I thank thee. Lead me on.   *Exeunt*

1.3   *Enter Sir Toby Belch and Maria*

SIR TOBY What a plague means my niece to take the death
of her brother thus? I am sure care's an enemy to life.

MARIA By my troth, Sir Toby, you must come in earlier
o' nights. Your cousin, my lady, takes great exceptions
to your ill hours.   5

SIR TOBY Why, let her except, before excepted.

MARIA Ay, but you must confine yourself within the
modest limits of order.

SIR TOBY Confine? I'll confine myself no finer than I am.
These clothes are good enough to drink in, and so be
these boots too; an they be not, let them hang
themselves in their own straps.

MARIA That quaffing and drinking will undo you. I heard
my lady talk of it yesterday, and of a foolish knight
that you brought in one night here to be her wooer. 15

SIR TOBY Who, Sir Andrew Aguecheek?

MARIA Ay, he.

SIR TOBY He's as tall a man as any's in Illyria.

MARIA What's that to th' purpose?

SIR TOBY Why, he has three thousand ducats a year.   20

MARIA Ay, but he'll have but a year in all these ducats.
He's a very fool, and a prodigal.

SIR TOBY Fie that you'll say so! He plays o'th' viol-de-
gamboys, and speaks three or four languages word for
word without book, and hath all the good gifts of
nature.   26

MARIA He hath indeed, almost natural, for besides that
he's a fool, he's a great quarreller, and but that he

nath the gift of a coward to allay the gust he hath in
quarrelling, 'tis thought among the prudent he would
quickly have the gift of a grave.   31

SIR TOBY By this hand, they are scoundrels and sub-
stractors that say so of him. Who are they?

MARIA They that add, moreover, he's drunk nightly in
your company.   35

SIR TOBY With drinking healths to my niece. I'll drink to
her as long as there is a passage in my throat and
drink in Illyria. He's a coward and a coistrel that will
not drink to my niece till his brains turn o'th' toe, like
a parish top. What wench, *Castiliano, vulgo*, for here
comes Sir Andrew Agueface.   41

Enter Sir Andrew Aguecheek

SIR ANDREW Sir Toby Belch! How now, Sir Toby Belch?

SIR TOBY Sweet Sir Andrew.

SIR ANDREW (*to Maria*) Bless you, fair shrew.

MARIA And you too, sir.   45

SIR TOBY Accost, Sir Andrew, accost.

SIR ANDREW What's that?

SIR TOBY My niece's chambermaid.

SIR ANDREW Good Mistress Accost, I desire better
acquaintance.   50

MARIA My name is Mary, sir.

SIR ANDREW Good Mistress Mary Accost.

SIR TOBY You mistake, knight. 'Accost' is front her, board
her, woo her, assail her.

SIR ANDREW By my troth, I would not undertake her in
this company. Is that the meaning of 'accost'?   56

MARIA Fare you well, gentlemen.

SIR TOBY An thou let part so, Sir Andrew, would thou
mightst never draw sword again.   59

SIR ANDREW An you part so, mistress, I would I might
never draw sword again. Fair lady, do you think you
have fools in hand?

MARIA Sir, I have not you by th' hand.

SIR ANDREW Marry, but you shall have, and here's my
hand.   65

MARIA (*taking his hand*) Now sir, thought is free. I pray
you, bring your hand to th' buttery-bar, and let it
drink.

SIR ANDREW Wherefore, sweetheart? What's your metaphor?   70

MARIA It's dry, sir.

SIR ANDREW Why, I think so. I am not such an ass but I
can keep my hand dry. But what's your jest?

MARIA A dry jest, sir.

SIR ANDREW Are you full of them?   75

MARIA Ay, sir, I have them at my fingers' ends. Marry,
now I let go your hand I am barren.   *Exit*

SIR TOBY O knight, thou lackest a cup of canary. When
did I see thee so put down?   79

SIR ANDREW Never in your life, I think, unless you see
canary put me down. Methinks sometimes I have no
more wit than a Christian or an ordinary man has;
but I am a great eater of beef, and I believe that does
harm to my wit.

SIR TOBY No question.   85

SIR ANDREW An I thought that, I'd forswear it. I'll ride
home tomorrow, Sir Toby.

SIR TOBY *Pourquoi*, my dear knight?

SIR ANDREW What is 'Pourquoi'? Do, or not do? I would
I had bestowed that time in the tongues that I have
in fencing, dancing, and bear-baiting. O, had I but
followed the arts!

SIR TOBY Then hadst thou had an excellent head of hair.

SIR ANDREW Why, would that have mended my hair?

SIR TOBY Past question, for thou seest it will not curl by
nature.   96

SIR ANDREW But it becomes me well enough, does't not?

SIR TOBY Excellent, it hangs like flax on a distaff, and I
hope to see a housewife take thee between her legs and
spin it off.   100

SIR ANDREW Faith, I'll home tomorrow, Sir Toby. Your
niece will not be seen, or if she be, it's four to one
she'll none of me. The Count himself here hard by woos
her.   104

SIR TOBY She'll none o'th' Count. She'll not match above
her degree, neither in estate, years, nor wit, I have
heard her swear't. Tut, there's life in't, man.

SIR ANDREW I'll stay a month longer. I am a fellow o'th'
strangest mind i'th' world. I delight in masques and
revels sometimes altogether.   110

SIR TOBY Art thou good at these kickshawses, knight?

SIR ANDREW As any man in Illyria, whatsoever he be,
under the degree of my betters; and yet I will not
compare with an old man.

SIR TOBY What is thy excellence in a galliard, knight? 115

SIR ANDREW Faith, I can cut a caper.

SIR TOBY And I can cut the mutton to't.

SIR ANDREW And I think I have the back-trick simply as
strong as any man in Illyria.   119

SIR TOBY Wherefore are these things hid? Wherefore have
these gifts a curtain before 'em? Are they like to take
dust, like Mistress Mall's picture? Why dost thou not
go to church in a galliard, and come home in a coranto?
My very walk should be a jig. I would not so much as
make water but in a cinquepace. What dost thou mean?
Is it a world to hide virtues in? I did think by the
excellent constitution of thy leg it was formed under
the star of a galliard.

SIR ANDREW Ay, 'tis strong, and it does indifferent well
in a divers-coloured stock. Shall we set about some
revels?   131

SIR TOBY What shall we do else—were we not born under
Taurus?

SIR ANDREW Taurus? That's sides and heart.

SIR TOBY No, sir, it is legs and thighs: let me see thee
caper.   136

⌈*Sir Andrew capers*⌉

Ha, higher! Ha ha, excellent.   *Exeunt*

1.4   *Enter Valentine, and Viola (as Cesario) in man's
attire*

VALENTINE If the Duke continue these favours towards
you, Cesario, you are like to be much advanced. He
hath known you but three days, and already you are
no stranger.   4

VIOLA You either fear his humour or my negligence, that
you call in question the continuance of his love. Is he
inconstant, sir, in his favours?

VALENTINE No, believe me.

Enter the Duke, Curio, and attendants

VIOLA I thank you. Here comes the Count.

ORSINO Who saw Cesario, ho?   10

VIOLA On your attendance, my lord, here.

ORSINO (*to Curio and attendants*)

Stand you a while aloof. (*To Viola*) Cesario,
Thou know'st no less but all. I have unclasped
To thee the book even of my secret soul.
Therefore, good youth, address thy gait unto her,   15
Be not denied access, stand at her doors,
And tell them there thy fixèd foot shall grow
Till thou have audience.

VIOLA   Sure, my noble lord,
If she be so abandoned to her sorrow
As it is spoke, she never will admit me.   20

ORSINO

Be clamorous, and leap all civil bounds,
Rather than make unprofited return.

VIOLA

Say I do speak with her, my lord, what then?

ORSINO

O then unfold the passion of my love,
Surprise her with discourse of my dear faith.   25
It shall become thee well to act my woes—
She will attend it better in thy youth
Than in a nuncio's of more grave aspect.

VIOLA

I think not so, my lord.

ORSINO   Dear lad, believe it;
For they shall yet belie thy happy years   30
That say thou art a man. Diana's lip
Is not more smooth and rubious; thy small pipe
Is as the maiden's organ, shrill and sound,
And all is semblative a woman's part.
I know thy constellation is right apt   35
For this affair. (*To Curio and attendants*) Some four or
five attend him.
All if you will, for I myself am best
When least in company. (*To Viola*) Prosper well in this
And thou shalt live as freely as thy lord,
To call his fortunes thine.

VIOLA   I'll do my best   40
To woo your lady—⌈*aside*⌉ yet a barful strife—
Whoe'er I woo, myself would be his wife.   *Exeunt*

1.5   *Enter Maria, and Feste, the clown*

MARIA Nay, either tell me where thou hast been or I will
not open my lips so wide as a bristle may enter in way
of thy excuse. My lady will hang thee for thy absence.

FESTE Let her hang me. He that is well hanged in this
world needs to fear no colours.   5

MARIA Make that good.

FESTE He shall see none to fear.

MARIA A good lenten answer. I can tell thee where that saying was born, of 'I fear no colours'.

FESTE Where, good Mistress Mary?   10

MARIA In the wars, and that may you be bold to say in your foolery.

FESTE Well, God give them wisdom that have it; and those that are fools, let them use their talents.

MARIA Yet you will be hanged for being so long absent, or to be turned away—is not that as good as a hanging to you?

FESTE Many a good hanging prevents a bad marriage; and for turning away, let summer bear it out.

MARIA You are resolute then?   20

FESTE Not so neither, but I am resolved on two points.

MARIA That if one break, the other will hold; or if both break, your gaskins fall.

FESTE Apt, in good faith, very apt. Well, go thy way. If Sir Toby would leave drinking thou wert as witty a piece of Eve's flesh as any in Illyria.   26

MARIA Peace, you rogue, no more o' that. Here comes my lady. Make your excuse wisely, you were best.

          Exit

          Enter Olivia, with Malvolio and attendants

FESTE ⌜*aside*⌝ Wit, an't be thy will, put me into good fooling! Those wits that think they have thee do very oft prove fools, and I that am sure I lack thee may pass for a wise man. For what says Quinapalus?—'Better a witty fool than a foolish wit.' (*To Olivia*) God bless thee, lady.

OLIVIA (*to attendants*) Take the fool away.   35

FESTE Do you not hear, fellows? Take away the lady.

OLIVIA Go to, you're a dry fool. I'll no more of you. Besides, you grow dishonest.

FESTE Two faults, madonna, that drink and good counsel will amend, for give the dry fool drink, then is the fool not dry; bid the dishonest man mend himself: if he mend, he is no longer dishonest; if he cannot, let the botcher mend him. Anything that's mended is but patched. Virtue that transgresses is but patched with sin, and sin that amends is but patched with virtue. If that this simple syllogism will serve, so. If it will not, what remedy? As there is no true cuckold but calamity, so beauty's a flower. The lady bade take away the fool, therefore I say again, take her away.

OLIVIA Sir, I bade them take away you.   50

FESTE Misprision in the highest degree! Lady, '*Cucullus non facit monachum*'—that's as much to say as I wear not motley in my brain. Good madonna, give me leave to prove you a fool.

OLIVIA Can you do it?   55

FESTE Dexteriously, good madonna.

OLIVIA Make your proof.

FESTE I must catechize you for it, madonna. Good my mouse of virtue, answer me.

OLIVIA Well, sir, for want of other idleness I'll bide your proof.   61

FESTE Good madonna, why mournest thou?

OLIVIA Good fool, for my brother's death.

FESTE I think his soul is in hell, madonna.

OLIVIA I know his soul is in heaven, fool.   65

FESTE The more fool, madonna, to mourn for your brother's soul, being in heaven. Take away the fool, gentlemen.

OLIVIA What think you of this fool, Malvolio? Doth he not mend?   70

MALVOLIO Yes, and shall do till the pangs of death shake him. Infirmity, that decays the wise, doth ever make the better fool.

FESTE God send you, sir, a speedy infirmity for the better increasing your folly. Sir Toby will be sworn that I am no fox, but he will not pass his word for twopence that you are no fool.

OLIVIA How say you to that, Malvolio?   78

MALVOLIO I marvel your ladyship takes delight in such a barren rascal. I saw him put down the other day with an ordinary fool that has no more brain than a stone. Look you now, he's out of his guard already. Unless you laugh and minister occasion to him, he is gagged. I protest I take these wise men that crow so at these set kind of fools no better than the fools' zanies.   85

OLIVIA O, you are sick of self-love, Malvolio, and taste with a distempered appetite. To be generous, guiltless, and of free disposition is to take those things for birdbolts that you deem cannon bullets. There is no slander in an allowed fool, though he do nothing but rail; nor no railing in a known discreet man, though he do nothing but reprove.

FESTE Now Mercury indue thee with leasing, for thou speakest well of fools.

          Enter Maria

MARIA Madam, there is at the gate a young gentleman much desires to speak with you.   96

OLIVIA From the Count Orsino, is it?

MARIA I know not, madam. 'Tis a fair young man, and well attended.

OLIVIA Who of my people hold him in delay?   100

MARIA Sir Toby, madam, your kinsman.

OLIVIA Fetch him off, I pray you, he speaks nothing but madman. Fie on him. Go you, Malvolio. If it be a suit from the Count, I am sick, or not at home—what you will to dismiss it.   *Exit Malvolio*

Now you see, sir, how your fooling grows old, and people dislike it.

FESTE Thou hast spoke for us, madonna, as if thy eldest son should be a fool, whose skull Jove cram with brains, for—here he comes—   110

          Enter Sir Toby

one of thy kin has a most weak *pia mater*.

OLIVIA By mine honour, half-drunk. What is he at the gate, cousin?

SIR TOBY A gentleman.

OLIVIA A gentleman? What gentleman?   115

SIR TOBY 'Tis a gentleman here. (*He belches*) A plague o' these pickle herring! (*To Feste*) How now, sot?

FESTE Good Sir Toby.

OLIVIA Cousin, cousin, how have you come so early by this lethargy?   120

SIR TOBY Lechery? I defy lechery. There's one at the gate.

OLIVIA Ay, marry, what is he?

SIR TOBY Let him be the devil an he will, I care not. Give me faith, say I. Well, it's all one.   *Exit*

OLIVIA What's a drunken man like, fool?   125

FESTE Like a drowned man, a fool, and a madman—one draught above heat makes him a fool, the second mads him, and a third drowns him.

OLIVIA Go thou and seek the coroner, and let him sit o' my coz, for he's in the third degree of drink, he's drowned. Go look after him.   131

FESTE He is but mad yet, madonna, and the fool shall look to the madman.   *Exit*

Enter Malvolio

MALVOLIO Madam, yon young fellow swears he will speak with you. I told him you were sick—he takes on him to understand so much, and therefore comes to speak with you. I told him you were asleep—he seems to have a foreknowledge of that too, and therefore comes to speak with you. What is to be said to him, lady? He's fortified against any denial.   140

OLIVIA Tell him he shall not speak with me.

MALVOLIO He's been told so, and he says he'll stand at your door like a sheriff's post, and be the supporter to a bench, but he'll speak with you.

OLIVIA What kind o' man is he?   145

MALVOLIO Why, of mankind.

OLIVIA What manner of man?

MALVOLIO Of very ill manner: he'll speak with you, will you or no.

OLIVIA Of what personage and years is he?   150

MALVOLIO Not yet old enough for a man, nor young enough for a boy; as a squash is before 'tis a peascod, or a codling when 'tis almost an apple. 'Tis with him in standing water between boy and man. He is very well-favoured, and he speaks very shrewishly. One would think his mother's milk were scarce out of him.

OLIVIA

Let him approach. Call in my gentlewoman.

MALVOLIO Gentlewoman, my lady calls.   *Exit*

Enter Maria

OLIVIA

Give me my veil. Come, throw it o'er my face. We'll once more hear Orsino's embassy.   160

Enter Viola as Cesario

VIOLA The honourable lady of the house, which is she?

OLIVIA Speak to me, I shall answer for her. Your will.

VIOLA Most radiant, exquisite, and unmatchable beauty. —I pray you, tell me if this be the lady of the house, for I never saw her. I would be loath to cast away my speech, for besides that it is excellently well penned, I have taken great pains to con it. Good beauties, let me sustain no scorn; I am very 'countable, even to the least sinister usage.

OLIVIA Whence came you, sir?   170

VIOLA I can say little more than I have studied, and that question's out of my part. Good gentle one, give me modest assurance if you be the lady of the house, that I may proceed in my speech.

OLIVIA Are you a comedian?   175

VIOLA No, my profound heart; and yet—by the very fangs of malice I swear—I am not that I play. Are you the lady of the house?

OLIVIA If I do not usurp myself, I am.   179

VIOLA Most certain if you are she you do usurp yourself, for what is yours to bestow is not yours to reserve. But this is from my commission. I will on with my speech in your praise, and then show you the heart of my message.

OLIVIA Come to what is important in't, I forgive you the praise.   186

VIOLA Alas, I took great pains to study it, and 'tis poetical.

OLIVIA It is the more like to be feigned, I pray you keep it in. I heard you were saucy at my gates, and allowed your approach rather to wonder at you than to hear you. If you be not mad, be gone. If you have reason, be brief. 'Tis not that time of moon with me to make one in so skipping a dialogue.

MARIA Will you hoist sail, sir? Here lies your way.   194

VIOLA No, good swabber, I am to hull here a little longer. (*To Olivia*) Some mollification for your giant, sweet lady. Tell me your mind, I am a messenger.

OLIVIA Sure, you have some hideous matter to deliver when the courtesy of it is so fearful. Speak your office.

VIOLA It alone concerns your ear. I bring no overture of war, no taxation of homage. I hold the olive in my hand. My words are as full of peace as matter.

OLIVIA Yet you began rudely. What are you? What would you?   204

VIOLA The rudeness that hath appeared in me have I learned from my entertainment. What I am and what I would are as secret as maidenhead; to your ears, divinity; to any others', profanation.

OLIVIA (*to Maria ⌜and attendants⌝*) Give us the place alone, we will hear this divinity.   210

Exeunt Maria ⌜and attendants⌝

Now sir, what is your text?

VIOLA Most sweet lady—

OLIVIA A comfortable doctrine, and much may be said of it. Where lies your text?

VIOLA In Orsino's bosom.   215

OLIVIA In his bosom? In what chapter of his bosom?

VIOLA To answer by the method, in the first of his heart.

OLIVIA O, I have read it. It is heresy. Have you no more to say?

VIOLA Good madam, let me see your face.   220

OLIVIA Have you any commission from your lord to negotiate with my face? You are now out of your text. But we will draw the curtain and show you the picture.

She unveils

Look you, sir, such a one I was this present. Is't not well done?   225

VIOLA Excellently done, if God did all.

OLIVIA 'Tis in grain, sir, 'twill endure wind and weather.

VIOLA

'Tis beauty truly blent, whose red and white
Nature's own sweet and cunning hand laid on.
Lady, you are the cruell'st she alive   230
If you will lead these graces to the grave
And leave the world no copy.

OLIVIA O sir, I will not be so hard-hearted. I will give out
divers schedules of my beauty. It shall be inventoried
and every particle and utensil labelled to my will, as,
item, two lips, indifferent red; *item*, two grey eyes, with
lids to them; *item*, one neck, one chin, and so forth.
Were you sent hither to praise me?

VIOLA

I see you what you are, you are too proud,
But if you were the devil, you are fair.   240
My lord and master loves you. O, such love
Could be but recompensed though you were crowned
The nonpareil of beauty.

OLIVIA   How does he love me?

VIOLA

With adorations, fertile tears,
With groans that thunder love, with sighs of fire.   245

OLIVIA

Your lord does know my mind, I cannot love him.
Yet I suppose him virtuous, know him noble,
Of great estate, of fresh and stainless youth,
In voices well divulged, free, learned, and valiant,
And in dimension and the shape of nature   250
A gracious person; but yet I cannot love him.
He might have took his answer long ago.

VIOLA

If I did love you in my master's flame,
With such a suff'ring, such a deadly life,
In your denial I would find no sense,   255
I would not understand it.

OLIVIA   Why, what would you?

VIOLA

Make me a willow cabin at your gate
And call upon my soul within the house,
Write loyal cantons of contemnèd love,
And sing them loud even in the dead of night;   260
Halloo your name to the reverberate hills,
And make the babbling gossip of the air
Cry out 'Olivia!' O, you should not rest
Between the elements of air and earth
But you should pity me.   265

OLIVIA You might do much.
What is your parentage?

VIOLA

Above my fortunes, yet my state is well.
I am a gentleman.

OLIVIA   Get you to your lord.
I cannot love him. Let him send no more,   270
Unless, perchance, you come to me again
To tell me how he takes it. Fare you well.
I thank you for your pains. (*Offering a purse*) Spend
this for me.

VIOLA

I am no fee'd post, lady. Keep your purse.
My master, not myself, lacks recompense.   275
Love make his heart of flint that you shall love,
And let your fervour, like my master's, be
Placed in contempt. Farewell, fair cruelty.   *Exit*

OLIVIA 'What is your parentage?'
'Above my fortunes, yet my state is well.   280
I am a gentleman.' I'll be sworn thou art.
Thy tongue, thy face, thy limbs, actions, and spirit
Do give thee five-fold blazon. Not too fast. Soft, soft—
Unless the master were the man. How now?
Even so quickly may one catch the plague?   285
Methinks I feel this youth's perfections
With an invisible and subtle stealth
To creep in at mine eyes. Well, let it be.
What ho, Malvolio.

    Enter Malvolio

MALVOLIO   Here, madam, at your service.

OLIVIA

Run after that same peevish messenger   290
The County's man. He left this ring behind him,
Would I or not. Tell him I'll none of it.
Desire him not to flatter with his lord,
Nor hold him up with hopes. I am not for him.
If that the youth will come this way tomorrow,   295
I'll give him reasons for't. Hie thee, Malvolio.

MALVOLIO Madam, I will.   *Exit at one door*

OLIVIA

I do I know not what, and fear to find
Mine eye too great a flatterer for my mind.
Fate, show thy force. Ourselves we do not owe.   300
What is decreed must be; and be this so.

    Exit at another door

2.1   *Enter Antonio and Sebastian*

ANTONIO Will you stay no longer, nor will you not that
I go with you?

SEBASTIAN By your patience, no. My stars shine darkly
over me. The malignancy of my fate might perhaps
distemper yours, therefore I shall crave of you your
leave that I may bear my evils alone. It were a bad
recompense for your love to lay any of them on you.

ANTONIO Let me yet know of you whither you are bound.

SEBASTIAN No, sooth, sir. My determinate voyage is mere
extravagancy. But I perceive in you so excellent a touch
of modesty that you will not extort from me what I am
willing to keep in. Therefore it charges me in manners
the rather to express myself. You must know of me
then, Antonio, my name is Sebastian, which I called
Roderigo. My father was that Sebastian of Messaline
whom I know you have heard of. He left behind him
myself and a sister, both born in an hour. If the heavens
had been pleased, would we had so ended. But you,
sir, altered that, for some hour before you took me
from the breach of the sea was my sister drowned.   20

ANTONIO Alas the day!

SEBASTIAN A lady, sir, though it was said she much

resembled me, was yet of many accounted beautiful. But though I could not with such estimable wonder over-far believe that, yet thus far I will boldly publish her: she bore a mind that envy could not but call fair. She is drowned already, sir, with salt water, though I seem to drown her remembrance again with more.

ANTONIO Pardon me, sir, your bad entertainment.

SEBASTIAN O good Antonio, forgive me your trouble.   30

ANTONIO If you will not murder me for my love, let me be your servant.

SEBASTIAN If you will not undo what you have done—that is, kill him whom you have recovered—desire it not. Fare ye well at once. My bosom is full of kindness, and I am yet so near the manners of my mother that upon the least occasion more mine eyes will tell tales of me. I am bound to the Count Orsino's court. Farewell.

⌈*Exit*⌉

ANTONIO

The gentleness of all the gods go with thee!
I have many enemies in Orsino's court,   40
Else would I very shortly see thee there.
But come what may, I do adore thee so
That danger shall seem sport, and I will go.   *Exit*

2.2   *Enter Viola as Cesario, and Malvolio, at several
doors*

MALVOLIO Were not you ev'n now with the Countess Olivia?

VIOLA Even now, sir, on a moderate pace, I have since arrived but hither.   4

MALVOLIO (*offering a ring*) She returns this ring to you, sir. You might have saved me my pains to have taken it away yourself. She adds, moreover, that you should put your lord into a desperate assurance she will none of him. And one thing more: that you be never so hardy to come again in his affairs, unless it be to report your lord's taking of this. Receive it so.   11

VIOLA

She took the ring of me. I'll none of it.

MALVOLIO Come, sir, you peevishly threw it to her, and her will is it should be so returned.

He throws the ring down

If it be worth stooping for, there it lies, in your eye; if not, be it his that finds it.   *Exit*

VIOLA (*picking up the ring*)

I left no ring with her. What means this lady?
Fortune forbid my outside have not charmed her.
She made good view of me, indeed so much
That straight methought her eyes had lost her tongue,
For she did speak in starts, distractedly.   21
She loves me, sure. The cunning of her passion
Invites me in this churlish messenger.
None of my lord's ring! Why, he sent her none.
I am the man. If it be so—as 'tis—   25
Poor lady, she were better love a dream!
Disguise, I see thou art a wickedness
Wherein the pregnant enemy does much.
How easy is it for the proper false
In women's waxen hearts to set their forms!   30

Alas, our frailty is the cause, not we,
For such as we are made of, such we be.
How will this fadge? My master loves her dearly,
And I, poor monster, fond as much on him,
And she, mistaken, seems to dote on me.   35
What will become of this? As I am man,
My state is desperate for my master's love.
As I am woman, now, alas the day,
What thriftless sighs shall poor Olivia breathe!
O time, thou must untangle this, not I.   40
It is too hard a knot for me t'untie.   *Exit*

2.3   *Enter Sir Toby and Sir Andrew*

SIR TOBY Approach, Sir Andrew. Not to be abed after midnight is to be up betimes, and *diliculo surgere*, thou knowest.

SIR ANDREW Nay, by my troth, I know not; but I know to be up late is to be up late.   5

SIR TOBY A false conclusion. I hate it as an unfilled can. To be up after midnight and to go to bed then is early; so that to go to bed after midnight is to go to bed betimes. Does not our lives consist of the four elements?

SIR ANDREW Faith, so they say, but I think it rather consists of eating and drinking.   11

SIR TOBY Thou'rt a scholar; let us therefore eat and drink. Marian, I say, a stoup of wine.

Enter Feste, the clown

SIR ANDREW Here comes the fool, i'faith.

FESTE How now, my hearts. Did you never see the picture of 'we three'?   16

SIR TOBY Welcome, ass. Now let's have a catch.

SIR ANDREW By my troth, the fool has an excellent breast. I had rather than forty shillings I had such a leg, and so sweet a breath to sing, as the fool has. In sooth, thou wast in very gracious fooling last night, when thou spokest of Pigrogromitus, of the Vapians passing the equinoctial of Queubus. 'Twas very good, i'faith. I sent thee sixpence for thy leman. Hadst it?   24

FESTE I did impeticos thy gratility; for Malvolio's nose is no whipstock. My lady has a white hand, and the Myrmidons are no bottle-ale houses.

SIR ANDREW Excellent! Why, this is the best fooling, when all is done. Now a song.

SIR TOBY (*to Feste*) Come on, there is sixpence for you. Let's have a song.   31

SIR ANDREW (*to Feste*) There's a testril of me, too. If one knight give a—

FESTE Would you have a love-song, or a song of good life?   35

SIR TOBY A love song, a love-song.

SIR ANDREW Ay, ay. I care not for good life.

FESTE (*sings*)

O mistress mine, where are you roaming?
O stay and hear, your true love's coming,
    That can sing both high and low.   40
Trip no further, pretty sweeting.
Journeys end in lovers meeting,
    Every wise man's son doth know.

SIR ANDREW Excellent good, i'faith.

SIR TOBY Good, good.   45

FESTE   What is love? 'Tis not hereafter,
           Present mirth hath present laughter.
              What's to come is still unsure.
           In delay there lies no plenty,
           Then come kiss me, sweet and twenty.   50
              Youth's a stuff will not endure.

SIR ANDREW A mellifluous voice, as I am true knight.

SIR TOBY A contagious breath.

SIR ANDREW Very sweet and contagious, i'faith.   54

SIR TOBY To hear by the nose, it is dulcet in contagion.
But shall we make the welkin dance indeed? Shall we
rouse the night-owl in a catch that will draw three
souls out of one weaver? Shall we do that?

SIR ANDREW An you love me, let's do't. I am dog at a
catch.   60

FESTE By'r Lady, sir, and some dogs will catch well.

SIR ANDREW Most certain. Let our catch be 'Thou knave'.

FESTE 'Hold thy peace, thou knave', knight. I shall be
constrained in't to call thee knave, knight.   64

SIR ANDREW 'Tis not the first time I have constrained one
to call me knave. Begin, fool. It begins 'Hold thy peace'.

FESTE I shall never begin if I hold my peace.

SIR ANDREW Good, i'faith. Come, begin.

They sing the catch.
Enter Maria

MARIA What a caterwauling do you keep here! If my
lady have not called up her steward Malvolio and bid
him turn you out of doors, never trust me.   71

SIR TOBY My lady's a Cathayan, we are politicians,
Malvolio's a Peg-o'-Ramsey, and 'Three merry men be
we'. Am not I consanguineous? Am I not of her blood?
Tilly-vally—'lady'! 'There dwelt a man in Babylon,
lady, lady.'   76

FESTE Beshrew me, the knight's in admirable fooling.

SIR ANDREW Ay, he does well enough if he be disposed,
and so do I, too. He does it with a better grace, but I
do it more natural.   80

SIR TOBY
'O' the twelfth day of December'—

MARIA For the love o' God, peace.

Enter Malvolio

MALVOLIO My masters, are you mad? Or what are you?
Have you no wit, manners, nor honesty, but to gabble
like tinkers at this time of night? Do ye make an
alehouse of my lady's house, that ye squeak out your
coziers' catches without any mitigation or remorse of
voice? Is there no respect of place, persons, nor time
in you?   89

SIR TOBY We did keep time, sir, in our catches. Sneck up!

MALVOLIO Sir Toby, I must be round with you. My lady
bade me tell you that though she harbours you as her
kinsman she's nothing allied to your disorders. If you
can separate yourself and your misdemeanours you are
welcome to the house. If not, an it would please you
to take leave of her she is very willing to bid you
farewell.

SIR TOBY
'Farewell, dear heart, since I must needs be gone.'

MARIA Nay, good Sir Toby.

FESTE
'His eyes do show his days are almost done.'   100

MALVOLIO Is't even so?

SIR TOBY
'But I will never die.'

FESTE
'Sir Toby, there you lie.'

MALVOLIO This is much credit to you.

SIR TOBY
'Shall I bid him go?'   105

FESTE
'What an if you do?'

SIR TOBY
'Shall I bid him go, and spare not?'

FESTE
'O no, no, no, no, you dare not.'

SIR TOBY Out o' tune, sir, ye lie. (*To Malvolio*) Art any
more than a steward? Dost thou think because thou
art virtuous there shall be no more cakes and ale? 111

FESTE Yes, by Saint Anne, and ginger shall be hot i'th'
mouth, too.

SIR TOBY Thou'rt i'th' right. (*To Malvolio*) Go, sir, rub
your chain with crumbs. (*To Maria*) A stoup of wine,
Maria.   116

MALVOLIO Mistress Mary, if you prized my lady's favour
at anything more than contempt you would not give
means for this uncivil rule. She shall know of it, by
this hand.   *Exit*

MARIA Go shake your ears.

SIR ANDREW 'Twere as good a deed as to drink when a
man's a-hungry to challenge him the field and then to
break promise with him, and make a fool of him.

SIR TOBY Do't, knight. I'll write thee a challenge, or I'll
deliver thy indignation to him by word of mouth.   126

MARIA Sweet Sir Toby, be patient for tonight. Since the
youth of the Count's was today with my lady she is
much out of quiet. For Monsieur Malvolio, let me alone
with him. If I do not gull him into a nayword and
make him a common recreation, do not think I have
wit enough to lie straight in my bed. I know I can do
it.

SIR TOBY Possess us, possess us, tell us something of him.

MARIA Marry, sir, sometimes he is a kind of puritan.

SIR ANDREW O, if I thought that I'd beat him like a dog.

SIR TOBY What, for being a puritan? Thy exquisite reason,
dear knight.

SIR ANDREW I have no exquisite reason for't, but I have
reason good enough.   140

MARIA The dev'l a puritan that he is, or anything
constantly but a time-pleaser, an affectioned ass that
cons state without book and utters it by great swathes;
the best persuaded of himself, so crammed, as he thinks,
with excellencies, that it is his grounds of faith that all
that look on him love him; and on that vice in him
will my revenge find notable cause to work.

SIR TOBY What wilt thou do?   148

MARIA I will drop in his way some obscure epistles of love, wherein by the colour of his beard, the shape of his leg, the manner of his gait, the expressure of his eye, forehead, and complexion, he shall find himself most feelingly personated. I can write very like my lady your niece; on a forgotten matter we can hardly make distinction of our hands.   155

SIR TOBY Excellent, I smell a device.

SIR ANDREW I have't in my nose too.

SIR TOBY He shall think by the letters that thou wilt drop that they come from my niece, and that she's in love with him.   160

MARIA My purpose is indeed a horse of that colour.

SIR ANDREW And your horse now would make him an ass.

MARIA Ass I doubt not.

SIR ANDREW O, 'twill be admirable.   165

MARIA Sport royal, I warrant you. I know my physic will work with him. I will plant you two—and let the fool make a third—where he shall find the letter. Observe his construction of it. For this night, to bed, and dream on the event. Farewell.   *Exit*

SIR TOBY Good night, Penthesilea.

SIR ANDREW Before me, she's a good wench.

SIR TOBY She's a beagle true bred, and one that adores me. What o' that?

SIR ANDREW I was adored once, too.   175

SIR TOBY Let's to bed, knight. Thou hadst need send for more money.

SIR ANDREW If I cannot recover your niece, I am a foul way out.

SIR TOBY Send for money, knight. If thou hast her not i'th' end, call me cut.   181

SIR ANDREW If I do not, never trust me, take it how you will.

SIR TOBY Come, come, I'll go burn some sack, 'tis too late to go to bed now. Come knight, come knight.   185
   Exeunt

2.4   *Enter the Duke, Viola as Cesario, Curio, and others*

ORSINO
Give me some music. Now good morrow, friends.
Now good Cesario, but that piece of song,
That old and antic song we heard last night.
Methought it did relieve my passion much,
More than light airs and recollected terms   5
Of these most brisk and giddy-pacèd times.
Come, but one verse.

CURIO He is not here, so please your lordship, that should sing it.

ORSINO Who was it?   10

CURIO Feste the jester, my lord, a fool that the lady Olivia's father took much delight in. He is about the house.

ORSINO
Seek him out, and play the tune the while.   *Exit Curio*
   Music plays
(*To Viola*) Come hither, boy. If ever thou shalt love,
In the sweet pangs of it remember me;   15

For such as I am, all true lovers are,
Unstaid and skittish in all motions else
Save in the constant image of the creature
That is beloved. How dost thou like this tune?

VIOLA
It gives a very echo to the seat   20
Where love is thronèd.

ORSINO   Thou dost speak masterly.
My life upon't, young though thou art thine eye
Hath stayed upon some favour that it loves.
Hath it not, boy?

VIOLA   A little, by your favour.

ORSINO
What kind of woman is't?

VIOLA   Of your complexion.   25

ORSINO
She is not worth thee then. What years, i'faith?

VIOLA About your years, my lord.

ORSINO
Too old, by heaven. Let still the woman take
An elder than herself. So wears she to him;
So sways she level in her husband's heart.   30
For, boy, however we do praise ourselves,
Our fancies are more giddy and unfirm,
More longing, wavering, sooner lost and worn,
Than women's are.

VIOLA   I think it well, my lord.

ORSINO
Then let thy love be younger than thyself,   35
Or thy affection cannot hold the bent;
For women are as roses, whose fair flower
Being once displayed, doth fall that very hour.

VIOLA
And so they are. Alas that they are so:
To die even when they to perfection grow.   40
   Enter Curio and Feste the clown

ORSINO (*to Feste*)
O fellow, come, the song we had last night.
Mark it, Cesario, it is old and plain.
The spinsters, and the knitters in the sun,
And the free maids that weave their thread with bones,
Do use to chant it. It is silly sooth,   45
And dallies with the innocence of love,
Like the old age.

FESTE Are you ready, sir?

ORSINO I prithee, sing.
   Music

FESTE (*sings*)
Come away, come away death,   50
  And in sad cypress let me be laid.
Fie away, fie away breath,
  I am slain by a fair cruel maid.
My shroud of white, stuck all with yew,
  O prepare it.   55
My part of death no one so true
  Did share it.

Not a flower, not a flower sweet
  On my black coffin let there be strewn.
Not a friend, not a friend greet   60
  My poor corpse, where my bones shall be thrown.
A thousand thousand sighs to save,
  Lay me O where
Sad true lover never find my grave,
  To weep there.   65

DUKE (*giving money*) There's for thy pains.
FESTE No pains, sir. I take pleasure in singing, sir.
ORSINO I'll pay thy pleasure then.
FESTE Truly, sir, and pleasure will be paid, one time or
  another.   70
ORSINO Give me now leave to leave thee.
FESTE Now the melancholy god protect thee, and the
tailor make, thy doublet of changeable taffeta, for thy
mind is a very opal. I would have men of such constancy
put to sea, that their business might be everything,
and their intent everywhere, for that's it that always
makes a good voyage of nothing. Farewell.   *Exit*
ORSINO
  Let all the rest give place: *Exeunt Curio and others*
                       Once more, Cesario,
  Get thee to yon same sovereign cruelty.
  Tell her my love, more noble than the world,   80
  Prizes not quantity of dirty lands.
  The parts that fortune hath bestowed upon her
  Tell her I hold as giddily as fortune;
  But 'tis that miracle and queen of gems
  That nature pranks her in attracts my soul.   85
VIOLA
  But if she cannot love you, sir?
ORSINO
  I cannot be so answered.
VIOLA   Sooth, but you must.
  Say that some lady, as perhaps there is,
  Hath for your love as great a pang of heart
  As you have for Olivia. You cannot love her.   90
  You tell her so. Must she not then be answered?
ORSINO There is no woman's sides
  Can bide the beating of so strong a passion
  As love doth give my heart; no woman's heart
  So big, to hold so much. They lack retention.   95
  Alas, their love may be called appetite,
  No motion of the liver, but the palate,
  That suffer surfeit, cloyment, and revolt.
  But mine is all as hungry as the sea,
  And can digest as much. Make no compare   100
  Between that love a woman can bear me
  And that I owe Olivia.
VIOLA Ay, but I know—
ORSINO What dost thou know?
VIOLA
  Too well what love women to men may owe.   105
  In faith, they are as true of heart as we.
  My father had a daughter loved a man
  As it might be, perhaps, were I a woman
  I should your lordship.
ORSINO   And what's her history?

VIOLA
  A blank, my lord. She never told her love,   110
  But let concealment, like a worm i'th' bud,
  Feed on her damask cheek. She pined in thought,
  And with a green and yellow melancholy
  She sat like patience on a monument,
  Smiling at grief. Was not this love indeed?   115
  We men may say more, swear more, but indeed
  Our shows are more than will; for still we prove
  Much in our vows, but little in our love.
ORSINO
  But died thy sister of her love, my boy?
VIOLA
  I am all the daughters of my father's house,   120
  And all the brothers too; and yet I know not.
  Sir, shall I to this lady?
ORSINO   Ay, that's the theme,
  To her in haste. Give her this jewel. Say
  My love can give no place, bide no denay.
                          Exeunt severally

2.5   *Enter Sir Toby, Sir Andrew, and Fabian*
SIR TOBY Come thy ways, Signor Fabian.
FABIAN Nay, I'll come. If I lose a scruple of this sport let
  me be boiled to death with melancholy.
SIR TOBY Wouldst thou not be glad to have the niggardly
  rascally sheep-biter come by some notable shame?   5
FABIAN I would exult, man. You know he brought me
  out o' favour with my lady about a bear-baiting here.
SIR TOBY To anger him we'll have the bear again, and
  we will fool him black and blue, shall we not, Sir
  Andrew?   10
SIR ANDREW An we do not, it is pity of our lives.
    Enter Maria with a letter
SIR TOBY Here comes the little villain. How now, my metal
  of India?
MARIA Get ye all three into the box-tree. Malvolio's
  coming down this walk. He has been yonder i' the sun
  practising behaviour to his own shadow this half-hour.
  Observe him, for the love of mockery, for I know this
  letter will make a contemplative idiot of him. Close, in
  the name of jesting!   19
    The men hide. Maria places the letter
  Lie thou there, for here comes the trout that must be
  caught with tickling.   *Exit*
    Enter Malvolio
MALVOLIO 'Tis but fortune, all is fortune. Maria once told
  me she did affect me, and I have heard herself come
  thus near, that should she fancy it should be one of
  my complexion. Besides, she uses me with a more
  exalted respect than anyone else that follows her. What
  should I think on't?
SIR TOBY Here's an overweening rogue.
FABIAN O, peace! Contemplation makes a rare turkeycock
  of him—how he jets under his advanced plumes!   30
SIR ANDREW 'Slight, I could so beat the rogue.
SIR TOBY Peace, I say.
MALVOLIO To be Count Malvolio!
SIR TOBY Ah, rogue.

SIR ANDREW Pistol him, pistol him. 35
SIR TOBY Peace, peace.
MALVOLIO There is example for't: the Lady of the Strachey married the yeoman of the wardrobe.
SIR ANDREW Fie on him, Jezebel.
FABIAN O peace, now he's deeply in. Look how imagination blows him. 41
MALVOLIO Having been three months married to her, sitting in my state—
SIR TOBY O for a stone-bow to hit him in the eye! 44
MALVOLIO Calling my officers about me, in my branched velvet gown, having come from a day-bed where I have left Olivia sleeping—
SIR TOBY Fire and brimstone!
FABIAN O peace, peace. 49
MALVOLIO And then to have the humour of state and—after a demure travel of regard, telling them I know my place, as I would they should do theirs—to ask for my kinsman Toby.
SIR TOBY Bolts and shackles!
FABIAN O peace, peace, peace, now, now. 55
MALVOLIO Seven of my people with an obedient start make out for him. I frown the while, and perchance wind up my watch, or play with my—(touching his chain) some rich jewel. Toby approaches; curtsies there to me. 60
SIR TOBY Shall this fellow live?
FABIAN Though our silence be drawn from us with cars, yet peace.
MALVOLIO I extend my hand to him thus, quenching my familiar smile with an austere regard of control— 65
SIR TOBY And does not Toby take you a blow o' the lips, then?
MALVOLIO Saying 'Cousin Toby, my fortunes, having cast me on your niece, give me this prerogative of speech'—
SIR TOBY What, what! 70
MALVOLIO 'You must amend your drunkenness.'
SIR TOBY Out, scab.
FABIAN Nay, patience, or we break the sinews of our plot.
MALVOLIO 'Besides, you waste the treasure of your time with a foolish knight'— 75
SIR ANDREW That's me, I warrant you.
MALVOLIO 'One Sir Andrew.'
SIR ANDREW I knew 'twas I, for many do call me fool.
MALVOLIO (seeing the letter) What employment have we here? 80
FABIAN Now is the woodcock near the gin.
SIR TOBY O peace, and the spirit of humours intimate reading aloud to him.
MALVOLIO (taking up the letter) By my life, this is my lady's hand. These be her very c's, her u's, and her t's, and thus makes she her great P's. It is in contempt of question her hand.
SIR ANDREW Her c's, her u's, and her t's? Why that?
MALVOLIO (reads) 'To the unknown beloved, this, and my good wishes.' Her very phrases! (Opening the letter) By your leave, wax—soft, and the impressure her Lucrece, with which she uses to seal—'tis my lady. To whom should this be?

FABIAN This wins him, liver and all.
MALVOLIO   'Jove knows I love, 95
      But who?
    Lips do not move,
      No man must know.'
'No man must know.' What follows? The numbers altered. 'No man must know.' If this should be thee, Malvolio? 101
SIR TOBY Marry, hang thee, brock.
MALVOLIO
    'I may command where I adore,
      But silence like a Lucrece knife
    With bloodless stroke my heart doth gore. 105
      M.O.A.I. doth sway my life.'
FABIAN A fustian riddle.
SIR TOBY Excellent wench, say I.
MALVOLIO 'M.O.A.I. doth sway my life.' Nay, but first let me see, let me see, let me see. 110
FABIAN What dish o' poison has she dressed him!
SIR TOBY And with what wing the staniel checks at it!
MALVOLIO 'I may command where I adore.' Why, she may command me. I serve her, she is my lady. Why, this is evident to any formal capacity. There is no obstruction in this. And the end—what should that alphabetical position portend? If I could make that resemble something in me. Softly—'M.O.A.I.'
SIR TOBY O ay, make up that, he is now at a cold scent.
FABIAN Sowter will cry upon't for all this, though it be as rank as a fox. 121
MALVOLIO 'M.' Malvolio—'M'—why, that begins my name.
FABIAN Did not I say he would work it out? The cur is excellent at faults. 125
MALVOLIO 'M.' But then there is no consonancy in the sequel. That suffers under probation. 'A' should follow, but 'O' does.
FABIAN And 'O' shall end, I hope.
SIR TOBY Ay, or I'll cudgel him, and make him cry 'O!'
MALVOLIO And then 'I' comes behind. 131
FABIAN Ay, an you had any eye behind you you might see more detraction at your heels than fortunes before you. 134
MALVOLIO 'M.O.A.I.' This simulation is not as the former; and yet to crush this a little, it would bow to me, for every one of these letters are in my name. Soft, here follows prose: 'If this fall into thy hand, revolve. In my stars I am above thee, but be not afraid of greatness. Some are born great, some achieve greatness, and some have greatness thrust upon 'em. Thy fates open their hands, let thy blood and spirit embrace them, and to inure thyself to what thou art like to be, cast thy humble slough, and appear fresh. Be opposite with a kinsman, surly with servants. Let thy tongue tang arguments of state; put thyself into the trick of singularity. She thus advises thee that sighs for thee. Remember who commended thy yellow stockings, and wished to see thee ever cross-gartered. I say remember, go to, thou art made if thou desirest to be so; if not, let me see thee a steward still, the fellow of servants,

and not worthy to touch Fortune's fingers. Farewell.
She that would alter services with thee,   153
          The Fortunate-Unhappy.'
Daylight and champaign discovers not more. This is
open. I will be proud, I will read politic authors, I will
baffle Sir Toby, I will wash off gross acquaintance, I
will be point-device the very man. I do not now fool
myself, to let imagination jade me; for every reason
excites to this, that my lady loves me. She did commend
my yellow stockings of late, she did praise my leg,
being cross-gartered, and in this she manifests herself
to my love, and with a kind of injunction drives me to
these habits of her liking. I thank my stars, I am happy.
I will be strange, stout, in yellow stockings, and cross-
gartered, even with the swiftness of putting on. Jove
and my stars be praised. Here is yet a postscript. 'Thou
canst not choose but know who I am. If thou
entertainest my love, let it appear in thy smiling, thy
smiles become thee well. Therefore in my presence still
smile, dear my sweet, I prithee.' Jove, I thank thee. I
will smile, I will do everything that thou wilt have me.
                              Exit
    Sir Toby, Sir Andrew, and Fabian come from hiding
FABIAN I will not give my part of this sport for a pension
    of thousands to be paid from the Sophy.
SIR TOBY I could marry this wench for this device.   175
SIR ANDREW So could I, too.
SIR TOBY And ask no other dowry with her but such
    another jest.
          Enter Maria
SIR ANDREW Nor I neither.
FABIAN Here comes my noble gull-catcher.   180
SIR TOBY (*to Maria*) Wilt thou set thy foot o' my neck?
SIR ANDREW (*to Maria*) Or o' mine either?
SIR TOBY (*to Maria*) Shall I play my freedom at tray-trip,
    and become thy bondslave?
SIR ANDREW (*to Maria*) I'faith, or I either?   185
SIR TOBY (*to Maria*) Why, thou hast put him in such a
    dream that when the image of it leaves him, he must
    run mad.
MARIA Nay, but say true, does it work upon him?
SIR TOBY Like aqua vitae with a midwife.   190
MARIA If you will then see the fruits of the sport, mark
    his first approach before my lady. He will come to her
    in yellow stockings, and 'tis a colour she abhors, and
    cross-gartered, a fashion she detests; and he will smile
    upon her, which will now be so unsuitable to her
    disposition, being addicted to a melancholy as she is,
    that it cannot but turn him into a notable contempt.
    If you will see it, follow me.
SIR TOBY To the gates of Tartar, thou most excellent devil
    of wit.   200
SIR ANDREW I'll make one, too.   *Exeunt*

3.1   *Enter Viola as Cesario and Feste the clown, with*
       ⌈*pipe and*⌉ *tabor*
VIOLA Save thee, friend, and thy music. Dost thou live by
    thy tabor?

FESTE No, sir, I live by the church.
VIOLA Art thou a churchman?
FESTE No such matter, sir. I do live by the church for I
    do live at my house, and my house doth stand by the
    church.
VIOLA So thou mayst say the king lies by a beggar if a
    beggar dwell near him, or the church stands by thy
    tabor if thy tabor stand by the church.   10
FESTE You have said, sir. To see this age!—A sentence is
    but a cheverel glove to a good wit, how quickly the
    wrong side may be turned outward.
VIOLA Nay, that's certain. They that dally nicely with
    words may quickly make them wanton.   15
FESTE I would therefore my sister had had no name, sir.
VIOLA Why, man?
FESTE Why, sir, her name's a word, and to dally with
    that word might make my sister wanton. But indeed,
    words are very rascals since bonds disgraced them. 20
VIOLA Thy reason, man?
FESTE Troth, sir, I can yield you none without words, and
    words are grown so false I am loath to prove reason
    with them.
VIOLA I warrant thou art a merry fellow, and carest for
    nothing.   26
FESTE Not so, sir, I do care for something; but in my
    conscience, sir, I do not care for you. If that be to care
    for nothing, sir, I would it would make you invisible.
VIOLA Art not thou the Lady Olivia's fool?   30
FESTE No indeed, sir, the Lady Olivia has no folly, she
    will keep no fool, sir, till she be married, and fools are
    as like husbands as pilchards are to herrings—the
    husband's the bigger. I am indeed not her fool, but her
    corrupter of words.   35
VIOLA I saw thee late at the Count Orsino's.
FESTE Foolery, sir, does walk about the orb like the sun,
    it shines everywhere. I would be sorry, sir, but the fool
    should be as oft with your master as with my mistress.
    I think I saw your wisdom there.   40
VIOLA Nay, an thou pass upon me, I'll no more with
    thee. (*Giving money*) Hold, there's expenses for thee.
FESTE Now Jove in his next commodity of hair send thee
    a beard.   44
VIOLA By my troth I'll tell thee, I am almost sick for one,
    though I would not have it grow on *my* chin. Is thy
    lady within?
FESTE Would not a pair of these have bred, sir?
VIOLA Yes, being kept together and put to use.
FESTE I would play Lord Pandarus of Phrygia, sir, to bring
    a Cressida to this Troilus.   51
VIOLA (*giving money*) I understand you, sir, 'tis well
    begged.
FESTE The matter I hope is not great, sir; begging but a
    beggar—Cressida was a beggar. My lady is within, sir.
    I will conster to them whence you come. Who you are
    and what you would are out of my welkin—I might
    say 'element', but the word is over-worn.   *Exit*
VIOLA
    This fellow is wise enough to play the fool,

And to do that well craves a kind of wit.   60
He must observe their mood on whom he jests,
The quality of persons, and the time,
And, like the haggard, check at every feather
That comes before his eye. This is a practice
As full of labour as a wise man's art,   65
For folly that he wisely shows is fit,
But wise men, folly-fall'n, quite taint their wit.
    Enter Sir Toby and Sir Andrew
SIR TOBY Save you, gentleman.
VIOLA And you, sir.
SIR ANDREW *Dieu vous garde, monsieur.*   70
VIOLA *Et vous aussi, votre serviteur.*
SIR ANDREW I hope, sir, you are, and I am yours.
SIR TOBY Will you encounter the house? My niece is
desirous you should enter if your trade be to her.
VIOLA I am bound to your niece, sir: I mean she is the
list of my voyage.   76
SIR TOBY Taste your legs, sir, put them to motion.
VIOLA My legs do better understand me, sir, than I
understand what you mean by bidding me taste my
legs.   80
SIR TOBY I mean to go, sir, to enter.
VIOLA I will answer you with gait and entrance.
    Enter Olivia, and Maria, her gentlewoman
But we are prevented. (*To Olivia*) Most excellent accom-
plished lady, the heavens rain odours on you.
SIR ANDREW (*to Sir Toby*) That youth's a rare courtier;
'rain odours'—well.   86
VIOLA My matter hath no voice, lady, but to your own
most pregnant and vouchsafed ear.
SIR ANDREW (*to Sir Toby*) 'Odours', 'pregnant', and
'vouchsafed'—I'll get 'em all three all ready.   90
OLIVIA Let the garden door be shut, and leave me to my
hearing.   *Exeunt Sir Toby, Sir Andrew, and Maria*
Give me your hand, sir.
VIOLA
My duty, madam, and most humble service.
OLIVIA What is your name?   95
VIOLA
Cesario is your servant's name, fair princess.
OLIVIA
My servant, sir? 'Twas never merry world
Since lowly feigning was called compliment.
You're servant to the Count Orsino, youth.
VIOLA
And he is yours, and his must needs be yours.   100
Your servant's servant is *your* servant, madam.
OLIVIA
For him, I think not on him. For his thoughts,
Would they were blanks rather than filled with me.
VIOLA
Madam, I come to whet your gentle thoughts
On his behalf.
OLIVIA   O by your leave, I pray you.   105
I bade you never speak again of him;
But would you undertake another suit,

I had rather hear you to solicit that
Than music from the spheres.
VIOLA   Dear lady—
OLIVIA
Give me leave, beseech you. I did send,   110
After the last enchantment you did here,
A ring in chase of you. So did I abuse
Myself, my servant, and I fear me you.
Under your hard construction must I sit,
To force that on you in a shameful cunning   115
Which you knew none of yours. What might you
    think?
Have you not set mine honour at the stake
And baited it with all th'unmuzzled thoughts
That tyrannous heart can think? To one of your
    receiving
Enough is shown. A cypress, not a bosom,   120
Hides my heart. So let me hear you speak.
VIOLA
I pity you.
OLIVIA   That's a degree to love.
VIOLA
No, not a grece, for 'tis a vulgar proof
That very oft we pity enemies.
OLIVIA
Why then, methinks 'tis time to smile again.   125
O world, how apt the poor are to be proud!
If one should be a prey, how much the better
To fall before the lion than the wolf!
    Clock strikes
The clock upbraids me with the waste of time.
Be not afraid, good youth, I will not have you;   130
And yet when wit and youth is come to harvest
Your wife is like to reap a proper man.
There lies your way, due west.
VIOLA   Then westward ho!
Grace and good disposition attend your ladyship.
You'll nothing, madam, to my lord by me?   135
OLIVIA
Stay. I prithee tell me what thou think'st of me.
VIOLA
That you do think you are not what you are.
OLIVIA
If I think so, I think the same of you.
VIOLA
Then think you right, I am not what I am.
OLIVIA
I would you were as I would have you be.   140
VIOLA
Would it be better, madam, than I am?
I wish it might, for now I am your fool.
OLIVIA (*aside*)
O, what a deal of scorn looks beautiful
In the contempt and anger of his lip!
A murd'rous guilt shows not itself more soon   145
Than love that would seem hid. Love's night is noon.
(*To Viola*) Cesario, by the roses of the spring,

By maidhood, honour, truth, and everything,
I love thee so that, maugre all thy pride,
Nor wit nor reason can my passion hide.   150
Do not extort thy reasons from this clause,
For that I woo, thou therefore hast no cause.
But rather reason thus with reason fetter:
Love sought is good, but given unsought, is better.

VIOLA
By innocence I swear, and by my youth,   155
I have one heart, one bosom, and one truth,
And that no woman has, nor never none
Shall mistress be of it save I alone.
And so adieu, good madam. Never more
Will I my master's tears to you deplore.   160

OLIVIA
Yet come again, for thou perhaps mayst move
That heart which now abhors, to like his love.

Exeunt ⌈severally⌉

3.2   *Enter Sir Toby, Sir Andrew, and Fabian*
SIR ANDREW No, faith, I'll not stay a jot longer.
SIR TOBY Thy reason, dear venom, give thy reason.
FABIAN You must needs yield your reason, Sir Andrew.
SIR ANDREW Marry, I saw your niece do more favours to
the Count's servingman than ever she bestowed upon
me. I saw't i'th' orchard.   6
SIR TOBY Did she see thee the while, old boy? Tell me
that.
SIR ANDREW As plain as I see you now.
FABIAN This was a great argument of love in her toward
you.   11
SIR ANDREW 'Slight, will you make an ass o' me?
FABIAN I will prove it legitimate, sir, upon the oaths of
judgement and reason.
SIR TOBY And they have been grand-jurymen since before
Noah was a sailor.   16
FABIAN She did show favour to the youth in your sight
only to exasperate you, to awake your dormouse valour,
to put fire in your heart and brimstone in your liver.
You should then have accosted her, and with some
excellent jests, fire-new from the mint, you should have
banged the youth into dumbness. This was looked for
at your hand, and this was balked. The double gilt of
this opportunity you let time wash off, and you are
now sailed into the north of my lady's opinion, where
you will hang like an icicle on a Dutchman's beard
unless you do redeem it by some laudable attempt
either of valour or policy.   28
SIR ANDREW An't be any way, it must be with valour, for
policy I hate. I had as lief be a Brownist as a politician.
SIR TOBY Why then, build me thy fortunes upon the basis
of valour. Challenge me the Count's youth to fight with
him, hurt him in eleven places. My niece shall take
note of it; and assure thyself, there is no love-broker
in the world can more prevail in man's commendation
with woman than report of valour.   36
FABIAN There is no way but this, Sir Andrew.

SIR ANDREW Will either of you bear me a challenge to
him?   39
SIR TOBY Go, write it in a martial hand, be curst and
brief. It is no matter how witty so it be eloquent and
full of invention. Taunt him with the licence of ink. If
thou 'thou'st' him some thrice, it shall not be amiss,
and as many lies as will lie in thy sheet of paper,
although the sheet were big enough for the bed of
Ware, in England, set 'em down, go about it. Let there
be gall enough in thy ink; though thou write with a
goose-pen, no matter. About it.
SIR ANDREW Where shall I find you?   49
SIR TOBY We'll call thee at the cubiculo. Go.

Exit Sir Andrew

FABIAN This is a dear manikin to you, Sir Toby.
SIR TOBY I have been dear to him, lad, some two thousand
strong or so.
FABIAN We shall have a rare letter from him; but you'll
not deliver't.   55
SIR TOBY Never trust me then; and by all means stir on
the youth to an answer. I think oxen and wain-ropes
cannot hale them together. For Andrew, if he were
opened and you find so much blood in his liver as will
clog the foot of a flea, I'll eat the rest of th'anatomy.
FABIAN And his opposite, the youth, bears in his visage
no great presage of cruelty.   62

Enter Maria

SIR TOBY Look where the youngest wren of nine comes.
MARIA If you desire the spleen, and will laugh yourselves
into stitches, follow me. Yon gull Malvolio is turned
heathen, a very renegado, for there is no Christian that
means to be saved by believing rightly can ever believe
such impossible passages of grossness. He's in yellow
stockings.
SIR TOBY And cross-gartered?   70
MARIA Most villainously, like a pedant that keeps a school
i'th' church. I have dogged him like his murderer. He
does obey every point of the letter that I dropped to
betray him. He does smile his face into more lines than
is in the new map with the augmentation of the Indies.
You have not seen such a thing as 'tis. I can hardly
forbear hurling things at him. I know my lady will
strike him. If she do, he'll smile, and take't for a great
favour.   79
SIR TOBY Come bring us, bring us where he is.   *Exeunt*

3.3   *Enter Sebastian and Antonio*
SEBASTIAN
I would not by my will have troubled you,
But since you make your pleasure of your pains
I will no further chide you.
ANTONIO
I could not stay behind you. My desire,
More sharp than filèd steel, did spur me forth,   5
And not all love to see you—though so much
As might have drawn one to a longer voyage—
But jealousy what might befall your travel,

Being skilless in these parts, which to a stranger,
Unguided and unfriended, often prove   10
Rough and unhospitable. My willing love
The rather by these arguments of fear
Set forth in your pursuit.
SEBASTIAN   My kind Antonio,
I can no other answer make but thanks,
And thanks; and ever oft good turns   15
Are shuffled off with such uncurrent pay.
But were my worth as is my conscience firm,
You should find better dealing. What's to do?
Shall we go see the relics of this town?
ANTONIO
Tomorrow, sir. Best first go see your lodging.   20
SEBASTIAN
I am not weary, and 'tis long to night.
I pray you let us satisfy our eyes
With the memorials and the things of fame
That do renown this city.
ANTONIO   Would you'd pardon me.
I do not without danger walk these streets.   25
Once in a sea-fight 'gainst the Count his galleys
I did some service, of such note indeed
That were I ta'en here it would scarce be answered.
SEBASTIAN
Belike you slew great number of his people.
ANTONIO
Th'offence is not of such a bloody nature,   30
Albeit the quality of the time and quarrel
Might well have given us bloody argument.
It might have since been answered in repaying
What we took from them, which for traffic's sake
Most of our city did. Only myself stood out,   35
For which if I be latchèd in this place
I shall pay dear.
SEBASTIAN   Do not then walk too open.
ANTONIO
It doth not fit me. Hold, sir, here's my purse.
In the south suburbs at the Elephant
Is best to lodge. I will bespeak our diet   40
Whiles you beguile the time and feed your knowledge
With viewing of the town. There shall you have me.
SEBASTIAN Why I your purse?
ANTONIO
Haply your eye shall light upon some toy
You have desire to purchase; and your store   45
I think is not for idle markets, sir.
SEBASTIAN
I'll be your purse-bearer, and leave you
For an hour.
ANTONIO   To th' Elephant.
SEBASTIAN   I do remember.
                              Exeunt severally

3.4   *Enter Olivia and Maria*
OLIVIA (*aside*)
I have sent after him, he says he'll come.

How shall I feast him? What bestow of him?
For youth is bought more oft than begged or
    borrowed.
I speak too loud.
(*To Maria*) Where's Malvolio? He is sad and civil,   5
And suits well for a servant with my fortunes.
Where is Malvolio?
MARIA He's coming, madam, but in very strange manner.
He is sure possessed, madam.
OLIVIA
Why, what's the matter? Does he rave?   10
MARIA No, madam, he does nothing but smile. Your
ladyship were best to have some guard about you if he
come, for sure the man is tainted in's wits.
OLIVIA
Go call him hither.   *Exit Maria*
              I am as mad as he,
If sad and merry madness equal be.   15
    Enter Malvolio, cross-gartered and wearing yellow
    stockings, with Maria
How now, Malvolio?
MALVOLIO Sweet lady, ho, ho!
OLIVIA
Smil'st thou? I sent for thee upon a sad occasion.
MALVOLIO Sad, lady? I could be sad. This does make some
obstruction in the blood, this cross-gartering, but what
of that? If it please the eye of one, it is with me as the
very true sonnet is, 'Please one, and please all'.   22
⌈OLIVIA⌉
Why, how dost thou, man? What is the matter with
    thee?
MALVOLIO Not black in my mind, though yellow in my
legs. It did come to his hands, and commands shall be
executed. I think we do know the sweet roman hand.
OLIVIA
Wilt thou go to bed, Malvolio?
MALVOLIO (*kissing his hand*) To bed? 'Ay, sweetheart, and
I'll come to thee.'
OLIVIA God comfort thee. Why dost thou smile so, and
kiss thy hand so oft?   31
MARIA How do you, Malvolio?
MALVOLIO At your request?—yes, nightingales answer
daws.
MARIA Why appear you with this ridiculous boldness
before my lady?   36
MALVOLIO 'Be not afraid of greatness'—'twas well writ.
OLIVIA What meanest thou by that, Malvolio?
MALVOLIO 'Some are born great'—
OLIVIA Ha?   40
MALVOLIO 'Some achieve greatness'—
OLIVIA What sayst thou?
MALVOLIO 'And some have greatness thrust upon them.'
OLIVIA Heaven restore thee.
MALVOLIO 'Remember who commended thy yellow
stockings'—   46
OLIVIA 'Thy yellow stockings'?
MALVOLIO 'And wished to see thee cross-gartered.'

OLIVIA 'Cross-gartered'?

MALVOLIO 'Go to, thou art made, if thou desirest to be so.'   51

OLIVIA Am I made?

MALVOLIO 'If not, let me see thee a servant still.'

OLIVIA Why, this is very midsummer madness.   54

Enter a Servant

SERVANT Madam, the young gentleman of the Count Orsino's is returned. I could hardly entreat him back. He attends your ladyship's pleasure.

OLIVIA I'll come to him.   *Exit Servant*
Good Maria, let this fellow be looked to. Where's my cousin Toby? Let some of my people have a special care of him, I would not have him miscarry for the half of my dowry.   *Exeunt Olivia and Maria, severally*

MALVOLIO O ho, do you come near me now? No worse man than Sir Toby to look to me. This concurs directly with the letter, she sends him on purpose, that I may appear stubborn to him, for she incites me to that in the letter. 'Cast thy humble slough,' says she, 'be opposite with a kinsman, surly with servants, let thy tongue tang arguments of state, put thyself into the trick of singularity', and consequently sets down the manner how, as a sad face, a reverend carriage, a slow tongue, in the habit of some sir of note, and so forth. I have limed her, but it is Jove's doing, and Jove make me thankful. And when she went away now, 'let this fellow be looked to'. Fellow!—not 'Malvolio', nor after my degree, but 'fellow'. Why, everything adheres together that no dram of a scruple, no scruple of a scruple, no obstacle, no incredulous or unsafe circumstance—what can be said?—nothing that can be can come between me and the full prospect of my hopes. Well, Jove, not I, is the doer of this, and he is to be thanked.

Enter Sir Toby, Fabian, and Maria

SIR TOBY Which way is he, in the name of sanctity? If all the devils of hell be drawn in little, and Legion himself possessed him, yet I'll speak to him.   85

FABIAN Here he is, here he is. (*To Malvolio*) How is't with you, sir? How is't with you, man?

MALVOLIO Go off, I discard you. Let me enjoy my private. Go off.   89

MARIA Lo, how hollow the fiend speaks within him. Did not I tell you? Sir Toby, my lady prays you to have a care of him.

MALVOLIO Aha, does she so?

SIR TOBY Go to, go to. Peace, peace, we must deal gently with him. Let me alone. How do you, Malvolio? How is't with you? What, man, defy the devil. Consider, he's an enemy to mankind.

MALVOLIO Do you know what you say?

MARIA La you, an you speak ill of the devil, how he takes it at heart. Pray God he be not bewitched.   100

FABIAN Carry his water to th' wise woman.

MARIA Marry, and it shall be done tomorrow morning, if I live. My lady would not lose him for more than I'll say.

MALVOLIO How now, mistress?   105

MARIA O Lord!

SIR TOBY Prithee hold thy peace, this is not the way. Do you not see you move him? Let me alone with him.

FABIAN No way but gentleness, gently, gently. The fiend is rough, and will not be roughly used.   110

SIR TOBY Why how now, my bawcock? How dost thou, chuck?

MALVOLIO Sir!

SIR TOBY Ay, biddy, come with me. What man, 'tis not for gravity to play at cherry-pit with Satan. Hang him, foul collier.   116

MARIA Get him to say his prayers. Good Sir Toby, get him to pray.

MALVOLIO My prayers, minx?   119

MARIA No, I warrant you, he will not hear of godliness.

MALVOLIO Go hang yourselves, all. You are idle shallow things, I am not of your element. You shall know more hereafter.   *Exit*

SIR TOBY Is't possible?

FABIAN If this were played upon a stage, now, I could condemn it as an improbable fiction.   126

SIR TOBY His very genius hath taken the infection of the device, man.

MARIA Nay, pursue him now, lest the device take air and taint.   130

FABIAN Why, we shall make him mad indeed.

MARIA The house will be the quieter.

SIR TOBY Come, we'll have him in a dark room and bound. My niece is already in the belief that he's mad. We may carry it thus for our pleasure and his penance till our very pastime, tired out of breath, prompt us to have mercy on him, at which time we will bring the device to the bar and crown thee for a finder of madmen. But see, but see.

Enter Sir Andrew with a paper

FABIAN More matter for a May morning.   140

SIR ANDREW Here's the challenge, read it. I warrant there's vinegar and pepper in't.

FABIAN Is't so saucy?

SIR ANDREW Ay—is't? I warrant him. Do but read.

SIR TOBY Give me.   145

(*Reads*) 'Youth, whatsoever thou art, thou art but a scurvy fellow.'

FABIAN Good, and valiant.

SIR TOBY 'Wonder not, nor admire not in thy mind why I do call thee so, for I will show thee no reason for't.'

FABIAN A good note, that keeps you from the blow of the law.

SIR TOBY 'Thou comest to the Lady Olivia, and in my sight she uses thee kindly; but thou liest in thy throat, that is not the matter I challenge thee for.'   155

FABIAN Very brief, and to exceeding good sense (*aside*) -less.

SIR TOBY 'I will waylay thee going home, where if it be thy chance to kill me'—

FABIAN Good.   160

SIR TOBY 'Thou killest me like a rogue and a villain.'

FABIAN Still you keep o'th' windy side of the law—good.

SIR TOBY 'Fare thee well, and God have mercy upon one of our souls. He may have mercy upon mine, but my hope is better, and so look to thyself. 165
Thy friend as thou usest him, and thy sworn enemy,
                              Andrew Aguecheek.'
If this letter move him not, his legs cannot. I'll give't him. 169

MARIA You may have very fit occasion for't. He is now in some commerce with my lady, and will by and by depart.

SIR TOBY Go, Sir Andrew. Scout me for him at the corner of the orchard like a bum-baily. So soon as ever thou seest him, draw, and as thou drawest, swear horrible, for it comes to pass oft that a terrible oath, with a swaggering accent sharply twanged off, gives manhood more approbation than ever proof itself would have earned him. Away. 179

SIR ANDREW Nay, let me alone for swearing.   Exit

SIR TOBY Now will not I deliver his letter, for the behaviour of the young gentleman gives him out to be of good capacity and breeding. His employment between his lord and my niece confirms no less. Therefore this letter, being so excellently ignorant, will breed no terror in the youth. He will find it comes from a clodpoll. But, sir, I will deliver his challenge by word of mouth, set upon Aguecheek a notable report of valour, and drive the gentleman—as I know his youth will aptly receive it—into a most hideous opinion of his rage, skill, fury, and impetuosity. This will so fright them both that they will kill one another by the look, like cockatrices.

Enter Olivia, and Viola as Cesario

FABIAN Here he comes with your niece. Give them way till he take leave, and presently after him.

SIR TOBY I will meditate the while upon some horrid message for a challenge. 196

Exeunt Sir Toby, Fabian, and Maria

OLIVIA
I have said too much unto a heart of stone,
And laid mine honour too unchary out.
There's something in me that reproves my fault,
But such a headstrong potent fault it is   200
That it but mocks reproof.

VIOLA   With the same 'haviour
That your passion bears goes on my master's griefs.

OLIVIA (*giving a jewel*)
Here, wear this jewel for me, 'tis my picture—
Refuse it not, it hath no tongue to vex you—
And I beseech you come again tomorrow.   205
What shall you ask of me that I'll deny,
That honour, saved, may upon asking give?

VIOLA
Nothing but this: your true love for my master.

OLIVIA
How with mine honour may I give him that
Which I have given to you?

VIOLA   I will acquit you.   210

OLIVIA
Well, come again tomorrow. Fare thee well.
A fiend like thee might bear my soul to hell.   *Exit*

Enter Sir Toby and Fabian

SIR TOBY Gentleman, God save thee.

VIOLA And you, sir.   214

SIR TOBY That defence thou hast, betake thee to't. Of what nature the wrongs are thou hast done him, I know not, but thy intercepter, full of despite, bloody as the hunter, attends thee at the orchard end. Dismount thy tuck, be yare in thy preparation, for thy assailant is quick, skilful, and deadly.   220

VIOLA You mistake, sir, I am sure no man hath any quarrel to me. My remembrance is very free and clear from any image of offence done to any man.

SIR TOBY You'll find it otherwise, I assure you. Therefore, if you hold your life at any price, betake you to your guard, for your opposite hath in him what youth, strength, skill, and wrath can furnish man withal.

VIOLA I pray you, sir, what is he?   228

SIR TOBY He is knight dubbed with unhatched rapier and on carpet consideration, but he is a devil in private brawl. Souls and bodies hath he divorced three, and his incensement at this moment is so implacable that satisfaction can be none but by pangs of death and sepulchre. Hob nob is his word, give't or take't.   234

VIOLA I will return again into the house and desire some conduct of the lady. I am no fighter. I have heard of some kind of men that put quarrels purposely on others, to taste their valour. Belike this is a man of that quirk.

SIR TOBY Sir, no. His indignation derives itself out of a very competent injury, therefore get you on, and give him his desire. Back you shall not to the house unless you undertake that with me which with as much safety you might answer him. Therefore on, or strip your sword stark naked, for meddle you must, that's certain, or forswear to wear iron about you.   245

VIOLA This is as uncivil as strange. I beseech you do me this courteous office, as to know of the knight what my offence to him is. It is something of my negligence, nothing of my purpose.

SIR TOBY I will do so. Signor Fabian, stay you by this gentleman till my return.   *Exit*

VIOLA Pray you, sir, do you know of this matter?

FABIAN I know the knight is incensed against you even to a mortal arbitrement, but nothing of the circumstance more.   255

VIOLA I beseech you, what manner of man is he?

FABIAN Nothing of that wonderful promise to read him by his form as you are like to find him in the proof of his valour. He is indeed, sir, the most skilful, bloody, and fatal opposite that you could possibly have found in any part of Illyria. Will you walk towards him, I will make your peace with him if I can.   262

VIOLA I shall be much bound to you for't. I am one that had rather go with Sir Priest than Sir Knight—I care not who knows so much of my mettle.   ⌈*Exeunt*⌉

Enter Sir Toby and Sir Andrew

SIR TOBY Why, man, he's a very devil, I have not seen
such a virago. I had a pass with him, rapier, scabbard,
and all, and he gives me the stuck-in with such a
mortal motion that it is inevitable, and on the answer,
he pays you as surely as your feet hits the ground they
step on. They say he has been fencer to the Sophy. 271

SIR ANDREW Pox on't, I'll not meddle with him.

SIR TOBY Ay, but he will not now be pacified, Fabian can
scarce hold him yonder.   274

SIR ANDREW Plague on't, an I thought he had been valiant
and so cunning in fence I'd have seen him damned ere
I'd have challenged him. Let him let the matter slip
and I'll give him my horse, grey Capulet.

SIR TOBY I'll make the motion. Stand here, make a good
show on't—this shall end without the perdition of souls.
(*Aside*) Marry, I'll ride your horse as well as I ride you.

Enter Fabian, and Viola as Cesario

⌈*Aside to Fabian*⌉ I have his horse to take up the quarrel,
I have persuaded him the youth's a devil.

FABIAN (*aside to Sir Toby*) He is as horribly conceited of
him, and pants and looks pale as if a bear were at his
heels.   286

SIR TOBY (*to Viola*) There's no remedy, sir, he will fight
with you for's oath' sake. Marry, he hath better
bethought him of his quarrel, and he finds that now
scarce to be worth talking of. Therefore draw for the
supportance of his vow, he protests he will not hurt
you.

VIOLA (*aside*) Pray God defend me. A little thing would
make me tell them how much I lack of a man.   294

FABIAN (*to Sir Andrew*) Give ground if you see him furious.

SIR TOBY Come, Sir Andrew, there's no remedy, the
gentleman will for his honour's sake have one bout
with you, he cannot by the duello avoid it, but he has
promised me, as he is a gentleman and a soldier, he
will not hurt you. Come on, to't.   300

SIR ANDREW Pray God he keep his oath.

Enter Antonio

VIOLA
I do assure you 'tis against my will.

Sir Andrew and Viola draw their swords

ANTONIO (*drawing his sword, to Sir Andrew*)
Put up your sword. If this young gentleman
Have done offence, I take the fault on me.
If you offend him, I for him defy you.   305

SIR TOBY You, sir? Why, what are you?

ANTONIO
One, sir, that for his love dares yet do more
Than you have heard him brag to you he will.

SIR TOBY (*drawing his sword*) Nay, if you be an undertaker,
I am for you.   310

Enter Officers

FABIAN O, good Sir Toby, hold. Here come the officers.

SIR TOBY (*to Antonio*) I'll be with you anon.

VIOLA (*to Sir Andrew*) Pray, sir, put your sword up if you
please.

SIR ANDREW Marry will I, sir, and for that I promised you
I'll be as good as my word. He will bear you easily,
and reins well.

Sir Andrew and Viola put up their swords

FIRST OFFICER This is the man, do thy office.

SECOND OFFICER Antonio, I arrest thee at the suit of Count
Orsino.   320

ANTONIO You do mistake me, sir.

FIRST OFFICER
No, sir, no jot. I know your favour well,
Though now you have no seacap on your head.
(*To Second Officer*) Take him away, he knows I know
him well.

ANTONIO
I must obey. (*To Viola*) This comes with seeking you.
But there's no remedy, I shall answer it.   326
What will you do now my necessity
Makes me to ask you for my purse? It grieves me
Much more for what I cannot do for you
Than what befalls myself. You stand amazed,   330
But be of comfort.

SECOND OFFICER   Come, sir, away.

ANTONIO (*to Viola*)
I must entreat of you some of that money.

VIOLA What money, sir?
For the fair kindness you have showed me here,
And part being prompted by your present trouble, 335
Out of my lean and low ability
I'll lend you something. My having is not much.
I'll make division of my present with you.
Hold, (*offering money*) there's half my coffer.

ANTONIO   Will you deny me now?
Is't possible that my deserts to you   340
Can lack persuasion? Do not tempt my misery,
Lest that it make me so unsound a man
As to upbraid you with those kindnesses
That I have done for you.

VIOLA   I know of none,
Nor know I you by voice, or any feature.   345
I hate ingratitude more in a man
Than lying, vainness, babbling drunkenness,
Or any taint of vice whose strong corruption
Inhabits our frail blood.

ANTONIO   O heavens themselves!

SECOND OFFICER Come, sir, I pray you go.   350

ANTONIO
Let me speak a little. This youth that you see here
I snatched one half out of the jaws of death,
Relieved him with such sanctity of love,
And to his image, which methought did promise
Most venerable worth, did I devotion.   355

FIRST OFFICER
What's that to us? The time goes by, away.

ANTONIO
But O, how vile an idol proves this god!
Thou hast, Sebastian, done good feature shame.
In nature there's no blemish but the mind.

None can be called deformed but the unkind.   360
Virtue is beauty, but the beauteous evil
Are empty trunks o'er-flourished by the devil.
FIRST OFFICER
The man grows mad, away with him. Come, come, sir.
ANTONIO Lead me on.   *Exit with Officers*
VIOLA (*aside*)
Methinks his words do from such passion fly   365
That he believes himself. So do not I.
Prove true, imagination, O prove true,
That I, dear brother, be now ta'en for you!
SIR TOBY Come hither, knight. Come hither, Fabian. We'll
whisper o'er a couplet or two of most sage saws.   370
          They stand aside
VIOLA
He named Sebastian. I my brother know
Yet living in my glass. Even such and so
In favour was my brother, and he went
Still in this fashion, colour, ornament,
For him I imitate. O, if it prove,   375
Tempests are kind, and salt waves fresh in love!   *Exit*
SIR TOBY (*to Sir Andrew*) A very dishonest, paltry boy, and
more a coward than a hare. His dishonesty appears in
leaving his friend here in necessity, and denying him;
and for his cowardship, ask Fabian.   380
FABIAN A coward, a most devout coward, religious in it.
SIR ANDREW 'Slid, I'll after him again, and beat him.
SIR TOBY Do, cuff him soundly, but never draw thy sword.
SIR ANDREW An I do not—   *Exit*
FABIAN Come, let's see the event.   385
SIR TOBY I dare lay any money 'twill be nothing yet.
          Exeunt

4.1   *Enter Sebastian and Feste, the clown*
FESTE Will you make me believe that I am not sent for
you?
SEBASTIAN
Go to, go to, thou art a foolish fellow,
Let me be clear of thee.   4
FESTE Well held out, i'faith! No, I do not know you, nor
I am not sent to you by my lady to bid you come speak
with her, nor your name is not Master Cesario, nor
this is not my nose, neither. Nothing that is so, is so.
SEBASTIAN
I prithee vent thy folly somewhere else,
Thou know'st not me.   10
FESTE Vent my folly! He has heard that word of some
great man, and now applies it to a fool. Vent my folly—
I am afraid this great lubber the world will prove a
cockney. I prithee now ungird thy strangeness, and tell
me what I shall 'vent' to my lady? Shall I 'vent' to her
that thou art coming?   16
SEBASTIAN
I prithee, foolish Greek, depart from me.
There's money for thee. If you tarry longer
I shall give worse payment.   19
FESTE By my troth, thou hast an open hand. These wise

men that give fools money get themselves a good report,
after fourteen years' purchase.
          Enter Sir Andrew, Sir Toby, and Fabian
SIR ANDREW (*to Sebastian*) Now, sir, have I met you again?
(*Striking him*) There's for you.
SEBASTIAN ⌈*striking Sir Andrew with his dagger*⌉
Why, there's for thee, and there, and there.   25
Are all the people mad?
SIR TOBY (*to Sebastian, holding him back*) Hold, sir, or I'll
throw your dagger o'er the house.
FESTE This will I tell my lady straight, I would not be in
some of your coats for twopence.   *Exit*
SIR TOBY Come on, sir, hold.   31
SIR ANDREW Nay, let him alone, I'll go another way to
work with him. I'll have an action of battery against
him if there be any law in Illyria. Though I struck him
first, yet it's no matter for that.   35
SEBASTIAN Let go thy hand.
SIR TOBY Come, sir, I will not let you go. Come, my young
soldier, put up your iron. You are well fleshed. Come
on.
SEBASTIAN (*freeing himself*)
I will be free from thee. What wouldst thou now?   40
If thou dar'st tempt me further, draw thy sword.
SIR TOBY What, what? Nay then, I must have an ounce
or two of this malapert blood from you.
          Sir Toby and Sebastian draw their swords.
          Enter Olivia
OLIVIA
Hold, Toby, on thy life I charge thee hold.
SIR TOBY Madam.   45
OLIVIA
Will it be ever thus? Ungracious wretch,
Fit for the mountains and the barbarous caves,
Where manners ne'er were preached—out of my sight!
Be not offended, dear Cesario.
(*To Sir Toby*) Rudesby, be gone.
          Exeunt Sir Toby, Sir Andrew, and Fabian
                    I prithee, gentle friend,
Let thy fair wisdom, not thy passion sway   51
In this uncivil and unjust extent
Against thy peace. Go with me to my house,
And hear thou there how many fruitless pranks
This ruffian hath botched up, that thou thereby   55
Mayst smile at this. Thou shalt not choose but go.
Do not deny. Beshrew his soul for me,
He started one poor heart of mine in thee.
SEBASTIAN
What relish is in this? How runs the stream?
Or I am mad, or else this is a dream.   60
Let fancy still my sense in Lethe steep.
If it be thus to dream, still let me sleep.
OLIVIA
Nay, come, I prithee, would thou'dst be ruled by me.
SEBASTIAN
Madam, I will.
OLIVIA   O, say so, and so be.   *Exeunt*

4.2 *Enter Maria carrying a gown and false beard, and Feste, the clown*

MARIA Nay, I prithee put on this gown and this beard, make him believe thou art Sir Topas the curate. Do it quickly. I'll call Sir Toby the whilst.   *Exit*

FESTE Well, I'll put it on, and I will dissemble myself in't, and I would I were the first that ever dissembled in such a gown.   6

He disguises himself

I am not tall enough to become the function well, nor lean enough to be thought a good student, but to be said 'an honest man and a good housekeeper' goes as fairly as to say 'a careful man and a great scholar'. The competitors enter.   11

Enter Sir Toby and Maria

SIR TOBY Jove bless thee, Master Parson.

FESTE *Bonos dies*, Sir Toby, for, as the old hermit of Prague, that never saw pen and ink, very wittily said to a niece of King Gorboduc, 'That that is, is.' So I, being Master Parson, am Master Parson; for what is 'that' but 'that', and 'is' but 'is'?

SIR TOBY To him, Sir Topas.

FESTE What ho, I say, peace in this prison.

SIR TOBY The knave counterfeits well—a good knave.   20

Malvolio within

MALVOLIO Who calls there?

FESTE Sir Topas the curate, who comes to visit Malvolio the lunatic.

MALVOLIO Sir Topas, Sir Topas, good Sir Topas, go to my lady.   25

FESTE Out, hyperbolical fiend, how vexest thou this man! Talkest thou nothing but of ladies?

SIR TOBY Well said, Master Parson.

MALVOLIO Sir Topas, never was man thus wronged. Good Sir Topas, do not think I am mad. They have laid me here in hideous darkness.   31

FESTE Fie, thou dishonest Satan—I call thee by the most modest terms, for I am one of those gentle ones that will use the devil himself with courtesy. Sayst thou that house is dark?   35

MALVOLIO As hell, Sir Topas.

FESTE Why, it hath bay windows transparent as barricadoes, and the clerestories toward the south-north are as lustrous as ebony, and yet complainest thou of obstruction?   40

MALVOLIO I am not mad, Sir Topas; I say to you this house is dark.

FESTE Madman, thou errest. I say there is no darkness but ignorance, in which thou art more puzzled than the Egyptians in their fog.   45

MALVOLIO I say this house is as dark as ignorance, though ignorance were as dark as hell; and I say there was never man thus abused. I am no more mad than you are. Make the trial of it in any constant question.

FESTE What is the opinion of Pythagoras concerning wildfowl?   51

MALVOLIO That the soul of our grandam might haply inhabit a bird.

FESTE What thinkest thou of his opinion?

MALVOLIO I think nobly of the soul, and no way approve his opinion.   56

FESTE Fare thee well. Remain thou still in darkness. Thou shalt hold th'opinion of Pythagoras ere I will allow of thy wits, and fear to kill a woodcock lest thou dispossess the soul of thy grandam. Fare thee well.   60

MALVOLIO Sir Topas, Sir Topas!

SIR TOBY My most exquisite Sir Topas.

FESTE Nay, I am for all waters.

MARIA Thou mightst have done this without thy beard and gown, he sees thee not.   65

SIR TOBY (*to Feste*) To him in thine own voice, and bring me word how thou findest him. I would we were well rid of this knavery. If he may be conveniently delivered, I would he were, for I am now so far in offence with my niece that I cannot pursue with any safety this sport to the upshot. ⌈*To Maria*⌉ Come by and by to my chamber.   *Exit* ⌈*with Maria*⌉

FESTE (*sings*)   'Hey Robin, jolly Robin,
                           Tell me how thy lady does.'

MALVOLIO Fool!   75

FESTE   'My lady is unkind, pardie.'

MALVOLIO Fool!

FESTE   'Alas, why is she so?'

MALVOLIO Fool, I say!

FESTE   'She loves another.'   80
                   Who calls, ha?

MALVOLIO Good fool, as ever thou wilt deserve well at my hand, help me to a candle and pen, ink, and paper. As I am a gentleman, I will live to be thankful to thee for't.   85

FESTE Master Malvolio?

MALVOLIO Ay, good fool.

FESTE Alas, sir, how fell you besides your five wits?

MALVOLIO Fool, there was never man so notoriously abused. I am as well in my wits, fool, as thou art.   90

FESTE But as well? Then you are mad indeed, if you be no better in your wits than a fool.

MALVOLIO They have here propertied me, keep me in darkness, send ministers to me, asses, and do all they can to face me out of my wits.   95

FESTE Advise you what you say, the minister is here. (*As Sir Topas*) Malvolio, Malvolio, thy wits the heavens restore. Endeavour thyself to sleep, and leave thy vain bibble-babble.

MALVOLIO Sir Topas.   100

FESTE (*as Sir Topas*) Maintain no words with him, good fellow. (*As himself*) Who I, sir? Not I, sir. God b'wi' you, good Sir Topas. (*As Sir Topas*) Marry, amen. (*As himself*) I will, sir, I will.

MALVOLIO Fool, fool, fool, I say.   105

FESTE Alas, sir, be patient. What say you, sir? I am shent for speaking to you.

MALVOLIO Good fool, help me to some light and some paper. I tell thee I am as well in my wits as any man in Illyria.   110

FESTE Well-a-day that you were, sir.

MALVOLIO By this hand, I am. Good fool, some ink, paper,
and light, and convey what I will set down to my lady.
It shall advantage thee more than ever the bearing of
letter did.   115
FESTE I will help you to't. But tell me true, are you not
mad indeed, or do you but counterfeit?
MALVOLIO Believe me, I am not, I tell thee true.
FESTE Nay, I'll ne'er believe a madman till I see his brains.
I will fetch you light, and paper, and ink.   120
MALVOLIO Fool, I'll requite it in the highest degree. I
prithee, be gone.
FESTE   I am gone, sir,
                            And anon, sir,
                              I'll be with you again,   125
                            In a trice,
                            Like to the old Vice,
                              Your need to sustain,
                            Who with dagger of lath
                            In his rage and his wrath   130
                              Cries 'Aha,' to the devil,
                            Like a mad lad,
                            'Pare thy nails, dad,
                              Adieu, goodman devil.'   *Exit*

4.3 *Enter Sebastian*
SEBASTIAN
This is the air, that is the glorious sun.
This pearl she gave me, I do feel't and see't,
And though 'tis wonder that enwraps me thus,
Yet 'tis not madness. Where's Antonio then?
I could not find him at the Elephant,   5
Yet there he was, and there I found this credit,
That he did range the town to seek me out.
His counsel now might do me golden service,
For though my soul disputes well with my sense
That this may be some error but no madness,   10
Yet doth this accident and flood of fortune
So far exceed all instance, all discourse,
That I am ready to distrust mine eyes
And wrangle with my reason that persuades me
To any other trust but that I am mad,   15
Or else the lady's mad. Yet if 'twere so
She could not sway her house, command her
    followers,
Take and give back affairs and their dispatch
With such a smooth, discreet, and stable bearing
As I perceive she does. There's something in't   20
That is deceivable. But here the lady comes.
    Enter Olivia and a Priest
OLIVIA
Blame not this haste of mine. If you mean well
Now go with me, and with this holy man,
Into the chantry by. There before him,
And underneath that consecrated roof,   25
Plight me the full assurance of your faith,
That my most jealous and too doubtful soul
May live at peace. He shall conceal it
Whiles you are willing it shall come to note,

What time we will our celebration keep   30
According to my birth. What do you say?
SEBASTIAN
I'll follow this good man, and go with you,
And having sworn truth, ever will be true.
OLIVIA
Then lead the way, good father, and heavens so shine
That they may fairly note this act of mine.   *Exeunt*

5.1 *Enter Feste the clown and Fabian*
FABIAN Now, as thou lovest me, let me see his letter.
FESTE Good Master Fabian, grant me another request.
FABIAN Anything.
FESTE Do not desire to see this letter.
FABIAN This is to give a dog, and in recompense desire
my dog again.   6
    Enter the Duke, Viola as Cesario, Curio, and lords
ORSINO
Belong you to the Lady Olivia, friends?
FESTE Ay, sir, we are some of her trappings.
ORSINO
I know thee well. How dost thou, my good fellow?
FESTE Truly, sir, the better for my foes and the worse for
my friends.   11
ORSINO
Just the contrary—the better for thy friends.
FESTE No, sir, the worse.
ORSINO How can that be?   14
FESTE Marry, sir, they praise me, and make an ass of me.
Now my foes tell me plainly I am an ass, so that by
my foes, sir, I profit in the knowledge of myself, and
by my friends I am abused; so that, conclusions to be
as kisses, if your four negatives make your two
affirmatives, why then the worse for my friends and
the better for my foes.   21
ORSINO Why, this is excellent.
FESTE By my troth, sir, no, though it please you to be
one of my friends.
ORSINO (*giving money*)
Thou shalt not be the worse for me. There's gold.   25
FESTE But that it would be double-dealing, sir, I would
you could make it another.
ORSINO O, you give me ill counsel.
FESTE Put your grace in your pocket, sir, for this once,
and let your flesh and blood obey it.   30
ORSINO Well, I will be so much a sinner to be a double-
dealer. (*Giving money*) There's another.
FESTE *Primo, secundo, tertio* is a good play, and the old
saying is 'The third pays for all'. The triplex, sir, is a
good tripping measure, or the bells of Saint Bennet, sir,
may put you in mind—'one, two, three'.   36
ORSINO You can fool no more money out of me at this
throw. If you will let your lady know I am here to
speak with her, and bring her along with you, it may
awake my bounty further.   40
FESTE Marry, sir, lullaby to your bounty till I come again.
I go, sir, but I would not have you to think that my
desire of having is the sin of covetousness. But as you

say, sir, let your bounty take a nap, I will awake it
anon.   *Exit*
    Enter Antonio and Officers
VIOLA
Here comes the man, sir, that did rescue me.   46
ORSINO
That face of his I do remember well,
Yet when I saw it last it was besmeared
As black as Vulcan in the smoke of war.
A baubling vessel was he captain of,   50
For shallow draught and bulk unprizable,
With which such scatheful grapple did he make
With the most noble bottom of our fleet
That very envy and the tongue of loss
Cried fame and honour on him. What's the matter? 55
FIRST OFFICER
Orsino, this is that Antonio
That took the *Phoenix* and her freight from Candy,
And this is he that did the *Tiger* board
When your young nephew Titus lost his leg.
Here in the streets, desperate of shame and state,   60
In private brabble did we apprehend him.
VIOLA
He did me kindness, sir, drew on my side,
But in conclusion put strange speech upon me.
I know not what 'twas but distraction.
ORSINO *(to Antonio)*
Notable pirate, thou salt-water thief,   65
What foolish boldness brought thee to their mercies
Whom thou in terms so bloody and so dear
Hast made thine enemies?
ANTONIO   Orsino, noble sir,
Be pleased that I shake off these names you give me.
Antonio never yet was thief or pirate,   70
Though, I confess, on base and ground enough
Orsino's enemy. A witchcraft drew me hither.
That most ingrateful boy there by your side
From the rude sea's enragèd and foamy mouth
Did I redeem. A wreck past hope he was.   75
His life I gave him, and did thereto add
My love without retention or restraint,
All his in dedication. For his sake
Did I expose myself, pure for his love,
Into the danger of this adverse town,   80
Drew to defend him when he was beset,
Where being apprehended, his false cunning—
Not meaning to partake with me in danger—
Taught him to face me out of his acquaintance,
And grew a twenty years' removèd thing   85
While one would wink, denied me mine own purse,
Which I had recommended to his use
Not half an hour before.
VIOLA How can this be?
ORSINO When came he to this town?   90
ANTONIO
Today, my lord, and for three months before,
No int'rim, not a minute's vacancy,
Both day and night did we keep company.

    Enter Olivia and attendants
ORSINO
Here comes the Countess. Now heaven walks on
    earth.
But for thee, fellow—fellow, thy words are madness.
Three months this youth hath tended upon me.   96
But more of that anon. Take him aside.
OLIVIA
What would my lord, but that he may not have,
Wherein Olivia may seem serviceable?
Cesario, you do not keep promise with me.   100
VIOLA Madam—
ORSINO Gracious Olivia—
OLIVIA
What do you say, Cesario? Good my lord—
VIOLA
My lord would speak, my duty hushes me.
OLIVIA
If it be aught to the old tune, my lord,   105
It is as fat and fulsome to mine ear
As howling after music.
ORSINO Still so cruel?
OLIVIA Still so constant, lord.
ORSINO
What, to perverseness? You uncivil lady,   110
To whose ingrate and unauspicious altars
My soul the faithfull'st off'rings hath breathed out
That e'er devotion tendered—what shall I do?
OLIVIA
Even what it please my lord that shall become him.
ORSINO
Why should I not, had I the heart to do it,   115
Like to th' Egyptian thief, at point of death
Kill what I love—a savage jealousy
That sometime savours nobly. But hear me this:
Since you to non-regardance cast my faith,
And that I partly know the instrument   120
That screws me from my true place in your favour,
Live you the marble-breasted tyrant still.
But this your minion, whom I know you love,
And whom, by heaven I swear, I tender dearly,
Him will I tear out of that cruel eye   125
Where he sits crownèd in his master's spite.
(To Viola) Come, boy, with me. My thoughts are ripe
    in mischief.
I'll sacrifice the lamb that I do love
To spite a raven's heart within a dove.
VIOLA
And I most jocund, apt, and willingly   130
To do you rest a thousand deaths would die.
OLIVIA
Where goes Cesario?
VIOLA   After him I love
More than I love these eyes, more than my life,
More by all mores than e'er I shall love wife.
If I do feign, you witnesses above,   135
Punish my life for tainting of my love.

OLIVIA
Ay me detested, how am I beguiled!
VIOLA
Who does beguile you? Who does do you wrong?
OLIVIA
Hast thou forgot thyself? Is it so long?
Call forth the holy father.   *Exit an attendant*
ORSINO (*to Viola*)   Come, away.   140
OLIVIA
Whither, my lord? Cesario, husband, stay.
ORSINO
Husband?
OLIVIA   Ay, husband. Can he that deny?
ORSINO (*to Viola*)
Her husband, sirrah?
VIOLA   No, my lord, not I.
OLIVIA
Alas, it is the baseness of thy fear
That makes thee strangle thy propriety.   145
Fear not, Cesario, take thy fortunes up,
Be that thou know'st thou art, and then thou art
As great as that thou fear'st.
        Enter the Priest
        O welcome, father.
Father, I charge thee by thy reverence
Here to unfold—though lately we intended   150
To keep in darkness what occasion now
Reveals before 'tis ripe—what thou dost know
Hath newly passed between this youth and me.
PRIEST
A contract of eternal bond of love,
Confirmed by mutual joinder of your hands,   155
Attested by the holy close of lips,
Strengthened by interchangement of your rings,
And all the ceremony of this compact
Sealed in my function, by my testimony;
Since when, my watch hath told me, toward my grave
I have travelled but two hours.   161
ORSINO (*to Viola*)
O thou dissembling cub, what wilt thou be
When time hath sowed a grizzle on thy case?
Or will not else thy craft so quickly grow
That thine own trip shall be thine overthrow?   165
Farewell, and take her, but direct thy feet
Where thou and I henceforth may never meet.
VIOLA
My lord, I do protest.
OLIVIA   O, do not swear!
Hold little faith, though thou hast too much fear.
        Enter Sir Andrew
SIR ANDREW For the love of God, a surgeon—send one
presently to Sir Toby.   171
OLIVIA What's the matter?
SIR ANDREW He's broke my head across, and has given
Sir Toby a bloody coxcomb, too. For the love of God,
your help! I had rather than forty pound I were at
home.   176
OLIVIA Who has done this, Sir Andrew?

SIR ANDREW The Count's gentleman, one Cesario. We
took him for a coward, but he's the very devil
incarnate.   180
ORSINO My gentleman, Cesario?
SIR ANDREW 'Od's lifelings, here he is. (*To Viola*) You broke
my head for nothing, and that that I did I was set on
to do't by Sir Toby.
VIOLA
Why do you speak to me? I never hurt you.   185
You drew your sword upon me without cause,
But I bespake you fair, and hurt you not.
        Enter Sir Toby and Feste, the clown
SIR ANDREW If a bloody coxcomb be a hurt you have hurt
me. I think you set nothing by a bloody coxcomb. Here
comes Sir Toby, halting. You shall hear more; but if
he had not been in drink he would have tickled you
othergates than he did.
ORSINO (*to Sir Toby*)
How now, gentleman? How is't with you?
SIR TOBY That's all one, he's hurt me, and there's th'end
on't. (*To Feste*) Sot, didst see Dick Surgeon, sot?   195
FESTE O, he's drunk, Sir Toby, an hour agone. His eyes
were set at eight i'th' morning.
SIR TOBY Then he's a rogue, and a passy-measures pavan.
I hate a drunken rogue.
OLIVIA
Away with him! Who hath made this havoc with
them?   200
SIR ANDREW I'll help you, Sir Toby, because we'll be
dressed together.
SIR TOBY Will *you* help—an ass-head, and a coxcomb,
and a knave; a thin-faced knave, a gull?
OLIVIA
Get him to bed, and let his hurt be looked to.   · 205
        Exeunt Sir Toby, Sir Andrew, Feste, and Fabian
        Enter Sebastian
SEBASTIAN (*to Olivia*)
I am sorry, madam, I have hurt your kinsman,
But had it been the brother of my blood
I must have done no less with wit and safety.
You throw a strange regard upon me, and by that
I do perceive it hath offended you.   210
Pardon me, sweet one, even for the vows
We made each other but so late ago.
ORSINO
One face, one voice, one habit, and two persons,
A natural perspective, that is and is not.
SEBASTIAN
Antonio! O, my dear Antonio,   215
How have the hours racked and tortured me
Since I have lost thee!
ANTONIO Sebastian are you?
SEBASTIAN Fear'st thou that, Antonio?
ANTONIO
How have you made division of yourself?   220
An apple cleft in two is not more twin
Than these two creatures. Which is Sebastian?
OLIVIA Most wonderful!

743

SEBASTIAN (*seeing Viola*)
Do I stand there? I never had a brother,
Nor can there be that deity in my nature   225
Of here and everywhere. I had a sister,
Whom the blind waves and surges have devoured.
Of charity, what kin are you to me?
What countryman? What name? What parentage?
VIOLA
Of Messaline. Sebastian was my father.   230
Such a Sebastian was my brother, too.
So went he suited to his watery tomb.
If spirits can assume both form and suit
You come to fright us.
SEBASTIAN   A spirit I am indeed,
But am in that dimension grossly clad   235
Which from the womb I did participate.
Were you a woman, as the rest goes even,
I should my tears let fall upon your cheek
And say 'Thrice welcome, drownèd Viola.'
VIOLA
My father had a mole upon his brow.   240
SEBASTIAN And so had mine.
VIOLA
And died that day when Viola from her birth
Had numbered thirteen years.
SEBASTIAN
O, that record is lively in my soul.
He finishèd indeed his mortal act   245
That day that made my sister thirteen years.
VIOLA
If nothing lets to make us happy both
But this my masculine usurped attire,
Do not embrace me till each circumstance
Of place, time, fortune do cohere and jump   250
That I am Viola, which to confirm
I'll bring you to a captain in this town
Where lie my maiden weeds, by whose gentle help
I was preserved to serve this noble count.
All the occurrence of my fortune since   255
Hath been between this lady and this lord.
SEBASTIAN (*to Olivia*)
So comes it, lady, you have been mistook.
But nature to her bias drew in that.
You would have been contracted to a maid,
Nor are you therein, by my life, deceived.   260
You are betrothed both to a maid and man.
ORSINO (*to Olivia*)
Be not amazed. Right noble is his blood.
If this be so, as yet the glass seems true,
I shall have share in this most happy wreck.
(*To Viola*) Boy, thou hast said to me a thousand times
Thou never shouldst love woman like to me.   266
VIOLA
And all those sayings will I overswear,
And all those swearings keep as true in soul
As doth that orbèd continent the fire
That severs day from night.
ORSINO   Give me thy hand,   270
And let me see thee in thy woman's weeds.

VIOLA
The captain that did bring me first on shore
Hath my maid's garments. He upon some action
Is now in durance, at Malvolio's suit,
A gentleman and follower of my lady's.   275
OLIVIA
He shall enlarge him. Fetch Malvolio hither—
And yet, alas, now I remember me,
They say, poor gentleman, he's much distraught.
Enter Feste the clown with a letter, and Fabian
A most extracting frenzy of mine own
From my remembrance clearly banished his.   280
How does he, sirrah?
FESTE Truly, madam, he holds Beelzebub at the stave's
end as well as a man in his case may do. He's here
writ a letter to you. I should have given't you today
morning. But as a madman's epistles are no gospels,
so it skills not much when they are delivered.   286
OLIVIA Open't and read it.
FESTE Look then to be well edified when the fool delivers
the madman. (*Reads*) 'By the Lord, madam'—
OLIVIA How now, art thou mad?   290
FESTE No, madam, I do but read madness. An your
ladyship will have it as it ought to be you must allow
vox.
OLIVIA Prithee, read i'thy right wits.   294
FESTE So I do, madonna, but to read his right wits is to
read thus. Therefore perpend, my princess, and give
ear.
OLIVIA (*to Fabian*) Read it you, sirrah.
Feste gives the letter to Fabian
FABIAN (*reads*) 'By the Lord, madam, you wrong me, and
the world shall know it. Though you have put me into
darkness and given your drunken cousin rule over me,
yet have I the benefit of my senses as well as your
ladyship. I have your own letter that induced me to
the semblance I put on, with the which I doubt not
but to do myself much right or you much shame. Think
of me as you please. I leave my duty a little unthought
of, and speak out of my injury.
                    The madly-used Malvolio.'
OLIVIA Did he write this?
FESTE Ay, madam.   310
ORSINO
This savours not much of distraction.
OLIVIA
See him delivered, Fabian, bring him hither.
My lord, so please you—these things further thought
    on—
To think me as well a sister as a wife,
One day shall crown th'alliance on't, so please you,
Here at my house and at my proper cost.   316
ORSINO
Madam, I am most apt t'embrace your offer.
(*To Viola*) Your master quits you, and for your service
    done him
So much against the mettle of your sex,
So far beneath your soft and tender breeding,   320
And since you called me master for so long,

Here is my hand. You shall from this time be
Your master's mistress.
OLIVIA (*to Viola*)   A sister, you are she.
          Enter Malvolio
ORSINO
  Is this the madman?
OLIVIA   Ay, my lord, this same.
  How now, Malvolio?
MALVOLIO   Madam, you have done me wrong,
  Notorious wrong.
OLIVIA   Have I, Malvolio? No.   326
MALVOLIO (*showing a letter*)
  Lady, you have. Pray you peruse that letter.
  You must not now deny it is your hand.
  Write from it if you can, in hand or phrase,
  Or say 'tis not your seal, not your invention.   330
  You can say none of this. Well, grant it then,
  And tell me in the modesty of honour
  Why you have given me such clear lights of favour,
  Bade me come smiling and cross-gartered to you,
  To put on yellow stockings, and to frown   335
  Upon Sir Toby and the lighter people,
  And acting this in an obedient hope,
  Why have you suffered me to be imprisoned,
  Kept in a dark house, visited by the priest,
  And made the most notorious geck and gull   340
  That e'er invention played on? Tell me why?
OLIVIA
  Alas, Malvolio, this is not my writing,
  Though I confess much like the character,
  But out of question, 'tis Maria's hand.
  And now I do bethink me, it was she   345
  First told me thou wast mad; then cam'st in smiling,
  And in such forms which here were presupposed
  Upon thee in the letter. Prithee be content;
  This practice hath most shrewdly passed upon thee,
  But when we know the grounds and authors of it
  Thou shalt be both the plaintiff and the judge   351
  Of thine own cause.
FABIAN   Good madam, hear me speak,
  And let no quarrel nor no brawl to come
  Taint the condition of this present hour,
  Which I have wondered at. In hope it shall not,   355
  Most freely I confess myself and Toby
  Set this device against Malvolio here
  Upon some stubborn and uncourteous parts
  We had conceived against him. Maria writ
  The letter, at Sir Toby's great importance,   360
  In recompense whereof he hath married her.
  How with a sportful malice it was followed
  May rather pluck on laughter than revenge

If that the injuries be justly weighed
  That have on both sides passed.   365
OLIVIA (*to Malvolio*)
  Alas, poor fool, how have they baffled thee!
FESTE Why, 'Some are born great, some achieve great-
  ness, and some have greatness thrown upon them.' I
  was one, sir, in this interlude, one Sir Topas, sir; but
  that's all one. 'By the Lord, fool, I am not mad'—but
  do you remember, 'Madam, why laugh you at such a
  barren rascal, an you smile not, he's gagged'—and
  thus the whirligig of time brings in his revenges.
MALVOLIO I'll be revenged on the whole pack of you.
                                                    Exit
OLIVIA
  He hath been most notoriously abused.   375
ORSINO
  Pursue him, and entreat him to a peace.
  He hath not told us of the captain yet.
                                    ⌈*Exit one or more*⌉
  When that is known, and golden time convents,
  A solemn combination shall be made
  Of our dear souls. Meantime, sweet sister,   380
  We will not part from hence. Cesario, come—
  For so you shall be while you are a man;
  But when in other habits you are seen,
  Orsino's mistress, and his fancy's queen.
                                    Exeunt all but Feste
FESTE (*sings*)
  When that I was and a little tiny boy,   385
    With hey, ho, the wind and the rain,
  A foolish thing was but a toy,
    For the rain it raineth every day.

  But when I came to man's estate,
    With hey, ho, the wind and the rain,   390
  'Gainst knaves and thieves men shut their gate,
    For the rain it raineth every day.

  But when I came, alas, to wive,
    With hey, ho, the wind and the rain,
  By swaggering could I never thrive,   395
    For the rain it raineth every day.

  But when I came unto my beds,
    With hey, ho, the wind and the rain,
  With tosspots still had drunken heads,
    For the rain it raineth every day.   400

  A great while ago the world begun,
    With hey ho, the wind and the rain,
  But that's all one, our play is done,
    And we'll strive to please you every day.   *Exit*

TROILUS AND CRESSIDA

Troilus and Cressida, first heard of in a Stationers' Register entry of 7 February 1603, was probably written within the previous eighteen months. This entry did not result in publication; the play was re-entered on 28 January 1609, and a quarto appeared during that year. The version printed in the 1623 Folio adds a Prologue, and has many variations in dialogue. It includes the epilogue spoken by Pandarus (which we print as an Additional Passage), but certain features of the text suggest that it does so by accident, and that the epilogue had been marked for omission. Our text is based in substance on the Folio in the belief that this represents the play in its later, revised form.

The story of the siege of Troy was the main subject of one of the greatest surviving works of classical literature, Homer's *Iliad*; probably Shakespeare read George Chapman's 1598 translation of Books 1-2 and 7-11. It also figures prominently in Virgil's *Aeneid* and Ovid's *Metamorphoses*, both of which Shakespeare knew well. The war between Greece and Troy had been provoked by the abduction of the Grecian Helen (better, if confusingly, known as Helen of Troy) by the Trojan hero Paris, son of King Priam. Shakespeare's play opens when the Greek forces, led by Menelaus' brother Agamemnon, have already been besieging Troy for seven years. Shakespeare concentrates on the opposition between the Greek hero Achilles and the Trojan Hector. In the Folio, *Troilus and Cressida* is printed among the tragedies; if there is a tragic hero, it is Hector.

Shakespeare also shows how the war caused by one love affair destroys another. The stories of the love between the Trojan Troilus and the Grecian Cressida, encouraged by her uncle Pandarus, and of Cressida's desertion of Troilus for the Greek Diomedes, are medieval additions to the heroic narrative. Chaucer's long poem *Troilus and Criseyde* was already a classic, and Shakespeare would also have known Robert Henryson's continuation, *The Testament of Cresseid*, in which Cressida, deserted by Diomedes, dwindles into a leprous beggar.

Troilus and Cressida is a demanding play, Shakespeare's third longest, highly philosophical in tone and with an exceptionally learned vocabulary. Possibly (as has often been conjectured) he wrote it for private performance; the 1603 Stationers' Register entry says it had been acted by the King's Men, and the original title-page of the 1609 quarto repeats this claim, but while the edition was being printed this title-page was replaced by one that does not mention performance, and an epistle was added claiming that it was 'a new play, never staled with the stage, never clapper-clawed with the palms of the vulgar'. An adaptation by John Dryden of 1679 was successfully acted from time to time for half a century, but the first verified performance of Shakespeare's play was in Germany in 1898, and that was heavily adapted. *Troilus and Cressida* has come into its own in the twentieth century, when its deflation of heroes, its radical questioning of human values (especially in relation to love and war), and its remorseless examination of the frailty of human aspirations in the face of the destructive powers of time have seemed particularly apposite to modern intellectual and ethical preoccupations.

THE PERSONS OF THE PLAY

PROLOGUE

Trojans

PRIAM, King of Troy

HECTOR ⎫
DEIPHOBUS ⎪
HELENUS, a priest ⎬ his sons
PARIS ⎪
TROILUS ⎪
MARGARETON, a bastard ⎭

CASSANDRA, Priam's daughter, a prophetess

ANDROMACHE, wife of Hector

AENEAS ⎫ commanders
ANTENOR ⎭

PANDARUS, a lord

CRESSIDA, his niece

CALCHAS, her father, who has joined the Greeks

HELEN, wife of Menelaus, now living with Paris

ALEXANDER, servant of Cressida

Servants of Troilus, musicians, soldiers, attendants

Greeks

AGAMEMNON, Commander-in-Chief

MENELAUS, his brother

NESTOR

ULYSSES

ACHILLES

PATROCLUS, his companion

DIOMEDES

AJAX

THERSITES

MYRMIDONS, soldiers of Achilles

Servants of Diomedes, soldiers

Troilus and Cressida

Prologue *Enter the Prologue armed*

PROLOGUE

In Troy there lies the scene. From isles of Greece
The princes orgulous, their high blood chafed,
Have to the port of Athens sent their ships,
Fraught with the ministers and instruments
Of cruel war. Sixty and nine, that wore   5
Their crownets regal, from th'Athenian bay
Put forth toward Phrygia, and their vow is made
To ransack Troy, within whose strong immures
The ravished Helen, Menelaus' queen,
With wanton Paris sleeps—and that's the quarrel. 10
To Tenedos they come,
And the deep-drawing barques do there disgorge
Their warlike freightage; now on Dardan plains
The fresh and yet unbruisèd Greeks do pitch
Their brave pavilions. Priam's six-gated city—   15
Dardan and Timbria, Helias, Chetas, Troien,
And Antenorides—with massy staples
And corresponsive and full-filling bolts
Spar up the sons of Troy.
Now expectation, tickling skittish spirits   20
On one and other side, Trojan and Greek,
Sets all on hazard. And hither am I come,
A Prologue armed—but not in confidence
Of author's pen or actor's voice, but suited
In like conditions as our argument—   25
To tell you, fair beholders, that our play
Leaps o'er the vaunt and firstlings of those broils,
Beginning in the middle, starting thence away
To what may be digested in a play.
Like or find fault; do as your pleasures are;   30
Now, good or bad, 'tis but the chance of war. *Exit*

1.1   *Enter Pandarus, and Troilus armed*

TROILUS

Call here my varlet. I'll unarm again.
Why should I war without the walls of Troy
That find such cruel battle here within?
Each Trojan that is master of his heart,
Let him to field—Troilus, alas, hath none.   5

PANDARUS Will this gear ne'er be mended?

TROILUS

The Greeks are strong, and skilful to their strength,
Fierce to their skill, and to their fierceness valiant.
But I am weaker than a woman's tear,
Tamer than sleep, fonder than ignorance,   10
Less valiant than the virgin in the night,
And skilless as unpractised infancy.

PANDARUS Well, I have told you enough of this. For my
part, I'll not meddle nor make no farther. He that will
have a cake out of the wheat must tarry the grinding.

TROILUS Have I not tarried?   16

PANDARUS Ay, the grinding; but you must tarry the
boulting.

TROILUS Have I not tarried?

PANDARUS Ay, the boulting; but you must tarry the
leavening.   21

TROILUS Still have I tarried.

PANDARUS Ay, to the leavening; but here's yet in the
word 'hereafter' the kneading, the making of the cake,
the heating the oven, and the baking—nay, you must
stay the cooling too, or ye may chance burn your lips.

TROILUS

Patience herself, what goddess e'er she be,
Doth lesser blench at suff'rance than I do.
At Priam's royal table do I sit
And when fair Cressid comes into my thoughts—   30
So, traitor! 'When she comes'? When is she thence?

PANDARUS Well, she looked yesternight fairer than ever I
saw her look, or any woman else.

TROILUS

I was about to tell thee: when my heart,
As wedgèd with a sigh, would rive in twain,   35
Lest Hector or my father should perceive me
I have, as when the sun doth light askance,
Buried this sigh in wrinkle of a smile.
But sorrow that is couched in seeming gladness
Is like that mirth fate turns to sudden sadness.   40

PANDARUS An her hair were not somewhat darker than
Helen's—well, go to, there were no more comparison
between the women. But, for my part, she is my
kinswoman; I would not, as they term it, 'praise' her.
But I would somebody had heard her talk yesterday,
as I did. I will not dispraise your sister Cassandra's wit,
but—

TROILUS

O Pandarus! I tell thee, Pandarus,
When I do tell thee 'There my hopes lie drowned',
Reply not in how many fathoms deep   50
They lie endrenched. I tell thee I am mad
In Cressid's love; thou answer'st 'She is fair',
Pourest in the open ulcer of my heart
Her eyes, her hair, her cheek, her gait, her voice;
Handlest in thy discourse, O, that her hand,   55
In whose comparison all whites are ink
Writing their own reproach, to whose soft seizure
The cygnet's down is harsh, and spirit of sense
Hard as the palm of ploughman. This thou tell'st me—
As true thou tell'st me—when I say I love her.   60
But saying thus, instead of oil and balm
Thou lay'st in every gash that love hath given me
The knife that made it.

PANDARUS I speak no more than truth.

TROILUS Thou dost not speak so much.   65

PANDARUS Faith, I'll not meddle in it. Let her be as she

is. If she be fair, 'tis the better for her; an she be not,
she has the mends in her own hands.

TROILUS Good Pandarus, how now, Pandarus!   69

PANDARUS I have had my labour for my travail. Ill thought
on of her and ill thought on of you. Gone between and
between, but small thanks for my labour.

TROILUS
What, art thou angry, Pandarus? What, with me?

PANDARUS Because she's kin to me, therefore she's not so
fair as Helen. An she were not kin to me, she would
be as fair o' Friday as Helen is on Sunday. But what
care I? I care not an she were a blackamoor. 'Tis all
one to me.

TROILUS Say I she is not fair?   79

PANDARUS I do not care whether you do or no. She's a
fool to stay behind her father. Let her to the Greeks—
and so I'll tell her the next time I see her. For my part,
I'll meddle nor make no more i'th' matter.

TROILUS Pandarus—

PANDARUS Not I.   85

TROILUS Sweet Pandarus—

PANDARUS Pray you, speak no more to me. I will leave
all as I found it. And there an end.   *Exit*

          Alarum

TROILUS
Peace, you ungracious clamours! Peace, rude sounds!
Fools on both sides. Helen must needs be fair   90
When with your blood you daily paint her thus.
I cannot fight upon this argument.
It is too starved a subject for my sword.
But Pandarus—O gods, how do you plague me!
I cannot come to Cressid but by Pandar,   95
And he's as tetchy to be wooed to woo
As she is stubborn-chaste against all suit.
Tell me, Apollo, for thy Daphne's love,
What Cressid is, what Pandar, and what we?
Her bed is India; there she lies, a pearl.   100
Between our Ilium and where she resides
Let it be called the wild and wand'ring flood,
Ourself the merchant, and this sailing Pandar
Our doubtful hope, our convoy, and our barque.

          Alarum. Enter Aeneas

AENEAS
How now, Prince Troilus? Wherefore not afield?   105

TROILUS
Because not there. This woman's answer sorts,
For womanish it is to be from thence.
What news, Aeneas, from the field today?

AENEAS
That Paris is returnèd home, and hurt.

TROILUS
By whom, Aeneas?

AENEAS   Troilus, by Menelaus.   110

TROILUS
Let Paris bleed, 'tis but a scar to scorn:
Paris is gored with Menelaus' horn.

          Alarum

AENEAS
Hark what good sport is out of town today.

TROILUS
Better at home, if 'would I might' were 'may'.
But to the sport abroad—are you bound thither?   115

AENEAS
In all swift haste.

TROILUS   Come, go we then together.   *Exeunt*

1.2   *Enter ⌈above⌉ Cressida and her servant Alexander*

CRESSIDA
Who were those went by?

ALEXANDER   Queen Hecuba and Helen.

CRESSIDA
And whither go they?

ALEXANDER   Up to the eastern tower,
Whose height commands as subject all the vale,
To see the battle. Hector, whose patience
Is as a virtue fixed, today was moved.   5
He chid Andromache and struck his armourer
And, like as there were husbandry in war,
Before the sun rose he was harnessed light,
And to the field goes he, where every flower
Did as a prophet weep what it foresaw   10
In Hector's wrath.

CRESSIDA   What was his cause of anger?

ALEXANDER
The noise goes this: there is among the Greeks
A lord of Trojan blood, nephew to Hector;
They call him Ajax.

CRESSIDA   Good, and what of him?

ALEXANDER
They say he is a very man *per se*,   15
And stands alone.

CRESSIDA   So do all men
Unless they are drunk, sick, or have no legs.

ALEXANDER This man, lady, hath robbed many beasts of
their particular additions: he is as valiant as the lion,
churlish as the bear, slow as the elephant—a man into
whom nature hath so crowded humours that his valour
is crushed into folly, his folly farced with discretion.
There is no man hath a virtue that he hath not a
glimpse of, nor any man an attaint but he carries some
stain of it. He is melancholy without cause and merry
against the hair; he hath the joints of everything, but
everything so out of joint that he is a gouty Briareus,
many hands and no use, or purblind Argus, all eyes
and no sight.

CRESSIDA But how should this man that makes me smile
make Hector angry?   31

ALEXANDER They say he yesterday coped Hector in the
battle and struck him down, the disdain and shame
whereof hath ever since kept Hector fasting and waking.

CRESSIDA Who comes here?   35

ALEXANDER Madam, your uncle Pandarus.

          ⌈Enter Pandarus above⌉

CRESSIDA Hector's a gallant man.

ALEXANDER As may be in the world, lady.

PANDARUS What's that? What's that?

CRESSIDA Good morrow, uncle Pandarus.   40

PANDARUS Good morrow, cousin Cressid. What do you talk of?—Good morrow, Alexander.—How do you, cousin? When were you at Ilium?

CRESSIDA This morning, uncle.   44

PANDARUS What were you talking of when I came? Was Hector armed and gone ere ye came to Ilium? Helen was not up, was she?

CRESSIDA
Hector was gone but Helen was not up?

PANDARUS E'en so. Hector was stirring early.

CRESSIDA
That were we talking of, and of his anger.   50

PANDARUS Was he angry?

CRESSIDA So he says here.

PANDARUS True, he was so. I know the cause too. He'll lay about him today, I can tell them that. And there's Troilus will not come far behind him. Let them take heed of Troilus, I can tell them that too.   56

CRESSIDA What, is he angry too?

PANDARUS Who, Troilus? Troilus is the better man of the two.

CRESSIDA
O Jupiter! There's no comparison.   60

PANDARUS What, not between Troilus and Hector? Do you know a man if you see him?

CRESSIDA
Ay, if I ever saw him before and knew him.

PANDARUS Well, I say Troilus is Troilus.

CRESSIDA
Then you say as I say, for I am sure   65
He is not Hector.

PANDARUS No, nor Hector is not Troilus, in some degrees.

CRESSIDA
'Tis just to each of them: he is himself.

PANDARUS Himself? Alas, poor Troilus, I would he were.

CRESSIDA So he is.   70

PANDARUS Condition I had gone barefoot to India.

CRESSIDA He is not Hector.

PANDARUS Himself? No, he's not himself. Would a were himself! Well, the gods are above, time must friend or end. Well, Troilus, well, I would my heart were in her body. No, Hector is not a better man than Troilus. 76

CRESSIDA Excuse me.

PANDARUS He is elder.

CRESSIDA Pardon me, pardon me.   79

PANDARUS Th'other's not come to't. You shall tell me another tale when th'other's come to't. Hector shall not have his will this year.

CRESSIDA
He shall not need it if he have his own.

PANDARUS Nor his qualities.

CRESSIDA No matter.   85

PANDARUS Nor his beauty.

CRESSIDA
'Twould not become him; his own's better.

PANDARUS You have no judgement, niece. Helen herself swore th'other day that Troilus for a brown favour, for so 'tis, I must confess—not brown neither—   90

CRESSIDA No, but brown.

PANDARUS Faith, to say truth, brown and not brown.

CRESSIDA To say the truth, true and not true.

PANDARUS She praised his complexion above Paris'.

CRESSIDA Why, Paris hath colour enough.   95

PANDARUS So he has.

CRESSIDA Then Troilus should have too much. If she praised him above, his complexion is higher than his; he having colour enough, and the other higher, is too flaming a praise for a good complexion. I had as lief Helen's golden tongue had commended Troilus for a copper nose.

PANDARUS I swear to you, I think Helen loves him better than Paris.

CRESSIDA Then she's a merry Greek indeed.   105

PANDARUS Nay, I am sure she does. She came to him th'other day into the compassed window, and you know he has not past three or four hairs on his chin—

CRESSIDA Indeed, a tapster's arithmetic may soon bring his particulars therein to a total.   110

PANDARUS Why, he is very young—and yet will he within three pound lift as much as his brother Hector.

CRESSIDA Is he so young a man and so old a lifter?

PANDARUS But to prove to you that Helen loves him: she came and puts me her white hand to his cloven chin.

CRESSIDA Juno have mercy! How came it cloven?   116

PANDARUS Why, you know, 'tis dimpled. I think his smiling becomes him better than any man in all Phrygia.

CRESSIDA O he smiles valiantly.   120

PANDARUS Does he not?

CRESSIDA O yes, an't were a cloud in autumn.

PANDARUS Why, go to then. But to prove to you that Helen loves Troilus—

CRESSIDA Troilus will stand to the proof if you'll prove it so.   126

PANDARUS Troilus? Why, he esteems her no more than I esteem an addle egg.

CRESSIDA If you love an addle egg as well as you love an idle head you would eat chickens i'th' shell.   130

PANDARUS I cannot choose but laugh to think how she tickled his chin. Indeed, she has a marvellous white hand, I must needs confess—

CRESSIDA Without the rack.

PANDARUS And she takes upon her to spy a white hair on his chin.   136

CRESSIDA Alas, poor chin! Many a wart is richer.

PANDARUS But there was such laughing! Queen Hecuba laughed that her eyes ran o'er.

CRESSIDA With millstones.   140

PANDARUS And Cassandra laughed.

CRESSIDA But there was a more temperate fire under the pot of her eyes—or did her eyes run o'er too?

PANDARUS And Hector laughed.

CRESSIDA At what was all this laughing?   145

PANDARUS Marry, at the white hair that Helen spied on Troilus' chin.

CRESSIDA An't had been a green hair I should have laughed too.

PANDARUS They laughed not so much at the hair as at his pretty answer.   151

CRESSIDA What was his answer?

PANDARUS Quoth she, 'Here's but two-and-fifty hairs on your chin, and one of them is white.'

CRESSIDA This is her question.   155

PANDARUS That's true, make no question of that. 'Two-and-fifty hairs,' quoth he, 'and one white? That white hair is my father, and all the rest are his sons.' 'Jupiter!' quoth she, 'which of these hairs is Paris my husband?' 'The forked one,' quoth he, 'pluck't out and give it him.' But there was such laughing, and Helen so blushed and Paris so chafed and all the rest so laughed, that it passed.

CRESSIDA So let it now, for it has been a great while going by.   165

PANDARUS Well, cousin, I told you a thing yesterday. Think on't.

CRESSIDA So I do.

PANDARUS I'll be sworn 'tis true. He will weep you an't were a man born in April.   170

CRESSIDA And I'll spring up in his tears an't were a nettle against May.

A retreat is sounded

PANDARUS Hark, they are coming from the field. Shall we stand up here and see them as they pass toward Ilium? Good niece, do, sweet niece Cressida.   175

CRESSIDA At your pleasure.

PANDARUS Here, here, here's an excellent place, here we may see most bravely. I'll tell you them all by their names as they pass by, but mark Troilus above the rest.   180

Enter Aeneas passing by ⌈below⌉

CRESSIDA Speak not so loud.

PANDARUS That's Aeneas. Is not that a brave man? He's one of the flowers of Troy, I can tell you. But mark Troilus; you shall see anon.

Enter Antenor passing by ⌈below⌉

CRESSIDA Who's that?   185

PANDARUS That's Antenor. He has a shrewd wit, I can tell you, and he's a man good enough. He's one o'th' soundest judgements in Troy whosoever, and a proper man of person. When comes Troilus? I'll show you Troilus anon. If he see me you shall see him nod at me.   191

CRESSIDA Will he give you the nod?

PANDARUS You shall see.

CRESSIDA If he do, the rich shall have more.   194

Enter Hector passing by ⌈below⌉

PANDARUS That's Hector, that, that, look you, that. There's a fellow!—Go thy way, Hector!—There's a brave man, niece. O brave Hector! Look how he looks. There's a countenance. Is't not a brave man?

CRESSIDA O a brave man.

PANDARUS Is a not? It does a man's heart good. Look you what hacks are on his helmet. Look you yonder, do you see? Look you there. There's no jesting. There's laying on, take't off who will, as they say. There be hacks.

CRESSIDA Be those with swords?   205

Enter Paris passing by ⌈below⌉

PANDARUS Swords, anything, he cares not. An the devil come to him it's all one. By God's lid it does one's heart good. Yonder comes Paris, yonder comes Paris. Look ye yonder, niece. Is't not a gallant man too? Is't not? Why, this is brave now. Who said he came hurt home today? He's not hurt. Why, this will do Helen's heart good now, ha! Would I could see Troilus now. You shall see Troilus anon.

Enter Helenus passing by ⌈below⌉

CRESSIDA Who's that?   214

PANDARUS That's Helenus. I marvel where Troilus is. That's Helenus. I think he went not forth today. That's Helenus.

CRESSIDA Can Helenus fight, uncle?

PANDARUS Helenus? No—yes, he'll fight indifferent well. I marvel where Troilus is.   220

⌈*A Shout*⌉

Hark, do you not hear the people cry 'Troilus'? Helenus is a priest.

Enter Troilus passing by ⌈below⌉

CRESSIDA What sneaking fellow comes yonder?

PANDARUS Where? Yonder? That's Deiphobus.—'Tis Troilus! There's a man, niece, h'm? Brave Troilus, the prince of chivalry!   226

CRESSIDA Peace, for shame, peace.

PANDARUS Mark him, note him. O brave Troilus! Look well upon him, niece. Look you how his sword is bloodied and his helm more hacked than Hector's, and how he looks and how he goes. O admirable youth! He ne'er saw three-and-twenty. —Go thy way, Troilus, go thy way!—Had I a sister were a grace, or a daughter a goddess, he should take his choice. O admirable man! Paris? Paris is dirt to him, and I warrant Helen to change would give an eye to boot.   236

Enter common soldiers passing by ⌈below⌉

CRESSIDA Here comes more.

PANDARUS Asses, fools, dolts. Chaff and bran, chaff and bran. Porridge after meat. I could live and die i'th' eyes of Troilus. Ne'er look, ne'er look, the eagles are gone. Crows and daws, crows and daws. I had rather be such a man as Troilus than Agamemnon and all Greece.

CRESSIDA There is among the Greeks Achilles, a better man than Troilus.

PANDARUS Achilles? A drayman, a porter, a very camel.

CRESSIDA Well, well.   246

PANDARUS Well, well? Why, have you any discretion? Have you any eyes? Do you know what a man is? Is not birth, beauty, good shape, discourse, manhood, learning, gentleness, virtue, youth, liberality, and so forth, the spice and salt that season a man?   251

CRESSIDA Ay, a minced man—and then to be baked with
no date in the pie, for then the man's date is out.
PANDARUS You are such another woman! One knows not
at what ward you lie.   255
CRESSIDA Upon my back to defend my belly, upon my wit
to defend my wiles, upon my secrecy to defend mine
honesty, my mask to defend my beauty, and you to
defend all these—and at all these wards I lie at a
thousand watches.   260
PANDARUS Say one of your watches.
CRESSIDA 'Nay, I'll watch you for that'—and that's one
of the chiefest of them too. If I cannot ward what I
would not have hit, I can watch you for telling how I
took the blow—unless it swell past hiding, and then
it's past watching.   266
PANDARUS You are such another!
        Enter Boy
BOY Sir, my lord would instantly speak with you.
PANDARUS Where?
BOY At your own house.   270
PANDARUS Good boy, tell him I come.   *Exit Boy*
    I doubt he be hurt. Fare ye well, good niece.
CRESSIDA Adieu, uncle.
PANDARUS I'll be with you, niece, by and by.
CRESSIDA To bring, uncle?   275
PANDARUS Ay, a token from Troilus.
CRESSIDA By the same token, you are a bawd.
                Exeunt Pandarus ⌈and Alexander⌉
    Words, vows, gifts, tears, and love's full sacrifice
    He offers in another's enterprise;
    But more in Troilus thousandfold I see   280
    Than in the glass of Pandar's praise may be.
    Yet hold I off. Women are angels, wooing;
    Things won are done. Joy's soul lies in the doing.
    That she beloved knows naught that knows him not this:
    Men price the thing ungained more than it is.   285
    That she was never yet that ever knew
    Love got so sweet as when desire did sue.
    Therefore this maxim out of love I teach:
    Achievement is command; ungained, beseech.   289
    Then though my heart's contents firm love doth bear,
    Nothing of that shall from mine eyes appear.   *Exit*

1.3   *Sennet. Enter Agamemnon, Nestor, Ulysses,*
          Diomedes, and Menelaus, with others
AGAMEMNON
    Princes, what grief hath set the jaundice on your
        cheeks?
    The ample proposition that hope makes
    In all designs begun on earth below
    Fails in the promised largeness. Checks and disasters
    Grow in the veins of actions highest reared,   5
    As knots, by the conflux of meeting sap,
    Infects the sound pine and diverts his grain
    Tortive and errant from his course of growth.
    Nor, princes, is it matter new to us
    That we come short of our suppose so far   10
    That after seven years' siege yet Troy walls stand,

    Sith every action that hath gone before,
    Whereof we have record, trial did draw
    Bias and thwart, not answering the aim
    And that unbodied figure of the thought   15
    That gave't surmisèd shape. Why then, you princes,
    Do you with cheeks abashed behold our works,
    And think them shames, which are indeed naught else
    But the protractive trials of great Jove
    To find persistive constancy in men?   20
    The fineness of which mettle is not found
    In fortune's love—for then the bold and coward,
    The wise and fool, the artist and unread,
    The hard and soft, seem all affined and kin.
    But in the wind and tempest of her frown   25
    Distinction with a loud and powerful fan,
    Puffing at all, winnows the light away,
    And what hath mass or matter by itself
    Lies rich in virtue and unminglèd.
NESTOR
    With due observance of thy godly seat,   30
    Great Agamemnon, Nestor shall apply
    Thy latest words. In the reproof of chance
    Lies the true proof of men. The sea being smooth,
    How many shallow bauble-boats dare sail
    Upon her patient breast, making their way   35
    With those of nobler bulk!
    But let the ruffian Boreas once enrage
    The gentle Thetis, and anon behold
    The strong-ribbed barque through liquid mountains
        cut,
    Bounding between the two moist elements   40
    Like Perseus' horse. Where's then the saucy boat
    Whose weak untimbered sides but even now
    Co-rivalled greatness? Either to harbour fled,
    Or made a toast for Neptune. Even so
    Doth valour's show and valour's worth divide   45
    In storms of fortune. For in her ray and brightness
    The herd hath more annoyance by the breese
    Than by the tiger; but when the splitting wind
    Makes flexible the knees of knotted oaks
    And flies flee under shade, why then the thing of
        courage,   50
    As roused with rage, with rage doth sympathize,
    And with an accent tuned in selfsame key
    Retorts to chiding fortune.
ULYSSES   Agamemnon,
    Thou great commander, nerve and bone of Greece,
    Heart of our numbers, soul and only spirit   55
    In whom the tempers and the minds of all
    Should be shut up, hear what Ulysses speaks.
    Besides th'applause and approbation
    The which, (*to Agamemnon*) most mighty for thy place
        and sway,
    And thou, (*to Nestor*) most reverend for thy stretched-
        out life,   60
    I give to both your speeches—which were such
    As, Agamemnon, every hand of Greece
    Should hold up high in brass, and such again

As, venerable Nestor, hatched in silver,
Should with a bond of air, strong as the axle-tree   65
On which the heavens ride, knit all Greeks' ears
To his experienced tongue—yet let it please both,
Thou (to Agamemnon) great, and (to Nestor) wise, to
    hear Ulysses speak.

AGAMEMNON
Speak, Prince of Ithaca, and be't of less expect
That matter needless, of importless burden,   70
Divide thy lips, than we are confident
When rank Thersites opes his mastic jaws
We shall hear music, wit, and oracle.

ULYSSES
Troy, yet upon his basis, had been down
And the great Hector's sword had lacked a master   75
But for these instances:
The specialty of rule hath been neglected.
And look how many Grecian tents do stand
Hollow upon this plain: so many hollow factions.
When that the general is not like the hive   80
To whom the foragers shall all repair,
What honey is expected? Degree being vizarded,
Th'unworthiest shows as fairly in the masque
⌈   ⌉.
The heavens themselves, the planets, and this centre
Observe degree, priority, and place,   86
Infixture, course, proportion, season, form,
Office and custom, in all line of order.
And therefore is the glorious planet Sol
In noble eminence enthroned and sphered   90
Amidst the other, whose med'cinable eye
Corrects the ill aspects of planets evil
And posts like the commandment of a king,
Sans check, to good and bad. But when the planets
In evil mixture to disorder wander,   95
What plagues and what portents, what mutiny?
What raging of the sea, shaking of earth?
Commotion in the winds, frights, changes, horrors
Divert and crack, rend and deracinate
The unity and married calm of states   100
Quite from their fixture. O when degree is shaked,
Which is the ladder to all high designs,
The enterprise is sick. How could communities,
Degrees in schools, and brotherhoods in cities,
Peaceful commerce from dividable shores,   105
The primogenity and due of birth,
Prerogative of age, crowns, sceptres, laurels,
But by degree stand in authentic place?
Take but degree away, untune that string,
And hark what discord follows. Each thing meets   110
In mere oppugnancy. The bounded waters
Should lift their bosoms higher than the shores
And make a sop of all this solid globe;
Strength should be lord of imbecility,
And the rude son should strike his father dead.   115
Force should be right—or rather, right and wrong,
Between whose endless jar justice resides,
Should lose their names, and so should justice too.

Then everything includes itself in power,
Power into will, will into appetite;   120
And appetite, an universal wolf,
So doubly seconded with will and power,
Must make perforce an universal prey,
And last eat up himself. Great Agamemnon,
This chaos, when degree is suffocate,   125
Follows the choking.
And this neglection of degree it is
That by a pace goes backward in a purpose
It hath to climb. The general's disdained
By him one step below; he, by the next;   130
That next, by him beneath. So every step,
Exampled by the first pace that is sick
Of his superior, grows to an envious fever
Of pale and bloodless emulation.
And 'tis this fever that keeps Troy on foot,   135
Not her own sinews. To end a tale of length:
Troy in our weakness lives, not in her strength.

NESTOR
Most wisely hath Ulysses here discovered
The fever whereof all our power is sick.

AGAMEMNON
The nature of the sickness found, Ulysses,   140
What is the remedy?

ULYSSES
The great Achilles, whom opinion crowns
The sinew and the forehand of our host,
Having his ear full of his airy fame
Grows dainty of his worth, and in his tent   145
Lies mocking our designs. With him Patroclus
Upon a lazy bed the livelong day
Breaks scurrile jests
And, with ridiculous and awkward action
Which, slanderer, he 'imitation' calls,   150
He pageants us. Sometime, great Agamemnon,
Thy topless deputation he puts on,
And like a strutting player, whose conceit
Lies in his hamstring and doth think it rich
To hear the wooden dialogue and sound   155
'Twixt his stretched footing and the scaffoldage,
Such to-be-pitied and o'er-wrested seeming
He acts thy greatness in. And when he speaks
'Tis like a chime a-mending, with terms unsquared
Which from the tongue of roaring Typhon dropped 160
Would seem hyperboles. At this fusty stuff
The large Achilles on his pressed bed lolling
From his deep chest laughs out a loud applause,
Cries 'Excellent! 'Tis Agamemnon just.
Now play me Nestor, hem and stroke thy beard,   165
As he being dressed to some oration.'
That's done as near as the extremest ends
Of parallels, as like as Vulcan and his wife.
Yet god Achilles still cries, 'Excellent!
'Tis Nestor right. Now play him me, Patroclus,   170
Arming to answer in a night alarm'.
And then forsooth the faint defects of age
Must be the scene of mirth: to cough and spit,

And with a palsy, fumbling on his gorget,
Shake in and out the rivet. And at this sport   175
Sir Valour dies, cries, 'O enough, Patroclus!
Or give me ribs of steel. I shall split all
In pleasure of my spleen.' And in this fashion
All our abilities, gifts, natures, shapes,
Severals and generals of grace exact,   180
Achievements, plots, orders, preventions,
Excitements to the field or speech for truce,
Success or loss, what is or is not, serves
As stuff for these two to make paradoxes.

NESTOR
And in the imitation of these twain   185
Who, as Ulysses says, opinion crowns
With an imperial voice, many are infect.
Ajax is grown self-willed and bears his head
In such a rein, in full as proud a place
As broad Achilles, and keeps his tent like him,   190
Makes factious feasts, rails on our state of war
Bold as an oracle, and sets Thersites,
A slave whose gall coins slanders like a mint,
To match us in comparisons with dirt,
To weaken and discredit our exposure,   195
How rank so ever rounded in with danger.

ULYSSES
They tax our policy and call it cowardice,
Count wisdom as no member of the war,
Forestall prescience and esteem no act
But that of hand. The still and mental parts   200
That do contrive how many hands shall strike
When fitness calls them on, and know by measure
Of their observant toil the enemy's weight,
Why, this hath not a finger's dignity.
They call this 'bed-work', 'mapp'ry', 'closet war'.   205
So that the ram that batters down the wall,
For the great swinge and rudeness of his poise
They place before his hand that made the engine,
Or those that with the finesse of their souls
By reason guide his execution.   210

NESTOR
Let this be granted, and Achilles' horse
Makes many Thetis' sons.
     Tucket
AGAMEMNON   What trumpet?
Look, Menelaus.
MENELAUS
From Troy.
     Enter Aeneas ⌈and a trumpeter⌉
AGAMEMNON   What would you fore our tent?
AENEAS
Is this great Agamemnon's tent I pray you?   215
AGAMEMNON   Even this.
AENEAS
May one that is a herald and a prince
Do a fair message to his kingly ears?
AGAMEMNON
With surety stronger than Achilles' arm,

Fore all the Greekish heads, which with one voice   220
Call Agamemnon heart and general.
AENEAS
Fair leave and large security. How may
A stranger to those most imperial looks
Know them from eyes of other mortals?
AGAMEMNON   How?
AENEAS
Ay, I ask that I might waken reverence   225
And on the cheek be ready with a blush
Modest as morning when she coldly eyes
The youthful Phoebus.
Which is that god in office, guiding men?
Which is the high and mighty Agamemnon?   230
AGAMEMNON (*to the Greeks*)
This Trojan scorns us, or the men of Troy
Are ceremonious courtiers.
AENEAS
Courtiers as free, as debonair, unarmed,
As bending angels—that's their fame in peace.
But when they would seem soldiers they have galls,
Good arms, strong joints, true swords—and great
     Jove's acorn   236
Nothing so full of heart. But peace, Aeneas,
Peace, Trojan; lay thy finger on thy lips.
The worthiness of praise distains his worth,
If that the praised himself bring the praise forth.   240
But what, repining, the enemy commends,
That breath fame blows; that praise, sole pure,
     transcends.
AGAMEMNON
Sir, you of Troy, call you yourself Aeneas?
AENEAS
Ay, Greek, that is my name.
AGAMEMNON   What's your affair, I pray you?
AENEAS
Sir, pardon, 'tis for Agamemnon's ears.   245
AGAMEMNON
He hears naught privately that comes from Troy.
AENEAS
Nor I from Troy come not to whisper him.
I bring a trumpet to awake his ear,
To set his sense on the attentive bent,
And then to speak.
AGAMEMNON   Speak frankly as the wind.   250
It is not Agamemnon's sleeping hour.
That thou shalt know, Trojan, he is awake,
He tells thee so himself.
AENEAS   Trumpet, blow loud.
Send thy brass voice through all these lazy tents,
And every Greek of mettle let him know   255
What Troy means fairly shall be spoke aloud.
     The trumpet sounds
We have, great Agamemnon, here in Troy
A prince called Hector—Priam is his father—
Who in this dull and long-continued truce
Is resty grown. He bade me take a trumpet   260

And to this purpose speak: 'Kings, princes, lords,
If there be one among the fair'st of Greece
That holds his honour higher than his ease,
That seeks his praise more than he fears his peril,
That knows his valour and knows not his fear,   265
That loves his mistress more than in confession
With truant vows to her own lips he loves,
And dare avow her beauty and her worth
In other arms than hers—to him this challenge.
Hector in view of Trojans and of Greeks   270
Shall make it good, or do his best to do it:
He hath a lady wiser, fairer, truer,
Than ever Greek did compass in his arms,
And will tomorrow with his trumpet call
Midway between your tents and walls of Troy   275
To rouse a Grecian that is true in love.
If any come, Hector shall honour him.
If none, he'll say in Troy when he retires
The Grecian dames are sunburnt and not worth
The splinter of a lance.' Even so much.   280

AGAMEMNON
This shall be told our lovers, Lord Aeneas.
If none of them have soul in such a kind,
We left them all at home. But we are soldiers,
And may that soldier a mere recreant prove
That means not, hath not, or is not in love.   285
If then one is, or hath, or means to be,
That one meets Hector. If none else, I'll be he.

NESTOR (*to Aeneas*)
Tell him of Nestor, one that was a man
When Hector's grandsire sucked. He is old now,
But if there be not in our Grecian mould   290
One noble man that hath one spark of fire
To answer for his love, tell him from me
I'll hide my silver beard in a gold beaver
And in my vambrace put this withered brawn,
And meeting him will tell him that my lady   295
Was fairer than his grandam, and as chaste
As may be in the world. His youth in flood,
I'll prove this truth with my three drops of blood.

AENEAS
Now heavens forbid such scarcity of youth.

ULYSSES Amen.   300

AGAMEMNON
Fair Lord Aeneas, let me touch your hand.
To our pavilion shall I lead you first.
Achilles shall have word of this intent;
So shall each lord of Greece, from tent to tent.
Yourself shall feast with us before you go,   305
And find the welcome of a noble foe.

Exeunt all but Ulysses and Nestor

ULYSSES
Nestor!

NESTOR   What says Ulysses?

ULYSSES   I have a young
Conception in my brain; be you my time
To bring it to some shape.

NESTOR   What is't?

ULYSSES   This 'tis:

Blunt wedges rive hard knots. The seeded pride   310
That hath to this maturity blown up
In rank Achilles must or now be cropped
Or, shedding, breed a nursery of like evil
To overbulk us all.

NESTOR   Well, and how?

ULYSSES
This challenge that the gallant Hector sends,   315
However it is spread in general name,
Relates in purpose only to Achilles.

NESTOR
The purpose is perspicuous, even as substance
Whose grossness little characters sum up.
And, in the publication, make no strain   320
But that Achilles, were his brain as barren
As banks of Libya—though, Apollo knows,
'Tis dry enough—will with great speed of judgement,
Ay with celerity, find Hector's purpose
Pointing on him.   325

ULYSSES
And wake him to the answer, think you?

NESTOR
Yes, 'tis most meet. Who may you else oppose,
That can from Hector bring his honour off,
If not Achilles? Though't be a sportful combat,
Yet in this trial much opinion dwells,   330
For here the Trojans taste our dear'st repute
With their fin'st palate. And trust to me, Ulysses,
Our imputation shall be oddly poised
In this wild action: for the success,
Although particular, shall give a scantling   335
Of good or bad unto the general—
And in such indices, although small pricks
To their subsequent volumes, there is seen
The baby figure of the giant mass
Of things to come at large. It is supposed   340
He that meets Hector issues from our choice,
And choice, being mutual act of all our souls,
Makes merit her election, and doth boil,
As 'twere, from forth us all a man distilled
Out of our virtues—who miscarrying,   345
What heart from hence receives the conqu'ring part
To steel a strong opinion to themselves?
Which entertained, limbs are e'en his instruments,
In no less working than are swords and bows
Directive by the limbs.

ULYSSES   Give pardon to my speech: 350
Therefore 'tis meet Achilles meet not Hector.
Let us like merchants show our foulest wares
And think perchance they'll sell. If not,
The lustre of the better yet to show
Shall show the better. Do not consent   355
That ever Hector and Achilles meet,
For both our honour and our shame in this
Are dogged with two strange followers.

NESTOR
I see them not with my old eyes. What are they?

ULYSSES
What glory our Achilles shares from Hector,   360

Were he not proud we all should wear with him.
But he already is too insolent,
And we were better parch in Afric sun
Than in the pride and salt scorn of his eyes,
Should he scape Hector fair. If he were foiled,   365
Why then we did our main opinion crush
In taint of our best man. No, make a lott'ry,
And by device let blockish Ajax draw
The sort to fight with Hector. Among ourselves
Give him allowance as the worthier man—   370
For that will physic the great Myrmidon,
Who broils in loud applause, and make him fall
His crest, that prouder than blue Iris bends.
If the dull brainless Ajax come safe off,
We'll dress him up in voices; if he fail,   375
Yet go we under our opinion still
That we have better men. But hit or miss,
Our project's life this shape of sense assumes:
Ajax employed plucks down Achilles' plumes.

NESTOR
Now, Ulysses, I begin to relish thy advice,   380
And I will give a taste of it forthwith
To Agamemnon. Go we to him straight.
Two curs shall tame each other; pride alone
Must tarre the mastiffs on, as 'twere their bone.

                                                 Exeunt

2.1 *Enter Ajax and Thersites*

AJAX Thersites.
THERSITES Agamemnon—how if he had boils, full, all
over, generally?
AJAX Thersites.   4
THERSITES And those boils did run? Say so, did not the
General run then? Were not that a botchy core?
AJAX Dog.
THERSITES Then there would come some matter from him.
I see none now.
AJAX Thou bitch-wolf's son, canst thou not hear? Feel
then.   11
        He strikes Thersites
THERSITES The plague of Greece upon thee, thou mongrel
beef-witted lord!
AJAX Speak then, thou unsifted leaven, speak! I will beat
thee into handsomeness.   15
THERSITES I shall sooner rail thee into wit and holiness.
But I think this horse will sooner con an oration than
thou learn a prayer without book.
        ⌜*Ajax strikes him*⌝
Thou canst strike, canst thou? A red murrain o' thy
jade's tricks.   20
AJAX Toad's stool!
        ⌜*He strikes Thersites*⌝
Learn me the proclamation.
THERSITES Dost thou think I have no sense, thou strikest
me thus?
AJAX The proclamation.   25
THERSITES Thou art proclaimed a fool, I think.

AJAX Do not, porcupine, do not. My fingers itch.
THERSITES I would thou didst itch from head to foot. An
I had the scratching of thee, I would make thee the
loathsomest scab in Greece.   30
AJAX I say, the proclamation.
THERSITES Thou grumblest and railest every hour on
Achilles, and thou art as full of envy at his greatness
as Cerberus is at Proserpina's beauty, ay, that thou
barkest at him.   35
AJAX Mistress Thersites.
THERSITES Thou shouldst strike him.
AJAX Cobloaf.
THERSITES He would pun thee into shivers with his fist,
as a sailor breaks a biscuit.   40
AJAX You whoreson cur.
        ⌜*He strikes Thersites*⌝
THERSITES Do! Do!
AJAX Thou stool for a witch.
        ⌜*He strikes Thersites*⌝
THERSITES Ay, do, do! Thou sodden-witted lord, thou hast
in thy skull no more brain than I have in mine elbows.
An *asnico* may tutor thee. Thou scurvy valiant ass,
thou art here but to thrash Trojans, and thou art
bought and sold among those of any wit like a barbarian
slave. If thou use to beat me, I will begin at thy heel
and tell what thou art by inches, thou thing of no
bowels, thou.   51
AJAX You dog.
THERSITES You scurvy lord.
AJAX You cur.
        ⌜*He strikes Thersites*⌝
THERSITES Mars his idiot! Do, rudeness! Do, camel, do,
do!   56
        Enter Achilles and Patroclus
ACHILLES
Why, how now, Ajax? Wherefore do ye thus?
How now, Thersites? What's the matter, man?
THERSITES You see him there? Do you?
ACHILLES Ay. What's the matter?   60
THERSITES Nay, look upon him.
ACHILLES So I do. What's the matter?
THERSITES Nay, but regard him well.
ACHILLES 'Well'? Why, I do so.
THERSITES But yet you look not well upon him. For
whosomever you take him to be, he is Ajax.   66
ACHILLES I know that, fool.
THERSITES Ay, but 'that fool' knows not himself.
AJAX Therefore I beat thee.   69
THERSITES Lo, lo, lo, lo, what modicums of wit he utters.
His evasions have ears thus long. I have bobbed his
brain more than he has beat my bones. I will buy nine
sparrows for a penny, and his *pia mater* is not worth
the ninth part of a sparrow. This lord, Achilles—Ajax,
who wears his wit in his belly and his guts in his
head—I'll tell you what I say of him.   76
ACHILLES What?
THERSITES I say, this Ajax—

⌈Ajax threatens to strike him⌉

ACHILLES Nay, good Ajax.

THERSITES Has not so much wit—   80

⌈Ajax threatens to strike him⌉

ACHILLES (*to Ajax*) Nay, I must hold you.

THERSITES As will stop the eye of Helen's needle, for whom
he comes to fight.

ACHILLES Peace, fool.

THERSITES I would have peace and quietness, but the fool
will not. He, there, that he, look you there.   86

AJAX O thou damned cur I shall—

ACHILLES (*to Ajax*) Will you set your wit to a fool's?

THERSITES No, I warrant you, for a fool's will shame it.

PATROCLUS Good words, Thersites.   90

ACHILLES (*to Ajax*) What's the quarrel?

AJAX I bade the vile owl go learn me the tenor of the
proclamation, and he rails upon me.

THERSITES I serve thee not.

AJAX Well, go to, go to.   95

THERSITES I serve here voluntary.

ACHILLES Your last service was sufferance. 'Twas not
voluntary: no man is beaten voluntary. Ajax was here
the voluntary, and you as under an impress.   99

THERSITES E'en so. A great deal of your wit, too, lies in
your sinews, or else there be liars. Hector shall have a
great catch an a knock out either of your brains. A
were as good crack a fusty nut with no kernel.

ACHILLES What, with me too, Thersites?   104

THERSITES There's Ulysses and old Nestor, whose wit was
mouldy ere your grandsires had nails on their toes,
yoke you like draught oxen and make you plough up
the war.

ACHILLES What? What?

THERSITES Yes, good sooth. To Achilles! To, Ajax, to—

AJAX I shall cut out your tongue.   111

THERSITES 'Tis no matter. I shall speak as much wit as
thou afterwards.

PATROCLUS No more words, Thersites, peace.

THERSITES I will hold my peace when Achilles' brach bids
me, shall I?   116

ACHILLES There's for you, Patroclus.

THERSITES I will see you hanged like clodpolls ere I come
any more to your tents. I will keep where there is wit
stirring, and leave the faction of fools.   *Exit*

PATROCLUS A good riddance.   121

ACHILLES (*to Ajax*)
Marry, this, sir, is proclaimed through all our host:
That Hector, by the fifth hour of the sun,
Will with a trumpet 'twixt our tents and Troy
Tomorrow morning call some knight to arms   125
That hath a stomach, and such a one that dare
Maintain—I know not what. 'Tis trash. Farewell.

AJAX Farewell. Who shall answer him?

ACHILLES
I know not. 'Tis put to lott'ry. Otherwise,   129
He knew his man.   *⌈Exeunt Achilles and Patroclus⌉*

AJAX O, meaning you? I will go learn more of it. *⌈Exit⌉*

2.2   *⌈Sennet.⌉ Enter King Priam, Hector, Troilus, Paris,*
and Helenus

PRIAM
After so many hours, lives, speeches spent,
Thus once again says Nestor from the Greeks:
'Deliver Helen, and all damage else—
As honour, loss of time, travail, expense,
Wounds, friends, and what else dear that is consumed
In hot digestion of this cormorant war—   6
Shall be struck off.' Hector, what say you to't?

HECTOR
Though no man lesser fears the Greeks than I,
As far as toucheth my particular, yet, dread Priam,
There is no lady of more softer bowels,   10
More spongy to suck in the sense of fear,
More ready to cry out, 'Who knows what follows?'
Than Hector is. The wound of peace is surety,
Surety secure; but modest doubt is called
The beacon of the wise, the tent that searches   15
To th' bottom of the worst. Let Helen go.
Since the first sword was drawn about this question,
Every tithe-soul, 'mongst many thousand dimes,
Hath been as dear as Helen—I mean, of ours.
If we have lost so many tenths of ours   20
To guard a thing not ours—nor worth to us,
Had it our name, the value of one ten—
What merit's in that reason which denies
The yielding of her up?

TROILUS   Fie, fie, my brother!
Weigh you the worth and honour of a king   25
So great as our dread father in a scale
Of common ounces? Will you with counters sum
The past-proportion of his infinite,
And buckle in a waist most fathomless
With spans and inches so diminutive   30
As fears and reasons? Fie, for godly shame!

HELENUS
No marvel though you bite so sharp at reasons,
You are so empty of them. Should not our father
Bear the great sway of his affairs with reason
Because your speech hath none that tells him so?   35

TROILUS
You are for dreams and slumbers, brother priest.
You fur your gloves with 'reason'. Here are your
reasons:
You know an enemy intends you harm,
You know a sword employed is perilous,
And reason flies the object of all harm.   40
Who marvels then, when Helenus beholds
A Grecian and his sword, if he do set
The very wings of reason to his heels
And fly like chidden Mercury from Jove,
Or like a star disorbed? Nay, if we talk of reason,   45
Let's shut our gates and sleep. Manhood and honour
Should have hare hearts, would they but fat their
thoughts
With this crammed reason. Reason and respect
Make livers pale and lustihood deject.

HECTOR
Brother, she is not worth what she doth cost   50
The holding.
TROILUS   What's aught but as 'tis valued?
HECTOR
But value dwells not in particular will.
It holds his estimate and dignity
As well wherein 'tis precious of itself
As in the prizer. 'Tis mad idolatry   55
To make the service greater than the god;
And the will dotes that is inclinable
To what infectiously itself affects
Without some image of th'affected merit.
TROILUS
I take today a wife, and my election   60
Is led on in the conduct of my will;
My will enkindled by mine eyes and ears,
Two traded pilots 'twixt the dangerous shores
Of will and judgement. How may I avoid—
Although my will distaste what it elected—   65
The wife I chose? There can be no evasion
To blench from this and to stand firm by honour.
We turn not back the silks upon the merchant
When we have spoiled them; nor the remainder viands
We do not throw in unrespective sewer   70
Because we now are full. It was thought meet
Paris should do some vengeance on the Greeks.
Your breath of full consent bellied his sails;
The seas and winds, old wranglers, took a truce
And did him service. He touched the ports desired,   75
And for an old aunt whom the Greeks held captive
He brought a Grecian queen, whose youth and
     freshness
Wrinkles Apollo's and makes stale the morning.
Why keep we her? The Grecians keep our aunt.
Is she worth keeping? Why, she is a pearl   80
Whose price hath launched above a thousand ships
And turned crowned kings to merchants.
If you'll avouch 'twas wisdom Paris went—
As you must needs, for you all cried, 'Go, go!';
If you'll confess he brought home noble prize—   85
As you must needs, for you all clapped your hands
And cried, 'Inestimable!'—why do you now
The issue of your proper wisdoms rate,
And do a deed that never fortune did:
Beggar the estimation which you prized   90
Richer than sea and land? O theft most base,
That we have stol'n what we do fear to keep!
But thieves unworthy of a thing so stol'n,
That in their country did them that disgrace
We fear to warrant in our native place.   95
CASSANDRA ⌈within⌉
Cry, Trojans, cry!
PRIAM   What noise? What shriek is this?
TROILUS
'Tis our mad sister. I do know her voice.
CASSANDRA ⌈within⌉ Cry, Trojans!
HECTOR It is Cassandra.

⌈Enter Cassandra raving, with her hair about her
     ears⌉
CASSANDRA
Cry, Trojans, cry! Lend me ten thousand eyes   100
And I will fill them with prophetic tears.
HECTOR Peace, sister, peace.
CASSANDRA
Virgins and boys, mid-age, and wrinkled old,
Soft infancy that nothing canst but cry,
Add to my clamours. Let us pay betimes   105
A moiety of that mass of moan to come.
Cry, Trojans, cry! Practise your eyes with tears.
Troy must not be, nor goodly Ilium stand.
Our firebrand brother, Paris, burns us all.
Cry, Trojans, cry! Ah Helen, and ah woe!   110
Cry, cry 'Troy burns!'—or else let Helen go.   Exit
HECTOR
Now, youthful Troilus, do not these high strains
Of divination in our sister work
Some touches of remorse? Or is your blood
So madly hot that no discourse of reason,   115
Nor fear of bad success in a bad cause,
Can qualify the same?
TROILUS   Why, brother Hector,
We may not think the justness of each act
Such and no other than the event doth form it,
Nor once deject the courage of our minds   120
Because Cassandra's mad. Her brainsick raptures
Cannot distaste the goodness of a quarrel
Which hath our several honours all engaged
To make it gracious. For my private part,
I am no more touched than all Priam's sons.   125
And Jove forbid there should be done amongst us
Such things as might offend the weakest spleen
To fight for and maintain.
PARIS
Else might the world convince of levity
As well my undertakings as your counsels.   130
But I attest the gods, your full consent
Gave wings to my propension and cut off
All fears attending on so dire a project.
For what, alas, can these my single arms?
What propugnation is in one man's valour   135
To stand the push and enmity of those
This quarrel would excite? Yet I protest,
Were I alone to pass the difficulties
And had as ample power as I have will,
Paris should ne'er retract what he hath done   140
Nor faint in the pursuit.
PRIAM   Paris, you speak
Like one besotted on your sweet delights.
You have the honey still, but these the gall.
So to be valiant is no praise at all.
PARIS
Sir, I propose not merely to myself   145
The pleasures such a beauty brings with it,
But I would have the soil of her fair rape
Wiped off in honourable keeping her.

What treason were it to the ransacked queen,
Disgrace to your great worths, and shame to me,   150
Now to deliver her possession up
On terms of base compulsion? Can it be
That so degenerate a strain as this
Should once set footing in your generous bosoms?
There's not the meanest spirit on our party   155
Without a heart to dare or sword to draw
When Helen is defended; nor none so noble
Whose life were ill bestowed or death unfamed
Where Helen is the subject. Then I say:
Well may we fight for her whom we know well   160
The world's large spaces cannot parallel.

HECTOR
Paris and Troilus, you have both said well,
But on the cause and question now in hand
Have glossed but superficially—not much
Unlike young men, whom•Aristotle thought   165
Unfit to hear moral philosophy.
The reasons you allege do more conduce
To the hot passion of distempered blood
Than to make up a free determination
'Twixt right and wrong; for pleasure and revenge   170
Have ears more deaf than adders to the voice
Of any true decision. Nature craves
All dues be rendered to their owners. Now,
What nearer debt in all humanity
Than wife is to the husband? If this law   175
Of nature be corrupted through affection,
And that great minds, of partial indulgence
To their benumbèd wills, resist the same,
There is a law in each well-ordered nation
To curb those raging appetites that are   180
Most disobedient and refractory.
If Helen then be wife to Sparta's king,
As it is known she is, these moral laws
Of nature and of nations speak aloud
To have her back returned. Thus to persist   185
In doing wrong extenuates not wrong,
But makes it much more heavy. Hector's opinion
Is this in way of truth—yet ne'ertheless,
My sprightly brethren, I propend to you
In resolution to keep Helen still;   190
For 'tis a cause that hath no mean dependence
Upon our joint and several dignities.

TROILUS
Why, there you touched the life of our design.
Were it not glory that we more affected
Than the performance of our heaving spleens,   195
I would not wish a drop of Trojan blood
Spent more in her defence. But, worthy Hector,
She is a theme of honour and renown,
A spur to valiant and magnanimous deeds,
Whose present courage may beat down our foes,   200
And fame in time to come canonize us—
For I presume brave Hector would not lose
So rich advantage of a promised glory

As smiles upon the forehead of this action
For the wide world's revenue.

HECTOR   I am yours,   205
You valiant offspring of great Priamus.
I have a roisting challenge sent amongst
The dull and factious nobles of the Greeks
Will shriek amazement to their drowsy spirits.
I was advertised their great general slept   210
Whilst emulation in the army crept;
This I presume will wake him.   ⌜Flourish.⌝ Exeunt

2.3   Enter Thersites

THERSITES How now, Thersites? What, lost in the
labyrinth of thy fury? Shall the elephant Ajax carry it
thus? He beats me and I rail at him. O worthy
satisfaction! Would it were otherwise: that I could beat
him whilst he railed at me. 'Sfoot, I'll learn to conjure
and raise devils but I'll see some issue of my spiteful
execrations. Then there's Achilles: a rare engineer. If
Troy be not taken till these two undermine it, the walls
will stand till they fall of themselves. O thou great
thunder-darter of Olympus, forget that thou art Jove,
the king of gods; and Mercury, lose all the serpentine
craft of thy caduceus, if ye take not that little, little,
less than little wit from them that they have—which
short-armed ignorance itself knows is so abundant-
scarce it will not in circumvention deliver a fly from a
spider without drawing their massy irons and cutting
the web. After this, the vengeance on the whole camp—
or rather, the Neapolitan bone-ache, for that methinks
is the curse dependent on those that war for a placket.
I have said my prayers, and devil Envy say 'Amen'.—
What ho! My lord Achilles!   21
      Enter Patroclus ⌜at the door to the tent⌝
PATROCLUS Who's there? Thersites? Good Thersites, come
in and rail.   ⌜Exit⌝
THERSITES If I could ha' remembered a gilt counterfeit,
thou wouldst not have slipped out of my contemplation;
but it is no matter. Thyself upon thyself! The common
curse of mankind, folly and ignorance, be thine in great
revenue! Heaven bless thee from a tutor, and discipline
come not near thee! Let thy blood be thy direction till
thy death! Then if she that lays thee out says thou art
a fair corpse, I'll be sworn and sworn upon't she never
shrouded any but lazars.   32
      ⌜Enter Patroclus⌝
Amen.—Where's Achilles?
PATROCLUS What, art thou devout? Wast thou in prayer?
THERSITES Ay. The heavens hear me!   35
PATROCLUS Amen.
      Enter Achilles
ACHILLES Who's there?
PATROCLUS Thersites, my lord.
ACHILLES Where? Where? O where?—Art thou come?
Why, my cheese, my digestion, why hast thou not
served thyself into my table so many meals? Come:
what's Agamemnon?   42

THERSITES Thy commander, Achilles.—Then tell me, Patroclus, what's Achilles?

PATROCLUS Thy lord, Thersites. Then tell me, I pray thee, what's Thersites?   46

THERSITES Thy knower, Patroclus. Then tell me, Patroclus, what art thou?

PATROCLUS Thou mayst tell, that knowest.

ACHILLES O tell, tell.   50

THERSITES I'll decline the whole question. Agamemnon commands Achilles, Achilles is my lord, I am Patroclus' knower, and Patroclus is a fool.

PATROCLUS You rascal.

THERSITES Peace, fool, I have not done.   55

ACHILLES (to Patroclus) He is a privileged man.—Proceed, Thersites.

THERSITES Agamemnon is a fool, Achilles is a fool, Thersites is a fool, and as aforesaid Patroclus is a fool.

ACHILLES Derive this. Come.   60

THERSITES Agamemnon is a fool to offer to command Achilles; Achilles is a fool to be commanded of Agamemnon; Thersites is a fool to serve such a fool; and Patroclus is a fool positive.

PATROCLUS Why am I a fool?   65

THERSITES Make that demand to the Creator. It suffices me thou art. Look you, who comes here?

Enter Agamemnon, Ulysses, Nestor, Diomedes, Ajax, and Calchas

ACHILLES Patroclus, I'll speak with nobody.—Come in with me, Thersites.   *Exit*

THERSITES Here is such patchery, such juggling and such knavery. All the argument is a whore and a cuckold. A good quarrel to draw emulous factions and bleed to death upon. Now the dry serpigo on the subject, and war and lechery confound all.   *Exit*

AGAMEMNON (to Patroclus) Where is Achilles?   75

PATROCLUS

Within his tent; but ill-disposed, my lord.

AGAMEMNON

Let it be known to him that we are here.
He faced our messengers, and we lay by
Our appertainments, visiting of him.
Let him be told so, lest perchance he think   80
We dare not move the question of our place,
Or know not what we are.

PATROCLUS   I shall so say to him.
⌐*Exit*⌐

ULYSSES

We saw him at the opening of his tent.
He is not sick.   84

AJAX Yes, lion-sick: sick of proud heart. You may call it 'melancholy' if you will favour the man, but by my head 'tis pride. But why? Why? Let him show us the cause. ⌐*To Agamemnon*⌐ A word, my lord.
⌐*Ajax and Agamemnon talk apart*⌐

NESTOR What moves Ajax thus to bay at him?

ULYSSES Achilles hath inveigled his fool from him.   90

NESTOR Who? Thersites?

ULYSSES He.

NESTOR Then will Ajax lack matter, if he have lost his argument.

ULYSSES No, you see, he *is* his argument that *has* his argument: Achilles.   96

NESTOR All the better—their fraction is more our wish than their faction. But it was a strong council that a fool could disunite.

ULYSSES The amity that wisdom knits not, folly may easily untie.   101

Enter Patroclus

Here comes Patroclus.

NESTOR No Achilles with him.

ULYSSES The elephant hath joints, but none for courtesy: his legs are legs for necessity, not for flexure.   105

PATROCLUS (to Agamemnon)

Achilles bids me say he is much sorry
If anything more than your sport and pleasure
Did move your greatness and this noble state
To call upon him. He hopes it is no other
But for your health and your digestion's sake: 110
An after-dinner's breath.

AGAMEMNON   Hear you, Patroclus.
We are too well acquainted with these answers.
But his evasion, winged thus swift with scorn,
Cannot outfly our apprehensions.
Much attribute he hath, and much the reason   115
Why we ascribe it to him. Yet all his virtues,
Not virtuously on his own part beheld,
Do in our eyes begin to lose their gloss,
Yea, and like fair fruit in an unwholesome dish
Are like to rot untasted. Go and tell him   120
We come to speak with him—and you shall not sin
If you do say we think him over-proud
And under-honest, in self-assumption greater
Than in the note of judgement. And worthier than himself
Here tend the savage strangeness he puts on,   125
Disguise the holy strength of their command,
And underwrite in an observing kind
His humorous predominance—yea, watch
His pettish lunes, his ebbs, his flows, as if
The passage and whole carriage of this action   130
Rode on his tide. Go tell him this, and add
That if he overhold his price so much
We'll none of him, but let him, like an engine
Not portable, lie under this report:
'Bring action hither, this cannot go to war.'   135
A stirring dwarf we do allowance give
Before a sleeping giant. Tell him so.

PATROCLUS

I shall, and bring his answer presently.

AGAMEMNON

In second voice we'll not be satisfied;
We come to speak with him.—Ulysses, enter you.   140
         Exit Ulysses ⌐*with Patroclus*⌐

AJAX What is he more than another?

AGAMEMNON No more than what he thinks he is.

AJAX Is he so much? Do you not think he thinks himself
a better man than I am?
AGAMEMNON No question.   145
AJAX Will you subscribe his thought, and say he is?
AGAMEMNON No, noble Ajax. You are as strong, as
valiant, as wise, no less noble, much more gentle, and
altogether more tractable.
AJAX Why should a man be proud? How doth pride
grow? I know not what it is.   151
AGAMEMNON Your mind is the clearer, Ajax, and your
virtues the fairer. He that is proud eats up himself.
Pride is his own glass, his own trumpet, his own
chronicle—and whatever praises itself but in the deed
devours the deed in the praise.   156

    Enter Ulysses

AJAX I do hate a proud man as I hate the engendering
of toads.
NESTOR (*aside*) Yet he loves himself. Is't not strange?
ULYSSES
Achilles will not to the field tomorrow.   160
AGAMEMNON
What's his excuse?
ULYSSES   He doth rely on none,
But carries on the stream of his dispose
Without observance or respect of any,
In will peculiar and in self-admission.
AGAMEMNON
Why, will he not, upon our fair request,   165
Untent his person and share the air with us?
ULYSSES
Things small as nothing, for request's sake only,
He makes important. Possessed he is with greatness,
And speaks not to himself but with a pride
That quarrels at self-breath. Imagined worth   170
Holds in his blood such swoll'n and hot discourse
That 'twixt his mental and his active parts
Kingdomed Achilles in commotion rages
And batters 'gainst himself. What should I say?
He is so plaguy proud that the death tokens of it   175
Cry 'No recovery'.
AGAMEMNON   Let Ajax go to him.
(*To Ajax*) Dear lord, go you and greet him in his tent.
'Tis said he holds you well and will be led,
At your request, a little from himself.
ULYSSES
O Agamemnon, let it not be so.   180
We'll consecrate the steps that Ajax makes
When they go from Achilles. Shall the proud lord
That bastes his arrogance with his own seam
And never suffers matter of the world
Enter his thoughts, save such as do revolve   185
And ruminate himself—shall he be worshipped
Of that we hold an idol more than he?
No, this thrice-worthy and right valiant lord
Must not so stale his palm, nobly acquired,
Nor by my will assubjugate his merit,   190
As amply titled as Achilles' is,

By going to Achilles—
That were to enlard his fat-already pride
And add more coals to Cancer when he burns
With entertaining great Hyperion.   195
This lord go to him? Jupiter forbid,
And say in thunder 'Achilles, go to him'.
NESTOR (*aside to Diomedes*)
O this is well. He rubs the vein of him.
DIOMEDES (*aside to Nestor*)
And how his silence drinks up this applause.
AJAX
If I go to him, with my armèd fist   200
I'll pash him o'er the face.
AGAMEMNON   O no, you shall not go.
AJAX
An a be proud with me, I'll feeze his pride.
Let me go to him.
ULYSSES
Not for the worth that hangs upon our quarrel.
AJAX A paltry insolent fellow.   205
NESTOR (*aside*) How he describes himself!
AJAX Can he not be sociable?
ULYSSES (*aside*) The raven chides blackness.
AJAX I'll let his humour's blood.
AGAMEMNON (*aside*) He will be the physician that should
be the patient.   211
AJAX An all men were o' my mind—
ULYSSES (*aside*) Wit would be out of fashion.
AJAX A should not bear it so. A should eat swords first.
Shall pride carry it?   215
NESTOR (*aside*) An 't would, you'd carry half.
⌈AJAX⌉ A would have ten shares.
⌈ULYSSES⌉ (*aside*) I will knead him; I'll make him supple.
He's not yet through warm.
NESTOR (*aside*) Farce him with praises. Pour in, pour in!
His ambition is dry.   221
ULYSSES (*to Agamemnon*)
My lord, you feed too much on this dislike.
NESTOR (*to Agamemnon*)
Our noble general, do not do so.
DIOMEDES (*to Agamemnon*)
You must prepare to fight without Achilles.
ULYSSES
Why, 'tis this naming of him does him harm.   225
Here is a man—but 'tis before his face.
I will be silent.
NESTOR   Wherefore should you so?
He is not emulous, as Achilles is.
ULYSSES
Know the whole world he is as valiant—
AJAX A whoreson dog, that shall palter thus with us—
would he were a Trojan!   231
NESTOR
What a vice were it in Ajax now—
ULYSSES
If he were proud—
DIOMEDES   Or covetous of praise—

ULYSSES
  Ay, or surly borne—
DIOMEDES   Or strange, or self-affected.
ULYSSES (*to Ajax*)
  Thank the heavens, lord, thou art of sweet composure.
  Praise him that got thee, she that gave thee suck. 236
  Famed be thy tutor, and thy parts of nature
  Thrice famed beyond, beyond all erudition.
  But he that disciplined thine arms to fight—
  Let Mars divide eternity in twain,   240
  And give him half. And for thy vigour,
  Bull-bearing Milo his addition yield
  To sinewy Ajax. I will not praise thy wisdom,
  Which like a bourn, a pale, a shore confines
  Thy spacious and dilated parts. Here's Nestor,   245
  Instructed by the antiquary times:
  He must, he is, he cannot but be, wise.
  But pardon, father Nestor: were your days
  As green as Ajax', and your brain so tempered,
  You should not have the eminence of him,   250
  But be as Ajax.
AJAX   Shall I call you father?
ULYSSES
  Ay, my good son.
DIOMEDES   Be ruled by him, Lord Ajax.
ULYSSES (*to Agamemnon*)
  There is no tarrying here: the hart Achilles
  Keeps thicket. Please it our great general
  To call together all his state of war.   255
  Fresh kings are come today to Troy; tomorrow
  We must with all our main of power stand fast.
  And here's a lord, come knights from east to west
  And cull their flower, Ajax shall cope the best.
AGAMEMNON
  Go we to counsel. Let Achilles sleep.   260
  Light boats sail swift, though greater hulks draw
      deep.   *Exeunt*

3.1   *Music sounds within. Enter Pandarus ⌈at one door⌉
      and a Servant ⌈at another door⌉*

PANDARUS Friend? You. Pray you, a word. Do not you
  follow the young Lord Paris?
SERVANT Ay, sir, when he goes before me.
PANDARUS You depend upon him, I mean.
SERVANT Sir, I do depend upon the Lord.   5
PANDARUS You depend upon a notable gentleman; I must
  needs praise him.
SERVANT The Lord be praised!
PANDARUS You know me—do you not?
SERVANT Faith, sir, superficially.   10
PANDARUS Friend, know me better. I am the Lord
  Pandarus.
SERVANT I hope I shall know your honour better.
PANDARUS I do desire it.
SERVANT You are in the state of grace?   15
PANDARUS Grace? Not so, friend. 'Honour' and 'lordship'
  are my titles. What music is this?

SERVANT I do but partly know, sir. It is music in parts.
PANDARUS Know you the musicians?
SERVANT Wholly, sir.   20
PANDARUS Who play they to?
SERVANT To the hearers, sir.
PANDARUS At whose pleasure, friend?
SERVANT At mine, sir, and theirs that love music.
PANDARUS 'Command' I mean, friend.   25
SERVANT Who shall I command, sir?
PANDARUS Friend, we understand not one another. I am
  too courtly and thou too cunning. At whose request
  do these men play?   29
SERVANT That's to't indeed, sir. Marry, sir, at the request
  of Paris my lord, who's there in person; with him, the
  mortal Venus, the heart-blood of beauty, love's visible
  soul—
PANDARUS Who, my cousin Cressida?
SERVANT No, sir, Helen. Could not you find out that by
  her attributes?   36
PANDARUS It should seem, fellow, that thou hast not seen
  the Lady Cressid. I come to speak with Paris from the
  Prince Troilus. I will make a complimental assault upon
  him, for my business seethes.   40
SERVANT Sodden business! There's a stewed phrase,
  indeed.
      Enter Paris and Helen, attended ⌈by musicians⌉
PANDARUS Fair be to you, my lord, and to all this fair
  company. Fair desires in all fair measure fairly guide
  them—especially to you, fair Queen. Fair thoughts be
  your fair pillow.   46
HELEN Dear lord, you are full of fair words.
PANDARUS You speak your fair pleasure, sweet Queen. (*To
  Paris*) Fair prince, here is good broken music. 49
PARIS You have broke it, cousin, and by my life you shall
  make it whole again. You shall piece it out with a piece
  of your performance.—Nell, he is full of harmony.
PANDARUS Truly, lady, no.
HELEN O sir.
      ⌈*She tickles him*⌉
PANDARUS Rude, in sooth, in good sooth very rude.   55
PARIS Well said, my lord. Will you say so in fits?
PANDARUS I have business to my lord, dear Queen.—My
  lord, will you vouchsafe me a word?
HELEN Nay, this shall not hedge us out. We'll hear you
  sing, certainly.   60
PANDARUS Well, sweet Queen, you are pleasant with
  me.—But marry, thus, my lord: my dear lord and most
  esteemed friend, your brother Troilus—
HELEN My lord Pandarus, honey-sweet lord.
PANDARUS Go to, sweet Queen, go to!—commends himself
  most affectionately to you.   66
HELEN You shall not bob us out of our melody. If you do,
  our melancholy upon your head.
PANDARUS Sweet Queen, sweet Queen, that's a sweet
  Queen. Ay, faith—   70
HELEN And to make a sweet lady sad is a sour offence.
PANDARUS Nay, that shall not serve your turn; that shall

it not, in truth, la. Nay, I care not for such words. No,
no.—And, my lord, he desires you that, if the King call
for him at supper, you will make his excuse.   75
HELEN My lord Pandarus.
PANDARUS What says my sweet Queen, my very very
sweet Queen?
PARIS What exploit's in hand? Where sups he tonight?
HELEN Nay, but my lord—   80
PANDARUS What says my sweet Queen? My cousin will
fall out with you.
HELEN (to Paris) You must not know where he sups.
PARIS I'll lay my life, with my dispenser Cressida.
PANDARUS No, no! No such matter. You are wide. Come,
your dispenser is sick.   86
PARIS Well, I'll make 's excuse.
PANDARUS Ay, good my lord. Why should you say
Cressida? No, your poor dispenser's sick.
PARIS 'I spy.'   90
PANDARUS You spy? What do you spy?— ⌈To a musician⌉
Come, give me an instrument.—Now, sweet Queen.
HELEN Why, this is kindly done!
PANDARUS My niece is horrible in love with a thing you
have, sweet Queen.   95
HELEN She shall have it, my lord—if it be not my lord
Paris.
PANDARUS He? No, she'll none of him. They two are
twain.   99
HELEN Falling in, after falling out, may make them three.
PANDARUS Come, come, I'll hear no more of this. I'll sing
you a song now.
HELEN Ay, ay, prithee. Now by my troth, sweet lord, thou
hast a fine forehead.
⌈She strokes his forehead⌉
PANDARUS Ay, you may, you may.   105
HELEN Let thy song be love. 'This love will undo us all.'
O Cupid, Cupid, Cupid!
PANDARUS Love? Ay, that it shall, i'faith.
PARIS Ay, good now, 'Love, love, nothing but love'.
PANDARUS In good truth, it begins so.   110
(Sings)
    Love, love, nothing but love, still love, still more!
        For O love's bow
        Shoots buck and doe.
        The shaft confounds
        Not that it wounds,   115
    But tickles still the sore.

    These lovers cry 'O! O!', they die.
        Yet that which seems the wound to kill
    Doth turn 'O! O!' to 'ha ha he!'
        So dying love lives still.   120
        'O! O!' a while, but 'ha ha ha!'
        'O! O!' groans out for 'ha ha ha!'—

Heigh-ho.
HELEN In love—ay, faith, to the very tip of the nose. 124
PARIS He eats nothing but doves, love, and that breeds
hot blood, and hot blood begets hot thoughts, and hot
thoughts beget hot deeds, and hot deeds is love.

PANDARUS Is this the generation of love: hot blood, hot
thoughts, and hot deeds? Why, they are vipers. Is love
a generation of vipers?   130
⌈Alarum⌉
Sweet lord, who's afield today?
PARIS Hector, Deiphobus, Helenus, Antenor, and all the
gallantry of Troy. I would fain have armed today, but
my Nell would not have it so. How chance my brother
Troilus went not?   135
HELEN He hangs the lip at something. You know all, Lord
Pandarus.
PANDARUS Not I, honey-sweet Queen. I long to hear how
they sped today.—You'll remember your brother's
excuse?   140
PARIS To a hair.
PANDARUS Farewell, sweet Queen.
HELEN Commend me to your niece.
PANDARUS I will, sweet Queen.   Exit
    Sound a retreat
PARIS
They're come from field. Let us to Priam's hall   145
To greet the warriors. Sweet Helen, I must woo you
To help unarm our Hector. His stubborn buckles,
With these your white enchanting fingers touched,
Shall more obey than to the edge of steel
Or force of Greekish sinews. You shall do more   150
Than all the island kings: disarm great Hector.
HELEN
'Twill make us proud to be his servant, Paris;
Yea, what he shall receive of us in duty
Gives us more palm in beauty than we have—
Yea, overshines ourself.
PARIS   Sweet above thought, I love thee!
    Exeunt

3.2   Enter Pandarus ⌈at one door⌉ and Troilus' man ⌈at
       another door⌉
PANDARUS How now, where's thy master? At my cousin
Cressida's?
MAN No, sir, he stays for you to conduct him thither.
    Enter Troilus
PANDARUS O here he comes.—How now, how now?
TROILUS Sirrah, walk off.   Exit Man
PANDARUS Have you seen my cousin?   6
TROILUS
No, Pandarus, I stalk about her door
Like a strange soul upon the Stygian banks
Staying for waftage. O be thou my Charon,
And give me swift transportance to those fields   10
Where I may wallow in the lily beds
Proposed for the deserver. O gentle Pandar,
From Cupid's shoulder pluck his painted wings
And fly with me to Cressid.   14
PANDARUS Walk here i'th' orchard. I'll bring her straight.
    Exit
TROILUS
I am giddy. Expectation whirls me round.
Th'imaginary relish is so sweet
That it enchants my sense. What will it be

When that the wat'ry palates taste indeed
Love's thrice-repurèd nectar? Death, I fear me,   20
Swooning destruction, or some joy too fine,
Too subtle-potent, tuned too sharp in sweetness
For the capacity of my ruder powers.
I fear it much, and I do fear besides
That I shall lose distinction in my joys,   25
As doth a battle when they charge on heaps
The enemy flying.

Enter Pandarus

PANDARUS She's making her ready. She'll come straight.
You must be witty now. She does so blush, and fetches
her wind so short as if she were frayed with a spirit.
I'll fetch her. It is the prettiest villain! She fetches her
breath as short as a new-ta'en sparrow.   *Exit*

TROILUS
Even such a passion doth embrace my bosom.
My heart beats thicker than a feverous pulse,
And all my powers do their bestowing lose,   35
Like vassalage at unawares encount'ring
The eye of majesty.

Enter Pandarus, with Cressida ⌈veiled⌉

PANDARUS (*to Cressida*) Come, come, what need you blush?
Shame's a baby. (*To Troilus*) Here she is now. Swear
the oaths now to her that you have sworn to me. (*To
Cressida*) What, are you gone again? You must be
watched ere you be made tame, must you? Come your
ways, come your ways. An you draw backward, we'll
put you i'th' thills. (*To Troilus*) Why do you not speak
to her? (*To Cressida*) Come, draw this curtain, and let's
see your picture. ⌈*He unveils her*⌉ Alas the day! How
loath you are to offend daylight! An't were dark, you'd
close sooner. So, so. (*To Troilus*) Rub on, and kiss the
mistress. (*They kiss*) How now, a kiss in fee farm! Build
there, carpenter, the air is sweet. Nay, you shall fight
your hearts out ere I part you. The falcon as the tercel,
for all the ducks i'th' river. Go to, go to.
TROILUS You have bereft me of all words, lady.   53
PANDARUS Words pay no debts; give her deeds. But she'll
bereave you o'th' deeds too, if she call your activity in
question. (*They kiss*) What, billing again? Here's 'in
witness whereof the parties interchangeably'. Come in,
come in. I'll go get a fire.   *Exit*
CRESSIDA Will you walk in, my lord?   59
TROILUS O Cressida, how often have I wished me thus.
CRESSIDA Wished, my lord? The gods grant—O, my lord!
TROILUS What should they grant? What makes this pretty
abruption? What too-curious dreg espies my sweet lady
in the fountain of our love?   64
CRESSIDA More dregs than water, if my fears have eyes.
TROILUS Fears make devils of cherubims; they never see
truly.
CRESSIDA Blind fear, that seeing reason leads, finds safer
footing than blind reason, stumbling without fear. To
fear the worst oft cures the worse.   70
TROILUS O let my lady apprehend no fear. In all Cupid's
pageant there is presented no monster.
CRESSIDA Nor nothing monstrous neither?

TROILUS Nothing but our undertakings, when we vow to
weep seas, live in fire, eat rocks, tame tigers, thinking
it harder for our mistress to devise imposition enough
than for us to undergo any difficulty imposed. This is
the monstruosity in love, lady—that the will is infinite
and the execution confined; that the desire is boundless
and the act a slave to limit.   80
CRESSIDA They say all lovers swear more performance
than they are able, and yet reserve an ability that they
never perform: vowing more than the perfection of ten,
and discharging less than the tenth part of one. They
that have the voice of lions and the act of hares, are
they not monsters?   86
TROILUS Are there such? Such are not we. Praise us as
we are tasted; allow us as we prove. Our head shall
go bare till merit crown it. No perfection in reversion
shall have a praise in present. We will not name desert
before his birth, and being born his addition shall be
humble. Few words to fair faith. Troilus shall be such
to Cressid as what envy can say worst shall be a mock
for his truth; and what truth can speak truest, not
truer than Troilus.   95
CRESSIDA Will you walk in, my lord?

Enter Pandarus

PANDARUS What, blushing still? Have you not done
talking yet?
CRESSIDA Well, uncle, what folly I commit I dedicate to
you.   100
PANDARUS I thank you for that. If my lord get a boy of
you, you'll give him me. Be true to my lord. If he
flinch, chide me for it.
TROILUS (*to Cressida*) You know now your hostages: your
uncle's word and my firm faith.   105
PANDARUS Nay, I'll give my word for her too. Our kindred,
though they be long ere they are wooed, they are
constant being won. They are burrs, I can tell you:
they'll stick where they are thrown.
CRESSIDA
Boldness comes to me now, and brings me heart.   110
Prince Troilus, I have loved you night and day
For many weary months.
TROILUS
Why was my Cressid then so hard to win?
CRESSIDA
Hard to seem won; but I was won, my lord,
With the first glance that ever—pardon me: 115
If I confess much, you will play the tyrant.
I love you now, but till now not so much
But I might master it. In faith, I lie:
My thoughts were like unbridled children, grown
Too headstrong for their mother. See, we fools!   120
Why have I blabbed? Who shall be true to us,
When we are so unsecret to ourselves?
But though I loved you well, I wooed you not—
And yet, good faith, I wished myself a man,
Or that we women had men's privilege   125
Of speaking first. Sweet, bid me hold my tongue,
For in this rapture I shall surely speak

The thing I shall repent. See, see, your silence,
Cunning in dumbness, in my weakness draws
My soul of counsel from me. Stop my mouth.   130
TROILUS
And shall, albeit sweet music issues thence.
    He kisses her
PANDARUS Pretty, i' faith.
CRESSIDA (*to Troilus*)
My lord, I do beseech you pardon me.
'Twas not my purpose thus to beg a kiss.
I am ashamed. O heavens, what have I done?   135
For this time I will take my leave, my lord.
TROILUS Your leave, sweet Cressid?
PANDARUS Leave? An you take leave till tomorrow
morning—
CRESSIDA
Pray you, content you.
TROILUS   What offends you, lady?   140
CRESSIDA Sir, mine own company.
TROILUS You cannot shun yourself.
CRESSIDA Let me go and try.
I have a kind of self resides with you—
But an unkind self, that itself will leave   145
To be another's fool. Where is my wit?
I would be gone. I speak I know not what.
TROILUS
Well know they what they speak that speak so wisely.
CRESSIDA
Perchance, my lord, I show more craft than love,
And fell so roundly to a large confession   150
To angle for your thoughts. But you are wise,
Or else you love not—for to be wise and love
Exceeds man's might: that dwells with gods above.
TROILUS
O that I thought it could be in a woman—
As, if it can, I will presume in you—   155
To feed for aye her lamp and flames of love,
To keep her constancy in plight and youth,
Outliving beauty's outward, with a mind
That doth renew swifter than blood decays;
Or that persuasion could but thus convince me   160
That my integrity and truth to you
Might be affronted with the match and weight
Of such a winnowed purity in love.
How were I then uplifted! But alas,
I am as true as truth's simplicity,   165
And simpler than the infancy of truth.
CRESSIDA
In that I'll war with you.
TROILUS   O virtuous fight,
When right with right wars who shall be most right.
True swains in love shall in the world to come
Approve their truth by Troilus. When their rhymes,170
Full of protest, of oath and big compare,
Wants similes, truth tired with iteration—
'As true as steel, as plantage to the moon,
As sun to day, as turtle to her mate,
As iron to adamant, as earth to th' centre'—   175

Yet, after all comparisons of truth,
As truth's authentic author to be cited,
'As true as Troilus' shall crown up the verse
And sanctify the numbers.
CRESSIDA   Prophet may you be!
If I be false, or swerve a hair from truth,   180
When time is old and hath forgot itself,
When water drops have worn the stones of Troy
And blind oblivion swallowed cities up,
And mighty states characterless are grated
To dusty nothing, yet let memory   185
From false to false among false maids in love
Upbraid my falsehood. When they've said, 'as false
As air, as water, wind or sandy earth,
As fox to lamb, or wolf to heifer's calf,
Pard to the hind, or stepdame to her son',   190
Yea, let them say, to stick the heart of falsehood,
'As false as Cressid'.
PANDARUS Go to, a bargain made. Seal it, seal it. I'll be
the witness. Here I hold your hand; here, my cousin's.
If ever you prove false one to another, since I have
taken such pain to bring you together, let all pitiful
goers-between be called to the world's end after my
name: call them all panders. Let all constant men be
Troiluses, all false women Cressids, and all brokers-
between panders. Say 'Amen'.   200
TROILUS Amen.
CRESSIDA Amen.
PANDARUS Amen. Whereupon I will show you a chamber
with a bed—which bed, because it shall not speak of
your pretty encounters, press it to death. Away!   205
                    Exeunt Troilus and Cressida
And Cupid grant all tongue-tied maidens here
Bed, chamber, pander to provide this gear.   *Exit*

3.3   *Flourish. Enter Ulysses, Diomedes, Nestor,*
        Agamemnon, Menelaus, Ajax, and Calchas
CALCHAS
Now, princes, for the service I have done you,
Th'advantage of the time prompts me aloud
To call for recompense. Appear it to your mind
That through the sight I bear in things to come
I have abandoned Troy, left my profession,   5
Incurred a traitor's name, exposed myself
From certain and possessed conveniences
To doubtful fortunes, sequest'ring from me all
That time, acquaintance, custom, and condition
Made tame and most familiar to my nature,   10
And here to do you service am become
As new into the world, strange, unacquainted.
I do beseech you, as in way of taste,
To give me now a little benefit
Out of those many registered in promise   15
Which you say live to come in my behalf.
AGAMEMNON
What wouldst thou of us, Trojan? Make demand.
CALCHAS
You have a Trojan prisoner called Antenor,

Yesterday took. Troy holds him very dear.
Oft have you—often have you thanks therefor—   20
Desired my Cressid in right great exchange,
Whom Troy hath still denied. But this Antenor
I know is such a wrest in their affairs
That their negotiations all must slack,
Wanting his manage, and they will almost   25
Give us a prince of blood, a son of Priam,
In change of him. Let him be sent, great princes,
And he shall buy my daughter, and her presence
Shall quite strike off all service I have done
In most accepted pain.

AGAMEMNON   Let Diomedes bear him,   30
And bring us Cressid hither; Calchas shall have
What he requests of us. Good Diomed,
Furnish you fairly for this interchange;
Withal bring word if Hector will tomorrow
Be answered in his challenge. Ajax is ready.   35

DIOMEDES
This shall I undertake, and 'tis a burden
Which I am proud to bear.   *Exit with Calchas*
        Enter Achilles and Patroclus in their tent

ULYSSES
Achilles stands i'th' entrance of his tent.
Please it our general pass strangely by him,
As if he were forgot; and, princes all,   40
Lay negligent and loose regard upon him.
I will come last. 'Tis like he'll question me
Why such unplausive eyes are bent, why turned on
        him.
If so, I have derision medicinable
To use between your strangeness and his pride,   45
Which his own will shall have desire to drink.
It may do good. Pride hath no other glass
To show itself but pride; for supple knees
Feed arrogance and are the proud man's fees.

AGAMEMNON
We'll execute your purpose and put on   50
A form of strangeness as we pass along.
So do each lord, and either greet him not
Or else disdainfully, which shall shake him more
Than if not looked on. I will lead the way.
        They pass by the tent, in turn

ACHILLES
What, comes the general to speak with me?   55
You know my mind: I'll fight no more 'gainst Troy.

AGAMEMNON (*to Nestor*)
What says Achilles? Would he aught with us?

NESTOR (*to Achilles*)
Would you, my lord, aught with the general?

ACHILLES   No.

NESTOR (*to Agamemnon*)
Nothing, my lord.

AGAMEMNON   The better.
            ⌈*Exeunt Agamemnon and Nestor*⌉

ACHILLES ⌈*to Menelaus*⌉   Good day, good day.   59

MENELAUS How do you? How do you?   ⌈*Exit*⌉

ACHILLES (*to Patroclus*)
What, does the cuckold scorn me?

AJAX   How now, Patroclus?

ACHILLES
Good morrow, Ajax.

AJAX   Ha?

ACHILLES   Good morrow.

AJAX Ay, and good next day too.   *Exit*

ACHILLES (*to Patroclus*)
What mean these fellows? Know they not Achilles?

PATROCLUS
They pass by strangely. They were used to bend,   65
To send their smiles before them to Achilles,
To come as humbly as they use to creep
To holy altars.

ACHILLES   What, am I poor of late?
'Tis certain, greatness once fall'n out with fortune
Must fall out with men too. What the declined is   70
He shall as soon read in the eyes of others
As feel in his own fall; for men, like butterflies,
Show not their mealy wings but to the summer,
And not a man, for being simply man,
Hath any honour, but honour for those honours   75
That are without him—as place, riches, and favour:
Prizes of accident as oft as merit;
Which, when they fall, as being slippery standers—
The love that leaned on them, as slippery too—
Doth one pluck down another, and together   80
Die in the fall. But 'tis not so with me.
Fortune and I are friends. I do enjoy
At ample point all that I did possess,
Save these men's looks—who do methinks find out
Something not worth in me such rich beholding   85
As they have often given. Here is Ulysses;
I'll interrupt his reading. How now, Ulysses?

ULYSSES Now, great Thetis' son.

ACHILLES What are you reading?

ULYSSES A strange fellow here   90
Writes me that man, how dearly ever parted,
How much in having, or without or in,
Cannot make boast to have that which he hath,
Nor feels not what he owes, but by reflection—
As when his virtues, shining upon others,   95
Heat them, and they retort that heat again
To the first givers.

ACHILLES   This is not strange, Ulysses.
The beauty that is borne here in the face
The bearer knows not, but commends itself
To others' eyes. Nor doth the eye itself,   100
That most pure spirit of sense, behold itself,
Not going from itself; but eye to eye opposed
Salutes each other with each other's form.
For speculation turns not to itself
Till it hath travelled and is mirrored there   105
Where it may see itself. This is not strange at all.

ULYSSES
I do not strain at the position—

It is familiar—but at the author's drift;
Who in his circumstance expressly proves
That no man is the lord of anything, 110
Though in and of him there be much consisting,
Till he communicate his parts to others.
Nor doth he of himself know them for aught
Till he behold them formèd in th'applause
Where they're extended—who, like an arch, reverb'rate
The voice again; or, like a gate of steel 116
Fronting the sun, receives and renders back
His figure and his heat. I was much rapt in this,
And apprehended here immediately
The unknown Ajax. 120
Heavens, what a man is there! A very horse,
That has he knows not what. Nature, what things
　　there are,
Most abject in regard and dear in use.
What things again, most dear in the esteem
And poor in worth. Now shall we see tomorrow 125
An act that very chance doth throw upon him.
Ajax renowned? O heavens, what some men do,
While some men leave to do.
How some men creep in skittish Fortune's hall
Whiles others play the idiots in her eyes; 130
How one man eats into another's pride
While pride is fasting in his wantonness.
To see these Grecian lords! Why, even already
They clap the lubber Ajax on the shoulder,
As if his foot were on brave Hector's breast 135
And great Troy shrinking.
ACHILLES 　　　　　　I do believe it,
For they passed by me as misers do by beggars,
Neither gave to me good word nor look.
What, are my deeds forgot?
ULYSSES 　　　　　　Time hath, my lord,
A wallet at his back, wherein he puts 140
Alms for oblivion, a great-sized monster
Of ingratitudes. Those scraps are good deeds past,
Which are devoured as fast as they are made,
Forgot as soon as done. Perseverance, dear my lord,
Keeps honour bright. To have done is to hang 145
Quite out of fashion, like a rusty mail
In monumental mock'ry. Take the instant way,
For honour travels in a strait so narrow,
Where one but goes abreast. Keep then the path,
For emulation hath a thousand sons 150
That one by one pursue: if you give way,
Or hedge aside from the direct forthright,
Like to an entered tide they all rush by
And leave you hindmost;
Or, like a gallant horse fall'n in first rank, 155
Lie there for pavement to the abject rear,
O'errun and trampled on. Then what they do in
　　present,
Though less than yours in past, must o'ertop yours.
For Time is like a fashionable host,
That slightly shakes his parting guest by th' hand 160
And, with his arms outstretched as he would fly,

Grasps in the comer. Welcome ever smiles,
And Farewell goes out sighing. O let not virtue seek
Remuneration for the thing it was;
For beauty, wit, 165
High birth, vigour of bone, desert in service,
Love, friendship, charity, are subjects all
To envious and calumniating time.
One touch of nature makes the whole world kin—
That all with one consent praise new-born gauds, 170
Though they are made and moulded of things past,
And give to dust that is a little gilt
More laud than gilt o'er-dusted.
The present eye praises the present object.
Then marvel not, thou great and complete man, 175
That all the Greeks begin to worship Ajax,
Since things in motion sooner catch the eye
Than what not stirs. The cry went once on thee,
And still it might, and yet it may again,
If thou wouldst not entomb thyself alive 180
And case thy reputation in thy tent,
Whose glorious deeds but in these fields of late
Made emulous missions 'mongst the gods themselves,
And drove great Mars to faction.
ACHILLES 　　　　　　Of this my privacy
I have strong reasons.
ULYSSES 　　　　　　But 'gainst your privacy 185
The reasons are more potent and heroical.
'Tis known, Achilles, that you are in love
With one of Priam's daughters.
ACHILLES 　　　　　　Ha? Known?
ULYSSES 　　　　　　Is that a wonder?
The providence that's in a watchful state
Knows almost every grain of Pluto's gold, 190
Finds bottom in th'uncomprehensive deeps,
Keeps place with aught, and almost like the gods
Do infant thoughts unveil in their dumb cradles.
There is a mystery, with whom relation
Durst never meddle, in the soul of state, 195
Which hath an operation more divine
Than breath or pen can give expressure to.
All the commerce that you have had with Troy
As perfectly is ours as yours, my lord;
And better would it fit Achilles much 200
To throw down Hector than Polyxena.
But it must grieve young Pyrrhus now at home,
When fame shall in his island sound her trump
And all the Greekish girls shall tripping sing,
'Great Hector's sister did Achilles win, 205
But our great Ajax bravely beat down *him*'.
Farewell, my lord. I as your lover speak.
The fool slides o'er the ice that you should break.
　　　　　　　　　　　　　　　　　　　Exit

PATROCLUS
To this effect, Achilles, have I moved you.
A woman impudent and mannish grown 210
Is not more loathed than an effeminate man
In time of action. I stand condemned for this.
They think my little stomach to the war

And your great love to me restrains you thus.
Sweet, rouse yourself, and the weak wanton Cupid
Shall from your neck unloose his amorous fold   216
And like a dew-drop from the lion's mane
Be shook to air.
ACHILLES   Shall Ajax fight with Hector?
PATROCLUS
Ay, and perhaps receive much honour by him.
ACHILLES
I see my reputation is at stake.   220
My fame is shrewdly gored.
PATROCLUS   O then beware:
Those wounds heal ill that men do give themselves.
Omission to do what is necessary
Seals a commission to a blank of danger,
And danger like an ague subtly taints   225
Even then when we sit idly in the sun.
ACHILLES
Go call Thersites hither, sweet Patroclus.
I'll send the fool to Ajax, and desire him
T'invite the Trojan lords after the combat
To see us here unarmed. I have a woman's longing,
An appetite that I am sick withal,   231
To see great Hector in his weeds of peace,
    Enter Thersites
To talk with him and to behold his visage
Even to my full of view.—A labour saved.
THERSITES A wonder!   235
ACHILLES What?
THERSITES Ajax goes up and down the field, as asking for
himself.
ACHILLES How so?   239
THERSITES He must fight singly tomorrow with Hector,
and is so prophetically proud of an heroical cudgelling
that he raves in saying nothing.
ACHILLES How can that be?   243
THERSITES Why, a stalks up and down like a peacock—a
stride and a stand; ruminates like an hostess that hath
no arithmetic but her brain to set down her reckoning;
bites his lip with a politic regard, as who should say
'There were wit in this head, an't would out'—and so
there is; but it lies as coldly in him as fire in a flint,
which will not show without knocking. The man's
undone for ever, for if Hector break not his neck i'th'
combat he'll break't himself in vainglory. He knows
not me. I said, 'Good morrow, Ajax', and he replies,
'Thanks, Agamemnon'. What think you of this man
that takes me for the General? He's grown a very land-
fish, languageless, a monster. A plague of opinion! A
man may wear it on both sides like a leather jerkin.
ACHILLES Thou must be my ambassador to him, Thersites.
THERSITES Who, I? Why, he'll answer nobody. He
professes not answering. Speaking is for beggars. He
wears his tongue in's arms. I will put on his presence.
Let Patroclus make demands to me. You shall see the
pageant of Ajax.   263
ACHILLES To him, Patroclus. Tell him I humbly desire the
valiant Ajax to invite the most valorous Hector to come

unarmed to my tent, and to procure safe-conduct for
his person of the magnanimous and most illustrious
six-or-seven-times-honoured captain-general of the
Grecian army, Agamemnon; et cetera. Do this.
PATROCLUS (*to Thersites*) Jove bless great Ajax!   270
THERSITES H'm.
PATROCLUS I come from the worthy Achilles—
THERSITES Ha?
PATROCLUS Who most humbly desires you to invite Hector
to his tent—   275
THERSITES H'm!
PATROCLUS And to procure safe-conduct from Aga-
memnon.
THERSITES Agamemnon?
PATROCLUS Ay, my lord.   280
THERSITES Ha!
PATROCLUS What say you to't?
THERSITES God b'wi' you, with all my heart.
PATROCLUS Your answer, sir?   284
THERSITES If tomorrow be a fair day, by eleven o'clock it
will go one way or other. Howsoever, he shall pay for
me ere he has me.
PATROCLUS Your answer, sir?
THERSITES Fare ye well, with all my heart.
ACHILLES Why, but he is not in this tune, is he?   290
THERSITES No, but he's out o' tune thus. What music will
be in him when Hector has knocked out his brains, I
know not. But I am feared none, unless the fiddler
Apollo get his sinews to make catlings on.
ACHILLES
Come, thou shalt bear a letter to him straight.   295
THERSITES Let me carry another to his horse, for that's
the more capable creature.
ACHILLES
My mind is troubled like a fountain stirred,
And I myself see not the bottom of it.
                    Exit with Patroclus
THERSITES Would the fountain of your mind were clear
again, that I might water an ass at it. I had rather be
a tick in a sheep than such a valiant ignorance.   *Exit*

4.1   *Enter at one door Aeneas with a torch; at another*
        Paris, Deiphobus, Antenor, and Diomedes the
        Grecian, with torch-bearers
PARIS See, ho! Who is that there?
DEIPHOBUS It is the Lord Aeneas.
AENEAS Is the Prince there in person?
    Had I so good occasion to lie long
    As you, Prince Paris, nothing but heavenly business   5
    Should rob my bed-mate of my company.
DIOMEDES
    That's my mind too. Good morrow, Lord Aeneas.
PARIS
    A valiant Greek, Aeneas, take his hand.
    Witness the process of your speech, wherein
    You told how Diomed e'en a whole week by days   10
    Did haunt you in the field.
AENEAS (*to Diomedes*)   Health to you, valiant sir,

During all question of the gentle truce.
But when I meet you armed, as black defiance
As heart can think or courage execute.
DIOMEDES
The one and other Diomed embraces.   15
Our bloods are now in calm; and so long, health.
But when contention and occasion meet,
By Jove I'll play the hunter for thy life
With all my force, pursuit, and policy.
AENEAS
And thou shalt hunt a lion that will fly   20
With his face backward. In humane gentleness,
Welcome to Troy. Now by Anchises' life,
Welcome indeed! By Venus' hand I swear
No man alive can love in such a sort
The thing he means to kill more excellently.   25
DIOMEDES
We sympathize. Jove, let Aeneas live—
If to my sword his fate be not the glory—
A thousand complete courses of the sun;
But, in mine emulous honour, let him die
With every joint a wound—and that, tomorrow.   30
AENEAS We know each other well.
DIOMEDES
We do, and long to know each other worse.
PARIS
This is the most despitefull'st gentle greeting,
The noblest hateful love, that e'er I heard of.
What business, lord, so early?   35
AENEAS
I was sent for to the King; but why, I know not.
PARIS
His purpose meets you: 'twas to bring this Greek
To Calchas' house, and there to render him,
For the enfreed Antenor, the fair Cressid.
Let's have your company, or if you please   40
Haste there before us. ⌈Aside⌉ I constantly do think—
Or rather, call my thought a certain knowledge—
My brother Troilus lodges there tonight.
Rouse him and give him note of our approach,
With the whole quality wherefore. I fear   45
We shall be much unwelcome.
AENEAS ⌈aside⌉   That I assure you.
Troilus had rather Troy were borne to Greece
Than Cressid borne from Troy.
PARIS ⌈aside⌉   There is no help.
The bitter disposition of the time
Will have it so.   50
⌈Aloud⌉ On, lord, we'll follow you.
AENEAS Good morrow all.   Exit
PARIS
And tell me, noble Diomed—faith, tell me true,
Even in the soul of sound good-fellowship—
Who in your thoughts merits fair Helen most,   55
Myself or Menelaus?
DIOMEDES   Both alike.
He merits well to have her that doth seek her,
Not making any scruple of her soilure,

With such a hell of pain and world of charge;
And you as well to keep her that defend her,   60
Not palating the taste of her dishonour,
With such a costly loss of wealth and friends.
He like a puling cuckold would drink up
The lees and dregs of a flat 'tamèd piece;
You like a lecher out of whorish loins   65
Are pleased to breed out your inheritors.
Both merits poised, each weighs nor less nor more,
But he as he: which heavier for a whore?
PARIS
You are too bitter to your countrywoman.
DIOMEDES
She's bitter to her country. Hear me, Paris.   70
For every false drop in her bawdy veins
A Grecian's life hath sunk; for every scruple
Of her contaminated carrion weight
A Trojan hath been slain. Since she could speak
She hath not given so many good words breath   75
As, for her, Greeks and Trojans suffered death.
PARIS
Fair Diomed, you do as chapmen do:
Dispraise the thing that you desire to buy.
But we in silence hold this virtue well:
We'll but commend what we intend to sell.—   80
Here lies our way.   Exeunt

4.2   *Enter Troilus and Cressida*
TROILUS
Dear, trouble not yourself. The morn is cold.
CRESSIDA
Then, sweet my lord, I'll call mine uncle down.
He shall unbolt the gates.
TROILUS   Trouble him not.
To bed, to bed! Sleep lull those pretty eyes
And give as soft attachment to thy senses   5
As to infants empty of all thought.
CRESSIDA Good morrow, then.
TROILUS I prithee now, to bed.
CRESSIDA Are you aweary of me?
TROILUS
O Cressida! But that the busy day,   10
Waked by the lark, hath roused the ribald crows,
And dreaming night will hide our joys no longer,
I would not from thee.
CRESSIDA   Night hath been too brief.
TROILUS
Beshrew the witch! With venomous wights she stays
As hideously as hell, but flies the grasps of love   15
With wings more momentary-swift than thought.
You will catch cold and curse me.
CRESSIDA Prithee, tarry. You men will never tarry.
O foolish Cressid! I might have still held off,
And then you would have tarried.—Hark, there's one
up.   20
⌈She veils herself⌉
PANDARUS (*within*) What's all the doors open here?
TROILUS It is your uncle.

CRESSIDA
A pestilence on him! Now will he be mocking.
I shall have such a life.   24
    ⌈Enter Pandarus⌉
PANDARUS How now, how now, how go maidenheads?
(To Cressida) Here, you, maid! Where's my cousin
Cressid?
CRESSIDA ⌈unveiling⌉
Go hang yourself. You naughty, mocking uncle!
You bring me to do—and then you flout me too.
PANDARUS To do what? To do what?—Let her say what.—
What have I brought you to do?   31
CRESSIDA
Come, come, beshrew your heart. You'll ne'er be
    good,
Nor suffer others.
PANDARUS Ha ha! Alas, poor wretch. Ah, poor capocchia,
hast not slept tonight? Would he not—a naughty
man—let it sleep? A bugbear take him.   36
CRESSIDA (to Troilus)
Did not I tell you? Would he were knocked i'th' head.
    ⌈One knocks within⌉
Who's that at door?—Good uncle, go and see.—
My lord, come you again into my chamber.
You smile and mock me, as if I meant naughtily.   40
TROILUS Ha ha!
CRESSIDA
Come, you are deceived, I think of no such thing.
    One knocks within
How earnestly they knock! Pray you come in.
I would not for half Troy have you seen here.
    Exeunt ⌈Troilus and Cressida⌉
PANDARUS Who's there? What's the matter? Will you
beat down the door?   46
    He opens the door. ⌈Enter Aeneas⌉
How now, what's the matter?
AENEAS Good morrow, lord, good morrow.
PANDARUS
Who's there? My Lord Aeneas? By my troth,
I knew you not. What news with you so early?   50
AENEAS
Is not Prince Troilus here?
PANDARUS   Here? What should he do here?
AENEAS
Come, he is here, my lord. Do not deny him.
It doth import him much to speak with me.
PANDARUS Is he here, say you? It's more than I know,
I'll be sworn. For my own part, I came in late. What
should he do here?   56
AENEAS
Whoa! Nay, then. Come, come, you'll do him wrong
Ere you are ware. You'll be so true to him
To be false to him. Do not you know of him,   59
But yet go fetch him hither. Go.   ⌈Exit Pandarus⌉
    Enter Troilus
TROILUS How now, what's the matter?
AENEAS
My lord, I scarce have leisure to salute you,

My matter is so rash. There is at hand
Paris your brother and Deiphobus,
The Grecian Diomed, and our Antenor   65
Delivered to us—and for him forthwith,
Ere the first sacrifice, within this hour,
We must give up to Diomedes' hand
The Lady Cressida.
TROILUS   Is it so concluded?
AENEAS
By Priam and the general state of Troy.   70
They are at hand, and ready to effect it.
TROILUS How my achievements mock me.
I will go meet them—and, my Lord Aeneas,
We met by chance: you did not find me here.
AENEAS
Good, good, my lord: the secrecies of nature   75
Have not more gift in taciturnity.   Exeunt

4.3   Enter Pandarus and Cressida
PANDARUS Is't possible? No sooner got but lost. The devil
take Antenor! The young prince will go mad. A plague
upon Antenor! I would they had broke 's neck.
CRESSIDA How now? What's the matter? Who was here?
PANDARUS Ah, ah!   5
CRESSIDA Why sigh you so profoundly? Where's my lord?
Gone? Tell me, sweet uncle, what's the matter?
PANDARUS Would I were as deep under the earth as I am
above.
CRESSIDA O the gods! What's the matter?   10
PANDARUS Pray thee, get thee in. Would thou hadst ne'er
been born. I knew thou wouldst be his death. O poor
gentleman! A plague upon Antenor!
CRESSIDA Good uncle, I beseech you on my knees; I
beseech you, what's the matter?   15
PANDARUS Thou must be gone, wench, thou must be
gone. Thou art changed for Antenor. Thou must to thy
father, and be gone from Troilus. 'Twill be his death.
'Twill be his bane. He cannot bear it.
CRESSIDA
O you immortal gods! I will not go.   20
PANDARUS Thou must.
CRESSIDA
I will not, uncle. I have forgot my father.
I know no touch of consanguinity,
No kin, no love, no blood, no soul, so near me
As the sweet Troilus. O you gods divine,   25
Make Cressid's name the very crown of falsehood
If ever she leave Troilus. Time, force, and death
Do to this body what extremity you can,
But the strong base and building of my love
Is as the very centre of the earth,   30
Drawing all things to it. I'll go in and weep—
PANDARUS Do, do.
CRESSIDA
Tear my bright hair, and scratch my praisèd cheeks,
Crack my clear voice with sobs, and break my heart
With sounding 'Troilus'. I will not go from Troy.   35
                                                    Exeunt

4.4 *Enter Paris, Troilus, Aeneas, Deiphobus, Antenor,*
      and Diomedes

PARIS

It is great morning, and the hour prefixed
Of her delivery to this valiant Greek
Comes fast upon us. Good my brother Troilus,
Tell you the lady what she is to do,
And haste her to the purpose.

TROILUS   Walk into her house. 5
I'll bring her to the Grecian presently—
And to his hand when I deliver her,
Think it an altar, and thy brother Troilus
A priest, there off'ring to it his own heart.

PARIS I know what 'tis to love,   10
And would, as I shall pity, I could help.—
Please you walk in, my lords?   ⌜*Exeunt*⌝

4.5 *Enter Pandarus and Cressida*

PANDARUS Be moderate, be moderate.

CRESSIDA

Why tell you me of moderation?
The grief is fine, full, perfect that I taste,
And violenteth in a sense as strong
As that which causeth it. How can I moderate it? 5
If I could temporize with my affection
Or brew it to a weak and colder palate,
The like allayment could I give my grief.
My love admits no qualifying dross;
No more my grief, in such a precious loss.   10
      Enter Troilus

PANDARUS Here, here, here he comes. Ah, sweet ducks!

CRESSIDA (*embracing him*) O Troilus, Troilus!

PANDARUS What a pair of spectacles is here! Let me
embrace you too. 'O heart', as the goodly saying is,
      'O heart, heavy heart,   15
         Why sigh'st thou without breaking?'
where he answers again
      'Because thou canst not ease thy smart
         By friendship nor by speaking.'   19
There was never a truer rhyme. Let us cast away
nothing, for we may live to have need of such a verse.
We see it, we see it. How now, lambs?

TROILUS

Cressid, I love thee in so strained a purity
That the blest gods, as angry with my fancy—
More bright in zeal than the devotion which   25
Cold lips blow to their deities—take thee from me.

CRESSIDA Have the gods envy?

PANDARUS Ay, ay, ay, ay, 'tis too plain a case.

CRESSIDA

And is it true that I must go from Troy?

TROILUS

A hateful truth.

CRESSIDA   What, and from Troilus too?   30

TROILUS

From Troy and Troilus.

CRESSIDA   Is't possible?

TROILUS

And suddenly—where injury of chance
Puts back leave-taking, jostles roughly by
All time of pause, rudely beguiles our lips
Of all rejoindure, forcibly prevents   35
Our locked embrasures, strangles our dear vows
Even in the birth of our own labouring breath.
We two, that with so many thousand sighs
Did buy each other, must poorly sell ourselves
With the rude brevity and discharge of one.   40
Injurious Time now with a robber's haste
Crams his rich thiev'ry up, he knows not how.
As many farewells as be stars in heaven,
With distinct breath and consigned kisses to them,
He fumbles up into a loose adieu   45
And scants us with a single famished kiss,
Distasted with the salt of broken tears.
      Enter Aeneas

AENEAS My lord, is the lady ready?

TROILUS (*to Cressida*)

Hark, you are called. Some say the *genius* so
Cries 'Come!' to him that instantly must die.   50
⌜*To Pandarus*⌝ Bid them have patience. She shall come
anon.

PANDARUS Where are my tears? Rain, to lay this wind,
or my heart will be blown up by the root.
      ⌜*Exit with Aeneas*⌝

CRESSIDA

I must then to the Grecians.

TROILUS   No remedy.

CRESSIDA

A woeful Cressid 'mongst the merry Greeks!   55
When shall we see again?

TROILUS

Hear me, my love: be thou but true of heart—

CRESSIDA

I true? How now! What wicked deem is this?

TROILUS

Nay, we must use expostulation kindly,
For it is parting from us.   60
I speak not 'Be thou true' as fearing thee—
For I will throw my glove to Death himself
That there's no maculation in thy heart—
But 'Be thou true' say I, to fashion in
My sequent protestation: 'Be thou true,   65
And I will see thee'.

CRESSIDA

O you shall be exposed, my lord, to dangers
As infinite as imminent. But I'll be true.

TROILUS

And I'll grow friend with danger. Wear this sleeve.

CRESSIDA

And you this glove. When shall I see you?   70

TROILUS

I will corrupt the Grecian sentinels
To give thee nightly visitation.
But yet, be true.

CRESSIDA O heavens! 'Be true' again!
TROILUS Hear why I speak it, love.   75
  The Grecian youths are full of quality,
  Their loving well composed, with gifts of nature
    flowing,
  And swelling o'er with arts and exercise.
  How novelty may move, and parts with person,
  Alas, a kind of godly jealousy—   80
  Which I beseech you call a virtuous sin—
  Makes me afeard.
CRESSIDA O heavens, you love me not!
TROILUS Die I a villain then!
  In this I do not call your faith in question   85
  So mainly as my merit. I cannot sing,
  Nor heel the high lavolt, nor sweeten talk,
  Nor play at subtle games—fair virtues all,
  To which the Grecians are most prompt and
    pregnant.
  But I can tell that in each grace of these   90
  There lurks a still and dumb-discoursive devil
  That tempts most cunningly. But be not tempted.
CRESSIDA Do you think I will?
TROILUS
  No, but something may be done that we will not,
  And sometimes we are devils to ourselves,   95
  When we will tempt the frailty of our powers,
  Presuming on their changeful potency.
AENEAS (within)
  Nay, good my lord!
TROILUS   Come, kiss, and let us part.
PARIS ⌈at the door⌉
  Brother Troilus?
TROILUS   Good brother, come you hither,
  And bring Aeneas and the Grecian with you.   100
                               ⌈Exit Paris⌉
CRESSIDA My lord, will you be true?
TROILUS
  Who, I? Alas, it is my vice, my fault.
  Whiles others fish with craft for great opinion,
  I with great truth catch mere simplicity;
  Whilst some with cunning gild their copper crowns,
  With truth and plainness I do wear mine bare.   106
    Enter Paris, Aeneas, Antenor, Deiphobus, and
    Diomedes
  Fear not my truth. The moral of my wit
  Is 'plain and true!'; there's all the reach of it.—
  Welcome, Sir Diomed. Here is the lady
  Which for Antenor we deliver you.   110
  At the port, lord, I'll give her to thy hand,
  And by the way possess thee what she is.
  Entreat her fair, and by my soul, fair Greek,
  If e'er thou stand at mercy of my sword,
  Name Cressid, and thy life shall be as safe   115
  As Priam is in Ilium.
DIOMEDES   Fair Lady Cressid,
  So please you, save the thanks this prince expects.
  The lustre in your eye, heaven in your cheek,
  Pleads your fair usage; and to Diomed

  You shall be mistress, and command him wholly.   120
TROILUS
  Grecian, thou dost not use me courteously,
  To shame the zeal of my petition towards thee
  In praising her. I tell thee, lord of Greece,
  She is as far high-soaring o'er thy praises
  As thou unworthy to be called her servant.   125
  I charge thee use her well, even for my charge;
  For, by the dreadful Pluto, if thou dost not,
  Though the great bulk Achilles be thy guard
  I'll cut thy throat.
DIOMEDES   O be not moved, Prince Troilus.
  Let me be privileged by my place and message   130
  To be a speaker free. When I am hence
  I'll answer to my lust. And know you, lord,
  I'll nothing do on charge. To her own worth
  She shall be prized; but that you say 'Be't so',
  I'll speak it in my spirit and honour 'No!'   135
TROILUS
  Come, to the port.—I'll tell thee, Diomed,
  This brave shall oft make thee to hide thy head.—
  Lady, give me your hand, and as we walk
  To our own selves bend we our needful talk.
        Exeunt Troilus, Cressida, and Diomedes.
    A trumpet sounds
PARIS
  Hark, Hector's trumpet.
AENEAS   How have we spent this morning?
  The Prince must think me tardy and remiss,   141
  That swore to ride before him in the field.
PARIS
  'Tis Troilus' fault. Come, come to field with him.
DEIPHOBUS Let us make ready straight.
AENEAS
  Yea, with a bridegroom's fresh alacrity   145
  Let us address to tend on Hector's heels.
  The glory of our Troy doth this day lie
  On his fair worth and single chivalry.   Exeunt

4.6   *Enter Ajax armed, Achilles, Patroclus, Agamemnon,*
    Menelaus, Ulysses, Nestor, a trumpeter, and others
AGAMEMNON
  Here art thou in appointment fresh and fair,
  Anticipating time with starting courage.
  Give with thy trumpet a loud note to Troy,
  Thou dreadful Ajax, that the appallèd air
  May pierce the head of the great combatant   5
  And hale him hither.
AJAX   Thou trumpet, there's my purse.
    He gives him money
  Now crack thy lungs and split thy brazen pipe.
  Blow, villain, till thy spherèd bias cheek
  Outswell the colic of puffed Aquilon.
  Come, stretch thy chest and let thy eyes spout blood;
  Thou blow'st for Hector.   11
    ⌈The trumpet sounds⌉
ULYSSES No trumpet answers.
ACHILLES 'Tis but early days.

AGAMEMNON
Is not yond Diomed with Calchas' daughter?
ULYSSES
'Tis he. I ken the manner of his gait.   15
He rises on the toe: that spirit of his
In aspiration lifts him from the earth.
          Enter Diomedes and Cressida
AGAMEMNON (*to Diomedes*)
Is this the Lady Cressid?
DIOMEDES   Even she.
AGAMEMNON
Most dearly welcome to the Greeks, sweet lady.
          He kisses her
NESTOR (*to Cressida*)
Our General doth salute you with a kiss.   20
ULYSSES
Yet is the kindness but particular;
'Twere better she were kissed in general.
NESTOR
And very courtly counsel. I'll begin.
          He kisses her
So much for Nestor.
ACHILLES
I'll take that winter from your lips, fair lady.   25
          He kisses her
Achilles bids you welcome.
MENELAUS (*to Cressida*)
I had good argument for kissing once.
PATROCLUS
But that's no argument for kissing now;
For thus ⌜*stepping between them*⌝ popped Paris in his
          hardiment,
And parted thus you and your argument.   30
          He kisses her
ULYSSES ⌜*aside*⌝
O deadly gall, and theme of all our scorns!
For which we lose our heads to gild his horns.
PATROCLUS (*to Cressida*)
The first was Menelaus' kiss; this, mine.
Patroclus kisses you.
          He kisses her again
MENELAUS   O this is trim.
PATROCLUS (*to Cressida*)
Paris and I kiss evermore for him.   35
MENELAUS
I'll have my kiss, sir.—Lady, by your leave.
CRESSIDA
In kissing do you render or receive?
⌜MENELAUS⌝
Both take and give.
CRESSIDA   I'll make my match to live,
The kiss you take is better than you give.
Therefore no kiss.   40
MENELAUS
I'll give you boot: I'll give you three for one.
CRESSIDA
You are an odd man: give even or give none.
MENELAUS
An odd man, lady? Every man is odd.

CRESSIDA
No, Paris is not—for you know 'tis true
That you are odd, and he is even with you.   45
MENELAUS
You fillip me o'th' head.
CRESSIDA   No, I'll be sworn.
ULYSSES
It were no match, your nail against his horn.
May I, sweet lady, beg a kiss of you?
CRESSIDA
You may.
ULYSSES   I do desire it.
CRESSIDA   Why, beg too.
ULYSSES
Why then, for Venus' sake, give me a kiss,   50
When Helen is a maid again, and his—
CRESSIDA
I am your debtor; claim it when 'tis due.
ULYSSES
Never's my day, and then a kiss of you.
DIOMEDES
Lady, a word. I'll bring you to your father.
          ⌜*They talk apart*⌝
NESTOR
A woman of quick sense.
ULYSSES   Fie, fie upon her!   55
There's language in her eye, her cheek, her lip;
Nay, her foot speaks. Her wanton spirits look out
At every joint and motive of her body.
O these encounterers so glib of tongue,
That give accosting welcome ere it comes,   60
And wide unclasp the tables of their thoughts
To every ticklish reader, set them down
For sluttish spoils of opportunity
And daughters of the game.
          ⌜*Exeunt Diomedes and Cressida*⌝
          Flourish
ALL The Trojans' trumpet.   65
          Enter all of Troy: Hector ⌜*armed*⌝, *Paris, Aeneas,*
          Helenus, and attendants, among them Troilus
AGAMEMNON Yonder comes the troop.
AENEAS ⌜*coming forward*⌝
Hail, all you state of Greece! What shall be done
To him that victory commands? Or do you purpose
A victor shall be known? Will you the knights
Shall to the edge of all extremity   70
Pursue each other, or shall they be divided
By any voice or order of the field?
Hector bade ask.
AGAMEMNON   Which way would Hector have it?
AENEAS
He cares not; he'll obey conditions.
⌜ACHILLES⌝
'Tis done like Hector—but securely done,   75
A little proudly, and great deal disprising
The knight opposed.
AENEAS   If not Achilles, sir,
What is your name?
ACHILLES   If not Achilles, nothing.

AENEAS
Therefore Achilles. But whate'er, know this:
In the extremity of great and little,   80
Valour and pride excel themselves in Hector,
The one almost as infinite as all,
The other blank as nothing. Weigh him well,
And that which looks like pride is courtesy.
This Ajax is half made of Hector's blood,   85
In love whereof half Hector stays at home.
Half heart, half hand, half Hector comes to seek
This blended knight, half Trojan and half Greek.

ACHILLES
A maiden battle, then? O I perceive you.
                Enter Diomedes

AGAMEMNON
Here is Sir Diomed.—Go, gentle knight,   90
Stand by our Ajax. As you and Lord Aeneas
Consent upon the order of their fight,
So be it: either to the uttermost
Or else a breath.
        ⌈*Exeunt Ajax, Diomedes, Hector, and Aeneas*⌉
                The combatants being kin
Half stints their strife before their strokes begin.   95
ULYSSES They are opposed already.

AGAMEMNON
What Trojan is that same that looks so heavy?

ULYSSES
The youngest son of Priam, a true knight:
They call him Troilus.
Not yet mature, yet matchless-firm of word,   100
Speaking in deeds and deedless in his tongue;
Not soon provoked, nor being provoked soon calmed;
His heart and hand both open and both free.
For what he has he gives; what thinks, he shows;
Yet gives he not till judgement guide his bounty,   105
Nor dignifies an impare thought with breath.
Manly as Hector but more dangerous,
For Hector in his blaze of wrath subscribes
To tender objects, but he in heat of action
Is more vindicative than jealous love.   110
They call him Troilus, and on him erect
A second hope as fairly built as Hector.
Thus says Aeneas, one that knows the youth
Even to his inches, and with private soul
Did in great Ilium thus translate him to me.   115
                Alarum

AGAMEMNON They are in action.
NESTOR Now, Ajax, hold thine own!
TROILUS Hector, thou sleep'st! Awake thee!

AGAMEMNON
His blows are well disposed. There, Ajax!   ⌈*Exeunt*⌉

4.7 ⌈*Enter Hector and Ajax fighting, and Aeneas and
        Diomedes interposing.*⌉ *Trumpets cease*

DIOMEDES
You must no more.
AENEAS   Princes, enough, so please you.

AJAX
I am not warm yet. Let us fight again.

DIOMEDES
As Hector pleases.
HECTOR   Why then will I no more.—
Thou art, great lord, my father's sister's son,
A cousin-german to great Priam's seed.   5
The obligation of our blood forbids
A gory emulation 'twixt us twain.
Were thy commixtion Greek and Trojan so
That thou couldst say 'This hand is Grecian all,
And this is Trojan; the sinews of this leg   10
All Greek, and this all Troy; my mother's blood
Runs on the dexter cheek, and this sinister
Bounds in my father's,' by Jove multipotent
Thou shouldst not bear from me a Greekish member
Wherein my sword had not impressure made   15
Of our rank feud. But the just gods gainsay
That any drop thou borrowed'st from thy mother,
My sacred aunt, should by my mortal sword
Be drained. Let me embrace thee, Ajax.
By him that thunders, thou hast lusty arms.   20
Hector would have them fall upon him thus.
Cousin, all honour to thee.
AJAX   I thank thee, Hector.
Thou art too gentle and too free a man.
I came to kill thee, cousin, and bear hence
A great addition earnèd in thy death.   25

HECTOR
Not Neoptolemus so mirable,
On whose bright crest Fame with her loud'st oyez
Cries 'This is he!', could promise to himself
A thought of added honour torn from Hector.

AENEAS
There is expectance here from both the sides   30
What further you will do.
HECTOR   We'll answer it:
The issue is embracement.—Ajax, farewell.

AJAX
If I might in entreaties find success,
As seld I have the chance, I would desire
My famous cousin to our Grecian tents.   35

DIOMEDES
'Tis Agamemnon's wish—and great Achilles
Doth long to see unarmed the valiant Hector.

HECTOR
Aeneas, call my brother Troilus to me,
And signify this loving interview
To the expecters of our Trojan part.   40
Desire them home.   ⌈*Exit Aeneas*⌉
                Give me thy hand, my cousin.
I will go eat with thee, and see your knights.
        *Enter Agamemnon and the rest: Aeneas, Ulysses,
        Menelaus, Nestor, Achilles, Patroclus, Troilus, and
        others*

AJAX
Great Agamemnon comes to meet us here.
HECTOR (*to Aeneas*)
The worthiest of them, tell me name by name.
But for Achilles, mine own searching eyes   45
Shall find him by his large and portly size.

AGAMEMNON (*embracing him*)
Worthy of arms, as welcome as to one
That would be rid of such an enemy.
But that's no welcome. Understand more clear:
What's past and what's to come is strewed with husks
And formless ruin of oblivion,   51
But in this extant moment faith and troth,
Strained purely from all hollow bias-drawing,
Bids thee with most divine integrity
From heart of very heart, 'Great Hector, welcome!' 55
HECTOR
I thank thee, most imperious Agamemnon.
AGAMEMNON ⌈*to Troilus*⌉
My well-famed lord of Troy, no less to you.
MENELAUS
Let me confirm my princely brother's greeting.
You brace of warlike brothers, welcome hither.
⌈*He embraces Hector and Troilus*⌉
HECTOR (*to Aeneas*)
Who must we answer?
AENEAS   The noble Menelaus.   60
HECTOR
O, you, my lord! By Mars his gauntlet, thanks.
Mock not that I affect th'untraded oath.
Your quondam wife swears still by Venus' glove.
She's well, but bade me not commend her to you.
MENELAUS
Name her not now, sir. She's a deadly theme.   65
HECTOR O, pardon. I offend.
NESTOR
I have, thou gallant Trojan, seen thee oft,
Labouring for destiny, make cruel way
Through ranks of Greekish youth, and I have seen thee
As hot as Perseus spur thy Phrygian steed,   70
And seen thee scorning forfeits and subduements,
When thou hast hung th'advancèd sword i'th' air,
Not letting it decline on the declined,
That I have said unto my standers-by,
'Lo, Jupiter is yonder, dealing life'.   75
And I have seen thee pause and take thy breath,
When that a ring of Greeks have hemmed thee in,
Like an Olympian, wrestling. This have I seen;
But this thy countenance, still locked in steel,
I never saw till now. I knew thy grandsire   80
And once fought with him. He was a soldier good,
But—by great Mars, the captain of us all—
Never like thee. Let an old man embrace thee;
And, worthy warrior, welcome to our tents.
He embraces Hector
AENEAS (*to Hector*) 'Tis the old Nestor.   85
HECTOR
Let me embrace thee, good old chronicle,
That hast so long walked hand in hand with time.
Most reverend Nestor, I am glad to clasp thee.
NESTOR
I would my arms could match thee in contention
As they contend with thee in courtesy.   90
HECTOR I would they could.

NESTOR
Ha! By this white beard I'd fight with thee tomorrow.
Well, welcome, welcome! I have seen the time.
ULYSSES
I wonder now how yonder city stands
When we have here her base and pillar by us?   95
HECTOR
I know your favour, Lord Ulysses, well.
Ah, sir, there's many a Greek and Trojan dead
Since first I saw yourself and Diomed
In Ilium on your Greekish embassy.
ULYSSES
Sir, I foretold you then what would ensue.   100
My prophecy is but half his journey yet;
For yonder walls that pertly front your town,
Yon towers whose wanton tops do buss the clouds,
Must kiss their own feet.
HECTOR   I must not believe you.
There they stand yet, and modestly I think   105
The fall of every Phrygian stone will cost
A drop of Grecian blood. The end crowns all,
And that old common arbitrator Time
Will one day end it.
ULYSSES   So to him we leave it.
Most gentle and most valiant Hector, welcome. 110
⌈*He embraces him*⌉
After the General, I beseech you next
To feast with me and see me at my tent.
ACHILLES
I shall forestall thee, Lord Ulysses. ⌈*To Hector*⌉ Thou!
Now, Hector, I have fed mine eyes on thee.
I have with exact view perused thee, Hector,   115
And quoted joint by joint.
HECTOR Is this Achilles?
ACHILLES I am Achilles.
HECTOR
Stand fair, I pray thee, let me look on thee.
ACHILLES
Behold thy fill.
HECTOR   Nay, I have done already.   120
ACHILLES
Thou art too brief. I will the second time,
As I would buy thee, view thee limb by limb.
HECTOR
O, like a book of sport thou'lt read me o'er.
But there's more in me than thou understand'st.
Why dost thou so oppress me with thine eye?   125
ACHILLES
Tell me, you heavens, in which part of his body
Shall I destroy him—whether there, or there, or
          there—
That I may give the local wound a name,
And make distinct the very breach whereout
Hector's great spirit flew? Answer me, heavens. 130
HECTOR
It would discredit the blest gods, proud man,
To answer such a question. Stand again.
Think'st thou to catch my life so pleasantly

As to prenominate in nice conjecture
Where thou wilt hit me dead?
ACHILLES　　　　　　　　　　　I tell thee, yea.　　135
HECTOR
　Wert thou the oracle to tell me so,
　I'd not believe thee. Henceforth guard thee well.
　For I'll not kill thee there, nor there, nor there,
　But, by the forge that stithied Mars his helm,
　I'll kill thee everywhere, yea, o'er and o'er.—　140
　You wisest Grecians, pardon me this brag:
　His insolence draws folly from my lips.
　But I'll endeavour deeds to match these words,
　Or may I never—
AJAX　　　　　　　Do not chafe thee, cousin.—
　And you, Achilles, let these threats alone,　145
　Till accident or purpose bring you to't.
　You may have every day enough of Hector,
　If you have stomach. The general state, I fear,
　Can scarce entreat you to be odd with him.
HECTOR (to Achilles)
　I pray you, let us see you in the field.　150
　We have had pelting wars since you refused
　The Grecians' cause.
ACHILLES　　　　　　　Dost thou entreat me, Hector?
　Tomorrow do I meet thee, fell as death;
　Tonight, all friends.
HECTOR　　　　　　　Thy hand upon that match.
AGAMEMNON
　First, all you peers of Greece, go to my tent.　155
　There in the full convive you. Afterwards,
　As Hector's leisure and your bounties shall
　Concur together, severally entreat him.
　Beat loud the taborins, let the trumpets blow,
　That this great soldier may his welcome know.　160
　　Flourish. Exeunt all but Troilus and Ulysses
TROILUS
　My Lord Ulysses, tell me, I beseech you,
　In what place of the field doth Calchas keep?
ULYSSES
　At Menelaus' tent, most princely Troilus.
　There Diomed doth feast with him tonight—
　Who neither looks on heaven nor on earth,　165
　But gives all gaze and bent of amorous view
　On the fair Cressid.
TROILUS
　Shall I, sweet lord, be bound to you so much,
　After we part from Agamemnon's tent,
　To bring me thither?
ULYSSES　　　　　　You shall command me, sir.　170
　As gentle tell me, of what honour was
　This Cressida in Troy? Had she no lover there
　That wails her absence?
TROILUS
　O sir, to such as boasting show their scars
　A mock is due. Will you walk on, my lord?　175
　She was beloved, she loved; she is, and doth.
　But still sweet love is food for fortune's tooth.　Exeunt

5.1　　Enter Achilles and Patroclus
ACHILLES
　I'll heat his blood with Greekish wine tonight,
　Which with my scimitar I'll cool tomorrow.
　Patroclus, let us feast him to the height.
PATROCLUS
　Here comes Thersites.
　　Enter Thersites
ACHILLES　　　　　　How now, thou core of envy,
　Thou crusty botch of nature, what's the news?　5
THERSITES Why, thou picture of what thou seemest, and
　idol of idiot-worshippers, here's a letter for thee.
ACHILLES From whence, fragment?
THERSITES Why, thou full dish of fool, from Troy.
　　Achilles reads the letter
PATROCLUS Who keeps the tent now?　10
THERSITES The surgeon's box or the patient's wound.
PATROCLUS Well said, adversity. And what need these
　tricks?
THERSITES Prithee be silent, boy. I profit not by thy talk.
　Thou art thought to be Achilles' male varlet.　15
PATROCLUS 'Male varlet', you rogue? What's that?
THERSITES Why, his masculine whore. Now the rotten
　diseases of the south, guts-griping, ruptures, catarrhs,
　loads o' gravel i'th' back, lethargies, cold palsies, and
　the like, take and take again such preposterous
　discoveries!　21
PATROCLUS Why, thou damnable box of envy thou, what
　mean'st thou to curse thus?
THERSITES Do I curse thee?
PATROCLUS Why, no, you ruinous butt, you whoreson
　indistinguishable cur, no.　26
THERSITES No? Why art thou then exasperate? Thou idle
　immaterial skein of sleave-silk, thou green sarsenet flap
　for a sore eye, thou tassel of a prodigal's purse, thou!
　Ah, how the poor world is pestered with such waterflies!
　Diminutives of nature.　31
PATROCLUS Out, gall!
THERSITES Finch egg!
ACHILLES
　My sweet Patroclus, I am thwarted quite
　From my great purpose in tomorrow's battle.　35
　Here is a letter from Queen Hecuba,
　A token from her daughter, my fair love,
　Both taxing me, and gaging me to keep
　An oath that I have sworn. I will not break it.
　Fall, Greeks; fail, fame; honour, or go or stay.　40
　My major vow lies here; this I'll obey.—
　Come, come, Thersites, help to trim my tent.
　This night in banqueting must all be spent.—
　Away, Patroclus.　　Exeunt Achilles and Patroclus
THERSITES With too much blood and too little brain these
　two may run mad, but if with too much brain and too
　little blood they do, I'll be a curer of madmen. Here's
　Agamemnon: an honest fellow enough, and one that
　loves quails, but he has not so much brain as ear-wax.
　And the goodly transformation of Jupiter there, his
　brother the bull, the primitive statue and oblique

memorial of cuckolds, a thrifty shoeing-horn in a chain, hanging at his brother's leg: to what form but that he is should wit larded with malice and malice farced with wit turn him to? To an ass were nothing: he is both ass and ox. To an ox were nothing: he is both ox and ass. To be a dog, a mule, a cat, a fitchew, a toad, a lizard, an owl, a puttock, or a herring without a roe, I would not care; but to be Menelaus!—I would conspire against destiny. Ask me not what I would be if I were not Thersites, for I care not to be the louse of a lazar, so I were not Menelaus.—Hey-day, sprites and fires.

Enter Hector, Ajax, Agamemnon, Ulysses, Nestor, Menelaus, Troilus, and Diomedes, with lights

AGAMEMNON
We go wrong, we go wrong.

AJAX   No, yonder 'tis:
There, where we see the light.

HECTOR   I trouble you.   65

AJAX
No, not a whit.

Enter Achilles

ULYSSES   Here comes himself to guide you.

ACHILLES
Welcome, brave Hector. Welcome, princes all.

AGAMEMNON (*to Hector*)
So now, fair prince of Troy, I bid good night.
Ajax commands the guard to tend on you.

HECTOR
Thanks and good night to the Greeks' general.   70

MENELAUS
Good night, my lord.

HECTOR   Good night, sweet Lord Menelaus.

THERSITES (*aside*) Sweet draught! 'Sweet', quoth a? Sweet sink, sweet sewer.

ACHILLES
Good night and welcome both at once, to those
That go or tarry.   75

AGAMEMNON Good night.

Exeunt Agamemnon and Menelaus

ACHILLES
Old Nestor tarries, and you too, Diomed.
Keep Hector company an hour or two.

DIOMEDES
I cannot, lord. I have important business
The tide whereof is now.—Good night, great Hector.

HECTOR Give me your hand.   81

ULYSSES (*aside to Troilus*)
Follow his torch, he goes to Calchas' tent.
I'll keep you company.

TROILUS (*aside*)   Sweet sir, you honour me.

HECTOR (*to Diomedes*)
And so good night.

ACHILLES   Come, come, enter my tent.   84

Exeunt Diomedes, followed by Ulysses and Troilus, at one door; and Achilles, Hector, Ajax, and Nestor at another door

THERSITES That same Diomed's a false-hearted rogue, a most unjust knave. I will no more trust him when he leers than I will a serpent when he hisses. He will spend his mouth and promise like Brabbler the hound, but when he performs astronomers foretell it: that is prodigious, there will come some change. The sun borrows of the moon when Diomed keeps his word. I will rather leave to see Hector than not to dog him. They say he keeps a Trojan drab, and uses the traitor Calchas his tent. I'll after.—Nothing but lechery! All incontinent varlets!   *Exit*

5.2   *Enter Diomedes*

DIOMEDES What, are you up here? Ho! Speak!

CALCHAS ⌈*at the door*⌉ Who calls?

DIOMEDES Diomed. Calchas, I think. Where's your daughter?

CALCHAS ⌈*at the door*⌉ She comes to you.   5

Enter Troilus and Ulysses, unseen

ULYSSES (*aside*)
Stand where the torch may not discover us.

TROILUS (*aside*)
Cressid comes forth to him.

Enter Cressida

DIOMEDES   How now, my charge?

CRESSIDA
Now, my sweet guardian. Hark, a word with you.

She whispers to him.

⌈*Enter Thersites, unseen*⌉

TROILUS (*aside*) Yea, so familiar?

ULYSSES (*aside*) She will sing any man at first sight.   10

THERSITES (*aside*) And any man may sing her, if he can take her clef. She's noted.

DIOMEDES Will you remember?

CRESSIDA Remember? Yes.

DIOMEDES Nay, but do then,   15
And let your mind be coupled with your words.

TROILUS (*aside*) What should she remember?

ULYSSES (*aside*) List!

CRESSIDA
Sweet honey Greek, tempt me no more to folly.

THERSITES (*aside*) Roguery.   20

DIOMEDES Nay, then!

CRESSIDA I'll tell you what—

DIOMEDES
Fo, fo! Come, tell a pin. You are forsworn.

CRESSIDA
In faith, I cannot. What would you have me do?

THERSITES (*aside*) A juggling trick: to be secretly open.   25

DIOMEDES
What did you swear you would bestow on me?

CRESSIDA
I prithee, do not hold me to mine oath.
Bid me do anything but that, sweet Greek.

DIOMEDES Good night.

TROILUS (*aside*)
Hold, patience!

ULYSSES (*aside*)   How now, Trojan?

CRESSIDA   Diomed.   30

DIOMEDES
No, no, good night. I'll be your fool no more.

TROILUS (*aside*) Thy better must.
CRESSIDA Hark, one word in your ear.
She whispers to him
TROILUS (*aside*) O plague and madness!
ULYSSES (*aside*)
  You are movèd, Prince. Let us depart, I pray you, 35
  Lest your displeasure should enlarge itself
  To wrathful terms. This place is dangerous,
  The time right deadly. I beseech you go.
TROILUS (*aside*)
  Behold, I pray you.
ULYSSES (*aside*)   Nay, good my lord, go off.
  You flow to great distraction. Come, my lord. 40
TROILUS (*aside*)
  I prithee, stay.
ULYSSES (*aside*)   You have not patience. Come.
TROILUS (*aside*)
  I pray you, stay. By hell and all hell's torments,
  I will not speak a word.
DIOMEDES   And so good night.
CRESSIDA
  Nay, but you part in anger.
TROILUS (*aside*)   Doth that grieve thee?
  O withered truth!
ULYSSES (*aside*)   Why, how now, lord?
TROILUS (*aside*)   By Jove, 45
  I will be patient.
  ⌈*Diomedes starts to go*⌉
CRESSIDA Guardian! Why, Greek!
DIOMEDES Fo, fo! Adieu. You palter.
CRESSIDA
  In faith, I do not. Come hither once again.
ULYSSES (*aside*)
  You shake, my lord, at something. Will you go? 50
  You will break out.
TROILUS (*aside*)   She strokes his cheek.
ULYSSES (*aside*)   Come, come.
TROILUS (*aside*)
  Nay, stay. By Jove, I will not speak a word.
  There is between my will and all offences
  A guard of patience. Stay a little while. 54
THERSITES (*aside*) How the devil Luxury with his fat rump
  and potato finger tickles these together! Fry, lechery,
  fry.
DIOMEDES But will you then?
CRESSIDA
  In faith, I will, la. Never trust me else.
DIOMEDES
  Give me some token for the surety of it. 60
CRESSIDA I'll fetch you one.   *Exit*
ULYSSES (*aside*) You have sworn patience.
TROILUS (*aside*) Fear me not, sweet lord.
  I will not be myself, nor have cognition
  Of what I feel. I am all patience. 65
  Enter Cressida with Troilus' sleeve
THERSITES (*aside*) Now the pledge! Now, now, now.
CRESSIDA Here Diomed, keep this sleeve.
TROILUS (*aside*) O beauty, where is thy faith?

ULYSSES (*aside*) My lord.
TROILUS (*aside*)
  I will be patient; outwardly I will. 70
CRESSIDA
  You look upon that sleeve. Behold it well.
  He loved me—O false wench!—give't me again.
  She takes it back
DIOMEDES Whose was't?
CRESSIDA
  It is no matter, now I ha't again.
  I will not meet with you tomorrow night. 75
  I prithee, Diomed, visit me no more.
THERSITES (*aside*) Now she sharpens. Well said, whetstone.
DIOMEDES I shall have it.
CRESSIDA What, this?
DIOMEDES Ay, that. 80
CRESSIDA
  O all you gods! O pretty pretty pledge!
  Thy master now lies thinking on his bed
  Of thee and me, and sighs, and takes my glove
  And gives memorial dainty kisses to it—
⌈DIOMEDES⌉
  As I kiss thee.
  ⌈*He snatches the sleeve*⌉
⌈CRESSIDA⌉   Nay, do not snatch it from me. 85
  He that takes that doth take my heart withal.
DIOMEDES
  I had your heart before; this follows it.
TROILUS (*aside*) I did swear patience.
CRESSIDA
  You shall not have it, Diomed. Faith, you shall not.
  I'll give you something else.
DIOMEDES   I will have this. Whose was it?
CRESSIDA
  It is no matter.
DIOMEDES   Come, tell me whose it was? 91
CRESSIDA
  'Twas one's that loved me better than you will.
  But now you have it, take it.
DIOMEDES   Whose was it?
CRESSIDA
  By all Diana's waiting-women yond,
  And by herself, I will not tell you whose. 95
DIOMEDES
  Tomorrow will I wear it on my helm,
  And grieve his spirit that dares not challenge it.
TROILUS (*aside*)
  Wert thou the devil and wor'st it on thy horn,
  It should be challenged.
CRESSIDA
  Well, well, 'tis done, 'tis past—and yet it is not. 100
  I will not keep my word.
DIOMEDES   Why then, farewell.
  Thou never shalt mock Diomed again.
CRESSIDA
  You shall not go. One cannot speak a word
  But it straight starts you.
DIOMEDES   I do not like this fooling.

⌈TROILUS⌉ (*aside*)
  Nor I, by Pluto—but that that likes not you   105
  Pleases me best.
DIOMEDES   What, shall I come? The hour—
CRESSIDA
  Ay, come. O Jove, do come. I shall be plagued.
DIOMEDES
  Farewell till then.
CRESSIDA   Good night. I prithee, come.
                           Exit Diomedes
  Troilus, farewell. One eye yet looks on thee,
  But with my heart the other eye doth see.   110
  Ah, poor our sex! This fault in us I find:
  The error of our eye directs our mind.
  What error leads must err. O then conclude:
  Minds swayed by eyes are full of turpitude.   *Exit*
THERSITES (*aside*)
  A proof of strength she could not publish more   115
  Unless she said, 'My mind is now turned whore'.
ULYSSES
  All's done, my lord.
TROILUS   It is.
ULYSSES   Why stay we then?
TROILUS
  To make a recordation to my soul
  Of every syllable that here was spoke.
  But if I tell how these two did co-act,   120
  Shall I not lie in publishing a truth?
  Sith yet there is a credence in my heart,
  An esperance so obstinately strong,
  That doth invert th'attest of eyes and ears,
  As if those organs had deceptious functions   125
  Created only to calumniate.
  Was Cressid here?
ULYSSES   I cannot conjure, Trojan.
TROILUS
  She was not, sure.
ULYSSES   Most sure, she was.
TROILUS
  Why, my negation hath no taste of madness.
ULYSSES
  Nor mine, my lord. Cressid was here but now.   130
TROILUS
  Let it not be believed, for womanhood.
  Think: we had mothers. Do not give advantage
  To stubborn critics, apt without a theme
  For depravation to square the general sex
  By Cressid's rule. Rather, think this not Cressid. 135
ULYSSES
  What hath she done, Prince, that can soil our mothers?
TROILUS
  Nothing at all, unless that this were she.
THERSITES (*aside*) Will a swagger himself out on's own
  eyes?
TROILUS
  This, she? No, this is Diomed's Cressida.   140
  If beauty have a soul, this is not she.
  If souls guide vows, if vows be sanctimonies,

  If sanctimony be the gods' delight,
  If there be rule in unity itself,
  This is not she. O madness of discourse,   145
  That cause sets up with and against thyself!
  Bifold authority, where reason can revolt
  Without perdition, and loss assume all reason
  Without revolt! This is and is not Cressid.
  Within my soul there doth conduce a fight   150
  Of this strange nature, that a thing inseparate
  Divides more wider than the sky and earth,
  And yet the spacious breadth of this division
  Admits no orifex for a point as subtle
  As Ariachne's broken woof to enter.   155
  Instance, O instance, strong as Pluto's gates:
  Cressid is mine, tied with the bonds of heaven.
  Instance, O instance, strong as heaven itself:
  The bonds of heaven are slipped, dissolved, and loosed,
  And with another knot, five-finger-tied,   160
  The fractions of her faith, orts of her love,
  The fragments, scraps, the bits and greasy relics
  Of her o'er-eaten faith, are bound to Diomed.
ULYSSES
  May worthy Troilus e'en be half attached
  With that which here his passion doth express?   165
TROILUS
  Ay, Greek, and that shall be divulgèd well
  In characters as red as Mars his heart
  Inflamed with Venus. Never did young man fancy
  With so eternal and so fixed a soul.
  Hark, Greek: as much as I do Cressid love,   170
  So much by weight hate I her Diomed.
  That sleeve is mine that he'll bear in his helm.
  Were it a casque composed by Vulcan's skill,
  My sword should bite it. Not the dreadful spout
  Which shipmen do the hurricano call,   175
  Constringed in mass by the almighty sun,
  Shall dizzy with more clamour Neptune's ear
  In his descent, than shall my prompted sword
  Falling on Diomed.
THERSITES (*aside*) He'll tickle it for his concupy.   180
TROILUS
  O Cressid, O false Cressid! False, false, false.
  Let all untruths stand by thy stainèd name,
  And they'll seem glorious.
ULYSSES   O contain yourself.
  Your passion draws ears hither.
            Enter Aeneas
AENEAS (*to Troilus*)
  I have been seeking you this hour, my lord.   185
  Hector by this is arming him in Troy.
  Ajax your guard stays to conduct you home.
TROILUS
  Have with you, Prince.—My courteous lord, adieu.—
  Farewell, revolted fair; and Diomed,
  Stand fast and wear a castle on thy head.   190
ULYSSES
  I'll bring you to the gates.
TROILUS   Accept distracted thanks.
          Exeunt Troilus, Aeneas, and Ulysses

THERSITES Would I could meet that rogue Diomed! I would croak like a raven. I would bode, I would bode. Patroclus will give me anything for the intelligence of this whore. The parrot will not do more for an almond than he for a commodious drab. Lechery, lechery, still wars and lechery! Nothing else holds fashion. A burning devil take them!   *Exit*

5.3   *Enter Hector armed, and Andromache*

ANDROMACHE
When was my lord so much ungently tempered
To stop his ears against admonishment?
Unarm, unarm, and do not fight today.

HECTOR
You train me to offend you. Get you in.
By all the everlasting gods, I'll go.   5

ANDROMACHE
My dreams will sure prove ominous to the day.

HECTOR
No more, I say.
              Enter Cassandra

CASSANDRA   Where is my brother Hector?

ANDROMACHE
Here, sister, armed and bloody in intent.
Consort with me in loud and dear petition,
Pursue we him on knees—for I have dreamed   10
Of bloody turbulence, and this whole night
Hath nothing been but shapes and forms of slaughter.

CASSANDRA
O 'tis true.

HECTOR   Ho! Bid my trumpet sound.

CASSANDRA
No notes of sally, for the heavens, sweet brother.

HECTOR
Begone, I say. The gods have heard me swear.   15

CASSANDRA
The gods are deaf to hot and peevish vows.
They are polluted off'rings, more abhorred
Than spotted livers in the sacrifice.

ANDROMACHE (*to Hector*)
O, be persuaded. Do not count it holy
To hurt by being just. It is as lawful,   20
For we would give much, to use violent thefts,
And rob in the behalf of charity.

CASSANDRA
It is the purpose that makes strong the vow,
But vows to every purpose must not hold.
Unarm, sweet Hector.

HECTOR   Hold you still, I say.   25
Mine honour keeps the weather of my fate.
Life every man holds dear, but the dear man
Holds honour far more precious-dear than life.
              Enter Troilus, armed
How now, young man, mean'st thou to fight today?

ANDROMACHE ⌈*aside*⌉
Cassandra, call my father to persuade. *Exit Cassandra*

HECTOR
No, faith, young Troilus. Doff thy harness, youth.   31
I am today i'th' vein of chivalry.

Let grow thy sinews till their knots be strong,
And tempt not yet the brushes of the war.
Unarm thee, go—and doubt thou not, brave boy,   35
I'll stand today for thee and me and Troy.

TROILUS
Brother, you have a vice of mercy in you,
Which better fits a lion than a man.

HECTOR
What vice is that? Good Troilus, chide me for it.

TROILUS
When many times the captive Grecian falls   40
Even in the fan and wind of your fair sword,
You bid them rise and live.

HECTOR O 'tis fair play.

TROILUS Fool's play, by heaven, Hector.

HECTOR How now! How now!   45

TROILUS For th' love of all the gods,
Let's leave the hermit pity with our mother
And, when we have our armours buckled on,
The venomed vengeance ride upon our swords,
Spur them to ruthful work, rein them from ruth.   50

HECTOR
Fie, savage, fie!

TROILUS   Hector, then 'tis wars.

HECTOR
Troilus, I would not have you fight today.

TROILUS Who should withhold me?
Not fate, obedience, nor the hand of Mars
Beck'ning with fiery truncheon my retire,   55
Not Priamus and Hecuba on knees,
Their eyes o'er-gallèd with recourse of tears,
Nor you, my brother, with your true sword drawn
Opposed to hinder me, should stop my way
But by my ruin.   60
              Enter Priam and Cassandra

CASSANDRA
Lay hold upon him, Priam, hold him fast.
He is thy crutch: now if thou loose thy stay,
Thou on him leaning and all Troy on thee,
Fall all together.

PRIAM   Come, Hector, come. Go back.
Thy wife hath dreamt, thy mother hath had visions,
Cassandra doth foresee, and I myself   66
Am like a prophet suddenly enrapt
To tell thee that this day is ominous.
Therefore come back.

HECTOR   Aeneas is afield,
And I do stand engaged to many Greeks,   70
Even in the faith of valour, to appear
This morning to them.

PRIAM Ay, but thou shalt not go.

HECTOR ⌈*kneeling*⌉ I must not break my faith.
You know me dutiful; therefore, dear sire,   75
Let me not shame respect, but give me leave
To take that course, by your consent and voice,
Which you do here forbid me, royal Priam.

CASSANDRA
O Priam, yield not to him.

ANDROMACHE   Do not, dear father.

HECTOR
Andromache, I am offended with you.   80
Upon the love you bear me, get you in.
                                        Exit Andromache

TROILUS
This foolish, dreaming, superstitious girl
Makes all these bodements.

CASSANDRA   O farewell, dear Hector.
Look how thou diest; look how thy eye turns pale;
Look how thy wounds do bleed at many vents.   85
Hark how Troy roars, how Hecuba cries out,
How poor Andromache shrills her dolours forth.
Behold: distraction, frenzy, and amazement
Like witless antics one another meet,
And all cry 'Hector, Hector's dead, O Hector!'   90

TROILUS Away, away!

CASSANDRA
Farewell. Yet soft: Hector, I take my leave.
Thou dost thyself and all our Troy deceive.   *Exit*

HECTOR *(to Priam)*
You are amazed, my liege, at her exclaim.
Go in and cheer the town. We'll forth and fight,   95
Do deeds of praise, and tell you them at night.

PRIAM
Farewell. The gods with safety stand about thee.
                Exeunt Priam and Hector severally. Alarum

TROILUS
They are at it, hark! Proud Diomed, believe
I come to lose my arm or win my sleeve.
                                    Enter Pandarus

PANDARUS Do you hear, my lord, do you hear?   100

TROILUS What now?

PANDARUS Here's a letter come from yon poor girl.

TROILUS Let me read.
                        Troilus reads the letter

PANDARUS A whoreson phthisic, a whoreson rascally
phthisic so troubles me, and the foolish fortune of this
girl, and what one thing, what another, that I shall
leave you one o' these days. And I have a rheum in
mine eyes too, and such an ache in my bones that
unless a man were cursed I cannot tell what to think
on't.—What says she there?   110

TROILUS *(tearing the letter)*
Words, words, mere words, no matter from the heart.
Th'effect doth operate another way.
Go, wind, to wind: there turn and change together.
My love with words and errors still she feeds,
But edifies another with her deeds.   115

PANDARUS Why, but hear you—

TROILUS
Hence, broker-lackey! Ignomy and shame
Pursue thy life, and live aye with thy name.
                                    Exeunt severally

5.4   *Alarum. Enter Thersites* ⌜*in*⌝ *excursions*

THERSITES Now they are clapper-clawing one another. I'll
go look on. That dissembling abominable varlet Diomed
has got that same scurvy doting foolish young knave's

sleeve of Troy there in his helm. I would fain see them
meet, that that same young Trojan ass that loves the
whore there might send that Greekish whoremasterly
villain with the sleeve back to the dissembling luxurious
drab of a sleeveless errand. O'th' t'other side, the policy
of those crafty swearing rascals—that stale old mouse-
eaten dry cheese Nestor and that same dog-fox
Ulysses—is proved not worth a blackberry. They set
me up in policy that mongrel cur Ajax against that
dog of as bad a kind Achilles. And now is the cur Ajax
prouder than the cur Achilles, and will not arm today—
whereupon the Grecians began to proclaim barbarism,
and policy grows into an ill opinion.   16
                Enter Diomedes, followed by Troilus
Soft, here comes sleeve and t'other.

TROILUS *(to Diomedes)*
Fly not, for shouldst thou take the river Styx
I would swim after.

DIOMEDES   Thou dost miscall retire.
I do not fly, but advantageous care   20
Withdrew me from the odds of multitude. Have at
   thee!
                                    They fight

THERSITES Hold thy whore, Grecian! Now for thy whore,
Trojan! Now the sleeve, now the sleeve!
                    Exit Diomedes ⌜*driving in*⌝ *Troilus*
                        Enter Hector ⌜*behind*⌝

HECTOR
What art thou, Greek? Art thou for Hector's match?
Art thou of blood and honour?   25

THERSITES No, no, I am a rascal, a scurvy railing knave,
a very filthy rogue.

HECTOR I do believe thee: live.

THERSITES God-a-mercy, that thou wilt believe me—
                                        ⌜*Exit Hector*⌝
but a plague break thy neck for frighting me. What's
become of the wenching rogues? I think they have
swallowed one another. I would laugh at that miracle—
yet in a sort lechery eats itself. I'll seek them.   *Exit*

5.5   *Enter Diomedes and Servants*

DIOMEDES
Go, go, my servant, take thou Troilus' horse.
Present the fair steed to my Lady Cressid.
Fellow, commend my service to her beauty.
Tell her I have chastised the amorous Trojan,
And am her knight by proof.

SERVANT   I go, my lord.   *Exit*
                                Enter Agamemnon

AGAMEMNON
Renew, renew! The fierce Polydamas   6
Hath beat down Menon; bastard Margareton
Hath Doreus prisoner,
And stands colossus-wise waving his beam
Upon the pashèd corpses of the kings   10
Epistropus and Cedius; Polixenes is slain,
Amphimacus and Thoas deadly hurt,
Patroclus ta'en or slain, and Palamedes

Sore hurt and bruised; the dreadful sagittary
Appals our numbers. Haste we, Diomed,   15
To reinforcement, or we perish all.
   Enter Nestor ⌈with Patroclus' body⌉
NESTOR
  Go, bear Patroclus' body to Achilles,
  And bid the snail-paced Ajax arm for shame.
            ⌈Exit one or more with the body⌉
  There is a thousand Hectors in the field.
  Now here he fights on Galathe his horse,   20
  And there lacks work; anon he's there afoot,
  And there they fly or die, like scalèd schools
  Before the belching whale. Then is he yonder,
  And there the strawy Greeks, ripe for his edge,
  Fall down before him like the mower's swath.   25
  Here, there, and everywhere he leaves and takes,
  Dexterity so obeying appetite
  That what he will he does, and does so much
  That proof is called impossibility.
   Enter Ulysses
ULYSSES
  O courage, courage, princes! Great Achilles   30
  Is arming, weeping, cursing, vowing vengeance.
  Patroclus' wounds have roused his drowsy blood,
  Together with his mangled Myrmidons,
  That noseless, handless, hacked and chipped come to
    him
  Crying on Hector. Ajax hath lost a friend   35
  And foams at mouth, and he is armed and at it,
  Roaring for Troilus—who hath done today
  Mad and fantastic execution,
  Engaging and redeeming of himself
  With such a careless force and forceless care   40
  As if that luck, in very spite of cunning,
  Bade him win all.
   Enter Ajax
AJAX Troilus, thou coward Troilus!   *Exit*
DIOMEDES Ay, there, there!   *⌈Exit⌉*
NESTOR So, so, we draw together.   45
   Enter Achilles
ACHILLES Where is this Hector?
  Come, come, thou brave boy-queller, show thy face.
  Know what it is to meet Achilles angry.
  Hector! Where's Hector? I will none but Hector.
                  ⌈Exeunt⌉

5.6 *Enter Ajax*
AJAX
  Troilus, thou coward Troilus! Show thy head!
   Enter Diomedes
DIOMEDES
  Troilus, I say! Where's Troilus?
AJAX   What wouldst thou?
DIOMEDES I would correct him.
AJAX
  Were I the general, thou shouldst have my office
  Ere that correction.—Troilus, I say! What, Troilus!   5

   Enter Troilus
TROILUS
  O traitor Diomed! Turn thy false face, thou traitor,
  And pay the life thou ow'st me for my horse.
DIOMEDES Ha, art thou there?
AJAX
  I'll fight with him alone. Stand, Diomed.
DIOMEDES
  He is my prize; I will not look upon.   10
TROILUS
  Come, both you cogging Greeks, have at you both!
   They fight.
   Enter Hector
HECTOR
  Yea, Troilus? O well fought, my youngest brother!
      Exit Troilus ⌈driving Diomedes and Ajax in⌉
   Enter Achilles ⌈behind⌉
ACHILLES
  Now do I see thee.—Ha! Have at thee, Hector.
   They fight. ⌈Achilles is bested⌉
HECTOR Pause, if thou wilt.
ACHILLES
  I do disdain thy courtesy, proud Trojan.   15
  Be happy that my arms are out of use.
  My rest and negligence befriends thee now;
  But thou anon shalt here of me again.
  Till when, go seek thy fortune.   *Exit*
HECTOR   Fare thee well.
  I would have been much more a fresher man   20
  Had I expected thee.
   Enter Troilus ⌈in haste⌉
             How now, my brother?
TROILUS
  Ajax hath ta'en Aeneas. Shall it be?
  No, by the flame of yonder glorious heaven,
  He shall not carry him. I'll be ta'en too,
  Or bring him off. Fate, hear me what I say: 25
  I reck not though thou end my life today.   *Exit*
   Enter one in sumptuous armour
HECTOR
  Stand, stand, thou Greek! Thou art a goodly mark.
  No? Wilt thou not? I like thy armour well.
  I'll frush it and unlock the rivets all,
  But I'll be master of it.   *⌈Exit one in armour⌉*
             Wilt thou not, beast, abide?   30
  Why then, fly on; I'll hunt thee for thy hide.   *Exit*

5.7 *Enter Achilles with Myrmidons*
ACHILLES
  Come here about me, you my Myrmidons.
  Mark what I say. Attend me where I wheel;
  Strike not a stroke, but keep yourselves in breath,
  And when I have the bloody Hector found,
  Empale him with your weapons round about.   5
  In fellest manner execute your arms.
  Follow me, sirs, and my proceedings eye.
  It is decreed Hector the great must die.   *Exeunt*

5.8　　*Enter Menelaus and Paris, fighting, ⌜then⌝ Thersites*

THERSITES The cuckold and the cuckold-maker are at it.—
Now, bull! Now, dog! 'Loo, Paris, 'loo! Now, my
double-horned Spartan! 'Loo, Paris, 'loo! The bull has
the game. Ware horns, ho!

Exit Menelaus ⌜driving in⌝ Paris
Enter Bastard ⌜behind⌝

BASTARD Turn, slave, and fight.　　　　　　　　　　　5

THERSITES What art thou?

BASTARD A bastard son of Priam's.

THERSITES I am a bastard, too. I love bastards. I am
bastard begot, bastard instructed, bastard in mind,
bastard in valour, in everything illegitimate. One bear
will not bite another, and wherefore should one
bastard? Take heed: the quarrel's most ominous to us.
If the son of a whore fight for a whore, he tempts
judgement. Farewell, bastard.　　　　　　⌜*Exit*⌝

BASTARD The devil take thee, coward.　　　　　*Exit*

5.9　　*Enter Hector ⌜dragging⌝ the one in sumptuous*
armour

HECTOR ⌜*taking off the helmet*⌝
Most putrefièd core, so fair without,
Thy goodly armour thus hath cost thy life.
Now is my day's work done. I'll take good breath.
Rest, sword: thou hast thy fill of blood and death.
He disarms.
Enter Achilles and his Myrmidons, surrounding
Hector

ACHILLES
Look, Hector, how the sun begins to set,　　　　　5
How ugly night comes breathing at his heels.
Even with the veil and dark'ning of the sun
To close the day up, Hector's life is done.

HECTOR
I am unarmed. Forgo this vantage, Greek.

ACHILLES
Strike, fellows, strike! This is the man I seek.　　10
⌜*The Myrmidons*⌝ *kill Hector*
So, Ilium, fall thou. Now, Troy, sink down.
Here lies thy heart, thy sinews, and thy bone.—
On, Myrmidons, and cry you all amain,
'Achilles hath the mighty Hector slain!'
A retreat is sounded
Hark, a retire upon our Grecian part.　　　　　　15
⌜*Another retreat is sounded*⌝

A MYRMIDON
The Trojan trumpets sound the like, my lord.

ACHILLES
The dragon wing of night o'erspreads the earth
And, stickler-like, the armies separates.
My half-supped sword, that frankly would have fed,
Pleased with this dainty bait, thus goes to bed.　20
He sheathes his sword
Come, tie his body to my horse's tail.
Along the field I will the Trojan trail.
Exeunt, dragging the bodies

5.10　　*A retreat is sounded. Enter Agamemnon, Ajax,*
Menelaus, Nestor, Diomedes, and the rest,
marching. ⌜A shout within⌝

AGAMEMNON
Hark, hark! What shout is that?

NESTOR　　　　　　　　　　　　Peace, drums.

MYRMIDONS (*within*)　　　　　　　　　　　Achilles!
Achilles! Hector's slain! Achilles!

DIOMEDES
The bruit is: Hector's slain, and by Achilles.

AJAX
If it be so, yet bragless let it be.
Great Hector was a man as good as he.　　　　　5

AGAMEMNON
March patiently along. Let one be sent
To pray Achilles see us at our tent.
If in his death the gods have us befriended,
Great Troy is ours, and our sharp wars are ended.
Exeunt ⌜marching⌝

5.11　　*Enter Aeneas, Paris, Antenor, and Deiphobus*

AENEAS
Stand, ho! Yet are we masters of the field.
Never go home; here starve we out the night.
Enter Troilus

TROILUS
Hector is slain.

ALL THE OTHERS　Hector? The gods forbid.

TROILUS
He's dead, and at the murderer's horse's tail
In beastly sort dragged through the shameful field.　5
Frown on, you heavens; effect your rage with speed;
Sit, gods, upon your thrones, and smite at Troy.
I say, at once: let your brief plagues be mercy,
And linger not our sure destructions on.

AENEAS
My lord, you do discomfort all the host.　　　　10

TROILUS
You understand me not that tell me so.
I do not speak of flight, of fear of death,
But dare all imminence that gods and men
Address their dangers in. Hector is gone.
Who shall tell Priam so, or Hecuba?　　　　　　15
Let him that will a screech-owl aye be called
Go into Troy and say their Hector's dead.
There is a word will Priam turn to stone,
Make wells and Niobes of the maids and wives,
Cold statues of the youth, and in a word　　　　20
Scare Troy out of itself. But march away.
Hector is dead; there is no more to say.
Stay yet.—You vile abominable tents
Thus proudly pitched upon our Phrygian plains,
Let Titan rise as early as he dare,　　　　　　　25
I'll through and through you! And thou great-sized
　　coward,
No space of earth shall sunder our two hates.
I'll haunt thee like a wicked conscience still,

That mouldeth goblins swift as frenzy's thoughts.
Strike a free march! To Troy with comfort go: 30

Hope of revenge shall hide our inward woe.
                                                    ⌜Exeunt marching⌝

ADDITIONAL PASSAGES

A. The Quarto (below) gives a more elaborate version of
Thersites' speech at 5.1.17–21.

THERSITES Why, his masculine whore. Now the rotten
  diseases of the south, the guts-griping, ruptures, loads
  o' gravel in the back, lethargies, cold palsies, raw
  eyes, dirt-rotten livers, wheezing lungs, bladders full of
  impostume, sciaticas, lime-kilns i'th' palm, incurable
  bone-ache, and the rivelled fee-simple of the tetter, take
  and take again such preposterous discoveries.

B. The Quarto gives a different ending to the play (which
the Folio inadvertently repeats).

        Enter Pandarus
PANDARUS But hear you, hear you.
TROILUS
  Hence, broker-lackey. ⌜Strikes him⌝ Ignomy and shame
  Pursue thy life, and live aye with thy name.
                                Exeunt all but Pandarus
PANDARUS A goodly medicine for my aching bones. O
  world, world, world!—thus is the poor agent despised.

O traitors and bawds, how earnestly are you set a
work, and how ill requited! Why should our endeavour
be so desired and the performance so loathed? What
verse for it? What instance for it? Let me see,
        Full merrily the humble-bee doth sing   10
        Till he hath lost his honey and his sting,
        And being once subdued in armèd tail,
        Sweet honey and sweet notes together fail.
Good traders in the flesh, set this in your painted cloths:
        As many as be here of Pandar's hall,   15
Your eyes, half out, weep out at Pandar's fall.
Or if you cannot weep, yet give some groans,
Though not for me, yet for your aching bones.
Brethren and sisters of the hold-door trade,
Some two months hence my will shall here be made. 20
It should be now, but that my fear is this:
Some gallèd goose of Winchester would hiss.
Till then I'll sweat and seek about for eases,
And at that time bequeath you my diseases.   Exit

MEASURE FOR MEASURE

Measure for Measure, first printed in the 1623 Folio, was performed at court on 26 December 1604. Plague had caused London's theatres to be closed from May 1603 to April 1604; the play was probably written and first acted during 1604. Dislocations and other features of the text as printed suggest that it may have undergone adaptation after Shakespeare's death. Someone—perhaps Thomas Middleton, to judge by the style—seems to have supplied a new, seedy opening to Act 1, Scene 2; and an adapter seems also to have altered 3.1.517-4.1.63 by transposing the Duke's two soliloquies, by introducing a stanza from a popular song, and by supplying dialogue to follow it. We print the text in what we believe to be its adapted form; a conjectural reconstruction of Shakespeare's original version of the adapted sections is given in the Additional Passages.

The story of a woman who, in seeking to save the life of a male relative, arouses the lust of a man in authority was an ancient one that reached literary form in the mid sixteenth century. Shakespeare may have known the prose version in Giambattista Cinzio Giraldi's *Gli Ecatommiti* (1565, translated into French in 1583) and the same author's play *Epitia* (1573, published in 1583), but his main source was George Whetstone's unsuccessful, unperformed two-part tragicomedy *Promos and Cassandra*, published in 1578.

Shakespeare's title comes from Saint Matthew's account of Christ's Sermon on the Mount: 'with what measure ye mete, it shall be measured to you again'. The title is not expressive of the play's morality, but it alerts the spectator to Shakespeare's exploration of moral issues. His heroine, Isabella, is not merely, as in Whetstone, a virtuous young maiden: she is about to enter a nunnery. Her brother, Claudio, has not, as in Whetstone, been accused (however unjustly) of rape: his union with the girl (Juliet) he has made pregnant has been ratified by a betrothal ceremony, and lacks only the church's formal blessing. So Angelo, deputizing for the absent Duke of Vienna, seems peculiarly harsh in attempting to enforce the city's laws against fornication by insisting on Claudio's execution; and Angelo's hypocrisy in demanding Isabella's chastity in return for her brother's life seems correspondingly greater. By adding the character of Mariana, to whom Angelo himself had once been betrothed, and by employing the traditional motif of the 'bed-trick', by which Mariana substitutes for Isabella in Angelo's bed, Shakespeare permits Isabella both to retain her virtue and to forgive Angelo without marrying him.

Although *Measure for Measure*, like *The Merchant of Venice*, is much concerned with justice and mercy, its more explicit concern with sex and death along with the intense emotional reality, at least in the earlier part of the play, of its portrayal of Angelo, Isabella, and Claudio, creates a deeper seriousness of tone which takes it out of the world of romantic comedy into that of tragicomedy or, as the twentieth-century label has it, 'problem play'. Its low-life characters inhabit a diseased world of brothels and prisons, but there is a life-enhancing quality in their frank acknowledgement of sexuality; and the Duke's manipulation of events casts a tinge of romance over the play's later scenes.

Measure for Measure's subtle and passionate exploration of issues of sexual morality, of the uses and abuses of power, has given it a special appeal in the later part of the twentieth century. Each of the 'good' characters fails in some respect; none of the 'bad' ones lacks some redeeming quality; all are, in the last analysis, 'desperately mortal' (4.2.148).

THE PERSONS OF THE PLAY

Vincentio, the DUKE of Vienna
ANGELO, appointed his deputy
ESCALUS, an old lord, appointed Angelo's secondary

CLAUDIO, a young gentleman
JULIET, betrothed to Claudio
ISABELLA, Claudio's sister, novice to a sisterhood of nuns

LUCIO, 'a fantastic'
Two other such GENTLEMEN
FROTH, a foolish gentleman
MISTRESS OVERDONE, a bawd
POMPEY, her clownish servant

A PROVOST
ELBOW, a simple constable
A JUSTICE
ABHORSON, an executioner
BARNARDINE, a dissolute condemned prisoner

MARIANA, betrothed to Angelo
A BOY, attendant on Mariana

FRIAR PETER
FRANCESCA, a nun

VARRIUS, a lord, friend to the Duke

Lords, officers, citizens, servants

Measure for Measure

1.1 *Enter the Duke, Escalus, and other lords*

DUKE Escalus.

ESCALUS My lord.

DUKE
Of government the properties to unfold
Would seem in me t'affect speech and discourse,
Since I am put to know that your own science   5
Exceeds in that the lists of all advice
My strength can give you. Then no more remains
But this: to your sufficiency, as your worth is able,
And let them work. The nature of our people,
Our city's institutions and the terms   10
For common justice, you're as pregnant in
As art and practice hath enrichèd any
That we remember.
    He gives Escalus papers
                There is our commission,
From which we would not have you warp.
(To a lord)   Call hither,
I say bid come before us, Angelo.   *Exit lord*
(To Escalus) What figure of us think you he will
    bear?—   16
For you must know we have with special soul
Elected him our absence to supply,
Lent him our terror, dressed him with our love,
And given his deputation all the organs   20
Of our own power. What think you of it?

ESCALUS
If any in Vienna be of worth
To undergo such ample grace and honour,
It is Lord Angelo.
    Enter Angelo

DUKE   Look where he comes.

ANGELO
Always obedient to your grace's will,   25
I come to know your pleasure.

DUKE   Angelo,
There is a kind of character in thy life
That to th'observer doth thy history
Fully unfold. Thyself and thy belongings
Are not thine own so proper as to waste   30
Thyself upon thy virtues, they on thee.
Heaven doth with us as we with torches do,
Not light them for themselves; for if our virtues
Did not go forth of us, 'twere all alike
As if we had them not. Spirits are not finely touched
But to fine issues; nor nature never lends   36
The smallest scruple of her excellence
But, like a thrifty goddess, she determines
Herself the glory of a creditor,
Both thanks and use. But I do bend my speech   40
To one that can my part in him advertise.

Hold therefore, Angelo.
In our remove be thou at full ourself.
Mortality and mercy in Vienna
Live in thy tongue and heart. Old Escalus,   45
Though first in question, is thy secondary.
Take thy commission.

ANGELO   Now good my lord,
Let there be some more test made of my metal
Before so noble and so great a figure
Be stamped upon it.

DUKE   No more evasion.   50
We have with leavened and preparèd choice
Proceeded to you; therefore take your honours.
    ⌜Angelo takes his commission⌝
Our haste from hence is of so quick condition
That it prefers itself, and leaves unquestioned
Matters of needful value. We shall write to you   55
As time and our concernings shall importune,
How it goes with us; and do look to know
What doth befall you here. So fare you well.
To th' hopeful execution do I leave you
Of your commissions.

ANGELO   Yet give leave, my lord,   60
That we may bring you something on the way.

DUKE My haste may not admit it;
Nor need you, on mine honour, have to do
With any scruple. Your scope is as mine own,
So to enforce or qualify the laws   65
As to your soul seems good. Give me your hand.
I'll privily away. I love the people,
But do not like to stage me to their eyes.
Though it do well, I do not relish well
Their loud applause and *aves* vehement;   70
Nor do I think the man of safe discretion
That does affect it. Once more, fare you well.

ANGELO
The heavens give safety to your purposes!

ESCALUS
Lead forth and bring you back in happiness!

DUKE I thank you. Fare you well.

ESCALUS
I shall desire you, sir, to give me leave
To have free speech with you; and it concerns me
To look into the bottom of my place.
A power I have, but of what strength and nature
I am not yet instructed.   80

ANGELO
'Tis so with me. Let us withdraw together,
And we may soon our satisfaction have
Touching that point.

ESCALUS   I'll wait upon your honour.
                        Exeunt

1.2 *Enter Lucio, and two other Gentlemen*

LUCIO If the Duke with the other dukes come not to composition with the King of Hungary, why then, all the dukes fall upon the King.

FIRST GENTLEMAN Heaven grant us its peace, but not the King of Hungary's!   5

SECOND GENTLEMAN Amen.

LUCIO Thou concludest like the sanctimonious pirate, that went to sea with the Ten Commandments, but scraped one out of the table.

SECOND GENTLEMAN 'Thou shalt not steal'?   10

LUCIO Ay, that he razed.

FIRST GENTLEMAN Why, 'twas a commandment to command the captain and all the rest from their functions: they put forth to steal. There's not a soldier of us all that in the thanksgiving before meat do relish the petition well that prays for peace.   16

SECOND GENTLEMAN I never heard any soldier dislike it.

LUCIO I believe thee, for I think thou never wast where grace was said.

SECOND GENTLEMAN No? A dozen times at least.   20

FIRST GENTLEMAN What, in metre?

LUCIO In any proportion, or in any language.

FIRST GENTLEMAN I think, or in any religion.

LUCIO Ay, why not? Grace is grace despite of all controversy; as for example, thou thyself art a wicked villain despite of all grace.   26

FIRST GENTLEMAN Well, there went but a pair of shears between us.

LUCIO I grant—as there may between the lists and the velvet. Thou art the list.   30

FIRST GENTLEMAN And thou the velvet. Thou art good velvet, thou'rt a three-piled piece, I warrant thee. I had as lief be a list of an English kersey as be piled as thou art pilled, for a French velvet. Do I speak feelingly now?

LUCIO I think thou dost, and indeed with most painful feeling of thy speech. I will out of thine own confession learn to begin thy health, but whilst I live forget to drink after thee.

FIRST GENTLEMAN I think I have done myself wrong, have I not?   40

SECOND GENTLEMAN Yes, that thou hast, whether thou art tainted or free.

Enter Mistress Overdone

LUCIO Behold, behold, where Madam Mitigation comes! I have purchased as many diseases under her roof as come to—   45

SECOND GENTLEMAN To what, I pray?

LUCIO Judge.

SECOND GENTLEMAN To three thousand dolours a year?

FIRST GENTLEMAN Ay, and more.

LUCIO A French crown more.   50

FIRST GENTLEMAN Thou art always figuring diseases in me, but thou art full of error—I am sound.

LUCIO Nay not, as one would say, healthy, but so sound as things that are hollow—thy bones are hollow, impiety has made a feast of thee.   55

FIRST GENTLEMAN (*to Mistress Overdone*) How now, which of your hips has the most profound sciatica?

MISTRESS OVERDONE Well, well! There's one yonder arrested and carried to prison was worth five thousand of you all.   60

SECOND GENTLEMAN Who's that, I pray thee?

MISTRESS OVERDONE Marry sir, that's Claudio, Signor Claudio.

FIRST GENTLEMAN Claudio to prison? 'Tis not so.   64

MISTRESS OVERDONE Nay, but I know 'tis so. I saw him arrested, saw him carried away; and, which is more, within these three days his head to be chopped off.

LUCIO But after all this fooling, I would not have it so. Art thou sure of this?

MISTRESS OVERDONE I am too sure of it, and it is for getting Madame Julietta with child.   71

LUCIO Believe me, this may be. He promised to meet me two hours since and he was ever precise in promise-keeping.

SECOND GENTLEMAN Besides, you know, it draws something near to the speech we had to such a purpose.   76

FIRST GENTLEMAN But most of all agreeing with the proclamation.

LUCIO Away; let's go learn the truth of it.

Exeunt Lucio and Gentlemen

MISTRESS OVERDONE Thus, what with the war, what with the sweat, what with the gallows, and what with poverty, I am custom-shrunk.   82

Enter Pompey

How now, what's the news with you?

POMPEY You have not heard of the proclamation, have you?   85

MISTRESS OVERDONE What proclamation, man?

POMPEY All houses in the suburbs of Vienna must be plucked down.

MISTRESS OVERDONE And what shall become of those in the city?   90

POMPEY They shall stand for seed. They had gone down too, but that a wise burgher put in for them.

MISTRESS OVERDONE But shall all our houses of resort in the suburbs be pulled down?

POMPEY To the ground, mistress.   95

MISTRESS OVERDONE Why, here's a change indeed in the commonwealth. What shall become of me?

POMPEY Come, fear not you. Good counsellors lack no clients. Though you change your place, you need not change your trade. I'll be your tapster still. Courage, there will be pity taken on you. You that have worn your eyes almost out in the service, you will be considered.   103

⌈*A noise within*⌉

MISTRESS OVERDONE What's to do here, Thomas Tapster? Let's withdraw!   105

Enter the Provost, Claudio, Juliet, and officers; Lucio and the two Gentlemen

POMPEY Here comes Signor Claudio, led by the Provost to prison; and there's Madame Juliet.

Exeunt Mistress Overdone and Pompey

CLAUDIO (*to the Provost*)
Fellow, why dost thou show me thus to th' world?
Bear me to prison, where I am committed.

PROVOST
  I do it not in evil disposition,   110
  But from Lord Angelo by special charge.
CLAUDIO
  Thus can the demigod Authority
  Make us pay down for our offence, by weight,
  The bonds of heaven. On whom it will, it will;
  On whom it will not, so; yet still 'tis just.   115
LUCIO
  Why, how now, Claudio? Whence comes this
    restraint?
CLAUDIO
  From too much liberty, my Lucio, liberty.
  As surfeit is the father of much fast,
  So every scope, by the immoderate use,
  Turns to restraint. Our natures do pursue,   120
  Like rats that raven down their proper bane,
  A thirsty evil; and when we drink, we die.
LUCIO If I could speak so wisely under an arrest, I would
  send for certain of my creditors. And yet, to say the
  truth, I had as lief have the foppery of freedom as the
  morality of imprisonment. What's thy offence, Claudio?
CLAUDIO
  What but to speak of would offend again.   127
LUCIO
  What, is't murder?
CLAUDIO   No.
LUCIO   ·   Lechery?
CLAUDIO   Call it so.
PROVOST Away, sir; you must go.
CLAUDIO
  One word, good friend.
    ⌜The Provost shows assent⌝
               Lucio, a word with you.   130
LUCIO A hundred, if they'll do you any good.
    ⌜Claudio and Lucio speak apart⌝
  Is lechery so looked after?
CLAUDIO
  Thus stands it with me. Upon a true contract,
  I got possession of Julietta's bed.
  You know the lady; she is fast my wife,   135
  Save that we do the denunciation lack
  Of outward order. This we came not to
  Only for propagation of a dower
  Remaining in the coffer of her friends,
  From whom we thought it meet to hide our love   140
  Till time had made them for us. But it chances
  The stealth of our most mutual entertainment
  With character too gross is writ on Juliet.
LUCIO
  With child, perhaps?
CLAUDIO   Unhapp'ly even so.
  And the new deputy now for the Duke—   145
  Whether it be the fault and glimpse of newness,
  Or whether that the body public be
  A horse whereon the governor doth ride,
  Who, newly in the seat, that it may know
  He can command, lets it straight feel the spur—   150

  Whether the tyranny be in his place,
  Or in his eminence that fills it up—
  I stagger in. But this new governor
  Awakes me all the enrollèd penalties
  Which have, like unscoured armour, hung by th' wall
  So long that fourteen zodiacs have gone round,   156
  And none of them been worn; and, for a name,
  Now puts the drowsy and neglected act
  Freshly on me. 'Tis surely for a name.   159
LUCIO I warrant it is; and thy head stands so tickle on
  thy shoulders that a milkmaid, if she be in love, may
  sigh it off. Send after the Duke, and appeal to him.
CLAUDIO
  I have done so, but he's not to be found.
  I prithee, Lucio, do me this kind service.
  This day my sister should the cloister enter,   165
  And there receive her approbation.
  Acquaint her with the danger of my state.
  Implore her in my voice that she make friends
  To the strict deputy. Bid herself assay him.
  I have great hope in that, for in her youth   170
  There is a prone and speechless dialect
  Such as move men; beside, she hath prosperous art
  When she will play with reason and discourse,
  And well she can persuade.   174
LUCIO I pray she may—as well for the encouragement of
  thy like, which else would stand under grievous
  imposition, as for the enjoying of thy life, who I would
  be sorry should be thus foolishly lost at a game of tick-
  tack. I'll to her.
CLAUDIO I thank you, good friend Lucio.   180
LUCIO Within two hours.
CLAUDIO Come, officer; away.
            Exeunt ⌜Lucio and gentlemen at one door;
         Claudio, Juliet, Provost, and officers at another⌝

1.3   *Enter the Duke and a Friar*
DUKE
  No, holy father, throw away that thought.
  Believe not that the dribbling dart of love
  Can pierce a complete bosom. Why I desire thee
  To give me secret harbour hath a purpose
  More grave and wrinkled than the aims and ends   5
  Of burning youth.
FRIAR   May your grace speak of it?
DUKE
  My holy sir, none better knows than you
  How I have ever loved the life removed,
  And held in idle price to haunt assemblies
  Where youth and cost a witless bravery keeps.   10
  I have delivered to Lord Angelo—
  A man of stricture and firm abstinence—
  My absolute power and place here in Vienna;
  And he supposes me travelled to Poland—
  For so I have strewed it in the common ear,   15
  And so it is received. Now, pious sir,
  You will demand of me why I do this.
FRIAR Gladly, my lord.

DUKE
  We have strict statutes and most biting laws,
  The needful bits and curbs to headstrong weeds,   20
  Which for this fourteen years we have let slip;
  Even like an o'ergrown lion in a cave
  That goes not out to prey. Now, as fond fathers,
  Having bound up the threat'ning twigs of birch
  Only to stick it in their children's sight   25
  For terror, not to use, in time the rod
  More mocked becomes than feared: so our decrees,
  Dead to infliction, to themselves are dead;
  And Liberty plucks Justice by the nose,
  The baby beats the nurse, and quite athwart   30
  Goes all decorum.
FRIAR   It rested in your grace
  To unloose this tied-up Justice when you pleased,
  And it in you more dreadful would have seemed
  Than in Lord Angelo.
DUKE   I do fear, too dreadful.
  Sith 'twas my fault to give the people scope,   35
  'Twould be my tyranny to strike and gall them
  For what I bid them do—for we bid this be done
  When evil deeds have their permissive pass,
  And not the punishment. Therefore indeed, my father,
  I have on Angelo imposed the office,   40
  Who may in th'ambush of my name strike home,
  And yet my nature never in the fight
  T'allow in slander. And to behold his sway,
  I will as 'twere a brother of your order
  Visit both prince and people. Therefore, I prithee,   45
  Supply me with the habit, and instruct me
  How I may formally in person bear
  Like a true friar. More reasons for this action
  At our more leisure shall I render you.
  Only this one: Lord Angelo is precise,   50
  Stands at a guard with envy, scarce confesses
  That his blood flows, or that his appetite
  Is more to bread than stone. Hence shall we see
  If power change purpose, what our seemers be.
                                                  Exeunt

1.4   *Enter Isabella, and Francesca, a nun*
ISABELLA
  And have you nuns no farther privileges?
FRANCESCA Are not these large enough?
ISABELLA
  Yes, truly. I speak not as desiring more,
  But rather wishing a more strict restraint
  Upon the sisterhood, the votarists of Saint Clare.   5
LUCIO (*within*)
  Ho, peace be in this place!
ISABELLA ⌈*to Francesca*⌉   Who's that which calls?
FRANCESCA
  It is a man's voice. Gentle Isabella.
  Turn you the key, and know his business of him.
  You may, I may not; you are yet unsworn.
  When you have vowed, you must not speak with men
  But in the presence of the prioress.   11

Then if you speak, you must not show your face;
  Or if you show your face, you must not speak.
            Lucio calls within
  He calls again. I pray you answer him.
            ⌈*She stands aside*⌉
ISABELLA
  Peace and prosperity! Who is't that calls?   15
            She opens the door.
            Enter Lucio
LUCIO
  Hail, virgin, if you be—as those cheek-roses
  Proclaim you are no less. Can you so stead me
  As bring me to the sight of Isabella,
  A novice of this place, and the fair sister
  To her unhappy brother Claudio?   20
ISABELLA
  Why her unhappy brother? Let me ask,
  The rather for I now must make you know
  I am that Isabella, and his sister.
LUCIO
  Gentle and fair, your brother kindly greets you.
  Not to be weary with you, he's in prison.   25
ISABELLA Woe me! For what?
LUCIO
  For that which, if myself might be his judge,
  He should receive his punishment in thanks.
  He hath got his friend with child.
ISABELLA   Sir, make me not your story.
LUCIO
  'Tis true. I would not—though 'tis my familiar sin   30
  With maids to seem the lapwing, and to jest
  Tongue far from heart—play with all virgins so.
  I hold you as a thing enskied and sainted
  By your renouncement, an immortal spirit,
  And to be talked with in sincerity   35
  As with a saint.
ISABELLA
  You do blaspheme the good in mocking me.
LUCIO
  Do not believe it. Fewness and truth, 'tis thus:
  Your brother and his lover have embraced.
  As those that feed grow full, as blossoming time   40
  That from the seedness the bare fallow brings
  To teeming foison, even so her plenteous womb
  Expresseth his full tilth and husbandry.
ISABELLA
  Someone with child by him? My cousin Juliet?
LUCIO Is she your cousin?   45
ISABELLA
  Adoptedly, as schoolmaids change their names
  By vain though apt affection.
LUCIO   She it is.
ISABELLA
  O, let him marry her!
LUCIO   This is the point.
  The Duke is very strangely gone from hence;
  Bore many gentlemen—myself being one—   50
  In hand and hope of action; but we do learn,

By those that know the very nerves of state,
His giving out were of an infinite distance
From his true-meant design. Upon his place,
And with full line of his authority,   55
Governs Lord Angelo—a man whose blood
Is very snow-broth; one who never feels
The wanton stings and motions of the sense,
But doth rebate and blunt his natural edge
With profits of the mind, study, and fast.   60
He, to give fear to use and liberty,
Which have for long run by the hideous law
As mice by lions, hath picked out an act
Under whose heavy sense your brother's life
Falls into forfeit. He arrests him on it,   65
And follows close the rigour of the statute
To make him an example. All hope is gone,
Unless you have the grace by your fair prayer
To soften Angelo. And that's my pith
Of business 'twixt you and your poor brother.   70

ISABELLA
Doth he so seek his life?

LUCIO   Has censured him already,
And, as I hear, the Provost hath a warrant
For's execution.

ISABELLA   Alas, what poor
Ability's in me to do him good?

LUCIO Assay the power you have.   75

ISABELLA My power? Alas, I doubt.

LUCIO Our doubts are traitors,
And makes us lose the good we oft might win,
By fearing to attempt. Go to Lord Angelo;
And let him learn to know, when maidens sue,   80
Men give like gods, but when they weep and kneel,
All their petitions are as freely theirs
As they themselves would owe them.

ISABELLA   I'll see what I can do.

LUCIO
But speedily.

ISABELLA   I will about it straight,
No longer staying but to give the Mother   85
Notice of my affair. I humbly thank you.
Commend me to my brother. Soon at night
I'll send him certain word of my success.

LUCIO
I take my leave of you.

ISABELLA   Good sir, adieu.
        Exeunt ⌈Isabella and Francesca at one door,
                        Lucio at another door⌉

                        ❦

2.1   *Enter Angelo, Escalus, and servants; a Justice*

ANGELO
We must not make a scarecrow of the law,
Setting it up to fear the birds of prey,
And let it keep one shape till custom make it
Their perch, and not their terror.

ESCALUS   Ay, but yet
Let us be keen, and rather cut a little   5

Than fall and bruise to death. Alas, this gentleman
Whom I would save had a most noble father.
Let but your honour know—
Whom I believe to be most strait in virtue—
That in the working of your own affections,   10
Had time cohered with place, or place with wishing,
Or that the resolute acting of your blood
Could have attained th'effect of your own purpose—
Whether you had not sometime in your life
Erred in this point which now you censure him,   15
And pulled the law upon you.

ANGELO
'Tis one thing to be tempted, Escalus,
Another thing to fall. I not deny
The jury passing on the prisoner's life
May in the sworn twelve have a thief or two   20
Guiltier than him they try. What knows the law
That thieves do pass on thieves? What's open made to justice,
That justice seizes. 'Tis very pregnant:
The jewel that we find, we stoop and take't
Because we see it, but what we do not see   25
We tread upon and never think of it.
You may not so extenuate his offence
For I have had such faults; but rather tell me,
When I that censure him do so offend,
Let mine own judgement pattern out my death,   30
And nothing come in partial. Sir, he must die.

ESCALUS
Be it as your wisdom will.

ANGELO   Where is the Provost?
        Enter Provost

PROVOST
Here, if it like your honour.

ANGELO   See that Claudio
Be execute by nine tomorrow morning.
Bring him his confessor, let him be prepared,   35
For that's the utmost of his pilgrimage.   *Exit Provost*

ESCALUS
Well, heaven forgive him, and forgive us all!
Some rise by sin, and some by virtue fall.
Some run from brakes of vice, and answer none;
And some condemnèd for a fault alone.   40
        Enter Elbow, Froth, Pompey, and officers

ELBOW Come, bring them away. If these be good people
in a commonweal, that do nothing but use their abuses
in common houses, I know no law. Bring them away.

ANGELO
How now, sir? What's your name? And what's the
matter?   44

ELBOW If it please your honour, I am the poor Duke's
constable, and my name is Elbow. I do lean upon
justice, sir; and do bring in here before your good
honour two notorious benefactors.

ANGELO
Benefactors? Well! What benefactors are they?
Are they not malefactors?   50

ELBOW If it please your honour, I know not well what

they are; but precise villains they are, that I am sure of, and void of all profanation in the world that good Christians ought to have.

ESCALUS (*to Angelo*)
This comes off well; here's a wise officer!   55

ANGELO Go to, what quality are they of? Elbow is your name? Why dost thou not speak, Elbow?

POMPEY He cannot, sir; he's out at elbow.

ANGELO What are you, sir?   59

ELBOW He, sir? A tapster, sir, parcel bawd; one that serves a bad woman whose house, sir, was, as they say, plucked down in the suburbs; and now she professes a hot-house, which I think is a very ill house too.

ESCALUS How know you that?   65

ELBOW My wife, sir, whom I detest before heaven and your honour—

ESCALUS How, thy wife?

ELBOW Ay, sir, whom I thank heaven is an honest woman—   70

ESCALUS Dost thou detest her therefor?

ELBOW I say, sir, I will detest myself also, as well as she, that this house, if it be not a bawd's house, it is pity of her life, for it is a naughty house.

ESCALUS How dost thou know that, constable?   75

ELBOW Marry, sir, by my wife, who, if she had been a woman cardinally given, might have been accused in fornication, adultery, and all uncleanliness there.

ESCALUS By the woman's means?

ELBOW Ay, sir, by Mistress Overdone's means. But as she spit in his face, so she defied him.   81

POMPEY (*to Escalus*) Sir, if it please your honour, this is not so.

ELBOW Prove it before these varlets here, thou honourable man, prove it.   85

ESCALUS (*to Angelo*) Do you hear how he misplaces?

POMPEY Sir, she came in great with child, and longing— saving your honour's reverence—for stewed prunes. Sir, we had but two in the house, which at that very distant time stood, as it were, in a fruit dish—a dish of some threepence; your honours have seen such dishes; they are not china dishes, but very good dishes.

ESCALUS Go to, go to, no matter for the dish, sir.   93

POMPEY No, indeed, sir, not of a pin; you are therein in the right. But to the point. As I say, this Mistress Elbow, being, as I say, with child, and being great-bellied, and longing, as I said, for prunes; and having but two in the dish, as I said, Master Froth here, this very man, having eaten the rest, as I said, and, as I say, paying for them very honestly; for, as you know, Master Froth, I could not give you threepence again.   101

FROTH No, indeed.

POMPEY Very well. You being, then, if you be remembered, cracking the stones of the foresaid prunes—

FROTH Ay, so I did indeed.   105

POMPEY Why, very well.—I telling you then, if you be remembered, that such a one and such a one were past

cure of the thing you wot of, unless they kept very good diet, as I told you—

FROTH All this is true.   110

POMPEY Why, very well then—

ESCALUS Come, you are a tedious fool. To the purpose. What was done to Elbow's wife that he hath cause to complain of? Come me to what was done to her.

POMPEY Sir, your honour cannot come to that yet.   115

ESCALUS No, sir, nor I mean it not.

POMPEY Sir, but you shall come to it, by your honour's leave. And I beseech you, look into Master Froth here, sir, a man of fourscore pound a year, whose father died at Hallowmas—was't not at Hallowmas, Master Froth?

FROTH All Hallow Eve.   121

POMPEY Why, very well. I hope here be truths. He, sir, sitting, as I say, in a lower chair, sir—'twas in the Bunch of Grapes, where indeed you have a delight to sit, have you not?   125

FROTH I have so, because it is an open room, and good for winter.

POMPEY Why, very well then. I hope here be truths.

ANGELO
This will last out a night in Russia,
When nights are longest there. (*To Escalus*) I'll take my leave,   130
And leave you to the hearing of the cause,
Hoping you'll find good cause to whip them all.

ESCALUS
I think no less. Good morrow to your lordship.
                                                                   Exit Angelo
Now, sir, come on, what was done to Elbow's wife, once more?   135

POMPEY Once, sir? There was nothing done to her once.

ELBOW I beseech you, sir, ask him what this man did to my wife.

POMPEY I beseech your honour, ask me.

ESCALUS Well, sir, what did this gentleman to her?   140

POMPEY I beseech you, sir, look in this gentleman's face. Good Master Froth, look upon his honour. 'Tis for a good purpose. Doth your honour mark his face?

ESCALUS Ay, sir, very well.

POMPEY Nay, I beseech you, mark it well.   145

ESCALUS Well, I do so.

POMPEY Doth your honour see any harm in his face?

ESCALUS Why, no.

POMPEY I'll be supposed upon a book his face is the worst thing about him. Good, then—if his face be the worst thing about him, how could Master Froth do the constable's wife any harm? I would know that of your honour.   153

ESCALUS He's in the right, constable; what say you to it?

ELBOW First, an it like you, the house is a respected house; next, this is a respected fellow; and his mistress is a respected woman.

POMPEY (*to Escalus*) By this hand, sir, his wife is a more respected person than any of us all.   159

ELBOW Varlet, thou liest; thou liest, wicked varlet. The

time is yet to come that she was ever respected with
man, woman, or child.

POMPEY Sir, she was respected with him before he married
with her.

ESCALUS Which is the wiser here, justice or iniquity? (*To
Elbow*) Is this true? 166

ELBOW (*to Pompey*) O thou caitiff, O thou varlet, O thou
wicked Hannibal! I respected with her before I was
married to her? (*To Escalus*) If ever I was respected
with her, or she with me, let not your worship think
me the poor Duke's officer. (*To Pompey*) Prove this,
thou wicked Hannibal, or I'll have mine action of
battery on thee.

ESCALUS If he took you a box o'th' ear you might have
your action of slander too. 175

ELBOW Marry, I thank your good worship for it. What
is't your worship's pleasure I shall do with this wicked
caitiff?

ESCALUS Truly, officer, because he hath some offences in
him that thou wouldst discover if thou couldst, let him
continue in his courses till thou knowest what they
are. 182

ELBOW Marry, I thank your worship for it.—Thou seest,
thou wicked varlet now, what's come upon thee. Thou
art to continue now, thou varlet, thou art to continue.

ESCALUS (*to Froth*) Where were you born, friend? 186

FROTH Here in Vienna, sir.

ESCALUS Are you of fourscore pounds a year?

FROTH Yes, an't please you, sir.

ESCALUS So. (*To Pompey*) What trade are you of, sir? 190

POMPEY A tapster, a poor widow's tapster.

ESCALUS Your mistress's name?

POMPEY Mistress Overdone.

ESCALUS Hath she had any more than one husband?

POMPEY Nine, sir—Overdone by the last. 195

ESCALUS Nine?—Come hither to me, Master Froth. Master
Froth, I would not have you acquainted with tapsters.
They will draw you, Master Froth, and you will hang
them. Get you gone, and let me hear no more of you.

FROTH I thank your worship. For mine own part, I never
come into any room in a tap-house but I am drawn in.

ESCALUS Well, no more of it, Master Froth. Farewell. 202

                                        Exit Froth

Come you hither to me, Master Tapster. What's your
name, Master Tapster?

POMPEY Pompey. 205

ESCALUS What else?

POMPEY Bum, sir.

ESCALUS Troth, and your bum is the greatest thing about
you; so that, in the beastliest sense, you are Pompey
the Great. Pompey, you are partly a bawd, Pompey,
howsoever you colour it in being a tapster, are you
not? Come, tell me true; it shall be the better for you.

POMPEY Truly, sir, I am a poor fellow that would live.

ESCALUS How would you live, Pompey? By being a bawd?
What do you think of the trade, Pompey? Is it a lawful
trade? 216

POMPEY If the law would allow it, sir.

ESCALUS But the law will not allow it, Pompey; nor it
shall not be allowed in Vienna.

POMPEY Does your worship mean to geld and spay all the
youth of the city? 221

ESCALUS No, Pompey.

POMPEY Truly, sir, in my poor opinion they will to't then.
If your worship will take order for the drabs and the
knaves, you need not to fear the bawds. 225

ESCALUS There is pretty orders beginning, I can tell you.
It is but heading and hanging.

POMPEY If you head and hang all that offend that way
but for ten year together, you'll be glad to give out a
commission for more heads. If this law hold in Vienna
ten year, I'll rent the fairest house in it after threepence
a bay. If you live to see this come to pass, say Pompey
told you so. 233

ESCALUS Thank you, good Pompey; and in requital of
your prophecy, hark you. I advise you, let me not find
you before me again upon any complaint whatsoever;
no, not for dwelling where you do. If I do, Pompey, I
shall beat you to your tent, and prove a shrewd Caesar
to you; in plain dealing, Pompey, I shall have you
whipped. So for this time, Pompey, fare you well. 240

POMPEY I thank your worship for your good counsel;
⌜*aside*⌝ but I shall follow it as the flesh and fortune shall
better determine.

Whip me? No, no; let carman whip his jade. 244
The valiant heart's not whipped out of his trade. *Exit*

ESCALUS Come hither to me, Master Elbow; come hither,
Master Constable. How long have you been in this
place of constable?

ELBOW Seven year and a half, sir. 249

ESCALUS I thought, by the readiness in the office, you had
continued in it some time. You say seven years
together?

ELBOW And a half, sir.

ESCALUS Alas, it hath been great pains to you. They do
you wrong to put you so oft upon't. Are there not men
in your ward sufficient to serve it? 256

ELBOW Faith, sir, few of any wit in such matters. As they
are chosen, they are glad to choose me for them. I do
it for some piece of money, and go through with all.

ESCALUS Look you bring me in the names of some six or
seven, the most sufficient of your parish. 261

ELBOW To your worship's house, sir?

ESCALUS To my house. Fare you well.

                            Exit Elbow with officers

What's o'clock, think you?

JUSTICE Eleven, sir. 265

ESCALUS I pray you home to dinner with me.

JUSTICE I humbly thank you.

ESCALUS
  It grieves me for the death of Claudio,
  But there's no remedy.

JUSTICE Lord Angelo is severe. 270

ESCALUS It is but needful.

Mercy is not itself that oft looks so.
Pardon is still the nurse of second woe.
But yet, poor Claudio! There is no remedy.　274
Come, sir.　　　　　　　　　　　*Exeunt*

2.2　*Enter the Provost and a Servant*
SERVANT
He's hearing of a cause; he will come straight.
I'll tell him of you.
PROVOST　　　　　　Pray you do.　　*Exit Servant*
　　　　　　　　　I'll know
His pleasure; maybe he will relent. Alas,
He hath but as offended in a dream.
All sects, all ages, smack of this vice; and he　5
To die for't!
　　　Enter Angelo
ANGELO　　　Now, what's the matter, Provost?
PROVOST
Is it your will Claudio shall die tomorrow?
ANGELO
Did not I tell thee yea? Hadst thou not order?
Why dost thou ask again?
PROVOST　　　　　　Lest I might be too rash.
Under your good correction, I have seen　10
When after execution judgement hath
Repented o'er his doom.
ANGELO　　　　　　Go to; let that be mine.
Do you your office, or give up your place,
And you shall well be spared.
PROVOST　　　　　　I crave your honour's pardon.
What shall be done, sir, with the groaning Juliet?　15
She's very near her hour.
ANGELO　　　　　　Dispose of her
To some more fitter place, and that with speed.
　　　Enter Servant
SERVANT
Here is the sister of the man condemned
Desires access to you.
ANGELO　　　　　　Hath he a sister?
PROVOST
Ay, my good lord; a very virtuous maid,　20
And to be shortly of a sisterhood,
If not already.
ANGELO　　Well, let her be admitted.　*Exit Servant*
See you the fornicatress be removed.
Let her have needful but not lavish means.
There shall be order for't.
　　　Enter Lucio and Isabella
PROVOST　　　　　　God save your honour.　25
ANGELO
Stay a little while. (*To Isabella*) You're welcome.
What's your will?
ISABELLA
I am a woeful suitor to your honour.
Please but your honour hear me.
ANGELO　　　　　　Well, what's your suit?
ISABELLA
There is a vice that most I do abhor,

And most desire should meet the blow of justice,　30
For which I would not plead, but that I must;
For which I must not plead, but that I am
At war 'twixt will and will not.
ANGELO　　　　　　Well, the matter?
ISABELLA
I have a brother is condemned to die.
I do beseech you, let it be his fault,　35
And not my brother.
PROVOST (*aside*)　　Heaven give thee moving graces!
ANGELO
Condemn the fault, and not the actor of it?
Why, every fault's condemned ere it be done.
Mine were the very cipher of a function,
To fine the faults whose fine stands in record,　40
And let go by the actor.
ISABELLA　　　　　O just but severe law!
I had a brother, then. Heaven keep your honour.
LUCIO (*aside to Isabella*)
Give't not o'er so. To him again; entreat him.
Kneel down before him; hang upon his gown.
You are too cold. If you should need a pin,　45
You could not with more tame a tongue desire it.
To him, I say!
ISABELLA (*to Angelo*) Must he needs die?
ANGELO Maiden, no remedy.
ISABELLA
Yes, I do think that you might pardon him,　50
And neither heaven nor man grieve at the mercy.
ANGELO
I will not do't.
ISABELLA　　　But can you if you would?
ANGELO
Look what I will not, that I cannot do.
ISABELLA
But might you do't, and do the world no wrong,
If so your heart were touched with that remorse　55
As mine is to him?
ANGELO He's sentenced; 'tis too late.
LUCIO (*aside to Isabella*) You are too cold.
ISABELLA
Too late? Why, no; I that do speak a word
May call it again. Well, believe this,　60
No ceremony that to great ones 'longs,
Not the king's crown, nor the deputed sword,
The marshal's truncheon, nor the judge's robe,
Become them with one half so good a grace
As mercy does.　65
If he had been as you and you as he,
You would have slipped like him, but he, like you,
Would not have been so stern.
ANGELO　　　　　　Pray you be gone.
ISABELLA
I would to heaven I had your potency,
And you were Isabel! Should it then be thus?　70
No; I would tell what 'twere to be a judge,
And what a prisoner.
LUCIO (*aside to Isabella*) Ay, touch him; there's the vein.

ANGELO
Your brother is a forfeit of the law,
And you but waste your words.
ISABELLA   Alas, alas!
Why, all the souls that were were forfeit once,   75
And He that might the vantage best have took
Found out the remedy. How would you be
If He which is the top of judgement should
But judge you as you are? O, think on that,
And mercy then will breathe within your lips,   80
Like man new made.
ANGELO   Be you content, fair maid.
It is the law, not I, condemn your brother.
Were he my kinsman, brother, or my son,
It should be thus with him. He must die tomorrow.
ISABELLA
Tomorrow? O, that's sudden! Spare him, spare him! 85
He's not prepared for death. Even for our kitchens
We kill the fowl of season. Shall we serve heaven
With less respect than we do minister
To our gross selves? Good good my lord, bethink you:
Who is it that hath died for this offence?   90
There's many have committed it.
LUCIO (aside)   Ay, well said.
ANGELO
The law hath not been dead, though it hath slept.
Those many had not dared to do that evil
If the first that did th'edict infringe
Had answered for his deed. Now 'tis awake,   95
Takes note of what is done, and, like a prophet,
Looks in a glass that shows what future evils,
Either raw, or by remissness new conceived
And so in progress to be hatched and born,
Are now to have no successive degrees,   100
But ere they live, to end.
ISABELLA   Yet show some pity.
ANGELO
I show it most of all when I show justice,
For then I pity those I do not know
Which a dismissed offence would after gall,
And do him right that, answering one foul wrong, 105
Lives not to act another. Be satisfied.
Your brother dies tomorrow. Be content.
ISABELLA
So you must be the first that gives this sentence,
And he that suffers. O, it is excellent
To have a giant's strength, but it is tyrannous   110
To use it like a giant.
LUCIO (aside to Isabella) That's well said.
ISABELLA Could great men thunder
As Jove himself does, Jove would never be quiet,
For every pelting petty officer   115
Would use his heaven for thunder, nothing but
      thunder.
Merciful heaven,
Thou rather with thy sharp and sulphurous bolt
Split'st the unwedgeable and gnarlèd oak
Than the soft myrtle. But man, proud man,   120
Dressed in a little brief authority,

Most ignorant of what he's most assured,
His glassy essence, like an angry ape
Plays such fantastic tricks before high heaven
As makes the angels weep, who, with our spleens, 125
Would all themselves laugh mortal.
LUCIO (aside to Isabella)
O, to him, to him, wench! He will relent.
He's coming; I perceive't.
PROVOST (aside)   Pray heaven she win him!
ISABELLA
We cannot weigh our brother with ourself.
Great men may jest with saints; 'tis wit in them, 130
But in the less, foul profanation.
LUCIO (aside to Isabella) Thou'rt i'th' right, girl. More o'
that.
ISABELLA
That in the captain's but a choleric word,
Which in the soldier is flat blasphemy.   135
LUCIO (aside to Isabella) Art advised o' that? More on't.
ANGELO
Why do you put these sayings upon me?
ISABELLA
Because authority, though it err like others,
Hath yet a kind of medicine in itself
That skins the vice o'th' top. Go to your bosom;   140
Knock there, and ask your heart what it doth know
That's like my brother's fault. If it confess
A natural guiltiness, such as is his,
Let it not sound a thought upon your tongue
Against my brother's life.
ANGELO (aside)   She speaks, and 'tis such sense
That my sense breeds with it. (To Isabella) Fare you 146
well.
ISABELLA Gentle my lord, turn back.
ANGELO
I will bethink me. Come again tomorrow.
ISABELLA
Hark how I'll bribe you; good my lord, turn back.
ANGELO How, bribe me?   150
ISABELLA
Ay, with such gifts that heaven shall share with you.
LUCIO (aside to Isabella) You had marred all else.
ISABELLA
Not with fond shekels of the tested gold,
Or stones, whose rate are either rich or poor
As fancy values them; but with true prayers,   155
That shall be up at heaven and enter there
Ere sunrise, prayers from preservèd souls,
From fasting maids whose minds are dedicate
To nothing temporal.
ANGELO Well, come to me tomorrow.   160
LUCIO (aside to Isabella) Go to; 'tis well; away.
ISABELLA Heaven keep your honour safe.
ANGELO (aside) Amen;
For I am that way going to temptation,
Where prayer is crossed.
ISABELLA   At what hour tomorrow 165
Shall I attend your lordship?
ANGELO   At any time fore noon.

ISABELLA
  God save your honour.
ANGELO (*aside*)   From thee; even from thy virtue.
                    Exeunt Isabella, Lucio, and Provost
  What's this? What's this? Is this her fault or mine?
  The tempter or the tempted, who sins most, ha?
  Not she; nor doth she tempt; but it is I   170
  That, lying by the violet in the sun,
  Do, as the carrion does, not as the flower,
  Corrupt with virtuous season. Can it be
  That modesty may more betray our sense
  Than woman's lightness? Having waste ground enough,
  Shall we desire to raze the sanctuary,   176
  And pitch our evils there? O, fie, fie, fie!
  What dost thou, or what art thou, Angelo?
  Dost thou desire her foully for those things
  That make her good? O, let her brother live!   180
  Thieves for their robbery have authority,
  When judges steal themselves. What, do I love her,
  That I desire to hear her speak again,
  And feast upon her eyes? What is't I dream on?
  O cunning enemy, that, to catch a saint,   185
  With saints dost bait thy hook! Most dangerous
  Is that temptation that doth goad us on
  To sin in loving virtue. Never could the strumpet,
  With all her double vigour—art and nature—
  Once stir my temper; but this virtuous maid   190
  Subdues me quite. Ever till now
  When men were fond, I smiled, and wondered how.
                                        Exit

2.3 *Enter ⌈at one door⌉ the Duke, disguised as a friar,*
       and ⌈at another door⌉ the Provost
DUKE
  Hail to you, Provost!—so I think you are.
PROVOST
  I am the Provost. What's your will, good friar?
DUKE
  Bound by my charity and my blest order,
  I come to visit the afflicted spirits
  Here in the prison. Do me the common right   5
  To let me see them, and to make me know
  The nature of their crimes, that I may minister
  To them accordingly.
PROVOST
  I would do more than that, if more were needful.
                    Enter Juliet
  Look, here comes one, a gentlewoman of mine,   10
  Who, falling in the flaws of her own youth,
  Hath blistered her report. She is with child,
  And he that got it, sentenced—a young man
  More fit to do another such offence
  Than die for this.   15
DUKE When must he die?
PROVOST As I do think, tomorrow.
       (*To Juliet*) I have provided for you. Stay a while,
  And you shall be conducted.
DUKE
  Repent you, fair one, of the sin you carry?   20

JULIET
  I do, and bear the shame most patiently.
DUKE
  I'll teach you how you shall arraign your conscience,
  And try your penitence if it be sound
  Or hollowly put on.
JULIET I'll gladly learn.   25
DUKE Love you the man that wronged you?
JULIET
  Yes, as I love the woman that wronged him.
DUKE
  So then it seems your most offenceful act
  Was mutually committed?
JULIET   Mutually.
DUKE
  Then was your sin of heavier kind than his.   30
JULIET
  I do confess it and repent it, father.
DUKE
  'Tis meet so, daughter. But lest you do repent
  As that the sin hath brought you to this shame—
  Which sorrow is always toward ourselves, not heaven,
  Showing we would not spare heaven as we love it,   35
  But as we stand in fear—
JULIET
  I do repent me as it is an evil,
  And take the shame with joy.
DUKE   There rest.
  Your partner, as I hear, must die tomorrow,
  And I am going with instruction to him.   40
  Grace go with you. *Benedicite!*   *Exit*
JULIET
  Must die tomorrow? O injurious law,
  That respites me a life whose very comfort
  Is still a dying horror!
PROVOST   'Tis pity of him.   *Exeunt*

2.4 *Enter Angelo*
ANGELO
  When I would pray and think, I think and pray
  To several subjects: heaven hath my empty words,
  Whilst my invention, hearing not my tongue,
  Anchors on Isabel; God in my mouth,
  As if I did but only chew his name,   5
  And in my heart the strong and swelling evil
  Of my conception. The state whereon I studied
  Is like a good thing, being often read,
  Grown seared and tedious. Yea, my gravity,
  Wherein—let no man hear me—I take pride,   10
  Could I with boot change for an idle plume
  Which the air beats in vain. O place, O form,
  How often dost thou with thy case, thy habit,
  Wrench awe from fools, and tie the wiser souls
  To thy false seeming! Blood, thou art blood.   15
  Let's write 'good angel' on the devil's horn—
  'Tis now the devil's crest.
          Enter Servant
                    How now? Who's there?

SERVANT One Isabel, a sister, desires access to you.

ANGELO
    Teach her the way.   *Exit Servant*
             O heavens,
    Why does my blood thus muster to my heart,   20
    Making both it unable for itself,
    And dispossessing all my other parts
    Of necessary fitness?
    So play the foolish throngs with one that swoons—
    Come all to help him, and so stop the air   25
    By which he should revive—and even so
    The general subject to a well-wished king
    Quit their own part and, in obsequious fondness,
    Crowd to his presence, where their untaught love
    Must needs appear offence.
      Enter Isabella
                 How now, fair maid?   30

ISABELLA I am come to know your pleasure.

ANGELO (*aside*)
    That you might know it would much better please me
    Than to demand what 'tis. (*To Isabella*) Your brother
    cannot live.

ISABELLA Even so. Heaven keep your honour.

ANGELO
    Yet may he live a while, and it may be   35
    As long as you or I. Yet he must die.

ISABELLA Under your sentence?

ANGELO Yea.

ISABELLA
    When, I beseech you?—that in his reprieve,
    Longer or shorter, he may be so fitted   40
    That his soul sicken not.

ANGELO
    Ha, fie, these filthy vices! It were as good
    To pardon him that hath from nature stolen
    A man already made, as to remit
    Their saucy sweetness that do coin God's image   45
    In stamps that are forbid. 'Tis all as easy
    Falsely to take away a life true made
    As to put metal in restrainèd moulds,
    To make a false one.

ISABELLA
    'Tis set down so in heaven, but not in earth.   50

ANGELO
    Say you so? Then I shall pose you quickly.
    Which had you rather: that the most just law
    Now took your brother's life, or, to redeem him,
    Give up your body to such sweet uncleanness
    As she that he hath stained?

ISABELLA   Sir, believe this.   55
    I had rather give my body than my soul.

ANGELO
    I talk not of your soul. Our compelled sins
    Stand more for number than for account.

ISABELLA   How say you?

ANGELO
    Nay, I'll not warrant that, for I can speak
    Against the thing I say. Answer to this.   60

    I now, the voice of the recorded law,
    Pronounce a sentence on your brother's life.
    Might there not be a charity in sin
    To save this brother's life?

ISABELLA   Please you to do't,
    I'll take it as a peril to my soul   65
    It is no sin at all, but charity.

ANGELO
    Pleased you to do't at peril of your soul
    Were equal poise of sin and charity.

ISABELLA
    That I do beg his life, if it be sin,
    Heaven let me bear it. You granting of my suit,   70
    If that be sin, I'll make it my morn prayer
    To have it added to the faults of mine,
    And nothing of your answer.

ANGELO   Nay, but hear me.
    Your sense pursues not mine. Either you are ignorant,
    Or seem so craftily, and that's not good.   75

ISABELLA
    Let me be ignorant, and in nothing good
    But graciously to know I am no better.

ANGELO
    Thus wisdom wishes to appear most bright
    When it doth tax itself: as these black masks
    Proclaim an enshield beauty ten times louder   80
    Than beauty could, displayed. But mark me.
    To be receivèd plain, I'll speak more gross.
    Your brother is to die.

ISABELLA So.

ANGELO
    And his offence is so, as it appears,   85
    Accountant to the law upon that pain.

ISABELLA True.

ANGELO
    Admit no other way to save his life—
    As I subscribe not that nor any other—
    But, in the loss of question, that you his sister,   90
    Finding yourself desired of such a person
    Whose credit with the judge, or own great place,
    Could fetch your brother from the manacles
    Of the all-binding law, and that there were
    No earthly mean to save him, but that either   95
    You must lay down the treasures of your body
    To this supposed, or else to let him suffer—
    What would you do?

ISABELLA
    As much for my poor brother as myself.
    That is, were I under the terms of death,   100
    Th'impression of keen whips I'd wear as rubies,
    And strip myself to death as to a bed
    That longing have been sick for, ere I'd yield
    My body up to shame.

ANGELO Then must your brother die.   105

ISABELLA And 'twere the cheaper way.
    Better it were a brother died at once
    Than that a sister, by redeeming him,
    Should die for ever.

ANGELO

Were not you then as cruel as the sentence   110
That you have slandered so?

ISABELLA

Ignominy in ransom and free pardon
Are of two houses; lawful mercy
Is nothing kin to foul redemption.

ANGELO

You seemed of late to make the law a tyrant,   115
And rather proved the sliding of your brother
A merriment than a vice.

ISABELLA

O pardon me, my lord. It oft falls out
To have what we would have, we speak not what we
     mean.
I something do excuse the thing I hate   120
For his advantage that I dearly love.

ANGELO

We are all frail.

ISABELLA   Else let my brother die—
If not a federy, but only he,
Owe and succeed thy weakness.

ANGELO   Nay, women are frail too.

ISABELLA

Ay, as the glasses where they view themselves,   125
Which are as easy broke as they make forms.
Women? Help, heaven! Men their creation mar
In profiting by them. Nay, call us ten times frail,
For we are soft as our complexions are,
And credulous to false prints.

ANGELO   I think it well,   130
And from this testimony of your own sex,
Since I suppose we are made to be no stronger
Than faults may shake our frames, let me be bold.
I do arrest your words. Be that you are;
That is, a woman. If you be more, you're none.   135
If you be one, as you are well expressed
By all external warrants, show it now,
By putting on the destined livery.

ISABELLA

I have no tongue but one. Gentle my lord,
Let me entreat you speak the former language.   140

ANGELO Plainly conceive, I love you.

ISABELLA

My brother did love Juliet,
And you tell me that he shall die for it.

ANGELO

He shall not, Isabel, if you give me love.

ISABELLA

I know your virtue hath a licence in't,   145
Which seems a little fouler than it is,
To pluck on others.

ANGELO   Believe me, on mine honour,
My words express my purpose.

ISABELLA

Ha, little honour to be much believed,
And most pernicious purpose! Seeming, seeming!   150
I will proclaim thee, Angelo; look for't.

Sign me a present pardon for my brother,
Or with an outstretched throat I'll tell the world aloud
What man thou art.

ANGELO   Who will believe thee, Isabel?
My unsoiled name, th'austereness of my life,   155
My vouch against you, and my place i'th' state,
Will so your accusation overweigh
That you shall stifle in your own report,
And smell of calumny. I have begun,
And now I give my sensual race the rein.   160
Fit thy consent to my sharp appetite.
Lay by all nicety and prolixious blushes
That banish what they sue for. Redeem thy brother
By yielding up thy body to my will,
Or else he must not only die the death,   165
But thy unkindness shall his death draw out
To ling'ring sufferance. Answer me tomorrow,
Or by the affection that now guides me most,
I'll prove a tyrant to him. As for you,
Say what you can, my false o'erweighs your true.   170
                                                Exit

ISABELLA

To whom should I complain? Did I tell this,
Who would believe me? O perilous mouths,
That bear in them one and the selfsame tongue
Either of condemnation or approof,
Bidding the law make curtsy to their will,   175
Hooking both right and wrong to th'appetite,
To follow as it draws! I'll to my brother.
Though he hath fall'n by prompture of the blood,
Yet hath he in him such a mind of honour
That had he twenty heads to tender down   180
On twenty bloody blocks, he'd yield them up
Before his sister should her body stoop
To such abhorred pollution.
Then Isabel live chaste, and brother die:
More than our brother is our chastity.   185
I'll tell him yet of Angelo's request,
And fit his mind to death, for his soul's rest.   *Exit*

                       ✥

3.1   *Enter the Duke, disguised as a friar, Claudio, and*
        the Provost

DUKE

So then you hope of pardon from Lord Angelo?

CLAUDIO

The miserable have no other medicine
But only hope.
I've hope to live, and am prepared to die.

DUKE

Be absolute for death. Either death or life   5
Shall thereby be the sweeter. Reason thus with life.
If I do lose thee, I do lose a thing
That none but fools would keep. A breath thou art,
Servile to all the skyey influences
That dost this habitation where thou keep'st   10
Hourly afflict. Merely thou art death's fool,
For him thou labour'st by thy flight to shun,

And yet runn'st toward him still. Thou art not noble,
For all th'accommodations that thou bear'st
Are nursed by baseness. Thou'rt by no means valiant,
For thou dost fear the soft and tender fork   16
Of a poor worm. Thy best of rest is sleep,
And that thou oft provok'st, yet grossly fear'st
Thy death, which is no more. Thou art not thyself,
For thou exist'st on many a thousand grains   20
That issue out of dust. Happy thou art not,
For what thou hast not, still thou striv'st to get,
And what thou hast, forget'st. Thou art not certain,
For thy complexion shifts to strange effects
After the moon. If thou art rich, thou'rt poor,   25
For like an ass whose back with ingots bows,
Thou bear'st thy heavy riches but a journey,
And death unloads thee. Friend hast thou none,
For thine own bowels, which do call thee sire,
The mere effusion of thy proper loins,   30
Do curse the gout, serpigo, and the rheum,
For ending thee no sooner. Thou hast nor youth nor
          age,
But as it were an after-dinner's sleep
Dreaming on both; for all thy blessèd youth
Becomes as agèd, and doth beg the alms   35
Of palsied eld; and when thou art old and rich,
Thou hast neither heat, affection, limb, nor beauty,
To make thy riches pleasant. What's in this
That bears the name of life? Yet in this life
Lie hid more thousand deaths; yet death we fear   40
That makes these odds all even.
CLAUDIO   I humbly thank you.
To sue to live, I find I seek to die,
And seeking death, find life. Let it come on.
ISABELLA (*within*)
What ho! Peace here, grace, and good company!   44
PROVOST
Who's there? Come in; the wish deserves a welcome.
DUKE (*to Claudio*)
Dear sir, ere long I'll visit you again.
CLAUDIO Most holy sir, I thank you.
          Enter Isabella
ISABELLA
My business is a word or two with Claudio.
PROVOST
And very welcome. Look, signor, here's your sister.
DUKE
Provost, a word with you.
PROVOST   As many as you please.   50
          The Duke and Provost draw aside
DUKE
Bring me to hear them speak where I may be
          concealed.
          They conceal themselves
CLAUDIO Now sister, what's the comfort?   \
ISABELLA
Why, as all comforts are: most good, most good
          indeed.
Lord Angelo, having affairs to heaven,

Intends you for his swift ambassador,   55
Where you shall be an everlasting leiger.
Therefore your best appointment make with speed.
Tomorrow you set on.
CLAUDIO   Is there no remedy?
ISABELLA
None but such remedy as, to save a head,
To cleave a heart in twain.   60
CLAUDIO But is there any?
ISABELLA Yes, brother, you may live.
There is a devilish mercy in the judge,
If you'll implore it, that will free your life,
But fetter you till death.
CLAUDIO   Perpetual durance?   65
ISABELLA
Ay, just, perpetual durance; a restraint,
Though all the world's vastidity you had,
To a determined scope.
CLAUDIO   But in what nature?
ISABELLA
In such a one as you consenting to't
Would bark your honour from that trunk you bear,   70
And leave you naked.
CLAUDIO   Let me know the point.
ISABELLA
O, I do fear thee, Claudio, and I quake
Lest thou a feverous life shouldst entertain,
And six or seven winters more respect
Than a perpetual honour. Dar'st thou die?   75
The sense of death is most in apprehension,
And the poor beetle that we tread upon
In corporal sufferance finds a pang as great
As when a giant dies.
CLAUDIO   Why give you me this shame?
Think you I can a resolution fetch   80
From flow'ry tenderness? If I must die,
I will encounter darkness as a bride,
And hug it in mine arms.
ISABELLA
There spake my brother; there my father's grave
Did utter forth a voice. Yes, thou must die.   85
Thou art too noble to conserve a life
In base appliances. This outward-sainted deputy,
Whose settled visage and deliberate word
Nips youth i'th' head and follies doth enew
As falcon doth the fowl, is yet a devil.   90
His filth within being cast, he would appear
A pond as deep as hell.
CLAUDIO   The precise Angelo?
ISABELLA
O, 'tis the cunning livery of hell
The damnedest body to invest and cover
In precise guards! Dost thou think, Claudio: 95
If I would yield him my virginity,
Thou might'st be freed!
CLAUDIO   O heavens, it cannot be!
ISABELLA
Yes, he would give't thee, from this rank offence,

So to offend him still. This night's the time
That I should do what I abhor to name,　　　　100
Or else thou diest tomorrow.
CLAUDIO Thou shalt not do't.
ISABELLA O, were it but my life,
I'd throw it down for your deliverance
As frankly as a pin.
CLAUDIO　　　　Thanks, dear Isabel.　　　　105
ISABELLA
Be ready, Claudio, for your death tomorrow.
CLAUDIO
Yes. Has he affections in him
That thus can make him bite the law by th' nose
When he would force it? Sure it is no sin,
Or of the deadly seven it is the least.　　　　110
ISABELLA Which is the least?
CLAUDIO
If it were damnable, he being so wise,
Why would he for the momentary trick
Be perdurably fined? O Isabel!
ISABELLA What says my brother?　　　　115
CLAUDIO Death is a fearful thing.
ISABELLA And shamèd life a hateful.
CLAUDIO
Ay, but to die, and go we know not where;
To lie in cold obstruction, and to rot;
This sensible warm motion to become　　　　120
A kneaded clod, and the dilated spirit
To bathe in fiery floods, or to reside
In thrilling region of thick-ribbèd ice;
To be imprisoned in the viewless winds,
And blown with restless violence round about　　　125
The pendent world; or to be worse than worst
Of those that lawless and incertain thought
Imagine howling—'tis too horrible!
The weariest and most loathèd worldly life
That age, ache, penury, and imprisonment　　　130
Can lay on nature is a paradise
To what we fear of death.
ISABELLA Alas, alas!
CLAUDIO Sweet sister, let me live.
What sin you do to save a brother's life,　　　135
Nature dispenses with the deed so far
That it becomes a virtue.
ISABELLA　　　　O, you beast!
O faithless coward, O dishonest wretch,
Wilt thou be made a man out of my vice?
Is't not a kind of incest to take life　　　140
From thine own sister's shame? What should I think?
Heaven shield my mother played my father fair,
For such a warpèd slip of wilderness
Ne'er issued from his blood. Take my defiance,
Die, perish! Might but my bending down　　　145
Reprieve thee from thy fate, it should proceed.
I'll pray a thousand prayers for thy death,
No word to save thee.
CLAUDIO Nay, hear me, Isabel.
ISABELLA O fie, fie, fie!　　　　150
Thy sin's not accidental, but a trade.

Mercy to thee would prove itself a bawd.
'Tis best that thou diest quickly.
　　　⌈*She parts from Claudio*⌉
CLAUDIO O hear me, Isabella.
DUKE (*coming forward to Isabella*)
Vouchsafe a word, young sister, but one word.　　　155
ISABELLA What is your will?
DUKE Might you dispense with your leisure, I would by
and by have some speech with you. The satisfaction I
would require is likewise your own benefit.　　　159
ISABELLA I have no superfluous leisure; my stay must be
stolen out of other affairs; but I will attend you a while.
DUKE ⌈*standing aside with Claudio*⌉ Son, I have overheard
what hath passed between you and your sister. Angelo
had never the purpose to corrupt her; only he hath
made an assay of her virtue, to practise his judgement
with the disposition of natures. She, having the truth
of honour in her, hath made him that gracious denial
which he is most glad to receive. I am confessor to
Angelo, and I know this to be true. Therefore prepare
yourself to death. Do not falsify your resolution with
hopes that are fallible. Tomorrow you must die. Go to
your knees and make ready.
CLAUDIO Let me ask my sister pardon. I am so out of love
with life that I will sue to be rid of it.
DUKE Hold you there. Farewell.　　　175
　　　⌈*Claudio joins Isabella*⌉
Provost, a word with you.
PROVOST (*coming forward*) What's your will, father?
DUKE That now you are come, you will be gone. Leave
me a while with the maid. My mind promises with my
habit no loss shall touch her by my company.　　　180
PROVOST In good time.　　　　*Exit* ⌈*with Claudio*⌉
DUKE The hand that hath made you fair hath made you
good. The goodness that is cheap in beauty makes
beauty brief in goodness; but grace, being the soul of
your complexion, shall keep the body of it ever fair.
The assault that Angelo hath made to you fortune hath
conveyed to my understanding; and but that frailty
hath examples for his falling, I should wonder at
Angelo. How will you do to content this substitute, and
to save your brother?　　　190
ISABELLA I am now going to resolve him. I had rather
my brother die by the law than my son should be
unlawfully born. But O, how much is the good Duke
deceived in Angelo! If ever he return and I can speak
to him, I will open my lips in vain, or discover his
government.　　　196
DUKE That shall not be much amiss. Yet as the matter
now stands, he will avoid your accusation: he made
trial of you only. Therefore fasten your ear on my
advisings. To the love I have in doing good, a remedy
presents itself. I do make myself believe that you may
most uprighteously do a poor wronged lady a merited
benefit, redeem your brother from the angry law, do
no stain to your own gracious person, and much please
the absent Duke, if peradventure he shall ever return
to have hearing of this business.　　　206
ISABELLA Let me hear you speak farther. I have spirit to

do anything that appears not foul in the truth of my
spirit.   209
DUKE Virtue is bold, and goodness never fearful. Have you
not heard speak of Mariana, the sister of Frederick, the
great soldier who miscarried at sea?
ISABELLA I have heard of the lady, and good words went
with her name.   214
DUKE She should this Angelo have married, was affianced
to her oath, and the nuptial appointed; between which
time of the contract and limit of the solemnity, her
brother Frederick was wrecked at sea, having in that
perished vessel the dowry of his sister. But mark how
heavily this befell to the poor gentlewoman. There she
lost a noble and renowned brother, in his love toward
her ever most kind and natural; with him, the portion
and sinew of her fortune, her marriage dowry; with
both, her combinate husband, this well-seeming
Angelo.   225
ISABELLA Can this be so? Did Angelo so leave her?
DUKE Left her in her tears, and dried not one of them
with his comfort; swallowed his vows whole, pretending in her discoveries of dishonour; in few,
bestowed her on her own lamentation, which she yet
wears for his sake; and he, a marble to her tears, is
washed with them, but relents not.   232
ISABELLA What a merit were it in death to take this poor
maid from the world! What corruption in this life, that
it will let this man live! But how out of this can she
avail?   236
DUKE It is a rupture that you may easily heal, and the
cure of it not only saves your brother, but keeps you
from dishonour in doing it.
ISABELLA Show me how, good father.   240
DUKE This forenamed maid hath yet in her the
continuance of her first affection. His unjust unkindness, that in all reason should have quenched her love,
hath, like an impediment in the current, made it more
violent and unruly. Go you to Angelo, answer his
requiring with a plausible obedience, agree with his
demands to the point; only refer yourself to this
advantage: first, that your stay with him may not be
long; that the time may have all shadow and silence
in it; and the place answer to convenience. This being
granted in course, and now follows all. We shall advise
this wronged maid to stead up your appointment, go
in your place. If the encounter acknowledge itself
hereafter, it may compel him to her recompense; and
hear, by this is your brother saved, your honour
untainted, the poor Mariana advantaged, and the
corrupt deputy scaled. The maid will I frame and make
fit for his attempt. If you think well to carry this, as
you may, the doubleness of the benefit defends the
deceit from reproof. What think you of it?   260
ISABELLA The image of it gives me content already, and
I trust it will grow to a most prosperous perfection.
DUKE It lies much in your holding up. Haste you speedily
to Angelo. If for this night he entreat you to his bed,
give him promise of satisfaction. I will presently to
Saint Luke's; there at the moated grange resides this

dejected Mariana. At that place call upon me; and
dispatch with Angelo, that it may be quickly.
ISABELLA I thank you for this comfort. Fare you well,
good father.   Exit

Enter Elbow, Clown, and officers

ELBOW Nay, if there be no remedy for it but that you will
needs buy and sell men and women like beasts, we
shall have all the world drink brown and white bastard.
DUKE O heavens, what stuff is here?   274
POMPEY 'Twas never merry world since, of two usuries,
the merriest was put down, and the worser allowed by
order of law, a furred gown to keep him warm—and
furred with fox on lambskins too, to signify that craft,
being richer than innocency, stands for the facing.
ELBOW Come your way, sir.—Bless you, good father friar.
DUKE And you, good brother father. What offence hath
this man made you, sir?   282
ELBOW Marry, sir, he hath offended the law; and, sir, we
take him to be a thief, too, sir, for we have found upon
him, sir, a strange picklock, which we have sent to the
deputy.
DUKE (*to Pompey*)
Fie, sirrah, a bawd, a wicked bawd!
The evil that thou causest to be done,
That is thy means to live. Do thou but think
What 'tis to cram a maw or clothe a back   290
From such a filthy vice. Say to thyself,
'From their abominable and beastly touches
I drink, I eat, array myself, and live'.
Canst thou believe thy living is a life,
So stinkingly depending? Go mend, go mend.   295
POMPEY Indeed it does stink in some sort, sir. But yet, sir,
I would prove—
DUKE
Nay, if the devil have given thee proofs for sin,
Thou wilt prove his.—Take him to prison, officer.
Correction and instruction must both work   300
Ere this rude beast will profit.
ELBOW He must before the deputy, sir; he has given him
warning. The deputy cannot abide a whoremaster. If
he be a whoremonger and comes before him, he were
as good go a mile on his errand.   305
DUKE
That we were all as some would seem to be—
Free from our faults, or faults from seeming free.
ELBOW His neck will come to your waist: a cord, sir.

Enter Lucio

POMPEY I spy comfort, I cry bail. Here's a gentleman, and
a friend of mine.   310
LUCIO How now, noble Pompey? What, at the wheels of
Caesar? Art thou led in triumph? What, is there none
of Pygmalion's images newly made woman to be had
now, for putting the hand in the pocket and extracting
clutched? What reply, ha? What sayst thou to this
tune, matter, and method? Is't not drowned i'th' last
rain, ha? What sayst thou, trot? Is the world as it was,
man? Which is the way? Is it sad and few words? Or
how? The trick of it?
DUKE Still thus and thus; still worse!   320

LUCIO How doth my dear morsel thy mistress? Procures she still, ha?

POMPEY Troth, sir, she hath eaten up all her beef, and she is herself in the tub. 324

LUCIO Why, 'tis good, it is the right of it, it must be so. Ever your fresh whore and your powdered bawd; an unshunned consequence, it must be so. Art going to prison, Pompey?

POMPEY Yes, faith, sir.

LUCIO Why 'tis not amiss, Pompey. Farewell. Go; say I sent thee thither. For debt, Pompey, or how? 331

ELBOW For being a bawd, for being a bawd.

LUCIO Well then, imprison him. If imprisonment be the due of a bawd, why, 'tis his right. Bawd is he doubtless, and of antiquity too—bawd born. Farewell, good Pompey. Commend me to the prison, Pompey. You will turn good husband now, Pompey; you will keep the house.

POMPEY I hope, sir, your good worship will be my bail?

LUCIO No, indeed, will I not, Pompey; it is not the wear. I will pray, Pompey, to increase your bondage. If you take it not patiently, why, your mettle is the more. Adieu, trusty Pompey.—Bless you, friar.

DUKE And you.

LUCIO Does Bridget paint still, Pompey, ha? 345

ELBOW (to Pompey) Come your ways, sir, come.

POMPEY (to Lucio) You will not bail me then, sir?

LUCIO Then, Pompey, nor now.—What news abroad, friar, what news?

ELBOW (to Pompey) Come your ways, sir, come. 350

LUCIO Go to kennel, Pompey, go.

Exeunt Elbow, Pompey, and officers

What news, friar, of the Duke?

DUKE I know none. Can you tell me of any?

LUCIO Some say he is with the Emperor of Russia; other some, he is in Rome. But where is he, think you? 355

DUKE I know not where; but wheresoever, I wish him well.

LUCIO It was a mad, fantastical trick of him to steal from the state, and usurp the beggary he was never born to. Lord Angelo dukes it well in his absence; he puts transgression to't. 361

DUKE He does well in't.

LUCIO A little more lenity to lechery would do no harm in him. Something too crabbed that way, friar.

DUKE It is too general a vice, and severity must cure it.

LUCIO Yes, in good sooth, the vice is of a great kindred, it is well allied. But it is impossible to extirp it quite, friar, till eating and drinking be put down. They say this Angelo was not made by man and woman, after this downright way of creation. Is it true, think you?

DUKE How should he be made, then? 371

LUCIO Some report a sea-maid spawned him, some that he was begot between two stockfishes. But it is certain that when he makes water his urine is congealed ice; that I know to be true. And he is a motion ungenerative; that's infallible. 376

DUKE You are pleasant, sir, and speak apace.

LUCIO Why, what a ruthless thing is this in him, for the rebellion of a codpiece to take away the life of a man! Would the Duke that is absent have done this? Ere he would have hanged a man for the getting a hundred bastards, he would have paid for the nursing a thousand. He had some feeling of the sport, he knew the service, and that instructed him to mercy.

DUKE I never heard the absent Duke much detected for women; he was not inclined that way. 386

LUCIO O sir, you are deceived.

DUKE 'Tis not possible.

LUCIO Who, not the Duke? Yes, your beggar of fifty; and his use was to put a ducat in her clack-dish. The Duke had crochets in him. He would be drunk too, that let me inform you. 392

DUKE You do him wrong, surely.

LUCIO Sir, I was an inward of his. A shy fellow was the Duke, and I believe I know the cause of his withdrawing.

DUKE What, I prithee, might be the cause? 396

LUCIO No, pardon, 'tis a secret must be locked within the teeth and the lips. But this I can let you understand. The greater file of the subject held the Duke to be wise.

DUKE Wise? Why, no question but he was. 400

LUCIO A very superficial, ignorant, unweighing fellow.

DUKE Either this is envy in you, folly, or mistaking. The very stream of his life, and the business he hath helmed, must, upon a warranted need, give him a better proclamation. Let him be but testimonied in his own bringings-forth, and he shall appear to the envious a scholar, a statesman, and a soldier. Therefore you speak unskilfully, or, if your knowledge be more, it is much darkened in your malice.

LUCIO Sir, I know him and I love him. 410

DUKE Love talks with better knowledge, and knowledge with dearer love.

LUCIO Come, sir, I know what I know.

DUKE I can hardly believe that, since you know not what you speak. But if ever the Duke return, as our prayers are he may, let me desire you to make your answer before him. If it be honest you have spoke, you have courage to maintain it. I am bound to call upon you; and I pray you, your name? 419

LUCIO Sir, my name is Lucio, well known to the Duke.

DUKE He shall know you better, sir, if I may live to report you.

LUCIO I fear you not.

DUKE O, you hope the Duke will return no more, or you imagine me too unhurtful an opposite. But indeed I can do you little harm; you'll forswear this again. 426

LUCIO I'll be hanged first. Thou art deceived in me, friar. But no more of this. Canst thou tell if Claudio die tomorrow or no?

DUKE Why should he die, sir? 430

LUCIO Why? For filling a bottle with a tundish. I would the Duke we talk of were returned again; this ungenitured agent will unpeople the province with continency. Sparrows must not build in his house-eaves, because they are lecherous. The Duke yet would have dark deeds darkly answered: he would never bring them to light. Would he were returned. Marry, this Claudio is condemned for untrussing. Farewell, good friar. I prithee pray for me. The Duke, I say to thee again, would eat mutton on Fridays. He's not past it yet, and, I say to thee, he would mouth with a beggar, though she smelt brown bread and garlic. Say that I said so. Farewell.   *Exit*

DUKE
No might nor greatness in mortality
Can censure scape; back-wounding calumny   45
The whitest virtue strikes. What king so strong
Can tie the gall up in the slanderous tongue?
        Enter Escalus, the Provost, and Mistress Overdone
But who comes here?

ESCALUS (*to the Provost*) Go, away with her to prison.

MISTRESS OVERDONE Good my lord, be good to me. Your honour is accounted a merciful man, good my lord.

ESCALUS Double and treble admonition, and still forfeit in the same kind! This would make mercy swear and play the tyrant.

PROVOST A bawd of eleven years' continuance, may it please your honour.   456

MISTRESS OVERDONE My lord, this is one Lucio's information against me. Mistress Kate Keepdown was with child by him in the Duke's time; he promised her marriage. His child is a year and a quarter old come Philip and Jacob. I have kept it myself; and see how he goes about to abuse me.   462

ESCALUS That fellow is a fellow of much licence. Let him be called before us. Away with her to prison. Go to, no more words. Provost, my brother Angelo will not be altered; Claudio must die tomorrow. Let him be furnished with divines, and have all charitable preparation. If my brother wrought by my pity, it should not be so with him.

PROVOST So please you, this friar hath been with him and advised him for th'entertainment of death.   471
        ⌈*Exeunt Provost and Mistress Overdone*⌉

ESCALUS Good even, good father.

DUKE Bliss and goodness on you.

ESCALUS Of whence are you?

DUKE
Not of this country, though my chance is now   475
To use it for my time. I am a brother
Of gracious order, late come from the See
In special business from his Holiness.

ESCALUS What news abroad i'th' world?

DUKE None, but that there is so great a fever on goodness that the dissolution of it must cure it. Novelty is only in request, and it is as dangerous to be aged in any kind of course as it is virtuous to be inconstant in any undertaking. There is scarce truth enough alive to make societies secure, but security enough to make fellowships accursed. Much upon this riddle runs the wisdom of the world. This news is old enough, yet it is every day's news. I pray you, sir, of what disposition was the Duke?   489

ESCALUS One that, above all other strifes, contended especially to know himself.   491

DUKE What pleasure was he given to?

ESCALUS Rather rejoicing to see another merry than merry at anything which professed to make him rejoice; a gentleman of all temperance. But leave we him to his events, with a prayer they may prove prosperous, and let me desire to know how you find Claudio prepared. I am made to understand that you have lent him visitation.   499

DUKE He professes to have received no sinister measure from his judge, but most willingly humbles himself to the determination of justice. Yet had he framed to himself, by the instruction of his frailty, many deceiving promises of life, which I, by my good leisure, have discredited to him; and now is he resolved to die.   505

ESCALUS You have paid the heavens your function, and the prisoner the very debt of your calling. I have laboured for the poor gentleman to the extremest shore of my modesty, but my brother-justice have I found so severe that he hath forced me to tell him he is indeed Justice.   511

DUKE If his own life answer the straitness of his proceeding, it shall become him well; wherein if he chance to fail, he hath sentenced himself.

ESCALUS I am going to visit the prisoner. Fare you well.

DUKE Peace be with you.   *Exit Escalus*
He who the sword of heaven will bear
Should be as holy as severe,
Pattern in himself to know,
Grace to stand, and virtue go,   520
More nor less to others paying
Than by self-offences weighing.
Shame to him whose cruel striking
Kills for faults of his own liking!
Twice treble shame on Angelo,   525
To weed my vice, and let his grow!
O, what may man within him hide,
Though angel on the outward side!
How may likeness made in crimes
Make my practice on the times   530
To draw with idle spiders' strings
Most ponderous and substantial things?
Craft against vice I must apply.
With Angelo tonight shall lie
His old betrothèd but despisèd.   535
So disguise shall, by th' disguisèd,
Pay with falsehood false exacting,
And perform an old contracting.   *Exit*

❀

4.1   *Mariana ⌈discovered⌉ with a Boy singing*

BOY
Take, O take those lips away
    That so sweetly were forsworn,
And those eyes, the break of day
    Lights that do mislead the morn;
But my kisses bring again, bring again,   5
Seals of love, though sealed in vain, sealed in vain.

Enter the Duke, disguised as a friar

MARIANA
Break off thy song, and haste thee quick away.
Here comes a man of comfort, whose advice
Hath often stilled my brawling discontent.   *Exit Boy*
I cry you mercy, sir, and well could wish   10
You had not found me here so musical.
Let me excuse me, and believe me so:
My mirth it much displeased, but pleased my woe.

DUKE
'Tis good; though music oft hath such a charm
To make bad good, and good provoke to harm.   15
I pray you tell me, hath anybody enquired for me here
today? Much upon this time have I promised here to
meet.

MARIANA You have not been enquired after; I have sat
here all day.   20
Enter Isabella

DUKE I do constantly believe you; the time is come even
now. I shall crave your forbearance a little. Maybe I
will call upon you anon, for some advantage to yourself.

MARIANA I am always bound to you.   *Exit*

DUKE Very well met, and welcome.   25
What is the news from this good deputy?

ISABELLA
He hath a garden circummured with brick,
Whose western side is with a vineyard backed;
And to that vineyard is a plankèd gate,
That makes his opening with this bigger key.   30
This other doth command a little door
Which from the vineyard to the garden leads.
There have I made my promise
Upon the heavy middle of the night
To call upon him.   35

DUKE
But shall you on your knowledge find this way?

ISABELLA
I have ta'en a due and wary note upon't.
With whispering and most guilty diligence,
In action all of precept, he did show me
The way twice o'er.

DUKE   Are there no other tokens   40
Between you 'greed concerning her observance?

ISABELLA
No, none, but only a repair i'th' dark,
And that I have possessed him my most stay
Can be but brief, for I have made him know
I have a servant comes with me along   45
That stays upon me, whose persuasion is
I come about my brother.

DUKE   'Tis well borne up.
I have not yet made known to Mariana
A word of this.—What ho, within! Come forth!
Enter Mariana
(*To Mariana*) I pray you be acquainted with this maid.
She comes to do you good.

ISABELLA   I do desire the like.   51

DUKE (*to Mariana*)
Do you persuade yourself that I respect you?

MARIANA
Good friar, I know you do, and so have found it.

DUKE
Take then this your companion by the hand,
Who hath a story ready for your ear.   55
I shall attend your leisure; but make haste,
The vaporous night approaches.

MARIANA (*to Isabella*)   Will't please you walk aside?
⌐*Exeunt Mariana and Isabella*⌐

DUKE
O place and greatness, millions of false eyes
Are stuck upon thee; volumes of report
Run with their false and most contrarious quest   60
Upon thy doings; thousand escapes of wit
Make thee the father of their idle dream,
And rack thee in their fancies.
⌐*Enter Mariana and Isabella*⌐
          Welcome. How agreed?

ISABELLA
She'll take the enterprise upon her, father,
If you advise it.

DUKE   It is not my consent,   65
But my entreaty too.

ISABELLA (*to Mariana*) Little have you to say
When you depart from him but, soft and low,
'Remember now my brother'.

MARIANA   Fear me not.

DUKE
Nor, gentle daughter, fear you not at all.
He is your husband on a pre-contract.   70
To bring you thus together 'tis no sin,
Sith that the justice of your title to him
Doth flourish the deceit. Come, let us go.
Our corn's to reap, for yet our tilth's to sow.   *Exeunt*

4.2   *Enter the Provost and Pompey*

PROVOST Come hither, sirrah. Can you cut off a man's
head?

POMPEY If the man be a bachelor, sir, I can; but if he be
a married man, he's his wife's head, and I can never
cut off a woman's head.   5

PROVOST Come, sir, leave me your snatches, and yield me
a direct answer. Tomorrow morning are to die Claudio
and Barnardine. Here is in our prison a common
executioner, who in his office lacks a helper. If you will
take it on you to assist him, it shall redeem you from
your gyves; if not, you shall have your full time of
imprisonment, and your deliverance with an unpitied
whipping; for you have been a notorious bawd.   13

POMPEY Sir, I have been an unlawful bawd time out of
mind, but yet I will be content to be a lawful hangman.
I would be glad to receive some instruction from my
fellow partner.

PROVOST What ho, Abhorson! Where's Abhorson there?
Enter Abhorson

ABHORSON Do you call, sir?   19

PROVOST Sirrah, here's a fellow will help you tomorrow
in your execution. If you think it meet, compound with
him by the year, and let him abide here with you; if
not, use him for the present, and dismiss him. He
cannot plead his estimation with you; he hath been a
bawd.   25
ABHORSON A bawd, sir? Fie upon him, he will discredit
our mystery.
PROVOST Go to, sir, you weigh equally; a feather will turn
the scale.   *Exit*
POMPEY Pray, sir, by your good favour—for surely, sir, a
good favour you have, but that you have a hanging
look—do you call, sir, your occupation a mystery?
ABHORSON Ay, sir, a mystery.   33
POMPEY Painting, sir, I have heard say is a mystery; and
your whores, sir, being members of my occupation,
using painting, do prove my occupation a mystery. But
what mystery there should be in hanging, if I should
be hanged I cannot imagine.
ABHORSON Sir, it is a mystery.
POMPEY Proof.   40
ABHORSON Every true man's apparel fits your thief—
POMPEY If it be too little for your thief, your true man
thinks it big enough. If it be too big for your thief, your
thief thinks it little enough. So every true man's apparel
fits your thief.   45
        Enter Provost
PROVOST Are you agreed?
POMPEY Sir, I will serve him, for I do find your hangman
is a more penitent trade than your bawd—he doth
oftener ask forgiveness.
PROVOST (*to Abhorson*) You, sirrah, provide your block and
your axe tomorrow, four o'clock.   51
ABHORSON (*to Pompey*) Come on, bawd, I will instruct thee
in my trade. Follow.
POMPEY I do desire to learn, sir, and I hope, if you have
occasion to use me for your own turn, you shall find
me yare. For truly, sir, for your kindness I owe you a
good turn.   57
PROVOST
Call hither Barnardine and Claudio.
                        Exeunt Abhorson and Pompey
Th'one has my pity; not a jot the other,
Being a murderer, though he were my brother.   60
        Enter Claudio
Look, here's the warrant, Claudio, for thy death.
'Tis now dead midnight, and by eight tomorrow
Thou must be made immortal. Where's Barnardine?
CLAUDIO
As fast locked up in sleep as guiltless labour
When it lies starkly in the travailer's bones.   65
He will not wake.
PROVOST   Who can do good on him?
Well, go prepare yourself.
        Knocking within
                        But hark, what noise?
Heaven give your spirits comfort!   *Exit Claudio*
        ⌜*Knocking again*⌝
                        By and by!

I hope it is some pardon or reprieve
For the most gentle Claudio.
        Enter the Duke, disguised as a friar
                        Welcome, father.   70
DUKE
The best and wholesom'st spirits of the night
Envelop you, good Provost! Who called here of late?
PROVOST None since the curfew rung.
DUKE Not Isabel?
PROVOST No.   75
DUKE They will then, ere't be long.
PROVOST What comfort is for Claudio?
DUKE There's some in hope.
PROVOST It is a bitter deputy.
DUKE
Not so, not so; his life is paralleled   80
Even with the stroke and line of his great justice.
He doth with holy abstinence subdue
That in himself which he spurs on his power
To qualify in others. Were he mealed with that
Which he corrects, then were he tyrannous;   85
But this being so, he's just.
        Knocking within
                        Now are they come.
        ⌜*The Provost goes to a door*⌝
This is a gentle Provost. Seldom when
The steelèd jailer is the friend of men.
        Knocking within
(*To Provost*) How now, what noise? That spirit's
possessed with haste
That wounds th'unlisting postern with these strokes.
PROVOST
There he must stay until the officer   91
Arise to let him in. He is called up.
DUKE
Have you no countermand for Claudio yet,
But he must die tomorrow?
PROVOST   None, sir, none.
DUKE
As near the dawning, Provost, as it is,   95
You shall hear more ere morning.
PROVOST   Happily
You something know, yet I believe there comes
No countermand. No such example have we;
Besides, upon the very siege of justice
Lord Angelo hath to the public ear   100
Professed the contrary.
        Enter a Messenger
This is his lordship's man.
⌜DUKE⌝ And here comes Claudio's pardon.
MESSENGER (*giving a paper to Provost*) My lord hath sent
you this note, and by me this further charge: that you
swerve not from the smallest article of it, neither in
time, matter, or other circumstance. Good morrow;
for, as I take it, it is almost day.
PROVOST I shall obey him.   *Exit Messenger*
DUKE (*aside*)
This is his pardon, purchased by such sin   110
For which the pardoner himself is in.

Hence hath offence his quick celerity,
When it is borne in high authority.
When vice makes mercy, mercy's so extended
That for the fault's love is th'offender friended.—   115
Now sir, what news?

PROVOST I told you: Lord Angelo, belike thinking me
remiss in mine office, awakens me with this unwonted
putting-on; methinks strangely, for he hath not used
it before.   120

DUKE Pray you let's hear.

⌜PROVOST⌝ (*reading the letter*) 'Whatsoever you may hear
to the contrary, let Claudio be executed by four of the
clock, and in the afternoon Barnardine. For my better
satisfaction, let me have Claudio's head sent me by five.
Let this be duly performed, with a thought that more
depends on it than we must yet deliver. Thus fail not
to do your office, as you will answer it at your peril.'
What say you to this, sir?

DUKE What is that Barnardine, who is to be executed in
th'afternoon?   131

PROVOST A Bohemian born, but here nursed up and bred;
one that is a prisoner nine years old.

DUKE How came it that the absent Duke had not either
delivered him to his liberty or executed him? I have
heard it was ever his manner to do so.   136

PROVOST His friends still wrought reprieves for him; and
indeed his fact, till now in the government of Lord
Angelo, came not to an undoubtful proof.

DUKE It is now apparent?   140

PROVOST Most manifest, and not denied by himself.

DUKE Hath he borne himself penitently in prison? How
seems he to be touched?

PROVOST A man that apprehends death no more dreadfully
but as a drunken sleep; careless, reckless, and fearless
of what's past, present, or to come; insensible of
mortality, and desperately mortal.   147

DUKE He wants advice.

PROVOST He will hear none. He hath evermore had the
liberty of the prison. Give him leave to escape hence,
he would not. Drunk many times a day, if not many
days entirely drunk. We have very oft awaked him as
if to carry him to execution, and showed him a seeming
warrant for it; it hath not moved him at all.   154

DUKE More of him anon. There is written in your brow,
Provost, honesty and constancy. If I read it not truly,
my ancient skill beguiles me. But in the boldness of my
cunning, I will lay myself in hazard. Claudio, whom
here you have warrant to execute, is no greater forfeit
to the law than Angelo who hath sentenced him. To
make you understand this in a manifested effect, I crave
but four days' respite, for the which you are to do me
both a present and a dangerous courtesy.

PROVOST Pray sir, in what?

DUKE In the delaying death.   165

PROVOST Alack, how may I do it, having the hour limited,
and an express command under penalty to deliver his
head in the view of Angelo? I may make my case as
Claudio's to cross this in the smallest.

DUKE By the vow of mine order, I warrant you, if my
instructions may be your guide, let this Barnardine be
this morning executed, and his head borne to Angelo.

PROVOST Angelo hath seen them both, and will discover
the favour.   174

DUKE O, death's a great disguiser, and you may add to
it. Shave the head and tie the beard, and say it was
the desire of the penitent to be so bared before his
death; you know the course is common. If anything
fall to you upon this more than thanks and good
fortune, by the saint whom I profess, I will plead against
it with my life.   181

PROVOST Pardon me, good father, it is against my oath.

DUKE Were you sworn to the Duke or to the deputy?

PROVOST To him and to his substitutes.

DUKE You will think you have made no offence if the
Duke avouch the justice of your dealing?   186

PROVOST But what likelihood is in that?

DUKE Not a resemblance, but a certainty. Yet since I see
you fearful, that neither my coat, integrity, nor
persuasion can with ease attempt you, I will go further
than I meant, to pluck all fears out of you. (*Showing a
letter*) Look you, sir, here is the hand and seal of the
Duke. You know the character, I doubt not, and the
signet is not strange to you?

PROVOST I know them both.   195

DUKE The contents of this is the return of the Duke. You
shall anon over-read it at your pleasure, where you
shall find within these two days he will be here. This
is a thing that Angelo knows not, for he this very day
receives letters of strange tenor, perchance of the Duke's
death, perchance entering into some monastery; but
by chance nothing of what is writ. Look, th'unfolding
star calls up the shepherd. Put not yourself into
amazement how these things should be. All difficulties
are but easy when they are known. Call your
executioner, and off with Barnardine's head. I will give
him a present shrift, and advise him for a better place.
Yet you are amazed; but this shall absolutely resolve
you. Come away, it is almost clear dawn.   *Exeunt*

4.3   *Enter Pompey*

POMPEY I am as well acquainted here as I was in our
house of profession. One would think it were Mistress
Overdone's own house, for here be many of her old
customers. First, here's young Master Rash; he's in for
a commodity of brown paper and old ginger, nine score
and seventeen pounds, of which he made five marks
ready money. Marry, then ginger was not much in
request, for the old women were all dead. Then is there
here one Master Caper, at the suit of Master Threepile
the mercer, for some four suits of peach-coloured satin,
which now peaches him a beggar. Then have we here
young Dizzy, and young Master Deepvow, and Master
Copperspur and Master Starve-lackey the rapier and
dagger man, and young Drop-hair that killed lusty
Pudding, and Master Forthright the tilter, and brave
Master Shoe-tie the great traveller, and wild Half-can

that stabbed Pots, and I think forty more, all great
doers in our trade, and are now 'for the Lord's sake'.
  Enter Abhorson
ABHORSON Sirrah, bring Barnardine hither.
POMPEY Master Barnardine! You must rise and be hanged,
 Master Barnardine!   21
ABHORSON What ho, Barnardine!
BARNARDINE (*within*) A pox o' your throats! Who makes
 that noise there? What are you?
POMPEY Your friends, sir; the hangman. You must be so
 good, sir, to rise and be put to death.   26
BARNARDINE Away, you rogue, away! I am sleepy.
ABHORSON Tell him he must awake, and that quickly too.
POMPEY Pray, Master Barnardine, awake till you are
 executed, and sleep afterwards.   30
ABHORSON Go in to him and fetch him out.
POMPEY He is coming, sir, he is coming. I hear his straw
 rustle.
ABHORSON Is the axe upon the block, sirrah?
POMPEY Very ready, sir.   35
  Enter Barnardine
BARNARDINE How now, Abhorson, what's the news with
 you?
ABHORSON Truly, sir, I would desire you to clap into your
 prayers, for, look you, the warrant's come.
BARNARDINE You rogue, I have been drinking all night. I
 am not fitted for't.   41
POMPEY O, the better, sir; for he that drinks all night,
 and is hanged betimes in the morning, may sleep the
 sounder all the next day.
  Enter the Duke, disguised as a friar
ABHORSON (*to Barnardine*) Look you, sir, here comes your
 ghostly father. Do we jest now, think you?   46
DUKE (*to Barnardine*) Sir, induced by my charity, and
 hearing how hastily you are to depart, I am come to
 advise you, comfort you, and pray with you.   49
BARNARDINE Friar, not I. I have been drinking hard all
 night, and I will have more time to prepare me, or
 they shall beat out my brains with billets. I will not
 consent to die this day, that's certain.
DUKE
 O sir, you must; and therefore, I beseech you,
 Look forward on the journey you shall go.   55
BARNARDINE I swear I will not die today, for any man's
 persuasion.
DUKE But hear you—
BARNARDINE Not a word. If you have anything to say to
 me, come to my ward, for thence will not I today. 60
              Exit
DUKE
 Unfit to live or die. O gravel heart!
 After him, fellows; bring him to the block.
      Exeunt Abhorson and Pompey
  Enter Provost
PROVOST
 Now, sir, how do you find the prisoner?
DUKE
 A creature unprepared, unmeet for death;

 And to transport him in the mind he is   65
 Were damnable.
PROVOST   Here in the prison, father,
 There died this morning of a cruel fever
 One Ragusine, a most notorious pirate,
 A man of Claudio's years, his beard and head
 Just of his colour. What if we do omit   70
 This reprobate till he were well inclined,
 And satisfy the deputy with the visage
 Of Ragusine, more like to Claudio?
DUKE
 O, 'tis an accident that heaven provides.
 Dispatch it presently; the hour draws on   75
 Prefixed by Angelo. See this be done,
 And sent according to command, whiles I
 Persuade this rude wretch willingly to die.
PROVOST
 This shall be done, good father, presently.
 But Barnardine must die this afternoon;   80
 And how shall we continue Claudio,
 To save me from the danger that might come
 If he were known alive?
DUKE   Let this be done:
 Put them in secret holds, both Barnardine and Claudio.
 Ere twice the sun hath made his journal greeting 85
 To yonder generation, you shall find
 Your safety manifested.
PROVOST   I am your free dependant.
DUKE
 Quick, dispatch, and send the head to Angelo.
            Exit Provost
 Now will I write letters to Angelo—
 The Provost, he shall bear them—whose contents 90
 Shall witness to him I am near at home,
 And that by great injunctions I am bound
 To enter publicly. Him I'll desire
 To meet me at the consecrated fount
 A league below the city, and from thence,   95
 By cold gradation and well-balanced form,
 We shall proceed with Angelo.
  Enter the Provost, with Ragusine's head
PROVOST
 Here is the head; I'll carry it myself.
DUKE
 Convenient is it. Make a swift return,
 For I would commune with you of such things 100
 That want no ear but yours.
PROVOST I'll make all speed.
ISABELLA (*within*) Peace, ho, be here!
DUKE
 The tongue of Isabel. She's come to know
 If yet her brother's pardon be come hither; 105
 But I will keep her ignorant of her good,
 To make her heavenly comforts of despair
 When it is least expected.
ISABELLA ⌈*within*⌉   Ho, by your leave!
  ⌈*Enter Isabella*⌉
DUKE
 Good morning to you, fair and gracious daughter.

ISABELLA
  The better, given me by so holy a man.   110
  Hath yet the deputy sent my brother's pardon?
DUKE
  He hath released him, Isabel, from the world.
  His head is off and sent to Angelo.
ISABELLA
  Nay, but it is not so.
DUKE   It is no other.
  Show your wisdom, daughter, in your close patience.
ISABELLA
  O, I will to him and pluck out his eyes!   116
DUKE
  You shall not be admitted to his sight.
ISABELLA (*weeping*)
  Unhappy Claudio! Wretched Isabel!
  Injurious world! Most damnèd Angelo!
DUKE
  This nor hurts him, nor profits you a jot.   120
  Forbear it, therefore; give your cause to heaven.
  Mark what I say, which you shall find
  By every syllable a faithful verity.
  The Duke comes home tomorrow—nay, dry your
      eyes—
  One of our convent, and his confessor,   125
  Gives me this instance. Already he hath carried
  Notice to Escalus and Angelo,
  Who do prepare to meet him at the gates,
  There to give up their power. If you can pace your
      wisdom
  In that good path that I would wish it go,   130
  And you shall have your bosom on this wretch,
  Grace of the Duke, revenges to your heart,
  And general honour.
ISABELLA   I am directed by you.
DUKE
  This letter, then, to Friar Peter give.
  'Tis that he sent me of the Duke's return.   135
  Say by this token I desire his company
  At Mariana's house tonight. Her cause and yours
  I'll perfect him withal, and he shall bring you
  Before the Duke, and to the head of Angelo
  Accuse him home and home. For my poor self,   140
  I am combinèd by a sacred vow,
  And shall be absent. (*Giving the letter*) Wend you with
      this letter.
  Command these fretting waters from your eyes
  With a light heart. Trust not my holy order
  If I pervert your course.
      Enter Lucio
                Who's here?
LUCIO   Good even.   145
  Friar, where's the Provost?
DUKE   Not within, sir.
LUCIO O pretty Isabella, I am pale at mine heart to see
  thine eyes so red. Thou must be patient. I am fain to
  dine and sup with water and bran; I dare not for my

head fill my belly; one fruitful meal would set me to't.
But they say the Duke will be here tomorrow. By my
troth, Isabel, I loved thy brother. If the old fantastical
Duke of dark corners had been at home, he had lived.
      ⌈*Exit Isabella*⌉
DUKE Sir, the Duke is marvellous little beholden to your
  reports; but the best is, he lives not in them.   155
LUCIO Friar, thou knowest not the Duke so well as I do.
  He's a better woodman than thou tak'st him for.
DUKE Well, you'll answer this one day. Fare ye well.
LUCIO Nay, tarry, I'll go along with thee. I can tell thee
  pretty tales of the Duke.   160
DUKE You have told me too many of him already, sir, if
  they be true; if not true, none were enough.
LUCIO I was once before him for getting a wench with
  child.
DUKE Did you such a thing?   165
LUCIO Yes, marry, did I; but I was fain to forswear it.
  They would else have married me to the rotten medlar.
DUKE Sir, your company is fairer than honest. Rest you
  well.   169
LUCIO By my troth, I'll go with thee to the lane's end. If
  bawdy talk offend you, we'll have very little of it. Nay,
  friar, I am a kind of burr; I shall stick.   *Exeunt*

4.4 *Enter Angelo and Escalus*
ESCALUS Every letter he hath writ hath disvouched other.
ANGELO In most uneven and distracted manner. His
  actions show much like to madness. Pray heaven his
  wisdom be not tainted. And why meet him at the gates,
  and redeliver our authorities there?   5
ESCALUS I guess not.
ANGELO And why should we proclaim it in an hour before
  his entering, that if any crave redress of injustice, they
  should exhibit their petitions in the street?   9
ESCALUS He shows his reason for that—to have a dispatch
  of complaints, and to deliver us from devices hereafter,
  which shall then have no power to stand against us.
ANGELO
  Well, I beseech you let it be proclaimed.
  Betimes i'th' morn I'll call you at your house.
  Give notice to such men of sort and suit   15
  As are to meet him.
ESCALUS I shall, sir. Fare you well.
ANGELO Good night.   *Exit Escalus*
  This deed unshapes me quite, makes me unpregnant
  And dull to all proceedings. A deflowered maid,   20
  And by an eminent body that enforced
  The law against it! But that her tender shame
  Will not proclaim against her maiden loss,
  How might she tongue me! Yet reason dares her no,
  For my authority bears off a credent bulk,   25
  That no particular scandal once can touch
  But it confounds the breather. He should have lived,
  Save that his riotous youth, with dangerous sense,
  Might in the times to come have ta'en revenge
  By so receiving a dishonoured life   30

With ransom of such shame. Would yet he had lived.
Alack, when once our grace we have forgot,
Nothing goes right; we would, and we would not.
                                                        Exit

4.5   *Enter the Duke, in his own habit, and Friar Peter*
DUKE
These letters at fit time deliver me.
The Provost knows our purpose and our plot.
The matter being afoot, keep your instruction,
And hold you ever to our special drift,
Though sometimes you do blench from this to that   5
As cause doth minister. Go call at Flavio's house,
And tell him where I stay. Give the like notice
To Valentinus, Rowland, and to Crassus,
And bid them bring the trumpets to the gate.
But send me Flavius first.
FRIAR   It shall be speeded well.   10
                                                        Exit

        Enter Varrius
DUKE
I thank thee, Varrius; thou hast made good haste.
Come, we will walk. There's other of our friends
Will greet us here anon. My gentle Varrius!   *Exeunt*

4.6   *Enter Isabella and Mariana*
ISABELLA
To speak so indirectly I am loath—
I would say the truth, but to accuse him so,
That is your part—yet I am advised to do it,
He says, to veil full purpose.
MARIANA   Be ruled by him.
ISABELLA
Besides, he tells me that if peradventure   5
He speak against me on the adverse side,
I should not think it strange, for 'tis a physic
That's bitter to sweet end.
        Enter Friar Peter
MARIANA I would Friar Peter—
ISABELLA O, peace; the friar is come.   10
FRIAR PETER
Come, I have found you out a stand most fit,
Where you may have such vantage on the Duke
He shall not pass you. Twice have the trumpets
        sounded.
The generous and gravest citizens
Have hent the gates, and very near upon   15
The Duke is ent'ring; therefore hence, away.   *Exeunt*

                    ❀

5.1   *Enter ⌈at one door⌉ the Duke, Varrius, and lords,*
        ⌈at another door⌉ Angelo, Escalus, Lucio, citizens,
        ⌈and officers⌉
DUKE (*to Angelo*)
My very worthy cousin, fairly met.
   (*To Escalus*) Our old and faithful friend, we are glad to
   see you.

ANGELO *and* ESCALUS
Happy return be to your royal grace.
DUKE
Many and hearty thankings to you both.
We have made enquiry of you, and we hear   5
Such goodness of your justice that our soul
Cannot but yield you forth to public thanks,
Forerunning more requital.
ANGELO   You make my bonds still greater.
DUKE
O, your desert speaks loud, and I should wrong it
To lock it in the wards of covert bosom,   10
When it deserves with characters of brass
A forted residence 'gainst the tooth of time
And razure of oblivion. Give me your hand,
And let the subject see, to make them know
That outward courtesies would fain proclaim   15
Favours that keep within. Come, Escalus,
You must walk by us on our other hand,
And good supporters are you.
        ⌈*They walk forward.*⌉
        Enter Friar Peter and Isabella
FRIAR PETER
Now is your time. Speak loud, and kneel before him.
ISABELLA (*kneeling*)
Justice, O royal Duke! Vail your regard   20
Upon a wronged—I would fain have said, a maid.
O worthy prince, dishonour not your eye
By throwing it on any other object,
Till you have heard me in my true complaint,
And given me justice, justice, justice, justice!   25
DUKE
Relate your wrongs. In what? By whom? Be brief.
Here is Lord Angelo shall give you justice.
Reveal yourself to him.
ISABELLA   O worthy Duke,
You bid me seek redemption of the devil.
Hear me yourself, for that which I must speak   30
Must either punish me, not being believed,
Or wring redress from you. Hear me, O hear me, hear!
ANGELO
My lord, her wits, I fear me, are not firm.
She hath been a suitor to me for her brother,
Cut off by course of justice.
ISABELLA ⌈*standing*⌉   By course of justice!   35
ANGELO
And she will speak most bitterly and strange.
ISABELLA
Most strange, but yet most truly, will I speak.
That Angelo's forsworn, is it not strange?
That Angelo's a murderer, is't not strange?
That Angelo is an adulterous thief,   40
An hypocrite, a virgin-violator,
Is it not strange, and strange?
DUKE   Nay, it is ten times strange!
ISABELLA
It is not truer he is Angelo

Than this is all as true as it is strange.
Nay, it is ten times true, for truth is truth   45
To th'end of reck'ning.
DUKE   Away with her. Poor soul,
She speaks this in th'infirmity of sense.
ISABELLA
O prince, I conjure thee, as thou believ'st
There is another comfort than this world,
That thou neglect me not with that opinion   50
That I am touched with madness. Make not
    impossible
That which but seems unlike. 'Tis not impossible
But one, the wicked'st caitiff on the ground,
May seem as shy, as grave, as just, as absolute,
As Angelo; even so may Angelo,   55
In all his dressings, characts, titles, forms,
Be an arch-villain. Believe it, royal prince,
If he be less, he's nothing; but he's more,
Had I more name for badness.
DUKE   By mine honesty,
If she be mad, as I believe no other,   60
Her madness hath the oddest frame of sense,
Such a dependency of thing on thing
As e'er I heard in madness.
ISABELLA   O gracious Duke,
Harp not on that, nor do not banish reason
For inequality; but let your reason serve   65
To make the truth appear where it seems hid,
And hide the false seems true.
DUKE   Many that are not mad
Have sure more lack of reason. What would you say?
ISABELLA
I am the sister of one Claudio,
Condemned upon the act of fornication   70
To lose his head, condemned by Angelo.
I, in probation of a sisterhood,
Was sent to by my brother, one Lucio
As then the messenger.
LUCIO   That's I, an't like your grace.
I came to her from Claudio, and desired her   75
To try her gracious fortune with Lord Angelo
For her poor brother's pardon.
ISABELLA   That's he indeed.
DUKE (to Lucio)
You were not bid to speak.
LUCIO   No, my good lord,
Nor wished to hold my peace.
DUKE
I wish you now, then. Pray you take note of it;   80
And when you have a business for yourself,
Pray heaven you then be perfect.
LUCIO   I warrant your honour.
DUKE
The warrant's for yourself; take heed to't.
ISABELLA
This gentleman told somewhat of my tale—
LUCIO Right.   85

DUKE
It may be right, but you are i'the wrong
To speak before your time. (To Isabella) Proceed.
ISABELLA   I went
To this pernicious caitiff deputy—
DUKE
That's somewhat madly spoken.
ISABELLA   Pardon it;
The phrase is to the matter.
DUKE   Mended again.   90
The matter; proceed.
ISABELLA
In brief, to set the needless process by,
How I persuaded, how I prayed and kneeled,
How he refelled me, and how I replied—
For this was of much length—the vile conclusion   95
I now begin with grief and shame to utter.
He would not, but by gift of my chaste body
To his concupiscible intemperate lust,
Release my brother; and after much debatement,
My sisterly remorse confutes mine honour,   100
And I did yield to him. But the next morn betimes,
His purpose surfeiting, he sends a warrant
For my poor brother's head.
DUKE   This is most likely!
ISABELLA
O, that it were as like as it is true!
DUKE
By heaven, fond wretch, thou know'st not what thou
    speak'st,   105
Or else thou art suborned against his honour
In hateful practice. First, his integrity
Stands without blemish. Next, it imports no reason
That with such vehemency he should pursue
Faults proper to himself. If he had so offended,   110
He would have weighed thy brother by himself,
And not have cut him off. Someone hath set you on.
Confess the truth, and say by whose advice
Thou cam'st here to complain.
ISABELLA   And is this all?
Then, O you blessèd ministers above,   115
Keep me in patience, and with ripened time
Unfold the evil which is here wrapped up
In countenance! Heaven shield your grace from woe,
As I, thus wronged, hence unbelievèd go.
DUKE
I know you'd fain be gone. An officer!   120
To prison with her.
          An officer guards Isabella
                          Shall we thus permit
A blasting and a scandalous breath to fall
On him so near us? This needs must be a practice.
Who knew of your intent and coming hither?
ISABELLA
One that I would were here, Friar Lodowick.   125
                          ⌈Exit, guarded⌉
DUKE
A ghostly father, belike. Who knows that Lodowick?

LUCIO
My lord, I know him. 'Tis a meddling friar;
I do not like the man. Had he been lay, my lord,
For certain words he spake against your grace
In your retirement, I had swinged him soundly.   130
DUKE
Words against me? This' a good friar, belike!
And to set on this wretched woman here
Against our substitute! Let this friar be found.
                    ⌜Exit one or more⌝
LUCIO
But yesternight, my lord, she and that friar,
I saw them at the prison. A saucy friar,   135
A very scurvy fellow.
FRIAR PETER   Blessed be your royal grace!
I have stood by, my lord, and I have heard
Your royal ear abused. First hath this woman
Most wrongfully accused your substitute,
Who is as free from touch or soil with her   140
As she from one ungot.
DUKE   We did believe no less.
Know you that Friar Lodowick that she speaks of?
FRIAR PETER
I know him for a man divine and holy,
Not scurvy, nor a temporary meddler,
As he's reported by this gentleman;   145
And, on my trust, a man that never yet
Did, as he vouches, misreport your grace.
LUCIO My lord, most villainously; believe it.
FRIAR PETER
Well, he in time may come to clear himself;
But at this instant he is sick, my lord,   150
Of a strange fever. Upon his mere request,
Being come to knowledge that there was complaint
Intended 'gainst Lord Angelo, came I hither
To speak, as from his mouth, what he doth know
Is true and false, and what he with his oath   155
And all probation will make up full clear
Whensoever he's convented. First, for this woman:
To justify this worthy nobleman,
So vulgarly and personally accused,
Her shall you hear disprovèd to her eyes,   160
Till she herself confess it.
DUKE   Good friar, let's hear it.
                    ⌜Exit Friar Peter⌝
Do you not smile at this, Lord Angelo?
O heaven, the vanity of wretched fools!
Give us some seats.
       ⌜Seats are brought in⌝
               Come, cousin Angelo,
In this I'll be impartial; be you judge   165
Of your own cause.
       The Duke and Angelo sit.
       Enter ⌜Friar Peter, and⌝ Mariana, veiled
               Is this the witness, friar?
First let her show her face, and after speak.
MARIANA
Pardon, my lord, I will not show my face
Until my husband bid me.

DUKE What, are you married?   170
MARIANA No, my lord.
DUKE Are you a maid?
MARIANA No, my lord.
DUKE A widow then?
MARIANA Neither, my lord.   175
DUKE Why, you are nothing then; neither maid, widow,
nor wife!
LUCIO My lord, she may be a punk, for many of them are
neither maid, widow, nor wife.
DUKE Silence that fellow. I would he had some cause to
prattle for himself.
LUCIO Well, my lord.
MARIANA
My lord, I do confess I ne'er was married,
And I confess besides, I am no maid.
I have known my husband, yet my husband   185
Knows not that ever he knew me.
LUCIO He was drunk then, my lord, it can be no better.
DUKE For the benefit of silence, would thou wert so too.
LUCIO Well, my lord.
DUKE
This is no witness for Lord Angelo.   190
MARIANA Now I come to't, my lord.
She that accuses him of fornication
In self-same manner doth accuse my husband,
And charges him, my lord, with such a time
When I'll depose I had him in mine arms   195
With all th'effect of love.
ANGELO   Charges she more than me?
MARIANA
Not that I know.
DUKE   No? You say your husband.
MARIANA
Why just, my lord, and that is Angelo,
Who thinks he knows that he ne'er knew my body,
But knows, he thinks, that he knows Isabel's.   200
ANGELO
This is a strange abuse. Let's see thy face.
MARIANA (unveiling)
My husband bids me; now I will unmask.
This is that face, thou cruel Angelo,
Which once thou swor'st was worth the looking on.
This is the hand which, with a vowed contract,   205
Was fast belocked in thine. This is the body
That took away the match from Isabel,
And did supply thee at thy garden-house
In her imagined person.
DUKE (to Angelo) Know you this woman?   210
LUCIO Carnally, she says.
DUKE Sirrah, no more!
LUCIO Enough, my lord.
ANGELO
My lord, I must confess I know this woman;
And five years since there was some speech of
               marriage   215
Betwixt myself and her, which was broke off,
Partly for that her promisèd proportions
Came short of composition, but in chief

For that her reputation was disvalued
In levity; since which time of five years   220
I never spake with her, saw her, nor heard from her,
Upon my faith and honour.

MARIANA [*kneeling before the Duke*] Noble prince,
  As there comes light from heaven, and words from
    breath,
  As there is sense in truth, and truth in virtue,
  I am affianced this man's wife, as strongly   225
  As words could make up vows. And, my good lord,
  But Tuesday night last gone, in's garden-house,
  He knew me as a wife. As this is true,
  Let me in safety raise me from my knees,
  Or else forever be confixèd here,   230
  A marble monument.

ANGELO   I did but smile till now.
  Now, good my lord, give me the scope of justice.
  My patience here is touched. I do perceive
  These poor informal women are no more
  But instruments of some more mightier member   235
  That sets them on. Let me have way, my lord,
  To find this practice out.

DUKE (*standing*)   Ay, with my heart,
  And punish them even to your height of pleasure.—
  Thou foolish friar, and thou pernicious woman
  Compact with her that's gone, think'st thou thy
    oaths,   240
  Though they would swear down each particular
    saint,
  Were testimonies against his worth and credit
  That's sealed in approbation? You, Lord Escalus,
  Sit with my cousin; lend him your kind pains
  To find out this abuse, whence 'tis derived.   245
  There is another friar that set them on.
  Let him be sent for.
          Escalus sits

FRIAR PETER
  Would he were here, my lord, for he indeed
  Hath set the women on to this complaint.
  Your Provost knows the place where he abides,   250
  And he may fetch him.

DUKE (*to one or more*)   Go, do it instantly.
          Exit one or more
  (*To Angelo*) And you, my noble and well-warranted
    cousin,
  Whom it concerns to hear this matter forth,
  Do with your injuries as seems you best
  In any chastisement. I for a while will leave you,   255
  But stir not you till you have well determined
  Upon these slanderers.

ESCALUS   My lord, we'll do it throughly.
          Exit Duke
  Signor Lucio, did not you say you knew that Friar
  Lodowick to be a dishonest person?   259

LUCIO *Cucullus non facit monachum*: honest in nothing but
  in his clothes; and one that hath spoke most villainous
  speeches of the Duke.

ESCALUS We shall entreat you to abide here till he come,

and enforce them against him. We shall find this friar
a notable fellow.   265

LUCIO As any in Vienna, on my word.

ESCALUS Call that same Isabel here once again; I would
  speak with her.   *Exit one or more*
  (*To Angelo*) Pray you, my lord, give me leave to question.
  You shall see how I'll handle her.   270

LUCIO Not better than he, by her own report.

ESCALUS Say you?

LUCIO Marry, sir, I think if you handled her privately, she
  would sooner confess; perchance publicly she'll be
  ashamed.   275

ESCALUS I will go darkly to work with her.

LUCIO That's the way, for women are light at midnight.
          Enter Isabella, guarded

ESCALUS (*to Isabella*) Come on, mistress, here's a gentlewoman denies all that you have said.
          *Enter the Duke, disguised as a friar, hooded, and the
          Provost*

LUCIO My lord, here comes the rascal I spoke of, here
  with the Provost.   281

ESCALUS In very good time. Speak not you to him till we
  call upon you.

LUCIO Mum.   284

ESCALUS (*to the Duke*) Come, sir, did you set these women
  on to slander Lord Angelo? They have confessed you
  did.

DUKE 'Tis false.

ESCALUS How! Know you where you are?

DUKE
  Respect to your great place, and let the devil   290
  Be sometime honoured fore his burning throne.
  Where is the Duke? 'Tis he should hear me speak.

ESCALUS
  The Duke's in us, and we will hear you speak.
  Look you speak justly.

DUKE   Boldly at least.
  (*To Isabella and Mariana*)   But O, poor souls,
  Come you to seek the lamb here of the fox,   295
  Good night to your redress! Is the Duke gone?
  Then is your cause gone too. The Duke's unjust
  Thus to retort your manifest appeal,
  And put your trial in the villain's mouth
  Which here you come to accuse.   300

LUCIO
  This is the rascal, this is he I spoke of.

ESCALUS
  Why, thou unreverend and unhallowed friar,
  Is't not enough thou hast suborned these women
  To accuse this worthy man but, in foul mouth,
  And in the witness of his proper ear,   305
  To call him villain, and then to glance from him
  To th' Duke himself, to tax him with injustice?
  Take him hence; to th' rack with him. We'll touse you
  Joint by joint—but we will know his purpose.
  What, 'unjust'?

DUKE   Be not so hot. The Duke   310
  Dare no more stretch this finger of mine than he

Dare rack his own. His subject am I not,
Nor here provincial. My business in this state
Made me a looker-on here in Vienna,
Where I have seen corruption boil and bubble   315
Till it o'errun the stew; laws for all faults,
But faults so countenanced that the strong statutes
Stand like the forfeits in a barber's shop,
As much in mock as mark.

ESCALUS Slander to th' state!   320
Away with him to prison.

ANGELO
What can you vouch against him, Signor Lucio?
Is this the man that you did tell us of?

LUCIO 'Tis he, my lord.—Come hither, goodman Bald-
pate. Do you know me?   325

DUKE I remember you, sir, by the sound of your voice. I
met you at the prison, in the absence of the Duke.

LUCIO O, did you so? And do you remember what you
said of the Duke?

DUKE Most notedly, sir.   330

LUCIO Do you so, sir? And was the Duke a fleshmonger,
a fool, and a coward, as you then reported him to be?

DUKE You must, sir, change persons with me ere you
make that my report. You indeed spoke so of him, and
much more, much worse.   335

LUCIO O, thou damnable fellow! Did not I pluck thee by
the nose for thy speeches?

DUKE I protest I love the Duke as I love myself.

ANGELO Hark how the villain would close now, after his
treasonable abuses.   340

ESCALUS Such a fellow is not to be talked withal. Away
with him to prison. Where is the Provost? Away with
him to prison. Lay bolts enough upon him. Let him
speak no more. Away with those giglets too, and with
the other confederate companion.   345

⌈Mariana is raised to her feet, and is guarded.⌉
The Provost makes to seize the Duke

DUKE Stay, sir, stay a while.

ANGELO What, resists he? Help him, Lucio.

LUCIO (to the Duke) Come, sir; come, sir; come, sir! Foh,
sir! Why, you bald-pated lying rascal, you must be
hooded, must you? Show your knave's visage, with a
pox to you! Show your sheep-biting face, and be hanged
an hour! Will't not off?   352

He pulls off the friar's hood, and discovers the Duke.
⌈Angelo and Escalus rise⌉

DUKE
Thou art the first knave that e'er madest a duke.
First, Provost, let me bail these gentle three.   354
(To Lucio) Sneak not away, sir, for the friar and you
Must have a word anon. (To one or more) Lay hold on
him.

LUCIO This may prove worse than hanging.

DUKE (to Escalus)
What you have spoke, I pardon. Sit you down.
We'll borrow place of him.
⌈Escalus sits⌉
(To Angelo)   Sir, by your leave.

⌈He takes Angelo's seat⌉
Hast thou or word or wit or impudence   360
That yet can do thee office? If thou hast,
Rely upon it till my tale be heard,
And hold no longer out.

ANGELO   O my dread lord,
I should be guiltier than my guiltiness
To think I can be undiscernible,   365
When I perceive your grace, like power divine,
Hath looked upon my passes. Then, good prince,
No longer session hold upon my shame,
But let my trial be mine own confession.
Immediate sentence then, and sequent death,   370
Is all the grace I beg.

DUKE   Come hither, Mariana.
(To Angelo) Say, wast thou e'er contracted to this
woman?

ANGELO I was, my lord.

DUKE
Go, take her hence and marry her instantly.
Do you the office, friar; which consummate,   375
Return him here again. Go with him, Provost.

Exeunt Angelo, Mariana, Friar Peter, and the
Provost

ESCALUS
My lord, I am more amazed at his dishonour
Than at the strangeness of it.

DUKE   Come hither, Isabel.
Your friar is now your prince. As I was then
Advertising and holy to your business,   380
Not changing heart with habit I am still
Attorneyed at your service.

ISABELLA   O, give me pardon,
That I, your vassal, have employed and pained
Your unknown sovereignty.

DUKE   You are pardoned, Isabel.
And now, dear maid, be you as free to us.   385
Your brother's death I know sits at your heart,
And you may marvel why I obscured myself,
Labouring to save his life, and would not rather
Make rash remonstrance of my hidden power
Than let him so be lost. O most kind maid,   390
It was the swift celerity of his death,
Which I did think with slower foot came on,
That brained my purpose. But peace be with him!
That life is better life, past fearing death,
Than that which lives to fear. Make it your comfort,
So happy is your brother.

ISABELLA   I do, my lord.   396

Enter Angelo, Mariana, Friar Peter, and the Provost

DUKE
For this new-married man approaching here,
Whose salt imagination yet hath wronged
Your well-defended honour, you must pardon
For Mariana's sake; but as he adjudged your
brother—   400
Being criminal in double violation
Of sacred chastity and of promise-breach,

Thereon dependent, for your brother's life—
The very mercy of the law cries out
Most audible, even from his proper tongue,   405
'An Angelo for Claudio, death for death'.
Haste still pays haste, and leisure answers leisure;
Like doth quit like, and measure still for measure.
Then, Angelo, thy fault's thus manifested,
Which, though thou wouldst deny, denies thee
     vantage.   410
We do condemn thee to the very block
Where Claudio stooped to death, and with like haste.
Away with him.

MARIANA   O my most gracious lord,
I hope you will not mock me with a husband!

DUKE
It is your husband mocked you with a husband.   415
Consenting to the safeguard of your honour,
I thought your marriage fit; else imputation,
For that he knew you, might reproach your life,
And choke your good to come. For his possessions,
Although by confiscation they are ours,   420
We do enstate and widow you with all,
To buy you a better husband.

MARIANA   O my dear lord,
I crave no other, nor no better man.

DUKE
Never crave him; we are definitive.

MARIANA
Gentle my liege—

DUKE   You do but lose your labour.—   425
Away with him to death. (To Lucio) Now, sir, to you.

MARIANA (kneeling) .
O my good lord!—Sweet Isabel, take my part;
Lend me your knees, and all my life to come
I'll lend you all my life to do you service.

DUKE
Against all sense you do importune her.   430
Should she kneel down in mercy of this fact,
Her brother's ghost his pavèd bed would break,
And take her hence in horror.

MARIANA   Isabel,
Sweet Isabel, do yet but kneel by me.
Hold up your hands; say nothing; I'll speak all.   435
They say best men are moulded out of faults,
And, for the most, become much more the better
For being a little bad. So may my husband.
O Isabel, will you not lend a knee?

DUKE
He dies for Claudio's death.

ISABELLA (kneeling)   Most bounteous sir,   440
Look, if it please you, on this man condemned
As if my brother lived. I partly think
A due sincerity governed his deeds,
Till he did look on me. Since it is so,
Let him not die. My brother had but justice,   445
In that he did the thing for which he died.
For Angelo,
His act did not o'ertake his bad intent,

And must be buried but as an intent
That perished by the way. Thoughts are no subjects,
Intents but merely thoughts.

MARIANA   Merely, my lord.   451

DUKE
Your suit's unprofitable. Stand up, I say.
     ⌈Mariana and Isabella stand⌉
I have bethought me of another fault.
Provost, how came it Claudio was beheaded
At an unusual hour?

PROVOST   It was commanded so.   455

DUKE
Had you a special warrant for the deed?

PROVOST
No, my good lord, it was by private message.

DUKE
For which I do discharge you of your office.
Give up your keys.

PROVOST   Pardon me, noble lord.
I thought it was a fault, but knew it not,   460
Yet did repent me after more advice;
For testimony whereof one in the prison
That should by private order else have died
I have reserved alive.

DUKE What's he?   465

PROVOST His name is Barnardine.

DUKE
I would thou hadst done so by Claudio.
Go fetch him hither. Let me look upon him.
                                        Exit Provost

ESCALUS
I am sorry one so learned and so wise
As you, Lord Angelo, have still appeared,   470
Should slip so grossly, both in the heat of blood
And lack of tempered judgement afterward.

ANGELO
I am sorry that such sorrow I procure,
And so deep sticks it in my penitent heart
That I crave death more willingly than mercy.   475
'Tis my deserving, and I do entreat it.
     Enter Barnardine and the Provost; Claudio,
     muffled, and Juliet

DUKE
Which is that Barnardine?

PROVOST   This, my lord.

DUKE
There was a friar told me of this man.
(To Barnardine) Sirrah, thou art said to have a
     stubborn soul
That apprehends no further than this world,   480
And squar'st thy life according. Thou'rt condemned;
But, for those earthly faults, I quit them all,
And pray thee take this mercy to provide
For better times to come.—Friar, advise him.
I leave him to your hand. (To Provost) What muffled
     fellow's that?   485

PROVOST
This is another prisoner that I saved,

Who should have died when Claudio lost his head,
As like almost to Claudio as himself.
  He unmuffles Claudio
DUKE (*to Isabella*)
 If he be like your brother, for his sake
 Is he pardoned; and for your lovely sake   490
 Give me your hand, and say you will be mine.
 He is my brother too. But fitter time for that.
 By this Lord Angelo perceives he's safe.
 Methinks I see a quick'ning in his eye.
 Well, Angelo, your evil quits you well.   495
 Look that you love your wife, her worth worth yours.
 I find an apt remission in myself;
 And yet here's one in place I cannot pardon.
 (*To Lucio*) You, sirrah, that knew me for a fool, a
  coward,
 One all of luxury, an ass, a madman,   500
 Wherein have I so deserved of you
 That you extol me thus?
LUCIO Faith, my lord, I spoke it but according to the trick.
 If you will hang me for it, you may; but I had rather
 it would please you I might be whipped.   505
DUKE Whipped first, sir, and hanged after.
 Proclaim it, Provost, round about the city,
 If any woman wronged by this lewd fellow,
 As I have heard him swear himself there's one
 Whom he begot with child, let her appear,   510
 And he shall marry her. The nuptial finished,
 Let him be whipped and hanged.

LUCIO I beseech your highness, do not marry me to a
 whore. Your highness said even now I made you a
 duke; good my lord, do not recompense me in making
 me a cuckold.   516
DUKE
 Upon mine honour, thou shalt marry her.
 Thy slanders I forgive, and therewithal
 Remit thy other forfeits.—Take him to prison,
 And see our pleasure herein executed.   520
LUCIO Marrying a punk, my lord, is pressing to death,
 whipping, and hanging.
DUKE Slandering a prince deserves it.
      ⌐*Exit Lucio guarded*⌐
 She, Claudio, that you wronged, look you restore.
 Joy to you, Mariana. Love her, Angelo.   525
 I have confessed her, and I know her virtue.
 Thanks, good friend Escalus, for thy much goodness.
 There's more behind that is more gratulate.
 Thanks, Provost, for thy care and secrecy.
 We shall employ thee in a worthier place.   530
 Forgive him, Angelo, that brought you home
 The head of Ragusine for Claudio's.
 Th'offence pardons itself. Dear Isabel,
 I have a motion much imports your good,
 Whereto, if you'll a willing ear incline,   535
 What's mine is yours, and what is yours is mine.
 (*To all*) So bring us to our palace, where we'll show
 What's yet behind that's meet you all should know.
            Exeunt

ADDITIONAL PASSAGES

The text of *Measure for Measure* given in this edition is
probably that of an adapted version made for
Shakespeare's company after his death. Adaptation seems
to have affected two passages, printed below as we believe
Shakespeare to have written them.

A. 1.2.0.1–116

A.2–9 (. . . by him') are lines which the adapter (whom
we believe to be Thomas Middleton) evidently intended
to be replaced by 1.2.56–79 of the play as we print it.
The adapter must have contributed all of 1.2.0.1–83,
which in the earliest and subsequent printed texts precede
the discussion between the Clown (Pompey) and the Bawd
(Mistress Overdone) about Claudio's arrest. Lucio's entry
alone at l. 40.1 below, some eleven lines after his re-entry
with the two Gentlemen and the Provost's party in the
adapted text, probably represents Shakespeare's original
intention. In his version, Juliet, present but silent in the
adapted text both in 1.2 and 5.1, probably did not appear
in either scene; accordingly, the words 'and there's
Madam Juliet' (1.2.107) must also be the reviser's work,
and do not appear below.

 Enter Pompey and Mistress Overdone, ⌐*meeting*⌐
MISTRESS OVERDONE How now, what's the news with you?

POMPEY Yonder man is carried to prison.
MISTRESS OVERDONE Well! What has he done?
POMPEY A woman.
MISTRESS OVERDONE But what's his offence?   5
POMPEY Groping for trouts in a peculiar river.
MISTRESS OVERDONE What, is there a maid with child by
 him?
POMPEY No, but there's a woman with maid by him: you
 have not heard of the proclamation, have you?   10
MISTRESS OVERDONE What proclamation, man?
POMPEY All houses in the suburbs of Vienna must be
 plucked down.
MISTRESS OVERDONE And what shall become of those in
 the city?   15
POMPEY They shall stand for seed. They had gone down
 too, but that a wise burgher put in for them.
MISTRESS OVERDONE But shall all our houses of resort in
 the suburbs be pulled down?
POMPEY To the ground, mistress.   20
MISTRESS OVERDONE Why, here's a change indeed in the
 commonwealth. What shall become of me?
POMPEY Come, fear not you. Good counsellors lack no
 clients. Though you change your place, you need not
 change your trade. I'll be your tapster still. Courage,

there will be pity taken on you. You that have worn your eyes almost out in the service, you will be considered.

⌈*A noise within*⌉

MISTRESS OVERDONE What's to do here, Thomas Tapster? Let's withdraw!　　　　　　　　　　　　　　30

Enter the Provost and Claudio

POMPEY Here comes Signor Claudio, led by the Provost to prison.　　　　　*Exeunt Mistress Overdone and Pompey*

CLAUDIO
Fellow, why dost thou show me thus to th' world?
Bear me to prison, where I am committed.

PROVOST
I do it not in evil disposition,　　　　　　　35
But from Lord Angelo by special charge.

CLAUDIO
Thus can the demigod Authority
Make us pay down for our offence, by weight,
The bonds of heaven. On whom it will, it will;
On whom it will not, so; yet still 'tis just.　　40

⌈*Enter Lucio*⌉

LUCIO
Why, how now, Claudio? Whence comes this restraint?

B. 3.1.515–4.1.65

Before revision there would have been no act-break and no song; the lines immediately following the song would also have been absent. The Duke's soliloquies 'He who the sword of heaven will bear' and 'O place and greatness' have evidently been transposed in revision; in the original, the end of 'O place and greatness' would have led straight on to the Duke's meeting with Isabella and then Mariana.

ESCALUS I am going to visit the prisoner. Fare you well.

DUKE Peace be with you.　　　　　　　*Exit Escalus*
O place and greatness, millions of false eyes
Are stuck upon thee; volumes of report
Run with their false and most contrarious quest　5
Upon thy doings; thousand escapes of wit
Make thee the father of their idle dream,
And rack thee in their fancies.

Enter Isabella

　　　　　　　　Very well met.
What is the news from this good deputy?

ISABELLA
He hath a garden circummured with brick,　　10
Whose western side is with a vineyard backed;
And to that vineyard is a planchèd gate,
That makes his opening with this bigger key.
This other doth command a little door
Which from the vineyard to the garden leads.　15
There have I made my promise
Upon the heavy middle of the night
To call upon him.

DUKE
But shall you on your knowledge find this way?

ISABELLA
I have ta'en a due and wary note upon't.　　20

With whispering and most guilty diligence,
In action all of precept, he did show me
The way twice o'er.

DUKE　　　　　　　Are there no other tokens
Between you 'greed concerning her observance?

ISABELLA
No, none, but only a repair i'th' dark,　　　25
And that I have possessed him my most stay
Can be but brief, for I have made him know
I have a servant comes with me along
That stays upon me, whose persuasion is
I come about my brother.

DUKE　　　　　　　　'Tis well borne up.　　30
I have not yet made known to Mariana
A word of this.—What ho, within! Come forth!

Enter Mariana

(*To Mariana*) I pray you be acquainted with this maid.
She comes to do you good.

ISABELLA　　　　　I do desire the like.

DUKE (*to Mariana*)
Do you persuade yourself that I respect you?　35

MARIANA
Good friar, I know you do, and so have found it.

DUKE
Take then this your companion by the hand,
Who hath a story ready for your ear.
I shall attend your leisure; but make haste,
The vaporous night approaches.

MARIANA　　　　　Will't please you walk aside.

⌈*Exeunt Mariana and Isabella*⌉

DUKE
He who the sword of heaven will bear
Should be as holy as severe,
Pattern in himself to know,
Grace to stand, and virtue go,
More nor less to others paying　　　　　45
Than by self-offences weighing.
Shame to him whose cruel striking
Kills for faults of his own liking!
Twice treble shame on Angelo,
To weed my vice, and let his grow!　　　50
O, what may man within him hide,
Though angel on the outward side!
How may likeness made in crimes
Make my practice on the times
To draw with idle spiders' strings　　　55
Most ponderous and substantial things?
Craft against vice I must apply.
With Angelo tonight shall lie
His old betrothed but despisèd.
So disguise shall, by th' disguisèd,　　　60
Pay with falsehood false exacting,
And perform an old contracting.

⌈*Enter Mariana and Isabella*⌉

Welcome. How agreed?

ISABELLA
She'll take the enterprise upon her, father,
If you advise it.　　　　　　　　　　65

ALL'S WELL THAT ENDS WELL

All's Well That Ends Well, first printed in the 1623 Folio, is often paired with *Measure for Measure*. Though we lack external evidence as to its date of composition, internal evidence suggests that it, too, is an early Jacobean play. Like *Measure for Measure*, it places its central characters in more painful situations than those in which the heroes and heroines of the earlier, more romantic comedies usually find themselves. The touching ardour with which Helen, 'a poor physician's daughter', pursues the young Bertram, son of her guardian the Countess of Rousillon, creates embarrassments for both of them. When the King whose illness she cures by her semi-magical skills brings about their marriage as a reward, Bertram's flight to the wars seems to destroy all her chances of happiness. She achieves consummation of the marriage only by the ruse (resembling Isabella's 'bed-trick' in *Measure for Measure*) of substituting herself for the Florentine maiden Diana whom Bertram believes himself to be seducing. The play's conclusion, in which the deception is exposed and Bertram is shamed into acknowledging Helen as his wife, offers only a tentatively happy ending.

Shakespeare based the story of Bertram and Helen on a tale from Boccaccio's *Decameron* either in the original or in the version included in William Painter's *Palace of Pleasure* (1566-7, revised 1575). But he created several important characters, including the Countess and the old Lord, Lafeu. He also invented the accompanying action exposing the roguery of Bertram's flashy friend Paroles, a man of words (as his name indicates) descending from the braggart soldier of Roman comedy.

Versions of the play performed in the eighteenth and nineteenth centuries, mostly emphasizing either the comedy of Paroles or the sentimental appeal of Helen, had little success; but some twentieth-century productions have shown it in a more favourable light, demonstrating, for example, that the role of the Countess is (in Bernard Shaw's words) 'the most beautiful old woman's part ever written', that the discomfiture of Paroles provides comedy that is subtle as well as highly laughable, and that the relationship of Bertram and Helen is profoundly convincing in its emotional reality.

THE PERSONS OF THE PLAY

The Dowager COUNTESS of Roussillon

BERTRAM, Count of Roussillon, her son

HELEN, an orphan, attending on the Countess

LAVATCH, a Clown, the Countess's servant

REYNALDO, the Countess's steward

PAROLES, Bertram's companion

The KING of France

LAFEU, an old lord

FIRST LORD DUMAINE
SECOND LORD DUMAINE
} brothers

INTERPRETER, a French soldier

An AUSTRINGER

The DUKE of Florence

WIDOW Capilet

DIANA, her daughter

MARIANA, a friend of the Widow

Lords, attendants, soldiers, citizens

All's Well That Ends Well

1.1 *Enter young Bertram Count of Roussillon, his mother the Countess, Helen, and Lord Lafeu, all in black*

COUNTESS In delivering my son from me I bury a second husband.

BERTRAM And I in going, madam, weep o'er my father's death anew; but I must attend his majesty's command, to whom I am now in ward, evermore in subjection. 5

LAFEU You shall find of the King a husband, madam; you, sir, a father. He that so generally is at all times good must of necessity hold his virtue to you, whose worthiness would stir it up where it wanted rather than lack it where there is such abundance. 10

COUNTESS What hope is there of his majesty's amendment?

LAFEU He hath abandoned his physicians, madam, under whose practices he hath persecuted time with hope, and finds no other advantage in the process but only the losing of hope by time. 15

COUNTESS This young gentlewoman had a father—O that 'had': how sad a passage 'tis!—whose skill was almost as great as his honesty; had it stretched so far, would have made nature immortal, and death should have play for lack of work. Would for the King's sake he were living. I think it would be the death of the King's disease.

LAFEU How called you the man you speak of, madam?

COUNTESS He was famous, sir, in his profession, and it was his great right to be so: Gérard de Narbonne. 25

LAFEU He was excellent indeed, madam. The King very lately spoke of him, admiringly and mournfully. He was skilful enough to have lived still, if knowledge could be set up against mortality.

BERTRAM What is it, my good lord, the King languishes of? 31

LAFEU A fistula, my lord.

BERTRAM I heard not of it before.

LAFEU I would it were not notorious.—Was this gentlewoman the daughter of Gérard de Narbonne? 35

COUNTESS His sole child, my lord, and bequeathed to my overlooking. I have those hopes of her good that her education promises; her dispositions she inherits, which makes fair gifts fairer—for where an unclean mind carries virtuous qualities, there commendations go with pity: they are virtues and traitors too. In her they are the better for their simpleness. She derives her honesty and achieves her goodness. 43

LAFEU Your commendations, madam, get from her tears.

COUNTESS 'Tis the best brine a maiden can season her praise in. The remembrance of her father never approaches her heart but the tyranny of her sorrows takes all livelihood from her cheek.—No more of this, Helen. Go to, no more, lest it be rather thought you affect a sorrow than to have— 50

HELEN I do affect a sorrow indeed, but I have it too.

LAFEU Moderate lamentation is the right of the dead, excessive grief the enemy to the living.

COUNTESS If the living be not enemy to the grief, the excess makes it soon mortal. 55

BERTRAM (*kneeling*) Madam, I desire your holy wishes.

LAFEU How understand we that?

COUNTESS
Be thou blessed, Bertram, and succeed thy father
In manners as in shape. Thy blood and virtue
Contend for empire in thee, and thy goodness 60
Share with thy birthright. Love all, trust a few,
Do wrong to none. Be able for thine enemy
Rather in power than use, and keep thy friend
Under thy own life's key. Be checked for silence
But never taxed for speech. What heaven more will 65
That thee may furnish and my prayers pluck down,
Fall on thy head. Farewell. (*To Lafeu*) My lord,
'Tis an unseasoned courtier. Good my lord,
Advise him.

LAFEU   He cannot want the best
That shall attend his love. 70

COUNTESS Heaven bless him!—Farewell, Bertram.

BERTRAM (*rising*) The best wishes that can be forged in
your thoughts be servants to you.   ⌈*Exit Countess*⌉
(*To Helen*) Be comfortable to my mother, your mistress,
and make much of her. 75

LAFEU Farewell, pretty lady. You must hold the credit of your father.   *Exeunt Bertram and Lafeu*

HELEN
O were that all! I think not on my father,
And these great tears grace his remembrance more
Than those I shed for him. What was he like? 80
I have forgot him. My imagination
Carries no favour in't but Bertram's.
I am undone. There is no living, none,
If Bertram be away. 'Twere all one
That I should love a bright particular star 85
And think to wed it, he is so above me.
In his bright radiance and collateral light
Must I be comforted, not in his sphere.
Th'ambition in my love thus plagues itself.
The hind that would be mated by the lion 90
Must die for love. 'Twas pretty, though a plague,
To see him every hour, to sit and draw
His archèd brows, his hawking eye, his curls,
In our heart's table—heart too capable
Of every line and trick of his sweet favour. 95
But now he's gone, and my idolatrous fancy
Must sanctify his relics. Who comes here?
          Enter Paroles
One that goes with him. I love him for his sake—
And yet I know him a notorious liar,
Think him a great way fool, solely a coward. 100
Yet these fixed evils sit so fit in him

That they take place when virtue's steely bones
Looks bleak i'th' cold wind. Withal, full oft we see
Cold wisdom waiting on superfluous folly.
PAROLES Save you, fair queen.   105
HELEN And you, monarch.
PAROLES No.
HELEN And no.
PAROLES Are you meditating on virginity?   109
HELEN Ay. You have some stain of soldier in you, let me
ask you a question. Man is enemy to virginity: how
may we barricado it against him?   112
PAROLES Keep him out.
HELEN But he assails, and our virginity, though valiant
in the defence, yet is weak. Unfold to us some warlike
resistance.   116
PAROLES There is none. Man, setting down before you,
will undermine you and blow you up.
HELEN Bless our poor virginity from underminers and
blowers-up. Is there no military policy how virgins
might blow up men?   121
PAROLES Virginity being blown down, man will quicklier
be blown up. Marry, in blowing him down again, with
the breach yourselves made you lose your city. It is
not politic in the commonwealth of nature to preserve
virginity. Loss of virginity is rational increase, and there
was never virgin got till virginity was first lost. That
you were made of is mettle to make virgins. Virginity
by being once lost may be ten times found; by being
ever kept it is ever lost. 'Tis too cold a companion,
away with't.   131
HELEN I will stand for't a little, though therefore I die a
virgin.
PAROLES There's little can be said in't. 'Tis against the
rule of nature. To speak on the part of virginity is to
accuse your mothers, which is most infallible
disobedience. He that hangs himself is a virgin: virginity
murders itself, and should be buried in highways, out
of all sanctified limit, as a desperate offendress against
nature. Virginity breeds mites, much like a cheese;
consumes itself to the very paring, and so dies with
feeding his own stomach. Besides, virginity is peevish,
proud, idle, made of self-love—which is the most
inhibited sin in the canon. Keep it not, you cannot
choose but lose by't. Out with't! Within t'one year it
will make itself two, which is a goodly increase, and
the principal itself not much the worse. Away with't.
HELEN How might one do, sir, to lose it to her own liking?
PAROLES Let me see. Marry, ill, to like him that ne'er it
likes. 'Tis a commodity will lose the gloss with lying:
the longer kept, the less worth. Off with't while 'tis
vendible. Answer the time of request. Virginity like an
old courtier wears her cap out of fashion, richly suited
but unsuitable, just like the brooch and the toothpick,
which wear not now. Your date is better in your pie
and your porridge than in your cheek, and your
virginity, your old virginity, is like one of our French
withered pears: it looks ill, it eats drily, marry, 'tis a
withered pear—it was formerly better, marry, yet 'tis
a withered pear. Will you anything with it?   160

HELEN Not my virginity, yet . . .
There shall your master have a thousand loves,
A mother and a mistress and a friend,
A phoenix, captain, and an enemy,
A guide, a goddess, and a sovereign,   165
A counsellor, a traitress, and a dear:
His humble ambition, proud humility,
His jarring concord and his discord dulcet,
His faith, his sweet disaster, with a world
Of pretty fond adoptious christendoms   170
That blinking Cupid gossips. Now shall he—
I know not what he shall. God send him well.
The court's a learning place, and he is one—
PAROLES What one, i'faith?
HELEN That I wish well. 'Tis pity.   175
PAROLES What's pity?
HELEN
That wishing well had not a body in't
Which might be felt, that we, the poorer born,
Whose baser stars do shut us up in wishes,
Might with effects of them follow our friends   180
And show what we alone must think, which never
Returns us thanks.
          Enter a Page
PAGE
Monsieur Paroles, my lord calls for you.   ⌈*Exit*⌉
PAROLES Little Helen, farewell. If I can remember thee I
will think of thee at court.   185
HELEN Monsieur Paroles, you were born under a
charitable star.
PAROLES Under Mars, I.
HELEN I especially think *under* Mars.
PAROLES Why '*under* Mars'?   190
HELEN The wars hath so kept you under that you must
needs be born under Mars.
PAROLES When he was predominant.
HELEN When he was retrograde, I think rather.
PAROLES Why think you so?   195
HELEN You go so much backward when you fight.
PAROLES That's for advantage.
HELEN So is running away, when fear proposes the safety.
But the composition that your valour and fear makes
in you is a virtue of a good wing, and I like the wear
well.   201
PAROLES I am so full of businesses I cannot answer thee
acutely. I will return perfect courtier, in the which my
instruction shall serve to naturalize thee, so thou wilt
be capable of a courtier's counsel and understand what
advice shall thrust upon thee; else thou diest in thine
unthankfulness, and thine ignorance makes thee away.
Farewell. When thou hast leisure say thy prayers;
when thou hast none remember thy friends. Get thee
a good husband and use him as he uses thee. So
farewell.   *Exit*
HELEN
Our remedies oft in ourselves do lie
Which we ascribe to heaven. The fated sky
Gives us free scope, only doth backward pull
Our slow designs when we ourselves are dull.   215

What power is it which mounts my love so high,
That makes me see and cannot feed mine eye?
The mightiest space in fortune nature brings
To join like likes and kiss like native things.
Impossible be strange attempts to those   220
That weigh their pains in sense and do suppose
What hath been cannot be. Who ever strove
To show her merit that did miss her love?
The King's disease—my project may deceive me,
But my intents are fixed and will not leave me.   *Exit*

1.2   *A flourish of cornetts. Enter the King of France*
       with letters, the two Lords Dumaine, ⌈and divers
       attendants⌉

KING
The Florentines and Sienese are by th'ears,
Have fought with equal fortune, and continue
A braving war.
FIRST LORD DUMAINE   So 'tis reported, sir.
KING
Nay, 'tis most credible: we here receive it
A certainty vouched from our cousin Austria,   5
With caution that the Florentine will move us
For speedy aid—wherein our dearest friend
Prejudicates the business, and would seem
To have us make denial.
FIRST LORD DUMAINE   His love and wisdom
Approved so to your majesty may plead   10
For amplest credence.
KING   He hath armed our answer,
And Florence is denied before he comes.
Yet for our gentlemen that mean to see
The Tuscan service, freely have they leave
To stand on either part.
SECOND LORD DUMAINE   It well may serve   15
A nursery to our gentry, who are sick
For breathing and exploit.
KING   What's he comes here?
       Enter Bertram, Lafeu, and Paroles
FIRST LORD DUMAINE
It is the Count Roussillon, my good lord,
Young Bertram.
KING (*to Bertram*) Youth, thou bear'st thy father's face.
Frank nature, rather curious than in haste,   20
Hath well composed thee. Thy father's moral parts
Mayst thou inherit, too. Welcome to Paris.
BERTRAM
My thanks and duty are your majesty's.
KING
I would I had that corporal soundness now
As when thy father and myself in friendship   25
First tried our soldiership. He did look far
Into the service of the time, and was
Disciped of the bravest. He lasted long,
But on us both did haggish age steal on,
And wore us out of act. It much repairs me   30
To talk of your good father. In his youth
He had the wit which I can well observe
Today in our young lords, but they may jest

Till their own scorn return to them unnoted
Ere they can hide their levity in honour.   35
So like a courtier, contempt nor bitterness
Were in his pride or sharpness; if they were
His equal had awaked them, and his honour—
Clock to itself—knew the true minute when
Exception bid him speak, and at this time   40
His tongue obeyed his hand. Who were below him
He used as creatures of another place,
And bowed his eminent top to their low ranks,
Making them proud of his humility,
In their poor praise he humbled. Such a man   45
Might be a copy to these younger times,
Which followed well would demonstrate them now
But goers-backward.
BERTRAM   His good remembrance, sir,
Lies richer in your thoughts than on his tomb.
So in approof lives not his epitaph   50
As in your royal speech.
KING
Would I were with him! He would always say—
Methinks I hear him now; his plausive words
He scattered not in ears, but grafted them
To grow there and to bear. 'Let me not live'—   55
This his good melancholy oft began
On the catastrophe and heel of pastime,
When it was out—'Let me not live', quoth he,
'After my flame lacks oil, to be the snuff
Of younger spirits, whose apprehensive senses   60
All but new things disdain, whose judgements are
Mere fathers of their garments, whose constancies
Expire before their fashions.' This he wished.
I after him do after him wish too,
Since I nor wax nor honey can bring home,   65
I quickly were dissolvèd from my hive
To give some labourers room.
SECOND LORD DUMAINE   You're lovèd, sir.
They that least lend it you shall lack you first.
KING
I fill a place, I know't.—How long is't, Count,
Since the physician at your father's died?   70
He was much famed.
BERTRAM   Some six months since, my lord.
KING
If he were living I would try him yet.—
Lend me an arm.—The rest have worn me out
With several applications. Nature and sickness
Debate it at their leisure. Welcome, Count.   75
My son's no dearer.
BERTRAM   Thank your majesty.
                              ⌈*Flourish.*⌉ *Exeunt*

1.3   *Enter the Countess, Reynaldo her steward, and*
       ⌈*behind*⌉ *Lavatch her clown*
COUNTESS I will now hear. What say you of this gentlewoman?
REYNALDO Madam, the care I have had to even your
content I wish might be found in the calendar of my
past endeavours, for then we wound our modesty and

make foul the clearness of our deservings, when of ourselves we publish them.

COUNTESS What does this knave here? (*To Lavatch*) Get you gone, sirrah. The complaints I have heard of you I do not all believe. 'Tis my slowness that I do not, for I know you lack not folly to commit them and have ability enough to make such knaveries yours.   12

LAVATCH 'Tis not unknown to you, madam, I am a poor fellow.

COUNTESS Well, sir?   15

LAVATCH No, madam, 'tis not so well that I am poor, though many of the rich are damned. But if I may have your ladyship's good will to go to the world, Isbel the woman and I will do as we may.

COUNTESS Wilt thou needs be a beggar?   20

LAVATCH I do beg your good will in this case.

COUNTESS In what case?

LAVATCH In Isbel's case and mine own. Service is no heritage, and I think I shall never have the blessing of God till I have issue o' my body, for they say bairns are blessings.

COUNTESS Tell me thy reason why thou wilt marry.   27

LAVATCH My poor body, madam, requires it. I am driven on by the flesh, and he must needs go that the devil drives.   30

COUNTESS Is this all your worship's reason?

LAVATCH Faith, madam, I have other holy reasons, such as they are.

COUNTESS May the world know them?   34

LAVATCH I have been, madam, a wicked creature, as you—and all flesh and blood—are, and indeed I do marry that I may repent.

COUNTESS Thy marriage sooner than thy wickedness.

LAVATCH I am out o' friends, madam, and I hope to have friends for my wife's sake.   40

COUNTESS Such friends are thine enemies, knave.

LAVATCH You're shallow, madam—in great friends, for the knaves come to do that for me which I am aweary of. He that ears my land spares my team, and gives me leave to in the crop. If I be his cuckold, he's my drudge. He that comforts my wife is the cherisher of my flesh and blood; he that cherishes my flesh and blood loves my flesh and blood; he that loves my flesh and blood is my friend; *ergo*, he that kisses my wife is my friend. If men could be contented to be what they are, there were no fear in marriage. For young Chairbonne the puritan and old Poisson the papist, howsome'er their hearts are severed in religion, their heads are both one: they may jowl horns together like any deer i'th' herd.   55

COUNTESS Wilt thou ever be a foul-mouthed and calumnious knave?

LAVATCH A prophet? Ay, madam, and I speak the truth the next way.

⌈*He sings*⌉

    For I the ballad will repeat,   60
      Which men full true shall find:
    Your marriage comes by destiny,
      Your cuckoo sings by kind.

COUNTESS Get you gone, sir. I'll talk with you more anon.

REYNALDO May it please you, madam, that he bid Helen come to you? Of her I am to speak.   66

COUNTESS (*to Lavatch*) Sirrah, tell my gentlewoman I would speak with her. Helen, I mean.

LAVATCH ⌈*sings*⌉

    'Was this fair face the cause', quoth she,
    'Why the Grecians sackèd Troy?   70
    Fond done, done fond. Was this King Priam's joy?'
    With that she sighèd as she stood,
    With that she sighèd as she stood,
      And gave this sentence then:
    'Among nine bad if one be good,   75
    Among nine bad if one be good,
      There's yet one good in ten.'

COUNTESS What, 'one good in ten'? You corrupt the song, sirrah.   79

LAVATCH One good *woman* in ten, madam, which is a purifying o'th' song. Would God would serve the world so all the year! We'd find no fault with the tithe-woman if I were the parson. One in ten, quoth a? An we might have a good woman born but ere every blazing star, or at an earthquake, 'twould mend the lottery well. A man may draw his heart out ere a pluck one.   87

COUNTESS You'll be gone, sir knave, and do as I command you.

LAVATCH That man should be at woman's command, and yet no hurt done! Though honesty be no puritan, yet it will do no hurt; it will wear the surplice of humility over the black gown of a big heart. I am going, forsooth. The business is for Helen to come hither.   *Exit*

COUNTESS Well now.   95

REYNALDO I know, madam, you love your gentlewoman entirely.

COUNTESS Faith, I do. Her father bequeathed her to me, and she herself without other advantage may lawfully make title to as much love as she finds. There is more owing her than is paid, and more shall be paid her than she'll demand.   102

REYNALDO Madam, I was very late more near her than I think she wished me. Alone she was, and did communicate to herself, her own words to her own ears; she thought, I dare vow for her, they touched not any stranger sense. Her matter was, she loved your son. Fortune, she said, was no goddess, that had put such difference betwixt their two estates; Love no god, that would not extend his might only where qualities were level; Dian no queen of virgins, that would suffer her poor knight surprised without rescue in the first assault or ransom afterward. This she delivered in the most bitter touch of sorrow that e'er I heard virgin exclaim in; which I held my duty speedily to acquaint you withal, sithence in the loss that may happen it concerns you something to know it.   117

COUNTESS You have discharged this honestly. Keep it to yourself. Many likelihoods informed me of this before, which hung so tott'ring in the balance that I could neither believe nor misdoubt. Pray you, leave me. Stall

this in your bosom, and I thank you for your honest
care. I will speak with you further anon.

Exit Steward

Enter Helen

COUNTESS *(aside)*

Even so it was with me when I was young.   124
    If ever we are nature's, these are ours: this thorn
Doth to our rose of youth rightly belong.
    Our blood to us, this to our blood is born;
It is the show and seal of nature's truth,
Where love's strong passion is impressed in youth.
By our remembrances of days foregone,   130
Such were our faults—or then we thought them
    none.
Her eye is sick on't. I observe her now.

HELEN

What is your pleasure, madam?

COUNTESS   You know, Helen,
I am a mother to you.

HELEN

Mine honourable mistress.

COUNTESS   Nay, a mother.   135
Why not a mother? When I said 'a mother',
Methought you saw a serpent. What's in 'mother'
That you start at it? I say I am your mother,
And put you in the catalogue of those
That were enwombèd mine. 'Tis often seen   140
Adoption strives with nature, and choice breeds
A native slip to us from foreign seeds.
You ne'er oppressed me with a mother's groan,
Yet I express to you a mother's care.
God's mercy, maiden! Does it curd thy blood   145
To say I am thy mother? What's the matter,
That this distempered messenger of wet,
The many-coloured Iris, rounds thine eye?
Why, that you are my daughter?

HELEN   That I am not.

COUNTESS

I say I am your mother.

HELEN   Pardon, madam.   150
The Count Roussillon cannot be my brother.
I am from humble, he from honoured name;
No note upon my parents, his all noble.
My master, my dear lord he is, and I
His servant live and will his vassal die.   155
He must not be my brother.

COUNTESS   Nor I your mother?

HELEN

You are my mother, madam. Would you were—
So that my lord your son were not my brother—
Indeed my mother! Or were you both our mothers
I care no more for than I do for heaven,   160
So I were not his sister. Can 't no other
But, I your daughter, he must be my brother?

COUNTESS

Yes, Helen, you might be my daughter-in-law.
God shield you mean it not! 'Daughter' and 'mother'
So strive upon your pulse. What, pale again?   165
My fear hath catched your fondness. Now I see

The myst'ry of your loneliness, and find
Your salt tears' head. Now to all sense 'tis gross:
You love my son. Invention is ashamed
Against the proclamation of thy passion   170
To say thou dost not. Therefore tell me true,
But tell me then 'tis so—for look, thy cheeks
Confess it t'one to th'other, and thine eyes
See it so grossly shown in thy behaviours
That in their kind they speak it. Only sin   175
And hellish obstinacy tie thy tongue,
That truth should be suspected. Speak, is't so?
If it be so you have wound a goodly clew;
If it be not, forswear't. Howe'er, I charge thee,
As heaven shall work in me for thine avail,   180
To tell me truly.

HELEN   Good madam, pardon me.

COUNTESS

Do you love my son?

HELEN   Your pardon, noble mistress.

COUNTESS

Love you my son?

HELEN   Do not you love him, madam?

COUNTESS

Go not about. My love hath in't a bond
Whereof the world takes note. Come, come, disclose
The state of your affection, for your passions   186
Have to the full appeached.

HELEN   Then I confess,
Here on my knee, before high heaven and you,
That before you and next unto high heaven
I love your son.   190
My friends were poor but honest; so's my love.
Be not offended, for it hurts not him
That he is loved of me. I follow him not
By any token of presumptuous suit,
Nor would I have him till I do deserve him,   195
Yet never know how that desert should be.
I know I love in vain, strive against hope;
Yet in this captious and intenable sieve
I still pour in the waters of my love
And lack not to lose still. Thus, Indian-like,   200
Religious in mine error, I adore
The sun that looks upon his worshipper
But knows of him no more. My dearest madam,
Let not your hate encounter with my love
For loving where you do; but if yourself,   205
Whose agèd honour cites a virtuous youth,
Did ever in so true a flame of liking
Wish chastely and love dearly, that your Dian
Was both herself and Love, O then give pity
To her whose state is such that cannot choose   210
But lend and give where she is sure to lose,
That seeks to find not that her search implies,
But riddle-like lives sweetly where she dies.

COUNTESS

Had you not lately an intent—speak truly—
To go to Paris?   215

HELEN Madam, I had.

COUNTESS Wherefore? Tell true.

HELEN
  I will tell truth, by grace itself I swear.
  You know my father left me some prescriptions
  Of rare and proved effects, such as his reading   220
  And manifest experience had collected
  For general sovereignty, and that he willed me
  In heedfull'st reservation to bestow them,
  As notes whose faculties inclusive were
  More than they were in note. Amongst the rest   225
  There is a remedy, approved, set down,
  To cure the desperate languishings whereof
  The King is rendered lost.
COUNTESS   This was your motive
  For Paris, was it? Speak.
HELEN
  My lord your son made me to think of this,   230
  Else Paris and the medicine and the King
  Had from the conversation of my thoughts
  Haply been absent then.
COUNTESS   But think you, Helen,
  If you should tender your supposèd aid,
  He would receive it? He and his physicians   235
  Are of a mind: he, that they cannot help him;
  They, that they cannot help. How shall they credit
  A poor unlearnèd virgin, when the schools,
  Embowelled of their doctrine, have left off
  The danger to itself?
HELEN   There's something in't   240
  More than my father's skill, which was the great'st
  Of his profession, that his good receipt
  Shall for my legacy be sanctified
  By th' luckiest stars in heaven, and would your
    honour
  But give me leave to try success, I'd venture   245
  The well-lost life of mine on his grace's cure
  By such a day, an hour.
COUNTESS Dost thou believe't?
HELEN Ay, madam, knowingly.
COUNTESS
  Why, Helen, thou shalt have my leave and love,   250
  Means and attendants, and my loving greetings
  To those of mine in court. I'll stay at home
  And pray God's blessing into thy attempt.
  Be gone tomorrow, and be sure of this:
  What I can help thee to, thou shalt not miss.   *Exeunt*

2.1 *Flourish of cornetts. Enter the King ⌈carried in a*
    chair⌉, with the two Lords Dumaine, divers young
    lords taking leave for the Florentine war, and
    Bertram and Paroles
KING
  Farewell, young lords. These warlike principles
  Do not throw from you. And you, my lords, farewell.
  Share the advice betwixt you; if both gain all,
  The gift doth stretch itself as 'tis received,
  And is enough for both.
FIRST LORD DUMAINE   'Tis our hope, sir,   5
  After well-entered soldiers, to return
  And find your grace in health.

KING
  No, no, it cannot be—and yet my heart
  Will not confess he owes the malady
  That doth my life besiege. Farewell, young lords.   10
  Whether I live or die, be you the sons
  Of worthy Frenchmen; let higher Italy—
  Those bated that inherit but the fall
  Of the last monarchy—see that you come
  Not to woo honour but to wed it. When   15
  The bravest questant shrinks, find what you seek,
  That fame may cry you loud. I say farewell.
FIRST LORD DUMAINE
  Health at your bidding serve your majesty.
KING
  Those girls of Italy, take heed of them.
  They say our French lack language to deny   20
  If they demand. Beware of being captives
  Before you serve.
BOTH LORDS DUMAINE Our hearts receive your warnings.
KING Farewell.—Come hither to me.
    ⌈*Some lords stand aside with the King*⌉
FIRST LORD DUMAINE (*to Bertram*)
  O my sweet lord, that you will stay behind us.
PAROLES
  'Tis not his fault, the spark.
SECOND LORD DUMAINE   O 'tis brave wars.   25
PAROLES
  Most admirable! I have seen those wars.
BERTRAM
  I am commanded here, and kept a coil with
  'Too young' and 'the next year' and ''tis too early'.
PAROLES
  An thy mind stand to't, boy, steal away bravely.
BERTRAM
  I shall stay here the forehorse to a smock,   30
  Creaking my shoes on the plain masonry,
  Till honour be bought up, and no sword worn
  But one to dance with. By heaven, I'll steal away.
FIRST LORD DUMAINE
  There's honour in the theft.
PAROLES   Commit it, Count.
SECOND LORD DUMAINE
  I am your accessary. And so, farewell.   35
BERTRAM I grow to you,
  And our parting is a tortured body.
FIRST LORD DUMAINE
  Farewell, captain.
SECOND LORD DUMAINE Sweet Monsieur Paroles.
PAROLES Noble heroes, my sword and yours are kin. Good
  sparks and lustrous, a word, good mettles. You shall
  find in the regiment of the Spinii one Captain Spurio,
  with his cicatrice, an emblem of war, here on his
  sinister cheek. It was this very sword entrenched it.
  Say to him I live, and observe his reports for me.
FIRST LORD DUMAINE We shall, noble captain.   45
PAROLES Mars dote on you for his novices.
                        Exeunt both Lords Dumaine
  (*To Bertram*) What will ye do?
BERTRAM Stay the King.

PAROLES Use a more spacious ceremony to the noble lords.
You have restrained yourself within the list of too cold
an adieu. Be more expressive to them, for they wear
themselves in the cap of the time, there do muster true
gait; eat, speak, and move under the influence of the
most received star—and though the devil lead the
measure, such are to be followed. After them, and take
a more dilated farewell.   56
BERTRAM And I will do so.
PAROLES Worthy fellows, and like to prove most sinewy
sword-men.   *Exeunt ⌜Bertram and Paroles⌝*
         Enter Lafeu to the King
LAFEU *(kneeling)*
Pardon, my lord, for me and for my tidings.   60
KING I'll fee thee to stand up.
LAFEU *(rising)*
Then here's a man stands that has bought his pardon.
I would you had kneeled, my lord, to ask me mercy,
And that at my bidding you could so stand up.
KING
I would I had, so I had broke thy pate   65
And asked thee mercy for't.
LAFEU   Good faith, across!
But my good lord, 'tis thus: will you be cured
Of your infirmity?
KING   No.
LAFEU   O will you eat
No grapes, my royal fox? Yes, but you will,
My noble grapes, an if my royal fox   70
Could reach them. I have seen a medicine
That's able to breathe life into a stone,
Quicken a rock, and make you dance canary
With sprightly fire and motion; whose simple touch
Is powerful to araise King Pépin, nay,   75
To give great Charlemagne a pen in's hand,
And write to her a love-line.
KING   What 'her' is this?
LAFEU
Why, Doctor She. My lord, there's one arrived,
If you will see her. Now by my faith and honour,
If seriously I may convey my thoughts   80
In this my light deliverance, I have spoke
With one that in her sex, her years, profession,
Wisdom and constancy, hath amazed me more
Than I dare blame my weakness. Will you see her—
For that is her demand—and know her business?   85
That done, laugh well at me.
KING   Now, good Lafeu,
Bring in the admiration, that we with thee
May spend our wonder too, or take off thine
By wond'ring how thou took'st it.
LAFEU   Nay, I'll fit you,
And not be all day neither.   90
         ⌜*He goes to the door*⌝
KING
Thus he his special nothing ever prologues.
LAFEU *(to Helen, within)* Nay, come your ways.
         Enter Helen ⌜*disguised*⌝
KING This haste hath wings indeed.

LAFEU *(to Helen)* Nay, come your ways.
This is his majesty. Say your mind to him.   95
A traitor you do look like, but such traitors
His majesty seldom fears. I am Cressid's uncle,
That dare leave two together. Fare you well.
         Exeunt ⌜*all but the King and Helen*⌝
KING
Now, fair one, does your business follow us?
HELEN
Ay, my good lord. Gérard de Narbonne was my father;
In what he did profess, well found.
KING   I knew him.   101
HELEN
The rather will I spare my praises towards him;
Knowing him is enough. On's bed of death
Many receipts he gave me, chiefly one
Which, as the dearest issue of his practice,   105
And of his old experience th'only darling,
He bade me store up as a triple eye
Safer than mine own two, more dear. I have so,
And hearing your high majesty is touched
With that malignant cause wherein the honour   110
Of my dear father's gift stands chief in power,
I come to tender it and my appliance
With all bound humbleness.
KING   We thank you, maiden,
But may not be so credulous of cure,
When our most learnèd doctors leave us, and   115
The congregated College have concluded
That labouring art can never ransom nature
From her inaidable estate. I say we must not
So stain our judgement or corrupt our hope,
To prostitute our past-cure malady   120
To empirics, or to dissever so
Our great self and our credit, to esteem
A senseless help, when help past sense we deem.
HELEN
My duty then shall pay me for my pains.
I will no more enforce mine office on you,   125
Humbly entreating from your royal thoughts
A modest one to bear me back again.
KING
I cannot give thee less, to be called grateful.
Thou thought'st to help me, and such thanks I give
As one near death to those that wish him live.   130
But what at full I know, thou know'st no part;
I knowing all my peril, thou no art.
HELEN
What I can do can do no hurt to try,
Since you set up your rest 'gainst remedy.
He that of greatest works is finisher   135
Oft does them by the weakest minister.
So holy writ in babes hath judgement shown
When judges have been babes; great floods have
         flow'n
From simple sources, and great seas have dried.
When miracles have by th' great'st been denied   140
⌜   ⌝
Oft expectation fails, and most oft there

Where most it promises, and oft it hits
Where hope is coldest and despair most fits.

KING
I must not hear thee. Fare thee well, kind maid.   145
Thy pains, not used, must by thyself be paid:
Proffers not took reap thanks for their reward.

HELEN
Inspirèd merit so by breath is barred.
It is not so with him that all things knows
As 'tis with us that square our guess by shows;   150
But most it is presumption in us when
The help of heaven we count the act of men.
Dear sir, to my endeavours give consent.
Of heaven, not me, make an experiment.
I am not an impostor, that proclaim   155
Myself against the level of mine aim,
But know I think, and think I know most sure,
My art is not past power, nor you past cure.

KING
Art thou so confident? Within what space
Hop'st thou my cure?

HELEN   The great'st grace lending grace,
Ere twice the horses of the sun shall bring   161
Their fiery coacher his diurnal ring,
Ere twice in murk and occidental damp
Moist Hesperus hath quenched her sleepy lamp,
Or four-and-twenty times the pilot's glass   165
Hath told the thievish minutes how they pass,
What is infirm from your sound parts shall fly,
Health shall live free, and sickness freely die.

KING
Upon thy certainty and confidence
What dar'st thou venture?

HELEN   Tax of impudence,   170
A strumpet's boldness, a divulgèd shame;
Traduced by odious ballads, my maiden's name
Seared otherwise, nay—worse of worst—extended
With vilest torture, let my life be ended.

KING
Methinks in thee some blessèd spirit doth speak,   175
His powerful sound within an organ weak;
And what impossibility would slay
In common sense, sense saves another way.
Thy life is dear, for all that life can rate
Worth name of life in thee hath estimate: 180
Youth, beauty, wisdom, courage, all
That happiness and prime can happy call.
Thou this to hazard needs must intimate
Skill infinite, or monstrous desperate.
Sweet practiser, thy physic I will try,   185
That ministers thine own death if I die.

HELEN
If I break time, or flinch in property
Of what I spoke, unpitied let me die,
And well deserved. Not helping, death's my fee.
But if I help, what do you promise me?   190

KING
Make thy demand.

HELEN   But will you make it even?

KING
Ay, by my sceptre and my hopes of heaven.

HELEN
Then shalt thou give me with thy kingly hand
What husband in thy power I will command.
Exempted be from me the arrogance   195
To choose from forth the royal blood of France,
My low and humble name to propagate
With any branch or image of thy state;
But such a one, thy vassal, whom I know
Is free for me to ask, thee to bestow.   200

KING
Here is my hand. The premises observed,
Thy will by my performance shall be served.
So make the choice of thy own time, for I,
Thy resolved patient, on thee still rely.
More should I question thee, and more I must,   205
Though more to know could not be more to trust:
From whence thou cam'st, how tended on—but rest
Unquestioned welcome, and undoubted blessed.—
Give me some help here, ho! If thou proceed
As high as word, my deed shall match thy deed.   210
        Flourish. Exeunt the King, ⌈carried⌉, and Helen

2.2   *Enter the Countess and Lavatch the clown*

COUNTESS Come on, sir. I shall now put you to the height
of your breeding.

LAVATCH I will show myself highly fed and lowly taught.
I know my business is but to the court.   4

COUNTESS 'To the court'? Why, what place make you
special, when you put off that with such contempt?
'But to the court'!

LAVATCH Truly, madam, if God have lent a man any
manners he may easily put it off at court. He that
cannot make a leg, put off's cap, kiss his hand, and
say nothing, has neither leg, hands, lip, nor cap, and
indeed such a fellow, to say precisely, were not for the
court. But for me, I have an answer will serve all men.

COUNTESS Marry, that's a bountiful answer that fits all
questions.   15

LAVATCH It is like a barber's chair that fits all buttocks:
the pin-buttock, the quatch-buttock, the brawn-
buttock, or any buttock.

COUNTESS Will your answer serve fit to all questions?   19

LAVATCH As fit as ten groats is for the hand of an attorney,
as your French crown for your taffeta punk, as Tib's
rush for Tom's forefinger, as a pancake for Shrove
Tuesday, a morris for May Day, as the nail to his hole,
the cuckold to his horn, as a scolding quean to a
wrangling knave, as the nun's lip to the friar's mouth,
nay as the pudding to his skin.   26

COUNTESS Have you, I say, an answer of such fitness for
all questions?

LAVATCH From beyond your duke to beneath your constable, it will fit any question.   30

COUNTESS It must be an answer of most monstrous size
that must fit all demands.

LAVATCH But a trifle neither, in good faith, if the learned
should speak truth of it. Here it is, and all that belongs

to't. Ask me if I am a courtier. It shall do you no harm
to learn.   36
COUNTESS To be young again, if we could! I will be a fool
in question, hoping to be the wiser by your answer. I
pray you, sir, are you a courtier?
LAVATCH O Lord, sir!—There's a simple putting off. More,
more, a hundred of them.   41
COUNTESS Sir, I am a poor friend of yours that loves you.
LAVATCH O Lord, sir!—Thick, thick, spare not me.
COUNTESS I think, sir, you can eat none of this homely
meat.   45
LAVATCH O Lord, sir!—Nay, put me to't, I warrant you.
COUNTESS You were lately whipped, sir, as I think.
LAVATCH O Lord, sir!—Spare not me.
COUNTESS Do you cry 'O Lord, sir!' at your whipping, and
'spare not me'? Indeed, your 'O Lord, sir!' is very
sequent to your whipping. You would answer very well
to a whipping, if you were but bound to't.   52
LAVATCH I ne'er had worse luck in my life in my 'O Lord,
sir!' I see things may serve long, but not serve ever.
COUNTESS I play the noble housewife with the time, to
entertain it so merrily with a fool.   56
LAVATCH O Lord, sir!—Why, there't serves well again.
COUNTESS
   An end, sir! To your business: give Helen this,
      She gives him a letter
   And urge her to a present answer back.
   Commend me to my kinsmen and my son.   60
   This is not much.
LAVATCH Not much commendation to them?
COUNTESS Not much employment for you. You understand
me.
LAVATCH Most fruitfully. I am there before my legs.
COUNTESS Haste you again.   *Exeunt severally*

2.3   *Enter Bertram, Lafeu ⌈with a ballad⌉, and Paroles*
LAFEU They say miracles are past, and we have our
philosophical persons to make modern and familiar
things supernatural and causeless. Hence is it that we
make trifles of terrors, ensconcing ourselves into
seeming knowledge when we should submit ourselves
to an unknown fear.   6
PAROLES Why, 'tis the rarest argument of wonder that
hath shot out in our latter times.
BERTRAM And so 'tis.
LAFEU To be relinquished of the artists—   10
PAROLES So I say—both of Galen and Paracelsus.
LAFEU Of all the learned and authentic Fellows—
PAROLES Right, so I say.
LAFEU That gave him out incurable—
PAROLES Why, there 'tis, so say I too.   15
LAFEU Not to be helped.
PAROLES Right, as 'twere a man assured of a—
LAFEU Uncertain life and sure death.
PAROLES Just, you say well, so would I have said.
LAFEU I may truly say it is a novelty to the world.   20
PAROLES It is indeed. If you will have it in showing, you
shall read it in ⌈*pointing to the ballad*⌉ what-do-ye-call
there.

LAFEU ⌈*reads*⌉ 'A showing of a heavenly effect in an earthly
actor.'   25
PAROLES That's it, I would have said the very same.
LAFEU Why, your dolphin is not lustier. Fore me, I speak
in respect—
PAROLES Nay, 'tis strange, 'tis very strange, that is the
brief and the tedious of it, and he's of a most facinorous
spirit that will not acknowledge it to be the—   31
LAFEU Very hand of heaven.
PAROLES Ay, so I say.
LAFEU In a most weak—   34
PAROLES And debile minister great power, great trans-
cendence, which should indeed give us a further use
to be made than alone the recov'ry of the king, as to
be—
LAFEU Generally thankful.
      Enter the King, Helen, and attendants
PAROLES I would have said it, you say well. Here comes
the King.   41
LAFEU *Lustig*, as the Dutchman says. I'll like a maid the
better whilst I have a tooth in my head.
      ⌈*The King and Helen dance*⌉
Why, he's able to lead her a coranto.
PAROLES *Mort du vinaigre*, is not this Helen?   45
LAFEU Fore God, I think so.
KING
   Go call before me all the lords in court.
                                          Exit one or more
   Sit, my preserver, by thy patient's side,
      ⌈*The King and Helen sit*⌉
   And with this healthful hand whose banished sense
   Thou hast repealed, a second time receive   50
   The confirmation of my promised gift,
   Which but attends thy naming.
      Enter four Lords
   Fair maid, send forth thine eye. This youthful parcel
   Of noble bachelors stand at my bestowing,
   O'er whom both sovereign power and father's voice   55
   I have to use. Thy frank election make.
   Thou hast power to choose, and they none to forsake.
HELEN
   To each of you one fair and virtuous mistress
   Fall when love please. Marry, to each but one.
LAFEU (*aside*)
   I'd give bay Curtal and his furniture   60
   My mouth no more were broken than these boys',
   And writ as little beard.
KING (*to Helen*)   Peruse them well.
   Not one of these but had a noble father.
HELEN Gentlemen,
   Heaven hath through me restored the King to health.
⌈ALL BUT HELEN⌉
   We understand it, and thank heaven for you.   66
HELEN
   I am a simple maid, and therein wealthiest
   That I protest I simply am a maid.—
   Please it your majesty, I have done already.
   The blushes in my cheeks thus whisper me: 70
   'We blush that thou shouldst choose; but, be refused,

Let the white death sit on thy cheek for ever,
We'll ne'er come there again.'
KING   Make choice and see.
Who shuns thy love shuns all his love in me.
HELEN (*rising*)
Now, Dian, from thy altar do I fly,   75
And to imperial Love, that god most high,
Do my sighs stream.
     ⌈*She addresses her to a Lord*⌉
           Sir, will you hear my suit?
FIRST LORD
And grant it.
HELEN   Thanks, sir. All the rest is mute.
LAFEU (*aside*) I had rather be in this choice than throw
ambs-ace for my life.   80
HELEN (*to another Lord*)
The honour, sir, that flames in your fair eyes,
Before I speak, too threat'ningly replies.
Love make your fortunes twenty times above
Her that so wishes, and her humble love.
SECOND LORD
No better, if you please.
HELEN   My wish receive,   85
Which great Love grant. And so I take my leave.
LAFEU (*aside*) Do all they deny her? An they were sons of
mine I'd have them whipped, or I would send them to
th' Turk to make eunuchs of.
HELEN (*to another Lord*)
Be not afraid that I your hand should take;   90
I'll never do you wrong for your own sake.
Blessing upon your vows, and in your bed
Find fairer fortune, if you ever wed.
LAFEU (*aside*) These boys are boys of ice, they'll none have
her. Sure they are bastards to the English, the French
ne'er got 'em.   96
HELEN (*to another Lord*)
You are too young, too happy, and too good
To make yourself a son out of my blood.
FOURTH LORD Fair one, I think not so.   99
LAFEU (*aside*) There's one grape yet. I am sure thy father
drunk wine, but if thou beest not an ass I am a youth
of fourteen. I have known thee already.
HELEN (*to Bertram*)
I dare not say I take you, but I give
Me and my service ever whilst I live
Into your guiding power.—This is the man.   105
KING
Why then, young Bertram, take her, she's thy wife.
BERTRAM
My wife, my liege? I shall beseech your highness,
In such a business give me leave to use
The help of mine own eyes.
KING   Know'st thou not, Bertram,
What she has done for me?
BERTRAM   Yes, my good lord,   110
But never hope to know why I should marry her.
KING
Thou know'st she has raised me from my sickly bed.

BERTRAM
But follows it, my lord, to bring me down
Must answer for your raising? I know her well:
She had her breeding at my father's charge.   115
A poor physician's daughter, my wife? Disdain
Rather corrupt me ever.
KING
'Tis only title thou disdain'st in her, the which
I can build up. Strange is it that our bloods,
Of colour, weight, and heat, poured all together,   120
Would quite confound distinction, yet stands off
In differences so mighty. If she be
All that is virtuous, save what thou dislik'st—
'A poor physician's daughter'—thou dislik'st
Of virtue for the name. But do not so.   125
From lowest place when virtuous things proceed,
The place is dignified by th' doer's deed.
Where great additions swell's, and virtue none,
It is a dropsied honour. Good alone
Is good without a name, vileness is so: 130
The property by what it is should go,
Not by the title. She is young, wise, fair.
In these to nature she's immediate heir,
And these breed honour. That is honour's scorn
Which challenges itself as honour's born   135
And is not like the sire; honours thrive
When rather from our acts we them derive
Than our foregoers. The mere word's a slave,
Debauched on every tomb, on every grave
A lying trophy, and as oft is dumb   140
Where dust and dammed oblivion is the tomb
Of honoured bones indeed. What should be said?
If thou canst like this creature as a maid,
I can create the rest. Virtue and she
Is her own dower; honour and wealth from me.   145
BERTRAM
I cannot love her, nor will strive to do't.
KING
Thou wrong'st thyself. If thou shouldst strive to
   choose—
HELEN
That you are well restored, my lord, I'm glad.
Let the rest go.
KING
My honour's at the stake, which to defeat   150
I must produce my power. Here, take her hand,
Proud, scornful boy, unworthy this good gift,
That dost in vile misprision shackle up
My love and her desert; that canst not dream
We, poising us in her defective scale,   155
Shall weigh thee to the beam; that wilt not know
It is in us to plant thine honour where
We please to have it grow. Check thy contempt;
Obey our will, which travails in thy good;
Believe not thy disdain, but presently   160
Do thine own fortunes that obedient right
Which both thy duty owes and our power claims,
Or I will throw thee from my care for ever

Into the staggers and the careless lapse
Of youth and ignorance, both my revenge and hate
Loosing upon thee in the name of justice   166
Without all terms of pity. Speak. Thine answer.
BERTRAM (*kneeling*)
Pardon, my gracious lord, for I submit
My fancy to your eyes. When I consider
What great creation and what dole of honour   170
Flies where you bid it, I find that she, which late
Was in my nobler thoughts most base, is now
The praisèd of the King; who, so ennobled,
Is as 'twere born so.
KING   Take her by the hand
And tell her she is thine; to whom I promise   175
A counterpoise, if not to thy estate
A balance more replete.
BERTRAM (*rising*)   I take her hand.
KING
Good fortune and the favour of the King
Smile upon this contract, whose ceremony
Shall seem expedient on the now-born brief,   180
And be performed tonight. The solemn feast
Shall more attend upon the coming space,
Expecting absent friends. As thou lov'st her
Thy love's to me religious; else, does err.
                    ⌈*Flourish.*⌉ *Exeunt all but Paroles and Lafeu,*
                    who stay behind, commenting on this wedding
LAFEU Do you hear, monsieur? A word with you.   185
PAROLES Your pleasure, sir.
LAFEU Your lord and master did well to make his
recantation.
PAROLES Recantation? My lord? My master?
LAFEU Ay. Is it not a language I speak?   190
PAROLES A most harsh one, and not to be understood
without bloody succeeding. My master?
LAFEU Are you companion to the Count Roussillon?
PAROLES To any count, to all counts, to what is man.
LAFEU To what is count's man; count's master is of
another style.   196
PAROLES You are too old, sir. Let it satisfy you, you are
too old.
LAFEU I must tell thee, sirrah, I write 'Man', to which
title age cannot bring thee.   200
PAROLES What I dare too well do I dare not do.
LAFEU I did think thee for two ordinaries to be a pretty
wise fellow. Thou didst make tolerable vent of thy
travel; it might pass. Yet the scarves and the bannerets
about thee did manifoldly dissuade me from believing
thee a vessel of too great a burden. I have now found
thee; when I lose thee again I care not. Yet art thou
good for nothing but taking up, and that thou'rt scarce
worth.
PAROLES Hadst thou not the privilege of antiquity upon
thee—   211
LAFEU Do not plunge thyself too far in anger, lest thou
hasten thy trial, which if—Lord have mercy on thee
for a hen! So, my good window of lattice, fare thee

well. Thy casement I need not open, for I look through
thee. Give me thy hand.   216
PAROLES My lord, you give me most egregious indignity.
LAFEU Ay, with all my heart, and thou art worthy of it.
PAROLES I have not, my lord, deserved it.
LAFEU Yes, good faith, every dram of it, and I will not
bate thee a scruple.   221
PAROLES Well, I shall be wiser.
LAFEU E'en as soon as thou canst, for thou hast to pull
at a smack o'th' contrary. If ever thou beest bound in
thy scarf and beaten thou shall find what it is to be
proud of thy bondage. I have a desire to hold my
acquaintance with thee, or rather my knowledge, that
I may say in the default, 'He is a man I know'.   228
PAROLES My lord, you do me most insupportable vexation.
LAFEU I would it were hell-pains for thy sake, and my
poor doing eternal; for doing I am past, as I will by
thee, in what motion age will give me leave.   *Exit*
PAROLES Well, thou hast a son shall take this disgrace off
me. Scurvy, old, filthy, scurvy lord. Well, I must be
patient. There is no fettering of authority. I'll beat him,
by my life, if I can meet him with any convenience,
an he were double and double a lord. I'll have no more
pity of his age than I would have of—I'll beat him, an
if I could but meet him again.   239
          Enter Lafeu
LAFEU Sirrah, your lord and master's married. There's
news for you: you have a new mistress.
PAROLES I most unfeignedly beseech your lordship to make
some reservation of your wrongs. He is my good lord;
whom I serve above is my master.
LAFEU Who? God?   245
PAROLES Ay, sir.
LAFEU The devil it is that's thy master. Why dost thou
garter up thy arms o' this fashion? Dost make hose of
thy sleeves? Do other servants so? Thou wert best set
thy lower part where thy nose stands. By mine honour,
if I were but two hours younger I'd beat thee. Methink'st
thou art a general offence and every man should beat
thee. I think thou wast created for men to breathe
themselves upon thee.   254
PAROLES This is hard and undeserved measure, my lord.
LAFEU Go to, sir. You were beaten in Italy for picking a
kernel out of a pomegranate, you are a vagabond and
no true traveller, you are more saucy with lords and
honourable personages than the commission of your
birth and virtue gives you heraldry. You are not worth
another word, else I'd call you knave. I leave you. 261
                    Exit
PAROLES Good, very good, it is so then. Good, very good,
let it be concealed awhile.
          ⌈*Enter Bertram*⌉
BERTRAM
Undone and forfeited to cares for ever.
PAROLES What's the matter, sweetheart?   265
BERTRAM
Although before the solemn priest I have sworn,
I will not bed her.

PAROLES What, what, sweetheart?

BERTRAM
O my Paroles, they have married me.
I'll to the Tuscan wars and never bed her.   270

PAROLES
France is a dog-hole, and it no more merits
The tread of a man's foot. To th' wars!

BERTRAM
There's letters from my mother. What th'import is
I know not yet.

PAROLES
Ay, that would be known. To th' wars, my boy, to th'
    wars!   275
He wears his honour in a box unseen
That hugs his kicky-wicky here at home,
Spending his manly marrow in her arms,
Which should sustain the bound and high curvet
Of Mars's fiery steed. To other regions!   280
France is a stable, we that dwell in't jades.
Therefore to th' war.

BERTRAM
It shall be so. I'll send her to my house,
Acquaint my mother with my hate to her,
And wherefore I am fled, write to the King   285
That which I durst not speak. His present gift
Shall furnish me to those Italian fields
Where noble fellows strike. Wars is no strife
To the dark house and the detested wife.

PAROLES
Will this *capriccio* hold in thee? Art sure?   290

BERTRAM
Go with me to my chamber and advise me.
I'll send her straight away. Tomorrow
I'll to the wars, she to her single sorrow.

PAROLES
Why, these balls bound, there's noise in it. 'Tis hard:
A young man married is a man that's marred.   295
Therefore away, and leave her bravely. Go.
The King has done you wrong, but hush 'tis so.
                                          Exeunt

2.4   *Enter Helen reading a letter, and Lavatch the clown*

HELEN
My mother greets me kindly. Is she well?

LAVATCH She is not well, but yet she has her health. She's
very merry, but yet she is not well. But thanks be given
she's very well and wants nothing i'th' world. But yet
she is not well.   5

HELEN
If she be very well, what does she ail
That she's not very well?

LAVATCH Truly, she's very well indeed, but for two things.

HELEN What two things?   9

LAVATCH One, that she's not in heaven, whither God send
her quickly. The other, that she's in earth, from whence
God send her quickly.
        Enter Paroles

PAROLES Bless you, my fortunate lady.

HELEN
I hope, sir, I have your good will to have
Mine own good fortunes.   15

PAROLES You had my prayers to lead them on, and to
keep them on have them still.—O my knave, how does
my old lady?

LAVATCH So that you had her wrinkles and I her money,
I would she did as you say.   20

PAROLES Why, I say nothing.

LAVATCH Marry, you are the wiser man, for many a
man's tongue shakes out his master's undoing. To say
nothing, to do nothing, to know nothing, and to have
nothing, is to be a great part of your title, which is
within a very little of nothing.   26

PAROLES Away, thou'rt a knave.

LAVATCH You should have said, sir, 'Before a knave,
thou'rt a knave'—that's 'Before me, thou'rt a knave'.
This had been truth, sir.   30

PAROLES Go to, thou art a witty fool. I have found thee.

LAVATCH Did you find me in yourself, sir, or were you
taught to find me?

⌐PAROLES⌐ In myself, knave.   34

LAVATCH The search, sir, was profitable, and much fool
may you find in you, even to the world's pleasure and
the increase of laughter.

PAROLES (*to Helen*) A good knave, i'faith, and well fed.
Madam, my lord will go away tonight.
A very serious business calls on him.   40
The great prerogative and rite of love,
Which as your due time claims, he does acknowledge,
But puts it off to a compelled restraint:
Whose want and whose delay is strewed with sweets,
Which they distil now in the curbèd time,   45
To make the coming hour o'erflow with joy,
And pleasure drown the brim.

HELEN   What's his will else?

PAROLES
That you will take your instant leave o'th' King,
And make this haste as your own good proceeding,
Strengthened with what apology you think   50
May make it probable need.

HELEN   What more commands he?

PAROLES
That having this obtained, you presently
Attend his further pleasure.

HELEN   In everything
I wait upon his will.

PAROLES   I shall report it so.   54

HELEN I pray you.   ⌐*Exit Paroles at one door*⌐
Come, sirrah.   *Exeunt* ⌐*at another door*⌐

2.5   *Enter Lafeu and Bertram*

LAFEU But I hope your lordship thinks not him a soldier.

BERTRAM Yes, my lord, and of very valiant approof.

LAFEU You have it from his own deliverance.

BERTRAM And by other warranted testimony.

LAFEU Then my dial goes not true. I took this lark for a
bunting.   6

BERTRAM I do assure you, my lord, he is very great in
knowledge, and accordingly valiant.   8
LAFEU I have then sinned against his experience and
transgressed against his valour—and my state that way
is dangerous, since I cannot yet find in my heart to
repent. Here he comes. I pray you make us friends. I
will pursue the amity.

Enter Paroles

PAROLES (*to Bertram*) These things shall be done, sir.
LAFEU (*to Bertram*) Pray you, sir, who's his tailor?   15
PAROLES Sir!
LAFEU O, I know him well. Ay, 'Sir', he; 'Sir' 's a good
workman, a very good tailor.
BERTRAM (*aside to Paroles*) Is she gone to the King?
PAROLES She is.   20
BERTRAM Will she away tonight?
PAROLES As you'll have her.
BERTRAM
I have writ my letters, casketed my treasure,
Given order for our horses, and tonight,
When I should take possession of the bride,   25
End ere I do begin.
LAFEU (*aside*) A good traveller is something at the latter
end of a dinner, but one that lies three-thirds and uses
a known truth to pass a thousand nothings with,
should be once heard and thrice beaten. (*To Paroles*)
God save you, captain.   31
BERTRAM (*to Paroles*) Is there any unkindness between my
lord and you, monsieur?
PAROLES I know not how I have deserved to run into my
lord's displeasure.   35
LAFEU You have made shift to run into't, boots and spurs
and all, like him that leaped into the custard, and out
of it you'll run again, rather than suffer question for
your residence.
BERTRAM It may be you have mistaken him, my lord.   40
LAFEU And shall do so ever, though I took him at's
prayers. Fare you well, my lord, and believe this of me:
there can be no kernel in this light nut. The soul of
this man is his clothes. Trust him not in matter of
heavy consequence. I have kept of them tame, and
know their natures.—Farewell, monsieur. I have
spoken better of you than you have wit or will to
deserve at my hand, but we must do good against evil.
                                                  Exit
PAROLES An idle lord, I swear.
BERTRAM I think not so.   50
PAROLES Why, do you not know him?
BERTRAM
Yes, I do know him well, and common speech
Gives him a worthy pass. Here comes my clog.

Enter Helen, ⌈attended⌉

HELEN
I have, sir, as I was commanded from you,
Spoke with the King, and have procured his leave   55
For present parting; only he desires
Some private speech with you.
BERTRAM   I shall obey his will.

You must not marvel, Helen, at my course,
Which holds not colour with the time, nor does
The ministration and requirèd office   60
On my particular. Prepared I was not
For such a business, therefore am I found
So much unsettled. This drives me to entreat you
That presently you take your way for home,
And rather muse than ask why I entreat you,   65
For my respects are better than they seem,
And my appointments have in them a need
Greater than shows itself at the first view
To you that know them not. This to my mother.
                  He gives her a letter
'Twill be two days ere I shall see you, so   70
I leave you to your wisdom.
HELEN   Sir, I can nothing say
But that I am your most obedient servant.
BERTRAM
Come, come, no more of that.
HELEN   And ever shall
With true observance seek to eke out that
Wherein toward me my homely stars have failed   75
To equal my great fortune.
BERTRAM   Let that go.
My haste is very great. Farewell. Hie home.
HELEN
Pray sir, your pardon.
BERTRAM   Well, what would you say?
HELEN
I am not worthy of the wealth I owe,
Nor dare I say 'tis mine—and yet it is—   80
But like a timorous thief most fain would steal
What law does vouch mine own.
BERTRAM   What would you have?
HELEN
Something, and scarce so much: nothing indeed.
I would not tell you what I would, my lord. Faith,
yes:
Strangers and foes do sunder and not kiss.   85
BERTRAM
I pray you, stay not, but in haste to horse.
HELEN
I shall not break your bidding, good my lord.—
Where are my other men?—Monsieur, farewell.
     Exeunt Helen ⌈and attendants at one door⌉
BERTRAM
Go thou toward home, where I will never come
Whilst I can shake my sword or hear the drum.—   90
Away, and for our flight.
PAROLES   Bravely. *Coraggio!*
                 Exeunt ⌈at another door⌉

3.1 *Flourish of trumpets. Enter the Duke of Florence*
        and the two Lords Dumaine, with a troop of
        soldiers

DUKE
So that from point to point now have you heard
The fundamental reasons of this war,

Whose great decision hath much blood let forth,
And more thirsts after.
FIRST LORD DUMAINE   Holy seems the quarrel
Upon your grace's part; black and fearful   5
On the opposer.
DUKE
Therefore we marvel much our cousin France
Would in so just a business shut his bosom
Against our borrowing prayers.
SECOND LORD DUMAINE   Good my lord,
The reasons of our state I cannot yield   10
But like a common and an outward man
That the great figure of a council frames
By self-unable motion; therefore dare not
Say what I think of it, since I have found
Myself in my incertain grounds to fail   15
As often as I guessed.
DUKE   Be it his pleasure.
FIRST LORD DUMAINE
But I am sure the younger of our nation,
That surfeit on their ease, will day by day
Come here for physic.
DUKE   Welcome shall they be,
And all the honours that can fly from us   20
Shall on them settle. You know your places well;
When better fall, for your avails they fell.
Tomorrow to the field.   *Flourish. Exeunt*

3.2   *Enter the Countess with a letter, and Lavatch*
COUNTESS It hath happened all as I would have had it,
save that he comes not along with her.
LAVATCH By my troth, I take my young lord to be a very
melancholy man.
COUNTESS By what observance, I pray you?   5
LAVATCH Why, he will look upon his boot and sing, mend
the ruff and sing, ask questions and sing, pick his teeth
and sing. I know a man that had this trick of
melancholy sold a goodly manor for a song.
COUNTESS Let me see what he writes, and when he means
to come.   11
   She opens the letter and reads
LAVATCH (*aside*) I have no mind to Isbel since I was at
court. Our old lings and our Isbels o'th' country are
nothing like your old ling and your Isbels o'th' court.
The brains of my Cupid's knocked out, and I begin to
love as an old man loves money: with no stomach.   16
COUNTESS What have we here?
LAVATCH E'en that you have there.   *Exit*
COUNTESS (*reads the letter aloud*) 'I have sent you a
daughter-in-law. She hath recovered the King and
undone me. I have wedded her, not bedded her, and
sworn to make the "not" eternal. You shall hear I am
run away; know it before the report come. If there be
breadth enough in the world I will hold a long distance.
My duty to you.   25
                    Your unfortunate son,
                         Bertram.'
This is not well, rash and unbridled boy,
To fly the favours of so good a King,

To pluck his indignation on thy head   30
By the misprizing of a maid too virtuous
For the contempt of empire.
   Enter Lavatch
LAVATCH O madam, yonder is heavy news within,
between two soldiers and my young lady.
COUNTESS What is the matter?   35
LAVATCH Nay, there is some comfort in the news, some
comfort. Your son will not be killed so soon as I thought
he would.
COUNTESS Why should he be killed?   39
LAVATCH So say I, madam—if he run away, as I hear he
does. The danger is in standing to't; that's the loss of
men, though it be the getting of children. Here they
come will tell you more. For my part, I only heard
your son was run away.   *Exit*
   Enter Helen with a letter, and the two Lords
   Dumaine
SECOND LORD DUMAINE (*to the Countess*)
Save you, good madam.   45
HELEN
Madam, my lord is gone, for ever gone.
FIRST LORD DUMAINE Do not say so.
COUNTESS (*to Helen*)
Think upon patience.—Pray you, gentlemen,
I have felt so many quirks of joy and grief
That the first face of neither on the start   50
Can woman me unto't. Where is my son, I pray you?
FIRST LORD DUMAINE
Madam, he's gone to serve the Duke of Florence.
We met him thitherward, for thence we came,
And, after some dispatch in hand at court,
Thither we bend again.   55
HELEN
Look on his letter, madam: here's my passport.
   She reads aloud
'When thou canst get the ring upon my finger, which
never shall come off, and show me a child begotten of
thy body that I am father to, then call me husband;
but in such a "then" I write a "never".'   60
This is a dreadful sentence.
COUNTESS
Brought you this letter, gentlemen?
FIRST LORD DUMAINE   Ay, madam,
And for the contents' sake are sorry for our pains.
COUNTESS
I prithee, lady, have a better cheer.
If thou engrossest all the griefs are thine   65
Thou robb'st me of a moiety. He was my son,
But I do wash his name out of my blood,
And thou art all my child.—Towards Florence is he?
FIRST LORD DUMAINE
Ay, madam.
COUNTESS   And to be a soldier?
FIRST LORD DUMAINE
Such is his noble purpose, and—believe't—   70
The Duke will lay upon him all the honour
That good convenience claims.
COUNTESS   Return you thither?

SECOND LORD DUMAINE
 Ay, madam, with the swiftest wing of speed.
HELEN 'Till I have no wife, I have nothing in France.'
 'Tis bitter.   75
COUNTESS Find you that there?
HELEN Ay, madam.
SECOND LORD DUMAINE
 'Tis but the boldness of his hand,
 Haply, which his heart was not consenting to.
COUNTESS
 Nothing in France until he have no wife?   80
 There's nothing here that is too good for him
 But only she, and she deserves a lord
 That twenty such rude boys might tend upon
 And call her, hourly, mistress. Who was with him?
SECOND LORD DUMAINE
 A servant only, and a gentleman   85
 Which I have sometime known.
COUNTESS Paroles, was it not?
SECOND LORD DUMAINE Ay, my good lady, he.
COUNTESS
 A very tainted fellow, and full of wickedness.
 My son corrupts a well-derivèd nature   90
 With his inducement.
SECOND LORD DUMAINE   Indeed, good lady,
 The fellow has a deal of that too much,
 Which holds him much to have.
COUNTESS   You're welcome, gentlemen.
 I will entreat you when you see my son
 To tell him that his sword can never win   95
 The honour that he loses. More I'll entreat you
 Written to bear along.
FIRST LORD DUMAINE   We serve you, madam,
 In that and all your worthiest affairs.
COUNTESS
 Not so, but as we change our courtesies.
 Will you draw near?   Exeunt all but Helen
HELEN 'Till I have no wife I have nothing in France.'
 Nothing in France until he has no wife.
 Thou shalt have none, Roussillon, none in France;
 Then hast thou all again. Poor lord, is't I
 That chase thee from thy country and expose   105
 Those tender limbs of thine to the event
 Of the none-sparing war? And is it I
 That drive thee from the sportive court, where thou
 Wast shot at with fair eyes, to be the mark
 Of smoky muskets? O you leaden messengers   110
 That ride upon the violent speed of fire,
 Fly with false aim, cleave the still-piecing air
 That sings with piercing, do not touch my lord.
 Whoever shoots at him, I set him there.
 Whoever charges on his forward breast,   115
 I am the caitiff that do hold him to't,
 And though I kill him not, I am the cause
 His death was so effected. Better 'twere
 I met the ravin lion when he roared
 With sharp constraint of hunger; better 'twere   120
 That all the miseries which nature owes

Were mine at once. No, come thou home, Roussillon,
 Whence honour but of danger wins a scar,
 As oft it loses all. I will be gone;
 My being here it is that holds thee hence.   125
 Shall I stay here to do't? No, no, although
 The air of paradise did fan the house
 And angels officed all. I will be gone,
 That pitiful rumour may report my flight
 To consolate thine ear. Come night, end day;   130
 For with the dark, poor thief, I'll steal away.   Exit

3.3   Flourish of trumpets. Enter the Duke of Florence,
       Bertram, a drummer and trumpeters, soldiers, and
       Paroles
DUKE (to Bertram)
 The general of our horse thou art, and we,
 Great in our hope, lay our best love and credence
 Upon thy promising fortune.
BERTRAM   Sir, it is
 A charge too heavy for my strength, but yet
 We'll strive to bear it for your worthy sake   5
 To th'extreme edge of hazard.
DUKE   Then go thou forth,
 And Fortune play upon thy prosperous helm
 As thy auspicious mistress.
BERTRAM   This very day,
 Great Mars, I put myself into thy file.
 Make me but like my thoughts, and I shall prove   10
 A lover of thy drum, hater of love.   Exeunt

3.4   Enter the Countess and Reynaldo her steward, with
       a letter
COUNTESS
 Alas! And would you take the letter of her?
 Might you not know she would do as she has done,
 By sending me a letter? Read it again.
REYNALDO (reads the letter)
 'I am Saint Jaques' pilgrim, thither gone.
   Ambitious love hath so in me offended   5
 That barefoot plod I the cold ground upon
   With sainted vow my faults to have amended.
 Write, write, that from the bloody course of war
   My dearest master, your dear son, may hie.
 Bless him at home in peace, whilst I from far   10
   His name with zealous fervour sanctify.
 His taken labours bid him me forgive;
   I, his despiteful Juno, sent him forth
 From courtly friends, with camping foes to live,
   Where death and danger dogs the heels of worth. 15
 He is too good and fair for death and me;
   Whom I myself embrace to set him free.'
COUNTESS
 Ah, what sharp stings are in her mildest words!
 Reynaldo, you did never lack advice so much
 As letting her pass so. Had I spoke with her,   20
 I could have well diverted her intents,
 Which thus she hath prevented.
REYNALDO   Pardon me, madam.

If I had given you this at over-night
She might have been o'erta'en—and yet she writes
Pursuit would be but vain.

COUNTESS   What angel shall   25
Bless this unworthy husband? He cannot thrive
Unless her prayers, whom heaven delights to hear
And loves to grant, reprieve him from the wrath
Of greatest justice. Write, write, Reynaldo,
To this unworthy husband of his wife.   30
Let every word weigh heavy of her worth,
That he does weigh too light; my greatest grief,
Though little he do feel it, set down sharply.
Dispatch the most convenient messenger.
When haply he shall hear that she is gone,   35
He will return, and hope I may that she,
Hearing so much, will speed her foot again,
Led hither by pure love. Which of them both
Is dearest to me I have no skill in sense
To make distinction. Provide this messenger.   40
My heart is heavy and mine age is weak;
Grief would have tears, and sorrow bids me speak.
                                          Exeunt

3.5   *A tucket afar off. Enter an old Widow, her daughter*
          Diana, and Mariana, with other Florentine citizens

WIDOW Nay, come, for if they do approach the city we
shall lose all the sight.

DIANA They say the French Count has done most
honourable service.

WIDOW It is reported that he has taken their greatest
commander, and that with his own hand he slew the
Duke's brother. (*Tucket*) We have lost our labour; they
are gone a contrary way. Hark. You may know by
their trumpets.   9

MARIANA Come, let's return again, and suffice ourselves
with the report of it.—Well, Diana, take heed of this
French earl. The honour of a maid is her name, and
no legacy is so rich as honesty.

WIDOW (*to Diana*) I have told my neighbour how you have
been solicited by a gentleman, his companion.   15

MARIANA I know that knave, hang him! One Paroles. A
filthy officer he is in those suggestions for the young
earl. Beware of them, Diana; their promises, entice-
ments, oaths, tokens, and all their engines of lust,
are not the things they go under. Many a maid hath
been seduced by them; and the misery is, example,
that so terrible shows in the wreck of maidenhood,
cannot for all that dissuade succession, but that they
are limed with the twigs that threatens them. I hope I
need not to advise you further, but I hope your own
grace will keep you where you are, though there were
no further danger known but the modesty which is so
lost.   28

DIANA You shall not need to fear me.
          Enter Helen dressed as a pilgrim

WIDOW I hope so. Look, here comes a pilgrim. I know she
will lie at my house; thither they send one another.
I'll question her.
God save you, pilgrim. Whither are you bound?

HELEN To Saint Jaques le Grand.
Where do the palmers lodge, I do beseech you?   35
WIDOW
At the 'Saint Francis' here beside the port.
HELEN
Is this the way?
WIDOW   Ay, marry, is't.
          Sound of a march, far off
Hark you, they come this way. If you will tarry,
Holy pilgrim, but till the troops come by,
I will conduct you where you shall be lodged,   40
The rather for I think I know your hostess
As ample as myself.
HELEN Is it yourself?
WIDOW If you shall please so, pilgrim.
HELEN
I thank you, and will stay upon your leisure.   45
WIDOW
You came, I think, from France?
HELEN   I did so.
WIDOW
Here you shall see a countryman of yours
That has done worthy service.
HELEN   His name, I pray you?
DIANA
The Count Roussillon. Know you such a one?
HELEN
But by the ear, that hears most nobly of him;   50
His face I know not.
DIANA   Whatsome'er he is,
He's bravely taken here. He stole from France,
As 'tis reported; for the King had married him
Against his liking. Think you it is so?
HELEN
Ay, surely, mere the truth. I know his lady.   55
DIANA
There is a gentleman that serves the Count
Reports but coarsely of her.
HELEN   What's his name?
DIANA
Monsieur Paroles.
HELEN   O, I believe with him:
In argument of praise, or to the worth
Of the great Count himself, she is too mean   60
To have her name repeated. All her deserving
Is a reservèd honesty, and that
I have not heard examined.
DIANA   Alas, poor lady.
'Tis a hard bondage to become the wife
Of a detesting lord.   65
WIDOW
I warr'nt, good creature, wheresoe'er she is
Her heart weighs sadly. This young maid might do her
A shrewd turn if she pleased.
HELEN   How do you mean?
Maybe the amorous Count solicits her
In the unlawful purpose.
WIDOW   He does indeed,   70
And brokes with all that can in such a suit

Corrupt the tender honour of a maid.
But she is armed for him, and keeps her guard
In honestest defence.
MARIANA The gods forbid else.   75
    ⌈Enter, with drummer and colours, Bertram,
    Paroles, and the whole army⌉
WIDOW So, now they come.
That is Antonio, the Duke's eldest son;
That, Escalus.
HELEN   Which is the Frenchman?
DIANA   He—
That with the plume. 'Tis a most gallant fellow.
I would he loved his wife. If he were honester   80
He were much goodlier. Is't not
A handsome gentleman?
HELEN I like him well.
DIANA 'Tis pity he is not honest.
Yond's that same knave that leads him to those
    places.   85
Were I his lady, I would poison
That vile rascal.
HELEN   Which is he?
DIANA   That jackanapes
With scarves. Why is he melancholy?
HELEN Perchance he's hurt i'th' battle.
PAROLES (aside) Lose our drum? Well.   90
MARIANA He's shrewdly vexed at something.
Look, he has spied us.
WIDOW (to Paroles)   Marry, hang you!
MARIANA (to Paroles)
And your courtesy, for a ring-carrier.
                    Exeunt Bertram, Paroles, and the army
WIDOW
The troop is past. Come, pilgrim, I will bring you
Where you shall host. Of enjoined penitents   95
There's four or five to great Saint Jaques bound
Already at my house.
HELEN   I humbly thank you.
Please it this matron and this gentle maid
To eat with us tonight, the charge and thanking
Shall be for me. And to requite you further,   100
I will bestow some precepts of this virgin
Worthy the note.
WIDOW and MARIANA We'll take your offer kindly.
                                        Exeunt

3.6   *Enter Bertram and the two Captains Dumaine*
SECOND LORD DUMAINE (*to Bertram*) Nay, good my lord,
put him to't. Let him have his way.
FIRST LORD DUMAINE (*to Bertram*) If your lordship find him
not a hilding, hold me no more in your respect.
SECOND LORD DUMAINE (*to Bertram*) On my life, my lord, a
bubble.   6
BERTRAM Do you think I am so far deceived in him?
SECOND LORD DUMAINE Believe it, my lord. In mine own
direct knowledge—without any malice, but to speak of
him as my kinsman—he's a most notable coward, an
infinite and endless liar, an hourly promise-breaker,

the owner of no one good quality worthy your lordship's
entertainment.
FIRST LORD DUMAINE (*to Bertram*) It were fit you knew
him, lest reposing too far in his virtue, which he hath
not, he might at some great and trusty business, in a
main danger, fail you.   17
BERTRAM I would I knew in what particular action to try
him.
FIRST LORD DUMAINE None better than to let him fetch off
his drum, which you hear him so confidently undertake
to do.   22
SECOND LORD DUMAINE (*to Bertram*) I, with a troop of
Florentines, will suddenly surprise him. Such I will
have whom I am sure he knows not from the enemy;
we will bind and hoodwink him so, that he shall
suppose no other but that he is carried into the laager
of the adversary's when we bring him to our own tents.
Be but your lordship present at his examination: if he
do not, for the promise of his life and in the highest
compulsion of base fear, offer to betray you, and deliver
all the intelligence in his power against you, and trust
with the divine forfeit of his soul upon oath, never trust
my judgement in anything.   34
FIRST LORD DUMAINE (*to Bertram*) O, for the love of laughter,
let him fetch his drum. He says he has a stratagem
for't. When your lordship sees the bottom of his success
in't, and to what metal this counterfeit lump of ore
will be melted, if you give him not John Drum's
entertainment, your inclining cannot be removed. Here
he comes.   41
    Enter Paroles
SECOND LORD DUMAINE O ⌈aside⌉ for the love of laughter
⌈aloud⌉ hinder not the honour of his design; let him
fetch off his drum in any hand.
BERTRAM (*to Paroles*) How now, monsieur? This drum
sticks sorely in your disposition.   46
FIRST LORD DUMAINE A pox on't, let it go. 'Tis but a drum.
PAROLES But a drum? Is't but a drum? A drum so lost!
There was excellent command: to charge in with our
horse upon our own wings and to rend our own
soldiers!   51
FIRST LORD DUMAINE That was not to be blamed in the
command of the service. It was a disaster of war that
Caesar himself could not have prevented, if he had
been there to command.   55
BERTRAM Well, we cannot greatly condemn our success.
Some dishonour we had in the loss of that drum, but
it is not to be recovered.
PAROLES It might have been recovered.
BERTRAM It might, but it is not now.   60
PAROLES It *is* to be recovered. But that the merit of service
is seldom attributed to the true and exact performer, I
would have that drum or another, or 'hic iacet'.
BERTRAM Why, if you have a stomach, to't, monsieur. If
you think your mystery in stratagem can bring this
instrument of honour again into his native quarter, be
magnanimous in the enterprise and go on. I will grace
the attempt for a worthy exploit. If you speed well in

it, the Duke shall both speak of it and extend to you
what further becomes his greatness, even to the utmost
syllable of your worthiness.   71

PAROLES By the hand of a soldier, I will undertake it.

BERTRAM But you must not now slumber in it.

PAROLES I'll about it this evening, and I will presently
pen down my dilemmas, encourage myself in my
certainty, put myself into my mortal preparation; and
by midnight look to hear further from me.

BERTRAM May I be bold to acquaint his grace you are
gone about it?

PAROLES I know not what the success will be, my lord,
but the attempt I vow.   81

BERTRAM I know thou'rt valiant, and to the possibility of
thy soldiership will subscribe for thee. Farewell.

PAROLES I love not many words.   *Exit*

SECOND LORD DUMAINE No more than a fish loves water.
(*To Bertram*) Is not this a strange fellow, my lord, that
so confidently seems to undertake this business, which
he knows is not to be done? Damns himself to do, and
dares better be damned than to do't.   89

FIRST LORD DUMAINE (*to Bertram*) You do not know him,
my lord, as we do. Certain it is that he will steal himself
into a man's favour, and for a week escape a great
deal of discoveries, but when you find him out, you
have him ever after.   94

BERTRAM Why, do you think he will make no deed at all
of this that so seriously he does address himself unto?

SECOND LORD DUMAINE None in the world, but return with
an invention, and clap upon you two or three probable
lies. But we have almost embosked him. You shall see
his fall tonight; for indeed he is not for your lordship's
respect.   101

FIRST LORD DUMAINE (*to Bertram*) We'll make you some
sport with the fox ere we case him. He was first smoked
by the old Lord Lafeu. When his disguise and he is
parted, tell me what a sprat you shall find him, which
you shall see this very night.   106

SECOND LORD DUMAINE
I must go look my twigs. He shall be caught.

BERTRAM
Your brother, he shall go along with me.

⌈SECOND⌉ LORD DUMAINE As't please your lordship. I'll leave
you.   *Exit*

BERTRAM
Now will I lead you to the house, and show you   111
The lass I spoke of.

⌈FIRST⌉ LORD DUMAINE But you say she's honest.

BERTRAM
That's all the fault. I spoke with her but once
And found her wondrous cold, but I sent to her
By this same coxcomb that we have i'th' wind   115
Tokens and letters, which she did re-send,
And this is all I have done. She's a fair creature.
Will you go see her?

⌈FIRST⌉ LORD DUMAINE With all my heart, my lord.

                                              Exeunt

3.7   *Enter Helen and the Widow*

HELEN
If you misdoubt me that I am not she,
I know not how I shall assure you further
But I shall lose the grounds I work upon.

WIDOW
Though my estate be fall'n, I was well born,
Nothing acquainted with these businesses,   5
And would not put my reputation now
In any staining act.

HELEN   Nor would I wish you.
First give me trust the Count he is my husband,
And what to your sworn counsel I have spoken
Is so from word to word, and then you cannot,   10
By the good aid that I of you shall borrow,
Err in bestowing it.

WIDOW   I should believe you,
For you have showed me that which well approves
You're great in fortune.

HELEN   Take this purse of gold,
And let me buy your friendly help thus far,   15
Which I will over-pay, and pay again
When I have found it. The Count he woos your
        daughter,
Lays down his wanton siege before her beauty,
Resolved to carry her. Let her in fine consent,
As we'll direct her how 'tis best to bear it.   20
Now his important blood will naught deny
That she'll demand. A ring the County wears,
That downward hath succeeded in his house
From son to son some four or five descents
Since the first father wore it. This ring he holds   25
In most rich choice; yet in his idle fire
To buy his will it would not seem too dear,
Howe'er repented after.

WIDOW
Now I see the bottom of your purpose.

HELEN
You see it lawful then. It is no more   30
But that your daughter ere she seems as won
Desires this ring; appoints him an encounter;
In fine, delivers me to fill the time,
Herself most chastely absent. After,
To marry her I'll add three thousand crowns   35
To what is passed already.

WIDOW   I have yielded.
Instruct my daughter how she shall persever,
That time and place with this deceit so lawful
May prove coherent. Every night he comes
With musics of all sorts, and songs composed   40
To her unworthiness. It nothing steads us
To chide him from our eaves, for he persists
As if his life lay on't.

HELEN   Why then tonight
Let us essay our plot, which if it speed
Is wicked meaning in a lawful deed   45

And lawful meaning in a wicked act,
Where both not sin, and yet a sinful fact.
But let's about it.   *Exeunt*

4.1   *Enter ⌈Second Lord Dumaine⌉, with five or six other*
            soldiers, in ambush
⌈SECOND⌉ LORD DUMAINE He can come no other way but
by this hedge corner. When you sally upon him, speak
what terrible language you will. Though you under-
stand it not yourselves, no matter, for we must not
seem to understand him, unless some one among us,
whom we must produce for an interpreter.   6
INTERPRETER Good captain, let me be th'interpreter.
⌈SECOND⌉ LORD DUMAINE Art not acquainted with him?
Knows he not thy voice?
INTERPRETER No, sir, I warrant you.   10
⌈SECOND⌉ LORD DUMAINE But what linsey-woolsey hast
thou to speak to us again?
INTERPRETER E'en such as you speak to me.
⌈SECOND⌉ LORD DUMAINE He must think us some band of
strangers i'th' adversary's entertainment. Now he hath
a smack of all neighbouring languages, therefore we
must every one be a man of his own fancy. Not to
know what we speak one to another, so we seem to
know, is to know straight our purpose: choughs'
language, gabble enough and good enough. As for you,
interpreter, you must seem very politic. But couch, ho!
Here he comes, to beguile two hours in a sleep, and
then to return and swear the lies he forges.   23
            They hide. Enter Paroles. ⌈Clock strikes⌉
PAROLES Ten o'clock. Within these three hours 'twill be
time enough to go home. What shall I say I have done?
It must be a very plausive invention that carries it.
They begin to smoke me, and disgraces have of late
knocked too often at my door. I find my tongue is too
foolhardy, but my heart hath the fear of Mars before
it, and of his creatures, not daring the reports of my
tongue.   31
⌈SECOND⌉ LORD DUMAINE (*aside*) This is the first truth that
e'er thine own tongue was guilty of.
PAROLES What the devil should move me to undertake
the recovery of this drum, being not ignorant of the
impossibility, and knowing I had no such purpose? I
must give myself some hurts, and say I got them in
exploit. Yet slight ones will not carry it. They will say,
'Came you off with so little?' And great ones I dare
not give. Wherefore, what's the instance? Tongue, I
must put you into a butter-woman's mouth, and buy
myself another of Bajazet's mute, if you prattle me into
these perils.
⌈SECOND⌉ LORD DUMAINE (*aside*) Is it possible he should
know what he is, and be that he is?   45
PAROLES I would the cutting of my garments would serve
the turn, or the breaking of my Spanish sword.
⌈SECOND⌉ LORD DUMAINE (*aside*) We cannot afford you so.
PAROLES Or the baring of my beard, and to say it was in
stratagem.   50

⌈SECOND⌉ LORD DUMAINE (*aside*) 'Twould not do.
PAROLES Or to drown my clothes, and say I was stripped.
⌈SECOND⌉ LORD DUMAINE (*aside*) Hardly serve.
PAROLES Though I swore I leapt from the window of the
citadel?   55
⌈SECOND⌉ LORD DUMAINE (*aside*) How deep?
PAROLES Thirty fathom.
⌈SECOND⌉ LORD DUMAINE (*aside*) Three great oaths would
scarce make that be believed.
PAROLES I would I had any drum of the enemy's. I would
swear I recovered it.   61
⌈SECOND⌉ LORD DUMAINE (*aside*) You shall hear one anon.
PAROLES A drum now of the enemy's—
            Alarum within. ⌈The ambush rushes forth⌉
⌈SECOND⌉ LORD DUMAINE *Throca movousus, cargo, cargo,*
cargo.   65
⌈SOLDIERS⌉ (*severally*) *Cargo, cargo, cargo, villianda par corbo,*
cargo.
            ⌈*They seize and blindfold him*⌉
PAROLES
O ransom, ransom, do not hide mine eyes.
INTERPRETER *Boskos thromuldo boskos.*
PAROLES
I know you are the Moscows regiment,   70
And I shall lose my life for want of language.
If there be here German or Dane, Low Dutch,
Italian, or French, let him speak to me,
I'll discover that which shall undo the Florentine.
INTERPRETER *Boskos vauvado.*—   75
I understand thee, and can speak thy tongue.—
Kerelybonto.—Sir,
Betake thee to thy faith, for seventeen poniards
Are at thy bosom.
PAROLES   O!
INTERPRETER   O pray, pray, pray!—
Manka revania dulche?   80
⌈SECOND⌉ LORD DUMAINE
Oscorbidulchos volivorco.
INTERPRETER
The general is content to spare thee yet,
And, hoodwinked as thou art, will lead thee on
To gather from thee. Haply thou mayst inform
Something to save thy life.
PAROLES   O let me live,   85
And all the secrets of our camp I'll show,
Their force, their purposes; nay, I'll speak that
Which you will wonder at.
INTERPRETER   But wilt thou faithfully?
PAROLES
If I do not, damn me.
INTERPRETER   *Acordo linta.*—
Come on, thou art granted space.   90
            Exeunt all but ⌈Second⌉ Lord Dumaine
                                and a Soldier
      A short alarum within
⌈SECOND⌉ LORD DUMAINE
Go tell the Count Roussillon and my brother

We have caught the woodcock, and will keep him
    muffled
Till we do hear from them.
SOLDIER   Captain, I will.
⌈SECOND⌉ LORD DUMAINE
A will betray us all unto ourselves.
Inform on that.
SOLDIER   So I will, sir.   95
⌈SECOND⌉ LORD DUMAINE
Till then I'll keep him dark and safely locked.
                     Exeunt severally

4.2 *Enter Bertram and the maid called Diana*
BERTRAM
They told me that your name was Fontibel.
DIANA
No, my good lord, Diana.
BERTRAM   Titled goddess,
And worth it, with addition. But, fair soul,
In your fine frame hath love no quality?
If the quick fire of youth light not your mind,   5
You are no maiden but a monument.
When you are dead you should be such a one
As you are now, for you are cold and stern,
And now you should be as your mother was
When your sweet self was got.   10
DIANA She then was honest.
BERTRAM So should you be.
DIANA   No.
My mother did but duty; such, my lord,
As you owe to your wife.
BERTRAM   No more o' that.   15
I prithee do not strive against my vows.
I was compelled to her, but I love thee
By love's own sweet constraint, and will for ever
Do thee all rights of service.
DIANA   Ay, so you serve us
Till we serve you. But when you have our roses, 20
You barely leave our thorns to prick ourselves,
And mock us with our bareness.
BERTRAM   How have I sworn!
DIANA
'Tis not the many oaths that makes the truth,
But the plain single vow that is vowed true.
What is not holy, that we swear not by,   25
But take the high'st to witness; then pray you, tell me,
If I should swear by Jove's great attributes
I loved you dearly, would you believe my oaths
When I did love you ill? This has no holding,
To swear by him whom I protest to love   30
That I will work against him. Therefore your oaths
Are words and poor conditions but unsealed,
At least in my opinion.
BERTRAM   Change it, change it.
Be not so holy-cruel. Love is holy,
And my integrity ne'er knew the crafts   35
That you do charge men with. Stand no more off,

But give thyself unto my sick desires,
Who then recovers. Say thou art mine, and ever
My love as it begins shall so persever.
DIANA
I see that men make toys e'en such a surance   40
That we'll forsake ourselves. Give me that ring.
BERTRAM
I'll lend it thee, my dear, but have no power
To give it from me.
DIANA   Will you not, my lord?
BERTRAM
It is an honour 'longing to our house,
Bequeathèd down from many ancestors,   45
Which were the greatest obloquy i'th' world
In me to lose.
DIANA   Mine honour's such a ring.
My chastity's the jewel of our house,
Bequeathèd down from many ancestors,
Which were the greatest obloquy i'th' world   50
In me to lose. Thus your own proper wisdom
Brings in the champion Honour on my part
Against your vain assault.
BERTRAM   Here, take my ring.
My house, mine honour, yea my life be thine,
And I'll be bid by thee.   55
DIANA
When midnight comes, knock at my chamber window.
I'll order take my mother shall not hear.
Now will I charge you in the bond of truth,
When you have conquered my yet maiden bed,
Remain there but an hour, nor speak to me—   60
My reasons are most strong, and you shall know them
When back again this ring shall be delivered—
And on your finger in the night I'll put
Another ring that, what in time proceeds,
May token to the future our past deeds.   65
Adieu till then; then, fail not. You have won
A wife of me, though there my hope be done.
BERTRAM
A heaven on earth I have won by wooing thee.
DIANA
For which live long to thank both heaven and me.
You may so in the end.   ⌈*Exit Bertram*⌉
My mother told me just how he would woo,
As if she sat in's heart. She says all men
Have the like oaths. He had sworn to marry me
When his wife's dead; therefore I'll lie with him
When I am buried. Since Frenchmen are so braid, 75
Marry that will; I live and die a maid.
Only, in this disguise I think't no sin
To cozen him that would unjustly win.   *Exit*

4.3 *Enter the two Captains Dumaine and some two or*
      three soldiers
FIRST LORD DUMAINE You have not given him his mother's
    letter?
SECOND LORD DUMAINE I have delivered it an hour since.

There is something in't that stings his nature, for on
the reading it he changed almost into another man.   5
FIRST LORD DUMAINE He has much worthy blame laid
upon him for shaking off so good a wife and so sweet
a lady.
SECOND LORD DUMAINE Especially he hath incurred the
everlasting displeasure of the King, who had even tuned
his bounty to sing happiness to him. I will tell you a
thing, but you shall let it dwell darkly with you.   12
FIRST LORD DUMAINE When you have spoken it 'tis dead,
and I am the grave of it.   14
SECOND LORD DUMAINE He hath perverted a young gentlewoman here in Florence of a most chaste renown, and
this night he fleshes his will in the spoil of her honour.
He hath given her his monumental ring, and thinks
himself made in the unchaste composition.
FIRST LORD DUMAINE Now God delay our rebellion! As we
are ourselves, what things are we.   21
SECOND LORD DUMAINE Merely our own traitors. And as in
the common course of all treasons we still see them
reveal themselves till they attain to their abhorred ends,
so he that in this action contrives against his own
nobility, in his proper stream o'erflows himself.   26
FIRST LORD DUMAINE Is it not meant damnable in us to be
trumpeters of our unlawful intents? We shall not then
have his company tonight?
SECOND LORD DUMAINE Not till after midnight, for he is
dieted to his hour.   31
FIRST LORD DUMAINE That approaches apace. I would
gladly have him see his company anatomized, that he
might take a measure of his own judgements, wherein
so curiously he had set this counterfeit.   35
SECOND LORD DUMAINE We will not meddle with him till
he come, for his presence must be the whip of the
other.
FIRST LORD DUMAINE In the mean time, what hear you of
these wars?   40
SECOND LORD DUMAINE I hear there is an overture of peace.
FIRST LORD DUMAINE Nay, I assure you, a peace concluded.
SECOND LORD DUMAINE What will Count Roussillon do
then? Will he travel higher, or return again into
France?   45
FIRST LORD DUMAINE I perceive by this demand you are
not altogether of his council.
SECOND LORD DUMAINE Let it be forbid, sir; so should I be
a great deal of his act.   49
FIRST LORD DUMAINE Sir, his wife some two months since
fled from his house. Her pretence is a pilgrimage to
Saint Jaques le Grand, which holy undertaking with
most austere sanctimony she accomplished, and there
residing, the tenderness of her nature became as a prey
to her grief: in fine, made a groan of her last breath,
and now she sings in heaven.   56
SECOND LORD DUMAINE How is this justified?
FIRST LORD DUMAINE The stronger part of it by her own
letters, which makes her story true even to the point
of her death. Her death itself, which could not be her

office to say is come, was faithfully confirmed by the
rector of the place.
SECOND LORD DUMAINE Hath the Count all this intelligence?
FIRST LORD DUMAINE Ay, and the particular confirmations,
point from point, to the full arming of the verity.   65
SECOND LORD DUMAINE I am heartily sorry that he'll be
glad of this.
FIRST LORD DUMAINE How mightily sometimes we make
us comforts of our losses.   69
SECOND LORD DUMAINE And how mightily some other times
we drown our gain in tears. The great dignity that his
valour hath here acquired for him shall at home be
encountered with a shame as ample.
FIRST LORD DUMAINE The web of our life is of a mingled
yarn, good and ill together. Our virtues would be proud
if our faults whipped them not, and our crimes would
despair if they were not cherished by our virtues.   77
Enter a Servant
How now? Where's your master?
SERVANT He met the Duke in the street, sir, of whom he
hath taken a solemn leave. His lordship will next
morning for France. The Duke hath offered him letters
of commendations to the King.   82
SECOND LORD DUMAINE They shall be no more than needful
there, if they were more than they can commend.
Enter Bertram
⌜FIRST LORD DUMAINE⌝ They cannot be too sweet for the
King's tartness. Here's his lordship now. How now, my
lord, is't not after midnight?
BERTRAM I have tonight dispatched sixteen businesses, a
month's length apiece. By an abstract of success: I
have *congéd* with the Duke, done my adieu with his
nearest, buried a wife, mourned for her, writ to my
lady mother I am returning, entertained my convoy,
and between these main parcels of dispatch affected
many nicer needs. The last was the greatest, but that
I have not ended yet.   95
SECOND LORD DUMAINE If the business be of any difficulty,
and this morning your departure hence, it requires
haste of your lordship.
BERTRAM I mean the business is not ended, as fearing to
hear of it hereafter. But shall we have this dialogue
between the Fool and the Soldier? Come, bring forth
this counterfeit model, has deceived me like a double-
meaning prophesier.
SECOND LORD DUMAINE Bring him forth.
Exit one or more
He's sat i'th' stocks all night, poor gallant knave.   105
BERTRAM No matter, his heels have deserved it in usurping
his spurs so long. How does he carry himself?
SECOND LORD DUMAINE I have told your lordship already,
the stocks carry him. But to answer you as you would
be understood, he weeps like a wench that had shed
her milk. He hath confessed himself to Morgan, whom
he supposes to be a friar, from the time of his remembrance to this very instant disaster of his setting i'th'
stocks. And what think you he hath confessed?   114

BERTRAM Nothing of me, has a? 115

SECOND LORD DUMAINE His confession is taken, and it shall be read to his face. If your lordship be in't, as I believe you are, you must have the patience to hear it.

Enter Paroles ⌈guarded and⌉ blindfolded, with the Interpreter

BERTRAM A plague upon him! Muffled! He can say nothing of me. 120

⌈FIRST LORD DUMAINE⌉ (*aside to Bertram*) Hush, hush.

⌈SECOND⌉ LORD DUMAINE (*aside to Bertram*) Hoodman comes. (*Aloud*) Porto tartarossa.

INTERPRETER (*to Paroles*) He calls for the tortures. What will you say without 'em? 125

PAROLES I will confess what I know without constraint. If ye pinch me like a pasty I can say no more.

INTERPRETER ⸌Bosko chimurcho.

⌈SECOND⌉ LORD DUMAINE Boblibindo chicurmurco.

INTERPRETER You are a merciful general.—Our general bids you answer to what I shall ask you out of a note.

PAROLES And truly, as I hope to live.

INTERPRETER ⌈reads⌉ 'First demand of him how many horse the Duke is strong.'—What say you to that? 134

PAROLES Five or six thousand, but very weak and unserviceable. The troops are all scattered and the commanders very poor rogues, upon my reputation and credit, and as I hope to live.

INTERPRETER Shall I set down your answer so?

PAROLES Do. I'll take the sacrament on't, how and which way you will. 141

⌈FIRST LORD DUMAINE⌉ (*aside*) All's one to him.

BERTRAM (*aside*) What a past-saving slave is this!

FIRST LORD DUMAINE (*aside*) You're deceived, my lord. This is Monsieur Paroles, the 'gallant militarist'—that was his own phrase—that had the whole theoric of war in the knot of his scarf, and the practice in the chape of his dagger.

SECOND LORD DUMAINE (*aside*) I will never trust a man again for keeping his sword clean, nor believe he can have everything in him by wearing his apparel neatly.

INTERPRETER (*to Paroles*) Well, that's set down. 152

PAROLES 'Five or six thousand horse,' I said—I will say true—'or thereabouts' set down, for I'll speak truth.

FIRST LORD DUMAINE (*aside*) He's very near the truth in this. 156

BERTRAM (*aside*) But I con him no thanks for't in the nature he delivers it.

PAROLES 'Poor rogues', I pray you say.

INTERPRETER Well, that's set down. 160

PAROLES I humbly thank you, sir. A truth's a truth. The rogues are marvellous poor.

INTERPRETER ⌈reads⌉ 'Demand of him of what strength they are a-foot.'—What say you to that? 164

PAROLES By my troth, sir, if I were to die this present hour, I will tell true. Let me see, Spurio a hundred and fifty; Sebastian so many; Corambus so many; Jaques so many; Guillaume, Cosmo, Lodowick, and Gratii, two hundred fifty each; mine own company, Chitopher, Vaumond, Bentii, two hundred fifty each. So that the muster file, rotten and sound, upon my life amounts not to fifteen thousand poll, half of which dare not shake the snow from off their cassocks lest they shake themselves to pieces.

BERTRAM (*aside*) What shall be done to him? 175

FIRST LORD DUMAINE (*aside*) Nothing, but let him have thanks. (*To Interpreter*) Demand of him my condition, and what credit I have with the Duke.

INTERPRETER (*to Paroles*) Well, that's set down. ⌈Reads⌉ 'You shall demand of him, whether one Captain Dumaine be i'th' camp, a Frenchman; what his reputation is with the Duke; what his valour, honesty, and expertness in wars; or whether he thinks it were not possible with well-weighing sums of gold to corrupt him to a revolt.'—What say you to this? What do you know of it?' 186

PAROLES I beseech you let me answer to the particular of the inter'gatories. Demand them singly.

INTERPRETER Do you know this Captain Dumaine? 189

PAROLES I know him. A was a botcher's prentice in Paris, from whence he was whipped for getting the sheriff's fool with child—a dumb innocent that could not say him nay.

BERTRAM (*aside to First Lord Dumaine*) Nay, by your leave, hold your hands, though I know his brains are forfeit to the next tile that falls. 196

INTERPRETER Well, is this captain in the Duke of Florence's camp?

PAROLES Upon my knowledge he is, and lousy.

FIRST LORD DUMAINE (*aside*) Nay, look not so upon me: we shall hear of your lordship anon. 201

INTERPRETER What is his reputation with the Duke?

PAROLES The Duke knows him for no other but a poor officer of mine, and writ to me this other day to turn him out o'th' band. I think I have his letter in my pocket. 206

INTERPRETER Marry, we'll search.

PAROLES In good sadness, I do not know. Either it is there, or it is upon a file with the Duke's other letters in my tent. 210

INTERPRETER Here 'tis, here's a paper. Shall I read it to you?

PAROLES I do not know if it be it or no.

BERTRAM (*aside*) Our interpreter does it well.

FIRST LORD DUMAINE (*aside*) Excellently. 215

INTERPRETER (*reads the letter*)
'Dian, the Count's a fool, and full of gold.'

PAROLES That is not the Duke's letter, sir. That is an advertisement to a proper maid in Florence, one Diana, to take heed of the allurement of one Count Roussillon, a foolish idle boy, but for all that very ruttish. I pray you, sir, put it up again. 222

INTERPRETER Nay, I'll read it first, by your favour.

PAROLES My meaning in't, I protest, was very honest in the behalf of the maid, for I knew the young Count to be a dangerous and lascivious boy, who is a whale to virginity, and devours up all the fry it finds. 227

BERTRAM (*aside*) Damnable both-sides rogue.

INTERPRETER (*reads*)
'When he swears oaths, bid him drop gold, and take it.
　After he scores he never pays the score.　　　　230
Half-won is match well made; match, and well make it.
He ne'er pays after-debts, take it before.
And say a soldier, Dian, told thee this:
Men are to mell with, boys are not to kiss.
For count of this, the Count's a fool, I know it,　235
Who pays before, but not when he does owe it.
　　Thine, as he vowed to thee in thine ear,
　　　　　　　　　　　　　　　　Paroles.'
BERTRAM (*aside*) He shall be whipped through the army
with this rhyme in's forehead.　　　　　　　　240
SECOND LORD DUMAINE (*aside*) This is your devoted friend,
sir, the manifold linguist and the armipotent soldier.
BERTRAM (*aside*) I could endure anything before but a cat,
and now he's a cat to me.
INTERPRETER I perceive, sir, by the general's looks, we
shall be fain to hang you.　　　　　　　　　246
PAROLES My life, sir, in any case! Not that I am afraid to
die, but that, my offences being many, I would repent
out the remainder of nature. Let me live, sir, in a
dungeon, i'th' stocks, or anywhere, so I may live.　250
INTERPRETER We'll see what may be done, so you confess
freely. Therefore once more to this Captain Dumaine.
You have answered to his reputation with the Duke,
and to his valour. What is his honesty?　　　254
PAROLES He will steal, sir, an egg out of a cloister. For
rapes and ravishments he parallels Nessus. He professes
not keeping of oaths; in breaking 'em he is stronger
than Hercules. He will lie, sir, with such volubility that
you would think truth were a fool. Drunkenness is his
best virtue, for he will be swine-drunk, and in his sleep
he does little harm, save to his bedclothes; but they
about him know his conditions, and lay him in straw.
I have but little more to say, sir, of his honesty. He has
everything that an honest man should not have; what
an honest man should have, he has nothing.　　265
FIRST LORD DUMAINE (*aside*) I begin to love him for this.
BERTRAM (*aside*) For this description of thine honesty? A
pox upon him! For me, he's more and more a cat.
INTERPRETER What say you to his expertness in war?　269
PAROLES Faith, sir, he's led the drum before the English
tragedians. To belie him I will not, and more of his
soldiership I know not, except in that country he had
the honour to be the officer at a place there called Mile
End, to instruct for the doubling of files. I would do the
man what honour I can, but of this I am not certain.
FIRST LORD DUMAINE (*aside*) He hath out-villained villainy
so far that the rarity redeems him.
BERTRAM (*aside*) A pox on him! He's a cat still.
INTERPRETER His qualities being at this poor price, I need
not to ask you if gold will corrupt him to revolt.　280
PAROLES Sir, for a *quart d'écu* he will sell the fee-simple of
his salvation, the inheritance of it, and cut th'entail
from all remainders, and a perpetual succession for it
perpetually.
INTERPRETER What's his brother, the other Captain
Dumaine?　　　　　　　　　　　　　　286

SECOND LORD DUMAINE (*aside*) Why does he ask him of me?
INTERPRETER What's he?
PAROLES E'en a crow o'th' same nest. Not altogether so
great as the first in goodness, but greater a great deal
in evil. He excels his brother for a coward, yet his
brother is reputed one of the best that is. In a retreat
he outruns any lackey; marry, in coming on he has
the cramp.
INTERPRETER If your life be saved will you undertake to
betray the Florentine?　　　　　　　　　　　296
PAROLES Ay, and the captain of his horse, Count
Roussillon.
INTERPRETER I'll whisper with the general and know his
pleasure.　　　　　　　　　　　　　　300
PAROLES I'll no more drumming. A plague of all drums!
Only to seem to deserve well, and to beguile the
supposition of that lascivious young boy, the Count,
have I run into this danger. Yet who would have
suspected an ambush where I was taken?　　305
INTERPRETER There is no remedy, sir, but you must die.
The general says you that have so traitorously
discovered the secrets of your army, and made such
pestiferous reports of men very nobly held, can serve
the world for no honest use; therefore you must die.—
Come, headsman, off with his head.　　　　311
PAROLES O Lord, sir!—Let me live, or let me see my death!
INTERPRETER That shall you, and take your leave of all
your friends.
　　　　　He unmuffles Paroles
So, look about you. Know you any here?　　　315
BERTRAM Good morrow, noble captain.
SECOND LORD DUMAINE God bless you, Captain Paroles.
FIRST LORD DUMAINE God save you, noble captain.
SECOND LORD DUMAINE Captain, what greeting will you to
my Lord Lafeu? I am for France.　　　　　320
FIRST LORD DUMAINE Good captain, will you give me a
copy of the sonnet you writ to Diana in behalf of the
Count Roussillon? An I were not a very coward I'd
compel it of you. But fare you well.
　　　　　　　　Exeunt all but Paroles and Interpreter
INTERPRETER You are undone, captain—all but your scarf;
that has a knot on't yet.　　　　　　　　　326
PAROLES Who cannot be crushed with a plot?
INTERPRETER If you could find out a country where but
women were that had received so much shame, you
might begin an impudent nation. Fare ye well, sir. I
am for France too. We shall speak of you there.　*Exit*
PAROLES
Yet am I thankful. If my heart were great
'Twould burst at this. Captain I'll be no more,
But I will eat and drink and sleep as soft
As captain shall. Simply the thing I am　　　335
Shall make me live. Who knows himself a braggart,
Let him fear this, for it will come to pass
That every braggart shall be found an ass.
Rust, sword; cool, blushes; and Paroles live
Safest in shame; being fooled, by fool'ry thrive.　340
There's place and means for every man alive.
I'll after them.　　　　　　　　　　　　*Exit*

4.4 *Enter Helen, the Widow, and Diana*

HELEN

That you may well perceive I have not wronged you,
One of the greatest in the Christian world
Shall be my surety; fore whose throne 'tis needful,
Ere I can perfect mine intents, to kneel.
Time was, I did him a desirèd office   5
Dear almost as his life; which gratitude
Through flinty Tartar's bosom would peep forth
And answer 'Thanks'. I duly am informed
His grace is at Marseilles, to which place
We have convenient convoy. You must know   10
I am supposèd dead. The army breaking,
My husband hies him home, where, heaven aiding,
And by the leave of my good lord the King,
We'll be before our welcome.

WIDOW   Gentle madam,
You never had a servant to whose trust   15
Your business was more welcome.

HELEN   Nor you, mistress,
Ever a friend whose thoughts more truly labour
To recompense your love. Doubt not but heaven
Hath brought me up to be your daughter's dower,
As it hath fated her to be my motive   20
And helper to a husband. But O, strange men,
That can such sweet use make of what they hate,
When saucy trusting of the cozened thoughts
Defiles the pitchy night; so lust doth play
With what it loathes, for that which is away.   25
But more of this hereafter. You, Diana,
Under my poor instructions yet must suffer
Something in my behalf.

DIANA   Let death and honesty
Go with your impositions, I am yours,
Upon your will to suffer.

HELEN   Yet, I pray you.—   30
But with that word the time will bring on summer,
When briers shall have leaves as well as thorns
And be as sweet as sharp. We must away,
Our wagon is prepared, and time revives us.
All's well that ends well; still the fine's the crown.   35
Whate'er the course, the end is the renown.   *Exeunt*

4.5 *Enter Lavatch, the old Countess, and Lafeu*

LAFEU No, no, no, your son was misled with a snipped-
taffeta fellow there, whose villainous saffron would
have made all the unbaked and doughy youth of a
nation in his colour. Else, your daughter-in-law had
been alive at this hour, and your son here at home,
more advanced by the King than by that red-tailed
humble-bee I speak of.   7

COUNTESS I would a had not known him. It was the death
of the most virtuous gentlewoman that ever nature
had praise for creating. If she had partaken of my flesh
and cost me the dearest groans of a mother I could not
have owed her a more rooted love.   12

LAFEU 'Twas a good lady, 'twas a good lady. We may
pick a thousand salads ere we light on such another
herb.   15

LAVATCH Indeed, sir, she was the sweet marjoram of the
salad, or rather the herb of grace.

LAFEU They are not grass, you knave, they are nose-
herbs.

LAVATCH I am no great Nebuchadnezzar, sir, I have not
much skill in grace.   21

LAFEU Whether dost thou profess thyself, a knave or a
fool?

LAVATCH A fool, sir, at a woman's service, and a knave
at a man's.   25

LAFEU Your distinction?

LAVATCH I would cozen the man of his wife and do his
service.

LAFEU So you were a knave at his service indeed.

LAVATCH And I would give his wife my bauble, sir, to do
her service.   31

LAFEU I will subscribe for thee, thou art both knave and
fool.

LAVATCH At your service.

LAFEU No, no, no.   35

LAVATCH Why, sir, if I cannot serve you I can serve as
great a prince as you are.

LAFEU Who's that? A Frenchman?

LAVATCH Faith, sir, a has an English name, but his
phys'namy is more hotter in France than there.   40

LAFEU What prince is that?

LAVATCH The Black Prince, sir, alias the prince of
darkness, alias the devil.

LAFEU Hold thee, there's my purse. I give thee not this
to suggest thee from thy master thou talk'st of; serve
him still.   46

LAVATCH I am a woodland fellow, sir, that always loved
a great fire, and the master I speak of ever keeps a
good fire. But since he is the prince of the world, let
the nobility remain in's court; I am for the house with
the narrow gate, which I take to be too little for pomp
to enter. Some that humble themselves may, but the
many will be too chill and tender, and they'll be for
the flow'ry way that leads to the broad gate and the
great fire.   55

LAFEU Go thy ways. I begin to be aweary of thee, and I
tell thee so before, because I would not fall out with
thee. Go thy ways. Let my horses be well looked to,
without any tricks.   59

LAVATCH If I put any tricks upon 'em, sir, they shall be
jades' tricks, which are their own right by the law of
nature.   *Exit*

LAFEU A shrewd knave and an unhappy.

COUNTESS So a is. My lord that's gone made himself much
sport out of him; by his authority he remains here,
which he thinks is a patent for his sauciness, and
indeed he has no pace, but runs where he will.   67

LAFEU I like him well, 'tis not amiss. And I was about to
tell you, since I heard of the good lady's death and
that my lord your son was upon his return home, I

moved the King my master to speak in the behalf of
my daughter; which, in the minority of them both, his
majesty out of a self-gracious remembrance did first
propose. His highness hath promised me to do it; and
to stop up the displeasure he hath conceived against
your son, there is no fitter matter. How does your
ladyship like it?   77
COUNTESS With very much content, my lord, and I wish
it happily effected.
LAFEU His highness comes post from Marseilles, of as able
body as when he numbered thirty. A will be here
tomorrow, or I am deceived by him that in such
intelligence hath seldom failed.   83
COUNTESS It rejoices me that I hope I shall see him ere I
die. I have letters that my son will be here tonight. I
shall beseech your lordship to remain with me till they
meet together.
LAFEU Madam, I was thinking with what manners I might
safely be admitted.   89
COUNTESS You need but plead your honourable privilege.
LAFEU Lady, of that I have made a bold charter, but, I
thank my God, it holds yet.

Enter Lavatch

LAVATCH O madam, yonder's my lord your son with a
patch of velvet on's face. Whether there be a scar
under't or no, the velvet knows; but 'tis a goodly patch
of velvet. His left cheek is a cheek of two pile and a
half, but his right cheek is worn bare.   97
LAFEU A scar nobly got, or a noble scar, is a good liv'ry
of honour. So belike is that.
LAVATCH But it is your carbonadoed face.   100
LAFEU (*to the Countess*) Let us go see your son, I pray you.
I long to talk with the young noble soldier.
LAVATCH Faith, there's a dozen of 'em, with delicate fine
hats, and most courteous feathers, which bow the head
and nod at every man.   *Exeunt*

5.1   *Enter Helen, the Widow, and Diana, with two*
           attendants

HELEN
But this exceeding posting day and night
Must wear your spirits low. We cannot help it.
But since you have made the days and nights as one
To wear your gentle limbs in my affairs,
Be bold you do so grow in my requital   5
As nothing can unroot you.

Enter a Gentleman Austringer

                          In happy time!
This man may help me to his majesty's ear,
If he would spend his power.—God save you, sir.
GENTLEMAN And you.
HELEN
Sir, I have seen you in the court of France.   10
GENTLEMAN I have been sometimes there.
HELEN
I do presume, sir, that you are not fall'n
From the report that goes upon your goodness,

And therefore, goaded with most sharp occasions
Which lay nice manners by, I put you to   15
The use of your own virtues, for the which
I shall continue thankful.
GENTLEMAN   What's your will?
HELEN That it will please you
To give this poor petition to the King,
And aid me with that store of power you have   20
To come into his presence.
GENTLEMAN The King's not here.
HELEN Not here, sir?
GENTLEMAN   Not indeed.
He hence removed last night, and with more haste   25
Than is his use.
WIDOW Lord, how we lose our pains.
HELEN All's well that ends well yet,
Though time seem so adverse, and means unfit.—
I do beseech you, whither is he gone?   30
GENTLEMAN
Marry, as I take it, to Roussillon,
Whither I am going.
HELEN   I do beseech you, sir,
Since you are like to see the King before me,
Commend the paper to his gracious hand,
Which I presume shall render you no blame,   35
But rather make you thank your pains for it.
I will come after you with what good speed
Our means will make us means.
GENTLEMAN (*taking the paper*)   This I'll do for you.
HELEN
And you shall find yourself to be well thanked,
Whate'er falls more. We must to horse again.—   40
Go, go, provide.   *Exeunt severally*

5.2   *Enter Lavatch and Paroles, with a letter*

PAROLES Good Master Lavatch, give my Lord Lafeu this
letter. I have ere now, sir, been better known to you,
when I have held familiarity with fresher clothes. But
I am now, sir, muddied in Fortune's mood, and smell
somewhat strong of her strong displeasure.   5
LAVATCH Truly, Fortune's displeasure is but sluttish if it
smell so strongly as thou speakest of. I will henceforth
eat no fish of Fortune's butt'ring. Prithee allow the
wind.
PAROLES Nay, you need not to stop your nose, sir, I spake
but by a metaphor.   11
LAVATCH Indeed, sir, if your metaphor stink I will stop
my nose, or against any man's metaphor. Prithee get
thee further.
PAROLES Pray you, sir, deliver me this paper.   15
LAVATCH Foh, prithee stand away. A paper from Fortune's
close-stool to give to a nobleman! Look, here he comes
himself.

Enter Lafeu

Here is a pur of Fortune's, sir, or of Fortune's cat—but
not a musk-cat—that has fallen into the unclean fish-
pond of her displeasure and, as he says, is muddied

withal. Pray you, sir, use the carp as you may, for he looks like a poor, decayed, ingenious, foolish, rascally knave. I do pity his distress in my similes of comfort, and leave him to your lordship.   *Exit*

PAROLES My lord, I am a man whom Fortune hath cruelly scratched.   27

LAFEU And what would you have me to do? 'Tis too late to pare her nails now. Wherein have you played the knave with Fortune that she should scratch you, who of herself is a good lady and would not have knaves thrive long under her? There's a *quart d'écu* for you. Let the justices make you and Fortune friends; I am for other business.

PAROLES I beseech your honour to hear me one single word—   36

LAFEU You beg a single penny more. Come, you shall ha't. Save your word.

PAROLES My name, my good lord, is Paroles.

LAFEU You beg more than one word then. Cox my passion! Give me your hand. How does your drum?   41

PAROLES O my good lord, you were the first that found me.

LAFEU Was I, in sooth? And I was the first that lost thee.

PAROLES It lies in you, my lord, to bring me in some grace, for you did bring me out.   46

LAFEU Out upon thee, knave! Dost thou put upon me at once both the office of God and the devil? One brings thee in grace, and the other brings thee out.

        Trumpets sound

The King's coming; I know by his trumpets. Sirrah, enquire further after me. I had talk of you last night. Though you are a fool and a knave, you shall eat. Go to, follow.

PAROLES I praise God for you.   ⌈*Exeunt*⌉

5.3   *Flourish of trumpets. Enter the King, the old*
        Countess, Lafeu, and attendants

KING
We lost a jewel of her, and our esteem
Was made much poorer by it. But your son,
As mad in folly, lacked the sense to know
Her estimation home.

COUNTESS   'Tis past, my liege,
And I beseech your majesty to make it   5
Natural rebellion done i'th' blade of youth,
When oil and fire, too strong for reason's force,
O'erbears it and burns on.

KING   My honoured lady,
I have forgiven and forgotten all,
Though my revenges were high bent upon him   10
And watched the time to shoot.

LAFEU   This I must say—
But first I beg my pardon—the young lord
Did to his majesty, his mother, and his lady
Offence of mighty note, but to himself
The greatest wrong of all. He lost a wife   15
Whose beauty did astonish the survey

Of richest eyes, whose words all ears took captive,
Whose dear perfection hearts that scorned to serve
Humbly called mistress.

KING   Praising what is lost
Makes the remembrance dear. Well, call him hither.   20
We are reconciled, and the first view shall kill
All repetition. Let him not ask our pardon.
The nature of his great offence is dead,
And deeper than oblivion we do bury
Th'incensing relics of it. Let him approach   25
A stranger, no offender; and inform him
So 'tis our will he should.

ATTENDANT   I shall, my liege.   *Exit*

KING (*to Lafeu*)
What says he to your daughter? Have you spoke?

LAFEU
All that he is hath reference to your highness.

KING
Then shall we have a match. I have letters sent me 30
That sets him high in fame.
        Enter Bertram ⌈*with a patch of velvet on his left*
        cheek, and kneels⌉

LAFEU He looks well on't.

KING (*to Bertram*) I am not a day of season,
For thou mayst see a sunshine and a hail
In me at once. But to the brightest beams   35
Distracted clouds give way; so stand thou forth.
The time is fair again.

BERTRAM   My high-repented blames,
Dear sovereign, pardon to me.

KING   All is whole.
Not one word more of the consumèd time.
Let's take the instant by the forward top,   40
For we are old, and on our quick'st decrees
Th'inaudible and noiseless foot of time
Steals ere we can effect them. You remember
The daughter of this lord?

BERTRAM
Admiringly, my liege. At first   45
I stuck my choice upon her, ere my heart
Durst make too bold a herald of my tongue;
Where, the impression of mine eye enfixing,
Contempt his scornful perspective did lend me,
Which warped the line of every other favour,   50
Stained a fair colour or expressed it stolen,
Extended or contracted all proportions
To a most hideous object. Thence it came
That she whom all men praised and whom myself,
Since I have lost, have loved, was in mine eye   55
The dust that did offend it.

KING   Well excused.
That thou didst love her strikes some scores away
From the great count. But love that comes too late,
Like a remorseful pardon slowly carried,
To the grace-sender turns a sour offence,   60
Crying, 'That's good that's gone.' Our rash faults
Make trivial price of serious things we have,
Not knowing them until we know their grave.

Oft our displeasures, to ourselves unjust,
Destroy our friends and after weep their dust. 65
Our own love waking cries to see what's done,
While shameful hate sleeps out the afternoon.
Be this sweet Helen's knell, and now forget her.
Send forth your amorous token for fair Maudlin.
The main consents are had, and here we'll stay 70
To see our widower's second marriage day.
⌈COUNTESS⌉
Which better than the first, O dear heaven, bless!
Or ere they meet, in me, O nature, cease.
LAFEU (*to Bertram*)
Come on, my son, in whom my house's name
Must be digested, give a favour from you 75
To sparkle in the spirits of my daughter,
That she may quickly come.
          Bertram gives Lafeu a ring
                              By my old beard
And ev'ry hair that's on't, Helen that's dead
Was a sweet creature. Such a ring as this,
The last that ere I took her leave at court, 80
I saw upon her finger.
BERTRAM   Hers it was not.
KING
Now pray you let me see it; for mine eye,
While I was speaking, oft was fastened to't.
          Lafeu gives him the ring
This ring was mine, and when I gave it Helen
I bade her, if her fortunes ever stood 85
Necessitied to help, that by this token
I would relieve her. Had you that craft to reave her
Of what should stead her most?
BERTRAM   My gracious sovereign,
Howe'er it pleases you to take it so,
The ring was never hers.
COUNTESS   Son, on my life 90
I have seen her wear it, and she reckoned it
At her life's rate.
LAFEU   I am sure I saw her wear it.
BERTRAM
You are deceived, my lord, she never saw it.
In Florence was it from a casement thrown me,
Wrapped in a paper which contained the name 95
Of her that threw it. Noble she was, and thought
I stood ingaged. But when I had subscribed
To mine own fortune, and informed her fully
I could not answer in that course of honour
As she had made the overture, she ceased 100
In heavy satisfaction, and would never
Receive the ring again.
KING   Plutus himself,
That knows the tinct and multiplying med'cine,
Hath not in nature's mystery more science
Than I have in this ring. 'Twas mine, 'twas Helen's,
Whoever gave it you. Then if you know 106
That you are well acquainted with yourself,
Confess 'twas hers, and by what rough enforcement

You got it from her. She called the saints to surety
That she would never put it from her finger 110
Unless she gave it to yourself in bed,
Where you have never come, or sent it us
Upon her great disaster.
BERTRAM   She never saw it.
KING
Thou speak'st it falsely, as I love mine honour,
And mak'st conjectural fears to come into me 115
Which I would fain shut out. If it should prove
That thou art so inhuman—'twill not prove so.
And yet I know not. Thou didst hate her deadly,
And she is dead, which nothing but to close
Her eyes myself could win me to believe, 120
More than to see this ring.—Take him away.
My fore-past proofs, howe'er the matter fall,
Shall tax my fears of little vanity,
Having vainly feared too little. Away with him.
We'll sift this matter further.
BERTRAM   If you shall prove 125
This ring was ever hers, you shall as easy
Prove that I husbanded her bed in Florence,
Where yet she never was.   *Exit guarded*
          Enter the Gentleman Austringer with a paper
KING I am wrapped in dismal thinkings.
GENTLEMAN Gracious sovereign, 130
Whether I have been to blame or no, I know not.
Here's a petition from a Florentine
Who hath for four or five removes come short
To tender it herself. I undertook it,
Vanquished thereto by the fair grace and speech 135
Of the poor suppliant, who by this I know
Is here attending. Her business looks in her
With an importing visage, and she told me
In a sweet verbal brief it did concern
Your highness with herself. 140
⌈KING⌉ (*reads a letter*) 'Upon his many protestations to
marry me when his wife was dead, I blush to say it,
he won me. Now is the Count Roussillon a widower,
his vows are forfeited to me, and my honour's paid to
him. He stole from Florence, taking no leave, and I
follow him to his country for justice. Grant it me, O
King! In you it best lies; otherwise a seducer flourishes
and a poor maid is undone.
                              Diana Capilet.'
LAFEU I will buy me a son-in-law in a fair, and toll for
this. I'll none of him.
KING
The heavens have thought well on thee, Lafeu,
To bring forth this discov'ry.—Seek these suitors.
Go speedily and bring again the Count.
                              Exit one or more
I am afeard the life of Helen, lady, 155
Was foully snatched.
          ⌈*Enter Bertram guarded*⌉
COUNTESS   Now justice on the doers!
KING (*to Bertram*)
I wonder, sir, since wives are monsters to you,

And that you fly them as you swear them lordship,
Yet you desire to marry.

Enter the Widow and Diana

         What woman's that?

DIANA
I am, my lord, a wretched Florentine,   160
Derivèd from the ancient Capilet.
My suit, as I do understand, you know,
And therefore know how far I may be pitied.

WIDOW (*to the King*)
I am her mother, sir, whose age and honour
Both suffer under this complaint we bring,   165
And both shall cease without your remedy.

KING
Come hither, Count. Do you know these women?

BERTRAM
My lord, I neither can nor will deny
But that I know them. Do they charge me further?

DIANA
Why do you look so strange upon your wife?   170

BERTRAM (*to the King*)
 She's none of mine, my lord.

DIANA   If you shall marry
You give away this hand, and that is mine;
You give away heaven's vows, and those are mine;
You give away myself, which is known mine,
For I by vow am so embodied yours   175
That she which marries you must marry me,
Either both or none.

LAFEU (*to Bertram*) Your reputation comes too short for
my daughter, you are no husband for her.

BERTRAM (*to the King*)
My lord, this is a fond and desp'rate creature   180
Whom sometime I have laughed with. Let your
  highness
Lay a more noble thought upon mine honour
Than for to think that I would sink it here.

KING
Sir, for my thoughts, you have them ill to friend
Till your deeds gain them. Fairer prove your honour
Than in my thought it lies.

DIANA   Good my lord,   186
Ask him upon his oath if he does think
He had not my virginity.

KING What sayst thou to her?

BERTRAM She's impudent, my lord,   190
And was a common gamester to the camp.

DIANA (*to the King*)
He does me wrong, my lord. If I were so
He might have bought me at a common price.
Do not believe him. O behold this ring,
Whose high respect and rich validity   195
Did lack a parallel; yet for all that
He gave it to a commoner o'th' camp,
If I be one.

COUNTESS   He blushes and 'tis hit.
Of six preceding ancestors, that gem;

Conferred by testament to th' sequent issue   200
Hath it been owed and worn. This is his wife.
That ring's a thousand proofs.

KING (*to Diana*)   Methought you said
You saw one here in court could witness it.

DIANA
I did, my lord, but loath am to produce
So bad an instrument. His name's Paroles.   205

LAFEU
I saw the man today, if man he be.

KING
Find him and bring him hither.   *Exit one*

BERTRAM   What of him?
He's quoted for a most perfidious slave
With all the spots o'th' world taxed and debauched,
Whose nature sickens but to speak a truth.   210
Am I or that or this for what he'll utter,
That will speak anything?

KING   She hath that ring of yours.

BERTRAM
I think she has. Certain it is I liked her
And boarded her i'th' wanton way of youth.
She knew her distance and did angle for me,   215
Madding my eagerness with her restraint,
As all impediments in fancy's course
Are motives of more fancy; and in fine
Her inf'nite cunning with her modern grace
Subdued me to her rate. She got the ring,   220
And I had that which my inferior might
At market price have bought.

DIANA   I must be patient.
You that have turned off a first so noble wife
May justly diet me. I pray you yet—
Since you lack virtue I will lose a husband—   225
Send for your ring, I will return it home,
And give me mine again.

BERTRAM I have it not.

KING (*to Diana*) What ring was yours, I pray you?

DIANA
Sir, much like the same upon your finger.   230

KING
Know you this ring? This ring was his of late.

DIANA
And this was it I gave him being abed.

KING
The story then goes false you threw it him
Out of a casement?

DIANA   I have spoke the truth.

Enter Paroles

BERTRAM (*to the King*)
My lord, I do confess the ring was hers.   235

KING
You boggle shrewdly; every feather starts you.—
Is this the man you speak of?

DIANA   Ay, my lord.

KING (*to Paroles*)
Tell me, sirrah—but tell me true, I charge you,

Not fearing the displeasure of your master,
Which on your just proceeding I'll keep off—   240
By him and by this woman here what know you?

PAROLES So please your majesty, my master hath been
an honourable gentleman. Tricks he hath had in him
which gentlemen have.

KING
Come, come, to th' purpose. Did he love this woman?

PAROLES Faith, sir, he did love her, but how?   246

KING How, I pray you?

PAROLES He did love her, sir, as a gentleman loves a
woman.

KING How is that?   250

PAROLES He loved her, sir, and loved her not.

KING As thou art a knave and no knave. What an
equivocal companion is this!

PAROLES I am a poor man, and at your majesty's
command.   255

LAFEU (to the King) He's a good drum, my lord, but a
naughty orator.

DIANA (to Paroles) Do you know he promised me marriage?

PAROLES Faith, I know more than I'll speak.

KING But wilt thou not speak all thou know'st?   260

PAROLES Yes, so please your majesty. I did go between
them, as I said; but more than that, he loved her, for
indeed he was mad for her and talked of Satan and of
limbo and of Furies and I know not what. Yet I was
in that credit with them at that time that I knew of
their going to bed and of other motions, as promising
her marriage and things which would derive me ill will
to speak of. Therefore I will not speak what I know.

KING Thou hast spoken all already, unless thou canst say
they are married. But thou art too fine in thy evidence,
therefore stand aside.—   271
This ring you say was yours.

DIANA   Ay, my good lord.

KING
Where did you buy it? Or who gave it you?

DIANA
It was not given me, nor I did not buy it.

KING
Who lent it you?

DIANA   It was not lent me neither.   275

KING
Where did you find it then?

DIANA   I found it not.

KING
If it were yours by none of all these ways,
How could you give it him?

DIANA   I never gave it him.

LAFEU (to the King) This woman's an easy glove, my lord,
she goes off and on at pleasure.   280

KING (to Diana)
This ring was mine. I gave it his first wife.

DIANA
It might be yours or hers for aught I know.

KING (to attendants)
Take her away, I do not like her now.

To prison with her. And away with him.—
Unless thou tell'st me where thou hadst this ring   285
Thou diest within this hour.

DIANA   I'll never tell you.

KING (to attendants)
Take her away.

DIANA   I'll put in bail, my liege.

KING
I think thee now some common customer.

DIANA
By Jove, if ever I knew man 'twas you.

KING
Wherefore hast thou accused him all this while?   290

DIANA
Because he's guilty, and he is not guilty.
He knows I am no maid, and he'll swear to't;
I'll swear I am a maid, and he knows not.
Great King, I am no strumpet; by my life,
I am either maid or else this old man's wife.   295

KING (to attendants)
She does abuse our ears. To prison with her.

DIANA
Good mother, fetch my bail.   Exit Widow
Stay, royal sir.
The jeweller that owes the ring is sent for,
And he shall surety me. But for this lord,
Who hath abused me as he knows himself,   300
Though yet he never harmed me, here I quit him.
He knows himself my bed he hath defiled,
And at that time he got his wife with child.
Dead though she be she feels her young one kick.
So there's my riddle; one that's dead is quick.   305
And now behold the meaning.
    Enter Helen and the Widow

KING   Is there no exorcist
Beguiles the truer office of mine eyes?
Is't real that I see?

HELEN   No, my good lord,
'Tis but the shadow of a wife you see,
The name and not the thing.

BERTRAM   Both, both. O, pardon!

HELEN
O, my good lord, when I was like this maid   311
I found you wondrous kind. There is your ring.
And, look you, here's your letter. This it says:
'When from my finger you can get this ring,
And are by me with child,' et cetera. This is done.   315
Will you be mine now you are doubly won?

BERTRAM (to the King)
If she, my liege, can make me know this clearly
I'll love her dearly, ever ever dearly.

HELEN
If it appear not plain and prove untrue,
Deadly divorce step between me and you.—   320
O my dear mother, do I see you living?

LAFEU
Mine eyes smell onions, I shall weep anon.
(To Paroles) Good Tom Drum, lend me a handkerchief.

So, I thank thee. Wait on me home, I'll make sport
with thee. Let thy curtsies alone, they are scurvy ones.

KING (*to Helen*)

Let us from point to point this story know   326
To make the even truth in pleasure flow.
(*To Diana*) If thou be'st yet a fresh uncroppèd flower,
Choose thou thy husband and I'll pay thy dower.
For I can guess that by thy honest aid   330
Thou kept'st a wife herself, thyself a maid.
Of that and all the progress more and less
Resolvèdly more leisure shall express.

All yet seems well; and if it end so meet,
The bitter past, more welcome is the sweet.   335

Flourish of trumpets

Epilogue

The King's a beggar now the play is done.
All is well ended if this suit be won:
That you express content, which we will pay
With strife to please you, day exceeding day.
Ours be your patience then, and yours our parts: 5
Your gentle hands lend us, and take our hearts.

Exeunt

PERICLES

BY WILLIAM SHAKESPEARE AND GEORGE WILKINS
A RECONSTRUCTED TEXT

ON 20 May 1608 *Pericles* was entered on the Stationers' Register to Edward Blount; but he did not publish it. Probably the players allowed him to license it in the hope of preventing its publication by anyone else, for it was one of the most popular plays of the period. Its success was exploited, also in 1608, by the publication of a novel, by George Wilkins, 'The *Painful Adventures of Pericles Prince of Tyre*, Being the True History of the Play of *Pericles*, as it was lately presented by the worthy and ancient poet John Gower'. The play itself appeared in print in the following year, with an ascription to Shakespeare, but in a manifestly corrupt text that gives every sign of having been put together from memory. This quarto was several times reprinted; but the play was not included in the 1623 Folio (perhaps because Heminges and Condell knew that Shakespeare was responsible for only part of it).

In putting together *The Painful Adventures*, Wilkins drew on an earlier version of the tale, *The Pattern of Painful Adventures*, by Laurence Twine, written in the mid-1570s and re-printed in 1607. Twine's book is also a source of the play, which draws too on the story of Apollonius of Tyre as told by John Gower in his *Confessio Amantis*, and, to a lesser extent, on Sir Philip Sidney's *Arcadia*. Wilkins not only incorporated verbatim passages from Twine's book, he also drew heavily on *Pericles* itself. Since the play text is so corrupt, it is quite likely that Wilkins reports parts of it both more accurately and more fully than the quarto. And he may have had special qualifications for doing so. He was a dramatist whose popular play *The Miseries of Enforced Marriage* had been performed by Shakespeare's company. *Pericles* has usually been regarded as either a collaborative play or one in which Shakespeare revised a pre-existing script. Our edition is based on the hypothesis (not new) that Wilkins was its joint author. Our attempt to reconstruct the play draws more heavily than is usual on Wilkins's novel, especially in the first nine scenes (which he probably wrote); in general, because of its obvious corruption, the original text is more freely emended than usual. So that readers may experience the play as originally printed, an unemended reprint of the 1609 quarto is given in our original-spelling edition. The deficiencies of the text are in part compensated for by the survival of an unusual amount of relevant visual material, reproduced overleaf.

The complex textual background of *Pericles* should not be allowed to draw attention away from the merits of this dramatic romance, which we hope will be more apparent as the result of our treatment of the text. If the original play had survived, it might well have been as highly valued as *The Winter's Tale* or *The Tempest*; as it is, it contains some hauntingly beautiful episodes, above all that in Scene 21 in which Marina, Pericles' long-lost daughter, draws him out of the comatose state to which his sufferings have reduced him.

The true History of the Play of *Pericles*, as it was lately presented by the worthy and an-cient Poet *John Gower*.

John Gower

The Description of John Gower

Large he was; his height was long;
Broad of breast; his limbs were strong,
But colour pale, and wan his look—
Such have they that plyen their book.
His head was grey and quaintly shorn.
Neatly was his beard worn.
His visage grave, stern and grim.
Cato was most like to him.
His bonnet was a hat of blue;
His sleeves straight of that same hue.
A surcoat of a tawny dye
Hung in pleats over his thigh;
A breech, close unto his dock,
Handsomed with a long stock.
Pricked before were his shoon;
He wore such as others doone.
A bag of red by his side,
And by that his napkin tied.
Thus John Gower did appear,
Quaint attired, as you hear.

10. From the title-page of *The Painful Adventures of Pericles Prince of Tyre* (1608), by George Wilkins; artist unknown. Since Gower is not a character in Wilkins's novel, the choice of woodcut undoubtedly reflects both the play's popularity and Gower's own impact in early performances, and it is as likely to reflect the visual detail of performance as any early title-page. The sprig of laurel (or posy) in Gower's left hand is symbolic of his poetic status.

11. From *Greene's Vision* (1592), sig. C1r-C1v; probably by Robert Greene. The description here fits reasonably well the *Painful Adventures* title-page, though the woodcut does not contain the 'bag of red', 'napkin', or tight-fitting 'breech'.

Me pompæ prouexit apex.
The desire of renowne hath promoted me, or set me forward.

Qui me alit, me extinguit.
He that nourisheth me, killeth me.

12. Severed heads displayed on the gate of London Bridge, from an etching by Claes Jan Visscher (1616). In the play's sources, and *Painful Adventures*, the heads of previous suitors (Sc. 1) are placed on the 'gate' of Antioch. In performance they could have been thrust out on poles from the upper stage; but the timing and method of their display is not clear.

13. From *The Heroical Devices of M. Claudius Paradin*, translated by P.S. (1591), sig. V3. This is the source for the impresa of the Third Knight, in Sc. 6.

14. From *The Heroical Devices of M. Claudius Paradin*, translated by P.S. (1591), sig. Z3. This is the source for the impresa of the Fourth Knight, in Sc. 6.

16. A miniature of Diana by Isaac Oliver (1615): the dress is yellow, the scarf a gauzy pink-white, the cloak over her right shoulder blue; the leaf-shaped brooch topped by the crescent moon, gold. In Samuel Daniel's masque *The Vision of the Twelve Goddesses* (1604), 'Diana, in a green mantle embroidered with silver half moons, and a crescent of pearl on her head, presents a bow and quiver' (sig. A5). The 'crescent of pearl'—an ornamental crescent moon, also detectable in Jones's sketch—can be seen in many emblematic representations of the goddess.

15. An Inigo Jones sketch of Diana, probably for Ben Jonson's masque *Time Vindicated* (1623). The goddess of chastity appeared as a character in court entertainments, masques, and plays, and her representation was governed by iconographic convention. As goddess of hunting, she was most often identified by her 'silver bow' (21.234). In Thomas Heywood's *The Golden Age* (1611), stage directions refer to '*Diana's bow*' (sig. E1ᵛ) and her '*buskins*' (sig. E3ᵛ); her '*nymphs*' explicitly, and by inference she, have '*garlands on their heads, and javelins in their hands . . . bows and quivers*' (sig. D3ᵛ). The bow, quiver, and javelin, all visible in Jones's sketch, were commonplace in emblematic representations. As a huntress, Diana could naturally be envisaged in a chariot: in Aurelian Townshend's masque *Albion's Triumph* (1631), she descends 'in her chariot' (pp. 2, 12); in *Time Vindicated*, 'Diana descends' (l. 446). Such descents for deities were used in the public theatres, too, usually in a chair or chariot (21.224.2).

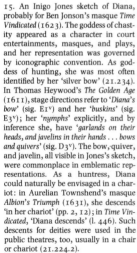

17. For the pastoral *Florimène* (1635), Inigo Jones designed two scenic views of 'The Temple of Diana' (see l. 22.17.1). Though such scenes were not used in the public theatres in Shakespeare's time, the columns supporting the overhanging roof of the public stage (see General Introduction, pp. xxv–xxvii) could have created a scenic effect roughly similar to Jones's recessed classical temple. Statues were also available as props in the public theatre; in *Pericles*, as in *The Winter's Tale*, the statue could have been impersonated by an actor on a pedestal. Whether or not a statue was visible, the temple could be identified by an altar (as in *The Two Noble Kinsmen*).

THE PERSONS OF THE PLAY

John GOWER, the Presenter

ANTIOCHUS, King of Antioch
His DAUGHTER
THALIART, a villain

PERICLES, Prince of Tyre
HELICANUS ⎫
AESCHINES ⎬ two grave counsellors of Tyre
MARINA, Pericles' daughter

CLEON, Governor of Tarsus
DIONIZA, his wife
LEONINE, a murderer

KING SIMONIDES, of Pentapolis
THAISA, his daughter
Three FISHERMEN, his subjects

Five PRINCES, suitors of Thaisa
A MARSHAL
LICHORIDA, Thaisa's nurse

CERIMON, a physician of Ephesus
PHILEMON, his servant

LYSIMACHUS, Governor of Mytilene
A BAWD
A PANDER
BOULT, a leno

DIANA, goddess of chastity

Lords, ladies, pages, messengers, sailors, gentlemen

A Reconstructed Text of
Pericles, Prince of Tyre

Sc. 1 *Enter Gower as Prologue*

GOWER

To sing a song that old was sung
From ashes ancient Gower is come,
Assuming man's infirmities
To glad your ear and please your eyes.
It hath been sung at festivals, 5
On ember-eves and holy-ales,
And lords and ladies in their lives
Have read it for restoratives.
The purchase is to make men glorious,
Et bonum quo antiquius eo melius. 10
If you, born in these latter times
When wit's more ripe, accept my rhymes,
And that to hear an old man sing
May to your wishes pleasure bring,
I life would wish, and that I might 15
Waste it for you like taper-light.
This' Antioch, then; Antiochus the Great
Built up this city for his chiefest seat,
The fairest in all Syria.
I tell you what mine authors say. 20
This king unto him took a fere
Who died, and left a female heir
So buxom, blithe, and full of face
As heav'n had lent her all his grace,
With whom the father liking took, 25
And her to incest did provoke.
Bad child, worse father, to entice his own
To evil should be done by none.
By custom what they did begin
Was with long use account' no sin. 30
The beauty of this sinful dame
Made many princes thither frame
To seek her as a bedfellow,
In marriage pleasures playfellow,
Which to prevent he made a law 35
To keep her still, and men in awe,
That whoso asked her for his wife,
His riddle told not, lost his life.
So for her many a wight did die,
⌜*A row of heads is revealed*⌝
As yon grim looks do testify. 40
What now ensues, to th' judgement of your eye
I give, my cause who best can justify. *Exit*
⌜*Sennet.*⌝ *Enter King Antiochus, Prince Pericles, and*
⌜*lords and peers in their richest ornaments*⌝

ANTIOCHUS

Young Prince of Tyre, you have at large received
The danger of the task you undertake.

PERICLES

I have, Antiochus, and with a soul 45
Emboldened with the glory of her praise
Think death no hazard in this enterprise.

ANTIOCHUS Music!

Music sounds

Bring in our daughter, clothèd like a bride
Fit for th'embracements ev'n of Jove himself, 50
At whose conception, till Lucina reigned,
Nature this dowry gave to glad her presence:
The senate-house of planets all did sit,
In her their best perfections to knit.

Enter Antiochus' Daughter

PERICLES

See where she comes, apparelled like the spring, 55
Graces her subjects, and her thoughts the king
Of ev'ry virtue gives renown to men;
Her face the book of praises, where is read
Nothing but curious pleasures, as from thence
Sorrow were ever razed and testy wrath 60
Could never be her mild companion.
You gods that made me man, and sway in love,
That have inflamed desire in my breast
To taste the fruit of yon celestial tree
Or die in the adventure, be my helps, 65
As I am son and servant to your will,
To compass such a boundless happiness.

ANTIOCHUS Prince Pericles—

PERICLES

That would be son to great Antiochus.

ANTIOCHUS

Before thee stands this fair Hesperides, 70
With golden fruit, but dang'rous to be touched,
⌜*He gestures towards the heads*⌝
For death-like dragons here affright thee hard.
⌜*He gestures towards his daughter*⌝
Her heav'n-like face enticeth thee to view
Her countless glory, which desert must gain;
And which without desert, because thine eye 75
Presumes to reach, all the whole heap must die.
Yon sometimes famous princes, like thyself
Drawn by report, advent'rous by desire,
Tell thee with speechless tongues and semblants
bloodless
That without covering save yon field of stars 80
Here they stand, martyrs slain in Cupid's wars,
And with dead cheeks advise thee to desist
From going on death's net, whom none resist.

PERICLES

Antiochus, I thank thee, who hath taught

My frail mortality to know itself, 85
And by those fearful objects to prepare
This body, like to them, to what I must;
For death remembered should be like a mirror
Who tells us life's but breath, to trust it error.
I'll make my will then, and, as sick men do, 90
Who know the world, see heav'n, but feeling woe
Grip not at earthly joys as erst they did,
So I bequeath a happy peace to you
And all good men, as ev'ry prince should do;
My riches to the earth from whence they came, 95
(To the Daughter) But my unspotted fire of love to you.
(To Antiochus) Thus ready for the way of life or death,
I wait the sharpest blow, Antiochus.

ANTIOCHUS
Scorning advice, read the conclusion then,
⌈*He angrily throws down the riddle*⌉
Which read and not expounded, 'tis decreed, 100
As these before thee, thou thyself shalt bleed.

DAUGHTER *(to Pericles)*
Of all 'sayed yet, mayst thou prove prosperous;
Of all 'sayed yet, I wish thee happiness.

PERICLES
Like a bold champion I assume the lists,
Nor ask advice of any other thought 105
But faithfulness and courage.
⌈*He takes up and*⌉ *reads aloud the riddle*
I am no viper, yet I feed
On mother's flesh which did me breed.
I sought a husband, in which labour
I found that kindness in a father. 110
He's father, son, and husband mild;
I mother, wife, and yet his child.
How this may be and yet in two,
As you will live resolve it you.
Sharp physic is the last. ⌈*Aside*⌉ But O, you powers 115
That gives heav'n countless eyes to view men's acts,
Why cloud they not their sights perpetually
If this be true which makes me pale to read it?
⌈*He gazes on the Daughter*⌉
Fair glass of light, I loved you, and could still,
Were not this glorious casket stored with ill. 120
But I must tell you now my thoughts revolt,
For he's no man on whom perfections wait
That, knowing sin within, will touch the gate.
You're a fair viol, and your sense the strings
Who, fingered to make man his lawful music, 125
Would draw heav'n down and all the gods to hearken,
But, being played upon before your time,
Hell only danceth at so harsh a chime.
Good sooth, I care not for you.

ANTIOCHUS
Prince Pericles, touch not, upon thy life, 130
For that's an article within our law
As dang'rous as the rest. Your time's expired.
Either expound now, or receive your sentence.

PERICLES Great King,
Few love to hear the sins they love to act. 135

'Twould braid yourself too near for me to tell it.
Who has a book of all that monarchs do,
He's more secure to keep it shut than shown,
For vice repeated, like the wand'ring wind,
Blows dust in others' eyes to spread itself; 140
And yet the end of all is bought thus dear,
The breath is gone, and the sore eyes see clear
To stop the air would hurt them. The blind mole casts
Copped hills towards heav'n to tell the earth is thronged
By man's oppression, and the poor worm doth die for't.
Kings are earth's gods; in vice their law's their will,
And if Jove stray, who dares say Jove doth ill? 147
It is enough you know, and it is fit,
What being more known grows worse, to smother it.
All love the womb that their first being bred; 150
Then give my tongue like leave to love my head.

ANTIOCHUS *(aside)*
Heav'n, that I had thy head! He's found the meaning.
But I will gloze with him. —Young Prince of Tyre,
Though by the tenor of our strict edict,
Your exposition misinterpreting, 155
We might proceed to cancel of your days,
Yet hope, succeeding from so fair a tree
As your fair self, doth tune us otherwise.
Forty days longer we do respite you,
If by which time our secret be undone, 160
This mercy shows we'll joy in such a son.
And until then your entertain shall be
As doth befit your worth and our degree.
⌈*Flourish.*⌉ *Exeunt all but Pericles*

PERICLES
How courtesy would seem to cover sin
When what is done is like an hypocrite, 165
The which is good in nothing but in sight.
If it be true that I interpret false,
Then were it certain you were not so bad
As with foul incest to abuse your soul,
Where now you're both a father and a son 170
By your uncomely claspings with your child—
Which pleasures fits a husband, not a father—
And she, an eater of her mother's flesh,
By the defiling of her parents' bed,
And both like serpents are, who though they feed 175
On sweetest flowers, yet they poison breed.
Antioch, farewell, for wisdom sees those men
Blush not in actions blacker than the night
Will 'schew no course to keep them from the light.
One sin, I know, another doth provoke. 180
Murder's as near to lust as flame to smoke.
Poison and treason are the hands of sin,
Ay, and the targets to put off the shame.
Then, lest my life be cropped to keep you clear, 184
By flight I'll shun the danger which I fear. *Exit*

Enter Antiochus

ANTIOCHUS
He hath found the meaning, for the which we mean
To have his head. He must not live
To trumpet forth my infamy, nor tell the world

Antiochus doth sin in such a loathèd manner,
And therefore instantly this prince must die,   190
For by his fall my honour must keep high.
Who attends us there?

Enter Thaliart

THALIART   Doth your highness call?
ANTIOCHUS
Thaliart, you are of our chamber, Thaliart,
And to your secrecy our mind partakes
Her private actions. For your faithfulness   195
We will advance you, Thaliart. Behold,
Here's poison, and here's gold.
We hate the Prince of Tyre, and thou must kill him.
It fits thee not to ask the reason. Why?
Because we bid it. Say, is it done?   200
THALIART My lord, 'tis done.
ANTIOCHUS Enough.

Enter a Messenger hastily

Let your breath cool yourself, telling your haste.
MESSENGER
Your majesty, Prince Pericles is fled.   ⌈*Exit*⌉
ANTIOCHUS (*to Thaliart*)
As thou wilt live, fly after; like an arrow   205
Shot from a well-experienced archer hits
The mark his eye doth level at, so thou
Never return unless it be to say
'Your majesty, Prince Pericles is dead.'
THALIART
If I can get him in my pistol's length   210
I'll make him sure enough. Farewell, your highness.
ANTIOCHUS
Thaliart, adieu.   ⌈*Exit Thaliart*⌉
Till Pericles be dead
My heart can lend no succour to my head.
                    Exit. ⌈*The heads are concealed*⌉

Sc. 2 *Enter Pericles, distempered, with his lords*
PERICLES
Let none disturb us.   *Exeunt lords*
                    Why should this change of thoughts,
The sad companion, dull-eyed melancholy,
Be my so used a guest as not an hour
In the day's glorious walk or peaceful night,
The tomb where grief should sleep, can breed me
      quiet?   5
Here pleasures court mine eyes, and mine eyes shun
      them,
And danger, which I feared, 's at Antioch,
Whose arm seems far too short to hit me here.
Yet neither pleasure's art can joy my spirits,
Nor yet care's author's distance comfort me.   10
Then it is thus: the passions of the mind,
That have their first conception by misdread,
Have after-nourishment and life by care,
And what was first but fear what might be done
Grows elder now, and cares it be not done.   15
And so with me. The great Antiochus,

'Gainst whom I am too little to contend,
Since he's so great can make his will his act,
Will think me speaking though I swear to silence,
Nor boots it me to say I honour him   20
If he suspect I may dishonour him.
And what may make him blush in being known,
He'll stop the course by which it might be known.
With hostile forces he'll o'erspread the land,
And with th'ostent of war will look so huge   25
Amazement shall drive courage from the state,
Our men be vanquished ere they do resist,
And subjects punished that ne'er thought offence,
Which care of them, not pity of myself,
Who am no more but as the tops of trees   30
Which fence the roots they grow by and defend them,
Makes both my body pine and soul to languish,
And punish that before that he would punish.

*Enter all the Lords, among them old Helicanus, to
Pericles*

FIRST LORD
Joy and all comfort in your sacred breast!
SECOND LORD
And keep your mind peaceful and comfortable.   35
HELICANUS
Peace, peace, and give experience tongue.
(*To Pericles*) You do not well so to abuse yourself,
To waste your body here with pining sorrow,
Upon whose safety doth depend the lives
And the prosperity of a whole kingdom.   40
'Tis ill in you to do it, and no less
Ill in your council not to contradict it.
They do abuse tne King that flatter him,
For flatt'ry is the bellows blows up sin;
The thing the which is flattered, but a spark,   45
To which that wind gives heat and stronger glowing;
Whereas reproof, obedient and in order,
Fits kings as they are men, for they may err.
When Signor Sooth here does proclaim a peace
He flatters you, makes war upon your life.   50
                    ⌈*He kneels*⌉
Prince, pardon me, or strike me if you please.
I cannot be much lower than my knees.
PERICLES
All leave us else; but let your cares o'erlook
What shipping and what lading's in our haven,
And then return to us.   *Exeunt Lords*
                    Helicane, thou   55
Hast movèd us. What seest thou in our looks?
HELICANUS An angry brow, dread lord.
PERICLES
If there be such a dart in princes' frowns,
How durst thy tongue move anger to our brows?
HELICANUS
How dares the plants look up to heav'n from whence
They have their nourishment?   61
PERICLES
Thou knowest I have pow'r to take thy life from thee.

HELICANUS
I have ground the axe myself; do you but strike the
    blow.

PERICLES ⌈lifting him up⌉
Rise, prithee, rise. Sit down. Thou art no flatterer,
I thank thee for it, and the heav'ns forbid   65
That kings should let their ears hear their faults hid.
Fit counsellor and servant for a prince,
Who by thy wisdom mak'st a prince thy servant,
What wouldst thou have me do?

HELICANUS   To bear with patience
Such griefs as you do lay upon yourself.   70

PERICLES
Thou speak'st like a physician, Helicanus,
That ministers a potion unto me
That thou wouldst tremble to receive thyself.
Attend me, then. I went to Antioch,
Where, as thou know'st, against the face of death   75
I sought the purchase of a glorious beauty
From whence an issue I might propagate,
As children are heav'n's blessings: to parents,
    objects;
Are arms to princes, and bring joys to subjects.
Her face was to mine eye beyond all wonder,   80
The rest—hark in thine ear—as black as incest,
Which by my knowledge found, the sinful father
Seemed not to strike, but smooth. But thou know'st
    this,
'Tis time to fear when tyrants seems to kiss;
Which fear so grew in me I hither fled   85
Under the covering of careful night,
Who seemed my good protector, and being here
Bethought me what was past, what might succeed.
I knew him tyrannous, and tyrants' fears
Decrease not, but grow faster than the years.   90
And should he doubt—as doubt no doubt he doth—
That I should open to the list'ning air
How many worthy princes' bloods were shed
To keep his bed of blackness unlaid ope,
To lop that doubt he'll fill this land with arms,   95
And make pretence of wrong that I have done him,
When all for mine—if I may call—offence
Must feel war's blow, who spares not innocence;
Which love to all, of which thyself art one,
Who now reproved'st me for't—

HELICANUS   Alas, sir.   100

PERICLES
Drew sleep out of mine eyes, blood from my cheeks,
Musings into my mind, with thousand doubts,
How I might stop this tempest ere it came,
And, finding little comfort to relieve them,
I thought it princely charity to grieve them.   105

HELICANUS
Well, my lord, since you have giv'n me leave to speak,
Freely will I speak. Antiochus you fear,
And justly too, I think, you fear the tyrant,
Who either by public war or private treason

Will take away your life.   110
Therefore, my lord, go travel for a while,
Till that his rage and anger be forgot,
Or destinies do cut his thread of life.
Your rule direct to any; if to me,
Day serves not light more faithful than I'll be.   115

PERICLES I do not doubt thy faith,
But should he in my absence wrong thy liberties?

HELICANUS
We'll mingle our bloods together in the earth
From whence we had our being and our birth.

PERICLES
Tyre, I now look from thee then, and to Tarsus   120
Intend my travel, where I'll hear from thee,
And by whose letters I'll dispose myself.
The care I had and have of subjects' good
On thee I lay, whose wisdom's strength can bear it.
I'll take thy word for faith, not ask thine oath;   125
Who shuns not to break one will sure crack both.
But in our orbs we'll live so round and safe
That time of both this truth shall ne'er convince:
Thou showed'st a subject's shine, I a true prince.
                            Exeunt

Sc. 3   *Enter Thaliart*

THALIART So this is Tyre, and this the court. Here must
I kill King Pericles, and if I do it and am caught I am
like to be hanged abroad, but if I do it not, I am sure
to be hanged at home. 'Tis dangerous. Well, I perceive
he was a wise fellow and had good discretion that,
being bid to ask what he would of the King, desired he
might know none of his secrets. Now do I see he had
some reason for't, for if a king bid a man be a villain,
he's bound by the indenture of his oath to be one.
Hush, here comes the lords of Tyre.

    Enter Helicanus and Aeschines, with other lords

HELICANUS
You shall not need, my fellow peers of Tyre,
Further to question of your King's departure.
His sealed commission left in trust with me
Does speak sufficiently he's gone to travel.

THALIART (*aside*) How? The King gone?   15

HELICANUS
If further yet you will be satisfied
Why, as it were unlicensed of your loves,
He would depart, I'll give some light unto you.
Being at Antioch—

THALIART (*aside*)   What from Antioch?

HELICANUS
Royal Antiochus, on what cause I know not,   20
Took some displeasure at him—at least he judged so—
And doubting lest that he had erred or sinned,
To show his sorrow he'd correct himself;
So puts himself unto the ship-man's toil,
With whom each minute threatens life or death.   25

THALIART (*aside*)
Well, I perceive I shall not be hanged now,

Although I would.
But since he's gone, the King's ears it must please
He scaped the land to perish on the seas.
I'll present myself.—Peace to the lords of Tyre.   30
Lord Thaliart am I, of Antioch.

⌈HELICANUS⌉
Lord Thaliart of Antioch is welcome.

THALIART
From King Antiochus I come
With message unto princely Pericles,
But since my landing I have understood   35
Your lord's betook himself to unknown travels.
Now my message must return from whence it came.

HELICANUS
We have no reason to enquire it,
Commended to our master, not to us.
Yet ere you shall depart, this we desire: 40
As friends to Antioch, we may feast in Tyre.   *Exeunt*

Sc. 4 *Enter Cleon, the Governor of Tarsus, with Dionyza*
       his wife, and others

CLEON
My Dionyza, shall we rest us here
And, by relating tales of others' griefs,
See if 'twill teach us to forget our own?

DIONYZA
That were to blow at fire in hope to quench it,
For who digs hills because they do aspire   5
Throws down one mountain to cast up a higher.
O my distressèd lord, e'en such our griefs are;
Here they're but felt and seen with midges' eyes,
But like to groves, being topped they higher rise.

CLEON O Dionyza,   10
Who wanteth food and will not say he wants it,
Or can conceal his hunger till he famish?
Our tongues our sorrows dictate to sound deep
Our woes into the air, and our eyes to weep
Till lungs fetch breath that may proclaim them louder,
That, if heav'n slumber while their creatures want, 16
They may awake their helps to comfort them.
I'll then discourse our woes, felt sev'ral years,
And, wanting breath to speak, help me with tears.

DIONYZA As you think best, sir.   20

CLEON
This Tarsus o'er which I have the government,
A city o'er whom plenty held full hand,
For riches strewed herself ev'n in the streets,
Whose tow'rs bore heads so high they kissed the clouds,
And strangers ne'er beheld but wondered at,   25
Whose men and dames so jetted and adorned
Like one another's glass to trim them by;
Their tables were stored full to glad the sight,
And not so much to feed on as delight.
All poverty was scorned, and pride so great   30
The name of help grew odious to repeat.

DIONYZA O, 'tis too true.

CLEON
But see what heav'n can do by this our change.

Those mouths who but of late earth, sea, and air
Were all too little to content and please,   35
Although they gave their creatures in abundance,
As houses are defiled for want of use,
They are now starved for want of exercise.
Those palates who, not yet two summers younger,
Must have inventions to delight the taste   40
Would now be glad of bread and beg for it.
Those mothers who to nuzzle up their babes
Thought naught too curious are ready now
To eat those little darlings whom they loved.
So sharp are hunger's teeth that man and wife   45
Draw lots who first shall die to lengthen life.
Here weeping stands a lord, there lies a lady dying,
Here many sink, yet those which see them fall
Have scarce strength left to give them burial.
Is not this true?   50

DIONYZA
Our cheeks and hollow eyes do witness it.

CLEON
O, let those cities that of plenty's cup
And her prosperities so largely taste
With their superfluous riots, heed these tears!
The misery of Tarsus may be theirs.   55

Enter a ⌈fainting⌉ Lord of Tarsus ⌈slowly⌉

LORD Where's the Lord Governor?

CLEON
Here. Speak out thy sorrows which thou bring'st in
haste,
For comfort is too far for us t'expect.

LORD
We have descried upon our neighbouring shore
A portly sail of ships make hitherward.   60

CLEON I thought as much.
One sorrow never comes but brings an heir
That may succeed as his inheritor,
And so in ours. Some neighbour nation,
Taking advantage of our misery,   65
Hath stuffed these hollow vessels with their power
To beat us down, the which are down already,
And make a conquest of unhappy men,
Whereas no glory's got to overcome.

LORD
That's the least fear, for by the semblance   70
Of their white flags displayed they bring us peace,
And come to us as favourers, not foes.

CLEON
Thou speak'st like him's untutored to repeat;
Who makes the fairest show means most deceit.
But bring they what they will and what they can, 75
What need we fear?
Our grave's the low'st, and we are half-way there.
Go tell their gen'ral we attend him here
To know for what he comes, and whence he comes.

LORD I go, my lord.   *Exit*

CLEON
Welcome is peace, if he on peace consist;   81
If wars, we are unable to resist.

Enter ⌈the Lord again conducting⌉ Pericles with
attendants

PERICLES (*to Cleon*)

Lord Governor, for so we hear you are,
Let not our ships and number of our men
Be like a beacon fixed t'amaze your eyes.   85
We have heard your miseries as far as Tyre,
Since entering your unshut gates have witnessed
The widowed desolation of your streets;
Nor come we to add sorrow to your hearts,
But to relieve them of their heavy load;   90
And these our ships, you happily may think
Are like the Trojan horse was fraught within
With bloody veins importing overthrow,
Are stored with corn to make your needy bread,
And give them life whom hunger starved half dead. 95

ALL OF TARSUS ⌈*falling on their knees and weeping*⌉

The gods of Greece protect you, and we'll pray for you!

PERICLES Arise, I pray you, rise.

We do not look for reverence but for love,
And harbourage for me, my ships and men.

CLEON

The which when any shall not gratify,   100
Or pay you with unthankfulness in thought,
Be it our wives, our children, or ourselves,
The curse of heav'n and men succeed their evils!
Till when—the which I hope shall ne'er be seen—
Your grace is welcome to our town and us.   105

PERICLES

Which welcome we'll accept, feast here a while,
Until our stars that frown lend us a smile.   *Exeunt*

Sc. 5   *Enter Gower*

GOWER

Here have you seen a mighty king
His child, iwis, to incest bring;
A better prince and benign lord
Prove awe-full both in deed and word.
Be quiet then, as men should be,   5
Till he hath passed necessity.
I'll show you those in trouble's reign,
Losing a mite, a mountain gain.
The good in conversation,
To whom I give my benison,   10
Is still at Tarsus where each man
Thinks all is writ he speken can,
And to remember what he does
His statue build to make him glorious.
But tidings to the contrary   15
Are brought your eyes. What need speak I?
          Dumb show.
Enter at one door Pericles talking with Cleon, all
the train with them. Enter at another door a
gentleman with a letter to Pericles. Pericles shows
the letter to Cleon. Pericles gives the messenger a
reward, and knights him. Exeunt with their trains
Pericles at one door and Cleon at another
Good Helicane that stayed at home,

Not to eat honey like a drone
From others' labours, for that he strive
To killen bad, keep good alive,   20
And to fulfil his prince' desire
Sent word of all that haps in Tyre;
How Thaliart came full bent with sin
And hid intent to murdren him,
And that in Tarsus was not best   25
Longer for him to make his rest.
He deeming so put forth to seas,
Where when men been there's seldom ease,
For now the wind begins to blow;
Thunder above and deeps below   30
Makes such unquiet that the ship
Should house him safe is wrecked and split,
And he, good prince, having all lost,
By waves from coast to coast is tossed.
All perishen of man, of pelf,   35
Ne aught escapend but himself,
Till fortune, tired with doing bad,
Threw him ashore to give him glad.
          ⌈*Enter Pericles wet and half-naked*⌉
And here he comes. What shall be next
Pardon old Gower; this 'longs the text.   *Exit*
          ⌈*Thunder and lightning*⌉

PERICLES

Yet cease your ire, you angry stars of heaven!   41
Wind, rain, and thunder, remember earthly man
Is but a substance that must yield to you,
And I, as fits my nature, do obey you.
Alas, the seas hath cast me on the rocks,   45
Washed me from shore to shore, and left my breath
Nothing to think on but ensuing death.
Let it suffice the greatness of your powers
To have bereft a prince of all his fortunes,
And, having thrown him from your wat'ry grave,   50
Here to have death in peace is all he'll crave.
          ⌈*He sits.*⌉
          Enter two poor Fishermen: one the Master, the
          other his man

MASTER ⌈*calling*⌉ What ho, Pilch!

SECOND FISHERMAN ⌈*calling*⌉ Ha, come and bring away the
nets.

MASTER ⌈*calling*⌉ What, Patchbreech, I say!   55
          ⌈*Enter a Third rough Fisherman with a hood upon*
          his head and a filthy leathern pelt upon his back,
          unseemly clad, and homely to behold. He brings nets
          to dry and repair⌉

THIRD FISHERMAN What say you, master?

MASTER Look how thou stirrest now. Come away, or I'll
fetch th' with a wanion.

THIRD FISHERMAN Faith, master, I am thinking of the poor
men that were cast away before us even now.   60

MASTER Alas, poor souls, it grieved my heart to hear what
pitiful cries they made to us to help them when, well-
a-day, we could scarce help ourselves.

THIRD FISHERMAN Nay, master, said not I as much when
I saw the porpoise how he bounced and tumbled? They

say they're half fish, half flesh. A plague on them, they
ne'er come but I look to be washed. Master, I marvel
how the fishes live in the sea.   68
MASTER Why, as men do a-land—the great ones eat up
the little ones. I can compare our rich misers to nothing
so fitly as to a whale: a plays and tumbles, driving the
poor fry before him, and at last devours them all at a
mouthful. Such whales have I heard on o'th' land, who
never leave gaping till they swallowed the whole parish:
church, steeple, bells, and all.   75
PERICLES (aside) A pretty moral.
THIRD FISHERMAN But, master, if I had been the sexton,
I would have been that day in the belfry.
SECOND FISHERMAN Why, man?   79
THIRD FISHERMAN Because he should have swallowed me,
too, and when I had been in his belly I would have
kept such a jangling of the bells that he should never
have left till he cast bells, steeple, church, and parish
up again. But if the good King Simonides were of my
mind—   85
PERICLES (aside) Simonides?
THIRD FISHERMAN We would purge the land of these
drones that rob the bee of her honey.
PERICLES (aside)
  How from the finny subject of the sea
  These fishers tell th'infirmities of men,   90
  And from their wat'ry empire recollect
  All that may men approve or men detect!
  ⌜Coming forward⌝ Peace be at your labour, honest
      fishermen.
SECOND FISHERMAN Honest, good fellow? What's that? If
it be a day fits you, scratch't out of the calendar, and
nobody look after it.   96
PERICLES
  May see the sea hath cast upon your coast—
SECOND FISHERMAN What a drunken knave was the sea
to cast thee in our way!
PERICLES
  A man, whom both the waters and the wind   100
  In that vast tennis-court hath made the ball
  For them to play upon, entreats you pity him.
  He asks of you that never used to beg.
MASTER No, friend, cannot you beg? Here's them in our
country of Greece gets more with begging than we can
do with working.   106
SECOND FISHERMAN Canst thou catch any fishes, then?
PERICLES I never practised it.
SECOND FISHERMAN Nay, then thou wilt starve, sure; for
here's nothing to be got nowadays unless thou canst
fish for't.   111
PERICLES
  What I have been, I have forgot to know,
  But what I am, want teaches me to think on:
  A man thronged up with cold; my veins are chill,
  And have no more of life than may suffice   115
  To give my tongue that heat to crave your help,
  Which if you shall refuse, when I am dead,
  For that I am a man, pray see me burièd.
      ⌜He falls down⌝

MASTER Die, quotha? Now, gods forbid't an I have a gown
here! ⌜To Pericles, lifting him up from the ground⌝ Come,
put it on, keep thee warm. Now, afore me, a handsome
fellow! Come, thou shalt go home, and we'll have flesh
for holidays, fish for fasting-days, and moreo'er
puddings and flapjacks, and thou shalt be welcome.
PERICLES I thank you, sir.   125
SECOND FISHERMAN Hark you, my friend, you said you
could not beg?
PERICLES I did but crave.
SECOND FISHERMAN But crave? Then I'll turn craver too,
an so I shall scape whipping.   130
PERICLES Why, are all your beggars whipped, then?
SECOND FISHERMAN O, not all, my friend, not all; for if all
your beggars were whipped I would wish no better
office than to be beadle.
MASTER Thine office, knave—   135
SECOND FISHERMAN Is to draw up the other nets. I'll go.
                          Exit with Third Fisherman
PERICLES (aside)
  How well this honest mirth becomes their labour!
MASTER ⌜seating himself by Pericles⌝ Hark you, sir, do you
know where ye are?
PERICLES Not well.   140
MASTER Why, I'll tell you. This is called Pentapolis, and
our king the good Simonides.
PERICLES
  'The good Simonides' do you call him?
MASTER Ay, sir, and he deserves so to be called for his
peaceable reign and good government.   145
PERICLES
  He is a happy king, since from his subjects
  He gains the name of good by his government.
  How far is his court distant from this shore?
MASTER Marry, sir, some half a day's journey. And I'll
tell you, he hath a fair daughter, and tomorrow is her
birthday, and there are princes and knights come from
all parts of the world to joust and tourney for her love.
PERICLES
  Were but my fortunes answerable
  To my desires I could wish to make one there.   154
MASTER O, sir, things must be as they may, and what a
man cannot get himself, he may lawfully deal for with
his wife's soul.
      Enter the other two Fishermen drawing up a net
SECOND FISHERMAN Help, master, help! Here's a fish hangs
in the net like a poor man's right in the law; 'twill
hardly come out.   160
      ⌜Before help comes, up comes their prize⌝
  Ha, bots on't, 'tis come at last, and 'tis turned to a
  rusty armour.
PERICLES
  An armour, friends? I pray you let me see it.
  (Aside) Thanks, fortune, yet that after all thy crosses
  Thou giv'st me somewhat to repair my losses,   165
  And though it was mine own, part of my heritage
  Which my dead father did bequeath to me
  With this strict charge ev'n as he left his life:
  'Keep it, my Pericles; it hath been a shield

'Twixt me and death,' and pointed to this brace,   170
'For that it saved me, keep it. In like necessity,
The which the Gods forfend, the same may defend thee.'
It kept where I kept, I so dearly loved it,
Till the rough seas that spares not any man
Took it in rage, though calmed have giv'n't again. 175
I thank thee for't. My shipwreck now's no ill,
Since I have here my father gave in 's will.

MASTER What mean you, sir?

PERICLES
To beg of you, kind friends, this coat of worth,
For it was sometime target to a king.   180
I know it by this mark. He loved me dearly,
And for his sake I wish the having of it,
And that you'd guide me to your sov'reign's court,
Where with't I may appear a gentleman.
And if that ever my low fortune's better,   185
I'll pay your bounties, till then rest your debtor.

MASTER Why, wilt thou tourney for the lady?

PERICLES
I'll show the virtue I have learned in arms.

MASTER Why, d'ye take it, and the gods give thee good
   on't!   190

SECOND FISHERMAN Ay, but hark you, my friend, 'twas
   we that made up this garment through the rough
   seams of the waters. There are certain condolements,
   certain vails. I hope, sir, if you thrive, you'll remember
   from whence you had this.   195

PERICLES Believe't, I will.
By your furtherance I'm clothed in steel,
And spite of all the rapture of the sea
This jewel holds his building on my arm.
Unto thy value I will mount myself   200
Upon a courser whose delightsome steps
Shall make the gazer joy to see him tread.
Only, my friends, I yet am unprovided
Of a pair of bases.   204

SECOND FISHERMAN We'll sure provide. Thou shalt have
   my best gown to make thee a pair, and I'll bring thee
   to the court myself.

PERICLES
Then honour be but equal to my will,
This day I'll rise, or else add ill to ill.

           Exeunt with nets and armour

Sc. 6 ⌈*Sennet.*⌉ *Enter King Simonides and Thaisa, with*
     Lords in attendance, ⌈*and sit on two thrones*⌉

KING SIMONIDES
Are the knights ready to begin the triumph?

FIRST LORD They are, my liege,
And stay your coming to present themselves.

KING SIMONIDES
Return them we are ready; and our daughter,
In honour of whose birth these triumphs are,   5
Sits here like beauty's child, whom nature gat
For men to see and, seeing, wonder at.   ⌈*Exit one*⌉

THAISA
It pleaseth you, my father, to express
My commendations great, whose merit's less.

KING SIMONIDES
It's fit it should be so, for princes are   10
A model which heav'n makes like to itself.
As jewels lose their glory if neglected,
So princes their renown, if not respected.
'Tis now your office, daughter, to entertain
The labour of each knight in his device.   15

THAISA
Which, to preserve mine honour, I'll perform.
     ⌈*Flourish.*⌉ *The first knight passes by* ⌈*richly armed,*
     and his page before him, bearing his device on his
     shield, delivers it to the Lady Thaisa⌉

KING SIMONIDES
Who is the first that doth prefer himself?

THAISA
A knight of Sparta, my renownèd father,
And the device he bears upon his shield
Is a black Ethiop reaching at the sun.   20
The word, *Lux tua vita mihi.*
     ⌈*She presents it to the King*⌉

KING SIMONIDES
He loves you well that holds his life of you.
     ⌈*He returns it to the page, who exits with the first*
     knight.⌉
     ⌈*Flourish.*⌉ *The second knight passes by* ⌈*richly*
     armed, and his page before him, bearing his device
     on his shield, delivers it to the Lady Thaisa⌉
Who is the second that presents himself?

THAISA
A prince of Macedon, my royal father,
And the device he bears upon his shield   25
An armèd knight that's conquered by a lady.
The motto thus: *Piùe per dolcezza che per forza.*
     ⌈*She presents it to the King*⌉

KING SIMONIDES
You win him more by lenity than force.
     ⌈*He returns it to the page, who exits with the*
     second knight.⌉
     ⌈*Flourish.*⌉ *The third knight passes by* ⌈*richly armed,*
     and his page before him, bearing his device on his
     shield, delivers it to the Lady Thaisa⌉
And what's the third?

THAISA   The third of Antioch,
And his device a wreath of chivalry.   30
The word, *Me pompae provexit apex.*
     ⌈*She presents it to the King*⌉

KING SIMONIDES
Desire of renown he doth devise,
The which hath drawn him to this enterprise.
     ⌈*He returns it to the page, who exits with the third*
     knight.⌉
     ⌈*Flourish.*⌉ *The fourth knight passes by* ⌈*richly*
     armed, and his page before him, bearing his device
     on his shield, delivers it to the Lady Thaisa⌉
What is the fourth?

THAISA   A knight of Athens bearing
A burning torch that's turnèd upside down.   35
The word, *Qui me alit me extinguit.*
     ⌈*She presents it to the King*⌉

KING SIMONIDES
Which shows that beauty hath this power and will,
Which can as well inflame as it can kill.
⌜*He returns it to the page, who exits with the fourth knight.*⌝
⌜*Flourish.*⌝ *The fifth Knight passes by* ⌜*richly armed, and his page before him, bearing his device on his shield, delivers it to the Lady Thaisa*⌝
And who the fifth?

THAISA   The fifth, a prince of Corinth,
Presents an hand environèd with clouds,   40
Holding out gold that's by the touchstone tried.
The motto thus: *Sic spectanda fides.*
⌜*She presents it to the King*⌝

KING SIMONIDES
So faith is to be looked into.
⌜*He returns it to the page, who exits with the fifth knight.*⌝
⌜*Flourish.*⌝ *The sixth knight, Pericles, in a rusty armour, who, having neither page to deliver his shield nor shield to deliver, presents his device unto the Lady Thaisa*
And what's the sixth and last, the which the knight himself
With such a graceful courtesy delivereth?   45

THAISA
He seems to be a stranger, but his present is
A withered branch that's only green at top.
The motto, *In hac spe vivo.*

KING SIMONIDES
From the dejected state wherein he is
He hopes by you his fortunes yet may flourish.   50

FIRST LORD
He had need mean better than his outward show
Can any way speak in his just commend,
For by his rusty outside he appears
T'have practised more the whipstock than the lance.

SECOND LORD
He well may be a stranger, for he comes   55
Unto an honoured triumph strangely furnished.

THIRD LORD
And on set purpose let his armour rust
Until this day, to scour it in the dust.

KING SIMONIDES
Opinion's but a fool, that makes us scan
The outward habit for the inward man.   60
⌜*Cornetts*⌝
But stay, the knights are coming. We will withdraw
Into the gallery.   ⌜*Exeunt*⌝
⌜*Cornetts and*⌝ *great shouts* ⌜*within*⌝, *and all cry*
'The mean knight!'

Sc. 7 ⌜*A stately banquet is brought in.*⌝ *Enter King Simonides, Thaisa* ⌜*and their train at one door*⌝, *and* ⌜*at another door*⌝ *a Marshal* ⌜*conducting*⌝ *Pericles and the other knights from tilting*
KING SIMONIDES (*to the knights*)
To say you're welcome were superfluous.

To place upon the volume of your deeds
As in a title page your worth in arms
Were more than you expect, or more than's fit,
Since every worth in show commends itself.   5
Prepare for mirth, for mirth becomes a feast.
You're princes, and my guests.

THAISA (*to Pericles*)   But you, my knight and guest;
To whom this wreath of victory I give,
And crown you king of this day's happiness.

PERICLES
'Tis more by fortune, lady, than my merit.   10

KING SIMONIDES
Call it by what you will, the day is yours,
And here I hope is none that envies it.
In framing artists art hath thus decreed,
To make some good, but others to exceed.
You are her laboured scholar. (*To Thaisa*) Come,
    queen o'th' feast—   15
For, daughter, so you are—here take your place.
(*To Marshal*) Marshal the rest as they deserve their
    grace.

KNIGHTS
We are honoured much by good Simonides.

KING SIMONIDES
Your presence glads our days; honour we love,
For who hates honour hates the gods above.   20

MARSHAL (*to Pericles*)
Sir, yonder is your place.

PERICLES   Some other is more fit.

FIRST KNIGHT
Contend not, sir, for we are gentlemen
Have neither in our hearts nor outward eyes
Envied the great, nor shall the low despise.

PERICLES
You are right courteous knights.

KING SIMONIDES   Sit, sir, sit.   25
⌜*Pericles sits directly over against the King and Thaisa. The guests feed apace. Pericles sits still and eats nothing*⌝
[*Aside*] By Jove I wonder, that is king of thoughts,
These cates distaste me, he but thought upon.

THAISA ⌜*aside*⌝
By Juno, that is queen of marriage,
I am amazed all viands that I eat
Do seem unsavoury, wishing him my meat.   30
⌜*To the King*⌝ Sure he's a gallant gentleman.

KING SIMONIDES
He's but a country gentleman.
He's done no more than other knights have done.
He's broke a staff or so, so let it pass.

THAISA ⌜*aside*⌝
To me he seems like diamond to glass.   35

PERICLES ⌜*aside*⌝
Yon king's to me like to my father's picture,
Which tells me in what glory once he was—
Had princes sit like stars about his throne,
And he the sun for them to reverence.
None that beheld him but like lesser lights   40

Did vail their crowns to his supremacy;
Where now his son's a glow-worm in the night,
The which hath fire in darkness, none in light;
Whereby I see that time's the king of men;
He's both their parent and he is their grave,   45
And gives them what he will, not what they crave.
KING SIMONIDES What, are you merry, knights?
⌈THE OTHER KNIGHTS⌉
Who can be other in this royal presence?
KING SIMONIDES
Here with a cup that's stored unto the brim,
As you do love, full to your mistress' lips,   50
We drink this health to you.
⌈THE OTHER KNIGHTS⌉   We thank your grace.
KING SIMONIDES
Yet pause a while. Yon knight doth sit too
    melancholy,
As if the entertainment in our court
Had not a show might countervail his worth.
Note it not you, Thaisa?
THAISA   What is't to me, my father? 55
KING SIMONIDES
O, attend, my daughter. Princes in this
Should live like gods above, who freely give
To everyone that come to honour them.
And princes not so doing are like gnats
Which make a sound but, killed, are wondered at. 60
Therefore to make his entertain more sweet,
Here bear this standing-bowl of wine to him.
THAISA
Alas, my father, it befits not me
Unto a stranger knight to be so bold.
He may my proffer take for an offence,   65
Since men take women's gifts for impudence.
KING SIMONIDES
How? Do as I bid you, or you'll move me else.
THAISA (aside)
Now, by the gods, he could not please me better.
KING SIMONIDES
Furthermore, tell him we desire to know
Of whence he is, his name and parentage.   70
    ⌈Thaisa bears the cup to Pericles⌉
THAISA
The King my father, sir, has drunk to you,
Wishing it so much blood unto your life.
PERICLES
I thank both him and you, and pledge him freely.
    He pledges the King
THAISA
And further he desires to know of you
Of whence you are, your name and parentage.   75
PERICLES
A gentleman of Tyre, my name Pericles,
My education been in arts and arms,
Who, looking for adventures in the world,
Was by the rough unconstant seas bereft
Unfortunately both of ships and men,   80
And after shipwreck driven upon this shore.

    ⌈Thaisa returns to the King⌉
THAISA
He thanks your grace, names himself Pericles,
A gentleman of Tyre, who, seeking adventures,
Was solely by misfortune of the seas
Bereft of ships and men, cast on this shore.   85
KING SIMONIDES
Now by the gods I pity his mishaps,
And will awake him from his melancholy.
    ⌈Simonides, rising from his state, goes forthwith and
    embraces Pericles⌉
Be cheered, for what misfortune hath impaired you of,
Fortune by my help can repair to you.
My self and country both shall be your friends,   90
And presently a goodly milk-white steed
And golden spurs I first bestow upon you,
The prizes due your merit, and ordained
For this day's enterprise.
PERICLES
Your kingly courtesy I thankfully accept.   95
KING SIMONIDES
Come, gentlemen, we sit too long on trifles,
And waste the time which looks for other revels.
Ev'n in your armours, as you are addressed,
Your limbs will well-become a soldier's dance.
I will not have excuse with saying this,   100
'Loud music is too harsh for ladies' heads',
Since they love men in arms as well as beds.
    The knights dance
So this was well asked, 'twas so well performed.
Come, here's a lady that wants breathing too.
(To Pericles) And I have heard, sir, that the knights of
    Tyre   105
Are excellent in making ladies trip,
And that their measures are as excellent.
PERICLES
In those that practise them they are, my lord.
KING SIMONIDES
O, that's as much as you would be denied
Of your fair courtesy. Unclasp, unclasp.   110
    They dance
Thanks, gentlemen, to all. All have done well,
(To Pericles) But you the best.—Lights, pages, to
    conduct
These knights unto their sev'ral lodgings.—Yours, sir,
We have giv'n order should be next our own.
PERICLES I am at your grace's pleasure.   115
KING SIMONIDES
Princes, it is too late to talk of love,
And that's the mark I know you level at.
Therefore each one betake him to his rest;
Tomorrow all for speeding do their best.
                                Exeunt ⌈severally⌉

Sc. 8 Enter Helicanus and Aeschines
HELICANUS
No, Aeschines, know this of me:
Antiochus from incest lived not free,

For which the most high gods, not minding longer
To hold the vengeance that they had in store
Due to this heinous capital offence,   5
Even in the height and pride of all his glory,
When he was seated in a chariot
Of an inestimable value, and
His daughter with him, both apparelled all in jewels,
A fire from heaven came and shrivelled up   10
Their bodies e'en to loathing, for they so stunk
That all those eyes adored them ere their fall
Scorn now their hands should give them burial.
AESCHINES
'Twas very strange.
HELICANUS   And yet but justice, for though
This king were great, his greatness was no guard   15
To bar heav'n's shaft, but sin had his reward.
AESCHINES 'Tis very true.
            Enter three Lords, and stand aside
FIRST LORD
See, not a man in private conference
Or council has respect with him but he.
SECOND LORD
It shall no longer grieve without reproof.   20
THIRD LORD
And cursed be he that will not second it.
FIRST LORD
Follow me, then.—Lord Helicane, a word.
HELICANUS
With me? And welcome. Happy day, my lords.
FIRST LORD
Know that our griefs are risen to the top,
And now at length they overflow their banks.   25
HELICANUS
Your griefs? For what? Wrong not your prince you
            love.
FIRST LORD
Wrong not yourself, then, noble Helicane,
But if the prince do live, let us salute him
Or know what ground's made happy by his step,
And be resolved he lives to govern us,   30
Or dead, give 's cause to mourn his funeral
And leave us to our free election.
SECOND LORD
Whose death indeed's the strongest in our censure,
And knowing this—kingdoms without a head,
Like goodly buildings left without a roof,   35
Soon fall to utter ruin—your noble self,
That best know how to rule and how to reign,
We thus submit unto as sovereign.
ALL ⌐*kneeling*⌐ Live, noble Helicane!
HELICANUS
By honour's cause, forbear your suffrages.   40
If that you love Prince Pericles, forbear.
            ⌐*The lords rise*⌐
Take I your wish I leap into the seas
Where's hourly trouble for a minute's ease,
But if I cannot win you to this love,
A twelvemonth longer then let me entreat you   45

Further to bear the absence of your king;
If in which time expired he not return,
I shall with agèd patience bear your yoke.
Go, seek your noble prince like noble subjects,
And in your search spend your adventurous worth, 50
Whom if you find and win unto return,
You shall like diamonds sit about his crown.
FIRST LORD
To wisdom he's a fool that will not yield,
And since Lord Helicane enjoineth us,
We with our travels will endeavour us.   55
If in the world he live we'll seek him out;
If in his grave he rest, we'll find him there.
HELICANUS
Then you love us, we you, and we'll clasp hands.
When peers thus knit, a kingdom ever stands.   *Exeunt*

Sc. 8a *Enter Pericles with Gentlemen with lights*
FIRST GENTLEMAN
Here is your lodging, sir.
PERICLES   Pray leave me private.
Only for instant solace pleasure me
With some delightful instrument, with which,
And with my former practice, I intend
To pass away the tediousness of night,   5
Though slumbers were more fitting.
FIRST GENTLEMAN   Presently.
                    Exit First Gentleman
SECOND GENTLEMAN
Your will's obeyed in all things, for our master
Commanded you be disobeyed in nothing.
        Enter First Gentleman with a stringed instrument
PERICLES
I thank you. Now betake you to your pillows,
And to the nourishment of quiet sleep.   10
                    Exeunt Gentlemen
        Pericles plays and sings
Day—that hath still that sovereignty to draw back
The empire of the night, though for a while
In darkness she usurp—brings morning on.
I will go give his grace that salutation
Morning requires of me.   *Exit with instrument*

Sc. 9 *Enter King Simonides at one door reading of a
        letter, the Knights enter ⌐at another door⌐ and meet
        him*
FIRST KNIGHT
Good morrow to the good Simonides.
KING SIMONIDES
Knights, from my daughter this I let you know:
That for this twelvemonth she'll not undertake
A married life. Her reason to herself
Is only known, which from her none can get.   5
SECOND KNIGHT
May we not have access to her, my lord?
KING SIMONIDES
Faith, by no means. It is impossible,
She hath so strictly tied her to her chamber.

One twelve moons more she'll wear Diana's liv'ry.
This by the eye of Cynthia hath she vowed,   10
And on her virgin honour will not break it.
THIRD KNIGHT
Loath to bid farewell, we take our leaves.
                                        Exeunt Knights
KING SIMONIDES
So, they are well dispatched. Now to my daughter's
    letter.
She tells me here she'll wed the stranger knight,
Or never more to view nor day nor light.   15
I like that well. Nay, how absolute she's in't,
Not minding whether I dislike or no!
Mistress, t'is well, I do commend your choice,
And will no longer have it be delayed.
        Enter Pericles
Soft, here he comes. I must dissemble that   20
In show, I have determined on in heart.
PERICLES
All fortune to the good Simonides.
KING SIMONIDES
To you as much, sir. I am beholden to you
For your sweet music this last night. My ears,
I do protest, were never better fed   25
With such delightful pleasing harmony.
PERICLES
It is your grace's pleasure to commend,
Not my desert.
KING SIMONIDES Sir, you are music's master.
PERICLES
The worst of all her scholars, my good lord.
KING SIMONIDES
Let me ask you one thing. What think you of my
    daughter?   30
PERICLES
A most virtuous princess.
KING SIMONIDES   And fair, too, is she not?
PERICLES
As a fair day in summer; wondrous fair.
KING SIMONIDES
My daughter, sir, thinks very well of you;
So well indeed that you must be her master
And she will be your scholar; therefore look to it.   35
PERICLES
I am unworthy for her schoolmaster.
KING SIMONIDES
She thinks not so. Peruse this writing else.
        He gives the letter to Pericles, who reads
PERICLES (*aside*)
What's here?—a letter that she loves the knight of
    Tyre?
'Tis the King's subtlety to have my life.
        ⌈*He prostrates himself at the King's feet*⌉
O, seek not to entrap me, gracious lord,   40
A stranger and distressèd gentleman
That never aimed so high to love your daughter,
But bent all offices to honour her.

Never did thought of mine levy offence,
Nor never did my actions yet commence   45
A deed might gain her love or your displeasure.
KING SIMONIDES
Thou liest like a traitor.
PERICLES   Traitor?
KING SIMONIDES   Ay, traitor,
That thus disguised art stol'n into my court
With witchcraft of thy actions to bewitch
The yielding spirit of my tender child.   50
PERICLES ⌈*rising*⌉
Who calls me traitor, unless it be the King,
Ev'n in his bosom I will write the lie.
KING SIMONIDES (*aside*)
Now, by the gods, I do applaud his courage.
PERICLES
My actions are as noble as my blood,
That never relished of a base descent.   55
I came unto your court in search of honour,
And not to be a rebel to your state;
And he that otherwise accounts of me,
This sword shall prove he's honour's enemy.
KING SIMONIDES
I shall prove otherwise, since both your practice   60
And her consent therein is evident
There, by my daughter's hand, as she can witness.
        Enter Thaisa
PERICLES (*to Thaisa*)
Then as you are as virtuous as fair,
By what you hope of heaven or desire
By your best wishes here i'th' world fulfilled,   65
Resolve your angry father if my tongue
Did e'er solicit, or my hand subscribe
To any syllable made love to you.
THAISA Why, sir, say if you had,
Who takes offence at that would make me glad?   70
KING SIMONIDES
How, minion, are you so peremptory?
(*Aside*) I am glad on't.—Is this a fit match for you?
A straggling Theseus, born we know not where,
One that hath neither blood nor merit
For thee to hope for, or himself to challenge   75
Of thy perfections e'en the least allowance.
THAISA (*kneeling*)
Suppose his birth were base, when that his life
Shows that he is not so, yet he hath virtue,
The very ground of all nobility,
Enough to make him noble. I entreat you   80
To remember that I am in love,
The power of which love cannot be confined
By th' power of your will. Most royal father,
What with my pen I have in secret written
With my tongue now I openly confirm,   85
Which is I have no life but in his love,
Nor any being but in joying of his worth.
KING SIMONIDES
Equals to equals, good to good is joined.

This not being so, the bavin of your mind
In rashness kindled must again be quenched,   90
Or purchase our displeasure.—And for you, sir,
First learn to know I banish you my court,
And yet I scorn our rage should stoop so low.
For your ambition, sir, I'll have your life.

THAISA (to Pericles)
For every drop of blood he sheds of yours   95
He'll draw another from his only child.

KING SIMONIDES
I'll tame you, yea, I'll bring you in subjection.
Will you not having my consent
Bestow your love and your affections
Upon a stranger?—(aside) who for aught I know   100
May be, nor can I think the contrary,
As great in blood as I myself.
            ⌈He catches Thaisa rashly by the hand⌉
Therefore hear you, mistress: either frame your will to
            mine—
            ⌈He catches Pericles rashly by the hand⌉
And you, sir, hear you: either be ruled by me—
Or I shall make you
            ⌈He claps their hands together⌉
                          man and wife.   105
Nay, come, your hands and lips must seal it too,
            Pericles and Thaisa kiss
And being joined, I'll thus your hopes destroy,
            ⌈He parts them⌉
And for your further grief, God give you joy.
What, are you pleased?

THAISA   Yes, (to Pericles) if you love me, sir.

PERICLES
Ev'n as my life my blood that fosters it.   110

KING SIMONIDES
What, are you both agreed?

PERICLES and THAISA   Yes, if't please your majesty.

KING SIMONIDES
It pleaseth me so well that I will see you wed,
Then with what haste you can, get you to bed.
                                              Exeunt

Sc. 10 Enter Gower

GOWER
Now sleep y-slackèd hath the rout,
No din but snores the house about,
Made louder by the o'erfed breast
Of this most pompous marriage feast.
The cat with eyne of burning coal   5
Now couches fore the mouse's hole,
And crickets sing at th'oven's mouth
As the blither for their drouth.
Hymen hath brought the bride to bed,
Where by the loss of maidenhead   10
A babe is moulded. Be attent,
And time that is so briefly spent
With your fine fancies quaintly eche.
What's dumb in show, I'll plain with speech.

            Dumb show.
Enter Pericles and Simonides at one door with
attendants. A messenger comes ⌈hastily⌉ in to them,
kneels, and gives Pericles a letter. Pericles shows it
Simonides; the lords kneel to him. Then enter
Thaisa with child, with Lychorida, a nurse. The
King shows her the letter. She rejoices. She and
Pericles take leave of her father and depart with
Lychorida at one door; Simonides ⌈and attendants⌉
depart at another
By many a dern and painful perch   15
Of Pericles the care-full search,
By the four opposing coigns
Which the world together joins,
Is made with all due diligence
That horse and sail and high expense   20
Can stead the quest. At last from Tyre
Fame answering the most strange enquire,
To th' court of King Simonides
Are letters brought, the tenor these:
Antiochus and his daughter dead,   25
The men of Tyrus on the head
Of Helicanus would set on
The crown of Tyre, but he will none.
The mutiny here he hastes t'appease,
Says to 'em if King Pericles   30
Come not home in twice six moons
He, obedient to their dooms,
Will take the crown. The sum of this
Brought hither to Pentapolis
Y-ravishèd the regions round,   35
And everyone with claps can sound
'Our heir-apparent is a king!
Who dreamt, who thought of such a thing?'
Brief he must hence depart to Tyre;
His queen with child makes her desire—   40
Which who shall cross?—along to go.
Omit we all their dole and woe.
Lychorida her nurse she takes,
And so to sea. Their vessel shakes
On Neptune's billow. Half the flood   45
Hath their keel cut, but fortune's mood
Varies again. The grizzled north
Disgorges such a tempest forth
That as a duck for life that dives,
So up and down the poor ship drives.   50
The lady shrieks, and well-a-near
Does fall in travail with her fear,
And what ensues in this fell storm
Shall for itself itself perform;
I nill relate; action may   55
Conveniently the rest convey,
Which might not what by me is told.
In your imagination hold
This stage the ship, upon whose deck
The sea-tossed Pericles appears to speke.   Exit   60

Sc. 11 ⌐*Thunder and lightning.*⌐ *Enter Pericles a-shipboard*
PERICLES
The god of this great vast rebuke these surges
Which wash both heav'n and hell; and thou that hast
Upon the winds command, bind them in brass,
Having called them from the deep. O still
Thy deaf'ning dreadful thunders, gently quench   5
Thy nimble sulph'rous flashes.—O, ho, Lychorida!
How does my queen?—Thou stormest venomously.
Wilt thou spit all thyself? The seaman's whistle
Is as a whisper in the ears of death,
Unheard.—Lychorida!—Lucina, O!   10
Divinest patroness, and midwife gentle
To those that cry by night, convey thy deity
Aboard our dancing boat, make swift the pangs
Of my queen's travails!—Now, Lychorida.
          Enter Lychorida with an infant
LYCHORIDA
Here is a thing too young for such a place,   15
Who, if it had conceit, would die, as I
Am like to do. Take in your arms this piece
Of your dead queen.
PERICLES   How, how, Lychorida?
LYCHORIDA
Patience, good sir, do not assist the storm.
Here's all that is left living of your queen,   20
A little daughter. For the sake of it
Be manly, and take comfort.
PERICLES   O you gods!
Why do you make us love your goodly gifts,
And snatch them straight away? We here below
Recall not what we give, and therein may   25
Use honour with you.
LYCHORIDA   Patience, good sir,
E'en for this charge.
          She gives him the infant. ⌐*Pericles, looking*
          mournfully upon it, shakes his head, and weeps⌐
PERICLES   Now mild may be thy life,
For a more blust'rous birth had never babe;
Quiet and gentle thy conditions, for
Thou art the rudeliest welcome to this world   30
That e'er was prince's child; happy what follows.
Thou hast as chiding a nativity
As fire, air, water, earth, and heav'n can make
To herald thee from th' womb. Poor inch of nature,
Ev'n at the first thy loss is more than can   35
Thy partage quit with all thou canst find here.
Now the good gods throw their best eyes upon't.
          Enter ⌐*the Master*⌐ *and a Sailor*
⌐MASTER⌐ What, courage, sir! God save you.
PERICLES
Courage enough, I do not fear the flaw;
It hath done to me its worst. Yet for the love   40
Of this poor infant, this fresh new seafarer,
I would it would be quiet.
⌐MASTER⌐ (*calling*) Slack the bow-lines, there.—Thou wilt
not, wilt thou? Blow, and split thyself.
SAILOR But searoom, and the brine and cloudy billow kiss
the moon, I care not.   46

⌐MASTER⌐ (*to Pericles*) Sir, your queen must overboard.
The sea works high, the wind is loud, and will not lie
till the ship be cleared of the dead.
PERICLES
That's but your superstition.   50
⌐MASTER⌐ Pardon us, sir; with us at sea it hath been still
observed, and we are strong in custom. Therefore briefly
yield 'er, for she must overboard straight.
PERICLES
As you think meet. Most wretched queen!
LYCHORIDA   Here she lies, sir.
          She ⌐*draws the curtains and discovers*⌐ *the body of*
          Thaisa in a ⌐*bed. Pericles gives Lychorida the infant*⌐
PERICLES (*to Thaisa*)
A terrible childbed hast thou had, my dear,   55
No light, no fire. Th'unfriendly elements
Forgot thee utterly, nor have I time
To give thee hallowed to thy grave, but straight
Must cast thee, scarcely coffined, in the ooze,
Where, for a monument upon thy bones   60
And aye-remaining lamps, the belching whale
And humming water must o'erwhelm thy corpse,
Lying with simple shells.—O Lychorida,
Bid Nestor bring me spices, ink, and paper,
My casket and my jewels, and bid Nicander   65
Bring me the satin coffer. Lay the babe
Upon the pillow. Hie thee whiles I say
A priestly farewell to her. Suddenly, woman.
                    Exit Lychorida
⌐SAILOR⌐ Sir, we have a chest beneath the hatches caulked
and bitumed ready.   70
PERICLES
I thank thee. ⌐*To the Master*⌐ Mariner, say, what coast
is this?
⌐MASTER⌐
We are near Tarsus.
PERICLES   Thither, gentle mariner,
Alter thy course from Tyre. When canst thou reach it?
⌐MASTER⌐
By break of day, if the wind cease.
PERICLES   Make for Tarsus.
There will I visit Cleon, for the babe   75
Cannot hold out to Tyrus. There I'll leave it
At careful nursing. Go thy ways, good mariner.
I'll bring the body presently.
          ⌐*Exit Master at one door and Sailor beneath*
          the hatches. Exit Pericles to Thaisa,
          closing the curtains⌐

Sc. 12 *Enter Lord Cerimon with a* ⌐*poor man and a*⌐
          servant
CERIMON
Philemon, ho!
          Enter Philemon
PHILEMON   Doth my lord call?
CERIMON
Get fire and meat for those poor men.
                    ⌐*Exit Philemon*⌐
'T'as been a turbulent and stormy night.

SERVANT
I have seen many, but such a night as this
Till now I ne'er endured.   5
CERIMON
Your master will be dead ere you return.
There's nothing can be ministered in nature
That can recover him. ⌈*To poor man*⌉ Give this to th'
    pothecary
And tell me how it works.
                    ⌈*Exeunt poor man and servant*⌉
        Enter two Gentlemen
FIRST GENTLEMAN   Good morrow.
SECOND GENTLEMAN
Good morrow to your lordship.
CERIMON   Gentlemen,   10
Why do you stir so early?
FIRST GENTLEMAN   Sir,
Our lodgings, standing bleak upon the sea,
Shook as the earth did quake.
The very principals did seem to rend
And all to topple. Pure surprise and fear   15
Made me to quit the house.
SECOND GENTLEMAN
That is the cause we trouble you so early;
'Tis not our husbandry.
CERIMON   O, you say well.
FIRST GENTLEMAN
But I much marvel that your lordship should,
Having rich tire about you, at this hour   20
Shake off the golden slumber of repose. 'Tis most
    strange,
Nature to be so conversant with pain,
Being thereto not compelled.
CERIMON   I held it ever
Virtue and cunning were endowments greater
Than nobleness and riches. Careless heirs   25
May the two latter darken and dispend,
But immortality attends the former,
Making a man a god. 'Tis known I ever
Have studied physic, through which secret art,
By turning o'er authorities, I have,   30
Together with my practice, made familiar
To me and to my aid the blest infusions
That dwells in vegetives, in metals, stones, .
And so can speak of the disturbances
That nature works, and of her cures, which doth
    give me   35
A more content and cause of true delight
Than to be thirsty after tott'ring honour,
Or tie my pleasure up in silken bags
To glad the fool and death.
SECOND GENTLEMAN   Your honour has
Through Ephesus poured forth your charity,   40
And hundreds call themselves your creatures who by
    you
Have been restored. And not alone your knowledge,
Your personal pain, but e'en your purse still open
Hath built Lord Cerimon such strong renown
As time shall never—   45

Enter ⌈*Philemon and one or*⌉ *two with a chest*
⌈PHILEMON⌉ So, lift there.
CERIMON What's that?
⌈PHILEMON⌉ Sir, even now
The sea tossed up upon our shore this chest.
'Tis off some wreck.
CERIMON   Set't down. Let's look upon't.   50
SECOND GENTLEMAN
'Tis like a coffin, sir.
CERIMON   Whate'er it be,
'Tis wondrous heavy.—Did the sea cast it up?
⌈PHILEMON⌉
I never saw so huge a billow, sir,
Or a more eager.
CERIMON   Wrench it open straight.
        The others start to work
If the sea's stomach be o'ercharged with gold   55
'Tis by a good constraint of queasy fortune
It belches upon us.
SECOND GENTLEMAN   'Tis so, my lord.
CERIMON
How close 'tis caulked and bitumed!
        ⌈*They force the lid*⌉
                        Soft, it smells
Most sweetly in my sense.
SECOND GENTLEMAN   A delicate odour.
CERIMON
As ever hit my nostril. So, up with it.   60
        They take the lid off
O you most potent gods! What's here—a corpse?
SECOND GENTLEMAN
Most strange.
CERIMON   Shrouded in cloth of state, and crowned,
Balmed and entreasured with full bags of spices.
A passport, too!
        He takes a paper from the chest
Apollo perfect me i'th' characters.   65
    'Here I give to understand,
    If e'er this coffin drives a-land,
    I, King Pericles, have lost
    This queen worth all our mundane cost.
    Who finds her, give her burying;   70
    She was the daughter of a king.
    Besides this treasure for a fee,
    The gods requite his charity.'
If thou liv'st, Pericles, thou hast a heart
That even cracks for woe. This chanced tonight.   75
SECOND GENTLEMAN
Most likely, sir.
CERIMON   Nay, certainly tonight,
For look how fresh she looks. They were too rash
That threw her in the sea. Make a fire within.
Fetch hither all my boxes in my closet.
                        ⌈*Exit Philemon*⌉
Death may usurp on nature many hours,   80
And yet the fire of life kindle again
The o'erpressed spirits. I have heard
Of an Egyptian nine hours dead
Who was by good appliances recovered.

Enter ⌈Philemon⌉ with napkins and fire
Well said, well said, the fire and cloths.   85
The still and woeful music that we have,
Cause it to sound, beseech you.
       Music
                              The vial once more.
How thou stirr'st, thou block! The music there!
I pray you give her air. Gentlemen,
This queen will live. Nature awakes, a warmth   90
Breathes out of her. She hath not been entranced
Above five hours. See how she 'gins to blow
Into life's flow'r again.
FIRST GENTLEMAN   The heavens
Through you increase our wonder, and set up
Your fame for ever.
CERIMON   She is alive. Behold,   95
Her eyelids, cases to those heav'nly jewels
Which Pericles hath lost,
Begin to part their fringes of bright gold.
The diamonds of a most praisèd water
Doth appear to make the world twice rich.—Live,   100
And make us weep to hear your fate, fair creature,
Rare as you seem to be.
       She moves
THAISA   O dear Diana,
Where am I? Where's my lord? What world is this?
SECOND GENTLEMAN
Is not this strange?
FIRST GENTLEMAN   Most rare.
CERIMON   Hush, gentle neighbours.
Lend me your hands. To the next chamber bear her.
Get linen. Now this matter must be looked to,   106
For her relapse is mortal. Come, come,
And Aesculapius guide us.
                    They carry her away. Exeunt

Sc. 13 *Enter Pericles at Tarsus, with Cleon and Dionyza,*
       and Lychorida with a babe
PERICLES
Most honoured Cleon, I must needs be gone.
My twelve months are expired, and Tyrus stands
In a litigious peace. You and your lady
Take from my heart all thankfulness. The gods
Make up the rest upon you!
CLEON   Your strokes of fortune,   5
Though they hurt you mortally, yet glance
Full woundingly on us.
DIONYZA   O your sweet queen!
That the strict fates had pleased you'd brought her
       hither
T'have blessed mine eyes with her!
PERICLES   We cannot but obey
The pow'rs above us. Should I rage and roar   10
As doth the sea she lies in, yet the end
Must be as 'tis. My gentle babe Marina,
Whom for she was born at sea I have named so,
Here I charge your charity withal, and leave her

The infant of your care, beseeching you   15
To give her princely training, that she may be
Mannered as she is born.
CLEON   Fear not, my lord, but think
Your grace, that fed my country with your corn—
For which the people's pray'rs still fall upon you—
Must in your child be thought on. If neglection   20
Should therein make me vile, the common body
By you relieved would force me to my duty.
But if to that my nature need a spur,
The gods revenge it upon me and mine
To t'1' end of generation.
PERICLES   I believe you.   25
Your honour and your goodness teach me to't
Without your vows.—Till she be married, madam,
By bright Diana, whom we honour all,
Unscissored shall this hair of mine remain,
Though I show ill in't. So I take my leave.   30
Good madam, make me blessèd in your care
In bringing up my child.
DIONYZA   I have one myself,
Who shall not be more dear to my respect
Than yours, my lord.
PERICLES   Madam, my thanks and prayers.
CLEON
We'll bring your grace e'en to the edge o'th' shore,   35
Then give you up to th' masted Neptune and
The gentlest winds of heaven.
PERICLES
I will embrace your offer.—Come, dear'st madam.—
O, no tears, Lychorida, no tears.
Look to your little mistress, on whose grace   40
You may depend hereafter.—Come, my lord.   *Exeunt*

Sc. 14 *Enter Cerimon and Thaisa*
CERIMON
Madam, this letter and some certain jewels
Lay with you in your coffer, which are all
At your command. Know you the character?
THAISA
It is my lord's. That I was shipped at sea
I well remember, ev'n on my eaning time,   5
But whether there delivered, by th' holy gods
I cannot rightly say. But since King Pericles,
My wedded lord, I ne'er shall see again,
A vestal liv'ry will I take me to,
And never more have joy.   10
CERIMON
Madam, if this you purpose as ye speak,
Diana's temple is not distant far,
Where till your date expire you may abide.
Moreover, if you please a niece of mine
Shall there attend you.   15
THAISA
My recompense is thanks, that's all,
Yet my good will is great, though the gift small.
                              Exeunt

Sc. 15 *Enter Gower*

GOWER
Imagine Pericles arriued at Tyre,
Welcomed and settled to his own desire.
His woeful queen we leave at Ephesus,
Unto Diana there 's a votaress.
  Now to Marina bend your mind, 5
  Whom our fast-growing scene must find
  At Tarsus, and by Cleon trained
  In music, letters; who hath gained
  Of education all the grace,
  Which makes her both the heart and place 10
  Of gen'ral wonder. But, alack,
  That monster envy, oft the wrack
  Of earnèd praise, Marina's life
  Seeks to take off by treason's knife,
  And in this kind our Cleon has 15
  One daughter, and a full-grown lass
  E'en ripe for marriage-rite. This maid
  Hight Philoten, and it is said
  For certain in our story she
  Would ever with Marina be, 20
  Be't when they weaved the sleided silk
  With fingers long, small, white as milk;
  Or when she would with sharp nee'le wound
  The cambric which she made more sound
  By hurting it, or when to th' lute 25
  She sung, and made the night bird mute,
  That still records with moan; or when
  She would with rich and constant pen
  Vail to her mistress Dian. Still
  This Philoten contends in skill 30
  With absolute Marina; so
  With dove of Paphos might the crow
  Vie feathers white. Marina gets
  All praises which are paid as debts,
  And not as given. This so darks 35
  In Philoten all graceful marks
  That Cleon's wife with envy rare
  A present murder does prepare
  For good Marina, that her daughter
  Might stand peerless by this slaughter. 40
  The sooner her vile thoughts to stead
  Lychorida, our nurse, is dead,
  ⌈*A tomb is revealed*⌉
  And cursèd Dionyza hath
  The pregnant instrument of wrath
  Pressed for this blow. Th'unborn event 45
  I do commend to your content,
  Only I carry wingèd Time
  Post on the lame feet of my rhyme,
  Which never could I so convey
  Unless your thoughts went on my way. 50
  ⌈*Enter Dionyza with Leonine*⌉
  Dionyza does appear,
  With Leonine, a murderer.

DIONYZA
  Thy oath remember. Thou hast sworn to do't.

'Tis but a blow, which never shall be known.
Thou canst not do a thing i'th' world so soon 55
To yield thee so much profit. Let not conscience,
Which is but cold, or fanning love thy bosom
Unflame too nicely, nor let pity, which
E'en women have cast off, melt thee; but be
A soldier to thy purpose.

LEONINE   I will do't; 60
  But yet she is a goodly creature.

DIONYZA
The fitter then the gods should have her.
    Enter Marina ⌈*to the tomb*⌉ *with a basket of flowers*
Here she comes, weeping her only nurse's death.
Thou art resolved.

LEONINE   I am resolved.

MARINA
No, I will rob Tellus of her weed 65
To strew thy grave with flow'rs. The yellows, blues,
The purple violets and marigolds
Shall as a carpet hang upon thy tomb
While summer days doth last. Ay me, poor maid,
Born in a tempest when my mother died, 70
This world to me is but a ceaseless storm
Whirring me from my friends.

DIONYZA
How now, Marina, why do you keep alone?
How chance my daughter is not with you?
Do not consume your blood with sorrowing. 75
Have you a nurse of me. Lord, how your favour
Is changed with this unprofitable woe!
Give me your flowers. Come, o'er the sea margin
Walk with Leonine. The air is piercing there,
And quick; it sharps the stomach. Come, Leonine, 80
Take her by th' arm. Walk with her.

MARINA   No, I pray you,
  I'll not bereave you of your servant.

DIONYZA   Come, come,
I love the King your father and yourself
With more than foreign heart. We ev'ry day
Expect him here. When he shall come and find 85
Our paragon to all reports thus blasted,
He will repent the breadth of his great voyage,
Blame both my lord and me, that we have taken
No care to your best courses. Go, I pray you,
Walk and be cheerful once again; resume 90
That excellent complexion which did steal
The eyes of young and old. Care not for me.
I can go home alone.

MARINA   Well, I will go,
  But truly I have no desire to it.

DIONYZA
Nay, I know 'tis good for you. Walk half an hour, 95
Leonine, at the least; remember
What I have said.

LEONINE   I warr'nt you, madam.

DIONYZA (*to Marina*)
  I'll leave you, my sweet lady, for a while.

Pray you walk softly, do not heat your blood.
What, I must have care of you!
MARINA   My thanks, sweet madam.
                                            Exit Dionyza
Is this wind westerly that blows?
LEONINE   South-west.   101
MARINA
When I was born the wind was north.
LEONINE   Was't so?
MARINA
My father, as nurse says, did never fear,
But cried 'Good seamen' to the mariners,
Galling his kingly hands with haling ropes,   105
And, clasping to the mast, endured a sea
That almost burst the deck.
LEONINE When was this?
MARINA When I was born.
Never was waves nor wind more violent.   110
Once from the ladder tackle washes off
A canvas-climber. 'Ha!' says one, 'wolt out?'
And with a dropping industry they skip
From stem to stern. The boatswain whistles, and
The master calls and trebles their confusion. 115
LEONINE Come, say your prayers.
MARINA What mean you?
LEONINE
If you require a little space for prayer
I grant it. Pray, but be not tedious.
The gods are quick of ear, and I am sworn   120
To do my work with haste.
MARINA   Why would you kill me?
LEONINE
To satisfy my lady.
MARINA   Why would she have me killed?
Now, as I can remember, by my troth
I never did her hurt in all my life.
I never spake bad word, nor did ill turn   125
To any living creature. Believe me, la.
I never killed a mouse nor hurt a fly.
I trod once on a worm against my will,
But I wept for it. How have I offended
Wherein my death might yield her any profit   130
Or my life imply her danger?
LEONINE   My commission
Is not to reason of the deed, but do't.
MARINA
You will not do't for all the world, I hope.
You are well favoured, and your looks foreshow
You have a gentle heart. I saw you lately   135
When you caught hurt in parting two that fought.
Good sooth, it showed well in you. Do so now.
Your lady seeks my life. Come you between,
And save poor me, the weaker.
LEONINE ⌈*drawing out his sword*⌉ I am sworn,
And will dispatch.   140
        Enter Pirates ⌈*running*⌉
FIRST PIRATE Hold, villain.
        Leonine runs away ⌈*and hides behind the tomb*⌉

SECOND PIRATE A prize, a prize.
THIRD PIRATE Half-part, mates, half-part. Come, let's have
her aboard suddenly.
                        Exeunt Pirates ⌈*carrying*⌉ *Marina*
        Leonine ⌈*steals back*⌉
LEONINE
These roguing thieves serve the great pirate Valdes.
An they have seized Marina, let her go.   146
There's no hope she'll return. I'll swear she's dead
And thrown into the sea; but I'll see further.
Perhaps they will but please themselves upon her,
Not carry her aboard. If she remain,   150
Whom they have ravished must by me be slain.
                        Exit. ⌈*The tomb is concealed*⌉

Sc. 16 ⌈*A brothel sign.*⌉ *Enter the Pander, his wife the*
        Bawd, and their man Boult
PANDER Boult.
BOULT Sir.
PANDER Search the market narrowly. Mytilene is full of
gallants. We lose too much money this mart by being
wenchless.   5
BAWD We were never so much out of creatures. We have
but poor three, and they can do no more than they
can do, and they with continual action are even as
good as rotten.   9
PANDER Therefore let's have fresh ones, whate'er we pay
for them. If there be not a conscience to be used in
every trade, we shall never prosper.
BAWD Thou sayst true. 'Tis not our bringing up of poor
bastards—as I think I have brought up some eleven—
BOULT Ay, to eleven, and brought them down again. But
shall I search the market?   16
BAWD What else, man? The stuff we have, a strong wind
will blow it to pieces, they are so pitifully sodden.
PANDER Thou sayst true. They're too unwholesome, o'
conscience. The poor Transylvanian is dead that lay
with the little baggage.   21
BOULT Ay, she quickly pooped him, she made him roast
meat for worms. But I'll go search the market.   *Exit*
PANDER Three or four thousand chequins were as pretty
a proportion to live quietly, and so give over.   25
BAWD Why to give over, I pray you? Is it a shame to get
when we are old?
PANDER O, our credit comes not in like the commodity,
nor the commodity wages not with the danger. Therefore if in our youths we could pick up some pretty
estate, 'twere not amiss to keep our door hatched.
Besides, the sore terms we stand upon with the gods
will be strong with us for giving o'er.
BAWD Come, other sorts offend as well as we.   34
PANDER As well as we? Ay, and better too; we offend
worse. Neither is our profession any mystery, it's no
calling. But here comes Boult.
        Enter Boult with the Pirates and Marina
BOULT ⌈*to the Pirates*⌉ Come your ways, my masters, you
say she's a virgin?
A PIRATE O sir, we doubt it not.   40

BOULT (*to Pander*) Master, I have gone through for this piece you see. If you like her, so; if not, I have lost my earnest.

BAWD Boult, has she any qualities? 44

BOULT She has a good face, speaks well, and has excellent good clothes. There's no farther necessity of qualities can make her be refused.

BAWD What's her price, Boult? 48

BOULT I cannot be bated one doit of a hundred sesterces.

PANDER (*to Pirates*) Well, follow me, my masters. You shall have your money presently. (*To Bawd*) Wife, take her in, instruct her what she has to do, that she may not be raw in her entertainment.

Exeunt Pander and Pirates

BAWD Boult, take you the marks of her, the colour of her hair, complexion, height, her age, with warrant of her virginity, and cry 'He that will give most shall have her first.' Such a maidenhead were no cheap thing if men were as they have been. Get this done as I command you. 59

BOULT Performance shall follow. *Exit*

MARINA
Alack that Leonine was so slack, so slow.
He should have struck, not spoke; or that these pirates,
Not enough barbarous, had but o'erboard thrown me
To seek my mother.

BAWD Why lament you, pretty one? 65

MARINA That I am pretty.

BAWD Come, the gods have done their part in you.

MARINA I accuse them not.

BAWD You are light into my hands, where you are like to live. 70

MARINA The more my fault
To scape his hands where I was like to die.

BAWD Ay, and you shall live in pleasure.

MARINA No. 74

BAWD Yes, indeed shall you, and taste gentlemen of all fashions. You shall fare well. You shall have the difference of all complexions. What, do you stop your ears?

MARINA Are you a woman? 79

BAWD What would you have me be an I be not a woman?

MARINA
An honest woman, or not a woman.

BAWD Marry, whip the gosling! I think I shall have something to do with you. Come, you're a young foolish sapling, and must be bowed as I would have you.

MARINA The gods defend me! 85

BAWD If it please the gods to defend you by men, then men must comfort you, men must feed you, men must stir you up.

Enter Boult

Now, sir, hast thou cried her through the market? 89

BOULT I have cried her almost to the number of her hairs. I have drawn her picture with my voice.

BAWD And I prithee tell me, how dost thou find the inclination of the people, especially of the younger sort?

BOULT Faith, they listened to me as they would have hearkened to their fathers' testament. There was a Spaniard's mouth watered as he went to bed to her very description. 97

BAWD We shall have him here tomorrow with his best ruff on.

BOULT Tonight, tonight. But mistress, do you know the French knight that cowers i' the hams? 101

BAWD Who, Monsieur Veroles?

BOULT Ay, he. He offered to cut a caper at the proclamation, but he made a groan at it, and swore he would see her tomorrow. 105

BAWD Well, well, as for him, he brought his disease hither. Here he does but repair it. I know he will come in our shadow to scatter his crowns of the sun.

BOULT Well, if we had of every nation a traveller, we should lodge them all with this sign. 110

BAWD (*to Marina*) Pray you, come hither a while. You have fortunes coming upon you. Mark me, you must seem to do that fearfully which you commit willingly, to despise profit where you have most gain. To weep that you live as ye do makes pity in your lovers. Seldom but that pity begets you a good opinion, and that opinion a mere profit.

MARINA I understand you not.

BOULT (*to Bawd*) O, take her home, mistress, take her home. These blushes of hers must be quenched with some present practice. 121

BAWD Thou sayst true, i'faith, so they must, for your bride goes to that with shame which is her way to go with warrant.

BOULT Faith, some do and some do not. But mistress, if I have bargained for the joint— 126

BAWD Thou mayst cut a morsel off the spit.

BOULT I may so.

BAWD Who should deny it? (*To Marina*) Come, young one, I like the manner of your garments well. 130

BOULT Ay, by my faith, they shall not be changed yet.

BAWD (*giving him money*) Boult, spend thou that in the town. Report what a sojourner we have. You'll lose nothing by custom. When nature framed this piece she meant thee a good turn. Therefore say what a paragon she is, and thou reapest the harvest out of thine own setting forth.

BOULT I warrant you, mistress, thunder shall not so awake the beds of eels as my giving out her beauty stirs up the lewdly inclined. I'll bring home some tonight. 140
⌈*Exit*⌉

BAWD Come your ways, follow me.

MARINA
If fires be hot, knives sharp, or waters deep,
Untied I still my virgin knot will keep.
Diana aid my purpose. 144

BAWD What have we to do with Diana? Pray you, will you go with me? *Exeunt.* ⌈*The sign is removed*⌉

Sc. 17 *Enter* ⌈*in mourning garments*⌉ *Cleon and Dionyza*
DIONYZA
Why, are you foolish? Can it be undone?

CLEON

    O Dionyza, such a piece of slaughter
    The sun and moon ne'er looked upon.

DIONYZA

    I think you'll turn a child again.

CLEON

    Were I chief lord of all this spacious world   5
    I'd give it to undo the deed. A lady
    Much less in blood than virtue, yet a princess
    To equal any single crown o'th' earth
    I'th' justice of compare. O villain Leonine,
    Whom thou hast poisoned too,   10
    If thou hadst drunk to him 't'ad been a kindness
    Becoming well thy fact. What canst thou say
    When noble Pericles demands his child?

DIONYZA

    That she is dead. Nurses are not the fates.
    To foster is not ever to preserve.   15
    She died at night. I'll say so. Who can cross it,
    Unless you play the pious innocent
    And, for an honest attribute, cry out
    'She died by foul play.'

CLEON   O, go to. Well, well,
    Of all the faults beneath the heav'ns the gods   20
    Do like this worst.

DIONYZA   Be one of those that thinks
    The petty wrens of Tarsus will fly hence
    And open this to Pericles. I do shame
    To think of what a noble strain you are,
    And of how cowed a spirit.

CLEON   To such proceeding   25
    Whoever but his approbation added,
    Though not his prime consent, he did not flow
    From honourable sources.

DIONYZA   Be it so, then.
    Yet none does know but you how she came dead,
    Nor none can know, Leonine being gone.   30
    She did distain my child, and stood between
    Her and her fortunes. None would look on her,
    But cast their gazes on Marina's face
    Whilst ours was blurted at, and held a malkin
    Not worth the time of day. It pierced me through,   35
    And though you call my course unnatural,
    You not your child well loving, yet I find
    It greets me as an enterprise of kindness
    Performed to your sole daughter.

CLEON Heavens forgive it.   40

DIONYZA And as for Pericles,
    What should he say? We wept after her hearse,
    And yet we mourn. Her monument
    Is almost finished, and her epitaphs
    In glitt'ring golden characters express   45
    A gen'ral praise to her and care in us,
    At whose expense 'tis done.

CLEON   Thou art like the harpy,
    Which, to betray, dost, with thine angel face,
    Seize in thine eagle talons.

DIONYZA

    Ye're like one that superstitiously   50
    Do swear to th' gods that winter kills the flies,
    But yet I know you'll do as I advise.   *Exeunt*

Sc. 18 *Enter Gower*

GOWER

    Thus time we waste, and long leagues make we short,
    Sail seas in cockles, have and wish but for't,
    Making to take imagination
    From bourn to bourn, region to region.
    By you being pardoned, we commit no crime   5
    To use one language in each sev'ral clime
    Where our scene seems to live. I do beseech you
    To learn of me, who stand i'th' gaps to teach you
    The stages of our story: Pericles
    Is now again thwarting the wayward seas,   10
    Attended on by many a lord and knight,
    To see his daughter, all his life's delight.
    Old Helicanus goes along. Behind
    Is left to govern, if you bear in mind,
    Old Aeschines, whom Helicanus late   15
    Advanced in Tyre to great and high estate.
    Well sailing ships and bounteous winds have brought
    This king to Tarsus—think his pilot thought;
    So with his steerage shall your thoughts go on—
    To fetch his daughter home, who first is gone.   20
    Like motes and shadows see them move a while;
    Your ears unto your eyes I'll reconcile.

               Dumb show.

    Enter Pericles at one door with all his train, Cleon
    and Dionyza ⌈in mourning garments⌉ at the other.
    Cleon ⌈draws the curtain and⌉ shows Pericles the
    tomb, whereat Pericles makes lamentation, puts on
    sack-cloth, and in a mighty passion departs,
    followed by his train. Cleon and Dionyza depart at
    the other door

    See how belief may suffer by foul show.
    This borrowed passion stands for true-owed woe,
    And Pericles, in sorrow all devoured,   25
    With sighs shot through, and biggest tears o'ershow'red,
    Leaves Tarsus, and again embarks. He swears
    Never to wash his face nor cut his hairs.
    He puts on sack-cloth, and to sea. He bears
    A tempest which his mortal vessel tears,   30
    And yet he rides it out. Now please you wit
    The epitaph is for Marina writ
    By wicked Dionyza.

      He reads Marina's epitaph on the tomb
    'The fairest, sweetest, best lies here,
    Who withered in her spring of year.   35
    In nature's garden, though by growth a bud,
    She was the chiefest flower: she was good.'
    No visor does become black villainy
    So well as soft and tender flattery.
    Let Pericles believe his daughter's dead   40
    And bear his courses to be orderèd

By Lady Fortune, while our scene must play
His daughter's woe and heavy well-a-day
In her unholy service. Patience then,   44
And think you now are all in Mytilene.   *Exit*

Sc. 19 ⌈*A brothel sign.*⌉ *Enter two Gentlemen*

FIRST GENTLEMAN Did you ever hear the like?

SECOND GENTLEMAN No, nor never shall do in such a place
as this, she being once gone.

FIRST GENTLEMAN But to have divinity preached there—
did you ever dream of such a thing?   5

SECOND GENTLEMAN No, no. Come, I am for no more
bawdy houses. Shall 's go hear the vestals sing?

FIRST GENTLEMAN I'll do anything now that is virtuous,
but I am out of the road of rutting for ever.   *Exeunt*

Enter Pander, Bawd, and Boult

PANDER Well, I had rather than twice the worth of her
she had ne'er come here.   11

BAWD Fie, fie upon her, she's able to freeze the god
Priapus and undo the whole of generation. We must
either get her ravished or be rid of her. When she
should do for clients her fitment and do me the kindness
of our profession, she has me her quirks, her reasons,
her master reasons, her prayers, her knees, that she
would make a puritan of the devil if he should cheapen
a kiss of her.

BOULT Faith, I must ravish her, or she'll disfurnish us of
all our cavalleria and make our swearers priests.   21

PANDER Now, the pox upon her green-sickness for me.

BAWD Faith, there's no way to be rid on't but by the way
to the pox.

Enter Lysimachus, disguised

Here comes the Lord Lysimachus, disguised.   25

BOULT We should have both lord and loon if the peevish
baggage would but give way to custom.

LYSIMACHUS How now, how a dozen of virginities?

BAWD Now, the gods to-bless your honour!

BOULT I am glad to see your honour in good health.   30

LYSIMACHUS You may so. 'Tis the better for you that your
resorters stand upon sound legs. How now, wholesome
iniquity have you, that a man may deal withal and
defy the surgeon?

BAWD We have here one, sir, if she would—but there
never came her like in Mytilene.   36

LYSIMACHUS If she'd do the deed of darkness, thou wouldst
say.

BAWD Your honour knows what 'tis to say well enough.

LYSIMACHUS Well, call forth, call forth.   ⌈*Exit Pander*⌉

BOULT For flesh and blood, sir, white and red, you shall
see a rose. And she were a rose indeed, if she had but—

LYSIMACHUS What, prithee?

BOULT O sir, I can be modest.

LYSIMACHUS That dignifies the renown of a bawd no less
than it gives a good report to a noble to be chaste.   46

⌈*Enter Pander with Marina*⌉

BAWD Here comes that which grows to the stalk, never
plucked yet, I can assure you. Is she not a fair creature?

LYSIMACHUS Faith, she would serve after a long voyage
at sea. Well, there's for you. Leave us.   50

⌈*He pays the Bawd*⌉

BAWD I beseech your honour give me leave: a word, and
I'll have done presently.

LYSIMACHUS I beseech you, do.

BAWD (*aside to Marina*) First, I would have you note this
is an honourable man.   55

MARINA I desire to find him so, that I may honourably
know him.

BAWD Next, he's the governor of this country, and a man
whom I am bound to.   59

MARINA If he govern the country you are bound to him
indeed, but how honourable he is in that, I know not.

BAWD Pray you, without any more virginal fencing, will
you use him kindly? He will line your apron with gold.

MARINA What he will do graciously I will thankfully
receive.   65

LYSIMACHUS (*to Bawd*) Ha' you done?

BAWD My lord, she's not paced yet. You must take some
pains to work her to your manège. (*To Boult and Pander*)
Come, we will leave his honour and hers together. Go
thy ways.   *Exeunt Pander, Bawd, and Boult*

LYSIMACHUS
Fair one, how long have you been at this trade?

MARINA What trade, sir?

LYSIMACHUS
I cannot name it but I shall offend.

MARINA
I cannot be offended with my trade.
Please you to name it.

LYSIMACHUS   How long have you been   75
Of this profession?

MARINA   E'er since I can remember.

LYSIMACHUS
Did you go to't so young? Were you a gamester
At five, or seven?

MARINA   Earlier too, sir,
If now I be one.

LYSIMACHUS   Why, the house you dwell in
Proclaimeth you a creature of sale.   80

MARINA
And do you know this house to be a place
Of such resort and will come into it?
I hear say you're of honourable blood,
And are the governor of this whole province.

LYSIMACHUS
What, hath your principal informed you who I am? 85

MARINA
Who is my principal?

LYSIMACHUS   Why, your herb-woman;
She that sets seeds of shame, roots of iniquity.

⌈*Marina weeps*⌉

O, you've heard something of my pow'r, and so
Stand off aloof for a more serious wooing.
But I protest to thee,   90
Pretty one, my authority can wink

At blemishes, or can on faults look friendly;
Or my displeasure punish at my pleasure,
From which displeasure, not thy beauty shall
Privilege thee, nor my affection, which 95
Hath drawn me here, abate with further ling'ring.
Come bring me to some private place. Come, come.

MARINA
Let not authority, which teaches you
To govern others, be the means to make you
Misgovern much yourself. 100
If you were born to honour, show it now;
If put upon you, make the judgement good
That thought you worthy of it. What reason's in
Your justice, who hath power over all,
To undo any? If you take from me 105
Mine honour, you're like him that makes a gap
Into forbidden ground, whom after
Too many enter, and of all their evils
Yourself are guilty. My life is yet unspotted;
My chastity unstainèd ev'n in thought. 110
Then if your violence deface this building,
The workmanship of heav'n, you do kill your honour,
Abuse your justice, and impoverish me.
My yet good lord, if there be fire before me,
Must I straight fly and burn myself? Suppose this
  house— 115
Which too too many feel such houses are—
Should be the doctor's patrimony, and
The surgeon's feeding; follows it, that I
Must needs infect myself to give them maint'nance?

LYSIMACHUS
How's this, how's this? Some more. Be sage.

MARINA ⌈kneeling⌉   For me
That am a maid, though most ungentle fortune 121
Have franked me in this sty, where since I came
Diseases have been sold dearer than physic—
That the gods would set me free from this unhallowed
  place,
Though they did change me to the meanest bird 125
That flies i'th' purer air!

LYSIMACHUS ⌈moved⌉   I did not think
Thou couldst have spoke so well, ne'er dreamt thou
  couldst.
  ⌈He lifts her up with his hands⌉
Though I brought hither a corrupted mind,
Thy speech hath altered it,
  ⌈He wipes the wet from her eyes⌉
      and my foul thoughts
Thy tears so well hath laved that they're now white.
I came here meaning but to pay the price, 131
A piece of gold for thy virginity,
Here's twenty to relieve thine honesty.
Persever still in that clear way thou goest,
And the gods strengthen thee.

MARINA   The good gods preserve you!

LYSIMACHUS
The very doors and windows savour vilely. 136
Fare thee well. Thou art a piece of virtue,

The best wrought up that ever nature made,
And I doubt not thy training hath been noble.
A curse upon him, die he like a thief, 140
That robs thee of thy honour. Hold, here's more gold.
If thou dost hear from me, it shall be for thy good.
  ⌈Enter Boult standing ready at the door, making his
  obeisance unto him as Lysimachus should go out⌉

BOULT I beseech your honour, one piece for me.

LYSIMACHUS
Avaunt, thou damnèd door-keeper!
Your house, but for this virgin that doth prop it, 145
Would sink and overwhelm you. Away.   Exit

BOULT How's this? We must take another course with
you. If your peevish chastity, which is not worth a
breakfast in the cheapest country under the cope, shall
undo a whole household, let me be gelded like a spaniel.
Come your ways. 151

MARINA Whither would you have me?

BOULT I must have your maidenhead taken off, or the
common executioner shall do it. We'll have no more
gentlemen driven away. Come your ways, I say. 155
  Enter Bawd and Pander

BAWD How now, what's the matter?

BOULT Worse and worse, mistress, she has here spoken
holy words to the Lord Lysimachus.

BAWD O, abominable!

BOULT She makes our profession as it were to stink afore
the face of the gods. 161

BAWD Marry hang her up for ever!

BOULT The nobleman would have dealt with her like a
nobleman, and she sent him away as cold as a snowball,
saying his prayers, too. 165

⌈PANDER⌉ Boult, take her away. Use her at thy pleasure.
Crack the ice of her virginity, and make the rest
malleable.

BOULT An if she were a thornier piece of ground than she
is, she shall be ploughed. 170

MARINA Hark, hark, you gods!

BAWD She conjures. Away with her! Would she had never
come within my doors.—Marry, hang you!—She's born
to undo us.—Will you not go the way of womenkind?
Marry, come up, my dish of chastity with rosemary
and bays. Exeunt Bawd and Pander

BOULT ⌈catching her rashly by the hand⌉ Come, mistress,
come your way with me.

MARINA Whither wilt thou have me?

BOULT To take from you the jewel you hold so dear. 180

MARINA Prithee, tell me one thing first.

BOULT Come, now, your one thing.

MARINA
What canst thou wish thine enemy to be?

BOULT Why, I could wish him to be my master, or rather
my mistress. 185

MARINA
Neither of these can be so bad as thou art,
Since they do better thee in their command.
Thou hold'st a place the painèd'st fiend of hell
Would not in reputation change with thee,

Thou damnèd doorkeeper to ev'ry coistrel   190
That comes enquiring for his Tib.
To th' choleric fisting of ev'ry rogue
Thy ear is liable. Thy food is such
As hath been belched on by infected lungs.   194
BOULT What would you have me do? Go to the wars,
would you, where a man may serve seven years for
the loss of a leg, and have not money enough in the
end to buy him a wooden one?
MARINA
Do anything but this thou dost. Empty
Old receptacles or common sew'rs of filth,   200
Serve by indenture to the public hangman—
Any of these are yet better than this.
For what thou professest a baboon, could he speak,
Would own a name too dear. Here's gold for thee.
If that thy master would make gain by me,   205
Proclaim that I can sing, weave, sew, and dance,
With other virtues which I'll keep from boast,
And I will undertake all these to teach.
I doubt not but this populous city will
Yield many scholars.   210
BOULT But can you teach all this you speak of?
MARINA
Prove that I cannot, take me home again
And prostitute me to the basest groom
That doth frequent your house.
BOULT Well, I will see what I can do for thee. If I can
place thee, I will.   216
MARINA But amongst honest women.
BOULT Faith, my acquaintance lies little amongst them;
but since my master and mistress hath bought you,
there's no going but by their consent. Therefore I will
make them acquainted with your purpose, and I doubt
not but I shall find them tractable enough. Come, I'll
do for thee what I can. Come your ways.
Exeunt. ⌈*The sign is removed*⌉

Sc. 20 *Enter Gower*
GOWER
Marina thus the brothel scapes, and chances
     Into an honest house, our story says.
She sings like one immortal, and she dances
     As goddess-like to her admirèd lays.
Deep clerks she dumbs, and with her nee'le composes
     Nature's own shape, of bud, bird, branch, or berry,
That e'en her art sisters the natural roses.   7
     Her inkle, silk, twin with the rubied cherry;
That pupils lacks she none of noble race,
     Who pour their bounty on her, and her gain   10
She gives the cursèd Bawd. Here we her place,
     And to her father turn our thoughts again.
We left him on the sea. Waves there him tossed,
     Whence, driven tofore the winds, he is arrived
Here where his daughter dwells, and on this coast   15
Suppose him now at anchor. The city strived
God Neptune's annual feast to keep, from whence
     Lysimachus our Tyrian ship espies,

His banners sable, trimmed with rich expense;
     And to him in his barge with fervour hies.   20
In your supposing once more put your sight;
     Of heavy Pericles think this the barque,
Where what is done in action, more if might,
     Shall be discovered. Please you sit and hark.   *Exit*

Sc. 21 *Enter Helicanus* ⌈*above; below, enter*⌉ *to him at the*
     first door two Sailors, ⌈*one of Tyre, the other of*
     Mytilene⌉
SAILOR OF TYRE (*to Sailor of Mytilene*)
Lord Helicanus can resolve you, sir.
(*To Helicanus*) There is a barge put off from Mytilene.
In it, Lysimachus, the governor,
Who craves to come aboard. What is your will?
HELICANUS
That he have his.   ⌈*Exit Sailor of Mytilene at first door*⌉
                         Call up some gentlemen.   5
                                        ⌈*Exit Helicanus above*⌉
⌈SAILOR OF TYRE⌉
Ho, my lord calls!
          Enter ⌈*from below the stage*⌉ *two or three*
          Gentlemen; ⌈*to them, enter Helicanus*⌉
FIRST GENTLEMAN   What is your lordship's pleasure?
HELICANUS
Gentlemen, some of worth would come aboard.
I pray you, greet him fairly.
          Enter Lysimachus ⌈*at first door, with the Sailor and*
          Lords of Mytilene⌉
⌈SAILOR OF MYTILENE⌉ (*to Lysimachus*)
This is the man that can in aught resolve you.
LYSIMACHUS (*to Helicanus*)
Hail, reverend sir; the gods preserve you!   10
HELICANUS
And you, sir, to outlive the age I am,
And die as I would do.
LYSIMACHUS   You wish me well.
I am the governor of Mytilene;
Being on shore, honouring of Neptune's triumphs,
Seeing this goodly vessel ride before us,   15
I made to it to know of whence you are.
HELICANUS
Our vessel is of Tyre, in it our king,
A man who for this three months hath not spoken
To anyone, nor taken sustenance
But to prorogue his grief.   20
LYSIMACHUS
Upon what ground grew his distemp'rature?
HELICANUS
'Twould be too tedious to tell it over,
But the main grief springs from the precious loss
Of a belovèd daughter and a wife.
LYSIMACHUS
May we not see him?
HELICANUS   See him, sir, you may,   25
But bootless is your sight. He will not speak
To any.
LYSIMACHUS Let me yet obtain my wish.

HELICANUS
Behold him.
⌈*Helicanus draws a curtain, revealing Pericles lying*
upon a couch with a long overgrown beard, diffused
hair, undecent nails on his fingers, and attired in
sack-cloth⌉
                This was a goodly person
Till the disaster of one mortal night
Drove him to this.   30
LYSIMACHUS (*to Pericles*)
Sir, King, all hail. Hail, royal sir.
⌈*Pericles shrinks himself down upon his pillow*⌉
HELICANUS
It is in vain. He will not speak to you.
LORD OF MYTILENE
Sir, we have a maid in Mytilene I durst wager
Would win some words of him.
LYSIMACHUS   'Tis well bethought.
She questionless, with her sweet harmony   35
And other choice attractions, would alarum
And make a batt'ry through his deafened ports,
Which now are midway stopped. She in all happy,
As the fair'st of all, among her fellow maids
Dwells now i'th' leafy shelter that abuts   40
Against the island's side. Go fetch her hither.
                                              ⌈*Exit Lord*⌉
HELICANUS
Sure, all effectless; yet nothing we'll omit
That bears recov'ry's name. But since your kindness
We have stretched thus far, let us beseech you
That for our gold we may provision have,   45
Wherein we are not destitute for want,
But weary for the staleness.
LYSIMACHUS   O sir, a courtesy
Which if we should deny, the most just gods
For every graft would send a caterpillar,
And so inflict our province. Yet once more   50
Let me entreat to know at large the cause
Of your king's sorrow.
HELICANUS   Sit, sir. I will recount it.
⌈*Enter Lord with Marina and another maid*⌉
But see, I am prevented.
LYSIMACHUS
O, here's the lady that I sent for.—
Welcome, fair one.—Is't not a goodly presence?   55
HELICANUS She's a gallant lady.
LYSIMACHUS
She's such a one that, were I well assured
Came of gentle kind or noble stock, I'd wish
No better choice to think me rarely wed.—
Fair one, all goodness that consists in bounty   60
Expect e'en here, where is a kingly patient;
If that thy prosperous and artificial feat
Can draw him but to answer thee in aught,
Thy sacred physic shall receive such pay
As thy desires can wish.
MARINA   Sir, I will use   65

My utmost skill in his recure, provided
That none but I and my companion maid
Be suffered to come near him.
LYSIMACHUS (*to the others*)   Let us leave her,
And the gods prosper her.   ⌈*The men stand aside*⌉
        The Song
LYSIMACHUS ⌈*coming forward*⌉ Marked he your music?
⌈MAID⌉
No, nor looked on us.
LYSIMACHUS (*to the others*) See, she will speak to him. 70
MARINA (*to Pericles*)
Hail, sir; my lord, lend ear.
PERICLES Hmh, ha!
        ⌈*He roughly repulses her*⌉
MARINA   I am a maid,
My lord, that ne'er before invited eyes,
But have been gazed on like a comet. She speaks, 75
My lord, that maybe hath endured a grief
Might equal yours, if both were justly weighed.
Though wayward fortune did malign my state,
My derivation was from ancestors
Who stood equivalent with mighty kings,   80
But time hath rooted out my parentage,
And to the world and awkward casualties
Bound me in servitude. (*Aside*) I will desist.
But there is something glows upon my cheek,
And whispers in mine ear 'Stay till he speak.'   85
PERICLES
My fortunes, parentage, good parentage,
To equal mine? Was it not thus? What say you?
MARINA
I said if you did know my parentage,
My lord, you would not do me violence.
PERICLES
I do think so. Pray you, turn your eyes upon me.   90
You're like something that—whát countrywoman?
Here of these shores?
MARINA   No, nor of any shores,
Yet I was mortally brought forth, and am
No other than I seem.
PERICLES ⌈*aside*⌉
I am great with woe, and shall deliver weeping.   95
My dearest wife was like this maid, and such
My daughter might have been. My queen's square
                                              brows,
Her stature to an inch, as wand-like straight,
As silver-voiced, her eyes as jewel-like,
And cased as richly, in pace another Juno,   100
Who starves the ears she feeds, and makes them
                                              hungry
The more she gives them speech.—Where do you live?
MARINA
Where I am but a stranger. From the deck
You may discern the place.
PERICLES   Where were you bred,
And how achieved you these endowments which   105
You make more rich to owe?
MARINA   If I should tell

My history, it would seem like lies
Disdained in the reporting.
PERICLES   Prithee speak.
Falseness cannot come from thee, for thou look'st
Modest as justice, and thou seem'st a palace   110
For the crowned truth to dwell in. I will believe thee,
And make my senses credit thy relation
To points that seem impossible. Thou show'st
Like one I loved indeed. What were thy friends?
Didst thou not say, when I did push thee back—   115
Which was when I perceived thee—that thou cam'st
From good descending?
MARINA   So indeed I did.
PERICLES
Report thy parentage. I think thou said'st
Thou hadst been tossed from wrong to injury,
And that thou thought'st thy griefs might equal mine,
If both were opened.
MARINA   Some such thing I said,   121
And said no more but what my circumstance
Did warrant me was likely.
PERICLES   Tell thy story.
If thine considered prove the thousandth part
Of my endurance, thou art a man, and I   125
Have suffered like a girl. Yet thou dost look
Like patience gazing on kings' graves, and smiling
Extremity out of act. What were thy friends?
How lost thou them? Thy name, my most kind virgin?
Recount, I do beseech thee. Come, sit by me.   130
She sits
MARINA
My name, sir, is Marina.
PERICLES   O, I am mocked,
And thou by some incensèd god sent hither
To make the world to laugh at me.
MARINA   Patience, good sir,
Or here I'll cease.
PERICLES   Nay, I'll be patient.
Thou little know'st how thou dost startle me   135
To call thyself Marina.
MARINA   The name
Was given me by one that had some power:
My father, and a king.
PERICLES   How, a king's daughter,
And called Marina?
MARINA   You said you would believe me,
But not to be a troubler of your peace   140
I will end here.
PERICLES   But are you flesh and blood?
Have you a working pulse and are no fairy?
Motion as well? Speak on. Where were you born,
And wherefore called Marina?
MARINA   Called Marina
For I was born at sea.
PERICLES   At sea? What mother?   145
MARINA
My mother was the daughter of a king,
Who died when I was born, as my good nurse
Lychorida hath oft recounted weeping.

PERICLES
O, stop there a little! ⌈*Aside*⌉ This is the rarest dream
That e'er dulled sleep did mock sad fools withal.   150
This cannot be my daughter, buried. Well.
(*To Marina*) Where were you bred? I'll hear you more
to th' bottom
Of your story, and never interrupt you.
MARINA
You will scarce believe me. 'Twere best I did give o'er.
PERICLES
I will believe you by the syllable   155
Of what you shall deliver. Yet give me leave.
How came you in these parts? Where were you bred?
MARINA
The King my father did in Tarsus leave me,
Till cruel Cleon, with his wicked wife,
Did seek to murder me, and wooed a villain   160
To attempt the deed; who having drawn to do't,
A crew of pirates came and rescued me.
To Mytilene they brought me. But, good sir,
What will you of me? Why do you weep? It may be
You think me an impostor. No, good faith,   165
I am the daughter to King Pericles,
If good King Pericles be.
PERICLES ⌈*rising*⌉ Ho, Helicanus!
HELICANUS (*coming forward*) Calls my lord?
PERICLES
Thou art a grave and noble counsellor,   170
Most wise in gen'ral. Tell me if thou canst
What this maid is, or what is like to be,
That thus hath made me weep.
HELICANUS   I know not.
But here's the regent, sir, of Mytilene
Speaks nobly of her.
LYSIMACHUS   She would never tell   175
Her parentage. Being demanded that,
She would sit still and weep.
PERICLES
O Helicanus, strike me, honoured sir,
Give me a gash, put me to present pain,
Lest this great sea of joys rushing upon me   180
O'erbear the shores of my mortality
And drown me with their sweetness! (*To Marina*) O,
come hither,
⌈*Marina stands*⌉
Thou that begett'st him that did thee beget,
Thou that wast born at sea, buried at Tarsus,
And found at sea again!—O Helicanus,   185
Down on thy knees, thank the holy gods as loud
As thunder threatens us, this is Marina!
(*To Marina*) What was thy mother's name? Tell me
but that,
For truth can never be confirmed enough,
Though doubts did ever sleep.
MARINA   First, sir, I pray,   190
What is your title?
PERICLES   I am Pericles
Of Tyre. But tell me now my drowned queen's name.

As in the rest thou hast been godlike perfect,
So prove but true in that, thou art my daughter,
The heir of kingdoms, and another life   195
To Pericles thy father.
MARINA ⌐kneeling¬   Is it no more
To be your daughter than to say my mother's name?
Thaisa was my mother, who did end
The minute I began.
PERICLES
Now blessing on thee! Rise. Thou art my child.   200
⌐Marina stands. He kisses her¬
⌐To attendants¬ Give me fresh garments.—Mine own,
Helicanus!
Not dead at Tarsus, as she should have been
By savage Cleon. She shall tell thee all,
When thou shalt kneel and justify in knowledge
She is thy very princess. Who is this?   205
HELICANUS
Sir, 'tis the governor of Mytilene,
Who, hearing of your melancholy state,
Did come to see you.
PERICLES (to Lysimachus) I embrace you, sir.—
Give me my robes.
⌐He is attired in fresh robes¬
                I am wild in my beholding.
O heavens, bless my girl!
⌐Celestial music¬
                But hark, what music?   210
Tell Helicanus, my Marina, tell him
O'er point by point, for yet he seems to doubt,
How sure you are my daughter. But what music?
HELICANUS My lord, I hear none.
PERICLES
None? The music of the spheres! List, my Marina. 215
LYSIMACHUS (aside to the others)
It is not good to cross him. Give him way.
PERICLES Rar'st sounds. Do ye not hear?
LYSIMACHUS Music, my lord?
PERICLES I hear most heav'nly music.
It raps me unto list'ning, and thick slumber   220
Hangs upon mine eyelids. Let me rest.
    He sleeps
LYSIMACHUS
A pillow for his head.
⌐To Marina and others¬ Companion friends,
If this but answer to my just belief
I'll well remember you. So leave him all.
                    Exeunt all but Pericles
    Diana ⌐descends from the heavens¬
DIANA
My temple stands in Ephesus. Hie thee thither,   225
And do upon mine altar sacrifice.
There when my maiden priests are met together,
At large discourse thy fortunes in this wise:
With a full voice before the people all,
Reveal how thou at sea didst lose thy wife.   230
To mourn thy crosses, with thy daughter's, call
And give them repetition to the life.

Perform my bidding, or thou liv'st in woe;
Do't, and rest happy, by my silver bow.
Awake, and tell thy dream.   235
            ⌐Diana ascends into the heavens¬
PERICLES
Celestial Dian, goddess argentine,
I will obey thee. (Calling) Helicanus!
    Enter Helicanus, Lysimachus, and Marina
HELICANUS   Sir?
PERICLES
My purpose was for Tarsus, there to strike
Th'inhospitable Cleon, but I am
For other service first. Toward Ephesus   240
Turn our blown sails. Eftsoons I'll tell thee why.
                            ⌐Exit Helicanus¬
Shall we refresh us, sir, upon your shore,
And give you gold for such provision
As our intents will need?
LYSIMACHUS   With all my heart, sir,
And when you come ashore I have a suit.   245
PERICLES
You shall prevail, were it to woo my daughter,
For it seems you have been noble towards her.
LYSIMACHUS
Sir, lend me your arm.
PERICLES   Come, my Marina.
    ⌐Exit Pericles with Lysimachus at one arm,
        Marina at the other¬

Sc. 22 Enter Gower
GOWER
Now our sands are almost run;
More a little, and then dumb.
This my last boon give me,
For such kindness must relieve me,
That you aptly will suppose   5
What pageantry, what feats, what shows,
What minstrelsy and pretty din
The regent made in Mytilene
To greet the King. So well he thrived
That he is promised to be wived   10
To fair Marina, but in no wise
Till he had done his sacrifice
As Dian bade, whereto being bound
The int'rim, pray you, all confound.
In feathered briefness sails are filled,   15
And wishes fall out as they're willed.
At Ephesus the temple see:
⌐An altar, Thaisa and other vestals are revealed¬
Our king, and all his company.
    ⌐Enter Pericles, Marina, Lysimachus, Helicanus,
    Cerimon, with attendants¬
That he can hither come so soon
Is by your fancies' thankful doom.   20
    ⌐Gower stands aside¬
PERICLES
Hail, Dian. To perform thy just command
I here confess myself the King of Tyre,
Who, frighted from my country, did espouse

The fair Thaisa
 ⌈*Thaisa starts*⌉
      at Pentapolis.
At sea in childbed died she, but brought forth   25
A maid child called Marina, who, O goddess,
Wears yet thy silver liv'ry. She at Tarsus
Was nursed with Cleon, whom at fourteen years
He sought to murder, but her better stars
Bore her to Mytilene, 'gainst whose shore riding   30
Her fortunes brought the maid aboard our barque,
Where, by her own most clear remembrance, she
Made known herself my daughter.
THAISA   Voice and favour—
You are, you are—O royal Pericles!
      She falls
PERICLES
What means the nun? She dies. Help, gentlemen!   35
CERIMON Noble sir,
If you have told Diana's altar true,
This is your wife.
PERICLES   Reverend appearer, no.
I threw her overboard with these same arms.
CERIMON
Upon this coast, I warr'nt you.
PERICLES   'Tis most certain.   40
CERIMON
Look to the lady. O, she's but o'erjoyed.
Early one blustering morn this lady
Was thrown upon this shore. I oped the coffin,
Found there rich jewels, recovered her, and placed her
Here in Diana's temple.
PERICLES   May we see them?   45
CERIMON
Great sir, they shall be brought you to my house,
Whither I invite you. Look, Thaisa is
Recoverèd.
THAISA   O, let me look upon him!
If he be none of mine, my sanctity
Will to my sense bend no licentious ear,   50
But curb it, spite of seeing. O, my lord,
Are you not Pericles? Like him you spake,
Like him you are. Did you not name a tempest,
A birth and death?
PERICLES The voice of dead Thaisa!   55
THAISA That Thaisa
Am I, supposèd dead and drowned.
PERICLES ⌈*taking Thaisa's hand*⌉ Immortal Dian!
THAISA Now I know you better.
When we with tears parted Pentapolis,   60
The King my father gave you such a ring.
PERICLES
This, this! No more, you gods. Your present kindness
Makes my past miseries sports; you shall do well
That on the touching of her lips I may
Melt, and no more be seen.—O come, be buried   65
A second time within these arms.
      ⌈*They embrace and kiss*⌉
MARINA (*kneeling to Thaisa*)   My heart
Leaps to be gone into my mother's bosom.

PERICLES
Look who kneels here: flesh of thy flesh, Thaisa,
Thy burden at the sea, and called Marina
For she was yielded there.
THAISA ⌈*embracing Marina*⌉ Blessed, and mine own!   70
HELICANUS ⌈*kneeling to Thaisa*⌉
Hail, madam, and my queen.
THAISA   I know you not.
PERICLES
You have heard me say, when I did fly from Tyre,
I left behind an ancient substitute.
Can you remember what I called the man?
I have named him oft.   75
THAISA 'Twas Helicanus then.
PERICLES Still confirmation.
Embrace him, dear Thaisa; this is he.
Now do I long to hear how you were found,
How possibly preserved, and who to thank—   80
Besides the gods—for this great miracle.
THAISA
Lord Cerimon, my lord. This is the man
Through whom the gods have shown their pow'r,
      that can
From first to last resolve you.
PERICLES (*to Cerimon*)   Reverend sir,
The gods can have no mortal officer   85
More like a god than you. Will you deliver
How this dead queen re-lives?
CERIMON   I will, my lord.
Beseech you, first go with me to my house,
Where shall be shown you all was found with her,
And told how in this temple she came placed,   90
No needful thing omitted.
PERICLES   Pure Diana,
I bless thee for thy vision, and will offer
Nightly oblations to thee.—Beloved Thaisa,
This prince, the fair betrothèd of your daughter,
At Pentapolis shall marry her.   95
(*To Marina*) And now this ornament
Makes me look dismal will I clip to form,
And what this fourteen years no razor touched,
To grace thy marriage day I'll beautify.
THAISA
Lord Cerimon hath letters of good credit,   100
Sir, from Pentapolis: my father's dead.
PERICLES
Heav'n make a star of him! Yet there, my queen,
We'll celebrate their nuptials, and ourselves
Will in that kingdom spend our following days.
Our son and daughter shall in Tyrus reign.—   105
Lord Cerimon, we do our longing stay
To hear the rest untold. Sir, lead 's the way.
      Exeunt ⌈*all but Gower*⌉
GOWER
In Antiochus and his daughter you have heard
Of monstrous lust the due and just reward;
In Pericles, his queen, and daughter seen,   110
Although assailed with fortune fierce and keen,

Virtue preserved from fell destruction's blast,
Led on by heav'n, and crowned with joy at last.
In Helicanus may you well descry
A figure of truth, of faith, of loyalty.   115
In reverend Cerimon there well appears
The worth that learnèd charity aye wears.
For wicked Cleon and his wife, when fame
Had spread their cursèd deed to th' honoured name

Of Pericles, to rage the city turn,   120
That him and his they in his palace burn.
The gods for murder seemèd so content
To punish that, although not done, but meant.
So on your patience evermore attending,
New joy wait on you. Here our play has ending.   125
                                                        Exit

ADDITIONAL PASSAGE

Q gives this more expansive version of Marina's Epitaph
(18.34–7):

   'The fairest, sweetest, best lies here,
   Who withered in her spring of year.
   She was of Tyrus the King's daughter,
   On whom foul death hath made this slaughter.

Marina was she called, and at her birth   5
Thetis, being proud, swallowed some part o'th' earth;
Therefore the earth, fearing to be o'erflowed,
Hath Thetis' birth-child on the heav'ns bestowed,
Wherefore she does, and swears she'll never stint,
Make raging batt'ry upon shores of flint.'   10

THE WINTER'S TALE

THE astrologer Simon Forman saw *The Winter's Tale* at the Globe on 15 May 1611. Just how much earlier the play was written is not certainly known. During the sheep-shearing feast in Act 4, twelve countrymen perform a satyrs' dance that three of them are said to have already 'danced before the King'. This is not necessarily a topical reference, but satyrs danced in Ben Jonson's *Masque of Oberon*, performed before King James on 1 January 1611. It seems likely that this dance was incorporated in *The Winter's Tale* (just as, later, another masque dance seems to have been transferred to *The Two Noble Kinsmen*). But it occurs in a self-contained passage that may well have been added after Shakespeare wrote the play itself. *The Winter's Tale*, first printed in the 1623 Folio, is usually thought to have been written after *Cymbeline*, but stylistic evidence places it before that play, perhaps in 1609-10.

A mid sixteenth-century book classes 'winter tales' along with 'old wives' tales'; Shakespeare's title prepared his audiences for a tale of romantic improbability, one to be wondered at rather than believed; and within the play itself characters compare its events to 'an old tale' (5.2.61; 5.3.118). The comparison is just: Shakespeare is dramatizing a story by his old rival Robert Greene, published as *Pandosto: The Triumph of Time* in or before 1588. This gave Shakespeare his plot outline, of a king (Leontes) who believes his wife (Hermione) to have committed adultery with another king (Polixenes), his boyhood friend, and who casts off his new-born daughter (Perdita—the lost one) in the belief that she is his friend's bastard. In both versions the baby is brought up as a shepherdess, falls in love with her supposed father's son (Florizel in the play), and returns to her real father's court where she is at last recognized as his daughter. In both versions, too, the wife's innocence is demonstrated by the pronouncement of the Delphic oracle, and her husband passes the period of his daughter's absence in penitence; but Shakespeare alters the ending of his source story, bringing it into line with the conventions of romance. He adopts Greene's tripartite structure, but greatly develops it, adding for instance Leontes' steward Antigonus and his redoubtable wife Paulina, along with the comic rogue Autolycus, 'snapper-up of unconsidered trifles'.

The intensity of poetic suffering with which Leontes expresses his irrational jealousy is matched by the lyrical rapture of the love episodes between Florizel and Perdita. In both verse and prose *The Winter's Tale* shows Shakespeare's verbal powers at their greatest, and his theatrical mastery is apparent in, for example, Hermione's trial (3.1) and the daring final scene in which time brings about its triumph.

THE PERSONS OF THE PLAY

LEONTES, King of Sicily

HERMIONE, his wife

MAMILLIUS, his son

PERDITA, his daughter

CAMILLO ⎫
ANTIGONUS ⎪
CLEOMENES ⎬ Lords at Leontes's court
DION ⎭

PAULINA, Antigonus's wife

EMILIA, a lady attending on Hermione

A JAILER

A MARINER

Other Lords and Gentlemen, Ladies, Officers, and Servants at Leontes's court

POLIXENES, King of Bohemia

FLORIZEL, his son, in love with Perdita; known as Doricles

ARCHIDAMUS, a Bohemian lord

AUTOLYCUS, a rogue, once in the service of Florizel

CLOWN, his son

MOPSA ⎫
DORCAS ⎬ shepherdesses

SERVANT of the Old Shepherd

Other Shepherds and Shepherdesses

Twelve countrymen disguised as satyrs

TIME, as chorus

The Winter's Tale

1.1 *Enter Camillo and Archidamus*

ARCHIDAMUS If you shall chance, Camillo, to visit Bohemia
on the like occasion whereon my services are now on
foot, you shall see, as I have said, great difference
betwixt our Bohemia and your Sicilia.   4

CAMILLO I think this coming summer the King of Sicilia
means to pay Bohemia the visitation which he justly
owes him.

ARCHIDAMUS Wherein our entertainment shall shame us,
we will be justified in our loves; for indeed—

CAMILLO Beseech you—   10

ARCHIDAMUS Verily, I speak it in the freedom of my
knowledge. We cannot with such magnificence—in so
rare—I know not what to say.—We will give you sleepy
drinks, that your senses, unintelligent of our
insufficience, may, though they cannot praise us, as
little accuse us.   16

CAMILLO You pay a great deal too dear for what's given
freely.

ARCHIDAMUS Believe me, I speak as my understanding
instructs me, and as mine honesty puts it to utterance.

CAMILLO Sicilia cannot show himself over-kind to
Bohemia. They were trained together in their
childhoods, and there rooted betwixt them then such
an affection which cannot choose but branch now.
Since their more mature dignities and royal necessities
made separation of their society, their encounters—
though not personal—hath been royally attorneyed
with interchange of gifts, letters, loving embassies, that
they have seemed to be together, though absent; shook
hands as over a vast; and embraced as it were from
the ends of opposed winds. The heavens continue their
loves.   32

ARCHIDAMUS I think there is not in the world either malice
or matter to alter it. You have an unspeakable comfort
of your young prince, Mamillius. It is a gentleman of
the greatest promise that ever came into my note.   36

CAMILLO· I very well agree with you in the hopes of him.
It is a gallant child; one that, indeed, physics the
subject, makes old hearts fresh. They that went on
crutches ere he was born desire yet their life to see him
a man.   41

ARCHIDAMUS Would they else be content to die?

CAMILLO Yes—if there were no other excuse why they
should desire to live.   44

ARCHIDAMUS If the King had no son they would desire to
live on crutches till he had one.   *Exeunt*

1.2 *Enter Leontes, Hermione, Mamillius, Polixenes, and*
⌈*Camillo*⌉

POLIXENES
Nine changes of the wat'ry star hath been
The shepherd's note since we have left our throne
Without a burden. Time as long again
Would be filled up, my brother, with our thanks,
And yet we should for perpetuity   5
Go hence in debt. And therefore, like a cipher,
Yet standing in rich place, I multiply
With one 'We thank you' many thousands more
That go before it.

LEONTES   Stay your thanks a while,
And pay them when you part.

POLIXENES   Sir, that's tomorrow.   10
I am questioned by my fears of what may chance
Or breed upon our absence, that may blow
No sneaping winds at home to make us say
'This is put forth too truly.' Besides, I have stayed
To tire your royalty.

LEONTES   We are tougher, brother,   15
Than you can put us to't.

POLIXENES   No longer stay.

LEONTES
One sennight longer.

POLIXENES   Very sooth, tomorrow.

LEONTES
We'll part the time between's, then; and in that
I'll no gainsaying.

POLIXENES   Press me not, beseech you, so.
There is no tongue that moves, none, none i'th' world
So soon as yours, could win me. So it should now,   21
Were there necessity in your request, although
'Twere needful I denied it. My affairs
Do even drag me homeward; which to hinder
Were, in your love, a whip to me; my stay   25
To you a charge and trouble. To save both,
Farewell, our brother.

LEONTES   Tongue-tied, our queen? Speak you.

HERMIONE
I had thought, sir, to have held my peace until
You had drawn oaths from him not to stay. You, sir,
Charge him too coldly. Tell him you are sure   30
All in Bohemia's well. This satisfaction
The bygone day proclaimed. Say this to him,
He's beat from his best ward.

LEONTES·   Well said, Hermione!

HERMIONE
To tell he longs to see his son were strong.
But let him say so then, and let him go.   35
But let him swear so and he shall not stay,
We'll thwack him hence with distaffs.
(To Polixenes) Yet of your royal presence I'll adventure
The borrow of a week. When at Bohemia
You take my lord, I'll give him my commission   40
To let him there a month behind the gest
Prefixed for's parting.—Yet, good deed, Leontes,
I love thee not a jar o'th' clock behind
What lady she her lord.—You'll stay?

POLIXENES   No, madam.

HERMIONE Nay, but you will? 45

POLIXENES I may not, verily.

HERMIONE Verily?
You put me off with limber vows. But I,
Though you would seek t'unsphere the stars with
    oaths,
Should yet say 'Sir, no going.' Verily 50
You shall not go. A lady's 'verily''s
As potent as a lord's. Will you go yet?
Force me to keep you as a prisoner,
Not like a guest: so you shall pay your fees
When you depart, and save your thanks. How say
    you? 55
My prisoner? or my guest? By your dread 'verily',
One of them you shall be.

POLIXENES   Your guest then, madam.
To be your prisoner should import offending,
Which is for me less easy to commit
Than you to punish.

HERMIONE   Not your jailer then, 60
But your kind hostess. Come, I'll question you
Of my lord's tricks and yours when you were boys.
You were pretty lordings then?

POLIXENES   We were, fair Queen,
Two lads that thought there was no more behind
But such a day tomorrow as today, 65
And to be boy eternal.

HERMIONE Was not my lord
The verier wag o'th' two?

POLIXENES
We were as twinned lambs that did frisk i'th' sun,
And bleat the one at th'other. What we changed 70
Was innocence for innocence. We knew not
The doctrine of ill-doing, nor dreamed
That any did. Had we pursued that life,
And our weak spirits ne'er been higher reared
With stronger blood, we should have answered
    heaven 75
Boldly, 'Not guilty', the imposition cleared
Hereditary ours.

HERMIONE   By this we gather
You have tripped since.

POLIXENES   O my most sacred lady,
Temptations have since then been born to's; for
In those unfledged days was my wife a girl. 80
Your precious self had then not crossed the eyes
Of my young playfellow.

HERMIONE   Grace to boot!
Of this make no conclusion, lest you say
Your queen and I are devils. Yet go on.
Th'offences we have made you do we'll answer, 85
If you first sinned with us, and that with us
You did continue fault, and that you slipped not
With any but with us.

LEONTES   Is he won yet?

HERMIONE
He'll stay, my lord.

LEONTES   At my request he would not.

Hermione, my dearest, thou never spok'st 90
To better purpose.

HERMIONE   Never?

LEONTES   Never but once.

HERMIONE
What, have I twice said well? When was't before?
I prithee tell me. Cram's with praise, and make's
As fat as tame things. One good deed dying tongueless
Slaughters a thousand waiting upon that. 95
Our praises are our wages. You may ride's
With one soft kiss a thousand furlongs ere
With spur we heat an acre. But to th' goal.
My last good deed was to entreat his stay.
What was my first? It has an elder sister, 100
Or I mistake you. O, would her name were Grace!
But once before I spoke to th' purpose? When?
Nay, let me have't. I long.

LEONTES   Why, that was when
Three crabbèd months had soured themselves to death
Ere I could make thee open thy white hand 105
And clap thyself my love. Then didst thou utter,
'I am yours for ever.'

HERMIONE   'Tis grace indeed.
Why lo you now; I have spoke to th' purpose twice.
The one for ever earned a royal husband;
Th'other, for some while a friend.
    ⌜She gives her hand to Polixenes.⌝
    They stand aside

LEONTES (aside)   Too hot, too hot: 110
To mingle friendship farre is mingling bloods.
I have tremor cordis on me. My heart dances,
But not for joy, not joy. This entertainment
May a free face put on, derive a liberty
From heartiness, from bounty, fertile bosom, 115
And well become the agent. 'T may, I grant.
But to be paddling palms and pinching fingers,
As now they are, and making practised smiles
As in a looking-glass; and then to sigh, as 'twere
The mort o'th' deer—O, that is entertainment 120
My bosom likes not, nor my brows.—Mamillius,
Art thou my boy?

MAMILLIUS   Ay, my good lord.

LEONTES   I'fecks,
Why, that's my bawcock. What? Hast smutched thy
    nose?
They say it is a copy out of mine. Come, captain,
We must be neat—not neat, but cleanly, captain. 125
And yet the steer, the heifer, and the calf
Are all called neat.—Still virginalling
Upon his palm?—How now, you wanton calf—
Art thou my calf?

MAMILLIUS   Yes, if you will, my lord.

LEONTES
Thou want'st a rough pash and the shoots that I have,
To be full like me. Yet they say we are 131
Almost as like as eggs. Women say so,
That will say anything. But were they false
As o'er-dyed blacks, as wind, as waters, false
As dice are to be wished by one that fixes 135

No bourn 'twixt his and mine, yet were it true
To say this boy were like me. Come, sir page,
Look on me with your welkin eye. Sweet villain,
Most dear'st, my collop! Can thy dam—may't be?—
Affection, thy intention stabs the centre.   140
Thou dost make possible things not so held,
Communicat'st with dreams—how can this be?—
With what's unreal thou coactive art,
And fellow'st nothing. Then 'tis very credent
Thou mayst co-join with something, and thou dost—
And that beyond commission; and I find it—   146
And that to the infection of my brains
And hard'ning of my brows.
POLIXENES   What means Sicilia?
HERMIONE
He something seems unsettled.
POLIXENES   How, my lord!
LEONTES
What cheer? How is't with you, best brother?
HERMIONE   You look
As if you held a brow of much distraction.   151
Are you moved, my lord?
LEONTES   No, in good earnest.
How sometimes nature will betray its folly,
Its tenderness, and make itself a pastime
To harder bosoms! Looking on the lines   155
Of my boy's face, methoughts I did recoil
Twenty-three years, and saw myself unbreeched,
In my green velvet coat; my dagger muzzled,
Lest it should bite its master, and so prove,
As ornament oft does, too dangerous.   160
How like, methought, I then was to this kernel,
This squash, this gentleman.—Mine honest friend,
Will you take eggs for money?
MAMILLIUS   No, my lord, I'll fight.
LEONTES
You will? Why, happy man be's dole!—My brother,
Are you so fond of your young prince as we   165
Do seem to be of ours?
POLIXENES   If at home, sir,
He's all my exercise, my mirth, my matter;
Now my sworn friend, and then mine enemy;
My parasite, my soldier, statesman, all.
He makes a July's day short as December,   170
And with his varying childness cures in me
Thoughts that would thick my blood.
LEONTES   So stands this squire
Officed with me. We two will walk, my lord,
And leave you to your graver steps. Hermione,
How thou lov'st us show in our brother's welcome.
Let what is dear in Sicily be cheap.   176
Next to thyself and my young rover, he's
Apparent to my heart.
HERMIONE   If you would seek us,
We are yours i'th' garden. Shall's attend you there?
LEONTES
To your own bents dispose you. You'll be found,   180
Be you beneath the sky. (*Aside*) I am angling now,

Though you perceive me not how I give line.
Go to, go to!
How she holds up the neb, the bill to him,
And arms her with the boldness of a wife   185
To her allowing husband!
          Exeunt Polixenes and Hermione
          Gone already.
Inch-thick, knee-deep, o'er head and ears a forked
   one!—
Go play, boy, play. Thy mother plays, and I
Play too; but so disgraced a part, whose issue
Will hiss me to my grave. Contempt and clamour   190
Will be my knell. Go play, boy, play. There have been,
Or I am much deceived, cuckolds ere now,
And many a man there is, even at this present,
Now, while I speak this, holds his wife by th'arm,
That little thinks she has been sluiced in's absence,   195
And his pond fished by his next neighbour, by
Sir Smile, his neighbour. Nay, there's comfort in't,
Whiles other men have gates, and those gates opened,
As mine, against their will. Should all despair
That have revolted wives, the tenth of mankind   200
Would hang themselves. Physic for't there's none.
It is a bawdy planet, that will strike
Where 'tis predominant; and 'tis powerful. Think it:
From east, west, north, and south, be it concluded,
No barricado for a belly. Know't,   205
It will let in and out the enemy
With bag and baggage. Many thousand on's
Have the disease and feel't not.—How now, boy?
MAMILLIUS
I am like you, they say.
LEONTES   Why, that's some comfort.
What, Camillo there!
CAMILLO ⌈*coming forward*⌉ Ay, my good lord.   210
LEONTES
Go play, Mamillius, thou'rt an honest man.
          Exit Mamillius
Camillo, this great sir will yet stay longer.
CAMILLO
You had much ado to make his anchor hold.
When you cast out, it still came home.
LEONTES   Didst note it?
CAMILLO
He would not stay at your petitions, made   215
His business more material.
LEONTES   Didst perceive it?
(*Aside*) They're here with me already, whisp'ring,
   rounding,
'Sicilia is a so-forth'. 'Tis far gone
When I shall gust it last.—How came't, Camillo,
That he did stay?
CAMILLO   At the good Queen's entreaty.   220
LEONTES
'At the Queen's' be't. 'Good' should be pertinent,
But so it is, it is not. Was this taken
By any understanding pate but thine?
For thy conceit is soaking, will draw in

More than the common blocks. Not noted, is't,   225
But of the finer natures? By some severals
Of head-piece extraordinary? Lower messes
Perchance are to this business purblind? Say.

CAMILLO
Business, my lord? I think most understand
Bohemia stays here longer.   230

LEONTES Ha?

CAMILLO Stays here longer.

LEONTES Ay, but why?

CAMILLO
To satisfy your highness, and the entreaties
Of our most gracious mistress.

LEONTES   Satisfy?   235
Th'entreaties of your mistress? Satisfy?
Let that suffice. I have trusted thee, Camillo,
With all the near'st things to my heart, as well
My chamber-counsels, wherein, priest-like, thou
Hast cleansed my bosom, I from thee departed   240
Thy penitent reformed. But we have been
Deceived in thy integrity, deceived
In that which seems so.

CAMILLO   Be it forbid, my lord.

LEONTES
To bide upon't: thou art not honest; or
If thou inclin'st that way, thou art a coward,   245
Which hoxes honesty behind, restraining
From course required. Or else thou must be counted
A servant grafted in my serious trust
And therein negligent, or else a fool
That seest a game played home, the rich stake drawn,
And tak'st it all for jest.

CAMILLO   My gracious lord,   251
I may be negligent, foolish, and fearful.
In every one of these no man is free,
But that his negligence, his folly, fear,
Among the infinite doings of the world   255
Sometime puts forth. In your affairs, my lord,
If ever I were wilful-negligent,
It was my folly. If industriously
I played the fool, it was my negligence,
Not weighing well the end. If ever fearful   260
To do a thing where I the issue doubted,
Whereof the execution did cry out
Against the non-performance, 'twas a fear
Which oft infects the wisest. These, my lord,
Are such allowed infirmities that honesty   265
Is never free of. But beseech your grace
Be plainer with me, let me know my trespass
By its own visage. If I then deny it,
'Tis none of mine.

LEONTES   Ha' not you seen, Camillo—
But that's past doubt; you have, or your eye-glass   270
Is thicker than a cuckold's horn—or heard—
For, to a vision so apparent, rumour
Cannot be mute—or thought—for cogitation
Resides not in that man that does not think—
My wife is slippery? If thou wilt confess—   275

Or else be impudently negative
To have nor eyes, nor ears, nor thought—then say
My wife's a hobby-horse, deserves a name
As rank as any flax-wench that puts to
Before her troth-plight. Say't, and justify't.   280

CAMILLO
I would not be a stander-by to hear
My sovereign mistress clouded so without
My present vengeance taken. 'Shrew my heart,
You never spoke what did become you less
Than this, which to reiterate were sin   285
As deep as that, though true.

LEONTES   •   Is whispering nothing?
Is leaning cheek to cheek? Is meeting noses?
Kissing with inside lip? Stopping the career
Of laughter with a sigh?—a note infallible
Of breaking honesty. Horsing foot on foot?   290
Skulking in corners? Wishing clocks more swift,
Hours minutes, noon midnight? And all eyes
Blind with the pin and web but theirs, theirs only,
That would unseen be wicked? Is this nothing?
Why then the world and all that's in't is nothing,   295
The covering sky is nothing, Bohemia nothing,
My wife is nothing, nor nothing have these nothings
If this be nothing.

CAMILLO   Good my lord, be cured
Of this diseased opinion, and betimes,
For 'tis most dangerous.

LEONTES   Say it be, 'tis true.   300

CAMILLO
No, no, my lord.

LEONTES   It is. You lie, you lie.
I say thou liest, Camillo, and I hate thee,
Pronounce thee a gross lout, a mindless slave,
Or else a hovering temporizer, that
Canst with thine eyes at once see good and evil,   305
Inclining to them both. Were my wife's liver
Infected as her life, she would not live
The running of one glass.

CAMILLO   Who does infect her?

LEONTES
Why, he that wears her like her medal, hanging
About his neck, Bohemia, who, if I   310
Had servants true about me, that bare eyes
To see alike mine honour as their profits,
Their own particular thrifts, they would do that
Which should undo more doing. Ay, and thou
His cupbearer, whom I from meaner form   315
Have benched, and reared to worship, who mayst see
Plainly as heaven sees earth and earth sees heaven,
How I am galled, mightst bespice a cup
To give mine enemy a lasting wink,
Which draught to me were cordial.

CAMILLO   Sir, my lord,   320
I could do this, and that with no rash potion,
But with a ling'ring dram, that should not work
Maliciously, like poison. But I cannot
Believe this crack to be in my dread mistress,

So sovereignly being honourable.   325
I have loved thee—
LEONTES   Make that thy question, and go rot!
Dost think I am so muddy, so unsettled,
To appoint myself in this vexation?
Sully the purity and whiteness of my sheets—
Which to preserve is sleep, which being spotted   330
Is goads, thorns, nettles, tails of wasps—
Give scandal to the blood o'th' prince, my son—
Who I do think is mine, and love as mine—
Without ripe moving to't? Would I do this?
Could man so blench?
CAMILLO   I must believe you, sir.   335
I do, and will fetch off Bohemia for't,
Provided that when he's removed your highness
Will take again your queen as yours at first,
Even for your son's sake, and thereby for sealing
The injury of tongues in courts and kingdoms   340
Known and allied to yours.
LEONTES   Thou dost advise me
Even so as I mine own course have set down.
I'll give no blemish to her honour, none.
CAMILLO
My lord, go then, and with a countenance as clear
As friendship wears at feasts, keep with Bohemia   345
And with your queen. I am his cupbearer.
If from me he have wholesome beverage,
Account me not your servant.
LEONTES   This is all.
Do't, and thou hast the one half of my heart;
Do't not, thou splitt'st thine own.
CAMILLO   I'll do't, my lord.   350
LEONTES
I will seem friendly, as thou hast advised me.   *Exit*
CAMILLO
O miserable lady. But for me,
What case stand I in? I must be the poisoner
Of good Polixenes, and my ground to do't
Is the obedience to a master—one   355
Who in rebellion with himself, will have
All that are his so too. To do this deed,
Promotion follows. If I could find example
Of thousands that had struck anointed kings
And flourished after, I'd not do't. But since   360
Nor brass, nor stone, nor parchment bears not one,
Let villainy itself forswear't. I must
Forsake the court. To do't, or no, is certain
To me a break-neck.
            Enter Polixenes
                    Happy star reign now!
Here comes Bohemia.
POLIXENES (*aside*)   This is strange. Methinks   365
My favour here begins to warp. Not speak?—
Good day, Camillo.
CAMILLO   Hail, most royal sir.
POLIXENES
What is the news i'th' court?
CAMILLO   None rare, my lord.

POLIXENES
The King hath on him such a countenance
As he had lost some province, and a region   370
Loved as he loves himself. Even now I met him
With customary compliment, when he,
Wafting his eyes to th' contrary, and falling
A lip of much contempt, speeds from me, and
So leaves me to consider what is breeding   375
That changes thus his manners.
CAMILLO   I dare not know, my lord.
POLIXENES
How, 'dare not'? Do not? Do you know, and dare not?
Be intelligent to me. 'Tis thereabouts.
For to yourself what you do know you must,
And cannot say you 'dare not'. Good Camillo,   380
Your changed complexions are to me a mirror
Which shows me mine changed, too; for I must be
A party in this alteration, finding
Myself thus altered with't.
CAMILLO   There is a sickness
Which puts some of us in distemper, but   385
I cannot name th' disease, and it is caught
Of you that yet are well.
POLIXENES   How caught of me?
Make me not sighted like the basilisk.
I have looked on thousands who have sped the better
By my regard, but killed none so. Camillo,   390
As you are certainly a gentleman, thereto
Clerk-like experienced, which no less adorns
Our gentry than our parents' noble names,
In whose success we are gentle: I beseech you,
If you know aught which does behove my knowledge
Thereof to be informed, imprison't not   396
In ignorant concealment.
CAMILLO   I may not answer.
POLIXENES
A sickness caught of me, and yet I well?
I must be answered. Dost thou hear, Camillo,
I conjure thee, by all the parts of man   400
Which honour does acknowledge, whereof the least
Is not this suit of mine, that thou declare
What incidency thou dost guess of harm
Is creeping toward me; how far off, how near,
Which way to be prevented, if to be;   405
If not, how best to bear it.
CAMILLO   Sir, I will tell you,
Since I am charged in honour, and by him
That I think honourable. Therefore mark my counsel,
Which must be e'en as swiftly followed as
I mean to utter it; or both yourself and me   410
Cry lost, and so good night!
POLIXENES   On, good Camillo.
CAMILLO
I am appointed him to murder you.
POLIXENES
By whom, Camillo?
CAMILLO   By the King.
POLIXENES   For what?

CAMILLO
He thinks, nay, with all confidence he swears
As he had seen't, or been an instrument   415
To vice you to't, that you have touched his queen
Forbiddenly.

POLIXENES   O, then my best blood turn
To an infected jelly, and my name
Be yoked with his that did betray the Best!
Turn then my freshest reputation to   420
A savour that may strike the dullest nostril
Where I arrive, and my approach be shunned,
Nay hated, too, worse than the great'st infection
That e'er was heard or read.

CAMILLO   Swear his thought over
By each particular star in heaven, and   425
By all their influences, you may as well
Forbid the sea for to obey the moon
As or by oath remove or counsel shake
The fabric of his folly, whose foundation
Is piled upon his faith, and will continue   430
The standing of his body.

POLIXENES   How should this grow?

CAMILLO
I know not, but I am sure 'tis safer to
Avoid what's grown than question how 'tis born.
If therefore you dare trust my honesty,
That lies enclosèd in this trunk which you   435
Shall bear along impawned, away tonight!
Your followers I will whisper to the business,
And will by twos and threes at several posterns
Clear them o'th' city. For myself, I'll put
My fortunes to your service, which are here   440
By this discovery lost. Be not uncertain,
For by the honour of my parents, I
Have uttered truth; which if you seek to prove,
I dare not stand by; nor shall you be safer
Than one condemnèd by the King's own mouth,   445
Thereon his execution sworn.

POLIXENES   I do believe thee,
I saw his heart in's face. Give me thy hand.
Be pilot to me, and thy places shall
Still neighbour mine. My ships are ready, and
My people did expect my hence departure   450
Two days ago. This jealousy
Is for a precious creature. As she's rare
Must it be great; and as his person's mighty
Must it be violent; and as he does conceive
He is dishonoured by a man which ever   455
Professed to him, why, his revenges must
In that be made more bitter. Fear o'ershades me.
Good expedition be my friend and comfort
The gracious Queen, part of his theme, but nothing
Of his ill-ta'en suspicion. Come, Camillo,   460
I will respect thee as a father if
Thou bear'st my life off hence. Let us avoid.

CAMILLO
It is in mine authority to command

The keys of all the posterns. Please your highness 464
To take the urgent hour. Come, sir, away.   *Exeunt*

❀

2.1   *Enter Hermione, Mamillius, and Ladies*
HERMIONE
Take the boy to you. He so troubles me
'Tis past enduring.

FIRST LADY   Come, my gracious lord,
Shall I be your play-fellow?

MAMILLIUS No, I'll none of you.

FIRST LADY Why, my sweet lord?   5
MAMILLIUS
You'll kiss me hard, and speak to me as if
I were a baby still. (*To Second Lady*) I love you better.

SECOND LADY
And why so, my lord?

MAMILLIUS   Not for because
Your brows are blacker—yet black brows they say
Become some women best, so that there be not   10
Too much hair there, but in a semicircle,
Or a half-moon made with a pen.

SECOND LADY   Who taught 'this?
MAMILLIUS
I learned it out of women's faces. Pray now,
What colour are your eyebrows?

FIRST LADY   Blue, my lord.
MAMILLIUS
Nay, that's a mock. I have seen a lady's nose   15
That has been blue, but not her eyebrows.

FIRST LADY   Hark ye,
The Queen your mother rounds apace. We shall
Present our services to a fine new prince
One of these days, and then you'd wanton with us,
If we would have you.

SECOND LADY   She is spread of late   20
Into a goodly bulk, good time encounter her.

HERMIONE
What wisdom stirs amongst you? Come sir, now
I am for you again. Pray you sit by us,
And tell's a tale.

MAMILLIUS Merry or sad shall't be?   25
HERMIONE As merry as you will.

MAMILLIUS
A sad tale's best for winter. I have one
Of sprites and goblins.

HERMIONE   Let's have that, good sir.
Come on, sit down, come on, and do your best
To fright me with your sprites. You're powerful at it.30

MAMILLIUS
There was a man—

HERMIONE   Nay, come sit down, then on.
MAMILLIUS (*sitting*)
Dwelt by a churchyard.—I will tell it softly,
Yon crickets shall not hear it.

HERMIONE
Come on then, and give't me in mine ear.

Enter apart Leontes, Antigonus, and Lords

LEONTES
Was he met there? His train? Camillo with him?   35

A LORD
Behind the tuft of pines I met them. Never
Saw I men scour so on their way. I eyed them
Even to their ships.

LEONTES   How blest am I
In my just censure, in my true opinion!
Alack, for lesser knowledge—how accursed   40
In being so blest! There may be in the cup
A spider steeped, and one may drink, depart,
And yet partake no venom, for his knowledge
Is not infected; but if one present
Th'abhorred ingredient to his eye, make known   45
How he hath drunk, he cracks his gorge, his sides,
With violent hefts. I have drunk, and seen the spider.
Camillo was his help in this, his pander.
There is a plot against my life, my crown.
All's true that is mistrusted. That false villain   50
Whom I employed was pre-employed by him.
He has discovered my design, and I
Remain a pinched thing, yea, a very trick
For them to play at will. How came the posterns
So easily open?

A LORD   By his great authority,   55
Which often hath no less prevailed than so
On your command.

LEONTES   I know't too well.
(To Hermione) Give me the boy. I am glad you did not
nurse him.
Though he does bear some signs of me, yet you
Have too much blood in him.

HERMIONE   What is this? Sport?   60

LEONTES *(to a Lord)*
Bear the boy hence. He shall not come about her.
Away with him, and let her sport herself
With that she's big with, *(to Hermione)* for 'tis
Polixenes
Has made thee swell thus.   *Exit one with Mamillius*

HERMIONE   But I'd say he had not,
And I'll be sworn you would believe my saying,   65
Howe'er you lean to th' nayward.

LEONTES   You, my lords,
Look on her, mark her well. Be but about
To say she is a goodly lady, and
The justice of your hearts will thereto add
''Tis pity she's not honest, honourable.'   70
Praise her but for this her without-door form—
Which on my faith deserves high speech—and
straight
The shrug, the 'hum' or 'ha', these petty brands
That calumny doth use—O, I am out,
That mercy does, for calumny will sear   75
Virtue itself—these shrugs, these 'hum's and 'ha's',
When you have said she's goodly, come between
Ere you can say she's honest. But be't known

From him that has most cause to grieve it should be,
She's an adultress.

HERMIONE   Should a villain say so,   80
The most replenished villain in the world,
He were as much more villain. You, my lord,
Do but mistake.

LEONTES   You have mistook, my lady—
Polixenes for Leontes. O, thou thing,
Which I'll not call a creature of thy place   85
Lest barbarism, making me the precedent,
Should a like language use to all degrees,
And mannerly distinguishment leave out
Betwixt the prince and beggar. I have said
She's an adultress, I have said with whom.   90
More, she's a traitor, and Camillo is
A federary with her, and one that knows
What she should shame to know herself,
But with her most vile principal: that she's
A bed-swerver, even as bad as those   95
That vulgars give bold'st titles; ay, and privy
To this their late escape.

HERMIONE   No, by my life,
Privy to none of this. How will this grieve you
When you shall come to clearer knowledge, that
You thus have published me? Gentle my lord,   100
You scarce can right me throughly then to say
You did mistake.

LEONTES   No. If I mistake
In those foundations which I build upon,
The centre is not big enough to bear
A schoolboy's top.—Away with her to prison!   105
He who shall speak for her is afar-off guilty,
But that he speaks.

HERMIONE   There's some ill planet reigns.
I must be patient till the heavens look
With an aspect more favourable. Good my lords,
I am not prone to weeping, as our sex   110
Commonly are; the want of which vain dew
Perchance shall dry your pities. But I have
That honourable grief lodged here which burns
Worse than tears drown. Beseech you all, my lords,
With thoughts so qualified as your charities   115
Shall best instruct you, measure me; and so
The King's will be performed.

LEONTES   Shall I be heard?

HERMIONE
Who is't that goes with me? Beseech your highness
My women may be with me, for you see
My plight requires it.—Do not weep, good fools,   120
There is no cause. When you shall know your
mistress
Has deserved prison, then abound in tears
As I come out. This action I now go on
Is for my better grace.—Adieu, my lord.
I never wished to see you sorry; now   125
I trust I shall. My women, come, you have leave.

LEONTES Go, do our bidding. Hence!

Exit Hermione, guarded, with Ladies

A LORD
  Beseech your highness, call the Queen again.
ANTIGONUS (*to Leontes*)
  Be certain what you do, sir, lest your justice
  Prove violence, in the which three great ones suffer—
  Yourself, your queen, your son.
A LORD (*to Leontes*)   For her, my lord, 131
  I dare my life lay down, and will do't, sir,
  Please you t'accept it, that the Queen is spotless
  I'th' eyes of heaven and to you—I mean
  In this which you accuse her.
ANTIGONUS (*to Leontes*)   If it prove 135
  She's otherwise, I'll keep my stables where
  I lodge my wife, I'll go in couples with her;
  Than when I feel and see her, no farther trust her.
  For every inch of woman in the world,
  Ay, every dram of woman's flesh is false 140
  If she be.
LEONTES Hold your peaces.
A LORD   Good my lord—
ANTIGONUS (*to Leontes*)
  It is for you we speak, not for ourselves.
  You are abused, and by some putter-on
  That will be damned for't. Would I knew the villain—
  I would land-damn him. Be she honour-flawed— 145
  I have three daughters: the eldest is eleven;
  The second and the third nine and some five;
  If this prove true, they'll pay for't. By mine honour,
  I'll geld 'em all. Fourteen they shall not see,
  To bring false generations. They are co-heirs, 150
  And I had rather glib myself than they
  Should not produce fair issue.
LEONTES   Cease, no more!
  You smell this business with a sense as cold
  As is a dead man's nose. But I do see't and feel't
  As you feel doing thus; and see withal 155
  The instruments that feel.
ANTIGONUS   If it be so,
  We need no grave to bury honesty;
  There's not a grain of it the face to sweeten
  Of the whole dungy earth.
LEONTES   What? Lack I credit?
A LORD
  I had rather you did lack than I, my lord, 160
  Upon this ground; and more it would content me
  To have her honour true than your suspicion,
  Be blamed for't how you might.
LEONTES   Why, what need we
  Commune with you of this, but rather follow
  Our forceful instigation? Our prerogative 165
  Calls not your counsels, but our natural goodness
  Imparts this; which, if you—or stupefied
  Or seeming so in skill—cannot or will not
  Relish a truth like us, inform yourselves
  We need no more of your advice. The matter, 170
  The loss, the gain, the ord'ring on't, is all
  Properly ours.
ANTIGONUS   And I wish, my liege,

  You had only in your silent judgement tried it
  Without more overture.
LEONTES   How could that be?
  Either thou art most ignorant by age 175
  Or thou wert born a fool. Camillo's flight
  Added to their familiarity,
  Which was as gross as ever touched conjecture
  That lacked sight only, naught for approbation
  But only seeing, all other circumstances 180
  Made up to th' deed—doth push on this proceeding.
  Yet for a greater confirmation—
  For in an act of this importance 'twere
  Most piteous to be wild—I have dispatched in post
  To sacred Delphos, to Apollo's temple, 185
  Cleomenes and Dion, whom you know
  Of stuffed sufficiency. Now from the oracle
  They will bring all, whose spiritual counsel had
  Shall stop or spur me. Have I done well?
A LORD Well done, my lord. 190
LEONTES
  Though I am satisfied, and need no more
  Than what I know, yet shall the oracle
  Give rest to th' minds of others such as he,
  Whose ignorant credulity will not
  Come up to th' truth. So have we thought it good 195
  From our free person she should be confined,
  Lest that the treachery of the two fled hence
  Be left her to perform. Come, follow us.
  We are to speak in public; for this business
  Will raise us all.
ANTIGONUS (*aside*) To laughter, as I take it, 200
  If the good truth were known.   *Exeunt*

2.2   *Enter Paulina, a Gentleman, and attendants*
PAULINA
  The keeper of the prison, call to him.
  Let him have knowledge who I am.   *Exit Gentleman*
                    Good lady,
  No court in Europe is too good for thee.
  What dost thou then in prison?
    Enter Jailer and Gentleman
                    Now, good sir,
  You know me, do you not?
JAILER   For a worthy lady, 5
  And one who much I honour.
PAULINA Pray you then,
  Conduct me to the Queen.
JAILER
  I may not, madam. To the contrary
  I have express commandment.
PAULINA   Here's ado, 10
  To lock up honesty and honour from
  Th'access of gentle visitors. Is't lawful, pray you,
  To see her women? Any of them? Emilia?
JAILER So please you, madam,
  To put apart these your attendants, I 15
  Shall bring Emilia forth.

PAULINA I pray now call her.—
  Withdraw yourselves.
           Exeunt Gentleman and attendants
JAILER And, madam,
  I must be present at your conference.   20
PAULINA Well, be't so, prithee.   *Exit Jailer*
  Here's such ado, to make no stain a stain
  As passes colouring.
      Enter Jailer and Emilia
              Dear gentlewoman,
  How fares our gracious lady?
EMILIA
  As well as one so great and so forlorn   25
  May hold together. On her frights and griefs,
  Which never tender lady hath borne greater,
  She is, something before her time, delivered.
PAULINA
  A boy?
EMILIA   A daughter, and a goodly babe,
  Lusty, and like to live. The Queen receives   30
  Much comfort in't; says, 'My poor prisoner,
  I am innocent as you.'
PAULINA   I dare be sworn.
  These dangerous, unsafe lunes i'th' King, beshrew
    them!
  He must be told on't, and he shall. The office
  Becomes a woman best. I'll take't upon me.   35
  If I prove honey-mouthed, let my tongue blister,
  And never to my red-looked anger be
  The trumpet any more. Pray you, Emilia,
  Commend my best obedience to the Queen.
  If she dares trust me with her little babe   40
  I'll show't the King, and undertake to be
  Her advocate to th' loud'st. We do not know
  How he may soften at the sight o'th' child.
  The silence often of pure innocence
  Persuades when speaking fails.
EMILIA   Most worthy madam, 45
  Your honour and your goodness is so evident
  That your free undertaking cannot miss
  A thriving issue. There is no lady living
  So meet for this great errand. Please your ladyship
  To visit the next room, I'll presently   50
  Acquaint the Queen of your most noble offer,
  Who but today hammered of this design
  But durst not tempt a minister of honour
  Lest she should be denied.
PAULINA   Tell her, Emilia,
  I'll use that tongue I have. If wit flow from't   55
  As boldness from my bosom, let't not be doubted
  I shall do good.
EMILIA   Now be you blest for it!
  I'll to the Queen. Please you come something nearer.
JAILER
  Madam, if't please the Queen to send the babe
  I know not what I shall incur to pass it,   60
  Having no warrant.
PAULINA   You need not fear it, sir.

This child was prisoner to the womb, and is
By law and process of great nature thence
Freed and enfranchised, not a party to
The anger of the King, nor guilty of—   65
If any be—the trespass of the Queen.
JAILER I do believe it.
PAULINA
  Do not you fear. Upon mine honour,
  I will stand twixt you and danger.   *Exeunt*

2.3   *Enter Leontes*

LEONTES
  Nor night nor day, no rest! It is but weakness
  To bear the matter thus, mere weakness. If
  The cause were not in being—part o'th' cause,
  She, th'adultress; for the harlot King
  Is quite beyond mine arm, out of the blank   5
  And level of my brain, plot-proof; but she
  I can hook to me. Say that she were gone,
  Given to the fire, a moiety of my rest
  Might come to me again. Who's there?
       Enter a Servant
SERVANT   My lord.
LEONTES
  How does the boy?
SERVANT   He took good rest tonight.   10
  'Tis hoped his sickness is discharged.
LEONTES To see his nobleness!
  Conceiving the dishonour of his mother
  He straight declined, drooped, took it deeply,
  Fastened and fixed the shame on't in himself;   15
  Threw off his spirit, his appetite, his sleep,
  And downright languished. Leave me solely. Go,
  See how he fares.   *Exit Servant*
             Fie, fie, no thought of him.
  The very thought of my revenges that way
  Recoil upon me. In himself too mighty,   20
  And in his parties, his alliance. Let him be
  Until a time may serve. For present vengeance,
  Take it on her. Camillo and Polixenes
  Laugh at me, make their pastime at my sorrow.
  They should not laugh if I could reach them, nor   25
  Shall she, within my power.
      Enter Paulina, carrying a babe, with Antigonus,
      Lords, and the Servant, trying to restrain her
A LORD   You must not enter.
PAULINA
  Nay rather, good my lords, be second to me.
  Fear you his tyrannous passion more, alas,
  Than the Queen's life?—a gracious, innocent soul,
  More free than he is jealous.
ANTIGONUS   That's enough.   30
SERVANT
  Madam, he hath not slept tonight, commanded
  None should come at him.
PAULINA   Not so hot, good sir.
  I come to bring him sleep. 'Tis such as you,
  That creep like shadows by him, and do sigh

At each his needless heavings, such as you   35
Nourish the cause of his awaking. I
Do come with words as medicinal as true,
Honest as either, to purge him of that humour
That presses him from sleep.
LEONTES   What noise there, ho?
PAULINA
No noise, my lord, but needful conference   40
About some gossips for your highness.
LEONTES   How?
Away with that audacious lady! Antigonus,
I charged thee that she should not come about me.
I knew she would.
ANTIGONUS   I told her so, my lord,
On your displeasure's peril and on mine,   45
She should not visit you.
LEONTES   What, canst not rule her?
PAULINA
From all dishonesty he can. In this,
Unless he take the course that you have done—
Commit me for committing honour—trust it,
He shall not rule me.
ANTIGONUS   La you now, you hear.   50
When she will take the rein I let her run,
But she'll not stumble.
PAULINA (to Leontes)   Good my liege, I come—
And I beseech you hear me, who professes
Myself your loyal servant, your physician,
Your most obedient counsellor; yet that dares   55
Less appear so in comforting your evils
Than such as most seem yours—I say, I come
From your good queen.
LEONTES Good queen?
PAULINA
Good queen, my lord, good queen, I say good queen,
And would by combat make her good, so were I   61
A man, the worst about you.
LEONTES (to Lords)   Force her hence.
PAULINA
Let him that makes but trifles of his eyes
First hand me. On mine own accord, I'll off.
But first I'll do my errand. The good Queen—   65
For she is good—hath brought you forth a daughter—
Here 'tis—commends it to your blessing.
    She lays down the babe
LEONTES   Out!
A mankind witch! Hence with her, out o'door—
A most intelligencing bawd.
PAULINA   Not so.
I am as ignorant in that as you   70
In so entitling me, and no less honest
Than you are mad, which is enough, I'll warrant,
As this world goes, to pass for honest.
LEONTES (to Lords)   Traitors,
Will you not push her out?
(To Antigonus)   Give her the bastard.
Thou dotard, thou art woman-tired, unroosted   75

By thy Dame Partlet here. Take up the bastard,
Take't up, I say. Give't to thy crone.
PAULINA (to Antigonus)   For ever
Unvenerable be thy hands if thou
Tak'st up the princess by that forcèd baseness
Which he has put upon't.
LEONTES   He dreads his wife.   80
PAULINA
So I would you did. Then 'twere past all doubt
You'd call your children yours.
LEONTES   A nest of traitors.
ANTIGONUS
I am none, by this good light.
PAULINA   Nor I, nor any
But one that's here, and that's himself, for he
The sacred honour of himself, his queen's,   85
His hopeful son's, his babe's, betrays to slander,
Whose sting is sharper than the sword's; and will
    not—
For as the case now stands, it is a curse
He cannot be compelled to't—once remove
The root of his opinion, which is rotten   90
As ever oak or stone was sound.
LEONTES (to Lords)   A callat
Of boundless tongue, who late hath beat her husband,
And now baits me! This brat is none of mine.
It is the issue of Polixenes.
Hence with it, and together with the dam   95
Commit them to the fire.
PAULINA   It is yours,
And might we lay th'old proverb to your charge,
So like you 'tis the worse. Behold, my lords,
Although the print be little, the whole matter
And copy of the father: eye, nose, lip,   100
The trick of's frown, his forehead, nay, the valley,
The pretty dimples of his chin and cheek, his smiles,
The very mould and frame of hand, nail, finger.
And thou good goddess Nature, which hast made it
So like to him that got it, if thou hast   105
The ordering of the mind too, 'mongst all colours
No yellow in't, lest she suspect, as he does,
Her children not her husband's.
LEONTES (to Antigonus)   A gross hag!—
And lozel, thou art worthy to be hanged,
That wilt not stay her tongue.
ANTIGONUS   Hang all the husbands
That cannot do that feat, you'll leave yourself   111
Hardly one subject.
LEONTES   Once more, take her hence.
PAULINA
A most unworthy and unnatural lord
Can do no more.
LEONTES   I'll ha' thee burnt.
PAULINA   I care not.
It is an heretic that makes the fire,   115
Not she which burns in't. I'll not call you tyrant;
But this most cruel usage of your queen—

Not able to produce more accusation
Than your own weak-hinged fancy—something savours
Of tyranny, and will ignoble make you,   120
Yea, scandalous to the world.

LEONTES (*to Antigonus*)   On your allegiance,
Out of the chamber with her! Were I a tyrant,
Where were her life? She durst not call me so
If she did know me one. Away with her!

PAULINA
I pray you do not push me, I'll be gone.   125
Look to your babe, my lord; 'tis yours. Jove send her
A better guiding spirit. What needs these hands?
You that are thus so tender o'er his follies
Will never do him good, not one of you.
So, so. Farewell, we are gone.   *Exit*

LEONTES (*to Antigonus*)
Thou, traitor, hast set on thy wife to this.   131
My child? Away with't! Even thou, that hast
A heart so tender o'er it, take it hence
And see it instantly consumed with fire.
Even thou, and none but thou. Take it up straight.   135
Within this hour bring me word 'tis done,
And by good testimony, or I'll seize thy life,
With what thou else call'st thine. If thou refuse
And wilt encounter with my wrath, say so.
The bastard brains with these my proper hands   140
Shall I dash out. Go, take it to the fire;
For thou set'st on thy wife.

ANTIGONUS   I did not, sir.
These lords, my noble fellows, if they please
Can clear me in't.

LORDS   We can. My royal liege,
He is not guilty of her coming hither.   145

LEONTES You're liars all.

A LORD
Beseech your highness, give us better credit.
We have always truly served you, and beseech
So to esteem of us. And on our knees we beg,
As recompense of our dear services   150
Past and to come, that you do change this purpose
Which, being so horrible, so bloody, must
Lead on to some foul issue. We all kneel.

LEONTES
I am a feather for each wind that blows.
Shall I live on, to see this bastard kneel   155
And call me father? Better burn it now
Than curse it then. But be it. Let it live.
It shall not neither.
(*To Antigonus*)   You, sir, come you hither,
You that have been so tenderly officious
With Lady Margery your midwife there,   160
To save this bastard's life—for 'tis a bastard,
So sure as this beard's grey. What will you adventure
To save this brat's life?

ANTIGONUS   Anything, my lord,
That my ability may undergo,
And nobleness impose. At least thus much,   165

I'll pawn the little blood which I have left
To save the innocent; anything possible.

LEONTES
It shall be possible. Swear by this sword
Thou wilt perform my bidding.

ANTIGONUS   I will, my lord.

LEONTES
Mark, and perform it. Seest thou? For the fail   170
Of any point in't shall not only be
Death to thyself but to thy lewd-tongued wife,
Whom for this time we pardon. We enjoin thee,
As thou art liegeman to us, that thou carry
This female bastard hence, and that thou bear it   175
To some remote and desert place, quite out
Of our dominions; and that there thou leave it,
Without more mercy, to it own protection
And favour of the climate. As by strange fortune
It came to us, I do in justice charge thee,   180
On thy soul's peril and thy body's torture,
That thou commend it strangely to some place
Where chance may nurse or end it. Take it up.

ANTIGONUS
I swear to do this, though a present death
Had been more merciful. Come on, poor babe,   185
Some powerful spirit instruct the kites and ravens
To be thy nurses. Wolves and bears, they say,
Casting their savageness aside, have done
Like offices of pity. Sir, be prosperous
In more than this deed does require; (*to the babe*) and
    blessing   190
Against this cruelty, fight on thy side,
Poor thing, condemned to loss.   *Exit with the babe*

LEONTES   No, I'll not rear
Another's issue.
    Enter a Servant

SERVANT   Please your highness, posts
From those you sent to th'oracle are come
An hour since. Cleomenes and Dion,   195
Being well arrived from Delphos, are both landed,
Hasting to th' court.

A LORD (*to Leontes*)   So please you, sir, their speed
Hath been beyond account.

LEONTES   Twenty-three days
They have been absent. 'Tis good speed, foretells
The great Apollo suddenly will have   200
The truth of this appear. Prepare you, lords.
Summon a session, that we may arraign
Our most disloyal lady; for as she hath
Been publicly accused, so shall she have
A just and open trial. While she lives   205
My heart will be a burden to me. Leave me,
And think upon my bidding.   *Exeunt severally*

❀

3.1   *Enter Cleomenes and Dion*

CLEOMENES
The climate's delicate, the air most sweet;

Fertile the isle, the temple much surpassing
The common praise it bears.
DION   I shall report,
For most it caught me, the celestial habits—
Methinks I so should term them—and the reverence 5
Of the grave wearers. O, the sacrifice—
How ceremonious, solemn, and unearthly
It was i'th' off'ring!
CLEOMENES   But of all, the burst
And the ear-deaf'ning voice o'th' oracle,
Kin to Jove's thunder, so surprised my sense 10
That I was nothing.
DION   If th'event o'th' journey
Prove as successful to the Queen—O, be't so!—
As it hath been to us rare, pleasant, speedy,
The time is worth the use on't.
CLEOMENES   Great Apollo
Turn all to th' best! These proclamations, 15
So forcing faults upon Hermione,
I little like.
DION   The violent carriage of it
Will clear or end the business. When the oracle,
Thus by Apollo's great divine sealed up,
Shall the contents discover, something rare 20
Even then will rush to knowledge. Go. Fresh horses!
And gracious be the issue.   *Exeunt*

3.2   *Enter Leontes, Lords, and Officers*
LEONTES
This sessions, to our great grief we pronounce,
Even pushes 'gainst our heart: the party tried
The daughter of a king, our wife, and one
Of us too much beloved. Let us be cleared
Of being tyrannous since we so openly 5
Proceed in justice, which shall have due course
Even to the guilt or the purgation.
Produce the prisoner.
OFFICER   It is his highness' pleasure
That the Queen appear in person here in court.
    Enter Hermione guarded, with Paulina and Ladies
Silence.   10
LEONTES Read the indictment.
OFFICER (*reads*) Hermione, queen to the worthy Leontes,
King of Sicilia, thou art here accused and arraigned of
high treason in committing adultery with Polixenes,
King of Bohemia, and conspiring with Camillo to take
away the life of our sovereign lord the King, thy royal
husband; the pretence whereof being by circumstances
partly laid open, thou, Hermione, contrary to the faith
and allegiance of a true subject, didst counsel and aid
them for their better safety to fly away by night. 20
HERMIONE
Since what I am to say must be but that
Which contradicts my accusation, and
The testimony on my part no other
But what comes from myself, it shall scarce boot me
To say 'Not guilty'. Mine integrity 25
Being counted falsehood shall, as I express it,

Be so received. But thus: if powers divine
Behold our human actions—as they do—
I doubt not then but innocence shall make
False accusation blush, and tyranny   30
Tremble at patience. You, my lord, best know—
Who least will seem to do so—my past life
Hath been as continent, as chaste, as true
As I am now unhappy; which is more
Than history can pattern, though devised   35
And played to take spectators. For behold me,
A fellow of the royal bed, which owe
A moiety of the throne; a great king's daughter,
The mother to a hopeful prince, here standing
To prate and talk for life and honour, fore   40
Who please to come and hear. For life, I prize it
As I weigh grief, which I would spare. For honour,
'Tis a derivative from me to mine,
And only that I stand for. I appeal
To your own conscience, sir, before Polixenes   45
Came to your court how I was in your grace,
How merited to be so; since he came,
With what encounter so uncurrent I
Have strained t'appear thus. If one jot beyond
The bound of honour, or in act or will   50
That way inclining, hardened be the hearts
Of all that hear me, and my near'st of kin
Cry 'Fie' upon my grave.
LEONTES   I ne'er heard yet
That any of these bolder vices wanted
Less impudence to gainsay what they did   55
Than to perform it first.
HERMIONE   That's true enough,
Though 'tis a saying, sir, not due to me.
LEONTES
You will not own it.
HERMIONE   More than mistress of
Which comes to me in name of fault, I must not
At all acknowledge. For Polixenes,   60
With whom I am accused, I do confess
I loved him as in honour he required;
With such a kind of love as might become
A lady like me; with a love, even such,
So, and no other, as yourself commanded;   65
Which not to have done I think had been in me
Both disobedience and ingratitude
To you and toward your friend, whose love had spoke
Even since it could speak, from an infant, freely
That it was yours. Now for conspiracy,   70
I know not how it tastes, though it be dished
For me to try how. All I know of it
Is that Camillo was an honest man;
And why he left your court, the gods themselves,
Wotting no more than I, are ignorant.   75
LEONTES
You knew of his departure, as you know
What you have underta'en to do in's absence.
HERMIONE Sir,
You speak a language that I understand not.

My life stands in the level of your dreams, 80
Which I'll lay down.
LEONTES   Your actions are my 'dreams'.
You had a bastard by Polixenes,
And I but dreamed it. As you were past all shame—
Those of your fact are so—so past all truth;
Which to deny concerns more than avails; for as 85
Thy brat hath been cast out, like to itself,
No father owning it—which is indeed
More criminal in thee than it—so thou
Shalt feel our justice, in whose easiest passage
Look for no less than death.
HERMIONE   Sir, spare your threats. 90
The bug which you would fright me with, I seek.
To me can life be no commodity.
The crown and comfort of my life, your favour,
I do give lost, for I do feel it gone
But know not how it went. My second joy, 95
And first fruits of my body, from his presence
I am barred, like one infectious. My third comfort,
Starred most unluckily, is from my breast,
The innocent milk in it most innocent mouth,
Haled out to murder; myself on every post 100
Proclaimed a strumpet, with immodest hatred
The childbed privilege denied, which 'longs
To women of all fashion; lastly, hurried
Here, to this place, i'th' open air, before
I have got strength of limit. Now, my liege, 105
Tell me what blessings I have here alive,
That I should fear to die. Therefore proceed.
But yet hear this—mistake me not—no life,
I prize it not a straw; but for mine honour,
Which I would free: if I shall be condemned 110
Upon surmises, all proofs sleeping else
But what your jealousies awake, I tell you
'Tis rigour, and not law. Your honours all,
I do refer me to the oracle.
Apollo be my judge.
A LORD   This your request 115
Is altogether just. Therefore bring forth,
And in Apollo's name, his oracle.
     ⌈*Exeunt certain Officers*⌉
HERMIONE
The Emperor of Russia was my father.
O that he were alive, and here beholding
His daughter's trial; that he did but see 120
The flatness of my misery—yet with eyes
Of pity, not revenge.
  ⌈*Enter Officers with Cleomenes and Dion*⌉
OFFICER
You here shall swear upon this sword of justice
That you, Cleomenes and Dion, have
Been both at Delphos, and from thence have brought
This sealed-up oracle, by the hand delivered 126
Of great Apollo's priest; and that since then
You have not dared to break the holy seal,
Nor read the secrets in't.
CLEOMENES *and* DION All this we swear. 130

LEONTES Break up the seals, and read.
OFFICER (*reads*) Hermione is chaste, Polixenes blameless,
Camillo a true subject, Leontes a jealous tyrant, his
innocent babe truly begotten, and the King shall live
without an heir if that which is lost be not found. 135
LORDS
Now blessèd be the great Apollo!
HERMIONE   Praised!
LEONTES Hast thou read truth?
OFFICER
Ay, my lord, even so as it is here set down.
LEONTES
There is no truth at all i'th' oracle.
The sessions shall proceed. This is mere falsehood. 140
   Enter a Servant
SERVANT
My lord the King! The King!
LEONTES   What is the business?
SERVANT
O sir, I shall be hated to report it.
The prince your son, with mere conceit and fear
Of the Queen's speed, is gone.
LEONTES   How, 'gone'?
SERVANT   Is dead.
LEONTES
Apollo's angry, and the heavens themselves 145
Do strike at my injustice.
   Hermione falls to the ground
     How now there?
PAULINA
This news is mortal to the Queen. Look down
And see what death is doing.
LEONTES   Take her hence.
Her heart is but o'ercharged. She will recover.
I have too much believed mine own suspicion. 150
Beseech you, tenderly apply to her
Some remedies for life.
  Exeunt Paulina and Ladies, carrying Hermione
    Apollo, pardon
My great profaneness 'gainst thine oracle.
I'll reconcile me to Polixenes,
New woo my queen, recall the good Camillo, 155
Whom I proclaim a man of truth, of mercy;
For being transported by my jealousies
To bloody thoughts and to revenge, I chose
Camillo for the minister to poison
My friend Polixenes, which had been done, 160
But that the good mind of Camillo tardied
My swift command. Though I with death and with
Reward did threaten and encourage him,
Not doing it, and being done, he, most humane
And filled with honour, to my kingly guest 165
Unclasped my practice, quit his fortunes here—
Which you knew great—and to the certain hazard
Of all incertainties himself commended,
No richer than his honour. How he glisters
Through my rust! And how his piety 170
Does my deeds make the blacker!

Enter Paulina

PAULINA   Woe the while!
O cut my lace, lest my heart, cracking it,
Break too.

A LORD   What fit is this, good lady?

PAULINA (*to Leontes*)
What studied torments, tyrant, hast for me?
What wheels, racks, fires? What flaying, boiling   175
In leads or oils? What old or newer torture
Must I receive, whose every word deserves
To taste of thy most worst? Thy tyranny,
Together working with thy jealousies—
Fancies too weak for boys, too green and idle   180
For girls of nine—O think what they have done,
And then run mad indeed, stark mad, for all
Thy bygone fooleries were but spices of it.
That thou betrayed'st Polixenes, 'twas nothing.
That did but show thee, of a fool, inconstant,   185
And damnable ingrateful. Nor was't much
Thou wouldst have poisoned good Camillo's honour
To have him kill a king—poor trespasses,
More monstrous standing by, whereof I reckon
The casting forth to crows thy baby daughter   190
To be or none or little, though a devil
Would have shed water out of fire ere done't.
Nor is't directly laid to thee the death
Of the young prince, whose honourable thoughts—
Thoughts high for one so tender—cleft the heart   195
That could conceive a gross and foolish sire
Blemished his gracious dam. This is not, no,
Laid to thy answer. But the last—O lords,
When I have said, cry woe! The Queen, the Queen,
The sweet'st, dear'st creature's dead, and vengeance
    for't
Not dropped down yet.   200

A LORD   The higher powers forbid!

PAULINA
I say she's dead. I'll swear't. If word nor oath
Prevail not, go and see. If you can bring
Tincture or lustre in her lip, her eye,
Heat outwardly or breath within, I'll serve you   205
As I would do the gods. But O thou tyrant,
Do not repent these things, for they are heavier
Than all thy woes can stir. Therefore betake thee
To nothing but despair. A thousand knees,
Ten thousand years together, naked, fasting,   210
Upon a barren mountain, and still winter
In storm perpetual, could not move the gods
To look that way thou wert.

LEONTES   Go on, go on.
Thou canst not speak too much. I have deserved
All tongues to talk their bitt'rest.

A LORD (*to Paulina*)   Say no more.   215
Howe'er the business goes, you have made fault
I'th' boldness of your speech.

PAULINA   I am sorry for't.
All faults I make, when I shall come to know them

I do repent. Alas, I have showed too much
The rashness of a woman. He is touched   220
To th' noble heart. What's gone and what's past help
Should be past grief.
(*To Leontes*)   Do not receive affliction
At my petition. I beseech you, rather
Let me be punished, that have minded you
Of what you should forget. Now, good my liege,   225
Sir, royal sir, forgive a foolish woman.
The love I bore your queen—lo, fool again!
I'll speak of her no more, nor of your children.
I'll not remember you of my own lord,
Who is lost too. Take your patience to you,   230
And I'll say nothing.

LEONTES   Thou didst speak but well
When most the truth, which I receive much better
Than to be pitied of thee. Prithee bring me
To the dead bodies of my queen and son.
One grave shall be for both. Upon them shall   235
The causes of their death appear, unto
Our shame perpetual. Once a day I'll visit
The chapel where they lie, and tears shed there
Shall be my recreation. So long as nature
Will bear up with this exercise, so long   240
I daily vow to use it. Come, and lead me
To these sorrows.   *Exeunt*

3.3   *Enter Antigonus, carrying the babe, with a Mariner*

ANTIGONUS
Thou art perfect then our ship hath touched upon
The deserts of Bohemia?

MARINER   Ay, my lord, and fear
We have landed in ill time. The skies look grimly
And threaten present blusters. In my conscience,
The heavens with that we have in hand are angry,   5
And frown upon's.

ANTIGONUS
Their sacred wills be done. Go get aboard.
Look to thy barque. I'll not be long before
I call upon thee.

MARINER   Make your best haste, and go not
Too far i'th' land. 'Tis like to be loud weather.   10
Besides, this place is famous for the creatures
Of prey that keep upon't.

ANTIGONUS   Go thou away.
I'll follow instantly.

MARINER   I am glad at heart
To be so rid o'th' business.   *Exit*

ANTIGONUS   Come, poor babe.
I have heard, but not believed, the spirits o'th' dead
May walk again. If such thing be, thy mother   16
Appeared to me last night, for ne'er was dream
So like a waking. To me comes a creature,
Sometimes her head on one side, some another.
I never saw a vessel of like sorrow,   20
So filled and so becoming. In pure white robes
Like very sanctity she did approach

My cabin where I lay, thrice bowed before me,
And, gasping to begin some speech, her eyes
Became two spouts. The fury spent, anon   25
Did this break from her: 'Good Antigonus,
Since fate, against thy better disposition,
Hath made thy person for the thrower-out
Of my poor babe according to thine oath,
Places remote enough are in Bohemia.   30
There weep, and leave it crying; and for the babe
Is counted lost for ever, Perdita
I prithee call't. For this ungentle business
Put on thee by my lord, thou ne'er shalt see
Thy wife Paulina more.' And so with shrieks   35
She melted into air. Affrighted much,
I did in time collect myself, and thought
This was so, and no slumber. Dreams are toys,
Yet for this once, yea superstitiously,
I will be squared by this. I do believe   40
Hermione hath suffered death, and that
Apollo would—this being indeed the issue
Of King Polixenes—it should here be laid,
Either for life or death, upon the earth
Of its right father. Blossom, speed thee well!   45
He lays down the babe and a scroll
There lie, and there thy character.
He lays down a box

                There these,
Which may, if fortune please, both breed thee, pretty,
And still rest thine.
    ⌈*Thunder*⌉
            The storm begins. Poor wretch,
That for thy mother's fault art thus exposed
To loss and what may follow! Weep I cannot,   50
But my heart bleeds, and most accursed am I
To be by oath enjoined to this. Farewell.
The day frowns more and more. Thou'rt like to have
A lullaby too rough. I never saw
The heavens so dim by day. A savage clamour!   55
Well may I get aboard. This is the chase.
I am gone for ever!   *Exit, pursued by a bear*
Enter an Old Shepherd
OLD SHEPHERD I would there were no age between ten
and three-and-twenty, or that youth would sleep out
the rest; for there is nothing in the between but getting
wenches with child, wronging the ancientry, stealing,
fighting—hark you now, would any but these boiled-
brains of nineteen and two-and-twenty hunt this
weather? They have scared away two of my best sheep,
which I fear the wolf will sooner find than the master.
If anywhere I have them, 'tis by the seaside, browsing
of ivy. Good luck, an't be thy will!   67
He sees the babe
What have we here? Mercy on's, a bairn! A very pretty
bairn. A boy or a child, I wonder? A pretty one, a very
pretty one. Sure some scape. Though I am not bookish,
yet I can read 'waiting-gentlewoman' in the scape. This
has been some stair-work, some trunk-work, some
behind-door-work. They were warmer that got this

than the poor thing is here. I'll take it up for pity; yet
I'll tarry till my son come. He hallooed but even now.
Whoa-ho-hoa!   76
Enter Clown
CLOWN Hilloa, loa!
OLD SHEPHERD What, art so near? If thou'lt see a thing
to talk on when thou art dead and rotten, come hither.
What ail'st thou, man?   80
CLOWN I have seen two such sights, by sea and by land!
But I am not to say it is a sea, for it is now the sky.
Betwixt the firmament and it you cannot thrust a
bodkin's point.
OLD SHEPHERD Why, boy, how is it?   85
CLOWN I would you did but see how it chafes, how it
rages, how it takes up the shore. But that's not to the
point. O, the most piteous cry of the poor souls!
Sometimes to see 'em, and not to see 'em; now the
ship boring the moon with her mainmast, and anon
swallowed with yeast and froth, as you'd thrust a cork
into a hogshead. And then for the land-service, to see
how the bear tore out his shoulder-bone, how he cried
to me for help, and said his name was Antigonus, a
nobleman! But to make an end of the ship—to see how
the sea flap-dragoned it! But first, how the poor souls
roared, and the sea mocked them, and how the poor
gentleman roared, and the bear mocked him, both
roaring louder than the sea or weather.
OLD SHEPHERD Name of mercy, when was this, boy? 100
CLOWN Now, now. I have not winked since I saw these
sights. The men are not yet cold under water, nor the
bear half dined on the gentleman. He's at it now.
OLD SHEPHERD Would I had been by to have helped the
old man!   105
CLOWN I would you had been by the ship side, to have
helped her. There your charity would have lacked
footing.
OLD SHEPHERD Heavy matters, heavy matters. But look
thee here, boy. Now bless thyself. Thou metst with
things dying, I with things new-born. Here's a sight
for thee. Look thee, a bearing-cloth for a squire's child.
He points to the box
Look thee here, take up, take up, boy. Open't. So, let's
see. It was told me I should be rich by the fairies. This
is some changeling. Open't. What's within, boy? 115
CLOWN (*opening the box*) You're a made old man. If the
sins of your youth are forgiven you, you're well to live.
Gold, all gold!
OLD SHEPHERD This is fairy gold, boy, and 'twill prove so.
Up with't, keep it close. Home, home, the next way.
We are lucky, boy, and to be so still requires nothing
but secrecy. Let my sheep go. Come, good boy, the next
way home.   123
CLOWN Go you the next way with your findings. I'll go
see if the bear be gone from the gentleman, and how
much he hath eaten. They are never curst but when
they are hungry. If there be any of him left, I'll bury
it.
OLD SHEPHERD That's a good deed. If thou mayst discern

by that which is left of him what he is, fetch me to th'
sight of him.　　131
CLOWN Marry will I; and you shall help to put him i'th'
ground.
OLD SHEPHERD 'Tis a lucky day, boy, and we'll do good
deeds on't.　　*Exeunt*

4.1　*Enter Time, the Chorus*
TIME
　I that please some, try all; both joy and terror
　Of good and bad; that makes and unfolds error,
　Now take upon me in the name of Time
　To use my wings. Impute it not a crime
　To me or my swift passage that I slide　　5
　O'er sixteen years and leave the growth untried
　Of that wide gap, since it is in my power
　To o'erthrow law, and in one self-born hour
　To plant and o'erwhelm custom. Let me pass
　The same I am ere ancient'st order was　　10
　Or what is now received. I witness to
　The times that brought them in; so shall I do
　To th' freshest things now reigning, and make stale
　The glistering of this present as my tale
　Now seems to it. Your patience this allowing,　　15
　I turn my glass, and give my scene such growing
　As you had slept between. Leontes leaving
　Th'effects of his fond jealousies, so grieving
　That he shuts up himself, imagine me,
　Gentle spectators, that I now may be　　20
　In fair Bohemia, and remember well
　I mentionèd a son o'th' King's, which Florizel
　I now name to you; and with speed so pace
　To speak of Perdita, now grown in grace
　Equal with wond'ring. What of her ensues　　25
　I list not prophesy, but let Time's news
　Be known when 'tis brought forth. A shepherd's
　　daughter
　And what to her adheres, which follows after,
　Is th'argument of Time. Of this allow,
　If ever you have spent time worse ere now.　　30
　If never, yet that Time himself doth say
　He wishes earnestly you never may.　　*Exit*

4.2　*Enter Polixenes and Camillo*
POLIXENES I pray thee, good Camillo, be no more
importunate. 'Tis a sickness denying thee anything, a
death to grant this.　　3
CAMILLO It is sixteen years since I saw my country.
Though I have for the most part been aired abroad, I
desire to lay my bones there. Besides, the penitent King,
my master, hath sent for me, to whose feeling sorrows
I might be some allay—or I o'erween to think so—
which is another spur to my departure.　　9
POLIXENES As thou lov'st me, Camillo, wipe not out the
rest of thy services by leaving me now. The need I have
of thee thine own goodness hath made. Better not to
have had thee than thus to want thee. Thou, having

made me businesses which none without thee can
sufficiently manage, must either stay to execute them
thyself or take away with thee the very services thou
hast done; which if I have not enough considered—as
too much I cannot—to be more thankful to thee shall
be my study, and my profit therein, the heaping
friendships. Of that fatal country Sicilia, prithee speak
no more, whose very naming punishes me with the
remembrance of that penitent—as thou callest him—
and reconciled King my brother, whose loss of his most
precious queen and children are even now to be afresh
lamented. Say to me, when sawest thou the Prince
Florizel, my son? Kings are no less unhappy, their issue
not being gracious, than they are in losing them when
they have approved their virtues.　　28
CAMILLO Sir, it is three days since I saw the Prince. What
his happier affairs may be are to me unknown; but I
have missingly noted he is of late much retired from
court, and is less frequent to his princely exercises than
formerly he hath appeared.
POLIXENES I have considered so much, Camillo, and with
some care, so far that I have eyes under my service
which look upon his removedness, from whom I have
this intelligence: that he is seldom from the house of
a most homely shepherd, a man, they say, that from
very nothing, and beyond the imagination of his
neighbours, is grown into an unspeakable estate.　　40
CAMILLO I have heard, sir, of such a man, who hath a
daughter of most rare note. The report of her is extended
more than can be thought to begin from such a cottage.
POLIXENES That's likewise part of my intelligence; but, I
fear, the angle that plucks our son thither. Thou shalt
accompany us to the place, where we will, not
appearing what we are, have some question with the
shepherd; from whose simplicity I think it not uneasy
to get the cause of my son's resort thither. Prithee, be
my present partner in this business, and lay aside the
thoughts of Sicilia.　　51
CAMILLO I willingly obey your command.
POLIXENES My best Camillo! We must disguise ourselves.
　　　　　Exeunt

4.3　*Enter Autolycus singing*

AUTOLYCUS
　When daffodils begin to peer,
　　With heigh, the doxy over the dale,
　Why then comes in the sweet o'the year,
　　For the red blood reigns in the winter's pale.

　The white sheet bleaching on the hedge,　　5
　　With heigh, the sweet birds, O how they sing!
　Doth set my pugging tooth on edge,
　　For a quart of ale is a dish for a king.

　The lark, that tirra-lirra chants,
　　With heigh, with heigh, the thrush and the jay,
　Are summer songs for me and my aunts　　11
　　While we lie tumbling in the hay.

I have served Prince Florizel, and in my time wore three-pile, but now I am out of service.

> But shall I go mourn for that, my dear?   15
> The pale moon shines by night,
> And when I wander here and there
> I then do most go right.
>
> If tinkers may have leave to live,
> And bear the sow-skin budget,   20
> Then my account I well may give,
> And in the stocks avouch it.

My traffic is sheets. When the kite builds, look to lesser linen. My father named me Autolycus, who being, as I am, littered under Mercury, was likewise a snapper-up of unconsidered trifles. With die and drab I purchased this caparison, and my revenue is the silly cheat. Gallows and knock are too powerful on the highway. Beating and hanging are terrors to me. For the life to come, I sleep out the thought of it. A prize, a prize!   30

Enter Clown

CLOWN Let me see. Every 'leven wether tods, every tod yields pound and odd shilling. Fifteen hundred shorn, what comes the wool to?

AUTOLYCUS (*aside*) If the springe hold, the cock's mine.   34

CLOWN I cannot do't without counters. Let me see, what am I to buy for our sheep-shearing feast? Three pound of sugar, five pound of currants, rice—what will this sister of mine do with rice? But my father hath made her mistress of the feast, and she lays it on. She hath made me four-and-twenty nosegays for the shearers—three-man-song-men, all, and very good ones—but they are most of them means and basses, but one Puritan amongst them, and he sings psalms to hornpipes. I must have saffron to colour the warden pies; mace; dates, none—that's out of my note; nutmegs, seven; a race or two of ginger—but that I may beg; four pound of prunes, and as many of raisins o'th' sun.

AUTOLYCUS (*grovelling on the ground*) O, that ever I was born!   50

CLOWN I'th' name of me!

AUTOLYCUS O help me, help me! Pluck but off these rags, and then death, death!

CLOWN Alack, poor soul, thou hast need of more rags to lay on thee rather than have these off.   55

AUTOLYCUS O sir, the loathsomeness of them offend me more than the stripes I have received, which are mighty ones and millions.

CLOWN Alas, poor man, a million of beating may come to a great matter.   60

AUTOLYCUS I am robbed, sir, and beaten; my money and apparel ta'en from me, and these detestable things put upon me.

CLOWN What, by a horseman, or a footman?

AUTOLYCUS A footman, sweet sir, a footman.   65

CLOWN Indeed, he should be a footman, by the garments he has left with thee. If this be a horseman's coat it hath seen very hot service. Lend me thy hand, I'll help thee. Come, lend me thy hand.

He helps Autolycus up

AUTOLYCUS O, good sir, tenderly. O!   70

CLOWN Alas, poor soul!

AUTOLYCUS O, good sir, softly, good sir! I fear, sir, my shoulder-blade is out.

CLOWN How now? Canst stand?

AUTOLYCUS Softly, dear sir. Good sir, softly.   75

⌈*He picks the Clown's pocket*⌉

You ha' done me a charitable office.

CLOWN (*reaching for his purse*) Dost lack any money? I have a little money for thee.

AUTOLYCUS No, good sweet sir, no, I beseech you, sir. I have a kinsman not past three-quarters of a mile hence, unto whom I was going. I shall there have money, or anything I want. Offer me no money, I pray you. That kills my heart.   83

CLOWN What manner of fellow was he that robbed you?

AUTOLYCUS A fellow, sir, that I have known to go about with troll-madams. I knew him once a servant of the Prince. I cannot tell, good sir, for which of his virtues it was, but he was certainly whipped out of court.   89

CLOWN His vices, you would say. There's no virtue whipped out of the court. They cherish it to make it stay there; and yet it will no more but abide.

AUTOLYCUS Vices, I would say, sir. I know this man well. He hath been since an ape-bearer, then a process-server—a bailiff—then he compassed a motion of the Prodigal Son, and married a tinker's wife within a mile where my land and living lies, and having flown over many knavish professions, he settled only in rogue. Some call him Autolycus.

CLOWN Out upon him! Prig, for my life, prig! He haunts wakes, fairs, and bear-baitings.   101

AUTOLYCUS Very true, sir. He, sir, he. That's the rogue that put me into this apparel.

CLOWN Not a more cowardly rogue in all Bohemia. If you had but looked big and spit at him, he'd have run.   105

AUTOLYCUS I must confess to you, sir, I am no fighter. I am false of heart that way, and that he knew, I warrant him.

CLOWN How do you now?   109

AUTOLYCUS Sweet sir, much better than I was. I can stand, and walk. I will even take my leave of you, and pace softly towards my kinsman's.

CLOWN Shall I bring thee on the way?

AUTOLYCUS No, good-faced sir, no, sweet sir.

CLOWN Then fare thee well. I must go buy spices for our sheep-shearing.   116

AUTOLYCUS Prosper you, sweet sir.   *Exit the Clown*

Your purse is not hot enough to purchase your spice. I'll be with you at your sheep-shearing, too. If I make not this cheat bring out another, and the shearers prove sheep, let me be unrolled and my name put in the book of virtue.

(Sings) Jog on, jog on, the footpath way,
     And merrily hent the stile-a.
     A merry heart goes all the day,   125
     Your sad tires in a mile-a.   *Exit*

4.4 *Enter Florizel dressed as Doricles a countryman,*
   and Perdita as Queen of the Feast
FLORIZEL
These your unusual weeds to each part of you
Does give a life; no shepherdess, but Flora
Peering in April's front. This your sheep-shearing
Is as a meeting of the petty gods,
And you the queen on't.
PERDITA   Sir, my gracious lord, 5
To chide at your extremes it not becomes me—
O, pardon that I name them! Your high self,
The gracious mark o'th' land, you have obscured
With a swain's wearing, and me, poor lowly maid,
Most goddess-like pranked up. But that our feasts 10
In every mess have folly, and the feeders
Digest it with a custom, I should blush
To see you so attired; swoon, I think,
To show myself a glass.
FLORIZEL   I bless the time
When my good falcon made her flight across 15
Thy father's ground.
PERDITA   Now Jove afford you cause!
To me the difference forges dread; your greatness
Hath not been used to fear. Even now I tremble
To think your father by some accident
Should pass this way, as you did. O, the fates! 20
How would he look to see his work, so noble,
Vilely bound up? What would he say? Or how
Should I, in these my borrowed flaunts, behold
The sternness of his presence?
FLORIZEL   Apprehend
Nothing but jollity. The gods themselves, 25
Humbling their deities to love, have taken
The shapes of beasts upon them. Jupiter
Became a bull, and bellowed; the green Neptune
A ram, and bleated; and the fire-robed god,
Golden Apollo, a poor humble swain, 30
As I seem now. Their transformations
Were never for a piece of beauty rarer,
Nor in a way so chaste, since my desires
Run not before mine honour, nor my lusts
Burn hotter than my faith.
PERDITA   O, but sir, 35
Your resolution cannot hold when 'tis
Opposed, as it must be, by th' power of the King.
One of these two must be necessities,
Which then will speak that you must change this
  purpose,
Or I my life.
FLORIZEL   Thou dearest Perdita, 40
With these forced thoughts I prithee darken not
The mirth o'th' feast. Or I'll be thine, my fair,
Or not my father's. For I cannot be

Mine own, nor anything to any, if
I be not thine. To this I am most constant, 45
Though destiny say no. Be merry, gentle;
Strangle such thoughts as these with anything
That you behold the while. Your guests are coming.
Lift up your countenance as it were the day
Of celebration of that nuptial which 50
We two have sworn shall come.
PERDITA   O Lady Fortune,
Stand you auspicious!
FLORIZEL   See, your guests approach.
Address yourself to entertain them sprightly,
And let's be red with mirth.
  Enter the Old Shepherd, with Polixenes and Camillo,
  disguised, the Clown, Mopsa, Dorcas, and others
OLD SHEPHERD *(to Perdita)*
Fie, daughter, when my old wife lived, upon 55
This day she was both pantler, butler, cook,
Both dame and servant, welcomed all, served all,
Would sing her song and dance her turn, now here
At upper end o'th' table, now i'th' middle,
On his shoulder, and his, her face afire 60
With labour, and the thing she took to quench it
She would to each one sip. You are retired
As if you were a feasted one and not
The hostess of the meeting. Pray you bid
These unknown friends to's welcome, for it is 65
A way to make us better friends, more known.
Come, quench your blushes, and present yourself
That which you are, mistress o'th' feast. Come on,
And bid us welcome to your sheep-shearing,
As your good flock shall prosper.
PERDITA *(to Polixenes)*   Sir, welcome. 70
It is my father's will I should take on me
The hostess-ship o'th' day.
  (To Camillo)   You're welcome, sir.
Give me those flowers there, Dorcas. Reverend sirs,
For you there's rosemary and rue. These keep
Seeming and savour all the winter long. 75
Grace and remembrance be to you both,
And welcome to our shearing.
POLIXENES   Shepherdess,
A fair one are you. Well you fit our ages
With flowers of winter.
PERDITA   Sir, the year growing ancient,
Not yet on summer's death, nor on the birth 80
Of trembling winter, the fairest flowers o'th' season
Are our carnations and streaked gillyvors,
Which some call nature's bastards. Of that kind
Our rustic garden's barren, and I care not
To get slips of them.
POLIXENES   Wherefore, gentle maiden, 85
Do you neglect them?
PERDITA   For I have heard it said
There is an art which in their piedness shares
With great creating nature.
POLIXENES   Say there be,
Yet nature is made better by no mean

But nature makes that mean. So over that art   90
Which you say adds to nature is an art
That nature makes. You see, sweet maid, we marry
A gentler scion to the wildest stock,
And make conceive a bark of baser kind
By bud of nobler race. This is an art   95
Which does mend nature—change it rather; but
The art itself is nature.

PERDITA   So it is.

POLIXENES
Then make your garden rich in gillyvors,
And do not call them bastards.

PERDITA   I'll not put
The dibble in earth to set one slip of them,   100
No more than, were I painted, I would wish
This youth should say 'twere well, and only therefore
Desire to breed by me. Here's flowers for you:
Hot lavender, mints, savory, marjoram,
The marigold, that goes to bed wi'th' sun,   105
And with him rises, weeping. These are flowers
Of middle summer, and I think they are given
To men of middle age. You're very welcome.

    She gives them flowers

CAMILLO
I should leave grazing were I of your flock,
And only live by gazing.

PERDITA   Out, alas,   110
You'd be so lean that blasts of January
Would blow you through and through.
(To Florizel)   Now, my fair'st friend,
I would I had some flowers o'th' spring that might
Become your time of day; *(to Mopsa and Dorcas)* and
yours, and yours,
That wear upon your virgin branches yet   115
Your maidenheads growing. O Proserpina,
For the flowers now that, frighted, thou letst fall
From Dis's wagon!—daffodils,
That come before the swallow dares, and take
The winds of March with beauty; violets, dim,   120
But sweeter than the lids of Juno's eyes
Or Cytherea's breath; pale primroses,
That die unmarried ere they can behold
Bright Phoebus in his strength—a malady
Most incident to maids; bold oxlips, and   125
The crown imperial; lilies of all kinds,
The flower-de-luce being one. O, these I lack,
To make you garlands of, and my sweet friend,
To strew him o'er and o'er.

FLORIZEL   What, like a corpse?

PERDITA
No, like a bank, for love to lie and play on,   130
Not like a corpse—or if, not to be buried,
But quick and in mine arms. Come, take your flowers.
Methinks I play as I have seen them do
In Whitsun pastorals. Sure this robe of mine
Does change my disposition.

FLORIZEL   What you do   135
Still betters what is done. When you speak, sweet,

I'd have you do it ever; when you sing,
I'd have you buy and sell so, so give alms,
Pray so; and for the ord'ring your affairs,
To sing them too. When you do dance, I wish you   140
A wave o'th' sea, that you might ever do
Nothing but that, move still, still so,
And own no other function. Each your doing,
So singular in each particular,
Crowns what you are doing in the present deeds,   145
That all your acts are queens.

PERDITA   O Doricles,
Your praises are too large. But that your youth
And the true blood which peeps so fairly through't
Do plainly give you out an unstained shepherd,
With wisdom I might fear, my Doricles,   150
You wooed me the false way.

FLORIZEL   I think you have
As little skill to fear as I have purpose
To put you to't. But come, our dance, I pray;
Your hand, my Perdita. So turtles pair,
That never mean to part.

PERDITA   I'll swear for 'em.   155

POLIXENES *(to Camillo)*
This is the prettiest low-born lass that ever
Ran on the greensward. Nothing she does or seems
But smacks of something greater than herself,
Too noble for this place.

CAMILLO   He tells her something
That makes her blood look out. Good sooth, she is   160
The queen of curds and cream.

CLOWN   Come on, strike up!

DORCAS Mopsa must be your mistress. Marry, garlic to
mend her kissing with!

MOPSA Now, in good time!

CLOWN Not a word, a word, we stand upon our manners.
Come, strike up!   166

    Music. Here a dance of shepherds and shepherdesses

POLIXENES
Pray, good shepherd, what fair swain is this
Which dances with your daughter?

OLD SHEPHERD
They call him Doricles, and boasts himself
To have a worthy feeding; but I have it   170
Upon his own report, and I believe it.
He looks like sooth. He says he loves my daughter.
I think so, too, for never gazed the moon
Upon the water as he'll stand and read,
As 'twere, my daughter's eyes; and to be plain,   175
I think there is not half a kiss to choose
Who loves another best.

POLIXENES   She dances featly.

OLD SHEPHERD
So she does anything, though I report it
That should be silent. If young Doricles
Do light upon her, she shall bring him that   180
Which he not dreams of.

    Enter a Servant

SERVANT O, master, if you did but hear the pedlar at the

door, you would never dance again after a tabor and pipe. No, the bagpipe could not move you. He sings several tunes faster than you'll tell money. He utters them as he had eaten ballads, and all men's ears grew to his tunes.   187

CLOWN He could never come better. He shall come in. I love a ballad but even too well, if it be doleful matter merrily set down, or a very pleasant thing indeed, and sung lamentably.   191

SERVANT He hath songs for man or woman, of all sizes. No milliner can so fit his customers with gloves. He has the prettiest love songs for maids, so without bawdry, which is strange, with such delicate burdens of dildos and fadings, 'Jump her, and thump her'; and where some stretch-mouthed rascal would, as it were, mean mischief and break a foul gap into the matter, he makes the maid to answer, 'Whoop, do me no harm, good man'; puts him off, slights him, with 'Whoop, do me no harm, good man!'   201

POLIXENES This is a brave fellow.

CLOWN Believe me, thou talkest of an admirable conceited fellow. Has he any unbraided wares?   204

SERVANT He hath ribbons of all the colours i'th' rainbow; points more than all the lawyers in Bohemia can learnedly handle, though they come to him by th' gross; inkles, caddises, cambrics, lawns—why, he sings 'em over as they were gods or goddesses. You would think a smock were a she-angel, he so chants to the sleeve-hand and the work about the square on't.   211

CLOWN Prithee bring him in, and let him approach singing.

PERDITA Forewarn him that he use no scurrilous words in's tunes.   *Exit Servant*

CLOWN You have of these pedlars that have more in them than you'd think, sister.   217

PERDITA Ay, good brother, or go about to think.

Enter Autolycus, wearing a false beard, carrying his pack, and singing

AUTOLYCUS

    Lawn as white as driven snow,
    Cypress black as e'er was crow,   220
    Gloves as sweet as damask roses,
    Masks for faces, and for noses;
    Bugle-bracelet, necklace amber,
    Perfume for a lady's chamber;
    Golden coifs, and stomachers   225
    For my lads to give their dears;
    Pins and poking-sticks of steel,
    What maids lack from head to heel
    Come buy of me, come, come buy, come buy,
    Buy, lads, or else your lasses cry. Come buy!   230

CLOWN If I were not in love with Mopsa thou shouldst take no money of me, but being enthralled as I am, it will also be the bondage of certain ribbons and gloves.

MOPSA I was promised them against the feast, but they come not too late now.   235

DORCAS He hath promised you more than that, or there be liars.

MOPSA He hath paid you all he promised you. Maybe he has paid you more, which will shame you to give him again.   240

CLOWN Is there no manners left among maids? Will they wear their plackets where they should bear their faces? Is there not milking-time, when you are going to bed, or kiln-hole, to whistle of these secrets, but you must be tittle-tattling before all our guests? 'Tis well they are whispering. Clammer your tongues, and not a word more.   247

MOPSA I have done. Come, you promised me a tawdry-lace and a pair of sweet gloves.

CLOWN Have I not told thee how I was cozened by the way, and lost all my money?   251

AUTOLYCUS And indeed, sir, there are cozeners abroad, therefore it behoves men to be wary.

CLOWN Fear not thou, man, thou shalt lose nothing here.

AUTOLYCUS I hope so, sir, for I have about me many parcels of charge.   256

CLOWN What hast here? Ballads?

MOPSA Pray now, buy some. I love a ballad in print, alife, for then we are sure they are true.   259

AUTOLYCUS Here's one to a very doleful tune, how a usurer's wife was brought to bed of twenty money-bags at a burden, and how she longed to eat adders' heads and toads carbonadoed.

MOPSA Is it true, think you?

AUTOLYCUS Very true, and but a month old.   265

DORCAS Bless me from marrying a usurer!

AUTOLYCUS Here's the midwife's name to't, one Mistress Tail-Porter, and five or six honest wives' that were present. Why should I carry lies abroad?

MOPSA (*to Clown*) Pray you now, buy it.   270

CLOWN Come on, lay it by, and let's first see more ballads. We'll buy the other things anon.

AUTOLYCUS Here's another ballad, of a fish that appeared upon the coast on Wednesday the fourscore of April, forty thousand fathom above water, and sung this ballad against the hard hearts of maids. It was thought she was a woman, and was turned into a cold fish for she would not exchange flesh with one that loved her. The ballad is very pitiful, and as true.

DORCAS Is it true too, think you?   280

AUTOLYCUS Five justices' hands at it, and witnesses more than my pack will hold.

CLOWN Lay it by, too. Another.

AUTOLYCUS This is a merry ballad, but a very pretty one.

MOPSA Let's have some merry ones.   285

AUTOLYCUS Why, this is a passing merry one, and goes to the tune of 'Two Maids Wooing a Man'. There's scarce a maid westward but she sings it. 'Tis in request, I can tell you.

MOPSA We can both sing it. If thou'lt bear a part thou shalt hear; 'tis in three parts.   291

DORCAS We had the tune on't a month ago.

AUTOLYCUS I can bear my part, you must know, 'tis my occupation. Have at it with you.

They sing

AUTOLYCUS

 Get you hence, for I must go   295
 Where it fits not you to know.
DORCAS Whither?
MOPSA   O whither?
DORCAS   Whither?
MOPSA It becomes thy oath full well
 Thou to me thy secrets tell.
DORCAS Me let me go thither.   300
MOPSA Or thou go'st to th' grange or mill,
DORCAS If to either, thou dost ill.
AUTOLYCUS Neither.
DORCAS   What neither?
AUTOLYCUS   Neither.
DORCAS Thou hast sworn my love to be.
MOPSA Thou hast sworn it more to me.   305
 Then whither goest? Say, whither?

CLOWN We'll have this song out anon by ourselves. My father and the gentlemen are in sad talk, and we'll not trouble them. Come, bring away thy pack after me. Wenches, I'll buy for you both. Pedlar, let's have the first choice. Follow me, girls.   311
      Exit with Dorcas and Mopsa
AUTOLYCUS And you shall pay well for 'em.

(*Sings*) Will you buy any tape,
 Or lace for your cape,
 My dainty duck, my dear-a?   315
 Any silk, any thread,
 Any toys for your head,
 Of the new'st and fin'st, fin'st wear-a?
 Come to the pedlar,
 Money's a meddler,   320
 That doth utter all men's ware-a.   *Exit*

Enter Servant

SERVANT Master, there is three carters, three shepherds, three neatherds, three swineherds that have made themselves all men of hair. They call themselves saultiers, and they have a dance which the wenches say is a gallimaufry of gambols, because they are not in't. But they themselves are o'th' mind, if it be not too rough for some that know little but bowling, it will please plentifully.   329
OLD SHEPHERD Away. We'll none on't. Here has been too much homely foolery already. (*To Polixenes*) I know, sir, we weary you.
POLIXENES You weary those that refresh us. Pray, let's see these four threes of herdsmen.   334
SERVANT One three of them, by their own report, sir, hath danced before the King, and not the worst of the three but jumps twelve foot and a half by th' square.
OLD SHEPHERD Leave your prating. Since these good men are pleased, let them come in—but quickly, now.

SERVANT Why, they stay at door, sir.   340
 Here a dance of twelve satyrs
POLIXENES (*to the Old Shepherd*)
O, father, you'll know more of that hereafter.
(*To Camillo*) Is it not too far gone? 'Tis time to part them.
He's simple, and tells much.
(*To Florizel*)   How now, fair shepherd,
Your heart is full of something that does take
Your mind from feasting. Sooth, when I was young
And handed love as you do, I was wont   346
To load my she with knacks. I would have ransacked
The pedlar's silken treasury, and have poured it
To her acceptance. You have let him go,
And nothing marted with him. If your lass   350
Interpretation should abuse, and call this
Your lack of love or bounty, you were straited
For a reply, at least if you make a care
Of happy holding her.
FLORIZEL   Old sir, I know
She prizes not such trifles as these are.   355
The gifts she looks from me are packed and locked
Up in my heart, which I have given already,
But not delivered.
(*To Perdita*)   O, hear me breathe my life
Before this ancient sir, who, it should seem,
Hath sometime loved. I take thy hand, this hand   360
As soft as dove's down, and as white as it,
Or Ethiopian's tooth, or the fanned snow that's bolted
By th' northern blasts twice o'er.
POLIXENES   What follows this?
How prettily the young swain seems to wash
The hand was fair before! I have put you out.   365
But to your protestation. Let me hear
What you profess.
FLORIZEL   Do, and be witness to't.
POLIXENES
And this my neighbour too?
FLORIZEL   And he, and more
Than he; and men, the earth, the heavens, and all,
That were I crowned the most imperial monarch,   370
Thereof most worthy, were I the fairest youth
That ever made eye swerve, had force and knowledge
More than was ever man's, I would not prize them
Without her love; for her employ them all,
Commend them and condemn them to her service   375
Or to their own perdition.
POLIXENES   Fairly offered.
CAMILLO
This shows a sound affection.
OLD SHEPHERD   But, my daughter,
Say you the like to him?
PERDITA   I cannot speak
So well, nothing so well, no, nor mean better.
By th' pattern of mine own thoughts I cut out   380
The purity of his.
OLD SHEPHERD   Take hands, a bargain;

And, friends unknown, you shall bear witness to't.
I give my daughter to him, and will make
Her portion equal his.

FLORIZEL   O, that must be
I'th' virtue of your daughter. One being dead,   385
I shall have more than you can dream of yet,
Enough then for your wonder. But come on,
Contract us fore these witnesses.

OLD SHEPHERD   Come, your hand;
And, daughter, yours.

POLIXENES   Soft, swain, a while, beseech you.
Have you a father?   390

FLORIZEL I have. But what of him?

POLIXENES Knows he of this?

FLORIZEL He neither does nor shall.

POLIXENES Methinks a father
Is at the nuptial of his son a guest   395
That best becomes the table. Pray you once more,
Is not your father grown incapable
Of reasonable affairs? Is he not stupid
With age and alt'ring rheums? Can he speak, hear,
Know man from man? Dispute his own estate?   400
Lies he not bed-rid, and again does nothing
But what he did being childish?

FLORIZEL   No, good sir.
He has his health, and ampler strength indeed
Than most have of his age.

POLIXENES   By my white beard,
You offer him, if this be so, a wrong   405
Something unfilial. Reason my son
Should choose himself a wife, but as good reason
The father, all whose joy is nothing else
But fair posterity, should hold some counsel
In such a business.

FLORIZEL   I yield all this;   410
But for some other reasons, my grave sir,
Which 'tis not fit you know, I not acquaint
My father of this business.

POLIXENES   Let him know't.

FLORIZEL
He shall not.

POLIXENES   Prithee let him.

FLORIZEL   No, he must not.

OLD SHEPHERD
Let him, my son. He shall not need to grieve   415
At knowing of thy choice.

FLORIZEL   Come, come, he must not.
Mark our contract.

POLIXENES (removing his disguise)
                    Mark your divorce, young sir,
Whom son I dare not call. Thou art too base
To be acknowledged. Thou a sceptre's heir,
That thus affects a sheep-hook?
(To the Old Shepherd)   Thou, old traitor,   420
I am sorry that by hanging thee I can but
Shorten thy life one week.
(To Perdita)   And thou, fresh piece

Of excellent witchcraft, who of force must know
The royal fool thou cop'st with—

OLD SHEPHERD   O, my heart!

POLIXENES
I'll have thy beauty scratched with briers and made
More homely than thy state.
(To Florizel)   For thee, fond boy,   426
If I may ever know thou dost but sigh
That thou no more shalt see this knack, as never
I mean thou shalt, we'll bar thee from succession,
Not hold thee of our blood, no, not our kin,   430
Farre than Deucalion off. Mark thou my words.
Follow us to the court.
(To the Old Shepherd)   Thou churl, for this time,
Though full of our displeasure, yet we free thee
From the dead blow of it.
(To Perdita)   And you, enchantment,
Worthy enough a herdsman—yea, him too,   435
That makes himself, but for our honour therein,
Unworthy thee—if ever henceforth thou
These rural latches to his entrance open,
Or hoop his body more with thy embraces,
I will devise a death as cruel for thee   440
As thou art tender to't.   Exit

PERDITA   Even here undone.
I was not much afeard, for once or twice
I was about to speak, and tell him plainly
The selfsame sun that shines upon his court
Hides not his visage from our cottage, but   445
Looks on alike. Will't please you, sir, be gone?
I told you what would come of this. Beseech you,
Of your own state take care. This dream of mine
Being now awake, I'll queen it no inch farther,
But milk my ewes and weep.

CAMILLO (to the Old Shepherd)   Why, how now, father?
Speak ere thou diest.

OLD SHEPHERD   I cannot speak, nor think,   451
Nor dare to know that which I know.
(To Florizel)   O sir,
You have undone a man of fourscore-three,
That thought to fill his grave in quiet, yea,
To die upon the bed my father died,   455
To lie close by his honest bones. But now
Some hangman must put on my shroud, and lay me
Where no priest shovels in dust.
(To Perdita)   O cursed wretch,
That knew'st this was the Prince, and wouldst
          adventure
To mingle faith with him. Undone, undone!   460
If I might die within this hour, I have lived
To die when I desire.   Exit

FLORIZEL (to Perdita)   Why look you so upon me?
I am but sorry, not afeard; delayed,
But nothing altered. What I was, I am,
More straining on for plucking back, not following   465
My leash unwillingly.

CAMILLO   Gracious my lord,

You know your father's temper. At this time
He will allow no speech—which I do guess
You do not purpose to him; and as hardly
Will he endure your sight as yet, I fear.   470
Then till the fury of his highness settle,
Come not before him.

FLORIZEL   I not purpose it.
I think, Camillo?

CAMILLO   Even he, my lord.

PERDITA (to Florizel)
How often have I told you 'twould be thus?
How often said my dignity would last   475
But till 'twere known?

FLORIZEL   It cannot fail but by
The violation of my faith, and then
Let nature crush the sides o'th' earth together
And mar the seeds within. Lift up thy looks.
From my succession wipe me, father! I   480
Am heir to my affection.

CAMILLO   Be advised.

FLORIZEL
I am, and by my fancy. If my reason
Will thereto be obedient, I have reason.
If not, my senses, better pleased with madness,
Do bid it welcome.

CAMILLO   This is desperate, sir.   485

FLORIZEL
So call it. But it does fulfil my vow.
I needs must think it honesty. Camillo,
Not for Bohemia, nor the pomp that may
Be thereat gleaned; for all the sun sees, or
The close earth wombs, or the profound seas hides   490
In unknown fathoms, will I break my oath
To this my fair beloved. Therefore, I pray you,
As you have ever been my father's honoured friend,
When he shall miss me—as, in faith, I mean not
To see him any more—cast your good counsels   495
Upon his passion. Let myself and fortune
Tug for the time to come. This you may know,
And so deliver: I am put to sea
With her who here I cannot hold on shore;
And most opportune to her need, I have   500
A vessel rides fast by, but not prepared
For this design. What course I mean to hold
Shall nothing benefit your knowledge, nor
Concern me the reporting.

CAMILLO   O my lord,
I would your spirit were easier for advice,   505
Or stronger for your need.

FLORIZEL   Hark, Perdita—
(To Camillo) I'll hear you by and by.

CAMILLO (aside)   He's irremovable,
Resolved for flight. Now were I happy if
His going I could frame to serve my turn,
Save him from danger, do him love and honour,   510
Purchase the sight again of dear Sicilia

And that unhappy king, my master, whom
I so much thirst to see.

FLORIZEL   Now, good Camillo,
I am so fraught with curious business that
I leave out ceremony.

CAMILLO   Sir, I think   515
You have heard of my poor services i'th' love
That I have borne your father?

FLORIZEL   Very nobly
Have you deserved. It is my father's music
To speak your deeds, not little of his care
To have them recompensed as thought on.

CAMILLO   Well, my lord,
If you may please to think I love the King,   521
And through him what's nearest to him, which is
Your gracious self, embrace but my direction,
If your more ponderous and settled project
May suffer alteration. On mine honour,   525
I'll point you where you shall have such receiving
As shall become your highness, where you may
Enjoy your mistress—from the whom I see
There's no disjunction to be made but by,
As heavens forfend, your ruin—marry her,   530
And with my best endeavours in your absence
Your discontenting father strive to qualify
And bring him up to liking.

FLORIZEL   How, Camillo,
May this, almost a miracle, be done?—
That I may call thee something more than man,   535
And after that trust to thee.

CAMILLO   Have you thought on
A place whereto you'll go?

FLORIZEL   Not any yet.
But as th'unthought-on accident is guilty
To what we wildly do, so we profess
Ourselves to be the slaves of chance, and flies   540
Of every wind that blows.

CAMILLO   Then list to me.
This follows, if you will not change your purpose
But undergo this flight: make for Sicilia,
And there present yourself and your fair princess,
For so I see she must be, fore Leontes.   545
She shall be habited as it becomes
The partner of your bed. Methinks I see
Leontes opening his free arms and weeping
His welcomes forth; asks thee there 'Son, forgiveness!'
As 'twere i'th' father's person, kisses the hands   550
Of your fresh princess; o'er and o'er divides him
'Twixt his unkindness and his kindness. Th'one
He chides to hell, and bids the other grow
Faster than thought or time.

FLORIZEL   Worthy Camillo,
What colour for my visitation shall I   555
Hold up before him?

CAMILLO   Sent by the King your father
To greet him, and to give him comforts. Sir,
The manner of your bearing towards him, with

What you, as from your father, shall deliver—
Things known betwixt us three—I'll write you down,
The which shall point you forth at every sitting   561
What you must say, that he shall not perceive
But that you have your father's bosom there,
And speak his very heart.

FLORIZEL   I am bound to you.
There is some sap in this.

CAMILLO   A course more promising
Than a wild dedication of yourselves   566
To unpathed waters, undreamed shores; most certain,
To miseries enough—no hope to help you,
But as you shake off one, to take another;
Nothing so certain as your anchors, who   570
Do their best office if they can but stay you
Where you'll be loath to be. Besides, you know,
Prosperity's the very bond of love,
Whose fresh complexion and whose heart together
Affliction alters.

PERDITA   One of these is true.   575
I think affliction may subdue the cheek
But not take in the mind.

CAMILLO   Yea, say you so?
There shall not at your father's house these seven
    years
Be born another such.

FLORIZEL   My good Camillo,
She's as forward of her breeding as   580
She is i'th' rear our birth.

CAMILLO   I cannot say 'tis pity
She lacks instructions, for she seems a mistress
To most that teach.

PERDITA   Your pardon, sir. For this
I'll blush you thanks.

FLORIZEL   My prettiest Perdita!
But O, the thorns we stand upon! Camillo,   585
Preserver of my father, now of me,
The medicine of our house, how shall we do?
We are not furnished like Bohemia's son,
Nor shall appear so in Sicilia.

CAMILLO My lord,   590
Fear none of this. I think you know my fortunes
Do all lie there. It shall be so my care
To have you royally appointed as if
The scene you play were mine. For instance, sir,   594
That you may know you shall not want—one word.

They speak apart.
Enter Autolycus

AUTOLYCUS Ha, ha! What a fool honesty is, and trust—
his sworn brother—a very simple gentleman! I have
sold all my trumpery; not a counterfeit stone, not a
ribbon, glass, pomander, brooch, table-book, ballad,
knife, tape, glove, shoe-tie, bracelet, horn-ring to keep
my pack from fasting. They throng who should buy
first, as if my trinkets had been hallowed, and brought
a benediction to the buyer; by which means I saw
whose purse was best in picture; and what I saw, to

my good use I remembered. My clown, who wants but
something to be a reasonable man, grew so in love
with the wenches' song that he would not stir his
pettitoes till he had both tune and words, which so
drew the rest of the herd to me that all their other
senses stuck in ears. You might have pinched a placket,
it was senseless. 'Twas nothing to geld a codpiece of a
purse. I could have filed keys off that hung in chains.
No hearing, no feeling but my sir's song, and admiring
the nothing of it. So that in this time of lethargy I
picked and cut most of their festival purses, and had
not the old man come in with a hubbub against his
daughter and the King's son, and scared my choughs
from the chaff, I had not left a purse alive in the whole
army.

Camillo, Florizel, and Perdita come forward

CAMILLO
Nay, but my letters by this means being there   620
So soon as you arrive shall clear that doubt.

FLORIZEL
And those that you'll procure from King Leontes—

CAMILLO
Shall satisfy your father.

PERDITA   Happy be you!
All that you speak shows fair.

CAMILLO (*seeing Autolycus*)   Who have we here?
We'll make an instrument of this, omit   625
Nothing may give us aid.

AUTOLYCUS (*aside*) If they have overheard me now—why,
hanging!

CAMILLO How now, good fellow? Why shakest thou so?
Fear not, man. Here's no harm intended to thee.   630

AUTOLYCUS I am a poor fellow, sir.

CAMILLO Why, be so still. Here's nobody will steal that
from thee. Yet for the outside of thy poverty, we must
make an exchange. Therefore discase thee instantly—
thou must think there's a necessity in't—and change
garments with this gentleman. Though the pennyworth
on his side be the worst, yet hold thee, (*giving him
money*) there's some boot.

AUTOLYCUS I am a poor fellow, sir. (*Aside*) I know ye well
enough.   640

CAMILLO Nay prithee, dispatch—the gentleman is half
flayed already.

AUTOLYCUS Are you in earnest, sir? (*Aside*) I smell the
trick on't.

FLORIZEL Dispatch, I prithee.   645

AUTOLYCUS Indeed, I have had earnest, but I cannot with
conscience take it.

CAMILLO Unbuckle, unbuckle.

Florizel and Autolycus exchange clothes
(*To Perdita*) Fortunate mistress—let my prophecy
Come home to ye!—you must retire yourself   650
Into some covert, take your sweetheart's hat
And pluck it o'er your brows, muffle your face,
Dismantle you, and, as you can, dislikent
The truth of your own seeming, that you may—

For I do fear eyes—over to shipboard   655
Get undescried.
PERDITA   I see the play so lies
That I must bear a part.
CAMILLO   No remedy.
(To Florizel) Have you done there?
FLORIZEL   Should I now meet my father
He would not call me son.
CAMILLO   Nay, you shall have no hat.
He gives the hat to Perdita
Come, lady, come. Farewell, my friend.
AUTOLYCUS   Adieu, sir.   660
FLORIZEL
O Perdita, what have we twain forgot!
Pray you, a word.
They speak aside
CAMILLO *(aside)*
What I do next shall be to tell the King
Of this escape, and whither they are bound;
Wherein my hope is I shall so prevail   665
To force him after, in whose company
I shall re-view Sicilia, for whose sight
I have a woman's longing.
FLORIZEL   Fortune speed us!
Thus we set on, Camillo, to th' seaside.
CAMILLO The swifter speed the better.   670
          Exeunt Florizel, Perdita, and Camillo
AUTOLYCUS I understand the business, I hear it. To have
an open ear, a quick eye, and a nimble hand is
necessary for a cutpurse. A good nose is requisite also,
to smell out work for th'other senses. I see this is the
time that the unjust man doth thrive. What an
exchange had this been without boot! What a boot is
here with this exchange! Sure the gods do this year
connive at us, and we may do anything extempore.
The Prince himself is about a piece of iniquity, stealing
away from his father with his clog at his heels. If I
thought it were a piece of honesty to acquaint the King
withal, I would not do't. I hold it the more knavery to
conceal it, and therein am I constant to my profession.
*Enter the Clown and the Old Shepherd, carrying a
fardel and a box*
Aside, aside! Here is more matter for a hot brain. Every
lane's end, every shop, church, session, hanging, yields
a careful man work.   686
CLOWN See, see, what a man you are now! There is no
other way but to tell the King she's a changeling, and
none of your flesh and blood.
OLD SHEPHERD Nay, but hear me.   690
CLOWN Nay, but hear *me*.
OLD SHEPHERD Go to, then.
CLOWN She being none of your flesh and blood, your flesh
and blood has not offended the King, and so your flesh
and blood is not to be punished by him. Show those
things you found about her, those secret things, all but
what she has with her. This being done, let the law go
whistle, I warrant you.   698
OLD SHEPHERD I will tell the King all, every word, yea,

and his son's pranks, too, who, I may say, is no honest
man, neither to his father nor to me, to go about to
make me the King's brother-in-law.   702
CLOWN Indeed, brother-in-law was the farthest off you
could have been to him, and then your blood had been
the dearer by I know not how much an ounce.   705
AUTOLYCUS *(aside)* Very wisely, puppies.
OLD SHEPHERD Well, let us to the King. There is that in
this fardel will make him scratch his beard.
AUTOLYCUS *(aside)* I know not what impediment this
complaint may be to the flight of my master.   710
CLOWN Pray heartily he be at' palace.
AUTOLYCUS *(aside)* Though I am not naturally honest, I
am so sometimes by chance. Let me pocket up my
pedlar's excrement.
He removes his false beard
—How now, rustics, whither are you bound?   715
OLD SHEPHERD To th' palace, an it like your worship.
AUTOLYCUS Your affairs there? What? With whom? The
condition of that fardel? The place of your dwelling?
Your names? Your ages? Of what having, breeding,
and anything that is fitting to be known, discover.   720
CLOWN We are but plain fellows, sir.
AUTOLYCUS A lie, you are rough and hairy. Let me have
no lying. It becomes none but tradesmen, and they
often give us soldiers the lie, but we pay them for it
with stamped coin, not stabbing steel, therefore they
do not *give* us the lie.   726
CLOWN Your worship had like to have given us one if you
had not taken yourself with the manner.
OLD SHEPHERD Are you a courtier, an't like you, sir?   729
AUTOLYCUS Whether it like me or no, I am a courtier.
Seest thou not the air of the court in these enfoldings?
Hath not my gait in it the measure of the court?
Receives not thy nose court-odour from me? Reflect I
not on thy baseness court-contempt? Thinkest thou,
for that I insinuate to toze from thee thy business, I
am therefore no courtier? I am courtier cap-à-pie, and
one that will either push on or pluck back thy business
there. Whereupon I command thee to open thy affair.
OLD SHEPHERD My business, sir, is to the King.
AUTOLYCUS What advocate hast thou to him?   740
OLD SHEPHERD I know not, an't like you.
CLOWN *(aside to the Old Shepherd)* 'Advocate''s the court
word for a pheasant. Say you have none.
OLD SHEPHERD
None, sir. I have no pheasant, cock nor hen.
AUTOLYCUS *(aside)*
How blessed are we that are not simple men!   745
Yet nature might have made me as these are,
Therefore I will not disdain.
CLOWN This cannot be but a great courtier.
OLD SHEPHERD His garments are rich, but he wears them
not handsomely.   750
CLOWN He seems to be the more noble in being fantastical.
A great man, I'll warrant. I know by the picking on's
teeth.

AUTOLYCUS The fardel there, what's i'th' fardel? Wherefore
that box?　　　755

OLD SHEPHERD Sir, there lies such secrets in this fardel
and box which none must know but the King, and
which he shall know within this hour, if I may come
to th' speech of him.

AUTOLYCUS Age, thou hast lost thy labour.　　　760

OLD SHEPHERD Why, sir?

AUTOLYCUS The King is not at the palace, he is gone
aboard a new ship to purge melancholy and air himself;
for if thou beest capable of things serious, thou must
know the King is full of grief.　　　765

OLD SHEPHERD So 'tis said, sir; about his son, that should
have married a shepherd's daughter.

AUTOLYCUS If that shepherd be not in handfast, let him
fly. The curses he shall have, the tortures he shall feel,
will break the back of man, the heart of monster.　770

CLOWN Think you so, sir?

AUTOLYCUS Not he alone shall suffer what wit can make
heavy and vengeance bitter, but those that are germane
to him, though removed fifty times, shall all come
under the hangman, which, though it be great pity,
yet it is necessary. An old sheep-whistling rogue, a
ram-tender, to offer to have his daughter come into
grace! Some say he shall be stoned; but that death is
too soft for him, say I. Draw our throne into a
sheepcote? All deaths are too few, the sharpest too
easy.　　　781

CLOWN Has the old man e'er a son, sir, do you hear, an't
like you, sir?

AUTOLYCUS He has a son, who shall be flayed alive, then
'nointed over with honey, set on the head of a wasps'
nest, then stand till he be three-quarters-and-a-dram
dead, then recovered again with aqua-vitae, or some
other hot infusion, then, raw as he is, and in the hottest
day prognostication proclaims, shall he be set against
a brick wall, the sun looking with a southward eye
upon him, where he is to behold him with flies blown
to death. But what talk we of these traitorly rascals,
whose miseries are to be smiled at, their offences being
so capital? Tell me, for you seem to be honest plain
men, what you have to the King. Being something
gently considered, I'll bring you where he is aboard,
tender your persons to his presence, whisper him in
your behalfs, and if it be in man, besides the King, to
effect your suits, here is man shall do it.　　799

CLOWN (to the Old Shepherd) He seems to be of great
authority. Close with him, give him gold; and though
authority be a stubborn bear, yet he is oft led by the
nose with gold. Show the inside of your purse to the
outside of his hand, and no more ado. Remember—
'stoned', and 'flayed alive'.　　　805

OLD SHEPHERD An't please you, sir, to undertake the
business for us, here is that gold I have. I'll make it as
much more, and leave this young man in pawn till I
bring it you.

AUTOLYCUS After I have done what I promised?　810

OLD SHEPHERD Ay, sir.

AUTOLYCUS Well, give me the moiety. (To the Clown) Are
you a party in this business?

CLOWN In some sort, sir. But though my case be a pitiful
one, I hope I shall not be flayed out of it.　　815

AUTOLYCUS O, that's the case of the shepherd's son. Hang
him, he'll be made an example.

CLOWN (to the Old Shepherd) Comfort, good comfort. We
must to the King, and show our strange sights. He
must know 'tis none of your daughter, nor my sister.
We are gone else. (To Autolycus) Sir, I will give you as
much as this old man does when the business is
performed, and remain, as he says, your pawn till it
be brought you.　　　824

AUTOLYCUS I will trust you. Walk before toward the
seaside. Go on the right hand. I will but look upon the
hedge, and follow you.

CLOWN (to the Old Shepherd) We are blessed in this man,
as I may say, even blessed.　　　829

OLD SHEPHERD Let's before, as he bids us. He was provided
to do us good.　　　*Exit with the Clown*

AUTOLYCUS If I had a mind to be honest, I see fortune
would not suffer me. She drops booties in my mouth.
I am courted now with a double occasion: gold, and a
means to do the Prince my master good, which who
knows how that may turn back to my advancement?
I will bring these two moles, these blind ones, aboard
him. If he think it fit to shore them again, and that
the complaint they have to the King concerns him
nothing, let him call me rogue for being so far officious,
for I am proof against that title, and what shame else
belongs to't. To him will I present them. There may be
matter in it.　　　*Exit*

5.1　*Enter Leontes, Cleomenes, Dion, and Paulina*

CLEOMENES (to Leontes)
Sir, you have done enough, and have performed
A saint-like sorrow. No fault could you make
Which you have not redeemed, indeed, paid down
More penitence than done trespass. At the last
Do as the heavens have done, forget your evil.　5
With them, forgive yourself.

LEONTES　　　　　Whilst I remember
Her and her virtues I cannot forget
My blemishes in them, and so still think of
The wrong I did myself, which was so much
That heirless it hath made my kingdom, and　10
Destroyed the sweet'st companion that e'er man
Bred his hopes out of. True?

PAULINA　　　　　Too true, my lord.
If one by one you wedded all the world,
Or from the all that are took something good
To make a perfect woman, she you killed　15
Would be unparalleled.

LEONTES　　　　　I think so. Killed?
She I killed? I did so. But thou strik'st me

Sorely to say I did; it is as bitter
Upon thy tongue as in my thought. Now, good now,
Say so but seldom.

CLEOMENES   Not at all, good lady.   20
You might have spoke a thousand things that would
Have done the time more benefit, and graced
Your kindness better.

PAULINA   You are one of those
Would have him wed again.

DION   If you would not so
You pity not the state, nor the remembrance   25
Of his most sovereign name, consider little
What dangers, by his highness' fail of issue,
May drop upon his kingdom and devour
Incertain lookers-on. What were more holy
Than to rejoice the former queen is well?   30
What holier, than for royalty's repair,
For present comfort and for future good,
To bless the bed of majesty again
With a sweet fellow to't?

PAULINA   There is none worthy
Respecting her that's gone. Besides, the gods   35
Will have fulfilled their secret purposes.
For has not the divine Apollo said?
Is't not the tenor of his oracle
That King Leontes shall not have an heir
Till his lost child be found? Which that it shall   40
Is all as monstrous to our human reason
As my Antigonus to break his grave
And come again to me, who, on my life,
Did perish with the infant. 'Tis your counsel
My lord should to the heavens be contrary,   45
Oppose against their wills.
(To Leontes)   Care not for issue.
The crown will find an heir. Great Alexander
Left his to th' worthiest, so his successor
Was like to be the best.

LEONTES   Good Paulina,
Who hast the memory of Hermione,   50
I know, in honour—O, that ever I
Had squared me to thy counsel! Then even now
I might have looked upon my queen's full eyes,
Have taken treasure from her lips.

PAULINA   And left them
More rich for what they yielded.

LEONTES   Thou speak'st truth. 55
No more such wives, therefore no wife. One worse,
And better used, would make her sainted spirit
Again possess her corpse, and on this stage,
Where we offenders mourn, appear soul-vexed,
And begin, 'Why to me?'

PAULINA   Had she such power   60
She had just cause.

LEONTES   She had, and would incense me
To murder her I married.

PAULINA   I should so.
Were I the ghost that walked I'd bid you mark
Her eye, and tell me for what dull part in't

You chose her. Then I'd shriek that even your ears   65
Should rift to hear me, and the words that followed
Should be, 'Remember mine'.

LEONTES   Stars, stars,
And all eyes else, dead coals! Fear thou no wife.
I'll have no wife, Paulina.

PAULINA   Will you swear
Never to marry but by my free leave?   70

LEONTES
Never, Paulina, so be blest my spirit.

PAULINA
Then, good my lords, bear witness to his oath.

CLEOMENES
You tempt him over-much.

PAULINA   Unless another
As like Hermione as is her picture
Affront his eye—

CLEOMENES   Good madam, I have done.   75

PAULINA
Yet if my lord will marry—if you will, sir;
No remedy but you will—give me the office
To choose your queen. She shall not be so young
As was your former, but she shall be such
As, walked your first queen's ghost, it should take joy
To see her in your arms.

LEONTES   My true Paulina,   81
We shall not marry till thou bidd'st us.

PAULINA   That
Shall be when your first queen's again in breath.
Never till then.

Enter a Servant

SERVANT
One that gives out himself Prince Florizel,   85
Son of Polixenes, with his princess—she
The fairest I have yet beheld—desires access
To your high presence.

LEONTES   What with him? He comes not
Like to his father's greatness. His approach,
So out of circumstance and sudden, tells us   90
'Tis not a visitation framed, but forced
By need and accident. What train?

SERVANT   But few,
And those but mean.

LEONTES   His princess, say you, with him?

SERVANT
Ay, the most peerless piece of earth, I think,
That e'er the sun shone bright on.

PAULINA   O, Hermione,   95
As every present time doth boast itself
Above a better, gone, so must thy grave
Give way to what's seen now!
(To the Servant)   Sir, you yourself
Have said and writ so; but your writing now
Is colder than that theme. She had not been   100
Nor was not to be equalled—thus your verse
Flowed with her beauty once. 'Tis shrewdly ebbed
To say you have seen a better.

SERVANT   Pardon, madam.

The one I have almost forgot—your pardon!
The other, when she has obtained your eye,   105
Will have your tongue too. This is a creature,
Would she begin a sect, might quench the zeal
Of all professors else; make proselytes
Of who she but bid follow.

PAULINA   How? Not women!

SERVANT
Women will love her that she is a woman   110
More worth than any man; men, that she is
The rarest of all women.

LEONTES   Go, Cleomenes.
Yourself, assisted with your honoured friends,
Bring them to our embracement.   *Exit Cleomenes*
                   Still 'tis strange
He thus should steal upon us.

PAULINA   Had our prince,   115
Jewel of children, seen this hour, he had paired
Well with this lord. There was not full a month
Between their births.

LEONTES   Prithee no more, cease. Thou know'st
He dies to me again when talked of. Sure,
When I shall see this gentleman thy speeches   120
Will bring me to consider that which may
Unfurnish me of reason. They are come.

    Enter Florizel, Perdita, Cleomenes, and others
Your mother was most true to wedlock, Prince,
For she did print your royal father off,
Conceiving you. Were I but twenty-one,   125
Your father's image is so hit in you,
His very air, that I should call you brother,
As I did him, and speak of something wildly
By us performed before. Most dearly welcome,
And your fair princess—goddess! O, alas,   130
I lost a couple that 'twixt heaven and earth
Might thus have stood, begetting wonder, as
You, gracious couple, do; and then I lost—
All mine own folly—the society,
Amity too, of your brave father, whom,   135
Though bearing misery, I desire my life
Once more to look on him.

FLORIZEL   By his command
Have I here touched Sicilia, and from him
Give you all greetings that a king at friend
Can send his brother; and but infirmity,   140
Which waits upon worn times, hath something seized
His wished ability, he had himself
The lands and waters 'twixt your throne and his
Measured to look upon you, whom he loves—
He bade me say so—more than all the sceptres,   145
And those that bear them, living.

LEONTES   O, my brother!
Good gentleman, the wrongs I have done thee stir
Afresh within me, and these thy offices,
So rarely kind, are as interpreters
Of my behindhand slackness. Welcome hither,   150
As is the spring to th'earth! And hath he too

Exposed this paragon to th' fearful usage—
At least ungentle—of the dreadful Neptune
To greet a man not worth her pains, much less
Th'adventure of her person?

FLORIZEL   Good my lord,   155
She came from Libya.

LEONTES   Where the warlike Smalus,
That noble honoured lord, is feared and loved?

FLORIZEL
Most royal sir, from thence; from him whose daughter
His tears proclaimed his, parting with her. Thence,
A prosperous south wind friendly, we have crossed,
To execute the charge my father gave me   161
For visiting your highness. My best train
I have from your Sicilian shores dismissed;
Who for Bohemia bend, to signify
Not only my success in Libya, sir,   165
But my arrival, and my wife's, in safety
Here where we are.

LEONTES   The blessèd gods
Purge all infection from our air whilst you
Do climate here! You have a holy father,
A graceful gentleman, against whose person,   170
So sacred as it is, I have done sin,
For which the heavens, taking angry note,
Have left me issueless; and your father's blessed,
As he from heaven merits it, with you,
Worthy his goodness. What might I have been,   175
Might I a son and daughter now have looked on,
Such goodly things as you?

    Enter a Lord

LORD   Most noble sir,
That which I shall report will bear no credit
Were not the proof so nigh. Please you, great sir,
Bohemia greets you from himself by me;   180
Desires you to attach his son, who has,
His dignity and duty both cast off,
Fled from his father, from his hopes, and with
A shepherd's daughter.

LEONTES   Where's Bohemia? Speak.

LORD
Here in your city. I now came from him.   185
I speak amazedly, and it becomes
My marvel and my message. To your court
Whiles he was hast'ning—in the chase, it seems,
Of this fair couple—meets he on the way
The father of this seeming lady and   190
Her brother, having both their country quitted
With this young prince.

FLORIZEL   Camillo has betrayed me,
Whose honour and whose honesty till now
Endured all weathers.

LORD   Lay't so to his charge.
He's with the King your father.

LEONTES   Who, Camillo?   195

LORD
Camillo, sir. I spake with him, who now

Has these poor men in question. Never saw I
Wretches so quake. They kneel, they kiss the earth,
Forswear themselves as often as they speak.
Bohemia stops his ears, and threatens them   200
With divers deaths in death.

PERDITA   O, my poor father!
The heaven sets spies upon us, will not have
Our contract celebrated.

LEONTES   You are married?

FLORIZEL
We are not, sir, nor are we like to be.
The stars, I see, will kiss the valleys first.   205
The odds for high and low's alike.

LEONTES   My lord,
Is this the daughter of a king?

FLORIZEL   She is,
When once she is my wife.

LEONTES
That 'once', I see, by your good father's speed
Will come on very slowly. I am sorry,   210
Most sorry, you have broken from his liking
Where you were tied in duty; and as sorry
Your choice is not so rich in worth as beauty,
That you might well enjoy her.

FLORIZEL (to Perdita)   Dear, look up.
Though fortune, visible an enemy,   215
Should chase us with my father, power no jot
Hath she to change our loves.—Beseech you, sir,
Remember since you owed no more to time
Than I do now. With thought of such affections,
Step forth mine advocate. At your request   220
My father will grant precious things as trifles.

LEONTES
Would he do so, I'd beg your precious mistress,
Which he counts but a trifle.

PAULINA   Sir, my liege,
Your eye hath too much youth in't. Not a month
Fore your queen died she was more worth such gazes
Than what you look on now.

LEONTES   I thought of her   226
Even in these looks I made.
(To Florizel)   But your petition
Is yet unanswered. I will to your father.
Your honour not o'erthrown by your desires,
I am friend to them and you. Upon which errand   230
I now go toward him. Therefore follow me,
And mark what way I make. Come, good my lord.

                                        Exeunt

5.2   *Enter Autolycus and a Gentleman*

AUTOLYCUS Beseech you, sir, were you present at this
relation?

FIRST GENTLEMAN I was by at the opening of the fardel,
heard the old shepherd deliver the manner how he
found it; whereupon, after a little amazedness, we were
all commanded out of the chamber. Only this,
methought I heard the shepherd say he found the child.

AUTOLYCUS I would most gladly know the issue of it.   8

FIRST GENTLEMAN I make a broken delivery of the business,
but the changes I perceived in the King and Camillo
were very notes of admiration. They seemed almost,
with staring on one another, to tear the cases of their
eyes. There was speech in their dumbness, language in
their very gesture. They looked as they had heard of a
world ransomed, or one destroyed. A notable passion
of wonder appeared in them, but the wisest beholder,
that knew no more but seeing, could not say if
th'importance were joy or sorrow. But in the extremity
of the one, it must needs be.

                Enter another Gentleman

Here comes a gentleman that happily knows more. The
news, Ruggiero!   21

SECOND GENTLEMAN Nothing but bonfires. The oracle is
fulfilled. The King's daughter is found. Such a deal of
wonder is broken out within this hour, that ballad-
makers cannot be able to express it.   25

                Enter another Gentleman

Here comes the Lady Paulina's steward. He can deliver
you more.—How goes it now, sir? This news which is
called true is so like an old tale that the verity of it is
in strong suspicion. Has the King found his heir?   29

THIRD GENTLEMAN Most true, if ever truth were pregnant
by circumstance. That which you hear you'll swear
you see, there is such unity in the proofs. The mantle
of Queen Hermione's, her jewel about the neck of it,
the letters of Antigonus found with it, which they know
to be his character; the majesty of the creature, in
resemblance of the mother; the affection of nobleness
which nature shows above her breeding, and many
other evidences proclaim her with all certainty to be
the King's daughter. Did you see the meeting of the
two kings?   40

SECOND GENTLEMAN No.

THIRD GENTLEMAN Then have you lost a sight which was
to be seen, cannot be spoken of. There might you have
beheld one joy crown another, so and in such manner
that it seemed sorrow wept to take leave of them, for
their joy waded in tears. There was casting up of eyes,
holding up of hands, with countenance of such
distraction that they were to be known by garment,
not by favour. Our king being ready to leap out of
himself for joy of his found daughter, as if that joy
were now become a loss cries, 'O, thy mother, thy
mother!', then asks Bohemia forgiveness, then
embraces his son-in-law, then again worries he his
daughter with clipping her. Now he thanks the old
shepherd, which stands by like a weather-bitten conduit
of many kings' reigns. I never heard of such another
encounter, which lames report to follow it, and undoes
description to do it.

SECOND GENTLEMAN What, pray you, became of Antigonus, that carried hence the child?   60

THIRD GENTLEMAN Like an old tale still, which will have
matter to rehearse though credit be asleep and not an

ear open. He was torn to pieces with a bear. This avouches the shepherd's son, who has not only his innocence, which seems much, to justify him, but a handkerchief and rings of his, that Paulina knows. 66

FIRST GENTLEMAN What became of his barque and his followers?

THIRD GENTLEMAN Wrecked the same instant of their master's death, and in the view of the shepherd; so that all the instruments which aided to expose the child were even then lost when it was found. But O, the noble combat that 'twixt joy and sorrow was fought in Paulina! She had one eye declined for the loss of her husband, another elevated that the oracle was fulfilled. She lifted the Princess from the earth, and so locks her in embracing as if she would pin her to her heart, that she might no more be in danger of losing. 78

FIRST GENTLEMAN The dignity of this act was worth the audience of kings and princes, for by such was it acted.

THIRD GENTLEMAN One of the prettiest touches of all, and that which angled for mine eyes—caught the water, though not the fish—was when at the relation of the Queen's death, with the manner how she came to't bravely confessed and lamented by the King, how attentiveness wounded his daughter till from one sign of dolour to another she did, with an 'Alas', I would fain say bleed tears; for I am sure my heart wept blood. Who was most marble there changed colour. Some swooned, all sorrowed. If all the world could have seen't, the woe had been universal. 91

FIRST GENTLEMAN Are they returned to the court?

THIRD GENTLEMAN No. The Princess, hearing of her mother's statue, which is in the keeping of Paulina, a piece many years in doing, and now newly performed by that rare Italian master Giulio Romano, who, had he himself eternity and could put breath into his work, would beguile nature of her custom, so perfectly he is her ape. He so near to Hermione hath done Hermione that they say one would speak to her and stand in hope of answer. Thither with all greediness of affection are they gone, and there they intend to sup. 102

SECOND GENTLEMAN I thought she had some great matter there in hand, for she hath privately twice or thrice a day, ever since the death of Hermione, visited that removed house. Shall we thither, and with our company piece the rejoicing? 107

FIRST GENTLEMAN Who would be thence, that has the benefit of access? Every wink of an eye some new grace will be born. Our absence makes us unthrifty to our knowledge. Let's along.   *Exeunt Gentlemen*

AUTOLYCUS Now, had I not the dash of my former life in me, would preferment drop on my head. I brought the old man and his son aboard the Prince; told him I heard them talk of a fardel, and I know not what. But he at that time over-fond of the shepherd's daughter— so he then took her to be—who began to be much sea-sick, and himself little better, extremity of weather continuing, this mystery remained undiscovered. But 'tis all one to me, for had I been the finder-out of this secret it would not have relished among my other discredits. 122

Enter the Old Shepherd and the Clown, dressed as gentlemen

Here come those I have done good to against my will, and already appearing in the blossoms of their fortune.

OLD SHEPHERD Come, boy; I am past more children, but thy sons and daughters will be all gentlemen born. 126

CLOWN (*to Autolycus*) You are well met, sir. You denied to fight with me this other day because I was no gentleman born. See you these clothes? Say you see them not, and think me still no gentleman born. You were best say these robes are not gentlemen born. Give me the lie, do, and try whether I am not now a gentleman born.

AUTOLYCUS I know you are now, sir, a gentleman born.

CLOWN Ay, and have been so any time these four hours.

OLD SHEPHERD And so have I, boy. 136

CLOWN So you have; but I was a gentleman born before my father, for the King's son took me by the hand and called me brother; and then the two kings called my father brother; and then the Prince my brother and the Princess my sister called my father father; and so we wept; and there was the first gentleman-like tears that ever we shed.

OLD SHEPHERD We may live, son, to shed many more.

CLOWN Ay, or else 'twere hard luck, being in so preposterous estate as we are. 146

AUTOLYCUS I humbly beseech you, sir, to pardon me all the faults I have committed to your worship, and to give me your good report to the Prince my master.

OLD SHEPHERD Prithee, son, do, for we must be gentle now we are gentlemen. 151

CLOWN Thou wilt amend thy life?

AUTOLYCUS Ay, an it like your good worship.

CLOWN Give me thy hand. I will swear to the Prince thou art as honest a true fellow as any is in Bohemia. 155

OLD SHEPHERD You may say it, but not swear it.

CLOWN Not swear it now I am a gentleman? Let boors and franklins say it; I'll swear it.

OLD SHEPHERD How if it be false, son? 159

CLOWN If it be ne'er so false, a true gentleman may swear it in the behalf of his friend, (*to Autolycus*) and I'll swear to the Prince thou art a tall fellow of thy hands and that thou wilt not be drunk; but I know thou art no tall fellow of thy hands and that thou wilt be drunk; but I'll swear it, and I would thou wouldst be a tall fellow of thy hands. 166

AUTOLYCUS I will prove so, sir, to my power.

CLOWN Ay, by any means prove a tall fellow. If I do not wonder how thou dar'st venture to be drunk, not being a tall fellow, trust me not. 170

⌈*Flourish within*⌉

Hark, the kings and princes, our kindred, are going to see the Queen's picture. Come, follow us. We'll be thy good masters.   *Exeunt*

5.3   *Enter Leontes, Polixenes, Florizel, Perdita, Camillo,*
Paulina, Lords, and attendants

LEONTES
O grave and good Paulina, the great comfort
That I have had of thee!

PAULINA   What, sovereign sir,
I did not well, I meant well. All my services
You have paid home, but that you have vouchsafed
With your crowned brother and these young
    contracted   5
Heirs of your kingdoms my poor house to visit,
It is a surplus of your grace which never
My life may last to answer.

LEONTES   O Paulina,
We honour you with trouble. But we came
To see the statue of our queen. Your gallery   10
Have we passed through, not without much content
In many singularities; but we saw not
That which my daughter came to look upon,
The statue of her mother.

PAULINA   As she lived peerless,
So her dead likeness I do well believe   15
Excels what ever yet you looked upon,
Or hand of man hath done. Therefore I keep it
Lonely, apart. But here it is. Prepare
To see the life as lively mocked as ever
Still sleep mocked death. Behold, and say 'tis well.   20
    She draws a curtain and reveals the figure of
    Hermione, standing like a statue
I like your silence; it the more shows off
Your wonder. But yet speak; first you, my liege.
Comes it not something near?

LEONTES   Her natural posture.
Chide me, dear stone, that I may say indeed
Thou art Hermione; or rather, thou art she   25
In thy not chiding, for she was as tender
As infancy and grace. But yet, Paulina,
Hermione was not so much wrinkled, nothing
So agèd as this seems.

POLIXENES   O, not by much.

PAULINA
So much the more our carver's excellence,   30
Which lets go by some sixteen years, and makes her
As she lived now.

LEONTES   As now she might have done,
So much to my good comfort as it is
Now piercing to my soul. O, thus she stood,
Even with such life of majesty—warm life,   35
As now it coldly stands—when first I wooed her.
I am ashamed. Does not the stone rebuke me
For being more stone than it? O royal piece!
There's magic in thy majesty, which has
My evils conjured to remembrance, and   40
From thy admiring daughter took the spirits,
Standing like stone with thee.

PERDITA   And give me leave,
And do not say 'tis superstition, that
I kneel and then implore her blessing. Lady,

Dear Queen, that ended when I but began,   45
Give me that hand of yours to kiss.

PAULINA   O, patience!
The statue is but newly fixed; the colour's
Not dry.

CAMILLO (*to Leontes*)
My lord, your sorrow was too sore laid on,
Which sixteen winters cannot blow away,   50
So many summers dry. Scarce any joy
Did ever so long live; no sorrow
But killed itself much sooner.

POLIXENES (*to Leontes*)   Dear my brother,
Let him that was the cause of this have power
To take off so much grief from you as he   55
Will piece up in himself.

PAULINA (*to Leontes*)   Indeed, my lord,
If I had thought the sight of my poor image
Would thus have wrought you—for the stone is mine—
I'd not have showed it.
    She makes to draw the curtain

LEONTES   Do not draw the curtain.

PAULINA
No longer shall you gaze on't, lest your fancy   60
May think anon it moves.

LEONTES   Let be, let be!
Would I were dead but that methinks already.
What was he that did make it? See, my lord,
Would you not deem it breathed, and that those veins
Did verily bear blood?

POLIXENES   Masterly done.   65
The very life seems warm upon her lip.

LEONTES
The fixture of her eye has motion in't,
As we are mocked with art.

PAULINA   I'll draw the curtain.
My lord's almost so far transported that
He'll think anon it lives.

LEONTES   O sweet Paulina,   70
Make me to think so twenty years together.
No settled senses of the world can match
The pleasure of that madness. Let't alone.

PAULINA
I am sorry, sir, I have thus far stirred you; but
I could afflict you farther.

LEONTES   Do, Paulina,   75
For this affliction has a taste as sweet
As any cordial comfort. Still methinks
There is an air comes from her. What fine chisel
Could ever yet cut breath? Let no man mock me,
For I will kiss her.

PAULINA   Good my lord, forbear.   80
The ruddiness upon her lip is wet.
You'll mar it if you kiss it, stain your own
With oily painting. Shall I draw the curtain?

LEONTES
No, not these twenty years.

PERDITA   So long could I
Stand by, a looker-on.

PAULINA   Either forbear,   85

Quit presently the chapel, or resolve you
For more amazement. If you can behold it,
I'll make the statue move indeed, descend,
And take you by the hand. But then you'll think—
Which I protest against—I am assisted   90
By wicked powers.
LEONTES   What you can make her do
I am content to look on; what to speak,
I am content to hear; for 'tis as easy
To make her speak as move.
PAULINA   It is required
You do awake your faith. Then, all stand still.   95
Or those that think it is unlawful business
I am about, let them depart.
LEONTES   Proceed.
No foot shall stir.
PAULINA   Music; awake her; strike!
     Music
(*To Hermione*) 'Tis time. Descend. Be stone no more.
     Approach.
Strike all that look upon with marvel. Come,   100
I'll fill your grave up. Stir. Nay, come away.
Bequeath to death your numbness, for from him
Dear life redeems you.
(*To Leontes*)   You perceive she stirs.
     Hermione slowly descends
Start not. Her actions shall be holy as
You hear my spell is lawful. Do not shun her   105
Until you see her die again, for then
You kill her double. Nay, present your hand.
When she was young, you wooed her. Now, in age,
Is she become the suitor?
LEONTES   O, she's warm!
If this be magic, let it be an art   110
Lawful as eating.
POLIXENES She embraces him.
CAMILLO She hangs about his neck.
If she pertain to life, let her speak too.
POLIXENES
Ay, and make it manifest where she has lived,   115
Or how stol'n from the dead.
PAULINA   That she is living,
Were it but told you, should be hooted at
Like an old tale. But it appears she lives,

Though yet she speak not. Mark a little while.
(*To Perdita*) Please you to interpose, fair madam.
     Kneel,   120
And pray your mother's blessing.—Turn, good lady,
Our Perdita is found.
HERMIONE   You gods, look down,
And from your sacred vials pour your graces
Upon my daughter's head.—Tell me, mine own,
Where hast thou been preserved? Where lived? How
     found   125
Thy father's court? For thou shalt hear that I,
Knowing by Paulina that the oracle
Gave hope thou wast in being, have preserved
Myself to see the issue.
PAULINA   There's time enough for that,
Lest they desire upon this push to trouble   130
Your joys with like relation. Go together,
You precious winners all; your exultation
Partake to everyone. I, an old turtle,
Will wing me to some withered bough, and there
My mate, that's never to be found again,   135
Lament till I am lost.
LEONTES   O peace, Paulina!
Thou shouldst a husband take by my consent,
As I by thine a wife. This is a match,
And made between's by vows. Thou hast found mine,
But how is to be questioned, for I saw her,   140
As I thought, dead, and have in vain said many
A prayer upon her grave. I'll not seek far—
For him, I partly know his mind—to find thee
An honourable husband. Come, Camillo,
And take her by the hand, whose worth and honesty
Is richly noted, and here justified   146
By us, a pair of kings. Let's from this place.
(*To Hermione*) What, look upon my brother. Both your
     pardons,
That e'er I put between your holy looks
My ill suspicion. This' your son-in-law   150
And son unto the King, whom heavens directing
Is troth-plight to your daughter. Good Paulina,
Lead us from hence, where we may leisurely
Each one demand and answer to his part
Performed in this wide gap of time since first   155
We were dissevered. Hastily lead away.   *Exeunt*

CYMBELINE

Our first reference to *Cymbeline* is a note by the astrologer Simon Forman that he saw the play, probably not long before his death on 8 September 1611. He refers to the heroine as 'Innogen', and this name occurs in the sources; the form 'Imogen', found only in the Folio, appears to be a misprint. The play's courtly tone, and the masque-like quality of, particularly, the episode (5.5.186.1-2) in which Jupiter 'descends in thunder and lightning, sitting upon an eagle', and 'throws a thunderbolt', suggest that as Shakespeare wrote he may have had in mind the audiences and the stage equipment of the Blackfriars theatre, which his company used from the autumn of 1609; and stylistic evidence places the play about 1610-11. It was first printed in the 1623 Folio, as the last of the tragedies. In fact it is a tragicomedy, or a romance, telling a complex and implausible tale of events which cause the deaths of certain subsidiary characters (Cloten, and the Queen) and bring major characters (including the heroine, Innogen) close to death, but which are miraculously resolved in the reunions and reconciliations of the closing scene.

Shakespeare's plot reflects a wide range of reading. He took his title and setting from the name and reign of the legendary British king Cymbeline, or Cunobelinus, said to have reigned from 33 BC till shortly after the birth of Christ. *Cymbeline* is no chronicle history, but Shakespeare derived some ideas, and many of his characters' names, from accounts of early British history in Holinshed's *Chronicles* and elsewhere. Drawing partially, it seems, on an old play, *The Rare Triumphs of Love and Fortune* (acted 1582, printed 1589), he gives Cymbeline a daughter, Innogen, and a wicked second Queen with a loutish, vicious son, Cloten, whom she wishes to see on the throne in her husband's place. Cymbeline, disapproving of his daughter's marriage to 'a poor but worthy gentleman', Posthumus Leonatus, banishes him. The strand of plot showing the outcome of a wager that Posthumus, in Rome, lays on his wife's chastity is indebted, directly or indirectly, to Boccaccio's *Decameron*. Another old play, *Sir Clyomon and Clamydes* (printed in 1599), may have suggested the bizarre scene (4.2) in which Innogen mistakes Cloten's headless body for that of Posthumus; and Holinshed's *History of Scotland* supplied the episode in which Cymbeline's two sons, Guiderius and Arviragus, helped only by the old man (Belarius) who has brought them up in the wilds of Wales, defeat the entire Roman army.

The tone of *Cymbeline* has puzzled commentators. Its prose and verse style is frequently ornate, sometimes grotesque. Its characterization often seems deliberately artificial. Extremes are violently juxtaposed, most daringly when Innogen, supposed dead, is laid beside Cloten's headless body: the beauty of the verse in which she is mourned, and of the flowers strewn over the bodies, contrasts with the hideous spectacle of the headless corpse; her waking speech is one of Shakespeare's most thrillingly difficult challenges to his performers. The appearance of Jupiter lifts the action to a new level of even greater implausibility, preparing us for the extraordinary series of revelations by which the play advances to its impossibly happy ending. *Cymbeline* has been valued mostly for its portrayal of Innogen, ideal of womanhood to, especially, Victorian readers and theatre-goers. The play as a whole is a fantasy, an experimental exercise in virtuosity.

THE PERSONS OF THE PLAY

CYMBELINE, King of Britain

Princess INNOGEN, his daughter, later disguised as a man named Fidele

GUIDERIUS, known as Polydore } Cymbeline's sons, stolen by
ARVIRAGUS, known as Cadwal } Belarius

QUEEN, Cymbeline's wife, Innogen's stepmother

Lord CLOTEN, her son

BELARIUS, a banished lord, calling himself Morgan

CORNELIUS, a physician

HELEN, a lady attending on Innogen

Two LORDS attending on Cloten

Two GENTLEMEN

Two British CAPTAINS

Two JAILERS

POSTHUMUS Leonatus, a poor gentleman, Innogen's husband

PISANIO, his servant

FILARIO, a friend of Posthumus

GIACOMO, an Italian }
A FRENCHMAN } Filario's friends
A DUTCHMAN }
A SPANIARD }

Caius LUCIUS, ambassador from Rome, later General of the Roman forces

Two Roman SENATORS

Roman TRIBUNES

A Roman CAPTAIN

Philharmonus, a SOOTHSAYER

JUPITER

Ghost of SICILIUS Leonatus, father of Posthumus

Ghost of the MOTHER of Posthumus

Ghosts of the BROTHERS of Posthumus

Lords attending on Cymbeline, ladies attending on the Queen, musicians attending on Cloten, messengers, soldiers

Cymbeline, King of Britain

1.1 *Enter two Gentlemen*

FIRST GENTLEMAN
You do not meet a man but frowns. Our bloods
No more obey the heavens than our courtiers
Still seem as does the King.

SECOND GENTLEMAN   But what's the matter?

FIRST GENTLEMAN
His daughter, and the heir of 's kingdom, whom
He purposed to his wife's sole son—a widow   5
That late he married—hath referred herself
Unto a poor but worthy gentleman. She's wedded,
Her husband banished, she imprisoned. All
Is outward sorrow, though I think the King
Be touched at very heart.

SECOND GENTLEMAN   None but the King?   10

FIRST GENTLEMAN
He that hath lost her, too. So is the Queen,
That most desired the match. But not a courtier—
Although they wear their faces to the bent
Of the King's looks—hath a heart that is not
Glad of the thing they scowl at.

SECOND GENTLEMAN   And why so?   15

FIRST GENTLEMAN
He that hath missed the Princess is a thing
Too bad for bad report, and he that hath her—
I mean that married her—alack, good man,
And therefore banished!—is a creature such
As, to seek through the regions of the earth   20
For one his like, there would be something failing
In him that should compare. I do not think
So fair an outward and such stuff within
Endows a man but he.

SECOND GENTLEMAN   You speak him far.

FIRST GENTLEMAN
I do extend him, sir, within himself;   25
Crush him together rather than unfold
His measure duly.

SECOND GENTLEMAN   What's his name and birth?

FIRST GENTLEMAN
I cannot delve him to the root. His father
Was called Sicilius, who did join his honour
Against the Romans with Cassibelan   30
But had his titles by Tenantius, whom
He served with glory and admired success,
So gained the sur-addition 'Leonatus';
And had, besides this gentleman in question,
Two other sons who in the wars o'th' time   35
Died with their swords in hand; for which their father,
Then old and fond of issue, took such sorrow
That he quit being, and his gentle lady,
Big of this gentleman, our theme, deceased
As he was born. The King, he takes the babe   40
To his protection, calls him Posthumus Leonatus,
Breeds him, and makes him of his bedchamber;

Puts to him all the learnings that his time
Could make him the receiver of, which he took
As we do air, fast as 'twas ministered,   45
And in 's spring became a harvest; lived in court—
Which rare it is to do—most praised, most loved;
A sample to the youngest, to th' more mature
A glass that feated them, and to the graver
A child that guided dotards. To his mistress,   50
For whom he now is banished, her own price
Proclaims how she esteemed him and his virtue.
By her election may be truly read
What kind of man he is.

SECOND GENTLEMAN   I honour him
Even out of your report. But pray you tell me,   55
Is she sole child to th' King?

FIRST GENTLEMAN   His only child.
He had two sons—if this be worth your hearing,
Mark it: the eld'st of them at three years old,
I'th' swathing clothes the other, from their nursery
Were stol'n, and to this hour no guess in knowledge
Which way they went.   61

SECOND GENTLEMAN How long is this ago?

FIRST GENTLEMAN Some twenty years.

SECOND GENTLEMAN
That a king's children should be so conveyed,
So slackly guarded, and the search so slow   65
That could not trace them!

FIRST GENTLEMAN   Howsoe'er 'tis strange,
Or that the negligence may well be laughed at,
Yet is it true, sir.

SECOND GENTLEMAN I do well believe you.
Enter the Queen, Posthumus, and Innogen

FIRST GENTLEMAN
We must forbear. Here comes the gentleman,
The Queen and Princess.   *Exeunt the two Gentlemen*

QUEEN
No, be assured you shall not find me, daughter,
After the slander of most stepmothers,
Evil-eyed unto you. You're my prisoner, but
Your jailer shall deliver you the keys
That lock up your restraint. For you, Posthumus,   75
So soon as I can win th'offended King
I will be known your advocate. Marry, yet
The fire of rage is in him, and 'twere good
You leaned unto his sentence with what patience
Your wisdom may inform you.

POSTHUMUS   Please your highness,   80
I will from hence today.

QUEEN   You know the peril.
I'll fetch a turn about the garden, pitying
The pangs of barred affections, though the King
Hath charged you should not speak together.   *Exit*

INNOGEN
O dissembling courtesy! How fine this tyrant   85

Can tickle where she wounds! My dearest husband,
I something fear my father's wrath, but nothing—
Always reserved my holy duty—what
His rage can do on me. You must be gone,
And I shall here abide the hourly shot   90
Of angry eyes, not comforted to live
But that there is this jewel in the world
That I may see again.
POSTHUMUS   My queen, my mistress!
O lady, weep no more, lest I give cause
To be suspected of more tenderness   95
Than doth become a man. I will remain
The loyal'st husband that did e'er plight troth;
My residence in Rome at one Filario's,
Who to my father was a friend, to me
Known but by letter; thither write, my queen,   100
And with mine eyes I'll drink the words you send
Though ink be made of gall.
        Enter Queen
QUEEN   Be brief, I pray you.
If the King come, I shall incur I know not
How much of his displeasure. (*Aside*) Yet I'll move him
To walk this way. I never do him wrong   105
But he does buy my injuries, to be friends,
Pays dear for my offences.   *Exit*
POSTHUMUS   Should we be taking leave
As long a term as yet we have to live,
The loathness to depart would grow. Adieu.
INNOGEN Nay, stay a little.   110
Were you but riding forth to air yourself
Such parting were too petty. Look here, love:
This diamond was my mother's. Take it, heart;
        She gives him a ring
But keep it till you woo another wife
When Innogen is dead.
POSTHUMUS   How, how? Another?   115
You gentle gods, give me but this I have,
And cere up my embracements from a next
With bonds of death! Remain, remain thou here
        He puts on the ring
While sense can keep it on; and, sweetest, fairest,
As I my poor self did exchange for you   120
To your so infinite loss, so in our trifles
I still win of you. For my sake wear this.
        He gives her a bracelet
It is a manacle of love. I'll place it
Upon this fairest prisoner.
INNOGEN   O the gods!
When shall we see again?
        Enter Cymbeline and lords
POSTHUMUS   .   Alack, the King!   125
CYMBELINE
Thou basest thing, avoid hence, from my sight!
If after this command thou fraught the court
With thy unworthiness, thou diest. Away.
Thou'rt poison to my blood.
POSTHUMUS   The gods protect you,

And bless the good remainders of the court!   130
I am gone.   *Exit*
INNOGEN   There cannot be a pinch in death
More sharp than this is.
CYMBELINE   O disloyal thing,
That shouldst repair my youth, thou heap'st
A year's age on me.
INNOGEN   I beseech you, sir,
Harm not yourself with your vexation.   135
I am senseless of your wrath. A touch more rare
Subdues all pangs, all fears.
CYMBELINE   Past grace, obedience—
INNOGEN
Past hope and in despair: that way past grace.
CYMBELINE
That mightst have had the sole son of my queen!
INNOGEN
O blessèd that I might not! I chose an eagle   140
And did avoid a puttock.
CYMBELINE
Thou took'st a beggar, wouldst have made my throne
A seat for baseness.
INNOGEN   No, I rather added
A lustre to it.
CYMBELINE   O thou vile one!
INNOGEN   Sir,
It is your fault that I have loved Posthumus.   145
You bred him as my playfellow, and he is
A man worth any woman, over-buys me
Almost the sum he pays.
CYMBELINE   What, art thou mad?
INNOGEN
Almost, sir. Heaven restore me! Would I were
A neatherd's daughter, and my Leonatus   150
Our neighbour shepherd's son.
        Enter Queen
CYMBELINE   Thou foolish thing.
(*To Queen*) They were again together; you have done
Not after our command. (*To lords*) Away with her,
And pen her up.
QUEEN   Beseech your patience, peace,
Dear lady daughter, peace. Sweet sovereign,   155
Leave us to ourselves, and make yourself some
        comfort
Out of your best advice.
CYMBELINE   Nay, let her languish
A drop of blood a day, and, being aged,
Die of this folly.   *Exit with lords*
QUEEN   Fie, you must give way.
        Enter Pisanio
Here is your servant. How now, sir? What news? 160
PISANIO
My lord your son drew on my master.
QUEEN   Ha!
No harm, I trust, is done?
PISANIO   There might have been,
But that my master rather played than fought,

And had no help of anger. They were parted
By gentlemen at hand.
QUEEN   I am very glad on't.   165
INNOGEN
Your son's my father's friend; he takes his part
To draw upon an exile—O brave sir!
I would they were in Afric both together,
Myself by with a needle, that I might prick
The goer-back. (*To Pisanio*) Why came you from your
    master?   170
PISANIO
On his command. He would not suffer me
To bring him to the haven, left these notes
Of what commands I should be subject to
When't pleased you to employ me.
QUEEN   This hath been
Your faithful servant. I dare lay mine honour   175
He will remain so.
PISANIO I humbly thank your highness.
QUEEN Pray walk a while.   ⌜*Exit*⌝
INNOGEN
About some half hour hence, pray you speak with
    me.
You shall at least go see my lord aboard.   180
For this time leave me.   *Exeunt severally*

1.2   *Enter Cloten and two Lords*

FIRST LORD Sir, I would advise you to shift a shirt. The
    violence of action hath made you reek as a sacrifice.
    Where air comes out, air comes in. There's none abroad
    so wholesome as that you vent.
CLOTEN If my shirt were bloody, then to shift it. Have I
    hurt him?   6
SECOND LORD (*aside*) No, faith, not so much as his patience.
FIRST LORD Hurt him? His body's a passable carcass if he
    be not hurt. It is a thoroughfare for steel if he be not
    hurt.   10
SECOND LORD (*aside*) His steel was in debt—it went o'th'
    backside the town.
CLOTEN The villain would not stand me.
SECOND LORD (*aside*) No, but he fled forward still, toward
    your face.   15
FIRST LORD Stand you? You have land enough of your
    own, but he added to your having, gave you some
    ground.
SECOND LORD (*aside*) As many inches as you have oceans.
    Puppies!   20
CLOTEN I would they had not come between us.
SECOND LORD (*aside*) So would I, till you had measured
    how long a fool you were upon the ground.
CLOTEN And that she should love this fellow and refuse
    me!   25
SECOND LORD (*aside*) If it be a sin to make a true election,
    she is damned.
FIRST LORD Sir, as I told you always, her beauty and her
    brain go not together. She's a good sign, but I have
    seen small reflection of her wit.   30

SECOND LORD (*aside*) She shines not upon fools lest the
    reflection should hurt her.
CLOTEN Come, I'll to my chamber. Would there had been
    some hurt done.
SECOND LORD (*aside*) I wish not so, unless it had been the
    fall of an ass, which is no great hurt.   36
CLOTEN (*to Second Lord*) You'll go with us?
FIRST LORD I'll attend your lordship.
CLOTEN Nay, come, let's go together.   39
SECOND LORD Well, my lord.   *Exeunt*

1.3   *Enter Innogen and Pisanio*

INNOGEN
I would thou grew'st unto the shores o'th' haven
And questionedst every sail. If he should write
And I not have it, 'twere a paper lost
As offered mercy is. What was the last
That he spake to thee?
PISANIO   It was his queen, his queen.   5
INNOGEN
Then waved his handkerchief?
PISANIO   And kissed it, madam.
INNOGEN
Senseless linen, happier therein than I!
And that was all?
PISANIO   No, madam. For so long
As he could make me with this eye or ear
Distinguish him from others he did keep   10
The deck, with glove or hat or handkerchief
Still waving, as the fits and stirs of 's mind
Could best express how slow his soul sailed on,
How swift his ship.
INNOGEN   Thou shouldst have made him
As little as a crow, or less, ere left   15
To after-eye him.
PISANIO   Madam, so I did.
INNOGEN
I would have broke mine eye-strings, cracked them,
    but
To look upon him till the diminution
Of space had pointed him sharp as my needle;
Nay, followed him till he had melted from   20
The smallness of a gnat to air, and then
Have turned mine eye and wept. But, good Pisanio,
When shall we hear from him?
PISANIO Be assured, madam,
With his next vantage.   25
INNOGEN
I did not take my leave of him, but had
Most pretty things to say. Ere I could tell him
How I would think on him at certain hours,
Such thoughts and such, or I could make him swear
The shes of Italy should not betray   30
Mine interest and his honour, or have charged him
At the sixth hour of morn, at noon, at midnight
T'encounter me with orisons—for then
I am in heaven for him—or ere I could

Give him that parting kiss which I had set   35
Betwixt two charming words, comes in my father,
And, like the tyrannous breathing of the north,
Shakes all our buds from growing.
        Enter a Lady
LADY   The Queen, madam,
Desires your highness' company.
INNOGEN (*to Pisanio*)
Those things I bid you do, get them dispatched.   40
I will attend the Queen.
PISANIO   Madam, I shall.
        Exeunt Innogen and Lady at one door, Pisanio
                                at another

1.4   ⌈*A table brought out, with a banquet upon it.*⌉ *Enter*
        Filario, Giacomo, a Frenchman, a Dutchman, and a
        Spaniard
GIACOMO Believe it, sir, I have seen him in Britain. He
was then of a crescent note, expected to prove so worthy
as since he hath been allowed the name of. But I could
then have looked on him without the help of admiration,
though the catalogue of his endowments had been
tabled by his side and I to peruse him by items.   6
FILARIO You speak of him when he was less furnished
than now he is with that which makes him both
without and within.   9
FRENCHMAN I have seen him in France. We had very
many there could behold the sun with as firm eyes as
he.
GIACOMO This matter of marrying his king's daughter,
wherein he must be weighed rather by her value than
his own, words him, I doubt not, a great deal from the
matter.   16
FRENCHMAN And then his banishment.
GIACOMO Ay, and the approbation of those that weep this
lamentable divorce under her colours are wonderfully
to extend him, be it but to fortify her judgement, which
else an easy battery might lay flat for taking a beggar
without less quality. But how comes it he is to sojourn
with you? How creeps acquaintance?
FILARIO His father and I were soldiers together, to whom
I have been often bound for no less than my life.   25
        Enter Posthumus
Here comes the Briton. Let him be so entertained
amongst you as suits with gentlemen of your knowing
to a stranger of his quality. I beseech you all, be better
known to this gentleman, whom I commend to you as
a noble friend of mine. How worthy he is I will leave
to appear hereafter rather than story him in his own
hearing.
FRENCHMAN (*to Posthumus*) Sir, we have known together
in Orléans.   34
POSTHUMUS Since when I have been debtor to you for
courtesies which I will be ever to pay, and yet pay still.
FRENCHMAN Sir, you o'er-rate my poor kindness. I was
glad I did atone my countryman and you. It had been
pity you should have been put together with so mortal
a purpose as then each bore, upon importance of so
slight and trivial a nature.   41

POSTHUMUS By your pardon, sir, I was then a young
traveller, rather shunned to go even with what I heard
than in my every action to be guided by others'
experiences; but upon my mended judgement—if I
offend not to say it is mended—my quarrel was not
altogether slight.   47
FRENCHMAN Faith, yes, to be put to the arbitrement of
swords, and by such two that would by all likelihood
have confounded the one other, or have fallen both.
GIACOMO Can we with manners ask what was the
difference?   52
FRENCHMAN Safely, I think. 'Twas a contention in public,
which may without contradiction suffer the report. It
was much like an argument that fell out last night,
where each of us fell in praise of our country mistresses,
this gentleman at that time vouching—and upon
warrant of bloody affirmation—his to be more fair,
virtuous, wise, chaste, constant, qualified, and less
attemptable than any the rarest of our ladies in France.
GIACOMO That lady is not now living, or this gentleman's
opinion by this worn out.   62
POSTHUMUS She holds her virtue still, and I my mind.
GIACOMO You must not so far prefer her fore ours of Italy.
POSTHUMUS Being so far provoked as I was in France I
would abate her nothing, though I profess myself her
adorer, not her friend.   67
GIACOMO As fair and as good—a kind of hand-in-hand
comparison—had been something too fair and too good
for any lady in Britain. If she went before others I have
seen—as that diamond of yours outlustres many I have
beheld—I could not but believe she excelled many; but
I have not seen the most precious diamond that is, nor
you the lady.
POSTHUMUS I praised her as I rated her; so do I my stone.
GIACOMO What do you esteem it at?   76
POSTHUMUS More than the world enjoys.
GIACOMO Either your unparagoned mistress is dead, or
she's outprized by a trifle.   79
POSTHUMUS You are mistaken. The one may be sold or
given, or if there were wealth enough for the purchase
or merit for the gift. The other is not a thing for sale,
and only the gift of the gods.
GIACOMO Which the gods have given you?
POSTHUMUS Which, by their graces, I will keep.   85
GIACOMO You may wear her in title yours; but, you know,
strange fowl light upon neighbouring ponds. Your ring
may be stolen too; so your brace of unprizable
estimations, the one is but frail, and the other casual.
A cunning thief or a that-way accomplished courtier
would hazard the winning both of first and last.   91
POSTHUMUS Your Italy contains none so accomplished a
courtier to convince the honour of my mistress if in
the holding or loss of that you term her frail. I do
nothing doubt you have store of thieves; notwithstanding, I fear not my ring.   96
FILARIO Let us leave here, gentlemen.
POSTHUMUS Sir, with all my heart. This worthy signor, I
thank him, makes no stranger of me. We are familiar
at first.   100

GIACOMO With five times so much conversation I should
get ground of your fair mistress, make her go back
even to the yielding, had I admittance and opportunity
to friend.

POSTHUMUS No, no.   105

GIACOMO I dare thereupon pawn the moiety of my estate
to your ring, which in my opinion o'ervalues it
something. But I make my wager rather against your
confidence than her reputation, and, to bar your offence
herein too, I durst attempt it against any lady in the
world.   111

POSTHUMUS You are a great deal abused in too bold a
persuasion, and I doubt not you sustain what you're
worthy of by your attempt.

GIACOMO What's that?   115

POSTHUMUS A repulse; though your attempt, as you call
it, deserve more—a punishment, too.

FILARIO Gentlemen, enough of this. It came in too
suddenly. Let it die as it was born; and, I pray you, be
better acquainted.   120

GIACOMO Would I had put my estate and my neighbour's
on th'approbation of what I have spoke.

POSTHUMUS What lady would you choose to assail?

GIACOMO Yours, whom in constancy you think stands so
safe. I will lay you ten thousand ducats to your ring
that, commend me to the court where your lady is,
with no more advantage than the opportunity of a
second conference, and I will bring from thence that
honour of hers which you imagine so reserved.

POSTHUMUS I will wage against your gold, gold to it; my
ring I hold dear as my finger, 'tis part of it.   131

GIACOMO You are a friend, and therein the wiser. If you
buy ladies' flesh at a million a dram, you cannot
preserve it from tainting. But I see you have some
religion in you, that you fear.   135

POSTHUMUS This is but a custom in your tongue. You bear
a graver purpose, I hope.

GIACOMO I am the master of my speeches, and would
undergo what's spoken, I swear.   139

POSTHUMUS Will you? I shall but lend my diamond till
your return. Let there be covenants drawn between 's.
My mistress exceeds in goodness the hugeness of your
unworthy thinking. I dare you to this match. Here's
my ring.

FILARIO I will have it no lay.   145

GIACOMO By the gods, it is one. If I bring you no sufficient
testimony that I have enjoyed the dearest bodily part
of your mistress, my ten thousand ducats are yours;
so is your diamond too. If I come off and leave her in
such honour as you have trust in, she your jewel, this
your jewel, and my gold are yours, provided I have
your commendation for my more free entertainment.

POSTHUMUS I embrace these conditions; let us have articles
betwixt us. Only thus far you shall answer: if you make
your voyage upon her and give me directly to
understand you have prevailed, I am no further your
enemy; she is not worth our debate. If she remain
unseduced, you not making it appear otherwise, for

your ill opinion and th'assault you have made to her
chastity you shall answer me with your sword.   160

GIACOMO Your hand, a covenant. We will have these
things set down by lawful counsel, and straight away
for Britain, lest the bargain should catch cold and
starve. I will fetch my gold and have our two wagers
recorded.   165

POSTHUMUS Agreed.   ⌈*Exit with Giacomo*⌉

FRENCHMAN Will this hold, think you?

FILARIO Signor Giacomo will not from it. Pray let us
follow 'em.   *Exeunt.* ⌈*Table is removed*⌉

1.5 *Enter Queen, Ladies, and Cornelius, a doctor*

QUEEN
Whiles yet the dew's on ground, gather those flowers.
Make haste. Who has the note of them?

A LADY   I, madam.

QUEEN Dispatch.   *Exeunt Ladies*
Now, Master Doctor, have you brought those drugs?

CORNELIUS
Pleaseth your highness, ay. Here they are, madam.   5
He gives her a box
But I beseech your grace, without offence—
My conscience bids me ask—wherefore you have
Commanded of me these most poisonous compounds,
Which are the movers of a languishing death,
But though slow, deadly.

QUEEN   I wonder, doctor,   10
Thou ask'st me such a question. Have I not been
Thy pupil long? Hast thou not learned me how
To make perfumes, distil, preserve—yea, so
That our great King himself doth woo me oft
For my confections? Having thus far proceeded,   15
Unless thou think'st me devilish, is't not meet
That I did amplify my judgement in
Other conclusions? I will try the forces
Of these thy compounds on such creatures as
We count not worth the hanging, but none human,
To try the vigour of them, and apply   21
Allayments to their act, and by them gather
Their several virtues and effects.

CORNELIUS   Your highness
Shall from this practice but make hard your heart.
Besides, the seeing these effects will be   25
Both noisome and infectious.

QUEEN   O, content thee.
Enter Pisanio
(*Aside*) Here comes a flattering rascal; upon him
Will I first work. He's factor for his master,
And enemy to my son. (*Aloud*) How now, Pisanio?—
Doctor, your service for this time is ended.   30
Take your own way.

CORNELIUS (*aside*)   I do suspect you, madam.
But you shall do no harm.

QUEEN (*to Pisanio*)   Hark thee, a word.

CORNELIUS (*aside*)
I do not like her. She doth think she has
Strange ling'ring poisons. I do know her spirit,

And will not trust one of her malice with   35
A drug of such damned nature. Those she has
Will stupefy and dull the sense a while,
Which first, perchance, she'll prove on cats and dogs,
Then afterward up higher; but there is
No danger in what show of death it makes   40
More than the locking up the spirits a time,
To be more fresh, reviving. She is fooled
With a most false effect, and I the truer
So to be false with her.
QUEEN   No further service, doctor,
Until I send for thee.
CORNELIUS   I humbly take my leave.   Exit
QUEEN (to Pisanio)
Weeps she still, sayst thou? Dost thou think in time 46
She will not quench, and let instructions enter
Where folly now possesses? Do thou work.
When thou shalt bring me word she loves my son
I'll tell thee on the instant thou art then   50
As great as is thy master—greater, for
His fortunes all lie speechless, and his name
Is at last gasp. Return he cannot, nor
Continue where he is. To shift his being
Is to exchange one misery with another,   55
And every day that comes comes to decay
A day's work in him. What shalt thou expect
To be depender on a thing that leans,
Who cannot be new built nor has no friends
So much as but to prop him?
⌈She drops her box. He takes it up⌉
                            Thou tak'st up   60
Thou know'st not what; but take it for thy labour.
It is a thing I made which hath the King
Five times redeemed from death. I do not know
What is more cordial. Nay, I prithee take it.
It is an earnest of a farther good   65
That I mean to thee. Tell thy mistress how
The case stands with her; do't as from thyself.
Think what a chance thou changest on, but think
Thou hast thy mistress still; to boot, my son,
Who shall take notice of thee. I'll move the King   70
To any shape of thy preferment, such
As thou'lt desire; and then myself, I chiefly,
That set thee on to this desert, am bound
To load thy merit richly. Call my women.
Think on my words.   Exit Pisanio
                    A sly and constant knave,   75
Not to be shaked; the agent for his master,
And the remembrancer of her to hold .
The hand-fast to her lord. I have given him that
Which, if he take, shall quite unpeople her
Of liegers for her sweet, and which she after,   80
Except she bend her humour, shall be assured
To taste of too.
        Enter Pisanio and Ladies
                    So, so; well done, well done.
The violets, cowslips, and the primroses

Bear to my closet. Fare thee well, Pisanio.
Think on my words, Pisanio.
PISANIO   And shall do.   85
                            Exeunt Queen and Ladies
But when to my good lord I prove untrue,
I'll choke myself—there's all I'll do for you.   Exit

1.6   Enter Innogen
INNOGEN
A father cruel and a stepdame false,
A foolish suitor to a wedded lady
That hath her husband banished. O, that husband,
My supreme crown of grief, and those repeated
Vexations of it! Had I been thief-stol'n,   5
As my two brothers, happy; but most miserable
Is the desire that's glorious. Blest be those,
How mean soe'er, that have their honest wills,
Which seasons comfort.
        Enter Pisanio and Giacomo
                    Who may this be? Fie!
PISANIO
Madam, a noble gentleman of Rome   10
Comes from my lord with letters.
GIACOMO   Change you, madam?
The worthy Leonatus is in safety,
And greets your highness dearly.
        He gives her the letters
INNOGEN   Thanks, good sir.
You're kindly welcome.
        She reads the letters
GIACOMO (aside)
All of her that is out of door most rich!   15
If she be furnished with a mind so rare
She is alone, th'Arabian bird, and I
Have lost the wager. Boldness be my friend;
Arm me audacity from head to foot,
Or, like the Parthian, I shall flying fight;   20
Rather, directly fly.
INNOGEN (reads aloud) 'He is one of the noblest note, to
whose kindnesses I am most infinitely tied. Reflect upon
him accordingly, as you value
                            Your truest   25
                            Leonatus.'
(To Giacomo) So far I read aloud,
But even the very middle of my heart
Is warmed by th' rest, and takes it thankfully.
You are as welcome, worthy sir, as I   30
Have words to bid you, and shall find it so
In all that I can do.
GIACOMO   Thanks, fairest lady.
What, are men mad? Hath nature given them eyes
To see this vaulted arch and the rich crop
Of sea and land, which can distinguish 'twixt   35
The fiery orbs above and the twinned stones
Upon th'unnumbered beach, and can we not
Partition make with spectacles so precious
'Twixt fair and foul?
INNOGEN   What makes your admiration?

GIACOMO
  It cannot be i'th' eye—for apes and monkeys,   40
'Twixt two such shes, would chatter this way and
Contemn with mows the other; nor i'th' judgement,
For idiots in this case of favour would
Be wisely definite; nor i'th' appetite—
Sluttery, to such neat excellence opposed,   45
Should make desire vomit emptiness,
Not so allured to feed.
INNOGEN   What is the matter, trow?
GIACOMO The cloyèd will,
  That satiate yet unsatisfied desire, that tub   50
Both filled and running, ravening first the lamb,
Longs after for the garbage.
INNOGEN   What, dear sir,
  Thus raps you? Are you well?
GIACOMO
  Thanks, madam, well. (*To Pisanio*) Beseech you, sir,
Desire my man's abode where I did leave him.   55
He's strange and peevish.
PISANIO   I was going, sir,
  To give him welcome.   *Exit*
INNOGEN   Continues well my lord?
  His health, beseech you?
GIACOMO   Well, madam.
INNOGEN
  Is he disposed to mirth? I hope he is.
GIACOMO
  Exceeding pleasant, none a stranger there   60
So merry and so gamesome. He is called
The Briton Reveller.
INNOGEN   When he was here
  He did incline to sadness, and oft-times
Not knowing why.
GIACOMO   I never saw him sad.
  There is a Frenchman his companion, one   65
An eminent monsieur that, it seems, much loves
A Gallian girl at home. He furnaces
The thick sighs from him, whiles the jolly Briton—
Your lord, I mean—laughs from 's free lungs, cries 'O,
Can my sides hold, to think that man, who knows   70
By history, report or his own proof
What woman is, yea, what she cannot choose
But must be, will 's free hours languish
For assurèd bondage?'
INNOGEN   Will my lord say so?
GIACOMO
  Ay, madam, with his eyes in flood with laughter.   75
It is a recreation to be by
And hear him mock the Frenchman. But heavens
     know
Some men are much to blame.
INNOGEN   Not he, I hope.
GIACOMO
  Not he; but yet heaven's bounty towards him might
Be used more thankfully. In himself 'tis much;   80
In you, which I count his, beyond all talents.

Whilst I am bound to wonder, I am bound
To pity too.
INNOGEN   What do you pity, sir?
GIACOMO
  Two creatures heartily.
INNOGEN   Am I one, sir?
  You look on me; what wreck discern you in me   85
Deserves your pity?
GIACOMO   Lamentable! What,
  To hide me from the radiant sun, and solace
I'th' dungeon by a snuff?
INNOGEN   I pray you, sir,
  Deliver with more openness your answers
To my demands. Why do you pity me?   90
GIACOMO That others do—
  I was about to say enjoy your—but
It is an office of the gods to venge it,
Not mine to speak on't.
INNOGEN   You do seem to know
  Something of me, or what concerns me. Pray you,   95
Since doubting things go ill often hurts more
Than to be sure they do—for certainties
Either are past remedies, or, timely knowing,
The remedy then born—discover to me
What both you spur and stop.
GIACOMO   Had I this cheek   100
To bathe my lips upon; this hand whose touch,
Whose every touch, would force the feeler's soul
To th'oath of loyalty; this object which
Takes prisoner the wild motion of mine eye,
Firing it only here: should I, damned then,   105
Slaver with lips as common as the stairs
That mount the Capitol; join grips with hands
Made hard with hourly falsehood—falsehood as
With labour; then by-peeping in an eye
Base and illustrous as the smoky light   110
That's fed with stinking tallow—it were fit
That all the plagues of hell should at one time
Encounter such revolt.
INNOGEN   My lord, I fear,
  Has forgot Britain.
GIACOMO   And himself. Not I
  Inclined to this intelligence pronounce   115
The beggary of his change, but 'tis your graces
That from my mutest conscience to my tongue
Charms this report out.
INNOGEN   Let me hear no more.
GIACOMO
  O dearest soul, your cause doth strike my heart
With pity that doth make me sick. A lady   120
So fair, and fastened to an empery
Would make the great'st king double, to be partnered
With tomboys hired with that self exhibition
Which your own coffers yield; with diseased ventures
That play with all infirmities for gold   125
Which rottenness can lend to nature; such boiled stuff
As well might poison poison! Be revenged,

Or she that bore you was no queen, and you
Recoil from your great stock.

INNOGEN   Revenged?

How should I be revenged? If this be true—   130
As I have such a heart that both mine ears
Must not in haste abuse—if it be true,
How should I be revenged?

GIACOMO   Should he make me
Live like Diana's priest betwixt cold sheets
Whiles he is vaulting variable ramps,   135
In your despite, upon your purse—revenge it.
I dedicate myself to your sweet pleasure,
More noble than that runagate to your bed,
And will continue fast to your affection,
Still close as sure.

INNOGEN   What ho, Pisanio!   140

GIACOMO
Let me my service tender on your lips.

INNOGEN
Away, I do condemn mine ears that have
So long attended thee. If thou wert honourable
Thou wouldst have told this tale for virtue, not
For such an end thou seek'st, as base as strange.   145
Thou wrong'st a gentleman who is as far
From thy report as thou from honour, and
Solicit'st here a lady that disdains
Thee and the devil alike. What ho, Pisanio!
The King my father shall be made acquainted   150
Of thy assault. If he shall think it fit
A saucy stranger in his court to mart
As in a Romish stew, and to expound
His beastly mind to us, he hath a court
He little cares for, and a daughter who   155
He not respects at all. What ho, Pisanio!

GIACOMO
O happy Leonatus! I may say
The credit that thy lady hath of thee
Deserves thy trust, and thy most perfect goodness
Her assured credit. Blessèd live you long,   160
A lady to the worthiest sir that ever
Country called his; and you his mistress, only
For the most worthiest fit. Give me your pardon.
I have spoke this to know if your affiance
Were deeply rooted, and shall make your lord   165
That which he is new o'er; and he is one
The truest mannered, such a holy witch
That he enchants societies into him;
Half all men's hearts are his.

INNOGEN   You make amends.

GIACOMO
He sits 'mongst men like a descended god.   170
He hath a kind of honour sets him off
More than a mortal seeming. Be not angry,
Most mighty princess, that I have adventured
To try your taking of a false report, which hath
Honoured with confirmation your great judgement 175
In the election of a sir so rare

Which you know cannot err. The love I bear him
Made me to fan you thus, but the gods made you,
Unlike all others, chaffless. Pray, your pardon.

INNOGEN
All's well, sir. Take my power i'th' court for yours.

GIACOMO
My humble thanks. I had almost forgot   181
T'entreat your grace but in a small request,
And yet of moment too, for it concerns
Your lord; myself and other noble friends
Are partners in the business.

INNOGEN   Pray what is't?   185

GIACOMO
Some dozen Romans of us, and your lord—
Best feather of our wing—have mingled sums
To buy a present for the Emperor,
Which I, the factor for the rest, have done
In France. 'Tis plate of rare device, and jewels   190
Of rich and exquisite form; their value's great,
And I am something curious, being strange,
To have them in safe stowage. May it please you
To take them in protection?

INNOGEN   Willingly,
And pawn mine honour for their safety; since   195
My lord hath interest in them, I will keep them
In my bedchamber.

GIACOMO   They are in a trunk
Attended by my men. I will make bold
To send them to you, only for this night.
I must aboard tomorrow.

INNOGEN   O, no, no!   200

GIACOMO
Yes, I beseech, or I shall short my word
By length'ning my return. From Gallia
I crossed the seas on purpose and on promise
To see your grace.

INNOGEN   I thank you for your pains;
But not away tomorrow!

GIACOMO   O, I must, madam.   205
Therefore I shall beseech you, if you please
To greet your lord with writing, do't tonight.
I have outstood my time, which is material
To th' tender of our present.

INNOGEN   I will write.
Send your trunk to me, it shall safe be kept,   210
And truly yielded you. You're very welcome.

                              Exeunt severally

2.1   *Enter Cloten and the two Lords*

CLOTEN Was there ever man had such luck? When I
kissed the jack upon an upcast, to be hit away! I had
a hundred pound on't, and then a whoreson jackanapes
must take me up for swearing, as if I borrowed mine
oaths of him, and might not spend them at my pleasure.

FIRST LORD What got he by that? You have broke his
pate with your bowl.   7

SECOND LORD (*aside*) If his wit had been like him that broke it, it would have run all out.

CLOTEN When a gentleman is disposed to swear it is not for any standers-by to curtail his oaths, ha?   11

SECOND LORD No, my lord (*aside*)—nor crop the ears of them.

CLOTEN Whoreson dog! I give him satisfaction? Would he had been one of my rank.   15

SECOND LORD (*aside*) To have smelled like a fool.

CLOTEN I am not vexed more at anything in th'earth. A pox on't, I had rather not be so noble as I am. They dare not fight with me because of the Queen, my mother. Every jack-slave hath his bellyful of fighting, and I must go up and down like a cock that nobody can match.

SECOND LORD (*aside*) You are cock and capon too an you crow cock with your comb on.

CLOTEN Sayst thou?   25

SECOND LORD It is not fit your lordship should undertake every companion that you give offence to.

CLOTEN No, I know that, but it is fit I should commit offence to my inferiors.

SECOND LORD Ay, it is fit for your lordship only.   30

CLOTEN Why, so I say.

FIRST LORD Did you hear of a stranger that's come to court tonight?

CLOTEN A stranger, and I not know on't?

SECOND LORD (*aside*) He's a strange fellow himself and knows it not.   36

FIRST LORD There's an Italian come, and, 'tis thought, one of Leonatus' friends.

CLOTEN Leonatus? A banished rascal; and he's another, whatsoever he be. Who told you of this stranger?   40

FIRST LORD One of your lordship's pages.

CLOTEN Is it fit I went to look upon him? Is there no derogation in't?

SECOND LORD You cannot derogate, my lord.

CLOTEN Not easily, I think.   45

SECOND LORD (*aside*) You are a fool granted, therefore your issues, being foolish, do not derogate.

CLOTEN Come, I'll go see this Italian. What I have lost today at bowls I'll win tonight of him. Come, go.

SECOND LORD I'll attend your lordship.   50

Exeunt Cloten and First Lord

That such a crafty devil as is his mother
Should yield the world this ass!—a woman that
Bears all down with her brain, and this her son
Cannot take two from twenty, for his heart,
And leave eighteen. Alas, poor princess,   55
Thou divine Innogen, what thou endur'st,
Betwixt a father by thy stepdame governed,
A mother hourly coining plots, a wooer
More hateful than the foul expulsion is
Of thy dear husband, than that horrid act   60
Of the divorce he'd make! The heavens hold firm
The walls of thy dear honour, keep unshaked
That temple, thy fair mind, that thou mayst stand
T'enjoy thy banished lord and this great land!   *Exit*

2.2 *A trunk ⌈and arras⌉. A bed is ⌈thrust forth⌉ with Innogen in it, reading a book. Enter to her Helen, a lady*

INNOGEN
Who's there? My woman Helen?

HELEN   Please you, madam.

INNOGEN
What hour is it?

HELEN   Almost midnight, madam.

INNOGEN
I have read three hours then. Mine eyes are weak.
Fold down the leaf where I have left. To bed.
Take not away the taper; leave it burning,   5
And if thou canst awake by four o'th' clock,
I prithee call me. Sleep hath seized me wholly.
⌈*Exit Helen*⌉
To your protection I commend me, gods.
From fairies and the tempters of the night
Guard me, beseech ye.   10
She sleeps.
Giacomo comes from the trunk

GIACOMO
The crickets sing, and man's o'er-laboured sense
Repairs itself by rest. Our Tarquin thus
Did softly press the rushes ere he wakened
The chastity he wounded. Cytherea,
How bravely thou becom'st thy bed! Fresh lily,   15
And whiter than the sheets! That I might touch,
But kiss, one kiss! Rubies unparagoned,
How dearly they do't! 'Tis her breathing that
Perfumes the chamber thus. The flame o'th' taper
Bows toward her, and would underpeep her lids,   20
To see th'enclosèd lights, now canopied
Under these windows, white and azure-laced
With blue of heaven's own tinct. But my design—
To note the chamber. I will write all down.
He writes in his tables
Such and such pictures, there the window, such   25
Th'adornment of her bed, the arras, figures,
Why, such and such; and the contents o'th' story.
Ah, but some natural notes about her body
Above ten thousand meaner movables
Would testify t'enrich mine inventory.   30
O sleep, thou ape of death, lie dull upon her,
And be her sense but as a monument
Thus in a chapel lying. Come off, come off;
As slippery as the Gordian knot was hard.
He takes the bracelet from her arm
'Tis mine, and this will witness outwardly,   35
As strongly as the conscience does within,
To th' madding of her lord. On her left breast
A mole, cinque-spotted, like the crimson drops
I'th' bottom of a cowslip. Here's a voucher
Stronger than ever law could make. This secret   40
Will force him think I have picked the lock and ta'en
The treasure of her honour. No more. To what end?
Why should I write this down that's riveted,
Screwed to my memory? She hath been reading late,

The tale of Tereus. Here the leaf's turned down   45
Where Philomel gave up. I have enough.
To th' trunk again, and shut the spring of it.
Swift, swift, you dragons of the night, that dawning
May bare the raven's eye! I lodge in fear.
Though this' a heavenly angel, hell is here.   50
        Clock strikes
One, two, three. Time, time!
            Exit into the trunk. ⌈*The bed and trunk are
                                    removed*⌉

2.3   *Enter Cloten and the two Lords*

FIRST LORD Your lordship is the most patient man in loss,
    the most coldest that ever turned up ace.
CLOTEN It would make any man cold to lose.
FIRST LORD But not every man patient after the noble
    temper of your lordship. You are most hot and furious
    when you win.   6
CLOTEN Winning will put any man into courage. If I could
    get this foolish Innogen I should have gold enough. It's
    almost morning, is't not?
FIRST LORD Day, my lord.   10
CLOTEN I would this music would come. I am advised to
    give her music o' mornings; they say it will penetrate.
        Enter Musicians
Come on, tune. If you can penetrate her with your
fingering, so; we'll try with tongue too. If none will
do, let her remain; but I'll never give o'er. First, a very
excellent good-conceited thing; after, a wonderful sweet
air with admirable rich words to it; and then let her
consider.
        ⌈*Music*⌉

⌈MUSICIAN⌉ (*sings*)
    Hark, hark, the lark at heaven gate sings,
        And Phoebus gins arise,   20
    His steeds to water at those springs
        On chaliced flowers that lies,
    And winking Mary-buds begin to ope their golden eyes;
    With everything that pretty is, my lady sweet, arise,
        Arise, arise!   25

CLOTEN So, get you gone. If this penetrate I will consider
your music the better; if it do not, it is a vice in her
ears which horse hairs and calves' guts nor the voice
of unpaved eunuch to boot can never amend.
                    Exeunt Musicians
        Enter Cymbeline and the Queen
SECOND LORD Here comes the King.   30
CLOTEN I am glad I was up so late, for that's the reason
I was up so early. He cannot choose but take this
service I have done fatherly. Good morrow to your
majesty, and to my gracious mother.
CYMBELINE
    Attend you here the door of our stern daughter?   35
    Will she not forth?
CLOTEN I have assailed her with musics, but she
    vouchsafes no notice.

CYMBELINE
    The exile of her minion is too new.
    She hath not yet forgot him. Some more time   40
    Must wear the print of his remembrance out,
    And then she's yours.
QUEEN (*to Cloten*)   You are most bound to th' King,
    Who lets go by no vantages that may
    Prefer you to his daughter. Frame yourself
    To orderly solicits, and be friended   45
    With aptness of the season. Make denials
    Increase your services; so seem as if
    You were inspired to do those duties which
    You tender to her; that you in all obey her,
    Save when command to your dismission tends,   50
    And therein you are senseless.
CLOTEN   Senseless? Not so.
        Enter a Messenger
MESSENGER (*to Cymbeline*)
    So like you, sir, ambassadors from Rome;
    The one is Caius Lucius.
CYMBELINE   A worthy fellow,
    Albeit he comes on angry purpose now:
    But that's no fault of his. We must receive him   55
    According to the honour of his sender,
    And towards himself, his goodness forespent on us,
    We must extend our notice. Our dear son,
    When you have given good morning to your mistress,
    Attend the Queen and us. We shall have need   60
    T'employ you towards this Roman. Come, our queen.
                Exeunt all but Cloten
CLOTEN
    If she be up, I'll speak with her; if not,
    Let her lie still and dream.
        ⌈*He knocks*⌉
                    By your leave, ho!—
    I know her women are about her; what
    If I do line one of their hands? 'Tis gold   65
    Which buys admittance—oft it doth—yea, and makes
    Diana's rangers false themselves, yield up
    Their deer to th' stand o'th' stealer; and 'tis gold
    Which makes the true man killed and saves the thief,
    Nay, sometime hangs both thief and true man. What
    Can it not do and undo? I will make   71
    One of her women lawyer to me, for
    I yet not understand the case myself.—
    By your leave.
        Knocks. Enter a Lady
LADY
    Who's there that knocks?
CLOTEN   A gentleman.
LADY   No more?   75
CLOTEN
    Yes, and a gentlewoman's son.
LADY   That's more
    ⌈*Aside*⌉ Than some whose tailors are as dear as yours
    Can justly boast of. (*To him*) What's your lordship's
        pleasure?

CLOTEN
Your lady's person. Is she ready?

LADY   Ay.
⌈*Aside*⌉ To keep her chamber.

CLOTEN   There is gold for you.   80
Sell me your good report.

LADY
How, my good name?—or to report of you
What I shall think is good?
    Enter Innogen
                       The Princess.   ⌈*Exit*⌉

CLOTEN
Good morrow, fairest. Sister, your sweet hand.

INNOGEN
Good morrow, sir. You lay out too much pains   85
For purchasing but trouble. The thanks I give
Is telling you that I am poor of thanks,
And scarce can spare them.

CLOTEN   Still I swear I love you.

INNOGEN
If you but said so, 'twere as deep with me.
If you swear still, your recompense is still   90
That I regard it not.

CLOTEN   This is no answer.

INNOGEN
But that you shall not say I yield being silent,
I would not speak. I pray you, spare me. Faith,
I shall unfold equal discourtesy
To your best kindness. One of your great knowing   95
Should learn, being taught, forbearance.

CLOTEN
To leave you in your madness, 'twere my sin.
I will not.

INNOGEN   Fools cure not mad folks.

CLOTEN
Do you call me fool?

INNOGEN   As I am mad, I do.
If you'll be patient, I'll no more be mad;   100
That cures us both. I am much sorry, sir,
You put me to forget a lady's manners
By being so verbal; and learn now for all
That I, which know my heart, do here pronounce
By th' very truth of it: I care not for you,   105
And am so near the lack of charity
To accuse myself I hate you, which I had rather
You felt than make't my boast.

CLOTEN   You sin against
Obedience which you owe your father. For
The contract you pretend with that base wretch,   110
One bred of alms and fostered with cold dishes,
With scraps o'th' court, it is no contract, none.
And though it be allowed in meaner parties—
Yet who than he more mean?—to knit their souls,
On whom there is no more dependency   115
But brats and beggary, in self-figured knot,
Yet you are curbed from that enlargement by
The consequence o'th' crown, and must not foil
The precious note of it with a base slave,

A hilding for a livery, a squire's cloth,   120
A pantler—not so eminent.

INNOGEN   Profane fellow,
Wert thou the son of Jupiter, and no more
But what thou art besides, thou wert too base
To be his groom; thou wert dignified enough,
Even to the point of envy, if 'twere made   125
Comparative for your virtues to be styled
The under-hangman of his kingdom, and hated
For being preferred so well.

CLOTEN   The south-fog rot him!

INNOGEN
He never can meet more mischance than come
To be but named of thee. His meanest garment   130
That ever hath but clipped his body is dearer
In my respect than all the hairs above thee,
Were they all made such men. How now, Pisanio!
    Enter Pisanio

CLOTEN His garment? Now the devil—

INNOGEN (*to Pisanio*)
To Dorothy, my woman, hie thee presently.   135

CLOTEN
His garment?

INNOGEN (*to Pisanio*) I am sprited with a fool,
Frighted, and angered worse. Go bid my woman
Search for a jewel that too casually
Hath left mine arm. It was thy master's. 'Shrew me
If I would lose it for a revenue   140
Of any king's in Europe! I do think
I saw't this morning; confident I am
Last night 'twas on mine arm; I kissed it.
I hope it be not gone to tell my lord
That I kiss aught but he.

PISANIO   'Twill not be lost.   145

INNOGEN
I hope so. Go and search.   *Exit Pisanio*

CLOTEN   You have abused me.
'His meanest garment'?

INNOGEN   Ay, I said so, sir.
If you will make't an action, call witness to't.

CLOTEN
I will inform your father.

INNOGEN   Your mother too.
She's my good lady, and will conceive, I hope,   150
But the worst of me. So I leave you, sir,
To th' worst of discontent.   *Exit*

CLOTEN   I'll be revenged.
'His meanest garment'? Well!   *Exit*

2.4   *Enter Posthumus and Filario*

POSTHUMUS
Fear it not, sir. I would I were so sure
To win the King as I am bold her honour
Will remain hers.

FILARIO   What means do you make to him?

POSTHUMUS
Not any; but abide the change of time,
Quake in the present winter's state, and wish   5

That warmer days would come. In these seared hopes
I barely gratify your love; they failing,
I must die much your debtor.
FILARIO
    Your very goodness and your company
O'erpays all I can do. By this, your king   10
Hath heard of great Augustus. Caius Lucius
Will do 's commission throughly. And I think
He'll grant the tribute, send th'arrearages,
Ere look upon óur Romans, whose remembrance
Is yet fresh in their grief.
POSTHUMUS   I do believe,   15
Statist though I am none, nor like to be,
That this will prove a war, and you shall hear
The legions now in Gallia sooner landed
In our not-fearing Britain than have tidings
Of any penny tribute paid. Our countrymen   20
Are men more ordered than when Julius Caesar
Smiled at their lack of skill but found their courage
Worthy his frowning at. Their discipline,
Now wing-led with their courage, will make known
To their approvers they are people such   25
That mend upon the world.
    Enter Giacomo
FILARIO   See, Giacomo.
POSTHUMUS (*to Giacomo*)
The swiftest harts have posted you by land,
And winds of all the corners kissed your sails
To make your vessel nimble.
FILARIO (*to Giacomo*)   Welcome, sir.
POSTHUMUS (*to Giacomo*)
I hope the briefness of your answer made   30
The speediness of your return.
GIACOMO   Your lady is
One of the fair'st that I have looked upon—
POSTHUMUS
And therewithal the best, or let her beauty
Look through a casement to allure false hearts,
And be false with them.
GIACOMO   Here are letters for you.   35
POSTHUMUS
Their tenor good, I trust.
GIACOMO   'Tis very like.
    Posthumus reads the letters
⌈FILARIO⌉
Was Caius Lucius in the Briton court
When you were there?
GIACOMO   He was expected then,
But not approached.
POSTHUMUS   All is well yet.
Sparkles this stone as it was wont, or is't not   40
Too dull for your good wearing?
GIACOMO   If I had lost it
I should have lost the worth of it in gold.
I'll make a journey twice as far t'enjoy
A second night of such sweet shortness which
Was mine in Britain; for the ring is won.   45

POSTHUMUS
The stone's too hard to come by.
GIACOMO   Not a whit,
Your lady being so easy.
POSTHUMUS   Make not, sir,
Your loss your sport. I hope you know that we
Must not continue friends.
GIACOMO   Good sir, we must,
If you keep covenant. Had I not brought   50
The knowledge of your mistress home I grant
We were to question farther, but I now
Profess myself the winner of her honour,
Together with your ring, and not the wronger
Of her or you, having proceeded but   55
By both your wills.
POSTHUMUS   If you can make't apparent
That you have tasted her in bed, my hand
And ring is yours. If not, the foul opinion
You had of her pure honour gains or loses
Your sword or mine, or masterless leaves both   60
To who shall find them.
GIACOMO   Sir, my circumstances,
Being so near the truth as I will make them,
Must first induce you to believe; whose strength
I will confirm with oath, which I doubt not
You'll give me leave to spare when you shall find   65
You need it not.
POSTHUMUS   Proceed.
GIACOMO   First, her bedchamber—
Where I confess I slept not, but profess
Had that was well worth watching—it was hanged
With tapestry of silk and silver; the story
Proud Cleopatra when she met her Roman,   70
And Cydnus swelled above the banks, or for
The press of boats or pride: a piece of work
So bravely done, so rich, that it did strive
In workmanship and value; which I wondered
Could be so rarely and exactly wrought,   75
Such the true life on't was.
POSTHUMUS   This is true,
And this you might have heard of here, by me
Or by some other.
GIACOMO   More particulars
Must justify my knowledge.
POSTHUMUS   So they must,
Or do your honour injury.
GIACOMO   The chimney   80
Is south the chamber, and the chimney-piece
Chaste Dian bathing. Never saw I figures
So likely to report themselves; the cutter
Was as another nature; dumb, outwent her,
Motion and breath left out.
POSTHUMUS   This is a thing   85
Which you might from relation likewise reap,
Being, as it is, much spoke of.
GIACOMO   The roof o'th' chamber
With golden cherubins is fretted. Her andirons—
I had forgot them—were two winking Cupids

Of silver, each on one foot standing, nicely 90
Depending on their brands.
POSTHUMUS   This is her honour!
Let it be granted you have seen all this—and praise
Be given to your remembrance—the description
Of what is in her chamber nothing saves
The wager you have laid.
GIACOMO   Then, if you can 95
Be pale, I beg but leave to air this jewel. See!
He shows the bracelet
And now 'tis up again; it must be married
To that your diamond. I'll keep them.
POSTHUMUS   Jove!
Once more let me behold it. Is it that
Which I left with her?
GIACOMO   Sir, I thank her, that. 100
She stripped it from her arm. I see her yet.
Her pretty action did outsell her gift,
And yet enriched it too. She gave it me,
And said she prized it once.
POSTHUMUS   Maybe she plucked it off
To send it me.
GIACOMO   She writes so to you, doth she? 105
POSTHUMUS
O, no, no, no—'tis true! Here, take this too.
He gives Giacomo his ring
It is a basilisk unto mine eye,
Kills me to look on't. Let there be no honour
Where there is beauty, truth where semblance, love
Where there's another man. The vows of women 110
Of no more bondage be to where they are made
Than they are to their virtues, which is nothing!
O, above measure false!
FILARIO   Have patience, sir,
And take your ring again; 'tis not yet won.
It may be probable she lost it, or 115
Who knows if one her woman, being corrupted,
Hath stol'n it from her?
POSTHUMUS   Very true,
And so I hope he came by't. Back my ring.
He takes his ring again
Render to me some corporal sign about her
More evident than this; for this was stol'n. 120
GIACOMO
By Jupiter, I had it from her arm.
POSTHUMUS
Hark you, he swears, by Jupiter he swears.
'Tis true, nay, keep the ring, 'tis true. I am sure
She would not lose it. Her attendants are
All sworn and honourable. They induced to steal it?
And by a stranger? No, he hath enjoyed her. 126
The cognizance of her incontinency
Is this. She hath bought the name of whore thus
    dearly.
He gives Giacomo his ring
There, take thy hire, and all the fiends of hell
Divide themselves between you!
FILARIO   Sir, be patient. 130

This is not strong enough to be believed
Of one persuaded well of.
POSTHUMUS   Never talk on't.
She hath been colted by him.
GIACOMO   If you seek
For further satisfying, under her breast—
Worthy the pressing—lies a mole, right proud 135
Of that most delicate lodging. By my life,
I kissed it, and it gave me present hunger
To feed again, though full. You do remember
This stain upon her?
POSTHUMUS   Ay, and it doth confirm
Another stain as big as hell can hold, 140
Were there no more but it.
GIACOMO   Will you hear more?
POSTHUMUS
Spare your arithmetic, never count the turns.
Once, and a million!
GIACOMO   I'll be sworn.
POSTHUMUS   No swearing.
If you will swear you have not done't, you lie,
And I will kill thee if thou dost deny 145
Thou'st made me cuckold.
GIACOMO   I'll deny nothing.
POSTHUMUS
O that I had her here to tear her limb-meal!
I will go there and do't i'th' court, before
Her father. I'll do something.   *Exit*
FILARIO   Quite besides
The government of patience! You have won. 150
Let's follow and pervert the present wrath
He hath against himself.
GIACOMO   With all my heart.   *Exeunt*

2.5   *Enter Posthumus*

POSTHUMUS
Is there no way for men to be, but women
Must be half-workers? We are bastards all,
And that most venerable man which I
Did call my father was I know not where
When I was stamped. Some coiner with his tools 5
Made me a counterfeit; yet my mother seemed
The Dian of that time: so doth my wife
The nonpareil of this. O vengeance, vengeance!
Me of my lawful pleasure she restrained,
And prayed me oft forbearance; did it with 10
A pudency so rosy the sweet view on't
Might well have warmed old Saturn; that I thought
    her
As chaste as unsunned snow. O all the devils!
This yellow Giacomo in an hour—was't not?—
Or less—at first? Perchance he spoke not, but 15
Like a full-acorned boar, a German one,
Cried 'O!' and mounted; found no opposition
But what he looked for should oppose and she
Should from encounter guard. Could I find out
The woman's part in me—for there's no motion 20
That tends to vice in man but I affirm

It is the woman's part; be it lying, note it,
The woman's; flattering, hers; deceiving, hers;
Lust and rank thoughts, hers, hers; revenges, hers;
Ambitions, covetings, change of prides, disdain,   25
Nice longing, slanders, mutability,
All faults that man can name, nay, that hell knows,
Why, hers in part or all, but rather all—
For even to vice
They are not constant, but are changing still   30
One vice but of a minute old for one
Not half so old as that. I'll write against them,
Detest them, curse them, yet 'tis greater skill
In a true hate to pray they have their will.   34
The very devils cannot plague them better.   *Exit*

3.1   ⌈*Flourish.*⌉ *Enter in state Cymbeline, the Queen,*
         Cloten, and lords at one door, and at another,
         Caius Lucius and attendants
CYMBELINE
Now say, what would Augustus Caesar with us?
LUCIUS
When Julius Caesar—whose remembrance yet
Lives in men's eyes, and will to ears and tongues
Be theme and hearing ever—was in this Britain
And conquered it, Cassibelan, thine uncle,   5
Famous in Caesar's praises no whit less
Than in his feats deserving it, for him
And his succession granted Rome a tribute,
Yearly three thousand pounds, which by thee lately
Is left untendered.
QUEEN   And, to kill the marvel,   10
Shall be so ever.
CLOTEN   There will be many Caesars
Ere such another Julius. Britain's a world
By itself, and we will nothing pay
For wearing our own noses.
QUEEN   That opportunity
Which then they had to take from 's, to resume   15
We have again. Remember, sir, my liege,
The kings your ancestors, together with
The natural bravery of your isle, which stands
As Neptune's park, ribbed and paled in
With banks unscalable and roaring waters,   20
With sands that will not bear your enemies' boats,
But suck them up to th' topmast. A kind of conquest
Caesar made here, but made not here his brag
Of 'came and saw and overcame'. With shame—
The first that ever touched him—he was carried   25
From off our coast, twice beaten; and his shipping,
Poor ignorant baubles, on our terrible seas
Like eggshells moved upon their surges, cracked
As easily 'gainst our rocks; for joy whereof
The famed Cassibelan, who was once at point—   30
O giglot fortune!—to master Caesar's sword,
Made Lud's town with rejoicing fires bright,
And Britons strut with courage.

CLOTEN Come, there's no more tribute to be paid. Our
kingdom is stronger than it was at that time, and, as
I said, there is no more such Caesars. Other of them
may have crooked noses, but to owe such straight
arms, none.
CYMBELINE Son, let your mother end.   39
CLOTEN We have yet many among us can grip as hard
as Cassibelan. I do not say I am one, but I have a
hand. Why tribute? Why should we pay tribute? If
Caesar can hide the sun from us with a blanket, or put
the moon in his pocket, we will pay him tribute for
light; else, sir, no more tribute, pray you now.   45
CYMBELINE (*to Lucius*) You must know,
Till the injurious Romans did extort
This tribute from us we were free. Caesar's ambition,
Which swelled so much that it did almost stretch
The sides o'th' world, against all colour here   50
Did put the yoke upon 's, which to shake off
Becomes a warlike people, whom we reckon
Ourselves to be. We do say then to Caesar,
Our ancestor was that Mulmutius which
Ordained our laws, whose use the sword of Caesar   55
Hath too much mangled, whose repair and franchise
Shall by the power we hold be our good deed,
Though Rome be therefore angry. Mulmutius made
     our laws,
Who was the first of Britain which did put
His brows within a golden crown and called   60
Himself a king.
LUCIUS   I am sorry, Cymbeline,
That I am to pronounce Augustus Caesar—
Caesar, that hath more kings his servants than
Thyself domestic officers—thine enemy.
Receive it from me, then: war and confusion   65
In Caesar's name pronounce I 'gainst thee. Look
For fury not to be resisted. Thus defied,
I thank thee for myself.
CYMBELINE   Thou art welcome, Caius.
Thy Caesar knighted me; my youth I spent
Much under him; of him I gathered honour,   70
Which he to seek of me again perforce
Behoves me keep at utterance. I am perfect
That the Pannonians and Dalmatians for
Their liberties are now in arms, a precedent
Which not to read would show the Britons cold;   75
So Caesar shall not find them.
LUCIUS   Let proof speak.
CLOTEN His majesty bids you welcome. Make pastime with
us a day or two or longer. If you seek us afterwards in
other terms, you shall find us in our salt-water girdle.
If you beat us out of it, it is yours; if you fall in the
adventure, our crows shall fare the better for you; and
there's an end.
LUCIUS So, sir.
CYMBELINE
I know your master's pleasure, and he mine.   84
All the remain is 'Welcome'.   ⌈*Flourish.*⌉ *Exeunt*

3.2 *Enter Pisanio, reading of a letter*

PISANIO

How? Of adultery? Wherefore write you not
What monster's her accuser? Leonatus,
O master, what a strange infection
Is fall'n into thy ear! What false Italian,
As poisonous tongued as handed, hath prevailed   5
On thy too ready hearing? Disloyal? No.
She's punished for her truth, and undergoes,
More goddess-like than wife-like, such assaults
As would take in some virtue. O my master,
Thy mind to hers is now as low as were   10
Thy fortunes. How? That I should murder her,
Upon the love and truth and vows which I
Have made to thy command? I her? Her blood?
If it be so to do good service, never
Let me be counted serviceable. How look I,   15
That I should seem to lack humanity
So much as this fact comes to? (*Reads*) 'Do't. The letter
That I have sent her, by her own command
Shall give thee opportunity.' O damned paper,
Black as the ink that's on thee! Senseless bauble,   20
Art thou a fedary for this act, and look'st
So virgin-like without?
        Enter Innogen
                                Lo, here she comes.
I am ignorant in what I am commanded.

INNOGEN How now, Pisanio?

PISANIO

Madam, here is a letter from my lord.   25

INNOGEN

Who, thy lord that is my lord, Leonatus?
O learned indeed were that astronomer
That knew the stars as I his characters—
He'd lay the future open. You good gods,
Let what is here contained relish of love,   30
Of my lord's health, of his content—yet not
That we two are asunder; let that grieve him.
Some griefs are med'cinable; that is one of them,
For it doth physic love—of his content
All but in that. Good wax, thy leave. Blest be   35
You bees that make these locks of counsel! Lovers
And men in dangerous bonds pray not alike;
Though forfeiters you cast in prison, yet
You clasp young Cupid's tables. Good news, gods!
        She opens and reads the letter
'Justice and your father's wrath, should he take me in
his dominion, could not be so cruel to me as you, O
the dearest of creatures, would even renew me with
your eyes. Take notice that I am in Cambria, at Milford
Haven. What your own love will out of this advise you,
follow. So he wishes you all happiness, that remains
loyal to his vow, and your increasing in love,   46
                                Leonatus Posthumus.'
O for a horse with wings! Hear'st thou, Pisanio?
He is at Milford Haven. Read, and tell me
How far 'tis thither. If one of mean affairs   50
May plod it in a week, why may not I

Glide thither in a day? Then, true Pisanio,
Who long'st like me to see thy lord, who long'st—
O let me bate—but not like me—yet long'st
But in a fainter kind—O, not like me,   55
For mine's beyond beyond; say, and speak thick—
Love's counsellor should fill the bores of hearing,
To th' smothering of the sense—how far it is
To this same blessèd Milford. And by th' way
Tell me how Wales was made so happy as   60
T'inherit such a haven. But first of all,
How we may steal from hence; and for the gap
That we shall make in time from our hence-going
Till our return, to excuse; but first, how get hence.
Why should excuse be born or ere begot?   65
We'll talk of that hereafter. Prithee speak,
How many score of miles may we well ride
'Twixt hour and hour?

PISANIO   One score 'twixt sun and sun,
Madam, 's enough for you, and too much too.

INNOGEN

Why, one that rode to 's execution, man,   70
Could never go so slow. I have heard of riding wagers
Where horses have been nimbler than the sands
That run i'th' clock's behalf. But this is fool'ry.
Go bid my woman feign a sickness, say
She'll home to her father; and provide me presently
A riding-suit no costlier than would fit   76
A franklin's housewife.

PISANIO   Madam, you're best consider.

INNOGEN

I see before me, man. Nor here, nor here,
Nor what ensues, but have a fog in them
That I cannot look through. Away, I prithee,   80
Do as I bid thee. There's no more to say:
Accessible is none but Milford way.   *Exeunt*

3.3 *Enter Belarius, followed by Guiderius and
        Arviragus, ⌈from a cave in the woods⌉*

BELARIUS

A goodly day not to keep house with such
Whose roof's as low as ours. Stoop, boys; this gate
Instructs you how t'adore the heavens, and bows you
To a morning's holy office. The gates of monarchs
Are arched so high that giants may jet through   5
And keep their impious turbans on without
Good morrow to the sun. Hail, thou fair heaven!
We house i'th' rock, yet use thee not so hardly
As prouder livers do.

GUIDERIUS   Hail, heaven!

ARVIRAGUS   Hail, heaven!

BELARIUS

Now for our mountain sport. Up to yon hill,   10
Your legs are young; I'll tread these flats. Consider,
When you above perceive me like a crow,
That it is place which lessens and sets off,
And you may then revolve what tales I have told you
Of courts, of princes, of the tricks in war;   15
That service is not service, so being done,

But being so allowed. To apprehend thus
Draws us a profit from all things we see,
And often to our comfort shall we find
The sharded beetle in a safer hold   20
Than is the full-winged eagle. O, this life
Is nobler than attending for a check,
Richer than doing nothing for a bauble,
Prouder than rustling in unpaid-for silk;
Such gain the cap of him that makes 'em fine,   25
Yet keeps his book uncrossed. No life to ours.

GUIDERIUS
Out of your proof you speak. We, poor unfledged,
Have never winged from view o'th' nest, nor know
    not
What air's from home. Haply this life is best,
If quiet life be best; sweeter to you   30
That have a sharper known; well corresponding
With your stiff age, but unto us it is
A cell of ignorance, travelling abed,
A prison for a debtor, that not dares
To stride a limit.

ARVIRAGUS (to Belarius) What should we speak of   35
When we are old as you? When we shall hear
The rain and wind beat dark December, how,
In this our pinching cave, shall we discourse
The freezing hours away? We have seen nothing.
We are beastly: subtle as the fox for prey,   40
Like warlike as the wolf for what we eat.
Our valour is to chase what flies; our cage
We make a choir, as doth the prisoned bird,
And sing our bondage freely.

BELARIUS   How you speak!
Did you but know the city's usuries,   45
And felt them knowingly; the art o'th' court,
As hard to leave as keep, whose top to climb
Is certain falling, or so slipp'ry that
The fear's as bad as falling; the toil o'th' war,
A pain that only seems to seek out danger   50
I'th' name of fame and honour, which dies i'th' search
And hath as oft a sland'rous epitaph
As record of fair act; nay, many times
Doth ill deserve by doing well; what's worse,
Must curtsy at the censure. O boys, this story 55
The world may read in me. My body's marked
With Roman swords, and my report was once
First with the best of note. Cymbeline loved me,
And when a soldier was the theme my name
Was not far off. Then was I as a tree   60
Whose boughs did bend with fruit; but in one night
A storm or robbery, call it what you will,
Shook down my mellow hangings, nay, my leaves,
And left me bare to weather.

GUIDERIUS   Uncertain favour!

BELARIUS
My fault being nothing, as I have told you oft, 65
But that two villains, whose false oaths prevailed
Before my perfect honour, swore to Cymbeline

I was confederate with the Romans. So
Followed my banishment, and this twenty years
This rock and these demesnes have been my world, 70
Where I have lived at honest freedom, paid
More pious debts to heaven than in all
The fore-end of my time. But up to th' mountains!
This is not hunter's language. He that strikes
The venison first shall be the lord o'th' feast, 75
To him the other two shall minister,
And we will fear no poison which attends
In place of greater state. I'll meet you in the valleys.
                    Exeunt Guiderius and Arviragus
How hard it is to hide the sparks of nature!
These boys know little they are sons to th' King, 80
Nor Cymbeline dreams that they are alive.
They think they are mine, and though trained up
    thus meanly
I'th' cave wherein they bow, their thoughts do hit
The roofs of palaces, and nature prompts them
In simple and low things to prince it much   85
Beyond the trick of others. This Polydore,
The heir of Cymbeline and Britain, who
The King his father called Guiderius—Jove,
When on my three-foot stool I sit and tell
The warlike feats I have done, his spirits fly out 90
Into my story: say 'Thus mine enemy fell,
And thus I set my foot on 's neck', even then
The princely blood flows in his cheek, he sweats,
Strains his young nerves, and puts himself in posture
That acts my words. The younger brother, Cadwal, 95
Once Arviragus, in as like a figure
Strikes life into my speech, and shows much more
His own conceiving.
        ⌈A hunting-horn sounds⌉
                    Hark, the game is roused!
O Cymbeline, heaven and my conscience knows
Thou didst unjustly banish me, whereon   100
At three and two years old I stole these babes,
Thinking to bar thee of succession as
Thou reft'st me of my lands. Euriphile,
Thou wast their nurse; they took thee for their
    mother,
And every day do honour to her grave.   105
Myself, Belarius, that am Morgan called,
They take for natural father.
        ⌈A hunting-horn sounds⌉
                    The game is up.   Exit

3.4   Enter Pisanio, and Innogen in a riding-suit
INNOGEN
Thou told'st me when we came from horse the place
Was near at hand. Ne'er longed my mother so
To see me first as I have now. Pisanio, man,
Where is Posthumus? What is in thy mind
That makes thee stare thus? Wherefore breaks that
    sigh   5
From th'inward of thee? One but painted thus

Would be interpreted a thing perplexed
Beyond self-explication. Put thyself
Into a haviour of less fear, ere wildness
Vanquish my staider senses. What's the matter?   10
    Pisanio gives her a letter
Why tender'st thou that paper to me with
A look untender? If't be summer news,
Smile to't before; if winterly, thou need'st
But keep that count'nance still. My husband's hand?
That drug-damned Italy hath out-craftied him,   15
And he's at some hard point. Speak, man. Thy tongue
May take off some extremity which to read
Would be even mortal to me.
PISANIO   Please you read,
And you shall find me, wretched man, a thing
The most disdained of fortune.   20
INNOGEN (*reads*) 'Thy mistress, Pisanio, hath played the
strumpet in my bed, the testimonies whereof lies
bleeding in me. I speak not out of weak surmises but
from proof as strong as my grief and as certain as I
expect my revenge. That part thou, Pisanio, must act
for me, if thy faith be not tainted with the breach of
hers. Let thine own hands take away her life. I shall
give thee opportunity at Milford Haven. She hath my
letter for the purpose, where if thou fear to strike and
to make me certain it is done, thou art the pander to
her dishonour and equally to me disloyal.'   31
PISANIO (*aside*)
What shall I need to draw my sword? The paper
Hath cut her throat already. No, 'tis slander,
Whose edge is sharper than the sword, whose tongue
Outvenoms all the worms of Nile, whose breath   35
Rides on the posting winds and doth belie
All corners of the world. Kings, queens, and states,
Maids, matrons, nay, the secrets of the grave
This viperous slander enters. (*To Innogen*) What cheer,
    madam?
INNOGEN
False to his bed? What is it to be false?   40
To lie in watch there and to think on him?
To weep 'twixt clock and clock? If sleep charge nature,
To break it with a fearful dream of him
And cry myself awake? That's false to 's bed, is it?
PISANIO Alas, good lady.   45
INNOGEN
I false? Thy conscience witness, Giacomo,
Thou didst accuse him of incontinency.
Thou then lookedst like a villain; now, methinks,
Thy favour's good enough. Some jay of Italy,
Whose mother was her painting, hath betrayed him.
Poor I am stale, a garment out of fashion,   51
And for I am richer than to hang by th' walls
I must be ripped. To pieces with me! O,
Men's vows are women's traitors. All good seeming,
By thy revolt, O husband, shall be thought   55
Put on for villainy; not born where't grows,
But worn a bait for ladies.
PISANIO   Good madam, hear me.

INNOGEN
True honest men being heard like false Aeneas
Were in his time thought false, and Sinon's weeping
Did scandal many a holy tear, took pity   60
From most true wretchedness. So thou, Posthumus,
Wilt lay the leaven on all proper men.
Goodly and gallant shall be false and perjured
From thy great fail. (*To Pisanio*) Come, fellow, be thou
    honest,
Do thou thy master's bidding. When thou seest him,
A little witness my obedience. Look,   66
I draw the sword myself. Take it, and hit
The innocent mansion of my love, my heart.
Fear not, 'tis empty of all things but grief.
Thy master is not there, who was indeed   70
The riches of it. Do his bidding; strike.
Thou mayst be valiant in a better cause,
But now thou seem'st a coward.
PISANIO   Hence, vile instrument,
Thou shalt not damn my hand!
INNOGEN   Why, I must die,
And if I do not by thy hand thou art   75
No servant of thy master's. Against self-slaughter
There is a prohibition so divine
That cravens my weak hand. Come, here's my heart.
Something's afore't. Soft, soft, we'll no defence;
Obedient as the scabbard. What is here?   80
    She takes letters from her bosom
The scriptures of the loyal Leonatus,
All turned to heresy? Away, away,
Corrupters of my faith, you shall no more
Be stomachers to my heart. Thus may poor fools
Believe false teachers. Though those that are betrayed
Do feel the treason sharply, yet the traitor   86
Stands in worse case of woe. And thou, Posthumus,
That didst set up my disobedience 'gainst the King
My father, and make me put into contempt the suits
Of princely fellows, shalt hereafter find   90
It is no act of common passage but
A strain of rareness; and I grieve myself
To think, when thou shalt be disedged by her
That now thou tirest on, how thy memory
Will then be panged by me. (*To Pisanio*) Prithee,
    dispatch.   95
The lamb entreats the butcher. Where's thy knife?
Thou art too slow to do thy master's bidding
When I desire it too.
PISANIO   O gracious lady,
Since I received command to do this business
I have not slept one wink.
INNOGEN   Do't, and to bed, then.   100
PISANIO
I'll wake mine eyeballs out first.
INNOGEN   Wherefore then
Didst undertake it? Why hast thou abused
So many miles with a pretence?—this place,
Mine action, and thine own? Our horses' labour,
The time inviting thee? The perturbed court,   105

For my being absent, whereunto I never
Purpose return? Why hast thou gone so far
To be unbent when thou hast ta'en thy stand,
Th'elected deer before thee?
PISANIO   But to win time
To lose so bad employment, in the which   110
I have considered of a course. Good lady,
Hear me with patience.
INNOGEN   Talk thy tongue weary. Speak.
I have heard I am a strumpet, and mine ear,
Therein false struck, can take no greater wound,
Nor tent to bottom that. But speak.
PISANIO   Then, madam, 115
I thought you would not back again.
INNOGEN   Most like,
Bringing me here to kill me.
PISANIO   Not so, neither.
But if I were as wise as honest, then
My purpose would prove well. It cannot be
But that my master is abused. Some villain,   120
Ay, and singular in his art, hath done you both
This cursèd injury.
INNOGEN Some Roman courtesan.
PISANIO No, on my life.
I'll give but notice you are dead, and send him   125
Some bloody sign of it, for 'tis commanded
I should do so. You shall be missed at court,
And that will well confirm it.
INNOGEN   Why, good fellow,
What shall I do the while, where bide, how live,
Or in my life what comfort when I am   130
Dead to my husband?
PISANIO   If you'll back to th' court—
INNOGEN
No court, no father, nor no more ado
With that harsh, churlish, noble, simple nothing,
That Cloten, whose love suit hath been to me
As fearful as a siege.
PISANIO   If not at court,   135
Then not in Britain must you bide.
INNOGEN   Where then?
Hath Britain all the sun that shines? Day, night,
Are they not but in Britain? I'th' world's volume
Our Britain seems as of it but not in't,
In a great pool a swan's nest. Prithee, think   140
There's livers out of Britain.
PISANIO   I am most glad
You think of other place. Th'ambassador,
Lucius the Roman, comes to Milford Haven
Tomorrow. Now if you could wear a mind
Dark as your fortune is, and but disguise   145
That which t'appear itself must not yet be
But by self-danger, you should tread a course
Pretty and full of view; yea, haply near
The residence of Posthumus; so nigh, at least,
That though his actions were not visible, yet   150
Report should render him hourly to your ear
As truly as he moves.
INNOGEN   O, for such means,

Though peril to my modesty, not death on't,
I would adventure.
PISANIO   Well then, here's the point:
You must forget to be a woman; change   155
Command into obedience, fear and niceness—
The handmaids of all women, or more truly
Woman it pretty self—into a waggish courage,
Ready in gibes, quick-answered, saucy and
As quarrelous as the weasel. Nay, you must   160
Forget that rarest treasure of your cheek,
Exposing it—but O, the harder heart!—
Alack, no remedy—to the greedy touch
Of common-kissing Titan, and forget
Your laboursome and dainty trims wherein   165
You made great Juno angry.
INNOGEN   Nay, be brief.
I see into thy end, and am almost
A man already.
PISANIO   First, make yourself but like one.
Forethinking this, I have already fit—
'Tis in my cloak-bag—doublet, hat, hose, all   170
That answer to them. Would you in their serving,
And with what imitation you can borrow
From youth of such a season, fore noble Lucius
Present yourself, desire his service, tell him
Wherein you're happy—which will make him know
If that his head have ear in music—doubtless   176
With joy he will embrace you, for he's honourable,
And, doubling that, most holy. Your means abroad—
You have me, rich, and I will never fail
Beginning nor supplyment.
INNOGEN   Thou art all the comfort
The gods will diet me with. Prithee away.   181
There's more to be considered, but we'll even
All that good time will give us. This attempt
I am soldier to, and will abide it with
A prince's courage. Away, I prithee.   185
PISANIO
Well, madam, we must take a short farewell
Lest, being missed, I be suspected of
Your carriage from the court. My noble mistress,
Here is a box. I had it from the Queen.
What's in't is precious. If you are sick at sea   190
Or stomach-qualmed at land, a dram of this
Will drive away distemper. To some shade,
And fit you to your manhood. May the gods
Direct you to the best.
INNOGEN   Amen. I thank thee.

Exeunt severally

3.5 ⌜*Flourish.*⌝ *Enter Cymbeline, the Queen, Cloten,*
       Lucius, and lords
CYMBELINE (*to Lucius*)
Thus far, and so farewell.
LUCIUS   Thanks, royal sir.
My emperor hath wrote I must from hence;
And am right sorry that I must report ye
My master's enemy.
CYMBELINE   Our subjects, sir,

Will not endure his yoke, and for ourself   5
To show less sovereignty than they must needs
Appear unkinglike.
LUCIUS   So, sir, I desire of you
A conduct over land to Milford Haven.
(*To the Queen*) Madam, all joy befall your grace,
⌈*to Cloten*⌉ and you.
CYMBELINE
My lords, you are appointed for that office.   10
The due of honour in no point omit.
So farewell, noble Lucius.
LUCIUS   Your hand, my lord.
CLOTEN
Receive it friendly, but from this time forth
I wear it as your enemy.
LUCIUS   Sir, the event
Is yet to name the winner. Fare you well.   15
CYMBELINE
Leave not the worthy Lucius, good my lords,
Till he have crossed the Severn. Happiness.
                    Exeunt Lucius and lords
QUEEN
He goes hence frowning, but it honours us
That we have given him cause.
CLOTEN   'Tis all the better.
Your valiant Britons have their wishes in it.   20
CYMBELINE
Lucius hath wrote already to the Emperor
How it goes here. It fits us therefore ripely
Our chariots and our horsemen be in readiness.
The powers that he already hath in Gallia
Will soon be drawn to head, from whence he moves
His war for Britain.
QUEEN   'Tis not sleepy business,   26
But must be looked to speedily and strongly.
CYMBELINE
Our expectation that it would be thus
Hath made us forward. But, my gentle queen,
Where is our daughter? She hath not appeared   30
Before the Roman, nor to us hath tendered
The duty of the day. She looks us like
A thing more made of malice than of duty.
We have noted it. Call her before us, for
We have been too slight in sufferance.
                      Exit one or more
QUEEN   Royal sir,   35
Since the exile of Posthumus most retired
Hath her life been, the cure whereof, my lord,
'Tis time must do. Beseech your majesty
Forbear sharp speeches to her. She's a lady
So tender of rebukes that words are strokes,   40
And strokes death to her.
    Enter a Messenger
CYMBELINE   Where is she, sir? How
Can her contempt be answered?
MESSENGER   Please you, sir,
Her chambers are all locked, and there's no answer
That will be given to th' loud'st of noise we make.

QUEEN
My lord, when last I went to visit her   45
She prayed me to excuse her keeping close,
Whereto constrained by her infirmity,
She should that duty leave unpaid to you
Which daily she was bound to proffer. This
She wished me to make known, but our great court
Made me to blame in memory.
CYMBELINE   Her doors locked?   51
Not seen of late? Grant heavens that which I
Fear prove false.   *Exit*
QUEEN   Son, I say, follow the King.
CLOTEN
That man of hers, Pisanio, her old servant,
I have not seen these two days.
QUEEN   Go, look after.   55
                        Exit Cloten
Pisanio, thou that stand'st so for Posthumus!
He hath a drug of mine. I pray his absence
Proceed by swallowing that, for he believes
It is a thing most precious. But for her,
Where is she gone? Haply despair hath seized her,   60
Or, winged with fervour of her love, she's flown
To her desired Posthumus. Gone she is
To death or to dishonour, and my end
Can make good use of either. She being down,
I have the placing of the British crown.   65
    Enter Cloten
How now, my son?
CLOTEN   'Tis certain she is fled.
Go in and cheer the King. He rages, none
Dare come about him.
QUEEN   All the better. May
This night forestall him of the coming day.   *Exit*
CLOTEN
I love and hate her. For she's fair and royal,   70
And that she hath all courtly parts more exquisite
Than lady, ladies, woman—from every one
The best she hath, and she, of all compounded,
Outsells them all—I love her therefore; but
Disdaining me, and throwing favours on   75
The low Posthumus, slanders so her judgement
That what's else rare is choked; and in that point
I will conclude to hate her, nay, indeed,
To be revenged upon her. For when fools
Shall—
    Enter Pisanio
        Who is here? What, are you packing, sirrah?
Come hither. Ah, you precious pander! Villain,   81
Where is thy lady? In a word, or else
Thou art straightway with the fiends.
PISANIO   O good my lord!
CLOTEN
Where is thy lady?—or, by Jupiter,
I will not ask again. Close villain,   85
I'll have this secret from thy tongue or rip
Thy heart to find it. Is she with Posthumus,

From whose so many weights of baseness cannot
A dram of worth be drawn?
PISANIO   Alas, my lord,
How can she be with him? When was she missed?
He is in Rome.
CLOTEN   Where is she, sir? Come nearer.   91
No farther halting. Satisfy me home
What is become of her.
PISANIO O my all-worthy lord!
CLOTEN All-worthy villain,   95
Discover where thy mistress is at once,
At the next word. No more of 'worthy lord'.
Speak, or thy silence on the instant is
Thy condemnation and thy death.
PISANIO   Then, sir,
This paper is the history of my knowledge   100
Touching her flight.
        He gives Cloten a letter
CLOTEN   Let's see't. I will pursue her
Even to Augustus' throne.
PISANIO ⌈aside⌉   Or this or perish.
She's far enough, and what he learns by this
May prove his travel, not her danger.
CLOTEN   Hum!
PISANIO (aside)
I'll write to my lord she's dead. O Innogen,   105
Safe mayst thou wander, safe return again!
CLOTEN
Sirrah, is this letter true?
PISANIO   Sir, as I think.
CLOTEN It is Posthumus' hand; I know't. Sirrah, if thou
wouldst not be a villain but do me true service, undergo
those employments wherein I should have cause to use
thee with a serious industry—that is, what villainy
soe'er I bid thee do, to perform it directly and truly—I
would think thee an honest man. Thou shouldst neither
want my means for thy relief nor my voice for thy
preferment.   115
PISANIO Well, my good lord.
CLOTEN Wilt thou serve me? For since patiently and
constantly thou hast stuck to the bare fortune of that
beggar Posthumus, thou canst not in the course of
gratitude but be a diligent follower of mine. Wilt thou
serve me?   121
PISANIO Sir, I will.
CLOTEN Give me thy hand. Here's my purse. Hast any of
thy late master's garments in thy possession?
PISANIO I have, my lord, at my lodging the same suit he
wore when he took leave of my lady and mistress. 126
CLOTEN The first service thou dost me, fetch that suit
hither. Let it be thy first service. Go.
PISANIO I shall, my lord.   *Exit*
CLOTEN Meet thee at Milford Haven! I forgot to ask him
one thing; I'll remember't anon. Even there, thou
villain Posthumus, will I kill thee. I would these
garments were come. She said upon a time—the
bitterness of it I now belch from my heart—that she

held the very garment of Posthumus in more respect
than my noble and natural person, together with the
adornment of my qualities. With that suit upon my
back will I ravish her—first kill him, and in her eyes;
there shall she see my valour, which will then be a
torment to her contempt. He on the ground, my speech
of insultment ended on his dead body, and when my
lust hath dined—which, as I say, to vex her I will
execute in the clothes that she so praised—to the court
I'll knock her back, foot her home again. She hath
despised me rejoicingly, and I'll be merry in my revenge.
        Enter Pisanio with Posthumus' suit
Be those the garments?
PISANIO   Ay, my noble lord.   146
CLOTEN
How long is't since she went to Milford Haven?
PISANIO She can scarce be there yet.
CLOTEN Bring this apparel to my chamber. That is the
second thing that I have commanded thee. The third
is that thou wilt be a voluntary mute to my design. Be
but duteous, and true preferment shall tender itself to
thee. My revenge is now at Milford. Would I had wings
to follow it. Come, and be true.   *Exit*
PISANIO
Thou bidd'st me to my loss, for true to thee   155
Were to prove false, which I will never be
To him that is most true. To Milford go,
And find not her whom thou pursuest. Flow, flow,
You heavenly blessings, on her. This fool's speed   159
Be crossed with slowness; labour be his meed.   *Exit*

3.6   *Enter Innogen, dressed as a man, before the cave*
INNOGEN
I see a man's life is a tedious one.
I have tired myself, and for two nights together
Have made the ground my bed. I should be sick,
But that my resolution helps me. Milford,
When from the mountain-top Pisanio showed thee,
Thou wast within a ken. O Jove, I think   6
Foundations fly the wretched—such, I mean,
Where they should be relieved. Two beggars told me
I could not miss my way. Will poor folks lie,
That have afflictions on them, knowing 'tis   10
A punishment or trial? Yes. No wonder,
When rich ones scarce tell true. To lapse in fullness
Is sorer than to lie for need, and falsehood
Is worse in kings than beggars. My dear lord,
Thou art one o'th' false ones. Now I think on thee 15
My hunger's gone, but even before I was
At point to sink for food. But what is this?
Here is a path to't. 'Tis some savage hold.
I were best not call; I dare not call; yet famine,
Ere clean it o'erthrow nature, makes it valiant. 20
Plenty and peace breeds cowards, hardness ever
Of hardiness is mother. Ho! Who's here?
If anything that's civil, speak; if savage,
Take or lend. Ho! No answer? Then I'll enter.

Best draw my sword, and if mine enemy   25
But fear the sword like me he'll scarcely look on't.
Such a foe, good heavens!   *Exit into the cave*
Enter Belarius, Guiderius, and Arviragus

BELARIUS
You, Polydore, have proved best woodman and
Are master of the feast. Cadwal and I
Will play the cook and servant; 'tis our match.   30
The sweat of industry would dry and die
But for the end it works to. Come, our stomachs
Will make what's homely savoury. Weariness
Can snore upon the flint when resty sloth
Finds the down pillow hard. Now peace be here,   35
Poor house, that keep'st thyself.

GUIDERIUS   I am throughly weary.

ARVIRAGUS
I am weak with toil yet strong in appetite.

GUIDERIUS
There is cold meat i'th' cave. We'll browse on that
Whilst what we have killed be cooked.

BELARIUS (*looking into the cave*)   Stay, come not in.
But that it eats our victuals I should think   40
Here were a fairy.

GUIDERIUS   What's the matter, sir?

BELARIUS
By Jupiter, an angel—or, if not,
An earthly paragon. Behold divineness
No elder than a boy.
Enter Innogen from the cave, dressed as a man

INNOGEN   Good masters, harm me not.
Before I entered here I called, and thought   45
To have begged or bought what I have took. Good
    truth,
I have stol'n naught, nor would not, though I had
    found
Gold strewed i'th' floor. Here's money for my meat.
I would have left it on the board so soon
As I had made my meal, and parted   50
With prayers for the provider.

GUIDERIUS   Money, youth?

ARVIRAGUS
All gold and silver rather turn to dirt,
As 'tis no better reckoned but of those
Who worship dirty gods.

INNOGEN   I see you're angry.
Know, if you kill me for my fault, I should   55
Have died had I not made it.

BELARIUS   Whither bound?

INNOGEN
To Milford Haven.

BELARIUS   What's your name?

INNOGEN
Fidele, sir. I have a kinsman who
Is bound for Italy. He embarked at Milford,
To whom being going, almost spent with hunger,   60
I am fall'n in this offence.

BELARIUS   Prithee, fair youth,
Think us no churls, nor measure our good minds

By this rude place we live in. Well encountered.
'Tis almost night. You shall have better cheer
Ere you depart, and thanks to stay and eat it.   65
Boys, bid him welcome.

GUIDERIUS   Were you a woman, youth,
I should woo hard but be your groom in honesty,
Ay, bid for you as I'd buy.

ARVIRAGUS   I'll make't my comfort
He is a man, I'll love him as my brother.
(*To Innogen*) And such a welcome as I'd give to him
After long absence, such is yours. Most welcome.   71
Be sprightly, for you fall 'mongst friends.

INNOGEN   'Mongst friends
If brothers. (*Aside*) Would it had been so that they
Had been my father's sons. Then had my price
Been less, and so more equal ballasting   75
To thee, Posthumus.
The three men speak apart

BELARIUS   He wrings at some distress.

GUIDERIUS
Would I could free't.

ARVIRAGUS   Or I, whate'er it be,
What pain it cost, what danger. Gods!

BELARIUS   Hark, boys.
They whisper

INNOGEN (*aside*) Great men
That had a court no bigger than this cave,   80
That did attend themselves and had the virtue
Which their own conscience sealed them, laying by
That nothing-gift of differing multitudes,
Could not outpeer these twain. Pardon me, gods,
I'd change my sex to be companion with them,   85
Since Leonatus' false.

BELARIUS   It shall be so.
Boys, we'll go dress our hunt. Fair youth, come in
Discourse is heavy, fasting. When we have supped
We'll mannerly demand thee of thy story,
So far as thou wilt speak it.

GUIDERIUS   Pray draw near.   90

ARVIRAGUS
The night to th' owl and morn to th' lark less
    welcome.

INNOGEN Thanks, sir.

ARVIRAGUS I pray draw near.   *Exeunt into the cave*

3.7   *Enter two Roman Senators, and Tribunes*

FIRST SENATOR
This is the tenor of the Emperor's writ:
That since the common men are now in action
'Gainst the Pannonians and Dalmatians,
And that the legions now in Gallia are
Full weak to undertake our wars against   5
The fall'n-off Britons, that we do incite
The gentry to this business. He creates
Lucius pro-consul, and to you the tribunes,
For this immediate levy, he commends
His absolute commission. Long live Caesar!   10

A TRIBUNE
  Is Lucius general of the forces?
SECOND SENATOR   Ay.
A TRIBUNE
  Remaining now in Gallia?
FIRST SENATOR   With those legions
  Which I have spoke of, whereunto your levy
  Must be supplyant. The words of your commission
  Will tie you to the numbers and the time   15
  Of their dispatch.
A TRIBUNE   We will discharge our duty.   *Exeunt*

4.1 *Enter Cloten, in Posthumus' suit*

CLOTEN I am near to th' place where they should meet,
if Pisanio have mapped it truly. How fit his garments
serve me! Why should his mistress, who was made by
him that made the tailor, not be fit too?—the rather—
saving reverence of the word—for 'tis said a woman's
fitness comes by fits. Therein I must play the workman.
I dare speak it to myself, for it is not vainglory for a
man and his glass to confer in his own chamber. I
mean the lines of my body are as well drawn as his:
no less young, more strong, not beneath him in
fortunes, beyond him in the advantage of the time,
above him in birth, alike conversant in general services,
and more remarkable in single oppositions. Yet this
imperceiverant thing loves him in my despite. What
mortality is! Posthumus, thy head which now is
growing upon thy shoulders shall within this hour be
off, thy mistress enforced, thy garments cut to pieces
before thy face; and all this done, spurn her home to
her father, who may haply be a little angry for my so
rough usage; but my mother, having power of his
testiness, shall turn all into my commendations. My
horse is tied up safe. Out, sword, and to a sore purpose!
Fortune, put them into my hand. This is the very
description of their meeting-place, and the fellow dares
not deceive me.   *Exit*

4.2 *Enter Belarius, Guiderius, Arviragus, and Innogen
      dressed as a man, from the cave*

BELARIUS (*to Innogen*)
  You are not well. Remain here in the cave.
  We'll come to you from hunting.
ARVIRAGUS (*to Innogen*)   Brother, stay here.
  Are we not brothers?
INNOGEN   So man and man should be,
  But clay and clay differs in dignity,
  Whose dust is both alike. I am very sick.   5
GUIDERIUS (*to Belarius and Arviragus*)
  Go you to hunting. I'll abide with him.
INNOGEN
  So sick I am not, yet I am not well;
  But not so citizen a wanton as
  To seem to die ere sick. So please you, leave me.
  Stick to your journal course. The breach of custom 10
  Is breach of all. I am ill, but your being by me

Cannot amend me. Society is no comfort
To one not sociable. I am not very sick,
Since I can reason of it. Pray you, trust me here.
I'll rob none but myself; and let me die,   15
Stealing so poorly.
GUIDERIUS   I love thee: I have spoke it;
  How much the quantity, the weight as much,
  As I do love my father.
BELARIUS   What, how, how?
ARVIRAGUS
  If it be sin to say so, sir, I yoke me
  In my good brother's fault. I know not why   20
  I love this youth, and I have heard you say
  Love's reason's without reason. The bier at door
  And a demand who is't shall die, I'd say
  'My father, not this youth'.
BELARIUS (*aside*)   O noble strain!
  O worthiness of nature, breed of greatness!   25
  Cowards father cowards, and base things sire base.
  Nature hath meal and bran, contempt and grace.
  I'm not their father, yet who this should be
  Doth miracle itself, loved before me.
  (*Aloud*) 'Tis the ninth hour o'th' morn.
ARVIRAGUS (*to Innogen*)   Brother, farewell.
INNOGEN
  I wish ye sport.
ARVIRAGUS   You health.—So please you, sir.   31
INNOGEN (*aside*)
  These are kind creatures. Gods, what lies I have heard!
  Our courtiers say all's savage but at court.
  Experience, O thou disprov'st report!
  Th'imperious seas breeds monsters; for the dish   35
  Poor tributary rivers as sweet fish.
  I am sick still, heart-sick. Pisanio,
  I'll now taste of thy drug.
  ⌐*She swallows the drug.*⌐ *The men speak apart*
GUIDERIUS   I could not stir him.
  He said he was gentle but unfortunate,
  Dishonestly afflicted but yet honest.   40
ARVIRAGUS
  Thus did he answer me, yet said hereafter
  I might know more.
BELARIUS   To th' field, to th' field!
  (*To Innogen*) We'll leave you for this time. Go in and
    rest.
ARVIRAGUS (*to Innogen*)
  We'll not be long away.
BELARIUS (*to Innogen*)   Pray be not sick,
  For you must be our housewife.
INNOGEN   Well or ill,   45
  I am bound to you.   *Exit*
BELARIUS   And shalt be ever.
  This youth, howe'er distressed, appears hath had
  Good ancestors.
ARVIRAGUS How angel-like he sings!
GUIDERIUS But his neat cookery!   50
⌐BELARIUS⌐
  He cut our roots in characters,

And sauced our broths as Juno had been sick
And he her dieter.

ARVIRAGUS   Nobly he yokes
A smiling with a sigh, as if the sigh
Was that it was for not being such a smile;   55
The smile mocking the sigh that it would fly
From so divine a temple to commix
With winds that sailors rail at.

GUIDERIUS   I do note
That grief and patience, rooted in him both,
Mingle their spurs together.

ARVIRAGUS   Grow patience,   60
And let the stinking elder, grief, untwine
His perishing root with the increasing vine.

BELARIUS
It is great morning. Come away. Who's there?
Enter Cloten in Posthumus' suit

CLOTEN
I cannot find those runagates. That villain
Hath mocked me. I am faint.

BELARIUS (*aside to Arviragus and Guiderius*)
                            'Those runagates'?   65
Means he not us? I partly know him; 'tis
Cloten, the son o'th' Queen. I fear some ambush.
I saw him not these many years, and yet
I know 'tis he. We are held as outlaws. Hence!

GUIDERIUS (*aside to Arviragus and Belarius*)
He is but one. You and my brother search   70
What companies are near. Pray you, away.
Let me alone with him.
                            Exeunt Arviragus and Belarius

CLOTEN   Soft, what are you
That fly me thus? Some villain mountaineers?
I have heard of such. What slave art thou?

GUIDERIUS   A thing
More slavish did I ne'er than answering   75
A slave without a knock.

CLOTEN   Thou art a robber,
A law-breaker, a villain. Yield thee, thief.

GUIDERIUS
To who? To thee? What art thou? Have not I
An arm as big as thine, a heart as big?
Thy words, I grant, are bigger, for I wear not   80
My dagger in my mouth. Say what thou art,
Why I should yield to thee.

CLOTEN   Thou villain base,
Know'st me not by my clothes?

GUIDERIUS   No, nor thy tailor, rascal,
Who is thy grandfather. He made those clothes,
Which, as it seems, make thee.

CLOTEN   Thou precious varlet,
My tailor made them not.

GUIDERIUS   Hence, then, and thank   86
The man that gave them thee. Thou art some fool.
I am loath to beat thee.

CLOTEN   Thou injurious thief,
Hear but my name and tremble.

GUIDERIUS   What's thy name?

CLOTEN Cloten, thou villain.   90

GUIDERIUS
Cloten, thou double villain, be thy name,
I cannot tremble at it. Were it toad or adder, spider,
'Twould move me sooner.

CLOTEN   To thy further fear,
Nay, to thy mere confusion, thou shalt know
I am son to th' Queen.

GUIDERIUS   I am sorry for't, not seeming
So worthy as thy birth.

CLOTEN   Art not afeard?   96

GUIDERIUS
Those that I reverence, those I fear, the wise.
At fools I laugh, not fear them.

CLOTEN   Die the death.
When I have slain thee with my proper hand
I'll follow those that even now fled hence,   100
And on the gates of Lud's town set your heads.
Yield, rustic mountaineer.   *Fight and exeunt*
                            Enter Belarius and Arviragus

BELARIUS   No company's abroad?

ARVIRAGUS
None in the world. You did mistake him, sure.

BELARIUS
I cannot tell. Long is it since I saw him,
But time hath nothing blurred those lines of favour
Which then he wore. The snatches in his voice   106
And burst of speaking were as his. I am absolute
'Twas very Cloten.

ARVIRAGUS   In this place we left them.
I wish my brother make good time with him,
You say he is so fell.

BELARIUS   Being scarce made up,   110
I mean to man, he had not apprehension
Of roaring terrors; for defect of judgement
Is oft the cause of fear.
                            Enter Guiderius with Cloten's head
                                    But see, thy brother.

GUIDERIUS
This Cloten was a fool, an empty purse,
There was no money in't. Not Hercules   115
Could have knocked out his brains, for he had none.
Yet I not doing this, the fool had borne
My head as I do his.

BELARIUS   What hast thou done?

GUIDERIUS
I am perfect what: cut off one Cloten's head,
Son to the Queen after his own report,   120
Who called me traitor, mountaineer, and swore
With his own single hand he'd take us in,
Displace our heads where—thanks, ye gods—they
     grow,
And set them on Lud's town.

BELARIUS   We are all undone.

GUIDERIUS
Why, worthy father, what have we to lose   125
But that he swore to take, our lives? The law
Protects not us: then why should we be tender

To let an arrogant piece of flesh threat us,
Play judge and executioner all himself,
For we do fear the law? What company   130
Discover you abroad?
BELARIUS   No single soul
Can we set eye on, but in all safe reason
He must have some attendants. Though his humour
Was nothing but mutation, ay, and that
From one bad thing to worse, not frenzy,   135
Not absolute madness, could so far have raved
To bring him here alone. Although perhaps
It may be heard at court that such as we
Cave here, hunt here, are outlaws, and in time
May make some stronger head, the which he
     hearing—   140
As it is like him—might break out, and swear
He'd fetch us in, yet is't not probable
To come alone, either he so undertaking,
Or they so suffering. Then on good ground we fear
If we do fear this body hath a tail   145
More perilous than the head.
ARVIRAGUS   Let ord'nance
Come as the gods foresay it; howsoe'er,
My brother hath done well.
BELARIUS   I had no mind
To hunt this day. The boy Fidele's sickness
Did make my way long forth.
GUIDERIUS   With his own sword, 150
Which he did wave against my throat, I have ta'en
His head from him. I'll throw't into the creek
Behind our rock, and let it to the sea
And tell the fishes he's the Queen's son, Cloten.
That's all I reck.   Exit with Cloten's head
BELARIUS   I fear 'twill be revenged. 155
Would, Polydore, thou hadst not done't, though
     valour
Becomes thee well enough.
ARVIRAGUS   Would I had done't,
So the revenge alone pursued me. Polydore,
I love thee brotherly, but envy much
Thou hast robbed me of this deed. I would revenges
That possible strength might meet would seek us
     through   161
And put us to our answer.
BELARIUS   Well, 'tis done.
We'll hunt no more today, nor seek for danger
Where there's no profit. I prithee, to our rock.
You and Fidele play the cooks. I'll stay   165
Till hasty Polydore return, and bring him
To dinner presently.
ARVIRAGUS   Poor sick Fidele!
I'll willingly to him. To gain his colour
I'd let a parish of such Clotens blood,
And praise myself for charity.   Exit into the cave
BELARIUS   O thou goddess,   170
Thou divine Nature, how thyself thou blazon'st
In these two princely boys! They are as gentle

As zephyrs blowing below the violet,
Not wagging his sweet head; and yet as rough,
Their royal blood enchafed, as the rud'st wind 175
That by the top doth take the mountain pine
And make him stoop to th' vale. 'Tis wonder
That an invisible instinct should frame them
To royalty unlearned, honour untaught,
Civility not seen from other, valour   180
That wildly grows in them, but yields a crop
As if it had been sowed. Yet still it's strange
What Cloten's being here to us portends,
Or what his death will bring us.
     Enter Guiderius
GUIDERIUS   Where's my brother?
I have sent Cloten's clotpoll down the stream   185
In embassy to his mother. His body's hostage
For his return.
     Solemn music
BELARIUS   My ingenious instrument!—
Hark, Polydore, it sounds. But what occasion
Hath Cadwal now to give it motion? Hark!
GUIDERIUS
Is he at home?
BELARIUS   He went hence even now.   190
GUIDERIUS
What does he mean? Since death of my dear'st mother
It did not speak before. All solemn things
Should answer solemn accidents. The matter?
Triumphs for nothing and lamenting toys
Is jollity for apes and grief for boys.   195
Is Cadwal mad?
     Enter from the cave Arviragus with Innogen, dead,
     bearing her in his arms
BELARIUS   Look, here he comes,
And brings the dire occasion in his arms
Of what we blame him for.
ARVIRAGUS   The bird is dead
That we have made so much on. I had rather
Have skipped from sixteen years of age to sixty, 200
To have turned my leaping time into a crutch,
Than have seen this.
GUIDERIUS (to Innogen) O sweetest, fairest lily!
My brother wears thee not one half so well
As when thou grew'st thyself.
BELARIUS   O melancholy,
Who ever yet could sound thy bottom, find   205
The ooze to show what coast thy sluggish crare
Might easiliest harbour in? Thou blessèd thing,
Jove knows what man thou mightst have made; but I,
Thou diedst a most rare boy, of melancholy.
(To Arviragus) How found you him?
ARVIRAGUS   Stark, as you see,
Thus smiling as some fly had tickled slumber,   211
Not as death's dart being laughed at; his right cheek
Reposing on a cushion.
GUIDERIUS   Where?
ARVIRAGUS   O'th' floor,

His arms thus leagued. I thought he slept, and put
My clouted brogues from off my feet, whose rudeness
Answered my steps too loud.
GUIDERIUS   Why, he but sleeps.   216
If he be gone he'll make his grave a bed.
With female fairies will his tomb be haunted,
(*To Innogen*) And worms will not come to thee.
ARVIRAGUS (*to Innogen*)   With fairest flowers
Whilst summer lasts and I live here, Fidele,   220
I'll sweeten thy sad grave. Thou shalt not lack
The flower that's like thy face, pale primrose, nor
The azured harebell, like thy veins; no, nor
The leaf of eglantine, whom not to slander
Outsweetened not thy breath. The ruddock would   225
With charitable bill—O bill sore shaming
Those rich-left heirs that let their fathers lie
Without a monument!—bring thee all this,
Yea, and furred moss besides, when flowers are none,
To winter-gown thy corpse.
GUIDERIUS   Prithee, have done,   230
And do not play in wench-like words with that
Which is so serious. Let us bury him,
And not protract with admiration what
Is now due debt. To th' grave.
ARVIRAGUS   Say, where shall 's lay him?
GUIDERIUS
By good Euriphile, our mother.
ARVIRAGUS   Be't so,   235
And let us, Polydore, though now our voices·
Have got the mannish crack, sing him to th' ground
As once our mother; use like note and words,
Save that 'Euriphile' must be 'Fidele'.
GUIDERIUS Cadwal,   240
I cannot sing. I'll weep, and word it with thee,
For notes of sorrow out of tune are worse
Than priests and fanes that lie.
ARVIRAGUS   We'll speak it then.
BELARIUS
Great griefs, I see, medicine the less, for Cloten
Is quite forgot. He was a queen's son, boys,   245
And though he came our enemy, remember
Hé was paid for that. Though mean and mighty
    rotting
Together have one dust, yet reverence,
That angel of the world, doth make distinction
Of place 'tween high and low. Our foe was princely,
And though you took his life as being our foe,   251
Yet bury him as a prince.
GUIDERIUS   Pray you, fetch him hither.
Thersites' body is as good as Ajax'
When neither are alive.
ARVIRAGUS (*to Belarius*)   If you'll go fetch him,
We'll say our song the whilst.   *Exit Belarius*
                            Brother, begin.   255
GUIDERIUS
Nay, Cadwal, we must lay his head to th'east.
My father hath a reason for't.
ARVIRAGUS   'Tis true.

GUIDERIUS
Come on, then, and remove him.
ARVIRAGUS   So, begin.
GUIDERIUS
    Fear no more the heat o'th' sun,
        Nor the furious winter's rages.   260
    Thou thy worldly task hast done,
        Home art gone and ta'en thy wages.
    Golden lads and girls all must,
    As chimney-sweepers, come to dust.
ARVIRAGUS
    Fear no more the frown o'th' great,   265
        Thou art past the tyrant's stroke.
    Care no more to clothe and eat,
        To thee the reed is as the oak.
    The sceptre, learning, physic, must
    All follow this and come to dust.   270
GUIDERIUS
    Fear no more the lightning flash,
ARVIRAGUS   Nor th'all-dreaded thunder-stone.
GUIDERIUS
    Fear not slander, censure rash.
ARVIRAGUS   Thou hast finished joy and moan.
GUIDERIUS *and* ARVIRAGUS
    All lovers young, all lovers must   275
    Consign to thee and come to dust.
GUIDERIUS
    No exorcisor harm thee,
ARVIRAGUS
    Nor no witchcraft charm thee.
GUIDERIUS
    Ghost unlaid forbear thee.
ARVIRAGUS
    Nothing ill come near thee.   280
GUIDERIUS *and* ARVIRAGUS
    Quiet consummation have,
    And renownèd be thy grave.

    Enter Belarius with the body of Cloten in
    Posthumus' suit
GUIDERIUS
We have done our obsequies. Come, lay him down.
BELARIUS
Here's a few flowers, but 'bout midnight more;   284
The herbs that have on them cold dew o'th' night
Are strewings fitt'st for graves upon th'earth's face.
You were as flowers, now withered; even so
These herblets shall, which we upon you strow.
Come on, away; apart upon our knees
⌈   ⌉   290
The ground that gave them first has them again.
Their pleasures here are past, so is their pain.
    Exeunt Belarius, Arviragus, and Guiderius
INNOGEN (*awakes*)
Yes, sir, to Milford Haven. Which is the way?
I thank you. By yon bush? Pray, how far thither?
'Od's pitykins, can it be six mile yet?   295

I have gone all night. 'Faith, I'll lie down and sleep.
She sees Cloten
But soft, no bedfellow! O gods and goddesses!
These flowers are like the pleasures of the world,
This bloody man the care on't. I hope I dream,
For so I thought I was a cavekeeper,   300
And cook to honest creatures. But 'tis not so.
'Twas but a bolt of nothing, shot of nothing,
Which the brain makes of fumes. Our very eyes
Are sometimes like our judgements, blind. Good faith,
I tremble still with fear; but if there be   305
Yet left in heaven as small a drop of pity
As a wren's eye, feared gods, a part of it!
The dream's here still. Even when I wake it is
Without me as within me; not imagined, felt.
A headless man? The garments of Posthumus?   310
I know the shape of 's leg; this is his hand,
His foot Mercurial, his Martial thigh,
The brawns of Hercules; but his Jovial face—
Murder in heaven! How? 'Tis gone. Pisanio,
All curses madded Hecuba gave the Greeks,   315
And mine to boot, be darted on thee! Thou,
Conspired with that irregulous devil Cloten,
Hath here cut off my lord. To write and read
Be henceforth treacherous! Damned Pisanio
Hath with his forgèd letters—damned Pisanio—   320
From this most bravest vessel of the world
Struck the main-top! O Posthumus, alas,
Where is thy head? Where's that? Ay me, where's
    that?
Pisanio might have killed thee at the heart
And left thy head on. How should this be? Pisanio?
'Tis he and Cloten. Malice and lucre in them   326
Have laid this woe here. O, 'tis pregnant, pregnant!
The drug he gave me, which he said was precious
And cordial to me, have I not found it
Murd'rous to th' senses? That confirms it home.   330
This is Pisanio's deed, and Cloten—O,
Give colour to my pale cheek with thy blood,
That we the horrider may seem to those
Which chance to find us!
⌈*She smears her face with blood*⌉
                            O my lord, my lord!
⌈*She faints.*⌉
Enter Lucius, Roman Captains, and a Soothsayer
A ROMAN CAPTAIN (*to Lucius*)
To them the legions garrisoned in Gallia   335
After your will have crossed the sea, attending
You here at Milford Haven with your ships.
They are hence in readiness.
LUCIUS   But what from Rome?
A ROMAN CAPTAIN
The senate hath stirred up the confiners
And gentlemen of Italy, most willing spirits   340
That promise noble service, and they come
Under the conduct of bold Giacomo,
Siena's brother.
LUCIUS   When expect you them?

A ROMAN CAPTAIN
With the next benefit o'th' wind.
LUCIUS   This forwardness
Makes our hopes fair. Command our present numbers
Be mustered; bid the captains look to't.
                            ⌈*Exit one or more*⌉
(*To Soothsayer*)   Now, sir,   346
What have you dreamed of late of this war's purpose?
SOOTHSAYER
Last night the very gods showed me a vision—
I fast, and prayed for their intelligence—thus:
I saw Jove's bird, the Roman eagle, winged   350
From the spongy south to this part of the west,
There vanished in the sunbeams; which portends,
Unless my sins abuse my divination,
Success to th' Roman host.
LUCIUS   Dream often so,
And never false.
    He sees Cloten's body
                Soft, ho, what trunk is here   355
Without his top? The ruin speaks that sometime
It was a worthy building. How, a page?
Or dead or sleeping on him? But dead rather,
For nature doth abhor to make his bed
With the defunct, or sleep upon the dead.   360
Let's see the boy's face.
A ROMAN CAPTAIN   He's alive, my lord.
LUCIUS
He'll then instruct us of this body. Young one,
Inform us of thy fortunes, for it seems
They crave to be demanded. Who is this
Thou mak'st thy bloody pillow? Or who was he   365
That, otherwise than noble nature did,
Hath altered that good picture? What's thy interest
In this sad wreck? How came't? Who is't?
What art thou?
INNOGEN   I am nothing; or if not,
Nothing to be were better. This was my master,   370
A very valiant Briton, and a good,
That here by mountaineers lies slain. Alas,
There is no more such masters. I may wander
From east to occident, cry out for service,
Try many, all good; serve truly, never   375
Find such another master.
LUCIUS   'Lack, good youth,
Thou mov'st no less with thy complaining than
Thy master in bleeding. Say his name, good friend.
INNOGEN
Richard du Champ. (*Aside*) If I do lie and do
No harm by it, though the gods hear I hope   380
They'll pardon it. (*Aloud*) Say you, sir?
LUCIUS   Thy name?
INNOGEN   Fidele, sir.
LUCIUS
Thou dost approve thyself the very same.
Thy name well fits thy faith, thy faith thy name.
Wilt take thy chance with me? I will not say
Thou shalt be so well mastered, but be sure,   385

No less beloved. The Roman Emperor's letters
Sent by a consul to me should not sooner
Than thine own worth prefer thee. Go with me.

INNOGEN
I'll follow, sir. But first, an't please the gods,
I'll hide my master from the flies as deep   390
As these poor pickaxes can dig; and when
With wild-wood leaves and weeds I ha' strewed his
grave
And on it said a century of prayers,
Such as I can, twice o'er I'll weep and sigh,
And leaving so his service, follow you,   395
So please you entertain me.

LUCIUS   Ay, good youth,
And rather father thee than master thee. My friends,
The boy hath taught us manly duties. Let us
Find out the prettiest daisied plot we can,
And make him with our pikes and partisans   400
A grave. Come, arm him. Boy, he is preferred
By thee to us, and he shall be interred
As soldiers can. Be cheerful. Wipe thine eyes.
Some falls are means the happier to arise.
                         Exeunt with Cloten's body

4.3   *Enter Cymbeline, Lords, and Pisanio*
CYMBELINE
Again, and bring me word how 'tis with her.
                         Exit one or more
A fever with the absence of her son,
A madness of which her life's in danger—heavens,
How deeply you at once do touch me! Innogen,
The great part of my comfort, gone; my queen   5
Upon a desperate bed, and in a time
When fearful wars point at me; her son gone,
So needful for this present! It strikes me past
The hope of comfort. (*To Pisanio*) But for thee, fellow,
Who needs must know of her departure and   10
Dost seem so ignorant, we'll enforce it from thee
By a sharp torture.

PISANIO   Sir, my life is yours.
I humbly set it at your will. But for my mistress,
I nothing know where she remains, why gone,
Nor when she purposes return. Beseech your
highness,   15
Hold me your loyal servant.

A LORD   Good my liege,
The day that she was missing he was here.
I dare be bound he's true, and shall perform
All parts of his subjection loyally. For Cloten,
There wants no diligence in seeking him,   20
And will no doubt be found.

CYMBELINE   The time is troublesome.
(*To Pisanio*) We'll slip you for a season, but our jealousy
Does yet depend.

A LORD   So please your majesty,
The Roman legions, all from Gallia drawn,
Are landed on your coast with a supply   25
Of Roman gentlemen by the senate sent.

CYMBELINE
Now for the counsel of my son and queen!
I am amazed with matter.

A LORD   Good my liege,
Your preparation can affront no less
Than what you hear of. Come more, for more you're
ready.   30
The want is but to put those powers in motion
That long to move.

CYMBELINE   I thank you. Let's withdraw,
And meet the time as it seeks us. We fear not
What can from Italy annoy us, but
We grieve at chances here. Away.   35
                    Exeunt Cymbeline and Lords

PISANIO
I heard no letter from my master since
I wrote him Innogen was slain. 'Tis strange.
Nor hear I from my mistress, who did promise
To yield me often tidings. Neither know I
What is betid to Cloten, but remain   40
Perplexed in all. The heavens still must work.
Wherein I am false I am honest; not true, to be true.
These present wars shall find I love my country
Even to the note o'th' King, or I'll fall in them.
All other doubts, by time let them be cleared: 45
Fortune brings in some boats that are not steered.
                                              Exit

4.4   *Enter Belarius, Guiderius, and Arviragus*
GUIDERIUS
The noise is round about us.

BELARIUS   Let us from it.

ARVIRAGUS
What pleasure, sir, find we in life to lock it
From action and adventure?

GUIDERIUS   Nay, what hope
Have we in hiding us? This way the Romans
Must or for Britains slay us, or receive us   5
For barbarous and unnatural revolts
During their use, and slay us after.

BELARIUS   Sons,
We'll higher to the mountains; there secure us.
To the King's party there's no going. Newness
Of Cloten's death—we being not known, not mustered
Among the bands—may drive us to a render   11
Where we have lived, and so extort from 's that
Which we have done, whose answer would be death
Drawn on with torture.

GUIDERIUS   This is, sir, a doubt
In such a time nothing becoming you   15
Nor satisfying us.

ARVIRAGUS   It is not likely
That when they hear the Roman horses neigh,
Behold their quartered files, have both their eyes
And ears so cloyed importantly as now,
That they will waste their time upon our note,   20
To know from whence we are.

BELARIUS   O, I am known

Of many in the army. Many years,
Though Cloten then but young, you see, not wore him
From my remembrance. And besides, the King
Hath not deserved my service nor your loves, 25
Who find in my exile the want of breeding,
The certainty of this hard life; aye hopeless
To have the courtesy your cradle promised,
But to be still hot summer's tanlings, and
The shrinking slaves of winter.
GUIDERIUS   Than be so, 30
Better to cease to be. Pray, sir, to th'army.
I and my brother are not known; yourself
So out of thought, and thereto so oe'rgrown,
Cannot be questioned.
ARVIRAGUS   By this sun that shines,
I'll thither. What thing is't that I never 35
Did see man die, scarce ever looked on blood
But that of coward hares, hot goats, and venison,
Never bestrid a horse save one that had
A rider like myself, who ne'er wore rowel
Nor iron on his heel! I am ashamed 40
To look upon the holy sun, to have
The benefit of his blest beams, remaining
So long a poor unknown.
GUIDERIUS   By heavens, I'll go.
If you will bless me, sir, and give me leave,
I'll take the better care; but if you will not, 45
The hazard therefore due fall on me by
The hands of Romans.
ARVIRAGUS   So say I, amen.
BELARIUS
No reason I, since of your lives you set
So slight a valuation, should reserve
My cracked one to more care. Have with you, boys!
If in your country wars you chance to die, 51
That is my bed, too, lads, and there I'll lie.
Lead, lead. (*Aside*) The time seems long. Their blood
   thinks scorn
Till it fly out and show them princes born. *Exeunt*

❈

5.1 *Enter Posthumus, dressed as an Italian gentleman,*
   carrying a bloody cloth
POSTHUMUS
Yea, bloody cloth, I'll keep thee, for I once wished
Thou shouldst be coloured thus. You married ones,
If each of you should take this course, how many
Must murder wives much better than themselves
For wrying but a little! O Pisanio, 5
Every good servant does not all commands,
No bond but to do just ones. Gods, if you
Should have ta'en vengeance on my faults, I never
Had lived to put on this; so had you saved
The noble Innogen to repent, and struck 10
Me, wretch, more worth your vengeance. But alack,
You snatch some hence for little faults; that's love,
To have them fall no more. You some permit
To second ills with ills, each elder worse,
And make them dread ill, to the doer's thrift. 15

But Innogen is your own. Do your blest wills,
And make me blest to obey. I am brought hither
Among th'Italian gentry, and to fight
Against my lady's kingdom. 'Tis enough
That, Britain, I have killed thy mistress-piece; 20
I'll give no wound to thee. Therefore, good heavens,
Hear patiently my purpose. I'll disrobe me
Of these Italian weeds, and suit myself
As does a Briton peasant.
   ⌈*He disrobes himself*⌉
                    So I'll fight
Against the part I come with; so I'll die 25
For thee, O Innogen, even for whom my life
Is every breath a death; and, thus unknown,
Pitied nor hated, to the face of peril
Myself I'll dedicate. Let me make men know
More valour in me than my habits show. 30
Gods, put the strength o'th' Leonati in me.
To shame the guise o'th' world, I will begin
The fashion—less without and more within. *Exit*

5.2 ⌈*A march.*⌉ *Enter Lucius, Giacomo, and the Roman*
   army at one door, and the Briton army at another,
   Leonatus Posthumus following like a poor soldier.
   They march over and go out. ⌈*Alarums.*⌉
   Then enter again in skirmish Giacomo and
   Posthumus: he vanquisheth and disarmeth
   Giacomo, and then leaves him
GIACOMO
The heaviness and guilt within my bosom
Takes off my manhood. I have belied a lady,
The princess of this country, and the air on't
Revengingly enfeebles me; or could this carl,
A very drudge of nature's, have subdued me 5
In my profession? Knighthoods and honours borne
As I wear mine are titles but of scorn.
If that thy gentry, Britain, go before
This lout as he exceeds our lords, the odds 9
Is that we scarce are men and you are gods. *Exit*

5.3 *The battle continues.* ⌈*Alarums. Excursions. The*
   trumpets sound a retreat.⌉ *The Britons fly,*
   Cymbeline is taken. Then enter to his rescue
   Belarius, Guiderius, and Arviragus
BELARIUS
Stand, stand, we have th'advantage of the ground.
The lane is guarded. Nothing routs us but
The villainy of our fears.
GUIDERIUS *and* ARVIRAGUS   Stand, stand, and fight.
   Enter Posthumus like a poor soldier, and seconds
   the Britons. They rescue Cymbeline and exeunt

5.4 ⌈*The trumpets sound a retreat,*⌉ *then enter Lucius,*
   Giacomo, and Innogen
LUCIUS (*to Innogen*)
Away, boy, from the troops, and save thyself;
For friends kill friends, and the disorder's such
As war were hoodwinked.
GIACOMO   'Tis their fresh supplies.

LUCIUS
It is a day turned strangely. Or betimes   4
Let's reinforce, or fly.   *Exeunt*

5.5 *Enter Posthumus like a poor soldier, and a Briton*
        Lord

LORD
Cam'st thou from where they made the stand?
POSTHUMUS   I did,
Though you, it seems, come from the fliers.
LORD   Ay.
POSTHUMUS
No blame be to you, sir, for all was lost,
But that the heavens fought. The King himself
Of his wings destitute, the army broken,   5
And but the backs of Britons seen, all flying
Through a strait lane; the enemy full-hearted,
Lolling the tongue with slaught'ring, having work
More plentiful than tools to do't, struck down
Some mortally, some slightly touched, some falling 10
Merely through fear, that the strait pass was dammed
With dead men hurt behind, and cowards living
To die with lengthened shame.
LORD   Where was this lane?
POSTHUMUS
Close by the battle, ditched, and walled with turf;
Which gave advantage to an ancient soldier,   15
An honest one, I warrant, who deserved
So long a breeding as his white beard came to,
In doing this for 's country. Athwart the lane
He with two striplings—lads more like to run
The country base than to commit such slaughter;   20
With faces fit for masks, or rather fairer
Than those for preservation cased, or shame—
Made good the passage, cried to those that fled
'Our Britain's harts die flying, not her men.
To darkness fleet souls that fly backwards. Stand,   25
Or we are Romans, and will give you that
Like beasts which you shun beastly, and may save
But to look back in frown. Stand, stand.' These three,
Three thousand confident, in act as many—
For three performers are the file when all   30
The rest do nothing—with this word 'Stand, stand',
Accommodated by the place, more charming
With their own nobleness, which could have turned
A distaff to a lance, gilded pale looks;
Part shame, part spirit renewed, that some, turned
    coward   35
But by example—O, a sin in war,
Damned in the first beginners!—gan to look
The way that they did and to grin like lions
Upon the pikes o'th' hunters. Then began
A stop i'th' chaser, a retire. Anon   40
A rout, confusion thick; forthwith they fly
Chickens the way which they stooped eagles; slaves,
The strides they victors made; and now our cowards,
Like fragments in hard voyages, became   44
The life o'th' need. Having found the back door open

Of the unguarded hearts, heavens, how they wound!
Some slain before, some dying, some their friends
O'erborne i'th' former wave, ten chased by one,
Are now each one the slaughterman of twenty.
Those that would die or ere resist are grown   50
The mortal bugs o'th' field.
LORD   This was strange chance:
A narrow lane, an old man, and two boys.
POSTHUMUS
Nay, do not wonder at it. Yet you are made
Rather to wonder at the things you hear
Than to work any. Will you rhyme upon't,   55
And vent it for a mock'ry? Here is one:
'Two boys, an old man twice a boy, a lane,
Preserved the Britons, was the Romans' bane.'
LORD
Nay, be not angry, sir.
POSTHUMUS   'Lack, to what end?
Who dares not stand his foe, I'll be his friend,   60
For if he'll do as he is made to do,
I know he'll quickly fly my friendship too.
You have put me into rhyme.
LORD   Farewell; you're angry.
                                                 Exit
POSTHUMUS
Still going? This a lord? O noble misery,
To be i'th' field and ask 'What news?' of me!   65
Today how many would have given their honours
To have saved their carcasses—took heel to do't,
And yet died too! I, in mine own woe charmed,
Could not find death where I did hear him groan,
Nor feel him where he struck. Being an ugly monster,
'Tis strange he hides him in fresh cups, soft beds,   71
Sweet words, or hath more ministers than we
That draw his knives i'th' war. Well, I will find him;
For being now a favourer to the Briton,
No more a Briton, I have resumed again   75
The part I came in. Fight I will no more,
But yield me to the veriest hind that shall
Once touch my shoulder. Great the slaughter is
Here made by th' Roman; great the answer be
Britons must take. For me, my ransom's death,   80
On either side I come to spend my breath,
Which neither here I'll keep nor bear again,
But end it by some means for Innogen.
        Enter two Briton Captains, and soldiers
FIRST CAPTAIN
Great Jupiter be praised, Lucius is taken.
'Tis thought the old man and his sons were angels.
SECOND CAPTAIN
There was a fourth man, in a seely habit,   86
That gave th'affront with them.
FIRST CAPTAIN   So 'tis reported,
But none of 'em can be found. Stand, who's there?
POSTHUMUS A Roman,
Who had not now been drooping here if seconds   90
Had answered him.
SECOND CAPTAIN (*to soldiers*) Lay hands on him, a dog!

A leg of Rome shall not return to tell
What crows have pecked them here. He brags his
  service
As if he were of note. Bring him to th' King.
    [Flourish.] Enter Cymbeline [and his train],
    Belarius, Guiderius, Arviragus, Pisanio, and
    Roman captives. The Captains present Posthumus to
    Cymbeline, who delivers him over to a Jailer.
    Exeunt all but Posthumus and two Jailers, [who
    lock gyves on his legs]

FIRST JAILER
You shall not now be stol'n. You have locks upon you,
So graze as you find pasture.

SECOND JAILER   Ay, or a stomach.   96
                       Exeunt Jailers

POSTHUMUS
Most welcome, bondage, for thou art a way,
I think, to liberty. Yet am I better
Than one that's sick o'th' gout, since he had rather
Groan so in perpetuity than be cured   100
By th' sure physician, death, who is the key
T'unbar these locks. My conscience, thou art fettered
More than my shanks and wrists. You good gods give
  me
The penitent instrument to pick that bolt,
Then free for ever. Is't enough I am sorry?   105
So children temporal fathers do appease;
Gods are more full of mercy. Must I repent,
I cannot do it better than in gyves
Desired more than constrained. To satisfy,
If of my freedom 'tis the main part, take   110
No stricter render of me than my all.
I know you are more clement than vile men
Who of their broken debtors take a third,
A sixth, a tenth, letting them thrive again
On their abatement. That's not my desire.   115
For Innogen's dear life take mine, and though
'Tis not so dear, yet 'tis a life; you coined it.
'Tween man and man they weigh not every stamp;
Though light, take pieces for the figure's sake;
You rather mine, being yours. And so, great powers,
If you will make this audit, take this life,   121
And cancel these cold bonds. O Innogen,
I'll speak to thee in silence!
    He sleeps. Solemn music. Enter, as in an apparition,
    Sicilius Leonatus (father to Posthumus, an old
    man), attired like a warrior, leading in his hand an
    ancient matron, his wife, and mother to
    Posthumus, with music before them.
    Then, after other music, follows the two young
    Leonati, brothers to Posthumus, with wounds as
    they died in the wars. They circle Posthumus round
    as he lies sleeping

SICILIUS
No more, thou thunder-master, show
Thy spite on mortal flies.   125
With Mars fall out, with Juno chide,
  That thy adulteries
Rates and revenges.

Hath my poor boy done aught but well,
  Whose face I never saw?   130
I died whilst in the womb he stayed,
  Attending nature's law,
Whose father then—as men report
  Thou orphans' father art—
Thou shouldst have been, and shielded him   135
  From this earth-vexing smart.

MOTHER
Lucina lent not me her aid,
  But took me in my throes,
That from me was Posthumus ripped,
  Came crying 'mongst his foes,   140
A thing of pity.

SICILIUS
Great nature like his ancestry
  Moulded the stuff so fair
That he deserved the praise o'th' world
  As great Sicilius' heir.   145

FIRST BROTHER
When once he was mature for man,
  In Britain where was he
That could stand up his parallel,
  Or fruitful object be
In eye of Innogen, that best   150
  Could deem his dignity?

MOTHER
With marriage wherefore was he mocked,
  To be exiled, and thrown
From Leonati seat and cast
  From her his dearest one,   155
Sweet Innogen?

SICILIUS
Why did you suffer Giacomo,
  Slight thing of Italy,
To taint his nobler heart and brain
  With needless jealousy,   160
And to become the geck and scorn
  O'th' other's villainy?

SECOND BROTHER
ᵁor this from stiller seats we come,
  Our parents and us twain,
That striking in our country's cause   165
  Fell bravely and were slain,
Our fealty and Tenantius' right
  With honour to maintain.

FIRST BROTHER
Like hardiment Posthumus hath
  To Cymbeline performed.   170
Then, Jupiter, thou king of gods,
  Why hast thou thus adjourned
The graces for his merits due,
  Being all to dolours turned?

SICILIUS
Thy crystal window ope; look out;   175
  No longer exercise
Upon a valiant race thy harsh
  And potent injuries.

MOTHER

Since, Jupiter, our son is good,
   Take off his miseries.   180

SICILIUS

Peep through thy marble mansion. Help,
   Or we poor ghosts will cry
To th' shining synod of the rest
   Against thy deity.

BROTHERS

Help, Jupiter, or we appeal,   185
   And from thy justice fly.

Jupiter descends in thunder and lightning, sitting
upon an eagle. He throws a thunderbolt. The ghosts
fall on their knees

JUPITER

No more, you petty spirits of region low,
   Offend our hearing. Hush! How dare you ghosts
Accuse the thunderer, whose bolt, you know,
   Sky-planted, batters all rebelling coasts?   190
Poor shadows of Elysium, hence, and rest
   Upon your never-withering banks of flowers.
Be not with mortal accidents oppressed;
   No care of yours it is; you know 'tis ours.
Whom best I love, I cross, to make my gift,   195
   The more delayed, delighted. Be content.
Your low-laid son our godhead will uplift.
   His comforts thrive, his trials well are spent.
Our Jovial star reigned at his birth, and in
   Our temple was he married. Rise, and fade.   200
He shall be lord of Lady Innogen,
   And happier much by his affliction made.
This tablet lay upon his breast, wherein
   Our pleasure his full fortune doth confine.

He gives the ghosts a tablet which they lay upon
Posthumus' breast

And so away. No farther with your din   205
   Express impatience, lest you stir up mine.
Mount, eagle, to my palace crystalline.

He ascends into the heavens

SICILIUS

He came in thunder. His celestial breath
Was sulphurous to smell. The holy eagle
Stooped, as to foot us. His ascension is   210
More sweet than our blest fields. His royal bird
Preens the immortal wing and claws his beak
As when his god is pleased.

ALL THE GHOSTS   Thanks, Jupiter.

SICILIUS

The marble pavement closes, he is entered
His radiant roof. Away, and, to be blest,   215
Let us with care perform his great behest.

The ghosts vanish

Posthumus awakes

POSTHUMUS

Sleep, thou hast been a grandsire, and begot
A father to me; and thou hast created
A mother and two brothers. But, O scorn,   219
Gone! They went hence so soon as they were born,

And so I am awake. Poor wretches that depend
On greatness' favour dream as I have done,
Wake and find nothing. But, alas, I swerve.
Many dream not to find, neither deserve,
And yet are steeped in favours; so am I,   225
That have this golden chance and know not why.
What fairies haunt this ground? A book? O rare one,
Be not, as is our fangled world, a garment
Nobler than that it covers. Let thy effects
So follow to be most unlike our courtiers,   230
As good as promise.

   He reads

'Whenas a lion's whelp shall, to himself unknown,
without seeking find, and be embraced by a piece of
tender air; and when from a stately cedar shall be
lopped branches which, being dead many years, shall
after revive, be jointed to the old stock, and freshly
grow; then shall Posthumus end his miseries, Britain
be fortunate and flourish in peace and plenty.'
'Tis still a dream, or else such stuff as madmen
Tongue, and brain not; either both, or nothing,   240
Or senseless speaking, or a speaking such
As sense cannot untie. Be what it is,
The action of my life is like it, which I'll keep,
If but for sympathy.

   Enter Jailer

JAILER Come, sir, are you ready for death?   245

POSTHUMUS Over-roasted rather; ready long ago.

JAILER Hanging is the word, sir. If you be ready for that,
you are well cooked.

POSTHUMUS So, if I prove a good repast to the spectators,
the dish pays the shot.   250

JAILER A heavy reckoning for you, sir. But the comfort
is, you shall be called to no more payments, fear no
more tavern bills, which are as often the sadness of
parting as the procuring of mirth. You come in faint
for want of meat, depart reeling with too much drink,
sorry that you have paid too much and sorry that you
are paid too much; purse and brain both empty: the
brain the heavier for being too light, the purse too
light, being drawn of heaviness. Of this contradiction
you shall now be quit. O, the charity of a penny cord!
It sums up thousands in a trice. You have no true
debitor and creditor but it: of what's past, is, and to
come the discharge. Your neck, sir, is pen, book, and
counters; so the acquittance follows.

POSTHUMUS I am merrier to die than thou art to live. 265

JAILER Indeed, sir, he that sleeps feels not the toothache;
but a man that were to sleep your sleep, and a hangman
to help him to bed, I think he would change places
with his officer; for look you, sir, you know not which
way you shall go.   270

POSTHUMUS Yes, indeed do I, fellow.

JAILER Your death has eyes in 's head, then. I have not
seen him so pictured. You must either be directed by
some that take upon them to know, or take upon
yourself that which I am sure you do not know, or
jump the after-enquiry on your own peril; and how

you shall speed in your journey's end I think you'll
never return to tell on.

POSTHUMUS I tell thee, fellow, there are none want eyes
to direct them the way I am going but such as wink
and will not use them.   281

JAILER What an infinite mock is this, that a man should
have the best use of eyes to see the way of blindness!
I am sure hanging's the way of winking.

Enter a Messenger

MESSENGER Knock off his manacles, bring your prisoner
to the King.   286

POSTHUMUS Thou bring'st good news, I am called to be
made free.

JAILER I'll be hanged then.

POSTHUMUS Thou shalt be then freer than a jailer; no
bolts for the dead.   291

JAILER (*aside*) Unless a man would marry a gallows and
beget young gibbets, I never saw one so prone. Yet, on
my conscience, there are verier knaves desire to live,
for all he be a Roman; and there be some of them, too,
that die against their wills; so should I if I were one. I
would we were all of one mind, and one mind good. I
O, there were desolation of jailers and gallowses! I
speak against my present profit, but my wish hath a
preferment in't.   *Exeunt*

5.6 ⌈*Flourish.*⌉ *Enter Cymbeline, Belarius, Guiderius,*
Arviragus, Pisanio, and lords

CYMBELINE (*to Belarius, Guiderius, and Arviragus*)
Stand by my side, you whom the gods have made
Preservers of my throne. Woe is my heart
That the poor soldier that so richly fought,
Whose rags shamed gilded arms, whose naked breast
Stepped before targs of proof, cannot be found.   5
He shall be happy that can find him, if
Our grace can make him so.

BELARIUS   I never saw
Such noble fury in so poor a thing,
Such precious deeds in one that promised naught
But beggary and poor looks.

CYMBELINE   No tidings of him?   10

PISANIO
He hath been searched among the dead and living,
But no trace of him.

CYMBELINE   To my grief I am
The heir of his reward, which I will add
(*To Belarius, Guiderius, and Arviragus*)
To you, the liver, heart, and brain of Britain,   15
By whom I grant she lives. 'Tis now the time
To ask of whence you are. Report it.

BELARIUS   Sir,
In Cambria are we born, and gentlemen.
Further to boast were neither true nor modest,
Unless I add we are honest.

CYMBELINE   Bow your knees.   20
They kneel. He knights them
Arise, my knights o'th' battle. I create you

Companions to our person, and will fit you
With dignities becoming your estates.
Belarius, Guiderius, and Arviragus rise.
Enter Cornelius and Ladies
There's business in these faces. Why so sadly
Greet you our victory? You look like Romans,   25
And not o'th' court of Britain.

CORNELIUS   Hail, great King!
To sour your happiness I must report
The Queen is dead.

CYMBELINE   Who worse than a physician
Would this report become? But I consider
By medicine life may be prolonged, yet death   30
Will seize the doctor too. How ended she?

CORNELIUS
With horror, madly dying, like her life,
Which being cruel to the world, concluded
Most cruel to herself. What she confessed
I will report, so please you. These her women   35
Can trip me if I err, who with wet cheeks
Were present when she finished.

CYMBELINE   Prithee, say.

CORNELIUS
First, she confessed she never loved you, only
Affected greatness got by you, not you;
Married your royalty, was wife to your place,   40
Abhorred your person.

CYMBELINE   She alone knew this,
And but she spoke it dying, I would not
Believe her lips in opening it. Proceed.

CORNELIUS
Your daughter, whom she bore in hand to love
With such integrity, she did confess   45
Was as a scorpion to her sight, whose life,
But that her flight prevented it, she had
Ta'en off by poison.

CYMBELINE   O most delicate fiend!
Who is't can read a woman? Is there more?

CORNELIUS
More, sir, and worse. She did confess she had   50
For you a mortal mineral which, being took,
Should by the minute feed on life, and, ling'ring,
By inches waste you. In which time she purposed
By watching, weeping, tendance, kissing, to
O'ercome you with her show; and in fine,   55
When she had fit you with her craft, to work
Her son into th'adoption of the crown;
But failing of her end by his strange absence,
Grew shameless-desperate, opened in despite
Of heaven and men her purposes, repented   60
The evils she hatched were not effected; so
Despairing died.

CYMBELINE   Heard you all this, her women?
⌈LADIES⌉
We did, so please your highness.

CYMBELINE   Mine eyes
Were not in fault, for she was beautiful;

Mine ears that heard her flattery, nor my heart   65
That thought her like her seeming. It had been vicious
To have mistrusted her. Yet, O my daughter,
That it was folly in me thou mayst say,
And prove it in thy feeling. Heaven mend all!
> *Enter Lucius, Giacomo, Soothsayer, and other*
> *Roman prisoners, Posthumus behind, and Innogen*
> *dressed as a man, all guarded by Briton soldiers*
Thou com'st not, Caius, now for tribute. That   70
The Britons have razed out, though with the loss
Of many a bold one; whose kinsmen have made suit
That their good souls may be appeased with slaughter
Of you, their captives, which ourself have granted.
So think of your estate.   75
LUCIUS
Consider, sir, the chance of war. The day
Was yours by accident. Had it gone with us,
We should not, when the blood was cool, have
    threatened
Our prisoners with the sword. But since the gods
Will have it thus, that nothing but our lives   80
May be called ransom, let it come. Sufficeth
A Roman with a Roman's heart can suffer.
Augustus lives to think on't; and so much
For my peculiar care. This one thing only
I will entreat:
> *He presents Innogen to Cymbeline*
    my boy, a Briton born,   85
Let him be ransomed. Never master had
A page so kind, so duteous, diligent,
So tender over his occasions, true,
So feat, so nurse-like; let his virtue join
With my request, which I'll make bold your highness
Cannot deny. He hath done no Briton harm,   91
Though he have served a Roman. Save him, sir,
And spare no blood beside.
CYMBELINE   I have surely seen him.
His favour is familiar to me. Boy,
Thou hast looked thyself into my grace,   95
And art mine own. I know not why, wherefore,
To say 'Live, boy'. Ne'er thank thy master. Live,
And ask of Cymbeline what boon thou wilt
Fitting my bounty and thy state, I'll give it,
Yea, though thou do demand a prisoner   100
The noblest ta'en.
INNOGEN   I humbly thank your highness.
LUCIUS
I do not bid thee beg my life, good lad,
And yet I know thou wilt.
INNOGEN   No, no. Alack,
There's other work in hand. I see a thing
Bitter to me as death. Your life, good master,   105
Must shuffle for itself.
LUCIUS   The boy disdains me.
He leaves me, scorns me. Briefly die their joys
That place them on the truth of girls and boys.
Why stands he so perplexed?
CYMBELINE (*to Innogen*)   What wouldst thou, boy?

I love thee more and more; think more and more   110
What's best to ask. Know'st him thou look'st on?
    Speak,
Wilt have him live? Is he thy kin, thy friend?
INNOGEN
He is a Roman, no more kin to me
Than I to your highness, who, being born your vassal,
Am something nearer.
CYMBELINE   Wherefore ey'st him so?   115
INNOGEN
I'll tell you, sir, in private, if you please
To give me hearing.
CYMBELINE   Ay, with all my heart,
And lend my best attention. What's thy name?
INNOGEN
Fidele, sir.
CYMBELINE   Thou'rt my good youth, my page.
I'll be thy master. Walk with me, speak freely.   120
> *Cymbeline and Innogen speak apart*
BELARIUS (*aside to Guiderius and Arviragus*)
Is not this boy revived from death?
ARVIRAGUS   One sand another
Not more resembles that sweet rosy lad
Who died, and was Fidele. What think you?
GUIDERIUS The same dead thing alive.
BELARIUS
Peace, peace, see further. He eyes us not. Forbear.   125
Creatures may be alike. Were't he, I am sure
He would have spoke to us.
GUIDERIUS   But we see him dead.
BELARIUS
Be silent; let's see further.
PISANIO (*aside*)   It is my mistress.
Since she is living, let the time run on   129
To good or bad.
CYMBELINE (*to Innogen*) Come, stand thou by our side,
Make thy demand aloud. (*To Giacomo*) Sir, step you
    forth.
Give answer to this boy, and do it freely,
Or, by our greatness and the grace of it,
Which is our honour, bitter torture shall
Winnow the truth from falsehood.
(*To Innogen*)   On, speak to him.
INNOGEN
My boon is that this gentleman may render   136
Of whom he had this ring.
POSTHUMUS (*aside*)   What's that to him?
CYMBELINE (*to Giacomo*)
That diamond upon your finger, say,
How came it yours?
GIACOMO
Thou'lt torture me to leave unspoken that   140
Which to be spoke would torture thee.
CYMBELINE   How, me?
GIACOMO
I am glad to be constrained to utter that
Torments me to conceal. By villainy
I got this ring; 'twas Leonatus' jewel,

Whom thou didst banish; and, which more may
   grieve thee,   145
As it doth me, a nobler sir ne'er lived
'Twixt sky and ground. Wilt thou hear more, my lord?
CYMBELINE
All that belongs to this.
GIACOMO   That paragon thy daughter,
For whom my heart drops blood, and my false spirits
Quail to remember—give me leave, I faint.   150
CYMBELINE
My daughter? What of her? Renew thy strength.
I had rather thou shouldst live while nature will
Than die ere I hear more. Strive, man, and speak.
GIACOMO
Upon a time—unhappy was the clock
That struck the hour—it was in Rome—accursed   155
The mansion where—'twas at a feast—O, would
Our viands had been poisoned, or at least
Those which I heaved to head!—the good Posthumus—
What should I say?—he was too good to be
Where ill men were, and was the best of all   160
Amongst the rar'st of good ones—sitting sadly,
Hearing us praise our loves of Italy
For beauty that made barren the swelled boast
Of him that best could speak; for feature laming
The shrine of Venus or straight-pitched Minerva,   165
Postures beyond brief nature; for condition,
A shop of all the qualities that man
Loves woman for; besides that hook of wiving,
Fairness which strikes the eye—
CYMBELINE   I stand on fire.
Come to the matter.
GIACOMO   All too soon I shall,   170
Unless thou wouldst grieve quickly. This Posthumus,
Most like a noble lord in love and one
That had a royal lover, took his hint,
And not dispraising whom we praised—therein
He was as calm as virtue—he began   175
His mistress' picture, which by his tongue being made,
And then a mind put in't, either our brags
Were cracked of kitchen-trulls, or his description
Proved us unspeaking sots.
CYMBELINE   Nay, nay, to th' purpose.
GIACOMO
Your daughter's chastity—there it begins.   180
He spake of her as Dian had hot dreams
And she alone were cold, whereat I, wretch,
Made scruple of his praise, and wagered with him
Pieces of gold 'gainst this which then he wore
Upon his honoured finger, to attain   185
In suit the place of 's bed and win this ring
By hers and mine adultery. He, true knight,
No lesser of her honour confident
Than I did truly find her, stakes this ring—
And would so had it been a carbuncle   190
Of Phoebus' wheel, and might so safely had it
Been all the worth of 's car. Away to Britain
Post I in this design. Well may you, sir,

Remember me at court, where I was taught
Of your chaste daughter the wide difference   195
'Twixt amorous and villainous. Being thus quenched
Of hope, not longing, mine Italian brain
Gan in your duller Britain operate
Most vilely; for my vantage, excellent.
And, to be brief, my practice so prevailed   200
That I returned with simular proof enough
To make the noble Leonatus mad
By wounding his belief in her renown
With tokens thus and thus; averring notes
Of chamber-hanging, pictures, this her bracelet—
O cunning, how I got it!—nay, some marks   206
Of secret on her person, that he could not
But think her bond of chastity quite cracked,
I having ta'en the forfeit. Whereupon—
Methinks I see him now—
POSTHUMUS (coming forward) Ay, so thou dost,   210
Italian fiend! Ay me, most credulous fool,
Egregious murderer, thief, anything
That's due to all the villains past, in being,
To come! O, give me cord, or knife, or poison,
Some upright justicer! Thou, King, send out   215
For torturers ingenious. It is I
That all th'abhorrèd things o'th' earth amend
By being worse than they. I am Posthumus,
That killed thy daughter—villain-like, I lie:
That caused a lesser villain than myself,   220
A sacrilegious thief, to do't. The temple
Of virtue was she; yea, and she herself.
Spit and throw stones, cast mire upon me, set
The dogs o'th' street to bay me. Every villain
Be called Posthumus Leonatus, and   225
Be 'villain' less than 'twas! O Innogen!
My queen, my life, my wife, O Innogen,
Innogen, Innogen!
INNOGEN (approaching him) Peace, my lord. Hear, hear.
POSTHUMUS
Shall 's have a play of this? Thou scornful page,
There lie thy part.
       He strikes her down
PISANIO (coming forward) O gentlemen, help!   230
Mine and your mistress! O my lord Posthumus,
You ne'er killed Innogen till now. Help, help!
(To Innogen) Mine honoured lady.
CYMBELINE   Does the world go round?
POSTHUMUS
How comes these staggers on me?
PISANIO (to Innogen)   Wake, my mistress.
CYMBELINE
If this be so, the gods do mean to strike me   235
To death with mortal joy.
PISANIO (to Innogen) How fares my mistress?
INNOGEN O, get thee from my sight!
Thou gav'st me poison. Dangerous fellow, hence.   239
Breathe not where princes are.
CYMBELINE   The tune of Innogen.

PISANIO
Lady, the gods throw stones of sulphur on me if
That box I gave you was not thought by me
A precious thing. I had it from the Queen.

CYMBELINE
New matter still.

INNOGEN   It poisoned me.

CORNELIUS   O gods!
I left out one thing which the Queen confessed   245
(*To Pisanio*) Which must approve thee honest. 'If
          Pisanio
Have', said she, 'given his mistress that confection
Which I gave him for cordial, she is served
As I would serve a rat.'

CYMBELINE   What's this, Cornelius?

CORNELIUS
The Queen, sir, very oft importuned me   250
To temper poisons for her, still pretending
The satisfaction of her knowledge only
In killing creatures vile, as cats and dogs
Of no esteem. I, dreading that her purpose
Was of more danger, did compound for her   255
A certain stuff which, being ta'en, would cease
The present power of life, but in short time
All offices of nature should again
Do their due functions. (*To Innogen*) Have you ta'en
          of it?

INNOGEN
Most like I did, for I was dead.

BELARIUS (*aside to Guiderius and Arviragus*) My boys,   260
There was our error.

GUIDERIUS   This is sure Fidele.

INNOGEN (*to Posthumus*)
Why did you throw your wedded lady from you?
Think that you are upon a lock, and now
Throw me again.

          She throws her arms about his neck

POSTHUMUS   Hang there like fruit, my soul,
Till the tree die.

CYMBELINE (*to Innogen*) How now, my flesh, my child?
What, mak'st thou me a dullard in this act?   266
Wilt thou not speak to me?

INNOGEN (*kneeling*)   Your blessing, sir.

BELARIUS (*aside to Guiderius and Arviragus*)
Though you did love this youth, I blame ye not.
You had a motive for't.

CYMBELINE   My tears that fall
Prove holy water on thee!

          ⌈*He raises her*⌉

                              Innogen,   270
Thy mother's dead.

INNOGEN   I am sorry for't, my lord.

CYMBELINE
O, she was naught, and 'long of her it was
That we meet here so strangely. But her son
Is gone, we know not how nor where.

PISANIO   My lord,
Now fear is from me I'll speak truth. Lord Cloten,   275

Upon my lady's missing, came to me
With his sword drawn, foamed at the mouth, and
          swore
If I discovered not which way she was gone
It was my instant death. By accident
I had a feignèd letter of my master's   280
Then in my pocket, which directed him
To seek her on the mountains near to Milford,
Where in a frenzy, in my master's garments,
Which he enforced from me, away he posts
With unchaste purpose, and with oath to violate   285
My lady's honour. What became of him
I further know not.

GUIDERIUS   Let me end the story.
I slew him there.

CYMBELINE   Marry, the gods forfend!
I would not thy good deeds should from my lips
Pluck a hard sentence. Prithee, valiant youth,   290
Deny't again.

GUIDERIUS I have spoke it, and I did it.

CYMBELINE He was a prince.

GUIDERIUS
A most incivil one. The wrongs he did me
Were nothing prince-like, for he did provoke me   295
With language that would make me spurn the sea
If it could so roar to me. I cut off 's head,
And am right glad he is not standing here
To tell this tale of mine.

CYMBELINE   I am sorrow for thee.
By thine own tongue thou art condemned, and must
Endure our law. Thou'rt dead.

INNOGEN   That headless man   301
I thought had been my lord.

CYMBELINE (*to soldiers*)   Bind the offender,
And take him from our presence.

BELARIUS   Stay, sir King.
This boy is better than the man he slew,
As well descended as thyself, and hath   305
More of thee merited than a band of Clotens
Had ever scar for. Let his arms alone;
They were not born for bondage.

CYMBELINE   Why, old soldier,
Wilt thou undo the worth thou art unpaid for
By tasting of our wrath? How of descent   310
As good as we?

ARVIRAGUS   In that he spake too far.

CYMBELINE ⌈*to Belarius*⌉
And thou shalt die for't.

BELARIUS   We will die all three
But I will prove that two on 's are as good
As I have given out him. My sons, I must
For mine own part unfold a dangerous speech,   315
Though haply well for you.

ARVIRAGUS   Your danger's ours.

GUIDERIUS
And our good his.

BELARIUS   Have at it then. By leave,

Thou hadst, great King, a subject who
Was called Belarius.
CYMBELINE   What of him? He is
A banished traitor.
BELARIUS   He it is that hath   320
Assumed this age. Indeed, a banished man;
I know not how a traitor.
CYMBELINE (*to soldiers*)   Take him hence.
The whole world shall not save him.
BELARIUS   Not too hot.
First pay me for the nursing of thy sons,
And let it be confiscate all so soon   325
As I have received it.
CYMBELINE   Nursing of my sons?
ARVIRAGUS
I am too blunt and saucy. (*Kneeling*) Here's my knee.
Ere I arise I will prefer my sons,
Then spare not the old father. Mighty sir,
These two young gentlemen that call me father   330
And think they are my sons are none of mine.
They are the issue of your loins, my liege,
And blood of your begetting.
CYMBELINE   How, my issue?
BELARIUS
So sure as you your father's. I, old Morgan,
Am that Belarius whom you sometime banished.   335
Your pleasure was my mere offence, my punishment
Itself, and all my treason. That I suffered
Was all the harm I did. These gentle princes—
For such and so they are—these twenty years
Have I trained up. Those arts they have as I   340
Could put into them. My breeding was, sir,
As your highness knows. Their nurse Euriphile,
Whom for the theft I wedded, stole these children
Upon my banishment. I moved her to't,
Having received the punishment before   345
For that which I did then. Beaten for loyalty
Excited me to treason. Their dear loss,
The more of you 'twas felt, the more it shaped
Unto my end of stealing them. But, gracious sir,
Here are your sons again, and I must lose   350
Two of the sweet'st companions in the world.
The benediction of these covering heavens
Fall on their heads like dew, for they are worthy
To inlay heaven with stars.
CYMBELINE   Thou weep'st, and speak'st.
The service that you three have done is more   355
Unlike than this thou tell'st. I lost my children.
If these be they, I know not how to wish
A pair of worthier sons.
BELARIUS ⌈*rising*⌉   Be pleased a while.
This gentleman, whom I call Polydore,
Most worthy prince, as yours, is true Guiderius.   360
⌈*Guiderius kneels*⌉
This gentleman, my Cadwal, Arviragus,
Your younger princely son.
⌈*Arviragus kneels*⌉
                    He, sir, was lapped
In a most curious mantle wrought by th' hand

Of his queen mother, which for more probation
I can with ease produce.
CYMBELINE   Guiderius had   365
Upon his neck a mole, a sanguine star.
It was a mark of wonder.
BELARIUS   This is he,
Who hath upon him still that natural stamp.
It was wise nature's end in the donation
To be his evidence now.
CYMBELINE   O, what am I?   370
A mother to the birth of three? Ne'er mother
Rejoiced deliverance more. Blest pray you be,
That, after this strange starting from your orbs,
You may reign in them now!
          ⌈*Guiderius and Arviragus rise*⌉
                    O Innogen,
Thou hast lost by this a kingdom.
INNOGEN   No, my lord,   375
I have got two worlds by't. O my gentle brothers,
Have we thus met? O, never say hereafter
But I am truest speaker. You called me brother
When I was but your sister; I you brothers
When ye were so indeed.
CYMBELINE   Did you e'er meet?   380
ARVIRAGUS
Ay, my good lord.
GUIDERIUS   And at first meeting loved,
Continued so until we thought he died.
CORNELIUS
By the Queen's dram she swallowed.
CYMBELINE   O rare instinct!
When shall I hear all through? This fierce abridgement
Hath to it circumstantial branches which   385
Distinction should be rich in. Where? How lived you?
And when came you to serve our Roman captive?
How parted with your brothers? How first met them?
Why fled you from the court? And whither? These,
And your three motives to the battle, with   390
I know not how much more, should be demanded,
And all the other by-dependences,
From chance to chance. But nor the time nor place
Will serve our long inter'gatories. See,
Posthumus anchors upon Innogen,   395
And she, like harmless lightning, throws her eye
On him, her brothers, me, her master, hitting
Each object with a joy. The counterchange
Is severally in all. Let's quit this ground,
And smoke the temple with our sacrifices.   400
(*To Belarius*) Thou art my brother; so we'll hold thee
          ever.
INNOGEN (*to Belarius*)
You are my father too, and did relieve me
To see this gracious season.
CYMBELINE   All o'erjoyed,
Save these in bonds. Let them be joyful too,
For they shall taste our comfort.
INNOGEN (*to Lucius*)   My good master,   405
I will yet do you service.
LUCIUS   Happy be you!

CYMBELINE
The forlorn soldier that so nobly fought,
He would have well becomed this place, and graced
The thankings of a king.
POSTHUMUS   I am, sir,
The soldier that did company these three   410
In poor beseeming. 'Twas a fitment for
The purpose I then followed. That I was he,
Speak, Giacomo; I had you down, and might
Have made you finish.
GIACOMO (kneeling)   I am down again,
But now my heavy conscience sinks my knee   415
As then your force did. Take that life, beseech you,
Which I so often owe; but your ring first,
And here the bracelet of the truest princess
That ever swore her faith.
POSTHUMUS (raising him)   Kneel not to me.
The power that I have on you is to spare you,   420
The malice towards you to forgive you. Live,
And deal with others better.
CYMBELINE   Nobly doomed!
We'll learn our freeness of a son-in-law.
Pardon's the word to all.
ARVIRAGUS (to Posthumus)   You holp us, sir,
As you did mean indeed to be our brother.   425
Joyed are we that you are.
POSTHUMUS
Your servant, princes. (To Lucius) Good my lord of
   Rome,
Call forth your soothsayer. As I slept, methought
Great Jupiter, upon his eagle backed,
Appeared to me with other spritely shows   430
Of mine own kindred. When I waked I found
This label on my bosom, whose containing
Is so from sense in hardness that I can
Make no collection of it. Let him show
His skill in the construction.
LUCIUS   Philharmonus.   435
SOOTHSAYER
Here, my good lord.
LUCIUS   Read, and declare the meaning.
SOOTHSAYER (reads the tablet) 'Whenas a lion's whelp shall,
   to himself unknown, without seeking find, and be
   embraced by a piece of tender air; and when from a
   stately cedar shall be lopped branches which, being
   dead many years, shall after revive, be jointed to the
   old stock, and freshly grow: then shall Posthumus end
   his miseries, Britain be fortunate and flourish in peace
   and plenty.'
Thou, Leonatus, art the lion's whelp.   445

The fit and apt construction of thy name,
Being leo-natus, doth import so much.
(To Cymbeline) The piece of tender air thy virtuous
   daughter,
Which we call 'mollis aer'; and 'mollis aer'
We term it 'mulier', (to Posthumus) which 'mulier' I
   divine   450
Is this most constant wife, who even now,
Answering the letter of the oracle,
Unknown to you, unsought, were clipped about
With this most tender air.
CYMBELINE   This hath some seeming.
SOOTHSAYER
The lofty cedar, royal Cymbeline,   455
Personates thee, and thy lopped branches point
Thy two sons forth, who, by Belarius stol'n,
For many years thought dead, are now revived,
To the majestic cedar joined, whose issue
Promises Britain peace and plenty.
CYMBELINE   Well,   460
My peace we will begin; and, Caius Lucius,
Although the victor, we submit to Caesar
And to the Roman empire, promising
To pay our wonted tribute, from the which
We were dissuaded by our wicked queen,   465
Whom heavens in justice both on her and hers
Have laid most heavy hand.
SOOTHSAYER
The fingers of the powers above do tune
The harmony of this peace. The vision,
Which I made known to Lucius ere the stroke   470
Of this yet scarce-cold battle, at this instant
Is full accomplished. For the Roman eagle,
From south to west on wing soaring aloft,
Lessened herself, and in the beams o'th' sun
So vanished; which foreshowed our princely eagle 475
Th'imperial Caesar should again unite
His favour with the radiant Cymbeline,
Which shines here in the west.
CYMBELINE   Laud we the gods,
And let our crookèd smokes climb to their nostrils
From our blest altars. Publish we this peace   480
To all our subjects. Set we forward, let
A Roman and a British ensign wave
Friendly together. So through Lud's town march,
And in the temple of great Jupiter
Our peace we'll ratify, seal it with feasts.   485
Set on there. Never was a war did cease,
Ere bloody hands were washed, with such a peace.
                    ⌐Flourish.⌐ Exeunt ⌐in triumph⌐

THE TEMPEST

THE King's Men acted *The Tempest* before their patron, James I, at Whitehall on 1 November 1611. (It was also chosen for performance during the festivities for the marriage of James's daughter, Princess Elizabeth, to the Elector Palatine during the winter of 1612-13). Shakespeare's play takes place on a desert island somewhere between Tunis and Naples; he derived some details of it from his reading of travel literature, including accounts of an expedition of nine ships taking five hundred colonists from Plymouth to Virginia, which set sail in May 1609. On 29 July the flagship, the *Sea-Adventure*, was wrecked by a storm on the coast of the Bermudas. She was presumed lost, but on 23 May 1610 those aboard her arrived safely in Jamestown, Virginia, having found shelter on the island of Bermuda, where they were able to build the pinnaces in which they completed their journey. Accounts of the voyage soon reached England; the last-written that Shakespeare seems to have known is a letter by William Strachey, who was on the *Sea-Adventure*, dated 15 July 1610; though it was not published until 1625, it circulated in manuscript. So it seems clear that Shakespeare wrote *The Tempest* during the later part of 1610 or in 1611. It was first printed in the 1623 Folio, where it is the opening play.

Though other items of Shakespeare's reading—including both Arthur Golding's translation and Ovid's original *Metamorphoses* (closely echoed in Prospero's farewell to his magic), John Florio's translation of essays by Michel de Montaigne, and (less locally but no less pervasively) Virgil's *Aeneid*—certainly fed Shakespeare's imagination as he wrote *The Tempest*, he appears to have devised the main plot himself. Many of its elements are based on the familiar stuff of romance literature: the long-past shipwreck after a perilous voyage of Prospero and his daughter Miranda; the shipwreck, depicted in the opening scene, of Prospero's brother, Antonio, with Alonso, King of Naples, and others; the separation and estrangement of relatives—Antonio usurped Prospero's dukedom, and Alonso believes his son, Ferdinand, is drowned; the chaste love, subjected to trials, of the handsome Ferdinand and the beautiful Miranda; the influence of the supernatural exercised through Prospero's magic powers; and the final reunions and reconciliations along with the happy conclusion of the love affair. Shakespeare had employed such conventions from the beginning of his career in his comedies, and with especial concentration, shortly before he wrote *The Tempest*, in *Pericles*, *The Winter's Tale*, and *Cymbeline*. But whereas those plays unfold the events as they happen, taking us on a journey through time and space, in *The Tempest* (as elsewhere only in *The Comedy of Errors*) Shakespeare gives us only the end of the story, concentrating the action into a few hours and locating it in a single place, but informing us about the past, as in the long, romance-type narrative (1.2) in which Prospero tells Miranda of her childhood. The supernatural, a strong presence in all Shakespeare's late plays, is particularly pervasive in *The Tempest*; Prospero is a 'white' magician—a beneficent one—attended by the spirit Ariel and the sub-human Caliban, two of Shakespeare's most obviously symbolic characters; and a climax of the play is the supernaturally induced wedding masque that Prospero conjures up for the entertainment and edification of the young lovers, and which vanishes as he remembers Caliban's plot against his life.

THE PERSONS OF THE PLAY

PROSPERO, the rightful Duke of Milan

MIRANDA, his daughter

ANTONIO, his brother, the usurping Duke of Milan

ALONSO, King of Naples

SEBASTIAN, his brother

FERDINAND, Alonso's son

GONZALO, an honest old counsellor of Naples

ADRIAN } lords
FRANCISCO

ARIEL, an airy spirit attendant upon Prospero

CALIBAN, a savage and deformed native of the island, Prospero's slave

TRINCULO, Alonso's jester

STEFANO, Alonso's drunken butler

The MASTER of a ship

BOATSWAIN

MARINERS

SPIRITS

The Masque

Spirits appearing as:

IRIS

CERES

JUNO

Nymphs, reapers

The Tempest

1.1 *A tempestuous noise of thunder and lightning heard.*
Enter ⌜severally⌝ a Shipmaster and a Boatswain
MASTER Boatswain!
BOATSWAIN Here, Master. What cheer?
MASTER Good, speak to th' mariners. Fall to't yarely, or
we run ourselves aground. Bestir, bestir! *Exit*
Enter Mariners
BOATSWAIN Heigh, my hearts! Cheerly, cheerly, my hearts!
Yare, yare! Take in the topsail! Tend to th' Master's
whistle!—Blow till thou burst thy wind, if room enough.
Enter Alonso, Sebastian, Antonio, Ferdinand,
Gonzalo, and others
ALONSO Good Boatswain, have care. Where's the Master?
(To the Mariners) Play the men!
BOATSWAIN I pray now, keep below.   10
ANTONIO Where is the Master, Boatswain?
BOATSWAIN Do you not hear him? You mar our labour.
Keep your cabins; you do assist the storm.
GONZALO Nay, good, be patient.   14
BOATSWAIN When the sea is. Hence! What cares these
roarers for the name of king? To cabin! Silence; trouble
us not.
GONZALO Good, yet remember whom thou hast aboard.
BOATSWAIN None that I more love than myself. You are
a councillor; if you can command these elements to
silence and work peace of the present, we will not hand
a rope more. Use your authority. If you cannot, give
thanks you have lived so long and make yourself ready
in your cabin for the mischance of the hour, if it so
hap. *(To the Mariners)* Cheerly, good hearts! *(To Gonzalo)*
Out of our way, I say!   *Exit*
GONZALO I have great comfort from this fellow. Methinks
he hath no drowning mark upon him; his complexion
is perfect gallows. Stand fast, good Fate, to his hanging.
Make the rope of his destiny our cable, for our own
doth little advantage. If he be not born to be hanged,
our case is miserable.   *Exeunt ⌜Courtiers⌝*
Enter Boatswain
BOATSWAIN Down with the topmast! Yare! Lower, lower!
Bring her to try wi'th' main-course!
A cry within
A plague upon this howling! They are louder than the
weather, or our office.   36
Enter Sebastian, Antonio, and Gonzalo
Yet again? What do you here? Shall we give o'er and
drown? Have you a mind to sink?
SEBASTIAN A pox o'your throat, you bawling, blasphemous,
incharitable dog!   40
BOATSWAIN Work you, then.
ANTONIO Hang, cur, hang, you whoreson insolent noise-
maker. We are less afraid to be drowned than thou art.
⌜Exeunt Mariners⌝

GONZALO I'll warrant him for drowning, though the ship
were no stronger than a nutshell and as leaky as an
unstanched wench.   46
BOATSWAIN Lay her a-hold, a-hold! Set her two courses!
Off to sea again! Lay her off!
Enter Mariners, wet
MARINERS All lost! To prayers, to prayers! All lost!
⌜Exeunt Mariners⌝
BOATSWAIN What, must our mouths be cold?   50
GONZALO
The King and Prince at prayers! Let's assist them,
For our case is as theirs.
SEBASTIAN   I'm out of patience.
ANTONIO
We are merely cheated of our lives by drunkards.
This wide-chopped rascal—would thou mightst lie
drowning
The washing of ten tides.
GONZALO   He'll be hanged yet,   55
Though every drop of water swear against it
And gape at wid'st to glut him.
A confused noise within
MARINERS *(within)*   Mercy on us!
We split, we split! Farewell, my wife and children!
Farewell, brother! We split, we split, we split!
⌜Exit Boatswain⌝
ANTONIO
Let's all sink wi'th' King.
SEBASTIAN   Let's take leave of him.   60
Exeunt Antonio and Sebastian
GONZALO Now would I give a thousand furlongs of sea
for an acre of barren ground: long heath, broom, furze,
anything. The wills above be done, but I would fain
die a dry death.   *Exit*

1.2 *Enter Prospero ⌜in his magic cloak, with a staff⌝,*
and Miranda
MIRANDA
If by your art, my dearest father, you have
Put the wild waters in this roar, allay them.
The sky, it seems, would pour down stinking pitch,
But that the sea, mounting to th' welkin's cheek,
Dashes the fire out. O, I have sufferèd   5
With those that I saw suffer! A brave vessel,
Who had, no doubt, some noble creature in her,
Dashed all to pieces! O, the cry did knock
Against my very heart! Poor souls, they perished.
Had I been any god of power, I would   10
Have sunk the sea within the earth, or ere
It should the good ship so have swallowed and
The fraughting souls within her.
PROSPERO   Be collected.

No more amazement. Tell your piteous heart
There's no harm done.

MIRANDA   O woe the day!

PROSPERO   No harm.   15
I have done nothing but in care of thee,
Of thee, my dear one, thee, my daughter, who
Art ignorant of what thou art, naught knowing
Of whence I am, nor that I am more better
Than Prospero, master of a full poor cell   20
And thy no greater father.

MIRANDA   More to know
Did never meddle with my thoughts.

PROSPERO   'Tis time
I should inform thee farther. Lend thy hand,
And pluck my magic garment from me.
          Miranda removes Prospero's cloak, ⌈and he lays it
          on the ground⌉
                              So.
Lie there, my art.—Wipe thou thine eyes; have comfort.
The direful spectacle of the wreck, which touched   26
The very virtue of compassion in thee,
I have with such provision in mine art
So safely ordered that there is no soul—
No, not so much perdition as an hair   30
Betid to any creature in the vessel,
Which thou heard'st cry, which thou saw'st sink. Sit
     down,
For thou must now know farther.
          Miranda sits

MIRANDA   You have often
Begun to tell me what I am, but stopped
And left me to a bootless inquisition,   35
Concluding 'Stay; not yet'.

PROSPERO   The hour's now come.
The very minute bids thee ope thine ear,
Obey, and be attentive. Canst thou remember
A time before we came unto this cell?
I do not think thou canst, for then thou wast not   40
Out three years old.

MIRANDA   Certainly, sir, I can.

PROSPERO
By what? By any other house or person?
Of anything the image tell me that
Hath kept with thy remembrance.

MIRANDA   'Tis far off,
And rather like a dream than an assurance   45
That my remembrance warrants. Had I not
Four or five women once that tended me?

PROSPERO
Thou hadst, and more, Miranda. But how is it
That this lives in thy mind? What seest thou else
In the dark backward and abyss of time?   50
If thou rememb'rest aught ere thou cam'st here,
How thou cam'st here thou mayst.

MIRANDA   But that I do not.

PROSPERO
Twelve year since, Miranda, twelve year since,

Thy father was the Duke of Milan, and
A prince of power—

MIRANDA   Sir, are not you my father?   55

PROSPERO
Thy mother was a piece of virtue, and
She said thou wast my daughter; and thy father
Was Duke of Milan, and his only heir
And princess no worse issued.

MIRANDA   O the heavens!
What foul play had we that we came from thence?   60
Or blessèd was't we did?

PROSPERO   Both, both, my girl.
By foul play, as thou sayst, were we heaved thence,
But blessedly holp hither.

MIRANDA   O, my heart bleeds
To think o'th' teen that I have turned you to,
Which is from my remembrance. Please you, farther.   65

PROSPERO
My brother and thy uncle called Antonio—
I pray thee mark me, that a brother should
Be so perfidious—he whom next thyself
Of all the world I loved, and to him put
The manage of my state—as at that time   70
Through all the signories it was the first,
And Prospero the prime duke—being so reputed
In dignity, and for the liberal arts
Without a parallel—those being all my study,
The government I cast upon my brother,   75
And to my state grew stranger, being transported
And rapt in secret studies. Thy false uncle—
Dost thou attend me?

MIRANDA   Sir, most heedfully.

PROSPERO
Being once perfected how to grant suits,
How to deny them, who t'advance and who   80
To trash for over-topping, new created
The creatures that were mine, I say—or changed 'em
Or else new formed 'em; having both the key
Of officer and office, set all hearts i'th' state
To what tune pleased his ear, that now he was   85
The ivy which had hid my princely trunk
And sucked my verdure out on't. Thou attend'st not!

MIRANDA
O good sir, I do.

PROSPERO   I pray thee mark me.
I, thus neglecting worldly ends, all dedicated
To closeness and the bettering of my mind   90
With that which but by being so retired
O'er-priced all popular rate, in my false brother
Awaked an evil nature; and my trust,
Like a good parent, did beget of him
A falsehood, in its contrary as great   95
As my trust was, which had indeed no limit,
A confidence sans bound. He being thus lorded
Not only with what my revenue yielded
But what my power might else exact, like one
Who having into truth, by telling oft,   100

Made such a sinner of his memory
To credit his own lie, he did believe
He was indeed the Duke. Out o'th' substitution,
And executing th'outward face of royalty
With all prerogative, hence his ambition growing— 105
Dost thou hear?
MIRANDA   Your tale, sir, would cure deafness.
PROSPERO
To have no screen between this part he played
And him he played it for, he needs will be
Absolute Milan. Me, poor man—my library
Was dukedom large enough—of temporal royalties 110
He thinks me now incapable; confederates,
So dry he was for sway, wi'th' King of Naples
To give him annual tribute, do him homage,
Subject his coronet to his crown, and bend
The dukedom, yet unbowed—alas, poor Milan— 115
To most ignoble stooping.
MIRANDA   O the heavens!
PROSPERO
Mark his condition and th'event, then tell me
If this might be a brother.
MIRANDA   I should sin
To think but nobly of my grandmother.
Good wombs have borne bad sons.
PROSPERO   Now the condition.
This King of Naples, being an enemy   121
To me inveterate, hearkens my brother's suit;
Which was that he, in lieu o'th' premises
Of homage and I know not how much tribute,
Should presently extirpate me and mine   125
Out of the dukedom, and confer fair Milan,
With all the honours, on my brother. Whereon,
A treacherous army levied, one midnight
Fated to th' purpose did Antonio open
The gates of Milan; and, i'th' dead of darkness, 130
The ministers for th' purpose hurried thence
Me and thy crying self.
MIRANDA   Alack, for pity!
I, not rememb'ring how I cried out then,
Will cry it o'er again; it is a hint
That wrings mine eyes to't.
PROSPERO ⌜sitting⌝   Hear a little further, 135
And then I'll bring thee to the present business
Which now's upon's, without the which this story
Were most impertinent.
MIRANDA   Wherefore did they not
That hour destroy us?
PROSPERO   Well demanded, wench;
My tale provokes that question. Dear, they durst not,
So dear the love my people bore me; nor set   141
A mark so bloody on the business, but
With colours fairer painted their foul ends.
In few, they hurried us aboard a barque,
Bore us some leagues to sea, where they prepared 145
A rotten carcass of a butt, not rigged,
Nor tackle, sail, nor mast—the very rats
Instinctively have quit it. There they hoist us,

To cry to th' sea that roared to us, to sigh
To th'winds, whose pity, sighing back again,   150
Did us but loving wrong.
MIRANDA   Alack, what trouble
Was I then to you!
PROSPERO   O, a cherubin
Thou wast that did preserve me. Thou didst smile,
Infusèd with a fortitude from heaven,
When I have decked the sea with drops full salt, 155
Under my burden groaned; which raised in me
An undergoing stomach, to bear up
Against what should ensue.
MIRANDA How came we ashore?
PROSPERO By providence divine.   160
Some food we had, and some fresh water, that
A noble Neapolitan, Gonzalo,
Out of his charity—who being then appointed
Master of this design—did give us; with
Rich garments, linens, stuffs, and necessaries 165
Which since have steaded much. So, of his gentleness,
Knowing I loved my books, he furnished me
From mine own library with volumes that
I prize above my dukedom.
MIRANDA   Would I might
But ever see that man!
PROSPERO   Now I arise.   170
⌜He stands and puts on his cloak⌝
Sit still, and hear the last of our sea-sorrow.
Here in this island we arrived, and here
Have I thy schoolmaster made thee more profit
Than other princes can, that have more time
For vainer hours and tutors not so careful.   175
MIRANDA
Heavens thank you for't. And now I pray you, sir—
For still 'tis beating in my mind—your reason
For raising this sea-storm.
PROSPERO   Know thus far forth.
By accident most strange, bountiful Fortune,
Now my dear lady, hath mine enemies   180
Brought to this shore; and by my prescience
I find my zenith doth depend upon
A most auspicious star, whose influence
If now I court not, but omit, my fortunes
Will ever after droop. Here cease more questions. 185
Thou art inclined to sleep; 'tis a good dullness,
And give it way. I know thou canst not choose.
    Miranda sleeps
Come away, servant, come! I am ready now.
Approach, my Ariel, come!
    Enter Ariel
ARIEL
All hail, great master, grave sir, hail. I come 190
To answer thy best pleasure. Be't to fly,
To swim, to dive into the fire, to ride
On the curled clouds, to thy strong bidding task
Ariel and all his quality.
PROSPERO   Hast thou, spirit,
Performed to point the tempest that I bade thee? 195

ARIEL To every article.
    I boarded the King's ship. Now on the beak,
    Now in the waste, the deck, in every cabin,
    I flamed amazement. Sometime I'd divide,
    And burn in many places; on the top-mast,   200
    The yards, and bowsprit, would I flame distinctly;
    Then meet and join. Jove's lightning, the precursors
    O'th' dreadful thunderclaps, more momentary
    And sight-outrunning were not. The fire and cracks
    Of sulphurous roaring the most mighty Neptune   205
    Seem to besiege, and make his bold waves tremble,
    Yea, his dread trident shake.
PROSPERO   My brave spirit!
    Who was so firm, so constant, that this coil
    Would not infect his reason?
ARIEL   Not a soul
    But felt a fever of the mad, and played   210
    Some tricks of desperation. All but mariners
    Plunged in the foaming brine and quit the vessel,
    Then all afire with me. The King's son Ferdinand,
    With hair upstaring—then like reeds, not hair—
    Was the first man that leaped; cried 'Hell is empty,   215
    And all the devils are here'.
PROSPERO   Why, that's my spirit!
    But was not this nigh shore?
ARIEL   Close by, my master.
PROSPERO
    But are they, Ariel, safe?
ARIEL   Not a hair perished.
    On their sustaining garments not a blemish,
    But fresher than before. And, as thou bad'st me,   220
    In troops I have dispersed them 'bout the isle.
    The King's son have I landed by himself,
    Whom I left cooling of the air with sighs
    In an odd angle of the isle, and sitting,
    His arms in this sad knot.
PROSPERO   Of the King's ship,   225
    The mariners, say how thou hast disposed,
    And all the rest o'th' fleet.
ARIEL   Safely in harbour
    Is the King's ship, in the deep nook where once
    Thou called'st me up at midnight to fetch dew
    From the still-vexed Bermudas, there she's hid;   230
    The mariners all under hatches stowed,
    Who, with a charm joined to their suffered labour,
    I have left asleep. And for the rest o'th' fleet,
    Which I dispersed, they all have met again,
    And are upon the Mediterranean float   235
    Bound sadly home for Naples,
    Supposing that they saw the King's ship wrecked,
    And his great person perish.
PROSPERO   Ariel, thy charge
    Exactly is performed; but there's more work.
    What is the time o'th' day?
ARIEL   Past the mid season.   240
PROSPERO
    At least two glasses. The time 'twixt six and now
    Must by us both be spent most preciously.

ARIEL
    Is there more toil? Since thou dost give me pains,
    Let me remember thee what thou hast promised
    Which is not yet performed me.
PROSPERO   How now? Moody?   245
    What is't thou canst demand?
ARIEL   My liberty.
PROSPERO
    Before the time be out? No more!
ARIEL   I prithee,
    Remember I have done thee worthy service,
    Told thee no lies, made thee no mistakings, served
    Without or grudge or grumblings. Thou did promise
    To bate me a full year.
PROSPERO   Dost thou forget   251
    From what a torment I did free thee?
ARIEL   No.
PROSPERO
    Thou dost, and think'st it much to tread the ooze
    Of the salt deep,
    To run upon the sharp wind of the north,   255
    To do me business in the veins o'th' earth
    When it is baked with frost.
ARIEL   I do not, sir.
PROSPERO
    Thou liest, malignant thing. Hast thou forgot
    The foul witch Sycorax, who with age and envy
    Was grown into a hoop? Hast thou forgot her?   260
ARIEL
    No, sir.
PROSPERO Thou hast. Where was she born? Speak, tell
    me!
ARIEL
    Sir, in Algiers.
PROSPERO   O, was she so! I must
    Once in a month recount what thou hast been,
    Which thou forget'st. This damned witch Sycorax,   265
    For mischiefs manifold and sorceries terrible
    To enter human hearing, from Algiers
    Thou know'st was banished. For one thing she did
    They would not take her life. Is not this true?
ARIEL Ay, sir.   270
PROSPERO
    This blue-eyed hag was hither brought with child,
    And here was left by th' sailors. Thou, my slave,
    As thou report'st thyself, was then her servant;
    And for thou wast a spirit too delicate
    To act her earthy and abhorred commands,   275
    Refusing her grand hests, she did confine thee
    By help of her more potent ministers,
    And in her most unmitigable rage,
    Into a cloven pine; within which rift
    Imprisoned thou didst painfully remain   280
    A dozen years, within which space she died
    And left thee there, where thou didst vent thy groans
    As fast as mill-wheels strike. Then was this island—
    Save for the son that she did litter here,

A freckled whelp, hag-born—not honoured with   285
A human shape.
ARIEL   Yes, Caliban her son.
PROSPERO
Dull thing, I say so: he, that Caliban
Whom now I keep in service. Thou best know'st
What torment I did find thee in. Thy groans
Did make wolves howl, and penetrate the breasts   290
Of ever-angry bears; it was a torment
To lay upon the damned, which Sycorax
Could not again undo. It was mine art,
When I arrived and heard thee, that made gape
The pine and let thee out.
ARIEL   I thank thee, master.   295
PROSPERO
If thou more murmur'st, I will rend an oak,
And peg thee in his knotty entrails till
Thou hast howled away twelve winters.
ARIEL   Pardon, master.
I will be correspondent to command,
And do my spriting gently.   300
PROSPERO Do so, and after two days
I will discharge thee.
ARIEL   That's my noble master!
What shall I do? Say what, what shall I do?
PROSPERO
Go make thyself like to a nymph o'th' sea. Be subject
To no sight but thine and mine, invisible   305
To every eyeball else. Go take this shape,
And hither come in't. Go; hence with diligence!
                                    Exit Ariel
Awake, dear heart, awake! Thou hast slept well;
Awake.
MIRANDA (*awaking*) The strangeness of your story put
Heaviness in me.
PROSPERO   Shake it off. Come on;   310
We'll visit Caliban my slave, who never
Yields us kind answer.
MIRANDA   'Tis a villain, sir,
I do not love to look on.
PROSPERO   But as 'tis,
We cannot miss him. He does make our fire,
Fetch in our wood, and serves in offices   315
That profit us.—What ho! Slave, Caliban!
Thou earth, thou, speak!
CALIBAN (*within*)   There's wood enough within.
PROSPERO
Come forth, I say! There's other business for thee.
Come, thou tortoise! When?
            Enter Ariel, like a water-nymph
Fine apparition! My quaint Ariel,   320
Hark in thine ear.
            He whispers
ARIEL   My lord, it shall be done.   *Exit*
PROSPERO
Thou poisonous slave, got by the devil himself
Upon thy wicked dam, come forth!
            Enter Caliban

CALIBAN
As wicked dew as e'er my mother brushed
With raven's feather from unwholesome fen   325
Drop on you both! A southwest blow on ye,
And blister you all o'er!
PROSPERO
For this be sure tonight thou shalt have cramps,
Side-stitches that shall pen thy breath up. Urchins
Shall forth at vast of night, that they may work   330
All exercise on thee. Thou shalt be pinched
As thick as honeycomb, each pinch more stinging
Than bees that made 'em.
CALIBAN   I must eat my dinner.
This island's mine, by Sycorax my mother,   334
Which thou tak'st from me. When thou cam'st first,
Thou strok'st me and made much of me, wouldst give me
Water with berries in't, and teach me how
To name the bigger light, and how the less,
That burn by day and night; and then I loved thee,
And showed thee all the qualities o'th' isle,   340
The fresh springs, brine-pits, barren place and fertile—
Cursed be I that did so! All the charms
Of Sycorax, toads, beetles, bats, light on you;
For I am all the subjects that you have,
Which first was mine own king, and here you sty me
In this hard rock, whiles you do keep from me   346
The rest o'th' island.
PROSPERO   Thou most lying slave,
Whom stripes may move, not kindness! I have used
thee,
Filth as thou art, with human care, and lodged thee
In mine own cell, till thou didst seek to violate   350
The honour of my child.
CALIBAN
O ho, O ho! Would't had been done!
Thou didst prevent me; I had peopled else
This isle with Calibans.
MIRANDA   Abhorrèd slave,
Which any print of goodness wilt not take,   355
Being capable of all ill! I pitied thee,
Took pains to make thee speak, taught thee each hour
One thing or other. When thou didst not, savage,
Know thine own meaning, but wouldst gabble like
A thing most brutish, I endowed thy purposes   360
With words that made them known. But thy vile race,
Though thou didst learn, had that in't which good
            natures
Could not abide to be with; therefore wast thou
Deservedly confined into this rock,
Who hadst deserved more than a prison.   365
CALIBAN
You taught me language, and my profit on't
Is I know how to curse. The red plague rid you
For learning me your language!
PROSPERO   Hag-seed, hence!
Fetch us in fuel. And be quick, thou'rt best,
To answer other business.—Shrug'st thou, malice?
If thou neglect'st or dost unwillingly   371

What I command, I'll rack thee with old cramps,
Fill all thy bones with aches, make thee roar,
That beasts shall tremble at thy din.
CALIBAN   No, pray thee.
    (*Aside*) I must obey. His art is of such power   375
    It would control my dam's god Setebos,
    And make a vassal of him.
PROSPERO   So, slave, hence!
                             Exit Caliban
    Enter Ariel ⌈like a water-nymph⌉, playing and
    singing, invisible to Ferdinand, who follows.
    ⌈Prospero and Miranda stand aside⌉

                 Song

ARIEL   Come unto these yellow sands,
          And then take hands;
          Curtsied when you have and kissed—   380
          The wild waves whist—
          Foot it featly here and there,
          And, sweet sprites, bear
          The burden. Hark, hark.
⌈SPIRITS⌉ (*dispersedly within*)
          Bow-wow!   385
⌈ARIEL⌉   The watch-dogs bark.
⌈SPIRITS⌉ (*within*) Bow-wow!
ARIEL   Hark, hark, I hear
          The strain of strutting Chanticleer
          Cry 'cock-a-diddle-dow'.   390

FERDINAND
    Where should this music be? I'th' air or th'earth?
    It sounds no more; and sure it waits upon
    Some god o'th' island. Sitting on a bank,
    Weeping again the King my father's wreck,
    This music crept by me upon the waters,   395
    Allaying both their fury and my passion
    With its sweet air. Thence I have followed it—
    Or it hath drawn me rather. But 'tis gone.
    No, it begins again.

                 Song

ARIEL   Full fathom five thy father lies.   400
          Of his bones are coral made;
          Those are pearls that were his eyes;
          Nothing of him that doth fade
          But doth suffer a sea-change
          Into something rich and strange.   405
          Sea-nymphs hourly ring his knell:
⌈SPIRITS⌉ (*within*) Ding dong.
ARIEL   Hark, now I hear them.
⌈SPIRITS⌉ (*within*)   Ding-dong bell. ⌈*etc.*⌉

FERDINAND
    The ditty does remember my drowned father.
    This is no mortal business, nor no sound   410
    That the earth owes.
       ⌈*Music*⌉
            I hear it now above me.

PROSPERO (*to Miranda*)
    The fringèd curtains of thine eye advance,
    And say what thou seest yon.
MIRANDA   What is't? A spirit?
    Lord, how it looks about! Believe me, sir,
    It carries a brave form. But 'tis a spirit.   415
PROSPERO
    No, wench, it eats and sleeps, and hath such senses
    As we have, such. This gallant which thou seest
    Was in the wreck, and but he's something stained
    With grief, that's beauty's canker, thou mightst call him
    A goodly person. He hath lost his fellows,   420
    And strays about to find 'em.
MIRANDA   I might call him
    A thing divine, for nothing natural
    I ever saw so noble.
PROSPERO (*aside*)   It goes on, I see,
    As my soul prompts it. (*To Ariel*) Spirit, fine spirit, I'll
       free thee
    Within two days for this.
FERDINAND ⌈*aside*⌉   Most sure the goddess   425
    On whom these airs attend. (*To Miranda*) Vouchsafe
       my prayer
    May know if you remain upon this island,
    And that you will some good instruction give
    How I may bear me here. My prime request,
    Which I do last pronounce, is—O you wonder—   430
    If you be maid or no?
MIRANDA   No wonder, sir,
    But certainly a maid.
FERDINAND   My language! Heavens!
    I am the best of them that speak this speech,
    Were I but where 'tis spoken.
PROSPERO   How, the best?
    What wert thou if the King of Naples heard thee?   435
FERDINAND
    A single thing, as I am now that wonders
    To hear thee speak of Naples. He does hear me,
    And that he does I weep. Myself am Naples,
    Who with mine eyes, never since at ebb, beheld
    The King my father wrecked.
MIRANDA   Alack, for mercy!   440
FERDINAND
    Yes, faith, and all his lords, the Duke of Milan
    And his brave son being twain.
PROSPERO (*aside*)   The Duke of Milan
    And his more braver daughter could control thee,
    If now 'twere fit to do't. At the first sight
    They have changed eyes.—Delicate Ariel,   445
    I'll set thee free for this. (*To Ferdinand*) A word, good sir.
    I fear you have done yourself some wrong. A word.
MIRANDA (*aside*)
    Why speaks my father so ungently? This
    Is the third man that e'er I saw, the first
    That e'er I sighed for. Pity move my father   450
    To be inclined my way.
FERDINAND   O, if a virgin,

And your affection not gone forth, I'll make you
The Queen of Naples.

PROSPERO   Soft, sir! One word more.
(*Aside*) They are both in either's powers. But this swift
    business
I must uneasy make, lest too light winning   455
Make the prize light. (*To Ferdinand*) One word more. I
    charge thee
That thou attend me. Thou dost here usurp
The name thou ow'st not; and hast put thyself
Upon this island as a spy, to win it
From me the lord on't.

FERDINAND   No, as I am a man.   460

MIRANDA
There's nothing ill can dwell in such a temple.
If the ill spirit have so fair a house,
Good things will strive to dwell with't.

PROSPERO (*to Ferdinand*)   Follow me.
(*To Miranda*) Speak not you for him; he's a traitor.
    (*To Ferdinand*) Come!
I'll manacle thy neck and feet together.   465
Sea-water shalt thou drink; thy food shall be
The fresh-brook mussels, withered roots, and husks
Wherein the acorn cradled. Follow!

FERDINAND   No.
I will resist such entertainment till
Mine enemy has more power.
            He draws, and is charmed from moving

MIRANDA   O dear father,   470
Make not too rash a trial of him, for
He's gentle, and not fearful.

PROSPERO   What, I say,
My foot my tutor? Put thy sword up, traitor,
Who mak'st a show but dar'st not strike, thy
    conscience
Is so possessed with guilt. Come from thy ward,   475
For I can here disarm thee with this stick
And make thy weapon drop.

MIRANDA   Beseech you, father!

PROSPERO
Hence! Hang not on my garments.

MIRANDA   Sir, have pity.
I'll be his surety.

PROSPERO   Silence! One word more
Shall make me chide thee, if not hate thee. What,
An advocate for an impostor? Hush!   481
Thou think'st there is no more such shapes as he,
Having seen but him and Caliban. Foolish wench!
To th' most of men this is a Caliban,
And they to him are angels.

MIRANDA   My affections   485
Are then most humble. I have no ambition
To see a goodlier man.

PROSPERO (*to Ferdinand*) Come on; obey.
Thy nerves are in their infancy again,
And have no vigour in them.

FERDINAND   So they are.

My spirits, as in a dream, are all bound up.   490
My father's loss, the weakness which I feel,
The wreck of all my friends, nor this man's threats
To whom I am subdued, are but light to me,
Might I but through my prison once a day
Behold this maid. All corners else o'th' earth   495
Let liberty make use of; space enough
Have I in such a prison.

PROSPERO (*aside*)   It works. (*To Ferdinand*) Come on.—
Thou hast done well, fine Ariel. (*To Ferdinand*) Follow
    me.
(*To Ariel*) Hark what thou else shalt do me.

MIRANDA (*to Ferdinand*)   Be of comfort.
My father's of a better nature, sir,   500
Than he appears by speech. This is unwonted
Which now came from him.

PROSPERO (*to Ariel*)   Thou shalt be as free
As mountain winds; but then exactly do
All points of my command.

ARIEL To th' syllable.   505

PROSPERO (*to Ferdinand*)
Come, follow. (*To Miranda*) Speak not for him.   *Exeunt*

❦

2.1   *Enter Alonso, Sebastian, Antonio, Gonzalo, Adrian,*
        and Francisco

GONZALO (*to Alonso*)
Beseech you, sir, be merry. You have cause,
So have we all, of joy; for our escape
Is much beyond our loss. Our hint of woe
Is common; every day some sailor's wife,
The masters of some merchant, and the merchant,   5
Have just our theme of woe. But for the miracle,
I mean our preservation, few in millions
Can speak like us. Then wisely, good sir, weigh
Our sorrow with our comfort.

ALONSO   Prithee, peace.

SEBASTIAN (*to Antonio*) He receives comfort like cold
    porridge.   11

ANTONIO The visitor will not give him o'er so.

SEBASTIAN Look, he's winding up the watch of his wit.
    By and by it will strike.

GONZALO (*to Alonso*) Sir—   15

SEBASTIAN (*to Antonio*) One: tell.

GONZALO (*to Alonso*)
When every grief is entertained that's offered,
Comes to th'entertainer—

SEBASTIAN A dollar.

GONZALO Dolour comes to him indeed. You have spoken
    truer than you purposed.   21

SEBASTIAN You have taken it wiselier than I meant you
    should.

GONZALO (*to Alonso*) Therefore my lord—

ANTONIO (*to Sebastian*) Fie, what a spendthrift is he of his
    tongue!   26

ALONSO (*to Gonzalo*) I prithee, spare.

GONZALO Well, I have done. But yet—

SEBASTIAN (*to Antonio*) He will be talking.

ANTONIO Which of he or Adrian, for a good wager, first
begins to crow?   31

SEBASTIAN The old cock.

ANTONIO The cockerel.

SEBASTIAN Done. The wager?

ANTONIO A laughter.   35

SEBASTIAN A match!

ADRIAN (*to Gonzalo*) Though this island seem to be desert—

⌜ANTONIO⌝ (*to Sebastian*) Ha, ha, ha!

⌜SEBASTIAN⌝ So, you're paid.

ADRIAN Uninhabitable, and almost inaccessible—   40

SEBASTIAN (*to Antonio*) Yet—

ADRIAN Yet—

ANTONIO (*to Sebastian*) He could not miss't.

ADRIAN It must needs be of subtle, tender, and delicate
temperance.   45

ANTONIO (*to Sebastian*) Temperance was a delicate wench.

SEBASTIAN Ay, and a subtle, as he most learnedly
delivered.

ADRIAN (*to Gonzalo*) The air breathes upon us here most
sweetly.   50

SEBASTIAN (*to Antonio*) As if it had lungs, and rotten ones.

ANTONIO Or as 'twere perfumed by a fen.

GONZALO (*to Adrian*) Here is everything advantageous to
life.

ANTONIO (*to Sebastian*) True, save means to live.   55

SEBASTIAN Óf that there's none, or little.

GONZALO (*to Adrian*) How lush and lusty the grass looks!
How green!

ANTONIO The ground indeed is tawny.

SEBASTIAN With an eye of green in't.   60

ANTONIO He misses not much.

SEBASTIAN No, he doth but mistake the truth totally.

GONZALO (*to Adrian*) But the rarity of it is, which is indeed
almost beyond credit—

SEBASTIAN (*to Antonio*) As many vouched rarities are.   65

GONZALO (*to Adrian*) That our garments being, as they
were, drenched in the sea, hold notwithstanding their
freshness and glosses, being rather new-dyed than
stained with salt water.

ANTONIO (*to Sebastian*) If but one of his pockets could
speak, would it not say he lies?   71

SEBASTIAN Ay, or very falsely pocket up his report.

GONZALO (*to Adrian*) Methinks our garments are now as
fresh as when we put them on first in Afric, at the
marriage of the King's fair daughter Claribel to the
King of Tunis.   76

SEBASTIAN 'Twas a sweet marriage, and we prosper well
in our return.

ADRIAN Tunis was never graced before with such a
paragon to their queen.   80

GONZALO Not since widow Dido's time.

ANTONIO (*to Sebastian*) Widow? A pox o'that! How came
that 'widow' in? Widow Dido!

SEBASTIAN What if he had said 'widower Aeneas' too?
Good Lord, how you take it!   85

ADRIAN (*to Gonzalo*) 'Widow Dido' said you? You make
me study of that: she was of Carthage, not of Tunis.

GONZALO This Tunis, sir, was Carthage.

ADRIAN Carthage?

GONZALO I assure you, Carthage.   90

ANTONIO (*to Sebastian*) His word is more than the
miraculous harp.

SEBASTIAN He hath raised the wall, and houses too.

ANTONIO What impossible matter will he make easy next?

SEBASTIAN I think he will carry this island home in his
pocket, and give it his son for an apple.   96

ANTONIO And sowing the kernels of it in the sea, bring
forth more islands.

GONZALO (*to Adrian*) Ay.

ANTONIO (*to Sebastian*) Why, in good time.   100

GONZALO (*to Alonso*) Sir, we were talking that our garments
seem now as fresh as when we were at Tunis, at the
marriage of your daughter, who is now queen.

ANTONIO And the rarest that e'er came there.

SEBASTIAN Bate, I beseech you, widow Dido.   105

ANTONIO O, widow Dido? Ay, widow Dido.

GONZALO (*to Alonso*) Is not, sir, my doublet as fresh as the
first day I wore it? I mean in a sort.

ANTONIO (*to Sebastian*) That 'sort' was well fished for.

GONZALO (*to Alonso*) When I wore it at your daughter's
marriage.   111

ALONSO
You cram these words into mine ears against
The stomach of my sense. Would I had never
Married my daughter there! For, coming thence,
My son is lost; and, in my rate, she too,   115
Who is so far from Italy removed
I ne'er again shall see her. O thou mine heir
Of Naples and of Milan, what strange fish
Hath made his meal on thee?

FRANCISCO   Sir, he may live.
I saw him beat the surges under him   120
And ride upon their backs. He trod the water,
Whose enmity he flung aside, and breasted
The surge, most swoll'n, that met him. His bold head
'Bove the contentious waves he kept, and oared
Himself with his good arms in lusty stroke   125
To th' shore, that o'er his wave-worn basis bowed,
As stooping to relieve him. I not doubt
He came alive to land.

ALONSO   No, no; he's gone.

SEBASTIAN (*to Alonso*)
Sir, you may thank yourself for this great loss,
That would not bless our Europe with your daughter,
But rather loose her to an African,   131
Where she, at least, is banished from your eye,
Who hath cause to wet the grief on't.

ALONSO   Prithee, peace.

SEBASTIAN
You were kneeled to and importuned otherwise
By all of us, and the fair soul herself   135
Weighed between loathness and obedience at

Which end o'th' beam should bow. We have lost your
    son,
I fear, for ever. Milan and Naples have
More widows in them of this business' making
Than we bring men to comfort them. The fault's your
    own.   140
ALONSO
    So is the dear'st o'th' loss.
GONZALO   My lord Sebastian,
    The truth you speak doth lack some gentleness
    And time to speak it in. You rub the sore
    When you should bring the plaster.
SEBASTIAN (to Antonio) Very well.   145
ANTONIO And most chirurgeonly.
GONZALO (to Alonso)
    It is foul weather in us all, good sir,
    When you are cloudy.
SEBASTIAN (to Antonio)   Fowl weather?
ANTONIO   Very foul.
GONZALO (to Alonso)
    Had I plantation of this isle, my lord—
ANTONIO (to Sebastian)
    He'd sow't with nettle-seed.
SEBASTIAN   Or docks, or mallows.   150
GONZALO
    And were the king on't, what would I do?
SEBASTIAN (to Antonio) Scape being drunk, for want of
    wine.
GONZALO
    I'th' commonwealth I would by contraries
    Execute all things. For no kind of traffic
    Would I admit, no name of magistrate;   155
    Letters should not be known; riches, poverty,
    And use of service, none; contract, succession,
    Bourn, bound of land, tilth, vineyard, none;
    No use of metal, corn, or wine, or oil;
    No occupation, all men idle, all;   160
    And women too—but innocent and pure;
    No sovereignty—
SEBASTIAN (to Antonio) Yet he would be king on't.
ANTONIO The latter end of his commonwealth forgets the
    beginning.
GONZALO (to Alonso)
    All things in common nature should produce   165
    Without sweat or endeavour. Treason, felony,
    Sword, pike, knife, gun, or need of any engine,
    Would I not have; but nature should bring forth
    Of it own kind all foison, all abundance,
    To feed my innocent people.   170
SEBASTIAN (to Antonio) No marrying 'mong his subjects?
ANTONIO None, man, all idle: whores and knaves.
GONZALO (to Alonso)
    I would with such perfection govern, sir,
    T'excel the Golden Age.
SEBASTIAN   Save his majesty!
ANTONIO
    Long live Gonzalo!
GONZALO (to Alonso) And—do you mark me, sir?   175

ALONSO
    Prithee, no more. Thou dost talk nothing to me.
GONZALO I do well believe your highness, and did it to
    minister occasion to these gentlemen, who are of such
    sensible and nimble lungs that they always use to laugh
    at nothing.   180
ANTONIO 'Twas you we laughed at.
GONZALO Who, in this kind of merry fooling, am nothing
    to you. So you may continue, and laugh at nothing
    still.
ANTONIO What a blow was there given!   185
SEBASTIAN An it had not fallen flat-long.
GONZALO You are gentlemen of brave mettle. You would
    lift the moon out of her sphere, if she would continue
    in it five weeks without changing.
    Enter Ariel, invisible, playing solemn music
SEBASTIAN We would so, and then go a-bat-fowling.   190
ANTONIO (to Gonzalo) Nay, good my lord, be not angry.
GONZALO No, I warrant you, I will not adventure my
    discretion so weakly. Will you laugh me asleep? For I
    am very heavy.
ANTONIO Go sleep, and hear us.   195
    Gonzalo, Adrian, and Francisco sleep
ALONSO
    What, all so soon asleep? I wish mine eyes
    Would, with themselves, shut up my thoughts.—I find
    They are inclined to do so.
SEBASTIAN   Please you, sir,
    Do not omit the heavy offer of it.
    It seldom visits sorrow; when it doth,   200
    It is a comforter.
ANTONIO   We two, my lord,
    Will guard your person while you take your rest,
    And watch your safety.
ALONSO   Thank you. Wondrous heavy.
    He sleeps. ⌈Exit Ariel⌉
SEBASTIAN
    What a strange drowsiness possesses them!
ANTONIO
    It is the quality o'th' climate.
SEBASTIAN   Why   205
    Doth it not then our eyelids sink? I find
    Not myself disposed to sleep.
ANTONIO   Nor I; my spirits are nimble.
    They fell together all, as by consent;
    They dropped as by a thunderstroke. What might,
    Worthy Sebastian, O, what might—? No more!—   210
    And yet methinks I see it in thy face.
    What thou shouldst be th'occasion speaks thee, and
    My strong imagination sees a crown
    Dropping upon thy head.
SEBASTIAN   What, art thou waking?
ANTONIO
    Do you not hear me speak?
SEBASTIAN   I do, and surely   215
    It is a sleepy language, and thou speak'st
    Out of thy sleep. What is it thou didst say?
    This is a strange repose, to be asleep

With eyes wide open; standing, speaking, moving,
And yet so fast asleep.
ANTONIO   Noble Sebastian,   220
Thou letst thy fortune sleep, die rather; wink'st
Whiles thou art waking.
SEBASTIAN   Thou dost snore distinctly;
There's meaning in thy snores.
ANTONIO
I am more serious than my custom. You
Must be so too if heed me, which to do   225
Trebles thee o'er.
SEBASTIAN   Well, I am standing water.
ANTONIO
I'll teach you how to flow.
SEBASTIAN   Do so; to ebb
Hereditary sloth instructs me.
ANTONIO   O,
If you but knew how you the purpose cherish
Whiles thus you mock it; how in stripping it   230
You more invest it! Ebbing men, indeed,
Most often do so near the bottom run
By their own fear or sloth.
SEBASTIAN   Prithee, say on.
The setting of thine eye and cheek proclaim
A matter from thee, and a birth, indeed,   235
Which throes thee much to yield.
ANTONIO   Thus, sir.
Although this lord of weak remembrance, this,
Who shall be of as little memory
When he is earthed, hath here almost persuaded—
For he's a spirit of persuasion, only   240
Professes to persuade—the King his son's alive,
'Tis as impossible that he's undrowned
As he that sleeps here swims.
SEBASTIAN   I have no hope
That he's undrowned.
ANTONIO   O, out of that 'no hope'
What great hope have you! No hope that way is
Another way so high a hope that even   246
Ambition cannot pierce a wink beyond,
But doubt discovery there. Will you grant with me
That Ferdinand is drowned?
SEBASTIAN   He's gone.
ANTONIO   Then tell me,
Who's the next heir of Naples?
SEBASTIAN   Claribel.   250
ANTONIO
She that is Queen of Tunis; she that dwells
Ten leagues beyond man's life; she that from Naples
Can have no note—unless the sun were post—
The man i'th' moon's too slow—till new-born chins
Be rough and razorable; she that from whom   255
We all were sea-swallowed, though some cast again—
And by that destiny, to perform an act
Whereof what's past is prologue, what to come
In yours and my discharge.
SEBASTIAN   What stuff is this? How say you?

'Tis true my brother's daughter's Queen of Tunis;   260
So is she heir of Naples; 'twixt which regions
There is some space.
ANTONIO   A space whose every cubit
Seems to cry out 'How shall that Claribel
Measure us back to Naples? Keep in Tunis,
And let Sebastian wake.' Say this were death   265
That now hath seized them; why, they were no worse
Than now they are. There be that can rule Naples
As well as he that sleeps; lords that can prate
As amply and unnecessarily
As this Gonzalo; I myself could make   270
A chough of as deep chat. O, that you bore
The mind that I do, what a sleep were this
For your advancement! Do you understand me?
SEBASTIAN
Methinks I do.
ANTONIO   And how does your content
Tender your own good fortune?
SEBASTIAN   I remember   275
You did supplant your brother Prospero.
ANTONIO   True;
And look how well my garments sit upon me,
Much feater than before. My brother's servants
Were then my fellows; now they are my men.
SEBASTIAN But for your conscience.   280
ANTONIO
Ay, sir, where lies that? If 'twere a kibe
'Twould put me to my slipper; but I feel not
This deity in my bosom. Twenty consciences
That stand 'twixt me and Milan, candied be they,
And melt ere they molest. Here lies your brother,   285
No better than the earth he lies upon
If he were that which now he's like—that's dead;
Whom I with this obedient steel, three inches of it,
Can lay to bed for ever; whiles you, doing thus,
To the perpetual wink for aye might put   290
This ancient morsel, this Sir Prudence, who
Should not upbraid our course. For all the rest,
They'll take suggestion as a cat laps milk;
They'll tell the clock to any business that
We say befits the hour.
SEBASTIAN   Thy case, dear friend,   295
Shall be my precedent. As thou got'st Milan,
I'll come by Naples. Draw thy sword. One stroke
Shall free thee from the tribute which thou payest,
And I the King shall love thee.
ANTONIO   Draw together,
And when I rear my hand, do you the like   300
To fall it on Gonzalo.
          They draw
SEBASTIAN   O, but one word.
          Enter Ariel, invisible, with music
ARIEL (*to Gonzalo*)
My master through his art foresees the danger
That you his friend are in—and sends me forth,
For else his project dies, to keep them living.

He sings in Gonzalo's ear

> While you here do snoring lie,   305
> Open-eyed conspiracy
> His time doth take.
> If of life you keep a care,
> Shake off slumber, and beware.
> Awake, awake!   310

ANTONIO (*to Sebastian*)
Then let us both be sudden.

GONZALO (*awaking*)   Now good angels
Preserve the King!

ALONSO (*awaking*)
Why, how now? Ho, awake!
    The others awake
(*To Antonio and Sebastian*)   Why are you drawn?
(*To Gonzalo*) Wherefore this ghastly looking?

GONZALO   What's the matter?

SEBASTIAN
Whiles we stood here securing your repose,   315
Even now we heard a hollow burst of bellowing,
Like bulls, or rather lions. Did't not wake you?
It struck mine ear most terribly.

ALONSO   I heard nothing.

ANTONIO
O, 'twas a din to fright a monster's ear,
To make an earthquake! Sure it was the roar   320
Of a whole herd of lions.

ALONSO   Heard you this, Gonzalo?

GONZALO
Upon mine honour, sir, I heard a humming,
And that a strange one too, which did awake me.
I shaked you, sir, and cried. As mine eyes opened
I saw their weapons drawn. There was a noise,   325
That's verily. 'Tis best we stand upon our guard,
Or that we quit this place. Let's draw our weapons.

ALONSO
Lead off this ground, and let's make further search
For my poor son.

GONZALO   Heavens keep him from these beasts!
For he is sure i'th' island.

ALONSO   Lead away.   330
                    Exeunt all but Ariel

ARIEL
Prospero my lord shall know what I have done.
So, King, go safely on to seek thy son.   *Exit*

2.2   *Enter Caliban, wearing a gaberdine, and with a*
        burden of wood.

CALIBAN ⌈*throwing down his burden*⌉
All the infections that the sun sucks up
From bogs, fens, flats, on Prosper fall, and make him
By inch-meal a disease!
    ⌈*A noise of thunder heard*⌉
                His spirits hear me,
And yet I needs must curse. But they'll nor pinch,
Fright me with urchin-shows, pitch me i'th' mire,   5
Nor lead me like a fire-brand in the dark
Out of my way, unless he bid 'em. But

For every trifle are they set upon me;
Sometime like apes, that mow and chatter at me
And after bite me; then like hedgehogs, which   10
Lie tumbling in my barefoot way and mount
Their pricks at my footfall; sometime am I
All wound with adders, who with cloven tongues
Do hiss me into madness.
    Enter Trinculo
                Lo now, lo!
Here comes a spirit of his, and to torment me   15
For bringing wood in slowly. I'll fall flat.
Perchance he will not mind me.
    He lies down

TRINCULO Here's neither bush nor shrub to bear off any
weather at all, and another storm brewing. I hear it
sing i'th' wind. Yon same black cloud, yon huge one,
looks like a foul bombard that would shed his liquor.
If it should thunder as it did before, I know not where
to hide my head. Yon same cloud cannot choose but
fall by pailfuls. (*Seeing Caliban*) What have we here, a
man or a fish? Dead or alive?—A fish, he smells like
a fish; a very ancient and fish-like smell; a kind of not-
of-the-newest poor-john. A strange fish! Were I in
England now, as once I was, and had but this fish
painted, not a holiday-fool there but would give a piece
of silver. There would this monster make a man. Any
strange beast there makes a man. When they will not
give a doit to relieve a lame beggar, they will lay out
ten to see a dead Indian. Legged like a man, and his
fins like arms! Warm, o'my troth! I do now let loose
my opinion, hold it no longer. This is no fish, but an
islander that hath lately suffered by a thunderbolt.   36
    ⌈*Thunder*⌉
Alas, the storm is come again. My best way is to creep
under his gaberdine; there is no other shelter hereabout.
Misery acquaints a man with strange bedfellows. I will
here shroud till the dregs of the storm be past.   40
    He hides under Caliban's gaberdine.
    Enter Stefano, singing, with a wooden bottle in his
    hand

STEFANO   I shall no more to sea, to sea,
            Here shall I die ashore—
This is a very scurvy tune to sing at a man's funeral.
Well, here's my comfort.
    He drinks, then sings
        The master, the swabber, the boatswain, and I,   45
            The gunner and his mate,
        Loved Mall, Meg, and Marian, and Margery,
            But none of us cared for Kate.
            For she had a tongue with a tang,
            Would cry to a sailor 'Go hang!'   50
        She loved not the savour of tar nor of pitch,
        Yet a tailor might scratch her where'er she did itch.
            Then to sea, boys, and let her go hang!
            Then to sea, etc.
This is a scurvy tune, too. But here's my comfort.   55
    He drinks

CALIBAN (*to Trinculo*) Do not torment me! O!

STEFANO What's the matter? Have we devils here? Do you put tricks upon's with savages and men of Ind, ha? I have not scaped drowning to be afeard now of your four legs. For it hath been said: 'As proper a man as ever went on four legs cannot make him give ground.' And it shall be said so again, while Stefano breathes at' nostrils.

CALIBAN The spirit torments me. O!   64

STEFANO This is some monster of the isle with four legs, who hath got, as I take it, an ague. Where the devil should he learn our language? I will give him some relief, if it be but for that. If I can recover him and keep him tame and get to Naples with him, he's a present for any emperor that ever trod on neat's leather.

CALIBAN (to Trinculo) Do not torment me, prithee! I'll bring my wood home faster.   72

STEFANO He's in nis fit now, and does not talk after the wisest. He shall taste of my bottle. If he have never drunk wine afore, it will go near to remove his fit. If I can recover him and keep him tame, I will not take too much for him. He shall pay for him that hath him, and that soundly.

CALIBAN (to Trinculo) Thou dost me yet but little hurt. Thou wilt anon, I know it by thy trembling. Now Prosper works upon thee.   81

STEFANO Come on your ways. Open your mouth. Here is that which will give language to you, cat. Open your mouth. This will shake your shaking, I can tell you, and that soundly. You cannot tell who's your friend. Open your chaps again.   86

Caliban drinks

TRINCULO I should know that voice. It should be—but he is drowned, and these are devils. O, defend me!

STEFANO Four legs and two voices—a most delicate monster! His forward voice now is to speak well of his friend; his backward voice is to utter foul speeches and to detract. If all the wine in my bottle will recover him, I will help his ague. Come.

Caliban drinks

Amen. I will pour some in thy other mouth.

TRINCULO Stefano!   95

STEFANO Doth thy other mouth call me? Mercy, mercy! This is a devil, and no monster. I will leave him. I have no long spoon.

TRINCULO Stefano! If thou beest Stefano, touch me and speak to me, for I am Trinculo. Be not afeard. Thy good friend Trinculo.   101

STEFANO If thou beest Trinculo, come forth. I'll pull thee by the lesser legs. If any be Trinculo's legs, these are they.

He pulls out Trinculo by the legs

Thou art very Trinculo indeed! How cam'st thou to be the siege of this moon-calf? Can he vent Trinculos? 105

TRINCULO (rising) I took him to be killed with a thunderstroke. But art thou not drowned, Stefano? I hope now thou art not drowned. Is the storm overblown? I hid me under the dead moon-calf's gaberdine for fear of the storm. And art thou living, Stefano? O Stefano, two Neapolitans scaped!   111

⌈He dances Stefano round⌉

STEFANO Prithee, do not turn me about. My stomach is not constant.

CALIBAN
These be fine things, an if they be not spirits.
That's a brave god, and bears celestial liquor.   115
I will kneel to him.

⌈He kneels⌉

STEFANO (to Trinculo) How didst thou scape? How cam'st thou hither? Swear by this bottle how thou cam'st hither. I escaped upon a butt of sack which the sailors heaved o'erboard, by this bottle—which I made of the bark of a tree with mine own hands since I was cast ashore.

CALIBAN I'll swear upon that bottle to be thy true subject, for the liquor is not earthly.

STEFANO (offering Trinculo the bottle) Here. Swear then how thou escapedst.   126

TRINCULO Swum ashore, man, like a duck. I can swim like a duck, I'll be sworn.

STEFANO Here, kiss the book.

Trinculo drinks

Though thou canst swim like a duck, thou art made like a goose.   131

TRINCULO O Stefano, hast any more of this?

STEFANO The whole butt, man. My cellar is in a rock by th' seaside, where my wine is hid.

⌈Caliban rises⌉

How now, moon-calf? How does thine ague?   135

CALIBAN Hast thou not dropped from heaven?

STEFANO Out o'th' moon, I do assure thee. I was the man i'th' moon when time was.

CALIBAN
I have seen thee in her, and I do adore thee.   139
My mistress showed me thee, and thy dog and thy bush.

STEFANO Come, swear to that. Kiss the book. I will furnish it anon with new contents. Swear.

Caliban drinks

TRINCULO By this good light, this is a very shallow monster! I afeard of him? A very weak monster! The man i'th' moon? A most poor, credulous monster! Well drawn, monster, in good sooth!   146

CALIBAN (to Stefano)
I'll show thee every fertile inch o'th' island,
And I will kiss thy foot. I prithee, be my god.

TRINCULO By this light, a most perfidious and drunken monster! When's god's asleep, he'll rob his bottle. 150

CALIBAN (to Stefano)
I'll kiss thy foot. I'll swear myself thy subject.

STEFANO Come on then; down, and swear.

⌈Caliban kneels⌉

TRINCULO I shall laugh myself to death at this puppy-headed monster. A most scurvy monster! I could find in my heart to beat him—   155

STEFANO (to Caliban) Come, kiss.

⌈Caliban kisses his foot⌉

TRINCULO But that the poor monster's in drink. An abominable monster!

CALIBAN
I'll show thee the best springs; I'll pluck thee berries;
I'll fish for thee, and get thee wood enough.   160
A plague upon the tyrant that I serve!
I'll bear him no more sticks, but follow thee,
Thou wondrous man.
TRINCULO A most ridiculous monster, to make a wonder
of a poor drunkard!   165
CALIBAN (to Stefano)
I prithee, let me bring thee where crabs grow,
And I with my long nails will dig thee pig-nuts,
Show thee a jay's nest, and instruct thee how
To snare the nimble marmoset. I'll bring thee
To clust'ring filberts, and sometimes I'll get thee   170
Young seamews from the rock. Wilt thou go with
me?
STEFANO I prithee now, lead the way without any more
talking.—Trinculo, the King and all our company else
being drowned, we will inherit here.—Here, bear my
bottle.—Fellow Trinculo, we'll fill him by and by again.
CALIBAN (sings drunkenly) Farewell, master, farewell,
farewell!
TRINCULO A howling monster, a drunken monster!
CALIBAN (sings)
        No more dams I'll make for fish,
            Nor fetch in firing   180
        At requiring,
        Nor scrape trenchering, nor wash dish.
        'Ban, 'ban, Cacaliban
            Has a new master.—Get a new man!
    Freedom, high-day! High-day, freedom! Freedom, high-
    day, freedom!   186
STEFANO O brave monster! Lead the way.   Exeunt

❁

3.1   Enter Ferdinand, bearing a log
FERDINAND
There be some sports are painful, and their labour
Delight in them sets off. Some kinds of baseness
Are nobly undergone, and most poor matters
Point to rich ends. This my mean task
Would be as heavy to me as odious, but   5
The mistress which I serve quickens what's dead,
And makes my labours pleasures. O, she is
Ten times more gentle than her father's crabbed,
And he's composed of harshness. I must remove
Some thousands of these logs and pile them up,   10
Upon a sore injunction. My sweet mistress
Weeps when she sees me work, and says such
        baseness
Had never like executor. I forget,
But these sweet thoughts do even refresh my labours,
Most busil'est when I do it.
    Enter Miranda, and Prospero following at a distance
MIRANDA   Alas now, pray you   15
Work not so hard. I would the lightning had
Burnt up those logs that you are enjoined to pile.
Pray set it down, and rest you. When this burns

'Twill weep for having wearied you. My father
Is hard at study. Pray now, rest yourself.   20
He's safe for these three hours.
FERDINAND   O most dear mistress,
The sun will set before I shall discharge
What I must strive to do.
MIRANDA   If you'll sit down
I'll bear your logs the while. Pray give me that;
I'll carry it to the pile.
FERDINAND   No, precious creature.   25
I had rather crack my sinews, break my back,
Than you should such dishonour undergo
While I sit lazy by.
MIRANDA   It would become me
As well as it does you; and I should do it
With much more ease, for my good will is to it,   30
And yours it is against.
PROSPERO (aside)   Poor worm, thou art infected.
This visitation shows it.
MIRANDA (to Ferdinand)   You look wearily.
FERDINAND
No, noble mistress, 'tis fresh morning with me
When you are by at night. I do beseech you,
Chiefly that I might set it in my prayers,   35
What is your name?
MIRANDA   Miranda. O my father,
I have broke your hest to say so!
FERDINAND   Admired Miranda!
Indeed the top of admiration, worth
What's dearest to the world. Full many a lady
I have eyed with best regard, and many a time   40
Th'harmony of their tongues hath into bondage
Brought my too diligent ear. For several virtues
Have I liked several women; never any
With so full soul but some defect in her
Did quarrel with the noblest grace she owed   45
And put it to the foil. But you, O you,
So perfect and so peerless, are created
Of every creature's best.
MIRANDA   I do not know
One of my sex, no woman's face remember
Save from my glass mine own; nor have I seen   50
More that I may call men than you, good friend,
And my dear father. How features are abroad
I am skilless of; but, by my modesty,
The jewel in my dower, I would not wish
Any companion in the world but you;   55
Nor can imagination form a shape
Besides yourself to like of. But I prattle
Something too wildly, and my father's precepts
I therein do forget.
FERDINAND   I am in my condition
A prince, Miranda, I do think a king—   60
I would not so—and would no more endure
This wooden slavery than to suffer
The flesh-fly blow my mouth. Hear my soul speak.
The very instant that I saw you did
My heart fly to your service; there resides   65

To make me slave to it. And for your sake
Am I this patient log-man.

MIRANDA   Do you love me?

FERDINAND
O heaven, O earth, bear witness to this sound,
And crown what I profess with kind event
If I speak true! If hollowly, invert   70
What best is boded me to mischief! I,
Beyond all limit of what else i'th' world,
Do love, prize, honour you.

MIRANDA (weeping)   I am a fool
To weep at what I am glad of.

PROSPERO (aside)   Fair encounter
Of two most rare affections! Heavens rain grace   75
On that which breeds between 'em.

FERDINAND (to Miranda)   Wherefore weep you?

MIRANDA
At mine unworthiness, that dare not offer
What I desire to give, and much less take
What I shall die to want. But this is trifling,
And all the more it seeks to hide itself   80
The bigger bulk it shows. Hence, bashful cunning,
And prompt me, plain and holy innocence.
I am your wife, if you will marry me.
If not, I'll die your maid. To be your fellow
You may deny me, but I'll be your servant   85
Whether you will or no.

FERDINAND ⌜kneeling⌝   My mistress, dearest;
And I thus humble ever.

MIRANDA My husband then?

FERDINAND Ay, with a heart as willing
As bondage e'er of freedom. Here's my hand.   90

MIRANDA
And mine, with my heart in't. And now farewell
Till half an hour hence.

FERDINAND   A thousand thousand.

Exeunt severally Miranda and Ferdinand

PROSPERO
So glad of this as they I cannot be,
Who are surprised with all; but my rejoicing
At nothing can be more. I'll to my book,   95
For yet ere supper-time must I perform
Much business appertaining.   *Exit*

3.2 *Enter Caliban, Stefano, and Trinculo*

STEFANO (to Caliban) Tell not me. When the butt is out
we will drink water, not a drop before. Therefore bear
up and board 'em. Servant monster, drink to me.

TRINCULO Servant monster? The folly of this island! They
say there's but five upon this isle. We are three of
them; if th'other two be brained like us, the state
totters.

STEFANO Drink, servant monster, when I bid thee. Thy
eyes are almost set in thy head.

TRINCULO Where should they be set else? He were a brave
monster indeed if they were set in his tail.   11

STEFANO My man-monster hath drowned his tongue in
sack. For my part, the sea cannot drown me. I swam,

ere I could recover the shore, five and thirty leagues,
off and on. By this light, thou shalt be my lieutenant,
monster, or my standard.   16

TRINCULO Your lieutenant if you list; he's no standard.

STEFANO We'll not run, Monsieur Monster.

TRINCULO Nor go neither; but you'll lie like dogs, and yet
say nothing neither.   20

STEFANO Moon-calf, speak once in thy life, if thou beest
a good moon-calf.

CALIBAN
How does thy honour? Let me lick thy shoe.
I'll not serve him; he is not valiant.   24

TRINCULO Thou liest, most ignorant monster! I am in case
to jostle a constable. Why, thou debauched fish, thou,
was there ever man a coward that hath drunk so much
sack as I today? Wilt thou tell a monstrous lie, being
but half a fish and half a monster?

CALIBAN (to Stefano) Lo, how he mocks me! Wilt thou let
him, my lord?   31

TRINCULO 'Lord' quoth he? That a monster should be
such a natural!

CALIBAN (to Stefano)
Lo, lo, again! Bite him to death, I prithee.   34

STEFANO Trinculo, keep a good tongue in your head. If
you prove a mutineer, the next tree. The poor monster's
my subject, and he shall not suffer indignity.

CALIBAN
I thank my noble lord. Wilt thou be pleased
To hearken once again to the suit I made to thee?

STEFANO Marry, will I. Kneel and repeat it. I will stand,
and so shall Trinculo.   41

⌜*Caliban kneels.*⌝
Enter Ariel, invisible

CALIBAN As I told thee before, I am subject to a tyrant,
a sorcerer, that by his cunning hath cheated me of the
island.

ARIEL Thou liest.   45

CALIBAN (to Trinculo)
Thou liest, thou jesting monkey, thou.
I would my valiant master would destroy thee.
I do not lie.

STEFANO Trinculo, if you trouble him any more in's tale,
by this hand, I will supplant some of your teeth. 50

TRINCULO Why, I said nothing.

STEFANO Mum, then, and no more. (*To Caliban*) Proceed.

CALIBAN
I say by sorcery he got this isle;
From me he got it. If thy greatness will
Revenge it on him—for I know thou dar'st,   55
But this thing dare not—

STEFANO That's most certain.

CALIBAN
Thou shalt be lord of it, and I'll serve thee.

STEFANO How now shall this be compassed? Canst thou
bring me to the party?   60

CALIBAN
Yea, yea, my lord. I'll yield him thee asleep
Where thou mayst knock a nail into his head.

ARIEL Thou liest, thou canst not.

CALIBAN

What a pied ninny's this! (*To Trinculo*) Thou scurvy
    patch!

(*To Stefano*) I do beseech thy greatness give him blows,
And take his bottle from him. When that's gone   66
He shall drink naught but brine, for I'll not show him
Where the quick freshes are.

STEFANO Trinculo, run into no further danger. Interrupt
the monster one word further, and, by this hand, I'll
turn my mercy out o'doors and make a stockfish of
thee.

TRINCULO Why, what did I? I did nothing. I'll go farther
off.

STEFANO Didst thou not say he lied?   75

ARIEL Thou liest.

STEFANO Do I so? (*Striking Trinculo*) Take thou that. As
you like this, give me the lie another time.

TRINCULO I did not give the lie. Out o'your wits and
hearing too? A pox o'your bottle! This can sack and
drinking do. A murrain on your monster, and the devil
take your fingers.

CALIBAN Ha, ha, ha!

STEFANO Now forward with your tale. (*To Trinculo*)
Prithee, stand further off.   85

CALIBAN

Beat him enough; after a little time
I'll beat him too.

STEFANO (*to Trinculo*)

                    Stand farther. (*To Caliban*) Come, proceed.

CALIBAN

Why, as I told thee, 'tis a custom with him
I'th' afternoon to sleep. There thou mayst brain him,
Having first seized his books; or with a log   90
Batter his skull, or paunch him with a stake,
Or cut his weasand with thy knife. Remember
First to possess his books, for without them
He's but a sot as I am, nor hath not
One spirit to command—they all do hate him   95
As rootedly as I. Burn but his books.
He has brave utensils, for so he calls them,
Which when he has a house he'll deck withal.
And that most deeply to consider is
The beauty of his daughter. He himself   100
Calls her a nonpareil. I never saw a woman
But only Sycorax my dam and she,
But she as far surpasseth Sycorax
As great'st does least.

STEFANO   Is it so brave a lass?

CALIBAN

Ay, lord. She will become thy bed, I warrant,   105
And bring thee forth brave brood.

STEFANO Monster, I will kill this man. His daughter and
I will be king and queen—save our graces!—and
Trinculo and thyself shall be viceroys. Dost thou like
the plot, Trinculo?   110

TRINCULO Excellent.

STEFANO Give me thy hand. I am sorry I beat thee. But
while thou liv'st, keep a good tongue in thy head.

CALIBAN

Within this half hour will he be asleep.
Wilt thou destroy him then?   115

STEFANO Ay, on mine honour.

ARIEL (*aside*) This will I tell my master.

CALIBAN

Thou mak'st me merry; I am full of pleasure.
Let us be jocund. Will you troll the catch
You taught me but while-ere?   120

STEFANO At thy request, monster, I will do reason, any
reason.—Come on, Trinculo, let us sing.

(*Sings*)   Flout 'em and cout 'em,
                    And scout 'em and flout 'em,
                    Thought is free.   125

CALIBAN That's not the tune.

Ariel plays the tune on a tabor and pipe

STEFANO What is this same?

TRINCULO This is the tune of our catch, played by the
picture of Nobody.   129

STEFANO (*calls towards Ariel*) If thou beest a man, show
thyself in thy likeness. If thou beest a devil, take't as
thou list.

TRINCULO O, forgive me my sins!

STEFANO He that dies pays all debts. (*Calls*) I defy thee.—
Mercy upon us!   135

CALIBAN Art thou afeard?

STEFANO No, monster, not I.

CALIBAN

Be not afeard. The isle is full of noises,
Sounds, and sweet airs, that give delight and hurt
    not.
Sometimes a thousand twangling instruments   140
Will hum about mine ears, and sometime voices
That if I then had waked after long sleep
Will make me sleep again; and then in dreaming
The clouds methought would open and show riches
Ready to drop upon me, that when I waked   145
I cried to dream again.

STEFANO This will prove a brave kingdom to me, where
I shall have my music for nothing.

CALIBAN When Prospero is destroyed.   149

STEFANO That shall be by and by. I remember the story.

Exit Ariel, playing music

TRINCULO The sound is going away. Let's follow it, and
after do our work.

STEFANO Lead, monster; we'll follow.—I would I could
see this taborer. He lays it on.

TRINCULO (*to Caliban*) Wilt come? I'll follow Stefano.   155

Exeunt

3.3   *Enter Alonso, Sebastian, Antonio, Gonzalo, Adrian,*
and Francisco

GONZALO (*to Alonso*)

By'r la'kin, I can go no further, sir.
My old bones ache. Here's a maze trod indeed

Through forthrights and meanders. By your patience,
I needs must rest me.

ALONSO   Old lord, I cannot blame thee,
Who am myself attached with weariness   5
To th' dulling of my spirits. Sit down and rest.
Even here I will put off my hope, and keep it
No longer for my flatterer. He is drowned
Whom thus we stray to find, and the sea mocks
Our frustrate search on land. Well, let him go.   10
⌈*They sit*⌉

ANTONIO (*aside to Sebastian*)
I am right glad that he's so out of hope.
Do not for one repulse forgo the purpose
That you resolved t'effect.

SEBASTIAN (*aside to Antonio*) The next advantage
Will we take throughly.

ANTONIO (*aside to Sebastian*) Let it be tonight,
For now they are oppressed with travel. They   15
Will not nor cannot use such vigilance
As when they are fresh.

SEBASTIAN (*aside to Antonio*) I say tonight. No more.
Solemn and strange music. Enter Prospero on the
top, invisible

ALONSO
What harmony is this? My good friends, hark.

GONZALO Marvellous sweet music.
Enter spirits, in several strange shapes, bringing in
a table and a banquet, and dance about it with
gentle actions of salutations, and, inviting the King
and his companions to eat, they depart

ALONSO
Give us kind keepers, heavens! What were these?   20

SEBASTIAN
A living drollery. Now I will believe
That there are unicorns; that in Arabia
There is one tree, the phoenix' throne, one phoenix
At this hour reigning there.

ANTONIO   I'll believe both;
And what does else want credit come to me,   25
And I'll be sworn 'tis true. Travellers ne'er did lie,
Though fools at home condemn 'em.

GONZALO   If in Naples
I should report this now, would they believe me—
If I should say I saw such islanders?
For certes these are people of the island,   30
Who though they are of monstrous shape, yet note
Their manners are more gentle-kind than of
Our human generation you shall find
Many, nay, almost any.

PROSPERO (*aside*)   Honest lord,
Thou hast said well, for some of you there present   35
Are worse than devils.

ALONSO   I cannot too much muse.
Such shapes, such gesture, and such sound,
expressing—
Although they want the use of tongue—a kind
Of excellent dumb discourse.

PROSPERO (*aside*)   Praise in departing.

FRANCISCO
They vanished strangely.

SEBASTIAN   No matter, since   40
They have left their viands behind, for we have
stomachs.
Will't please you taste of what is here?

ALONSO   Not I.

GONZALO
Faith, sir, you need not fear. When we were boys,
Who would believe that there were mountaineers
Dewlapped like bulls, whose throats had hanging at 'em
Wallets of flesh? Or that there were such men   46
Whose heads stood in their breasts? Which now we
find
Each putter-out of five for one will bring us
Good warrant of.

ALONSO ⌈*rising*⌉   I will stand to and feed,
Although my last—no matter, since I feel   50
The best is past. Brother, my lord the Duke,
Stand to, and do as we.
⌈Alonso, Sebastian, and Antonio approach the table.⌉
Thunder and lightning. Ariel ⌈descends⌉ like a harpy,
claps his wings upon the table, and, with a quaint
device, the banquet vanishes

ARIEL
You are three men of sin, whom destiny—
That hath to instrument this lower world
And what is in't—the never-surfeited sea   55
Hath caused to belch up you, and on this island
Where man doth not inhabit, you 'mongst men
Being most unfit to live. I have made you mad,
And even with suchlike valour men hang and drown
Their proper selves.
Alonso, Sebastian, and Antonio draw
          You fools! I and my fellows   60
Are ministers of fate. The elements
Of whom your swords are tempered may as well
Wound the loud winds, or with bemocked-at stabs
Kill the still-closing waters, as diminish
One dowl that's in my plume. My fellow ministers
Are like invulnerable. If you could hurt,   66
Your swords are now too massy for your strengths
And will not be uplifted.
Alonso, Sebastian, and Antonio stand amazed
          But remember,
For that's my business to you, that you three
From Milan did supplant good Prospero;   70
Exposed unto the sea, which hath requit it,
Him and his innocent child; for which foul deed,
The powers, delaying not forgetting, have
Incensed the seas and shores, yea, all the creatures,
Against your peace. Thee of thy son, Alonso,   75
They have bereft, and do pronounce by me
Ling'ring perdition—worse than any death
Can be at once—shall step by step attend
You and your ways; whose wraths to guard you
from—
Which here in this most desolate isle else falls   80

Upon your heads—is nothing but heart's sorrow
And a clear life ensuing.
> *He ⌜ascends and⌝ vanishes in thunder. Then, to soft*
> *music, enter the spirits again, and dance with mocks*
> *and mows, and they depart, carrying out the table*

PROSPERO
Bravely the figure of this harpy hast thou
Performed, my Ariel; a grace it had devouring.
Of my instruction hast thou nothing bated   85
In what thou hadst to say. So with good life
And observation strange my meaner ministers
Their several kinds have done. My high charms work,
And these mine enemies are all knit up
In their distractions. They now are in my power;   90
And in these fits I leave them, while I visit
Young Ferdinand, whom they suppose is drowned,
And his and mine loved darling.   *Exit*
> ⌜*Gonzalo, Adrian, and Francisco go towards the others*⌝

GONZALO
I'th' name of something holy, sir, why stand you
In this strange stare?

ALONSO   O, it is monstrous, monstrous! 95
Methought the billows spoke and told me of it,
The winds did sing it to me, and the thunder,
That deep and dreadful organ-pipe, pronounced
The name of Prosper. It did bass my trespass.
Therefor my son i'th' ooze is bedded, and   100
I'll seek him deeper than e'er plummet sounded,
And with him there lie mudded.   *Exit*

SEBASTIAN   But one fiend at a time,
I'll fight their legions o'er.

ANTONIO   I'll be thy second.
> *Exeunt Sebastian and Antonio*

GONZALO
All three of them are desperate. Their great guilt,
Like poison given to work a great time after,   105
Now 'gins to bite the spirits. I do beseech you
That are of suppler joints, follow them swiftly,
And hinder them from what this ecstasy
May now provoke them to.

ADRIAN   Follow, I pray you. *Exeunt*

❦

4.1   *Enter Prospero, Ferdinand, and Miranda*

PROSPERO (*to Ferdinand*)
If I have too austerely punished you,
Your compensation makes amends, for I
Have given you here a third of mine own life—
Or that for which I live—who once again
I tender to thy hand. All thy vexations   5
Were but my trials of thy love, and thou
Hast strangely stood the test. Here, afore heaven,
I ratify this my rich gift. O Ferdinand,
Do not smile at me that I boast of her,
For thou shalt find she will outstrip all praise,   10
And make it halt behind her.

FERDINAND   I do believe it
Against an oracle.

PROSPERO
Then, as my gift and thine own acquisition
Worthily purchased, take my daughter. But
If thou dost break her virgin-knot before   15
All sanctimonious ceremonies may
With full and holy rite be ministered,
No sweet aspersion shall the heavens let fall
To make this contract grow; but barren hate,
Sour-eyed disdain, and discord, shall bestrew   20
The union of your bed with weeds so loathly
That you shall hate it both. Therefore take heed,
As Hymen's lamps shall light you.

FERDINAND   As I hope
For quiet days, fair issue, and long life
With such love as 'tis now, the murkiest den,   25
The most opportune place, the strong'st suggestion
Our worser genius can, shall never melt
Mine honour into lust to take away
The edge of that day's celebration;
When I shall think or Phoebus' steeds are foundered 30
Or night kept chained below.

PROSPERO   Fairly spoke.
Sit, then, and talk with her. She is thine own.
> *Ferdinand and Miranda sit and talk together*
What, Ariel, my industrious servant Ariel!
> *Enter Ariel*

ARIEL
What would my potent master? Here I am.

PROSPERO
Thou and thy meaner fellows your last service   35
Did worthily perform, and I must use you
In such another trick. Go bring the rabble,
O'er whom I give thee power, here to this place.
Incite them to quick motion, for I must
Bestow upon the eyes of this young couple   40
Some vanity of mine art. It is my promise,
And they expect it from me.

ARIEL   Presently?

PROSPERO Ay, with a twink.

ARIEL   Before you can say 'Come' and 'Go',
And breathe twice, and cry 'So, so',   45
Each one tripping on his toe
Will be here with mop and mow.
Do you love me, master? No?

PROSPERO
Dearly, my delicate Ariel. Do not approach
Till thou dost hear me call.

ARIEL   Well; I conceive.   *Exit*

PROSPERO (*to Ferdinand*)
Look thou be true. Do not give dalliance   51
Too much the rein. The strongest oaths are straw
To th' fire i'th' blood. Be more abstemious,
Or else, good night your vow.

FERDINAND   I warrant you, sir,
The white cold virgin snow upon my heart   55
Abates the ardour of my liver.

PROSPERO   Well.—
Now come, my Ariel! Bring a corollary

Rather than want a spirit. Appear, and pertly.
Soft music
(*To Ferdinand and Miranda*) No tongue, all eyes! Be silent.
Enter Iris

IRIS
Ceres, most bounteous lady, thy rich leas   60
Of wheat, rye, barley, vetches, oats, and peas;
Thy turfy mountains where live nibbling sheep,
And flat meads thatched with stover, them to keep;
Thy banks with peonied and twillèd brims
Which spongy April at thy hest betrims   65
To make cold nymphs chaste crowns; and thy broom-
      groves,
Whose shadow the dismissèd bachelor loves,
Being lass-lorn; thy pole-clipped vineyard,
And thy sea-marge, sterile and rocky-hard,
Where thou thyself dost air: the Queen o'th' Sky,   70
Whose wat'ry arch and messenger am I,
Bids thee leave these, and with her sovereign grace
      Juno ⌈appears in the air⌉
Here on this grass-plot, in this very place,
To come and sport.—Her peacocks fly amain.
Approach, rich Ceres, her to entertain.   75
      Enter ⌈Ariel as⌉ Ceres

CERES
Hail, many-coloured messenger, that ne'er
Dost disobey the wife of Jupiter;
Who with thy saffron wings upon my flowers
Diffusest honey-drops, refreshing showers,
And with each end of thy blue bow dost crown   80
My bosky acres and my unshrubbed down,
Rich scarf to my proud earth. Why hath thy queen
Summoned me hither to this short-grassed green?

IRIS
A contract of true love to celebrate,
And some donation freely to estate   85
On the blest lovers.

CERES   Tell me, heavenly bow,
If Venus or her son, as thou dost know,
Do now attend the Queen. Since they did plot
The means that dusky Dis my daughter got,
Her and her blind boy's scandalled company   90
I have forsworn.

IRIS   Of her society
Be not afraid. I met her deity
Cutting the clouds towards Paphos, and her son
Dove-drawn with her. Here thought they to have
      done
Some wanton charm upon this man and maid,   95
Whose vows are that no bed-right shall be paid
Till Hymen's torch be lighted—but in vain.
Mars's hot minion is returned again.
Her waspish-headed son has broke his arrows,
Swears he will shoot no more, but play with
      sparrows,   100
And be a boy right out.
      ⌈Music. Juno descends to the stage⌉

CERES   Highest queen of state,
Great Juno, comes; I know her by her gait.

JUNO
How does my bounteous sister? Go with me
To bless this twain, that they may prosperous be,
And honoured in their issue.   105
      ⌈Ceres joins Juno, and⌉ they sing

JUNO   Honour, riches, marriage-blessing,
                Long continuance and increasing,
                Hourly joys be still upon you.
                Juno sings her blessings on you.

⌈CERES⌉   Earth's increase, and foison plenty,   110
                Barns and garners never empty,
                Vines with clust'ring bunches growing,
                Plants with goodly burden bowing;
                Spring come to you at the farthest,
                In the very end of harvest.   115
                Scarcity and want shall shun you,
                Ceres' blessing so is on you.

FERDINAND
This is a most majestic vision, and
Harmonious charmingly. May I be bold
To think these spirits?

PROSPERO   Spirits, which by mine art   120
I have from their confines called to enact
My present fancies.

FERDINAND   Let me live here ever!
So rare a wondered father and a wise
Makes this place paradise.
      *Juno and Ceres whisper, and send Iris on
      employment*

PROSPERO   Sweet now, silence.
Juno and Ceres whisper seriously.   125
There's something else to do. Hush, and be mute,
Or else our spell is marred.

IRIS
You nymphs called naiads of the wind'ring brooks,
With your sedged crowns and ever-harmless looks,
Leave your crisp channels, and on this green land   130
Answer your summons; Juno does command.
Come, temperate nymphs, and help to celebrate
A contract of true love. Be not too late.
      Enter certain nymphs
You sunburned sicklemen, of August weary,
Come hither from the furrow and be merry;   135
Make holiday, your rye-straw hats put on,
And these fresh nymphs encounter every one
In country footing.
      *Enter certain reapers, properly habited. They join
      with the nymphs in a graceful dance; towards the
      end whereof Prospero starts suddenly, and speaks*

PROSPERO (*aside*)
I had forgot that foul conspiracy
Of the beast Caliban and his confederates   140
Against my life. The minute of their plot
Is almost come. (*To the spirits*) Well done! Avoid; no
      more!
      *To a strange, hollow, and confused noise, the spirits
      in the pageant heavily vanish.
      ⌈Ferdinand and Miranda rise⌉*

FERDINAND (*to Miranda*)
 This is strange. Your father's in some passion
 That works him strongly.
MIRANDA   Never till this day
 Saw I him touched with anger so distempered.   145
PROSPERO
 You do look, my son, in a moved sort,
 As if you were dismayed. Be cheerful, sir.
 Our revels now are ended. These our actors,
 As I foretold you, were all spirits, and
 Are melted into air, into thin air;   150
 And like the baseless fabric of this vision,
 The cloud-capped towers, the gorgeous palaces,
 The solemn temples, the great globe itself,
 Yea, all which it inherit, shall dissolve;
 And, like this insubstantial pageant faded,   155
 Leave not a rack behind. We are such stuff
 As dreams are made on, and our little life
 Is rounded with a sleep. Sir, I am vexed.
 Bear with my weakness. My old brain is troubled.
 Be not disturbed with my infirmity.   160
 If you be pleased, retire into my cell,
 And there repose. A turn or two I'll walk
 To still my beating mind.
FERDINAND *and* MIRANDA   We wish your peace.
                    Exeunt Ferdinand and Miranda
PROSPERO
 Come with a thought! I thank thee, Ariel. Come!
      Enter Ariel
ARIEL
 Thy thoughts I cleave to. What's thy pleasure?
PROSPERO   Spirit,
 We must prepare to meet with Caliban.   166
ARIEL
 Ay, my commander. When I presented Ceres
 I thought to have told thee of it, but I feared
 Lest I might anger thee.
PROSPERO
 Say again: where didst thou leave these varlets?   170
ARIEL
 I told you, sir, they were red-hot with drinking;
 So full of valour that they smote the air
 For breathing in their faces, beat the ground
 For kissing of their feet; yet always bending
 Towards their project. Then I beat my tabor,   175
 At which like unbacked colts they pricked their ears,
 Advanced their eyelids, lifted up their noses
 As they smelt music. So I charmed their ears
 That calf-like they my lowing followed, through
 Toothed briars, sharp furzes, pricking gorse, and
      thorns,   180
 Which entered their frail shins. At last I left them
 I'th' filthy-mantled pool beyond your cell,
 There dancing up to th' chins, that the foul lake
 O'er-stunk their feet.
PROSPERO   This was well done, my bird.
 Thy shape invisible retain thou still.   185

 The trumpery in my house, go bring it hither
 For stale to catch these thieves.
ARIEL   I go, I go.   *Exit*
PROSPERO
 A devil, a born devil, on whose nature
 Nurture can never stick; on whom my pains,
 Humanely taken, all, all lost, quite lost,   190
 And, as with age his body uglier grows,
 So his mind cankers. I will plague them all,
 Even to roaring.
      Enter Ariel, laden with glistening apparel, etc.
              Come, hang them on this lime.
      Ariel hangs up the apparel. ⌈*Exeunt Prospero and
      Ariel.*⌉
      Enter Caliban, Stefano, and Trinculo, all wet
CALIBAN
 Pray you, tread softly, that the blind mole may
 Not hear a foot fall. We now are near his cell.   195
STEFANO Monster, your fairy, which you say is a harmless
 fairy, has done little better than played the Jack with
 us.
TRINCULO Monster, I do smell all horse-piss, at which my
 nose is in great indignation.   200
STEFANO So is mine. Do you hear, monster? If I should
 take a displeasure against you, look you—
TRINCULO Thou wert but a lost monster.
CALIBAN
 Good my lord, give me thy favour still.
 Be patient, for the prize I'll bring thee to   205
 Shall hoodwink this mischance. Therefore speak softly.
 All's hushed as midnight yet.
TRINCULO Ay, but to lose our bottles in the pool!
STEFANO There is not only disgrace and dishonour in that,
 monster, but an infinite loss.   210
TRINCULO That's more to me than my wetting. Yet this is
 your harmless fairy, monster.
STEFANO I will fetch off my bottle, though I be o'er ears
 for my labour.
CALIBAN
 Prithee, my king, be quiet. Seest thou here;   215
 This is the mouth o'th' cell. No noise, and enter.
 Do that good mischief which may make this island
 Thine own for ever, and I thy Caliban
 For aye thy foot-licker.
STEFANO   Give me thy hand.
 I do begin to have bloody thoughts.   220
TRINCULO (*seeing the apparel*) O King Stefano, O peer! O
 worthy Stefano, look what a wardrobe here is for thee!
CALIBAN
 Let it alone, thou fool, it is but trash.
TRINCULO (*putting on a gown*) O ho, monster, we know
 what belongs to a frippery! O King Stefano!   225
STEFANO Put off that gown, Trinculo. By this hand, I'll
 have that gown.
TRINCULO Thy grace shall have it.
CALIBAN
 The dropsy drown this fool! What do you mean

To dote thus on such luggage? Let't alone,   230
And do the murder first. If he awake,
From toe to crown he'll fill our skins with pinches,
Make us strange stuff.

STEFANO Be you quiet, monster.—Mistress lime, is not
this my jerkin? Now is the jerkin under the line. Now,
jerkin, you are like to lose your hair and prove a bald
jerkin.

Stefano and Trinculo take garments

TRINCULO Do, do! We steal by line and level, an't like
your grace.   239

STEFANO I thank thee for that jest. Here's a garment for't.
Wit shall not go unrewarded while I am king of this
country. 'Steal by line and level' is an excellent pass
of pate. There's another garment for't.

TRINCULO Monster, come, put some lime upon your
fingers, and away with the rest.   245

CALIBAN
I will have none on't. We shall lose our time,
And all be turned to barnacles, or to apes
With foreheads villainous low.

STEFANO Monster, lay to your fingers. Help to bear this
away where my hogshead of wine is, or I'll turn you
out of my kingdom. Go to, carry this.   251

TRINCULO And this.

STEFANO Ay, and this.

They load Caliban with apparel.
A noise of hunters heard. Enter divers spirits in
shape of dogs and hounds, hunting them about;
Prospero and Ariel setting them on

PROSPERO
Hey, Mountain, hey!

ARIEL   Silver! There it goes, Silver!

PROSPERO
Fury, Fury! There, Tyrant, there! Hark, hark!   255
Exeunt Stefano, Trinculo, and Caliban, pursued
by spirits
(*To Ariel*) Go, charge my goblins that they grind their
joints
With dry convulsions, shorten up their sinews
With agèd cramps, and more pinch-spotted make
them
Than pard or cat o'mountain.

Cries within

ARIEL   Hark, they roar!

PROSPERO
Let them be hunted soundly. At this hour   260
Lies at my mercy all mine enemies.
Shortly shall all my labours end, and thou
Shalt have the air at freedom. For a little,
Follow, and do me service.   *Exeunt*

❀

5.1 *Enter Prospero, in his magic robes, and Ariel*

PROSPERO
Now does my project gather to a head.
My charms crack not, my spirits obey, and time
Goes upright with his carriage. How's the day?

ARIEL
On the sixth hour; at which time, my lord,
You said our work should cease.

PROSPERO   I did say so   5
When first I raised the tempest. Say, my spirit,
How fares the King and's followers?

ARIEL   Confined together
In the same fashion as you gave in charge,
Just as you left them; all prisoners, sir,
In the lime-grove which weather-fends your cell.   10
They cannot budge till your release. The King,
His brother, and yours, abide all three distracted,
And the remainder mourning over them,
Brimful of sorrow and dismay; but chiefly
Him that you termed, sir, the good old lord Gonzalo:
His tears run down his beard like winter's drops   16
From eaves of reeds. Your charm so strongly works 'em
That if you now beheld them your affections
Would become tender.

PROSPERO   Dost thou think so, spirit?

ARIEL
Mine would, sir, were I human.

PROSPERO   And mine shall.   20
Hast thou, which art but air, a touch, a feeling
Of their afflictions, and shall not myself,
One of their kind, that relish all as sharply
Passion as they, be kindlier moved than thou art?
Though with their high wrongs I am struck to th'
quick,   25
Yet with my nobler reason 'gainst my fury
Do I take part. The rarer action is
In virtue than in vengeance. They being penitent,
The sole drift of my purpose doth extend
Not a frown further. Go release them, Ariel.   30
My charms I'll break, their senses I'll restore,
And they shall be themselves.

ARIEL   I'll fetch them, sir.   *Exit*
⌐*Prospero draws a circle with his staff*⌐

PROSPERO
Ye elves of hills, brooks, standing lakes and groves,
And ye that on the sands with printless foot
Do chase the ebbing Neptune, and do fly him   35
When he comes back; you demi-puppets that
By moonshine do the green sour ringlets make
Whereof the ewe not bites; and you whose pastime
Is to make midnight mushrooms, that rejoice
To hear the solemn curfew; by whose aid,   40
Weak masters though ye be, I have bedimmed
The noontide sun, called forth the mutinous winds,
And 'twixt the green sea and the azured vault
Set roaring war—to the dread rattling thunder
Have I given fire, and rifted Jove's stout oak   45
With his own bolt; the strong-based promontory
Have I made shake, and by the spurs plucked up
The pine and cedar; graves at my command
Have waked their sleepers, oped, and let 'em forth
By my so potent art. But this rough magic   50
I here abjure. And when I have required

Some heavenly music—which even now I do—
To work mine end upon their senses that
This airy charm is for, I'll break my staff,
Bury it certain fathoms in the earth,   55
And deeper than did ever plummet sound
I'll drown my book.

Solemn music. Here enters first Ariel, invisible;
then Alonso, with a frantic gesture, attended by
Gonzalo; Sebastian and Antonio, in like manner,
attended by Adrian and Francisco. They all enter
the circle which Prospero had made, and there stand
charmed; which Prospero observing, speaks

(*To Alonso*) A solemn air, and the best comforter
To an unsettled fancy, cure thy brains,
Now useless, boiled within thy skull.

(*To Sebastian and Antonio*)   There stand,   60
For you are spell-stopped.—
Holy Gonzalo, honourable man,
Mine eyes, ev'n sociable to the show of thine,
Fall fellowly drops. (*Aside*) The charm dissolves apace,
And as the morning steals upon the night,   65
Melting the darkness, so their rising senses
Begin to chase the ignorant fumes that mantle
Their clearer reason.—O good Gonzalo,
My true preserver, and a loyal sir
To him thou follow'st, I will pay thy graces   70
Home both in word and deed.—Most cruelly
Didst thou, Alonso, use me and my daughter.
Thy brother was a furtherer in the act.—
Thou art pinched for't now, Sebastian.

(*To Antonio*)   Flesh and blood,
You, brother mine, that entertained ambition,   75
Expelled remorse and nature, whom, with Sebastian—
Whose inward pinches therefore are most strong,—
Would here have killed your king, I do forgive thee,
Unnatural though thou art. (*Aside*) Their understanding
Begins to swell, and the approaching tide   80
Will shortly fill the reasonable shores
That now lie foul and muddy. Not one of them
That yet looks on me, or would know me.—Ariel,
Fetch me the hat and rapier in my cell.
I will discase me, and myself present   85
As I was sometime Milan. Quickly, spirit!
Thou shalt ere long be free.

Ariel sings and helps to attire him as Duke of Milan

ARIEL   Where the bee sucks, there suck I:
In a cowslip's bell I lie;
There I couch when owls do cry.   90
On the bat's back I do fly
After summer merrily.
Merrily, merrily shall I live now
Under the blossom that hangs on the bow.
Merrily, merrily shall I live now   95
Under the blossom that hangs on the bow.

PROSPERO
Why, that's my dainty Ariel! I shall miss thee,
But yet thou shalt have freedom.—So, so, so.—
To the King's ship, invisible as thou art!

There shalt thou find the mariners asleep   100
Under the hatches. The Master and the Boatswain
Being awake, enforce them to this place,
And presently, I prithee.

ARIEL
I drink the air before me, and return
Or ere your pulse twice beat.   *Exit*

GONZALO
All torment, trouble, wonder, and amazement
Inhabits here. Some heavenly power guide us
Out of this fearful country!

PROSPERO   Behold, sir King,
The wrongèd Duke of Milan, Prospero.
For more assurance that a living prince   110
Does now speak to thee, I embrace thy body;
And to thee and thy company I bid
A hearty welcome.

He embraces Alonso

ALONSO   Whe'er thou beest he or no,
Or some enchanted trifle to abuse me,
As late I have been, I not know. Thy pulse   115
Beats as of flesh and blood; and since I saw thee
Th'affliction of my mind amends, with which
I fear a madness held me. This must crave—
An if this be at all—a most strange story.
Thy dukedom I resign, and do entreat   120
Thou pardon me my wrongs. But how should
Prospero
Be living and be here?

PROSPERO (*to Gonzalo*)   First, noble friend,
Let me embrace thine age, whose honour cannot
Be measured or confined.

He embraces Gonzalo

GONZALO   Whether this be
Or be not, I'll not swear.

PROSPERO   You do yet taste   125
Some subtleties o'th' isle that will not let you
Believe things certain.—Welcome, my friends all.
(*Aside to Sebastian and Antonio*)
But you, my brace of lords, were I so minded,
I here could pluck his highness' frown upon you
And justify you traitors. At this time   130
I will tell no tales.

SEBASTIAN (*to Antonio*) The devil speaks in him.

PROSPERO   No.
(*To Antonio*) For you, most wicked sir, whom to call
brother
Would even infect my mouth, I do forgive
Thy rankest fault, all of them, and require
My dukedom of thee, which perforce I know   135
Thou must restore.

ALONSO   If thou beest Prospero,
Give us particulars of thy preservation,
How thou hast met us here, whom three hours since
Were wrecked upon this shore, where I have lost—
How sharp the point of this remembrance is!—   140
My dear son Ferdinand.

PROSPERO   I am woe for't, sir.

ALONSO
  Irreparable is the loss, and patience
  Says it is past her cure.
PROSPERO   I rather think
  You have not sought her help, of whose soft grace
  For the like loss I have her sovereign aid,   145
  And rest myself content.
ALONSO   You the like loss?
PROSPERO
  As great to me as late; and supportable
  To make the dear loss have I means much weaker
  Than you may call to comfort you, for I
  Have lost my daughter.
ALONSO   A daughter?   150
  O heavens, that they were living both in Naples,
  The king and queen there! That they were, I wish
  Myself were mudded in that oozy bed
  Where my son lies. When did you lose your daughter?
PROSPERO
  In this last tempest. I perceive these lords   155
  At this encounter do so much admire
  That they devour their reason, and scarce think
  Their eyes do offices of truth, these words
  Are natural breath. But howsoe'er you have
  Been jostled from your senses, know for certain   160
  That I am Prospero, and that very Duke
  Which was thrust forth of Milan, who most strangely,
  Upon this shore where you were wrecked, was landed
  To be the lord on't. No more yet of this,
  For 'tis a chronicle of day by day,   165
  Not a relation for a breakfast, nor
  Befitting this first meeting. Welcome, sir.
  This cell's my court. Here have I few attendants,
  And subjects none abroad. Pray you, look in.
  My dukedom since you have given me again,   170
  I will requite you with as good a thing;
  At least bring forth a wonder to content ye
  As much as me my dukedom.
    Here Prospero discovers Ferdinand and Miranda,
    playing at chess
MIRANDA
  Sweet lord, you play me false.
FERDINAND No, my dearest love,   175
  I would not for the world.
MIRANDA
  Yes, for a score of kingdoms you should wrangle,
  An I would call it fair play.
ALONSO   If this prove
  A vision of the island, one dear son
  Shall I twice lose.
SEBASTIAN   A most high miracle.   180
FERDINAND (*coming forward*)
  Though the seas threaten, they are merciful.
  I have cursed them without cause.
    He kneels
ALONSO   Now all the blessings
  Of a glad father compass thee about.
  Arise and say how thou cam'st here.

    Ferdinand rises
MIRANDA (*coming forward*)   O wonder!
  How many goodly creatures are there here!   185
  How beauteous mankind is! O brave new world
  That has such people in't!
PROSPERO   'Tis new to thee.
ALONSO (*to Ferdinand*)
  What is this maid with whom thou wast at play?
  Your eld'st acquaintance cannot be three hours.
  Is she the goddess that hath severed us,   190
  And brought us thus together?
FERDINAND   Sir, she is mortal;
  But by immortal providence she's mine.
  I chose her when I could not ask my father
  For his advice, nor thought I had one. She
  Is daughter to this famous Duke of Milan,   195
  Of whom so often I have heard renown,
  But never saw before; of whom I have
  Received a second life; and second father
  This lady makes him to me.
ALONSO   I am hers.
  But O, how oddly will it sound, that I   200
  Must ask my child forgiveness!
PROSPERO   There, sir, stop.
  Let us not burden our remembrance with
  A heaviness that's gone.
GONZALO   I have inly wept,
  Or should have spoke ere this. Look down, you gods,
  And on this couple drop a blessèd crown,   205
  For it is you that have chalked forth the way
  Which brought us hither.
ALONSO   I say amen, Gonzalo.
GONZALO
  Was Milan thrust from Milan, that his issue
  Should become kings of Naples? O rejoice
  Beyond a common joy! And set it down   210
  With gold on lasting pillars: in one voyage
  Did Claribel her husband find at Tunis,
  And Ferdinand her brother found a wife
  Where he himself was lost; Prospero his dukedom
  In a poor isle; and all of us ourselves,   215
  When no man was his own.
ALONSO (*to Ferdinand and Miranda*) Give me your hands.
  Let grief and sorrow still embrace his heart
  That doth not wish you joy.
GONZALO   Be it so! Amen!
    Enter Ariel, with the Master and Boatswain
    amazedly following
  O look, sir, look, sir, here is more of us!
  I prophesied if a gallows were on land   220
  This fellow could not drown. (*To the Boatswain*) Now,
  blasphemy,
  That swear'st grace o'erboard: not an oath on shore?
  Hast thou no mouth by land? What is the news?
BOATSWAIN
  The best news is that we have safely found
  Our King and company. The next, our ship,   225
  Which but three glasses since we gave out split,

Is tight and yare and bravely rigged, as when
We first put out to sea.
ARIEL (*aside to Prospero*) Sir, all this service
Have I done since I went.
PROSPERO (*aside to Ariel*)   My tricksy spirit!
ALONSO
These are not natural events; they strengthen   230
From strange to stranger. Say, how came you hither?
BOATSWAIN
If I did think, sir, I were well awake
I'd strive to tell you. We were dead of sleep,
And—how we know not—all clapped under hatches,
Where but even now, with strange and several noises
Of roaring, shrieking, howling, jingling chains,   236
And more diversity of sounds, all horrible,
We were awaked; straightway at liberty;
Where we in all her trim freshly beheld
Our royal, good, and gallant ship, our Master   240
Cap'ring to eye her. On a trice, so please you,
Even in a dream, were we divided from them,
And were brought moping hither.
ARIEL (*aside to Prospero*)   Was't well done?
PROSPERO (*aside to Ariel*)
Bravely, my diligence. Thou shalt be free.
ALONSO
This is as strange a maze as e'er men trod,   245
And there is in this business more than nature
Was ever conduct of. Some oracle
Must rectify our knowledge.
PROSPERO   Sir, my liege,
Do not infest your mind with beating on
The strangeness of this business. At picked leisure,   250
Which shall be shortly, single I'll resolve you,
Which to you shall seem probable, of every
These happened accidents; till when be cheerful,
And think of each thing well. (*Aside to Ariel*) Come
    hither, spirit.
Set Caliban and his companions free.   255
Untie the spell.   *Exit Ariel*
(*To Alonso*)   How fares my gracious sir?
There are yet missing of your company
Some few odd lads that you remember not.
    *Enter Ariel, driving in Caliban, Stefano, and
    Trinculo, in their stolen apparel*
STEFANO Every man shift for all the rest, and let no man
    take care for himself, for all is but fortune. Coragio,
    bully-monster, coragio!   261
TRINCULO If these be true spies which I wear in my head,
    here's a goodly sight.
CALIBAN
O Setebos, these be brave spirits indeed!
How fine my master is! I am afraid   265
He will chastise me.
SEBASTIAN
Ha, ha! What things are these, my lord Antonio?
Will money buy 'em?
ANTONIO   Very like; one of them
Is a plain fish, and no doubt marketable.

PROSPERO
Mark but the badges of these men, my lords,   270
Then say if they be true. This misshapen knave,
His mother was a witch, and one so strong
That could control the moon, make flows and ebbs,
And deal in her command without her power.
These three have robbed me, and this demi-devil,   275
For he's a bastard one, had plotted with them
To take my life. Two of these fellows you
Must know and own. This thing of darkness I
Acknowledge mine.
CALIBAN   I shall be pinched to death.
ALONSO
Is not this Stefano, my drunken butler?   280
SEBASTIAN
He is drunk now. Where had he wine?
ALONSO
And Trinculo is reeling ripe. Where should they
Find this grand liquor that hath gilded 'em?
(*To Trinculo*) How cam'st thou in this pickle?
TRINCULO I have been in such a pickle since I saw you
    last that, I fear me, will never out of my bones. I shall
    not fear fly-blowing.
SEBASTIAN Why, how now, Stefano?
STEFANO O, touch me not! I am not Stefano, but a cramp.
PROSPERO You'd be king o'the isle, sirrah?   290
STEFANO I should have been a sore one, then.
ALONSO (*pointing to Caliban*) This is a strange thing as e'er
    I looked on.
PROSPERO
He is as disproportioned in his manners
As in his shape. (*To Caliban*) Go, sirrah, to my cell. 295
Take with you your companions. As you look
To have my pardon, trim it handsomely.
CALIBAN
Ay, that I will; and I'll be wise hereafter,
And seek for grace. What a thrice-double ass
Was I to take this drunkard for a god,   300
And worship this dull fool!
PROSPERO   Go to, away!   *Exit Caliban*
ALONSO (*to Stefano and Trinculo*)
Hence, and bestow your luggage where you found it.
SEBASTIAN Or stole it, rather.
                    Exeunt Stefano and Trinculo
PROSPERO (*to Alonso*)
Sir, I invite your highness and your train
To my poor cell, where you shall take your rest   305
For this one night; which part of it I'll waste
With such discourse as I not doubt shall make it
Go quick away: the story of my life,
And the particular accidents gone by
Since I came to this isle. And in the morn   310
I'll bring you to your ship, and so to Naples,
Where I have hope to see the nuptial
Of these our dear-belovèd solemnized;
And thence retire me to my Milan, where
Every third thought shall be my grave.
ALONSO   I long   315

To hear the story of your life, which must
Take the ear strangely.
PROSPERO   I'll deliver all,
And promise you calm seas, auspicious gales,
And sail so expeditious that shall catch
Your royal fleet far off. (*Aside to Ariel*) My Ariel, chick,
That is thy charge. Then to the elements   321
Be free, and fare thou well.   *Exit Ariel*
               Please you, draw near.
               Exeunt ⌈all but Prospero⌉

Epilogue
PROSPERO
Now my charms are all o'erthrown,
And what strength I have's mine own,
Which is most faint. Now 'tis true
I must be here confined by you

Or sent to Naples. Let me not,   5
Since I have my dukedom got,
And pardoned the deceiver, dwell
In this bare island by your spell;
But release me from my bands
With the help of your good hands.   10
Gentle breath of yours my sails
Must fill, or else my project fails,
Which was to please. Now I want
Spirits to enforce, art to enchant;
And my ending is despair   15
Unless I be relieved by prayer,
Which pierces so, that it assaults
Mercy itself, and frees all faults.
As you from crimes would pardoned be,
Let your indulgence set me free.   20
            He awaits applause, then exit

CARDENIO

A BRIEF ACCOUNT

MANY plays acted in Shakespeare's time have failed to survive; they may easily include some that he wrote. The mystery of *Love's Labour's Won* is discussed elsewhere (p. 349). Certain manuscript records of the seventeenth century suggest that at least one other play in which he had a hand may have disappeared. On 9 September 1653 the London publisher Humphrey Moseley entered in the Stationers' Register a batch of plays including '*The History of Cardenio*, by Mr Fletcher and Shakespeare'. Cardenio is a character in Part One of Cervantes' *Don Quixote*, published in English translation in 1612. Two earlier allusions suggest that the King's Men owned a play on this subject at the time that Shakespeare was collaborating with John Fletcher (1579-1625). On 20 May 1613 the Privy Council authorized payment of £20 to John Heminges, as leader of the King's Men, for the presentation at court of six plays, one listed as 'Cardenno'. On 9 July of the same year Heminges received £6 13s. 4d. for his company's performance of a play 'called Cardenna' before the ambassador of the Duke of Savoy.

No more information about this play survives from the seventeenth century, but in 1728 Lewis Theobald published a play based on the story of Cardenio and called *Double Falsehood, or The Distrest Lovers*, which he claimed to have 'revised and adapted' from one 'written originally by W. Shakespeare'. It had been successfully produced at Drury Lane on 13 December 1727, and was given thirteen times up to 1 May 1728. Other performances are recorded in 1740, 1741, 1767 (when it was reprinted), 1770, and 1847. In 1770 a newspaper stated that 'the original manuscript' was 'treasured up in the Museum of Covent Garden Playhouse'; fire destroyed the theatre, including its library, in 1808.

Theobald claimed to own several manuscripts of an original play by Shakespeare, and remarked that some of his contemporaries thought the style was Fletcher's, not Shakespeare's. When he himself came to edit Shakespeare's plays he did not include either *Double Falsehood* or the play on which he claimed to have based it; he simply edited the plays of the First Folio, not adding either *Pericles* or *The Two Noble Kinsmen*, though he believed they were partly by Shakespeare. It is quite possible that *Double Falsehood* is based (however distantly) on a play of Shakespeare's time; if so, the play is likely to have been the one performed by the King's Men and ascribed by Moseley in 1653 to Fletcher and Shakespeare.

Double Falsehood is a tragicomedy; the characters' names differ from those in *Don Quixote*, and the story is varied. Henriquez rapes Violante, then falls in love with Leonora, loved by his friend Julio. Her parents agree to the marriage, but Julio interrupts the ceremony. Leonora (who had intended to kill herself) swoons and later takes sanctuary in a nunnery. Julio goes mad with desire for vengeance on his false friend; and the wronged Violante, disguised as a boy, joins a group of shepherds, and is almost raped by one of them. Henriquez's virtuous brother, Roderick, ignorant of his villainy, helps him to abduct Leonora. Leonora and Violante both denounce Henriquez to Roderick. Finally Henriquez repents and marries Violante, while Julio (now sane) marries Leonora.

Some of the motifs of *Double Falsehood*, such as the disguised heroine wronged by her lover and, particularly, the reuniting and reconciliation of parents with children, recall Shakespeare's late plays. But most of the dialogue seems un-Shakespearian. Though the play deserved its limited success, it is now no more than an interesting curiosity.

THE TWO NOBLE KINSMEN

BY JOHN FLETCHER AND WILLIAM SHAKESPEARE

WHEN it first appeared in print, in 1634, *The Two Noble Kinsmen* was stated to be 'by the memorable worthies of their time, Mr John Fletcher, and Mr William Shakespeare'. There is no reason to disbelieve this ascription: many plays of the period were not printed till long after they were acted, and there is other evidence that Shakespeare collaborated with Fletcher (1579-1625). The morris dance in Act 3, Scene 5, contains characters who also appear in Francis Beaumont's *Masque of the Inner Temple and Gray's Inn* performed before James I on 20 February 1613. Their dance was a great success with the King; probably the King's Men—some of whom may have taken part in the masque—decided to exploit its success by incorporating it in a play written soon afterwards, in the last year of Shakespeare's playwriting life.

The Two Noble Kinsmen, a tragicomedy of the kind that became popular during the last years of the first decade of the seventeenth century, is based on Chaucer's *Knight's Tale*, on which Shakespeare had already drawn for episodes of *A Midsummer Night's Dream*. It tells a romantic tale of the conflicting claims of love and friendship: the 'two noble kinsmen', Palamon and Arcite, are the closest of friends until each falls in love with Emilia, sister-in-law of Theseus, Duke of Athens. Their conflict is finally resolved by a formal combat with Emilia as the prize, in which the loser is to be executed. Arcite wins, and Palamon's head is on the block as news arrives that Arcite has been thrown from his horse. Dying, Arcite commends Emilia to his friend, and Theseus rounds off the play with a meditation on the paradoxes of fortune.

Studies of style suggest that Shakespeare was primarily responsible for the rhetorically and ritualistically impressive Act 1; for Act 2, Scene 1; Act 3, Scenes 1 and 2; and for most of Act 5 (Scene 4 excepted), which includes emblematically spectacular episodes related to his other late plays. Fletcher appears mainly to have written the scenes showing the rivalry of Palamon and Arcite along with the sub-plots concerned with the Jailer's daughter's love for Palamon and the rustics' entertainment for Theseus.

Though the play was adapted by William Davenant as *The Rivals* (1664), its first known performances since the seventeenth century were at the Old Vic in 1928; it has been played only occasionally since then, but was chosen to open the Swan Theatre in Stratford-upon-Avon in 1986. Critical interest, too, has been slight; but Shakespeare's contributions are entirely characteristic of his late style, and Fletcher's scenes are both touching and funny.

THE PERSONS OF THE PLAY

PROLOGUE

THESEUS, Duke of Athens

HIPPOLYTA, Queen of the Amazons, later wife of Theseus

EMILIA, her sister

PIRITHOUS, friend of Theseus

PALAMON   }   the two noble kinsmen, cousins, nephews of
ARCITE   }   Creon, the King of Thebes

Hymen, god of marriage

A BOY, who sings

ARTESIUS, an Athenian soldier

Three QUEENS, widows of kings killed in the siege of Thebes

VALERIUS, a Theban

A HERALD

WOMAN, attending Emilia

An Athenian GENTLEMAN

MESSENGERS

Six KNIGHTS, three attending Arcite and three Palamon

A SERVANT

A JAILER in charge of Theseus' prison

The JAILER'S DAUGHTER

The JAILER'S BROTHER

The WOOER of the Jailer's daughter

Two FRIENDS of the Jailer

A DOCTOR

Six COUNTRYMEN, one dressed as a babion, or baboon

Gerald, a SCHOOLMASTER

NELL, a country wench

Four other country wenches: Fritz, Madeline, Luce, and Barbara

Timothy, a TABORER

EPILOGUE

Nymphs, attendants, maids, executioner, guard

The Two Noble Kinsmen

Prologue *Flourish. Enter Prologue*

PROLOGUE

New plays and maidenheads are near akin:
Much followed both, for both much money giv'n
If they stand sound and well. And a good play,
Whose modest scenes blush on his marriage day
And shake to lose his honour, is like her   5
That after holy tie and first night's stir
Yet still is modesty, and still retains
More of the maid to sight than husband's pains.
We pray our play may be so, for I am sure
It has a noble breeder and a pure,   10
A learnèd, and a poet never went
More famous yet 'twixt Po and silver Trent.
Chaucer, of all admired, the story gives:
There constant to eternity it lives.
If we let fall the nobleness of this   15
And the first sound this child hear be a hiss,
How will it shake the bones of that good man,
And make him cry from under ground, 'O fan
From me the witless chaff of such a writer,
That blasts my bays and my famed works makes
          lighter   20
Than Robin Hood'? This is the fear we bring,
For to say truth, it were an endless thing
And too ambitious to aspire to him,
Weak as we are, and almost breathless swim
In this deep water. Do but you hold out   25
Your helping hands and we shall tack about
And something do to save us. You shall hear
Scenes, though below his art, may yet appear
Worth two hours' travail. To his bones, sweet sleep;
Content to you. If this play do not keep   30
A little dull time from us, we perceive
Our losses fall so thick we must needs leave.

Flourish. Exit

1.1 *Music. Enter Hymen with a torch burning, a Boy
in a white robe before, singing and strewing
flowers. After Hymen, a nymph encompassed in her
tresses, bearing a wheaten garland. Then Theseus
between two other nymphs with wheaten chaplets
on their heads. Then Hippolyta, the bride, led by
Pirithous and another holding a garland over her
head, her tresses likewise hanging. After her, Emilia
holding up her train. Then Artesius ⌈and other
attendants⌉*

BOY *(sings during procession)*

    Roses, their sharp spines being gone,
    Not royal in their smells alone,
        But in their hue;

Maiden pinks, of odour faint,
Daisies smell-less, yet most quaint,   5
    And sweet thyme true;

Primrose, first-born child of Ver,
Merry springtime's harbinger,
    With harebells dim;
Oxlips, in their cradles growing,   10
Marigolds, on deathbeds blowing,
    Lark's-heels trim;

All dear nature's children sweet,
Lie fore bride and bridegroom's feet,

He strews flowers

    Blessing their sense.   15
    Not an angel of the air,
    Bird melodious, or bird fair,
        Is absent hence.

    The crow, the sland'rous cuckoo, nor
    The boding raven, nor chough hoar,   20
        Nor chatt'ring pie,
    May on our bridehouse perch or sing,
    Or with them any discord bring,
        But from it fly.

*Enter three Queens in black, with veils stained, with
imperial crowns. The First Queen falls down at the
foot of Theseus; the Second falls down at the foot of
Hippolyta; the Third, before Emilia*

FIRST QUEEN *(to Theseus)*
    For pity's sake and true gentility's,   25
    Hear and respect me.
SECOND QUEEN *(to Hippolyta)* For your mother's sake,
    And as you wish your womb may thrive with fair ones,
    Hear and respect me.
THIRD QUEEN *(to Emilia)*
    Now for the love of him whom Jove hath marked
    The honour of your bed, and for the sake   30
    Of clear virginity, be advocate
    For us and our distresses. This good deed
    Shall raze you out o'th' Book of Trespasses
    All you are set down there.
THESEUS *(to First Queen)*
    Sad lady, rise.
HIPPOLYTA *(to Second Queen)* Stand up.
EMILIA *(to Third Queen)*   No knees to me.
    What woman I may stead that is distressed   36
    Does bind me to her.
THESEUS *(to First Queen)*
    What's your request? Deliver you for all.
FIRST QUEEN ⌈kneeling still⌉
    We are three queens whose sovereigns fell before

987

The wrath of cruel Creon; who endured   40
The beaks of ravens, talons of the kites,
And pecks of crows in the foul fields of Thebes.
He will not suffer us to burn their bones,
To urn their ashes, nor to take th'offence
Of mortal loathsomeness from the blest eye   45
Of holy Phoebus, but infects the winds
With stench of our slain lords. O pity, Duke!
Thou purger of the earth, draw thy feared sword
That does good turns to'th' world; give us the bones
Of our dead kings that we may chapel them;   50
And of thy boundless goodness take some note
That for our crownèd heads we have no roof,
Save this, which is the lion's and the bear's,
And vault to everything.
THESEUS   Pray you, kneel not:
I was transported with your speech, and suffered   55
Your knees to wrong themselves. I have heard the
          fortunes
Of your dead lords, which gives me such lamenting
As wakes my vengeance and revenge for 'em.
King Capaneus was your lord: the day
That he should marry you—at such a season   60
As now it is with me—I met your groom
By Mars's altar. You were that time fair,
Not Juno's mantle fairer than your tresses,
Nor in more bounty spread her. Your wheaten wreath
Was then nor threshed nor blasted; fortune at you   65
Dimpled her cheek with smiles; Hercules our
          kinsman—
Then weaker than your eyes—laid by his club.
He tumbled down upon his Nemean hide
And swore his sinews thawed. O grief and time,
Fearful consumers, you will all devour.   70
FIRST QUEEN ⌈kneeling still⌉ O, I hope some god,
Some god hath put his mercy in your manhood,
Whereto he'll infuse power and press you forth
Our undertaker.
THESEUS   O no knees, none, widow:
⌈The First Queen rises⌉
Unto the helmeted Bellona use them   75
And pray for me, your soldier. Troubled I am.
He turns away
SECOND QUEEN ⌈kneeling still⌉ Honoured Hippolyta,
Most dreaded Amazonian, that hast slain
The scythe-tusked boar, that with thy arm, as strong
As it is white, wast near to make the male   80
To thy sex captive, but that this, thy lord—
Born to uphold creation in that honour
First nature styled it in—shrunk thee into
The bound thou wast o'erflowing, at once subduing
Thy force and thy affection; soldieress,   85
That equally canst poise sternness with pity,
Whom now I know hast much more power on him
Than ever he had on thee, who ow'st his strength,
And his love too, who is a servant for
The tenor of thy speech; dear glass of ladies,   90
Bid him that we, whom flaming war doth scorch,

Under the shadow of his sword may cool us.
Require him he advance it o'er our heads.
Speak't in a woman's key, like such a woman
As any of us three. Weep ere you fail.   95
Lend us a knee:
But touch the ground for us no longer time
Than a dove's motion when the head's plucked off.
Tell him, if he i'th' blood-sized field lay swoll'n,
Showing the sun his teeth, grinning at the moon,   100
What you would do.
HIPPOLYTA   Poor lady, say no more.
I had as lief trace this good action with you
As that whereto I am going, and never yet
Went I so willing way. My lord is taken
Heart-deep with your distress. Let him consider.   105
I'll speak anon.
⌈The Second Queen rises⌉
THIRD QUEEN (kneeling ⌈still⌉ to Emilia)
          O, my petition was
Set down in ice, which by hot grief uncandied
Melts into drops; so sorrow, wanting form,
Is pressed with deeper matter.
EMILIA   Pray stand up:
Your grief is written in your cheek.
THIRD QUEEN   O woe,   110
You cannot read it there; there, through my tears,
Like wrinkled pebbles in a glassy stream,
You may behold 'em.
⌈The Third Queen rises⌉
          Lady, lady, alack—
He that will all the treasure know o'th' earth
Must know the centre too; he that will fish   115
For my least minnow, let him lead his line
To catch one at my heart. O, pardon me:
Extremity, that sharpens sundry wits,
Makes me a fool.
EMILIA   Pray you, say nothing, pray you.
Who cannot feel nor see the rain, being in't,   120
Knows neither wet nor dry. If that you were
The ground-piece of some painter, I would buy you
T'instruct me 'gainst a capital grief, indeed
Such heart-pierced demonstration; but, alas,
Being a natural sister of our sex,   125
Your sorrow beats so ardently upon me
That it shall make a counter-reflect 'gainst
My brother's heart, and warm it to some pity,
Though it were made of stone. Pray have good
          comfort.
THESEUS
Forward to th' temple. Leave not out a jot   130
O'th' sacred ceremony.
FIRST QUEEN   O, this celebration
Will longer last and be more costly than
Your suppliants' war. Remember that your fame
Knolls in the ear o'th' world: what you do quickly
Is not done rashly; your first thought is more   135
Than others' laboured meditance; your premeditating
More than their actions. But, O Jove, your actions,

Soon as they move, as ospreys do the fish,   138
Subdue before they touch. Think, dear Duke, think
What beds our slain kings have.
SECOND QUEEN   What griefs our beds,
That our dear lords have none.
THIRD QUEEN   None fit for th' dead.
Those that with cords, knives, drams, precipitance,
Weary of this world's light, have to themselves
Been death's most horrid agents, human grace
Affords them dust and shadow.
FIRST QUEEN   But our lords   145
Lie blist'ring fore the visitating sun,
And were good kings, when living.
THESEUS   It is true,
And I will give you comfort to give your dead lords
     graves,
The which to do must make some work with Creon.
FIRST QUEEN
And that work presents itself to th' doing.   150
Now 'twill take form, the heats are gone tomorrow.
Then, bootless toil must recompense itself
With its own sweat; now he's secure,
Not dreams we stand before your puissance
Rinsing our holy begging in our eyes   155
To make petition clear.
SECOND QUEEN   Now you may take him,
Drunk with his victory.
THIRD QUEEN   And his army full
Of bread and sloth.
THESEUS   Artesius, that best knowest
How to draw out, fit to this enterprise
The prim'st for this proceeding and the number   160
To carry such a business: forth and levy
Our worthiest instruments, whilst we dispatch
This grand act of our life, this daring deed
Of fate in wedlock.
FIRST QUEEN (to the other two Queens)
          Dowagers, take hands;
Let us be widows to our woes; delay   165
Commends us to a famishing hope.
ALL THREE QUEENS   Farewell.
SECOND QUEEN
We come unseasonably, but when could grief
Cull forth, as unpanged judgement can, fitt'st time
For best solicitation?
THESEUS   Why, good ladies,
This is a service whereto I am going   170
Greater than any war—it more imports me
Than all the actions that I have foregone,
Or futurely can cope.
FIRST QUEEN   The more proclaiming
Our suit shall be neglected when her arms,
Able to lock Jove from a synod, shall   175
By warranting moonlight corslet thee! O when
Her twinning cherries shall their sweetness fall
Upon thy tasteful lips, what wilt thou think
Of rotten kings or blubbered queens? What care
For what thou feel'st not, what thou feel'st being able
To make Mars spurn his drum? O, if thou couch   181

But one night with her, every hour in't will
Take hostage of thee for a hundred, and
Thou shalt remember nothing more than what
That banquet bids thee to.
HIPPOLYTA (to Theseus)   Though much unlike   185
You should be so transported, as much sorry
I should be such a suitor—yet I think
Did I not by th'abstaining of my joy,
Which breeds a deeper longing, cure their surfeit
That craves a present medicine, I should pluck   190
All ladies' scandal on me. ⌈Kneels⌉ Therefore, sir,
As I shall here make trial of my prayers,
Either presuming them to have some force,
Or sentencing for aye their vigour dumb,
Prorogue this business we are going about, and hang
Your shield afore your heart—about that neck   196
Which is my fee, and which I freely lend
To do these poor queens service.
ALL THREE QUEENS (to Emilia)   O, help now,
Our cause cries for your knee.
EMILIA (kneels to Theseus)   If you grant not
My sister her petition in that force   200
With that celerity and nature which
She makes it in, from henceforth I'll not dare
To ask you anything, nor be so hardy
Ever to take a husband.
THESEUS   Pray stand up.
          ⌈They rise⌉
I am entreating of myself to do   205
That which you kneel to have me.—Pirithous,
Lead on the bride: get you and pray the gods
For success and return; omit not anything
In the pretended celebration.—Queens,
Follow your soldier. (To Artesius) As before, hence you,
And at the banks of Aulis meet us with   211
The forces you can raise, where we shall find
The moiety of a number for a business
More bigger looked.   Exit Artesius
(To Hippolyta)   Since that our theme is haste,
I stamp this kiss upon thy current lip—   215
Sweet, keep it as my token. (To the wedding party) Set
     you forward,
For I will see you gone.
(To Emilia) Farewell, my beauteous sister.—Pirithous,
Keep the feast full: bate not an hour on't.
PIRITHOUS   Sir,
I'll follow you at heels. The feast's solemnity   220
Shall want till your return.
THESEUS   Cousin, I charge you
Budge not from Athens. We shall be returning
Ere you can end this feast, of which, I pray you,
Make no abatement.—Once more, farewell all.
          Exeunt Hippolyta, Emilia, Pirithous, and train
               towards the temple
FIRST QUEEN
Thus dost thou still make good the tongue o'th' world.
SECOND QUEEN
And earn'st a deity equal with Mars—   226
THIRD QUEEN If not above him, for

Thou being but mortal mak'st affections bend
To godlike honours; they themselves, some say,
Groan under such a mast'ry.
THESEUS   As we are men,   230
Thus should we do; being sensually subdued
We lose our human title. Good cheer, ladies.
Now turn we towards your comforts.
                                  ⌈Flourish.⌉ Exeunt

1.2   Enter Palamon and Arcite
ARCITE
Dear Palamon, dearer in love than blood,
And our prime cousin, yet unhardened in
The crimes of nature, let us leave the city,
Thebes, and the temptings in't, before we further
Sully our gloss of youth.   5
And here to keep in abstinence we shame
As in incontinence; for not to swim
I'th' aid o'th' current were almost to sink—
At least to frustrate striving; and to follow
The common stream 'twould bring us to an eddy   10
Where we should turn or drown; if labour through,
Our gain but life and weakness.
PALAMON   Your advice
Is cried up with example. What strange ruins
Since first we went to school may we perceive
Walking in Thebes? Scars and bare weeds   15
The gain o'th' martialist who did propound
To his bold ends honour and golden ingots,
Which though he won, he had not; and now flirted
By peace for whom he fought. Who then shall offer
To Mars's so-scorned altar? I do bleed   20
When such I meet, and wish great Juno would
Resume her ancient fit of jealousy
To get the soldier work, that peace might purge
For her repletion and retain anew
Her charitable heart, now hard and harsher   25
Than strife or war could be.
ARCITE   Are you not out?
Meet you no ruin but the soldier in
The cranks and turns of Thebes? You did begin
As if you met decays of many kinds.
Perceive you none that do arouse your pity   30
But th'unconsidered soldier?
PALAMON   Yes, I pity
Decays where'er I find them, but such most
That, sweating in an honourable toil,
Are paid with ice to cool 'em.
ARCITE   'Tis not this
I did begin to speak of. This is virtue,   35
Of no respect in Thebes. I spake of Thebes,
How dangerous, if we will keep our honours,
It is for our residing where every evil
Hath a good colour, where every seeming good's
A certain evil, where not to be ev'n jump   40
As they are here were to be strangers, and
Such things to be, mere monsters.
PALAMON   'Tis in our power,
Unless we fear that apes can tutor's, to

Be masters of our manners. What need I
Affect another's gait, which is not catching   45
Where there is faith? Or to be fond upon
Another's way of speech, when by mine own
I may be reasonably conceived—saved, too—
Speaking it truly? Why am I bound
By any generous bond to follow him   50
Follows his tailor, haply so long until
The followed make pursuit? Or let me know
Why mine own barber is unblest—with him
My poor chin, too—for 'tis not scissored just
To such a favourite's glass? What canon is there 55
That does command my rapier from my hip
To dangle't in my hand? Or to go tiptoe
Before the street be foul? Either I am
The fore-horse in the team or I am none
That draw i'th' sequent trace. These poor slight sores
Need not a plantain. That which rips my bosom   61
Almost to th' heart's—
ARCITE   Our uncle Creon.
PALAMON   He,
A most unbounded tyrant, whose successes
Makes heaven unfeared and villainy assured
Beyond its power there's nothing; almost puts   65
Faith in a fever, and deifies alone
Voluble chance; who only attributes
The faculties of other instruments
To his own nerves and act; commands men's service,
And what they win in't, boot and glory; one   70
That fears not to do harm, good dares not. Let
The blood of mine that's sib to him be sucked
From me with leeches. Let them break and fall
Off me with that corruption.
ARCITE   Clear-spirited cousin,
Let's leave his court that we may nothing share 75
Of his loud infamy: for our milk
Will relish of the pasture, and we must
Be vile or disobedient; not his kinsmen
In blood unless in quality.
PALAMON   Nothing truer.
I think the echoes of his shames have deafed   80
The ears of heav'nly justice. Widows' cries
Descend again into their throats and have not
                  Enter Valerius
Due audience of the gods—Valerius.
VALERIUS
The King calls for you; yet be leaden-footed
Till his great rage be off him. Phoebus, when   85
He broke his whipstock and exclaimed against
The horses of the sun, but whispered to
The loudness of his fury.
PALAMON   Small winds shake him.
But what's the matter?
VALERIUS
Theseus, who where he threats, appals, hath sent 90
Deadly defiance to him and pronounces
Ruin to Thebes, who is at hand to seal
The promise of his wrath.
ARCITE   Let him approach.

But that we fear the gods in him, he brings not
A jot of terror to us. Yet what man   95
Thirds his own worth—the case is each of ours—
When that his action's dregged with mind assured
'Tis bad he goes about.
PALAMON   Leave that unreasoned.
Our services stand now for Thebes, not Creon,
Yet to be neutral to him were dishonour,   100
Rebellious to oppose. Therefore we must
With him stand to the mercy of our fate,
Who hath bounded our last minute.
ARCITE   So we must.
Is't said this war's afoot? Or it shall be
On fail of some condition?
VALERIUS   'Tis in motion,   105
The intelligence of state came in the instant
With the defier.
PALAMON   Let's to the King, who, were he
A quarter carrier of that honour which
His enemy come in, the blood we venture
Should be as for our health, which were not spent, 110
Rather laid out for purchase. But, alas,
Our hands advanced before our hearts, what will
The fall o'th' stroke do damage?
ARCITE   Let th'event—
That never-erring arbitrator—tell us
When we know all ourselves, and let us follow   115
The becking of our chance.   *Exeunt*

1.3   *Enter Pirithous, Hippolyta, and Emilia*
PIRITHOUS
No further.
HIPPOLYTA   Sir, farewell. Repeat my wishes
To our great lord, of whose success I dare not
Make any timorous question; yet I wish him
Excess and overflow of power, an't might be,
To dure ill-dealing fortune. Speed to him;   5
Store never hurts good governors.
PIRITHOUS   Though I know
His ocean needs not my poor drops, yet they
Must yield their tribute there. (*To Emilia*) My precious
      maid,
Those best affections that the heavens infuse
In their best-tempered pieces keep enthroned   10
In your dear heart.
EMILIA   Thanks, sir. Remember me
To our all-royal brother, for whose speed
The great Bellona I'll solicit; and
Since in our terrene state petitions are not
Without gifts understood, I'll offer to her   15
What I shall be advised she likes. Our hearts
Are in his army, in his tent.
HIPPOLYTA   In's bosom.
We have been soldiers, and we cannot weep
When our friends don their helms, or put to sea,
Or tell of babes broached on the lance, or women   20
That have sod their infants in—and after eat them—
The brine they wept at killing 'em: then if

You stay to see of us such spinsters, we
Should hold you here forever.
PIRITHOUS   Peace be to you
As I pursue this war, which shall be then   25
Beyond further requiring.   *Exit Pirithous*
EMILIA   How his longing
Follows his friend! Since his depart, his sports,
Though craving seriousness and skill, passed slightly
His careless execution, where nor gain
Made him regard or loss consider, but   30
Playing one business in his hand, another
Directing in his head, his mind nurse equal
To these so diff'ring twins. Have you observed him
Since our great lord departed?
HIPPOLYTA   With much labour;
And I did love him for't. They two have cabined   35
In many as dangerous as poor a corner,
Peril and want contending; they have skiffed
Torrents whose roaring tyranny and power
I'th' least of these was dreadful, and they have
Fought out together where death's self was lodged; 40
Yet fate hath brought them off. Their knot of love,
Tied, weaved, entangled with so true, so long,
And with a finger of so deep a cunning,
May be outworn, never undone. I think
Theseus cannot be umpire to himself,   45
Cleaving his conscience into twain and doing
Each side like justice, which he loves best.
EMILIA   Doubtless
There is a best, and reason has no manners
To say it is not you. I was acquainted
Once with a time when I enjoyed a playfellow;   50
You were at wars when she the grave enriched,
Who made too proud the bed; took leave o'th'
      moon—
Which then looked pale at parting—when our count
Was each eleven.
HIPPOLYTA   'Twas Flavina.
EMILIA   Yes.
You talk of Pirithous' and Theseus' love: 55
Theirs has more ground, is more maturely seasoned,
More buckled with strong judgement, and their needs
The one of th'other may be said to water
Their intertangled roots of love; but I
And she I sigh and spoke of were things innocent,   60
Loved for we did, and like the elements,
That know not what, nor why, yet do effect
Rare issues by their operance, our souls
Did so to one another. What she liked
Was then of me approved; what not, condemned—   65
No more arraignment. The flower that I would pluck
And put between my breasts—O then but beginning
To swell about the blossom—she would long
Till she had such another, and commit it
To the like innocent cradle, where, phoenix-like,   70
They died in perfume. On my head no toy
But was her pattern. Her affections—pretty,
Though happily her careless wear—I followed

For my most serious decking. Had mine ear
Stol'n some new air, or at adventure hummed one, 75
From musical coinage, why, it was a note
Whereon her spirits would sojourn—rather dwell on—
And sing it in her slumbers. This rehearsal—
Which, seely innocence wots well, comes in
Like old emportment's bastard—has this end: 80
That the true love 'tween maid and maid may be
More than in sex dividual.

HIPPOLYTA　　　　　　　　You're out of breath,
And this high-speeded pace is but to say
That you shall never, like the maid Flavina,
Love any that's called man. 85

EMILIA I am sure I shall not.

HIPPOLYTA Now alack, weak sister,
I must no more believe thee in this point—
Though in't I know thou dost believe thyself—
Than I will trust a sickly appetite 90
That loathes even as it longs. But sure, my sister,
If I were ripe for your persuasion, you
Have said enough to shake me from the arm
Of the all-noble Theseus, for whose fortunes
I will now in and kneel, with great assurance 95
That we more than his Pirithous possess
The high throne in his heart.

EMILIA　　　　　　　　　　I am not
Against your faith, yet I continue mine.　　　*Exeunt*

1.4　　*Cornetts. A battle struck within. Then a retreat.*
　　　Flourish. Then enter Theseus, victor. The three
　　　Queens meet him and fall on their faces before him.
　　　⌈*Also enter a Herald, and attendants bearing*
　　　Palamon and Arcite on two hearses⌉

FIRST QUEEN (*to Theseus*)
　To thee no star be dark.

SECOND QUEEN (*to Theseus*)　Both heaven and earth
Friend thee for ever.

THIRD QUEEN (*to Theseus*) All the good that may
Be wished upon thy head, I cry 'Amen' to't.

THESEUS
Th'impartial gods, who from the mounted heavens
View us their mortal herd, behold who err 5
And in their time chastise. Go and find out
The bones of your dead lords and honour them
With treble ceremony: rather than a gap
Should be in their dear rites we would supply't.
But those we will depute which shall invest 10
You in your dignities, and even each thing
Our haste does leave imperfect. So adieu,
And heaven's good eyes look on you.
　　　　　　　　　　　　　Exeunt the Queens
　　　　　　　　　　　　　What are those?

HERALD
Men of great quality, as may be judged
By their appointment. Some of Thebes have told's 15
They are sisters' children, nephews to the King.

THESEUS
By th' helm of Mars I saw them in the war,
Like to a pair of lions smeared with prey,

Make lanes in troops aghast. I fixed my note
Constantly on them, for they were a mark 20
Worth a god's view. What prisoner was't that told me
When I enquired their names?

HERALD　　　　　　　　　Wi' leave, they're called
Arcite and Palamon.

THESEUS　　　　　　　'Tis right: those, those.
They are not dead?

HERALD
Nor in a state of life. Had they been taken 25
When their last hurts were given, 'twas possible
They might have been recovered. Yet they breathe,
And have the name of men.

THESEUS　　　　　　　　Then like men use 'em.
The very lees of such, millions of rates
Exceed the wine of others. All our surgeons 30
Convent in their behoof; our richest balms,
Rather than niggard, waste. Their lives concern us
Much more than Thebes is worth. Rather than have
　'em
Freed of this plight and in their morning state—
Sound and at liberty—I would 'em dead; 35
But forty-thousandfold we had rather have 'em
Prisoners to us, than death. Bear 'em speedily
From our kind air, to them unkind, and minister
What man to man may do—for our sake, more,
Since I have known frights, fury, friends' behests, 40
Love's provocations, zeal, a mistress' task,
Desire of liberty, a fever, madness,
Hath set a mark which nature could not reach to
Without some imposition, sickness in will
O'er-wrestling strength in reason. For our love 45
And great Apollo's mercy, all our best
Their best skill tender.—Lead into the city
Where, having bound things scattered, we will post
To Athens fore our army.　　　　*Flourish. Exeunt*

1.5　　*Music. Enter the three Queens with the hearses of*
　　　their lords in a funeral solemnity, with attendants

Song

Urns and odours, bring away,
Vapours, sighs, darken the day;
　Our dole more deadly looks than dying.
Balms and gums and heavy cheers,
Sacred vials filled with tears, 5
　And clamours through the wild air flying:

Come all sad and solemn shows,
That are quick-eyed pleasure's foes.
We convent naught else but woes,
We convent naught else but woes. 10

THIRD QUEEN
This funeral path brings to your household's grave—
Joy seize on you again, peace sleep with him.

SECOND QUEEN
And this to yours.

FIRST QUEEN　　　　Yours this way. Heavens lend
A thousand differing ways to one sure end.

THIRD QUEEN

This world's a city full of straying streets,   15
And death's the market-place where each one meets.

Exeunt severally

❈

2.1   *Enter the Jailer and the Wooer*

JAILER I may depart with little, while I live; something I
may cast to you, not much. Alas, the prison I keep,
though it be for great ones, yet they seldom come;
before one salmon you shall take a number of minnows.
I am given out to be better lined than it can appear to
me report is a true speaker. I would I were really that
I am delivered to be. Marry, what I have—be it what
it will—I will assure upon my daughter at the day of
my death.

WOOER Sir, I demand no more than your own offer, and
I will estate your daughter in what I have promised.   11

JAILER Well, we will talk more of this when the solemnity
is past. But have you a full promise of her?

Enter the Jailer's Daughter with rushes

When that shall be seen, I tender my consent.

WOOER I have, sir. Here she comes.   15

JAILER (*to Daughter*) Your friend and I have chanced to
name you here, upon the old business—but no more
of that now. So soon as the court hurry is over we will
have an end of it. I'th' mean time, look tenderly to the
two prisoners. I can tell you they are princes.   20

JAILER'S DAUGHTER These strewings are for their chamber.
'Tis pity they are in prison, and 'twere pity they should
be out. I do think they have patience to make any
adversity ashamed; the prison itself is proud of 'em,
and they have all the world in their chamber.   25

JAILER They are famed to be a pair of absolute men.

JAILER'S DAUGHTER By my troth, I think fame but stam-
mers 'em—they stand a grece above the reach of report.

JAILER I heard them reported in the battle to be the only
doers.   30

JAILER'S DAUGHTER Nay, most likely, for they are noble
sufferers. I marvel how they would have looked had
they been victors, that with such a constant nobility
enforce a freedom out of bondage, making misery their
mirth, and affliction a toy to jest at.   35

JAILER Do they so?

JAILER'S DAUGHTER It seems to me they have no more
sense of their captivity than I of ruling Athens. They
eat well, look merrily, discourse of many things, but
nothing of their own restraint and disasters. Yet
sometime a divided sigh—martyred as 'twere i'th'
deliverance—will break from one of them, when the
other presently gives it so sweet a rebuke that I could
wish myself a sigh to be so chid, or at least a sigher
to be comforted.   45

WOOER I never saw 'em.

JAILER The Duke himself came privately in the night,

Palamon and Arcite appear ⌈at a window⌉ above

and so did they. What the reason of it is I know not.
Look, yonder they are. That's Arcite looks out.

JAILER'S DAUGHTER No, sir, no—that's Palamon. Arcite is
the lower of the twain—(*pointing at Arcite*) you may
perceive a part of him.   52

JAILER Go to, leave your pointing. They would not make
us their object. Out of their sight.

JAILER'S DAUGHTER It is a holiday to look on them. Lord,
the difference of men!   *Exeunt*

2.2   *Enter Palamon and Arcite in prison, ⌈in shackles,
above⌉*

PALAMON

How do you, noble cousin?

ARCITE   How do you, sir?

PALAMON

Why, strong enough to laugh at misery
And bear the chance of war. Yet we are prisoners,
I fear, for ever, cousin.

ARCITE   I believe it,
And to that destiny have patiently   5
Laid up my hour to come.

PALAMON   O, cousin Arcite,
Where is Thebes now? Where is our noble country?
Where are our friends and kindreds? Never more
Must we behold those comforts, never see
The hardy youths strive for the games of honour,   10
Hung with the painted favours of their ladies,
Like tall ships under sail; then start amongst 'em
And, as an east wind, leave 'em all behind us,
Like lazy clouds, whilst Palamon and Arcite,
Even in the wagging of a wanton leg,   15
Outstripped the people's praises, won the garlands
Ere they have time to wish 'em ours. O never
Shall we two exercise, like twins of honour,
Our arms again and feel our fiery horses
Like proud seas under us. Our good swords, now—   20
Better the red-eyed god of war ne'er wore—
Ravished our sides, like age must run to rust
And deck the temples of those gods that hate us.
These hands shall never draw 'em out like lightning
To blast whole armies more.

ARCITE   No, Palamon,   25
Those hopes are prisoners with us. Here we are,
And here the graces of our youths must wither,
Like a too-timely spring. Here age must find us
And, which is heaviest, Palamon, unmarried—
The sweet embraces of a loving wife   30
Loaden with kisses, armed with thousand Cupids,
Shall never clasp our necks; no issue know us;
No figures of ourselves shall we e'er see
To glad our age, and, like young eagles, teach 'em
Boldly to gaze against bright arms and say,   35
'Remember what your fathers were, and conquer.'
The fair-eyed maids shall weep our banishments,
And in their songs curse ever-blinded fortune,
Till she for shame see what a wrong she has done
To youth and nature. This is all our world.   40
We shall know nothing here but one another,
Hear nothing but the clock that tells our woes.

The vine shall grow, but we shall never see it;
Summer shall come, and with her all delights,
But dead-cold winter must inhabit here still.   45
PALAMON
'Tis too true, Arcite. To our Theban hounds
That shook the agèd forest with their echoes,
No more now must we holler; no more shake
Our pointed javelins whilst the angry swine
Flies like a Parthian quiver from our rages,   50
Struck with our well-steeled darts. All valiant uses—
The food and nourishment of noble minds—
In us two here shall perish; we shall die—
Which is the curse of honour—lastly,
Children of grief and ignorance.
ARCITE   Yet, cousin,   55
Even from the bottom of these miseries,
From all that fortune can inflict upon us,
I see two comforts rising—two mere blessings,
If the gods please, to hold here a brave patience
And the enjoying of our griefs together.   60
Whilst Palamon is with me, let me perish
If I think this our prison.
PALAMON   Certainly
'Tis a main goodness, cousin, that our fortunes
Were twined together. 'Tis most true, two souls
Put in two noble bodies, let 'em suffer   65
The gall of hazard, so they grow together,
Will never sink; they must not, say they could.
A willing man dies sleeping and all's done.
ARCITE
Shall we make worthy uses of this place
That all men hate so much?
PALAMON   How, gentle cousin?   70
ARCITE
Let's think this prison holy sanctuary,
To keep us from corruption of worse men.
We are young, and yet desire the ways of honour
That liberty and common conversation,
The poison of pure spirits, might, like women,   75
Woo us to wander from. What worthy blessing
Can be, but our imaginations
May make it ours? And here being thus together,
We are an endless mine to one another:
We are one another's wife, ever begetting   80
New births of love; we are father, friends,
    acquaintance;
We are in one another, families—
I am your heir, and you are mine; this place
Is our inheritance: no hard oppressor
Dare take this from us. Here, with a little patience,   85
We shall live long and loving. No surfeits seek us—
The hand of war hurts none here, nor the seas
Swallow their youth. Were we at liberty
A wife might part us lawfully, or business;
Quarrels consume us; envy of ill men   90
Crave our acquaintance. I might sicken, cousin,
Where you should never know it, and so perish
Without your noble hand to close mine eyes,

Or prayers to the gods. A thousand chances,
Were we from hence, would sever us.
PALAMON   You have made me—
I thank you, cousin Arcite—almost wanton   96
With my captivity. What a misery
It is to live abroad, and everywhere!
'Tis like a beast, methinks. I find the court here;
I am sure, a more content; and all those pleasures
That woo the wills of men to vanity   101
I see through now, and am sufficient
To tell the world 'tis but a gaudy shadow,
That old Time, as he passes by, takes with him.
What had we been, old in the court of Creon,   105
Where sin is justice, lust and ignorance
The virtues of the great ones? Cousin Arcite,
Had not the loving gods found this place for us,
We had died as they do, ill old men, unwept,
And had their epitaphs, the people's curses.   110
Shall I say more?
ARCITE   I would hear you still.
PALAMON   Ye shall.
Is there record of any two that loved
Better than we do, Arcite?
ARCITE   Sure there cannot.
PALAMON
I do not think it possible our friendship
Should ever leave us.
ARCITE   Till our deaths it cannot,   115
    Enter Emilia and her Woman ⌈*below*⌉. *Palamon sees*
    Emilia and is silent
And after death our spirits shall be led
To those that love eternally. Speak on, sir.
EMILIA (*to her Woman*)
This garden has a world of pleasure in't.
What flower is this?
WOMAN   'Tis called narcissus, madam.
EMILIA
That was a fair boy, certain, but a fool   120
To love himself. Were there not maids enough?
ARCITE (*to Palamon*)
    Pray forward.
PALAMON   Yes.
EMILIA (*to her Woman*) Or were they all hard-hearted?
WOMAN
They could not be to one so fair.
EMILIA   Thou wouldst not.
WOMAN
I think I should not, madam.
EMILIA   That's a good wench—
But take heed to your kindness, though.
WOMAN   Why, madam?
EMILIA
Men are mad things.
ARCITE (*to Palamon*)   Will ye go forward, cousin?   126
EMILIA (*to her Woman*)
Canst not thou work such flowers in silk, wench?
WOMAN   Yes.
EMILIA
I'll have a gown full of 'em, and of these.

This is a pretty colour—will't not do
Rarely upon a skirt, wench?
WOMAN   Dainty, madam.   130
ARCITE (*to Palamon*)
Cousin, cousin, how do you, sir? Why, Palamon!
PALAMON
Never till now was I in prison, Arcite.
ARCITE
Why, what's the matter, man?
PALAMON   Behold and wonder!
   Arcite sees Emilia
By heaven, she is a goddess!
ARCITE   Ha!
PALAMON   Do reverence.
She is a goddess, Arcite.
EMILIA (*to her Woman*)   Of all flowers   135
Methinks a rose is best.
WOMAN   Why, gentle madam?
EMILIA
It is the very emblem of a maid—
For when the west wind courts her gently,
How modestly she blows, and paints the sun
With her chaste blushes! When the north comes near
   her,   140
Rude and impatient, then, like chastity,
She locks her beauties in her bud again,
And leaves him to base briers.
WOMAN   Yet, good madam,
Sometimes her modesty will blow so far
She falls for't—a maid,   145
· If she have any honour, would be loath
To take example by her.
EMILIA   Thou art wanton.
ARCITE (*to Palamon*)
She is wondrous fair.
PALAMON   She is all the beauty extant.
EMILIA (*to her Woman*)
The sun grows high—let's walk in. Keep these flowers.
We'll see how close art can come near their colours.
I am wondrous merry-hearted—I could laugh now.
WOMAN
I could lie down, I am sure.
EMILIA   And take one with you?
WOMAN
That's as we bargain, madam.
EMILIA   Well, agree then.   153
   Exeunt Emilia and her Woman
PALAMON
What think you of this beauty?
ARCITE   'Tis a rare one.
PALAMON
Is't but a rare one?
ARCITE   Yes, a matchless beauty.   155
PALAMON
Might not a man well lose himself and love her?
ARCITE
I cannot tell what you have done; I have,
Beshrew mine eyes for't. Now I feel my shackles.
PALAMON You love her then?

ARCITE Who would not?   160
PALAMON And desire her?
ARCITE Before my liberty.
PALAMON
I saw her first.
ARCITE   That's nothing.
PALAMON   But it shall be.
ARCITE
I saw her too.
PALAMON   Yes, but you must not love her.
ARCITE
I will not, as you do, to worship her   165
As she is heavenly and a blessèd goddess!
I love her as a woman, to enjoy her—
So both may love.
PALAMON   You shall not love at all.
ARCITE
Not love at all—who shall deny me?
PALAMON
I that first saw her, I that took possession   170
First with mine eye of all those beauties
In her revealed to mankind. If thou lov'st her,
Or entertain'st a hope to blast my wishes,
Thou art a traitor, Arcite, and a fellow
False as thy title to her. Friendship, blood,   175
And all the ties between us I disclaim,
If thou once think upon her.
ARCITE   Yes, I love her—
And if the lives of all my name lay on it,
I must do so. I love her with my soul—
If that will lose ye, farewell, Palamon!   180
I say again,
I love her, and in loving her maintain
I am as worthy and as free a lover,
And have as just a title to her beauty,
As any Palamon, or any living   185
That is a man's son.
PALAMON   Have I called thee friend?
ARCITE
Yes, and have found me so. Why are you moved
   thus?
Let me deal coldly with you. Am not I
Part of your blood, part of your soul? You have
   told me
That I was Palamon and you were Arcite.
PALAMON   Yes.   190
ARCITE
Am not I liable to those affections,
Those joys, griefs, angers, fears, my friend shall
   suffer?
PALAMON
Ye may be.
ARCITE   Why then would you deal so cunningly,
So strangely, so unlike a noble kinsman,
To love alone? Speak truly. Do you think me   195
Unworthy of her sight?
PALAMON   No, but unjust
If thou pursue that sight.
ARCITE   Because another

First sees the enemy, shall I stand still,
And let mine honour down, and never charge?
PALAMON
Yes, if he be but one.
ARCITE   But say that one   200
Had rather combat me?
PALAMON   Let that one say so,
And use thy freedom; else, if thou pursuest her,
Be as that cursèd man that hates his country,
A branded villain.
ARCITE   You are mad.
PALAMON   I must be.
Till thou art worthy, Arcite, it concerns me;   205
And in this madness if I hazard thee
And take thy life, I deal but truly.
ARCITE   Fie, sir.
You play the child extremely. I will love her,
I must, I ought to do so, and I dare—
And all this justly.
PALAMON   O, that now, that now   210
Thy false self and thy friend had but this fortune—
To be one hour at liberty and grasp
Our good swords in our hands! I would quickly teach
thee
What 'twere to filch affection from another.
Thou art baser in it than a cutpurse.   215
Put but thy head out of this window more
And, as I have a soul, I'll nail thy life to't.
ARCITE
Thou dar'st not, fool; thou canst not; thou art feeble.
Put my head out? I'll throw my body out
And leap the garden when I see her next,   220
          Enter the Jailer ⌈above⌉
And pitch between her arms to anger thee.
PALAMON
No more—the keeper's coming. I shall live
To knock thy brains out with my shackles.
ARCITE   Do.
JAILER
By your leave, gentlemen.
PALAMON   Now, honest keeper?
JAILER
Lord Arcite, you must presently to th' Duke.   225
The cause I know not yet.
ARCITE   I am ready, keeper.
JAILER
Prince Palamon, I must a while bereave you
Of your fair cousin's company.
                    Exeunt Arcite and the Jailer
PALAMON   And me, too,
Even when you please, of life. Why is he sent for?
It may be he shall marry her—he's goodly,   230
And like enough the Duke hath taken notice
Both of his blood and body. But his falsehood!
Why should a friend be treacherous? If that
Get him a wife so noble and so fair,
Let honest men ne'er love again. Once more   235

I would but see this fair one. Blessèd garden,
And fruit and flowers more blessèd, that still blossom
As her bright eyes shine on ye! Would I were,
For all the fortune of my life hereafter,
Yon little tree, yon blooming apricot—   240
How I would spread and fling my wanton arms
In at her window! I would bring her fruit
Fit for the gods to feed on; youth and pleasure
Still as she tasted should be doubled on her;
And if she be not heavenly, I would make her   245
So near the gods in nature they should fear her—
          Enter the Jailer ⌈above⌉
And then I am sure she would love me. How now,
          keeper,
Where's Arcite?
JAILER   Banished—Prince Pirithous
Obtained his liberty; but never more,
Upon his oath and life, must he set foot   250
Upon this kingdom.
PALAMON ⌈aside⌉   He's a blessèd man.
He shall see Thebes again, and call to arms
The bold young men that, when he bids 'em charge,
Fall on like fire. Arcite shall have a fortune,
If he dare make himself a worthy lover,   255
Yet in the field to strike a battle for her;
And if he lose her then, he's a cold coward.
How bravely may he bear himself to win her
If he be noble Arcite; thousand ways!
Were I at liberty I would do things   260
Of such a virtuous greatness that this lady,
This blushing virgin, should take manhood to her
And seek to ravish me.
JAILER   My lord, for you
I have this charge to—
PALAMON   To discharge my life.
JAILER
No, but from this place to remove your lordship—   265
The windows are too open.
PALAMON   Devils take 'em
That are so envious to me—prithee kill me.
JAILER
And hang for't afterward?
PALAMON   By this good light,
Had I a sword I would kill thee.
JAILER   Why, my lord?
PALAMON
Thou bring'st such pelting scurvy news continually,
Thou art not worthy life. I will not go.   271
JAILER
Indeed you must, my lord.
PALAMON   May I see the garden?
JAILER
No.
PALAMON Then I am resolved—I will not go.
JAILER
I must constrain you, then; and for you are dangerous,
I'll clap more irons on you.
PALAMON   Do, good keeper.   275

I'll shake 'em so ye shall not sleep:
I'll make ye a new morris. Must I go?

JAILER
There is no remedy.

PALAMON   Farewell, kind window.
May rude wind never hurt thee. O, my lady,
If ever thou hast felt what sorrow was,   280
Dream how I suffer. Come, now bury me.

Exeunt Palamon and the Jailer

2.3   *Enter Arcite*

ARCITE
Banished the kingdom? 'Tis a benefit,
A mercy I must thank 'em for; but banished
The free enjoying of that face I die for—
O, 'twas a studied punishment, a death
Beyond imagination; such a vengeance   5
That, were I old and wicked, all my sins
Could never pluck upon me. Palamon,
Thou hast the start now—thou shalt stay and see
Her bright eyes break each morning 'gainst thy
    window,
And let in life into thee. Thou shalt feed   10
Upon the sweetness of a noble beauty
That nature ne'er exceeded, nor ne'er shall.
Good gods! What happiness has Palamon!
Twenty to one he'll come to speak to her,
And if she be as gentle as she's fair,   15
I know she's his—he has a tongue will tame
Tempests and make the wild rocks wanton.
Come what can come,
The worst is death. I will not leave the kingdom.
I know mine own is but a heap of ruins,   20
And no redress there. If I go he has her.
I am resolved another shape shall make me,
Or end my fortunes. Either way I am happy—
I'll see her and be near her, or no more.

*Enter four Country People, one of whom carries a
garland before them. Arcite stands apart*

FIRST COUNTRYMAN
My masters, I'll be there—that's certain.   25

SECOND COUNTRYMAN And I'll be there.

THIRD COUNTRYMAN And I.

FOURTH COUNTRYMAN
Why then, have with ye, boys! 'Tis but a chiding—
Let the plough play today, I'll tickle't out
Of the jades' tails tomorrow.

FIRST COUNTRYMAN   I am sure   30
To have my wife as jealous as a turkey—
But that's all one. I'll go through, let her mumble.

SECOND COUNTRYMAN
Clap her aboard tomorrow night and stow her,
And all's made up again.

THIRD COUNTRYMAN   Ay, do but put
A fescue in her fist and you shall see her   35
Take a new lesson out and be a good wench.
Do we all hold against the maying?

FOURTH COUNTRYMAN
Hold? What should ail us?

THIRD COUNTRYMAN   Arcas will be there.

SECOND COUNTRYMAN And Sennois, and Rycas, and three
better lads ne'er danced under green tree; and ye know
what wenches, ha? But will the dainty dominie, the
schoolmaster, keep touch, do you think? For he does
all, ye know.   43

THIRD COUNTRYMAN He'll eat a hornbook ere he fail. Go
to, the matter's too far driven between him and the
tanner's daughter to let slip now, and she must see the
Duke, and she must dance too.   47

FOURTH COUNTRYMAN Shall we be lusty?

SECOND COUNTRYMAN All the boys in Athens blow wind
i'th' breech on's! And here I'll be and there I'll be, for
our town, and here again and there again—ha, boys,
hey for the weavers!

FIRST COUNTRYMAN This must be done i'th' woods.

FOURTH COUNTRYMAN O, pardon me.   54

SECOND COUNTRYMAN By any means, our thing of learning
said so; where he himself will edify the Duke most
parlously in our behalfs—he's excellent i'th' woods,
bring him to th' plains, his learning makes no cry.

THIRD COUNTRYMAN We'll see the sports, then every man
to's tackle—and, sweet companions, let's rehearse, by
any means, before the ladies see us, and do sweetly,
and God knows what may come on't.   62

FOURTH COUNTRYMAN Content—the sports once ended,
we'll perform. Away boys, and hold.

ARCITE (*coming forward*)
By your leaves, honest friends, pray you whither go
you?   65

FOURTH COUNTRYMAN
Whither? Why, what a question's that?

ARCITE Yet 'tis a question
To me that know not.

THIRD COUNTRYMAN   To the games, my friend.

SECOND COUNTRYMAN
Where were you bred, you know it not?

ARCITE   Not far, sir—
Are there such games today?

FIRST COUNTRYMAN   Yes, marry, are there, 70
And such as you never saw. The Duke himself
Will be in person there.

ARCITE   What pastimes are they?

SECOND COUNTRYMAN
Wrestling and running. (*To the others*) 'Tis a pretty
fellow.

THIRD COUNTRYMAN (*to Arcite*)
Thou wilt not go along?

ARCITE   Not yet, sir.

FOURTH COUNTRYMAN   Well, sir,
Take your own time. (*To the others*) Come, boys.

FIRST COUNTRYMAN   My mind misgives me—
This fellow has a vengeance trick o'th' hip: 76
Mark how his body's made for't.

SECOND COUNTRYMAN   I'll be hanged though

If he dare venture; hang him, plum porridge!
He wrestle? He roast eggs! Come, let's be gone, lads.
                              Exeunt the four Countrymen

ARCITE
This is an offered opportunity   80
  I durst not wish for. Well I could have wrestled—
The best men called it excellent—and run
Swifter than wind upon a field of corn,
Curling the wealthy ears, never flew. I'll venture,
And in some poor disguise be there. Who knows   85
Whether my brows may not be girt with garlands,
And happiness prefer me to a place
Where I may ever dwell in sight of her?   *Exit*

2.4   *Enter the Jailer's Daughter*

JAILER'S DAUGHTER
Why should I love this gentleman? 'Tis odds
He never will affect me. I am base,
My father the mean keeper of his prison,
And he a prince. To marry him is hopeless,
To be his whore is witless. Out upon't,   5
What pushes are we wenches driven to
When fifteen once has found us? First, I saw him;
I, seeing, thought he was a goodly man;
He has as much to please a woman in him—
If he please to bestow it so—as ever   10
These eyes yet looked on. Next, I pitied him,
And so would any young wench, o'my conscience,
That ever dreamed or vowed her maidenhead
To a young handsome man. Then, I loved him,
Extremely loved him, infinitely loved him—   15
And yet he had a cousin fair as he, too.
But in my heart was Palamon, and there,
Lord, what a coil he keeps! To hear him
Sing in an evening, what a heaven it is!
And yet his songs are sad ones. Fairer spoken   20
Was never gentleman. When I come in
To bring him water in a morning, first
He bows his noble body, then salutes me, thus:
'Fair, gentle maid, good morrow. May thy goodness
Get thee a happy husband.' Once he kissed me—   25
I loved my lips the better ten days after.
Would he would do so every day! He grieves much,
And me as much to see his misery.
What should I do to make him know I love him?
For I would fain enjoy him. Say I ventured   30
To set him free? What says the law then? Thus much
For law or kindred! I will do it,
And this night; ere tomorrow he shall love me.   *Exit*

2.5   *Short flourish of cornetts and shouts within. Enter*
        Theseus, Hippolyta, Pirithous, Emilia, Arcite
        disguised, with a garland, and attendants

THESEUS
You have done worthily. I have not seen
Since Hercules a man of tougher sinews.
Whate'er you are, you run the best and wrestle
That these times can allow.

ARCITE   I am proud to please you.

THESEUS
  What country bred you?

ARCITE   This—but far off, prince.   5

THESEUS
  Are you a gentleman?

ARCITE   My father said so,
And to those gentle uses gave me life.

THESEUS
  Are you his heir?

ARCITE   His youngest, sir.

THESEUS   Your father
Sure is a happy sire, then. What proves you?

ARCITE
A little of all noble qualities.   10
I could have kept a hawk and well have hollered
To a deep cry of dogs; I dare not praise
My feat in horsemanship, yet they that knew me
Would say it was my best piece; last and greatest,
I would be thought a soldier.

THESEUS   You are perfect.   15

PIRITHOUS
Upon my soul, a proper man.

EMILIA   He is so.

PIRITHOUS (*to Hippolyta*)
  How do you like him, lady?

HIPPOLYTA   I admire him.
I have not seen so young a man so noble—
If he say true—of his sort.

EMILIA   Believe
His mother was a wondrous handsome woman—   20
His face methinks goes that way.

HIPPOLYTA   But his body
And fiery mind illustrate a brave father.

PIRITHOUS
Mark how his virtue, like a hidden sun,
Breaks through his baser garments.

HIPPOLYTA   He's well got, sure.

THESEUS (*to Arcite*)
  What made you seek this place, sir?

ARCITE   Noble Theseus, 25
To purchase name and do my ablest service
To such a well-found wonder as thy worth,
For only in thy court of all the world
Dwells fair-eyed honour.

PIRITHOUS   All his words are worthy.

THESEUS (*to Arcite*)
Sir, we are much indebted to your travel,   30
Nor shall you lose your wish.—Pirithous,
Dispose of this fair gentleman.

PIRITHOUS   Thanks, Theseus.
(*To Arcite*) Whate'er you are, you're mine, and I shall
     give you
To a most noble service, to this lady,
This bright young virgin; pray observe her goodness.
You have honoured her fair birthday with your
     virtues,
                                                   36
And as your due you're hers. Kiss her fair hand, sir.

ARCITE
Sir, you're a noble giver. (*To Emilia*) Dearest beauty,

Thus let me seal my vowed faith.
    He kisses her hand
                    When your servant,
Your most unworthy creature, but offends you,   40
Command him die, he shall.
EMILIA   That were too cruel.
  If you deserve well, sir, I shall soon see't.
  You're mine, and somewhat better than your rank I'll
    use you.
PIRITHOUS (*to Arcite*)
  I'll see you furnished, and, because you say
  You are a horseman, I must needs entreat you   45
  This afternoon to ride—but 'tis a rough one.
ARCITE
  I like him better, prince—I shall not then
  Freeze in my saddle.
THESEUS (*to Hippolyta*) Sweet, you must be ready—
  And you, Emilia, ⌜*to Pirithous*⌝ and you, friend—and
    all,
  Tomorrow by the sun, to do observance   50
  To flow'ry May in Dian's wood. (*To Arcite*) Wait well,
    sir,
  Upon your mistress.—Emily, I hope
  He shall not go afoot.
EMILIA   That were a shame, sir,
  While I have horses. (*To Arcite*) Take your choice, and
    what
  You want, at any time, let me but know it.   55
  If you serve faithfully, I dare assure you,
  You'll find a loving mistress.
ARCITE   If I do not,
  Let me find that my father ever hated—
  Disgrace and blows.
THESEUS   Go, lead the way—you have won it.
  It shall be so: you shall receive all dues   60
  Fit for the honour you have won. 'Twere wrong else.
  (*To Emilia*) Sister, beshrew my heart, you have a
    servant
  That, if I were a woman, would be master.
  But you are wise.
EMILIA   I hope too wise for that, sir.
                      Flourish. Exeunt

2.6   *Enter the Jailer's Daughter*
JAILER'S DAUGHTER
  Let all the dukes and all the devils roar—
  He is at liberty! I have ventured for him,
  And out I have brought him. To a little wood
  A mile hence I have sent him, where a cedar
  Higher than all the rest spreads like a plane,   5
  Fast by a brook—and there he shall keep close
  Till I provide him files and food, for yet
  His iron bracelets are not off. O Love,
  What a stout-hearted child thou art! My father
  Durst better have endured cold iron than done it.   10
  I love him beyond love and beyond reason
  Or wit or safety. I have made him know it—
  I care not, I am desperate. If the law
  Find me and then condemn me for't, some wenches,

Some honest-hearted maids, will sing my dirge   15
And tell to memory my death was noble,
Dying almost a martyr. That way he takes,
I purpose, is my way too. Sure, he cannot
Be so unmanly as to leave me here.
If he do, maids will not so easily   20
Trust men again. And yet, he has not thanked me
For what I have done—no, not so much as kissed me—
And that, methinks, is not so well. Nor scarcely
Could I persuade him to become a free man,
He made such scruples of the wrong he did   25
To me and to my father. Yet, I hope
When he considers more, this love of mine
Will take more root within him. Let him do
What he will with me—so he use me kindly.
For use me, so he shall, or I'll proclaim him,   30
And to his face, no man. I'll presently
Provide him necessaries and pack my clothes up,
And where there is a patch of ground I'll venture,
So he be with me. By him, like a shadow,
I'll ever dwell. Within this hour the hubbub   35
Will be all o'er the prison—I am then
Kissing the man they look for. Farewell, father:
Get many more such prisoners and such daughters,
And shortly you may keep yourself. Now to him. *Exit*

               ✿

3.1   ⌜*A bush in place.*⌝ *Cornetts in sundry places. Noise*
      and hollering as of people a-Maying.
      Enter Arcite
ARCITE
  The Duke has lost Hippolyta—each took
  A several laund. This is a solemn rite
  They owe bloomed May, and the Athenians pay it
  To th' heart of ceremony. O, Queen Emilia,
  Fresher than May, sweeter   5
  Than her gold buttons on the boughs, or all
  Th'enamelled knacks o'th' mead or garden—yea,
  We challenge too the bank of any nymph
  That makes the stream seem flowers; thou, O jewel
  O'th' wood, o'th' world, hast likewise blessed a pace
  With thy sole presence in thy ⌜   11
                   ⌝ rumination
  That I, poor man, might eftsoons come between
  And chop on some cold thought. Thrice blessèd
    chance
  To drop on such a mistress, expectation   15
  Most guiltless on't! Tell me, O Lady Fortune,
  Next after Emily my sovereign, how far
  I may be proud. She takes strong note of me,
  Hath made me near her, and this beauteous morn,
  The prim'st of all the year, presents me with   20
  A brace of horses—two such steeds might well
  Be by a pair of kings backed, in a field
  That their crowns' titles tried. Alas, alas,
  Poor cousin Palamon, poor prisoner—thou
  So little dream'st upon my fortune that   25
  Thou think'st thyself the happier thing to be
  So near Emilia. Me thou deem'st at Thebes,

And therein wretched, although free. But if
Thou knew'st my mistress breathed on me, and that
I eared her language, lived in her eye—O, coz,   30
What passion would enclose thee!
    Enter Palamon as out of a bush with his shackles.
    He bends his fist at Arcite
PALAMON   Traitor kinsman,
Thou shouldst perceive my passion if these signs
Of prisonment were off me, and this hand
But owner of a sword. By all oaths in one,
I and the justice of my love would make thee   35
A confessed traitor. O thou most perfidious
That ever gently looked, the void'st of honour
That e'er bore gentle token, falsest cousin
That ever blood made kin—call'st thou her thine?
I'll prove it in my shackles, with these hands,   40
Void of appointment, that thou liest and art
A very thief in love, a chaffy lord
Not worth the name of villain. Had I a sword
And these house-clogs away—
ARCITE   Dear cousin Palamon—
PALAMON
Cozener Arcite, give me language such   45
As thou hast showed me feat.
ARCITE   Not finding in
The circuit of my breast any gross stuff
To form me like your blazon holds me to
This gentleness of answer—'tis your passion
That thus mistakes, the which, to you being enemy,
Cannot to me be kind. Honour and honesty   51
I cherish and depend on, howsoe'er
You skip them in me, and with them, fair coz,
I'll maintain my proceedings. Pray be pleased
To show in generous terms your griefs, since that   55
Your question's with your equal, who professes
To clear his own way with the mind and sword
Of a true gentleman.
PALAMON   That thou durst, Arcite!
ARCITE
My coz, my coz, you have been well advertised
How much I dare; you've seen me use my sword   60
Against th'advice of fear. Sure, of another
You would not hear me doubted, but your silence
Should break out, though i'th' sanctuary.
PALAMON   Sir,
I have seen you move in such a place which well
Might justify your manhood; you were called   65
A good knight and a bold. But the whole week's not
    fair
If any day it rain: their valiant temper
Men lose when they incline to treachery,
And then they fight like compelled bears—would fly
Were they not tied.
ARCITE   Kinsman, you might as well   70
Speak this and act it in your glass as to
His ear which now disdains you.
PALAMON   Come up to me,

Quit me of these cold gyves, give me a sword,
Though it be rusty, and the charity
Of one meal lend me. Come before me then,   75
A good sword in thy hand, and do but say
That Emily is thine—I will forgive
The trespass thou hast done me, yea, my life,
If then thou carry't; and brave souls in shades
That have died manly, which will seek of me   80
Some news from earth, they shall get none but this—
That thou art brave and noble.
ARCITE   Be content,
Again betake you to your hawthorn house.
With counsel of the night I will be here
With wholesome viands. These impediments   85
Will I file off. You shall have garments and
Perfumes to kill the smell o'th' prison. After,
When you shall stretch yourself and say but 'Arcite,
I am in plight', there shall be at your choice
Both sword and armour.
PALAMON   O, you heavens, dares any   90
So noble bear a guilty business! None
But only Arcite, therefore none but Arcite
In this kind is so bold.
ARCITE   Sweet Palamon.
PALAMON
I do embrace you and your offer—for
Your offer do't I only, sir; your person,   95
Without hypocrisy, I may not wish
    Wind horns within
More than my sword's edge on't.
ARCITE   You hear the horns—
Enter your muset lest this match between's
Be crossed ere met. Give me your hand, farewell.
I'll bring you every needful thing—I pray you,   100
Take comfort and be strong.
PALAMON   Pray hold your promise,
And do the deed with a bent brow. Most certain
You love me not—be rough with me and pour
This oil out of your language. By this air,
I could for each word give a cuff, my stomach   105
Not reconciled by reason.
ARCITE   Plainly spoken,
Yet—pardon me—hard language: when I spur
    Wind horns within
My horse I chide him not. Content and anger
In me have but one face. Hark, sir, they call
The scattered to the banquet. You must guess   110
I have an office there.
PALAMON   Sir, your attendance
Cannot please heaven, and I know your office
Unjustly is achieved.
ARCITE   'Tis a good title.
I am persuaded this question, sick between's,
By bleeding must be cured. I am a suitor   115
That to your sword you will bequeath this plea
And talk of it no more.
PALAMON   But this one word:

You are going now to gaze upon my mistress—
For note you, mine she is—
ARCITE   Nay then—
PALAMON   Nay, pray you—
You talk of feeding me to breed me strength—   120
You are going now to look upon a sun
That strengthens what it looks on. There you have
A vantage o'er me, but enjoy it till
I may enforce my remedy. Farewell.
          Exeunt severally, ⌈Palamon as into the bush⌉

3.2   *Enter the Jailer's Daughter, with a file*
JAILER'S DAUGHTER
He has mistook the brake I meant, is gone
After his fancy. 'Tis now wellnigh morning.
No matter—would it were perpetual night,
And darkness lord o'th' world. Hark, 'tis a wolf!
In me hath grief slain fear, and, but for one thing,   5
I care for nothing—and that's Palamon.
I reck not if the wolves would jaw me, so
He had this file. What if I hollered for him?
I cannot holler. If I whooped, what then?
If he not answered, I should call a wolf   10
And do him but that service. I have heard
Strange howls this livelong night—why may't not be
They have made prey of him? He has no weapons;
He cannot run; the jangling of his gyves
Might call fell things to listen, who have in them   15
A sense to know a man unarmed, and can
Smell where resistance is. I'll set it down
He's torn to pieces: they howled many together
And then they fed on him. So much for that.
Be bold to ring the bell. How stand I then?   20
All's chared when he is gone. No, no, I lie:
My father's to be hanged for his escape,
Myself to beg, if I prized life so much
As to deny my act—but that I would not,
Should I try death by dozens. I am moped—   25
Food took I none these two days,
Sipped some water. I have not closed mine eyes
Save when my lids scoured off their brine. Alas,
Dissolve, my life; let not my sense unsettle,
Lest I should drown or stab or hang myself.   30
O state of nature, fail together in me,
Since thy best props are warped. So which way now?
The best way is the next way to a grave,
Each errant step beside is torment. Lo,
The moon is down, the crickets chirp, the screech-owl
Calls in the dawn. All offices are done   36
Save what I fail in: but the point is this,
An end, and that is all.   *Exit*

**3.3   *Enter Arcite with a bundle containing meat, wine,
          and files***
ARCITE
I should be near the place. Ho, cousin Palamon!
          Enter Palamon ⌈as from the bush⌉

PALAMON
Arcite.
ARCITE   The same. I have brought you food and files.
Come forth and fear not, here's no Theseus.
PALAMON
Nor none so honest, Arcite.
ARCITE   That's no matter—
We'll argue that hereafter. Come, take courage—   5
You shall not die thus beastly. Here, sir, drink;
I know you are faint. Then I'll talk further with you.
PALAMON
Arcite, thou mightst now poison me.
ARCITE   I might—
But I must fear you first. Sit down and, good now,
No more of these vain parleys. Let us not,   10
Having our ancient reputation with us,
Make talk for fools and cowards. To your health, sir.
PALAMON
Do.
          ⌈*Arcite drinks*⌉
ARCITE Pray sit down, then, and let me entreat you,
By all the honesty and honour in you,
No mention of this woman—'twill disturb us.   15
We shall have time enough.
PALAMON   Well, sir, I'll pledge you.
          Palamon drinks
ARCITE
Drink a good hearty draught; it breeds good blood,
    man.
Do not you feel it thaw you?
PALAMON   Stay, I'll tell you
After a draught or two more.
          Palamon drinks
ARCITE   Spare it not—
The Duke has more, coz. Eat now.
PALAMON   Yes.
          Palamon eats
ARCITE   I am glad   20
You have so good a stomach.
PALAMON   I am gladder
I have so good meat to't.
ARCITE   Is't not mad, lodging
Here in the wild woods, cousin?
PALAMON   Yes, for them
That have wild consciences.
ARCITE   How tastes your victuals?
Your hunger needs no sauce, I see.
PALAMON   Not much.   25
But if it did, yours is too tart, sweet cousin.
What is this?
ARCITE   Venison.
PALAMON   'Tis a lusty meat—
Give me more wine. Here, Arcite, to the wenches
We have known in our days. ⌈*Drinking*⌉ The lord
    steward's daughter.
Do you remember her?
ARCITE   After you, coz.   30

PALAMON
  She loved a black-haired man.
ARCITE   She did so; well, sir.
PALAMON
  And I have heard some call him Arcite, and—
ARCITE
  Out with't, faith.
PALAMON   She met him in an arbour—
  What did she there, coz? Play o'th' virginals?
ARCITE
  Something she did, sir—
PALAMON   Made her groan a month for't—
  Or two, or three, or ten.
ARCITE   The marshal's sister   36
  Had her share too, as I remember, cousin,
  Else there be tales abroad. You'll pledge her?
PALAMON   Yes.
  [They drink]
ARCITE
  A pretty brown wench 'tis. There was a time
  When young men went a-hunting, and a wood,   40
  And a broad beech, and thereby hangs a tale—
  Heigh-ho!
PALAMON   For Emily, upon my life! Fool,
  Away with this strained mirth. I say again,
  That sigh was breathed for Emily. Base cousin,
  Dar'st thou break first?
ARCITE   You are wide.
PALAMON   By heaven and earth,
  There's nothing in thee honest.
ARCITE   Then I'll leave you—
  You are a beast now.
PALAMON   As thou mak'st me, traitor.   47
ARCITE (pointing to the bundle)
  There's all things needful: files and shirts and
      perfumes—
  I'll come again some two hours hence and bring
  That that shall quiet all.
PALAMON   A sword and armour.   50
ARCITE
  Fear me not. You are now too foul. Farewell.
  Get off your trinkets: you shall want naught.
PALAMON   Sirrah—
ARCITE
  I'll hear no more.   Exit
PALAMON   If he keep touch, he dies for't.
                      Exit [as into the bush]

3.4 Enter the Jailer's Daughter
JAILER'S DAUGHTER
  I am very cold, and all the stars are out too,
  The little stars and all, that look like aglets—
  The sun has seen my folly. Palamon!
  Alas, no, he's in heaven. Where am I now?
  Yonder's the sea and there's a ship—how't tumbles!
  And there's a rock lies watching under water—   6
  Now, now, it beats upon it—now, now, now,

There's a leak sprung, a sound one—how they cry!
Open her before the wind—you'll lose all else.
Up with a course or two and tack about, boys.   10
Good night, good night, you're gone. I am very
    hungry.
Would I could find a fine frog—he would tell me
News from all parts o'th' world, then would I make
A carrack of a cockle-shell, and sail
By east and north-east to the King of Pygmies,   15
For he tells fortunes rarely. Now my father,
Twenty to one, is trussed up in a trice
Tomorrow morning. I'll say never a word.

(She sings)
For I'll cut my green coat, a foot above my knee,
And I'll clip my yellow locks, an inch below mine eye,
  Hey nonny, nonny, nonny,   21
He s'buy me a white cut, forth for to ride,
And I'll go seek him, through the world that is so wide,
  Hey nonny, nonny, nonny.

O for a prick now, like a nightingale,   25
To put my breast against. I shall sleep like a top else.
                      Exit

3.5 Enter Gerald (a schoolmaster), five Countrymen, one
        of whom is dressed as a Babion, five Wenches, and
        Timothy, a taborer. All are attired as morris
        dancers
SCHOOLMASTER Fie, fie,
  What tediosity and disinsanity
  Is here among ye! Have my rudiments
  Been laboured so long with ye, milked unto ye,
  And, by a figure, even the very plum-broth   5
  And marrow of my understanding laid upon ye?
  And do you still cry 'where?' and 'how?' and
      'wherefore?'
  You most coarse frieze capacities, ye jean judgements,
  Have I said, 'thus let be', and 'there let be',
  And 'then let be', and no man understand me?   10
  Proh deum, medius fidius—ye are all dunces.
  Forwhy, here stand I. Here the Duke comes. There are
      you,
  Close in the thicket. The Duke appears. I meet him,
  And unto him I utter learnèd things
  And many figures. He hears, and nods, and hums,   15
  And then cries, 'Rare!', and I go forward. At length
  I fling my cap up—mark there—then do you,
  As once did Meleager and the boar,
  Break comely out before him, like true lovers,
  Cast yourselves in a body decently,   20
  And sweetly, by a figure, trace and turn, boys.
FIRST COUNTRYMAN
  And sweetly we will do it, master Gerald.
SECOND COUNTRYMAN
  Draw up the company. Where's the taborer?
THIRD COUNTRYMAN
  Why, Timothy!
TABORER   Here, my mad boys, have at ye!

SCHOOLMASTER
But I say, where's these women?
FOURTH COUNTRYMAN   Here's Friz and Madeline.
SECOND COUNTRYMAN
And little Luce with the white legs, and bouncing
   Barbara.   26
FIRST COUNTRYMAN
And freckled Nell, that never failed her master.
SCHOOLMASTER
Where be your ribbons, maids? Swim with your bodies
And carry it sweetly and deliverly,
And now and then a favour and a frisk.   30
NELL
Let us alone, sir.
SCHOOLMASTER   Where's the rest o'th' music?
THIRD COUNTRYMAN
Dispersed as you commanded.
SCHOOLMASTER   Couple, then,
And see what's wanting. Where's the babion?
(*To the Babion*) My friend, carry your tail without
   offence
Or scandal to the ladies; and be sure   35
You tumble with audacity and manhood,
And when you bark, do it with judgement.
BABION   Yes, sir.
SCHOOLMASTER
Quousque tandem? Here is a woman wanting!
FOURTH COUNTRYMAN
We may go whistle—all the fat's i'th' fire.
SCHOOLMASTER We have,   40
As learnèd authors utter, washed a tile;
We have been *fatuus*, and laboured vainly.
SECOND COUNTRYMAN
This is that scornful piece, that scurvy hilding
That gave her promise faithfully she would be here—
Cicely, the seamstress' daughter.   45
The next gloves that I give her shall be dogskin.
Nay, an she fail me once—you can tell, Arcas,
She swore by wine and bread she would not break.
SCHOOLMASTER An eel and woman,
A learnèd poet says, unless by th' tail   50
And with thy teeth thou hold, will either fail—
In manners this was false position.
FIRST COUNTRYMAN
A fire-ill take her! Does she flinch now?
THIRD COUNTRYMAN   What
Shall we determine, sir?
SCHOOLMASTER   Nothing;
Our business is become a nullity,   55
Yea, and a woeful and a piteous nullity.
FOURTH COUNTRYMAN
Now, when the credit of our town lay on it,
Now to be frampold, now to piss o'th' nettle!
Go thy ways—I'll remember thee, I'll fit thee!
   Enter the Jailer's Daughter

JAILER'S DAUGHTER (*sings*)
The *George Alow* came from the south,   60
   From the coast of Barbary-a;

And there he met with brave gallants of war,
   By one, by two, by three-a.
'Well hailed, well hailed, you jolly gallants,
   And whither now are you bound-a?   65
O let me have your company
   Till I come to the sound-a.'
There was three fools fell out about an owlet—
   The one he said it was an owl,
   The other he said nay,   70
   The third he said it was a hawk,
   And her bells were cut away.
THIRD COUNTRYMAN
There's a dainty madwoman, master,
Comes i'th' nick, as mad as a March hare.
If we can get her dance, we are made again.   75
I warrant her, she'll do the rarest gambols.
FIRST COUNTRYMAN
A madwoman? We are made, boys.
SCHOOLMASTER (*to the Jailer's Daughter*)
And are you mad, good woman?
JAILER'S DAUGHTER   I would be sorry else.
Give me your hand.
SCHOOLMASTER   Why?
JAILER'S DAUGHTER   I can tell your fortune.
   ⌈*She examines his hand*⌉
You are a fool. Tell ten—I have posed him. Buzz!   80
Friend, you must eat no white bread—if you do,
Your teeth will bleed extremely. Shall we dance, ho?
I know you—you're a tinker. Sirrah tinker,
Stop no more holes but what you should.
SCHOOLMASTER   *Dii boni*—
A tinker, damsel?
JAILER'S DAUGHTER   Or a conjurer—   85
Raise me a devil now and let him play
Qui passa o'th' bells and bones.
SCHOOLMASTER   Go, take her,
And fluently persuade her to a peace.
Et opus exegi, quod nec Iovis ira, nec ignis—
Strike up, and lead her in.
SECOND COUNTRYMAN   Come, lass, let's trip it.   90
JAILER'S DAUGHTER I'll lead.
THIRD COUNTRYMAN Do, do.
SCHOOLMASTER
Persuasively and cunningly—
   Wind horns within
               away, boys,
I hear the horns. Give me some meditation,
And mark your cue.
   Exeunt all but Gerald the Schoolmaster
         Pallas inspire me.   95
   Enter Theseus, Pirithous, Hippolyta, Emilia, Arcite,
   and train
THESEUS This way the stag took.
SCHOOLMASTER Stay and edify.
THESEUS What have we here?
PIRITHOUS
Some country sport, upon my life, sir.

THESEUS (*to the Schoolmaster*)
  Well, sir, go forward—we will edify.   100
  Ladies, sit down—we'll stay it.
    They sit: ⌐Theseus⌐ *in a chair, the others on stools*
SCHOOLMASTER
  Thou doughty Duke, all hail! All hail, sweet ladies.
THESEUS This is a cold beginning.
SCHOOLMASTER
  If you but favour, our country pastime made is.
  We are a few of those collected here,   105
  That ruder tongues distinguish 'villager';
  And to say verity, and not to fable,
  We are a merry rout, or else a rabble,
  Or company, or, by a figure, chorus,
  That fore thy dignity will dance a morris.   110
  And I, that am the rectifier of all,
  By title *pedagogus*, that let fall
  The birch upon the breeches of the small ones,
  And humble with a ferula the tall ones,
  Do here present this machine, or this frame;   115
  And dainty Duke, whose doughty dismal fame
  From Dis to Daedalus, from post to pillar,
  Is blown abroad, help me, thy poor well-willer,
  And with thy twinkling eyes, look right and straight
  Upon this mighty 'Moor'—of mickle weight—   120
  'Ice' now comes in, which, being glued together,
  Makes 'morris', and the cause that we came hither.
  The body of our sport, of no small study,
  I first appear, though rude, and raw, and muddy,
  To speak, before thy noble grace, this tenor   125
  At whose great feet I offer up my penner.
  The next, the Lord of May and Lady bright;
  The Chambermaid and Servingman, by night
  That seek out silent hanging; then mine Host
  And his fat Spouse, that welcomes, to their cost,   130
  The gallèd traveller, and with a beck'ning
  Informs the tapster to inflame the reck'ning;
  Then the beest-eating Clown; and next, the Fool;
  The babion with long tail and eke long tool,
  Cum multis aliis that make a dance—   135
  Say 'ay', and all shall presently advance.
THESEUS
  Ay, ay, by any means, dear dominie.
PIRITHOUS   Produce.
SCHOOLMASTER (*knocks for the dance*)
  Intrate filii, come forth and foot it.
    ⌐He flings up his cap.⌐ *Music.*
    ⌐The Schoolmaster ushers in
    May Lord,   *May Lady.*
    Servingman,   *Chambermaid.*
    A Country Clown,
      or Shepherd,   *Country Wench.*
    An Host,   *Hostess.*
    A He-babion,   *She-babion.*
    A He-fool,   *The Jailer's Daughter as*
                     She-fool.
    *All these persons apparelled to the life, the men
    issuing out of one door and the wenches from the
    other. They dance a morris⌐*

Ladies, if we have been merry,
And have pleased ye with a derry,   140
And a derry, and a down,
Say the schoolmaster's no clown.
Duke, if we have pleased thee too,
And have done as good boys should do,
Give us but a tree or twain   145
For a maypole, and again,
Ere another year run out,
We'll make thee laugh, and all this rout.
THESEUS
  Take twenty, dominie. (*To Hippolyta*) How does my
    sweetheart?
HIPPOLYTA
  Never so pleased, sir.
EMILIA   'Twas an excellent dance,   150
  And for a preface, I never heard a better.
THESEUS
  Schoolmaster, I thank you. One see 'em all rewarded.
PIRITHOUS
  And here's something to paint your pole withal.
    He gives them money
THESEUS Now to our sports again.
SCHOOLMASTER
            May the stag thou hunt'st stand long,   155
            And thy dogs be swift and strong;
            May they kill him without lets,
            And the ladies eat his dowsets.
              Exeunt Theseus and train. Wind horns within
  Come, we are all made. *Dii deaeque omnes,*   159
  Ye have danced rarely, wenches.   *Exeunt*

3.6   *Enter Palamon from the bush*
PALAMON
  About this hour my cousin gave his faith
  To visit me again, and with him bring
  Two swords and two good armours; if he fail,
  He's neither man nor soldier. When he left me,
  I did not think a week could have restored   5
  My lost strength to me, I was grown so low
  And crest-fall'n with my wants. I thank thee, Arcite,
  Thou art yet a fair foe, and I feel myself,
  With this refreshing, able once again
  To out-dure danger. To delay it longer   10
  Would make the world think, when it comes to
    hearing,
  That I lay fatting, like a swine, to fight,
  And not a soldier. Therefore this blest morning
  Shall be the last; and that sword he refuses,
  If it but hold, I kill him with; 'tis justice.   15
  So, love and fortune for me!
    Enter Arcite with two armours and two swords
                   O, good morrow.
ARCITE
  Good morrow, noble kinsman.
PALAMON   I have put you
  To too much pains, sir.
ARCITE   That too much, fair cousin,
  Is but a debt to honour, and my duty.

PALAMON
Would you were so in all, sir—I could wish ye   20
As kind a kinsman, as you force me find
A beneficial foe, that my embraces
Might thank ye, not my blows.

ARCITE   I shall think either,
Well done, a noble recompense.

PALAMON   Then I shall quit you.

ARCITE
Defy me in these fair terms, and you show   25
More than a mistress to me—no more anger,
As you love anything that's honourable.
We were not bred to talk, man. When we are armed
And both upon our guards, then let our fury,
Like meeting of two tides, fly strongly from us;   30
And then to whom the birthright of this beauty
Truly pertains—without upbraidings, scorns,
Despisings of our persons, and such poutings
Fitter for girls and schoolboys—will be seen,
And quickly, yours or mine. Will't please you arm,
sir?   35
Or, if you feel yourself not fitting yet,
And furnished with your old strength, I'll stay,
cousin,
And every day discourse you into health,
As I am spared. Your person I am friends with,
And I could wish I had not said I loved her,   40
Though I had died; but loving such a lady,
And justifying my love, I must not fly from't.

PALAMON
Arcite, thou art so brave an enemy
That no man but thy cousin's fit to kill thee.
I am well and lusty—choose your arms.

ARCITE   Choose you, sir.

PALAMON
Wilt thou exceed in all, or dost thou do it   46
To make me spare thee?

ARCITE   If you think so, cousin,
You are deceived, for as I am a soldier,
I will not spare you.

PALAMON   That's well said.

ARCITE   You'll find it.

PALAMON
Then as I am an honest man, and love   50
With all the justice of affection,
I'll pay thee soundly.
     He chooses one armour
            This I'll take.

ARCITE (*indicating the remaining armour*)
            That's mine, then.
I'll arm you first.

PALAMON   Do.
     Arcite arms Palamon
            Pray thee tell me, cousin,
Where gott'st thou this good armour?

ARCITE   'Tis the Duke's,
And to say true, I stole it. Do I pinch you?

PALAMON   No.   55

ARCITE
Is't not too heavy?

PALAMON   I have worn a lighter—
But I shall make it serve.

ARCITE   I'll buckle't close.

PALAMON
By any means.

ARCITE   You care not for a grand guard?

PALAMON
No, no, we'll use no horses. I perceive
You would fain be at that fight.

ARCITE   I am indifferent.   60

PALAMON
Faith, so am I. Good cousin, thrust the buckle
Through far enough.

ARCITE   I warrant you.

PALAMON   My casque now.

ARCITE
Will you fight bare-armed?

PALAMON   We shall be the nimbler.

ARCITE
But use your gauntlets, though—those are o'th' least.
Prithee take mine, good cousin.

PALAMON   Thank you, Arcite.   65
How do I look? Am I fall'n much away?

ARCITE
Faith, very little—love has used you kindly.

PALAMON
I'll warrant thee, I'll strike home.

ARCITE   Do, and spare not—
I'll give you cause, sweet cousin.

PALAMON   Now to you, sir.
     Palamon arms Arcite
Methinks this armour's very like that, Arcite,   70
Thou wor'st that day the three kings fell, but lighter.

ARCITE
That was a very good one, and that day,
I well remember, you outdid me, cousin.
I never saw such valour. When you charged
Upon the left wing of the enemy,   75
I spurred hard to come up, and under me
I had a right good horse.

PALAMON   You had indeed—
A bright bay, I remember.

ARCITE   Yes. But all
Was vainly laboured in me—you outwent me,
Nor could my wishes reach you. Yet a little   80
I did by imitation.

PALAMON   More by virtue—
You are modest, cousin.

ARCITE   When I saw you charge first,
Methought I heard a dreadful clap of thunder
Break from the troop.

PALAMON   But still before that flew
The lightning of your valour. Stay a little,   85
Is not this piece too strait?

ARCITE   No, no, 'tis well.

PALAMON
I would have nothing hurt thee but my sword—
A bruise would be dishonour.
ARCITE   Now I am perfect.
PALAMON
Stand off, then.
ARCITE   Take my sword; I hold it better.
PALAMON
I thank ye. No, keep it—your life lies on it.   90
Here's one—if it but hold, I ask no more
For all my hopes. My cause and honour guard me.
ARCITE
And me, my love.
          They bow several ways, then advance and stand
                    Is there aught else to say?
PALAMON
This only, and no more. Thou art mine aunt's son,
And that blood we desire to shed is mutual: 95
In me, thine, and in thee, mine. My sword
Is in my hand, and if thou kill'st me,
The gods and I forgive thee. If there be
A place prepared for those that sleep in honour,
I wish his weary soul that falls may win it.   100
Fight bravely, cousin. Give me thy noble hand.
ARCITE
Here, Palamon. This hand shall never more
Come near thee with such friendship.
PALAMON   I commend thee.
ARCITE
If I fall, curse me, and say I was a coward—
For none but such dare die in these just trials.   105
Once more farewell, my cousin.
PALAMON   Farewell, Arcite.
          Fight. Horns within; they stand
ARCITE
Lo, cousin, lo, our folly has undone us.
PALAMON   Why?
ARCITE
This is the Duke a-hunting, as I told you.
If we be found, we are wretched. O, retire,
For honour's sake, and safely, presently,   110
Into your bush again. Sir, we shall find
Too many hours to die. In, gentle cousin—
If you be seen, you perish instantly
For breaking prison, and I, if you reveal me,
For my contempt. Then all the world will scorn us,   115
And say we had a noble difference,
But base disposers of it.
PALAMON   No, no, cousin,
I will no more be hidden, nor put off
This great adventure to a second trial.
I know your cunning and I know your cause—   120
He that faints now, shame take him! Put thyself
Upon thy present guard—
ARCITE   You are not mad?
PALAMON
Or I will make th'advantage of this hour
Mine own, and what to come shall threaten me
I fear less than my fortune. Know, weak cousin,   125

I love Emilia, and in that I'll bury
Thee and all crosses else.
ARCITE   Then come what can come,
Thou shalt know, Palamon, I dare as well
Die as discourse or sleep. Only this fears me,
The law will have the honour of our ends.   130
Have at thy life!
PALAMON   Look to thine own well, Arcite!
          They fight again.
          Horns. Enter Theseus, Hippolyta, Emilia, Pirithous,
          and train. ⌈Theseus⌉ separates Palamon and Arcite
THESEUS
What ignorant and mad malicious traitors
Are you, that 'gainst the tenor of my laws
Are making battle, thus like knights appointed,
Without my leave and officers of arms?   135
By Castor, both shall die.
PALAMON   Hold thy word, Theseus.
We are certainly both traitors, both despisers
Of thee and of thy goodness. I am Palamon,
That cannot love thee, he that broke thy prison—
Think well what that deserves. And this is Arcite;   140
A bolder traitor never trod thy ground,
A falser ne'er seemed friend. This is the man
Was begged and banished; this is he contemns thee,
And what thou dar'st do; and in this disguise,
Against thine own edict, follows thy sister,   145
That fortunate bright star, the fair Emilia,
Whose servant—if there be a right in seeing
And first bequeathing of the soul to—justly
I am; and, which is more, dares think her his.
This treachery, like a most trusty lover,   150
I called him now to answer. If thou be'st
As thou art spoken, great and virtuous,
The true decider of all injuries,
Say, 'Fight again', and thou shalt see me, Theseus,
Do such a justice thou thyself wilt envy.   155
Then take my life—I'll woo thee to't.
PIRITHOUS   O heaven,
What more than man is this!
THESEUS   I have sworn.
ARCITE   We seek not
Thy breath of mercy, Theseus. 'Tis to me
A thing as soon to die as thee to say it,
And no more moved. Where this man calls me traitor
Let me say thus much—if in love be treason,   161
In service of so excellent a beauty,
As I love most, and in that faith will perish,
As I have brought my life here to confirm it,
As I have served her truest, worthiest,   165
As I dare kill this cousin that denies it,
So let me be most traitor and ye please me.
For scorning thy edict, Duke, ask that lady
Why she is fair, and why her eyes command me
Stay here to love her, and if she say, 'Traitor',   170
I am a villain fit to lie unburied.
PALAMON
Thou shalt have pity of us both, O Theseus,
If unto neither thou show mercy. Stop,

As thou art just, thy noble ear against us;
As thou art valiant, for thy cousin's soul,   175
Whose twelve strong labours crown his memory,
Let's die together, at one instant, Duke.
Only a little let him fall before me,
That I may tell my soul he shall not have her.

THESEUS
I grant your wish; for to say true, your cousin   180
Has ten times more offended, for I gave him
More mercy than you found, sir, your offences
Being no more than his. None here speak for 'em,
For ere the sun set both shall sleep for ever.

HIPPOLYTA (*to Emilia*)
Alas, the pity! Now or never, sister,   185
Speak, not to be denied. That face of yours
Will bear the curses else of after ages
For these lost cousins.

EMILIA   In my face, dear sister,
I find no anger to 'em, nor no ruin.
The misadventure of their own eyes kill 'em.   190
Yet that I will be woman and have pity,
⌈*She kneels*⌉
My knees shall grow to th' ground, but I'll get mercy.
Help me, dear sister—in a deed so virtuous
The powers of all women will be with us.
    Hippolyta kneels
Most royal brother—

HIPPOLYTA   Sir, by our tie of marriage—   195

EMILIA
By your own spotless honour—

HIPPOLYTA   By that faith,
That fair hand, and that honest heart you gave me—

EMILIA
By that you would have pity in another,
By your own virtues infinite—

HIPPOLYTA   By valour,
By all the chaste nights I have ever pleased you—   200

THESEUS
These are strange conjurings.

PIRITHOUS   Nay, then, I'll in too.
⌈*He kneels*⌉
By all our friendship, sir, by all our dangers,
By all you love most: wars, and this sweet lady—

EMILIA
By that you would have trembled to deny
A blushing maid—

HIPPOLYTA   By your own eyes, by strength—
In which you swore I went beyond all women,   206
Almost all men—and yet I yielded, Theseus—

PIRITHOUS
To crown all this, by your most noble soul,
Which cannot want due mercy, I beg first—

HIPPOLYTA
Next hear my prayers—

EMILIA   Last let me entreat, sir—   210

PIRITHOUS
For mercy.

HIPPOLYTA   Mercy.

EMILIA   Mercy on these princes.

THESEUS
Ye make my faith reel. Say I felt
Compassion to 'em both, how would you place it?
    ⌈*They rise*⌉

EMILIA
Upon their lives—but with their banishments.

THESEUS
You are a right woman, sister: you have pity,   215
But want the understanding where to use it.
If you desire their lives, invent a way
Safer than banishment. Can these two live,
And have the agony of love about 'em,
And not kill one another? Every day   220
They'd fight about you, hourly bring your honour
In public question with their swords. Be wise, then,
And here forget 'em. It concerns your credit
And my oath equally. I have said—they die.
Better they fall by th' law than one another.   225
Bow not my honour.

EMILIA   O my noble brother,
That oath was rashly made, and in your anger.
Your reason will not hold it. If such vows
Stand for express will, all the world must perish.
Beside, I have another oath 'gainst yours,   230
Of more authority, I am sure more love—
Not made in passion, neither, but good heed.

THESEUS
What is it, sister?

PIRITHOUS (*to Emilia*) Urge it home, brave lady.

EMILIA
That you would ne'er deny me anything
Fit for my modest suit and your free granting.   235
I tie you to your word now; if ye fail in't,
Think how you maim your honour—
For now I am set a-begging, sir. I am deaf
To all but your compassion—how their lives
Might breed the ruin of my name, opinion.   240
Shall anything that loves me perish for me?
That were a cruel wisdom: do men prune
The straight young boughs that blush with thousand blossoms
Because they may be rotten? O, Duke Theseus,
The goodly mothers that have groaned for these,   245
And all the longing maids that ever loved,
If your vow stand, shall curse me and my beauty,
And in their funeral songs for these two cousins
Despise my cruelty and cry woe worth me,
Till I am nothing but the scorn of women.   250
For heaven's sake, save their lives and banish 'em.

THESEUS
On what conditions?

EMILIA   Swear 'em never more
To make me their contention, or to know me,
To tread upon thy dukedom; and to be,
Wherever they shall travel, ever strangers   255
To one another.

PALAMON   I'll be cut a-pieces
Before I take this oath—forget I love her?

O all ye gods, despise me, then. Thy banishment
I not mislike, so we may fairly carry
Our swords and cause along—else, never trifle,   260
But take our lives, Duke. I must love, and will;
And for that love must and dare kill this cousin
On any piece the earth has.
THESEUS   Will you, Arcite,
Take these conditions?
PALAMON   He's a villain then.
PIRITHOUS   These are men!
ARCITE
No, never, Duke. 'Tis worse to me than begging,   265
To take my life so basely. Though I think
I never shall enjoy her, yet I'll preserve
The honour of affection and die for her,
Make death a devil.
THESEUS
What may be done? For now I feel compassion.   270
PIRITHOUS
Let it not fall again, sir.
THESEUS   Say, Emilia,
If one of them were dead—as one must—are you
Content to take the other to your husband?
They cannot both enjoy you. They are princes
As goodly as your own eyes, and as noble   275
As ever fame yet spoke of. Look upon 'em,
And if you can love, end this difference.
I give consent. (To Palamon and Arcite) Are you
content too, princes?
PALAMON and ARCITE
With all our souls.
THESEUS   He that she refuses
Must die, then.
PALAMON and ARCITE
                        Any death thou canst invent, Duke.   280
PALAMON
If I fall from that mouth, I fall with favour,
And lovers yet unborn shall bless my ashes.
ARCITE
If she refuse me, yet my grave will wed me,
And soldiers sing my epitaph.
THESEUS (to Emilia)   Make choice, then.
EMILIA
I cannot, sir. They are both too excellent.   285
For me, a hair shall never fall of these men.
HIPPOLYTA ⌜to Theseus⌝
  What will become of 'em?
THESEUS   Thus I ordain it,
And by mine honour once again it stands,
Or both shall die. (To Palamon and Arcite) You shall
both to your country,
And each within this month, accompanied   290
With three fair knights, appear again in this place,
In which I'll plant a pyramid; and whether,
Before us that are here, can force his cousin,
By fair and knightly strength, to touch the pillar,
He shall enjoy her; the other lose his head,   295
And all his friends; nor shall he grudge to fall,

Nor think he dies with interest in this lady.
Will this content ye?
PALAMON   Yes. Here, cousin Arcite,
I am friends again till that hour.
ARCITE   I embrace ye.
THESEUS (to Emilia)
Are you content, sister?
EMILIA   Yes, I must, sir,   300
Else both miscarry.
THESEUS (to Palamon and Arcite)
                        Come, shake hands again, then,
And take heed, as you are gentlemen, this quarrel
Sleep till the hour prefixed, and hold your course.
PALAMON
We dare not fail thee, Theseus.
THESEUS   Come, I'll give ye
Now usage like to princes and to friends.   305
When ye return, who wins I'll settle here,
Who loses, yet I'll weep upon his bier.
                        Exeunt. ⌜In the act-time the bush is removed⌝

4.1   Enter the Jailer and his Friend
JAILER
Hear you no more? Was nothing said of me
Concerning the escape of Palamon?
Good sir, remember.
FRIEND   Nothing that I heard,
For I came home before the business
Was fully ended. Yet I might perceive,   5
Ere I departed, a great likelihood
Of both their pardons: for Hippolyta
And fair-eyed Emily upon their knees
Begged with such handsome pity that the Duke,
Methought, stood staggering whether he should
follow   10
His rash oath or the sweet compassion
Of those two ladies; and to second them
That truly noble prince, Pirithous—
Half his own heart—set in too, that I hope
All shall be well. Neither heard I one question   15
Of your name or his scape.
                        Enter the Second Friend
JAILER   Pray heaven it hold so.
SECOND FRIEND
Be of good comfort, man. I bring you news,
Good news.
JAILER   They are welcome.
SECOND FRIEND   Palamon has cleared you,
And got your pardon, and discovered how
And by whose means he scaped—which was your
daughter's,   20
Whose pardon is procured too; and the prisoner,
Not to be held ungrateful to her goodness,
Has given a sum of money to her marriage—
A large one, I'll assure you.
JAILER   Ye are a good man,
And ever bring good news.
FIRST FRIEND   How was it ended?   25

SECOND FRIEND
Why, as it should be: they that ne'er begged,
But they prevailed, had their suits fairly granted—
The prisoners have their lives.

FIRST FRIEND   I knew 'twould be so.

SECOND FRIEND
But there be new conditions which you'll hear of   29
At better time.

JAILER   I hope they are good.

SECOND FRIEND   They are honourable—
How good they'll prove I know not.

    Enter the Wooer

FIRST FRIEND   'Twill be known.

WOOER
Alas, sir, where's your daughter?

JAILER   Why do you ask?

WOOER
O, sir, when did you see her?

SECOND FRIEND   How he looks!

JAILER
This morning.

WOOER   Was she well? Was she in health?
Sir, when did she sleep?

FIRST FRIEND   These are strange questions.

JAILER
I do not think she was very well: for now   36
You make me mind her, but this very day
I asked her questions and she answered me
So far from what she was, so childishly,
So sillily, as if she were a fool,   40
An innocent—and I was very angry.
But what of her, sir?

WOOER   Nothing, but my pity—
But you must know it, and as good by me
As by another that less loves her—

JAILER
Well, sir?

FIRST FRIEND Not right?

WOOER   No, sir, not well.

SECOND FRIEND   Not well?   45

WOOER
'Tis too true—she is mad.

FIRST FRIEND   It cannot be.

WOOER
Believe, you'll find it so.

JAILER   I half suspected
What you told me—the gods comfort her!
Either this was her love to Palamon,
Or fear of my miscarrying on his scape,   50
Or both.

WOOER   'Tis likely.

JAILER   But why all this haste, sir?

WOOER
I'll tell you quickly. As I late was angling
In the great lake that lies behind the palace,
From the far shore, thick set with reeds and sedges,
As patiently I was attending sport,   55
I heard a voice—a shrill one—and attentive
I gave my ear, when I might well perceive
'Twas one that sung, and by the smallness of it
A boy or woman. I then left my angle
To his own skill, came near, but yet perceived not   60
Who made the sound, the rushes and the reeds
Had so encompassed it. I laid me down
And listened to the words she sung, for then,
Through a small glade cut by the fishermen,
I saw it was your daughter.

JAILER   Pray go on, sir.   65

WOOER
She sung much, but no sense; only I heard her
Repeat this often—'Palamon is gone,
Is gone to th' wood to gather mulberries;
I'll find him out tomorrow.'

FIRST FRIEND   Pretty soul!

WOOER
'His shackles will betray him—he'll be taken,   70
And what shall I do then? I'll bring a bevy,
A hundred black-eyed maids that love as I do,
With chaplets on their heads of daffodillies,
With cherry lips and cheeks of damask roses,
And all we'll dance an antic fore the Duke   75
And beg his pardon.' Then she talked of you, sir—
That you must lose your head tomorrow morning,
And she must gather flowers to bury you,
And see the house made handsome. Then she sung
Nothing but 'willow, willow, willow', and between   80
Ever was 'Palamon, fair Palamon',
And 'Palamon was a tall young man'. The place
Was knee-deep where she sat; her careless tresses
A wreath of bull-rush rounded; about her stuck
Thousand freshwater flowers of several colours—   85
That she appeared, methought, like the fair nymph
That feeds the lake with waters, or as Iris
Newly dropped down from heaven. Rings she made
Of rushes that grew by, and to 'em spoke
The prettiest posies—'Thus our true love's tied',   90
'This you may lose, not me', and many a one.
And then she wept, and sung again, and sighed—
And with the same breath smiled and kissed her
    hand.

SECOND FRIEND
Alas, what pity it is!

WOOER   I made in to her:
She saw me and straight sought the flood—I saved
    her,   95
And set her safe to land, when presently
She slipped away and to the city made,
With such a cry and swiftness that, believe me,
She left me far behind her. Three or four
I saw from far off cross her—one of 'em   100
I knew to be your brother, where she stayed
And fell, scarce to be got away. I left them with her,

    Enter the Jailer's Brother, the Jailer's Daughter, and
    others

And hither came to tell you—here they are.

JAILER'S DAUGHTER (sings)
  'May you never more enjoy the light . . .'—
Is not this a fine song?
JAILER'S BROTHER   O, a very fine one.   105
JAILER'S DAUGHTER
  I can sing twenty more.
JAILER'S BROTHER   I think you can.
JAILER'S DAUGHTER
  Yes, truly can I—I can sing 'The Broom'
And 'Bonny Robin'—are not you a tailor?
JAILER'S BROTHER
  Yes.
JAILER'S DAUGHTER Where's my wedding gown?
JAILER'S BROTHER   I'll bring it tomorrow
JAILER'S DAUGHTER
  Do, very rarely—I must be abroad else,   110
To call the maids and pay the minstrels,
For I must lose my maidenhead by cocklight,
'Twill never thrive else. (Sings) 'O fair, O sweet . . .'
JAILER'S BROTHER ⌈to the Jailer⌉
  You must e'en take it patiently.
JAILER   'Tis true.
JAILER'S DAUGHTER
  Good ev'n, good men. Pray, did you ever hear   115
Of one young Palamon?
JAILER   Yes, wench, we know him.
JAILER'S DAUGHTER
  Is't not a fine young gentleman?
JAILER   'Tis, love.
JAILER'S BROTHER
  By no mean cross her, she is then distempered
Far worse than now she shows.
FIRST FRIEND (to the Jailer's Daughter)
             Yes, he's a fine man.
JAILER'S DAUGHTER
  O, is he so? You have a sister.
FIRST FRIEND   Yes.   120
JAILER'S DAUGHTER
  But she shall never have him, tell her so,
For a trick that I know. You'd best look to her,
For if she see him once, she's gone—she's done
And undone in an hour. All the young maids
Of our town are in love with him, but I laugh at 'em
And let 'em all alone. Is't not a wise course?
FIRST FRIEND   Yes. 126
JAILER'S DAUGHTER
  There is at least two hundred now with child by him,
There must be four; yet I keep close for all this,
Close as a cockle; and all these must be boys—
He has the trick on't—and at ten years old   130
They must be all gelt for musicians
And sing the wars of Theseus.
SECOND FRIEND   This is strange.
⌈JAILER'S BROTHER⌉
  As ever you heard, but say nothing.
FIRST FRIEND   No.
JAILER'S DAUGHTER
  They come from all parts of the dukedom to him.

I'll warrant ye, he had not so few last night   135
As twenty to dispatch. He'll tickle't up
In two hours, if his hand be in.
JAILER   She's lost
Past all cure.
JAILER'S BROTHER Heaven forbid, man!
JAILER'S DAUGHTER (to the Jailer)
  Come hither—you are a wise man.
FIRST FRIEND   Does she know him?
SECOND FRIEND
  No—would she did.
JAILER'S DAUGHTER   You are master of a ship?   140
JAILER
  Yes.
JAILER'S DAUGHTER Where's your compass?
JAILER   Here.
JAILER'S DAUGHTER   Set it to th' north.
And now direct your course to th' wood where
    Palamon
Lies longing for me. For the tackling,
Let me alone. Come, weigh, my hearts, cheerly all.
Uff, uff, uff! 'Tis up. The wind's fair. Top the bowline.
Out with the mainsail. Where's your whistle, master?
JAILER'S BROTHER Let's get her in.   147
JAILER
  Up to the top, boy!
JAILER'S BROTHER   Where's the pilot?
FIRST FRIEND   Here.
JAILER'S DAUGHTER
  What kenn'st thou?
SECOND FRIEND   A fair wood.
JAILER'S DAUGHTER   Bear for it, master.
  Tack about!   150
(Sings) 'When Cynthia with her borrowed light . . .'
                   Exeunt

4.2 ⌈Enter Emilia, with two pictures⌉
EMILIA
  Yet I may bind those wounds up that must open
And bleed to death for my sake else—I'll choose,
And end their strife. Two such young handsome men
Shall never fall for me; their weeping mothers
Following the dead cold ashes of their sons,   5
Shall never curse my cruelty. Good heaven,
What a sweet face has Arcite! If wise nature,
With all her best endowments, all those beauties
She sows into the births of noble bodies,
Were here a mortal woman and had in her   10
The coy denials of young maids, yet doubtless
She would run mad for this man. What an eye,
Of what a fiery sparkle and quick sweetness
Has this young prince! Here love himself sits smiling!
Just such another wanton Ganymede   15
Set Jove afire once, and enforced the god
Snatch up the goodly boy and set him by him,
A shining constellation. What a brow,
Of what a spacious majesty, he carries!
Arched like the great-eyed Juno's, but far sweeter,   20
Smoother than Pelops' shoulder! Fame and honour,

Methinks, from hence, as from a promontory
Pointed in heaven, should clap their wings and sing
To all the under world the loves and fights
Of gods, and such men near 'em. Palamon   25
Is but his foil; to him a mere dull shadow;
He's swart and meagre, of an eye as heavy
As if he had lost his mother; a still temper,
No stirring in him, no alacrity,
Of all this sprightly sharpness, not a smile.   30
Yet these that we count errors may become him:
Narcissus was a sad boy, but a heavenly.
O, who can find the bent of woman's fancy?
I am a fool, my reason is lost in me,
I have no choice, and I have lied so lewdly   35
That women ought to beat me. On my knees
I ask thy pardon, Palamon, thou art alone
And only beautiful, and these the eyes,
These the bright lamps of beauty, that command
And threaten love—and what young maid dare cross
   'em?   40
What a bold gravity, and yet inviting,
Has this brown manly face? O, love, this only
From this hour is complexion. Lie there, Arcite,
Thou art a changeling to him, a mere gypsy,
And this the noble body. I am sotted,   45
Utterly lost—my virgin's faith has fled me.
For if my brother, but even now, had asked me
Whether I loved, I had run mad for Arcite;
Now if my sister, more for Palamon.
Stand both together. Now come ask me, brother—   50
Alas, I know not; ask me now, sweet sister—
I may go look. What a mere child is fancy,
That having two fair gauds of equal sweetness,
Cannot distinguish, but must cry for both!
   ⌜Enter a Gentleman⌝
How now, sir?
GENTLEMAN   From the noble Duke your brother,   55
  Madam, I bring you news. The knights are come.
EMILIA
  To end the quarrel?
GENTLEMAN   Yes.
EMILIA   Would I might end first!
  What sins have I committed, chaste Diana,
  That my unspotted youth must now be soiled
  With blood of princes, and my chastity   60
  Be made the altar where the lives of lovers—
  Two greater and two better never yet
  Made mothers joy—must be the sacrifice
  To my unhappy beauty?
   Enter Theseus, Hippolyta, Pirithous, and attendants
THESEUS   Bring 'em in
  Quickly, by any means, I long to see 'em.   65
               Exit one or more
(To Emilia) Your two contending lovers are returned,
And with them their fair knights. Now, my fair sister,
You must love one of them.
EMILIA   I had rather both,
  So neither for my sake should fall untimely.

   Enter a Messenger
THESEUS
  Who saw 'em?
PIRITHOUS   I a while.
GENTLEMAN   And I.   70
THESEUS (to the Messenger)
  From whence come you, sir?
MESSENGER   From the knights.
THESEUS   Pray speak,
  You that have seen them, what they are.
MESSENGER   I will, sir,
  And truly what I think. Six braver spirits
  Than these they have brought, if we judge by the
    outside,
  I never saw nor read of. He that stands   75
  In the first place with Arcite, by his seeming,
  Should be a stout man; by his face, a prince.
  His very looks so say him: his complexion,
  Nearer a brown than black, stern and yet noble,
  Which shows him hardy, fearless, proud of dangers. 80
  The circles of his eyes show fire within him,
  And, as a heated lion, so he looks.
  His hair hangs long behind him, black and shining,
  Like ravens' wings. His shoulders, broad and strong;
  Armed long and round; and on his thigh a sword   85
  Hung by a curious baldric, when he frowns
  To seal his will with. Better, o' my conscience,
  Was never soldier's friend.
THESEUS Thou hast well described him.
PIRITHOUS Yet a great deal short,   90
  Methinks, of him that's first with Palamon.
THESEUS
  Pray speak him, friend.
PIRITHOUS   I guess he is a prince too,
  And, if it may be, greater—for his show
  Has all the ornament of honour in't.
  He's somewhat bigger than the knight he spoke of, 95
  But of a face far sweeter. His complexion
  Is as a ripe grape, ruddy. He has felt,
  Without doubt, what he fights for, and so apter
  To make this cause his own. In's face appears
  All the fair hopes of what he undertakes,   100
  And when he's angry, then a settled valour,
  Not tainted with extremes, runs through his body
  And guides his arm to brave things. Fear he cannot—
  He shows no such soft temper. His head's yellow,
  Hard-haired and curled, thick twined: like ivy tods,
  Not to undo with thunder. In his face   106
  The livery of the warlike maid appears,
  Pure red and white—for yet no beard has blessed
    him—
  And in his rolling eyes sits victory,
  As if she ever meant to court his valour.   110
  His nose stands high, a character of honour;
  His red lips, after fights, are fit for ladies.
EMILIA
  Must these men die too?
PIRITHOUS   When he speaks, his tongue

Sounds like a trumpet. All his lineaments
Are as a man would wish 'em—strong and clean. 115
He wears a well-steeled axe, the staff of gold.
His age, some five-and-twenty.
MESSENGER   There's another—
A little man, but of a tough soul, seeming
As great as any. Fairer promises
In such a body yet I never looked on. 120
PIRITHOUS
O, he that's freckle-faced?
MESSENGER   The same, my lord.
Are they not sweet ones?
PIRITHOUS   Yes, they are well.
MESSENGER   Methinks,
Being so few and well disposed, they show
Great and fine art in nature. He's white-haired—
Not wanton white, but such a manly colour 125
Next to an auburn, tough and nimble set,
Which shows an active soul. His arms are brawny,
Lined with strong sinews—to the shoulder piece
Gently they swell, like women new-conceived,
Which speaks him prone to labour, never fainting 130
Under the weight of arms; stout-hearted, still,
But when he stirs, a tiger. He's grey-eyed,
Which yields compassion where he conquers; sharp
To spy advantages, and where he finds 'em,
He's swift to make 'em his. He does no wrongs, 135
Nor takes none. He's round-faced, and when he smiles
He shows a lover; when he frowns, a soldier.
About his head he wears the winner's oak,
And in it stuck the favour of his lady.
His age, some six-and-thirty. In his hand 140
He bears a charging-staff embossed with silver.
THESEUS
Are they all thus?
PIRITHOUS   They are all the sons of honour.
THESEUS
Now as I have a soul, I long to see 'em.
(*To Hippolyta*) Lady, you shall see men fight now.
HIPPOLYTA   I wish it,
But not the cause, my lord. They would show 145
Bravely about the titles of two kingdoms—
'Tis pity love should be so tyrannous.
(*To Emilia*) O my soft-hearted sister, what think you?
Weep not till they weep blood. Wench, it must be.
THESEUS (*to Emilia*)
You have steeled 'em with your beauty.
(*To Pirithous*)   Honoured friend,
To you I give the field: pray order it 151
Fitting the persons that must use it.
PIRITHOUS   Yes, sir.
THESEUS
Come, I'll go visit 'em—I cannot stay,
Their fame has fired me so. Till they appear,
Good friend, be royal.
PIRITHOUS   There shall want no bravery. 155
EMILIA ⌈*aside*⌉
Poor wench, go weep—for whosoever wins
Loses a noble cousin for thy sins.   *Exeunt*

4.3   *Enter the Jailer, the Wooer, and the Doctor*
DOCTOR Her distraction is more at some time of the moon
than at other some, is it not?   2
JAILER She is continually in a harmless distemper: sleeps
little; altogether without appetite, save often drinking;
dreaming of another world, and a better; and what
broken piece of matter soe'er she's about, the name
'Palamon' lards it, that she farces every business
Enter the Jailer's Daughter
withal, fits it to every question. Look where she comes—
you shall perceive her behaviour.   9
They stand apart
JAILER'S DAUGHTER I have forgot it quite—the burden on't
was 'Down-a, down-a', and penned by no worse man
than Giraldo, Emilia's schoolmaster. He's as fantastical,
too, as ever he may go upon's legs—for in the next
world will Dido see Palamon, and then will she be out
of love with Aeneas.   15
DOCTOR What stuff's here? Poor soul.
JAILER E'en thus all day long.
JAILER'S DAUGHTER Now for this charm that I told you
of—you must bring a piece of silver on the tip of your
tongue, or no ferry: then, if it be your chance to come
where the blessed spirits are—there's a sight now! We
maids that have our livers perished, cracked to pieces
with love, we shall come there and do nothing all day
long but pick flowers with Proserpine. Then will I make
Palamon a nosegay, then let him mark me, then— 25
DOCTOR How prettily she's amiss! Note her a little further.
JAILER'S DAUGHTER Faith, I'll tell you: sometime we go to
barley-break, we of the blessed. Alas, 'tis a sore life
they have i'th' other place—such burning, frying,
boiling, hissing, howling, chattering, cursing—O they
have shrewd measure—take heed! If one be mad or
hang or drown themselves, thither they go, Jupiter
bless us, and there shall we be put in a cauldron of
lead and usurers' grease, amongst a whole million of
cutpurses, and there boil like a gammon of bacon that
will never be enough.   36
DOCTOR How her brain coins!
JAILER'S DAUGHTER Lords and courtiers that have got
maids with child—they are in this place. They shall
stand in fire up to the navel and in ice up to th' heart,
and there th'offending part burns, and the deceiving
part freezes—in truth a very grievous punishment as
one would think for such a trifle. Believe me, one would
marry a leprous witch to be rid on't, I'll assure you. 44
DOCTOR How she continues this fancy! 'Tis not an
engrafted madness, but a most thick and profound
melancholy.
JAILER'S DAUGHTER To hear there a proud lady and a
proud city wife howl together! I were a beast an I'd
call it good sport. One cries, 'O this smoke!', th'other,
'This fire!'; one cries, 'O that ever I did it behind the
arras!', and then howls—th'other curses a suing fellow
and her garden-house.   53
(*Sings*) 'I will be true, my stars, my fate . . .'
Exit Daughter

JAILER (*to the Doctor*) What think you of her, sir? 55

DOCTOR I think she has a perturbed mind, which I cannot
minister to.

JAILER Alas, what then?

DOCTOR Understand you she ever affected any man ere
she beheld Palamon? 60

JAILER I was once, sir, in great hope she had fixed her
liking on this gentleman, my friend.

WOOER I did think so too, and would account I had a
great penn'orth on't to give half my state that both
she and I, at this present, stood unfeignedly on the
same terms. 66

DOCTOR That intemperate surfeit of her eye hath distempered the other senses. They may return and settle
again to execute their preordained faculties, but they
are now in a most extravagant vagary. This you must
do: confine her to a place where the light may rather
seem to steal in than be permitted; take upon you,
young sir her friend, the name of Palamon; say you
come to eat with her and to commune of love. This
will catch her attention, for this her mind beats upon—
other objects that are inserted 'tween her mind and
eye become the pranks and friskins of her madness.
Sing to her such green songs of love as she says
Palamon hath sung in prison; come to her stuck in as
sweet flowers as the season is mistress of, and thereto
make an addition of some other compounded odours
which are grateful to the sense. All this shall become
Palamon, for Palamon can sing, and Palamon is sweet
and every good thing. Desire to eat with her, carve
her, drink to her, and still among intermingle your
petition of grace and acceptance into her favour. Learn
what maids have been her companions and playferes,
and let them repair to her, with Palamon in their
mouths, and appear with tokens as if they suggested
for him. It is a falsehood she is in, which is with
falsehoods to be combated. This may bring her to eat,
to sleep, and reduce what's now out of square in her
into their former law and regiment. I have seen it
approved, how many times I know not, but to make
the number more I have great hope in this. I will
between the passages of this project come in with my
appliance. Let us put it in execution, and hasten the
success, which doubt not will bring forth comfort. 98

Exeunt

5.1 ⌈*An altar prepared.*⌉ *Flourish. Enter Theseus,
Pirithous, Hippolyta, attendants*

THESEUS

Now let 'em enter and before the gods
Tender their holy prayers. Let the temples
Burn bright with sacred fires, and the altars
In hallowed clouds commend their swelling incense
To those above us. Let no due be wanting. 5

Flourish of cornetts

They have a noble work in hand, will honour
The very powers that love 'em.

Enter Palamon with his three Knights ⌈*at
one door*⌉, *and Arcite with his three Knights*
⌈*at the other door*⌉

PIRITHOUS   Sir, they enter.

THESEUS

You valiant and strong-hearted enemies,
You royal german foes that this day come
To blow that nearness out that flames between ye, 10
Lay by your anger for an hour and, dove-like,
Before the holy altars of your helpers,
The all-feared gods, bow down your stubborn bodies.
Your ire is more than mortal—so your help be;
And as the gods regard ye, fight with justice. 15
I'll leave you to your prayers, and betwixt ye
I part my wishes.

PIRITHOUS   Honour crown the worthiest.

Exit Theseus and his train

PALAMON (*to Arcite*)

The glass is running now that cannot finish
Till one of us expire. Think you but thus,
That were there aught in me which strove to show 20
Mine enemy in this business, were't one eye
Against another, arm oppressed by arm,
I would destroy th'offender—coz, I would,
Though parcel of myself. Then from this gather
How I should tender you.

ARCITE   I am in labour 25
To push your name, your ancient love, our kindred,
Out of my memory, and i'th' selfsame place
To seat something I would confound. So hoist we
The sails that must these vessels port even where
The heavenly limiter pleases.

PALAMON   You speak well. 30
Before I turn, let me embrace thee, cousin—
This I shall never do again.

ARCITE   One farewell.

PALAMON

Why, let it be so—farewell, coz.

ARCITE   Farewell, sir.

Exeunt Palamon and his three Knights

Knights, kinsmen, lovers—yea, my sacrifices,
True worshippers of Mars, whose spirit in you 35
Expels the seeds of fear and th'apprehension
Which still is father of it, go with me
Before the god of our profession. There
Require of him the hearts of lions and
The breath of tigers, yea, the fierceness too, 40
Yea, the speed also—to go on, I mean,
Else wish we to be snails. You know my prize
Must be dragged out of blood—force and great feat
Must put my garland on me, where she sticks,
The queen of flowers. Our intercession, then, 45
Must be to him that makes the camp a cistern
Brimmed with the blood of men—give me your aid,
And bend your spirits towards him.

They kneel before the altar, ⌈*fall on their faces, then
on their knees again*⌉

(*Praying to Mars*)   Thou mighty one,

That with thy power hast turned green Neptune into
    purple;
Whose havoc in vast field comets prewarn,   50
Unearthèd skulls proclaim; whose breath blows down
The teeming Ceres' foison; who dost pluck
With hand armipotent from forth blue clouds
The masoned turrets, that both mak'st and break'st
The stony girths of cities; me thy pupil,   55
Youngest follower of thy drum, instruct this day
With military skill, that to thy laud
I may advance my streamer, and by thee
Be styled the lord o'th' day. Give me, great Mars,
Some token of thy pleasure.   60

> *Here they fall on their faces, as formerly, and there*
> *is heard clanging of armour, with a short thunder,*
> *as the burst of a battle, whereupon they all rise and*
> *bow to the altar*

O great corrector of enormous times,
Shaker of o'er-rank states, thou grand decider
Of dusty and old titles, that heal'st with blood
The earth when it is sick, and cur'st the world
O'th' plurisy of people, I do take   65
Thy signs auspiciously, and in thy name,
To my design, march boldly. *(To his Knights)* Let us go.
     Exeunt

5.2   *Enter Palamon and his Knights with the former*
     observance
PALAMON *(to his Knights)*
Our stars must glister with new fire, or be
Today extinct. Our argument is love,
Which if the goddess of it grant, she gives
Victory too. Then blend your spirits with mine,
You whose free nobleness do make my cause   5
Your personal hazard. To the goddess Venus
Commend we our proceeding, and implore
Her power unto our party.

> *Here they kneel before the altar, ⌈fall on their faces*
> *then on their knees again⌉*

(Praying to Venus) Hail, sovereign queen of secrets,
    who hast power
To call the fiercest tyrant from his rage   10
And weep unto a girl; that hast the might,
Even with an eye-glance, to choke Mars's drum
And turn th'alarum to whispers; that canst make
A cripple flourish with his crutch, and cure him
Before Apollo; that mayst force the king   15
To be his subject's vassal, and induce
Stale gravity to dance; the polled bachelor
Whose youth, like wanton boys through bonfires,
Have skipped thy flame, at seventy thou canst catch
And make him to the scorn of his hoarse throat   20
Abuse young lays of love. What godlike power
Hast thou not power upon? To Phoebus thou
Add'st flames hotter than his—the heavenly fires
Did scorch his mortal son, thine him. The huntress,
All moist and cold, some say, began to throw   25
Her bow away and sigh. Take to thy grace
Me, thy vowed soldier, who do bear thy yoke

As 'twere a wreath of roses, yet is heavier
Than lead itself, stings more than nettles.
I have never been foul-mouthed against thy law;   30
Ne'er revealed secret, for I knew none; would not,
Had I kenned all that were. I never practised
Upon man's wife, nor would the libels read
Of liberal wits. I never at great feasts
Sought to betray a beauty, but have blushed   35
At simp'ring sirs that did. I have been harsh
To large confessors, and have hotly asked them
If they had mothers—I had one, a woman,
And women 'twere they wronged. I knew a man
Of eighty winters, this I told them, who   40
A lass of fourteen brided—'twas thy power
To put life into dust. The agèd cramp
Had screwed his square foot round,
The gout had knit his fingers into knots,
Torturing convulsions from his globy eyes   45
Had almost drawn their spheres, that what was life
In him seemed torture. This anatomy
Had by his young fair fere a boy, and I
Believed it was his, for she swore it was,
And who would not believe her? Brief—I am   50
To those that prate and have done, no companion;
To those that boast and have not, a defier;
To those that would and cannot, a rejoicer.
Yea, him I do not love that tells close offices
The foulest way, nor names concealments in   55
The boldest language. Such a one I am,
And vow that lover never yet made sigh
Truer than I. O, then, most soft sweet goddess,
Give me the victory of this question, which
Is true love's merit, and bless me with a sign   60
Of thy great pleasure.

> *Here music is heard, doves are seen to flutter. They*
> *fall again upon their faces, then on their knees*

O thou that from eleven to ninety reign'st
In mortal bosoms, whose chase is this world
And we in herds thy game, I give thee thanks
For this fair token, which, being laid unto   65
Mine innocent true heart, arms in assurance
My body to this business. *(To his Knights)* Let us rise
And bow before the goddess.
    They rise and bow
           Time comes on.   *Exeunt*

5.3   *Still music of recorders. Enter Emilia in white, her*
     hair about her shoulders, with a wheaten wreath;
     one in white holding up her train, her hair stuck
     with flowers; one before her carrying a silver hind
     in which is conveyed incense and sweet odours,
     which being set upon the altar, her maids standing
     apart, she sets fire to it. Then they curtsy and kneel
EMILIA *(praying to Diana)*
O sacred, shadowy, cold, and constant queen,
Abandoner of revels, mute contemplative,
Sweet, solitary, white as chaste, and pure
As wind-fanned snow, who to thy female knights
Allow'st no more blood than will make a blush,   5

Which is their order's robe: I here, thy priest,
Am humbled fore thine altar. O, vouchsafe
With that thy rare green eye, which never yet
Beheld thing maculate, look on thy virgin;
And, sacred silver mistress, lend thine ear—   10
Which ne'er heard scurril term, into whose port
Ne'er entered wanton sound—to my petition,
Seasoned with holy fear. This is my last
Of vestal office. I am bride-habited,
But maiden-hearted. A husband I have 'pointed,   15
But do not know him. Out of two, I should
Choose one and pray for his success, but I
Am guiltless of election. Of mine eyes
Were I to lose one, they are equal precious—
I could doom neither: that which perished should   20
Go to't unsentenced. Therefore, most modest queen,
He of the two pretenders that best loves me
And has the truest title in't, let him
Take off my wheaten garland, or else grant
The file and quality I hold I may   25
Continue in thy band.
    Here the hind vanishes under the altar and in the
    place ascends a rose tree having one rose upon it
(*To her women*) See what our general of ebbs and flows
Out from the bowels of her holy altar,
With sacred act, advances—but one rose!
If well inspired, this battle shall confound   30
Both these brave knights, and I a virgin flower
Must grow alone, unplucked.
    Here is heard a sudden twang of instruments and
    the rose falls from the tree
The flower is fall'n, the tree descends. (*To Diana*) O
    mistress,
Thou here dischargest me—I shall be gathered.
I think so, but I know not thine own will.   35
Unclasp thy mystery. ⌈*To her women*⌉ I hope she's
    pleased;
Her signs were gracious.   *They curtsy and exeunt*

5.4   *Enter the Doctor, the Jailer, and the Wooer in the*
    habit of Palamon
DOCTOR Has this advice I told you done any good upon
   her?
WOOER O, very much. The maids that kept her company
have half persuaded her that I am Palamon. Within
this half-hour she came smiling to me, and asked me
what I would eat, and when I would kiss her.   6
I told her presently, and kissed her twice.
DOCTOR
'Twas well done—twenty times had been far better,
For there the cure lies mainly.
WOOER   Then she told me
She would watch with me tonight, for well she knew
What hour my fit would take me.
DOCTOR   Let her do so,   11
And when your fit comes, fit her home,
And presently.
WOOER   She would have me sing.

DOCTOR
You did so?
WOOER   No.
DOCTOR   'Twas very ill done, then.
You should observe her every way.
WOOER   Alas,   15
I have no voice, sir, to confirm her that way.
DOCTOR
That's all one, if ye make a noise.
If she entreat again, do anything—
Lie with her if she ask you.
JAILER   Ho there, Doctor.
DOCTOR
Yes, in the way of cure.
JAILER   But first, by your leave,   20
I'th' way of honesty.
DOCTOR   That's but a niceness—
Ne'er cast your child away for honesty.
Cure her first this way, then if she will be honest,
She has the path before her.
JAILER   Thank ye, Doctor.
DOCTOR
Pray bring her in and let's see how she is.   25
JAILER
I will, and tell her her Palamon stays for her.
But, Doctor, methinks you are i'th' wrong still.
                     Exit Jailer
DOCTOR
Go, go. You fathers are fine fools—her honesty?
An we should give her physic till we find that—
WOOER
Why, do you think she is not honest, sir?   30
DOCTOR
How old is she?
WOOER   She's eighteen.
DOCTOR   She may be—
But that's all one. 'Tis nothing to our purpose.
Whate'er her father says, if you perceive
Her mood inclining that way that I spoke of,
Videlicet, the way of flesh—you have me?   35
WOOER
Yes, very well, sir.
DOCTOR   Please her appetite,
And do it home—it cures her, *ipso facto*,
The melancholy humour that infects her.
WOOER I am of your mind, Doctor.
    Enter the Jailer and his Daughter, ⌈mad⌉
DOCTOR
You'll find it so—she comes: pray humour her.   40
    ⌈*The Doctor and the Wooer stand apart*⌉
JAILER (*to his Daughter*)
Come, your love Palamon stays for you, child,
And has done this long hour, to visit you.
JAILER'S DAUGHTER
I thank him for his gentle patience.
He's a kind gentleman, and I am much bound to him.
Did you ne'er see the horse he gave me?
JAILER   Yes.   45

JAILER'S DAUGHTER
  How do you like him?
JAILER   He's a very fair one.
JAILER'S DAUGHTER
  You never saw him dance?
JAILER   No.
JAILER'S DAUGHTER   I have, often.
  He dances very finely, very comely,
  And, for a jig, come cut and long-tail to him,
  He turns ye like a top.
JAILER   That's fine, indeed.   50
JAILER'S DAUGHTER
  He'll dance the morris twenty mile an hour,
  And that will founder the best hobbyhorse,
  If I have any skill, in all the parish—
  And gallops to the tune of 'Light o' love'.
  What think you of this horse?
JAILER   Having these virtues   55
  I think he might be brought to play at tennis.
JAILER'S DAUGHTER
  Alas, that's nothing.
JAILER   Can he write and read too?
JAILER'S DAUGHTER
  A very fair hand, and casts himself th'accounts
  Of all his hay and provender. That ostler
  Must rise betime that cozens him. You know   60
  The chestnut mare the Duke has?
JAILER   Very well.
JAILER'S DAUGHTER
  She is horribly in love with him, poor beast,
  But he is like his master—coy and scornful.
JAILER
  What dowry has she?
JAILER'S DAUGHTER   Some two hundred bottles
  And twenty strike of oats, but he'll ne'er have her. 65
  He lisps in's neighing, able to entice
  A miller's mare. He'll be the death of her.
DOCTOR What stuff she utters!
JAILER Make curtsy—here your love comes.
WOOER (coming forward) Pretty soul,   70
  How do ye?
                    She curtsies
                    That's a fine maid, there's a curtsy.
JAILER'S DAUGHTER
  Yours to command, i'th' way of honesty—
  How far is't now to th' end o'th' world, my masters?
DOCTOR
  Why, a day's journey, wench.
JAILER'S DAUGHTER (to Wooer)   Will you go with me?
WOOER
  What shall we do there, wench?
JAILER'S DAUGHTER   Why, play at stool-ball—
  What is there else to do?
WOOER   I am content   76
  If we shall keep our wedding there.
JAILER'S DAUGHTER   'Tis true—
  For there, I will assure you, we shall find
  Some blind priest for the purpose that will venture

To marry us, for here they are nice, and foolish.   80
  Besides, my father must be hanged tomorrow,
  And that would be a blot i'th' business.
  Are not you Palamon?
WOOER   Do not you know me?
JAILER'S DAUGHTER
  Yes, but you care not for me. I have nothing
  But this poor petticoat and two coarse smocks.   85
WOOER
  That's all one—I will have you.
JAILER'S DAUGHTER   Will you surely?
WOOER
  Yes, by this fair hand, will I.
JAILER'S DAUGHTER   We'll to bed then.
WOOER
  E'en when you will.
                    He kisses her
JAILER'S DAUGHTER (rubbing off the kiss)
                    O, sir, you would fain be nibbling.
WOOER
  Why do you rub my kiss off?
JAILER'S DAUGHTER   'Tis a sweet one,
  And will perfume me finely against the wedding.   90
  (Indicating the Doctor) Is not this your cousin Arcite?
DOCTOR   Yes, sweetheart,
  And I am glad my cousin Palamon
  Has made so fair a choice.
JAILER'S DAUGHTER   Do you think he'll have me?
DOCTOR
  Yes, without doubt.
JAILER'S DAUGHTER (to the Jailer) Do you think so too?
JAILER   Yes.
JAILER'S DAUGHTER
  We shall have many children. ⌜To the Doctor⌝ Lord,
    how you're grown!   95
  My Palamon, I hope, will grow too, finely,
  Now he's at liberty. Alas, poor chicken,
  He was kept down with hard meat and ill lodging,
  But I'll kiss him up again.
                    Enter a Messenger
MESSENGER
  What do you here? You'll lose the noblest sight   100
  That e'er was seen.
JAILER   Are they i'th' field?
MESSENGER   They are—
  You bear a charge there too.
JAILER   I'll away straight.
  ⌜To the others⌝ I must e'en leave you here.
DOCTOR   Nay, we'll go with you—
  I will not lose the sight.
JAILER   How did you like her?
DOCTOR
  I'll warrant you, within these three or four days   105
  I'll make her right again.
                    ⌜Exit the Jailer with the Messenger⌝
  (To the Wooer)   You must not from her,
  But still preserve her in this way.
WOOER   I will.

DOCTOR
　Let's get her in.
WOOER (*to the Jailer's Daughter*)
　　　　Come, sweet, we'll go to dinner,
　And then we'll play at cards.
JAILER'S DAUGHTER　　　And shall we kiss too?
WOOER
　A hundred times.
JAILER'S DAUGHTER　And twenty.
WOOER　　　　　　　Ay, and twenty.　　110
JAILER'S DAUGHTER
　And then we'll sleep together.
DOCTOR (*to the Wooer*)　　Take her offer.
WOOER (*to the Jailer's Daughter*)
　Yes, marry, will we.
JAILER'S DAUGHTER　　But you shall not hurt me.
WOOER
　I will not, sweet.
JAILER'S DAUGHTER　If you do, love, I'll cry.　　*Exeunt*

5.5　*Flourish. Enter Theseus, Hippolyta, Emilia,*
　　　Pirithous, and some attendants

EMILIA
　I'll no step further.
PIRITHOUS　　　　Will you lose this sight?
EMILIA
　I had rather see a wren hawk at a fly
　Than this decision. Every blow that falls
　Threats a brave life; each stroke laments
　The place whereon it falls, and sounds more like　5
　A bell than blade. I will stay here.
　It is enough my hearing shall be punished
　With what shall happen, 'gainst the which there is
　No deafing, but to hear; not taint mine eye
　With dread sights it may shun.
PIRITHOUS (*to Theseus*)　　　Sir, my good lord,　10
　Your sister will no further.
THESEUS　　　　　　　O, she must.
　She shall see deeds of honour in their kind,
　Which sometime show well pencilled. Nature now
　Shall make and act the story, the belief
　Both sealed with eye and ear. (*To Emilia*) You must be
　present—　　15
　You are the victor's meed, the price and garland
　To crown the question's title.
EMILIA　　　　　　　Pardon me,
　If I were there I'd wink.
THESEUS　　　　　　　You must be there—
　This trial is, as 'twere, i'th' night, and you
　The only star to shine.
EMILIA　　　　　　I am extinct.　　20
　There is but envy in that light which shows
　The one the other. Darkness, which ever was
　The dam of horror, who does stand accursed
　Of many mortal millions, may even now,
　By casting her black mantle over both,　　25
　That neither could find other, get herself

Some part of a good name, and many a murder
Set off whereto she's guilty.
HIPPOLYTA　　　　　You must go.
EMILIA
　In faith, I will not.
THESEUS　　　　Why, the knights must kindle
　Their valour at your eye. Know, of this war　30
　You are the treasure, and must needs be by
　To give the service pay.
EMILIA　　　　　　Sir, pardon me—
　The title of a kingdom may be tried
　Out of itself.
THESEUS　　Well, well—then at your pleasure.
　Those that remain with you could wish their office　35
　To any of their enemies.
HIPPOLYTA　　　　　Farewell, sister.
　I am like to know your husband fore yourself,
　By some small start of time. He whom the gods
　Do of the two know best, I pray them he　39
　Be made your lot.　　*Exeunt all but Emilia*
　⌈*Emilia takes out two pictures, one from her right*
　side, and one from her left⌉
EMILIA
　Arcite is gently visaged, yet his eye
　Is like an engine bent or a sharp weapon
　In a soft sheath. Mercy and manly courage
　Are bedfellows in his visage. Palamon
　Has a most menacing aspect. His brow　　45
　Is graved and seems to bury what it frowns on,
　Yet sometime 'tis not so, but alters to
　The quality of his thoughts. Long time his eye
　Will dwell upon his object. Melancholy
　Becomes him nobly—so does Arcite's mirth.　50
　But Palamon's sadness is a kind of mirth,
　So mingled as if mirth did make him sad
　And sadness merry. Those darker humours that
　Stick misbecomingly on others, on them
　Live in fair dwelling.　　55
　　　Cornetts. Trumpets sound as to a charge
　Hark, how yon spurs to spirit do incite
　The princes to their proof. Arcite may win me,
　And yet may Palamon wound Arcite to
　The spoiling of his figure. O, what pity
　Enough for such a chance! If I were by　　60
　I might do hurt, for they would glance their eyes
　Toward my seat, and in that motion might
　Omit a ward or forfeit an offence
　Which craved that very time. It is much better
　　　Cornetts. A great cry and noise within, crying, 'A
　　　Palamon'
　I am not there. O better never born,　　65
　Than minister to such harm.
　　　Enter Servant
　　　　　　　What is the chance?
SERVANT　The cry's 'A Palamon'.
EMILIA
　Then he has won. 'Twas ever likely—

He looked all grace and success, and he is
Doubtless the prim'st of men. I prithee run   70
And tell me how it goes.
    Shout and cornetts, crying, 'A Palamon'
SERVANT   Still 'Palamon'.
EMILIA
Run and enquire.   *Exit Servant*
    ⌈*She speaks to the picture in her right hand*⌉
          Poor servant, thou hast lost.
Upon my right side still I wore thy picture,
Palamon's on the left. Why so, I know not.
I had no end in't, else chance would have it so.   75
    Another cry and shout within and cornetts
On the sinister side the heart lies—Palamon
Had the best-boding chance. This burst of clamour
Is sure the end o'th' combat.
    Enter Servant
SERVANT
They said that Palamon had Arcite's body
Within an inch o'th' pyramid—that the cry   80
Was general 'A Palamon'. But anon
Th'assistants made a brave redemption, and
The two bold titlers at this instant are
Hand to hand at it.
EMILIA   Were they metamorphosed
Both into one? O why? There were no woman   85
Worth so composed a man: their single share,
Their nobleness peculiar to them, gives
The prejudice of disparity, value's shortness,
To any lady breathing—
    Cornetts. Cry within, 'Arcite, Arcite'
             More exulting?
'Palamon' still?
SERVANT   Nay, now the sound is 'Arcite'.   90
EMILIA
I prithee, lay attention to the cry.
    Cornetts. A great shout and cry, 'Arcite, victory!'
Set both thine ears to th' business.
SERVANT   The cry is
'Arcite' and 'Victory'—hark, 'Arcite, victory!'
The combat's consummation is proclaimed
By the wind instruments.
EMILIA   Half sights saw   95
That Arcite was no babe. God's lid, his richness
And costliness of spirit looked through him—it could
No more be hid in him than fire in flax,
Than humble banks can go to law with waters
That drift winds force to raging. I did think   100
Good Palamon would miscarry, yet I knew not
Why I did think so. Our reasons are not prophets
When oft our fancies are. They are coming off—
Alas, poor Palamon.
    ⌈*She puts away the pictures.*⌉
    Cornetts. Enter Theseus, Hippolyta, Pirithous,
    Arcite as victor, and attendants
THESEUS
Lo, where our sister is in expectation,   105
Yet quaking and unsettled. Fairest Emily,
The gods by their divine arbitrament

Have given you this knight. He is a good one
As ever struck at head. ⌈*To Arcite and Emilia*⌉ Give me
    your hands.
    (*To Arcite*) Receive you her, (*to Emilia*) you him: (*to*
       both) be plighted with   110
A love that grows as you decay.
ARCITE   Emilia,
To buy you I have lost what's dearest to me
Save what is bought, and yet I purchase cheaply
As I do rate your value.
THESEUS (*to Emilia*)   O lovèd sister,
He speaks now of as brave a knight as e'er   115
Did spur a noble steed. Surely the gods
Would have him die a bachelor lest his race
Should show i'th' world too godlike. His behaviour
So charmed me that, methought, Alcides was
To him a sow of lead. If I could praise   120
Each part of him to th'all I have spoke, your Arcite
Did not lose by't; for he that was thus good,
Encountered yet his better. I have heard
Two emulous Philomels beat the ear o'th' night
With their contentious throats, now one the higher,
Anon the other, then again the first,   126
And by and by out-breasted, that the sense
Could not be judge between 'em—so it fared
Good space between these kinsmen, till heavens did
Make hardly one the winner. (*To Arcite*) Wear the
    garland   130
With joy that you have won.—For the subdued,
Give them our present justice, since I know
Their lives but pinch 'em. Let it here be done.
The scene's not for our seeing; go we hence
Right joyful, with some sorrow. (*To Arcite*) Arm your
    prize;   135
I know you will not lose her. Hippolyta,
I see one eye of yours conceives a tear,
The which it will deliver.
    Flourish
EMILIA   Is this winning?
O all you heavenly powers, where is your mercy?
But that your wills have said it must be so,   140
And charge me live to comfort this unfriended,
This miserable prince, that cuts away
A life more worthy from him than all women,
I should and would die too.
HIPPOLYTA   Infinite pity
That four such eyes should be so fixed on one   145
That two must needs be blind for't.
THESEUS   So it is.   *Exeunt*

5.6   *Enter, guarded, Palamon and his three Knights*
        pinioned; enter with them the Jailer and an
        executioner with block and axe
PALAMON
There's many a man alive that hath outlived
The love o'th' people; yea, i'th' selfsame state
Stands many a father with his child: some comfort
We have by so considering. We expire,
And not without men's pity; to live still,   5

Have their good wishes. We prevent
The loathsome misery of age, beguile
The gout and rheum that in lag hours attend
For grey approachers; we come towards the gods
Young and unwappered, not halting under crimes   10
Many and stale—that sure shall please the gods
Sooner than such, to give us nectar with 'em,
For we are more clear spirits. My dear kinsmen,
Whose lives for this poor comfort are laid down,
You have sold 'em too too cheap.

FIRST KNIGHT   What ending could be
Of more content? O'er us the victors have   16
Fortune, whose title is as momentary
As to us death is certain—a grain of honour
They not o'erweigh us.

SECOND KNIGHT   Let us bid farewell,
And with our patience anger tott'ring fortune,   20
Who at her certain'st reels.

THIRD KNIGHT   Come, who begins?

PALAMON
E'en he that led you to this banquet shall
Taste to you all. (*To the Jailer*) Aha, my friend, my
    friend,
Your gentle daughter gave me freedom once;
You'll see't done now for ever. Pray, how does she? 25
I heard she was not well; her kind of ill
Gave me some sorrow.

JAILER   Sir, she's well restored
And to be married shortly.

PALAMON   By my short life,
I am most glad on't. 'Tis the latest thing
I shall be glad of. Prithee, tell her so;   30
Commend me to her, and to piece her portion
Tender her this.

He gives his purse

FIRST KNIGHT   Nay, let's be offerers all.

SECOND KNIGHT
Is it a maid?

PALAMON   Verily, I think so—
A right good creature more to me deserving
Than I can quit or speak of.

ALL THREE KNIGHTS   Commend us to her.   35
They give their purses

JAILER
The gods requite you all, and make her thankful.

PALAMON
Adieu, and let my life be now as short
As my leave-taking.
He lies on the block

FIRST KNIGHT   Lead, courageous cousin.

SECOND *and* THIRD KNIGHTS We'll follow cheerfully.
A great noise within: crying, 'Run! Save! Hold!'
Enter in haste a Messenger

MESSENGER Hold! Hold! O, hold! Hold! Hold!   40
Enter Pirithous in haste

PIRITHOUS
Hold, ho! It is a cursèd haste you made
If you have done so quickly! Noble Palamon,

The gods will show their glory in a life
That thou art yet to lead.

PALAMON   Can that be,
When Venus, I have said, is false? How do things
    fare?   45

PIRITHOUS
Arise, great sir, and give the tidings ear
That are most rarely sweet and bitter.

PALAMON   What
Hath waked us from our dream?

PIRITHOUS   List, then: your cousin,
Mounted upon a steed that Emily
Did first bestow on him, a black one owing   50
Not a hair-worth of white—which some will say
Weakens his price and many will not buy
His goodness with this note; which superstition
Here finds allowance—on this horse is Arcite
Trotting the stones of Athens, which the calkins   55
Did rather tell than trample; for the horse
Would make his length a mile, if't pleased his rider
To put pride in him. As he thus went counting
The flinty pavement, dancing, as 'twere, to th' music
His own hooves made—for, as they say, from iron   60
Came music's origin—what envious flint,
Cold as old Saturn and like him possessed
With fire malevolent, darted a spark,
Or what fierce sulphur else, to this end made,
I comment not—the hot horse, hot as fire,   65
Took toy at this and fell to what disorder
His power could give his will; bounds; comes on end;
Forgets school-doing, being therein trained
And of kind manège; pig-like he whines
At the sharp rowel, which he frets at rather   70
Than any jot obeys; seeks all foul means
Of boist'rous and rough jad'ry to disseat
His lord, that kept it bravely. When naught served,
When neither curb would crack, girth break, nor
    diff'ring plunges
Disroot his rider whence he grew, but that   75
He kept him 'tween his legs, on his hind hooves—
On end he stands—
That Arcite's legs, being higher than his head,
Seemed with strange art to hang. His victor's wreath
Even then fell off his head; and presently   80
Backward the jade comes o'er and his full poise
Becomes the rider's load. Yet is he living;
But such a vessel 'tis that floats but for
The surge that next approaches. He much desires
To have some speech with you—lo, he appears.   85
Enter Theseus, Hippolyta, Emilia, and Arcite in a
chair borne by attendants

PALAMON
O miserable end of our alliance!
The gods are mighty. Arcite, if thy heart,
Thy worthy manly heart, be yet unbroken,
Give me thy last words. I am Palamon,
One that yet loves thee dying.

ARCITE   Take Emilia,   90

And with her all the world's joy. Reach thy hand—
Farewell—I have told my last hour. I was false,
Yet never treacherous. Forgive me, cousin—
One kiss from fair Emilia—(*they kiss*) 'tis done.
Take her; I die.   *He dies*
PALAMON   Thy brave soul seek Elysium.   95
EMILIA (*to Arcite's body*)
I'll close thine eyes, Prince. Blessèd souls be with thee.
Thou art a right good man, and, while I live,
This day I give to tears.
PALAMON   And I to honour.
THESEUS
In this place first you fought, e'en very here
I sundered you. Acknowledge to the gods   100
Our thanks that you are living.
His part is played, and, though it were too short,
He did it well. Your day is lengthened and
The blissful dew of heaven does arrouse you.
The powerful Venus well hath graced her altar,   105
And given you your love; our master, Mars,
Hath vouched his oracle, and to Arcite gave
The grace of the contention. So the deities
Have showed due justice.—Bear this hence.
                   ⌈*Exeunt attendants with Arcite's body*⌉
PALAMON   O cousin,
That we should things desire which do cost us   110
The loss of our desire! That naught could buy
Dear love, but loss of dear love!
THESEUS   Never fortune
Did play a subtler game—the conquered triumphs,
The victor has the loss. Yet in the passage
The gods have been most equal. Palamon,   115
Your kinsman hath confessed the right o'th' lady
Did lie in you, for you first saw her and
Even then proclaimed your fancy. He restored her
As your stol'n jewel, and desired your spirit
To send him hence forgiven. The gods my justice   120
Take from my hand, and they themselves become
The executioners. Lead your lady off,

And call your lovers from the stage of death,
Whom I adopt my friends. A day or two
Let us look sadly and give grace unto   125
The funeral of Arcite, in whose end
The visages of bridegrooms we'll put on
And smile with Palamon, for whom an hour,
But one hour since, I was as dearly sorry
As glad of Arcite, and am now as glad   130
As for him sorry. O you heavenly charmers,
What things you make of us! For what we lack
We laugh, for what we have, are sorry; still
Are children in some kind. Let us be thankful
For that which is, and with you leave dispute   135
That are above our question. Let's go off
And bear us like the time.   *Flourish. Exeunt*

Epilogue   *Enter Epilogue*
EPILOGUE
I would now ask ye how ye like the play,
But, as it is with schoolboys, cannot say.
I am cruel fearful. Pray yet stay awhile,
And let me look upon ye. No man smile?
Then it goes hard, I see. He that has   5
Loved a young handsome wench, then, show his
    face—
'Tis strange if none be here—and, if he will,
Against his conscience let him hiss and kill
Our market. 'Tis in vain, I see, to stay ye.
Have at the worst can come, then! Now, what say ye?
And yet mistake me not—I am not bold—   11
We have no such cause. If the tale we have told—
For 'tis no other—any way content ye,
For to that honest purpose it was meant ye,
We have our end; and ye shall have ere long,   15
I dare say, many a better to prolong
Your old loves to us. We and all our might
Rest at your service. Gentlemen, good night.
                           Flourish. Exit